Social Media Marketing:

Breakthroughs in Research and Practice

Information Resources Management Association
USA

Volume I

Published in the United States of America by
IGI Global
Business Science Reference (an imprint of IGI Global)
701 E. Chocolate Avenue
Hershey PA, USA 17033
Tel: 717-533-8845
Fax: 717-533-8661
E-mail: cust@igi-global.com
Web site: http://www.igi-global.com

Library of Congress Cataloging-in-Publication Data

Names: Information Resources Management Association, editor.
Title: Social media marketing: breakthroughs in research and practice / Information Resources Management Association, editor.
Description: Hershey : Business Science Reference, [2018]
Identifiers: LCCN 2017051838| ISBN 9781522556374 (hardcover) | ISBN 9781522556381 (ebook)
Subjects: LCSH: Social media. | Mass media and business.. | Relationship marketing. | Customer relations.
Classification: LCC HD59 .S626 2018 | DDC 651.8--dc23 LC record available at https://lccn.loc.gov/2017051838

British Cataloguing in Publication Data
A Cataloguing in Publication record for this book is available from the British Library.

For electronic access to this publication, please contact: eresources@igi-global.com.

List of Contributors

Table of Contents

Volume II

Section 3
Information Management and Analysis

Preface

The constant advancement of new business strategies, especially those centered around technology, can make it very difficult to stay competitive in the modern business era. That is why IGI Global is pleased to offer this two-volume comprehensive reference that will empower students, researchers, practitioners, consultants, and academicians in a variety of industries with a stronger understanding of one of these very important strategies, social media marketing.

This compilation is designed to act as a single reference source on conceptual, methodological, and technical aspects, and will provide insight into emerging topics including but not limited to consumer behavior, popularity prediction, social media campaigns, strategic planning, and emotional branding. The chapters within this publication are sure to provide readers with the tools necessary to brainstorm and execute robust marketing campaigns that will effectively engage their customer base. Through a variety of outlined techniques, their organizations can benefit from long-term market sustainability.

Social Media Marketing: Breakthroughs in Research and Practice is organized into five sections that provide comprehensive coverage of important topics. The sections are:

1. Adoption, Implementation, and Strategy;
2. Branding, Consumer Engagement, and CRM;
3. Information Management Analysis;
4. Industry-Specific; and
5. Politics and Government Organizations.

The following paragraphs provide a summary of what to expect from each of these designated sections within this invaluable reference source:

Section 1, "Adoption, Implementation, and Strategy," opens this extensive reference source by highlighting the latest trends in marketing communications and consumer-generated media. Through perspectives on viral marketing, social networking sites, and brand awareness, this section demonstrates the importance of advertising and branding for business performance and success. The presented research facilitates a better understanding of how the use of electronic word-of-mouth is shaping business audience outreach.

Section 2, "Branding, Consumer Engagement, and CRM," includes chapters on emerging innovations in brand management and engaging social media audiences. Including discussions on customer retention, purchase intention, and social media intelligence, this section presents research on the impact of competitive intelligence and social networking in building brand loyalty. This inclusive information assists in advancing current practices in consumer and strategic online engagement.

Section 3, "Information Management Analysis," presents coverage on social media metrics to enhance business intelligence and management. Through innovative discussions on demographic data, competitive intelligence, and big data analytics, this section highlights the changing landscape of social media mining and networking. These inclusive perspectives contribute to the available knowledge on the use of social sharing content analysis to predict trends and build brand equity.

Section 4, "Industry-Specific," discusses coverage and research perspectives on the use of social media marketing strategy across different industries such as educational institutions, the fashion industry, the airline industry, banking, and tourism. The presented research facilitates a comprehensive understanding of areas including but not limited to tourism destination marketing, customer influence, and user-centered museums.

Section 5, "Politics and Government Organizations," includes chapters on the use of political marketing in various regions. Including discussions on online petitions, web campaigns, and political public relations, this section presents research on the implementation of social media in political campaigns to promote political awareness and alleviate political scandals. This inclusive information assists in advancing current government social media practices.

Although the primary organization of the contents in this work is based on its five sections, offering a progression of coverage of the important concepts, methodologies, technologies, applications, social issues, and emerging trends, the reader can also identify specific contents by utilizing the extensive indexing system listed at the end.

Section 1

Adoption, Implementation, and Strategy

Chapter 1
The Emergence of Social Media as a Contemporary Marketing Practice

T. Solomon
Massey University, New Zealand

R. Peter
Massey University, New Zealand

ABSTRACT

In this era of rapid technological change, Social Media has emerged as a key marketing practice in the ICT sector in India. In this chapter, the authors examine the emergence of Social Media as a marketing practice, its application in Relationship Marketing and Market Research and the influence of these on Customer Satisfaction in a B2B market. This research integrates Social Media with the widely prevalent Marketing Management and Relationship Marketing paradigms. A web based survey was used to collect data from a sampling frame of ICT firms in India. Factor analysis evidenced the emergence of Social Media as a unique and distinct factor. It also clearly shows the use of Social Media for Relationship Marketing and Market Research purposes by these ICT firms. Multiple regression analysis showed a significant positive relationship between the independent variables - Social Media, Relationship Marketing and Market Research and the dependent variable Customer Satisfaction.

INTRODUCTION

There has been a revolutionary growth in the Information and Communication Technology (ICT) sector in India since 2001. According to a report prepared by the trade council of India (2014), the revenue of the country's ICT sector was valued at USD 108 billion and is expected to reach USD 220 billion by 2020. As of 2014 this sector had the highest relative share of 9.5% in the national gross domestic product (National Association of Software and Services Companies, 2015). ICT also contributes to economic growth, globalization, foreign exchange earnings, market diversification, employment generation and socio-cultural developments of the country (Ministry of Statistics & Programme Implementation, 2010).

DOI: 10.4018/978-1-5225-5637-4.ch001

The marketing of high technology products, such as the ICT products, differs significantly from the marketing of other low technology products (Mohr, Sengupta & Slater, 2010; Yadav, Swami & Pal, 2006; Traynor & Traynor, 2004). This difference is attributed to the volatile marketing environment of the high technology firms which is characterised by market uncertainty, technological uncertainty and competitive volatility (Mohr et al, 2010).

In spite of the widely acknowledged differences in marketing practices of the technology intensive firms, very little research has been undertaken to identify the strategic marketing practices that are adopted by these firms (Hills & Sarin, 2003). The gap in literature for the general theory development related to the marketing for HT firms has also been identified by Uslay, Malhotra and Citrin (2004). Their study noted the need for both conceptual and empirical research regarding the marketing practices of HT firms. This paper explores some of the marketing practices of ICT firms.

The use of social media in the B2B market clients is a relatively a new phenomenon and remains largely unexplored in literature (Järvinen, Tollinen, Karjaluoto & Jayawardhena, 2012; Schultz, Schwepker & Good, 2012). ICT firms have the technological competency to use online networks and their customers are proficient in internet use. These firms rely on the internet more than any other firms in the business sector. Hence engagement in social media platforms has become a strategic choice for the success of these firms. Because of the importance of the ICT firms to the Indian economy, Sarin (2012) also addressed the need for more research into the strategic marketing practices of these technology intensive firms.

The objective of this paper is to enhance the understanding of Social Media as a contemporary marketing practice. Further it also explores the link between Social Media, Relationship Marketing and Market Research and their influence on Customer Satisfaction in the Information and Communication Technology (ICT) firms in India. This is a part of a larger study in which the authors investigated the marketing practices of the ICT firms in India and their influence on Customer Satisfaction and Firm Performance. The specific research questions of this paper are:

1. Is there evidence to support that Social Media is a contemporary marketing practice?
2. Is there a nexus between Social Media, Relationship Marketing and Market Research practices of these ICT firms?
3. What is the influence of Social Media, Relationship Marketing and Market Research practices on Customer Satisfaction in these ICT firms?

THEORETICAL BACKGROUND

Lehtinen (2011) proposes that an integrated approach to marketing must be used to understand the strategic marketing practices of firms as most empirical research in marketing emphasize the combined use of transactional and relationship marketing approaches by firms. The two approaches were found to complement each other and it is difficult to separate them both in theory and in marketing practice. Coviello and Brodie (2000) concluded that in order to capture the scope of what is being practiced in firms the theoretical framework should include the full spectrum of marketing practices which include the elements of both transactional and relationship marketing practices. Further, Fruchter and Sigue (2005) also contend that marketing is about both exchange transactions and exchange relationships. Hence an integrated approach was used to develop the conceptual framework for this research study. A combination of the Marketing Management perspective and Relationship Marketing perspective were used to identify the marketing practices of the ICT firms in India and to understand the influence of these practices on Customer Satisfaction and Firm Performance. A brief note of the two different perspectives of marketing is discussed below.

Marketing Management Perspective

The Marketing Management school of thought evolved in the late 1950s and the 1960s was characterized by a decision-making approach to manage the marketing functions with an extended focus on customers. Drucker (1954) characterised marketing as a decision-making activity directed at satisfying customers at a profit by targeting a market and then making optimal decisions on the marketing mix or the 4ps. The focus of the firm is on managing the marketing mix decision variables– Product, Price, Promotion and Place (distribution) in order to attract customers. Segmentation and targeting, differentiation and positioning were also introduced in the marketing literature, during this period. Marketing Research also gained significance in marketing management practice as an instrument for aligning the firms' productive capabilities with the needs of the market place (Webster, 1992). Thus, the marketing management school formed a union between the "marketing concept" that firms exist to satisfy customer wants with the perspective of optimizing profit through the management of the marketing mix (Pels & Saren, 2009). The practices relating to the Marketing Management components lead to Customer Satisfaction resulting in higher firm performance (Slater, Hult & Olson, 2007). It is also acknowledged that application of strategic marketing management practices in high technology firms increased Customer Satisfaction (Mohr et al., 2010).

Relationship Marketing Theory

The services marketing discipline acquired a distinct position in the early 1970s, as more researchers began to emphasise the unique characteristics of the services (for example, see Shostack, 1977; Bessom & Jackson, 1975). Increasingly services became a part of the physical products and were mentioned as an important element of the augmented product dimension as noted by Kotler, Armstrong, Saunders and Wong (2000). Two major elements contributed to the development of the services marketing literature: firstly, services became an important source of corporate revenue and a major instrument of all economic activities. Secondly, service was introduced as a significant dimension of product differentiation and also as an important basis of competitive advantage (Constantinides, 2006). The advent of the services marketing perspective raised questions about the relevance and application of the traditional marketing management perspective to services marketing. The primary concern of such researchers was that that the marketing-mix approach did not include the modelling and the managing of the relationships between the service provider and the customers (Möller & Hallinen, 2000). The emphasis on the importance of the development and the maintenance of buyer-seller relationships led to the emergence of relationship marketing.

Also, since early 1980's there has been a significant increase of interest in theory, research and practice focusing on the buyer-seller relationships in marketing (Dwyer, Schurr & Oh, 1987; Lewin & Johnston, 1997). During these decades companies competing in both consumer and industrial markets sought the help of their suppliers to support them to achieve stronger competitive advantage by supplying them with higher quality products, improved services, and efficient distribution systems. Thus, they began to embrace co-operative buyer-seller relationships. Accordingly, the parties involved in the exchange attained and settled for lower total costs by working together to ensure efficient management of inventories, to share risks and to eliminate unnecessary tasks and procedures (Lewin & Johnston, 1997). These "discrete" market relationships were progressively displaced by closer, long-term relationships between the buyers and the sellers. (Lewin & Johnston, 1997).

The term "Relationship marketing" was first alluded to by Thomas in 1976 (cited by Harker & Egan, 2006). This term was explicitly used by Berry (1983) in the context of services marketing. Relationship marketing is described as attracting, maintaining and enhancing customer relationships. Servicing existing customers and selling to them is viewed to be just as important to long-term marketing success as acquiring new customers (Berry, 2002).

Although research identifies numerous factors associated with relationship marketing constructs the factors that were most cited are trust, commitment and communication. These three factors are consistently identified as significant for relationship marketing practice to be successful. Trust is recognised as the central component in all relational exchanges (Dwyer, Schurr & Oh, 1987; Lewin & Johnston, 1997). Trust exists when one party in the exchange process has confidence in an exchange partner's reliability and integrity. Also Dwyer et al. (1987) argue that trust provides a basis for future collaborations, which results in long term relationships among the partner firms. It is proposed that trust is the extent to which the customer believes that the vendor has intentions and motives beneficial to the customer and is concerned with creating positive outcomes for the customer

Commitment is the other major component of relational exchanges (Anderson & Weitz, 1992; Moorman, Zaltman & Deshpande, 1992). It is defined by Moorman, Zaltman and Deshpande, (1992) "as an enduring desire to maintain a valued relationship" (p. 316). Studies propose that relationship commitment is the crux of all successful working relationships and is also commended as an essential ingredient in successful long term relationships. It is posited that commitment increases with the ability of the exchange partners providing positive outcomes to one another in their relationship.

Communication is also an important aspect of successful relationships and a major antecedent to trust and commitment (Anderson & Narus, 1984; Mohr, Fisher & Nevin, 1996). Anderson and Narus describe communication as "formal and informal sharing of meaningful and timely information between firms' (1990, p.44). Empirical research from literature suggests that communication increases the level of trust between firms (Anderson & Narus, 1984; Anderson & Weitz, 1992). Along with the partners' ability to align their expectations and perceptions communication also helps build trust among partners by providing a mechanism that could be used to resolve conflicts (Arnett & Badrinarayanan, 2005).

Social Media

In the recent years, the radical technological advancements have a profound impact on the marketing practices that are adopted by firms (Ramaswamy & Namakumari, 2012). Developments in marketing are closely intertwined with the technological developments in the information and communication sector. Brady, Saren and Tzokas (2002) argued that marketing is context dependent and when one of the contextual element like the technological environment changes, it has a significant impact on the nature and scope of the marketing discipline. Hence the developments in technology were expected to have a radical impact on how marketing is being practiced in firms.

Among the various internet-based technologies, social media has dramatically influenced businesses and industries. Social connectivity through this online platform has become a key to marketing in firms (Geho & Dangelo, 2012). Firms have adapted themselves to harness this web technology and have adopted strategic approaches to use this online tool for the benefit of the firm.

Social media includes a variety of online information sharing platforms covering all social networking sites (for example, Facebook, LinkedIn and Myspace), creativity work-sharing sites (for example, YouTube and Flickr), collaborative websites such as Wikipedia and microblogging sites (for example, Twitter) (Mangold & Faulds, 2009). These platforms have revolutionised the ways firms relate to market place thus creating a new world of possibilities in all management practices in firms (Aral, Dellarocas & Godes, 2013; Schultz, Schwepker & Good, 2012).

In literature, there are numerous definitions for social media. In a broader sense, social media has been defined as the digital content and the network based interactions which are developed and maintained by and between people (Cohen, 2011). Two primary themes of social media use are highlighted in literature. They are digital content creation and network-based interactions. Many authors see the technologies relating to social media as a paradigm shift that have facilitated a culture of participation through users interacting and collectively creating and sharing knowledge over the internet (for e.g. Benson & Morgan, 2015; Vuori, 2012; Schneckenberg, 2009).

Being present in these online platforms provides significant benefits for firms. They acquire privileged access to customers, discover customer needs early and get increased customer referrals which results in generating revenue. It also provides close proximity to customers which helps to coordinate value co-creation and to deliver superior value through customer relationships, especially in the business-to-business market place (Agnihotri, Kothandaraman, kashyap & Singh, 2012; Vargo & Lusch, 2011; Plouffe & Barclay, 2007). Marketers are increasingly aware of the potential use of this online platform is becoming and have embraced the ability of these tools to assist in marketing practices in firms (Andzulis, Panagopoulos & Rapp, 2012). In this research, all those aspects of social media that are increasingly recognised to provide potential value to the firms in the business context are included in the study.

A steady increase in references in literature about the potential use of social media for marketing purposes in firms signals that social media is becoming a mainstream marketing strategy of the practitioners in firms. Agnihotri, Kothandaraman, Kashyap and Singh (2012) conceded that a practical understanding of how social media is deployed in firms for maximum benefits is still in its infancy, despite a large body of emerging literature in social media marketing. It has also been indicated that social media practioners seek best practices for contexts in which it is widely applicable.

According to Brennan and Croft (2012) and Naude and Holland (2004) the most successful marketing organisations in this era will be those that make the most effective use of information technology tools in developing their marketing strategy. As discussed, the latest tool to emerge that has a huge impact on the marketing practices of firms is social media. Hence social media was integrated into the theoretical framework along with the Marketing Management and the Relationship Marketing perspectives.

Social media not only facilitates firms to interact with their customers directly but also helps the firms to listen to what their customers say about them and their products and services, thereby enhancing the relationship between them. Because social media helps to know the pulse of the customer and deepens the relationship with customers, it is proposed in this study that it would influence customer satisfaction.

Market Research

Market research is posited as the heart of any marketing program in business-to-business markets (Zimmerman & Blythe, 2013). It includes the set of processes that are employed to obtain information about customer needs and market conditions (Vorhies, Harker & Rao, 1999). It is often used in firms for forecasting, developing trends, finding market potential and competitor analysis. Research related to product attributes and product acceptance also comes under the scope of market research in firms. Malhotra (2012) defined market research as "the systematic and objective identification, collection, analysis, dissemination and use of information that is undertaken to improve decision making related to identifying and solving problems in marketing" (p.5).

Market research is widely recognised as a major source of information for marketing decision making, as it serves as the link between the customers and the marketer (Hart & Diamantopoulos, 1993). It provides information that is necessary to identify and define marketing opportunities and problems and helps to develop, evaluate and refine marketing actions so that they can be made more effective (Malhotra, 2010). In high tech markets market research is consistently used to gather information from the marketplace, to incorporate customer needs into the product development and for the marketing process (Mohr et al., 2012).

In regards to market research it is necessary to understand: 1) whether any market research activity was conducted by the firms, 2) how market research information was generated by these firms and 3) what type of information was sought after by the ICT firms. Hart and Diamantopoulos (1993) suggested that primarily, it must be established as to whether market research is done by firms internally, by an in-house department and/or externally, through specialist agencies or external contractors. Relevant information can be collected by firms either by meeting customers formally or gathering the needed information through informal networks (Vorhies, Harker & Rao, 1999). Market research databases that are published online by large firms can also be sources of information (Brooksbank, 1991).

Market research is identified as a quality marketing practice in firms. It helps to identify customer needs. As firms meet these needs, the level of customer satisfaction increases, providing firms with the competitive advantage which is vital for their operations (Kuratko, Goodale & Hornsby 2001). Firms that lead in identifying customer needs have a superior understanding of the factors that affects customer purchase decisions and have strong marketing capability (Dutta, Narasimhan & Rajiv, 1999). These firms achieve better targeting and positioning of its products and services relative to the competitor's.

Customer Satisfaction

According to Gupta and Zeithaml (2006) customer satisfaction is defined essentially as the consumer's judgement that a product or service meets or fall short of expectations. Firms seek to improve and increase customer satisfaction, as satisfied customers ultimately lead to financial benefits to the firms who serve them (Ranaweera & Prabhu, 2003).

There is significant evidence in the marketing literature that customer satisfaction is an important driver of a firm's profitability. For example, Rust, Moorman, and Dickson (2002) report a positive impact of customer satisfaction on financial performance, such as return on investment and return on assets. A study on the personal computers industry by Smith and Wright (2004) suggests that the firm's ability to satisfy its customers provides a sustainable competitive advantage that allows higher average prices, higher sales growth and higher return on assets. Customer satisfaction is also recognised as one of the market assets that can be leveraged to produce superior financial performance (Clark, 1999).

In response to the competitive market place managers seek to improve organisational effectiveness by identifying organisational metrics which contribute to long term success (Sui-Hua, 2007). Sui-Hua contend that organisations are touting for continuous improvement strategies to stay ahead of the competition. In order to drive continuous improvement researchers are placing more importance on measuring organisational performance from the customer's perspective. A growing number of organisations are using customer satisfaction measures in developing, monitoring and evaluating product and service offerings (Anderson, Fornell & Lehmann, 1994). This is because the firm's ability to satisfy customers provides a sustainable competitive advantage which is necessary to operate in today's competitive global environment (Smith & Wright, 2004).

Customer satisfaction is a more fundamental indicator of firm's performance due to its link to behavioural and economic consequences that are beneficial to the firm. According to Gupta and Zeithaml (2006) customer satisfaction is expected to lead to repurchase behaviour (behavioural consequence), which translates into increased sales and profits (economic consequence). Also, customer satisfaction is the central element in the marketing exchange process (Martin-Consuegra, 2007). The marketing concept starts with a well-defined market, focuses on customer needs, coordinates all the activities that affect customers, and produces profit by satisfying customers (Kotler & Keller, 2009). In this study, Customer Satisfaction is measured from the firms' perspective (Hung & Wong, 2007).

METHODOLOGY

This section discusses the research design, data collection and sampling methods employed in this research. Sub-sections which describe the questionnaire design, sampling design, instrumentation and survey implementation are included in the discussion.

Exploratory research design was used in this research to obtain insights into the different marketing practices of the ICT firms in the Indian context. To achieve this, survey method of data collection was used for the study (Malhotra, 2010; McDaniel & Gates, 2010). The choice of the suitable survey method depends on the context of the specific research and the advantages of the chosen method over the other options. This study includes ICT firms and so the sample population has access to the internet. Hence web survey method was adopted for the study as it facilitates speedy data collection, geographical flexibility, less cost and there is less interviewer interference (Zikmund & Babin, 2012).

The sampling frame for this research comes from the list of registered online panel members of a reputed market research agency who provided the data collection services for this research. Managers were used as proxies for firms and the managers in all the 2983 firms were invited to participate in an online survey. A number of these ICT firms have offices in multiple locations in the country. In order to avoid duplication of data from the same company, respondents were required to specify the name of their firm. Only 187 respondents had provided this information yielding a response rate of 6.3%. Hence only these were considered in the data analysis. MacCallum, Widaman, Zhang and Hong (1999) and Tabachnick and Fidell (2013) indicated that a sample size in the range of 100-200 is acceptable with well determined factors. The sample used for the current study is 187, and is within this guideline.

A formal, well-structured questionnaire was used to obtain specific information. Structured questions were used in the questionnaire. Fixed alternative questions were used because it was easier for the respondents to answer and it enabled comparability of answers, facilitated coding, tabulation and interpretation of data (McDaniel & Gates, 2010; Hair, Black, Babin, Anderson & Tatham, 2006). To minimize the risk of comprehension and misinterpretation problems, definitions of key question concepts were made available to the web survey respondents (Peytchev, Conrad, Couper & Tourangeau, 2010). This helped the researcher to communicate the intended meaning of the key concepts in the questionnaire to the survey respondents, thereby increasing the accuracy of the responses. All key concepts were clearly defined in the questionnaire to improve the accuracy of the survey results.

In the web survey questionnaire, all the items for a construct were presented in the same page. This facilitated easy referencing to the definitions of the construct and to effectively lead the respondents through, to complete the questionnaire. All the questions and the definitions for the constructs were highlighted. A "progress bar" to indicate the percentage completion of the questionnaire was included in each page of the questionnaire. The "back button" option was added to assist respondents, if they want to go back and change the answers. The respondents were required to access a uniform resource locator (URL) to take the survey. Because of the save and continue option in the questionnaire, they also had the possibility of completing the survey at their convenience within the stipulated time frame of two weeks.

Likert scales were used in this study to evaluate the items. Accordingly a series of statements that expressed either a favourable or an unfavourable attitude were employed to assess the concept under study. The respondents were asked to indicate their level of disagreement or agreement with each statement. The anchor points were, 1=strongly disagree and 7 = strongly agree with 4 being the neutral point. Even though the assumption of equal intervals between the anchor points in Likert scales are debated in literature, the averages derived from these scales are found to be meaningful, thus rendering this type of scale closer to interval scale than to ordinal scale measurement (Meyers, Gamst & Guarino, 2013). Also multivariate analysis techniques like regression analysis are robust to deviations from equivalency of intervals between scale units and are not overly susceptible to relaxing interval data requirement. All the constructs were measured with a number of items and therefore a multi-item scale was used in this study. Using different items to measure the same concept provides a more accurate cumulative measure than single-item estimates. The respondents were asked to select from a limited number of ordered categories for each of the statements that measured the various constructs. A review of relevant literature and a series of informal discussions with the academic staff and experts in ICT firms guided the development of the survey instrument of this study.

The ten items identified for the relationship marketing construct were specifically aimed at measuring the different dimensions of relationships that exist between the exchange partners in the given context. In the literature four major dimensions of relationship marketing are identified - trust, commitment, communication and customer relationship orientation in firms. The scale items that were adapted to measure Relationship Marketing practices are —

RM1: In our organisation, retaining customers is considered to be a top priority (Jayachandran, Sharma, Kaufman & Raman, 2005);

RM2: In our organisation, customer relationships are considered to be a valuable asset (Jayachandran et al., 2005);

RM3: Our senior management emphasizes the importance of customer relationships (Jayachandran et al., 2005);

RM4: In our organisation, employees receive incentives based on customer satisfaction measures (Jayachandran et al., 2005);
RM5: We can rely on our firm to keep the promises that it makes to the customers (Lawson-Body, Willoughby & Logossah, 2010);
RM6: In our relationship with customers, our firm can be trusted at all times (Lawson-Body et al., 2010);
RM7: Our firm rewards employees who do their very best to solve customer problems (Lawson-Body et al., 2010);
RM8: We fulfil all obligations and promises we make to customers (Negi & Ketema, 2010);
RM9: We nmake significant investments (in terms of time and resources) in building relationship with our customers (Palmatier, Gopalakrishna & Houston, 2006); and
RM10: We are committed to establishing long term relationship with our customers (Sin, Yau, Chow, Lee & Lau, 2005).

Respondents were asked to indicate how market research information was gathered in their firm and what kinds of information were obtained. The following seven items were used to assess the Market Research practices of the ICT firms in India:

MR1: In our firm, we do a lot of in-house marketing research (Hart & Diamantopoulos, 1993; Jaworski & Kohli, 1993);
MR2: In our firm, we use external contractors to do market research for us (Hart & Diamantopoulos, 1993; Jaworski & Kohli, 1993);
MR3: In our firm, we meet our customers formally to find out their future requirements (Vorhies et al., 1999);
MR4: In our firm, we use the marketing research database that is published online by large firms (Vorhies et al., 1999);
MR5: In our firm, we collect relevant industry information through informal networks (Vorhies et al., 1999);
MR6: In our firm, we gather data to understand the market perception of our new products and services (Hart & Diamantopoulos, 1993); and
MR7: In our firm, we gather data regarding the customer acceptance of our products and services (Hart & Diamantopoulos, 1993).

The scale items for Social Media were drawn from literature and were not from previously established or published scales. All the eleven items captured the potential purposes of the use of social media by the ICT firms in India. The items are:

SM1: Managers in our firm actively participate in professional social networks (like Linked In) (Smith, 2009);
SM2: Our firm actively searches for market opportunities in user generated blogs in online communities (Smith, 2009; Moen, Madsen & Aspelund, 2008);
SM3: our firm constantly monitors social network sites for reviews of our products and services (Fisher, 2009; Moen, Endresen & Gavlen, 2003);
SM4: In our firm, we constantly check online networks to know about competitor's products and services (Moen, Madsen, & Aspelund, 2008);

SM5: We encourage our customers to participate in live and interactive discussion forums in our website (Moen et al., 2008; Deans, Gray, Ibbotson, Osborne & Knightbridge, 2003);
SM6: Our firm has increased efficiency in developing products due to online customer interaction at various stages of product development (Fisher, 2009; Moen et al., 2008; Deans et al., 2003);
SM7: Our constant interaction with customers through online networks has improved our customer relations (Moen et al., 2008; Deans et al., 2003);
SM8: There is a reduction in online customer support because of the information we provide through our online discussion forums (Fisher, 2009; Deans et al., 2003);
SM9: We use our online networks to explain our products/services to customers (Deans et al., 2003);
SM10: We use our online networks to facilitate endorsement of our product/services by customers (Pfeiffer & Zinnbauer, 2010); and
SM11: Our engagement in the online social networks help build our firm's reputation (Pfeiffer & Zinnbauer, 2010; Fisher, 2009; Moen et al., 2003).

In this study Customer Satisfaction was measured from the firm's perspective. The items include both the firm's assessment of Customer Satisfaction and the practices that they use to enhance Customer Satisfaction. The nine items are:

CS1: We get more clients/business through positive word of mouth from our existing customers (Szymanski & Henard, 2001);
CS2: Our customers frequently return for additional business to our firm (Makarem, Mudambi & Podoshen, 2009);
CS3: All departments are responsive to, and are integrated in serving customers (Hung & Wong, 2007);
CS4: We deliver the offering in the time frame that the customer desires or needs (Boyd, 2002);
CS5: We respond to customer complaints and suggestions without delay (Hung & Wong, 2007);
CS6: We have a system of conflict resolution that is fair to the customer and to us (Boyd, 2002);
CS7: Our firm responds quickly to changing customer requirements (Hung & Wong, 2007);
CS8: Our firm obtains feedback from our customers through formal review meetings (Makarem et al., 2007); and
CS9: We often rely on informal networks to assess the satisfaction of our customers with our products and services (Makarem et al., 2007).

Once the questionnaire was developed, it was pre-tested with a small group of respondents as suggested by Zikmund and Babin (2007). This facilitated pre-testing the questionnaire for clarity of questions, relevance and completeness which improved the face validity of the survey questionnaire. Further modifications to the questionnaire content, format, wording and response alternatives were

made based on the results of the pretest. Also, every effort was undertaken to develop the final questionnaire more respondent friendly.

The authors employed Exploratory Factor Analysis (EFA) and Multiple Regression analysis to test the proposed conceptual model. However, only the results pertaining to the marketing practices relating to Social Media, Relationship Marketing and Market Research are presented in this paper, since it brings out the nexus between these constructs.

RESULTS

EFA was used in this study to identify the underlying structure among the independent variables (IVs) in the analysis and to reduce their number to include only the most parsimonious sets of variables in the subsequent multiple regression analysis (Hair, Black, Babin & Anderson,2010). A significant score of .904 for the KMO measure of sampling adequacy and a Chi-square value of 5135.122 (significant at .000) rendered the data suitable for EFA. As recommended by de Winter and Dodou, (2012) principal axis factoring with oblique rotation (promax) was employed in this research study.

Eigen values were used to determine the number of factors to be extracted. Items with factor loadings less than .30 were deleted from the analysis. Single item factors were also excluded from the analysis from the standpoint of parsimony (Lawson-Body, Willoughby & Logossah, 2010). Items with squared multiple correlations less than .4 were excluded from the analysis (Anna & Osbourne, 2005). EFA resulted in a final instrument of 43 items representing 10 distinct factors. These 10 factors explained 72.36% of the variance. The tables below (Table 1, Table 2 and Table 3 present the EFA results for the three factors of interest, viz, Relationship Marketing practices, Market Research practices and Social Media practices, together with the squared multiple correlations (communalities) and the Cronbach's Alpha (coefficient of reliability).

Factor 1, 'Relationship Marketing Practices' explained 39% of the total variance and consisted of 10 items with factor loadings ranging from .513 to .821. It is interesting to note from the above table that some of the items that were used to assess the Social Media practices (SM5, SM6 & SM7) loaded under this factor. It appears therefore, that social media is effectively used by the ICT firms in India to improve relationship with customers by constant interaction with customers through online networks (SM7), to encourage customers to participate in live and interactive discussion forums (SM5) and to increase efficiency in developing products due to online customer interaction at various stages of product

Table 1. Factor 1: relationship marketing practices

Items	Factor Loadings	SMC*
RM10: We are committed to establish long term relationship with our customers	.821	.764
RM2: In our organization, customer relationships are considered to be a valuable asset	.750	.779
RM8: We fulfill all obligations and promises we make with customers.	.692	.689
SM7: Our constant interaction with customers through online networks has improved our customer relations.	.666	.635
SM5: We encourage our customers to participate in live and interactive discussion forums in our website.	.656	.642
RM5: We can rely on our firm to keep the promises that it makes to the customers	.646	.692
RM3: Our senior management emphasizes the importance of customer relationships	.633	.609
SM6: Our firm has increased efficiency in developing products due to online customer interaction at various stages of product development.	.602	.610
RM6: In our relationship with customers, our firm can be trusted at all times	.587	.685
RM9: We make significant investments (in terms of time and resources) in building relationship with our customers	.513	.638

*Squared Multiple Correlations; Cronbach's α: .920.

development (SM7). The results show that social media practices are prevalent in the ICT firms in India and are efficiently used by these firms to build relationships through effective communication.

Table 2 includes the four items that describe the Market Research practices that loaded under this factor. Once again it can be seen that the ICT firms tend to use social media for market research purposes. Along with using external contractors for market research, firms are found to use social media to know about the reviews of their firm's products and services (SM3) and to know about competitor's products and services (SM4). Also market opportunities are actively searched for in user generated blogs in online communities (SM2). Hence this factor is assigned the name 'Market Research Practices'.

Three items that pertain to Social Media loaded on to the third factor. These items explain the purposes of using social media by the ICT firms, for reasons other than for relationship marketing and marketing research. Social media is found to be used by the firms to facilitate endorsement of the firm's products (SM10), to explain the products and services to customers (SM9), and services by customers and to build firm's reputation (SM11).

As the next step, the summated scales for these three factors, viz, Relationship Marketing practices, Market Research practices and Social Media practices were computed. As recommended by Hair, Black, Babin & Anderson (2010), these summated scales were formed by combining the individual variables loading into a factor to compute the composite measure. The composite measure for Customer Satisfaction practices was also computed. These composite measures represent the new composite latent variables that were used in the subsequent regression analysis. The results of the regression analysis are presented below

A standard multiple regression was performed using the composite measures of the latent variables. The Dependent Variable – Customer Satisfaction was regressed against the Independent Variables (IVs) - Relationship Marketing practices, Market research practices and Social Media practices. Regression results presented here follow the pattern adopted by Tabachnick and Fidell (2013). The analysis yielded

Table 2. Factor 2: market research practices

Items	Factor Loadings	SMC*
SM3: Our firm constantly monitors social network sites for reviews of our products and services.	.793	.662
SM2: Our firm actively searches for market opportunities in user generated blogs in online communities.	.644	.656
MR2: Use external contractors to do market research for us	.513	.515
SM4: In our firm, we constantly check online networks to know about competitor's products and services.	.387	.545

*Squared Multiple Correlations; Cronbach's α: .806.

Table 3. Factor 3: social media practices

Items	Factor Loadings	SMC*
SM10: We use our online networks to facilitate endorsement of our product/services by customers	.813	.728
SM9: We use our online networks to explain our products/services to customers.	.666	.629
SM11: Our engagement in the online social networks helps build our firm's reputation.	.566	.660

*Squared Multiple Correlations; Cronbach's α: .825.

a statistically significant result. R (the multiple correlation coefficient) for regression was significantly different from zero, $F(3,183) = 96.228$, $p<.001$. The adjusted value of $R^2 = .606$ indicated that approximately 61% of the variability in Customer Satisfaction is influenced by the IVs chosen for this analysis. Relationship Marketing practices has the highest β value of .547 indicating that it has a strong positive influence on Customer Satisfaction. This is also supported by a highly significant t-value ($t = 8.483$, $p = .000$). Social Media practices has the next highest influence on Customer Satisfaction with $\beta = .185$, $t = 3.134$ and $p = .002$. This is followed by Market Research practices with $\beta = .155$; $t = 2.572$ and $p = .011$. The influence of Social Media and Market Research are also significant at $p < .01$.

FINDINGS AND IMPLICATIONS

Empirical evidence supports the emergence of Social Media as a unique and distinct marketing practice. Besides Social Media is also used by these firms for Relationship Marketing and Market Research purposes. Further, this study clearly indicates that the three marketing practices, viz, Relationship Marketing practices, Social Media practices and Market Research practices significantly influences Customer Satisfaction in these firms. Customer Satisfaction is widely accepted in literature as one of the major outcomes of all marketing activities. However, most of the empirical research supporting this proposition was conducted in the context of other countries and other industries. The current research extends the existing body of knowledge to include the ICT firms in the Indian context by providing incremental evidence in understanding how these three marketing practices enhances Customer Satisfaction in these firms.

The findings pertaining to the individual constructs are discussed below.

Relationship Marketing Practices

The three important elements of Relationship Marketing - trust, commitment and communication between the exchange partners were assessed in this research together with the customer relationship orientation in these firms. All three elements emerged as components of Relationship Marketing practices. Existing Relationship Marketing literature points out that retaining existing customer is more profitable, especially in the B2B sector. Hence managers and practitioners must put their efforts on being customer relationship orientated and to build trust and commitment with their customers through constant and consistent communication.

The importance of communicating and interacting with business-to-business customers to develop and maintain relationships through the use of Social Media is established in this research. Relationship Marketing literature posits communication as an integral element to enhance and maintain relationships with customers, especially in B2B firms. This research empirically establishes Social Media as an integral part of the firms' Relationship Marketing strategy. Managers need to use Social Media effectively to build and maintain relationships with customers. This can be accomplished through constant communication and interaction with customers.

Market Research Practices

The EFA results show that three items pertaining to Social Media loaded on to Market Research practices. The items clearly indicate the use of social media for market research purposes by the ICT firms in India. Firms use social media: to know about the reviews of their firm's products and services; to know about competitor's products and services, and to actively search for market

opportunities in user generated blogs in online communities. It is evident that the information available through Social Media is used by the ICT firms for market research purposes

Social networking capabilities enable firms to generate market knowledge which facilitates firms to develop and deploy information (Heirati, O'Cass & Ngo, 2013). The use of Social Media is a cost effective means to reach a wider audience in the market. Further an online presence creates and enhances product and/or brand awareness and builds brand reputation. Social Media needs to be leveraged for Market Research purposes by the ICT firms in India. Social Media tools need to be strategically used by practicing managers of these ICT firms to enhance their market research practices and to complement the objectives of strategic marketing in these firms.

Social Media Practices

The ICT firms in India employ distinctive Social Media practices. Social media is found to be used by the firms to facilitate endorsement of the firm's products, to explain the products and services to customers, and services by customers and to build firm's reputation. Managers of the ICT firms in India should diligently seek to establish these practices in their firms.

This research makes a distinct contribution to Social Media literature. It addresses the gap in literature by providing an understanding of the actual use of Social Media for commercial purposes by the B2B firms in the ICT sector in India. It provides empirical evidence to support that Social Media is effectively utilised for marketing purposes in these firms. Social Media technologies have been found to support other marketing practices such as Relationship Marketing and Market Research.

Practitioners need to encourage their firms to engage diligently in Social Media given the findings that it supports marketing practices in firms. Firms in this sector should leverage Social Media to facilitate Relationship Marketing and Market Research practices. Social Media practices were found to significantly influence Customer Satisfaction in the ICT firms in India. Therefore marketing practitioners should increasingly advocate the use of Social Media technologies to improve Customer Satisfaction in their firms. In this digital era the unparalleled speed of information diffusion through Social Media undoubtedly improves and enhances the success of firms that take advantage of Social Media technologies. Hence it would be advisable for managers in ICT firms to prioritise and use various Social Media platforms along with other Strategic Marketing Practices to enhance and increase Customer Satisfaction.

CONCLUSION

The results of EFA show that each construct was well defined by multiple indicator variables. This is further confirmed by the measures of reliability with Cronbach's α ranging from .806 to .902. The contribution of this study to theory development emerges from the valid operationalisation of Social Media as a construct that has hitherto not been considered. Social Media has emerged as a distinct and unique marketing practice in itself in B2B marketing. There is also evidence to support the use of Social Media for Relationship Marketing and Market Research purposes by the ICT firms in India. The nexus between Social Media, Relationship Marketing and Market Research can be clearly seen by the loading of items pertaining to Social Media in Relationship Marketing and Market Research. Finally all three latent variables have a significant positive influence on Customer Satisfaction. The present study draws its conclusions from the empirical testing of data from the ICT sector in India, which contributes significantly to the economic growth in India. In order to bring in Social Media into mainstream theory it will be necessary to undertake this research in other countries. We welcome researchers to undertake similar studies in other cultural and economic contexts.

REFERENCES

Agnihotri, R., Kothandaraman, P., Kashyap, R., & Singh, R. (2012). Bringing "Social" into Sales: The Impact of Salespeople's Social Media Use on Service Behaviors and Value Creation. *Journal of Personal Selling & Sales Management*, *32*(3), 333–348. doi:10.2753/PSS0885-3134320304

Anderson, E., & Weitz, B. (1992). The Use of Pledges to build and Sustain Commitment in Distribution Channels. *JMR, Journal of Marketing Research*, *29*(1), 18–34. doi:10.2307/3172490

Anderson, E. W., Fornell, C., & Lehmann, D. R. (1994). Customer Satisfaction, Market Share, and Profitability: Findings from Sweden. *Journal of Marketing*, *58*(3), 53–66. doi:10.2307/1252310

Anderson, J. C., & Narus, J. A. (1984). A Model of the Distributor's Perspective of Distributor- Manufacturer Working Relationships. *Journal of Marketing*, *48*(4), 62–74. doi:10.2307/1251511

Andzulis, J. M., Panagopoulos, N. G., & Rapp, A. (2012). A Review of Social Media and Implications for the Sales Process. *Journal of Personal Selling & Sales Management*, *32*(3), 305–316. doi:10.2753/PSS0885-3134320302

Aral, S., Dellarocas, C., & Godes, D. (2013). Social Media and Business Transformation: A Framework for Research. *Information Systems Research*, *24*(1), 3–14. doi:10.1287/isre.1120.0470

Arnett, D. B., & Badrinarayanan, V. (2005). Enhancing Customer-Needs--Driven CRM Strategies: Core Selling Teams, Knowledge Management Competence, and Relationship Marketing Competence. *Journal of Personal Selling & Sales Management*, *25*(4), 329–343.

Benson, V., & Morgan, S. (2015). *Implications of Social Media Use in Personal and Professional Settings*. Hershey, PA: IGI Global; doi:10.4018/978-1-4666-7401-1

Berry, L. L. (1983). *Relationship Marketing*. Paper presented at the Emerging Perspectives on Services Marketing, Chicago, IL.

Berry, L. L. (1995). Relationship Marketing of Services-Growing Interest, Emerging Perspectives. *Journal of the Academy of Marketing Science*, *23*(4), 236–245. doi:10.1177/009207039502300402

Bessom, R. M., & Jackson, D. W. Jr. (1975). Service Retailing: A Strategic Marketing Approach. *Journal of Retailing*, *51*(2), 75–85.

Boyd, A. (2002). The Goals, Questions, Indicators, Measures (GQIM) Approach to the Measurement of Customer Satisfaction with e-commerce Web sites. *Aslib Proceedings*, *54*(3), 177–187. doi:10.1108/00012530210441728

Brady, M., Saren, M., & Tzokas, N. (2002). *Integrating information technology into marketing practice - the IT reality of contemporary marketing practice*. Academic Press.

Brennan, R., & Croft, R. (2012). The use of social media in B2B marketing and branding: An Exploratory Study. *Journal of Customer Behaviour*, *11*(2), 101–115. doi:10.1362/147539212X13420906144552

Brooksbank, R. W. (1991). Successful Marketing Practice: A Literature Review and Checklist for Marketing Practitioners. *European Journal of Marketing*, *25*(5), 20–29. doi:10.1108/EUM0000000000619

Clark, B. H. (1999). Marketing Performance Measures: History and Interrelationships. *Journal of Marketing Management*, *15*(8), 711–732. doi:10.1362/026725799784772594

Cohen, C. (2011). Interconnections: Brand Reputation And Free Online Monitoring Tools. *Franchising World*, *43*(7), 18.

Constantinides, E. (2006). The Marketing Mix Revisited: Towards the 21st Century Marketing. *Journal of Marketing Management*, *22*(3/4), 407–438. doi:10.1362/026725706776861190

Coviello, N. E., & Brodie, R. J. (2001). Contemporary marketing practices of consumer and business- to-business firms: How different are they? *Journal of Business and Industrial Marketing*, *16*(5), 382–400. doi:10.1108/08858620110400223

Deans, K. R., Gray, B. J., Ibbotson, P., Osborne, P., & Knightbridge, K. (2003). Web Marketing Practices of Service Providers. *Service Industries Journal*, *23*(3), 82–102. doi:10.1080/714005119

Drucker, P. F. (1954). *The Practice of Management*. New York: Harper and Row.

Dutta, S., Narasimhan, O., & Rajiv, S. (1999). *Success in High-Technology Markets: Is Marketing Capability Critical?*. Academic Press.

Dwyer, F. R., Schurr, P. H., & Oh, S. (1987). Developing Buyer-Seller Relationships. *Journal of Marketing*, *51*(2), 11–27. doi:10.2307/1251126

Fisher, T. (2009). ROI in Social Media: A look at the Arguments. *Journal of Database Marketing & Customer Strategy Management*, *16*(3), 189–195. doi:10.1057/dbm.2009.16

Fruchter, G. E., & Sigué, S. P. (2005). Transactions vs. Relationships: What Should the Company Emphasize? *Journal of Service Research*, *8*(1), 18–36. doi:10.1177/1094670505276629

Geho, P. R., & Dangelo, J. (2012). The Evolution of Social Media as a Marketing Tool for Entrepreneurs. *Entrepreneurial Executive*, *17*, 61–68.

Gupta, S., & Zeithaml, V. (2006). Customer Metrics and Their Impact on Financial Performance. *Marketing Science*, *25*(6), 718–739. doi:10.1287/mksc.1060.0221

Hair, J. F., Black, W. C., Babin, B. J., & Anderson, R. E. (2010). *Multivariate data analysis* (7th ed.). Upper Saddle River, NJ: Pearson Prentice Hall.

Harker, M. J., & Egan, J. (2006). The Past, Present and Future of Relationship Marketing. *Journal of Marketing Management*, *22*(1/2), 215–242. doi:10.1362/026725706776022326

Hart, S., & Diamantopoulos, A. (1993). Marketing Research Activity and Company Performance: Evidence from Manufacturing Industry. *European Journal of Marketing*, *27*(5), 54–72. doi:10.1108/03090569310039723

Heirati, N., O'Cass, A., & Ngo, L. V. (2013). The Contingent Value of Marketing and Social Networking Capabilities in Firm Performance. *Journal of Strategic Marketing*, *21*(1), 82–98. doi:10.1080/0965254X.2012.742130

Hills, S. B., & Sarin, S. (2003). From Market Driven to Market Driving: An Alternate Paradigm for Marketing in High Technology Industries. *Journal of Marketing Theory and Practice*, *11*(3), 13–24. doi:10.1080/10696679.2003.11658498

Hung, H., & Wong, Y. H. (2007). Organisational Perception of Customer Satisfaction: Theories and Evidence. *Service Industries Journal*, *27*(4), 495–507. doi:10.1080/02642060701346540

Jaworski, B. J., & Kohli, A. K. (1993). Market Orientation - Antecedents and Consequences. *Journal of Marketing*, *57*(3), 53–70.

Jayachandran, S., Sharma, S., Kaufman, P., & Raman, P. (2005). The role of relational information processes and technology use in customer relationship management. *Journal of Marketing*, *69*(4), 177–192.

Kotler, P., Armstrong, G., Saunders, J., & Wong, V. (2000). *Principles of Marketing* (2d Russian Ed). Moscow: Williams Publishing House.

Kotler, P., & Keller, K. L. (2007). *Marketing Management*. Praha: Grada Publishing.

Kuratko, D. F., Goodale, J. C., & Hornsby, J. S. (2001). Quality Practices for a Competitive Advantage in Smaller Firms. *Journal of Small Business Management*, *39*(4), 293–311.

Lawson-Body, A., Willoughby, L., & Logossah, K. (2010). Developing an Instrument for Measuring E-Commerce Dimensions. *Journal of Computer Information Systems*, *51*(2), 2–13.

Lehtinen, U. (2011). Combining Mix and Relationship marketing. *Marketing Review*, *11*(2), 117–136.

Lewin, J. E., & Johnston, W. J. (1997). Relationship Marketing Theory in Practice: A Case Study. *Journal of Business Research*, *39*(1), 23–31.

Makarem, S. C., Mudambi, S. M., & Podoshen, J. S. (2009). Satisfaction in Technology-enabled Service Encounters. *Journal of Services Marketing*, *23*(2-3), 134–143. doi:10.1108/08876040910955143

Malhotra, N. K. (2010). *Marketing Research: An Applied Orientation* (6th ed.). Upper Saddle River, NJ: Pearson Education. doi:10.1108/S1548-6435(2010)6

Mangold, W. G., & Faulds, D. J. (2009). Social Media: The New Hybrid Element of the Promotion Mix. *Business Horizons*, *52*(4), 357–365. doi:10.1016/j.bushor.2009.03.002

McDaniel, C. D., & Gates, R. H. (2010). *Marketing Research Essentials* (7th ed.). Hoboken, NJ: John Wiley & Sons.

Meyers, L. S., Gamst, G., & Guarino, A. J. (n.d.). Applied multivariate Research: Design and Interpretation (2nd ed.). Thousand Oaks, CA: SAGE Publications.

Ministry of Statistics & Programme Implementation. India. (2011). *Value Addition and Employment Generation in the ICT Sector in India.* Retrieved from http://mospi.nic.in/mospi_new/upload/val_add_ict_21june11.pdf

Moen, O., Endresen, I., & Gavlen, M. (2003). Executive insights: Use of the Internet in International Marketing: A Case Study of Small Computer Software Firms. *Journal of International Marketing*, *11*(4), 129–149. doi:10.1509/jimk.11.4.129.20146

Moen, O., Madsen, T. K., & Aspelund, A. (2008). The Importance of the Internet in International Business-to-Business Markets. *International Marketing Review*, *25*(5), 487–503. doi:10.1108/02651330810904053

Mohr, J., Slater, S., & Sengupta, S. (2010). *Marketing of High-Technology Products and Innovations* (3rd ed.). Upper Saddle River, Prentice Hall.

Mohr, J. J., Fisher, R. J., & Nevin, J. R. (1996). Collaborative communication in interfirm relationships: Moderating effects of integration and. *Journal of Marketing*, *60*(3), 103. doi:10.2307/1251844

Möller, K., & Halinen, A. (2000). Relationship Marketing Theory: Its Roots and Direction. *Journal of Marketing Management*, *16*(1-3), 29–54. doi:10.1362/026725700785100460

Moorman, C., Zaltman, G., & Deshpande, R. (1992). Relationships Between Providers and Users of Market Research: The Dynamics of Trust Within and Between Organizations. *JMR, Journal of Marketing Research*, *29*(3), 314–328. doi:10.2307/3172742

National Association of Software and Services Companies. India. (2013). *Indian IT-BPO Industry.* Retrieved from http://www.nasscom.in/impact-indias-growth

Naudé, P., & Holland, C. P. (2004). The Role of Information and Communications Technology in Transforming Marketing Theory and Practice. *Journal of Business and Industrial Marketing*, *19*(3), 165–166. doi:10.1108/08858620410531298

Negi, R., & Ketema, E. (2010). Relationship Marketing and Customer Loyalty: The Ethiopian Mobile Communications Perspective. *International Journal of Mobile Marketing*, *5*(1), 113–124.

Palmatier, R. W., Gopalakrishna, S., & Houston, M. B. (2006). Returns on Business-To-Business Relationship Marketing Investments: Strategies For Leveraging Profits. *Marketing Science*, *25*(5), 477–493. doi:10.1287/mksc.1060.0209

Pels, J., Möller, K., & Saren, M. (2009). Do we really understand business marketing? Getting beyond the RM and BM matrimony. *Journal of Business and Industrial Marketing*, *24*(5/6), 322–336. doi:10.1108/08858620910966219

Peytchev, A., Conrad, F. G., Couper, M. P., & Tourangeau, R. (2010). Increasing Respondents' Use of Definitions in Web Surveys. *Journal of Official Statistics*, *26*(4), 633–650. PMID:23411499

Pfeiffer, M., & Zinnbauer, M. (2010). Can Old Media Enhance New Media?: How Traditional Advertising Pays off for an Online Social Network. *Journal of Advertising Research*, *50*(1), 42–49. doi:10.2501/S0021849910091166

Plouffe, C. R., & Barclay, D. W. (2007). Salesperson navigation: The Intraorganizational Dimension of the Sales Role. *Industrial Marketing Management*, *36*(4), 528–539. doi:10.1016/j.indmarman.2006.02.002

Ramaswamy, & Namakumari. (2013). *Marketing Management: Indian Context* (5th ed.). McGraw Hill Education (India) Private Limited.

Ranaweera, C., & Prabhu, J. (2003). On the relative importance of Customer Satisfaction and Trust as Determinants of Customer Retention and Positive Word Of Mouth. *Journal of Targeting. Measurement & Analysis for Marketing*, *12*(1), 82–90. doi:10.1057/palgrave.jt.5740100

Rust, R. T., Moorman, C., & Dickson, P. R. (2002). Getting Return on Quality: Revenue Expansion, Cost Reduction, or Both? *Journal of Marketing*, *66*(4), 7–24. doi:10.1509/jmkg.66.4.7.18515

Sarin, S. (2012). My Years with B2B Marketing in India: Reflections and Learnings from a Journey of 40 years. *Journal of Business and Industrial Marketing*, *27*(3), 160–168. doi:10.1108/08858621211207199

Schultz, R. J., Schwepker, C. H., & Good, D. J. (2012). An Exploratory Study of Social Media in Business-To-Business Selling: Salesperson Characteristics, Activities and Performance. *Marketing Management Journal*, *22*(2), 76–89.

Shostack, G. L. (1977). Breaking Free from Product Marketing. *Journal of Marketing*, *41*(2), 73–80.

Sin, L. Y. M., Tse, A. C. B., Yau, O. H. M., Chow, R. P. M., Lee, J. S. Y., & Lau, L. B. Y. (2005). Relationship Marketing Orientation: Scale Development and Cross-Cultural Validation. *Journal of Business Research*, *58*(2), 185–194.

Slater, S. F., Hult, G. T. M., & Olson, E. M. (2007). On the Importance of Matching Strategic Behavior and Target Market Selection to Business Strategy in High-Tech Markets. *Journal of the Academy of Marketing Science*, *35*(1), 5–17. doi:10.1007/s11747-006-0002-4

Smith, R. E., & Wright, W. F. (2004). Determinants of Customer Loyalty and Financial Performance. *Journal of Management Accounting Research*, *16*(1), 183–205. doi:10.2308/jmar.2004.16.1.183

Smith, T. (2009). The social Media Revolution. *International Journal of Market Research*, *51*(4), 559–561. doi:10.2501/S1470785309200773

Sui-Hua, Y. (2007). An Empirical Investigation on the Economic Consequences of Customer Satisfaction. *Total Quality Management & Business Excellence*, *18*(5), 555–569. doi:10.1080/14783360701240493

Szymanski, D. M., & Henard, D. H. (2001). Customer Satisfaction: A Meta-analysis of the Empirical Evidence. *Journal of the Academy of Marketing Science*, *29*(1), 16–35. doi:10.1177/0092070301291002

Tabachnick, B. G., & Fidel, L. S. (2013). *Using Multivariate Statistics* (6th ed.). Boston: Pearson Education.

Traynor, K., & Traynor, S. (2004). A Comparison of Marketing Approaches used by High-tech Firms: 1985 versus 2001. *Industrial Marketing Management*, *33*(5), 457–461. doi:10.1016/j.indmarman.2003.08.013

Uslay, C., Malhotra, N. K., & Citrin, A. V. (2004). Unique Marketing Challenges at the Frontiers of Technology: An Integrated Perspective. *International Journal of Technology Management*, *28*(1), 8–30. doi:10.1504/IJTM.2004.005050

Vargo, S. L., & Lusch, R. F. (2004). Evolving to a New Dominant Logic for Marketing. *Journal of Marketing*, *68*(1), 1–17. doi:10.1509/jmkg.68.1.1.24036

Vorhies, D. W., Harker, M., & Rao, C. P. (1999). The Capabilities and Performance Advantages of Market-driven Firms. *European Journal of Marketing*, *33*(11/12), 1171–1202. doi:10.1108/03090569910292339

Vuori, M. (2012). Exploring Uses of Social Media in a Global Corporation. *Journal of Systems and Information Technology*, *14*(2), 155–170. doi:10.1108/13287261211232171

Webster, J. F. E. (1992). The Changing role of Marketing in the Corporation. *Journal of Marketing*, *56*(4), 1. doi:10.2307/1251983

Yadav, N., Swami, S., & Pal, P. (2006). High Technology Marketing: Conceptualization and Case Study. *Vikalpa: The Journal for Decision Makers*, *31*(2), 57–74.

Zikmund, W. G., & Babin, B. J. (2012). Marketing Research (10th ed.). South-Western/Cengage Learning.

Zikmund, W. G., Babin, B. J., Carr, J. C., & Griffin, M. (2010). *Business Research Methods*. South-Western Cengage Learning.

Zimmerman, A. S., & Blythe, J. (2013). *Business to business marketing management: a global perspective* (2nd ed.). New York: Routledge.

This research was previously published in Analyzing the Strategic Role of Social Networking in Firm Growth and Productivity edited by Vladlena Benson, Ronald Tuninga, and George Saridakis, pages 314-333, copyright year 2017 by Business Science Reference (an imprint of IGI Global).

Chapter 2
Using Social Media Marketing for Competitive Advantage

Amir Manzoor
Bahria University, Pakistan

ABSTRACT

Social media provides companies innovative ways to market their products and services to their customers. The social media tools, such as Facebook, provides new ways to reach customers. With increasing number of people being connected to social media, businesses of all types are targeting social media as a new platform to reach their customers and strengthen customer relationships. Still, many companies are unsure as to how they can use social media for their advantage. There is lack of resources and fear of failure that hold many companies back from using social media in their marketing campaigns. Companies need a set of guidelines to understand how they can develop long-term, successful marketing strategies that involve social media as a significant component. This chapter analyzes use of social media marketing to suggest some ways companies can use social media to generate value both for them and their customers. This chapter also discusses how companies can develop a social media marketing strategy.

INTRODUCTION

Social Media

Social networking is a generally new idea. As such, social media experts keep on debating a legitimate meaning of the term, and choosing a universally accepted definition may be unimaginable (Solis, 2009). However, definitions from a few social media experts may help provide a reasonable definition—one that precisely portrays the core motivation behind social media.

According to Safko and Brake (2009), social media "refers to activities, practices, and behaviors among communities of people who gather online to share information, knowledge, and opinions using conversational media" (p. 6). According to Weinberg (2009), social media "relates to the sharing of information, experiences, and perspectives throughout community-oriented websites" (p. 1). Comm (2009) suggests that social media is "content that has been created by its audience" (p. 3). The Universal

DOI: 10.4018/978-1-5225-5637-4.ch002

McCann report (2008) suggests social media as "online applications, platforms and media which aim to facilitate interaction, collaboration, and the sharing of content" (p. 10).

The previous definitions, though depict different aspects of social media, fails to identify the essence of social media. Zarrella (2010) provides a basic definition of social media by suggesting that social media consists of online technologies that facilitate the creation and distribution of content. This compact and straightforward definition establishes the framework to properly understand additional aspects of social media.

Categories of Social Media

Social media includes a vast array of online resources each having unique features that appeal different people. In this chapter, we shall discuss some of the most important categories of social media such as social networking, blogging, microblogging, social news, social bookmarking, and media sharing.

Social Networking Site

According to Weinberg (2009), social networking sites and social networks "are generic terms for sites that are used to connect users with similar backgrounds and interests" (p. 149). Most social networks provide the same essential features such as an individual profile, the ability to include friends, photographs, and various ways to collaborate with friends. In general, there exist two categories of social networking sites: popular sites or niche sites. Popular sites, such as Facebook, attract a broader set of audience and have millions of active users. LinkedIn is another example of a general purpose popular site that attracts all types of professionals. In contrast, niche social networking sites, such as Sharecipe, attracts people interested in cooking. The site provides its users with many recipes and cooking tips. For the Love of Film (fan.tcm.com) is another niche site that is a place for movie lovers to gather. ActiveRain is another niche site that brings together land experts.

Blog

According to (Zarrella 2010), a blog is "a kind of substance administration framework that makes it simple for anybody to distribute short articles called posts" (p. 9). Blogs have become very popular recently due to the fat that virtually anyone with Internet access can start a blog using a variety of freely available tools (Safko & Brake, 2009). Mainstream blogging platforms include WordPress (http://wordpress.org), Movable Type (http://www.movabletype.com), and Google's Blogger (http://www.blogger.com). Some regular features of blogs include comments, which permits readers to leave remarks on various blog posts; the blogroll, a list of other suggested blogs; and Really Simple Syndication (RSS), an innovative technology that empowers users to effortlessly see summary of blog posts.

Microblog

A microblog is a kind of site in which posts have a restricted length. The essential example of a microblogging platform is Twitter, which restricts the length of every post to 140 characters. Numerous individuals mistakenly mention Twitter as a social networking site due to its similarities to prevalent social networking sites. Microblogging encourages concise discussions. Individuals consider microblogging valuable to share interesting web site links, make statements, and provide status updates (O'Reilly

& Milstein, 2009). Different examples of microblogging sites include Jaiku (http://www.jaiku.com), which is comparable to Twitter; and Yammer (http://www.yammer.com), an internal communication platform for enterprises.

Social News Site

On a social news site, users can submit and vote on content. It might be said, a social news website serves as a channel that filters compelling content from everyday content on the Web. When users discover content that interests them (for example, an article, feature, picture, and so forth.), they can submit the content to a social news site. In the event that the online community finds the content intriguing they will vote likewise and drive the content to a more visible place on the new website. At present, the most well known social news site is Digg (digg.com). Other famous social news sites are Reddit (reddit.com) and Mixx (mixx.com). These sites serve broad audience and cover extensive variety of subjects. There are numerous specialty social news sites, for example, Tip'd (tipd.com), which focuses on investment/finance and business, and Slashdot (slashdot.org), which focuses on science and innovation.

Social Bookmarking Site

A social bookmarking site is like a social news site. According to Zarrella (2010), for a social bookmarking site, "the value presented to users is focused on allowing them to collect and store interesting links they've found and may wish to revisit"(p. 103). Basically, users use web links or bookmarks to share organized content from the web. Voting on submitted bookmarks is used to determine the bookmarks which will be shown prominently on the bookmarking site. Social news sites and social bookmarking sites both focus on helping users find desired information. As such, individuals frequently confuse these two different types of sites. The most prevalent social bookmarking sites are Delicious (delicious.com) and StumbleUpon (stumbleupon.com). Diigo (diigo.com) is an specialty social bookmarking site which concentrates on collaboration and research.

Media-Sharing Site

A media-sharing site enables clients to upload video, images, podcasts and other forms of multimedia (Zarrella, 2010). This part of social media has is especially powerful through video-sharing sites, for example, YouTube (youtube.com). Photograph sharing sites, for example, Flickr (flickr.com), let users upload their own pictures and scan a large number of pictures that others have uploaded. Presentation-sharing sites, for example, SlideShare (slideshare.net), let users upload and share presentations. A typical feature of media-sharing sites is that a tag can be associated with a user's content. A tag is essentially a descriptive word that helps individuals find the content (Zarrella, 2010).

Significance of Social Media

To establish the impact and potential of social media, we can take example of the case of Iranian presidential elections of 2009. In June 2009, Iran was reeling from the political turmoil of a disputed presidential elections. Protestors had been pouring into the streets for a long time when a 26-year-old Iranian lady, Neda, chose to go to the anti-government rally in Tehran, the capital of Iran. Soon after touching base close to the scene of the rally, a shooter fired a shot that that struck in her heart. Neda died on the spot (Fathi, 2009).

The terrible story of Neda's sudden demise shortly went worldwide. More shockingly, the phenomenal coverage of her demise came not from professional journalists but individuals using social media. The publicity of this incident on social media was so extensive that traditional mainstream media eventually covered the story (Cashmore, 2009). The timeline of the events on social media made it possible to compile and report the events as they occurred (Parr, 2009).

The disruptive consequence of the Iranian election exhibited the extensive potential and impact of social media. In another case, the Australian Network Ten newsreader Natarsha Belling took to the airwaves to present the channel's current affair show Eyewitness News over the weekend, wearing a fetching 'phallic-shaped neckline' green jacket over her black top. Her act caused social media meltdown. It all started with Facebook user Ruben Haywood, and from there the comments just kept on coming. Social media was quick to respond after Facebook user Ruben Haywood posted a snap of the newsreader online – with some pointing out it was hard to 'unsee' Natarsha's top once you'd had a look. Within few days the show went on air, Natarsha Belling became the No. 1 trending Facebook topic and the post garnered more than 113,000 likes (Blidner, 2015).

By 2008, a very large number of Internet users were reading blogs, viewing multimedia content, and taking part in different types of social media (Universal McCann., 2008). In 2007, one in four online American adults visited social networking sites at least a month (Li & Bernoff, 2008). Facebook doubled its active users base to 400 million users by 2010 (Zuckerberg, 2010).

Social Media Marketing

Barefoot and Szabo (2010) offers a basic definition of social media marketing by saying that social media marketing is "using social media channels to promote your company and its products" (p. 13). An expanded definition provided by Weinberg (2009) describes social media marketing as "a process that empowers individuals to promote their websites, products, or services through online social channels and to communicate with and tap into a much larger community that may not have been available via traditional advertising channels" (p. 3). The focus of this definition on communication with the community is in line with Hunt (2009) who maintains that community marketing is synonymous with social media marketing.

The tremendous development of social media has numerous implications. One of these implications is the way social media transform business. Social media represents some genuine difficulties to organizations as clients and workers progressively rush to social media sites (Ross, 2009). Exceptionally compelling is the impact of social media on marketing. By 2014, social media marketing was expected to grow annually at a rate of 34%, outpacing all other forms of online marketing (VanBoskirk, 2009). The huge number of individuals utilizing social media sites provides one explanation behind this trend. Marketers now have a very large customer base. An alternate explanation is the users ability to engage in instant communication with other users. Unfortunately, for numerous organizations social media is still a mystery as they remain uncertain of how to integrate social media in their marketing efforts (Li & Bernoff, 2008).

Social media technologies continually change. However, the desire of companies to use social media for engaging in meaningful interactions with customers is yet a dream to come true for many companies. As such, the social media tools themselves could change but social media marketing principles would remain relevant for the time to come. One reason why many companies are reluctant to integrate social media in their marketing efforts is the examples of many failed social media marketing campaigns. These campaigns failed despite the availability of magnitude of resources and brought serious consequences for the companies. It is therefore crucial for companies to understand how they can develop a social media marketing campaign that will be successful in the long run and help companies create and capture value. The objective of this chapter is explore the social media marketing phenomenon and social media marketing principles. The chapter further explores ways companies can use to create and capture value using social media marketing and discuss how companies should formulate a social media marketing strategy.

CONSUMER AND BUSINESS ADOPTION OF SOCIAL MEDIA

There is a need to understand why consumers and businesses have enthusiastically adopted social media. Such an understanding would not only help to explain the social media phenomenon but also demonstrate the permanency of social media.

Reasons Behind Consumers Use of Social Media

The individual's desire to connect with other people and belong to a community is the most fundamental reason why people adopt social media. As Barefoot and Szabo (2010) notes "From [bulletin board systems] to chat rooms, forums, and blogs, human nature is at the heart of creating and building online communities" (p. 3). This reason applies to all forms of online communities. This trend is clearly demonstrated by the explosion of online communities. Barefoot and Szabo (2010) further notes that consumers now know the power social media has provided them to communicate, share, and collaborate with greater efficiency. The projects of open source web browser, such as Firefox, and open source operating systems, such as Ubuntu Linux, are developed and managed by online communities.

By relying on social networking to connect with loved ones, individuals build up an emotional and personal affection to social media. Chase (2009) notes that "If your experience with a social catalyst, be it either a brand or a website, is something that enhances your life or deepens your bonds with friends and associates, you will also become bonded with that social catalyst" (p. 285). Many a times, users don't understand their reliance on social media service until a blackout abruptly happens. As an interesting illustration, the US State Department asked Twitter and other online networking sites to put on hold their schedule maintenance in order avoid any downtime of these services during the crisis of Iranian presidential elections of 2009.

In this situation, getting information through the social media sites was the primary reason that forced US authorities to contact the social networking sites (Labott, 2009). Businesses must comprehend the idea that individuals appreciate utilizing social media fundamentally because its use satisfy their intrinsic desire to connect with other individuals. According to Powell (2009), the businesses bears the obligation of "comprehension that need, arranging it, and utilizing that code to better succeed in business" (p. 6).

An alternate explanation for the user acceptance of social media is the radical shift of power from the business to the customer. An indication of this critical shift was the dotcom bubble burst in late 2001. This dotcom bubble burst resulted in the emergence of Web 2.0. Basically, Web 2.0 technologies present interactive, dynamic, content as opposed to static content (Google, 2008). Earlier, users passively observed the Web; now they can actively contribute content to the Web through social media. Threadless (threadless.com), an online apparel store, figured out how to use the capability of online users to contribute content. The organization keeps up a flourishing online community of T-shirts designers. The members submit designs to Threadless, and other members vote in favor of their most favorite design. Threadless then takes the designs getting most votes and produces a limited quantity of these designs, offering T-shirts to the community that designed them. Members get involved by submitting shirt designs as well as by posting pictures, taking part in community, and writing slogans. Voting play a vital role in the community and members are encouraged to distinguish quality content from mundane content. The Threadless site serves as the nucleus for all these activities. The Threadless's methodology appears to have met expectations, particularly since it almost doubled its revenue and registered around half a minion users by 2009. (Hunt, 2009).

Media, used to be top-down, is another aspect of this power shift from business to consumer (Comm, 2009; Powell, 2009). Social media is making the media bottom-up and empowering media consumers to both create media and communicate with media creators (Szabo & Barefoot, 2010). Companies have historically relied on traditional media channels for their marketing efforts. According to Hunt (2009), these media channels present few potential problems such as too much advertising, lack of trust, and too many choices. The story of Thomas Hawke a blogger, is an illustration of this power shift into the hands of consumer. Thomas Hawk wrote a blog post about PriceRitePhoto when the company denied to ship him the camera he purchase if he didn't buy the accessories. His post sparked a firestorm of online criticism on PriceRitePhoto. The scale of criticism was so massive that traditional media giants, such as New York Times and Forbes, eventually covered this story. PriceRitePhoto went out of business shortly and all this happened because of the influence of just one blogger (Powell, 2009).

Organizations must comprehend that consumers are utilizing one another to discover what they need, when they need it, and how they need it. Li and Bernoff (2008) portray this phenomenon as the groundswell. A groundswell, according to Li and Bernoff (2008), is a "social trend in which people use technologies to get the things they need from each other, rather than from traditional institutions like corporations" (p. 9). Chase (2009) says, "the majority of our buying decisions have always been through word of mouth. However…thanks to the proliferation of online communities, our personal networks have gotten *bigger*, much bigger" (p. 36). The basic premise is that buyers are making purchase decisions in which friends recommendations have lot more weight than the product recommendations provided by the businesses.

Reasons Behind Businesses Use of Social Media

Business world now understand the intensity of social media use by the consumers. As a result, marketers have come up with a variety of reasons for engaging in social media marketing. Two reasons mentioned earlier are the large number of social media users and instant communication with the consumers. However, these two reasons need to be looked at great depth in order provide a more helpful explanation of social media phenomenon.

To start, more individuals are utilizing the Internet than ever before. BY 2009, there were more than 1.7 billion Internet users and this user base grew at a rate of 380% from year 2000 to 2009. People were spending more time than ever using Internet. According to Bloomberg (2009b), adult users were "spending an average of thirteen hours a week online" (p. 1). This was more than double the amount of time adult users spent in 2002. The influx of Internet users has sparked an exponential growth in social media users. As of 2009, there were about 625 million active users of social media. Out of these 625 millions users, 83% watched online videos, 71% visited a friend's page on a social networking site, and

63% crated a profile on social networking sites (Universal McCann., 2009). Forrester (2009) reported that "marketing budgets are following the innovation trail—social media spending in the US will grow from $716 million this year to more than $3.1 billion in 2014" (p. 1).

Marketing is about fulfilling people's needs. According to Weinberg (2009), 58% of individuals use Internet to address their problem and issues. Wikis and online repositories receive millions of visitors searching for answers. There exist an enormous opportunity to influence consumer purchase decisions. Take example of Home Depot, a US retailer of home improvement and construction products and services. Home Depot uses YouTube to share demonstrations of do-it-yourself home projects. The topics may include home improvement and energy efficiency. The Home Depot also make use of Twitter to deliver announcements and resolve customer queries. During the 2008 hurricane Gustav in USA, the Home Depot used Twitter to provide helpful safety information to the users (Weinberg, 2009).

Customers are already using Internet to engage in conversations about products, services, and brands. Participation in these conversations can be beneficial for companies (Zarrella, 2010). Active participation in these conversations can help companies attract customers and provide useful information to the customers (Hunt, 2009). Scott (2009) notes that "where organizations get into trouble is in failing to participate at all" (p. 121). Hewlett Packard (HP) made an intensive effort by hosting many executive blogs on industry-related topics. The objective of this effort was to stay in touch with its target customers. Using these blogs, HP was able to respond to customers through comments customers posted on these blogs. With these blogs, HP was able to build trust and encourage conversations with the customers by showing them that HP was willing to have conversation with them and listen to their concerns.

The financial barriers to social media marketing are not high and many social media tools are free even for businesses to use. Companies with limited budgets can run successful social media marketing campaigns. Blendtec, a manufacturer of blenders, used a $50 initial marketing budget to create a video series called 'Will it Blend?' The video series received millions of viewers in a short period of time (Weinberg, 2009).

CREATING AND CAPTURING VALUE WITH SOCIAL MEDIA

Companies use a variety of methods/techniques of creating and capturing value with social media. A wide variety of social media tools are available and companies can use them to reach their customers in many ways. Social media is like a large toolbox in which blogs, social networks, and social news sites are unique tools. These tools are most effective in different situations. It is important for marketers to learn the capabilities of each tool and when to use each tool. The practical experience of marketers is, therefore, very important for formulating a successful social media marketing campaign.

Principles of Social Media Marketing

Each social media marketing campaign is governed by certain principle. These principles relate to community, content, conversation, and transparency. Each principle is crucial in supporting the effectiveness of social media marketing. Social media cannot be truly social without conversations and without transparency these conversations cannot be constructive. Social media would not be a media if content is missing and this content cannot be relevant without a community (Perdue, 2010).

Community

A community should be the hub of company's social media marketing campaigns. This is important because social media marketing is about meaningful connections with groups of people and connecting with people having similar interests is important tool. According to Barefoot and Szabo (2010), "social media tools enable like- minded people—be they bird watchers, Québécois undertakers, or Vietnam veterans—to find each other. This is a key benefit of social media marketing" (p.7). Companies generally are more successful when they target specific online communities. Companies can either target existing communities or build a new online community around its products and services. To build a community, however, a core customer is important (Hunt, 2009). With increasing number of people publishing their preferences on social network sites, the markets served by the companies can become narrower. We can see the emergence of 'socialgraphics' i.e. the segmenting of people based on their memberships of groups, their preferences, their public wish lists, and the topics of their discussions with their friends and family.

Content

Social media are tools that facilitate the creation and distribution of content. When companies publish content using social media, they need to decide both the type and purpose of the content to be created. According to Safko and Brake (2009), there are four pillars of social media marketing strategies to engage in online communities. These four pillars are communication, collaboration, education, and entertainment (Perdue, 2010). Put it simply, content is the main element companies use to communicate with its customers, facilitate collaboration with customers, and educate/entertain the customers. A company also need to make significant efforts to develop creative content i.e. the type of content that attracts people and encourage them to share it with others (Scott, 2009). The 'Will it Blend' video series attracted a large number of people because it was based on providing people with information they needed in their daily lives. As Weinberg (2009) notes, "instead of making ads, think of making content" (p. 30).

Conversations

By nature, social media is interactive. A company can participate in online conversations and engage with online communities related to its products and services. This conversation and engagement is not meant to provide advertising and promotion but to provide information to the customers by answering questions, posting tips, or just make comments.

Transparency

According to principle of transparency, a company's participation in social media must be authentic. Weinberg (2009) notes that "when it comes to social media marketing, the rules of engagement are different. Altruism rules above all. Authentic online relationships can further your cause and help foster real relationships that can flourish offline" (p. 323). In its social media marketing, a company attempts for the ultimate transparency in all of its online interactions. Those companies who do not do so can end up distancing themselves from customer communities and lose their trust. In its every type or level of social media interaction, a company needs to keep focus on reaching out online communities, creating attractive content for the communities, participating in online conversations, and be transparent in all of its online interactions.

Techniques of Creating and Capturing Value Through Social Media

There are many techniques/methods marketers can use to develop profitable social media marketing campaigns. Not all methods result in direct sales but certainly do add value by providing indirect sales. All of these techniques/methods possess huge potential to have meaningful engagements with the customers.

Online Reputation Management

Online reputation management involves building a positive perception of a company's brands. It is achieved by interacting with customers and responding to negative perceptions about the company and its brands. Weinberg (2009) notes, "you can manage relationships, but you can't manage reputation" (p. 30). The online reputation management is important because the Internet has significantly enhanced people's ability to affect company's reputation. Scott (2009) notes that "the power of the Internet makes it easier for people to fall in love with you faster. But beware—it also makes it easier for them to fall out of love with you faster. It's a double-edged sword" (p. 11). Companies may adopt a passive approach to online reputation management. In passive approach, company simply ignores what people say about it online. However, this approach is not recommended. Companies can use social media to actively participate in online conversations related to company or its brands. Beal (2008) suggests that to monitor their reputation, companies should monitor their name, brands, company's executives, slogans, competitions, intellectual property etc. Monitoring so many things can be tricky. According to Brogan and Smith (2009), reputation management is "is a burgeoning field right now because the process of checking everything is so daunting that large companies often need entire smaller companies to deal with it" (p. 172). Many online tracking tools are available. Some are free while other are fee-based. Companies need to select those tools that best meet their needs. Some examples of free tools include Google Alerts and Technorati (a blog search engine). Some examples of commercial fe-based tools include Radian6, Trackur, and Buzzlogic. All these tools provide detailed dashboards that can aggregate real-time information and help in quick understanding of people perception of the company (Schawbel, 2009).

A good example of the power of effective online reputation management is a serious ethical failure at Network Solutions. Network Solutions is an Internet domain registrar company. In this case, Network Solutions bought those domain names that users searched on its website. Network Solutions did so with a hope that users would be forced to use its services to acquire those domain names. Such unethical behavior resulted in a very negative reputation and Network Solutions, in an attempt to regain customer trust, started to listen to, participate in, and add value to online communities of its customers. These efforts proved successful and during next six months company witnessed a significant decrease in negative comments and increase in positive comments about the company (Weinberg, 2009).

Brand Awareness

Social media marketing can also be used to increase brand awareness. Brand awareness may not necessarily result in immediate sales but can help increase future customer recall of company's products and services to make a purchase (Weinberg, 2009). According to Immediate Future (2008), active participation across social media sites positively impacts a company's brand awareness. Today, customers are expecting an established social media presence of their favorite companies. At the same times, customers are also continually coming across many companies on social media sites. According to Weinberg (2009), one of the major focuses of brand awareness is to simultaneously target multiple audience across various social media sites on which users spend time. However, social media presence of a company should be relevant to each online community they participate in. Companies should also increase their social media presence beyond popular social media sites to cover relevant niche social media sites (Weinberg, 2009). In social media, identity theft is now common place where someone claims a user name that should belong to someone else such as a company. KnowEm (knowem.com) is a service companies can use to prevent social media identity theft. Companies can also target influencers in online communities they participate in to increase brand awareness. Companies should be careful while deliberately transforming these influencers into their brand ambassadors. These brand ambassadors would be individuals passionate about the products and services of the company. The company can use these brand ambassadors to indirectly access potential customers in online communities they enter (Safko & Brake, 2009). Burger King, a famous fast food chain in USA, released a Facebook App called 'Whopper Sacrifice' in 2009. Users of the app were promised a free whopper if they remove ten of their Facebook friends from their account. As a result, users removed about 234,000 of their friends. Eventually, Facebook removed this app but by that time the app was already mentioned by more than 13,000 blogs around the globe. This example illustrates an unusual attempt by a company to increase its brand awareness using social media (Weinberg, 2009).

Social Capital Management

Social media marketing can increase a company's social capital. According to Powell (2009), social capital is "both the network of relationships you have and the access to resources provided therein" (p. 77). In other words, a company builds social capital by developing and maintaining relationships with its customers. One strong reason why companies should focus on increasing social capital and not the financial capital is that social capital can provide indirect and vital increase in financial capital (Powell, 2009). According to Hunt (2009), there are four important reasons for companies to focus on increasing social capital. First, meaningful customer relationships can develop into long-term customer loyalty. Second, the companies can spread word of mouth by having customers talk favorably about their products and services and company itself. Third, building relationships with customers online is relatively inexpensive. Fourth, the companies cannot afford to lag behind in increasing social capital while all their competitors are in the race to increase social capital. If a company lags behind in increasing social capital it can be difficult for the company to build customer loyalty because customers may already have established their loyalties. According to Hunt (2009), one way to raise social capital in an increasingly uncertain online world is "about recognizing how to find your community and potential community and interact on a level that will benefit everyone" (p. 282). Companies need to look genuine in their interaction with the online communities and provide compelling content. A US-based wine store 'Shopper's discount liquors' started a Wine Library TV video podcast. In less than three years since its start, the TV series became so successful that the wine store developed into a multi-million dollar global business and increased its employee base from ten to one hundred employees. This excellent example of raising social capital was made possible by listening to store customers and having conversations with them using social media (i.e. video podcasts). Viewers found the podcast series very interesting and within one year of its launch 15,000 downloads were made and each podcast received around hundred comments (Hunt, 2009).

Viral Marketing

Companies can also take advantage of viral marketing power of the social media. Viral marketing on social media sites revolves around the content created by companies. According to Powell (2009), whether or not that content will go viral depends on if "the content resonate with people enough that they want to share it with their friends?" (p. 93). To start a viral marketing campaign, a company first needs to identify those aspects of a product or service that resonate with people. According to Scott (2009), "If you can boil your message down to just its syrupy goodness, you can achieve lift—the irresistible force of millions of customers selling your product for you" (p. 43). The concept behind marketing is that companies use its own customers to promote its products and services. As Scott (2009) notes "potential customers are eager to hear from people like them, and they pay close attention to how others have been helped by a product or service" (p. 149). After determining a core concept of a product or service, a company must use some creative content to demonstrate that concept in an appealing way. Use of videos is very common for delivering content (Scott, 2009).

Approva is an enterprise software solution provider that deals in solutions to identify and prevent fraud. Approva started a company blog named 'Audit Trail' and posted a video celebrating fifth birthday of the Sarbanes-Oxley Act. The humorous video was enjoyed by many who understood the complexities of the act and were able to relate to the humor presented in the video. This video soon went viral and spread by many bloggers. During the first six months of the posting of video, Approva blog received many more visitors than the visitors to the Approva's official website (Scott, 2009).

Customer and Media Communication

Social media can be used by businesses to communicate with their customers as well as media. Use of social media for communication provides companies opportunities of personal communication with customers. Twitter is a popular microblogging tool to reach out customers in a personal way. According to O'Reilly and Milstein (2009), "the biggest opportunity Twitter gives you is the chance to show the personality and humanness behind your organization" (p. 197). Tools like Twitter can be used by companies to communicate with customers they previously communicated using traditional media. Companies can also open communication with bloggers because of their influence in the online world. Scott (2009) also recognizes importance of bloggers by noting that "bloggers are likely already talking about *your* organization, too. Why not cultivate a relationship with them?" (p. 98). Companies should remember that social media is not simply a platform to make product announcements but can also be used to participate in online conversations with the customers. Companies can also use social media to report problems or inform customers of resolution of issues (O'Reilly & Milstein, 2009). Companies can maintain close and direct communication with their loyal customers who can help promote the company and get the attention of mainstream media (Scott, 2009; Perdue, 2010). In 2007, Dell (dell.com) implemented IdeaStorm (ideastorm.com) as a platform to gather ideas from users. The IdeaStorm was implemented after a disaster that involved poor product performance. Dell used IdeaStorm to communicate with users and get their support. By 2008, IdeaStorm received over 7,000 ideas from users (Li & Bernoff, 2008).

Other Techniques/Methods

There are other techniques/methods available to create and capture value using social media. According to Hunt (2009), social media can be a good platform to market research because social media encourages a "continuous flow of information to and from your customers" (p.1). With increasing number of businesses establish social media presence, companies can use social media to monitor their competitors and review their social media tactics. Companies can also use social media to drive traffic to their websites and improve search engine visibility (Weinberg, 2009). Companies can use social media to get deeper insight of their target markets, discover new distribution channels, generate leads, find joint venture opportunities, and improve their customer service (Carleton, 2009; Perdue, 2010). Since social media is still at its nascent stages, companies should continue to look for innovative ways to use social media in their marketing efforts.

PRACTICAL/MANAGERIAL IMPLICATIONS AND RECOMMENDATIONS

Without a strategy to use social media marketing, an understanding of the social media phenomenon and ways of creating and capturing value with social media marketing would be of little value for companies. This strategy is needed in order provide coherence among different methods of creating and capturing value using social media marketing. Some preliminary considerations are also important before a company develop and use a social media marketing strategy.

First, companies should understand that social media marketing requires a significant investment of time. It would be unwise for a company to start with handful social media resources and hope to realize enormous returns. Second, social media marketing is complementary to traditional marketing. Social media marketing doesn't require companies to stop using traditional marketing methods (Barefoot & Szabo, 2010). There may be few exceptions where companies may be able to successfully rely on social media marketing alone. The marketer's goal should be to discover the best marketing mix-one that involves both traditional and social media marketing. Third, use of social media marketing may not get approval from all stakeholders of the company. This is because it empowers consumers. Therefore, a company must address any internal concerns about the use of social media first. In addition, many managers may see potential problems with employees using social media because they feel that employee could leak secret information through social media (Scott, 2009). Companies may opt to develop social computing guidelines for employees similar to the ones developed by IBM (IBM, 2011).

Developing the Strategy

Keeping these preliminary consideration in mind, companies should proceed to develop their social media marketing strategy. According to Li and Bernoff (2008), "technology is shifting so quickly—chasing it is like trying to jump on a speeding merry-go-round" (p. 67). Li and Burnoff (2008), further suggests that companies should focus their social media marketing strategy around four aspects: people, objectives, strategy, and technology.

People

It is important for companies to know who their customers are, what kinds of social media they are already using, and what they are most willing to do online using social media. Companies may still succeed without this knowledge but as Li and Burnoff (2008) points out that "you might also build a whole social networking strategy only to find that your customers are more likely to write reviews than join social networks" (p. 67) this customer knowledge would be necessary to build a strong foundation of social media marketing and gain competitive advantage.

Objectives

A company should have clearly defined objectives for its social media marketing campaign. These objectives could relate to the social media marketing methods used to create and capture value. However, one general objective of company's social media marketing campaign should be expanding the company's web presence (Barefoot & Szabo, 2010). In addition, companies may have specific short-term and long-term objectives (Zarrella, 2010).

Strategy

According to Li and Bernoff (2008), the strategy aspect of social media marketing answers the question "How do you want relationships with your customers to change?" (p. 68). The ultimate objective of company's social media marketing is to develop and sustain customer relationships. Li and Bernoff (2008) identified five basic strategies companies could use in their social media marketing campaigns. These include *listening* (i.e. knowing what the customers saying about your products and services), *talking* (i.e. using social media to communicate with customers), *energizing* (i.e. encouraging customers to become your), *supporting* (i.e. helping customers), and *embracing* (i.e. gain customer support to achieve company's goals).

Technology

This aspect refers to company's selection and use of technology to achieve its goals and reach customers. Companies should consider current and popular technologies. Companies must not forget that selection of technology or tool (such as Facebook) should not be solely based on familiarity with the technology or tool. According to Weinberg (2009), use of a single technology or tool in a social media marketing campaign with not produce optimal results. Companies should analyze a variety of available social media tools and choose the ones that will optimize company's performance in social media marketing campaign. According to Weinberg (2009), regardless of the type of tools used, a company should clearly identify itself on all social media sites that it participates in. Doing so, companies can promote their transparency in the online community and establish their identity and aims.

Integration of Tools

Since companies can have different combinations of customer, objectives, strategies, and technologies, their individual approaches to social media marketing can be different as well. However, a focus of social media marketing campaign of a company should be to integrate company's message across all social media platforms in order achieve coherence and success in their strategy. According to Zarrella (2010), "users of one kind of social media are likely to be users of other types; it makes sense to invite those who interact with you on Twitter to join your page on Facebook" (p. 199). Similarly, companies should operate a company blog that would become the central platform for their social media marketing campaign. This is because blogs can integrate with many types of social media platforms.

Social Media Marketing Metrics

To measure the success of the social media marketing campaigns, companies generally are eager to measure the ROI (Return on Investment) of the campaign. Companies should also consider using metrics in their social media marketing campaigns. A metric is a unit of measurement. Metrics can be classified into two broad categories: on-site metrics and off-site metrics. According to Zarrella (2010), "on- site metrics measure activity that takes place directly on your site, whereas off-site metrics measure activity that happens on other sites where you and your customers interact" (p. 207). Within these two categories, there can be many other metrics that can be used to measure the ROI of social media marketing campaign. According to Barefoot and Szabo (2010), companies should measure eight metrics namely visitors, incoming links, social network activity, conversations and contributions, references in the blogosphere, views on social media sites, RSS subscribers, and social bookmarking. For visitors, companies should know both number and types of visitors in order identify visitors that engage with company and its products. Analytic software, such as Google Analytics, can be used in this regard. More incoming links help establish a company's authority and expertise and stir up talks about up company. Social network activity can be measured by counting Friends on social media (such as Facebook friends or Twitter followers). Conversations and contributions can be measured by tracking the frequency and quality of customer interaction with the company. This interaction can occur through comments the customer post on company's blog, Facebook pages, Twitter followings etc. The purpose of this measurement is to ensure company's meaningful conversations with the target customer population. To keep track of references in the blogosphere, companies can measure the frequency with which other blogs provide reference to company's blog. It also involves analyzing whether these references actually result in customers conversations about company. Knowing both the number of conversations as well as the quality of conversations can be very helpful. To keep track of customer views on social media sites, companies can measure number of hits on the content posted to social media sites. For example, a company could measure how many times a video posted by the company on YouTube was watched by users or measure the number of Facebook likes on a post made by the company. To keep track of RSS subscribers, companies can use tools (such as FeedBurner) to count subscribers, track subscribers origin, and learn their preferences. With this information, a company can be in a better position to understand what people are looking for and deliver the appropriate content. Using social book marking sites, companies can measure the number of links about the company that users post to various social media sites. A low number may indicate a lack of customer interest in content posted by company.

FUTURE RESEARCH AREAS

There exist some additional social media categories that worth mentioning. These sites include rating and review sites, forums, and virtual worlds. Further research in these areas may yield helpful thoughts for social media marketing. However, organizations may get good advantage from concentrating on these forms of social media due to their tremendous prominence.

CONCLUSION

The phenomenon of social media is rapidly affecting all aspects of business and marketing is no exception. It is clear that a good grasp on meaning and capabilities of social media provide companies a decisive advantage in their marketing capabilities. Individuals are spending more time on the Internet and progressively spending their online time utilizing social networking. As communities of people establish and the force of social networking builds relentlessly, organizations must consider their active involvement. The companies who avoid doing as such or just defer progressing onto the social networking scene—are prone to pay a high cost. While a huge number of Internet users are rushing to social networking sites, organizations all over still struggle to discover methods for contacting them so as to grow their customer base. There exist variety of techniques to create and capture value using social media in marketing. However, building an effective social media marketing strategy based on four aspects i.e. people, objectives, strategy, and technology, is essential to gain the competitive advantage through social media marketing. Individuals change and technology changes but standards don't. Organizations who base their social media marketing campaigns on these four aspects can gain stability and progress in a business environment that is increasingly complex and challenging. This chapter contributes to the existing knowledge base of social media marketing and provide a practical approach to using social media marketing to better serve customers and gain competitive advantage.

REFERENCES

Barney, J. B. (1999). How a firm's capabilities affect boundary decisions. *Sloan Management Review*, *40*(3), 137–145.

Beal, A. (2008, April 10). 12 Reputations Every Company Should Monitor Online | Marketing Pilgrim. Retrieved from http://www.marketingpilgrim.com/2008/04/online-reputation-monitoring-campaign.html

Bharadwaj, A., El Sawy, O. A., Pavlou, P. A., & Venkatraman, N. (2013). Digital business strategy: Toward a next generation of insights. *Management Information Systems Quarterly*, *37*(2), 471–482.

Blidner, R. (2015, March 17). Australian news anchor goes viral with penis-shaped neckline. Retrieved from http://www.nydailynews.com/entertainment/tv/australian-news-anchor-viral-penis-shaped-neckline-article-1.2151861

Brogan, C., & Smith, J. (2010). *Trust Agents: Using the Web to Build Influence, Improve Reputation, and Earn Trust* (2nd ed.). Hoboken, N.J: Wiley.

Carleton, D. (2009, June 25). The Top 20 Business Reasons To Use Social Media Marketing. Retrieved from http://www.examiner.com/article/the-top-20-business-reasons-to-use-social-media-marketing

Cashmore, P. (2009, June 21). Neda: YouTube Video Too Distressing to Ignore. *Mashable.com.* Retrieved from http://mashable.com/2009/06/21/neda/

Cashmore, P. (n.d.). Neda: YouTube Video Too Distressing to Ignore. Retrieved July 29, 2014, from http://mashable.com/2009/06/21/neda/

The World Factbook. (2014). Central Intelligence Agency (CIA). Retrieved from https://www.cia.gov/library/publications/the-world-factbook/rankorder/2119rank.html

Chan, J. M., & Yazdanifard, R. (2014). How social media marketing can influence the profitability of an online company from a consumer point of view. *Journal of Research in Marketing*, *2*(2), 157–160. doi:10.17722/jorm.v2i2.55

Comm, J. (2010). *Twitter Power 2.0: How to Dominate Your Market One Tweet at a Time* (2nd ed.). Hoboken, NJ: Wiley.

Correia, A. (2013). Social Information: Gaining Competitive and Business Advantage Using Social Media Tools. *Online Information Review*, *37*(1), 151–152. doi:10.1108/14684521311311720

Fathi, N. (2009, June 23). In a Death Seen Around the World, a Symbol of Iranian Protests. *The New York Times*. Retrieved from http://www.nytimes.com/2009/06/23/world/middleeast/23neda.html

Fathi, N. (2009, June 23). In a Death Seen Around the World, a Symbol of Iranian Protests. *The New York Times*. Retrieved from http://www.nytimes.com/2009/06/23/world/middleeast/23neda.html

Forrester Marketing Forum: Social Technologies Allow For More. (2009a, April 24). *Bloomberg*. Retrieved from http://www.bloomberg.com/apps/news?pid=newsarchive&sid=ax9.YmVPxwMg

Forrester Research. (2009). Forrester marketing forum: Social technologies allow for more accessible innovation in down economy. Retrieved from http://www.forrester.com/ER/Press/Release/0,1769,1274,00.html

The top brands in social media report 2008. (2008). *Immediate Future*. Retrieved from http://www.immediatefuture.co.uk/the-top-brands-in-social-media-report-2008

Web 2.0: The new face of the Web. (2008). Google. Retrieved from www.google.com/a/help/intl/en/security/pdf/web_2_new_face.pdf

He, W., Zha, S., & Li, L. (2013). Social media competitive analysis and text mining: A case study in the pizza industry. *International Journal of Information Management*, *33*(3), 464–472. doi:10.1016/j.ijinfomgt.2013.01.001

Hunt, T. (2009). *The whuffie factor: Using the power of social networks to build your business*. Crown Pub.

Hunt, T. (2010a). *The power of social networking: Using the whuffie factor to build your business.* Crown Business.

Hunt, T. (2010b). *The Power of Social Networking: Using the Whuffie Factor to Build Your Business* (1st ed.). New York: Crown Business.

IBM Social Computing Guidelines [CT402]. (2011, August 3). *IBM.* Retrieved from http://www.ibm.com/blogs/zz/en/guidelines.html

IBM Social Computing Guidelines [CT402]. (2011, August 3). IBM. Retrieved from http://www.ibm.com/blogs/zz/en/guidelines.html

Internet Users Now Spending an Average of 13 Hours a Week Online. (2009b, December 23). *Bloomberg.* Retrieved from http://www.bloomberg.com/apps/news?pid=newsarchive&sid=aQrAoB85tDvs

Internet Users Spend an Average of 13 Hours a Week Online, Survey Finds. (2009). eWeek. Retrieved from http://www.eweek.com/c/a/Midmarket/Internet-Users-Spend-an-Average-of-13-Hours-a-Week-Online-Survey-Finds-485147

Internet Users Spend an Average of 13 Hours a Week Online, Survey Finds. (2009). eWeek. Retrieved from http://www.eweek.com/c/a/Midmarket/Internet-Users-Spend-an-Average-of-13-Hours-a-Week-Online-Survey-Finds-485147

Internet usage statistics: The Internet big picture. (2009). *Internet World Stats.* Retrieved from http://www.internetworldstats.com/stats.htm

Kogut, B. (1985). Designing global strategies: Comparative and competitive value added chains. *Sloan Management Review*, *26*(4).

Labott, E. (2009, June 16). State Department to Twitter: Keep Iranian tweets coming. Retrieved from http://ac360.blogs.cnn.com/2009/06/16/state-department-to-twitter-keep-iranian-tweets-coming/

Li, C. (2010). Groundswell. Winning in a world transformed by social technologies. *Strategic Direction, 26*(8).

Mangold, W. G., & Faulds, D. J. (2009). Social media: The new hybrid element of the promotion mix. *Business Horizons*, *52*(4), 357–365. doi:10.1016/j.bushor.2009.03.002

Michaelidou, N., Siamagka, N. T., & Christodoulides, G. (2011). Usage, barriers and measurement of social media marketing: An exploratory investigation of small and medium B2B brands. *Industrial Marketing Management*, *40*(7), 1153–1159. doi:10.1016/j.indmarman.2011.09.009

O'Reilly, T., & Milstein, S. (2009). *The twitter book.* O'Reilly Media, Inc.

Parr, B. (2009, June 21). #IranElection Crisis: A Social Media Timeline. *Mashable.com.* Retrieved from http://mashable.com/2009/06/21/iran-election-timeline/

Perdue, D. J. (2010). Social media marketing: Gaining a competitive advantage by reaching the masses (Paper 127). *Senior Honors Papers.*

Piskorski, M. J., Casciaro, T., & Kivel, M. (2013). Social Strategy: Why Social Media Platforms Work and How to Leverage them for Competitive Advantage. Princeton, NJ: Princeton University Press.

Powell, J. (2009). *33 Million people in the room: How to create, influence, and run a successful business with social networking*. Que Publishing.

Ross, J. (2009). A corporate guide for social media. Retrieved from http://www.forbes.com/2009/06/30/social-media-guidelines-intelligenttechnology-oreilly.html

Safko, L., & Brake, D. K. (2009). *The social media bible: Tactics, tools & strategies for business success*. Hoboken, NJ: John Wiley & Sons.

Schaupp, L. C., & Bélanger, F. (2014). The Value of Social Media for Small Businesses. *Journal of Information Systems*, *28*(1), 187–207. doi:10.2308/isys-50674

Schawbel, D. (2008, December 29). Top 10 Reputation Tracking Tools Worth Paying For. *Mashable.com*. Retrieved from http://mashable.com/2008/12/29/brand-reputation-monitoring-tools/

Scott, D. M. (2009). *World wide rave: Creating triggers that get millions of people to spread your ideas and share your stories*. Hoboken, NJ: John Wiley & Sons. doi:10.1002/9781118258286

Power to the people: Social media tracker wave 3. (2008). *Universal McCann*. Retrieved from http://www.universalmccann.com/Assets/UM%20Wave%203%20Final_20080505110444.pdf

Power to the people: Social media tracker wave 4. (2009). *Universal McCann*. Retrieved from http://universalmccann.bitecp.com/wave4/Wave4.pdf

VanBoskirk, S. (2009, July 7). Interactive marketing nears $55 billion; advertising overall delines. Retrieved from http://blogs.forrester.com/

Weinberg, T. (2009). The new community rules: Marketing on the social web. O'Reilly Sebastopol, CA.

Zarrella, D. (2010). *The social media marketing book*. O'Reilly Media, Inc.

Zuckerberg, M. (2009, April 8). 200 million strong. Retrieved from http://blog.facebook.com/blog.php?post=72353897130

Zuckerberg, M. (2010, February 4). Six years of making connections. Retrieved from http://blog.facebook.com/blog.php?post=287542162130

This research was previously published in Competitive Social Media Marketing Strategies edited by Wilson Ozuem and Gordon Bowen, pages 201-218, copyright year 2016 by Business Science Reference (an imprint of IGI Global).

Chapter 3
Social Networking Sites and Marketing Strategies

Ying Wu
University of Sussex, UK

Malcolm Stewart
University of Sussex, UK

Rebecca Liu
Lancaster University, UK

ABSTRACT

This chapter begins with an introduction to social networking. The opportunities and challenges of social network sites regarding marketing strategies are discussed and these provide a foundation for exploring viral marketing with regard to the development of online word-of-mouth activities on social networking sites. This chapter explores strategies for successful viral marketing and investigates strategic perspectives of social networking. We look into several types of social networking sites available for consumers to share and access information and experience such as Facebook and Twitter in the context of marketing strategy decision-making. The chapter concludes with an examination of the online marketing mix regarding social network marketing strategy development and a case study (Fiesta Movement Campaign) and methodology is also included to 'bridge the gap' between the academic theory in this chapter and an example showing how marketers in the industry have taken advantage of social networking sites to promote their business.

INTRODUCTION

Social networking sites have been big news for a while now. The popularity of social networking sites is increasing worldwide; marketers have been facing opportunities and challenges to develop strategies to apply this media as a channel to reach customers and potential customers alike. The success of a series of viral marketing campaigns has prompted a number of companies to engage in viral marketing on social networking websites such as Facebook and Twitter. Furthermore, nowadays few if any marketing

DOI: 10.4018/978-1-5225-5637-4.ch003

plans can be completed without a blending of the E-Marketing mix into the traditional mix to create an effective marketing strategy. The objectives of this chapter are:

- Evaluate the relevance of social networking sites to marketing.
- Identify the advantages and challenges of social networking sites to marketing.
- Identify the key differences between social networks marketing and traditional marketing.
- Identify the factors a company should consider for developing social networks marketing strategy.
- Relate viral marketing strategies to major social networking sites such as Facebook and Twitter.
- Apply marketing mix in the context of social networks marketing.
- Review Strategic Perspectives of Social Networking Sites.

BACKGROUND

A social networking site is a Web-based service for users to construct a public or private profile and to connect with other users for exchange of content and communication. Social network sites provide individuals platforms to construct a public or semi-public profile within a bounded system. People are able to connect with groups of other users whom they share a connection, and to view and visit their own list of virtual connections and those made by other individuals within the system. Social networking sites are significant because there is ongoing interaction between consumers and the community, and they facilitate low-cost communications that are asynchronous, interactive and instant

The first recognizable social network service website was launched in 1997, named SixDegrees.com. The name is based on the theory associated with actor Kevin Bacon that no person is separated by more than six degrees from another. SixDegrees.com allowed users to create profiles, list their Friends and, beginning in 1998, surf their Friends lists. In some form, each of these features existed before SixDegrees, for sure. For example, Profiles existed on most major dating sites and a lot of community sites. AIM and ICQ buddy lists supported lists of Friends, although those Friends were not visible to others. Classmates.com allowed people to affiliate with their high school or college and surf the network for others who were also affiliated, but users could not create profiles or list Friends until years later. CompuServe allowed members to share files and access news and events. But it also offered something few had ever experienced – true interaction. Nevertheless, SixDegrees was the first to combine these features.

At its peak, SixDegrees employed about 100 employees, and around 3,500,000 individuals had fully registered as its members. A tool to assist people to connect with and send messages to others is what SixDegrees promoted itself as. Although SixDegrees attracted millions of users, it failed to become a sustainable business. As a matter of fact, the service closed in 2000. Regarding the failure, its founder gives his opinion that SixDegrees was simply ahead of its time. While people were already flocking to the Internet, most did not have extended networks of friends who were online. There were complaints from early adopters that they had almost nothing to do after accepting Friend requests, and the majority of the users were not very interested in meeting people they did not know in their lives.

Nevertheless, the 2000s saw the explosive growth of social networks. Currently, Facebook is the most popular social networking site. Facebook is a social networking site allowing its users to create their own profiles, upload photos and videos, send messages to people and stay connected with friends, family and so on. Facebook was founded by Mark Zuckerberg with his college roommates and fellow Harvard University students Eduardo Saverin, Andrew McCollum, Dustin Moskovitz and Chris Hughes at Harvard University. Mark Zuckerberg was 23 studying psychology and as a passionate computer programmer, Mr. Zuckerberg had already developed a number of social-networking websites for fellow students before Facebook, which include Facemash, where people's attractiveness could be rated by users, and Coursematch that provide its users a platform to view people taking their degree.

The membership of Facebook was initially restricted to Harvard students, but by September 2006, it was open to everyone aged 13 and older with a registered email address. In the summer of 2004, Facebook was incorporated. Sean Parker, the entrepreneur who had been informally advising Zuckerberg, was appointed to be the company's president. In June 2004, Facebook moved its base of operations to California. The site remains free to join, and makes a profit through advertising revenue. In April, 2014, a new feature called FB Newswire was announced by Facebook and Storyful.

Twitter is one of the most popular online social networking sites and it provides microblogging services. Users are able to send and read brief 140-character maximum text messages called "tweets" on Twitter. Tweets that provide small bursts of information distinguish Twitter from other social networking sites. The site was created by Jack Dorsey, Evan Williams, Biz Stone and Noah Glass in March 2006 and launched July 2006. The 2007 South by Southwest Interactive Conference was the tipping point for the popularity of Twitter. Usage of Twitter had increased from 20,000 tweets per day to 60,000 tweets per day during the event. Feedback for Twitter was highly positive at the conference and it won the Festival Web Award prize. Rapid growth of the company was seen during these years. As of September 2013, 200 million users send over 400 million tweets daily, with nearly 60% of tweets sent from mobile devices, according to the company's data.

The brief history of social networking sites has been presented in Figure 1.

An introduction of the current major social networking sites is presented in Table 1.

Figure 1. Timeline of major social networking sites

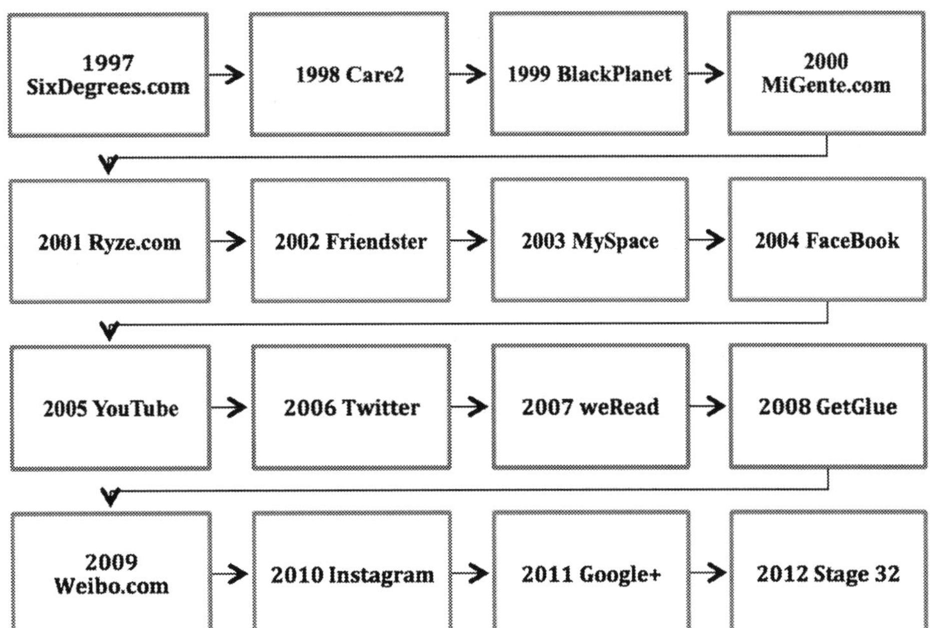

Table 1. Major networking sites

Social Networking Sites	Description	Date Launched	Global Alex Rank
Facebook	A social utility that connects people, to keep up with friends, upload photos, share links and videos.	February 2004	2
Youtube.com	YouTube is a video-sharing website. It allows billions of people to discover, watch and share originally created videos.	February 14, 2005	3
Twitter	Social networking and microblogging service utilising instant messaging, SMS or a web interface.	March 21, 2006	10
Linkedin	A networking tool to find connections to recommended job candidates, industry experts and business partners.	May 5, 2003	12
Weibo.com	A Chinese microblogging (weibo) website. Users are allowed to insert graphical emoticons or attach own image, music, video files in every post.	14 August 2009	16
Pinterest.com	Pinterest is an online pinboard: a place where you can post collections of things you love, and "follow" collections created by people with great taste.	March 2010	27
Instagram	An online mobile photo-sharing, video-sharing and social networking service.	October 6, 2010	32

Social networking sites typically allow users to build and maintain their networks of friends for all sorts of interactions. The core of a social networking site consists of personalized user profiles. Individual profiles are usually a combination of users' images (or avatars); lists of interests and music, book, and movie preferences; and links to affiliated profiles (friends). Different sites impose different levels of privacy in terms of what information is revealed through profile pages to nonaffiliated visitors and how far strangers versus friends can traverse through the network of a profile's friends. Profile holders acquire new friends by browsing and searching through the site and sending requests to be added as a friend.

Borgatti et al. (2009) note that social network studies include four basic tie types that also might refer to the design of social networks: proximities, relations, interactions, and flows (Table 2). Proximities represent shared physical or social spaces, such as physical distances or co-membership in groups, which provide opportunities for ties to form. Relations are ties that reflect persistent social connections between nodes, such as role-based connections (friends, family) or affective relations (likes, dislikes). Interactions include discrete, transitory relational events, such as having lunch or signing an agreement with another node. Relations should increase the probability of interactions, and interactions can create or change relations. Finally, flows refer to tangible and intangible material (e.g., money, goods, information, beliefs) that can move from one node to another when nodes interact (Borgatti 2005). This rich understanding of social ties is important, because social media expands the types of social connections that IT can support.

One main question facing contagion studies in social media networks pertains to how the features of the user profile influence the way content spreads across and affects others in a network. Ellison and boyd (2013) refer to three sources of content in the user profile—content type, digital activity trace, and third-party contributions.

Table 2. Types of dyadic phenomena (Kane, Alavi Labianca & Borgatti, 2014)

Name	Proximities	Social Relations	Interactions	Flows
Description	Shared space/time	Relational states	Relational events	What moves between nodes
Examples	Living in same city	Friends; boss	Talking; sending e-mail	Goods; information
Social media	Being on the same platform or in same group; location-based services (e.g., Foursquare)	Facebook friends, LinkedIn connections, Twitter followers	Messaging, e-mail, discussion boards	Twitter trends and re-tweeted content, social bookmarking systems

Firstly, the way in which content spread on the social networking platform may be influenced by the forms of content contained in the profile. Nowadays users are mostly able to create different types of information in their digital profiles, such as text, pictures, audios, videos, and hypermedia (e.g., links, tags).

With regard to text, users describe about themselves using words that are searchable and viewable towards other users; content with varieties of multimedia could cultivate greater social presence for users, which tends to be conducive to the effective transfer of information on digital platforms. The existence of hypermedia creates opportunities both inside and outside the social media platform for connecting the profile to other content, which therefore broadens the varieties of information presented on the platform. Moreover, it allows the network's content to have references towards other content, providing facilitates for sharing content with others but without sacrificing the possible richness and depth of that content for consumers.

In current technological settings of rapidly increased bandwidth as well as storage that make more types of content available, understanding how the type and amount of content provided by a digital profile influences the perceptions of others in the network is still poorly understood (Kane et al 2014).

Secondly, most conversations or posts on the social networking sites leave a digital trace, often including a record of content that the user has contributed (e.g., status updates), commented on (e.g., reacting to the status updates of others), viewed (e.g., automatically reporting what content was read), or interacted with (i.e., liked on Facebook).

Because of the digital trace features, or users' activity contained in the digital profile, digital profiles are increasingly augmented or even superseded. The digital trace may encourage certain types of behaviors in the network that might facilitate the flow of certain types of information. For instance, if the digital trace indicates that a trusted individual or a substantial proportion of the person's contacts have viewed particular content, it may encourage the focal user to view it as well, increasing the tendency toward herding behavior or the viral spread of information. It also may encourage users to act in ways specifically intended to influence their digital trace.

Thirdly, adding to or even modifying content in user profiles is sometimes applicable with the services provided by the social networking site. Certain users can post new content to others' profiles, link other content to profiles through tags, or comment on existing content in the profile. Individuals can post independent recommendations of others' work on LinkedIn, which may lead additional users to trust the profile information more. Furthermore, users may tag unflattering pictures of someone taken at an office holiday party. In that case it consequently becomes part of the user's profile and visible to others in the network, probably lowering that person's reputation. In an extreme case scenario, some users might even establish a fake profile, with or without the person's knowledge (Table 3).

Table 3. Digital profile features and their implications for social media networks (Kane et al 2014)

Feature	Description	Implications
Profile Content	The forms of digital information that a digital profile will support (e.g. text, multimedia, hypermedia).	Content richness is associated with the level of digital presence supported by an IT platform (Miranda and Saunders 2003).
Digital Trace	The types of data platforms collect and present about user behavior.	The types of data collected and associated with the profile will encourage certain types of behaviors and discourage others (Piskorski 2009).
Third-Party Contributions	Whether other members of the platform can contribute information to, edit, or create profiles for the user.	Users must consider the potential behavior of other users when making use (Burton-Jones & Gallivan 2007) and adoption (Venkatesh et al. 2003) decisions of social media platforms.
Authenticity	The degree to which the digital profile accurately reflects the user's offline identity.	Similar to anonymity, which influences how people interact using information systems (Sia et al., 2002), profiles introduce the possibility of pseudonymity, identities consistent in network but unrelated to offline identity.
Inverted Modality	Different types of users (e.g. individual, group, company) being represented by similar digital profiles.	Profiles will exhibit different capabilities, interests, and goals depending on the type of user it is intended to represent. Reverses traditional concepts of multimodality in social networks (Kane and Alavi 2008).

OPPORTUNITIES AND CHALLENGES OF SOCIAL NETWORKING SITES

Ubiquitous digitalization processes and their implications for online social relationships are driving a fundamental change in the development of social networking sites. Armed with tools that not only allow consumers to screen what media they see, but also to shape and contribute to it, consumers are seizing control. Marketers have no choice, but to reframe their perspectives and deliver engaging experiences that inform, educate, or entertain. Marketers are realizing that this new world is not about porting 15-second TV spots into websites. It is about defining an engaging concept and then using a variety of media to make it come to life, with personalization and accessibility that enables consumers to call it their own. Engagement means people want to spend time to interact during the marketing campaign-play, learn, share, and create, etc.

Networks that occur on and through social media sites will be shaped in part by the characteristics of those media, such that certain types of social interactions flourish while others do not. These social media platforms likely introduce differences in terms of how relationships form and develop and can introduce other differences back into the dynamics and outcomes of traditional, offline social networks.

There are a lot of challenges that are already causing some social networks to work inefficiently. Eventually, these problems could lose the networks a lot of customers, or even force the site to shut down. It is important to understand the most important problems, so perhaps they can be resolved in the future.

Studies state that social networking sites should serve certain purposes. This means that there should be something that connects the users to each other. Usually this is a common interest such as employers meeting employees, old school friends reconnecting, or users with shared hobbies. The problem that some of the current networks have is that they do not have anything that truly connects the users. People are just adding other people to their friend list without knowing them or having anything in common. This kind of activity might work for a while, but eventually it is bound to fail. Having hundreds of unknown people as friends is not going to work, if they don't have something to share with each other.

For instance, LinkedIn made their network to work as place for business and professional contacts. However, LinkedIn also has problems in keeping its customers interested. Many users try to add business contacts that are not connected to them in any way. This kind of behaviour leads to the exact same problems as in networks that serve a purpose. The only difference here is that the network actually has a purpose, but if it's not used properly, it won't work properly either. To combat this problem, there have been suggestions that people should follow a certain etiquette in the network. For example, one should only add friends or acquaintances that they have actually met or had some mutual business with.

Security related issues are also big challenges. There are privacy issues and vulnerabilities that can occur in the networks. When users are making communications with connected friends, they can be making information available at the meantime towards those individuals who intend to abuse it. There have already been a lot of cases where a user's private information has been acquired from social networks. This kind of information may get exploited in various ways, such as selling it to spammers, harassing the user and etc. Nevertheless, the most dangerous issue has been identity theft. There are millions of identity theft cases each year in Great Britain, United States and Canada, leading to huge financial losses.

Some of the social networks do have provided privacy control options, therefore users can choose what kind of information will be shown to which groups of people. Nevertheless, these privacy controls need to be improved. Currently at least Facebook is in the process of improving its privacy control over the content users want to share. Even if the privacy control is improved, there is still a problem that most people do not know or care about changing their privacy settings. For example, only 25 percent of Facebook users have actually used their privacy control options. This means that most people have default settings on, which often allow outsiders to see some or even all information about the user. Besides leaking information to other users, social networks can also give or sell information to third parties such as advertisers. Usually it is written in the site's privacy policy if information can be shared to others. Sometimes the privacy policy does not tell whether or not giving information is allowed, or the document can be very unclear about this. In these cases it might impossible for the user to forbid the usage of his/her personal information.

WOM ACTIVITIES AND VIRAL MARKETING STRATEGIES

WOM Activities

The term "word of mouth" (WOM) commonly refers to the flow of communications among consumers about products and services. Nowadays this is a world offering a plethora of product and service information from a wealth of sources; there has been a phenomenon that modern consumers have become less attentive to traditional advertising. Moreover, consumer evaluations and opinions of a product or service have become widely available and WOM plays an even more important role today in shaping consumers' attitudes and buying behaviors. As a matter of fact, WOM has been frequently cited as one of the most powerful forces in the marketplace.

The diffusion of WOM is also called "Buzz Marketing." It helps generate a ripple effect for marketing activities. The ripple effect has been identified as being able to significantly multiply or extend the effectiveness of advertising.

Regarded as an important but difficult to manage market force, WOM is believed to be able to complement and extend the effect of various advertising activities. As an instance, initial marketing activities such as advertisements and promotions trigger initial reactions as purchase activities, and subsequently that purchase experience triggers the spread of WOM, which means that customers share their experiences with others during that stage. The extent to which the effect of advertising is extended (or multiplied) by WOM is called "advertising ripple effect" caused by WOM (Figure 2). Another concept, which is similar to ripple effect, is called as the spillover effect of social interaction. The spillover effect of social interaction arises when a marketing activity directed toward an agent affects the behaviour of others in the agent's group via social interactions.

WOM can influence consumer behaviour and, consequently, increase the effectiveness of advertising activities. For example, using a customer lifetime value modelling approach; this had been tested by scholars on both theoretical and empirical perspectives. Hogan et al. (2004) found that in common situations, multiplier coefficients could be three or even greater. Furthermore, as aforementioned, firms are spending greater amounts of money on social network advertising in online environments.

Word-of-mouth marketing is a particularly prominent feature on the Internet. The Internet provides numerous venues for consumers to share their views, preferences, or experiences with others, as well as opportunities for firms to take advantage of WOM marketing. As one commentator stated: "Instead of tossing away millions of dollars on Superbowl advertisements, fledgling dot-com companies are trying to catch attention through much cheaper marketing strategies such as blogging and WOM campaigns".

Offline WOM is defined as face-to-face communication between participants. Offline WOM requires resenders and receivers to interact in real time, which is termed as "temporal synchronicity" by Hoffman and Novak (1996). These resenders and receivers must know each other, must have some form of social ties and must exchange information using verbal communication. Table 4 shows the characteristics and consequences of offline and online WOM diffusions.

Figure 2. Ripple effect of WOM activities (Huang, Cai, Tsang, & Zhou, 2011)

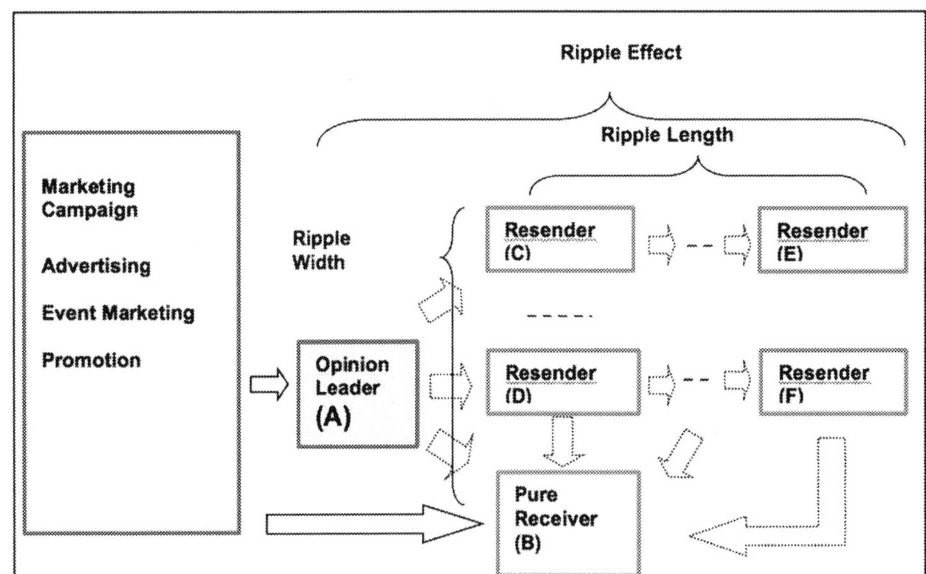

Table 4. Online marketing and offline marketing (Hoffman & Novak 1996; Huang et al, 2011)

	Offline WOM	Online WOM	
		One-to-one/many diffusion	Many-to-many diffusion
Characteristics			
Communication medium	Talk, telephone, meeting (letter)	E-mail, text chatting (voice chatting)	Discussion forums, blog
Form	Oral (written) communication	Written (oral) communication	Written communication
Synchronicity	Synchronous communication	Could be asynchronous/ synchronous	Could be asynchronous/ synchronous
Type of interaction	Face-to-face interaction/ direct	Virtual interaction/ indirect	Virtual interaction/ indirect
Format	Mostly linear communication	Linear or non-linear communication	Non-linear communication
Relationship between sender and receiver	Know each other/real social ties/limited receiver pool	Know each other (anonymous)/real (virtual) social ties/ bigger receiver pool	Generally anonymous virtual social ties/bigger receiver pool
Ease of transmission	Difficult to transmit	Easy to transmit/ forward	Easy to transmit/ forward
Consequence			
Ripple effect	Low ripple/multiplier effect (isolated WOM)	Middle ripple/multiplier effect (WOM flow)	High ripple/multiplier effect (WOM flow)
Focus	Focus on persuasive communication	Focus on persuasive communication	Focus on both persuasive and diffusive communication
Critical role	Opinion leaders as critical role	Opinion leaders as critical role	Resenders as critical role

Viral Marketing and Seeding Strategies

Viral marketing describes the kind of peer-to-peer communications in which individuals are encouraged to spread promotional messages within their social networks, with the relevant marketing information initially sent out deliberately by marketers to stimulate and capitalize on word-of-mouth (WOM) behaviors. These sorts of stimuli can be made up of various forms such as hyperlinks included in the posts on social networking sites, direct messages and e-mails; they are generally unsolicited, however, they are usually designed to be easily forwarded to a number of other individuals. These characteristics are similar to the parallel traits of infectious diseases and a lot of marketing concepts underlying viral marketing actually have been built on epidemiology research.

As a diffusion of information about the product or service and its adoption over the network, viral marketing has been studied in the context of the influence of social networks on innovation and product diffusion. These studies have been primarily based on small networks and mostly regarding a single product or service.

The marketers' ability to identify individuals with high Social Networking Potential (SNP) and formulate marketing messages that appeal to this segment of the population and have a high probability of being passed along is where the success of a viral marketing campaign lies in.

A user will become "infected" when a viral message reaches a "susceptible" user, (e.g. sign up for an account) and this infected user may pass the viral by infecting other susceptible users. A logistic curve for its growth is indicated by epidemiology whose initial segment appears exponential.

The initial stage of growth is approximately exponential; then, as saturation begins, the growth slows, and at maturity, growth stops (Figure 3).

Advantages of Viral Marketing

1. The viral campaign's communication depends more on the agents and their social networks and relatively does not require as much financial investments on promoting the product or the service itself. This is especially an advantage for products or services that are lack of previous accumulated reputation or fell short of competitive advantages competing with other highly branded product or services.
2. Allowing marketers to reach and influence the audience more effectively compared with the clutter of traditional advertising.
3. Viral campaigns can be very interactive. Participants of the campaigns do not receive the message passively. Instead, they spend time interacting with other participants and spreading proactively which will help participants remember the campaign and increase brand royalty.

Figure 3. Growth of viral marketing

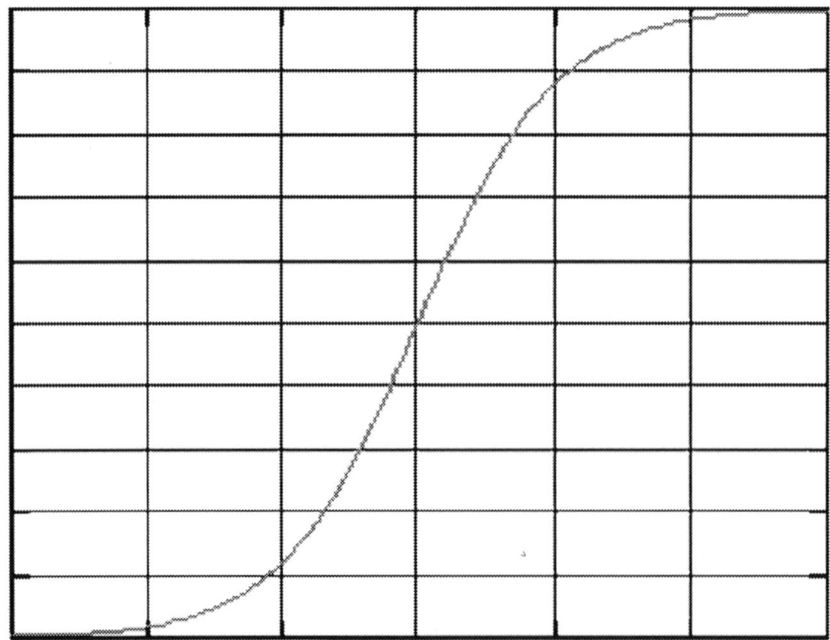

Disadvantages of Viral Marketing

Viral marketing by nature is more risky or controversial than traditional marketing. If the marketer seeds inappropriate groups of people, the campaign may fail to take off at the start. If a viral marketing campaign is carried out improperly such as keeping bombarding participants with frequent and repetitive requests, viral marketing can be irritating and sometimes a product or service can over praised which may cause disappointments and even create significant negative buzz.

Elements of a Viral Marketing Strategy

There are basically five elements that marketers can be included in a viral marketing strategy.

1. Provides valuable products or services as stimuli

To attract viral marketing campaign participants, "free" is a powerful and attractive word. A number of viral marketing programs give away certain products or services to people who join the programs on the social networking sites to attract attention and participants. It is vital for marketers to generate a groundswell of interest for a successful viral marketing campaign, and that can be started from giving away something free to participants.

2. Provides multiple platforms to facilitate the spread of marketing message

Viruses spread widely and rapidly when they are easy to transmit and in the right target groups of people. The agents and social networking platforms that present the marketing message should be easy to transfer, forward and replicate such as texts, e-mails, videos, and graphics on popular social networking sites. Viral marketing works on the Internet because instant communication has become increasingly easy and inexpensive. Digital format of information make copying simpler than other forms of information. From a marketing standpoint, it is essential to simplify your marketing message so it can be transmitted easily and without degradation.

3. Consider underlying motivations and behaviors

Viral marketing plans should take consumer behavior into consideration. The urge to communicate contributes to the developments of social networking sites and e-mail services. Design a marketing strategy that builds on common motivations and behaviors for its transmission is important.

4. Target the right audience

In order to get the word out, there should be well-connected participants of the viral marketing campaign that are potentially passionate about the product or service. It is important for marketers to look into the segments and target the right audience to create positive buzz.

One method of viral marketing involves seeding certain consumers within a population to encourage faster adoption of the product throughout the entire population. Seeding the original message is a key component of a viral campaign. Seeding is the act of planting the campaign with the initial group who will then go on to spread the campaign to others. The social networking sites provide a variety of options for seeding.

Seeding Strategies

The success of viral marketing campaigns is significantly dependent on the seeding strategies. According to Hinz et al (2011), marketers can achieve the highest number of referrals, across various settings, if they seed the message to hubs (high-degree seeding) or bridges (high-betweenness seeding) (Figure 4). The superiority of the high-degree seeding strategy does not rest on a higher conversion rate due to a higher persuasiveness of hubs but rather on the increased activity of hubs, which is in line with previous findings.

Based upon the central assumption that highly connected people are more difficult to influence than less connected people, as highly connected people are subject to the influence of too many others, there are a couple of research that suggests a low-degree seeding strategy. Hinz et al (2011) reject this assumption. They underline that hubs are more likely to engage because viral marketing works mostly through awareness caused by information transfer from previous adopters and through belief updating, especially for low-risk products. The low perceived risk means hubs do not hesitate before participating.

What's more, when social contagion occurs mostly at the awareness stage, the possible disproportionate persuasiveness of hubs is irrelevant. As long as it is at the awareness stage when the social contagion occurs through simple information transfer, hubs are not more persuasive than other nodes. In addition, for the group of participating customers, there is a negative influence of greater connectivity on the resulting influence domains. Although in epidemiology studies infectious diseases spread through hubs, research from Hinz et al. (2011) finds that well-connected people do not use their greater reach potential fully in a marketing setting. Spreading information is costly in terms of both time invested and the effort needed to capture attention of their peers. Furthermore, hubs may be less likely to reach other previously unaffected central actors, such that they are limited in their overall influence domain.

Thus in viral marketing settings, the compelling findings from sociology and epidemiology appear to have been incorrectly transferred to targeting strategies. Nevertheless, the social network remains a crucial determinant of optimal seeding strategies in practice because a social structure is much easier to observe and measure than communication intensity, quality, or frequency. Therefore, companies should use social network information about mutual relationships to determine their viral marketing strategy.

Figure 4. Hub bridge and fringe (Adapted from Hinz et al 2011)

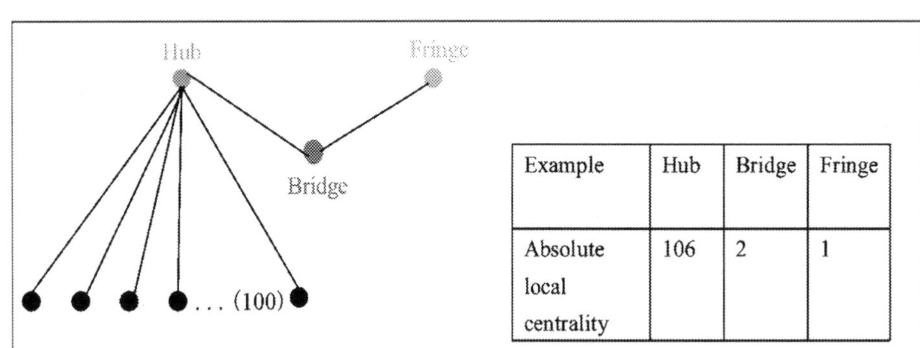

Example	Hub	Bridge	Fringe
Absolute local centrality	106	2	1

Highly connected persons should therefore get selected by marketers as initial seeds if it is to generate awareness or encourage transactions through their viral marketing campaigns. The reason is that the hubs provide better possibilities of spreading the viral message more widely. As long as the social contagion operates at the awareness stage through information transfer, hubs are not more persuasive. Thus, the sociometric measure of degree centrality cannot be used to identify persuasive seeding points. What seems more promising for this purpose is the use of demographics and product-related characteristics. Additionally, monetary incentives for referring strongly increase the spread of viral marketing messages, which supports the use of such incentives. Nevertheless, they would make viral marketing more costly than is commonly assumed.

STRATEGIC PERSPECTIVES OF SOCIAL NETWORKING SITES

The best strategies are now changing the drill-down dynamic by placing rich, interactive content where targets are likely to be and letting the users experience the full brand without leaving where they are. (David C. Edelman)

There are four core stages to building and running an online marketing strategy (Figure 5). Each of these stages runs into the next to deliver a complete social networking sites marketing campaign. These four stages deliver an ongoing digital strategy as the audience and brand perception evolves.

The foundation of any digital strategy is based upon business objectives. They are supposed be generic rather than specific at the planning stage, so as not to get overloaded with details. A good set of goals often comes down to these points:

- A good mix between internal goals and external goals.
- Goals are supposed to have come from more than one department. It will fall short if the strategy is only informed by the marketing or PR department.

Figure 5. Four core stages to building and running an online marketing strategy (Adapted from Third Wave, 2013)

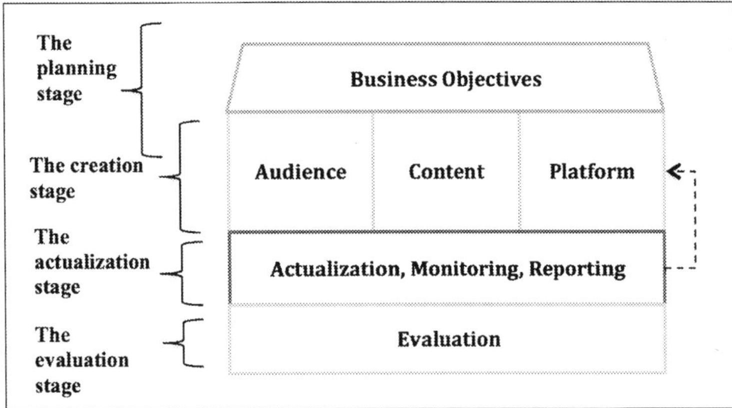

- The goals should be organized into different groups as short-term, middle-term and long- term ones so as to provide a good mix between actionable next steps, a plan and a vision.
- Goals should be quantifiable and measurable to the extent that is possible. If no metric is available, a new one should be established.

Whilst each brand will have specific aims and objectives of its own, they can normally be aligned to one of these four main groups:

- Consumer awareness and demand creation
- Direct consumer drive to retail and purchase
- Education and incentive within the retail space
- Process improvement through streamlined communications

Among the core propositions of modern social networking sites marketing strategies, there is the role reversal of the audience from being a non-participatory group into an engaged and lively medium through which further brand advocacy can take place. It is working with the brand audience in a positive engagement through social networking sites that can enable brand exposure to grow like snowball, but the flipside to this proposition is that negative experience is also broadcast to a wider sphere. Audience management is a key factor in the actualisation stage; however, to work with the brand audience the first step must be to identify and understand each of its segments.

The opportunity to segment activity into different spheres and places directly targeted to the location of the audience is one of the benefits of digital strategy. To be more specific, the personas need to be matching the aims of the digital strategy. Targeting activities in this way can be used to reduce cost whilst increasing efficiency and message for each of the channels based in these locations.

It is possible to apply demographic filters to major locations where digital strategy activities can take place from each of the personas defined. Often locations are applicable to multiple personas and demographics (e.g. Facebook, which is almost ubiquitous across western consumer audiences). Certain networks (e.g. Facebook, LinkedIn) provide a combination of demographic and interest segmentation that allows the development of highly personalised campaigns.

In order to build a suitable strategy for social networking sites, there are often several composite ideas that create a distinct channel (user journey). Each of these ideas shall be rated as follows:

- How does the idea match the needs of the audience?
- Which audience groups does the idea touch upon?
- Where do the ideas sit on the engagement path?
- How do the ideas interconnect (if required) to route the audience through to the final step of the engagement path?

Marketers can thereafter evaluate the value of the ideas themselves and a coherent picture of how users move through different ideas in a channel. Table 5 shows the social media marketing strategies involved in the aforementioned four core stages.

Table 5. Social media marketing strategies (Conyard, 2014)

Planning The planning of a digital strategy involves analysing the following:	Creation The creation stage is purely focused around campaign formalisation. This involves:	Actualization The actualization focuses on the delivery of the campaign, including:	Evaluation The evaluation of a digital strategy is imperative to learn the lessons of the campaign, including:
• The initial aims and expected returns • The background of the brand, present positioning and perception • The audience (broken down into key segments) • Audience locations and value of each audience segment against initial aims The planning stage deals purely in the analysis and identification of focus areas.	• Planning campaign elements based upon previous analysis • Creating key performance indicators per channel and estimating expected return per channel • Design and build of campaign elements / channels • Planning and establishing actualisation routes, communication flows and expectations The creation stage for each channel finishes on the launch of each channel.	• Building the engagement timeline • Engaging with the audience through the engagement loop • Sampling progress through a campaign and optimizing the campaign message • Recording salient information through each campaign step for evaluation The actualisation stage runs as a microcosm of the strategy as a whole and relies on rapid responses to tune the strategy.	• Evaluating fiscal achievement • Reviewing engagement and unexpected longer term benefits • Taking lessons on board to build stronger future campaigns • Scoring the strategy and the benefits that it has given Evaluation improves the effectiveness of future campaigns and strategies by becoming the key building block in planning them.

MAJOR SOCIAL NETWORKING SITES AND MARKETING STRATEGY DECISION MAKING

Facebook and Viral Marketing Strategies

The recent trend toward viral marketing has been fueled by the growing popularity of social network platforms such as Facebook, on which more than 1 billion connected consumers share marketing messages with a single click on their computers or mobile devices. Figure 6 shows the login page of Facebook. The resulting potential for viral marketing campaigns on Facebook is evident from popular examples such as FarmVille and Candy Crush Saga that reached as many as 100 million customers in just a few weeks.

Candy Crush is a successful case of social media sharing (Figure 7). If you want to play the game, you need to connect with your Facebook account. If you want to advance past a particular checkpoint, you need to get three Facebook friends who have downloaded the game to help you move on. If you run out of lives, you can ask Facebook friends for more.

The viral marketing success of products such as Candy Crush has attracted many firms to Facebook -not only game producers but also makers of primarily utilitarian products, whose value for consumers results more from their products' usefulness and less from the fun they offer. Marketing managers from all industries wonder whether they can replicate the success of FarmVille and similar products by simply imitating their approach-that is, encouraging consumers to broadcast unsolicited viral marketing messages to their Facebook friends and offering small incentives to convince the receiver to try and use the product.

Success stories about viral marketing campaigns on Facebook and similar platforms mostly involve products that fit well with the platforms' fun-oriented environments. However, not all products are fun oriented, and marketing literature abounds with examples illustrating that what works for one product does not necessarily work for all products. There is this ideal sharing mechanism uses incentives and suggests that customers recommend products to their friends rather than to strangers, according to previous research (Figure 8). It illustrates that sharing mechanisms that rely on unsolicited viral marketing

Figure 6. Facebook login page

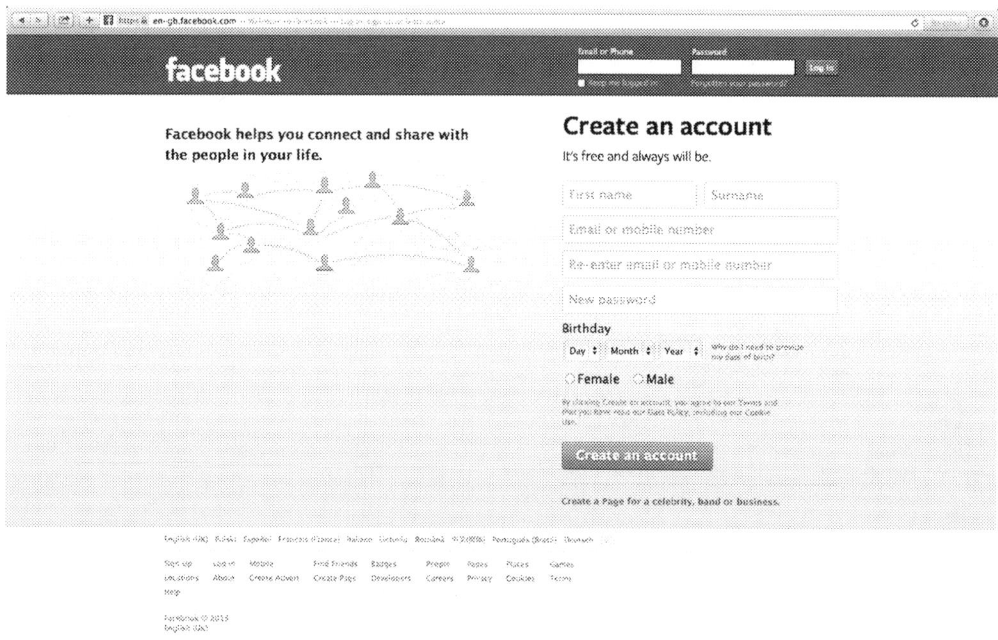

Figure 7. Candy Crush Saga

messages are as effective as sharing mechanisms that use solicited messages. That is to say, for low-utilitarian products, to follow the best-practice strategy of products such as Candy Crush and encourage unsolicited and incentivized broadcast messages from friends to spread viral marketing information are good advice for viral marketing campaigns on Facebook.

Elements of the model (Schulze et al., 2014) are explained in Table 6.

The aspects of viral marketing strategies for primarily utilitarian product and low-utilitarian products on Facebook presented in the model are, based on the research by Schulze, et al (2014):

1. Expressed interest of receivers.

For high-utilitarian products, when information processing follows the peripheral route, consumers rely more on heuristics and simple inferences. Unsolicited push messages are regarded by consumers as an indication suggesting that the product, compared with information they (actively) seek out, is of low quality and has low personal relevance. The thought is like this: "If the product was truly useful and of high quality, the company would not have to market it so aggressively ". On the other hand, if information processing follows a more central route, a much smaller negative effect or even none at all from unsolicited messages is expected. The effectiveness of sharing mechanisms that rely on unsolicited viral marketing messages for which the receiver has not expressed a prior interest (rather than solicited messages) is lower for high-utilitarian products than for low-utilitarian products.

Figure 8. The aspects of viral marketing strategies for primarily utilitarian product and low-utilitarian products on Facebook (adapted from Sciiuize, Sciiöler, & Skiera, 2014)

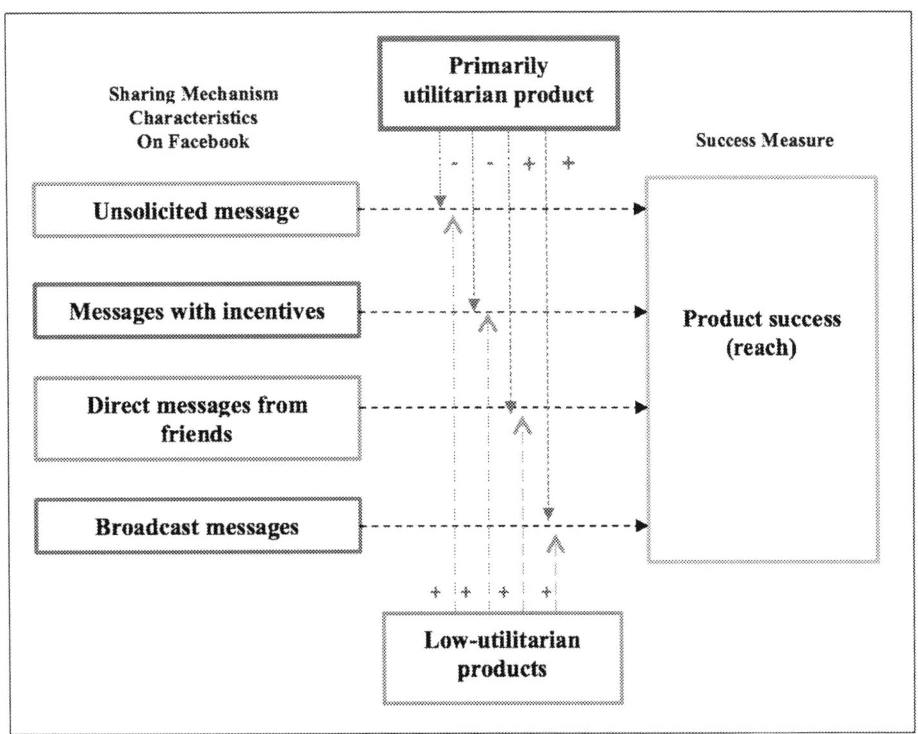

Table 6. Elements of the model (Adapted from Schulze et al., 2014)

Construct	Description	Example
Number of sharing mechanisms	Sharing mechanisms should encourage consumers to recommend product to their peers. Each sharing mechanism has four dimensions. Viral marketing campaigns can use several sharing mechanisms simultaneously but must rely on at least one.	Sharing mechanisms on Facebook include a post on a friend's timeline or a direct message to friends with incentives.
Unsolicited messages	Messages are unsolicited if receiver has not expressed interest in receiving the message	A viral message from a friend in the inbox that promotes, for example, a new game
Solicited messages	Messages are solicited if the message receiver has expressed an interest in receiving the message or has searched for it.	A Facebook user visits a friend's "About" page to see which apps the friend is using.
Messages with incentives	Incentives in viral marketing messages provide greater benefits for message receivers (compared with regular consumers) if they use the product.	A viral marketing message such as "Try Spotify now and get one month of premium membership for free!" offers an incentive to the receiver.
Messages without incentives	Without incentives, receivers of viral marketing messages have no benefit over regular consumers from using the product.	A viral marketing message such as "Try Spotify now and listen to music today!" does not offer a specific incentive to receiver.
Direct messages from friends	A direct message from a friend describes one-to-one communications (comparable to email) between direct (first-degree) contacts	Two befriended Facebook users can send each other messages to their Facebook inbox. Direct messages on Facebook require consumers to be direct, first-degree contacts.
Broadcast messages from strangers	Broadcast messages from strangers describe one-to-many communications between Facebook users who are not directly connected, such as second-degree contacts who share a common friend.	When a Facebook user posts a viral marketing message to a friend's timeline, that friend's contacts will see this message in their news feeds and view it as a broadcast message from a stranger.
Broadcast messages from friends	Broadcast messages from friends describe one-to-many communications between Facebook users who are direct (first-degree) contacts.	When a Facebook user posts a viral marketing message to her own timeline, her direct friends see this message in their news feeds as a broadcast message from a friend.
Primarily utilitarian products	A product is primarily utilitarian if its main purpose is to be effective, helpful, functional, and practical (rather than fun, exciting, and enjoyable).	Facebook apps that, for example, enable consumers to track their stock investments or find a new house. In the context of our study, we classify apps as primarily utilitarian if they belong to the business, money, utility, alerts, or politics categories.
Low-utilitarian products	Products that are fun oriented. They can be fun, exciting, and enjoyable.	Candy Crush Saga
Product success (reach)	Success of a viral marketing campaign is typically measured by its reach, or the number of individual consumers that took action after receiving the viral marketing message	We operationalized reach by the maximum (estimated) number of installations. The estimated reach for the Facebook app "Cities I've Visited" is approximately 10 million unique consumers

2. Message features.

Consumers do not actively evaluate the usefulness of an incentive included in a viral marketing message when information processing follows the peripheral route. As an alternative, they regard the incentive as a indication of inferior product quality. The thought is like this: "If the product were good, the company would not have to offer me an incentive". Therefore it reduces the effectiveness of the viral marketing message. At the same time, a positive effect is expected from incentives for less utilitarian products when consumers evaluate their usefulness more thoroughly. The effectiveness of sharing mechanisms that rely on viral marketing messages containing an incentive for the receiver to use the product (rather than no incentive) is lower for high-utilitarian products than for low-utilitarian products.

3. Communication exclusivity.

When information processing follows the peripheral route, consumers do not expend as much thought to elaborate on the merits of a broadcast message. Instead, they believe that the lack of a direct, individual message signals low personal relevance. The thought being "had my Facebook friend thought this were truly relevant for me, she would have sent me a direct message". In contrast, a significant difference between direct and broadcast messages from Facebook friends when consumers spend more thought evaluating the actual message is not expected, as they should for low-utilitarian products.

4. Sender-receiver relationship.

Consumers seeking fun and entertainment on Facebook rely on their friends for recommendations, because friends often have similar tastes and preferences. Thus, recommendations from friends are useful to consumers, regardless of whether they evaluate these recommendations on the basis of their objective, informational value (central route) or simply by following a heuristic (peripheral route). Viral marketing messages from friends that promote hedonic products are to be more effective than messages from strangers.

Consumers evaluate the quality of utilitarian products on the basis of their effectiveness, helpfulness, functionality, and usefulness. If they follow the peripheral route, they should value information from a competent, neutral, external source at least as much as information from a friend with similar views and experiences. Godes and Mayzlin (2009) support this notion, showing that word-of mouth recommendations from actual customers are equally effective whether they involve friends or strangers. Thus, for utilitarian products, messages from strangers can be as effective as messages from friends, but messages from strangers should be significantly less effective for less utilitarian products. The effectiveness of sharing mechanisms that rely on broadcast messages from strangers (rather than friends) is greater for high-utilitarian products than for low-utilitarian products.

Twitter and Marketing Strategies

Designed to be the "Short Message Service of the Internet" at start-up, Twitter was launched in July 2006. During the 2007 South by Southwest (SXSW) Festival in Austin, TX, a show- case of Twitter impressed the highly tech-savvy attendees. Since then, Twitter has entered a phase of rapid growth and gained popularity far beyond the technology industry insiders. Twitter is now one of the most vibrant online communities in the world. Figure 9 shows the online login page of Twitter.

On Twitter home pages are users' basic information, a list and number of who they are following, and another list and number of who is following them. The main part of the page is the "Tweets," the messages that the user has posted.

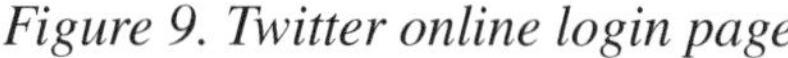

Figure 9. Twitter online login page

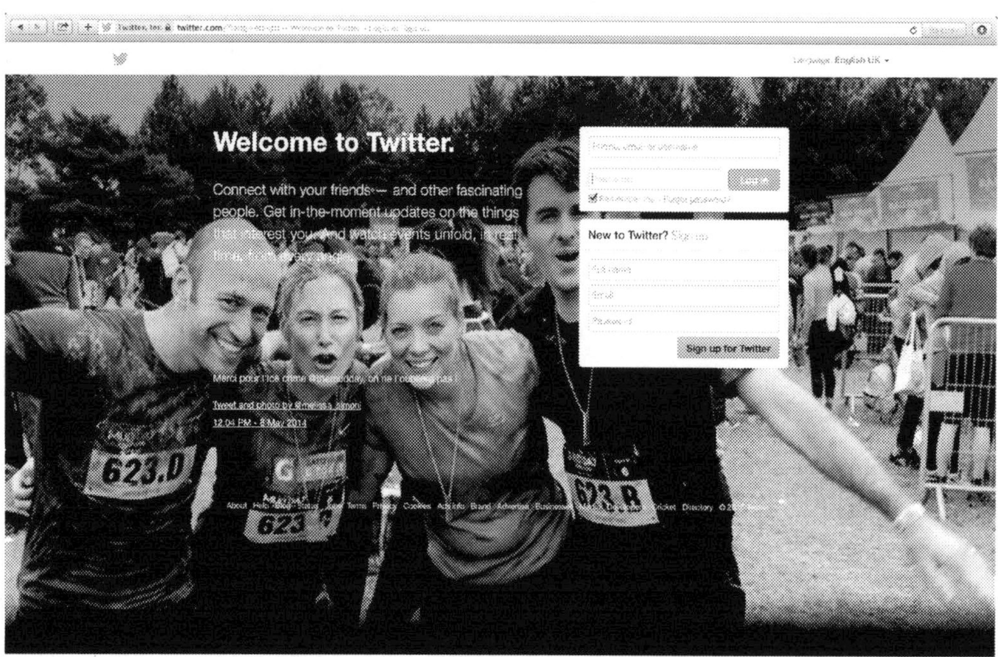

Twitter is an example of a social broadcasting site, where a broadcasting service and a social network organically constitute the technological infrastructure. Twitter users produce and consume informational content by authoring and reading tweets, which are text-based updates/ messages of up to 140 characters. Similar to content on most traditional mass media, tweets are by default open to the public. There is no restriction on consumption. Powered by its service, every Twitter user can be a content broadcaster and/ or a content consumer.

Twitter users are networked to each other through a following–follower relationship. A user's followers are those who subscribe to receive his or her tweets, and a user's followings are the users whose tweets he or she subscribes to receive. This following-follower relationship is the sole interpersonal link in the Twitter network. It is not only the pathway through which broadcasted content but also the channel of person-to-person communications, such as public reply and direct message. This relationship differs from friendship on Facebook or some other social network site in two respects: (1) the following– follower relationship on Twitter is relatively open in the sense that A following B does not require B's consent, and they usually do not map to real-world friendships as the ones on Facebook do; and (2) perhaps more importantly, the following–follower relationship is directed (A's following B does not imply B's following A) while friendship is undirected (A's being a friend of B implies B's being a friend of A). The existence of a large volume of loose and directed subscription relationships is thus a distinctive characteristic of a social broadcasting network.

An integral part of the Twitter experience includes the sharing of content. In addition to composing and posting tweets themselves, Twitter users can also retweet, in Twitter's terminology—other users', of whom are mostly their followings, tweets that they find are of particular (informational, entertaining, etc.) value. Retweeting spreads information by exposing a new audience to the content every time. In the meantime, because a retweet is simply a copy of the original tweet, retweeting is a special kind of sharing, and thus the author, content, and format of the shared information stay exactly the same as the original tweet. A "chain effect" can also be shown up because of retweeting: not only a tweet's author's followers, but also sharers' followers, and so on, can further retweet. That provides possibilities of spreading the content onto their respective networks and amplifying the audience of the content to a potentially massive scale (Lotan 2011). Therefore, a critical mechanism of information diffusion on Twitter is significantly lying in retweeting. Retweeting has been extremely popular on Twitter since it was introduced, thanks to the easy-to-use official retweet button and straightforward idea behind it.

The mechanism of retweeting can be graphically illustrated as illustrated in Figure 10, which is adapted from the research of Shi, Rui and Whinston (2014). The user who writes the original tweet is the author, and the author is denoted D in the figure. The other nodes represent other users who are linked to each other via the following–follower relationship, together forming a tiny community inside the Twitter world. If two users mutually follow each other, the line between them is solid (e.g., D and F, and we call F a bidirectional follower of D). Otherwise, if only one of them follows the other, the line between them is dashed, with an arrow pointing to the user followed (e.g., J follows D but D doesn't follow J, so that we call J a unidirectional follower of D). After R posts an update, if no one retweets it, only D's followers B, C, E, F, and J would receive it. But now assume that after reading the message, users F, C, and A retweet (retweeters are designated by shaded circles), thereby making H, I, M, and A, who are not immediate followers of D, receive a copy of the tweet. Then the new receivers could also retweet (as H and I do in the example), circulating the information more broadly on the network. One thing to note is that a retweet is also a content broadcast; because of the technology, a sharer cannot select a subgroup of his or her followers and only retweet to this subgroup.

To quantify the re-tweet influence, there exists two equations that can be used by social media marketers and researchers:

$$\text{Influence to buzz ratio} = \frac{\text{Avg. retweeted count}}{\text{Total references}}$$

Figure 10. An example of retweeting (Adapted from Shi, Rui & Whinston, 2014)

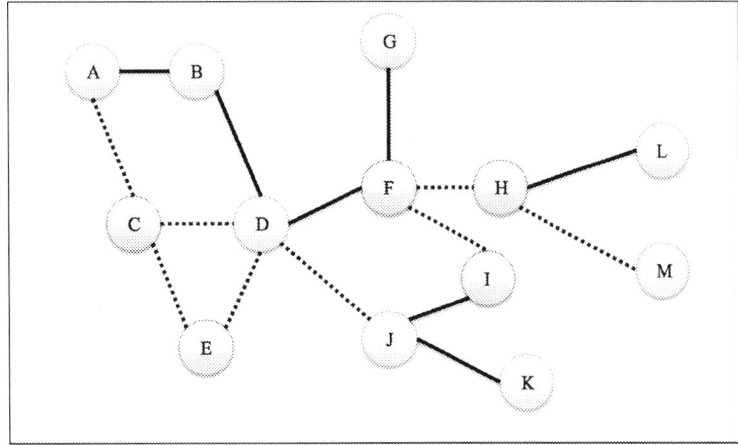

$$\text{Influence to audience ratio} = \frac{\text{Avg. retweeted count}}{\text{Total followers}}$$

The influence to buzz ratio reflects the degree to which a celebrity is able to drive content on the Twitter network, relative to the degree to which he or she receives attention by being widely discussed *(Rosenman, 2012)*. In this case, a high ratio may indicate that a person is perceived to be an interesting source of information, but that individual is not a very interesting topic to discuss about. A low ratio indicates that an individual is very interesting to talk about, however, his or her social media content is not very interesting in itself. One potential interpretation of this ratio is that it serves as a "conversion metric," indicating the degree to which celebrities are able to convert individuals who discuss them into individuals who retweet their content on social networks.

The influence to audience ratio provides a metric of how much a celebrity is able to drive content on the Twitter network, relative to the degree to which he or she is followed. A high ratio indicates that despite having comparatively few followers, an individual is still capable to propagate his content widely; this could be interpreted to mean that the content provided is particularly interesting or say, worthy, but that he or she has relatively few individuals who identify as explicit or fans." A low ratio could be seemed as meaning the opposite: that an individual has a lot of self-identified fans but does not produce exciting or intriguing content.

According to the research by Rosenman (2012), Comedians lead in the influence to buzz ratio, which may be interpreted as that they exert exceptionally large influence relative to the degree to which they are discussed on Twitter (as shown in Figure 11). Many of the comedians in the dataset of Rosenman (2012) tended to tweet jokes and humorous musings that possibly encouraged retweets due to that other Twitter users found them funny and interesting. As a matter of fact, one of the more heavily retweeted tweets in the dataset was from Conan O'Brien: "Thank God Beyonce had her baby and can go back to work. For the past 6 months that family's had to live entirely on Jay-Z's salary." It could be said that the humorous nature of these tweets more than likely encourage Twitter users to share them than a standard or normal tweet. The funniness of their tweets increases their "retweetability". And it means that comedians are less reliant on attracting buzz in order to get more retweets. At the other end of the spectrum, politicians seemed to be highly non-influential relative to the amount they are discussed in the study. According to Rosenman (2012), the reason could be that the data was collected during the period of the Republican presidential primaries, and most of the politicians in our dataset were seeking the Republican nomination. Thus, there was an extremely active conversation regarding these people on Twitter, but much of that discussion were focused on the politicians' campaigns and statements

Seeding strategy determines the initial set of targeted consumers chosen by the initiator of the viral marketing campaign. Seeding strategy falls entirely under the control of the initiator and can exploit social characteristics or observable network metrics, therefore it is essential for the success of viral marketing campaigns. When information about an underlying social network is available, seeding on the basis of this information, as typically captured by sociometric data, seems promising (Van den Bulte 2010)

According to Hinz et al. (2011), the low-degree seeding strategy is inferior to the other three seeding strategies and that both high-betweenness and high-degree seeding outperform the random seeding strategy but yield comparable results. The influential hypothesis has been adopted by the majority of previous research, which states that targeting opinion leaders and strongly connected members of social networks (i.e., hubs) is significant for the esurient of rapid diffusion.

Figure 11. Influence of different groups on Twitter (Rosenman, 2012)

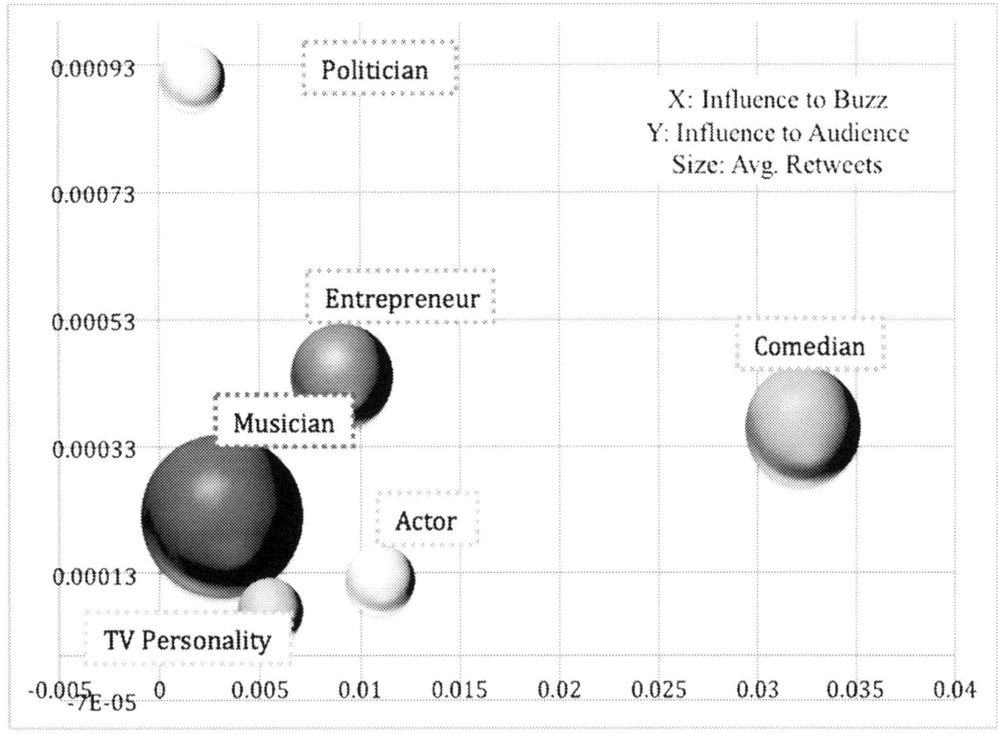

Using sociometric data to seed their viral marketing campaigns can improve the campaigns for marketers. Seeding the "right" consumers yields up to eight times more referrals than seeding the "wrong" ones. Compared with random seeding, seeding hubs and bridges can easily increase the number of successful referrals by more than half. Thus, it is essential for marketers to adopt an appropriate seeding strategy and use sociometric data to increase their profits. Therefore markets can take advantage of such seeding strategies to launch successful viral marketing campaigns on Twitter.

MARKETING MIX OF ONLINE MARKETING VIA SOCIAL NETWORKING SITES

Marketing mix is a concept that could be seemed as one of the most ubiquitous aspects of the marketing literature. The marketing mix (the 4P's of Product, Price, Place and Promotion) has persisted for more than 40 years. Nevertheless, marketers are forced to deal with a whole host of new marketing elements that have emerged from the online world of the internet, especially facing the rapid development of social networking sites.

The "marketing mix" and also its extension as the "retailing mix" are concepts that provide a standard vocabulary for the marketing community. At the beginning, the idea of a "marketing mix" was somewhat controversial. Ultimately a 4Ps depiction of the marketing mix became what today is one of the most standardized and universally accepted aspects of the marketing landscape.

There are several benefits for the marketing mix. Firstly, it provides a standardized vocabulary for the marketing community. The mix helps to categorize what would otherwise be potentially thousands of microelements in a full-blown marketing campaign into manageable macro-elements that can be the basis for the development and communication of a more macro marketing strategy. The marketing industry is organized into verticals around the elements of the marketing mix (e.g. Advertising, Direct Marketing, Pricing, Sales Promotion, Branding) with associated industry organizations, conferences, tradeshows, textbooks and academic courses. Since the marketing mix specifies the scope of marketing activities, it serves as the natural reference point for budget allocation. Vertical industries differ in the manner in which they allocate their marketing budget across the marketing mix.

In the virtual market place, the four elements of the mix are not detached from each other which is different from what they are like in the physical world (Table 7). They are heavily interrelated and for all intents and purposes jointly experienced by the online customer, being merely parts of the content of the Company Customer interface, better known as the Web Site. From the customer's perspective the Web depicts the very aspects likely to prompt his/her direct manner, as elements of the Web site-based reaction to the online offering, the 4Ps being merely customer experience. For Internet customers this a part of the site based Web Experience and as such experience will include many other elements simultaneously experienced by the customer.

Attempts of approaching the 4Ps in isolation in the Web environment is not a sound strategy according to the above 4Ps analysis. That is because online customers mostly experience them in a simultaneous and direct manner, as elements of the Web site-based customer experience.

Constantinides (2002) came up with the Web-Marketing Mix model (Figure 12). The Web-Marketing Mix identifies four online marketing strategic, operational, organisational and technical critical factors: the Scope (strategic issues), the Site (operational issues), the Synergy (integration into the physical processes) and the System (technical issues). These are illustrated in Table 8.

Thanks to the three-dimensional representation, Kalyanam & McIntyre (2002) have come up with a more complete taxonomy of the elements forming the mix, which can be seen in Figure 13. They have included the 4 Ps inside their $4P+P^2+C^2+S^3$ model in a wider operative context as illustrated in figure 13.

Table 7. Conventional 4 Ps (Constantinides, 2002)

Product	The Web site is the prime online product and brand of the online organisation. The customer should become aware, develop interest and be persuaded to search for the site / product before going on looking into the company's detailed online offering.
Price	The majority of commercial sites function as price for the company's physical product assortment. Besides that, the Web site is perceived by the online prospect and customer as a cost element (due to that connectivity transaction costs, time and opportunity cost). Although this costs will be in most cases lower than the cost of performing these activities physically, the customer will compare these with the often cost of finding other online competitors and doing business with them.
Promotion	The Web site is the promotional medium as well constantly as the promotional content. The communicational Internet can rapidly and emotional impact of the Web site is an important part of the Web experience and a major factor in attracting and retaining online customer
Place	For any form of online interaction–transaction, the Website is the counter, helpdesk and sales outlet where the actual commercial or non-commercial transaction takes place. Moreover for products delivered in digital form (music, information, software and online services) the site fulfills even the task of the physical distributor by allowing the product delivery online

Table 8. Elements of Web-Marketing Mix model (Constantinides, 2002)

SCOPE. This content of this element is of primarily strategic character and outlines the decisions to be made on four areas:	*i) Objectives.* Online strategic objectives do not essentially differ from the traditional ones and are subject to the same quality criteria. *ii) Market analysis.* Online clients can be persons with different buying motives, cultural backgrounds, needs, demographic, ethnographic or lifestyle profiles from the conventional customers. In case that market research data is not available, a number of initial, basic assumptions must be made as to the most likely profiles, needs, motives, attitudes and demographics of the potential Web customers. iii) *Internal analysis* It is likely that in some cases the outcome of the internal assessment will be a No-Go decision, due for example to the high degree of organizational disruption, low added value or extremely high expenditure against low expected benefits. iv) *Strategic role* Web marketers can choose between a number of generic strategic roles, the most common being the informational, educational, service oriented, promotional, relational and transactional ones.
Site The Website is the functional platform of communication, interaction and transaction with the online customers	Some of the common site objectives and tasks are: g) communicating and promoting the business image, labels and products/ services; h) providing company information to customers and stakeholders; i) effectively communicating the firm physical or virtual promotional activities j) providing customer service and helpdesk functionality in order to enhance the customer loyalty and retention k) providing sales leads and customer/ market data l) allowing customers to communicate and interact with the company as well as creating online content;
Synergy Synergy means the integrating processes necessary for realising the virtual organisation's objectives.	i) *The Front Office.* The Web industry usually refers to the front office, as the website itself. Utilising existing promotional activities and capitalising on embedded customer goodwill is economical, less time consuming and more effective than launching new promotional campaigns with the purpose of establishing new commercial concepts and brand identities. ii) *The Back Office.* Making existing organisational infrastructures available to the online operation is a more sensible option than crating new ones. Next to the obvious cost aspects, the online organisation is likely to benefit from economies of scale and learning effects. iii) *Third parties.* Success in the virtual marketplace often requires co-operation with Internet partners outside the organisation and its value system.
System	Web site administration, maintenance and service, Web site traffic and transaction data; Web server hosting and choice of the Internet Service Provider; Website construction. Content management; Site security, System backup and etc.

METHODOLOGY FOR CASE STUDY

The purpose of this section is to provide steps of strategic social network marketing for analysing real-life case study.

A pre-defined set of actions planed for implementing integrated marketing communications strategy (Madhavaram, Badrinarayanan, and McDonald, 2005) are illustrate in Figure 14.

Situation Analysis and Identification of Opportunities

According to Madhavaram et al, (2005) and Caemmerer (2009), the marketing team would need to analyse the market situation and also identify potential opportunities for the product or service first. That is to analyse the market situation and identify potential opportunities for the product or service. Therefore a thorough and effective research phase is required. Secondary and primary data are collected and analysed during the market research process (Figure 14).

Figure 12. Web-Marketing Mix model(Constantinides, 2002)

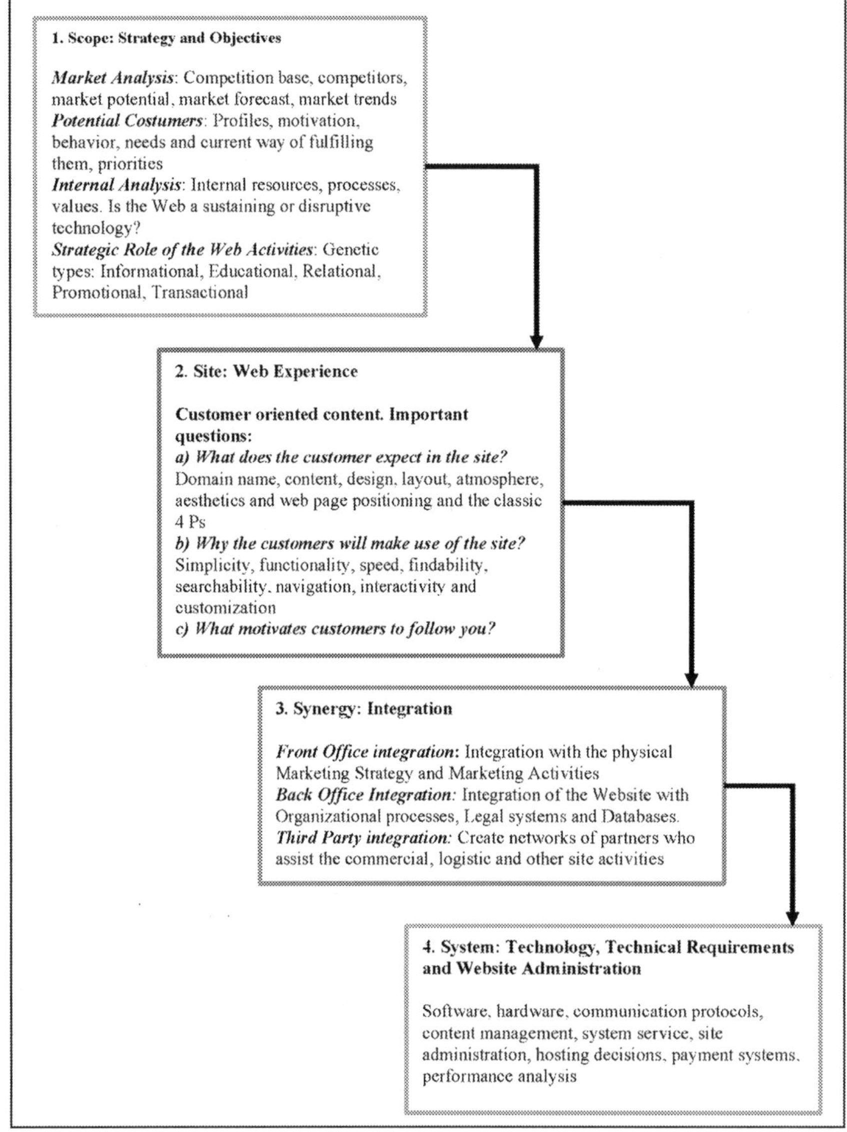

- *Secondary data.* Existing information that has been collected for other purposes. Generally, the start of a market research process is collecting such secondary data in order to establish a basic understanding of the situation. It is also for marketers to define problems and come up with objectives to continue the following primary research (Kotler et al., 1999; Wilson, 2006).

The advantages of secondary research are that it is generally easier, faster and cheaper to conduct than primary research. Moreover, secondary datasets sometimes provide data that an individual or a small organisation is not capable of collecting on its own. The information sometimes is not directly available for marketers or the information can cost too much financially to collect. Official statistics include data

Figure 13. The $4P+P^2+C^2+S^3$ model (Kalyanam & McIntyre, 2002)

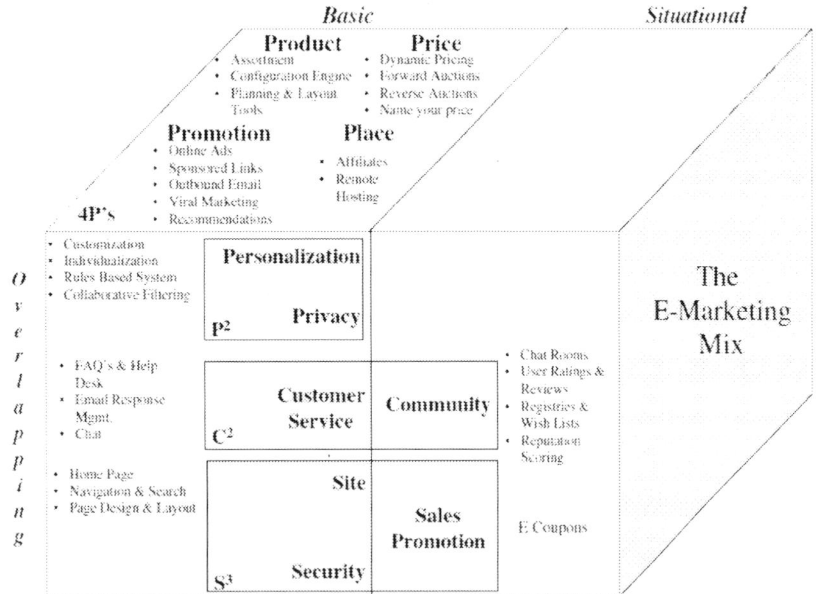

produced by the government or specialised agencies. In the case of Fiesta Movement Campaign by Ford, for example, the selection of social media and "agents" started with secondary data research.

- *Primary data.* Primary research involves activities that require going 'into the field'. Interviews, focus groups and questionnaire surveys can be included during the primary research.

Groups of individuals will be invited to discuss their opinions regarding a product or service over a given period of time in focus group activities. In this case, a interviewer will be leading the discussions to encourage participants to bring out their thoughts. Personal interviews are normally a face-to-face interview. The disadvantage of a personal interview is that it takes time to organize and it also could be financial costly. Telephone interviews provide opportunities to contact a great number of people during a short period of time. Nevertheless, the answers may be influenced by the interviewer and thus could be misleading. Postal surveys are posted and in the survey are mostly short questions. The disadvantage is that the response rates are normally very low and it also can take a very long time. In the case study, participants are picked based on both secondary and primary data.

Choosing the Marketing Communications Agency

After marketing communications opportunity and target group were identified, the marketing group still need to answer various questions (Caemmerer, 2009):

- What elements of the marketing communications mix should be used?
- What should the creative execution look like?
- How should the campaign be evaluated?

Figure 14. Stages in the planning and implementation of integrated marketing (Madhavaram et al, 2005; Caemmerer, 2009)

In order to answer these important questions, a brief that outlines key existing market data and campaign objectives needs to be created. The marketing team can also invite various marketing communications agencies to present their ideas and pitch for the account.

Selection of the Marketing Communications Mix and Creative Execution

In the case study of Fiesta Movement Campaign, the direct objective of the campaign is to increase these consumers' awareness of the Ford car Fiesta. There are tasks for the selected 'agents'. The agents are to complete the 'missions' and document their actions through various social media, conveying marketing message to the target audience - young, tech-savvy buyers.

Media Planning

The marketing team has to make decisions regarding which media channels to choose to reach the intended marketing communications objective. (Caemmerer, 2009). In the case study, a good mix of social media and social networking sites were used completing each other.

Campaign Evaluation and Success

In order to evaluate the efficiency and effectiveness of the marketing communications initiatives used by the marketing team, the marketing team or selected market research institutes should track consumers' attitudes towards the product or service during the period of campaign (Sherwood et al., 1989, Caemmerer, 2009).

Follow-Up

After the campaign was successful implemented, the marketing team should go back to the drawing board and create follow-up commercials for the product or service in order to ensure continuous exposure to and reinforcement of the communications message (Shapiro and Krishnan, 2001). In the case study, Ford also have created a series of follow-up promotions to reinforce the success of the Fiesta Movement Campaign.

CASE STUDY: FIESTA MOVEMENT CAMPAIGN

A successful social media marketing campaign which demonstrated the benefits of using established social networking channels was the Fiesta Movement Campaign by Ford in 2009 (Figure 15). Ford gave 100 hand-picked 20-30 year olds across the United States ford fetes for six calendar months and enquired them to complete a different "mission" every calendar month. The 100 participants were picked based on certain factors, especially their level of activity on social sites and with social media. These "agents" (social media influencers) delivered dinners from meals on wheels, eloped with the assist of the fete, and wrestled alligators among many other things. To document their adventures on Youtube, Flickr, Facebook, and Twitter pages which ford had created was required from the agents.

The Ford Fiesta Movement was regarded as an extremely successful social media campaign.

6.5 million views were generated from 700 videos produced by agents. Photos taken by the agents have accumulated more than 670,000 views. The campaign prompted over 50,000 U.S. consumers to request more information about the car, 973 of which did not already own a Ford vehicle. In the first six days of sales, Ford sold 10,000 units.

Since Ford wants to sell Fiestas to young, tech-savvy buyers, Ford benefit from consumers who are already familiar with popular social media websites to build awareness. In return, the agents get additional exposure from their association with Ford, and for 6 months, the 100 agents drive a new Ford Fiesta for free.

Figure 15. Fiesta Movement Campaign

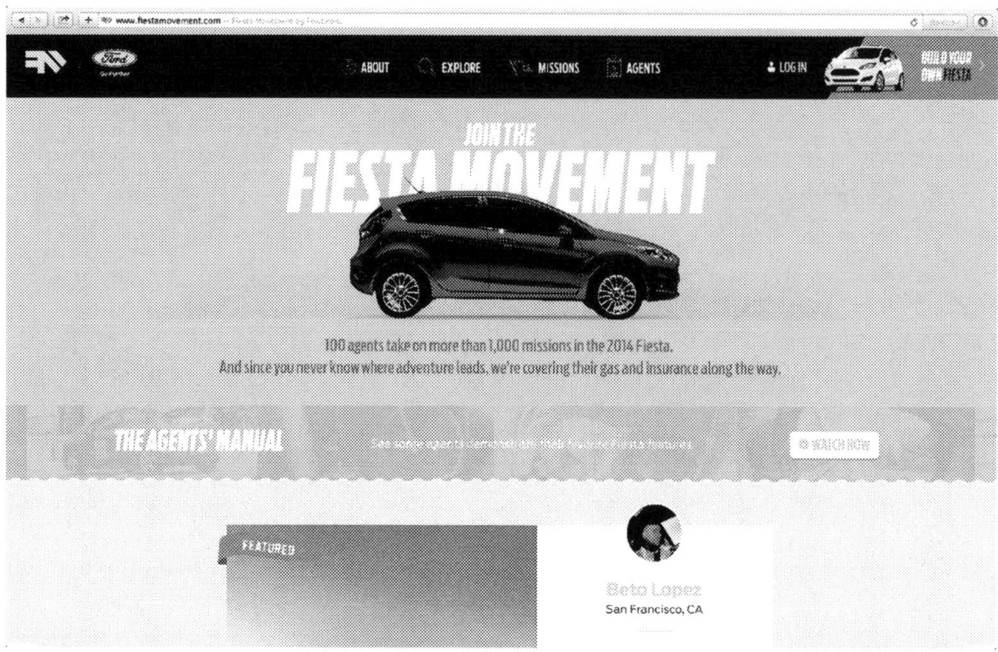

In 2014, Ford launches Fiesta 2014 via first completely user-generated campaign. Ford lets its customer to be entirely responsible for the 2014 Fiesta ad campaign. The company currently searches for 100 influencers whose voices and content generated in whatever form they prefer will be distributed by Ford.

"Fiesta was designed to reflect the individuality of the customer, so we feel the marketing efforts should give the reins to the people who will be driving it," says Jim Farley, Ford Motor Company executive vice president of Global Marketing, Sales and Service and Lincoln. "We have a fuel-efficient, tech-savvy and stylish car that doesn't sacrifice on performance – it truly has its own personality. That personality will come through in the stories and experiences of real people."

"Consumers – Millennials in particular – like being a part of the brands they feel represent them," says Keith Koeppen, Ford advertising and media manager. "This demographic is accustomed to creating content about their lives, so it just makes sense to give their creativity a bigger platform with greater scale."

Question

Describe the viral marketing approach used by Ford and explain the reasons behind the success of the Fiesta Movement Campaign.

FUTURE RESEARCH DIRECTIONS

So far, social networking sites use explicit representations of social networks primarily for visualization and browsing purposes. Yet, some research prototypes show that social networks are actually useful for more than just ego surfing to discover unexpected links in networks of friends. For example, some efforts are under way to examine email filtering and ranking based on social networks. Explicitly represented social networking information can also provide a means for assessing a piece of information's importance and relevance for many other kinds of information filtering (for example, in semantic attention management) and routing, in general.

At the moment social networks are mostly free of charge to users. However, it is possible that in the future some extra services will be added for a small price. For example, services such as personalized radio, premium account or improved security control could be offered to people who are willing to pay for them. It is hard to estimate what percentage of users would actually pay for these services, because they are accustomed themselves to getting everything for free. Nevertheless, it is plausible that the site owners will at least try to implement chargeable services to see if there is a market for them.

CONCLUSION

Social network studies include different tie types that are useful to evaluate interactions between members on social networking platforms. Currently, social networking sites are facing opportunities and challenges. As an important but hard to manage market force, WOM is believed to be able to complement and extend the effect of advertising. Viral campaigns work the Internet to deliver exposure via peer-to-peer endorsement and a good seeding strategy can greatly contribute to viral marketing campaign success. There is a growing popularity of social network platforms such as Facebook and Twitter different strategies could be applied to different social network platforms. Moreover, attempting to approach the 4Ps in isolation in the Web environment is not enough. The Web-Marketing Mix model, however, can be used for marketers to design a sound social media marketing strategy

Social networking sites provide additional channels to traditional marketing in the perspective of an integrated marketing communication strategy. Social networking sites are ideal for marketers to provide highly interactive and influential channels using combinations of words, videos, hyperlinks, hashtags and etc. These social networking sites also make information easily accessible for consumers who are already interested in the product or service. Moreover, social networking sites strategy can be highly reactive, e.g. responding to consumers' reviews and opinions.

The methodology section illustrated the steps for planning and implementation of integrated marketing communications. The case study demonstrates how the creative execution of Ford marketing campaign has successfully exploited the existing social networking sites.

REFERENCES

Borgatti, S. P. (2005). Centrality and Network Flow. *Social Networks*, *27*(1), 55–71. doi:10.1016/j.socnet.2004.11.008

Borgatti, S. P., & Cross, R. (2003). A Relational View of Information Seeking and Learning in Social Networks. *Management Science*, *49*(4), 432–445. doi:10.1287/mnsc.49.4.432.14428

Borgatti, S. P., Mehra, A., Brass, D. J., & Labianca, G. (2009). Network Analysis in the Social Sciences. *Science*, *323*(5916), 892–895. doi:10.1126/science.1165821 PMID:19213908

Burton-Jones, A., & Gallivan, M. J. (2007). Toward a Deeper Understanding of System Usage in Organizations: A Multilevel Perspective. *Management Information Systems Quarterly*, *31*(4), 657–679.

Caemmerer, B. (2009). The planning and implementation of integrated marketing communications. *Marketing Intelligence & Planning*, *27*(4), 524–538. doi:10.1108/02634500910964083

Christophe, V. D. B. (2010). Opportunities and Challenges in Studying Consumer Networks. *The Connected Consumer*, 7-35.

Constantinides, E. (2002). The 4S Web-Marketing Mix model. *Electronic Commerce Research and Applications*, *1*(1), 57–76. doi:10.1016/S1567-4223(02)00006-6

Conyard, R. (2014). Planning and Managing a Digital Strategy. *Red Ant*. Retrieved from www.redant.com

Ellison, N. B., & boyd, d. (2013). Sociality through Social Network Sites. In *The Oxford Handbook of Internet Studies*. Oxford, UK: Oxford University Press.

Hinz, O., Skiera, B., Barrot, C., & Becker, J. U. (2011). Seeding Strategies for Viral Marketing: An Empirical Comparison. *Journal of Marketing*, *75*(11), 55–71. doi:10.1509/jm.10.0088

Hoffman, D. L., & Thomas, P. N. (1996). Marketing in Hypermedia Computer-Mediated Environments: Conceptual Foundations. *Journal of Marketing*, *60*(7), 50–68. doi:10.2307/1251841

Hogan, J. E., Lemon, K. N., & Libai, B. (2004). Quantifying the ripple: Word-of-mouth and advertising effectiveness. *Journal of Advertising Research*, *44*(3), 271–280. doi:10.1017/S0021849904040243

Huang, M., Cai, F., Tsang, A. S. L., & Zhou, N. (2011). Making your online voice loud: The critical role of WOM information. *European Journal of Marketing*, *45*(7-8), 1277–1297. doi:10.1108/03090561111137714

Kalyanam, K., & McIntyre, S. (2002). The E-Marketing Mix: A Contribution of the E-Tailing Wars. *Journal of the Academy of Marketing Science*, *30*(4), 487–499. doi:10.1177/009207002236924

Kalyanam, K., & McIntyre, S. (2002). The E-marketing Mix: A Contribution of the E-Tailing Wars. *Academy of Marketing Science Journal*, *30*(4), 487–499. doi:10.1177/009207002236924

Kalyanam, K., & Shelby, M. (2007). Adaptive Experimentation in Interactive Marketing: The Case of Viral Marketing at Plaxo. *Journal of Interactive Marketing*, *21*(3), 72–85. doi:10.1002/dir.20086

Kane, G. C., & Alavi, M. (2008). Casting the Net: A Multimodal Network Perspective on User-System Interactions. *Information Systems Research*, *19*(3), 253–272. doi:10.1287/isre.1070.0158

Kane, G. C., Alavi, M., Labianca, G., & Borgatti, S. P. (2014). What's different about social media networks? A framework and Research Agenda. *MIS Quaterly*, *38*(1), 275–304.

Kane, G. C., Alavi, M., Labianca, G. J., & Borgatti, S. P. (2014). What's different about social media networks? A framework and research agenda. *Management Information Systems Quarterly*, *38*(1), 275–304.

Lotan, G. (2011). Breaking Bin Laden: Visualizing the Power of a Single Tweet. *Socialflow*. Retrieved from http://blog.socialflow.com/ post/5246404319/breaking-bin-laden-visualizing-the-power-of-a-single

Madhavaram, S., Badrinarayanan, V., & McDonald, R. (2005). Integrated marketing communication (IMC) and brand identity as critical components of brand equity strategy: A conceptual framework and research propositions. *Journal of Advertising*, *34*(4), 69–81. doi:10.1080/00913367.2005.10639213

Miranda, S. M., & Saunders, C. S. (2003). The Social Construction of Meaning: An Alternative Perspective on Information Sharing. *Information Systems Research*, *14*(1), 87–106. doi:10.1287/isre.14.1.87.14765

Miranda, S. M., & Saunders, C. S. (2003). The Social Construction of Meaning: An Alternative Perspective on Information Sharing. *Information Systems Research*, *14*(1), 87–106. doi:10.1287/isre.14.1.87.14765

Piskorski, M. J. (2009). *Networks as Covers: Evidence from Business and Social On-Line Networks*. Paper presented at the Academy of Management Annual Meeting, Chicago, IL.

Putnam, R. D. (1995). Tuning In, Tuning Out: The Strange Disappearance of Social Capital in America. *Political Science& Politics*, *28*(4), 664–683. doi:10.1017/S1049096500058856

Rosenman, E. T. R. (2012). *Retweets-but Not just Retweets: Quantifying and Predicting Influence on Twitter*. Retrieved from http://people.seas.harvard.edu/~mruberry/erosenmanthesis.pdf

Schulze, C., Bernd, S., & Thorsten, W. (2012). Linking Customer and Financial Metrics to Shareholder Value: The Leverage Effect in Customer-Based Valuation. *Journal of Marketing*, *76*(March), 17–32. doi:10.1509/jm.10.0280

Sciiuize, C., Sciiöler, L., & Skiera, B. (2014). Not All Fun and Games: Viral Marketing for Utilitarian Products. *Journal of Marketing*, *78*(1), 1–19. doi:10.1509/jm.11.0528

Shi, Z., Rui, H., & Whinston, A. B. (2014). Content Sharing in a Social Brocasting Environmen: Evidence from Twitter. *MIS Quaterly*, *38*(1), 123–142.

Sia, C. L., Tan, B. C. Y., & Wei, K. K. (2002). Group Polarization and Computer-Mediated Communication: Effects of Communication Cues, Social Presence, and Anonymity. *Information Systems Research*, *13*(1), 70–90. doi:10.1287/isre.13.1.70.92

Third Wave. (2013). *Social Media Strategy Framework*. Retrieved from http://thirdwaveberlin.com/ThirdWave-SocialMediaStrategyFramework.pdf

Venkatesh, V., Morris, M. G., Davis, G. B., & Davis, F. D. (2003). User Acceptance of Information Technology: Toward a Unified View. *Management Information Systems Quarterly*, *27*(3), 425–478.

KEY TERMS AND DEFINITIONS

Hubs: A segment construct in the Word-of-Mouth Network that indicate individuals who are the most well-connected in the local social networks.

Ripple Effect: A term to describe the effects generated by WOM activities, describing the spread of WOM.

Seeding Strategy: A form of marketing strategy that identifies specific customers and marketing towards them, so as to stimulate the internal dynamics of the market.

Social Networking Site: A service based on website for individuals to construct a public or private profile and to connect with other users for exchange of content and communication.

Viral Marketing: A type of peer-to-peer communication where people are encouraged to pass on promotional messages within their social networks.

Web-Marketing Mix: An alternative for conventional marketing mix which identifies online marketing strategic, operational, organizational and technical critical factors.

Word of Mouth (WOM): The flow of communications among consumers regarding products and services.

This research was previously published in the Handbook of Research on Integrating Social Media into Strategic Marketing edited by Nick Hajli, pages 207-239, copyright year 2015 by Business Science Reference (an imprint of IGI Global).

Chapter 4 Developing Marketing Strategy on Social Networks

Boris Milović
Union University, Serbia & Sava Kovacevic ad Vrbas, Serbia

ABSTRACT

Social networks have proven to be very convenient and effective medium for the spreading of marketing messages, advertising, branding and promotion of products and services. Social networks offer companies, nonprofit organizations, political parties etc. sending certain messages for free. In addition, they allow companies access to a wide range of characteristics of their users. Developing appropriate, the winning strategy for marketing in social media is a comprehensive, time-intensive process therefore it is important to know to manage their content. Social networks transform certain classical approaches to marketing. They provide creative and relatively easy way to increase public awareness of the company and its products, and facilitate obtaining feedback and decision making. These are sources of different information about users and groups that they've joined. The success itself of marketing performance on a social network depends on the readiness and training of organizations to perform on them.

INTRODUCTION

Research of the last few years points to the fact that people more often than not turn to social networks when looking for discounts and more affordable shopping and usually come in contact with brands promoting themselves on social websites in this manner. Advantage of social network marketing is, unlike traditional promotional channels, ads and sending promotional materials by mail, results of online social campaigns can be directly measured, which gives organizations far clearer insight in invested/gained ratio giving them plenty of information about consumers, clients and their needs and interests which they can use in the long run to create new, more efficient promotional campaigns to fortify and create a more complete business and marketing strategy.

Social networks are an online community of people which usually share a common interest or activity. They offer different ways for users to communicate with each other through blogs, e-mail, instant messaging and news containing valuable information for people in your network. Social networks are

DOI: 10.4018/978-1-5225-5637-4.ch004

powerful in their ability to ease communication. Social networks are becoming increasingly important part of media mix. Organizations are starting to treat them as traditional offline and online media (Peters, Chen, Kaplan, Ognibeni, & Koen, 2013). Social networks are affordable tools used to combine technology and social interactions with the use of words. These tools are mostly internet or mobile based. In the field of social networking, wide range of currently available applications can be used with the goal of connecting people, sharing resources, hosting multimedia conferences etc.

Attempts to hear the voice of consumers or users on social networks uses the advantage based on openness and honesty (Patino, Pitta, & Quinones, 2012). Users are willing to ask questions about important things and expect comments from people sharing the same interests or problems. Flow of information is open to the members of the community and represents conversation that member can follow.

They enable marketers to communicate with visitors, users and potential consumers. They personalize the brand and help to convey the message in a relaxed and conversational manner. Social networks help to inform consumers about the advertized product, about the company and what it offers. Relationship is created with people who otherwise probably wouldn't find out about the products and services or what the company represents. Social networks make a company "real" for the consumers. If the goal to be achieved is for the people to keep track of the company, then not only should newest products be discussed, but share its "personality" with them. It can be used for communication and providing interactions which consumers want (Lake).

Websites of social networks are starting to serve as a center on the web where large groups of people, usually with similar interests, gather together. Philosophy is simple: Make an appearance where target population spends time. Appearance benefits the company in several ways (Williams, 2009):

1. Exposure to the target group,
2. Interaction with the target group,
3. Sharing the business identity of the company.

This strategy of social marketing refers to the need for suitable branding and establishing appropriate strategies for user services.

Another reason for the use of social networks is that contents can be sent to those interested in receiving new information. Users subscribed to the news about the product or brand, are often offered several methods of informing. They can subscribe or unsubscribe with ease. Therefore, those connected to the company on social media are those most interested to find out more about the company, or what it offers.

Since it is easy for people to publish content, they can and will talk about the company brand – good or bad. To be a part of that conversation is extremely important and useful. One of the basic characteristics of social networks is fluidity of the virtual identity of its members. It means that variability of the community members' identity is simplified and frequent, due to the nature of the medium carrying the communication. Data offered are often unreliable and at the very least impossible to verify due to the fact that the members of the community rarely meet in person, in the real world. Consequence is that the most important facts about the other person (sex, age, appearance or race) which in direct or face to face communication are easily observed, in virtual networks they remain only unverified data which we accept with caution.

Social networks are usefull for influencing and monitoring consumer beliefs and views towards the product or brand. They can attract different groups of people and conversation can continue for years. Content in online communities can reflect great diversity of personal views, richer conversation and long term engagement of users. This type of social networks are appropriate tools for managing customer relationships, and simplifying establishing and maintaining relationships between users and the company. In using different types of social networks, different goals and ways in which the user reacts or uses these networks are observed (Weinberg & Pehlivan, 2011). Social networks are everywhere in business, thereby most of the companies are present on Facebook, Twitter etc, while connections between social media in the classroom and business are just starting to surface (Veeck & Hoger, 2014). Elements of social networks aren't replacing traditional goals but they secure improved and potentially more active appreciation of users' needs (Veeck & Hoger, 2014).

Marketers must involve media relations as part of their online strategy and thus maintain strong relationships with relevant users. Social networks are a good way to increase company reliability which will certainly give the company good ratings and better branding. Possibility to communicate with consumers gives the company results in the form of large credibility on the Internet. Generating contacts is yet another basis for the company to plunge into social network marketing. Since acquiring potential consumers is important for the success of the company, use of social network marketing helps to reach target potential consumers. There is no better way or cheaper way to announce a new product or service of the company than through social networks, which will ease spreading news about them. Social networks also influence generating large traffic on company's website.

ENGAGING USERS ON SOCIAL NETWORKS

Increased awareness of organizations about the importance of engaging users/members of social networks started together with the emergence of new technologies and tools which enable higher interactivity among individuals and organizations. The evolution of internet and especially emergence of social networks with their important characteristic of improving interaction between customers and salesmen has occupied the attention of managers searching for better understanding and servicing of their customers using these technologies and tools (Sashi, 2012). Number of users using social networks and chat applications is in constant increase and current data are given in Table 1.

Social networks enable more flexible engagement of consumers. This has to be taken as a priority since engaging users is crucial because it will help the company keep existing users and strengthen the credibility of the brand. Connecting to social networks means that the user becomes a participant and not just a visitor. Process of connecting is very important for success of social marketing and to establish successful social business practice. Connecting in social context indicates that the users have personal interest for what the company brings to the market. This refers to users, partners, employees, and all that can express and share their opinion or ideas on social networks (Evans & McKee, 2010). Social network marketing enables revealing user preferences, so that the organization can orient based on what the users want. Knowing user preferences means easier improvement of products and more efficient planning of marketing campaigns. Social networks can be useful for businesses in purely business purposes, although social network works at the individual level as well, individual business people can exercise individual contacts with other business people to achieve common goals.

World study about the use of social media published by UM "Social Media Tracker Wave 5" (2010) has determined that almost 75% of active internet users has used websites for social networking and that almost half of them has joined an online brand community. This points to the fact that the users are actively using online social media to communicate with companies. However, the use of social media

Table 1. Number of users on social networks and chats

Social Network	Users
Facebook	1.184 M
QQ	816 M
Q zone	632 M
Whatsapp	400 M
Google+	300 M
Wechat	272 M
Linkedln	259 M
Twitter	232 M
Tumblr	230 M
Tancent Weibo	220 M

Source: We Are Social, 2014.

is not uniform across the world. Recent data about the use of social media data imply that there are significant differences in ways social networks are used on a global level, what content is created and what "public wisdom" is shared (Singh, Lehnert, & Bostick, 2012).

Users of social networks want to connect with other users with similar interests and desires. Organizations are able to use this fact by creating an online community which will attract people with same views. These communities should focus on sharing interests and values. Success in social networks depends on the quality of content. Everything is reduced to engaging people and the key for success is good content which is placed on social networks. In social networks people create, read, keep, mark and share content. If content they value is not provided, it will not be published or shared again. Sharing the story online in the right place to the right people gives results. But first well thought out strategy should be created based on thorough research to achieve those results (Falkow, 2009).

Achieving goals such as profitability, good market position, income and sales, depends on satisfying users' needs and desires. Product purchase itself doesn't signify user engagement, rather that purchase should lead to other purchases of that product or other products of the same brand, or other products in the same rank of offered products by a single company (Sashi, 2012). Creating a loyal consumer is a process which not only depends on the purchase of products, but also on his satisfaction with those products. Repeat purchases of a single user leads to his connection to the brand, so in time the user gains emotional bond with the company and becomes its fan, which results in his engagement (connecting). These users will probably recommend the product to others through blogs, social networks, comments on websites and even add value by providing user generated content. User connecting expands traditional role of the user and involves them in the process of adding value helping managers to understand their needs, product development process, providing support for strategies and products, and become representatives of the product.

Users feel engaged when they can send feedback related to the product or organization. It comes in the form of criticism, accolades and useful suggestions. When considering the whole, this information contributes to the meaning of the online community in which sincere and open communication is encouraged and the engagement of users is increased (Mangold & Faulds, 2009). Users are motivated with desire to demonstrate their expertise and provide information for the others. By maintaining constant product quality, lower prices indicate better purchase decision. It is expected that the number of posts should be in negative connection with the price of the product in the early stages of user consideration. Consumers leaving their opinion on the Internet in early stages are probably going to be more constructive and less influenced by price than the wider mass of consumers. Posts that users leave today are connected to their satisfaction with the product. Since the same product quality is given, lower price leads to high satisfaction and with that higher user ratings. Although high price can mean product quality, which increases ratings, it also signifies higher discontent which decreases ratings. Except the price product quality also influences leaving of comments. Users satisfied with the quality will leave comments of praise and thus influence product rating. Leaving of comments will especially be informative and influential if the product being rated is of significantly lower or higher quality compared to its competition (Chen, Fay, & Wang, 2011).

People in online communities connected to the brand are involved together with the organization in creating values and in promotion of the brand itself, and also in maintaining social community centered around the brand. Online community brand positively influences on these practices of creating values (Laroche, Habibi, Richard, & Sankaramarayanan, 2012).

Marketing of social networks is highly demanding because it encourages users and organizations to be interactive. This gives the consumers a positive image of the product or service which the company offers, which can lead to increase in sales. Users try to find out everything they can about the product or service on company website. If their attempt to inform themselves fails, a lot of them will either give up or seek the information on social networks. Companies should enable their users to ask questions on social media, and to quickly provide answers to those questions. Also users should be asked to leave their thoughts about the products on social networks. More information posted about the product leads to more potential consumers. Social network platforms should be updated with news about the products as often as possible (Davis, 2012).

Social networks overcome flaws in corporate websites and have many advantages relative to other forms of marketing. Social network services enable almost instant communication with existing and potential users (Shelton, 2012). Unlike websites, where companies have to wait for the website to be visited, social networks enable companies to send information to interested parties. When the company updates information about the product, they can be sent to all users who subscribed to receive news about that product, and information can be sent around the world in a matter of seconds. Social networks give an appropriate manner to manage sales through distribution of coupons and discounts. Users also access social media through mobile phones, which means that companies advertising a product through social networks have constant access to their users.

IMPACT OF SOCIAL NETWORKS ON MARKETING STRATEGY

Proper appearance on social networks makes companies able to reach new customers, to maintain contact with existing customers and to become recognizable. Thanks to creative marketing campaigns on social networks, we can significantly improve their business, because someone who is different and creative in this field is very quickly becoming the well known brand. Social networks offer the possibility for thorough research practically free. It is possible to set goals and get return of investment, but one need to know the desired direction and what exactly needs to be achieved.

In online conversation it is possible to find out (Falkow, 2009):

- Who discusses the company?
- What do they say?
- Is it positive or negative?
- Where the conversation is taking place?
- Which groups discuss the company?
- What the competition does on social media?
- What is important about them?
- Which contents are relevant to users?
- Are there topics of interest that the company can provide content about?
- Which social websites have the most conversations?
- Who to connect with?
- Who influences these networks?
- Where are opportunities and threats?

As powerful tool of communication, social networks allow companies to reach their customers exactly where they spend the most time, at the same time raising awareness of its brand and expanding customer base. If this form of marketing is properly implemented, marketing on social networks may also increase the efficacy of other marketing techniques - including SEO - helps in building natural links, increases traffic sites, increasing brand awareness and consequently brand recognition.

Once this information is gathered, resources can be divided wisely, which means starting point is known, or on which social networks we should focus. Their significance and the size of this potential market are best illustrated by data in Table 2.

Social networks as noted are sources of direct marketing. Members of company groups or pages are usually people interested in products or services offered by the company, and especially for special offers and discounts. Promotion on social networks includes directly addressing the customers. It is necessary for the companies to create additional content – company blog, interactive Internet presentation, interesting articles, images and video material. Also, social networks are useful for fast development of existing and research and development of new markets.

SOME SIGNIFICANT FACTS ABOUT SOCIAL MEDIA

Social networks are dominant compared to all print media, radio and Television. This claim is supported by numerous facts. How significant are social networks and how wide their impact in 2016 is best illustrated by the following data (Mansfield, 2016):

- 97 percent of online adults aged 16-64 say they have visited or used a social network within the last month.
- Internet users have average of 7 social accounts, up from 3 in 2012.
- More than half of online adults (56 percent) use more than one of the five social media.
- 8 in 10 internet users globally visit/use social networks on their mobile devices.
- People are most likely to use social media in order to keep up with friends (43 percent) or news (41 percent), or to fill time (39 percent).

Table 2. Social network statistics

Social Network Statistics	Data
Total number of Facebook users worldwide	1.4 Billion
Total percentage of 18-24 year olds who already use social media	98%
Total percentage of people on Earth who use Facebook	11%
Total amount of minutes people spend on Facebook every month	700 billion
Average amount of time a person uses Facebook per month	15 hours 33 minutes
Total amount of people who access Facebook with phone	250 million
Total amount of websites that have integrated with Facebook	2.5 million
Total pieces of content shared on Facebook each month	70 billion
Total amount of unique YouTube users per month	490 million
Total amount of YouTube page views per month	92 billion
Total amount hours spent on YouTube per month	2.9 billion
Total amount of articles hosted by Wikipedia	17 million
Average pictures uploaded to Flickr per minute	3,000
Total amount of pictures hosted by Flickr	5 billion
Average amount of tweets per day	190 million
Percent of teenagers who log on to Facebook over 10 times per day	22%

Source: http://www.statisticbrain.com/social-networking-statistics/.

- Around 1 in every 3 minutes spent online is devoted to social networking and messaging, with digital consumers engaging for a daily average of 1 hour and 58 minutes.

Average daily time spent on social networks measured in 2015 in some countries is shown by Figure 1 (Bauer, 2016).

Figure 1. Time spent on social media
Source: We are social 2015.

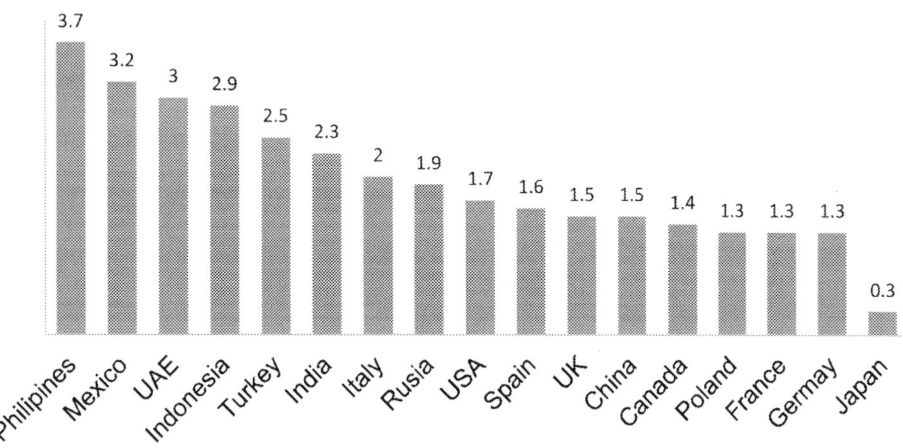

The characteristics of the Internet itself affect the marketing communications. Foremost is the availability of the Internet 24 hours, then multimedia communication, interactivity between the user and the company, "one on one" marketing. Thanks to the growing presence of the Internet companies began to invest large sums in with the marketing activities on it.

Social networking very popular among adult internet users in emerging and developing nations.

Social structure is composed of individuals who have specific types of interdependency, such as vision, ideas, friendship, financial interests, common interests, trust, knowledge and prestige.

New social networks "are springing up like mushrooms", and every day are increasingly popular. Mostly it comes to mobile applications. How it looks in different countries of the world is as shown in Figure 2.

Over 75% of all Internet users use social media. Social media sites used to be an auxiliary territory in Internetland, but it's become clear that these kinds of sites are now the bread and butter of modern Web activity. They make up a sizable portion of all Web traffic (Lee, 2015).

Social networks may be used in studies to be used in market segmentation, generating new ideas, testing a new concept, new product development, launching new brands, creating price and integrate marketing solutions. They can be used for a variety of marketing research, such as focus groups, panels, interviews etc

For younger users, Instagram is more important than Facebook and Twitter. While Facebook and Twitter are still the reigning leaders, their mainstream status means that the younger generation considers them "old school" (Lee, 2015). If we look this facts in wider contexts we can say that traditionally the for Ps of marketing is now five Ps, Price, Products, Place, Promotion and new one is People.

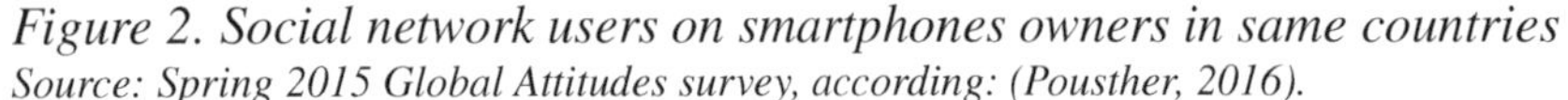

Figure 2. Social network users on smartphones owners in same countries
Source: Spring 2015 Global Attitudes survey, according: (Pousther, 2016).

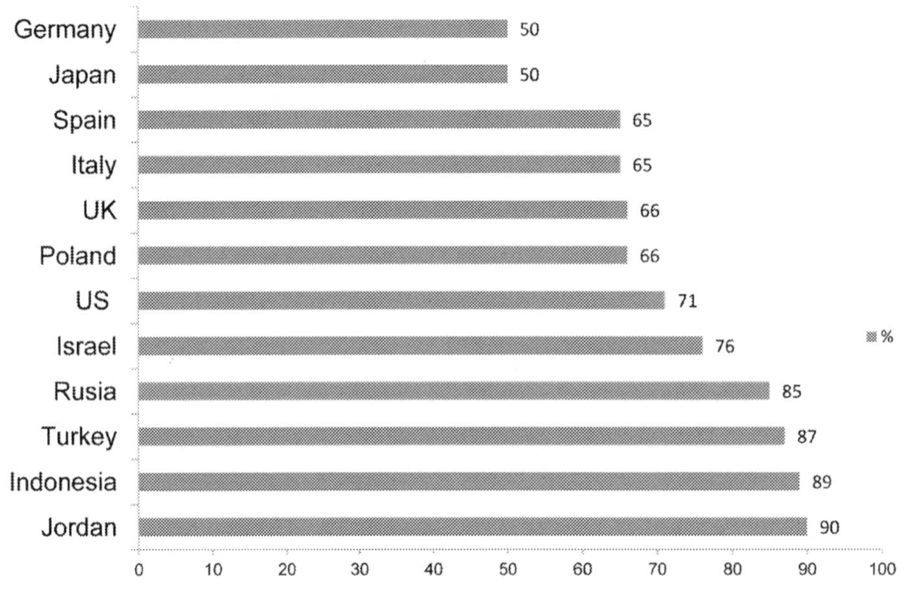

CONTENT MANAGEMENT STRATEGY

Thanks to social media, nature of communication has gone through significant changes in the last two decades and those changes aren't complete yet. In recent years social changes have led to a switch in focus from the group to the individual. Modern shopping process begins by consumers independently collected information about the product, whether surf the Internet or exchange views with each other on social networks. Customers are not interested in what the company wants to sell them, but they are interested in the benefits that they themselves receive. While older generations, used to linear offer of media content, still rely on classic media, for younger generations Social networks already cloud the border between personal interaction and professional business tools (Šiđanin, 2012). Users today focus on the web as their primary source of research, insight and information which condition decisions about shopping. Companies have to connect with users in places where they spend time online through relevant and intriguing content.

Information about the product, expert advice, relevant articles, as well as rating and reviews, are all examples of content used by leading companies. Efficient content management strategy is expanded beyond the pages of company website or blog in relevant social networks and communication channels, including marketing and PR (Bumgardner, 2011). Social network contents are perspective sources of data for analysts and decision makers about events, services, products and experiences of their consumers/users (Grljevic & Bošnjak, 2012). Social network content analysis includes monitoring preferences, intentions and interests of the consumers. Personalization of content through a content management helps brands to have greater visibility of the codes of their target groups, because the focus of today's consumers scattered, so that traditional marketing methods become obsolete.

The attitude of companies towards social networks are different. Companies who carefully create their own strategies of social networks have a huge advantage over others. They make interactive relationship with customers and they are able to communicate with customers and by respecting their wishes make them loyal.

Social media websites in addition to entertainment can be an efficient business technique for companies. With intensifying use of these websites, consumer behavior drastically changes, and social media contents which they generate are perspective sources of data for analysts and decision makers (Grljevic & Bošnjak, 2012). Business decision makers are still leaning to higher ROI marketing. Sometimes they don't understand that getting satisfactory results begins with consumer awareness. Creating awareness doesn't mean avoiding measures and return of investments (Bumgardner, 2011). Following elements can contribute to this:

- Promotions in the form of animated banners, images, interactive networks with audio and visual elements. Cookies and browser history is used here to determine: demographics and interests and to direct appropriate ads towards those individuals.
- Social networks are used to turn communication into interactive dialogues and to share content among people. They make shopping decisions based on information gathered on credible social websites among visitors with similar interests. Companies sharing educational contents and participate in relevant conversations have an opportunity to create awareness and increase advantage relative to competition.

- Internet search engine marketing – this forma of marketing is seen as a strategy of capturing existing queries. Appropriate sorting of keywords and phrases with user's intentions is a key factor in generating awareness and reaching users in the early stage of shopping. Marketers should identify and direct their attention on users which use general key phrases instead of those who use more specific phrases and those who use company name. With this strategy marketers have the possibility to reach a wider user population and with that advance their position on the market.

Products are mostly made to respond to user needs, which explain development of new products based on consumer tastes and preferences. Furthermore, products are branded in order to be made unique and more attractive to certain segments of the population (Bardfield, 2012). Content management strategy is creating a plan for the production, publication and distribution of useful and usable content. Companies witch planning this process must work to define not only the content to be published, but must first know and why they have and the time publish to achieve the target segment.

Companies use information about user profiles on social media as a means to discover which marketing messages would be best accepted by the users. User presence on social media reveals a large part of information about their preferences, needs and aspirations. Companies use information gathered from user profiles on social media to send targeted marketing material. Facebook applications can be used to send special offers based on user interests, desires and social connections on facebook. By personalizing marketing companies can generate large interest for their product or service, which will lead to increase in sales. Well planned social network program based on observation and understanding focus group will result in deeper relations with users and other interested parties.

DEFINING MARKET SEGMENT ON SOCIAL MEDIA

First users of social media networks were teen-agers and students, but today it is already used by people of all ages and different professions. Today, we count over hundreds service, and most importantly should be singled out Facebook, Instagram,Twitter, Google Plus, LinkedIn, Pinterest, Tumblr...Companies getting to know their target consumer group and implementing strategy to attract them is one of the key assignments of marketing on social networks. It is necessary to determine trends on your target market, characteristics, needs and social activities of target consumer and then research target group behavior on social networks. If the company already has an email base, it is possible to use it to find your target public with the help of services for finding friends on Facebook and Twitter or connections on LinkedIn. It is necessary to discover which social network is used by the target group to determine on which social networks the company should appear on. Just because Facebook is the most popular social network with the greatest user base in a certain country doesn't mean that target customers use this social network. Or, for example, if average users in one country doesn't use social network Google Plus, this doesn't mean that your target public doesn't belong to a group of Internet enthusiasts and technology addicts which are pretty active on this social network also.

Research phase of target market is of crucial importance in the process of strategy building of whose quality largely depends the success of marketing campaigns on social websites.

When identifying goals, who should the company reach with its marketing should be determined. Content quality should be considered and which groups it would attract the most. Some factors to consider are (cvent.com, 2012):

Table 3. Percent of people who use social networks

Social Networks	Percent Yes
Do you ever use / have a profile on… (Poll Taken in early 2012)	
Any social network	58%
Facebook	56%
LinkedIn	14%
Twitter	11%
Google+	9%

Source: http://www.statisticbrain.com/social-networking-statistics/.

- **Demographics:** Age, sex, geographic location, nationality, etc.
- **Key Words and Phrases:** Which business functions, industrial terms, user groups define target group?
- **Interest:** What motivates the target market? Which topics affect the most, or engage people in the company target group should be determined.
- **Social Behavior:** How the target market uses social networks? Are they active participants and probable to create user generated content? Will they criticize given content? Or are they passive participants which will read the comment but will not share it or comment upon it? Maybe they will join the group but will not participate actively in discussions. Identifying these behaviors by listening and observing social network channels.

Forming of a group itself is of importance for the company because it presents a market segment it speaks to or communicates with. Companies strive, as always, to adjust their market performance to the target segment on social network.

SUCCESS OF MARKETING ON SOCIAL NETWORKS

Social networks, as already mentioned, are a modern tool where the brand image of a company can be manifested daily in new words, multimedia and different interactions. The companies are able to create new content easily, while engaging directly with prospects, customers and peers one-on-one. Social media is an excellent way to introduce people to a brandnad it is a good way of attracting new customers. Social networks are the ideal platform for building and managing a positive online PR strategy. On social networks companies may meet everyone surfers, potential customers, partners, customers, consumers and even competitors.

Benefits for marketing on social networks are numerous and mostly gained at a very low cost. The use of social media to achieve given goals of a company to promote their products or services, communicologically viewed, is to design and conduct different methods of communication through chosen social media for achieving publicity. Through more advance use of social media company has the possibility to establish and manage a whole spectrum of action of corporate communication (Šiđanin, 2012). Return of investment (ROI) of marketing is defined by marketers inside the company when measuring multiple components of their social marketing initiatives. Starting from indicators related to social presence and ranges, marketers move beyond apparent growth of fans and followers and traffic on their websites for linking social initiative to lead the generation and sell. The most important indicators of return of investment in social network marketing are (State of Social Media Marketing, 2012):

- **Presence on Social Networks (Number of Followers and Fans):** Marketing on websites for social networking will increase awareness by increasing online presence of their products and brand. When the company creates the group or organizes a promotion on social networks, members are reminded of your brand and website with every interaction. Future customers decide which groups they wish to join and which information they want to get. This information is usually received well.
- **Increase Internet Traffic:** Communication, recommendations and other publications on websites for social networking often contain links. If the company is mentioned and the link is clearly stated, such publications direct traffic to your website, increasing the brand and product awareness. Due to the structure of social networking websites, these link are naturally aimed at potential clients interested in your company, products or services.
- **Social Mentioning of the Company Through the Platform/Increase Customer Loyalty:** if done properly, by promoting the company or products through construction of social network, customer loyalty can be improved greatly. If the participation is frequent and the firm is consistent and honest, it adds value by providing useful content, and it presents itself personally, it will greatly improve company reputation and build trust and credibility.
- **Sharing Social Conversations (Increasing Success of Newly Launched Products):** Social networks provide unique opportunity to make the polls about the product relevant for the community's desires and needs. Community can lead and participate in the process of product development. By giving them a say in the process company can increase loyalty and guarantee success when launching a new product.
- Social networking website users create their profiles as they join the network. These profiles must be very detailed, and their aim is to help users connect with others who share similar interests and activities. Profiles contain, not just basic information about the user, but information about their education, areas of technical expertise, publications, membership in other groups, geographic location and workplace (among other information). For marketing, this information is priceless, because it can be used to develop high targeted marketing message.
- Lead generation.
- Sales.

Success of marketing approach on social network depends on the training of employees in social media in organizations. This training must include not just focusing on the use of certain tools, but how to determine which tools to use and how to efficiently measure their use. By using internet technologies, social media management coordinates media campaign, manages consumer relations, improves trading and sales through channels of social media and acts as a representative for social integration of media in company strategy. Also, it creates contents which attract the attention of online users – consumers and encourages them to share on their social networks.

One of the key thing for a successful marketing platform on social networks is knowing your own business. Regardless of the size or the nature of the company, knowledge about company power, target market and information about products and services are key things of a successful marketing on social networks. Companies should be prepared to efficiently manage constantly changing appearance of social networks because each new day brings new forms of social networks (DiStaso, McCorkindale, & Wright, 2011).

Advancement in technologies has lead to dynamic growth of communication through interactive networks, especially Internet, enabling the flow of information involving user engagement and participation in real time. Equally important, for small and large organizations whose goals are to provide new and current information allowing a certain level of involvement of the target group. Internet as an efficient means of marketing used as part of marketing programs and social networks eases increase in achieving goals (Bhagat, Dutta, & Dutta, 2012). Development of the Internet as means of communication has triggered increase in sending of adapted messages in real time, user feedback and engagement. New forms of engagement such as Social networks give promising results which are widely used in order to separate the company from the competition and to establish special position in consumer awareness and chosen social community. Main idea (Bhagat, Dutta, & Dutta, 2012) is to encourage interaction on social media and promote the brand on the Internet, and with that create users loyal to the brand which finally become the driving force of promotion and the ambassadors for the product, or category in their social circles becomes integrated in their social life so deep that it is nearly impossible to separate. This achieves the end goal with greater results and long term community. Users start to treat the brand as part of their social community.

Although social networks as: Facebook and Twitter, give creative and relatively easy way to increase public awareness about the company and its products, these services carry with them certain risks. Main risk is unauthorized registration using a fake name or account name that involves company brand, practice called "brand theft". False user names can distribute false information about the company, redirect public to other companies or products, gather classified information, or simply prevent company owners to use them as logical user names for marketing purposes (Shelton, 2012).

Social networks are a growing market with a tendency of continued growth in the foreseeable future. While some companies have already established a strong presence on social networks, others are just beginning to see the reality of inevitability of presence. Opinion on social networks is much divided. Each company has its own opinion on social networks and their potential application, risk management strategy, etc. Risk awareness connected to social networks is very small. Many managers confirm the existence of risks on social networks, but those risks aren't well defined (Thompson, Hertzberg, & Sullivan, 2011). Managing structures or management governing risks and development of approach on social networks is, with many companies, still in the phase of development. As risks connected with social networks start to get more and more public attention, organizations will be able to respond with more determination to spotted risks.

CONCLUSION

The appearance of social networks greatly shake the world, especially in the field of communication, future Web eliminated needs for "face to face" interaction, allowing people connect regardless of the place where you are and the time in which to do so.

Modern organizations have less and less loyal clients, on the other hand offer of similar products or competition is greater so business itself is harder compared to earlier periods. Basic condition of survival and advancement of organizations is expanding customer base or users. Question arises in what way is this possible to achieve, and the solution lies precisely in the use of social networks as practical and relatively cheap solution. Basic advantage of social networks compared to classic channels of communication with customers is their availability, price, and large number of users. Social networks present powerful tools for communication – they enable efficient communication with current and potential clients, as well as communication inside the organization itself. Social networks have become integral part of everyday life for most people. Everybody uses Facebook, LinkedIn, Twitter, Youtube and other services for telecommunication with friends and colleagues, sharing family photographs, videos and other important parts of life. Still, those same people who privately like and tweet with friends and family, seem to forget that when they come to their workplace. Even though social networks offer clear possibilities for communication with consumers, majority of manager views them as a mystery or in best case scenario advertising channel. Integration with corporate information systems makes communication channels of social networks more efficient, within the company itself, as well as in relations with users. Adoption of forms of communication with users increases employee productivity, shortens production cycle, improves communication efficiency which as a consequence has increase in user satisfaction.

REFERENCES

Bardfield, L. (2012, March 1). *Applying a Social Marketing Framework to Salt Reduction*. Retrieved from http://www.paho.org/panamericanforum/wp-content/uploads/2012/08/APPLYING-A-SOCIAL-MARKETING-STRATEGY-TO-SALT-REDUCTION-_MARCH-2012.pdf

Bauer, R. (2016, October 02). Retrieved November 29, 2016, from http://blogs.worldbank.org/publicsphere/media-revolutions-time-spent-online-continues-rise

Bhagat, R. N., Dutta, M., & Dutta, B. K. (2012). Social Media Promotion: Role of IMC in Rising above the Clutter. *National Conference on Emerging Challenges for Sustainable Business 2012*, 1437-1451.

Bumgardner, K. (2011). *The Right Digital Marketing Mix*. Retrieved February 05, 2013, from websitebiz.com: http://www.websitebiz.com/resources/white-papers/right-digital-marketing-mix-b2b/

Burton, S., & Soboleva, A. (2011). Interactive or reactive? Marketing with Twitter. *Journal of Consumer Marketing*, *28*(7), 491–499. doi:10.1108/07363761111181473

Chen, Y., Fay, S., & Wangc, Q. (2011). The Role of Marketing in Social Media: How Online Consumer Reviews Evolve. *Journal of Interactive Marketing*, *25*(2), 85–94. doi:10.1016/j.intmar.2011.01.003

cvent.com. (2012). *Event Marketing 2.0 - How to Boost Attendance Through Social Media*. Retrieved February 05, 2013, from cvent.com: www.cvent.com/en/pdf/social-media-event-marketing-ebook.pdf

Davis, N. (2012). *How To Improve Your Social Media Marketing In 30 Minutes*. Retrieved February 05, 2013, from impactbnd.com: http://www.impactbnd.com/improve-social-media-marketing-30-minutes/

DiStaso, M. W., McCorkindale, T., & Wright, D. K. (2011). How public relations executives perceive and measure the impact of social media in their organizations. *Public Relations Review*, *37*(3), 325–328. doi:10.1016/j.pubrev.2011.06.005

Đukić, S. (2011). Uloga i značaj društvenih medija u komuniciranju vrednosti marke. *Marketing*, *42*(1), 17–26.

Evans, D., & McKee, J. (2010). *Social Media Marketing - The Next Generation of Business Engagement*. Indianapolis, IN: Wiley Publishing, Inc.

Falkow, S. (2009). *Social Media Strategy*. Pasadena, CA: Expansion Plus, Inc.

Lake, L. (n.d.). *Understanding the Role of Social Media in Marketing*. Retrieved February 05, 2013, from About.com: http://marketing.about.com/od/strategytutorials/a/socialmediamktg.htm

Laroche, M., Habibi, M. R., Richard, M.-O., & Sankaranarayanan, R. (2012). The effects of social media based brand communities on brand community markers, value creation practices, brand trust and brand loyalty. *Computers in Human Behavior*, *28*(5), 1755–1767. doi:10.1016/j.chb.2012.04.016

Lee, J. (2015, December 15). *12-social-media-facts-statistics-know-2016*. Retrieved October 27, 2016, from http://www.makeuseof.com/tag/12-social-media-facts-statistics-know-2016/

Madera, J. M. (2012). Using social networking websites as a selection tool: The role of selection process fairness and job pursuit intentions. *International Journal of Hospitality Management*, *31*(4), 1276–1282. doi:10.1016/j.ijhm.2012.03.008

Mangold, W. G., & Faulds, D. J. (2009). Social media: The new hybrid element of the promotion mix. *Business Horizons*, *52*(4), 357–365. doi:10.1016/j.bushor.2009.03.002

Mansfield, M. (2016, November 22). *Social media statistics 2016*. Retrieved November 29, 2016, from smallbiztrends.com: https://smallbiztrends.com/2016/11/social-media-statistics-2016.html

McCann, U. (2010, October 14). *Social Media Wave*. Retrieved January 25, 2014, from harrenmedia: http://www.slideshare.net/harrenmedia/social-media-wave-5-universal-mccann

Patino, A., Pitta, D. A., & Quinones, R. (2012). Social medias emerging importance in market research. *Journal of Consumer Marketing*, *29*(3), 233–237. doi:10.1108/07363761211221800

Peters, K., Chen, Y., Kaplan, A. M., Ognibeni, B., & Koen, P. (2013). Social Media Metrics — A Framework and Guidelines for Managing Social Media. *Journal of Interactive Marketing*, *27*(4), 281–298. doi:10.1016/j.intmar.2013.09.007

Pousther, J. (2016, February 22). *Social networking very popular among adult internet users in emerging and developing nations*. Retrieved October 28, 2016, from http://www.pewglobal.org/: http://www.pewglobal.org/2016/02/22/social-networking-very-popular-among-adult-internet-users-in-emerging-and-developing-nations/

Sashi, C. (2012). Customer engagement, buyer-seller relationships, and social media. *Management Decision*, *50*(2), 253–272. doi:10.1108/00251741211203551

Shelton, S. T. (2012). Threats to Brands From Social Media. *New York Law Journal*.

Singh, N., Lehnert, K., & Bostick, K. (2012). Global Social Media Usage: Insights Into Reaching Consumers Worldwide. *Thunderbird International Business Review*, *54*(5), 688–700. doi:10.1002/tie.21493

State of Social Media Marketing. (2012). Retrieved February 05, 2013, from awarenessnetworks.com: http://info.awarenessnetworks.com/rs/awarenessnetworks/images/The_State_of_Social_Marketing.pdf

Thompson, T. J., Hertzberg, J., & Sullivan, M. (2011). *Social media and its associated risks.* Retrieved February 03, 2013, from grantthornton.com: http://www.grantthornton.com/staticfiles/GTCom/Advisory/GRC/Social%20media%20and%20risk/social%20media_whitepaper%20-%20FINAL.PDF

Veeck, A., & Hoger, B. (2014). Tools for Monitoring Social Media: A Marketing research Project. *Marketing Education Review, 24*(1), 37–42.

We Are Social Ltd. (2014, January 1). *Global Digital Statistic.* Retrieved October 05, 2014, from We Are Social: http://wearesocial.net/blog/2014/01/social-digital-mobile-worldwide-2014/

Weinberg, B. D., & Pehlivan, E. (2011). Social spending: Managing the social media mix. *Business Horizons*, *54*(3), 275–282. doi:10.1016/j.bushor.2011.01.008

Williams, R. (2009). *What Is Social Media Marketing?* Retrieved February 10, 2013, from orangejack.com: http://orangejack.com/media/what-is-social-media-marketing.pdf

KEY TERMS AND DEFINITIONS

Brand: The most significant property of the company and their highest value. It represents everything that reminds us of a product or service. The entire success in the market lies in the reputation of a brand and collective knowledge about the company. Brand adds characteristics which in a way are different from a product or satisfying same needs. The best brands represent quality guarantee.

Content Management: Creating, adding, deleting and other editing text, graphics or multimedia Internet channels. Content Management Systems are being developed thanks to the progress of Internet technology and software solutions.

Internet Marketing: Different marketing activities that use the Internet as a channel marketing communications.

Market Segmentation: Needed to understand the market and choosing a market segment where we want to sell our products, i.e. group of persons or companies to which create a marketing mix (product, price, distribution and promotion). It implies division of the market into parts based on previously defined criteria. It is necessary to divide the market into homogenous groups of consumers which do not overlap with each other by criteria such as: product or service, distribution channels, consummation habits, purchase subtlety level, geographic, existing or new customers etc. Brand is valued in each segment and by summing the values of each individual segmented values we obtain the total value of a brand.

Marketing Strategy: Part of the strategy of the company. It is a process in which the company translates business strategy and goals in marketing. Once chosen marketing strategy is valid for all time. It changes over time, according to market changes. Marketing strategy enables the company to concentrate their limited resources on the best opportunities in the environment with the goal of expanding sales and reaching sustainable competitive advantage. By analyzing the competition, with detailed research of consumers and their decisions the company makes a long-term strategy for conquest of new and keeping existing consumers.

Segmentation: The process of sharing the consumer in a less homogeneous group.

Social Networks: Websites where you can create your profile, edit it, communicate with acquaintances and strangers, share content, and even advertising.

Strategy: A word borrowed from the military vocabulary that reflects the skill and ability of finding the right way to achieve the objective. Strategy defines ways to achieve your goals.

This research was previously published in Global Observations of the Influence of Culture on Consumer Buying Behavior edited by Sarmistha Sarma, pages 66-82, copyright year 2018 by Business Science Reference (an imprint of IGI Global).

Chapter 5
Marketing and Social Media

Reshu Goyal
Banasthali Vidhyapeeth, India

Praveen Dhyani
Banasthali Vidhyapeeth, India

Om Prakash Rishi
University of Kota, India

ABSTRACT

Time has changed and so does the world. Today everything has become as a matter of one click. With this effort we are trying to explore the new opportunities features and capabilities of the new compeers of Internet applicability known as Social Media or Web 2.0. The effort has been put in to use the internet, social media or web 2.0 as the tool for marketing issues or the strategic business decision making. The main aim is to seek social media, web 2.0 internet applications as the tool for marketing.

INTRODUCTION

Internet and its applications have enabled the firms to adapt and implement innovative form of interactions and compositions with real end users or rightly called as consumers (Ainscough & Luckett, 1996). To facilitate the study and have a close look as to the hindrances and the opportunities for the empirical implementation of the social media in the marketing strategies, Portugal data of 2000 firms was studied which revealed that firms are under both internal and external pressure to adopt digitalization of social content (Bayo-Moriones & Lera-López, 2007) Relationship-based interaction should go hand in hand with the customers, merging the traditional mode with the new technologies.

JOLT AND JERK FOR THE COMPANIES AND THE SOCIAL MEDIA

Customers at large are using the internet based social mode of communication at large which forces the majority of the concerns to charter with it as well. Initial mode of communications were e-mails,

DOI: 10.4018/978-1-5225-5637-4.ch005

direct marketing, telemarketing, informational websites, television, radio, and other interactive modes to share knowledge related to the company and the articles (Berthon, Pitt, Plangger & Shapiro, 2012), (Budden, Anthony, Budden, & Jones, 2011).Though initial means of communication served as the data or the information reaching larger number of people in short time but didn't promote the direct communication or interaction between the buyer and the seller. To track down the abiding collaborative and delightful friendship, substitute have to be sorted of? To effectuate it, word of mouth communication (facilitating the use of social networking sites) seemed to be of usage (Agarwal, 2009), (Ellison, Steinfield & Lampe, 2007), (Budden, Anthony, Budden, & Jones, 2011). Present technologies have become more customers oriented.

Actually, the initial boom or the first tide of the Internet application was not taken seriously by large, but rapid changing scenarios the situations have also changed and so does the application of the Internet. Even the companies with low capital and manpower strength go in for this form of media and communication sources maximum of the employees have sorted to have the blogs (Weinberg, Pehlivan, 2011, Barnard, 2012). Other side of the coin also says the same thing i.e. from the consumer front, also are readily accepting the mode of purchasing. Participation has increased with reduction in the price of the broadband and increase in concurrence by the consumers in the form of messaging, blogs, experience sharing etc. (Fisher, 2009) (See Figure 1 for the business plan in integration with the social media marketing).

EXPLAINING THE TERM WEB 2.0/SOCIAL MEDIA MARKETING

See Figure 2, showing various sources of social media from the pool of mediums. Web 2.0 is termed as the internet based application/s which is the collective formation of online portals, web interactions, open ended data/discussions which smoothens the communications, synergy of the customers and result in formation of business, marketing and strategic decisions if required. Web 2.0 also supports formation of congenial peer groups, free-flow of idea or knowledge and thus coming out with some important

Figure 1. Depicts the plan to be followed by the business personal for marketing in integration with social media

Source: Budden, Anthony, Budden, & Jones (2011)

Step-1-Listen	Step-2 Plan	Step-3 Strategy	Step-4-Tools
• Locate consumers • Assess their social activities • Look for small focused audience	• Define business objectives • How can your brands strengths be extended online?	• How and where will you do it? • How will the relationship with the consumers change? • Who will be leading this effort?	• Decide what social tools you will use • How will you monitor activities and measure success?

Figure 2. Shows the various sources of Social Media Marketing

Source: (http://www.zenithoptimedia.com/zenith/zenithoptimedia-releases-september-2012-advertising-expenditure-forecasts/)

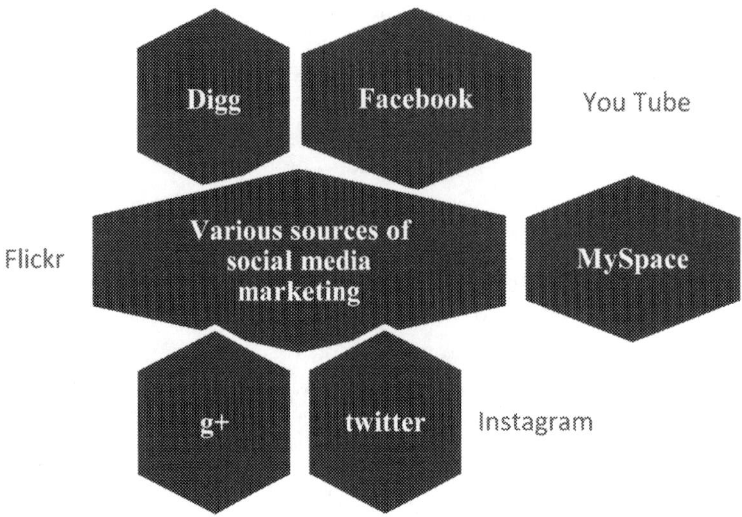

results or just the casual relationship building (Pitt, Berthon, Watson, & Zinkhan, 2002), (Union, 2009) (Study table 1 which showcases various applications of the social media in marketing, its social effects and the enabling technologies).

WEB 2.0, SOCIAL MEDIA AND MARKETING STRATEGIES

The way companies run their business, the way the people buy the products have changed with time. Thinking of the people and so the scenarios have modified to such an extent that being the part of this social fraternity have become the need of an hour. It has become an essence for the marketers and the business personals to understand what comes in with social media, or how to operate in sync with this

Table 1. Shows various applications of the social media in marketing, its social effects and the enabling technologies (Union, 2009)

Web 2.0 Dimensions		
Applications Types	**Social Effects**	**Enabling Technologies**
Blogs	Empowerment	Open Source
Social Networks (Content)	Participation	RSS
Communities Forums/Bulletin Boards	Openness	Wikis
Content Aggregators	Networking	Mashups
	Conversation	AJAX
	Community	
	Democratization/User Control	

form of businesses (Kondopoulos, 2011), (Rizzotti & Burkhart, 2010). It is not that application of social media in marketing would generate results; it is rather the correct usability of the medium to generate adequate results. Inabilities of the business personal to correctly use it still make it a trial and error medium of application into the business.

SPOTTING THE OUTLAY FOR THE SOCIAL MEDIA IMPLEMENTATION OR DIGITALIZATION

There is no canonical formula for decision making, as to how much a firm should spend on digital social media. It depends upon every firm and the peculiarity they possess which enclose (Figure 3).

Figure 3 depicts the reasons business uses in investing in social media and using it as a tool of marketing. Faster the benefits of the social media are growing, doubly it is being used by the firms to fill up their lockers. Dotingly the marketing director of a reputed firma said "investment in digital media is worthless, claiming that the most important factor for the involvement of companies in digital media is the very low investment required when compared with traditional media." (Ellison, Steinfield & Lampe, 2007), (Hoffman, & Fodor, 2010), (Mangold & Faulds, 2009). Notwithstanding the declarations and the statements made firms have still increased their investments in digital media up to 18%. With increasing importance and changing scenario studies and researchers believe that number would increase considerably (Kumar, Novak, & Tomkins, 2010). Statistics state that more than 81% of the participants plan to go in for this mode of marketing strategies. Records claim that where are the increase in the investment

Figure 3. Shows reasons for the business decisions firm takes when investing in social media and using it as a source for marketing
Source: Berthon, Pitt, Plangger and Shapiro (2012)

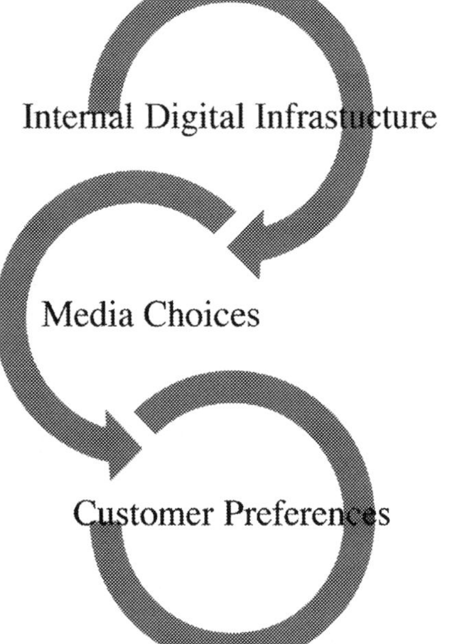

in traditional mode of the marketing is 4% which is far behind the increase in digital mode which ranges up to 14% by 2013(Hutchings, 2012), (Bayo-Moriones & Lera-López, 2007). Figures may reflect major changes with advent of mobile computing and app based technologies in 2015.

For any organization to succeed employees play a major role because they are the key stake holders in forming firms strategies. Firms are also focusing on such employees who are digitally equipped and the number is supposedly to increase to 45% ANACOM, 2012). (Berthon, Pitt, Plangger, & Shapiro, 2012).

After effects of the survey were two inevitable conclusions:

1. Digital media or social networking play grave role in business marketing and its relevance and utility is increasing with changing scenarios.
2. It has become critically important for the organizations to implement the digitization or the internet based mode of communications.

ASCERTAINING THE CAPABILITY OF SOCIAL MEDIA MARKETING

There are different views about measuring the return on investment of digital marketing. Some of the digital calculators have been proposed to measure return on investment like the model suggested by (Fisher, 2009), (Weinberg & Pehlivan, 2011), (Hoffman & Fodor, 2010) suggested different models to measure the income generated by digital marketing like measuring the competitors' actions, return on investment, brand awareness etc.

Overall the studies reveal that the kind of model to be adopted depends upon the firm's strategic decision making and the objectives which are core importance for the success of the firm.

NEED OF AN HOUR-SOCIAL MEDIA

Web or the Internet Applications have become the essence in right from conceptualization, movement and the establishment of the business activities. It has become the need of the hour and to gain the maximum competitive advantage the firms should instrument this mode of interaction and relationship building. To take full advantage of Internet, organizations have to adopt Internet to fullest that is from people communication to customer interaction, stakeholder's connections and finally make profit and sales. As the need and the usage of Internet and its applications is increasing with time so as its need is being felt by the customers (Berthon, Pitt & Watson, 1996), (Budden, Anthony, Budden, & Jones, 2011) and integration into marketing practices have been done.

Sinking with internet or creating the tech enabled firms does not appear overnight it needs whole lot of resource management, planning, management and administration with time. Lot of energy and efforts have to be put in to move from the traditional marketing methods to digital prone world but nothing is impossible.

REFERENCES

Agarwal, A. (2009). *Web 3.0 concepts explained in plain English*. Retrieved June 12,fromhttp://www.labnol.org/internet/web-3-concepts-explained/8908/

Ainscough, T., & Luckett, M. (1996). The Internet for the rest of us: Marketing on the World Wide Web. *Journal of Consumer Marketing*, *13*(2), 36–47. doi:10.1108/07363769610115393

ANACOM. (2012). InformaçãoEstatística do Serviço de Acesso à Internet: Vol. 3. *Trimestre de 2012*. Lisboa: ANACOM.

Barnard, J. (2012). *ZenithOptimedia releases September 2012 advertising expenditure forecast*. Retrieved January 4, 2013, from http://www.zenithoptimedia.com/zenith/zenithoptimedia-releases-september-2012-advertising-expenditure-forecasts/

Bayo-Moriones, A., & Lera-López, F. (2007). A firm-level analysis of determinants of ICT adoption in Spain. *Technovation*, *27*(6-7), 352–366. doi:10.1016/j.technovation.2007.01.003

Berthon, P., Pitt, L. F., & Watson, R. T. (1996). The World Wide Web as an advertising medium. *Journal of Advertising Research*, *36*(1), 43–54.

Berthon, P. R., Pitt, L. F., Plangger, K., & Shapiro, D. (2012). Marketing meets Web 2.0, social media, and creative consumers: Implications for international marketing strategy. *Business Horizons*, *55*(3), 261–271. doi:10.1016/j.bushor.2012.01.007

Brown, J., Broderick, A. J., & Lee, N. (2007). Word of mouth communication within online communities: Conceptualizing the online social network. *Journal of Interactive Marketing*, *21*(3), 2–20. doi:10.1002/dir.20082

Budden, C. B., Anthony, J. F., Budden, M. C., & Jones, M. A. (2011). Managing the evolution of a revolution: Marketing implications of Internet media usage among college students. *College Teaching Methods & Styles Journal*, *3*(3), 5–10. doi:10.19030/ctms.v3i3.5283

Eid, R., & El-Gohary, H. (2011). The impact of E-marketing use on small business enterprises marketing success. *Service Industries Journal*, *33*(1), 31–50. doi:10.1080/02642069.2011.594878

Ellison, N. B., Steinfield, C., & Lampe, C. (2007). The benefits of Facebook friends: Social capital and college students use of online social network sites. *Journal of Computer-Mediated Communication*, *12*(4), 1143–1168. doi:10.1111/j.1083-6101.2007.00367.x

Fisher, T. (2009). ROI in social media: A look at the arguments. *Journal of Database Marketing & Customer Strategy Management*, *16*(3), 189–195. doi:10.1057/dbm.2009.16

Hoffman, D. L., & Fodor, M. (2010). Can you measure the ROI of your social media marketing? *MIT Sloan Management Review*, *52*(1), 41–49.

Hutchings, C. (2012). Commercial use of Facebook and Twitter–risks and rewards. *Computer Fraud & Security*, *2012*(6), 19–20. doi:10.1016/S1361-3723(12)70065-9

Kaplan, A. M., & Haenlein, M. (2010). Users of the world, unite! The challenges and opportunities of social media. *Business Horizons*, *53*(1), 59–68. doi:10.1016/j.bushor.2009.09.003

Kondopoulos, D. (2011). Internet marketing advanced techniques for increased market share. *ChimicaOggi-Chemistry Today*, *29*(3), 9–12.

Kumar, R., Novak, J., & Tomkins, A. (2010). Structure and evolution of online social networks. In P. S. Yu, J. Han, & C. Faloutsos (Eds.), *Link mining: Models, algorithms, and applications* (pp. 337–357). New York: Springer. doi:10.1007/978-1-4419-6515-8_13

Lampe, C. A. C., Ellison, N., & Steinfield, C. (2007). A familiar face(book): Profile elements as signals in an online social network. *Proceedings of the SIGCHI Conference on Human Factors in Computing Systems*. doi:10.1145/1240624.1240695

Mangold, W. G., & Faulds, D. J. (2009). Social media: The new hybrid element of the promotion mix. *Business Horizons*, *52*(4), 357–365. doi:10.1016/j.bushor.2009.03.002

Pitt, L., Berthon, P., Watson, R., & Zinkhan, G. (2002). The Internet and the birth of real consumer power. *Business Horizons*, *45*(4), 7–14. doi:10.1016/S0007-6813(02)00220-3

Rizzotti, S., & Burkhart, H. (2010). useKit: a step towards the executable web s3.0. *Proceedings of the 19th International Conference on Worldwide Web*. doi:10.1145/1772690.1772861

Rodríguez-Ardura, I., Ryan, G., & Gretzel, U. (2012). Special issue on qualitative approaches to E-marketing and online consumer behaviour: Guest editors' introduction. *Journal of Theoretical and Applied Electronic Commerce Research*, (August), 2012.

Seybert, H. (2012). *Internet use in households and by individuals 2012*. Retrieved January 25, 2013, from http://epp.eurostat.ec.europa.eu/cache/ITY_OFFPUB/KS-SF-12-050/EN/KS-SF12-050-EN.PDF

Silva, J. M., MahfujurRahman, A. S. M., & El Saddik, A. (2008). Web 3.0: a vision for bridging the gap between real and virtual. *Proceeding of the 1st ACM International Workshop on Communicability Design and Evaluation in Cultural and Ecological Multimedia Systems*.

Union, I. T. (2009). *Media statistics: Mobile phone subscribers (most recent) by country*. Retrieved December 6, from http://www.NationMaster.com/graph/med_mob_pho-media-mobile-phones 17

Van Belleghem, S., Thijs, D., & De Ruyck, T. (2012). *Social Media around the World 2012*. Retrieved November 3, from http://www.slideshare.net/InSitesConsulting/social-media-around-the-world-2012-by-insites-consulting

Weinberg, B. D., & Pehlivan, E. (2011). Social spending: Managing the social media mix. *Business Horizons*, *54*(3), 275–282.

Whitla, P. (2009). Crowdsourcing and its application in marketing activities. *Contemporary Management Research*, *5*(1), 15–28.

This research was previously published in Maximizing Business Performance and Efficiency Through Intelligent Systems edited by Om Prakash Rishi and Anukrati Sharma, pages 191-199, copyright year 2017 by Business Science Reference (an imprint of IGI Global).

Chapter 6
Social Media as an Advertisement Tool:
Strategical Need of Being More Experiential

Füsun Topsümer
Ege University, Turkey

Dincer Yarkin
Gediz University, Turkey

ABSTRACT

Daily routine and time pressure have become the reason for ignoring social media advertisements; because of thousands of messages on Internet, and social media, consumers need more reliable and differentiated messages. Today's customer is looking for utilitarian and hedonic attributes in the content of advertisement. Otherwise they would interpret advertisements as "time loss." In this chapter, some suggestions are offered to companies as well as to the advertising agencies who should look for a new way of attracting customers to advertisement. Experiential components are becoming more and more vital, in advertisement as well as in marketing. Feel, sense, think, act, and relate as subjects of experiential marketing can be transferred into social media advertisements and touch consumer's heart for acquiring effective and efficient outcomes.

INTRODUCTION

The advertising landscape has changed dramatically in recent years, and nowhere is this more visible than it is online. The advertising industry has long sought to go where consumers go. Indeed the industry has followed consumers online, and even developed new forms of advertising to relate consumers in their virtual reality (Tuten, 2008, p.1)With millions of users worldwide, it raises the question of what types of people rely on these online social media tools in their interactions with others. Previous research has established three personality traits that are central to social media use: extraversion, neuroticism, and

DOI: 10.4018/978-1-5225-5637-4.ch006

openness to experience (Ross et al., 2009; Zywica & Danowski, 2008; as cited in Correa, Hinsley and Zuniga, 2010, p.247). The concept of Social Media is top of the agenda for many business executives today. Decision makers, as well as consultants, try to identify ways in which firms can make profitable use of applications such as Wikipedia, YouTube, Facebook, Second Life, and Twitter (Kaplan & Haenlein, 2010, p. 59). The social media phenomenon, can now significantly impact a firm's reputation, sales, and even survival. Yet, many executives eschew or ignore this form of media because they do not understand what it is, the various forms it can take, and how to engage with it and learn(Kietzmann, Hermkens, & Mc Charty, 2011, p. 254).Therefore we can see a new business opportunity as "social media specialists" deal and handle with the complexity of this platform.

According to Kim and Ko (2012), five constructs of perceived social media marketing activities of luxury fashion brands are entertainment, interaction, trendiness, customization, and word of mouth (p.1480) . Their effects on value equity, relationship equity, and brand equity are significantly positive. According to Urry (1990, p. 248) the images, videos, and films available through the various systems provide various messages that represent destinations and serve as mediators of tourist experiences. Urry (1990) argues: ''-people are tourists most of the time, whether they are literally mobile or only experience simulated mobility through the incredible fluidity of multiple signs and electronic images (as cited in Tussyadiah & Fesenmaier, 2009, p. 24).

Cultural aspects must be considered during advertising process in social media platform according to countries and local habitats of consumers as well. For example in the USA, the number of Facebook users is around 135 million people, while in Turkey, it is more than 30 million. When these two countries are compared, it is easily determined that time spent by people is different due to different cultural indicators.

Although it is clear that–for better or for worse–social media is very powerful, many executives are reluctant or unable to develop strategies and allocate resources to engage effectively with social media. Consequently, firms regularly ignore or mismanage the opportunities and threats presented by creative consumers (Berthon, Pitt, McCarthy, &Kates, 2007, as cited in Kietzmann, 2011).Providing experiential tools in social media advertisement applications and feedbacks behind this can eliminate threats. It can be understood from studies of Tussyadiah & Fesenmaier (2009) that perceived attractions, and tourists represent the informative roles of the videos for viewers at the reflective phase of experiences as a media for sharing and re-sharing experiences. Meanwhile, the category of travel stimuli represents how viewers are stimulated to have travel intention. Viewers' comments about the quality of videos (including pictures, audio, and editing in general) do not simply express personal appreciation of the directors' works; videos with good quality enable viewers to experience the tourist gaze with imaginative access in a more realistic sense(p.36).

It is found that individuals' personality traits – extraversion, emotional stability and openness to experiences– play a role in the uses of interactive social media. These results are consistent with previous studies conducted by Amichai-Hamburger and Ben-Artzi (2000, 2002, 2003), who tested how personality played a role in Internet use, and with studies that examined online applications that involved some degree of social interaction (Guadagno et al., 2008; Ross et al., 2009 as cited in Correa et al, 2010). Social media, especially social network sites, provide a virtual space for people to communicate through the Internet, which also might be an important agent of consumer socialization (Köhler et al. 2011; Lueg and Finney 2007; Lueg et al. 2006; Muratore 2008; Zhang and Daugherty 2009 as cited in Wang, Yu, & Wei 2012, p. 1999). Social media provide three conditions that encourage consumer socialization among peers online. First blogs, instant messaging, and social networking sites, second, increasing numbers of consumers visit social media websites to communicate with others and find information to help them make various consumption related decisions (Lueg et al. 2006). Third, social media facilitate education and information because they feature multitudes of friends or peers who act as socialization agents and provide vast product information and evaluations quickly (Gershoff & Johar 2006; Taylor, Lewin, & Strutton 2011).

BACKGROUND

"After creation of Usenet by Tom Truscott and Jim Ellis from Duke University, internet users were allowed to post messages". This system was the ancestor of the social media.In the beginning of 2000's My Space and Facebook came to world as networking platforms and they were called as "Social Media". Main forms of social media are social network sites, social virtual worlds, virtual game worlds, content communities and blogs (Kaplan & Haenlein, 2010).

Due to spending more and more time online and, changes in advertising landscape as a part of this new visual world, social media became new platform for creating, sharing, commenting for the communities.(Tuten,2008). Before integrating advertising implementations, rich and diverse nature of social media sites, different profiles of users should have been understood (Kietzmann, et al. 2011; Chu,2013). New forms of advertisement, should be adapted to social media platforms. Experience modules as sense, feel, think, act and relate (Schmit,1999) in social media advertisements can reach, and touch expectations of todays' customer.

BORN IN INTERNET PLATFORM: SOCIAL MEDIA

The internet is nearly 40 years old. Started in 1969 as the ARPANET, it was commissioned by U.S. Department of Defense's Advanced Research Projects Agency (ARPA) as a network for academic and military use (Strauss & Frost, 2009, p. 10).

1969: ARPANET commissioned by U.S. Department of Defense for academic and military use.
1975: First mailing list for the new computer network (first e-mail sent in 1965).
1979: USENET established to host discussions. First post in 1981. Later managed by GoogleGroups (800 million archived messages as of 2008).
1984: Number of connected computer host reaches 1000.
1987: Number of connected computer hosts reaches 10000.First e-mail connection with China.
1988: First virus, affects 10% of the 60000 hosts.
1993: Early Web sites appear and business and media take notice.
1994: Early web sites appear on hotwired.com "Jerry and David's Guide to the World Wide Web Appears (later named Yahoo!).
1995: eBay opens its doors and disrupts the classified advertising business.
2000: Napster.com shows the World that peer-to-peer networking can work.
2002: Running your own blog is now considered hip. Power begins to shift to users.
2003: Recording industry Association of America (RIAA) sues 261 people for illegal music downloading.

2004: 16% of the world's population uses the Internet. Businesses figure out how to be profitable with e-business models.
2007: 19% of the world's population is online. Internet usage in industrialized nations reaches maturity.

The first part of terminology, social, refers to the instinctual needs we have to connect with other human beings. The second part of that term refers to the media we use which we make those connections with other humans (Safko & Brake, 2010, p. 4).

Today, everything is social media. Some industry gurus claim that if you do not participate in Facebook, YouTube, and Second Life you are not part of cyberspace anymore (Kaplan & Haenlein, 2010, p. 67).But it is not enough to take place in Social media, some studies showed that, it is an obligation for companies to update themselves in virtual platform as real life. Internet users, naturally, needs more actual information. If they can not reach the needed information, their perception about the company will be negatively influenced.

SOCIAL MEDIA ADVERTISING STRATEGIES

Advertising, an essential component in the marketing of any business, has been around for a long time. People have been trying to influence other people since the dawn of human existence, utilizing whatever means and media they had at their disposal at the time (Ryan & Jones, 2012, p. 3)

Advertising is the one of the most crucial tool of promotion mix in the marketing context with the way of targeting potential or current audiences of a company or any organization. By advertising, organizations provide information about utilitarian as well as hedonic aspects of their products or services which they supplied. With the aim of ensuring customers about brand's identity, value proposition and position against competing brands, advertising is the simplest and relatively cheapest way of ad hoc communicating with target customers.

Advertising is commonly defined as paid, one-way promotional communication in any mass media (Tuten, 2008, p. 2).According to The American Marketing Association, -advertising is-, "the placement of announcements and persuasive messages in time or space purchased in any of the mass media by business, firms, nonprofit organizations, government agencies, and individuals who seek to inform and/or persuade members of a particular target market or audience about their products, services, organizations, or ideas". For Lee and Carlson (2006) advertising is paid, non-personal communication about and organization and its products or services that is transmitted to a target audience through mass media such as television, radio, newspapers, magazines, direct mail, outdoor displays, or mass-transit vehicles (p. 3).Since invention of radio, and after Television have been commonly used as advertising instruments because of providing audial and visual elements and which were more attracting for target audiences. But, advertising through social media can be one of the cheapest and most targeted forms of advertising (Curran, Graham and Temple 2011, p. 29)

Expenditures on advertising, even global crisis grow year by year. Please see Table 1, for the growth rate of social media advertisements.

"According to Zenith Media Agency advertising with mobile has the share of %31 in total advertising expenditures. Even, mobile advertising still has a small share in the industry, with the 14,3 billion $ of growth in this year, has captured % 2,8 of share from total advertising market with rapid growth. Zenith Media Agency guesses that in 2015 mobile advertising will have %6 of market share with 33,1

Table 1. Growth rate of the social media advertisements

	Year on Year % Growth at Current Prices	
	2013	2014
GLOBAL	**3.0 (3.7)**	**4.5 (5.0)**
NORTH AMERICA	**3.1 (3.5)**	**3.0 (4.0)**
USA	3.1 (3.5)	3.0 (4.0)
CANADA	3.4 (3.4)	3.3 (3.9)
WESTERN EUROPE	**-2.3 (-0.3)**	**1.4 (1.8)**
UK	3.6 (2.7)	5.0 (4.4)
GERMANY	-1.0 (0.0)	0.0 (1.0)
FRANCE	-3.3 (-0.4)	0.8 (0.7)
ITALY	-11.7 (-4.8)	-1.3 (0.4)
SPAIN	-9.7 (-8.4)	1.1 (1.2)
C&EE	**5.9 (6.4)**	**7.4 (7.6)**
RUSSIA	11.2 (11.3)	11.0 (10.9)
ASIA PACIFIC	**4.7 (5.3)**	**5.2 (6.2)**
AUSTRALIA	0.0 (1.5)	1.0 (1.4)
CHINA	6.9 (6.9)	7.9 (7.8)
JAPAN	1.3 (2.7)	1.0 (2.8)
LATIN AMERICA	**9.0 (9.1)**	**14.5 (14.8)**
BRAZIL	4.6 (9.4)	12.3 (17.2)
Figures in brackets show our previous forecasts from March 2013		

billion $s" (Monloss, 2014). "Only in U.S. social-media advertising spending may rise to $9.8 billion in 2016 from $3.8 billion last year, as companies seek to harness new tools that help reach people who interact online, researcher BIA/Kelsey said. Higher ad spending at Google Inc. (GOOG)'s YouTube and LinkedIn Corp. (LNKD) boosted BIA/Kelsey's forecast from six months ago. In November, BIA/Kelsey projected 2011 social-media advertising revenues would reach $3.4 billion -- $400 million less than the figure released today. "We've slightly accelerated our numbers for 2012 and 2013 because of the growth we've seen with social video, with YouTube as a driver," said Jed Williams, an analyst and program director at Chantilly, Virginia-based BIA/Kelsey. "YouTube will play an increasingly important role." The researcher bumped up its 2012 social-media advertising spending estimate by $200 million to $4.8 billion, Williams said in a phone interview. Next year's spending will reach $5.9 billion, up from the $5.8 billion BIA/Kelsey expected in November, he said" (http://www.bloomberg.com/news/2012-05-15/social-media-ad-spending-to-jump-to-9-8-billion-in-2016.htmlwith).

Social media provides a very different context for a message, and this may require some attention by the manager when considering media strategy with traditional media, the source of a brand's message is the advertiser. But with social media, much of the context concerning a brand is user-generated and under the control of the brand, including adverts (Percy & Elliot,2009, p. 11).

Functions of Social Media in the Context of Advertising

Social media is the umbrella term for web-based software and services that allow users to come together online and exchange, discuss, communicate and participate in any form of social interaction (Ryan & Jones,2012, p.152) Although it is clear that for better or worse social media is very powerful, many executives are reluctant or unable to develop strategies and allocate resources to engage effectively with social media(Kietzmann, et al, 2011, p. 242).

Today, consumers gain a new role with social media. Consumers are becoming "content creators" and, thus, functional consumers instead of just consuming, as in the past. Social media applications or tools that facilitate this are blogs, micro blogging applications (such as Twitter), social networking sites (such as Facebook), podcasts, and video and photo sharing sites (such as YouTube and Flickr) (Nadaraja & Yazdanifard, 2011)

With this rise in Social media, it appears that corporate communication has been democratized. The power has been taken from those in marketing and public relations by the individuals and communities that create, share, and consume blogs, tweets, Facebook entries, movies, pictures and so forth. (Kietzmann, et al, 2011, p 242).

Figure 1 illustrates a honeycomb of seven functional building blocks: identity, conversations, sharing, presence, relationships, reputation, and groups. Each block allows us to unpack and examine (1) a specific facet of social media user experience, and (2) its implications for firms. These building blocks are neither mutually exclusive, nor do they all have to be present in a social media activity. They are constructs that allow us to make sense of how different levels of social media functionality can be configured (Kietzmann et al., 2011, p. 243).

Figure 1. Honeycomb of Social Media. Source: (Kietzmann, Hermkens and Mc Charthy, 2011).

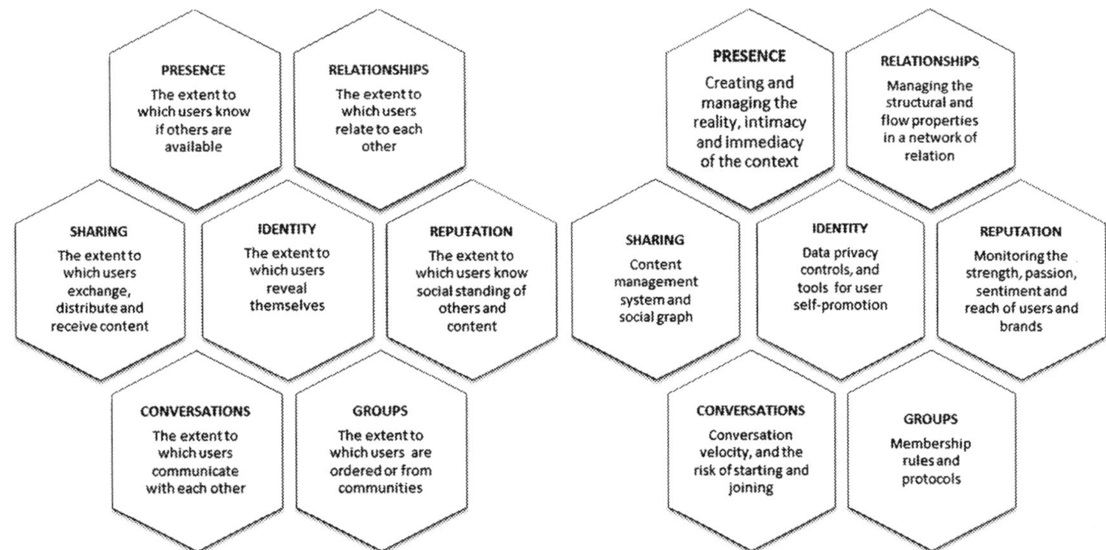

Strategic Opportunities of Social Media in the Context of Advertising

Social media provides different opportunities to the companies as blogs, social networking sites, virtual game worlds, content communities. All these subjects are means by which to meet existing and potential customers.

Collaborative projects enable the joint and simultaneous creation of content by many end users, within collaborative projects. One difference between wikis which allow users to add, remove and change text-based content and social bookmarking applications (Kaplan & Haenlein, 2010, p.62) Wikipedia from USA based, with more than 200 languages, eksisozluk.com from Turkey, are the examples of collaborative projects of social media.

Blogs are mainly used by individuals to share and transfer ideas in a personal manner. But according to reputation of blog, the number of audiences provide great marketing potential for the firms in a corporate base. Blogs are inexpensive; however, they can be effectively used as promotion tool.

Content communities are the individuals who are sharing interesting videos, speeches, and Power Point or pdf presentations. According to Kaplan & Haenlein (2010), "high popularity of content communities makes them a very attractive contact channel for many firms"(p.63).

Social network sites basically let users build up a group of friends with whom they can share things in all sorts of ways- from videos to articles, to games, to groups(Ryan and Jones, 2012:161).For example a new social network application Watt pad is a leader in this new storytelling environment, with more than two million writers producing 100,000 pieces of material a day for 20 million readers on an intricate international social network (http://www.nytimes.com/2014/03/24/technology/web-fiction-serialized-and-social.html.)

Understanding nature and content of social media is more crucial than ever for defining target groups. Main social media platforms can be seen on Table 2.

ADAPTING EXPERIENTIAL STRATEGIES ON SOCIAL MEDIA ADVERTISEMENTS

Experience is a group of private events that occur in response to some stimulation (e.g., as provided by marketing efforts before and after purchase) (Schmitt, 1999, p. 60). They do not only occur in physi-

Table 2.

Social Media	What Is It?	Examples
Reputation Aggregators	Databases allowing users to search for content	Google, Yahoo!, MSN, Tripadvisor.com
Blogs	Online multimedia journals with frequent updating	Technology: TypePad, Blogger, Wordpress. Site: Marketingpilgrim.com
Online communities	Sites offering Professional or user content and allowing members to upload content	CNN, Slate, Youtube, Google Groups, Flickr, Del.ici.ous, Wikipedia, Second Life
Social networks	Associations of internet users for social connection	Myspace, Facebook, Xing, LinkedIn

Source: Judy Strauss, Raymond Frost, "E-Marketing Management" Pearson International Edition, 2009 p.326

cal life but also may be seen in virtual life. With the rise of experiential marketing in the literature as well as in practical life, marketers, scholars gave strategic importance to this, fresh marketing concept. In their book "Welcome to Experience Economy" (1998) Pine II and Gilmore emphasized that goods and services were not enough for economic development, new form of economic output called "experiences" needed for value addiction for enterprises. According to Hirschmann and Hollbrook (1982) and Schmitt (1999), experience focused marketing concept provides new method for reaching and touching customers. Experiential marketing is the methodology that can provide a bridge between the old status quo of brands based on mass marketing, and the future of mass marketing that is based on personalized messages delivered to a consumer who can choose to engage brand on his or her own terms (Lenderman, 2006, p. 274).

Types of Experiences

Schmitt (1999), classified experiences as sense, feel, think, act and relate.

- **Sense:** The Sense module appeals to the senses with the objective of creating sensory experiences, through sight, sound, touch, taste and smell.
- **Feel:** Feel module appeals to customers' inner feelings and emotions with the objective of creating affective experiences that range from mildly positive moods linked to a brand (Schmitt 1999, p.61). Consumers' emotions have a significant influence on purchase and consumption decisions for a wide variety of products. A good example of this phenomenon can be found in the candy and snack market, where consumer responses are a product of a sizable number of emotion-laden situations that may be exploited in advertising strategy (Mizerski & White 1986, p. 57).The feel side was interpreted to represent products where the drive for purchase is ego gratification, social acceptance and sensory stimulation (Claeys, Swinnen & Abeeyes, 1995).
- **Think:** Think module appeals to the intellect with the objective of creating, cognitive, problem solving experiences that engage customers creatively.
- **Act:** Act module appeals to enriching customer lives by targeting their physical experiences, showing them alternative ways of doing things.
- **Relate:** Relate module contains aspects of Sense, Feel, Think, and Marketing modules. However relate marketing expands beyond the individual's personal, private feelings, thus relating the individual to something outside his/her private state. With this new initiative, Yatra.com aims to engage its target group through social networking websites such as Facebook, Twitter, Orkut and YouTube. It aims to optimally use the social media platform to listen to, engage, encourage and support customers through new innovative initiatives (Sharma & Sharma, 2011, p. 5).

Experiential Advertisement on Social Media

Marketing communication channels traditionally include advertising, direct mail, packaging and sales promotion along with the relatively more recent prominence of sponsorship, public relations; digital and live brand experiences (Smilansky, 2009, p.3) Social media advertising can be redesigned according to types of experiences. One or more variation of experiences should take place in the content of advertisements. Sense and feel, think, act and relate experiences are both or proper mix of them can be adapted to the social media advertisement according to expectations of target groups.

Social media as a communication platform, interactive in nature. According to Liu and Shrum's study (2002) interactivity was distinguished between two, as experiential and structural aspects of the construct. The structural aspect of interactivity refers to the hardwired opportunity of interactivity provided during an interaction, whereas the experiential aspect of interactivity is the interactivity of the communication process as perceived by the communication parties.

The first step in in creating effective advertising messages is to plan a message strategy-to decide what general message will be communicated to consumers (Kotler & Armstrong, 2002, p. 460).Demography, life style of target audiences must be considered, during creation of the message. Attractive, sensual and cognitive aspects are both being hung on messages without irritating them.

Recently, research in human–computer interaction has seen a shift in focus from transaction efficiency expense and effectiveness, to user engagement. Engagement task is the sense of being a part of a context, being aware of sensations, thought, and feelings (Lee & Benbasat 2003, p.242).

As individuals develop experience communicating with a specific communication partner, they may develop a knowledge base for that individual, enabling the encoding of messages tailored to that person, using cues relevant to him or her, and containing information having richer meaning for that communication partner(for instance, referring to shared experiences or using shared jargon) (Carlson & Zmud,1999, p. 156).

Consumers are no longer passive spectators of marketing activity – they expect to be active participants in brand conversations and campaigns. Experiential marketing fulfills this demand by taking engaging, interactive and memorable brand experiences directly to consumers – driving awareness, trial, conversations, content and generating a strong impact on purchase propensity (http://wallblog.co.uk/2012/10/16/the-perfect-threesome-social-media-mobile-and-experiential/).

Experiential marketing has been used in social media now to combine a consumer "experience" with a brand. Otherwise known as relationship marketing, it is a way to connect a customer to a brand emotionally, through a live event or stunt (http://www.toptensocialmedia.com/social-media-business/10-ways-experiential-marketing-has-been-used-in-social-media/).With the increased ownership and use of mobile devices, smartphones and tablets, consumers are more able to enhance and share their product experiences. Creating a unique experiential marketing campaign that inspires people's emotions, and allows them to share their experience in real time by engaging their online networks through social media, is a powerful method for increasing the reaching of your brand into the everyday lives of audiences (http://gimpactevents.com/2014/03/05/event-marketing-social-media). Results revealed that while extraversion and openness to experiences were positively related to social media use, emotional stability was a negative predictor, controlling for socio-demographics and life satisfaction (Correa, et al., 2010: 247).

FUTURE RESEARCH DIRECTIONS

According to Lendermann (2006), it became painfully obvious that consumers were not clicking on the banners, were not volunteering to provide personal information, and were not interacting with advertisers but actively avoiding them. Future research can detain a wider perspective in understanding the reason for those habits of consumers.

The advertisers are looking for innovative and differentiated ways of advertising in traditional and modern platforms as internet and social media. Experiential perspectives from Schmitt (1999)'s, Lenderman (2006)'s and Smilansky (2009)'s studies can be adapted to the social media advertising for attracting consumers. Therefore, future researchers can ask these questions: What kind of experiences can be presented to consumers by advertisements? How can networks, blogs, content communities provide experiential advertisements to consumers?

CONCLUSION

Consumers have experienced a significant transformation from being passive to active after rising of social media. Experience based advertisements should provide meanings to target audiences by attracting them in emotional way. Marketers, advertising agencies should consider nature of social media as differentiating from mass media with interactivity. Especially among young people who will be the future's adult sharing experiences and information on social media platforms have become more vital than ever. According to Kuhn (2013), the integration of social media with experiential marketing campaigns is highly beneficial to any brand: By allowing social media users to share their experiences with their friends, followers and connections, the reach and life span of any experiential campaign can be increased indefinitely. Opportunities to integrate social media into experiential marketing campaigns are vast and varied, allowing brands to appeal to a wide audience of social media users. Implementations about experiential marketing on social media should be related with the five modules of experiences as sense, feel, think, act and relate. These modules can be adapted to the social media advertisements according to nature of the product or service. This also will provide quite contribution to positioning strategies of companies. Experiential social media issues, have quite impact on the development of corporate image and corporate reputation (Yarkin, 2013).

REFERENCES

Brianna, B. (2014). *10 ways experiential marketing has been used in social media*. Retrieved from http://www.toptensocialmedia.com/social-media-business/10-ways-experiential-marketing-has-been-used-in-social-media/

Cacheux, B. (2014, May 8). *The perfect three some-social media, mobile, and experiential?* Retrieved from http://wallblog.co.uk/2012/10/16/the-perfect-threesome-social-media-mobile-and-experiential/

Carlson, J., & Zmud, R. W. (1999). Channel expansion theory and the experiential nature of media richness perceptions. *Academy of Management Journal*, *42*(2), 153–176. doi:10.2307/257090

Chu, S. C. (2013). Viral advertising in social media. *Journal of Interactive Advertising*, *12*(1), 30–43. doi:10.1080/15252019.2011.10722189

Claeys, C., Swinnen, A., & Abeele, P. V. (1995). Consumers' means-end chains for "think" and "feel" products. *Journal of Research in Marketing*, *12*(3), 193–208. doi:10.1016/0167-8116(95)00021-S

Correa, T., Hinsley, A. W., & Zuniga, G. H. (2010). Who interacts on the web? The intersection of users' personality and social media use. *Computers in Human Behavior*, *26*(2), 247–253. doi:10.1016/j.chb.2009.09.003

Curran, K., Graham, S., & Temple, C. (2011). Advertising on Facebook. *IJED*, *1*(1), 26–33.

Eyrich, N., Padman, M. L., & Sweeter, K. D. (2008). PR practitioners' use of social media tools and communication technology. *Public Relations Review*, *34*(4), 412–414. doi:10.1016/j.pubrev.2008.09.010

Kaplan, A. (2012). If you love something, let it go mobile: Mobile marketing and mobile socail media 4X4. *Business Horizons*, *55*(2), 129–139. doi:10.1016/j.bushor.2011.10.009

Kaplan, A., & Haenlein, M. (2010). Users of the world, unite! The challenges and opportunities of Social Media. *Business Horizons*, *53*(1), 59–68. doi:10.1016/j.bushor.2009.09.003

Kharif, O. (2014, May 1). *Social-media ad spending to jump to $9.8 billion in 2016*. Retrieved from http://www.bloomberg.com/news/2012-05-15/social-media-ad-spending-to-jump-to-9-8-billion-in-2016.html

Kietzmann, J. H., Hermkens, K., & McCharthy, I. P. (2011). Social Media? Get Serious! Understanding the functional building blocks of social media. *Business Horizons*, *54*(3), 241–251. doi:10.1016/j.bushor.2011.01.005

Kim, A. J., & Ko, E. (2012). Do social media marketing activities enhance customer equity?An empirical study of luxury fashion brand. *Journal of Business Research*, *65*(10), 1480–1486. doi:10.1016/j.jbusres.2011.10.014

Kuhn, M. (2014, May 8). *Experiential marketing and social media integration: A match made in heaven*. Retrieved from http://www.ambientmediaww.com/wordpress/?tag=experiential-marketing

Lee, M., & Johnson, C. (2006). *Principles of adverstising: A global perspective* (2nd ed.). The Haworth Press,Inc.

Lee, W., & Benbasat, I. (2003). Designing an electronic commerce interface: Attention and product memory as elicited by web design. *Electronic Commerce Research And Applications, Vol*, *2*(1), 240–253. doi:10.1016/S1567-4223(03)00026-7

Lenderman, M. (2006). *Experience the Message, how experiential marketing is changing the brand world*. New York: Carrol and Graf Publishers.

Mangold, G. W., & Faulds, D. J. (2009). Social media: The new hybrid element of the promotion mix. *Business Horizons*, *52*(4), 357–365. doi:10.1016/j.bushor.2009.03.002

Mizerski, R. W., & Dennis White, J. (1986). Understanding and using emotions in advertising. *Journal of Consumer Marketing*, *3*(4), 57–69. doi:10.1108/eb008180

Monloss, K. (2014, May 10). *Zenith optimedia expects ad spending to rise in each of the next 3 years growth due to the global economy's progress*. Retrieved from http://www.adweek.com/news/advertising-branding/zenithoptimedia-expects-ad-spending-rise-over-next-3-years-156837

Nadaraja, R., & Yazdanifard, R. (2012). *Social media advertising: Advantages and disadvantages*. Retrieved from http://scholar.google.com.tr/scholar?hl=tr&q=Nadaraja+and+Yazdanifard&btnG=&lr=

Percy, L., & Rosenbaum, E. R. (2009). *Strategic advertising planning*. Oxford University Press.

Ryan, D., & Jones, C. (2012). *Understanding digital marketing*. Kogan Page.

Safko, L., & Brake, D. K. (2009). *The social media bible: Tactics, tools, and strategies for business success*. Hoboken, NJ: John Wiley and Sons.

Sharma, R., & Sharma, V. (2011). Experiential marketing: A contemporary marketing. *International Journal of Management and Strategy*, *3*(4), 1–10.

Strauss, J., & Frost, R. (2009). *E-marketing*. Pearson Education International.

Tussyadiah, I. P., & Fesenmaier, D. R. (2009). Mediating tourist experiences. *Access to Places via Shared Videos, 36*(1), 24-40.

Tuten, T. L. (2008). *Advertising 2.0: Social media marketing in a web 2.0 world*. London: Praeger Publishers.

Wang, X., Chunling, Y., & Yujie, W. (2012). Social media peer communication and impacts of purchase intentions: A consumer socialization framework. *Journal of Interactive Marketing*, *26*(4), 198–208. doi:10.1016/j.intmar.2011.11.004

Yarkın, D. (2013). *Deneyimsel Pazarlama Yaklaşımı ve Kurum İmajı İlişkisi*. (Unpublished doctoral dissertation). Dumlupınar Universitesi, Sosyal Bilimler Enstititüsü, Kütahya.

ADDITIONAL READING

Heitzler, C. D., Asbury, L. D., Stella, L., & Kusner, S. L. (2008). The VERB™ Campaign — Not About Health, All About Fun: Marketing Physical Activity to Children. *American Journal of Preventive Medicine*, *34*(6Supplement), 188–S193. doi:10.1016/j.amepre.2008.03.009 PMID:18471599

Petkus, E. Jr. (2004). Enhancing the application of experiential marketing in the arts. *International Journal of Nonprofit and Voluntary Sector Marketing*, *9*(1), 49–56. doi:10.1002/nvsm.232

Pine, J., & Gilmore, J. H. (1999). *The Experience Economy: Work Is Theatre& Every Business a Stage*. USA: Harvard Business Press.

Schmitt, B. (1999). Experiential Marketing: A New Framework for Design and Communications, *Design Management Journal (Former Series)* [Former Series]. *Design Management Journal*, *10*(2), 10–16.

Wei, Y., Song, P., & Rutherford, B. (2014). Corporate blogs, social media links and firm performance: A study of Fortune 500 Companies. *Journal of Digital & Social Media Marketing*, *2*(2), 159–175.

Yuan, Y. H., & Wu, C. K. (2008). Relationships among experiential marketing, experiential value, and customer satisfaction. *Journal of Hospitality & Tourism Research (Washington, D.C.)*, *32*(3), 387–410. doi:10.1177/1096348008317392

KEY TERMS AND DEFINITIONS

Act: Take action; do something.

Advertising: The activity or profession of producing advertisements for commercial products or services.

Experiential Marketing: A special marketing approach, focuses on customer experiences.

Feel: Be aware of (a person or object) through touching or being touched.

Internet: A global computer network providing a variety of information and communication facilities, consisting of interconnected networks using standardized communication protocols.

Relate: Make or show a connection between.

Sense: A faculty by which the body perceives an external stimulus; one of the faculties of sight, smell, hearing, taste, and touch.

Social Media: Websites and applications that enable users to create and share content or to participate in social networking.

Think: Have a particular belief or idea.

This research was previously published in the Handbook of Research on Effective Advertising Strategies in the Social Media Age edited by Nurdan Öncel Taşkıran and Recep Yılmaz, pages 52-63, copyright year 2015 by Business Science Reference (an imprint of IGI Global).

Chapter 7
Mastering Social Media in the Modern Business World

Kijpokin Kasemsap
Suan Sunandha Rajabhat University, Thailand

ABSTRACT

This chapter explains the overview of social media; the perspectives of social media marketing; social media and communication management; social media competence and knowledge sharing in modern business; social media applications in the tourism industry; social media applications in the health care industry; the multifaceted applications of social media platforms in modern business; and the importance of social media in the modern business world. The implementation of social media is required for modern organizations that seek to serve suppliers and customers, increase business performance, strengthen competitiveness, and achieve continuous success in the modern business world. The chapter argues that applying social media has the potential to enhance organizational performance and reach strategic goals in the social media age.

INTRODUCTION

Social media has rapidly grown in modern business (Kim, Koh, Cha, & Lee, 2015). Social media technologies are a variety of networked tools that encourage collaboration, communication, and productivity among social media users (Dabbagh & Kitsantas, 2012). Social media can be categorized into microblogs (e.g., personal blogs and Twitter), online communities or social networking sites (SNSs) (e.g., Facebook), pictures or video sharing applications (e.g., Flickr and YouTube), and dictionary-type applications, such as Wikipedia (Leung, Law, van Hoof, & Buhalis, 2013). Social media is viewed as a group of Internet-based applications that enable Internet users from all over the world to share ideas, thoughts, experiences, perspectives, information, and forge relationships (Chan & Guillet, 2011). Social media is an electronic communication platform that conveys content generated by the networks of users (Suh, 2015).

Rapid diffusion of social media forms the landscape of communication in contemporary society, with deep impact in markets and the functioning of businesses (Boudreau & Lakhani, 2013). Social media business practices reach a significant business awareness among firms (Aral, Dellarocas, & Godes, 2013).

DOI: 10.4018/978-1-5225-5637-4.ch007

Braojos-Gomez et al. (2015) stated that social media can be leveraged to improve the firm's business activities to create value. Social media represents one of the most important platforms for electronic commerce (e-commerce) (Lee & Phang, 2015). Social media is considered as the quick, cheap, and interactive channels for reaching targeted audiences (Valentini, 2015). Companies use social media to communicate with consumers, and the content of social media affects consumer's decision making in modern business (Zhang, 2015).

Social media has expanded the boundary of mediated relationships that social media user can experience (Lim, Hwang, Kim, & Biocca, 2015). Consumers can interact with social media during multiple stages of the consumption process, including information search, decision making, word of mouth (WOM), and the acquisition, use, and disposal of products and services (Filo, Lock, & Karg, 2015). This chapter aims to bridge the gap in the literature on the thorough literature consolidation of social media in the modern business world. The extant literature of social media provides a contribution to practitioners and researchers by describing the challenges and implications of social media in order to maximize the business impact of social media in modern business.

BACKGROUND

Social media has grown exponentially over the last few years (Duggan & Smith, 2014). Many organizations have used social media as channels for marketing and promotion because of their potential to reach the broad and diverse population across the globe (Wang, Chen, & Wang, 2010). While prior studies have demonstrated various benefits, such as fostering the user engagement, participation, knowledge reuse, and collective innovation (Majchrzak, Wagner, & Yates, 2013) toward understanding the social media's impacts and potential implications of their adoption for organizations remains a fertile research ground for information systems (IS) researchers (Jarvenpaa & Majchrzak, 2010). Firms with the higher development of information technology (IT) infrastructure capability can develop more easily the social media competence due to its greater experience leveraging IT to acquire and provide the appropriate information (Braojos-Gomez et al., 2015).

Although more attention is being paid to the potential negative and unanticipated consequences of social media (Champoux, Durgee, & McGlynn, 2012) and its role in social change (Mohajerani, Baptista, & Nandhakumar, 2015), social media is recognized as a technological remedy for addressing communication and social interaction problems in modern business (Granados & Gupta, 2013). Conceptualizing the dyadic nature and potential of social media in delivering both positive and negative effects is still under-explored (Baptista, Newell, & Currie, 2010). The effects of social media within an organization is a growing area of research (Leonardi, 2014), but still relatively under-theorized (Majchrzak et al., 2013).

Social media is an interactive, collaborative, instant form of communication, which transcends geographical boundaries and social isolation (Lawson & Cowling, 2015). Social media users can quickly interact with geographically dispersed people through the social media, which is an emerging topic in social presence research (Schroeder, 2002). Social media use is an increasingly popular activity for Internet users (Filo et al., 2015). Studies examining social media-related phenomena primarily take a view from the community levels (Miller & Tucker, 2013) considering how organizations interact with customers (Aral et al., 2013) and other external stakeholders (Oestreicher-Singer & Zalmanson, 2013).

CHALLENGES AND IMPLICATIONS OF SOCIAL MEDIA PLATFORMS

This section emphasizes the overview of social media; the perspectives of social media marketing; social media and communication management; social media competence and knowledge sharing in modern business; social media applications in the tourism industry; social media applications in the health care industry; the multifaceted applications of social media platforms in modern business; and the importance of social media in the modern business world.

Overview of Social Media

Social media is broadly used across the globe as a platform for communication, sharing and connecting individuals with their networks in unprecedented ways (Kaplan & Haenlein, 2010). Social media is an alternative communication space embedded with opportunities for free and equal participation (Demirhan & Cakır-Demirhan, 2015). Life on social media has incorporated into many people's daily life (Mou, Miller, & Fu, 2015). The technological development from the World Wide Web to the Web 2.0 has created a new online communication environment (Linke & Oliveira, 2015). Web 2.0 represents an ensemble of technological platforms which allow the interaction of the users by creating and sharing information and other different online materials (Georgescu & Popescul, 2015).

Within the business disciplines, much research has been conducted on how businesses can leverage social media to increase exposure, profits, and other business goals (Brooks, 2015). There is a growing body of research on the social media role in the process of political change in both developed countries (Anstead & Chadwick, 2012) and developing countries, in particular the Middle East (including Iran) (Shirky, 2011), Pakistan (Shaheen, 2008), China (Yang, 2009), and Malaysia (Smeltzer & Keddy, 2010). Social media supports the creation of extensive networks that are capable of organizing business action (Howard & Hussain, 2011).

Social media tools (e.g., Facebook, Twitter, YouTube, and blogs) have played an influential role in political mobilization in the high-profile social movements (Karagiannopoulos, 2012). Kaplan and Haenlein (2010) considered social media as the Internet-based applications complex that build on the ideological and technological foundations of the Web 2.0, which allows its users to generate contents (e.g., articles, pictures, drawings, and videos) and build relationships via exchange material and ideas. Social media is viewed as a firm-specific capability that positively influences a firm's performance (Wu, 2010). Social media technologies allow user-generated content and provide new opportunities and challenges for firms to transform their business (Dong & Wu, 2015).

The utilization of social media (Deans, 2011), such as microblogging (Zhang, Qu, Cody, & Wu, 2010), blogs (Lee, Hwang, & Lee, 2006), wikis (Yates, Wagner, & Majchrzak, 2010), and social networking platforms (Richter & Riemer, 2009) has changed work processes, activities, and the patterns of communication (Luo, Zhang, & Duan, 2013). Huang et al. (2014) found that the adoption of enterprise microblogging improves operational performance by increasing the marketing capability. With the popularity of SNSs (e.g., Facebook) and content-sharing websites (e.g., Flickr and YouTube), images on SNSs or content-sharing websites, called social images, become the dominating multimedia objects on the Internet (Niu, Hua, Tian, & Gao, 2015).

The adoption of social media to support the internal communication effectively broadens participation (Denyer, Parry, & Flowers, 2011) and interactive dialogue (Miles & Mangold, 2014). Employees use social media in various ways and for different purposes, including building and maintaining social ties via Linkedin or Facebook, sharing stories through blogging and microblogging, collaborating through shared sites, and sharing pictures on Instagram and videos on YouTube (Ali-Hassan, Nevo, & Wade, 2015). Won et al. (2015) indicated that social media has the potential to facilitate the documentation of the design process from collaborative idea generation through the testing and refinement in the design-based learning environments.

For a successful implementation of social media, firms should execute strategies based on mindful adoption, community building, and absorptive capability (Culnan, McHugh, & Ubillaga, 2010). Kietzmann et al. (2011) suggested that a firm must develop strategies that are congruent with different social media functionalities and the goals of the firm. The development of social media affords the extensive connectivity and the easy information exchange concerning copyright infringement (Carpenter, 2012). Wu et al. (2015) proposed four perspectives to detect the creation of rumors in microblogging platforms (i.e., the combination of features from the topics of the original message, the sentiments that are communicated in the responses, the observed patterns of message propagation, and the profiles of the users who transmit the messages).

Social media helps organizations create new business models, improve demand predictions, enable management practices, and enhance innovation, knowledge sharing, collaboration, and communication in modern business (Aral et al., 2013). Social media becomes relevant to the whole spectrum of organizational interactions with the public, from brand promotion to complaints, queries, campaigning, and participation in policy making (Trainor, Andzulis, Rapp, & Agnihotri, 2014). Current work on social media in organizations focuses on business engagement, mainly relationships with customers (McCarthy, Rowley, Ashworth, & Pioch, 2014) and information management models (Aladwani, 2014).

Contributions outside business engagement have either mapped online interactions with public sector (Mergel, 2013) and cultural organizations (Padilla-Meléndez & del Águila-Obra, 2013) or explored how non-profit organizations use social media to engage with stakeholder groups (Lovejoy & Saxton, 2012). Kietzmann et al. (2011) explained that the relevance of social media in participation and interactivity is evident as their different functionalities enable organizations to share information, construct identities, and network according to their purposes. Panagiotopoulos et al. (2015) stated that modern organizations are expected to develop a social media presence in order to enable them to share information and engage with the networked public.

Perspectives of Social Media Marketing

Business literature has recognized social media from the marketing capabilities' point of view (Kim et al., 2015) because companies have adopted social media for an effective marketing strategy (Kim & Ko, 2012). Social media marketing efforts need to be congruent and aligned with the different needs of social media users (Zhu & Chen, 2015). Congruence of advertisement and website content will decrease the feelings of intrusiveness and increase positive reactions toward advertising (Newman, Stem, & Sprott, 2004). McCoy et al. (2007) indicated that consumers develop such a negative attitude toward the advertising that they avoid them whenever possible.

Social media helps firms to build a positive corporate image through improving transparency and accountability when various stakeholders actively communicate online (Jones, Temperley, & Lima, 2009). WOM generated in the right social media platform by the right social media users enhances brand loyalty and firm's revenues (Kumar & Mirchandani, 2012). Electronic word of mouth (eWOM) is a critical component of social media (Jeong & Jang, 2011). Online communication through social media websites can reduce information asymmetry because online contents (e.g., eWOM) include a wide range of information about firms, such as new product information and user experiences with products and services (Gu, Park, & Konana, 2012).

Trainor et al. (2014) stated that social media and customer relationship management (CRM) develop capabilities to better serve customer needs in modern business. Customer value, customer satisfaction, and brand loyalty have mediated positive effect on CRM performance (Kasemsap, 2014a). CRM becomes one of the most important business strategies in the digital age, thus involving organizational capability of managing business interactions with customers in an effective manner (Kasemsap, 2015a). The capability of social media in building brand in the global marketplace is practically important in modern advertising (Kasemsap, 2015b).

Social media activities generated by consumers in brand communities are claimed to have a game-changing impact on interaction among brand entities and brand building (Luo, Zhang, & Liu, 2015). Rishika et al. (2013) indicated that customer participation in social media increases customers' shopping visits and customer profitability. Regarding user and marketer-generated content, the indirect comments of informative and persuasive customers has a stronger effect on purchase than firm messages (Goh, Heng, & Lin, 2013).

Social Media and Communication Management

Computer-mediated communication (CMC) can bring together individuals from far and wide to the same online space (Pavelko & Myrick, 2015). The introduction of Web 2.0 technology and social media has dramatically impacted the day-to-day activities of public relations practitioners, who need to master the digital tools for effective communication (Taylor & Perry, 2005). Although it is recognized that the speed at which new technology is adopted by organizations and considerable research has focused on the specific use of a single platform (Waters & Jamal, 2011), more knowledge is required about the professional use of social media tools in public relations through empirical and cross-cultural studies. Task characteristics facilitate the usage of social communication technologies to increase the task performance (Koo, Wati, & Jung, 2011).

Following the approach of new institutionalism applied to communication management and public relations (Sandhu, 2009), most of the research about social media in communication management has approached from a meso-level perspective. The meso-level is above the individual and below the general societal system and allows studying organizations in a broad perspective. The meso-level is studied from normative perspectives and produced rational arguments about benefits and recommendations for the optimal use of new media and tools and for managing the impact on organization of empowered stakeholders (Moreno, Navarro, Tench, & Zerfass, 2015). The key aspect for explaining online communication is the micro level of communication practitioners' social media usage and their general attitudes toward digital platforms (Moreno et al., 2015).

To improve the firm's internal communication, social media tools should increase emotional capital (Huy & Shipilov, 2012). Emerging technologies, advances in social media, and new communication platforms represent powerful tools for enhancing public participation (Lovejoy, Waters, & Saxton, 2012), communicating with the public, bypassing traditional gatekeepers (Wright & Hinson, 2009), repairing the reputation and preventing potential boycotts in crisis situations (Schultz, Utz, & Göritz, 2011), achieving higher organizational credibility (Yang & Lim, 2009), and empowering practitioners by improving their productivity and managing issues better (Sallot, Porter, & Acosta-Alzuru, 2004).

Regarding stakeholders, social media has changed the landscape for communications and empowered publics, who are able to post, share, and republish information easily (Porter, Sweetser, & Chung, 2009). This perspective forces organizations to build and maintain the positive relationships with active consumers, bloggers, community managers, and other gatekeepers on the social web (Moreno et al., 2015). Citizens practically recognize social media as a credible source of information that is free from the organizational, marketing, and economic imperatives faced by traditional journalism (Banning & Sweetser, 2007).

Social Media Competence and Knowledge Sharing in Modern Business

Although an increasing number of organizations implement social media as the method to enhance internal knowledge exchange, employees are not motivated to make use of new technologies (Behringer & Sassenberg, 2015). Social media has the potential to contribute to knowledge exchange in the organizational context (Grace, 2009). Technology use is at the essence of many models explaining the acceptance, impact, and success of information systems (Ali-Hassan, 2015). IT infrastructure capability can enable the firm to develop the social media competence (Braojos-Gomez et al., 2015). Suh et al. (2013) stated that IT infrastructure refers to the set of shared technical and human IT resources in the firm that acquire and provide the foundation for utilizing various IT applications.

Technical IT resources include servers, computers, laptops, operating systems, software, electronic communication networks (e.g., e-mail, Intranet, Extranet, and wireless devices), and shared customer databases (Aral & Weill, 2007). Human IT resources refer to the technical and business skills of IT managers and employees (Wang, Chen, & Benitez-Amado, 2015). The firm's technical IT resources, such as computers, laptops, operating systems and electronic communication networks (e.g., wireless devices) are the base to early adopt social media and develop the social media competence through time and experience (Crossan, Maurer, & White, 2011).

The innovative firms search for experimentation and pursue to develop new products which can persuade them to early adopt social media practices to absorb customers' ideas on new products and product improvements (Camison & Villar-Lopez, 2012), which can enable the development of a social media competence through accumulated knowledge and experience (Real, Roldan, & Leal, 2014). Product innovation strategies and knowledge management efficiently support each other and together to achieve planned goals in modern business (Kasemsap, 2016a). Organizations should promote a culture of knowledge management and organizational innovation regarding the use of open communication, shared support, and collaboration (Kasemsap, 2016b).

Social media is significant in everyday life and in learning (Chantanarungpak, 2015). Firms with a higher innovation management capability have more innovative managers and employees, which are more open, proactive and pioneer in using social media (Nambisan, Agarwal, & Tanniru, 1999) to develop the social media competence. Trust in other bloggers, trust in the economic benefit of sharing knowledge, and trust in the blog service provider positively affect the knowledge sharing in blogs (Chai & Kim, 2010). Zhao et al. (2012) indicated that familiarity, trust, and perceived similarity positively affect the sense of belonging, which influence the intention to get and share knowledge in the virtual communities. Virtual user communities can foster the creation of knowledge for innovation projects at the firm level (Mahr & Lievens, 2012).

Social media technology can enhance the improved organizational productivity by fostering the communication and collaboration of employees which aids knowledge transfer and makes organizations more profitable (Kasemsap, 2014b). Social media enables the creation of knowledge value chain to customize information and delivery for a technological business growth (Kasemsap, 2014c). Social media marks a huge range of the personalized cloud computing platforms and functions of interaction on the Web 2.0 (Bianco, 2009). Many benefits are achieved through the utilization of technologies, such as cloud computing and virtualization (Kasemsap, 2015c). Researchers and practitioners should recognize the significance of cloud computing toward gaining sustainable competitive advantage in global supply chain (Kasemsap, 2015d).

Breschi and Lissoni (2001) indicated that the social media tools, based on personal knowledge coming from common professional experience, are the main channels for the distribution and the creation of knowledge. The employee's self-confidence to share knowledge with others, the perceived enjoyment, and the reward expectations affect the knowledge sharing via the firm's weblogs (Papadopoulos, Stamati, & Nopparuch, 2013). By providing a channel where collective action and communication is conducted in real time (Gallaugher & Ransbotham, 2010), social media facilitates the collaboration (Deans, 2011) and the transfer of both explicit and tacit knowledge (Begel et al., 2010).

Social Media Applications in the Tourism Industry

When faced with new technology for tourism purposes, travelers use information searches in the Internet and gain valuable travel information from various social media sources (Chung & Koo, 2015). In terms of travel information, social media becomes an external source of information where users combine what they know with what they have acquired (Chung, Lee, & Han, 2015). IT-enhanced social media (Choi, 2013) in the tourism industry has become an essential tool for accessing various sources of tourist information (Sigala, Christou, & Gretzel, 2011). In the field of tourism, social media on information sharing (Lee, Reid, & Kim, 2012), information searching (Xiang & Gretzel, 2010), intention of using (Yoo & Gretzel, 2011), and marketing (Chan & Guillet, 2011) have been extensively researched.

Many social media tools enable users to publically exchange information, opinions, and experiences, and are broadly recognized by potential tourists as external information sources (Kaplan & Haenlein, 2010). It is crucial to understand the changes in social media technologies and travelers' behaviors that impact the creation, distribution, and accessibility of travel information (Xiang & Gretzel, 2010). In the tourism industry, travelers have basic motivations to choose several valuable destinations to visit; therefore they pursue information reliability through an intensive information search via social media (Hwang & Fesenmaier, 2011). The characteristics of tourism products make travel information essential in reducing the risk of purchasing tourism products (Tan & Chen, 2012). The potential tourists become self-advisors by referencing their own experience and knowledge, but when the internal source does not provide enough information, they use the external sources of information, such as the Internet, books, travel agencies, and acquaintances (Kim, Lehto, & Morrison, 2007).

Through social media, potential tourists can express their opinions, share information about tourism destinations, attractions, and activities, and make decisions based on this knowledge exchange (Ku, 2012). Social media is essential for restructuring the tourism industry (Xiang, Wober, & Fesenmaier, 2008). Social media is directly related to tourist behaviors, such as planning in the pre-travel stage, sharing experience in the on-travel stage, and recommending tourism products in the after-travel stage (Chung & Buhalis, 2008). Huang et al. (2010) studied the factors that encourage and discourage travel information sharing on SNSs, such as Facebook. Kang and Schuett (2013) explored the factors in sharing travel experiences on travel websites, delving into how social factors affect perceived enjoyment, travel planning, and travel experiences through the utilization of social media.

Social Media Applications in the Health Care Industry

Thackeray et al. (2012) stated that heath agencies and organizations have proven to be no exception for the uses of online social media. With low cost and high reach, increasing numbers of public health promotion campaigns have been deployed through online social media platforms (Cugelman, Thelwall, & Dawes, 2011). An increasing number of health campaigns and programs will be deployed and implemented via online social media platforms (Abroms & Lefebvre, 2009). Health campaigns via online social media platforms open up the two-way communication routes through which audiences can engage and participate (Heldman, Schindelar, & Weaver, 2013).

Linking via social media encourages health care practitioners to share case studies, ask for advice, and contribute professional opinions (Kaufman, 2012). With the ever-growing uses of social media for health campaigns, scholarly attention is paid to understand how audiences respond to campaign messages on social media platforms (Korda & Itani, 2013). Syred et al. (2014) indicated that the majority of studies on health campaigns look at the application and feasibility of popular social media websites, such as Facebook and Twitter.

YouTube offers an alternative, cost-effective platform for health campaign videos (Dutta, 2015). With the option of posting comments and replies, YouTube provides a space for social interaction and audience engagement (Dynel, 2014). Postings on YouTube reflect audience attitudes and feedback (Shapiro & Park, 2015). Audience response presented and shared on a social media platform are important to study because they influence the subsequent viewers' attitudes and opinions (Paek, Hove, & Jeon, 2013). Social media users look for the responses of others and are swayed by their comments (Shi, Messaris, & Cappella, 2014). Audience comments practically set the context for social influence (Cialdini & Golstein, 2004).

Multifaceted Applications of Social Media Platforms in Modern Business

With the advances in IT, social media technologies support a large volume of user-generated content that provides opportunities and challenges for business transformation (Jarvenpaa & Tuunainen, 2013). As firms increasingly leverage IT in various innovation activities (Dong & Yang, 2015), they can use a particular social media technology, such as online user innovation communities (OUICs) for open innovation by crowdsourcing the ideas about new products, services, and processes (Di Gangi & Wasko, 2009).

OUICs are valuable for crowdsourcing by enabling firms to collect large amount of user-generated ideas (Bayus, 2013). A better understanding of the ways in which firms increase their business value through the strategic use of OUICs has important implications on the business value of social media technologies, as recent studies on the business value of IT have switched the focus to the IT enablement of innovation (Bardhan, Krishnan, & Lin, 2013). OUICs provide a social media platform for user-generated ideas on innovation (Nambisan, 2013). In OUICs, firms can assign the internal employees as the idea partners to evaluate and select the posts and comments (Dong & Wu, 2015).

If a firm is unable to gain access to enough new ideas, it results in missed opportunities (Hansen & Birkinshaw, 2007). Sourcing external ideas from customers is a solution to extend the scope of search because customers are able to expect the shift of demand (Nambisan, 2002). Dell Incorporation (i.e., an innovative firm) learned to leverage social media by creating a social media platform to enable the innovative customers to participate in the research and development (R&D) processes of the firm (Di Gangi, Wasko, & Hooker, 2010). OUIC-enabled ideation capability can therefore collect ideas from outside the company by tapping into the opinions of end users (Nambisan, 2013). For example, Dell Incorporation has gathered more than 22,000 posts and 100,000 comments on new ideas from its OUIC IdeaStorm, which are related to its desktops and laptops, mobile devices, servers and storage, software, printers and ink, accessories, broadband and mobility, advertising and marketing, retail, and service (Dong & Wu, 2015).

The role of social media in business and in the IT industry focuses on various researches, such as marketing strategies (Cachia, Compano, & Da Costa, 2007), the changing relationship between businesses and marketplaces (Aral et al., 2013), and the reshaping of industries, such as health care (Hawn, 2009), news and publishing (Hong, 2012), and education (Moran et al., 2011). The advancement in the IT sector is a new generation of entrepreneurs who are starting new businesses using social media, often challenging the business models of traditional companies (Mohajerani et al., 2015). For example, an individual software developer can use social media to collaborate with people to establish the new applications and software development (Begel, DeLine, & Zimmermann, 2010). Large firms from IT industries are more likely to adopt social media tools (Sinclaire & Vogus, 2011).

Kim et al. (2012) evaluated the determinants of continuance and WOM intention in Korea's social media. Wu et al. (2013) reported how four dimensions of perceived interactivity (i.e., control, synchronicity, surveillance, and social bandwidth) affect the users' bridging and bonding social capital in Taiwan. Zhang et al. (2013) explored how product attitudes form on online review sites with social networks in China. Chen et al. (2013) discovered the influence structure of users in online social networks through the application of the Bayesian model on data from China's social media website Douban allowing consumers to share reviews on books, movies, and music. Utilizing Douban data, Phang et al. (2013) inspected the types of online social network structure that may increase user participation and promote their tendency to purchase the niche cultural products.

Goh et al. (2013) conducted empirical research measuring the differential impacts of user-generated content and marketer-generated content in social media on consumer purchases in Singapore. Kim et al. (2014) considered the impacts of social media sentiments on stock prices in the Korean financial market. Using Twitter data, Pervin et al. (2014) found that retweetability is significantly affected by amplifiers and information starters. Regarding virtual communities, user identification and satisfaction with the community are related to the participation in the community and promotion to non-members, which in turn increase the member loyalty to the community (Casalo, Flavian, & Guinaliu, 2010).

Importance of Social Media in the Modern Business World

Social media has become an important area of exploration for researchers interested in online technologies and their impacts on customers and businesses (Lee & Phang, 2015). At corporate level, social media enables the firm's proficiency to seize business opportunities and the reconfiguration of business resources (Wagner & Wagner, 2013). At operational level, firms leverage social media to improve their relationships with customers (in terms of product, brand, engagement, and firm) toward increasing the brand trust to lead to a greater customer loyalty and business value (Laroche, Habibi, & Richard, 2013). Kiron et al. (2012) indicated that business managers are the most interested managers in the use of social media for business activities.

As social media use has developed, businesses and brands have evolved practices to communicate with consumers and generate revenue through interactive online tools (Filo et al., 2015). Due to its ease of use, speed, and reach, social media is fast changing the public discourse in society and setting trends and agendas in topics that range from the environment and politics, to technology and the entertainment industry (Asur & Huberman, 2010). Social media becomes the foundation for social interactions and a regular part of the social structure of communities and organizations (Baptista, 2009), adapting the arrangement of communication and interaction (Hoffman & Fodor, 2010). The adoption of social media within modern organizations shifts processes and practices (Subramaniam, Nandhakumar, & Baptista, 2013) as it becomes embedded in decision making and community building in modern business (Culnan et al., 2010).

Social media supports the informational capitalization by spreading the information about the organization and by acquiring the valuable information of employees, suppliers, and clients (Georgescu & Popescul, 2015). Social media and conventional media have a strong interaction effect on stock market performance (Yu, Duan, & Cao, 2013). Firm's corporate image strategies enabled by social media improve financial performance (Schniederjans, Cao, & Schniederjans, 2013). Luo et al. (2013) indicated that social media predicts firm equity value better, faster, and more accurately than conventional online media (e.g., Google search).

The more flexible and adaptive nature of smaller organizations allows them to more quickly and fully appropriate the participative features and practices of social media as a platform for communication (Meske & Stieglitz, 2013) and collaboration (Zeiller & Schauer, 2011). By using the capabilities of social media to access richer information, small and medium-sized enterprises (SMEs) are able to change how they interact with and manage customers (Stockdale, Ahmed, & Scheepers, 2012). The affordances of social media enable entrepreneurs to facilitate the adoption of new business practices (Djelic & Ainamo, 2005). Social media users are more willing to participate in social media from firms with greater corporate social responsibility (Lee, Oh, & Kim, 2013).

Practitioners with a high level of social media usage give more importance to social media channels, the influence of social media on the internal and external stakeholders, and the relevance of key stakeholders along with a better self-estimation of competences (Moreno et al., 2015). Concerning social media competitive analysis and text mining, the pizza manufacturing firms leverage Facebook and Twitter to engage customers and build online communities (He, Zha, & Li, 2013). Social media enable the relationships among customers, products, and companies, which in turn increase their brand loyalty (Laroche et al., 2013).

Social media builds a platform that instantly allows customers to report satisfaction or dissatisfaction with services or products (Kim et al., 2015). Lee et al. (2012) introduced Starbuck's practice that it uses social media not only as tools for direct communication with its customers, but also as windows to obtain the first-hand suggestions and criticisms from those customers. Many companies across industries assign employees who monitor customer reviews that are posted on social media in order to manage customer feedback (Huang, Chou, & Lin, 2010). Managing consumers' feedback in social media is crucial and it can even destroy the business when poorly managed (Gelb & Sundaram, 2002).

FUTURE RESEARCH DIRECTIONS

The classification of the extant literature in the domains of social media will provide the potential opportunities for future research. Social media platforms (e.g., Facebook and Twitter) allow organizations to improve communication and productivity by disseminating information among different groups of employees in a more efficient manner. Facebook is one of the most powerful social media platforms in modern business. Facebook has helped to create a personal brand for many individuals and for businesses. The Internet of Things (IoT) is a system where the Internet is connected to the physical world via ubiquitous sensors. Utilizing the IoT can save consumers and companies a lot of time and money.

Web 2.0 is a technology that is associated with the web applications, which enables interactive user-centered design, interoperability, information sharing, and collaboration on the World Wide Web. The applications developed using Web 2.0 can be shared among a number of users through Internet and can be simultaneously used by numerous users. Web search engines (e.g., Google and Yahoo!) utilize computer algorithms to search the Internet and identify items that match the characters and keywords entered by a user. The relationships among social media platforms, the IoT, and web search engines will be the beneficial topics for future research directions.

CONCLUSION

This chapter highlighted the overview of social media; the perspectives of social media marketing; social media and communication management; social media competence and knowledge sharing in modern business; social media applications in the tourism industry; social media applications in the health care industry; the multifaceted applications of social media platforms in modern business; and the importance of social media in the modern business world. Social media plays a growing role in business communication and becomes important platforms for marketing and advertising. Social media offers a chance to redefine the delivery of service to customers, thus changing the way they think about a company's brands while considerably lowering service costs.

Social media has many benefits, such as the increased awareness of the organization, the increased traffic to website, the greater favorable perceptions of the brand, the better understanding of customer perceptions of their brand, the improved insights into target markets, and the improved identification of new product opportunities in modern business. Social media allows organizations to improve communication and productivity by disseminating information among the different groups of employees in a more efficient manner. The most obvious opportunity of utilizing social media is to generate business revenue through building a business community and advertising products within social media platforms.

When considering social media campaigns, social media users can try to attract followers with promotions. Social media is an important approach to attracting new customers, enhancing brand management, and promoting knowledge management in modern organizations. Using social media allows customers to connect and interact with business on a more personal level. Applying social media has the potential to enhance organizational performance and reach strategic goals in modern business.

REFERENCES

Abroms, L. C., & Lefebvre, R. C. (2009). Obama's wired campaign: Lessons for public health communication. *Journal of Health Communication, 14*(5), 415–423. doi:10.1080/10810730903033000

Aladwani, A. M. (2014). The 6As model of social content management. *International Journal of Information Management, 34*(2), 133–138. doi:10.1016/j.ijinfomgt.2013.12.004

Ali-Hassan, H., Nevo, D., & Wade, M. (2015). Linking dimensions of social media use to job performance: The role of social capital. *The Journal of Strategic Information Systems, 24*(2), 65–89. doi:10.1016/j.jsis.2015.03.001

Anstead, N., & Chadwick, A. (2012). *Parties, election campaigning, and the Internet: Toward a comparative institutional approach*. London, UK: Routledge.

Aral, S., Dellarocas, C., & Godes, D. (2013). Social media and business transformation: A framework for research. *Information Systems Research, 24*(1), 3–13. doi:10.1287/isre.1120.0470

Aral, S., & Weill, P. (2007). IT assets, organizational capabilities, and firm performance: How resource allocations and organizational differences explain performance variation. *Organization Science, 18*(5), 763–780. doi:10.1287/orsc.1070.0306

Banning, S. A., & Sweetser, K. D. (2007). How much do they think it affects them and whom do they believe?: Comparing the third-person effect and credibility of blogs and traditional media. *Communication Quarterly, 55*(4), 451–466. doi:10.1080/01463370701665114

Baptista, J. (2009). Institutionalisation as a process of interplay between technology and its organisational context of use. *Journal of Information Technology, 24*(4), 305–319. doi:10.1057/jit.2009.15

Baptista, J., Newell, S., & Currie, W. (2010). Paradoxical effects of institutionalization on the strategic awareness of technology in organizations. *The Journal of Strategic Information Systems, 19*(3), 171–183. doi:10.1016/j.jsis.2010.07.001

Bardhan, I., Krishnan, V., & Lin, S. (2013). Business value of information technology: Testing the interaction effect of IT and R&D on Tobin's Q. *Information Systems Research, 24*(4), 1147–1161. doi:10.1287/isre.2013.0481

Bayus, B. L. (2013). Crowdsourcing new product ideas over time: An analysis of the Dell IdeaStorm community. *Management Science, 59*(1), 226–244. doi:10.1287/mnsc.1120.1599

Begel, A., DeLine, R., & Zimmermann, T. (2010). *Social media for software engineering*. Paper presented at the 2010 FSE/SDP Workshop on the Future of Software Engineering Research (FoSER), Santa Fe, NM.

Behringer, N., & Sassenberg, K. (2015). Introducing social media for knowledge management: Determinants of employees' intentions to adopt new tools. *Computers in Human Behavior, 48*, 290–296. doi:10.1016/j.chb.2015.01.069

Bianco, J. S.Jamie Skye Bianco. (2009). Social networking and cloud computing: Precarious affordances for the "prosumer." *WSQ: Women's Studies Quarterly, 37*(1/2), 303–312. doi:10.1353/wsq.0.0146

Boudreau, K. J., & Lakhani, K. R. (2013). Using the crowd as an innovation partner. *Harvard Business Review*, *91*(4), 60–69.

Braojos-Gomez, J., Benitez-Amado, J., & Llorens-Montes, F. J. (2015). How do small firms learn to develop a social media competence? *International Journal of Information Management*, *35*(4), 443–458. doi:10.1016/j.ijinfomgt.2015.04.003

Breschi, S., & Lissoni, F. (2001). Knowledge spillovers and local innovation systems: A critical survey. *Industrial and Corporate Change*, *10*(4), 975–1005. doi:10.1093/icc/10.4.975

Brooks, S. (2015). Does personal social media usage affect efficiency and well-being? *Computers in Human Behavior*, *46*, 26–37. doi:10.1016/j.chb.2014.12.053

Cachia, R., Compano, R., & Da Costa, O. (2007). Grasping the potential of online social networks for foresight. *Technological Forecasting and Social Change*, *74*(8), 1179–1203. doi:10.1016/j.techfore.2007.05.006

Camison, C., & Villar-Lopez, A. (2012). On how firms located in and industrial district profit from knowledge spillovers: Adoption of an organic structure and innovation capabilities. *British Journal of Management*, *23*(3), 361–382. doi: 10.1111/j.1467-8551.2011.00745.x

Carpenter, C. (2012). Copyright infringement and the second generation of social media websites: Why Pinterest users should be protected from copyright infringement by the fair use defense. *Journal of Internet Law*, *16*(7), 9–21. doi: 10.2139/ssrn.2131483

Casalo, L. V., Flavian, C., & Guinaliu, M. (2010). Relationship quality, community promotion and brand loyalty in virtual communities: Evidence from free software communities. *International Journal of Information Management*, *30*(4), 357–367. doi:10.1016/j.ijinfomgt.2010.01.004

Chai, S., & Kim, M. (2010). What makes bloggers share knowledge? An investigation on the role of trust. *International Journal of Information Management*, *30*(5), 408–415. doi:10.1016/j.ijinfomgt.2010.02.005

Champoux, V., Durgee, J., & McGlynn, L. (2012). Corporate Facebook pages: When "fans" attack. *The Journal of Business Strategy*, *33*(2), 22–30. doi:10.1108/02756661211206717

Chan, N. L., & Guillet, B. D. (2011). Investigation of social media marketing: How does the hotel industry in Hong Kong perform in marketing on social media websites? *Journal of Travel & Tourism Marketing*, *28*(4), 345–368. doi:10.1080/10548408.2011.571571

Chang, H. L., & Chou, C. Y. (2012). *Shaping proactivity for firm performance: Evaluating the role of IT-enabled collaboration in small and medium enterprises*. Paper presented at the 16th Pacific Asia Conference on Information Systems (PACIS 2012), Ho Chi Minh City, Vietnam.

Chantanarungpak, K. (2015). Using e-portfolio on social media. *Procedia: Social and Behavioral Sciences*, *186*, 1275–1281. doi:10.1016/j.sbspro.2015.04.063

Chen, X., Wang, C., & Zhang, X. (2013). *All online friends are not created equal: Discovering influence structure in online social networks*. Paper presented at the Pacific Asia Conference on Information Systems (PACIS 2013), Jeju Island, South Korea.

Choi, S. (2013). An empirical study of social network service (SNS) continuance: Incorporating the customer value-satisfaction-loyalty model into the IS continuance model. *Asia Pacific Journal of Information Systems*, *23*(4), 1–28. doi:10.14329/apjis.2013.23.4.001

Chung, J. E. (2015). Antismoking campaign videos on YouTube and audience response: Application of social media assessment metrics. *Computers in Human Behavior*, *51*, 114–121. doi:10.1016/j.chb.2015.04.061

Chung, J. Y., & Buhalis, D. (2008). *A study of online travel community and Web 2.0: Factors affecting participation and attitude*. Paper presented at the ENTER 2008 Conference on eTourism, Innsbruck, Austria. doi:10.1007/978-3-211-77280-5_7

Chung, N., & Koo, C. (2015). The use of social media in travel information search. *Telematics and Informatics*, *32*(2), 215–229. doi:10.1016/j.tele.2014.08.005

Chung, N., Lee, S., & Han, H. (2015). Understanding communication types on travel information sharing in social media: A transactive memory systems perspective. *Telematics and Informatics*, *32*(4), 564–575. doi:10.1016/j.tele.2015.02.002

Cialdini, R., & Golstein, N. (2004). Social influence: Compliance and conformity. *Annual Review of Psychology*, *55*(1), 591–621. doi:10.1146/annurev.psych.55.090902.142015

Crossan, M. M., Maurer, C. C., & White, R. E. (2011). Reflections on the 2009 AMR decade award: Do we have a theory of organizational learning? *Academy of Management Review*, *36*(3), 446–460. doi:10.5465/amr.2010.0544

Cugelman, B., Thelwall, M., & Dawes, P. (2011). Online interventions for social marketing health behavior change campaigns: A meta-analysis of psychological architectures and adherence factors. *Journal of Medical Internet Research*, *13*(1), 84–107. doi:10.2196/jmir.1367

Culnan, M., McHugh, P., & Zubillaga, J. (2010). How large US companies can use Twitter and other social media to gain business value. *MIS Quarterly Executive*, *9*(4), 243–259.

Deans, P. C. (2011). The impact of social media on C-level roles. *MIS Quarterly Executive*, *10*(4), 187–200.

Demirhan, K., & Cakır-Demirhan, D. (2015). Gender and politics: Patriarchal discourse on social media. *Public Relations Review*, *41*(1), 308–310. doi:10.1016/j.pubrev.2014.11.010

Denyer, D., Parry, E., & Flowers, P. (2011). "Social", "open" and "participative"? Exploring personal experiences and organizational effects of Enterprise 2.0 use. *Long Range Planning*, *44*(5/6), 375–396. doi:10.1016/j.lrp.2011.09.007

Di Gangi, P. M., & Wasko, M. (2009). Steal my idea! Organizational adoption of user innovations from a user innovation community: A case study of Dell IdeaStorm. *Decision Support Systems*, *48*(1), 303–312. doi:10.1016/j.dss.2009.04.004

Di Gangi, P. M., Wasko, M. M., & Hooker, R. E. (2010). Getting customers' ideas to work for you: Learning from Dell how to succeed with online user innovation communities. *MIS Quarterly Executive*, *9*(4), 213–228.

Djelic, M. L., & Ainamo, A. (2005). The telecom industry as cultural industry? The transposition of fashion logics into the field of mobile telephony. *Research in the Sociology of Organizations*, *23*(1), 45–82. doi:10.1016/S0733-558X(05)23002-1

Dong, J. Q., & Wu, W. (2015). Business value of social media technologies: Evidence from online user innovation communities. *The Journal of Strategic Information Systems*, *24*(2), 113–127. doi:10.1016/j.jsis.2015.04.003

Dong, J. Q., & Yang, C. H. (2015). Information technology and organizational learning in knowledge alliances and networks: Evidence from U.S. pharmaceutical industry. *Information & Management*, *52*(1), 111–122. doi:10.1016/j.im.2014.10.010

Duggan, M., & Smith, A. (2014). *Social media update 2013*. Washington, DC: Pew Research Center.

Dutta, M. J. (2015). New communication technologies, social media, and public health. In R. Detels, M. Gulliford, Q. Karim, & C. Tan (Eds.), *Oxford textbook of global public health* (pp. 388–399). Oxford, UK: Oxford University Press. doi:10.1093/med/9780199661756.003.0102

Dynel, M. (2014). Participation framework underlying YouTube interaction. *Journal of Pragmatics*, *73*, 37–52. doi:10.1016/j.pragma.2014.04.001

Filo, K., Lock, D., & Karg, A. (2015). Sport and social media research: A review. *Sport Management Review*, *18*(2), 166–181. doi:10.1016/j.smr.2014.11.001

Gallaugher, J., & Ransbotham, S. (2010). Social media and customer dialog management at Starbucks. *MIS Quarterly Executive*, *9*(4), 197–212.

Gelb, B. D., & Sundaram, S. (2002). Adapting to word of mouse. *Business Horizons*, *45*(4), 21–25. doi:10.1016/S0007-6813(02)00222-7

Georgescu, M., & Popescul, D. (2015). Social media: The new paradigm of collaboration and communication for business environment. *Procedia Economics and Finance*, *20*, 277–282. doi:10.1016/S2212-5671(15)00075-1

Goh, K. Y., Heng, C. S., & Lin, Z. (2013). Social media brand community and consumer behavior: Quantifying the relative impact of user- and marketer-generated content. *Information Systems Research*, *24*(1), 88–107. doi:10.1287/isre.1120.0469

Grace, T. P. L. (2009). Wikis as a knowledge management tool. *Journal of Knowledge Management*, *13*(4), 64–74. doi:10.1108/13673270910971833

Granados, N., & Gupta, A. (2013). Transparency strategy: Competing with information in a digital world. *Management Information Systems Quarterly*, *37*(2), 637–641.

Gu, B., Park, J., & Konana, P. (2012). The impact of external word-of-mouth sources on retailer sales of high-involvement products. *Information Systems Research*, *23*(1), 182–196. doi:10.1287/isre.1100.0343

Hansen, R., & Birkinshaw, J. (2007). The innovation value chain. *Harvard Business Review*, *85*(6), 121–135.

Hawn, C. (2009). Take two aspirin and tweet me in the morning: How Twitter, Facebook, and other social media are reshaping health care. *Health Affairs*, *28*(2), 361–368. doi:10.1377/hlthaff.28.2.361

He, W., Zha, S., & Li, L. (2013). Social media competitive analysis and text mining: A case study in the pizza industry. *International Journal of Information Management*, *33*(3), 464–472. doi:10.1016/j.ijinfomgt.2013.01.001

Heldman, A. B., Schindelar, J., & Weaver, J. B. (2013). Social media engagement and public health communication: Implications for public health organizations being truly "social". *Public Health Reviews*, *35*(1), 1–18.

Hoffman, D. L., & Fodor, M. (2010). Can you measure the ROI of your social media marketing? *MIT Sloan Management Review*, *52*(1), 41–49.

Hong, S. (2012). Online news on Twitter: Newspapers' social media adoption and their online readership. *Information Economics and Policy*, *24*(1), 69–74. doi:10.1016/j.infoecopol.2012.01.004

Howard, P. N., & Hussain, M. M. (2011). The role of digital media. *Journal of Democracy*, *22*(3), 35–48. doi:10.1353/jod.2011.0041

Huang, C. Y., Chou, C. J., & Lin, P. C. (2010). Involvement theory in constructing bloggers' intention to purchase travel products. *Tourism Management*, *31*(4), 513–526. doi:10.1016/j.tourman.2009.06.003

Huang, J., Baptista, J., & Newell, S. (2015). Communicational ambidexterity as a new capability to manage social media communication within organizations. *The Journal of Strategic Information Systems*, *24*(2), 49–64. doi:10.1016/j.jsis.2015.03.002

Huang, J., Zhang, J., Li, Y., & Lv, Z. (2014). Business value of enterprise micro-blogging: Empirical study from Weibo.com in Sina. *Journal of Global Information Management*, *22*(3), 32–56. doi:10.4018/jgim.2014070102

Huang, Y., Basu, C., & Hsu, M. K. (2010). Exploring motivations of travel knowledge sharing on social network sites: An empirical investigation of U.S. college students. *Journal of Hospitality Marketing & Management*, *19*(7), 717–734. doi:10.1080/19368623.2010.508002

Huy, Q., & Shipilov, A. (2012). The key to social media success within organizations. *MIT Sloan Management Review*, *54*(1), 73–81.

Hwang, Y. H., & Fesenmaier, D. R. (2011). Unplanned tourist attraction visits by travellers. *Tourism Geographies: An International Journal of Tourism Space, Place and Environment*, *13*(3), 398–416. doi:10.1080/14616688.2011.570777

Jarvenpaa, S. L., & Majchrzak, A. (2010). Vigilant interaction in knowledge collaboration: Challenges of online user participation under ambivalence. *Information Systems Research*, *21*(4), 773–784. doi:10.1287/isre.1100.0320

Jarvenpaa, S. L., & Tuunainen, V. K. (2013). How Finnair socialized customers for service co-creation with social media. *MIS Quarterly Executive*, *12*(3), 125–136.

Jeong, E., & Jang, S. C. (2011). Restaurant experiences triggering positive electronic word-of-mouth (eWOM) motivations. *International Journal of Hospitality Management, 30*(2), 356–366. doi:10.1016/j.ijhm.2010.08.005

Jones, J., Temperley, B., & Lima, A. (2009). Corporate reputation in the era of Web 2. 0: The case of Primark. *Journal of Marketing Management, 25*(9/10), 927–939. doi:10.1362/026725709X479309

Kang, M., & Schuett, M. A. (2013). Determinants of sharing travel experiences in social media. *Journal of Travel & Tourism Marketing, 30*(1/2), 93–107. doi:10.1080/10548408.2013.751237

Kaplan, A., & Haenlein, M. (2010). Users of the world, unite! The challenges and opportunities of social media. *Business Horizons, 53*(1), 59–68. doi:10.1016/j.bushor.2009.09.003

Karagiannopoulos, V. (2012). The role of the internet in political struggles: Some conclusions from Iran and Egypt. *New Political Science, 34*(2), 151–171. doi:10.1080/07393148.2012.676394

Kasemsap, K. (2014a). The role of brand loyalty on CRM performance: An innovative framework for smart manufacturing. In Z. Luo (Ed.), *Smart manufacturing innovation and transformation: Interconnection and intelligence* (pp. 252–284). Hershey, PA: IGI Global. doi:10.4018/978-1-4666-5836-3.ch010

Kasemsap, K. (2014b). The role of social networking in global business environments. In P. Smith & T. Cockburn (Eds.), *Impact of emerging digital technologies on leadership in global business* (pp. 183–201). Hershey, PA: IGI Global. doi:10.4018/978-1-4666-6134-9.ch010

Kasemsap, K. (2014c). The role of social media in the knowledge-based organizations. In I. Lee (Ed.), *Integrating social media into business practice, applications, management, and models* (pp. 254–275). Hershey, PA: IGI Global. doi:10.4018/978-1-4666-6182-0.ch013

Kasemsap, K. (2015a). The role of customer relationship management in the global business environments. In T. Tsiakis (Ed.), *Trends and innovations in marketing information systems* (pp. 130–156). Hershey, PA: IGI Global. doi:10.4018/978-1-4666-8459-1.ch007

Kasemsap, K. (2015b). The role of social media in international advertising. In N. Taşkıran & R. Yılmaz (Eds.), *Handbook of research on effective advertising strategies in the social media age* (pp. 171–196). Hershey, PA: IGI Global. doi:10.4018/978-1-4666-8125-5.ch010

Kasemsap, K. (2015c). The role of cloud computing adoption in global business. In V. Chang, R. Walters, & G. Wills (Eds.), *Delivery and adoption of cloud computing services in contemporary organizations* (pp. 26–55). Hershey, PA: IGI Global. doi:10.4018/978-1-4666-8210-8.ch002

Kasemsap, K. (2015d). The role of cloud computing in global supply chain. In N. Rao (Ed.), Enterprise management strategies in the era of cloud computing (pp. 192–219). Hershey, PA: IGI Global. doi:10.4018/978-1-4666-8339-6.ch009

Kasemsap, K. (2016a). Creating product innovation strategies through knowledge management in global business. In A. Goel & P. Singhal (Eds.), *Product innovation through knowledge management and social media strategies* (pp. 330–357). Hershey, PA: IGI Global. doi:10.4018/978-1-4666-9607-5.ch015

Kasemsap, K. (2016b). The roles of knowledge management and organizational innovation in global business. In G. Jamil, J. Poças-Rascão, F. Ribeiro, & A. Malheiro da Silva (Eds.), *Handbook of research on information architecture and management in modern organizations* (pp. 130–153). Hershey, PA: IGI Global. doi:10.4018/978-1-4666-8637-3.ch006

Kaufman, M. B. (2012). Online communities for healthcare professionals can help improve communication, collaboration. *Formulary (Cleveland, Ohio)*, *47*(4), 161.

Kietzmann, J. H., Hermkens, K., McCarthy, I. P., & Silvestre, B. S. (2011). Social media? Get serious! Understanding the functional building blocks of social media. *Business Horizons*, *54*(3), 241–251. doi:10.1016/j.bushor.2011.01.005

Kim, A. J., & Ko, E. (2012). Do social media marketing activities enhance customer equity? An empirical study of luxury fashion brand. *Journal of Business Research*, *65*(10), 1480–1486. doi:10.1016/j.jbusres.2011.10.014

Kim, D. Y., Lehto, X. Y., & Morrison, A. M. (2007). Gender differences in online travel information search: Implications for marketing communications on the Internet. *Tourism Management*, *28*(2), 423–433. doi:10.1016/j.tourman.2006.04.001

Kim, H., Son, J., & Suh, K. (2012). Following firms on Twitter: Determinants of continuance and word-of-mouth intention. *Asia Pacific Journal of Information Systems*, *22*(3), 1–27. doi:10.5859/KAIS.2012.21.2.1

Kim, S., Koh, Y., Cha, J., & Lee, S. (2015). Effects of social media on firm value for U.S. restaurant companies. *International Journal of Hospitality Management*, *49*, 40–46. doi:10.1016/j.ijhm.2015.05.006

Kim, T., Jung, W. J., & Lee, S. Y. (2014). The analysis on the relationship between firms' exposures to SNS and stock prices in Korea. *Asia Pacific Journal of Information Systems*, *24*(2), 233–253. doi:10.14329/apjis.2014.24.2.233

Kiron, D., Palmer, D., Phillips, A. N., & Kruschwitz, N. (2012). What managers really think about social business. *MIT Sloan Management Review*, *53*(4), 51–60.

Koo, C., Wati, Y., & Jung, J. J. (2011). Examination of how social aspects moderate the relationship between task characteristics and usage of social communication technologies (SCTs) in organizations. *International Journal of Information Management*, *31*(5), 445–459. doi:10.1016/j.ijinfomgt.2011.01.003

Korda, H., & Itani, Z. (2013). Harnessing social media for health promotion and behavior change. *Health Promotion Practice*, *14*(1), 15–23. doi:10.1177/1524839911405850

Ku, E. (2012). Distributed fascinating knowledge over an online travel community. *International Journal of Tourism Research*, *16*(1), 33–43. doi:10.1002/jtr.1895

Kumar, V., & Mirchandani, R. (2012). Increasing the ROI of social media marketing. *MIT Sloan Management Review*, *54*(1), 55–61.

Laroche, M., Habibi, M. R., & Richard, M. O. (2013). To be or not to be in social media: How brand loyalty is affected by social media? *International Journal of Information Management*, *33*(1), 76–82. doi:10.1016/j.ijinfomgt.2012.07.003

Lawson, C., & Cowling, C. (2015). Social media: The next frontier for professional development in radiography. *Radiography, 21*(2), e74–e80. doi:10.1016/j.radi.2014.11.006

Lee, H., Reid, E., & Kim, W. G. (2012). Understanding knowledge sharing in online travel communities: Antecedents and the moderating effects of interaction modes. *Journal of Hospitality & Tourism Research (Washington, D.C.), 38*(2), 222–242. doi:10.1177/1096348012451454

Lee, K., Oh, W. Y., & Kim, N. (2013). Social media for socially responsible firms: Analysis of Fortune 500's Twitter profiles and their CSR/CSIR ratings. *Journal of Business Ethics, 118*(4), 791–806. doi:10.1007/s10551-013-1961-2

Lee, S., Hwang, T., & Lee, H. H. (2006). Corporate blogging strategies of the Fortune 500 companies. *Management Decision, 44*(3), 316–334. doi:10.1108/00251740610656232

Lee, S. Y. T., & Phang, C. W. (2015). Leveraging social media for electronic commerce in Asia: Research areas and opportunities. *Electronic Commerce Research and Applications, 14*(3), 145–149. doi:10.1016/j.elerap.2015.02.001

Lee, W., Xiong, L., & Hu, C. (2012). The effect of Facebook users' arousal and valence on intention to go to the festival: Applying an extension of the technology acceptance model. *International Journal of Hospitality Management, 31*(3), 819–827. doi:10.1016/j.ijhm.2011.09.018

Leonardi, P. M. (2014). Social media, knowledge sharing, and innovation: Toward a theory of communication visibility. *Information Systems Research, 25*(4), 796–816. doi:10.1287/isre.2014.0536

Leung, D., Law, R., van Hoof, H., & Buhalis, D. (2013). Social media in tourism and hospitality: A literature review. *Journal of Travel & Tourism Marketing, 30*(1/2), 3–22. doi:10.1080/10548408.2013.750919

Lim, J. S., Hwang, Y. C., Kim, S., & Biocca, F. A. (2015). How social media engagement leads to sports channel loyalty: Mediating roles of social presence and channel commitment. *Computers in Human Behavior, 46*, 158–167. doi:10.1016/j.chb.2015.01.013

Linke, A., & Oliveira, E. (2015). Quantity or quality? The professionalization of social media communication in Portugal and Germany: A comparison. *Public Relations Review, 41*(2), 305–307. doi:10.1016/j.pubrev.2014.11.018

Lovejoy, K., & Saxton, G. D. (2012). Information, community, and action: How nonprofit organizations use social media. *Journal of Computer-Mediated Communication, 17*(3), 337–353. doi:10.1111/j.1083-6101.2012.01576.x

Lovejoy, K., Waters, R. D., & Saxton, G. D. (2012). Engaging stakeholders through Twitter: How nonprofit organizations are getting more out of 140 characters or less. *Public Relations Review, 38*(2), 313–318. doi:10.1016/j.pubrev.2012.01.005

Luo, N., Zhang, M., & Liu, W. (2015). The effects of value co-creation practices on building harmonious brand community and achieving brand loyalty on social media in China. *Computers in Human Behavior, 48*, 492–499. doi:10.1016/j.chb.2015.02.020

Luo, X., Zhang, J., & Duan, W. (2013). Social media and firm equity value. *Information Systems Research, 24*(1), 146–163. doi:10.1287/isre.1120.0462

Mahr, D., & Lievens, A. (2012). Virtual lead user communities: Drivers of knowledge creation for innovation. *Research Policy*, *41*(1), 167–177. doi:10.1016/j.respol.2011.08.006

Majchrzak, A., Wagner, C., & Yates, D. (2013). The impact of shaping on knowledge reuse for organizational improvement with wikis. *Management Information Systems Quarterly*, *37*(2), 455–469.

McCarthy, J., Rowley, J., Ashworth, C. J., & Pioch, E. (2014). Managing brand presence through social media: The case of UK football clubs. *Internet Research*, *24*(2), 181–204. doi:10.1108/IntR-08-2012-0154

McCoy, S., Everard, A., Polak, P., & Galletta, D. F. (2007). The effects of online advertising. *Communications of the ACM*, *50*(3), 84–88. doi:10.1145/1226736.1226740

Mergel, I. (2013). A framework for interpreting social media interactions in the public sector. *Government Information Quarterly*, *30*(4), 327–334. doi:10.1016/j.giq.2013.05.015

Meske, C., & Stieglitz, S. (2013). Adoption and use of social media in small and medium-sized enterprises. In F. Harmsen & H. Proper (Eds.), *Practice-driven research on enterprise transformation* (pp. 61–75). Heidelberg, Germany: Springer–Verlag. doi:10.1007/978-3-642-38774-6_5

Miles, S. J., & Mangold, W. G. (2014). Employee voice: Untapped resource or social media time bomb? *Business Horizons*, *57*(3), 401–411. doi:10.1016/j.bushor.2013.12.011

Miller, A. R., & Tucker, C. (2013). Active social media management: The case of health care. *Information Systems Research*, *24*(1), 52–70. doi:10.1287/isre.1120.0466

Mohajerani, A., Baptista, J., & Nandhakumar, J. (2015). Exploring the role of social media in importing logics across social contexts: The case of IT SMEs in Iran. *Technological Forecasting and Social Change*, *95*, 16–31. doi:10.1016/j.techfore.2014.06.008

Moreno, A., Navarro, C., Tench, R., & Zerfass, A. (2015). Does social media usage matter? An analysis of online practices and digital media perceptions of communication practitioners in Europe. *Public Relations Review*, *41*(2), 242–253. doi:10.1016/j.pubrev.2014.12.006

Mou, Y., Miller, M., & Fu, H. (2015). Evaluating a target on social media: From the self-categorization perspective. *Computers in Human Behavior*, *49*, 451–459. doi:10.1016/j.chb.2015.03.031

Nambisan, S. (2002). Designing virtual customer environments for new product development: Toward a theory. *Academy of Management Review*, *27*(3), 392–413. doi: 10.5465/AMR.2002.7389914

Nambisan, S. (2013). Information technology and product/service innovation: A brief assessment and some suggestions for future research. *Journal of the Association for Information Systems*, *14*(4), 215–226.

Nambisan, S., Agarwal, R., & Tanniru, M. (1999). Organizational mechanisms for enhancing user innovation in information technology. *Management Information Systems Quarterly*, *23*(3), 365–395. doi:10.2307/249468

Newman, E. F., Stem, D. E. Jr, & Sprott, D. E. (2004). Banner advertisement and web site congruity effects on consumer web site perceptions. *Industrial Management & Data Systems*, *104*(3), 273–281. doi:10.1108/02635570410525816

Niu, Z., Hua, G., Tian, Q., & Gao, X. (2015). Visual topic network: Building better image representations for images in social media. *Computer Vision and Image Understanding*, *136*, 3–13. doi:10.1016/j.cviu.2015.01.010

Oestreicher-Singer, G., & Zalmanson, L. (2013). Content or community? A digital business strategy for content providers in the social age. *Management Information Systems Quarterly*, *37*(2), 591–616.

Paek, H. J., Hove, T., & Jeon, J. (2013). Social media for message testing: A multilevel approach to linking favorable viewer responses with message, producer, and viewer influence on YouTube. *Health Communication*, *28*(3), 226–236. doi:10.1080/10410236.2012.672912

Panagiotopoulos, P., Shan, L. C., Barnett, J., Regan, A., & McConnon, A. (2015). A framework of social media engagement: Case studies with food and consumer organisations in the UK and Ireland. *International Journal of Information Management*, *35*(4), 394–402. doi:10.1016/j.ijinfomgt.2015.02.006

Papadopoulos, T., Stamati, T., & Nopparuch, P. (2013). Exploring the determinants of knowledge sharing via employee weblogs. *International Journal of Information Management*, *33*(1), 133–146. doi:10.1016/j.ijinfomgt.2012.08.002

Pavelko, R. L., & Myrick, J. G. (2015). That's so OCD: The effects of disease trivialization via social media on user perceptions and impression formation. *Computers in Human Behavior*, *49*, 251–258. doi:10.1016/j.chb.2015.02.061

Pervin, N., Takeda, H., & Toriumi, F. (2014). *Factors affecting retweetability: An event-centric analysis on Twitter*. Paper presented at the International Conference on Information Systems (ICIS 2014), Atlanta, GA.

Phang, C. W., Zhang, C., & Sutanto, J. (2013). The influence of user interaction and participation in social media on the consumption intention of niche products. *Information & Management*, *50*(8), 661–672. doi:10.1016/j.im.2013.07.001

Porter, L. V., Sweetser, K. D., & Chung, D. (2009). The blogosphere and public relations: Investigating practitioners' roles and blog use. *Journal of Communication Management*, *13*(3), 250–267. doi:10.1108/13632540910976699

Real, J. C., Roldan, J. L., & Leal, A. (2014). From entrepreneurial orientation and learning orientation to business performance: Analysing the mediating role of organizational learning and the moderating effects of organizational size. *British Journal of Management*, *25*(2), 186–208. doi:10.1111/j.1467-8551.2012.00848.x

Richter, A., & Riemer, K. (2009). *Corporate social networking sites: Modes of use and appropriation through co-evolution*. Paper presented at the 20th Australasian Conference on Information Systems (ACIS 2009), Melbourne, Australia.

Rishika, R., Kumar, A., Janakiraman, R., & Bezawada, R. (2013). The effect of customers' social media participation on customer visit frequency and profitability: An empirical investigation. *Information Systems Research*, *54*(1), 108–127. doi:10.1287/isre.1120.0460

Sallot, L. M., Porter, L. V., & Acosta-Alzuru, C. (2004). Practitioners' web use and perceptions of their own roles and power: A qualitative study. *Public Relations Review*, *30*(3), 269–278. doi:10.1016/j.pubrev.2004.05.002

Sandhu, S. (2009). Strategic communication: An institutional perspective. *International Journal of Strategic Communication*, *3*(2), 72–92. doi:10.1080/15531180902805429

Schniederjans, D., Cao, E. S., & Schniederjans, M. (2013). Enhancing financial performance with social media: An impression management perspective. *Decision Support Systems*, *55*(4), 911–918. doi:10.1016/j.dss.2012.12.027

Schroeder, R. (2002). *Copresence and interaction in virtual environments: An overview of the range of issues*. Paper presented at the Fifth International Workshop on Presence, Porto, Portugal.

Schultz, F., Utz, S., & Göritz, A. (2011). Is the medium the message? Perceptions of and reactions to crisis communication via twitter, blogs and traditional media. *Public Relations Review*, *37*(1), 20–27. doi:10.1016/j.pubrev.2010.12.001

Shaheen, M. A. (2008). Use of social networks and information seeking behavior of students during political crises in Pakistan: A case study. *The International Information & Library Review*, *40*(3), 142–147. doi:10.1080/10572317.2008.10762774

Shapiro, M. A., & Park, H. W. (2015). More than entertainment: YouTube and public responses to the science of global warming and climate change. *Social Sciences Information. Information Sur les Sciences Sociales*, *54*(1), 115–145. doi:10.1177/0539018414554730

Shi, R., Messaris, P., & Cappella, J. N. (2014). Effects of online comments on smokers' perception of antismoking public service announcements. *Journal of Computer-Mediated Communication*, *19*(4), 975–990. doi:10.1111/jcc4.12057

Shirky, C. (2011). The political power of social media technology, the public sphere, and political change. *Foreign Affairs*, *90*(1), 28–41.

Sigala, M., Christou, E., & Gretzel, U. (2011). *Web 2.0 in travel, tourism and hospitality: Theory, practice and cases*. Farnham, UK: Ashgate Publishing.

Sinclaire, J. K., & Vogus, C. E. (2011). Adoption of social networking sites: An exploratory adaptive structuration perspective for global organizations. *Information Technology & Management*, *12*(4), 293–314. doi:10.1007/s10799-011-0086-5

Smeltzer, S., & Keddy, D. (2010). Won't you be my (political) friend? The changing Face(book) of socio-political contestation in Malaysia. *Canadian Journal of Development Studies*, *30*(3/4), 421–440.

Stockdale, R., Ahmed, A., & Scheepers, H. (2012). *Identifying business value from the use of social media: An SME perspective*. Paper presented at the 16th Pacific Asia Conference on Information Systems (PACIS 2012), Ho Chi Minh City, Vietnam.

Subramaniam, N., Nandhakumar, J., & Baptista, J. (2013). Exploring social network interactions in enterprise systems: The role of virtual co-presence. *Information Systems Journal*, *23*(6), 475–499. doi:10.1111/isj.12019

Suh, H., van Hillegersberg, J., Choi, J., & Chung, S. (2013). Effects of strategic alignment on IS success: The mediation role of IS investment in Korea. *Information Technology & Management*, *14*(1), 7–27. doi:10.1007/s10799-012-0144-7

Suh, J. H. (2015). Forecasting the daily outbreak of topic-level political risk from social media using hidden Markov model-based techniques. *Technological Forecasting and Social Change*, *94*(1), 115–132. doi:10.1016/j.techfore.2014.08.014

Syred, J., Naidoo, C., Woodhall, S. C., & Baraitser, P. (2014). Would you tell everyone this? Facebook conversations as health promotion interventions. *Journal of Medical Internet Research*, *16*(4), 148–156. doi:10.2196/jmir.3231

Tan, W. K., & Chen, T. H. (2012). The usage of online tourist information sources in tourist information search: An exploratory study. *Service Industries Journal*, *32*(3), 451–476. doi:10.1080/02642069.2010.529130

Taylor, M., & Perry, D. (2005). Diffusion of traditional and new media tactics in crisis communication. *Public Relations Review*, *31*(2), 209–217. doi:10.1016/j.pubrev.2005.02.018

Thackeray, R., Neiger, B. L., Smith, A. K., & van Wagenen, S. B. (2012). Adoption and use of social media among public health. *BMC Public Health*, *12*(1), 242–247. doi:10.1186/1471-2458-12-242

Trainor, K. J., Andzulis, J., Rapp, A., & Agnihotri, R. (2014). Social media technology usage and customer relationship performance: A capabilities-based examination of social CRM. *Journal of Business Research*, *67*(6), 1201–1208. doi:10.1016/j.jbusres.2013.05.002

Valentini, C. (2015). Is using social media "good" for the public relations profession? A critical reflection. *Public Relations Review*, *41*(2), 170–177. doi:10.1016/j.pubrev.2014.11.009

Wagner, D., & Wagner, H. (2013). *Online communities and dynamic capabilities: Across-case examination of sensing, seizing, and reconfiguration*. Paper presented at the 19th Americas Conference on Information Systems (AMCIS 2013), Chicago, IL.

Wang, C., Chen, W., & Wang, Y. (2012). Scalable influence maximization for independent cascade model in large-scale social networks. *Data Mining and Knowledge Discovery*, *25*(3), 545–576. doi:10.1007/s10618-012-0262-1

Wang, Y., Chen, Y., & Benitez-Amado, J. (2015). How information technology influences environmental performance: Empirical evidence from China. *International Journal of Information Management*, *35*(2), 160–170. doi:10.1016/j.ijinfomgt.2014.11.005

Waters, R. D., & Jamal, J. Y. (2011). Tweet, tweet, tweet: A content analysis of nonprofit organizations' Twitter updates. *Public Relations Review*, *37*(3), 321–324. doi:10.1016/j.pubrev.2011.03.002

Won, S. G. L., Evans, M. A., Carey, C., & Schnittka, C. G. (2015). Youth appropriation of social media for collaborative and facilitated design-based learning. *Computers in Human Behavior*, *50*, 385–391. doi:10.1016/j.chb.2015.04.017

Wright, D. K., & Hinson, M. D. (2009). An updated look at the impact of social media on public relations practice. *The Public Relations Journal*, *3*(2), 1–33.

Wu, K., Yang, S., & Zhu, K. Q. (2015). *False rumors detection on Sina Weibo by propagation structures*. Paper presented at the International Conference on Data Engineering (ICDE 2015), Seoul, South Korea. doi:10.1109/ICDE.2015.7113322

Wu, L. (2010). Applicability of the resource-based and dynamic-capability views under environmental volatility. *Journal of Business Research*, *63*(1), 27–31. doi:10.1016/j.jbusres.2009.01.007

Wu, L. L., Wang, Y. T., Su, Y. T., & Yeh, M. Y. (2013). *Cultivating social capital through interactivity on social network sites*. Paper presented at the Pacific Asia Conference on Information Systems (PACIS 2013), Jeju Island, South Korea.

Xiang, Z., & Gretzel, U. (2010). Role of social media in online travel information search. *Tourism Management*, *31*(2), 179–188. doi:10.1016/j.tourman.2009.02.016

Xiang, Z., Wober, K., & Fesenmaier, D. R. (2008). Representation of the online tourism domain in search engines. *Journal of Travel Research*, *47*(2), 137–150. doi:10.1177/0047287508321193

Yang, G. (2009). *The power of the Internet in China: Citizen activism online*. New York, NY: Columbia University Press.

Yang, S. U., & Lim, J. S. (2009). The effects of blog-mediated public relations (BMPR) on relational trust. *Journal of Public Relations Research*, *21*(3), 341–359. doi:10.1080/10627260802640773

Yates, D., Wagner, C., & Majchrzak, A. (2010). Factors affecting shapers of organizational wikis. *Journal of the American Society for Information Science and Technology*, *61*(3), 543–554. doi: 10.1002/asi.21266

Yoo, K. H., & Gretzel, U. (2011). Influence of personality on travel-related consumer-generated media creation. *Computers in Human Behavior*, *27*(2), 609–621. doi:10.1016/j.chb.2010.05.002

Yu, Y., Duan, W., & Cao, Q. (2013). The impact of social and conventional media on firm equity value: A sentiment analysis approach. *Decision Support Systems*, *55*(4), 919–926. doi:10.1016/j.dss.2012.12.028

Zeiller, M., & Schauer, B. (2011). *Adoption, motivation and success factors of social media for team collaboration in SMEs*. Paper presented at the 11th International Conference on Knowledge Management and Knowledge Technologies (i-KNOW 2011), Graz, Austria. doi:10.1145/2024288.2024294

Zhang, J. (2015). Voluntary information disclosure on social media. *Decision Support Systems*, *73*, 28–36. doi:10.1016/j.dss.2015.02.018

Zhang, J., Qu, Y., Cody, J., & Wu, Y. (2010). *A case study of micro-blogging in the enterprise: Use, value, and related issues*. Paper presented at the 28th Annual ACM Conference on Human Factors in Computing Systems (CHI 2010), Atlanta, GA.

Zhang, K., Zhao, S. J., & Lee, M. K. O. (2013). *Product attitude formation on online review sites with social networks*. Paper presented at the Pacific Asia Conference on Information Systems (PACIS 2013), Jeju Island, South Korea.

Zhao, L., Lu, Y., Wang, B., Chau, P. Y. K., & Zhang, L. (2012). Cultivating the sense of belonging and motivating user participation in virtual communities: A social capital perspective. *International Journal of Information Management*, *32*(6), 574–588. doi:10.1016/j.ijinfomgt.2012.02.006

Zhu, Y. Q., & Chen, H. G. (2015). Social media and human need satisfaction: Implications for social media marketing. *Business Horizons*, *58*(3), 335–345. doi:10.1016/j.bushor.2015.01.006

ADDITIONAL READING

Abril, P. S., Levin, A., & del Riego, A. (2012). Blurred boundaries: Social media privacy and the twenty-first century employee. *American Business Law Journal*, *49*(1), 63–124. doi:10.1111/j.1744-1714.2011.01127.x

Agerdal-Hjermind, A. (2014). Organizational blogging: A case study of a corporate weblog from an employee perspective. *Corporate Communications: An International Journal*, *19*(1), 34–51. doi:10.1108/CCIJ-09-2012-0066

Ali, H. (2011). Exchanging value within individuals' networks: Social support implications for health marketers. *Journal of Marketing Management*, *27*(3/4), 316–335. doi:10.1080/0267257X.2011.547075

Andre, P., Bernstein, M., & Luther, K. (2012). What makes a great tweet? *Harvard Business Review*, *90*(5), 36–37.

Babaesmailli, M., Arbabshirani, B., & Golmah, V. (2012). Integrating analytical network process and fuzzy logic to prioritize the strategies: A case study for tile manufacturing firm. *Expert Systems with Applications*, *39*(1), 925–935. doi:10.1016/j.eswa.2011.07.090

Baird, H. C., & Parasnis, G. (2011). From social media to social customer relationship management. *Strategy and Leadership*, *30*(5), 30–37. doi:10.1108/10878571111161507

Bertoni, M., & Chirumalla, K. (2011). Leveraging Web 2.0 in new product development: Lessons learned from a cross-company study. *Journal of Universal Computer Science*, *17*(4), 548–564. doi: 10.3217/jucs-017-04-0548

Brown, V. R., & Vaughn, E. D. (2012). The writing on the (Facebook) wall: The use of social network sites in hiring decisions. *Journal of Business and Psychology*, *26*(2), 219–225. doi:10.1007/s10869-011-9221-x

Chen, Y., Fay, S., & Wang, Q. (2011). The role of marketing in social media: How online consumer reviews evolve. *Journal of Interactive Marketing*, *25*(2), 85–94. doi:10.1016/j.intmar.2011.01.003

Chikandiwa, S. T., Contogiannis, E., & Jembere, E. (2013). The adoption of social media marketing in South African banks. *European Business Review*, *25*(4), 365–381. doi:10.1108/EBR-02-2013-0013

Gopsill, J. A., McAlpine, H. C., & Hicks, B. J. (2013). A social media framework to support engineering design communication. *Advanced Engineering Informatics*, *27*(4), 580–597. doi:10.1016/j.aei.2013.07.002

Green, E. (2011). Pushing the social media buttons. *Media Development*, *58*(1), 12–15.

Grieve, R., Indian, M., Witteveen, K., Tolan, G. A., & Marrington, J. (2013). Face-to-face or Facebook: Can social connectedness be derived online? *Computers in Human Behavior*, *29*(3), 604–609. doi:10.1016/j.chb.2012.11.017

Hall, R., & Lewis, S. (2014). Managing workplace bullying and social media policy: Implications for employee engagement. *Academy of Business Research Journal*, *1*, 128–138.

Hansen, D. L., Shneiderman, B., & Smith, M. A. (2011). *Analyzing social media networks with Nodexl*. Burlington, MA: Elsevier.

Hsu, Y. H., & Tsou, H. T. (2011). Understanding customer experiences in online blog environments. *International Journal of Information Management*, *31*(6), 510–523. doi:10.1016/j.ijinfomgt.2011.05.003

Hughes, D. J., Rowe, M., Batey, M., & Lee, A. (2011). A tale of two sites: Twitter vs. Facebook and the personality predictors. *Computers in Human Behavior*, *28*(2), 561–569. doi:10.1016/j.chb.2011.11.001

Kietzmann, J. H., Silvestre, B. S., McCarthy, I. P., & Pitt, L. F. (2012). Unpacking the social media phenomenon: Towards a research agenda. *Journal of Public Affairs*, *12*(2), 109–119. doi:10.1002/pa.1412

Kim, Y. A., & Ahmad, M. A. (2013). Trust, distrust and lack of confidence of users in online social media-sharing communities. *Knowledge-Based Systems*, *37*(1), 438–450. doi:10.1016/j.knosys.2012.09.002

Kuksov, D., Shachar, R., & Kangkang, W. (2013). Advertising and consumers' communications. *Marketing Science*, *32*(2), 294–309. doi:10.1287/mksc.1120.0753

Lau, R. Y. K., Xia, Y., & Ye, Y. (2014). A probabilistic generative model for mining cybercriminal networks from online social media. *IEEE Computational Intelligence Magazine*, *9*(1), 31–43. doi:10.1109/MCI.2013.2291689

Lee, T. Y., & BradLow, E. T. (2011). Automated marketing research using online customer reviews. *JMR, Journal of Marketing Research*, *48*(5), 881–894. doi:10.1509/jmkr.48.5.881

Moe, W. M., & Schweidel, D. A. (2012). Online product opinions: Incidence, evaluation, and evolution. *Marketing Science*, *31*(3), 372–386. doi:10.1287/mksc.1110.0662

Oh, O., Agrawal, M., & Rao, H. R. (2013). Community intelligence and social media services: A rumor theoretic analysis of tweets during social crises. *Management Information Systems Quarterly*, *37*(2), 407–426.

Okazaki, S., & Taylor, C. R. (2013). Social media and international advertising: Theoretical challenges and future directions. *International Marketing Review*, *30*(1), 56–71. doi:10.1108/02651331311298573

Onishi, H., & Manchanda, P. (2012). Marketing activity, blogging and sales. *International Journal of Research in Marketing*, *29*(3), 221–234. doi:10.1016/j.ijresmar.2011.11.003

Smock, A. D., Ellison, N. B., Lampe, C., & Wohn, D. Y. (2011). Facebook as a toolkit: A uses and gratification approach to unbundling feature use. *Computers in Human Behavior*, *27*(6), 2322–2329. doi:10.1016/j.chb.2011.07.011

Sun, M., Chen, Z. Y., & Fan, Z. P. (2014). A multi-task multi-kernel transfer learning method for customer response modeling in social media. *Procedia Computer Science*, *31*, 221–230. doi:10.1016/j.procs.2014.05.263

Wang, X., Yu, C., & Wei, Y. (2012). Social media peer communication and impacts on purchase intentions: A consumer socialization framework. *Journal of Interactive Marketing*, *26*(4), 198–208. doi:10.1016/j.intmar.2011.11.004

Yuan, Y., Zhao, X., Liao, Q., & Chi, C. (2013). The use of different information and communication technologies to support knowledge sharing in organizations: From e-mail to micro-blogging. *Journal of the American Society for Information Science and Technology*, *64*(8), 1659–1670. doi:10.1002/asi.22863

KEY TERMS AND DEFINITIONS

Blog: A website, similar to an online journal, that includes chronological entries made by individuals.

Business: The purchase and sale of goods in an attempt to make a profit.

Facebook: The name of a social networking service and website, launched in 2004.

Internet: A worldwide computer network that provides information on very many subjects and enables users to exchange messages.

Social Media: The website and application considered as collectively constituting a medium by which people share messages, photographs, and other information, especially in online communities or forums based on shared interests or backgrounds.

Technology: The use of scientific knowledge to solve practical problems, especially in industry and commerce.

Twitter: A website where people can post short messages about their current activities.

Website: The virtual location on World Wide Web, containing several subject-related web pages and data files accessible through a browser.

This research was previously published in Social Media Listening and Monitoring for Business Applications edited by N. Raghavendra Rao, pages 18-44, copyright year 2017 by Business Science Reference (an imprint of IGI Global).

Chapter 8
Does Social Media Marketing Improve Business Performance?

Tanses Yasemin Gülsoy
Beykent University, Turkey

ABSTRACT

The recent growth of social media, or consumer-generated media, has given rise to bidirectional communication between consumers and marketers. There is some evidence that the dialogue appears to help the business performance of companies by influencing, for example, product sales, consumer attitudes, and consumer decision-making. This chapter examines the evidence, with a particular focus on on-line consumer product reviews. Also investigated is the role trust plays in how marketing works in the social media. Managerial implications and research directions are indicated.

INTRODUCTION

A recent survey of American businesses suggests that almost one-third of the organizations surveyed do not know how much of their revenue was influenced by or attributed to social media (Demand Metric Research Corporation, 2014). In the face of the growing marketing expenditure in the social media, this professed ignorance by businesses appears surprising and calls to mind a well-publicized quotation by an advertiser that he knows half of the money he spends on advertising is wasted, but he simply does not know which half (Lane, King, & Russell, 2008, p. 204). With the increasing sophistication of the tools and techniques for measuring marketing effectiveness and advertising effectiveness, businesses can now track with more precision the return on their marketing communication expenditures in traditional media. The uncertainty still surrounding social media may well dissipate in time again with increasing sophistication of measurement tools and techniques. This chapter argues that already there is mounting evidence that social media marketing does improve business performance, and in various ways. This chapter aims to review the literature on social media to indicate the ways in which social media marketing improves business performance.

DOI: 10.4018/978-1-5225-5637-4.ch008

The remainder of this chapter is organized as follows: First, we distinguish social media marketing from marketing in the traditional media, beginning with the definition and scope of social media. We then review the theoretical framework governing social media marketing, focusing particularly on the reasons why consumers participate in social media, electronic word-of-mouth communication, and the role of trust in social media marketing. Next comes a review of the evidence on the impact of social media marketing on business performance. Concluding remarks, including managerial and research implications, are found in the last section.

WHAT IS SOCIAL MEDIA?

In this chapter we follow Kotler and Keller's (2012) definition of social media as "a means for consumers to share text, images, audio and video information with each other and with companies and vice versa" through the three main platforms of on-line communities and forums, bloggers, and social networks (such as Facebook, Twitter, and YouTube) (p. 568). Social media is the "umbrella term" for Web-based software and services that allow users to join one another on-line and "exchange, discuss, communicate, and participate in any form of social interaction" (Ryan & Jones, 2009, p. 152). A more technical definition is "a group of Internet-based applications that build on Web 2.0 technologies, employ web- and mobile-based technologies to support the creation and exchange of user-generated content" (Duan, 2013, p. 861). Kaplan and Haenlein (2010) suggest that the World Wide Web's growth increasingly into a social media platform can be seen as "an evolution back to the Internet's roots, since it re-transforms the World Wide Web to what it was initially created for; a platform to facilitate information exchange between users" (p. 60). Mobile devices such as certain types of cellular phones can also enable social networking through mobile components of Web sites and programs. Thus, mobile marketing which involves the delivery of direct marketing messages to mobile devices using wireless technologies (Fill, 2009, p. 739), may sometimes take on the features of social media marketing.

Many different types of social media exist, and these include forums and discussion sites, media sharing sites, reviews and ratings sites, social networking sites, social media submission sites, blogs, podcasts, micro-blogging, and "wikis" among others (Ryan & Jones, 2009, pp. 157-169). Some of these media such as "wikis", defined as Web sites that allow users to "add, remove, or otherwise edit and change content collectively" (Organisation for Economic Co-operation and Development, 2007, p. 33), are user-generated, but they do not allow for social interaction among different users.

Two types of on-line communities are distinguished by Porter and Donthu (2002, as cited in Katarivas, Bendit, & Rosenthal, 2014, p. 95): those founded by people with shared interests and those developed under the stimulus of a company. Important on-line communities include, besides social networking sites, entertainment communities, trading communities, education communities, scheduled events communities, advocacy communities, brand communities ("customer relationship management communities" on company Web sites that allow user posting), consumer communities, employee communities, and special topics communities (Strauss & Frost, 2009, p. 184).

Based on theories in the field of media research and social processes, Kaplan and Haenlein (2010) distinguish social media according to two dimensions: One dimension is composed of the characteristics of social presence and media richness, while the other dimension is composed again of two characteristics, self-presentation and self-disclosure. Based on their classification, virtual social worlds, for example, are high both on the dimension of social presence/media richness and on the dimension of self-presentation/

self-disclosure. In other words, these sites allow for a lot of information to be transmitted in a given time interval (media richness), and they enable a high degree of acoustic, visual, and physical contact to occur between the communication partners (social presence). At the same time, these sites allow for a lot of self-disclosure and self-presentation by users. According to the same classification, social networking sites allow for less social presence/media richness compared to virtual social worlds but score higher than blogs on the social presence/media richness dimension. On the other hand, social networking sites allow for more self-disclosure than, for example, content communities (Kaplan & Haenlein, 2010). Furthermore, there are differences among different vehicles of a social media platform. For example, different social networking sites may differ regarding ease of use or the restrictions they may impose upon the amount and type of content to be generated, for example. Such differences may in fact influence perceived benefits by users and consequently user loyalty (see for example Zhuang, Hsu, Brewer, & Xiao, 2013), which would have an effect on the business outcomes that may accrue to companies or brands marketing in the social media.

In the following section we will try to illustrate how marketing in these various types of social media differs from marketing in traditional media.

How Is Social Media Marketing Different From Marketing in the Traditional Media?

"Consumers are talking, just as they always have, only now they're talking online to more extensive groups of their peers. ... Marketing too is evolving rapidly to become more of a conversation than a lecture," note Ryan and Jones (2009, p. 151). Vargo and Lusch (2006, as cited in Vargo & Lusch, 2010, p. 227) in their call for a new marketing logic suggest that the concept of "promotion" or even the newer "integrated marketing communications" be replaced by dialogue. This emphasis on interactivity is also one of the fundamental tenets of social media marketing. Social media allow for real-time interactive communications.

Social media marketing differs from traditional marketing in several important dimensions. Perhaps the primary difference is the "control vs. contributions" dimension (Barker, Barker, Bormann, & Neher, 2013, p. 15). Unlike traditional marketing exchanges where the seller mainly controls the marketing mix decisions relating to product, price, place, and promotion, social media has shifted some of those decisions to customers, as noted by Sashi (2012, p. 267). For example, while traditional marketing seeks to control the content seen by the audience, social media marketers are more likely to host on-line discussions in which their brands may be compared to competitor brands. In their discussion of a proposed model of consumer navigation behavior in a hypermedia computer-mediated environment (of which they cite the World Wide Web as the main example), Hoffman and Novak (1996) differentiate marketing in this environment in the following words: "... in perhaps the most radical departure from traditional marketing environments – consumers can put product-related content in the medium" (p. 54). It is in effect their "egalitarian" nature that distinguishes social media most prominently from traditional media and other on-line media (Peters, Chen, Kaplan, Ognibeni, & Pauwels, 2013, p. 282).

Personalization of messages on a commercially feasible scale is another important feature of social media marketing in particular (Fill, 2009, p. 748) and digital communications in general. Another important difference is the trust-building that arises from two-way communication between the consumer and the company (Barker et al., 2013, p. 16) though trust appears to be not so easy to establish in the on-line environment. The section on trust in this chapter will explore this issue further.

Social media marketing differs from marketing in traditional media also by its greater ability to prompt customer action (Fill, 2009, p. 759). Digital media in general afford marketers the opportunity to engage consumers when they visit the marketer's Web site to play video games or take part in contests in an effort to build brand connections and encourage repeat visits to the site (Lane et al., 2008, p. 419-420). The growing managerial interest in customer engagement, as noted by Sashi (2012), has paralleled the emergence of new technologies and tools that enable greater interactivity among individuals and organizations.

"Engagement," as it is defined by the American Association of Advertising Agencies, the Association of National Advertisers, and the Advertising Research Foundation, is "turning on a prospect to a brand idea enhanced by the surrounding context" (Advertising Research Foundation, 2006). Other definitions have also been provided. For example, the Economist Intelligence Unit underlines the ability of companies to create "a deeper, more meaningful connection between the company and the customer, and one that endures over time" (Economist Intelligence Unit, 2007, p. 2). Yet another definition points to the formation of "deep connections with customers that drive purchase decisions, interaction, and participation over time" (Forrester Consulting, 2008, as cited in Sashi, 2012, p. 256). Sashi (2012) offers a customer engagement cycle with connection, interaction, satisfaction, retention, commitment, advocacy, and engagement as stages in the cycle and then develops a "customer engagement matrix" based on the degree of relational exchange and emotional bonds between buyer and seller. Research suggests that engagement with a Web site, in the sense that the Web site provides for the consumer utilitarian or intrinsic enjoyment, increases advertising effectiveness (Calder, Malthouse, & Schaedel, 2009).[1]

The opportunities for deeper engagement and interactivity suggest that social media may be used effectively to improve business performance. The following sections discuss the conceptual foundations of social media marketing and the means of measuring effectiveness of marketing and marketing communications efforts using social media.

CONCEPTUAL FRAMEWORK

Why Do People Participate in Social Media?

Theoretical explanations for why consumers participate in social media come from several different disciplines. The uses and gratifications theory of communication offers one explanation: People turn to media to satisfy their cognitive needs (by, for example, watching the television news), affective needs (to enjoy emotional, pleasant, or aesthetic experiences), "personal integrative" needs (to enhance credibility, confidence, and status), "social integrative" needs (to enhance connections with family and friends), and for "tension release," or escape and diversion (Katz, Gurevitch, and Haas, 1973, as cited in Grant, 2004: 397). Besides offering people diversion, defined as escaping from routines or daily problems, the media may also provide personal relationships (when people substitute the media for companionship), personal identity (which refers to how people use the media to reinforce their values), and surveillance (which is information about how the media will help the individual accomplish a goal) (McQuail, Blumler, & Brown, 1972, as cited in Grant, 2004, p. 397).

Social exchange theory, based on the assumption that people will form and sustain relationships if they believe that the benefits they derive from those relationships will exceed costs, provides another explanation (Homans, 1958). Balasubramanian and Mahajan (2001) draw mainly on neoclassical economic theory, which posits that people are rational utility maximizers, and social exchange theory to propose a conceptual framework within which the economic leverage of virtual communities may be discussed. Their main proposition is that consumers derive different kinds of utilities by engaging in word-of-mouth communications in a virtual community even while expending effort through providing communications, which becomes costlier as the individual contributes more. The total utilities derived by the individual minus costs as represented by the effort of contribution results in a total "social interaction utility" experienced by the individual (Balasubramanian & Mahajan, 2001, p. 125-126).

Social capital theory is also advanced as a way of explaining why people use social media (Chakraborty, Vishik, & Rao, 2013). The central proposition of social capital theory is that networks of relationships constitute a valuable resource for the individual, such as privileged access to information or opportunity, and significant social capital may be derived from membership in specific networks in the form of social status or reputation, as noted by Nahapiet and Ghoshal, for example (1998, p. 243). The desire to access social capital may be one reason, for example, for joining social networks, and differences in behavior patterns of different demographic groups may be predicted based on social capital theory (Chakraborty et al., 2013).

Bagozzi and Dholakia (2002) rely on attitude theory and social identity theory as well as motivational research to investigate the personal and group intentions of individuals for joining virtual communities. The authors base their argument on a significant aspect of on-line communities, which is what distinguishes them from their off-line counterparts: It is voluntary membership and participation, which the authors call "volitional choice" (p. 6), and this leads to "intentional social action" (p. 7). Their findings suggest that participation in virtual communities is a function both of positive anticipated emotions and desires and of social identity. Social identity theory suggests that increased contact with an organization leads to a sense of identification with the attributes and values of the organization so that customers start to define themselves in terms of those attributes and values (Bhattacharya, Rao, & Glynn, 1995, as cited in Bhattacharya & Bolton, 2000, p. 346).

The relationship marketing approach is also useful for explaining social media participation. Relationship marketing suggests that by encouraging consumer involvement in the design, development, and marketing processes of the company, marketers can achieve closer and more rewarding relationships with their consumers, who in turn will be more committed to the company's market offerings because consumers feel more empowered and more satisfied when they themselves can perform certain tasks that marketers would normally do for them (Sheth & Parvatiyar, 1995/2000, pp. 191-196). This argument suggests that promoting consumer involvement through the social media in the design, development, and marketing processes of the company will increase consumer empowerment, consumer satisfaction, and consequently commitment to the company's products and services. In fact, based on their observation of electronic forums, electronic bulletin boards, and electronic mail, Sheth and Parvatiyar (1995/2000, p. 197) predict that it will be easier in the future for marketers to engage consumers in relationships and to enhance those relationships. However, the authors predict at the same time that information technology will make it easier for customers to also terminate their relationship with the marketer.

Peters et al. (2013) draw on theories from sociology, psychology, and marketing to suggest the following motives for social media participation: intellectual value to be derived from co-creation and content quality, social value to be derived from activities on the platform and social ties, and cultural value to be derived from being part of the community.

Furthermore, differences of motives as well as other dissimilarities exist among users of social media. One study suggests that early users of the Internet had differing motives for posting on-line reviews in the social media than users of a decade later (Chen, Fay & Wang, 2011). The researchers show that while early users were more interested in demonstrating social status and expertise and were less price-sensitive, later users were more value-driven. Also, level of consumers' computer skills may determine whether and to what extent they participate in social media. A study suggests, for example, that consumers who are motivated to use discussion forums and who perceive themselves as skilled at navigating such forums on the Internet are more likely to engage in know-how exchange (Gruen, Osmonbekov, & Czaplewski, 2006). But, the pattern of communicative exchange on the Internet (please see the following section on electronic word-of-mouth communication) is predicated on other user characteristics: One study suggests that in consumer communities messages can originate from any member, but those who reply to the messages are usually possessed of greater social capital, and, as the author notes, greater expert power by implication (Dwyer, 2007, p. 72).

Kozinets (1999) divided members of "virtual communities of consumption" into four types according to the strength of their relations with the consumption activity and with the virtual community: tourists, minglers, devotees, and insiders. In this classification only insiders and devotees have a strong interest in and enthusiasm for the consumption activity. Insiders are distinguished from devotees by their strong social ties to the group. Thus, a variety of marketing strategies may be devised to convert tourists and minglers to devotees and insiders. Furthermore, insiders tend to wield the greatest influence in the group, and if their tastes change, may even convert others to their new passion and create a mass exodus. Hence, Kozinets' analysis emphasizes the importance of recognizing the "insiders" in order to deal with such situations.

Electronic Word-of-Mouth Communication

Often social media participation takes the form of providing word-of-mouth communication in various social media platforms. Word of mouth refers to consumer sharing of information about a product or promotion (American Marketing Association, 2014).

Several theories underlie the phenomenon of consumer word of mouth. Socialization theory points to the importance of social groups as a key socializing institution. Social group influence processes have been shown to involve compliance, identification, and internalization (Kelman, 1958, as cited in Wilkie, 1990, p. 433). Reference groups, the groups to which an individual would compare himself or herself to determine his or her social standing in the community, may exert an important influence on the individual under certain circumstances (Hyman, 1942, as cited in Wilkie, 1990, p. 433). Social power theory posits, for example, that some agents are complied with because the individual believes they have expert power, that is the agent wielding power is trusted as an expert in the area (French and Raven, 1959, as cited in Robbins & Judge, 2013, pp. 448-449). Others may have the power to bestow rewards or to inflict punishment so that the individual complies with their wishes either to win rewards or to avoid punishment. Others may hold power by virtue of the office they occupy (legitimate power), or they may possess certain personal characteristics so that others obey them out of a wish to identify with them, to be like them or to be liked by them (referent power) (Robbins & Judge, 2013, pp. 448-449).

The power of word-of-mouth communication in consumer behavior has long been recognized (Katz & Lazarsfeld, 1955). Consumer recommendations have power for three main reasons (Wilkie, 1990, p. 437): They usually have high source credibility as those reading the recommendations have no reason to think that as a fellow consumer, the author has any vested interest or any intentions to manipulate the reader. As noted by Dichter (1966, p. 148), the power of word-of-mouth communication lies mainly in the "*speaker's* lack of *material* interest" [Author's emphasis]. Secondly, consumer word of mouth is bidirectional, allowing for two-way communication. Thirdly, word-of-mouth communication enables vicarious trial.

An important factor in word-of-mouth communications is the source. In marketing communications the initiator of the communication can be a formal or an informal source. The marketer (either a for-profit or a not-for-profit organization) represents a formal source while an informal source was originally defined as a person giving product information or advice that the message receiver knows personally (Schiffman et al., 2010, p. 281). Today on-line social networks and other Web forums may also be considered as informal sources, as noted by Schiffman, Kanuk, and Wisenblit (2010, p. 281) while on-line sellers, on-line commercially linked third parties (such as comparison shopping Web sites) and non-commercially linked third parties (such as product or merchant assessment Web sites) as classified by Senecal and Nantel (2002, as cited in Senecal & Nantel, 2004, p. 160) can be considered as formal sources.

Another factor to be considered in word-of-mouth communications is the network structure. Three dimensions have been identified in on-line social networks, for example (Brown, Broderick, & Lee, 2007, as cited in Schiffman et al., 2010, p. 283): Tie strength, which refers to the degree of intimacy and frequency of contacts between the information seeker and the source; similarity among the group's members in terms of lifestyle and demographics; and source credibility, the perceived expertise of the source in the area where advice is sought.

The motives for providing positive word-of-mouth communication as outlined by Dichter (1966) are product involvement, self-involvement, other-involvement, and message-involvement. Product involvement is construed as the desire to express "strongly felt, gratifying experiences with a product or service which make the speaker 'flow over'" (p. 149). Self-involvement motives are varied; they include the desire to get attention, to show connoisseurship, to feel like a pioneer, to have inside information, to suggest status, to assert superiority, to seek confirmation of one's own judgement, or to spread the good word about the product or service. Other-involvement is the need to help another person and to share with another person the "enthusiasm in, and benefits of, things enjoyed" (p. 151). Finally, message-involvement refers to involvement with advertising messages that manifests itself through talking about the advertising or peppering one's speech with slogans or word play on advertising lines (p. 152). Motives cited for providing positive word-of-mouth communications by other researchers include besides altruism, product involvement, and self-enhancement, the desire to help the company, and motives cited for providing negative word of mouth include altruism, anxiety reduction, vengeance, and advice seeking (Sundaram, Mitra, & Webster, 1998).

Other researchers attribute provision of word-of-mouth communication to people's enjoyment of sharing information and their need to give advice (Smith, Coyle, Lightfoot, and Scott, 2007, as cited in Schiffman et al., 2010, p. 283).

By facilitating word-of-mouth communication and by enlarging its reach, Internet is changing the nature and power of this type of communication, as noted by Park and Lee (2009). Hennig-Thurau, Gwinner, Walsh, and Gremler (2004) have found that people participate in electronic word of mouth communications for primarily the following reasons: They seek social interaction, respond to economic incentives, desire to enhance their own self-worth, and are concerned about other consumers. The authors have segmented consumers based on motives for providing electronic word-of-mouth communications and identified the following groups: self-interested helpers, multiple-motive consumers, consumer advocates, and true altruists. Self-interested helpers are mainly driven by economic incentives. Consumer advocates appear to be driven by the single motive of helping other consumers while true altruists are motivated both by helping other consumers and by helping companies. Multiple-motive consumers, on the other hand, are motivated by a large number of factors, including the above-named motives but, in addition, others such as the desire to seek advice, to derive social benefits, and to vent negative feelings. Furthermore, one study points to the size of the audience with whom the message is shared (i.e., whether the receiver is one person vs a group of people) in shaping the motives of word of mouth (Barasch & Berger, 2014): The findings of the study suggest that when the receiver of the communication is just one person, the sender tends to share more useful content whereas with a group of people senders tend to share self-presentational content and avoid sharing content that makes them look bad.

The Role of Trust in Social Media Marketing

In his discussion of how to build trust in the marketing of services, Berry (1995/2000, p. 166) makes the following statement: "Companies seeking to build genuine relationships with customers must be willing to operate with a higher standard of conduct than just legality. Corporate practices that rob customers of self-esteem or justice may be legal, but they destroy trust and consequently the potential for relationship building." This statement underlines the importance of trust as an antecedent of relationship building, which goes to the heart of social media marketing.

Winning the consumer's trust in on-line environments is especially important, considering that perceptions of trust and risk have been found to be the major determinants of consumers' attitudes towards shopping on-line (e.g., Verhagen, Meents, & Tan, 2006, as cited in Schiffman et al., 2010, p. 203; Horrigan, 2008, as cited in Utz, Kerkhof, & van den Bos, 2012). Trust, however, reduces consumers' perceived risk in the electronic marketplace (e.g., Harridge-March, 2006).

Some of the risks associated with on-line shopping have been listed by Utz and colleagues (2012, pp. 49-50) as the following: Less information about the product is available as the buyer is not able to touch and feel the product; product and money are not exchanged immediately at the counter, with the seller usually shipping the product after receiving the payment; technical failures may inhibit smooth transactions; as many of these transactions are one-shot transactions with the buyer and seller often living in different places and not having much information about each other, the product might not be shipped at all, not be shipped on time, or a lower quality product might be shipped; and finally, the company might not handle complaints as quickly as the case would have been in a bricks-and-mortar shop environment, or might not respond to e-mail or phone calls at all. The consumer reservations regarding on-line purchasing point to the importance of building trust both in the brand and in the company for social media marketing efforts to be successful.

Trust is defined as "a willingness to rely on an exchange partner in whom one has confidence" (Moorman, Zaltman, & Deshpande, 1992, p. 315). Morgan and Hunt (1994) provide a commitment-trust theory of relationship marketing, which holds that commitment and trust are imperative to building cooperative marketing relationships. Trust in the Morgan and Hunt model is a major determinant of relationship commitment. Such cooperative marketing relationships based on trust and commitment yield important benefits to companies – a basic precept of relationship marketing.

Research has identified three characteristics of trust: integrity, benevolence, and ability (Mayer, Davis, & Schoorman, as cited in Robbins & Judge, 2013; Colquitt, Scott, & LePine, 2007, as cited in Robbins & Judge, 2013). Ability refers to an individual's technical and interpersonal knowledge and skills; integrity is honesty, truthfulness, and a person's consistency in word and deed while benevolence refers to having the other person's interests at heart even when they conflict with one's own interests

(Robbins & Judge, 2013, p. 423). In word-of-mouth communications when the sender of the message is perceived as having expertise, the influence of his or her word-of-mouth communication will be greater on the receiver's purchase decision (Bansal & Voyer, 2000). Peer recommendations in on-line environments serve as word of mouth, and research evidence suggests that the greater the trust in the peer recommender during on-line shopping experiences, the greater the perceived influence of the peer recommender on the choice decision, and the greater the expertise of a peer recommender, the greater the perceived trust of the recommender (Smith, Menon, & Sivakumar, 2005).

As trust is construed as an important antecedent in relationship building (Morgan and Hunt, 1994), relationship marketing lends itself to furnishing one of the conceptual foundations for direct marketing over the Internet (see for example Luo & Donthu, 2007; Wu, Chen, & Chung, 2010) and social media marketing (see for example Sashi, 2012). The benefits of relationship marketing derive from two basic arguments, as suggested by Sheth and Parvatiyar (1995/2000, p. 172): One of them is that retaining existing customers is more profitable to the firm than winning new customers. The other is that having loyal customers provides the firm with a competitive advantage. The authors note, however, that the firm can benefit from such advantages of relationship marketing "if, and only if, consumers are willing and able to engage in relationship patronage" (p. 172). The authors argue that the basic principle of relationship marketing is consumer choice reduction, which the consumer demonstrates by repeatedly purchasing from the same marketers and forgoing the opportunity to choose other marketers. Sheth and Parvatiyar contend that a cooperative relationship is not confined to repeat purchasing. They suggest along the lines of Webster (1992, as cited in Sheth & Parvatiyar, 1995/2000, p. 174) that when consumers are actively involved in the decisions of the company, these relationships become more valuable. This premise of relationship marketing underlies one of the primary arguments for engaging consumers in social media. "Any relationship that attempts to develop customer value through partnering activities is therefore likely to create greater bonding between consumers and marketers (their products, symbols, processes, stores, and people)," reason Sheth & Parvatiyar (1995/2000, p. 174), thus, consumers become more committed to the company and therefore they are less likely to patronize other marketers.

In buyer-seller relationships trust has been shown to be predicated on shared values, communication and satisfaction with the supplier (e.g., Morgan & Hunt, 1994; Selnes, 1998). Trust in the seller, once established, gives the customer a strong motivation for enhancing the scope of the relationship and increases customer commitment (e.g., Selnes, 1998; LaBahn & Kohli, 1997; Halinen, 1997).

Trust becomes especially important where purchase risks as perceived by the consumer are high. The main types of risks that consumers perceive when making product decisions include functional risk (the risk that the product will perform as expected), physical risk (that the product will constitute some physical danger to the consumer or to others), financial risk (the risk that the product will not be worth its cost), time risk (the risk that the time spent searching for the product will be wasted if the product does not perform as expected), psychological risk (the risk that a poor product choice will hurt the consumer's ego), and social risk (the risk that a poor product choice will cause social embarrassment) (Schiffman et al., 2010, p. 202).

Closely related to the concept of perceived risk is consumer involvement. Consumer involvement is the degree of personal relevance that the product or purchase holds for that consumer (Schiffman et al., 2010, p. 229). While high-involvement purchases are very important to the consumer in terms of perceived risk and therefore trigger extensive problem-solving and information processing by the consumer, low-involvement purchases result in very little information processing (Schiffman et al., 2010, p. 229). Senecal and Nantel (2004) have shown, for example, that the influence of on-line recommendation sources is moderated by product type, with consumers following on-line recommendations for experience products more than on-line recommendations for search products, suggesting the importance of consumer involvement and product category in the impact of on-line marketing communications.

An important determinant of consumer-perceived risk is product category, as suggested by the preceding discussion of consumer involvement. Services, because of their intangibility, usually represent more risk to the consumer as examining their quality before the purchase is normally difficult. The quality of some services can only be evaluated after the purchase, and some services do not lend themselves to quality evaluation even after the consumption (Zeithaml, 1981, as cited in Kotler & Keller, 2012: 379). As a result, consumers develop ways of handling perceived risk, and some of these coping strategies are to be brand-loyal, to rely on store image or brand image, or to seek information about the product and product category (Schiffman et al., 2010, pp. 202-203). One of the sources of information consulted to reduce perceived risk is word-of-mouth, and information from a source that is considered more trustworthy can lead to greater persuasiveness of that information (Wilson & Sherrell, 1993, as cited in Bickart & Schindler, 2001). Where word of mouth is so copious and easy to access as on the Internet, building trust through positive word of mouth becomes especially important for brands.

Trust features as an important element in brand equity. For instance, in Keller's (1993, 2008) customer-based brand equity, trust is embedded in various subdimensions, among them product reliability, durability, credibility, values, and heritage. "Brand credibility," which is part of the brand judgements dimension of brand equity, incorporates three components: perceived expertise, trustworthiness, and likeability (Keller, 2008, p. 68). Brand trustworthiness is defined as the qualities of being dependable and "keeping customer interests in mind" (Keller, 2008, p. 68).

The effects of store reputation on trust has been studied in the on-line shopping context, and a positive relationship has been indicated between store reputation and trust (e.g., Jarvenpaa, Tractinsky, and Vitale, 2000; Metzger, 2006, as cited in Utz et al., 2012). Utz and colleagues (2012), however, found that on-line store reviews by consumers have a stronger effect on perceived trustworthiness than store reputation. This is to be expected given that informal sources have higher credibility than formal ones. Electronic word of mouth is likely to have higher credibility with consumers than marketers' Web sites; Bickart and Schindler (2001), for example, suggest that on-line discussion forums are more effective in generating consumer interest in the product than are corporate Web sites.

Information shared by consumers with strong ties to each other is typically perceived as more trustworthy and therefore is more effective in leading to the desired behavior such as referral or adoption (Liu-Thompkins, 2012, as cited in Gensler, Völckner, Liu-Thompkins, & Wirtz, 2013). Therefore, satisfied consumers with strong ties to other consumers may be a brand's ally in risky purchases, as suggested by Gensler and colleagues (2013, p. 248).

Finally, differences exist among users of social media; information-sharing habits of older adults, for example, appear to be different and their information disclosure appears to be influenced by their friends (Chakraborty et al., 2013), carrying managerial implications for trust building with this demographic group.

Barker et al. (2013) note that social media involves "*earning permission* to join in *personal conversations* with *real people* who don't usually want to be the target of advertising" [Authors' emphasis] (p. 74). The practice of marketing to consumers only after having received their permission is referred to as "permission marketing." In his book on permission marketing Godin (1999, as cited in Kotler & Keller, 2012, p. 159) suggests that marketers can develop stronger consumer relationships by respecting consumers' wishes and sending messages only when the consumer expresses a willingness to become more involved with the brand. Such practices are fundamentally important in gaining the consumer's trust in on-line environments.

BUSINESS PERFORMANCE AND SOCIAL MEDIA

Business performance is traditionally evaluated through financial measures such as net income and return on investment, though a more balanced perspective of business performance integrates various dimensions of control that focus on customers, internal processes, employees, as well as financial indicators (Kaplan & Norton, 1996). Business performance is construed in this chapter primarily as marketing performance. To evaluate marketing performance, several types of marketing control are necessary (Kotler & Keller, 2012, p. 663): annual-plan control, profitability control, efficiency control, and strategic control. The annual-plan control involves monitoring the company's marketplace performance to determine serious deviations from predetermined objectives, uncover the reasons for the deviations, and make necessary corrections. For this purpose marketers use sales analysis, market share analysis, marketing expense-to-sales analysis, and financial analysis (Kotler & Keller, 2012, p. 663). In their discussion of the history of marketing metrics, Knowles and Ambler (2010) note that the measurement of marketing performance, and especially advertising, has traditionally focused on the impact on sales; however, with the broadening conception of business performance as a function not only of financial performance but also of other variables, marketing performance measurement has come to incorporate other measures, which may include such non-financial indicators as customer satisfaction, loyalty, and brand equity, or an output measure such as efficiency/effectiveness (pp. 383-384). Standards of measurement for sales may include sales growth, market share, and sales from new products. Distribution performance may also be measured using a variety of metrics such as number of outlets or share of shelf. Some customer-related performance measures focus on the customer's readiness to purchase (such as purchase intention or trial rate) while others are related to customer acquisition or customer retention (Kotler & Keller, 2012, p. 664). Profitability control involves measuring the profitability of products, territories, customer groups, market segments, trade channels, and order sizes (Kotler & Keller, 2012, p. 664). Efficiency control aims at pinpointing those elements of the marketing plan that could be managed more efficiently (Kotler & Keller, 2012, p. 664). Finally, strategic control involves periodically and comprehensively reexamining the marketing strategy and major marketing activities of a business, which may include profitability and efficiency analyses but also expand to ethical/social responsibility reviews (Kotler & Keller, 2012, p. 665).

Marketing effectiveness refers to the degree to which the marketing effort reaches its predetermined objectives (Clark, 2000), and marketing communication effectiveness is evaluated by a variety of brand awareness or advertising awareness metrics, recall, response rate, reach and frequency, and gross rating points (Kotler & Keller, 2012, p. 664).

Advertising effectiveness is the degree to which the advertising (a specific advertisement or the advertising campaign) reaches its predetermined goals, as specified by the advertiser (American Marketing Association, 2014). These goals may range from raising advertising awareness or brand awareness, to influencing attitudes and influencing sales (Lane et al., 2008). In fact, a considerable amount of research exists that points to the positive impact of advertising on business performance (see for example Jones, 1995; Broadbent, 2000) and brand equity (see for example Aaker & Biel, 1993). Advertising is one of the first industries to feel the brunt of economic contractions; therefore, it is especially important to point to research findings that suggest that firms that increase their advertising spending during recessions experience higher sales, market share, and earnings during and after the contraction (see, for example, Tellis & Tellis, 2009, for a review; for more recent evidence please see Özturan, Özsomer, & Pieters, 2014).

Some of the skepticism with which advertising is viewed stems from the difficulty of measuring its effectiveness. It should be noted, however, that measurement of advertising effectiveness had already reached a level of maturity in the early 1960s as evinced by the publication in 1963 of a book on the subject by Mc-Graw-Hill: *Measuring Advertising Effectiveness* (Lucas & Britt, 1963).[2] Furthermore, Bartels (1976) notes that during the decade of the 1960s sixteen books were published on the methodology, techniques, and testing of advertising (p. 48, pp. 269-271). In fact, in view of the relatively recent history of the Internet, already several models of measuring the effectiveness of on-line advertising have been proposed (see, for example, Baltas, 2003; Calder, Malthouse, & Schaedel, 2009; Kim, Kwon, & Chang, 2011; Song, Xu, Techatassanasoontorn, & Zhang, 2011).

Brand equity, regarded as "possibly the most important concept for marketing in the last 50 years" (Knowles & Ambler, 2000, p. 379), is also a key factor that needs to be included in discussions of marketing effectiveness as any marketing effort – and especially those in the social media – may conceivably have an impact on the firm's brand equity. In fact, the first companies to start monitoring the social media were public relations firms and advertising agencies who searched for negative comments posted in social media in an effort to defend their clients against potential public relations crises (FreshMinds Research, 2010, as cited in Barker et al., 2013, pp. 280-281); hence, those early efforts were directed at protecting the client's brand equity.

Brand equity measurement may take different forms depending on the orientation of the measurers. In their examination of the evolution of brand equity measurement Knowles and Ambler (2000, p. 386) note that in the 1990s while the brand valuation sector focused on establishing its methodologies and approaches, market research agencies developed ways to define and measure the non-financial version of brand equity. The non-financial version of brand equity measurement fell into two classes of metrics: consumer behavioral measures such as loyalty and market share and intermediate measures such as awareness and intention to purchase (Lehmann and Reibstein, 2006, as cited in Knowles and Ambler, 2000; Park & Srinivasan, 1994, as cited in Knowles & Ambler, 2000). As a multidimensional construct (Keller, 1993, 2008), brand equity has many sources, and in Keller's model these sources include six subdimensions: brand salience (the degree of relevance the brand has for the consumer and the awareness of the brand), brand performance, brand imagery, brand judgements, brand feelings, and brand resonance (separated into behavioral loyalty, attitudinal attachment, sense of community, and active engagement). All of these sources of brand equity may be influenced by social media marketing (see for example Gensler et al., 2013).

The use of social media as a marketing venue has given rise to the need to measure the marketing effectiveness of efforts in the social media. Such traditional measures as net number of transactions, net sales volume, net number of transacting customers, and average yield per transaction can be tracked also in the social media (Blanchard, 2011). Besides these metrics, businesses use also more medium-tailored indicators such as hits/visits/page views, repeat visits, number of followers or friends, conversion rates from visitor to buyer, on-line product or service ratings, and abandoned shopping carts among others (The CMO Survey, 2011, as cited in Barker et al., 2013, p. 284). The most popular social media quantitative measures appear to be the number of visitors/page views, number of fans/followers, and the traffic arriving at company Web sites from the social media sites (Social Media Usage, Attitudes, and Measurability, 2011, as cited in Barker et al., 2013, p. 285). Also recommended are site-specific metrics such as the percentage of growth in the number of followers within thirty days on Twitter, percentage increase in the number of "Likes" and percentage increase in the number of comments within six months, for example, on Facebook, or the percentage increase in the ratio of visitors' comments to posts within a specific time period such as six months on a corporate Web log, or blog (Barker et al., 2013, pp. 285-286). Some examples among a wide range of metrics suggested for measuring effectiveness of social media marketing efforts are number of downloads, number of "shares" per day, cost per engagement, click-through rates on specific links, number of unique visitors to the blog per day, and volume of mentions across channels (Baker et al., 2013, pp. 283-298; Brown & Fiorella, 2013, pp. 165-170; Blanchard, 2011, pp. 198-202; Macarthy, 2013, p. 224).

One of the key performance indicators of social media marketing is sentiment analysis (Wright, 2009, August 23, as cited in Barker et al., 2013, p. 287), which aims to determine the sentiment of a speaker or writer with respect to a specific topic (Liu, 2010, as cited in Yu, Duan, & Cao, 2013, p. 920). Sentiment analysis is the computational detection and study of opinions, emotions, and subjectivities in text (Yu et al., 2013, p. 921). It is typically measured as the ratio of either positive, neutral, or negative brand mentions to total brand mentions (Barker et al., 2013, p. 294).

Peters et al. (2013) suggest that effective management of social media is predicated on their effective measurement, and offer a theoretical framework to guide in the construction of appropriate metrics. Their framework includes motives, content, network structure, and social roles and interactions as they are manifested in the social media.

IMPACT OF SOCIAL MEDIA MARKETING ON BUSINESS PERFORMANCE: REVIEW OF THE EVIDENCE

The impact of marketing in the social media may be profound. "Social media allow consumers to become engaged with a brand at perhaps a deeper and broader level than ever before," argue Kotler and Keller (2012, p. 570) and recommend that marketers do "everything they can to encourage willing consumers to engage productively."

Some of the benefits marketers may enjoy by using social media are gaining feedback on marketing activities, favorably influencing consumers towards the company and the company's products, and ultimately, converting consumers to purchasers or achieving some other desired marketing objective. Next, we will review research on aspects of marketing performance that word of mouth communications and marketers' efforts in social media may impact.

Overall, some empirical studies suggest that social media marketing improves stock performance. For example, Yu and colleagues (2013) suggest that sentiment in the social media has a stronger impact on firm stock performance than conventional media. Schniederjans, Cao, and Schniederjans (2013) also argue that companies' use of social media (specifically, use of particular impression management strategies) improves financial performance, as measured by quarterly earnings per share. There is also some evidence that electronic retailers' activities in on-line communities improve their business performance, as measured by revenue and transaction volume (Qu, Wang, Wang, & Zhang, 2013). Consumers' consumption-related communication with peers on social media have been found to be positively associated with product attitude, product involvement, and purchase intentions (Wang, Yu, & Wei, 2012).

The majority of electronic word-of-mouth studies have focused on on-line consumer reviews made on e-commerce Web sites, discussion forums, or rating sites, one study has found (Cheung & Thadani,

2012, p. 462). On-line consumer reviews provide information, comments or evaluations of products, services, or companies. They may be found on the Web sites of electronic retailers, opinion Web sites, and on-line community sites. For instance, the product reviews on the Web site of the on-line retailer Amazon.com, which began offering consumers the option of posting their comments on products on its Web site as early as 1995, are regarded as one of the most successful features of the site (New York Times, 2004, as cited in Zhang, Ye, Law, & Li, 2010, p. 694).

There is increasing evidence that on-line word-of-mouth has a significant influence on purchase behavior as suggested, for example, by a *Wall Street Journal* survey that reported that 71% of on-line US adults use consumer reviews for their purchases and 42% of them trust such a source (Spors, 2006, as cited in Chen et al., 2011, p. 85). Previous research has established, for instance, that on-line product reviews have an influence on consumer behavior (e.g., Senecal & Nantel, 2004; Dellarocas, Zhang, & Awad, 2007; Vermeulen & Seegers, 2009; Park & Lee, 2009; Zhang, Craciun, & Shin, 2010). In one of the earlier studies, Chevalier and Mayzlin (2006) demonstrated that an improvement in a book's reviews on either of two on-line book-selling sites led to an increase in relative sales at that site. Duan, Gu, and Whinston (2008) provided evidence that the volume of on-line posting significantly influenced box-office movie revenues while Dhar and Chang (2009) found that future sales of music albums were positively correlated with the volume of blog posts about an album. Rui, Liu, and Whinston (2013) demonstrated that positive messages on the micro-blog Twitter ("tweets") were associated with higher movie sales. Furthermore, they showed that tweets whose authors had more followers had a significantly higher impact on movie revenue than tweet authors with fewer followers. Ye, Law, and Gu (2009) provided evidence that positive on-line reviews could significantly increase the number of bookings at a hotel while Zhang, Ye, Law, and Li (2010) showed that more positive consumer reviews of restaurants led to more visits to a restaurant's Web page.

Research also suggests that positive word of mouth increases sales while negative word of mouth decreases sales (e.g., Rui, Liu, & Whinston, 2013). There is, however, some research that suggests some product reviews are deceptive (for a literature review, please see Anderson and Simester, 2014). Positive on-line reviews appear to improve the awareness of lesser known brands more than that of well-known brands (Vermeulen & Seegers, 2009). Negative on-line product reviews, on the other hand, are found more useful by consumers than positive reviews (Sen & Lerman, 2007) for utilitarian products – rather than hedonic products (i.e., products that people consume to have sensory, fantasy, or emotive experiences; Hirschman and Holbrook, 1982, as cited in Wilkie, 1990, p. 163). Finally, consumer reviews of on-line stores appear to be more predictive of trustworthiness judgements than store reputation (Utz et al., 2012). Taken together, there is sufficient evidence that electronic word of mouth influences on-line consumer purchasing behavior.

Research also offers some insights into how electronic word of mouth operates. Gruen, Osmonbekov, and Czaplewski (2006) suggest that electronic word-of-mouth communication impacts the overall value of the firm's offering as perceived by the consumer. Senecal and Nantel (2004) have demonstrated that on-line recommendation sources influence consumers' on-line choices, and recommendations were less influential for search products – products whose quality may be evaluated before the purchase – than for experience products – products whose quality may be evaluated only after purchase (Zeithaml, 1981, as cited in Kotler and Keller, 2012, p. 379). Where quality is difficult or costly to evaluate before purchase and consumers undertake extensive decision making, again they appear to be more likely to seek out others' opinions, as noted by Chen, Fay, and Wang (2011). Furthermore, overall consumer rating appears to be positively related to objective quality, and that more postings are observed for extremely low- or extremely high-quality products than for products of moderate quality (Chen et al., 2011).

In the social media information presented on social networks or Web forums may have greater credibility than marketer-generated information. In fact, research evidence suggests that consumers prefer to use peer recommendation in on-line shopping rather than editorial recommendation, especially for hedonic (or less utilitarian) shopping goals (Smith, Menon, & Sivakumar, 2005).

A framework suggested by Yadav, de Valck, Hennig-Thurau, Hoffman, and Spann (2013) acknowledges the influence of various product characteristics on the outcomes of social commerce, which the authors define as "exchange-related activities that occur in, or are influenced by, an individual's social network in computer-mediated social environments, where the activities correspond to the need recognition, pre-purchase, purchase, and post-purchase stages of a focal exchange" (p. 312). The product characteristics incorporated into the framework are necessity vs luxury products, high-effort products (products that require greater purchasing effort) vs low-effort products, products consumed in private vs those consumed in public, single vs group purchase and consumption, self-consumption vs gifts, perceived risk, and perceived value. Platform characteristics are also included in the framework. Hence, a firm's presence and initiatives in social media are proposed to influence outcomes related to various stages of the consumer's buying decision process through product and platform characteristics.

Brand equity also appears to benefit from social media marketing. Brand fans tend to visit the store more, generate more positive word of mouth, and are more emotionally attached to the brand than non-brand fans (Dholakia & Durham, 2010). Brands' participation in brand communities lead to stronger loyalty and purchase intentions (Algesheimer, Borle, Dholakia, and Singh, 2010, as cited in Gensler et al., 2013: 246). Overall, social media marketing activities appear to have a positive impact on brand equity (Kim & Ko, 2012).

The above discussion is intended to suggest that the impact of marketing in the social media on business performance appears to be important and growing. This, however, should not overshadow the importance of marketing using traditional media. In fact, evidence suggests that new and traditional media work in synergy, enhancing each other's effectiveness (e.g., Onishi & Manchanda, 2012).

CONCLUSION: MANAGERIAL AND RESEARCH IMPLICATIONS FOR EFFECTIVE ADVERTISING STRATEGIES IN THE SOCIAL MEDIA AGE

Managerial Implications

From the growing body of evidence suggesting a positive impact on business performance of social media marketing, marketers may draw several inferences to improve their social media performance.

Perhaps the most significant of these is the role of two-way communication in building consumer trust. Berry (1995/2000) explicitly recommends that marketers "demonstrate their trustworthiness" (p. 164) by opening up the lines of communication. Social media may enhance relationship building through providing customer listening posts and feedback channels. For that purpose, some marketers include on their Web sites links to discussion forums related to the company's products or sponsor discussion forums on their corporate Web sites. It is imperative, however, that the marketer not censor negative reviews and abstain from manipulating the discussion other than by responding to the negative information submitted to the forum, as Bickart and Schindler (2001) caution. Another important implication for marketers here should be to focus on the virtual community rather than on the product by providing the right conditions for consumers to come together, as suggested by Bagozzi and Dholakia (2002).

Research suggests that electronic word-of-mouth communication is influential in purchasing behavior. Probably, the most evident implication of this finding is that marketers should seriously consider on-line product reviews by consumers, monitor them vigilantly by tracking consumer opinion Web sites, and respond especially to negative reviews by consumers through Web platforms to improve their products and customer service. This response should match the content of the complaint, and it is suggested that the employee involved in the service failure respond rather than the company spokesperson (Van Laer & de Ruyter, 2010, as cited in Gensler et al., 2013). An implication here for Web platform managers is to improve system design to make information provision easier, as suggested by Zhao, Stylianou, and Zheng (2013).

As lesser known brands appear to benefit more from positive word of mouth, marketers might include consumer reviews on their corporate Web sites to raise awareness of their brands. Another managerial implication is that marketers should try to make sure that the consumer sees the most helpful reviews, as suggested by Zhang, Craciun, and Shin (2010), especially where a large of number of reviews is available and sifting through them is difficult. Wang et al. (2012) suggest that social media Web sites should highlight the commonalities between the reviewer and reader to stimulate visitors' desire to learn more about a product or to think more about the product category.

Consumers differ in their motives for participating in social media, as indicated by various studies (e.g., Hennig-Thurau et al., 2004; Peters et al., 2013), which implies that strategies for encouraging word-of-mouth participation could be formulated based on a motive-based segmentation of composers of electronic word of mouth. Furthermore, consumers differ in their social media usage habits based on age, with older adults emerging as a group with distinct information sharing behavior (e.g., Chakraborty et al., 2013), leading to the implication that different social media marketing strategies are called for to reach this demographic group.

Product type also appears to be an important factor in determining on-line purchasing behavior. For instance, consumers appear to be more influenced by word of mouth concerning experience products than search products; consequently, marketers of experience products should especially encourage electronic word-of-mouth communication. Differences may exist regarding consumer goods based on the amount of purchasing effort required, whether the product is a necessity or a luxury, whether purchase or consumption occurs in private or public, perceived risk and perceived value associated with the product, as indicated in the framework by Yadav et al. (2013). Such differences also have managerial implications: For publicly consumed goods, for example, marketers can offer means that enable consumers to share on their social networks news of the purchase. Where the purchase is characterized by high perceived performance risk, for example, social media frequented by experts can be used to generate word of mouth, as suggested by Yadav et al. (2013).

The body of research delineated above suggests that marketing strategies should be tailored to different social media platforms as social media platforms differ in their ability of and capacity for enabling content generation (by placing restrictions for example on the amount or type of content to be generated). Consequently, marketing to brand communities should be different from marketing in social networking sites. The relative advantages and disadvantages of different social media platforms should be considered in the formulation of social media strategy while the different platforms should be integrated as closely as possible to maximize effectiveness. An implication for the managers of social media platforms is the importance of making the site more amenable to data mining (with user permission, of course, and without jeopardizing users' privacy) so that effectiveness of marketing efforts in a particular medium can be better gauged by marketers.

Research Implications

Implications for research into the relationship between social media marketing and business performance are many as this stream of research appears to be just emerging. For example, even though studies into electronic word-of-mouth communications are mushrooming, they appear to be fragmented with little effort at integrating the findings of prior work, as noted by Cheung and Thadani (2012). Consequently, one research direction indicated is an attempt at forging a meaningful conclusion from the various streams of research and adoption of a common framework for studying electronic word-of-mouth communications. Furthermore, electronic word of mouth may influence different products in different ways, as described for example by Senecal and Nantel (2004), and examination of how electronic word of mouth influences different products may enhance our understanding of the impact of social media marketing on business performance. Again, research may explore the influence of social media marketing as it relates to these different products and consumption/purchase situations. Research could also explore the impact of social media marketing across the consumer's various decision-making stages, as suggested by Yadav et al. (2013).

In fact, new methods of investigation are proposed to gain an in-depth understanding of virtual communities. Kozinets, who has developed the technique of "netnography," or the methodology of adapting traditional in-person ethnographic research techniques to the study of on-line cultures and communities (2006, p. 281), suggests that, in order to be able to generate knowledge, researchers studying virtual communities using netnography should immerse themselves in those virtual communities that they study, "just as must an ethnographer" (p. 286).

Though our understanding of how social media can be used to manage customer relationships, marketing communications, and branding is growing, more research into the various components of the communication process in different social media platforms is still needed to sharpen that understanding.

An important research direction appears to be examination of how cross-media exposure – consumers' exposure to the advertising in both traditional media and social media – works, and how word-of-mouth communications in social media interact with marketer-generated advertising in traditional media. (A small but growing body of research is already emerging. See, for example, Dinner, van Heerde, & Neslin, 2014.) This research stream could provide insights into how the two types of media should be combined to accomplish different marketing communications goals.

Research into social media marketing appears to grow with accelerating pace. With what we know about marketing and advertising effectiveness today, it is relatively easier to conjecture that tools for measuring the effectiveness of marketing and advertising in the social media will become ever more sophisticated in time. Therefore, we agree with Knowles and Ambler (2010) that the coming years will witness an increasing emphasis on the engagement and community dimensions of marketing as social media technologies enter the business mainstream.

REFERENCES

Aaker, D. A., & Biel, A. L. (Eds.). (1993). *Brand equity and advertising: Advertising's role in building strong brands*. Hillsdale, NJ: Lawrence Erlbaum Associates, Publishers.

Advertising Research Foundation. (2006). *Defining engagement initiative*. Retrieved on March 30, 2014, from http://thearf.org/research-arf-initiatives-defining-engagement

American Marketing Association. (2014). *Dictionary*. Retrieved on April 13, 2014, from https://www.ama.org/resources/Pages/Dictionary.aspx

Anderson, E. T., & Simester, D. I. (2014). Reviews without a purchase: Low ratings, loyal customers, and deception. *JMR, Journal of Marketing Research, 51*(3), 249–269. doi:10.1509/jmr.13.0209

Bagozzi, R. P., & Dholakia, U. M. (2002). Intentional social action in virtual communities. *Journal of Interactive Marketing, 16*(2), 2–21. doi:10.1002/dir.10006

Balasubramanian, S., & Mahajan, V. (2001). The economic leverage of the virtual community. *International Journal of Electronic Commerce, 5*(3), 103–138.

Baltas, G. (2003). Determinants of internet advertising effectiveness: An empirical study. *International Journal of Market Research, 45*(4), 505–513.

Bansal, H. S., & Voyer, P. A. (2000). Word-of-mouth processes within a services purchase decision context. *Journal of Service Research, 3*(2), 166–177. doi:10.1177/109467050032005

Barasch, A., & Berger, J. (2014). Broadcasting and narrowcasting: How audience size affects what people share. *JMR, Journal of Marketing Research, 51*(3), 286–299. doi:10.1509/jmr.13.0238

Barker, M., Barker, D., Bormann, N., & Neher, K. (2013). *Social media marketing: A strategic approach* (International edition). South-Western Cengage Learning.

Bartels, R. (1976). *The history of marketing thought* (2nd ed.). Columbus, OH: Grid, Inc.

Berry, L. L. (2000). Relationship marketing of services: Growing interest, emerging perspectives. In J.N. Sheth, & A. Parvatiyar (Eds.), Handbook of relationship marketing (pp. 149-170). Thousand Oaks, CA: Sage Publications Inc.

Bhattacharya, C. B., & Bolton, R. N. (2000). Relationship marketing in mass markets. In J. N. Sheth & A. Parvatiyar (Eds.), *Handbook of relationship marketing* (pp. 327–354). Thousand Oaks, CA: Sage Publications Inc. doi:10.4135/9781452231310.n12

Bickart, B., & Schindler, R. M. (2001). Internet forums as influential sources of consumer information. *Journal of Interactive Marketing, 15*(3), 31–40. doi:10.1002/dir.1014

Blanchard, O. (2011). Social media ROI: Managing and measuring social media efforts in your organization. Indianapolis, IN: Que.

Broadbent, S. (2000). What do advertisements really do for brands? *International Journal of Advertising, 19*(2), 147–165.

Brown, D., & Fiorella, S. (2013). Influence marketing: How to create, manage, and measure brand influencers in social media marketing. Indianapolis, IN: Que.

Calder, B.J., Malthouse, E., & Schaedel, U. (n.d.). An experimental study of the relationship between online engagement and advertising effectiveness. *Journal of Interactive Marketing, 23*, 321–331.

Chakraborty, R., Vishik, C., & Rao, H. R. (2013). Privacy preserving actions of older adults on social media: Exploring the behavior of opting out of information sharing. *Decision Support Systems*, *55*(4), 948–956. doi:10.1016/j.dss.2013.01.004

Chen, Y., Fay, S., & Wang, Q. (2011). The role of marketing in social media: How online consumer reviews evolve. *Journal of Interactive Marketing*, *25*(2), 85–94. doi:10.1016/j.intmar.2011.01.003

Cheung, C. M. K., & Thadani, D. R. (2012). The impact of electronic word-of-mouth communication: A literature analysis and integrative model. *Decision Support Systems*, *54*(1), 461–470. doi:10.1016/j.dss.2012.06.008

Chevalier, J. A., & Mayzlin, D. (2006). The effect of word of mouth on sales: Online book reviews. *JMR, Journal of Marketing Research*, *43*(3), 345–354. doi:10.1509/jmkr.43.3.345

Clark, B. H. (2000). Managerial perceptions of marketing performance: Efficiency, adaptability, effectiveness, and satisfaction. *Journal of Strategic Marketing*, *8*(1), 3–25. doi:10.1080/096525400346286

Dellarocas, C., Zhang, X. M., & Awad, N. F. (2007). Exploring the value of online product reviews in forecasting sales: The case of motion pictures. *Journal of Interactive Marketing*, *21*(4), 23–45. doi:10.1002/dir.20087

Demand Metric Research Corporation. (2014). *Social media analytics: Enabling and optimizing use cases with analytics*. Retrieved in February 2014 from http://www.demandmetric.com/content/social-media-analytics-benchmark-report

Dhar, V., & Chang, E. A. (2009). Does chatter matter? The impact of user-generated content on music sales. *Journal of Interactive Marketing*, *23*(4), 300–307. doi:10.1016/j.intmar.2009.07.004

Dholakia, U. M., & Durham, E. (2010). One café chain's Facebook experiment. *Harvard Business Review*, *88*(3), 26.

Dichter, E. (1966). How word-of-mouth advertising works. *Harvard Business Review*, (November-December): 147–166.

Dinner, I. M., van Heerde, H. J., & Neslin, S. A. (2014). Driving online and offline sales: The cross-channel effects of traditional, online display, and paid search advertising. *JMR, Journal of Marketing Research*, *51*(5), 527–545. doi:10.1509/jmr.11.0466

Duan, W. (2013). Special issue on social media: An editorial introduction. *Decision Support Systems*, *55*(4), 861–862. doi:10.1016/j.dss.2012.12.021

Duan, W., Gu, B., & Whinston, A. B. (2008). Do online reviews matter? An empirical investigation of panel data. *Decision Support Systems*, *45*(4), 1007–1016. doi:10.1016/j.dss.2008.04.001

Dwyer, P. (2007). Measuring the value of electronic word of mouth and its impact in consumer communities. *Journal of Interactive Marketing*, *21*(2), 63–79. doi:10.1002/dir.20078

Economist Intelligence Unit. (2007). *Beyond loyalty: Meeting the challenge of customer engagement, part 1*. Retrieved on May 9, 2014, from http://www.adobe.com/engagement/pdfs/partI.pdf

Fill, C. (2009). *Marketing communications: Interactivity, communities, and content* (5th ed.). Harlow, UK: Pearson Education Limited.

Gensler, S., Völckner, F., Liu-Thompkins, Y., & Wirtz, C. (2013). Managing brands in the social media environment. *Journal of Interactive Marketing*, *27*(4), 242–256. doi:10.1016/j.intmar.2013.09.004

Grant, R. (2004). Uses and gratifications theory. In R. West & L. H. Turner (Eds.), *Introducing communication theory: Analysis and application* (pp. 392–408). New York: McGraw-Hill.

Gruen, T. W., Osmonbekov, T., & Czaplewski, A. J. (2006). EWOM: The impact of customer-to-customer online know-how exchange on customer value and loyalty. *Journal of Business Research*, *59*(4), 449–456. doi:10.1016/j.jbusres.2005.10.004

Halinen, A. (1997). *Relationship marketing in professional services: A study of agency-client dynamics in the advertising sector*. London, UK: Routledge. doi:10.4324/9780203280775

Harridge-March, S. (2006). Can the building of trust overcome consumer perceived risk online? *Marketing Intelligence & Planning*, *24*(7), 746–761. doi:10.1108/02634500610711897

Hennig-Thurau, T., Gwinner, K. P., Walsh, G., & Gremler, D. D. (2004). Electronic word-of-mouth via consumer-opinion platforms: What motivates consumers to articulate themselves on the Internet? *Journal of Interactive Marketing*, *18*(1), 38–52. doi:10.1002/dir.10073

Hoffman, D. L., & Novak, T. P. (1996). Marketing in hypermedia computer-mediated environments: Conceptual foundations. *Journal of Marketing*, *60*(3), 50–68. doi:10.2307/1251841

Homans, G. C. (1958). Social behavior as exchange. *American Journal of Sociology*, *63*(6), 597–606. doi:10.1086/222355

Jarvenpaa, S. L., Tractinsky, N., & Vitale, M. (2000). Consumer trust in an Internet store. *Information Technology Management*, *1*(1-2), 45–71. doi:10.1023/A:1019104520776

Jones, J. P. (1995). *When ads work: New proof that advertising triggers sales*. New York, NY: Lexington Books.

Kaplan, A. M., & Haenlein, M. (2010). Users of the world, unite! The challenges and opportunities of social media. *Business Horizons*, *53*(1), 59–68. doi:10.1016/j.bushor.2009.09.003

Kaplan, R. S., & Norton, D. P. (1996). Using the balanced scorecard as a strategic management system. *Harvard Business Review*, (January-February), 75–85.

Katarivas, B. R., Bendit, R., & Rosenthal, B. (2014). Market research through on-line custom panel: Co-creation value and customer relationship. In A. Goyal (Ed.), *Innovations in services marketing and management: Strategies for emerging economies* (pp. 89–101). Hershey, PA: IGI Global. doi:10.4018/978-1-4666-4671-1.ch005

Katz, E., & Lazarsfeld, P. F. (1955). *Personal influence*. New York: Free Press of Glencoe.

Keller, K. L. (1993). Conceptualizing, measuring, and managing customer-based brand equity. *Journal of Marketing*, *57*(January), 1–22. doi:10.2307/1252054

Keller, K. L. (2008). *Strategic brand management: Building, measuring, and managing brand equity* (3rd ed.). Upper Saddle River, NJ: Pearson Prentice Hall.

Kim, A. J., & Ko, E. (2012). Do social media marketing activities enhance customer equity? An empirical study of luxury fashion brand. *Journal of Business Research*, *65*(10), 1480–1486. doi:10.1016/j.jbusres.2011.10.014

Kim, C., Kwon, K., & Chang, W. (2011). How to measure the effectiveness of online advertising in online marketplaces. *Expert Systems with Applications*, *38*(4), 4234–4243. doi:10.1016/j.eswa.2010.09.090

Knowles, J., & Ambler, T. (2010). Orientation and marketing metrics. In P. Maclaran, M. Saren, B. Stern, & M. Tadajewski (Eds.), *The Sage handbook of marketing theory* (pp. 379–396). London, UK: Sage Publications Ltd.

Kotler, P., & Keller, K. L. (2012). *Marketing management* (14th ed.). Essex, UK: Pearson Education Ltd.

Kozinets, R. V. (1999). E-tribalized marketing? The strategic implications of virtual communities of consumption. *European Management Journal*, *17*(3), 252–264. doi:10.1016/S0263-2373(99)00004-3

Kozinets, R. V. (2006). Click to connect: Netnography and tribal advertising. *Journal of Advertising Research*, *46*(September), 279–288. doi:10.2501/S0021849906060338

LaBahn, D. W., & Kohli, C. (1997). Maintaining client commitment in advertising agency-client relationships. *Industrial Marketing Management*, *26*(6), 497–508. doi:10.1016/S0019-8501(97)00025-4

Lane, W. R., King, K. W., & Russell, J. T. (2008). *Kleppner's advertising procedure* (17th ed.). Upper Saddle River, NJ: Pearson Prentice Hall.

Lucas, D. B., & Britt, S. H. (1963). *Measuring advertising effectiveness*. New York, NY: McGraw-Hill Book Company, Inc. doi:10.1037/13112-000

Luo, X., & Donthu, N. (2007). The role of cyber-intermediaries: A framework based on transaction cost analysis, agency, relationship marketing and social exchange theories. *Journal of Business and Industrial Marketing*, *22*(7), 452–458. doi:10.1108/08858620710828836

Macarthy, A. (2013). *500 social media marketing tips: Essential advice, hints, and strategy for business*. Andrew Macarthy.

Moorman, C., Zaltman, G., & Deshpande, R. (1992). Relationships between providers and users of market research: They dynamics of trust within and between organizations. *JMR, Journal of Marketing Research*, *29*(August), 314–328. doi:10.2307/3172742

Morgan, R. M., & Hunt, S. D. (1994). Commitment-trust theory of relationship marketing. *Journal of Marketing*, *58*(3), 20–38. doi:10.2307/1252308

Nahapiet, J., & Ghoshal, S. (1998). Social capital, intellectual capital, and the organizational advantage. *Academy of Management Review*, *23*(2), 242–266.

Onishi, H., & Manchanda, P. (2012). Marketing activity, blogging and sales. *International Journal of Research in Marketing*, *29*(3), 221–234. doi:10.1016/j.ijresmar.2011.11.003

Organisation for Economic Co-operation and Development (OECD). (2007). *Participative web and user-created content: Web 2.0, wikis, and social networking*. Retrieved in March 2014 from http://www.oecd-ilibrary.org/science-and-technology/participative-web-and-user-created-content_9789264037472-en

Özturan, P., Özsomer, A., & Pieters, R. (2014). The role of market orientation in advertising spending during economic collapse: The case of Turkey in 2001. *JMR, Journal of Marketing Research*, *51*(April), 139–152. doi:10.1509/jmr.11.0528

Park, C., & Lee, T. M. (2009). Antecedents of online reviews' usage and purchase influence: An empirical comparison of US and Korean consumers. *Journal of Interactive Marketing*, *23*(4), 332–340. doi:10.1016/j.intmar.2009.07.001

Peters, K., Chen, Y., Kaplan, A. M., Ognibeni, B., & Pauwels, K. (2013). Social media metrics: A framework and guidelines for managing social media. *Journal of Interactive Marketing*, *27*(4), 281–298. doi:10.1016/j.intmar.2013.09.007

Qu, Z., Wang, Y., Wang, S., & Zhang, Y. (2013). Implications of online social activities for e-tailers' business performance. *European Journal of Marketing*, *47*(8), 1190–1212. doi:10.1108/03090561311324282

Robbins, S. P., & Judge, T. A. (2013). *Organizational behavior* (15th ed.). Essex, UK: Pearson Education Limited.

Rui, H., Liu, Y., & Whinston, A. (2013). Whose and what chatter matters? The effect of tweets on movie sales. *Decision Support Systems*, *55*(4), 863–870. doi:10.1016/j.dss.2012.12.022

Ryan, D., & Jones, C. (2009). *Understanding digital marketing: Marketing strategies for engaging the digital generation*. London, UK: Kogan Page.

Sashi, C. M. (2012). Customer engagement, buyer-seller relationships, and social media. *Management Decision*, *50*(2), 253–272. doi:10.1108/00251741211203551

Schiffman, L. G., Kanuk, L. L., & Wisenblit, J. (2010). *Consumer behavior* (10th ed.). Upper Saddle River, NJ: Pearson.

Schniederjans, D., Cao, E. S., & Schniederjans, M. (2013). Enhancing financial performance with social media: An impression management perspective. *Decision Support Systems*, *55*(4), 911–918. doi:10.1016/j.dss.2012.12.027

Selnes, F. (1998). Antecedents and consequences of trust and satisfaction in buyer-seller relationships. *European Journal of Marketing*, *32*(3/4), 305–322. doi:10.1108/03090569810204580

Sen, S., & Lerman, D. (2007). Why are you telling me this? An examination into negative consumer reviews on the Web. *Journal of Interactive Marketing*, *21*(4), 76–94. doi:10.1002/dir.20090

Senecal, S., & Nantel, J. (2004). The influence of online product recommendations on consumers' online choices. *Journal of Retailing*, *80*(2), 159–169. doi:10.1016/j.jretai.2004.04.001

Sheth, J. N., & Parvatiyar, A. (2000). Relationship marketing in consumer markets: Antecedents and consequences. In J.N. Sheth & A. Parvatiyar (Eds.), Handbook of relationship marketing (pp. 171-207). Thousand Oaks, CA: Sage Publications Inc.

Smith, D., Menon, S., & Sivakumar, K. (2005). Online peer and editorial recommendations, trust, and choice in virtual markets. *Journal of Interactive Marketing*, *19*(3), 15–37. doi:10.1002/dir.20041

Song, P., Xu, H., Techatassanasoontorn, A., & Zhang, C. (2011). The influence of product integration on online advertising effectiveness. *Electronic Commerce Research and Applications*, *10*(3), 288–303. doi:10.1016/j.elerap.2010.09.003

Strauss, J., & Frost, R. (2009). *E-marketing* (5th ed.). Upper Saddle River, NJ: Pearson Prentice Hall.

Sundaram, D. S., Mitra, K., & Webster, C. (1998). Word-of-mouth communications: A motivational analysis. *Advances in Consumer Research. Association for Consumer Research (U. S.)*, *25*, 527–531.

Tellis, G. J., & Tellis, K. (2009). Research on advertising in a recession: A critical review and synthesis. *Journal of Advertising Research*, *49*(3), 304–327. doi:10.2501/S0021849909090400

Utz, S., Kerkhof, P., & van den Bos, J. (2012). Consumers rule: How consumer reviews influence perceived trustworthiness of online stores. *Electronic Commerce Research and Applications*, *11*(1), 49–58. doi:10.1016/j.elerap.2011.07.010

Vargo, S. L., & Lusch, R. F. (2010). A service-dominant logic for marketing. In P. Maclaran, M. Saren, B. Stern, & M. Tadajewski (Eds.), *The Sage handbook of marketing theory* (pp. 219–234). London, UK: Sage Publications Ltd.

Vermeulen, I. E., & Seegers, D. (2009). Tried and tested: The impact of online hotel reviews on consumer consideration. *Tourism Management*, *30*(1), 123–127. doi:10.1016/j.tourman.2008.04.008

Wang, X., Yu, C., & Wei, Y. (2012). Social media peer communication and impacts on purchase intentions: A consumer socialization framework. *Journal of Interactive Marketing*, *26*(4), 198–208. doi:10.1016/j.intmar.2011.11.004

Wilkie, W. (1990). *Consumer behavior* (2nd ed.). New York: John Wiley & Sons.

Wu, J.-J., Chen, Y.-H., & Chung, Y.-S. (2010). Trust factors influencing virtual community members: A study of transaction communities. *Journal of Business Research*, *63*(9-10), 1025–1032. doi:10.1016/j.jbusres.2009.03.022

Yadav, M. S., de Valck, K., Hennig-Thurau, T., Hoffman, D. L., & Spann, M. (2013). Social commerce: A contingency framework for assessing marketing potential. *Journal of Interactive Marketing*, *27*(4), 311–323. doi:10.1016/j.intmar.2013.09.001

Ye, Q., Law, R., & Gu, B. (2009). The impact of online user reviews on hotel room sales. *International Journal of Hospitality Management*, *28*(1), 180–182. doi:10.1016/j.ijhm.2008.06.011

Yu, Y., Duan, W., & Cao, Q. (2013). The impact of social and conventional media on firm equity value: A sentiment analysis approach. *Decision Support Systems*, *55*(4), 919–926. doi:10.1016/j.dss.2012.12.028

Zhang, J. Q., Craciun, G., & Shin, D. (2010). When does electronic word-of-mouth matter? A study of consumer product reviews. *Journal of Business Research*, *63*(12), 1336–1341. doi:10.1016/j.jbusres.2009.12.011

Zhang, Z., Ye, Q., Law, R., & Li, Y. (2010). The impact of e-word-of-mouth on the online popularity of restaurants: A comparison of consumer reviews and editor reviews. *International Journal of Hospitality Management*, *29*(4), 694–700. doi:10.1016/j.ijhm.2010.02.002

Zhao, K., Stylianou, A. C., & Zheng, Y. (2013). Predicting users' continuance intention in virtual communities: The dual intention-formation process. *Decision Support Systems*, *55*(4), 903–910. doi:10.1016/j.dss.2012.12.026

Zhuang, W., Hsu, M. K., Brewer, K. L., & Xiao, Q. (2013). Paradoxes of social networking sites: An empirical analysis. *Management Research Review*, *36*(1), 33–49. doi:10.1108/01409171311284576

KEY TERMS AND DEFINITIONS

Business Performance Indicator: Indicators such as market share and return on investment that give an indication of business performance.

Digital Marketing Strategy: Marketing strategy as it pertains to digital channels of communication.

Marketing Effectiveness: The extent to which a marketing activity or program reaches its predefined objectives.

On-Line Customer Review: Customer reviews of products posted on digital media such as marketers' Web sites or social media platforms.

Social Media: The on-line electronic media such as on-line communities and forums, blogs, and social networks through which consumers share information with each other and with companies. The companies also may use these platforms to share information with consumers. This definition is based on Kotler and Keller (2012: 568).

Social Media Marketing: Marketing activities performed through the use of social media.

Word-of-Mouth Communication: Communication shared by consumers about a product or promotion and the act of sharing such communication (based on the definition of the American Marketing Association, 2014).

ENDNOTES

1. In social media "audience engagement" is used as a performance indicator. For its measurement please see Barker et al. (2013: 289). Please see the section on social media and business performance for more examples of performance indicators used in social media marketing.
2. *Measuring Advertising Effectiveness* by Lucas and Britt (1963) contains two parts, the first one of which deals with the measurement of advertising messages while the second part is devoted to the measurement of advertising media, which contains a section on the optimization of media reach through mathematical programming (pp. 377-386). The book opens with the following observation, which serves to show that the meaning of advertising effectiveness had been taken to heart then and for more than half a century methods of increasing sophistication are being devised to measure it: "The purpose of an advertisement is to produce for the advertiser a profit in terms of money, reputation, good will, or understanding – or all of these" (p. 7).

This research was previously published in the Handbook of Research on Effective Advertising Strategies in the Social Media Age edited by Nurdan Öncel Taşkıran and Recep Yılmaz, pages 416-439, copyright year 2015 by Business Science Reference (an imprint of IGI Global).

Chapter 9
Developing a Hierarchy Model for Selection of Social Media Manager

Pi-Fang Hsu
Shih Hsin University, Taiwan

Yi-Wen Su
Shih Hsin University, Taiwan

Chia-Wen Tsai
Ming Chuan University, Taiwan

ABSTRACT

With the fast development of the Internet, communication tools are no longer limited to traditional media. Enterprises have become aware of the rapid emergence of social media in recent years. Social media marketing has become an important field that demands attention, especially its changing marketing strategies. It is necessary to designate a professional to manage the social media platforms of an enterprise to attract consumers. Hence this study develops a two-part model to assist employers in choosing the ideal social media manager. The first part derives criteria for choosing a social media manager by conducting a thorough literature review and employing the modified Delphi method. The second part applies the analytic hierarchy process to calculate and identify the best suited social media manager by ranking candidates according to the relative weights of the evaluation criteria. In addition, a renowned Taiwanese restaurant chain is used as an example, to demonstrate how a social media manager is selected by applying this model. The results show that enterprises emphasize social media capabilities, professional skills, innovation, personal characteristics, and social skills.

DOI: 10.4018/978-1-5225-5637-4.ch009

1. INTRODUCTION

With the ongoing development of technology, the Internet has become is one of the necessities of daily life and a crucial communication medium. The Internet not only eliminates the gap between people but also offers prompt and efficient global communication. It is both the easiest and fastest means of information exchange. In parallel with the development of the Internet, network application services or social media such as Facebook, Twitter, YouTube, and LinkedIn have become the latest trend. Kaplan and Haenlein (2010) define social media as "a group of Internet-based applications that build on the ideological and technological foundations of Web 2.0, and that allow the creation and exchange of user-generated content." Social media have substantially changed the way organizations, communities, and individuals communicate.

Studies show that the online world has gained considerable influence (e.g., Weinberg 2009). Social media provide automated social network platforms, including resources and sharing of information, experiences, and perspectives. It can take different forms such as forums, blogs, social networks, podcasts, virtual online games, and videos. According to Sterne (2010), there are six types of social media: forums and message boards, review and opinion sites, social networks, blogs, micro-blogs, and media sharing. Kietzmann et al. (2011) present a honeycomb framework that defines how social media services focus on some or all seven functional building blocks—identity, conversations, sharing, presence, relationships, reputation, and groups. For instance, the building blocks observed for Facebook users are relationships, identity, reputation, conversations, and presence.

As of September 2011, Facebook's global user statistics reached 700 million (Checkfacebook 2011). eMarketer.com, a famous marketing website, predicts that two out of three people will be users of social networking in 2014 (Willianson 2010). It is therefore reasonable to say that social media represent a revolutionary new trend that should be of interest to enterprises operating in the online space. Furthermore, 70% of marketers plan on increasing investment in social media marketing (eMarketer.com 2012). In fact, an increasing number of enterprises and marketers are using social media to boost their sales. Social media marketing is useful not only for generating sales but also for developing consumer relationships. The significant difference between traditional marketing and new media marketing is noteworthy.

According to the *European Journal of Social Psychology*, a key component in successful social media marketing is building "social authority." Social authority is created when an individual or organization establishes themselves as an "expert" in their given field or area, thereby becoming an influencer in that field or area (Brauer and Bourhis 2006). It is the process of "building social authority" that makes social media effective. Qualman (2010) showed that the marketer function has transformed from the creation and promotion of the message into listening and participation in response to current and potential customer needs. In other words, the business model is changing, requiring companies to restructure to cope with changes brought about by social media and influence.

Social media marketing has gained significant enterprise attention and continues to do so even today. However, some agencies' surveys show that enterprises are finding a dearth of professionals with the skills needed to manage their social media platforms. An investigation by the Economist Intelligence Unit (EIU) reveals that 84% of surveyed enterprises rated themselves "poor" in a social media platform operation. The investigation agency Alterian contacted 1500 members of marketing and media agencies, digital marketing companies, system integrators, and other businesses for a social media marketing survey. Its results showed that only 30% of marketers have the ability to analyze the content of social media dialogue or deal with social media crises. Also, it indicated that 38.6% use tracking tools to measure the social media conversation with consumers (FIND 2011). These numbers show that many enterprises have weaknesses in the area of social media.

The management of a social media operation is a new, specialized career. Not everyone is suited for the position or specializes in public interaction (Armano 2010). Lanz (2010) points out that an appropriate social media manager is key to a brand. The manager's personality has to passionately and creatively represent your brand. The right candidate should be digital media savvy and have social media knowledge and first-hand sales experience (Lavrusik 2011).

Evaluation and selection of a social media manager is a multi-criteria decision-making question. An enterprise should generally form a special selection team to make decisions. In the case of selecting a social media manager, experts and scholars should co-decide on who is best-suited for the position. More importantly, a procedure with a series of strict evaluation criteria is required to find the ideal social media manager. Therefore, this study creates a decision model for evaluating and selecting an ideal social media manager from the perspective of business owners. First, the modified Delphi method is applied to the summaries of overall opinions from experts to find the appropriate decision criteria. The Analytic Hierarchy Process (AHP) is applied to determine the relative weights of these criteria to rank the candidate and select the one best suited for the position. On the basis of these results, the study provides a valuable reference for enterprises needing social media manager.

2. METHODOLOGY

The study uses a two-fold methodology: the modified Delphi technique and AHP. The modified Delphi combines the opinions of experts. Then, using AHP, each criterion's weight and order of priority are determined. This decision method considers both quantitative and qualitative criteria and is suitable for this study's objective. The following describes the two-part methodology.

2.1. Modified Delphi Technique

The Delphi technique is a conventional forecasting approach that does not require large samples and can be applied to generate a professional consensus for ambiguous, complex, and contentious topics (Hartman 1981). The technique requires continuous written and oral discussion and feedback among anonymous experts on a particular topic. Anonymous experts offer professional experience, knowledge, skills, and opinions as well as exchange views with other experts until a consensus is reached (Hartman 1981). The Delphi method comprises the following steps: (1) select the experts, (2) perform a first-round survey, (3) provide feedback to the experts based on the previous survey and perform another survey, and (4) synthesize expert responses to describe the consensus. Step (3) is normally repeated until a uniform result is achieved for a particular topic. The modified Delphi method is a simplification of the above procedure (Delbecq et al. 1975).

This study adopts the modified Delphi technique to identify evaluation criteria for selecting a social media manager. The technique employs anonymous expert interviews and a survey of statistical outcomes regarding the research subject. Delbecq et al. (1975) suggested 5–9 individuals as the appropriate number of members in a Delphi technique panel. This study employed a decision-making group comprising nine experts.

2.2. Analytic Hierarchy Process

AHP is a decision method that decomposes a complex multi-criterion decision problem into a hierarchy (Saaty 1980). It is a measurement theory that prioritizes the hierarchy and consistency of judgmental data provided by a group of decision makers. AHP incorporates the evaluations of all decision makers into a final decision without having to elicit their utility functions on subjective and objective criteria, using pairwise comparisons of the alternatives (Saaty 1990).

While Dyer et al. (1992) applied AHP to media selection, Lin and Hsu (2003) used it to select an ideal Internet advertising network. Hsu et al. (2012) applied AHP to select the optimal video for city marketing. Hsu and Lin (2013) used AHP to develop a decision model for brand naming. Hsu et al. (2013) adopted AHP to select the optimal Korean dramas for commercial TV stations in Taiwan. The detailed calculation procedure follows.

2.2.1. Establishing the Hierarchy Structure

A complex issue can be addressed by decomposing the hierarchy structure. Given the inability of humans to simultaneously compare seven categories, each element of the hierarchy is assumed to not exceed seven elements. Under this limited condition, a reliable comparison and consistency can be ensured (Saaty 1980). The first hierarchy of the structure refers to the targeted goal. Beneath the last hierarchy are the choice projects or replacement alternatives and the middle hierarchies, which are the appraisal factors or criteria.

2.2.2. Computing Element Weight of Various Hierarchies

1. Establishment of pairwise comparison matrix A

Let $C_1, C_2, \ldots, C_n$ be the set of elements, while a_{ij} represents a quantified judgment on a pair of elements C_i, C_j. The relative importance of two elements is rated using a scale with the values 1, 3, 5, 7, and 9 (1 = equally important, 3 = slightly more important, 5 = strongly more important, 7 = demonstrably more important, 9 = absolutely more important). This yields an n-by-n matrix A as follows

$$A = \left[a_{ij}\right] = \begin{matrix} & C_1 & C_2 & \cdots & C_n \\ C_1 & 1 & a_{12} & \cdots & a_{1n} \\ C_2 & 1/a_{12} & 1 & \cdots & a_{2n} \\ \vdots & \vdots & \vdots & & \vdots \\ C_n & 1/a_{1n} & 1/a_{2n} & \cdots & 1 \end{matrix}, \tag{1}$$

where $a_{ii} = 1$ and $a_{ji} = 1/a_{ij}$, $i, j = 1, 2, \ldots, n$. In matrix A, the problem becomes one of assigning to the n elements $C_1, C_2, \ldots Cn$ a set of numerical weights $W_1, W_2, \ldots Wn$ that "reflect the recorded judgments." If A is a consistency matrix, the relations between weights W_i and judgments a_{ij} are simply given by $Wi/Wj = a_{ij}$ (for $i, j = 1, 2, \ldots, n$).

2. Eigenvalue and eigenvector

Saaty (1990) suggested that the largest eigenvalue λ_{max} will be

$$\lambda_{max} = \sum_{j=1}^{n} a_{ij} \frac{W_j}{W_i}. \tag{2}$$

If A is a consistency matrix, eigenvector X can be calculated by the formula (3):

$$(A - \lambda_{max} I) X = 0. \tag{3}$$

3. Consistency test

Saaty (1990) proposed utilizing consistency index (CI) and consistency ratio (CR) to check the consistency of the comparison matrix. CI and CR are defined as follows:

$$CI = (\lambda_{max} - n) / (n - 1), \tag{4}$$

$$CR = CI / RI, \tag{5}$$

where CI denotes the average consistency index over numerous random entries of same order reciprocal matrices. If CR≦0.1, the estimate is accepted; otherwise, a new comparison matrix is solicited until CR≦0.1.

2.2.3. Computing Overall Hierarchy Weight

After the weights are computed for various hierarchies and elements, the overall hierarchy weight is computed, ultimately allowing decision makers to select the optimal project.

3. MODEL AND APPLICATIONS

In this study, a model is developed for selecting the ideal social media manager from the perspective of business owners. The example used in this study is a renowned Taiwanese restaurant chain, which plans to select a social media manager. At first, a decision making team is formed internally with three members including the CEO, the marketing director, and the human resource manager. Then, according to the recommendations made by HR manager form screening of candidates resume, three candidates are invited to interview, as candidate A, candidate B, and candidate C in this study. The decision making team members then give scores to the three candidates according to their performance in each sub-criterion. The real data are obtained for the model developed in this study according to the following six steps.

Step 1: Define evaluation criteria for social media manager selection.

1. Designate the group of experts for defining the evaluation criteria

By applying the modified Delphi method, evaluation criteria for selecting a social media manager are determined by interviewing nine people with experience in selecting a social media manager or long-term experience with digital marketing. The interviewed experts are selected on the basis of the following conditions: (a) must hold a managerial or human resource position (b) must have experience in analyzing research topics, or (c) must have long-term experience with digital marketing or social media operation.

2. Review pertinent literature on major factors in selecting social media managers

The present marketing environment is becoming increasingly complicated, and to be successful, companies also need a social media marketing strategy. According to the related reference material, criteria of social media manager selection can be generalized into the following categories: personal qualities, professional skills, social skills, innovation and social media capabilities.

3. Confirm criteria for social media manager selection

A five point Likert scale is used to ensure that criteria weight surpasses the four scales above, which are listed as the important reference criteria. Nine experts determine the criterion for evaluation model establishment, and implement a modified Delphi method for reaching a consensus among experts and achieving uniform recognition. This study obtains five essential criteria and 21 sub-criteria after two rounds of survey results, as listed in Table 1.

The evaluation of weights is performed using the AHP questionnaire, whose design is based on the level structure shown in Figure 1. It is composed of three parts: (a) a question for the evaluation of the criteria weights (b) five questions for the evaluation of the weights of the minor principle, and (c) 21 questions for the pairwise comparison of substitute managers according to the 21 sub-criteria. The questions in the first and second parts are answered by the nine experts, which are tested using the modified Delphi method, while those in the third part are answered by the company's decision-making team members. This study assumed that the evaluation criteria are independent.

Step 2: Establish hierarchical structure.

The problem of social media manager selection is separated into four levels: (a) setting the goal of selecting the best suited social media manager (b) five evaluation criteria (c) 21 sub-criteria, and (d) the candidates themselves (Figure 1).

Step 3: Establish each factor of the pairwise comparison matrix.

Pairwise comparison matrices of criteria and sub-criteria for selecting social media manager are created. The geometric means of the weights given by the experts are calculated to summarize their opinions and make pairwise comparisons for the decision elements of different levels. According to

Table 1. Criteria and sub-criteria for selecting a social media manager

Criteria	Sub-Criteria	Description of Sub-Criteria	References
Personal qualities	Thirst for knowledge	Have the thirst for knowledge about all aspect of and those related to social media. Explore all possibilities	Grove (2009), Lanz (2010)
	Careful thought	Listen to and observe customers' comments on a social media platform and try to provide prompt responses	Sweeney (2011)
	Passion	Passionate about interaction, e.g., with customers, boss, and colleagues	Grove (2009), Gibson & Jagger (2009)
	Ambition	Set goals as well as assess and achieve them	Sweeney (2011)
	Curiosity	In social media, customer location is generally unknown. Must be curious at all times	Grove (2009), Gibson & Jagger (2009)
Professional skills	Writing ability	Must write effectively enough to inspire people to engage and comment	Sweeney (2011)
	Logical reasoning	Propose a plan based on clear logical thinking	Sweeney (2011)
	Strategic thinking	Have the ability to not only have a conversation with consumers but also set goals and estimate the outcome	Grove (2009), Gibson & Jagger (2009), Nerney (2009), Lanz (2010), Sweeney (2011)
	Executive power	Prompt in implementing a promotion strategy when faced with the rapid change in social media	Sweeney (2011)
	Ability to tackle ambiguity	Chart a clear trajectory under conditions of high uncertainty in the network	Expert opinion
Social skills	Effective communication	Have conversations on a social media platform effective enough to yield good results	Owyang (2007), Nerney (2009), Owyang (2007)
	People skills	Must be confident when facing the public and engaging in dialogue, whether in real life or on the Internet	Nerney (2009), Owyang (2007)
	Influence	Must exuberate power and influence when conversing with customers	Gibson & Jagger (2009)
	Team priority	Social media marketing strategy is implemented by a team. Must give the team priority and be willing to take onus	Nerney (2009)
Innovation	Innovative	Implement an innovative strategy	Gibson & Jagger (2009), Lanz (2010)
	Adventurous	Willing to try new things, media, and ideas	Gibson & Jagger (2009), Owyang (2007)
	Technologically savvy	Good at using all types of social media tools to improve communication	Nerney (2009)
	Creative	Inspire new ideas through social media platforms	Lanz (2010)
Social media capabilities	Activity level management	Must manage activity levels of social media, such as the rate of response to comments or the frequency of information announcements	Expert opinion
	Number of social media operations	Must have experience in operating social media tools or platforms	Expert opinion
	Duration of social media operation	Must have spent sufficient time in operating a social media tool or platform	Expert opinion

Figure 1. Hierarchical structure for selecting the ideal social media manager

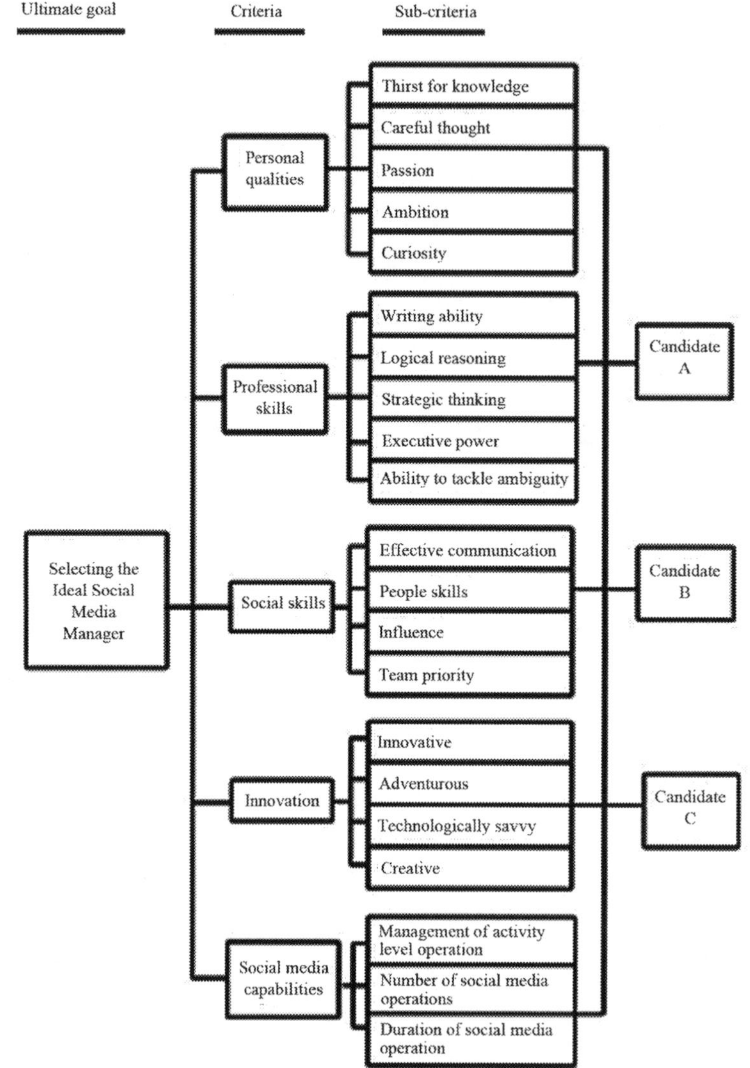

equation (1), pairwise comparison matrices can be obtained. The comparison matrix (Table 2) is used to calculate the eigenvectors using equations (2) and (3). Table 3 summarizes the eigenvectors for each criteria and sub-criteria.

Step 4: Perform consistency testing.

Equations (4) and (5) are used to calculate the criteria comparison matrix of consistency for each hierarchy (Tables 2 and 3). Results of the consistency test and CR of the comparison matrix for each of the nine experts are all smaller than 0.1, indicating "consistency." Furthermore, CR of the aggregate matrix is also smaller than 0.1.

Table 2. Aggregate pairwise comparison matrix for level-2 criteria

	Personal Qualities	Professional Skills	Social Skills	Innovation	Social Media Capabilities
Personal qualities	1.000	0.404	1.704	0.754	0.523
Professional skills	2.474	1.000	4.217	1.437	0.997
Social skills	0.587	0.237	1.000	0.250	0.236
Innovation	1.326	0.696	4.004	1.000	0.478
Social media capabilities	1.910	1.000	4.240	2.090	1.000
CR = 0.062; CI = 0.055; λ_{max} = 5.247					

Step 5: Calculate relative weights of elements at each level.

After summarizing the geometric means of the scores, the relative weights of the elements of each level are calculated by applying the eigenvector method according to equation (3). The results are listed in Table 3.

According to Table 3, the respective weights of the five evaluation criteria in order are social media capabilities (0.390), professional skills (0.186), innovation (0.216), personal qualities (0.133), and social skills (0.075).

Regarding the social media manager's personal qualities, the five sub-criteria are ordered as follows: thirst for knowledge (0.358), careful thought (0.201), passion (0.139), ambition (0.194), and curiosity (0.109). For the social media manager's professional skills, the five sub-criteria are ordered as follows: writing ability (0.093), logical reasoning (0.28), strategic thinking (0.28), executive power (0.23), and ability to tackle ambiguity (0.118). As for the social media manager's social skills, the four sub-criteria are ordered as follows: effective communication (0.349), people skills (0.265), influence (0.174), and team priority (0.212). Regarding the social media manager's innovation skills, the four sub-criteria are ordered as follows: innovative (0.388), adventurous (0.259), technologically savvy (0.157), and creative (0.197). Finally, for the social media manager's social media capabilities, the three sub-criteria are ordered as follows: management of activity level of social media operation (0.341), number of social media operations (0.164), and duration of social media operation (0.494).

Step 6: Calculate overall hierarchy weights for social media managers selection.

After calculating the weights of criteria of the different levels, the overall level weights are calculated. According to the weights of alternatives, the optimal case is finally determined.

From Table 4, for personal qualities, candidate A showed the best performance, followed by candidates C and B. Regarding professional skills, candidate B showed the highest performance, followed by candidates A and C. As for social skills, candidate A showed the highest scores, followed by candidates B and C. With respect to innovation, candidate A showed the best performance, followed by candidates B and C. Finally, regarding social media capabilities, candidate B showed the best performance, followed by candidates C and A.

When a company is choosing a social media manager, it will consider a person with experience in the social media world and social media capabilities. A social media manager must also be innovative

Table 3. Eigenvectors and weights of five criteria

Criteria	Criteria Weigh	Sub-Criteria	Weights of Sub-Criteria	Overall Level Weight	Consistency
Personal qualities	0.133	Thirst for knowledge	0.358	0.048	CR = 0.012 CI = 0.013 λ_{max} = 5.054
		Careful thought	0.201	0.027	
		Passion	0.139	0.018	
		Ambition	0.194	0.026	
		Curiosity	0.109	0.014	
Professional skills	0.186	Writing ability	0.093	0.017	CR = 0.015 CI = 0.016 λ_{max} = 5.065
		Logical reasoning	0.28	0.052	
		Strategic thinking	0.28	0.052	
		Executive power	0.23	0.043	
		Ability to tackle ambiguity	0.118	0.022	
Social skills	0.075	Effective communication	0.349	0.026	CR = 0.020 CI = 0.018 λ_{max} = 4.053
		People skills	0.265	0.020	
		Influence	0.174	0.013	
		Team priority	0.212	0.016	
Innovation	0.216	Innovative	0.388	0.084	CR = 0.005 CI = 0.004 λ_{max} = 4.013
		Adventurous	0.259	0.056	
		Technologically savvy	0.157	0.034	
		Creative	0.197	0.043	
Social media capabilities	0.390	Management of activity level of social media	0.341	0.133	CR = 0.039 CI = 0.023 λ_{max} = 3.045
		Number of social media operation	0.164	0.064	
		Duration of social media operation	0.495	0.193	

Table 4. Overall scores and ranking of three social media managers

Criteria	Weights of criteria	Candidate A	Candidate B	Candidate C
Personal qualities	0.133	0.481	0.254	0.265
Professional skills	0.186	0.227	0.586	0.187
Social skills	0.075	0.473	0.287	0.240
Innovation	0.216	0.491	0.28	0.228
Social media capabilities	0.390	0.260	0.398	0.342
Overall scores		0.349	0.380	0.270
Rank		2	1	3

and be able to propose marketing strategies that differ from those previously implemented. Moreover, a social media manager's professional skills must include the ability to chart clear trajectories when establishing connections with consumers. Finally, regarding personal qualities, "social skills" is considered important for the selection of a social media manager. As for the social media manager's total evaluation scores, which are the relative weights of managers, the ranking of the scores assigned to different social media managers is as follows: candidate B (0.380), candidate A (0.349), and candidate C (0.270). This confirms that candidate B is the most appropriate social media manager.

4. DISCUSSION AND CONCLUSION

Selecting an appropriate and ideal candidate to manage social media and implement a social media marketing strategy is a strategic corporate choice. Keeping this in mind, this study developed a decision-making model for corporations to select a best-suited social media manager. First, the research model applies the modified Delphi method to identify suitable assessment criteria for selecting the social media manager. Then, AHP is used to determine relative weights of the evaluation criteria, rank the alternatives, and select a social media manager. According to the rankings, business owners focus on the candidate's social media capabilities, professional skills, ability to innovate, personal qualities, and social skills. The result demonstrates that the most crucial criteria for selecting a social media manager are social media capabilities and professional skills. Social media substitute for traditional communications and establish close connections among people throughout the world. Although it continues to grow rapidly, business owners and marketers are still unprepared for this new trend. Furthermore, social media has been an indistinct area compared to traditional marketing.

In this study, a renowned Taiwanese restaurant chain is used as an example for the empirical development and analysis of this model. According to the research findings, after ranking alternative cases by their total scores, candidate B shows the best performance, followed by candidates A and C. Therefore, in the present analysis, candidate B identifies the ideal social media manager. The decision model developed in this study is a systematic and objective method for business owners to select a social media manager. It merely requires the entry of data on the candidate into the model according to corporate demands and market requirements. The social media manager with the highest score will be the optimal choice. In summary, corporations undoubtedly require a person who is prompt and possess experience in social media operations, including maintaining the involvement and loyalty of online communities. This model provides qualitative and quantitative measurements for business owners to select the most ideal and professional social media manager.

ACKNOWLEDGMENT

The author would like to thanks the National Science Council of the ROC for financially supporting this research under Contract No. NSC 101-2410-H-128-025.

REFERENCES

Armano, D. (2010). Fire your marketing manager and hire a community manager. Retrieved May 6, 2014 from: http://blogs.hbr.org/cs/2010/07/fire_your_marketing_manager_an.html

Brauer, M., & Bourhis, R. Y. (2006). Special issue: Social power. *European Journal of Social Psychology*, *36*(4), 601–616. doi:10.1002/ejsp.355

Checkfacebook. (2011). *Facebook online population*. Retrieved January 5, 2015 from: http://www.checkfacebook.com/

Delbecq, A. L., Van de Ven, A. H., & Gustafson, D. H. (1975). *Group techniques for program planning: a guide to nominal group and Delphi processes*. Scott, Foresman.

Dyer, R. F., Forman, E. H., & Mustfa, M. A. (1992). Decision support for media selection using the Analytic Hierarchy Process. *Journal of Advertising*, *21*(1), 59–72. doi:10.1080/00913367.1992.10673360

FIND. (2011). *Alterian survey: One-third of marketers cannot handle the problem of social media on brand awareness*. Retrieved January 5, 2015 from: http://www.find.org.tw/find/home.aspx?page=news&id=6284

Gibson, S., & Jagger, S. (2009). *Sociable! How social media is turning sales and marketing upside-down*. Charleston, SC: Booksurge.

Grove, V. J. (2009). *3 Qualities to look for when hiring a community manager*. Retrieved May 6, 2014 from: http://www.openforum.com/idea-hub/topics/technology/article/3-qualities-to-look-for-when-hiring-a-community-manager-jennifer-van-grove#aside_media

Hartman, A. (1981). Reaching consensus using the Delphi technique. *Educational Leadership*, *38*, 495–497.

Hsu, P. F., & Lin, F. L. (2013). Developing a decision model for brand naming using delphi method and Analytic Hierarchy Process. *Asia Pacific Journal of Marketing and Logistics*, *25*(2), 187–199. doi:10.1108/13555851311314013

Hsu, P. F., Lin, S. Y., & Tsai, C. W. (2013). Optimal selection of Korean dramas for commercial TV stations in Taiwan by using the AHP. *International Journal of E-Adoption*, *5*(2), 14–24. doi:10.4018/jea.2013040102

Hsu, P. F., Tsai, C. W., & Doong, S. W. (2012). Developing and implementing a model for selecting videos for city marketing. *International Journal of Customer Relationship Marketing and Management*, *3*(4), 50–64. doi:10.4018/jcrmm.2012100105

Kaplan, A. M., & Haenlein, M. (2010). Users of the world, unite! The challenges and opportunities of social media. *Business Horizons*, *53*(1), 59–68. doi:10.1016/j.bushor.2009.09.003

Kietzmann, J. H., Hermkens, K., McCarthy, I. P., & Silvestre, B. S. (2011). Social media? Get serious! Understanding the functional building blocks of social media. *Business Horizons*, *54*(3), 241–251. doi:10.1016/j.bushor.2011.01.005

Lanz, H. L. (2010). Introducing the newest member of your hotel marketing team: The social media manager. *HVS International Journal, Special section*, 1-3.

Lavrusik, V. (2011). The evolution of the social media manager: Social monetization manager? Retrieved May 5, 2014 from: http://mashable.com/2011/02/03/social-media-manager-social-monetization-manager/

Lin, C. T., & Hsu, P. F. (2003). Adopting an Analytic Hierarchy Process to select internet advertising networks. *Marketing Intelligence & Planning*, *21*(3), 183–191. doi:10.1108/02634500310474993

Nerney, C. (2009). 5 Qualities of a good social media manager. Retrieved May 5, 2014 from: http://socialtimes.com/5-qualities-of-a-good-social-media-manager_b51148

Owyang, J. (2007). The four tenets of the community manager. Retrieved May 5, 2014 from: http://www.web-strategist.com/blog/2007/11/25/the-four-tenets-of-the-community-manager/

Qualman, E. (2010). *Socialnomics: How social media transforms the way we live and do business*. New Jersey: John Wiley and Sons.

Saaty, T. L. (1980). *The Analytic Hierarchy Process*. New York: McGraw-Hill. Inc.

Saaty, T. L. (1990). How to make a decision: The Analytic Hierarchy Process. *European Journal of Operational Research*, *48*(1), 9–26. doi:10.1016/0377-2217(90)90057-I

Sterne, J. (2010). *Social media metrics: How to measure and optimize your marketing investment*. New Jersey: John Wiley & Sons, Inc.

Sweeney, M. (2011). What makes an exceptional social media manager? Retrieved May 5, 2014 from: http://socialmediatoday.com/mike-sweeney/275368/what-makes-exceptional-social-media-manager

Weinberg, T. (2009). *The new community rules: Marketing on the social web*. California, CA: O'Reilly.

Williamson, A. D. (2009). Social networks: Five consumer trends for 2009 Retrieved May 5, 2014 from: http://www.emarketer.com/Reports/All/Emarketer_2000644.aspx

This research was previously published in the International Journal of E-Adoption (IJEA), 7(1); edited by Sushil Sharma and Hayden Wimmer, pages 17-31, copyright year 2015 by IGI Publishing (an imprint of IGI Global).

Chapter 10
Analysing the Role of Social Media in Dialogue Marketing and Management as a Contemporary Franchising Local Area Marketing Technique

Geoffrey B. Webster
Central Queensland University, Australia

Margee Hume
Central Queensland University, Australia

ABSTRACT

The role of social media as a contemporary Local Area Marketing (LAM) technique in Dialogue Marketing is not clearly defined. Dialogue Marketing focuses on a structured approach of ongoing interactive communication to form relationships with people (Allan Steinmetz, 1997). According to Webster and Hume (2015) contemporary LAM techniques refer to using digital marketing to build relationships with local community. Problems facing franchise businesses include how to use Dialogue Marketing as a contemporary LAM technique to maximise local community connections as well as to build essential relationships. Advancing previous work in LAM, this study analyses social media's role as a contemporary LAM technique in Dialogue Marketing. It explores the use of Dialogue Management as a tool to enhance Dialogue Marketing for franchise businesses. It presents an integrated framework for the identification of social media adoption levels and how this can enhance franchise business success by providing an important contribution to the franchise industry sector. It concludes by offering a conceptual touchpoint channel model with a view to progressing discourse in the area and uniting current thinking.

DOI: 10.4018/978-1-5225-5637-4.ch010

RESEARCH RATIONALE

This research is significant in that it is not only exploring dialogue management strategy choices as contemporary franchise local area marketing (LAM) techniques in the social media platform hierarchy but also the extent to which dialogue marketing is embedded in social networking. It is also examining further the consistency of LAM techniques used to engage with their online communities.

This chapter will highlight how franchises create and retain their customers with social media using dialogue management strategies. This chapter examines 3 distinct problems. These problems include:

Problem 1: The lack of objective investigation into how franchises make dialogue management strategy choices for their contemporary LAM techniques: Often franchisees are provided with limited marketing training (Webster & Hume, 2015), resulting in poor or inadequate dialogue management strategy choices given their social media involvement. This research will advance discussion into this problem and highlight optimal strategy choices.

Problem 2: Lack of objective reporting into the extent franchises have embedded dialogue marketing into their social networking strategies. Social networking is typically undertaken at a franchisor level rather than at the franchisee level resulting in a standardised approach as opposed to a customised one.

Problem 3: The lack of an enhanced theoretical framework or model that incorporates the dialogue marketing process in the formation of relationships with customers and consumers: A proposed social media engagement model outlines the categories of the relationships but not specifically how dialogue marketing leads people to form relationships using social media platforms. This work will incorporate the notion of dialogue marketing and advance the model.

RESEARCH METHOD

As this work is initially exploratory, a qualitative approach was considered relevant to define the problems the researchers are seeking to examine (Boyce, 2002). The research aim encompassed undertaking exploratory research to ascertain the suitability of conducting a more robust examination and to enlarge the researcher's knowledge about the issues and problems described earlier (Kumar, 1996). An extensive literature review, incorporating 'internet' sources and 'academic business journal databases' was conducted. As Kumar (1996) points out, a literature review can assist a researcher in widening their base of knowledge for their area of research, offering focus and definition to the research problem as well as improving their research methodology. To search academic journal databases, keyword terms the researchers used included *social media engagement*, *touchpoints* and *social media measurement*. Internet search engines, 'Google' and 'Bing' were utilised by the researchers to unearth supplementary information, in particular, practitioner white papers, forum reviews, content articles, industry survey reports and advocacy group websites for the keyword terms, *customer engagement*, *content marketing*, *social analytics* and *touchpoints*.

Following the literature review pertaining to the topic areas, "Franchise Dialogue Marketing" and "Dialogue Marketing in Social Media", further information was collected through a structured observation. A structured observation was conducted in the shape of an internet marketing images review for the keyword, "touchpoints". The reason a structured observation method was considered as an approach for because it increased data reliability and lowers the chance of observer bias (Kinnear & Taylor, 1998). A convenience sampling methodology was employed to select the internet marketing images to study. In exploratory research situations, convenience or 'haphazard sampling' is the most preferred approach as it is easy as well as quick to implement and to administer, given tight deadlines (Zikmund, Ward, Lowe & Winzar, 2007). As the research aims to investigate how businesses, in particular franchise businesses embed dialogue marketing into their social networking strategies as well as to form and build relationships, the data analysis undertaken was a 'descriptive analysis' (Kinnear & Taylor, 1998) which was applicable given the nature of the research.

DATA COLLECTION

As described above, two instruments, a literature review and researcher observations were used to collect data on the role of social media in dialogue marketing and management. Reporting time constraints required only exploratory and descriptive research to be undertaken. Completing the literature review was important for a number of reasons. It brought focus and clarity to shaping the research problems as well as understanding the relationship between the existing body of knowledge on social media and dialogue marketing and identified gaps.

The second instrument was the recording of researcher observations from primary sources in the form of touchpoint images. Details about the first 31 images observed on the Google Images website were recorded. Image rankings based on image use frequency was the reason for selecting the first 31 touchpoint images. Given the exploratory nature of this research, data findings tabulations were limited to frequency and percentage distributions only without statistical analysis.

INTRODUCTION

In July 2010, Amazon, the giant American on-line book retailer sold more ebooks than paperbacks. Also, ebooks accounted for triple the number of sales of hardcovers according to Amazon CEO, Jeff Bezos. In the publishing industry, this was a huge milestone (Ostrow, 2011). Bradley Johnson (2014) from Ad Age, reported that in 2013, digital marketing accounted for 35.3% of all U.S. advertising agency revenue but this growth is slowing. Traditional marketing still has the dominant position with over 57% of advertising revenue with television advertising (40%) the significant player (Marketingcharts.com, April 2014). Traditional television viewing though especially amongst young American adults (18-24 year olds) remains in steady decline. Other age demographic groups, including 25-34 year olds, 35-49 year olds and 50-64 year olds appear to be reducing their levels of traditional television consumption as well (Marketingcharts.com, September 2014). In a recent IAB survey (2014), it is also reported that increases in digital video advertising will be funded by shifting money away from television advertising. It predicts that within five years, digital marketing will at least be the same as television. In the latest 2014 CMO Survey, respondents have indicated that social media spending would account for over 21% of a business's overall marketing budget within the next five years. This highlights at least a doubling of social media spending budgets in a five year period (CMOSurvey.org, 2014). So how does this paradigm shift relate to 'Dialogue Marketing'?

It was the 'digital revolution' that has made dialogue marketing possible. Dialogue marketing is firstly establishing the consumers attention, whilst at the same time, learning all about them including their motive or intent and then secondly to engage with them on an individual basis through various appropriate online experiences. Such engagement means developing experiences across a range of brand communication channels such as e-mails, point-of-purchase (POP), mobile messaging and social networks. The goal is to have the consumer create an emotional bond with the organisation's brand (Koreatimes.co.kr, 2013).

This chapter investigates the dialogue components of contemporary local area marketing (LAM) and how they are managed by businesses including franchises. The chapter will also analyse the reasons and causes of dialogue engagement levels used in social media and the contribution of this knowledge to further enhance a proposed theoretical social media engagement model. Understanding the role of dialogue management in social media to form online customer relationships is crucial in being able to further enhance this proposed theoretical social media engagement framework.

The objective of this research is to report on how businesses especially franchisees and their social media marketers market and manage dialogue within the social media context as a contemporary local area marketing (LAM) technique for building relationships with prospects and customers. This will provide a better understanding on how franchisees manage their online dialogue for different levels of engagement.

The intended contribution to the franchise industry specifically is to provide an integrated framework for the application of social media as a LAM and community based dialogue marketing technique to increase awareness and ultimately enhance franchise brand success using dialogue management strategies to engage with prospects and customers.

BACKGROUND

Dialogue Marketing is a term that refers to a structured approach of ongoing interactive communication to form relationships with people (Allan Steinmetz, 1997). Social networks are a key component in 'Dialogue Marketing' as it is this strategy that organisations leverage to induce sales with customer prospects (Financial-dictionary.thefreedictionary.com, 2012). Ellie Selby (2012) defines dialogue marketing also as social networking. She further states that of the 90% of businesses who use social media as their social networking tool, only 50% of them use it effectively. This assessment is supported by survey results from the CMO Survey conducted once every four years in conjunction with the American Duke University, Fuqua School of Business. From this survey, 45% of respondents believed social media had not had any significant impact on their business (CMOsurvey.org, 2014). This supports the research conducted by Webster and Hume (2015) into franchise businesses where they found that 77% of Australian franchises appeared to receive minimal benefits from their social media engagement. Cooper Smith from Business Insider (2014) also reported associated findings in a recent survey stating that only 23% of marketers thought their promotional social media efforts were effective. Negative social media feedback often stimulates further discussion on social networks which could have devastating consequences for franchise businesses (Corstjens & Umblijs, 2012). This may not be the major reason though. Sensis Yellow Pages Australia (2014, p.59) reported the main reasons why businesses did not have a social media presence were that, "it took too much time, it did not provide a return on investment, a feeling that it was too open to tampering as well as to adverse comments and there had been a lack of interest in it."

These reasons were echoed to much extent in the annual Digital Readiness Survey (Table 1) conducted by Chambers of Commerce and Industry Queensland (CCIQ) (2012) (2013), the top reason was "time and resources". A close second was "not relevant to my customers" but this was down 6.5% from last year, suggesting more businesses may have believed that social media is now more relevant. This is supported too by respondents indicating only a minimal positive change (+ 2%) to the "See little value" reason option. As for the reason "fear of negative exposure and feedback" receiving the largest positive percentage change (+9.5%), it was still ranked bottom of all the likely reasons.

According to Australian public relations specialist Rebecca Stalker (2010), franchise businesses in how they use social media, focus on strong word-of-mouth recommendations as well as enhancing and increasing brand awareness.

Findings from the annual CCIQ Digital Readiness Survey (2012) (2013), on how Queensland businesses use social media in their business (Table 2) would support Stalker's earlier assertion. 'Communication with clients', 'Marketing' and 'PR' have increased in significance and appear to be the stand-out likely reasons. According to Sensis Yellow Pages Australia (2014), for small to medium businesses the most common use of social media was to invite online comments, ratings or reviews whilst for large businesses it was for interactive communication with contacts or customers (Table 3). Of interest here for further research is the percentage of businesses offering incentives, coupons and discounts being the lowest even though consumers saw these as their key reason to connect.

In relation to 'social media for interactive communication', a survey of Australian franchise businesses (2012 Franchising Australia Report) into the most common social media communication methods used highlighted Facebook 63.5%, Franchisee intranet 58.7%, Twitter 38.9%, LinkedIn 27% and Posing

Table 1. Business Social Media non-usage

Survey Question: Why do you not use social media in your business?			
Response Option	**2012**	**2013**	**% Change**
See little value	25%	27.0%	+ 2%
Not relevant to my customers	45%	38.5%	- 6.5%
Time and resources	35%	41.0%	+ 6%
Don't understand social media	15%	22.6%	+ 7.6%
Fear of negative exposure and feedback	10%	19.5%	+ 9.5%

Table 2. Business Social Media usage

Survey Question: How do you use social media in your business?			
Response Option	**2012**	**2013**	**% Change**
Communication with clients	70%	75.0%	+ 5.0%
Communication with suppliers	20%	20.0%	-
Research/information gathering	40%	35.9%	- 4.1%
Marketing	70%	78.2%	+ 8.2%
PR	55%	61.5%	+ 6.5%
Communicate internally	20%	15%	- 5%

Table 3. 2014 Business use of Social Media (Sensis Yellow Pages Australia)

Key Reasons	Large	Medium	Small
Offer incentives to consumers via social media	41%	43%	28%
Use social media for interactive communication with customers and contacts	61%	55%	45%
Invite online comments, ratings and reviews on SM sites	53%	59%	46%

and responding to Franchisee blogs 14.3%. No details as to the emphasis of the communication was reported. Ironically, in the latest Franchising Australia Report (2014, p.3) on the topic of social media communication methods, there is no survey question or discussion even though there is a report subsection, *"Franchisor Online Communication & Sales Strategies"*. The focus is purely on online sales. This would suggest a gap in the understanding by franchise businesses as to what is social media and its rising power as a dialogue marketing tool.

SOCIAL MEDIA

Social media fundamentality is a form of two-way social communication that is evolving through new applications and categories (Nations, 2014). It's alive, organic and dynamic. Social media was defined early in its evolution as "a category of online media where people are talking, participating, sharing, networking, and bookmarking online. Most social media services encourage discussion, feedback, voting, comments, and sharing of information from all interested parties." (Jones, 2009) He suggested that social media used various conduits to develop two-conversations. These conduits included such categories as 'social news' (people reading and voting on news articles and topics), 'social sharing' (people creating and uploading content such as photos and videos), 'social networks' (people connecting and maintaining connections with family, friends, family as well as associates and social bookmarking' (people flagging interesting information and content and sharing these with other people.

Kaplan and Haenlein (2010) classified social media as a ranking by level of personal interaction:

1. Virtual social worlds (e.g. Second Life),
2. Virtual game worlds (e.g. World of Warcraft),
3. Social networking sites (e.g. Facebook),
4. Content communities (e.g. YouTube),
5. Blogs and microbloggs (e.g. Twitter),
6. Collaborative projects (e.g. Wikipedia).

This ranking suggested a higher emphasis on social media as a vehicle for social communities given its interactive conversational focus as opposed to a content one. A classic example of the power of social media community was when Dave Carroll used social media to complain about United Airlines breaking his guitar in 2008 The world quickly knew about that. For the global community, social media has shifted the scales and taken brand communication power away from organisations (Kietzmann, Hermkens, McCarthy, Silvestre, 2011). Organisations and businesses are increasing faced with the dilemma of embracing social media or ignoring it.

Kietzmann et al. (2011) argue that organisations have been hesitant to engage appropriately with social media. A possible reason for this could be their lack of understanding about social media ecology (Kaplan and Haenlein, 2010). For organisations to understand their social media audience and engagement needs, Kietzmann et al. (2011) developed a seven building block honeycomb (Table 4).

Each building block represents a specific social media function. By analysing the 'building blocks' of individual social media platforms and their implications, organisations can determine their applicability and suitability fit. This framework can also provide useful criteria in analysing the social media platform choices of organisations, specifically franchise businesses which will be the subject of future explanatory research.

Accompanying this framework is a set of guidelines, for organisations to navigate through the social media maze. Kietzmann et al. (2011) coincidently referred to these guidelines as their 4 C's, Cognize (review and identification of suitable social media platforms), Congruity (alignment of suitable social media platforms with organisational goals), Curate (management of social media engagement by level and frequency of involvement) and Chase (monitoring the social media environment for changes that would impact on the organisation.) These guidelines are meant to provide the foundations for the monitoring, understanding and responding to actions generated from those target social media sites that form the basis of an organisation's social media strategy. These four steps coincidently appear to model the PDCA continuous improvement cycle process developed by quality management experts, Edwards Deming and Walter Shewhart (Pearson, Larson & Gray, 2013).

With the predicted rise in digital marketing as reported earlier, so marketing budgets will change to reflect increases in spending on social media spending. For example, according to the 2014 Sensis Yellow Pages Australia Report, social media spending in 2014 was as an average, $4,560 for small businesses (16% of marketing budget) and $38,800 (12% of marketing budget). In 2013, for small business it was $1,970 (15% of marketing budget) and for medium sized businesses it was $11,780 (9% of marketing budget) (2014 Sensis Yellow Pages Australia Report).

An important characteristic of any effective social media strategy is measurability. When it comes to how well Australian businesses measure the success of social media investment, the statistics are

Table 4. The Honeycomb of Social Media (Kietzmann, Hermkens, McCarthy, Silvestre, 2011, p. 243)

Functionality	Description	Implications
Conversations	The extent to which users communicate with each other	Conversation velocity, and the risks of sharing and joining
Groups	The extent to which users are ordered or form communities	Membership rules and protocols
Identity	The extent to which users reveal themselves	Data privacy controls, and tools for user self-promotion
Presence	The extent to which users know if others are available	Creating and managing the reality, intimacy and immediacy of the content
Relationships	The extent to which users relate to each other	Managing the structural and flow properties in a network of relationships
Reputation	The extent to which users know the social standing of others and content	Monitoring the strength, passion, sentiment, and reach of users and brands
Sharing	The extent to which users exchange, distribute and receive content	Content management system and social graph

shocking. Only 17% of small businesses and 28% of medium businesses explicitly measure their social media investment returns. The most frequent measure used by these businesses was to monitor the level of social media responses. Most of these businesses however did not know what the level was. The other concern raised as well in the 2014 Sensis Yellow Pages Australia Report apart from the majority of businesses not formally measuring their social media ROI, many also were not clear as to the ingredients of a successful social media strategy. From these findings, there appears to be gap of knowledge in this area that warrants further investigation.

Without suitable metrics, it is hard to monitor its effectiveness (Willis, 2011). According to Natalie Burg of Forbes (2013), no social media return-on-investment (ROI) measurement is perfect or comprehensive but it is possible. The key is to use a combination of methods such as metric tools, interactions and traffic analysis over time to develop suitable benchmarks against which future social media strategies and efforts can be measured (CMOsurvey.org, 2014). This means better integration of data, strategies, automation technologies and analytics tools in the form of Dialogue Management (Koreatimes.co.kr, 2013). In relation to 'metrics', one of the interesting trends identified in the CMO survey (2014) is that businesses are now shifting away from pure 'financial' metrics such as sales level, revenue per customer, customer retention costs and profit per customer toward more referral and text measures ('soft' metrics) such as hits per page, number of followers or friends, repeat visits and buzz indicators (web mentions)

Dialogue management in a marketing context involves monitoring various social media platforms to identify how people are engaging in communication and conversations. In other words, identifying what and how the dialogue is being used. With social media, it's all about the relationship and the quality of that relationship. In a social media context therefore, dialogue management involves using various dialogue marketing techniques to leverage marketing strategies. For franchise businesses, this would mean embedding dialogue management into their franchise marketing efforts.

Franchise Marketing is the dialogue of a franchise business's most important relationship, which is the one between themselves and their customers (Franchisemarketingsystems.com, 2014). An issue often raised by franchisee's that affect this dialogue, is the social media restrictions and lack of marketing support provided by franchisor's to their local operations. These social media restrictions make it hard for the local franchise business to drive customer engagement, local awareness, the feeling of belonging and connectedness as well as prospect traffic. (Rubin, 2014)

DIALOGUE MARKETING

Dialogue Marketing according to Allan Steinmetz (1997, p.1), is "a structured program of ongoing two-way communication". He explains that it works due to its roots in human nature, i.e. people are more likely to communicate with those people who they know and trust. Even though the communication will be highly customized, there are 4 stages to dialogue marketing, these being:

Stage 1: Recognise the business.
Stage 2: Know the business.
Stage 3: Want to use the business.
Stage 4: Maintain an ongoing relationship with the business (Steinmetz, 1997).

These stages align closely to the customer strategy stages outlined by McColl-Kennedy & Keil (2000) for developing and building customer loyalty. The key element with the customer strategy stages methodology is the understanding of customer retention economics, sometimes described as "customer-focussed marketing". Being "customer-centric" means focussing on customer outcomes through achieving customer satisfaction and loyalty. Creating, maintaining and enhancing customer relationships are the essence of the relationship marketing process (Kotler, Brown, Adam, Burton & Armstrong, 2007). Table 5 outlines the integration of dialogue marketing stages to both the social media categories (Nations, 2014) and relationship marketing process. (Webster & Hume, 2015).

Nations (2014) social media categories definitions are:

- **Social Media:** Two-way social communication between people,
- **Social Networking:** People connecting and staying in touch with friends, relatives and colleagues,
- **Social News:** People reading and voting on news topics and articles,
- **Social Bookmarking:** People finding, flagging and sharing online information,
- **Social Sharing:** People creating, uploading and sharing their creations, and
- **Wiki Authoring:** People collaboratively adding and editing articles for websites and/or databases.

Customer-centric focused businesses using technology are able to more easily identify, differentiate and engage with their customers as well as communicate more personally with them (Stone and Jacobs, 2001, p.49). Technology in this sense includes online channels that support the overall customer relationship strategy (Petersen, Grone, Kammer, Kirscheneder, 2010, p.4).

To investigate the role of Dialogue Marketing further, it is important to also consider its rise to prominence as a marketing concept. According to Tahir Wafi (2014), initially there was the Marketing Mix concept originally developed by Borden (1964) which consisted of 14 elements. Jerome McCarthy refined to the concept to 4 P's (Product, Price, Place and Promotion) which subsequently appeared in a book by Philip Kotler, 'Principles of Marketing' published in 1967. The first marketing mix concept to offer a customer-centric approach was developed by Lauterborn (1990).

To understand the shifts in consumer behaviour coinciding with the rise in consumer power, Bob Lauterborn proposed a consumer marketing mix model, the '4 C's'. He reasoned that marketers needed to view the marketing mix from the consumer's perspective, i.e. 'walking in their shoes'. This meant

Table 5. Social Media dialogue marketing relationship strategies

Dialogue Marketing Stage	Recognise the Business	Know the Business	Want to Use the Business	Maintain Business Relationship
Social Media Category	*Customer Awareness*	*Customer Acquisition*	*Customer Retention/ Service*	*Customer Loyalty*
Social Media	√	√	√	√
Social Networking	√	√	√	√
Social News		√	√	√
Social Bookmarking			√	√
Social Sharing				√
Wiki Authoring				√

describing, 'product' in terms of 'consumer needs and wants', 'price' as the 'cost' to satisfy consumers wants and needs, 'place' as in the 'convenience' for consumers to buy and 'promotion' being the 'communication' marketers have with consumers. Lauterborn himself says, "All good advertising creates a dialogue".

So how could dialogue marketing be used by businesses to build relationships, add value to the experience and lead to product recommendations? Steinmetz (1997) has outlined 10 guiding principles behind successful dialogue marketing. These principles are:

- Develop a clear objectives statement
- Ensure consumers can select their own entry points
- Create a channel where consumers can respond and share information about themselves
- Don't be in a rush
- Appreciate the benefit and value of the interaction
- Continue maintaining contact
- Adopt a sequenced approach with the communication
- Based on consumer information gained, customise responses and modify tactics to suit
- Ensure the marketing database is comprehensive for dialogue marketing
- Be creative with the communication.

Table 6 compares the two marketing mix concepts with Dialogue Marketing principles and how they align. Between the Lauterborn model and the Steinmetz model, there appears to be quite a strong correlation. In understanding consumer's wants and needs, this would require businesses to 'listen'. Customised responses would be the outcome of the data collected. The cost of a successful outcome is not only money but 'time' for the customer to feel satisfied with the outcome. Steinmetz believed that customer satisfaction could be gauged through maintaining regular communication with the customer. He also believed that by providing multiple entry points and a variety of channels through which to communication was possible accentuated consumer 'convenience.' It's about making it easy for the customer to eventually buy. To maintain ongoing 'communication' also means not letting the message and the content get stale in the eyes of the consumer. Regular communication involves a systematic approach. Steinmetz's underlying premise for the dialogue marketing model was that people tended to interact more with those they already knew and trusted.

The premise, according to Steinmetz (1997) of what makes dialogue marketing work is the basic human nature principle. A relationship is built up over time through communication leading to a form of

Table 6. Marketing mix elements comparison

4 Marketing Mix P's	4 Marketing Mix C's	Dialogue Marketing Principles
Product	Consumer Wants & Needs	Objectives, Customised responses, Comprehensive data
Price	Consumer's Cost to Satisfy	Time, Contact continuity
Place	Convenience to Buy	Entry points, Channels
Promotion	Communication	Sequenced approach, Creativity
Source: McCarthy (1964)	Source: Lauterborn (1990)	Source: Steinmetz (1997)

behavioural response. In advertising this is referred to as the 'Hierarchy of Effects Model' (or purchase funnel), one of the traditional learning response hierarchy models (Belch, Belch, Kerr & Powell, 2009).

DIGITAL MARKETING MIX

In the ongoing refinement of the marketing mix concept, various contemporary models incorporating 'digital marketing' have emerged. Digital Marketing involves using various digital media, such as email, mobile phones and social networks for promotional purposes (Inwise.com, 2011). Contemporary LAM techniques used by franchise businesses include email, mobile and search engine marketing, online advertising, forums and directories as well as blogs (Webster & Hume, 2015). These techniques are in essence, digital media channels forming part of the 'digital marketing mix'.

So what would constitute the 'digital marketing mix' and what would be its elements? Various models have been proposed to describe such a mix. In 2005, the SIVA model was created by Dev and Schultz. This was enhanced to the SAVE model in 2013 by Richard Ettensen, Eduardo Conrado and Jonathon Knowles and has since then been gaining marketing practitioner traction.

The key SAVE model elements are:

- **Solutions:** Offerings defined by needs met,
- **Access:** Integrated cross-channel presence that takes into account the customer's complete purchase journey,
- **Value:** Benefits received relative to purchase price, and
- **Education:** Providing information relevant to customer's specific needs at every purchase cycle point.

The SAVE model was originally developed to explain the B2B market and the only difference between SIVA and SAVE was that the earlier model emphasises 'Information' instead of 'Education'. Information in this context related to one-way communication whereas with 'Education', the wording is two-way, meaning that information is given and received with feedback and recommendations being included to close the customer purchase cycle (Wafi, 2014).

Several years prior to the SAVE model, Fetherstonhaugh (2009) developed his 4E's model in response to what he saw as the 'information age' and improvements in technology. His 4E's model related to:

- **Experience:** How the product makes the consumer feel,
- **Everyplace:** Trialling new methods of distribution,
- **Exchange:** Perception of product value, rather than cost to buy, and
- **Evangelism:** Belief in the product, sharing the emotion with others.

Although his model was primarily designed to explain 'e-commerce', it could also be applied in non-technological environments (Wafi, 2014). Interestingly, in these contemporary marketing concept models, social media appears is not specifically mentioned even though the 4E's and SAVE models were developed after the advent of social media. In 2013, Leslie Nuccio developed the '4C's of Social Media Marketing Model specifically for social media. The elements in this 4C's model include:

- **Communities:** Social communities made up of intertwined social networks with common interests,
- **Conversations:** Social conversations around personal community interests,
- **Channels:** Various social media channels, and
- **Campaigns:** Social media campaigns.

With this model, the common thread appears to be the emphasis on information sharing and the value of the information being shared through reciprocity. For a business, the success of its social media would depend on choosing the right social media channels to conduct the ideal conversations. Successful social media strategies involve closely aligning social media community interests with relevant business goals and then fostering the right conversations that will be reciprocated by the community (Siddiqi, 2014).

In Table 7, the two digital marketing mix models are compared to the 4C's Social Media Marketing model. There appears to be an effective synergy of stages, however with social media there is the level of engagement context. In this regard, the Social Media Honeycomb framework (Keitzmann, et. al., 2011) might be a viable option but would warrant further research. Wafi (2014) believes that the SAVE model aligns with the relationship management concept because, as it steps customers through the purchase process, the relationship is continually being built. It could be argued that the 4 E's and SAVE models are not purely 'customer-centric' as there is a product emphasis in the initial stages, 'Experience' and 'Solutions' in contrast to the business engaging with its customer community first with the 4C's Social Media model. Even in the 'Value' and 'Exchange' stages, the notion of a business justifying product value appears to be at odds with fostering community interests.

Reciprocity is often the provision of first-party referrals or endorsements as part of the feedback process, as well as third-party testimonials from reliable sources. In a social media context, this would be considered 'social bookmarking' (Webster & Hume 2015). Conversations begin and are maintained, through reciprocity and sharing. At the core of the 4C's of Social Media Marketing is the sales funnel, the same one described by Lauterborn (1990), or otherwise known as the "Hierarchy of Effects model (Belch, Belch, Kerr & Powell, 2009).

HIERARCHY OF EFFECTS MODEL

Being the basis for both Steinmetz's Dialogue Marketing model (1997) and Nuccio's 4C's of Social Media Marketing model (2013), why does the Hierarchy of Effects model still have appeal as a concept? Interestingly, as reported by Belch et al. (2009) this model is also the foundation for the measuring the

Table 7. Digital marketing mix model comparison

4 E's Model	SAVE Model	4 Social Media Marketing C's
Experience	Solutions	Communities
Everyplace	Access	Channels
Exchange	Value	Campaigns
Evangelism	Education	Conversations
Source: Fetherstonhaugh (2009)	Source: Ettensen, et. al. (2013)	Source: Nuccio (2013)

effects of advertising in many decision making processes as well as for setting objectives. Lavidge and Steiner (1961) who developed the Hierarchy of Effects model discussed how each the three functions of advertising, 1) awareness and knowledge, 2) liking and preference and 3) conviction and purchase directly aligned with each of three psychological behavioural components, a) cognitive (thoughts), b) affective (emotions) and c) conative (motives). They likened their process to a flight of stairs and the evaluation as to the effectiveness of advertising would indicate measures of progression on the staircase. The logic behind the staircase analogy, Lavidge and Steiner (1961) claim is that the effects of advertising are cumulative and therefore measurement needs to consider the residual 'long-term' effects.

Leslie Nuccio (2013) in the 4C's of Social Media Marketing explains this process as the customer purchase funnel, similarly with six steps, these being: awareness, consideration, preference, purchase, loyalty and advocacy. It is part of relationship marketing which is a nurturing type model. That is, marketers need to be aware online customers will require numerous 'touches' and 'impressions' before they feel comfortable to purchase. Nuccio refers to this as 'social dialogue marketing' or in its basic form, word-of-mouth sharing. The 4C's of Social Media Marketing model was developed to provide an approach to transition from traditional marketing to social media marketing. The first step in this transition is 'social listening' which involves using social media technologies and tools (i.e. social media networks) to understand more about the target community to be pursued. This information is then used to generate meaningful and appropriate word-of-mouth conversations that can be easily shared.

Social media networks emit enhanced persona through the provision of current, authentic and focussed communication tailored to the receiver according to Artegic.com (2014), a German digital marketing firm. For businesses to embrace online dialogue marketing, they need to be open to criticism and see it as an opportunity for improvement. In the social media space, this means being a good 'listener' and tailoring personalised responses as part of two-way communication. Interestingly, Artegic.com describes the engagement process as being customer-centred. They explain the approach as one where relevant 'teaser' information is provided through social networks, encouraging people to engage through subscribing, opting-in or signing up to get the 'full version'. Another approach is to embed reward incentives for engagement, such as competition prizes directly into the specific social media platforms to elicit this engagement. In terms of measurability, they recommend lead tracking from specific social media networks.

Leslie Nuccio (2013) contends that measuring social media success can best be achieved using 'action' oriented metrics, i.e. disguised clicks in the form of shares, emails, likes, tweets and other aptly named counts. This can be likened to 'impressions' used to measure performance in traditional public relations and advertising campaigns. Given that for brand recognition, as a heuristic, it has to be seen at least seven times before it makes an 'impression', tracking these is a good metric option.

According to Nuccio (2013), where social media comes its own as a method of communication is through the combination of the personal selling dialogue (information sharing) with the enormity of traditional broadcast advertising. Using 'impressions' in tandem with 'actions' forms the basis of 'social dialogue marketing' and makes compelling sense as an indicator of solid communication channel strategy (Nuccio 2013). This sounds straightforward in theory, however for Australian SME's measuring social media success is an issue. Could Dialogue Management be a solution?

DIALOGUE MANAGEMENT

Dialogue management involves identifying and monitoring how people engage in communication and conversations within the social media networking context. The emphasis is on determining the strength and quality of that relationship and how it's managed/leveraged. Technology is the key to driving dialogue management. In a recent Economist Intelligence Unit (2014, p.8) survey report titled, "Customer Service, Marketing and Technology: Mastering the Customer Journey", which surveyed 272 customer service and marketing executives, the 5 top technologies identified as changing the way businesses operate were:

1. Mobile Technology
2. Cloud Computing
3. Social Media
4. Big Data
5. E-Commerce

For mobile technology popularity, this reinforces the 2013 Australian research that reports the percentage of social media users who accessed their accounts on smartphones and tablets increased sharply in 2013. Up from 53% the previous year, sixty-seven percent of social users surveyed accessed their accounts via smartphone, which was the highest of all the devices (eMarketer.com, 2013). According to Don Springer of Oracle (clickzintel, 2014a) businesses using cloud computing only have to store and maintain the data that is essential to them. Data will be hosted in the cloud by third parties but with the business maintaining the data.

Cloud-based data services are rapidly gaining momentum in the market, with a choice of two delivery options, a) 'emerging': this option is an "appliance" service that provides a single, reliable source of accurate business data, alongside social information about accounts, leads, contacts, etc. The second option b) 'exchange' is where premium datasets are sold in exchange for providing a rich set of Web interfaces to ease data integration, like a 'market exchange'.

'Big data' is simply a term to describe the large volume of structure, semi-structured and un-structured data that is capable of being mined. (Rouse, 2014). E-commerce technologies relate to various internet reliant functions such as text messages, emails, shopping carts, data exchanges and web based services used to conduct business over the internet (Beal, 2014). For franchise businesses, ecommerce brings with it certain issues. For one, it can change brand awareness and perception and therefore significantly influence franchise brand value. For any franchise business, brand name is everything. Territory conflict is another issue for those franchise businesses that benefit from a designated territory. Internet sales from the franchisor or other franchise businesses is often viewed as 'unfair competition' and 'territory encroachment' (Perrigot & Penart, 2013).

This may only be a concern of the franchise businesses but not their customers. An emerging platform in ecommerce that has developed out of the popularity of social media is 'social commerce.' It's using social networking sites to share information socially (social sharing) with friends about their sales or intended purchases. Consultation with social communities for purchasing decision advice is also conducted by consumers. Website functions make it easy to share this information with friends as well. Such recommendation from friends are more valuable as it strongly influences a friend's online purchases (Liang, Ho, Li & Turtan, 2011).

For businesses, it's a matter of channeling this social commerce into a single source where it can be synthesised and analysed, i.e. converting this social media communication into 'social data'. This social data is then used to provide insights about the businesses social community, their contributions, history and activities (Gross, 2012). Listening to the social commerce is the first step in the 'social relationship management' process. It is hearing what people are saying about the business, its products and its people on various social media channels.

The social relationship management (SRM) process consists of 6 steps, Listen, Engage, Create, Publish, Manage and Analyse according to Oracle (clickzintel, 2014a, p.5). 'Engage' is where a business actually interacts with its fans and followers in ways prompting further community engagement, such as with questions, proving feedback to comments, and answering posts, etc. 'Create' is about developing resources, such as online content and web applications based on engagement feedback to maintain the engagement cycle. These resources are then published across social media channels. The 'Manage' step in the SRM process focuses on ensuring the business communicates with its community in a consistent manner. With the 'Analyse' step, its emphasis is on the metrics and outcomes and where can improve on social performance.

This is where the integration of social technologies within a CRM system becomes an effective business tool. According to Paul Greenberg from Oracle (clickzintel, 2014b, p.6) in response to customer's controlling conversations, 'social CRM' has emerged as a tool to engage customers in mutually beneficial interactive conversations. He states that, "social CRM is a philosophy and a business strategy supported by a technology platform, business rules and characteristics." Again, all good in theory but when it's reported that 75% of SMEs do not have a CRM system and only 39% have a digital marketing plan (CCIQ Digital Readiness Survey, 2013), then the goalposts blur. When it came to use of various technologies, nearly 60% of respondents who didn't indicated it was due to a lack of knowledge or understanding about them. They were unsure as to which technologies to adopt and they didn't know what they really wanted in terms of outcomes. On top of that, over 50% of businesses were worried about the shortage of digital skills to drive and manage these technologies. Given that 98% of all Australian businesses are responsible for their own online presence (Sensis Yellow Pages Australia, 2014), it would be reasonable to assume based on the various survey findings that they have become overwhelmed with all this current emphasis on technology.

A more holistic approach to identifying and monitoring how people engage in communication and conversations with businesses would be to analyse business contact points. Contact points for franchise businesses would be the LAM techniques, both traditional (direct marketing) and contemporary (digital marketing channels) they use to engage with their local community (Webster & Hume, 2015). For businesses in general, these contact points would be all those interactions (human and physical) where they keep in 'touch' with their customers during the life of their relationship (Bradbury & Coons, 2007).

TOUCHPOINTS

Given the focus of this chapter, contact points or 'touchpoints' will be viewed from a digital marketing channel perspective. Using the SRM process, how can businesses communicate with their communities in a consistent manner? It is contended that this could be achieved through Dialogue Marketing and an integrated customer loyalty strategy approach. Online marketing expert Joanna Lord (Bigdoor, 2014, p.16) believes that customer loyalty should start for a business when an online community member first discovers the business. At every step of the customer journey, businesses should be creating opportunities to seed customer loyalty. Alex Gonzalez (2014) agrees that online consumers are now more social about their purchasing decision making and are increasingly going online for their advice, ideas and inspiration. Consumers are now, "critics, experts, advocates and influencers" states Gonzalez, co-founder of Chatalog. Social media and content strategist Jay Baer (Convinceandconvert.com, 2014), suggests that the goal for businesses should be to increase the variety of ways they can connect with people who have an interest in them through maximising social connection 'touchpoints' to gain maximum connection possibilities.

According to J-P De Clerck (2014), it's more than just increasing the number of digital marketing channels, its aligning experiences, goals, intent/purpose, context and channels to some tangible value for the customer within a context where touchpoints are activated through interest. This he asserts is the basis for 'touchpoint marketing'. Rather than focussing on 'content' alone as the prime marketing strategy, De Clerck maintains it is understanding the confines as to why people engage, i.e. their individual customer experiences and the specific touchpoint relevance where a business should concentrate its marketing efforts. As De Clerck (2014) states, "consistent customer experiences across channels lead to recommendations, retention and loyalty." Touchpoints can be either direct, indirect or invisible. Examples of direct touchpoints would be having some personal experience with a business such as, 'filling in a form', or 'clicking on a link', i.e. direct contact. Indirect touchpoints are those social interactions, word-of-mouth and value sharing contributions whereas invisible are those experiences that are non-visible, i.e. from the other four senses (sound, taste, smell and feeling) that are sometimes passed off as being random or by chance.

So what makes up a touchpoint? From J-P De Clerck's (2014) perspective it involves subject (interacting with people), intent (purpose of the interaction), social object (interaction creation content), and context (social environment). These elements together become the catalyst for a common significance convergence where businesses have the opportunity for conversion. Gonzalez (2014) believes there are 8 touchpoints that consumers use as part of their online decision making process.

These 8 touchpoints he lists as are:

- **Discovery Platforms:** For product ideas and inspiration,
- **Influencers and Bloggers:** For trusted opinions from expert sources,
- **Affinity Groups and Communities:** For opinions/feedback from reliable third party sources,
- **Social Networks:** For opinions from most trusted friends,
- **Social Media Platforms:** For additional influencer perceptions,
- **Consumer Reviews:** Relevant purchaser comments,
- **Direct Communication:** Live business contact,
- **In-Store via Mobile:** Live purchase decision feedback.

Gambetti and Graffigna (2010) in their research on consumer engagement refer to context as the ninth touchpoint, 'Social Environment', i.e. locations where people socialise that can nurture the growth of consumer engagement. As these are 'consumer touchpoints', according to Li and Kannan (2014), they are typically consumer initiated in their search for information. Business initiated touchpoints on the other hand are business marketing strategies, such as targeting potential customers through email marketing or advertising.

Business initiated brand touchpoints according to Di Marca (2012) are those contact points that interface the customer with the business's brand. They are the 'moments of truth' in the battle to position a business's brand in the minds of consumers. Brand reputation and trust is built on customer's experiences with these touchpoints having the power to spark dialogue and build relationships by creating consistently motivating and positive images, emotions and associations.

What Are Brand Touchpoints?

Scott Davis and Tina Longoria (2003, p.1) define brand touchpoints as, "all the different ways a brand interacts with and makes an impression with customers, employees and other stakeholders. Every action, tactic and strategy your brand has with customers or stakeholders whether it's through advertising, a merchandising display or a customer service call, it is a brand touchpoint."

Davis and Longoria (2003) segment brand touchpoints by customer experience in terms of 'pre-purchase', 'purchase' or 'post-purchase'. Examples of brand touchpoints in these segments include:

- **Pre-Purchase:** Advertising, direct mail/samples, coupons and incentives, deals and coupons,
- **Purchase:** Sales people, store and shelf placement, P-O-P displays, packaging, and
- **Post-Purchase:** Loyalty programs, newsletters, customer service, product and package performance.

Michael Paffenback (n.d.) in his Touchpointers.com blog similarly views brand touchpoints in three stages, pre-purchase, purchase and post-purchase. Jonas Persson (2012) based his Brand Touchpoint Matrix, on the belief that brand touchpoints should lead customers through the: consider, evaluate, buy, enjoy/advocate/bond phases and create increasing levels of value as they travel along the 'consumer decision journey'.

Steve Yastrow (n.d.) suggests that brand touchpoints fall into four categories:

1. When customer learns about the product (brand),
2. When the customer goes through product buying process,
3. When the customer maintains and uses the product (brand), and
4. When the customer informs other people about the product (brand) or merely thinks doing so.

This he describes as the customer relationship lifecycle with the product.

What Are Customer Touchpoints?

SurveyMonkey.com (2014) define 'customer touchpoints' as a "brands point of customer contact, from start to finish". They go on to further define it as "any time a potential customer or customer comes in contact with your brand – before, during and after they purchase something from you". SurveyMonkey even provide a list of touchpoints under the categories of 'before purchase', 'during purchase' and 'after purchase'.

The major conclusions to be drawn from this discussion are that, a) 'brand touchpoints' and 'customer touchpoints are essentially the same thing, 'touchpoints', b) there appears to be marketing practitioner consensus over the categorising of touchpoints and c) touchpoint customer lifecycles appear to follow a customer loyalty approach. To further elaborate on touchpoint categories, Denise Lee Yohn (2013-14) groups the three brand touchpoint segments as 'interactions' with customers. Brand touchpoints such advertising and packaging she refers to as 'static'. Call centres and sales people Denise labels as 'people' touchpoints whilst social media and websites she denotes as 'interactive' touchpoints.

Touchpoints, Jeannie Walters (2013) claims are mistakenly described. Most touchpoints are in fact conduits or channels indicating the connection method, not the actual interaction undertaken. These touchpoint channels are business oriented not customer-centric focused. An example of the distinction between the two would be, touchpoint channel: 'social media', touchpoint: 'Facebook chat'. The touchpoint is the action or experience from engaging with the touchpoint channel.

An additional perspective to the defining of 'touchpoints', is this notion of touchpoint 'affective commitment'. Iglesias, Singh and Batista-Foguet (2011) argue consumers with increased experiences are more likely to develop heightened levels of customer loyalty due to their propensity for affective commitment. In their research they define affective commitment (Allen & Meyer 1990) as the level of consumer emotional attachment to a specific brand or business based on brand recognition. Wilson and Morgan (2011) refer to this as a 'state of resonance' brand consumer bond. They suggest that sense of intimacy generated stems from brands being human personified. Brand contact intimacy is therefore the emotional mirror existing where consumers also project and graft their own emotions onto brands. Valued brand experience, is what Jonas Persson (2012) considered were the keys to a businesses success which is in agreement with the Iglesias, Singh and Batista-Foguet assertions. Given the diversity of touchpoints, Yandav and Pavlou (2014) argue that even if the businesses offline and online emphasis differed in context, the consumer's underlying behavioural processes will most likely be similar.

So where is this leading to? Businesses when analysing the value of their touchpoints need to consider a) channel, b) action response and c) emotional attachment.

From an academic perspective, has there been any consistency in how marketing practitioners view 'touchpoints' or 'touchpoint channels'? For ease of continuing discussion, 'touchpoint channels' have been described under the term 'touchpoints'.

TOUCHPOINTS REVIEW

One of the authors, Geoff Webster conducted an internet review over 2 days analysing images for the keyword term, 'touchpoints' in Google images. As a convenience sample, he selected for his review the first 31 images that appeared. The review considered; a) industry focus, b) touchpoints present, c) touchpoint categories and d) theoretical model connectivity. Review observation questions included:

- Was there an industry focus present?
- How many touchpoints could be observed?
- Were these touchpoints categorised in some way?
- Was there reference to a theoretical model?

Where there was a reference to a theoretical model, appropriate identifications were sought. For 'Response Process', this included any of the Response Process models such as AIDA model and the Hierarchy of Effects model (Belch, Belch, Kerr & Powell, 2009). Steinmetz (1997) in describing his Dialogue Marketing Principles discussed earlier, notes that the centre of Dialogue Marketing is the Hierarchy of Effects model or 'Purchase Funnel'. With 'Decision Making Process', this included any of the purchase involvement and types of consumer decision making models (Neal, Quester and Hawkins,

2002). Relationship Marketing included any reference the customer relationship stages, awareness, acquisition, retention/service and loyalty emphasising a customer-centric approach as also earlier discussed.

In summary, from the Touchpoint Review (Table 8), 39% had an industry focus, 87% had a touchpoint presence, 48% had touchpoints categorised, and 32% were linked to theoretical models.

Industry Focus

It is noted that 61% were not industry specific, suggesting the images were to serve a generic purpose. The industries depicted also were quite diverse.

Touchpoints

Even though a significant number listed touchpoints (87%), there were still 13% that included no touchpoints even though the images were about touchpoints. The average number of touchpoints was just under 17 and the range was quite wide from 0 - 47. The nature of the specific touchpoints did vary widely from image to image and would provide excellent subject material for future research.

Touchpoint Categories

About half of the images (48%) had categorised their touchpoints. Similarly, the specific categories also varied widely across the image array additionally offering ideal data for future research.

Theoretical Model Connectivity

What is interesting here is that of the 32% that linked to a theoretical model only 2 images (6%) also had an industry focus. When identifying theoretical model connectivity, 60% (6) connected to the Decision Making Process, whilst 30% (3) connected to the 'Response Process' and 10% (1) only related to the Relationship Marketing Stages.

From the researcher's observations, the overwhelming emphasis with the touchpoints appears to be on a 'purchase' onus, i.e. response process and decision making process rather than one on 'relationship', i.e. relationship marketing stages. Also, of the images reviewed in Table 7, 19% (6) only indicated touchpoints and an additional 16% (5) had touchpoints and categories, making up a total of 35% of images being purely generic in nature meaning they relate to nothing specifically. This would indicate disconcerting fragmentation amongst marketing practitioners as to their interpretation and application of touchpoints. Further evidence of this divide is coming from marketing practitioners themselves where they distinguish between 'marketers' and 'modern marketers' as well as in the use of buzz phrases such marketing qualified leads, digital body language and lead scoring (clickzintel, 2014b).

Frequencies reported in the form of Yes/Number count.

In observing the touchpoint images, a significant proportion were depicted as being a a) pie/circle, b) mind map, c) matrix or d) cycle. Many of the images represented as a cycle included linkages to the customer strategy stages, i.e. the Hierarchy of Effects Model (Lavidge & Steiner, 1961) or more commonly the "Purchase Funnel". The descriptions of these customer strategy stages differed slightly image to image, but the contexts are essentially the same. A comparison of the first five cycle images with linked customer strategy stages has been compiled in Table 9 to highlight the similarities in descriptions.

Table 8. Touchpoints review

Image	Industry Focus	Touchpoints	Categories	Theoretical Model
1	-	24	√	Response Process
2	Small Business	18	√	-
3	Retail	17	-	-
4	-	10	-	-
5	-	4	√	-
6	-	17	-	-
7	-	17	√	Response Process
8	Supplier	-	-	-
9	-	8	-	Decision Making Process
10	Healthcare	4	√	-
11	-	33	√	-
12	Baby Care	16	√	-
13	-	11	-	-
14	Beer Brewing	21	√	Decision Making Process
15	-	10	√	-
16	Travel	8	-	-
17	-	47	√	Response Process
18	Finance	19	√	-
19	-	21	-	Decision Making Process
20	-	16	-	Decision Making Process
21	-	11	√	-
22	-	9	√	-
23	Small Business	9	-	-
24	Childcare	-	-	-
25	-	15	√	Decision Making Process
26	-	13	√	Relationship Marketing Stages
27	-	-	-	-
28	Furniture	23	-	Decision Making Process
29	-	33	-	-
30	Art	-	-	-
31	-	21	-	-
No.	**12**	**455**	**15**	**10**

The table also shows how these customer strategy stages fit within Steinmetz's (1997) Dialogue Marketing stages. From the observations it was noted that within the cycle images some of the touchpoints were repeated. This suggested a model for collating and categorising touchpoints on the basis of engagement was warranted.

Table 9. Touchpoint cycles comparison

Customer Strategy Stage Descriptions								Source
Pre-purchase				***Purchase***	***Post-purchase***			Michael Paffenback (n.d)
Awareness			Consideration	Purchase		Service	Loyalty	B2bstories.com
Awareness			Consideration	Purchase		Retention	Advocacy	Garymagnone.com
	Discover	Compare	Consider	Commit		Retain		Bigdoor.com
Awareness		Evaluation		Purchase	Usage	Repurchase	Advocacy	Ecommercemanagers.com
Awareness	Discovery			Engagement	Active client	Successful client	Refer	Nickmangham.wordpress.com
Recognise the business		***Know the business***		***Use the business***		***Maintain business relationship***		Steinmetz (1997)

PROPOSED TOUCHPOINT CHANNEL ENGAGEMENT MODEL

In the previous discussion about touchpoints and touchpoint channels, researchers were divided on how to categorise them. For example, Davis and Longoria (2003) suggested segmenting touchpoints by "experience". Denise Lee Yohn (2013-14) proposed that they should be segmented by "interactions". Li and Kannan (2014) and Di Marcia (2012) outlined classifying touchpoints by who "initiated" them. Webster and Hume (2015) when describing traditional and contemporary LAM techniques used by franchise businesses profiled touchpoints by their "type" as either physical or digital in form. De Clerck (2014) portrayed touchpoints as being "direct" or "indirect" by their engagement with people.

Based on the Jeannie Walters (2013) concept of touchpoint channels, a model to categorise these channels is proposed. The proposed Touchpoint Channel Engagement Model allows segmentation of touchpoint channels. With segmentation, a business can determine whether it has the correct mix and balance of touchpoint channels for engagement with its community. This requires a two step process. Step 1 involves creating an inventory list of a business's touchpoint channels. As an example, a touchpoint channel such as, 'Facebook' would be listed on the inventory list as shown in Table 10.

In Step 2, each of the "Touchpoint Channels" would be mapped to a "Touchpoint Channel Triangle" (Figure 1) on the basis of 'Type', 'Initiation' and 'Experience'. The 'Form' description would be denoted with the number of the touchpoint channel, i.e. 1I (Social Media – Facebook), 2D (Billboard). The intention is to develop a touchpoint channel mix based on engagement segmentation. With the touchpoint channel mix mapped, the Touchpoint Channel Triangle could then be used as a gap analysis tool to

Table 10. Touchpoint channel inventory list

No	Description	Form		Type		Initiation		Experience	
		Direct	**Indirect**	**Physical**	**Digital**	**Consumer**	**Business**	**Interactive**	**Static**
1	**Social Media – Facebook**		√		√	√		√	
2	**Billboard**	√		√			√		√

determine if businesses have the right balance of touchpoint channels. This would also form the basis for ongoing touchpoint channel testing.

This proposed model is theoretical only and field testing is yet to be undertaken. It is envisaged that this will occur as part of future research.

CONTRIBUTIONS OF THIS MODEL

This conceptual research furthers the discourse into the role of local area marketing techniques or more commonly known as touchpoints and how they relate to dialogue marketing and management. The particular emphasis was initially on franchise businesses with small to medium enterprises (SMEs) in the broader context, given the limited academic material available on LAM and social media engagement techniques for franchise businesses. It reflected on various areas of digital marketing including, marketing mix, digital revolution impacts on dialogue marketing, ROI emphasis shift from 'hard' to 'soft' metric options, functions of social media and implications, social media marketing mix alignment to Hierarchy of Effects Model, uptake of social customer relationship management strategies using dialogue management techniques, researching and reviewing touchpoints as a means of interactive community engagement and understanding dialogue marketing in the customer strategy process. It considered these theories as a system of relationships not previously examined and by doing so has conceptualised a new and original approach to touchpoints and community engagement. A touchpoint channel engagement model has been proposed integrating various touchpoint segmentation methods including by type, experience, initiation and form into an easy to understand triangular matrix that business can use as a map.

Continuing this study to analyse the role of Social Media in Dialogue Marketing as a contemporary Local Area Marketing (LAM) technique has enabled the authors to propose a model that may provide a missing link for marketing practitioners and advance the area of knowledge with respect to touchpoints.

Figure 1. Touchpoint channel triangle

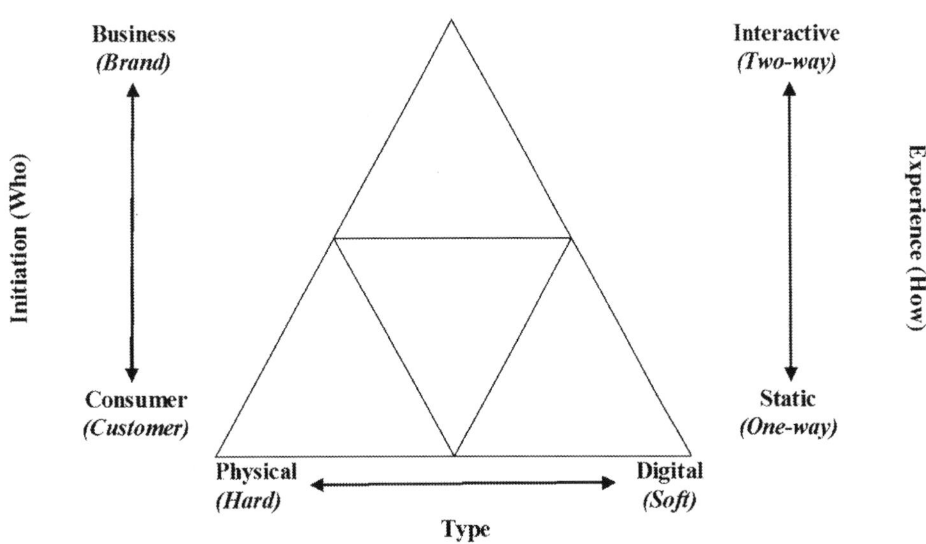

The study identified knowledge gaps in the application of touchpoints especially amongst marketing practitioners. Locating these voids has led to a better understanding of touchpoints and touchpoint channels. This now heightens the need for a consistent approach to classifying and categorising touchpoint channels and touchpoint engagement. The touchpoint review confirmed the reciprocity concept as to not only providing the basis for a business, in particular franchise businesses to identify their social media level standing but also outline gap opportunities to further engage with its community.

LIMITATIONS AND FUTURE RESEARCH DIRECTIONS

In reading this chapter, there were a number of limitations that should be taken into consideration. Firstly, qualitative research was limited to the perusing of topic related material including business industry white papers including marketing practitioner survey reports and academic journals as well as online touchpoint image convenience sample observations. Secondly, this work is theoretical only in nature with testing yet to occur. This is earmarked as future research.

Research into dialogue marketing identified that the stages were very similar to customer strategy stages as well as the Hierarchy of Effects Model, purchase funnel steps. This prompted a comparison of touchpoint cycles featuring customer strategy stages. From the sample, there were a number of images observed where touchpoints were associated with various customer strategy stages. Confirming the strength of these associations especially to social media categories could be the subject of future research. Several contemporary digital marketing mix concepts were compared with a potential social marketing mix being possibly identified. Another avenue for future research would be research into a digital marketing mix that incorporates social media as well as dialogue management technologies.

An online touchpoint image review was undertaken observing how touchpoints were represented. The review focused on what images were industry specific, the number of touchpoint examples listed, the relevance of touchpoint channel categories and justification linkages to decision inducing theoretical models, i.e. for sales, customer loyalty, decision making, etc. Of the 31 images observed, 61% had no industry focus, 52% did not listing touchpoints by category and 68% without being justified by a theoretical model. Given that this was a preliminary study, the findings suggest an inconsistent application and that further research to be undertaken. This research will include an investigation into social media touchpoint channel audience engagement and the implications on business through the application of the Social Media Honeycomb (Kietzmann, et. al., 2011).

Future research will be examining social media metrics especially to identify those that reflect social engagement trends and the most appropriate dialogue management technologies. Even though there is a trend toward referral and text measures for social media metrics, a goal for future research would be establish industry benchmarks. Industry benchmark metrics would provide a comparison when monitoring data on content engagement, conversations, touchpoint channels and social media campaigns. From a business perspective it's vital to understand which dialogue management technologies are more profitable. For a franchise business, it's important to know which touchpoints or local area marketing techniques and dialogue marketing strategies are working to build relationships as well as identifying any contact gaps. With social media marketing, it is understanding which touchpoint channels provide the best levels of engagement. Given that digital marketing expenditure and mobile broadband penetration increasing, knowing where to focus local area marketing efforts is essential for survival. The question would be then does digital marketing provide value to a business. It is estimated that by 2016, more internet searches will be undertaken by mobile devices than by desktop computers warranting increased research and understanding into dialogue management. From a cultural context, is there a trend to using regional based technologies (i.e. geographic based search engines) and how might such a development affect social media engagement? Future research into the impact of digital body language and its influence on touchpoints could be of benefit.

Determining the success of touchpoints to create emotional attachment with a brand or a business is currently a popular topic amongst marketing practitioners and warrants academic attention. A focus of this research would relate to the type of emotional attachment that has the most success in engaging people, i.e. is it emotional bonding through image association, brand persona, character personality or narrative. Typically it's connected with brand/product positioning. As a benchmark for emotional attachment, a recent development for franchise businesses, the Vende Social Franchise Social Index (FSI) ranks on a weekly basis how well franchise industry brands are engaging on social media sites such as Facebook and Twitter. Further research into the effectiveness of such indexes to flag trends when mapped against a social media marketing mix would be worthwhile.

Being able to map touchpoint channels is just one component in the process of measuring the value of customer contacts or engagement. Kaplan and Haenlein (2010) alluded to where business might go with their social media strategies in the future and that would be into virtual worlds. Given the sophistication of Enterprise Resource Planning (ERP) tools, it is not too implausible to think about simulated business environments in virtual worlds where business and marketing strategies are tested as well as new products and services being developed, all though the use of social media with real data (i.e. customer demographics and preferences). As for future social media research, there is no doubt it will continue.

CONCLUSION

This research furthers the discourse into the role of local area marketing techniques as it relates to dialogue marketing and management with particular emphasis on franchise businesses. The following conclusions can be drawn from this study. There is no standardised approach in the identification of a business's level of social media adoption. Marketing practitioners also appear to be divided over which applicable methods are applicable in determining appropriate touchpoint channels. There is an implicit assertion that dialogue marketing has consensus as a relationship building strategy. As technology evolves, especially mobile technology, dialogue management strategies such as online environmental diagnostic tools are becoming more prevalent as a preferred option to manage touchpoints. Although businesses are using touchpoints to engage with communities and customers, there appears to be minimal research into the value of these connections (i.e. frequency and level), albeit due to a lack of industry focus or theoretical supporting framework.

The chapter proposed a Touchpoint Channel Engagement Model (Touchpoint Channel Triangle) to better understand how businesses manage their dialogue and to identify potential contact gaps. This model provided linkages to the marking, digital marketing and social media mixes through the perceptual mapping of a business's touchpoints. Such mapping would enable testing of alternate touchpoint mixes to identify potential implications for business and determine suitable mix balances. For social media touchpoint testing, the use of the Social Media Honeycomb (Kietzmann, et. al., 2011) could be appropriate.

The chapter identified that digital marketing expenditure is trending upwards to the point of exceeding traditional marketing within the near future. The question for small to medium size businesses is how can they sustain and subsequently justify the associated cost increases to maintain their online presence. This chapter outlines areas for future research into social media including metrics benchmarks, the effects of mobile technology penetration and the subsequent impacts on digital marketing budgets. Any future research into Dialogue Marketing should also cover the personification of business brands and the creation of emotional attachment to prompt enhanced touchpoint engagement.

REFERENCES

Allen, N. J., & Meyer, J. P. (1990). The measurement and antecedents of affective, continuance and normative commitment to the organization. *Journal of Occupational Psychology*, 63(1).

Artegic.com. (2014). *What Social Media Can Do for Your Dialogue Marketing*. Retrieved from https://www.artegic.com/eCRM/0,215645635f6964092d0933333734/EN/news/d0.html

Beal, V. (2014). *Electronic Commerce (ecommerce)*. Retrieved from http://www.webopedia.com/TERM/E/electronic_commerce.html

Belch, G. E., Belch, M. A., Kerr, G., & Powell, I. (2009). *Advertising and Promotion: An Integrated Marketing Communication Perspective*. Sydney, Australia: McGraw Hill.

Bigdoor.com. (2014). *A Marketers Guide to Customer Loyalty*. Retrieved from http://bigdoor.com/resources/marketers-guide-to-customer-loyalty/

Borden, N. H. (1964). The Concept of the Marketing Mix. In G. Schwartz (Ed.), Science in Marketing. New York, NJ: John Wiley.

Boyce, J. (2002). *Market Research in Practice*. Sydney, Australia: McGraw Hill.

Bradbury, T., & Coons, D. (2007). *Customer Touchpoints – Your Brand in Action*. Retrieved from http://www.thesmartbuilder.com/whitepapers/SMART_Whitepaper_-_Touchpoints.pdf

Burg, N. (2013). *How to Measure Your Social Media Return on Investment*. Retrieved from http://www.forbes.com/sites/capitalonespark/2013/04/25/how-to-measure-your-social-media-return-on-investment/

Cciq.com.au. (2012). *2012 Digital Readiness Study*. Retrieved from http://www.cciq.com.au/assets/Documents/Digital/DigitalReadiness-Report-final-web.pdf

Cciq.com.au. (2013). *2013 Digital Readiness Survey*. Retrieved from http://www.cciq.com.au/industries/technology/digital-readiness-study/

Clickzintel.com. 2014a. *The Value of Social Data*. Retrieved from http://www.clickzintel.com/download/getting-true-value-social-20281

Clickzintel.com. 2014b. *Conversion: Along the Suspect to Advocate Journey*. Retrieved from http://www.clickzintel.com/abstract/conversion-suspect-advocate-journey-22997

CMOSurvey.org. (2014). *CMO Survey Report: Highlights and Insights, August 2014*. Retrieved from http://cmosurvey.org/files/2014/09/The_CMO_Survey-Highlights_and_Insights-Aug-2014.pdf

Convinceandconvert.com. (2014). *Social Circles Use Social Media to Build a Touchpoint Corral*. Retrieved from http://www.convinceandconvert.com/social-media-strategy/social-circles-use-social-media-to-build-a-touchpoint-corral/

Corstjens, M. & Umblijs, A. (2012). The Power of Evil – The Damage of Negative Social Media Strongly Outweigh Positive Contributions. *Journal of Advertising Research*, December, 52(4), 433-449.

Davis, S., & Longoria, T. (2003). *Harmonizing your Touchpoints*. Retrieved October 16, 2014, from https://www.prophet.com/downloads/articles/Harmonizing%20Your%20Touchpoints%20(SD%20TL).pdf

De Clerck, J.-P. (2014). *Is Touchpoint Marketing the Only Marketing Left?* Retrieved from http://www.i-scoop.eu/touchpoint-marketing-marketing-left/

Dimarca.com.au. (2012). *Build the Brand Experience Through Touch Points*. Retrieved from http://www.dimarca.com.au/brand-touch-points.aspx

Economist Intelligence Unit. (2014). *EIU Survey Report: Customer Service, Marketing and Technology: Mastering the Customer Journey*. Retrieved from http://www.cio.co.uk/cmsdata/whitepapers/3508924/Customer_service_marketing_and_technology_Mastering_the_customer_journey.pdf

eMarketer.com. (2014). *In Australia, Mobile Propels More Time Spent on Social*. Retrieved from http://www.emarketer.com/Articles/Print.aspx?R=1009951

Ettenson, R. Eduardo, C. & Knowles, J. (2013). Rethinking the 4Ps. *Harvard Business Review*, 91(1), 26.

Fetherstonhaugh, B. (2009). *The 4Ps are out, the 4Es are in*. OgilvyOne worldwide- New York, Retrieved from http//www.ogilvyone.com.ph/downloads/The4PsAreOutthe4EsAreIn.pdf

Financial-dictionary.thefreedictionary.com. (2014). *Dialogue Marketing*. Retrieved from http://financial-dictionary.thefreedictionary.com/Dialogue+Marketing

Franchise.edu.au. (2014). *2014 Franchising Australia Report*. Retrieved from https://www.franchise.edu.au/__data/assets/pdf_file/0009/657063/FranchisingAustralia2014_webversion.pdf?bustCache=93366477&webSyncID=ab0cfc4d-39e7-41ad-b380-0eda5d1b3503&sessionGUID=08846ed5-e354-4c7e-aa14-4a24feb9b611

Franchisemarketingsystems.com. (2014). *Franchise Marketing Systems will sell your franchise for you*. Retrieved from http://www.franchisemarketingsystems.com/services/franchise-sales/

Frazer, L., Weaven, S., & Bodey, K. (2012). *Franchising Australia 2012 Report*. Retrieved from http://www.franchise.org.au/images/FranchisingAustralia2012fullreport.pdf

Gambetti, R. C., & Graffigna, G. (2010). The concept of Engagement: A Systematic Analysis of the Ongoing Marketing Debate. *International Journal of Market Research, 52*(6), 801–826. doi:10.2501/S147078531020166

Gonzales, A. (2014). *The Eight Touchpoints of a Customers Consideration Phase*. Retrieved from http://www.marketingprofs.com/opinions/2014/24455/the-eight-touchpoints-of-a-customers-consideration-phase

Griffith.edu.au. (2012). *2012 Franchising Australia Report*. Retrieved from https://www.griffith.edu.au/__data/assets/pdf_file/0005/571793/Franchising-Australia-2012-full-report-compressed.pdf

Gross, T. S. (2012). *Social Relationship Management …Is In Your Future*. Retrieved from http://www.forbes.com/sites/prospernow/2012/02/20/social-relationship-management-is-in-your-future/

Iab.net. (2014). *Digital Content Newfronts: Video Ads Spend Study April 2014*. Retrieved from http://www.iab.net/media/file/2014_IAB_Digital_NewFronts.pdf

Iglesias, O., Singh, J., & Batista-Foguet, J. (2011). The role of brand experience and affective commitment in determining brand loyalty. *Journal of Brand Management*, *18*(8), 570–582. doi:10.1057/bm.2010.58

Inwise.com. (2011). *What is Digital Marketing?* Retrieved from http://www.inwise.com/about/what's-digital-marketing.aspx

Johnson, B. (2014). *Revenue, Staffing, Stocks and Digital Show Growth for Agencies in 2014 Report*. Retrieved from http://adage.com/article/agency-news/2014-agency-report-revenue-staffing-stocks-digital/292849/

Jones, R. (2009). *Social Media Marketing 101, Part 1*. Retrieved from http://sbinfocanada.about.com/gi/o.htm?zi=1/XJ&zTi=1&sdn=sbinfocanada&cdn=money&tm=1059&gps=451_10_1887_1024&f=00&tt=8&bt=6&bts=6&zu=http%3A//searchenginewatch.com/3632809

Kaplan, A. M., & Haenlein, M. (2010). Users of the world, unite! The challenges and opportunities of Social Media. *Business Horizons*, *53*(1), 59–68. doi:10.1016/j.bushor.2009.09.003

Kietzmann, J. H., Hermkens, K., McCarthy, I. P., & Silvestre, B. S. (2011). Social Media? Get serious! Understanding the functional building blocks of social media. *Business Horizons*, *54*(3), 241–251. doi:10.1016/j.bushor.2011.01.005

Kinnear, T. C., & Taylor, J. R. (1988). *Marketing Research: An Applied Approach* (3rd ed.). Singapore: McGraw Hill.

Koreatimes.co.kr. (2013). *Dialogue Marketing: Having a Two-way Conversation*. Retrieved from http://www.koreatimes.co.kr/www/news/biz/2014/03/331_131812.html

Kotler, P., Brown, L., Adam, S., Burton, S., & Armstrong, G. (2007). *Marketing* (7th ed.). Sydney, Australia: Pearson Education.

Kumar, R. (1996). *Research Methodology: A Step-by-Step Guide for Beginners*. Melbourne, Australia: Addison Wesley Longman.

Lauterborn, R. (1990). New Marketing Litany: 4Ps Passé; C-Words Take Over. *Advertising Age*, *61*(41), 26–28.

Lavidge, R. J., & Steiner, G. A. (1961). A Model for Predictive Measurements of Advertising Effectiveness. *Journal of Marketing*, *25*(6), 59–62. doi:10.2307/1248516

Lee Yahn, D. (2013). *Brand Touchpoint Wheel – Worksheet*. Retrieved from http://deniseleeyohn.com/wp-content/uploads/2013/12/WGBD-Download-Brand-Touchpoint-Wheel-Worksheet.pdf

Li, H., & Kannan, P. K. (2014). Attributing Conversions in a Multichannel Online Marketing Environment: An Empirical Model and a Field Experiment. *JMR, Journal of Marketing Research*, *51*(1), 40–56. doi:10.1509/jmr.13.0050

Liang, T., Ho, Y., Li, Y. & Turton E. (2011). What Drives Social Commerce: The Role of Social Support and Relationship Quality. *International Journal of Electronic Commerce,* 16(2), 69–90.

Marketingcharts.com. (2014a). *Marketing Budget Shifts from Traditional to Digital Media Might be Slowing*. Retrieved from http://www.marketingcharts.com/online/marketing-budget-shifts-from-traditional-to-digital-media-may-be-slowing-42159/

Marketingcharts.com. (2014b). *Are Young People Watching less TV?* Retrieved from http://www.marketingcharts.com/television/are-young-people-watching-less-tv-24817/

McColl-Kennedy, J. R., & Kiel, G. C. (2000). *Marketing – A Strategic Approach*. Melbourne, Australia: Nelson Thompson Learning.

Nations, D. (2014). *What is Social Media?* Retrieved from http://webtrends.about.com/od/web20/a/social-media.htm

Neal, C., Quester, P. G., & Hawkins, D. (2002). *Consumer Behaviour – Implications for Marketing Strategy* (3rd ed.). Sydney, Australia: McGraw-Hill Irwin.

Nuccio, L. (2013). *Social Dialogue Marketing Metrics Drives Word-of-Mouth*. Retrieved from http://www.meltwater.com/social-media-blog/social-dialogue-marketing/

Ostrow, A. (2011). *Kindle Books Now Outselling Paperbacks at Amazon*. Retrieved from http://mashable.com/2011/01/27/kindle-books-outselling-paperbacks/

Paffenback, M. (2011). *How To Identify Your Brand Touchpoints*. Retrieved from http://www.touchpointers.com/2011/10/11/how-to-identify-your-brand-touchpoints/

Pearson, N., Larson, E. W., & Gray, C. F. (2013). *Project Management in Practice* (1st ed.). Sydney, Australia: McGraw-Hill Education.

Perrigot, R., & Penard, T. (2013, Spring). Determinants of Economic Strategy in Franchising: A Resources –Based View in Franchising. *International Journal of Electronic Commerce*, *17*(3), 109–130. doi:10.2753/JEC1086-4415170305

Persson, J. (2012). *Brand Touchpoint Matrix*. Retrieved from http://brandtouchpointmatrix.com/

Petersen, M., Grone, F., Kammer, K., & Kirscheneder, J. (2010). *Multi-Channel Customer Management: Delighting Consumers, Driving Efficiency*. Retrieved from http://www.strategyand.pwc.com/media/uploads/Multi-Channel_Customer_Management.pdf

Rouse, M. (2014). *Big Data*. Retrieved from http://searchcloudcomputing.techtarget.com/definition/big-data-Big-Data

Rubin, G. (2014). *Effective National Marketing Policies for Your Local Franchisees*. Retrieved from http://www.franchising.com/articles/effective_national_marketing_policies_for_your_local_franchisees.html

Selby, E. (2014). *The Big Misunderstanding About Social Media Marketing*. Retrieved from http://www.maxxdesignblog.co.uk/integrated-marketing/social-media-marketing/social-media-berkshire/

Sensis.com.au. (2014). *Yellow Social Media Report*. Retrieved from https://www.sensis.com.au/content/dam/sas/PDFdirectory/Yellow-Social-Media-Report-2014.pdf

Siddiqi, A. (2014). *From Monologue to Dialogue With the Right Technology and the 4 C's of Social Media Marketing*. Retrieved from http://www.mediabuzz.com.sg/asian-emarketing/Social-Media/1855-from-monologue-to-dialogue-with-the-right-technology-and-the-four-cs-of-social-media-marketing

Smith, C. (2014). *One-Third of Marketers Generate a Return on Their Social Media Efforts*. Retrieved from http://www.businessinsider.com.au/one-third-of-marketers-generate-a-return-on-their-social-media-efforts-2014-1

Stalker, R. (2010). *The Rise and Rise of Social Media*. Retrieved from http://www.franchise.net.au/issues/the-rise-and-rise-of-social-media

Steinmetz, A. (1997). *The Art of Conversation: Dialogue Marketing and the Business-to-Business Relationship*. Retrieved from http://www.adlittle.com/downloads/tx_adlprism/1997_q4_27-32.pdf

Stone, R., & Jacobs, R. (2001). *Successful Direct Marketing Methods* (7th ed.). New York, NJ: McGraw Hill.

SurveyMonkey.com. (2014). *How To Identify Your Customer Touchpoints*. Retrieved October 17, 2014, from https://www.surveymonkey.com/blog/en/identify-customer-touchpoints/

Wafi, T. (2014). *From 4Ps to SAVE – A Theoretical Analysis of Various Marketing Mix Models*. Retrieved from http://www.academia.edu/3834304/FROM_4PS_TO_SAVE_A_THEORITICAL_ANALYSIS_OF_VARIOUS_MARKETING_MIX_MODELS

Walters, J. (2013). *What is a Customer Touchpoint?* Retrieved from http://360connext.com/customer-touchpoint/

Webster, G. B., & Hume, M. (2015). Defining the Role of Social Media as a Contemporary LAM Technique in Franchising. In G. Bowen & W. Ozuem (Eds.), *Computer-mediated strategies: social media and online brand communities* (pp. 223–251). Hershey, PA: IGI Global.

Willis, J. (2011). *8 Characteristics of Effective Social Media Campaigns*. Retrieved from http://www.searchenginepeople.com/blog/effective-social-media-campaigns.html

Wilson, J. J., & Morgan, J. E. (2011). Friends or Freeloaders? Encouraging brand conscience and introducing the concept of emotion-based consumer loss mitigation. *Journal of Brand Management*, *18*(9), 659–676. doi:10.1057/bm.2011.4

Yadav, M. S., & Pavlou, P. A. (2014). Marketing in Computer-Mediated Environments: Research Synthesis and New Directions. *Journal of Marketing*, *78*(1), 20–40. doi:10.1509/jm.12.0020

Yastrow, S. (n. d.). *Touchpoint Mapping Exercise*. Retrieved from http://www.yastrow.com/downloads/touchpoint-map.pdf

Zikmund, W. G., Ward, S., Lowe, B., & Winzar, H. (2007). *Marketing Research* (A. Pacific, Ed.). Melbourne, Australia: Thomson Learning.

ADDITIONAL READING

Harrison, F. (2013). Digging Deeper Down into the Empirical Generalization of Brand Recall: Adding Owned and Earned Media to Paid-Media Touchpoints. *Journal of Advertising Research*, *53*(2), 181–185. doi:10.2501/JAR-53-2-181-185

Trainor, K.J. (2012). Relating Social Media Technologies to Performance: A Capabilities-Based Perspective. *Journal of Personal Selling & Sales Management*, 32(3), 317-331.

Webcertain.com. (2014). *The Webcertain Global Mobile Report 2014*. Retrieved from http://internationaldigitalhub.com/en/publications/the-2014-webcertain-global-mobile-report

KEY TERMS AND DEFINITIONS

Brand Touchpoints: Points of contact where people interface with a business brand or product.

Consumer Touchpoints: Consumer initiated points of contact in search of information.

Dialogue Management: Identifying and monitoring of the dialogue people use to engage in communities as well as conversations and maneuvering this dialogue to build relationships.

Dialogue Marketing: A structured approach of ongoing interactive communication to form relationships with people.

Digital Marketing: The use of digital media channels and electronic devices to market products and services.

Social Commerce: Using social media to share information with friends about purchases or planned purchases.

Social Dialogue Marketing: The use of social media in a structured way to engage in ongoing interactive communication to form relationships with people.

Social Marketing: Maximising the connections with people who share a common interest through social media.

Social Relationship Management: Monitoring of a business's social media mentions to better manage their online presence.

This research was previously published in Competitive Social Media Marketing Strategies edited by Wilson Ozuem and Gordon Bowen, pages 20-49, copyright year 2016 by Business Science Reference (an imprint of IGI Global).

Chapter 11
Storytelling and Narrative Marketing in the Era of Social Media

Sonia Ferrari
University of Calabria, Italy

ABSTRACT

This chapter is focused on the elements that, in post modern era, have greatly changed our society, both in terms of buying and consumption habits and, more generally, in terms of lifestyles. This is mainly due to the Internet, which provides low cost, faster and interactive information and communication. As described in detail in the chapter, companies have been forced to adopt new marketing strategies and, thanks to the spread of social media and viral marketing, tools such as word of mouth and storytelling have become even more effective than in the past. But today companies need to use them in a different way, actively involving the consumers, because they attribute a greater value to a product if they participate in the process of creation of its image and elements of differentiation. If managed in an innovative way, focusing on sensory and transmedia aspects, storytelling becomes a very powerful Customer Relationship Marketing and image building medium and, above all, a source of enduring competitive advantage.

INTRODUCTION

Stories are an effective way to communicate and involve people. Storytelling is an important part of human culture in the field of entertainment and education (Zhou, Cheok, Pan & Li, 2004). It has always been a way to fascinate the public and has been used for many years in marketing and management (Mossberg, 2008). Through it companies create stories about products and brands in order to differentiate their offerings, make stronger and long lasting ties with their customers, and improve their images.

Storytelling can be defined as the "sharing of knowledge and experiences through narrative and anecdotes in order to communicate lessons, complex ideas, concepts, and causal connections" (Sole & Gray-Wilson, 1999, p. 6). It is a marketing tool with an increasing success; since the mid-90s it has been no longer just a communication instrument dedicated to children and an object of literary studies

DOI: 10.4018/978-1-5225-5637-4.ch011

used only for leisure (Salmon, 2008). In fact, thanks to the turn of marketing from a mass instrument to a rising attention towards the relationship marketing, today firms are more and more interested in creating strong and direct connections with every consumer, to facilitate the reciprocal generation of value and encourage customers' loyalty (Agren & Ölund, 2007). Very often for the customers the value and meaning of a brand are based on one or more stories (Aaker, 1991; Escalas, 2004; Keller, 1993).

In the last few years the success and popularity of social networks and all kinds of virtual communities, together with the wide popularity of Internet, the spread of communication, information and digital technologies and the increasing use of mobile media, have caused dramatic changes in business models in terms of communication strategies and decision-making processes (Garrigos-Simon, Lapiedra Alcami & Barbera Ribera, 2012; Hagel & Armstrong, 1997). In fact, the audience is now not a passive recipient of information and communication but an active creator of media content. Besides, because of the growing importance of social media, traditional advertising is every day becoming less important in marketing strategies. For companies it is increasingly relevant to dialogue with customers, even informally, through social networks; it is a means to know better their target market and interact with them, but also a way to create a different image from the traditional and institutional one.

As it will be illustrated in this chapter, the new ways to communicate is based on the Internet, the virtual reality, the augmented reality, the trigging of all senses, and the use of multiple media platforms. *Narrative marketing* becomes a better way to involve the audience and add value to products/services and brands. In fact, through it customers can know the story of the company and other background information about its offers and its social and environmental impact (Mödinger, 2011), being more and more engaged in the creation and spreading of fascinating plots, themes and characters.

Besides the social media has effects also on the value chain and structure of enterprises, creating new forms of competition. In fact, they are precious sources of information and knowledge sharing, but also sources of creativity and innovation. Through them people can add value to firms' offers, adapting them to new trends in market preferences, tastes and needs, fashion and styles, changes in social patterns, etc. They can become also powerful promotional vehicles.

STORYTELLING AND MARKETING IN POST-MODERN SOCIETY

During the so-called *narrative turn* storytelling became a very effective communication, control and power technique (Salmon, 2008), also thanks to the Internet. As just described, it gave life to the narrative marketing, which is a way to increase customer awareness and trust, together with companies' sales, but also a tool to immerse the consumer in atmospheres and feelings with a strong emotional involvement. The stories can strengthen ties with market and stakeholders, convey ideas, create and exploit brands and improve products/services/ companies' images. Storytelling is related to *word of mouth*, since a good story can generate a positive word of mouth for a company, especially in the field of services, where expectations' formation and performances' evaluations are more difficult processes.

There are advertising stories, as well as stories about products/services, brands, tourist destinations, companies, and also consumer stories (Escalas, 2004; Mossberg, 2008). They have to meet customers' expectations and preferences to generate a feeling of compatibility with the firms, their offers and their brands (Jensen, 1999). Frequently these stories are based on fiction, films, myths, legends, and/ or historic events.

Storytelling can trig and touch people emotionally, intellectually, spiritually, and physically (Agren & Ölund, 2007; Gabriel, 2000; Gummesson, 2004), entertaining and becoming an effective instrument of communication thanks to a high impact on individual memory. It is, together with dramaturgy, a way to offer experiences to customers, stimulating their imagination, entertaining them (Escalas, 2004; Mossberg, 2008) and satisfying their desire to live trigging holistic and unique experiences.

Referring to storytelling it is possible to talk of *immersion* and *absorption* in the experience. In fact, according to Pine and Gilmore (1999) the parameters used to identify the areas of experience are two: the type of guest participation (active or passive) and the kind of relationship between the customers and the environmental experience (immersion or absorption). In the immersion the person is mentally involved, while in the absorption the involvement is physical or virtual. The first situation occurs when the person lives the experience with the mind (e.g. in reading), while the second case involves the physical (or virtual) presence of the client, with a real access inside the experience. As described later, thanks to virtual reality and augmented reality today the recipient of storytelling initiatives can live even absorption experiences with multisensory stimulations. It means that the storytelling will not give just visual stimuli but also odours, sounds, music, touch and/or taste inputs to enjoy a stronger and memorable experience.

Therefore, storytelling becomes an instrument always more used by companies, which are trying to maximize their efforts to offer products and services able to provide emotionally, physically, mentally, socially, and spiritually engaging experiences (O' Sullivan & Spangler, 1998; Pine & Gilmore, 1999). The aim of these efforts is to differentiate their offerings and increase customers' loyalty, creating emotional bonds with the market and satisfying a greater need for enjoyment and fun.

To be unique and difficult to imitate, the story must have a strong connection with the life of the firm and its organization (Mossberg, 2008; Rosen, 2000). Advertising stories could be of different types. They suggest models to use the products and in the same time entertain the audience. In same case, the advertising narrative is a starting point for customers' self-generated stories, because it becomes a way to remember and relive personal experiences. The companies can encourage the rediscovery of memories, directly with specific instructions or indirectly by means of sound, music, images, smells, fragrances and photos; it is a way of influencing the audience through a new active narrative role connected to the product / service use (Escalas, 2004; Sujan, Bettam & Baumgartner, 1993).

WEB 2.0 AND WEB 3.0 ERAS: HOW COMMUNICATION IS CHANGING

Nowadays, thanks to the Internet, that is a source of cheap and easily accessible information and also an instrument of socialization and learning, consumers have a level of freedom not previously imaginable. As a consequence, consumers, highly active and participatory, have become more informed and more demanding than ever before, reducing the information asymmetry between supply and demand of goods and services.

After the stages of *information only* (Web 1.0) and *relational marketing* (Web 2.0, the era in which companies mainly sought to contact the users of their Websites), the Internet has now entered the period of the collaborative or semantic marketing (the Web 3.0). Supply and demand can meet in an interactive way and companies and their stakeholders seek to acquire knowledge not about the client but from the client and work with him/her to strengthen their images and brands. The Internet is no longer just an information tool: it has become a new dimension, allowing the firms to know better their customers and communicate more effectively, as well as to promote and market products, services, companies, and brands.

For this reason, today digital marketing is rapidly transforming the way companies communicate. A characteristic of the Web 2.0 is the *microcontent*, created by the Internet users, which put the consumer in a central location. Microcontent and social media have synergic and viral effects (Alexander & Levine, 2008), thanks to the spreading of content in different web platforms and with the continuous insertion of new elements added to the content by every new user and conversation.

The *open source content management system* connects people within communities that share interests, facilitating the dissemination of information and the collaboration between different subjects. In the beginning of the Web 3.0 era this gave rise to forms of communication that are no longer *one to one* or *one to many*, but rather *many to many* (Kotler, Kartajaya & Setiawan,2010; Rincon, 2012). In some cases, the customer can become the creator of a myth or a story about a product/service, a company, a brand or a tourist destination. If the firms are able to adequately address and enhance the user generated content these stories could represent out-and-out tools for storytelling, and the starting point of very effective advertising campaigns. Thanks to user-generated content the roles of those who exercise authority and who control have changed and innovative languages and new forms of storytelling have emerged (Sassoon, 2012).

Besides, the easy access to information and search makes researching for related content on the web effortless for the writers and readers of stories; for this reason the sharing and enriching of stories becomes easer and storytelling can be seen as a more and more powerful communication instrument for companies.

Ultimately the availability of innovative tools, such as platforms for the sharing of digital content, social commerce, blogs, social networks, forums, newsgroups and communities, that are independent information networks, enables the consumer to become a co-producer of communication, adapting it to her/his own tastes and needs (Escalas, 2004; Hagel & Armstrong, 1997).

In this new situation, marketing strategies are above all direct marketing initiatives, which act through personal not through mass media and consumers can provide companies an active feedback by means of co-produced communication (Bacile, Ye & Swilley, 2014). For the customer it is a way to live an interactive experience, creating a value for him/her and for the organization it is a competitive advantage. The consumer, now a *prosumer,* becomes a co-creator of value (Erragcha, 2014; Prahalad & Krishnan, 2008).

As a consequence, costumers have a greater power and companies no longer have control of their brands. The importance of advertising is decreasing and the influence, already very high, of the word of mouth is growing. For the companies, having their own website is not enough to maximize the results. It is essential, in fact, to be easily reached, communicate effectively with the target markets and create a trustful and interactive relationship with the market by means of a right Web Marketing strategy. The Web 3.0 is the era of the *collaborative marketing* (Kotler et al., 2010), in which firms need to cooperate with their shareholders, clients, employees, and partners and invite customers to participate in the development of products and communication. In Box 1 you can read about a promotion campaign of Tuscany Region based on the inputs of local people and residents.

EXPERIENTIAL AND MULTISENSORY TRANSMEDIA MARKETING

In the light of the foregoing, it appears that in the Web 3.0 age (in which the interaction is between computers and the aim is to process large quantities of data and information to obtain targeted knowledge) the consumer is no longer a passive recipient of one-sided communications and the storytelling has become

Box 1. Tuscany Faces: How to represent a place on the Web through its people

Would you like to put your work story and your picture on the Internet? It is possible thanks to www.tuscanyfaces.com, the website that collects the faces of the Tuscan people, by birth or adoption, immortalized during their daily activities. The project, conceived and edited by the Social Media Team of the Tuscany Region, intends to introduce the excellence and the peculiarities of the region through the faces of the people who live there. It is not an accident that the project began during the Feast of Tuscany: it wanted to be an homage to the original Tuscany, a tradition that marks the landscape, architecture, food and everything you see, not a natural beauty but the result of man's work.

There are people of all types in over 100 photos collected by the Social Media Team; next to each of them a brief caption (in Italian and English) summarizes the name, the craft and the history of the protagonists. "We want to tell the stories of people who somehow embody the 'Tuscany', of those who represent excellences in all areas: artistic, scientific, crafts, food and wine sectors. They are not necessarily people born in Tuscany, but people who have chosen to live there and be inspired by this land," said the team of the project.

Everyone can send his/her face, a photo and a story! In the Web they say: "You are Tuscany! If you're Tuscan by blood or soul, if you live in Tuscany or if you're an ambassador of the tuscan spirit in the world, tell us your story and send us your most bizarre photo (in the foreground or from the waist up)."

Source: adapted from: www.tuscanyfaces.com.

digital (Barassi & Treré, 2012; Carbone, Contreras, Hernandez & Gomez-Perez, 2012; Eftekhari & Zeynab, 2008; Garrigos-Simon et al., 2012; Mistilis, 2012). On the network the social media are means that consumers use to convey their stories that may include products and brands. These stories, because they have been generated by customers, are more credible, effective and engaging and can be used by companies as promotional tools, creating forms of communication based on storytelling (Alexander & Levine, 2008; Brake, 2014; Sassoon, 2008).

Another important aspect of the evolution of the web is the *social media* spread. Social media are the interactions among people in which they create, share, or exchange information and ideas in virtual communities and networks, creating forms of *viral communication.* Social media are instruments to create *modern tribes* or communities of fans of a product, a brand or an experience (Cova, 1995; Cova & Cova, 2002; Maffesoli, 1996). To get in touch with these groups, companies have to offer them elements that contribute to the rites of the tribe, creating myths, magic content, stories and more (Sassoon, 2012).

Studies on the evolution of communication in recent years pay particular attention to social media and virtual communities. They provide an interesting and fascinating environment in which every user can interact with others, together with highly enriching experiences; these experiences go far beyond the desire to exchange information about products/services, brands, and consumer experiences (Hagel III & Armstrong, 1997). Members of virtual communities seek, in fact, emotions and satisfaction of intrinsic needs. The community offers a trigging environment in which they can share experiences, memories, passions and / or consumption rituals, reliving memories of past experiences, being reassured, creating social bonds, daydreaming, receiving stimuli and experiencing moments of anticipation about future experiences, as well as enjoying their leisure time (Cova, 1995; Jansson, 2002; Maffesoli, 1996; Stamboulis & Skayannis, 2003; Tussyadiah & Fesenmaier, 2009). As a consequence, the Internet has become a virtual place in which to live and share experiences and emotions, a real *experientialscape.*

The *self-generated narrative*, thanks to the shared participation of social media members and the support of multimedia web instruments (such as sounds, music, videos, photos, etc.), can create more interesting and engaging stories. They are very important in the *experience society*, in which consumers are looking for products and services that intrigue and stimulate them; in effect, they are interested in emotionally and mentally enriching goods that grant holistic, unique and memorable consumption experiences (Addis & Holbrook, 2001; Holbrook & Hirschman, 1982; Schmitt, 1999).

As Pine and Gilmore (1999) state in their studies on this phenomenon, today the firms not only offer goods and services, but also emotions and unforgettable experiences (Ferrari, 2006; Pine & Gilmore, 1999). In fact, in their approach to marketing the companies have switched in recent decades from a focus on attributes / benefits sought by consumers to a higher concentration on brand policies (an approach in which the brand determines the image and has a symbolic value) and, finally, on aesthetic marketing (Schmitt & Simonson, 1997). This includes companies' marketing activities based on providing multi-sensory experiences, which aim to meet hedonistic needs. It is precisely the emotional aspect of contacts among companies, goods, services and customers that represents the challenge of *experiential marketing* (Schmitt, 1999, 2003). It has been neglected until few years ago and rediscovered today in the purchasing and consumption processes, mainly due to the contributions of Holbrook and Hirschman (1982),

Furthermore, companies can encourage consumers to "experience the experience" (Morgan, Lugosi & Ritchie, 2010, p. 130), creating stories that allow them to relive the moments of consumption; these stories can be the base of targeted storytelling activities. The case in Box 2 shows an example of storytelling of this type.

Experiential marketing aims to deliver memorable experiences of consumption and / or purchase primarily through sensory stimulation, not only visual but also the other senses, which today call for increased attention. These stimuli should aim to intensify the sensory interaction between enterprise and customer. In fact, according to Pine and Gilmore (1999), each product and service can be *sensorized*, as to say it is possible to increase the sensory stimuli perceived during its use or consumption, increasing the emphasis on the most important sense for every consumer.

Multisensory perceptions aim to transform the experience into a global and significant event for all the senses. In fact, by "multisensory experience we mean the receipt of experience in multiple sensory modalities including tastes, sounds, scents, tactile impressions and visual images" (Hirschman & Holbrook, 1982, p. 92).

The multi-sensory experiences can be developed by means of virtual reality, multimedia presentations, interactive techniques, fire-wire connections, haptic experiences, olfactory pathways, forms of sound art and other instruments. Information and communication technologies make it possible to use tools such as virtual and augmented reality, digital reproductions of objects, reconstructions of buildings and environments, which allow the users to immerse themselves in the atmosphere, feeling stronger and trigging sensory stimuli. These are very effective tools of communication, because they are not based on language codes but on interactivity, therefore on sensory stimuli (such as sounds, images, haptic experiences, etc.). The emergence of new media environments is the result of the spread of smart phones and

Box 2. How to tell in a multimedia way the traditional Italian ice cream: The experience of Sammontana's #sedicogelato

In 2013 the Italian historic producer of ice cream Sammontana invented a type of storytelling, called *#sedicogelato* (*#ifIsayicecream*), based on consumers' images, videos and texts, which were shared by social media. The communication project is based on the transmedia and social storytelling. The begging is a video, which tells the history of the family and the company. The short film *"La storia di un sorriso"* (The history of a smile), by Virgilio Villoresi, tells with images, leafing through the pages of an imaginary book, the seventy year old story of the firm that has started from a dairy shop. The smile is the main sign of the brand of Sammontana, the producer of the first family pack ice cream in the middle fifties. In the website they trigger the users' interactivity by means of the contest *"Se dico gelato"*, specially addressed to the young. In a multimedia platform the consumers are invited to share a brief text, an image or a video about their ice cream experience, through a mobile App, the website *"Se dico Gelato"* or FB *"Facebook del Gelataio"* (Facebook of the ice cream maker).
Source: adapted from www.sammontana.it.

tablet connected to the network, accessing multimedia innovative services and applications, favoured by the spread of wireless networks. Also the miniaturisation of augmented reality technologies, the availability of augmented reality on mobile devices and the augmented reality applications easy to use have helped the extensive utilization of augmented reality in the communication area (Pavlik & Bridges, 2013).

So innovative ways to immerse the user in storytelling, transforming it from a bi-dimensional to a three dimensional perspective, can be achieved through virtual and augmented realities. Through the use of these technologies, in fact, the recipient can experience the story in a real environment or in a virtual world but with the support of physical objects and with sensory stimuli, living it through the narrative (Bimber, Encarnacao & Schmalstieg, 2003). The AR-enhanced experience becomes more funny, trigging and interactive, adding the spatial dimension to the oral and written ones (Zhou et al., 2004).

STORYTELLING TOWARDS THE FUTURE

In this context, storytelling is more and more used by organizations as a tool to emotionally involve existing and potential customers. In fact, the power of emotional engagement may not lie in the object itself but in the drama and romance of the story of the encounter with the object (Picard & Robinson, 2012).

The Internet, a multimedia instrument, can be used to communicate in an innovative and more effective way, and is especially suited to experiential products and services, e.g. tourism or leisure (Ferrari, 2012). In fact, by means of video, audio, photos, augmented reality, three-dimensional and interactive maps, virtual tours, Webcams, GIS, Tags, printed materials downloaded, geological sites, online sale, GPS and smart phones, etc., the communication changes from unilateral push tools to interactive multiple channels. Besides, the contents of communication are becoming more and more complex and specific, depending on the identity and the character of the receiver and the context of the communication itself (Stavrakantonakis, Gagiu, Toma & Fensel, 2013).

With all these innovations, the Internet has also become a tool for a strong emotional involvement on the part of the potential customer, who, through it, can imagine and create her/his own consumer experience. In fact, the new web tools allow people to share the experience of consumption in real-time with other consumers, making their stories much more engaging, especially if they are inserted in the web during the experience, often with the support of photos, audios and/or videos.

Today people use multiple digital and no digital devises on different media, sometimes in the same moment. For this reason, and also because thanks to the web customers search for interactive and bidimensional dialogues, companies have to communicate in an innovative way. More and more the companies try to reach the customer through multiple communication media, adapting the message to their different characters. So the stories can be told by television, cinema, radio, books, interactive web sites, but also by alternate reality games, social media, and QR codes that allow to connect with web sites and download, for example, audios. In this way communication and storytelling become transmedia, because they use different media with various messages and stories. The same way of communicating is, in fact, impossible to adapt to a transmedia strategy that needs a specific message for every platform.

An instrument that leads in this direction is the *transmedia storytelling* (Jenkins, 2003; Scolari, 2009), which uses multiple new and traditional channels to spread the several components of a story across time. Every component tells a unique story in itself, which has been designed adapting it to the specificity of the medium used; all together these different parts create a more complete and fascinating story. Besides, every user can enrich the whole, adding elements such as new characters, a secondary plot, a contextualization, etc.

Usually the companies' storytelling is part of a creative project and it is difficult to distinguish promotion and marketing from artwork and creativity (Dena, 2009). The carrying on of entertainment projects for marketing scopes is called *content marketing* or *branded entertainment*.

Many important transmedia projects have been realized in occasion of the launch of a product or service (a film, a book, etc.) with the aim to promote it. See in Box 3 the case of the promotion of a tourist destination, Elba Island in Italy, by means of a transmedia storytelling initiative.

Really interesting is the case of transmedia storytelling of Harry Potter, the bestseller book character. Today there are different media and products on the theme of the books: films, video games, an interactive web site, the cinematographic studio tour, a theme park, social networks, web communities, merchandising, etc. The case of Harry Potter is not just a narrative series: it is now a *narrative brand* that expresses itself in different languages and business areas (Scolari, 2009). It is an example of business diversification started thanks to the storytelling that allowed the organization to reach new segments of the market. Besides, the studios and the theme park represent cases of *brandscapes*; they are themed immersive environments dedicated to a specific brand, that strengthen in sensory terms the brand and

Box 3. The case of #elbamovie: A transmedia storytelling project to promote a tourist destination

#elbamovie is an innovative cross-media storytelling project for an experiential tourist promotion of the Italian Elba Island. The main aim of the project is to reinforce the image of Elba, bringing together, in a new way, the expertise of storytelling and film production with the design of tourist experiences.

2014 is the Bicentenary Year of Napoleon at Elba, where he was exiled for one year. For this reason VisitElba decided to make a short artistic film to reappraise Napoleon from a modern point of view, underlining the beauty and the rich tourist amenities of the island, with a narrative slant that differs from a traditional publicity style. The film will be divided into four episodes, each eight minutes long, forming a web-series published on YouTube and Vimeo to be used for the Web communication of the island.

To increase the degree of involvement in the initiative, the entire process of production of the film will be published on the Elbamovie site, where you can find: videos of interviews to the producers, director and actors; images of the making of the film; photographs of the actors and the scenes; materials about the life experiences of the friends of the characters in Elbamovie.

As Maurizio Goetz, Destination Manager of Elba, points out, "We really believe a lot in this project. We decided to work together with independent video makers, to promote a story of independence, in harmony with the positioning chosen for communication regarding the island of Elba, which is based on an 'independent lifestyle". Andrea Rossi, Social Media & Marketing Manager for Elba, adds, "It's a new approach to tourism storytelling, in which the destination is the hub of an experiential narrative, which we believe will engross adventure lovers. We wanted to unite a strong tourist promotion asset with the creativity that a personality like Napoleon can unleash in the imagination of people all round the world. The goal is to do high profile, captivating and fascinating promotion – aimed at a very attentive audience – while at the same time highlighting the resources and great professional skills of this territory."

The project is based on four elements that characterises the experience: the story (that is set between the past and the present, allowing the audience to live a Napoleonic experience in a modern setting); the suspension between reality and fiction (which enables Elba's visitors to see the places where the film was made and enjoy all the experiential elements included in the narration that can be discovered on the island); the depth and variety of the transmedia storytelling experience (which can be lived uninterruptedly on various media and in the territory of Elba); the evolution of the narration project (which develops like a living organism through the nutrition supplied by the contribution of the audience. The characters in Elbamovie are imaginary, but their life experiences and friends are real).

The plot.

The Tyrant, a Spirit blinded by the desire for conquest, who wanted to conquer the entire Universe, is defeated and trapped in space and time. From that moment the Tyrant waits…

Elba – June 2014: Sara, impetuous and ambitious, is having a tough time with her boyfriend Leonardo. She helped a private French collector win an old artefact from Elba at an auction, an object of very ancient origin cast in iron from the mines.

Elba – June 1814: Napoleon has recently landed on the island. In the hall of his new residence, a shady character approaches him to pay his homage to the Emperor with a gift: an ancient iron medallion. The medallion creates a temporal bridge across this two-hundred-year gap.

The entire island, in 2014 and 1814, freezes while the Tyrant, from the depths of the earth, begins to struggle to free himself from his prison. Sara and Napoleon – in the body of Leonardo – have a few precious hours to try and save Elba and accidentally, the Universe as well.

Source: partially adapted from www.elbamovie.com. See also https://www.youtube.com/user/visitelbait.

the relationship with the company. For the opening of the theme park: The Wizarding World of Harry Potter in Florida, the newspaper USA Today created an augmented reality communication tool, printing a map of the world of the fictional character. In front of a webcamera Internet connected and with a specific software, this map became interactive and three dimensional on the computer screen.

So the transmedia storytelling can use the web, with the company website, but also different platforms, such as social networks, blogs, wikis, etc. The content must be visible not only on personal computers but also on tablets and smart phones. By means of QR codes users can be linked to online content to enrich their experiences, for example downloading sounds or music files. Other media can be comics, video games, mobile apps, books, e-books, newspapers, films, radio, and television. Companies must use different points of entry to reach various market segments and communicate in heterogeneous ways to exploit every sensory aspect of the story that they are telling to their customers. A well-known case of transmedia storytelling is that of the film The Matrix. In fact, the world of The Matrix comprises three franchise films, a series of comics, a series of anime movies, and a video game.

A hypothetical example of transmedia storytelling is described below (see Box 4). The story of a product is widespread on the web and its users can add their content by an interactive website. They can discuss and share the story on social media, enriching it with their photos, videos, comments, and reviews related to the consumer experience. In the product's package they can find a QR code that linked to the web provides auditory stimuli; a video game appeals to younger people and in magazines' advertising there is a fragrance that reinforces the brand image. The customers see the story in a video on YouTube; it is periodically changed according to the inputs of the users themselves through an app. The story is then narrated in an interactive comic e-book intended for the most loyal customers. The characters in the comic are also used for merchandising inspired by the theme of the story.

Every medium has its own narrative form, language and content. The use of different media platform makes the storytelling more interesting, fun, and easy to remember, and, if in line with the client's attitudes, also useful to create a strong and lasting relationship with the company.

But to be really involving the story must be immersive and participatory. Referring to these concepts, Rose (2011) speaks of *deep media* that offer experiences in which the users immerse themselves taking part in the stories. Rose refers especially to the Internet; it, while in the beginning was a new platform for old ways of telling stories, today represents an instrument for popularising an innovative type of storytelling. He explains that under the influence of the web "a new type of narrative is emerging – one that's told through many media at once in a way that's nonlinear, that's participatory and often gamelike, and that's designed above all to be immersive" (Rose, 2011, p. 18).

Some of the recipients, the fans of the product/ brand/ film etc., are more active than others and share the story, enriching it with their content. Therefore, the companies when conceiving a story must leave room for the fans' and users' generated content, to encourage the *fanfiction* (as to say the practice of adding elements to the story) (Bourdaa, 2012). Of course the content generated by consumers and fans is no more under the control of companies and it can represent a problem and a danger, but also a challenge.

In the Box below is described the case of *I love bees*, one of the more interesting examples of transmedia storytelling based on the launch of an alternate reality game and created to promote a videogame. An Alternate Reality Game (ARG) is an interactive story that links the web to the real word through transmedia storytelling (Sassoon, 2012). The players can change the game, which is normally based on a mystery, interacting directly with the game characters. For this reason the plot and the end of the story are just in part pre-programmed: in some way the users influence them. The alternate reality game uses different media, such as emails, blogs and telephone, but the core is that of the Internet; however the

Box 4. I love bees: A case of successful storytelling transmedia marketing

In 2004 the members of a videogame community received in their mail boxes a honey jar from someone that has to do with a web site: *I love bees.com….*
This was the beginning of *I love bees*, the core element of one of the most successful examples of viral marketing based on storytelling.
I love bees is a transmedia story based on an alternate reality game; it was created by the 42 Entertainment for the viral advertising campaign commissioned by Microsoft to promote the videogame *Halo 2*, the sequel of the Xbox game *Halo*. *I love bees* was a web-based interactive fiction that used websites, blogs, Mp3 recordings, emails, jpegs, and other platforms with the aim to create an immersive storytelling for *Halo 2*. The plot of the story was about the life of five people who live in the year 2552, before the invasion of the Covenant.
"The distributed fiction of I love bees was designed as a kind of investigative playground, in which players could collect, assemble and interpret thousands of different story pieces related to the Halo universe. By reconstructing and making sense of the fragmented fiction, the fans would collaboratively author a narrative bridge between the first Halo videogame and its sequel" (McGonigal, 2007, p.7). As the project's lead writer Sean Stewart explains: "Instead of telling a story, we would present the evidence of that story, and let the players tell it to themselves" (McGonigal, 2007, p.7). The players did not know the promotional scope of the game.
I love bees was launched in 2004. In the same year the first trailer of *Halo 2* briefly showed the alternate reality game's website, www.ilovebees.com. It seemed the modest blog of the beekeeper Dana, but soon it was possible to notice that it has been hacked by an artificial intelligence and showed strange messages, corrupted data and countdowns. Later the players discovered that the goal of the game was to find payphones, indicated by GPS coordinates on the website all across the United States, and wait for a call. These phones rang at certain times and a pre-recorded voice required to answer questions through numerical codes. The more the game went on the more the requests became strange: to make human pyramids, tell jokes, sing one's own favourite songs. As a reward to players who had arrived at the end of the game they were allowed to play *Halo 2* preview inside the cinema.
I love bees was based on the *Halo* fiction and was a radio drama delivered to users by means of an innovative medium for narrative marketing and storytelling: ringing payphones. It was not the first alternate reality game, but it is the most well-known, also because of the popularity of *Halo*. The alternate reality game was a great success in marketing terms and obtained great attention by the traditional media.
The participants trying to solve the mystery of the story have been about 750,000 and casual participants have been about 2.5 million. More than three million people visited the site during the 3 months of play. It won several awards and helped to raise awareness of the alternate reality game throughout the world. *I love bees* was a predecessor for *Iris*, the alternate reality game of *Halo 3*.
Its success is due to the players' curiosity about the backstory of the *Halo* universe and the immersive and funny experience offered to participants. "The main goal in producing the project as a commercial game was, of course, exciting entertainment through immersive storytelling" (McGonigal, 2007, p. 9).

storytelling is partially fiction and partially real life. Characters and clues are distributed on and off line. Normally it has a promotional scope.

CONCLUSION AND FUTURE RESEARCH DIRECTIONS

In conclusion, today thanks to user-generated content platforms such as social networks and blogs, there is no longer on the web a boundary between stories producers and those who benefit from them; besides, the roles of the subjects that exercise authority and those that control have changed and new languages and forms of storytelling have emerged (Sassoon, 2012).

The user-generated content, even if it reduces the organizations' ability to control, increases the creative potential of storytelling. Companies must, therefore, program specific and innovative marketing initiatives to stimulate these processes, trying to keep them, directly or indirectly, under control, in order to obtain valid and long lasting results.

Besides, the fast spread of multiple communication media needs greater attention in the planning of marketing strategies and the adoption of a transmedia approach, especially in storytelling. Today companies can no longer use in the same way the different communication platforms and need to adopt forms of transmedia marketing and storytelling. They have to plan strategically, taking into account the fact that the communication world is changing every day.

However, the idea of transmedia storytelling is an evolving concept; nowadays companies rarely understand its value and only few use it in order to reach its full potential. In the future, academic research could devote a greater commitment in studying this phenomenon, which is still poorly analysed in terms of its evolution and its implications in the management and marketing fields.

REFERENCES

Aaker, D. A. (1991). *Managing brand equity: Capitalizing on the value of a brand name*. New York: The Free Press.

Addis, M., & Holbrook, M. B. (2001). On the conceptual link between mass customisation and experiential consumption: An explosion of subjectivity. *Journal of Consumer Behaviour, 1*(1), 50–66. doi:10.1002/cb.53

Agren, M., & Ölund, M. (2007). *Storytelling. A Study of Marketing Communication in the Hospitality Industry* [Master's Thesis]. Jönköping International Business School, Jönköping University.

Alexander, B., & Levine, A. (2008). Web 2.0 Storytelling. Emergence of a New Genre. *EDUCAUSE Review, 43*(6), 41–56.

Bacile, T. J., Ye, C., & Swilley, E. (2014). From Firm-Controlled to Consumer-Contributed: Consumer Co-Production of Personal Media Marketing Communication. *Journal of Interactive Marketing, 28*(2), 117–133. doi:10.1016/j.intmar.2013.12.001

Barassi, V., & Treré, E. (2012). Does Web 3.0 come after Web 2.0? Deconstructing theoretical assumptions through practice. *New Media & Society, 14*(8), 1269–1285. doi:10.1177/1461444812445878

Bimber, O., Encarnacao, L. M., & Schmalstieg, D. (2003). The Virtual Showcase as a new Platform for Augmented Reality Digital Storytelling. Proceedings of *Eurographics Workshop on Virtual Environments*. doi:10.1145/769953.769964

Bourdaa, M. (2012). Transmedia: between augmented storytelling and immersive practices. *Ina Global. The review of creative industries and media.*

Brake, D. R. (2014). Are We All Online Content Creators Now? Web 2.0 and Digital Divides. *Journal of Computer-Mediated Communication, 19*(3), 591–609. doi:10.1111/jcc4.12042

Carbone, F., Contreras, J., Hernandez, J. Z., & Gomez-Perez, J. M. (2012). Open innovation in an Enterprise 3.0 framework: Three case studies. *Expert Systems with Applications, 39*(10), 8929–8939. doi:10.1016/j.eswa.2012.02.015

Cova, B. (1995). Community and consumption: towards a definition of the "linking value" of products and services. *Proceedings of the European marketing Academy Conference ESSEC*. Paris.

Cova, B. & Cova, V. (2002). Tribal marketing: The tribalisation of society and its impact on the conduct of marketing. *European Journal of Marketing, 36* (5), 595, 620.

Dena, C. (2009). *Transmedia practice: theorising the practice of expressing a fictional world across distinct media and environments*. PhD Thesis. Sydney: University of Sydney.

Eftekhari, M. H., & Zeynab, B. (2008). *Web 1.0 to Web 3.0 Evolution and Its Impact on Tourism Business Development*. Working paper.

Erragcha, N. (2014). Social networks as marketing tools. *British Journal of Marketing Studies*, *2*(1), 79–88.

Escalas, J. E. (2004). Narrative Processing: Building Consumer Connections to Brands. *Journal of Consumer Psychology*, *14*(1&2), 168–180. doi:10.1207/s15327663jcp1401&2_19

Ferrari, S. (2006). *Modelli gestionali per il turismo come esperienza. Emozioni e polisensorialità nel marketing delle imprese turistiche*. Padova: Cedam.

Ferrari, S. (2012). *Marketing del turismo. Consumatori, imprese e destinazioni nel nuovo millennio*. Padova: Cedam.

Gabriel, Y. (2000). *Storytelling in organizations: facts, fictions, and fantasies*. Oxford: Oxford University Press. doi:10.1093/acprof:oso/9780198290957.001.0001

Garrigos-Simon, F. J., Lapiedra Alcami, R., & Barbera Ribera, T. (2012). Social networks and Web 3.0: Their impact on the management and marketing of organizations. *Management Decision*, *50*(10), 1880–1890. doi:10.1108/00251741211279657

Gummesson, E. (2004). From one-to-one to many-to-many marketing. In Atverksekonomins Marknadsföring: Attse Marknadsföringen Genom Nätverksglasögon. Malmö: Liber ekonomi.

Hagel, J. III, & Armstrong, A. G. (1997). *Net Gain: Expanding Markets Through Virtual Communities*. Harvard, MA: Harvard Business School Press.

Hirschman, E. C., & Holbrook, M. B. (1982). Hedonic consumption: emerging concepts, methods and propositions, *Journal of Marketing, 46*, 92-101.

Holbrook, M. B., & Hirschman, E. C. (1982). The experiential aspects of consumption: Consumer fantasies, feelings, and fun. *The Journal of Consumer Research*, *9*, 132–140.

Jansson, A. (2002). Spatial Phantasmagoria. *European Journal of Communication*, *17*(4), 429–443. do i:10.1177/0267323102017004020l

Jenkins, H. (2003, November). Why the matrix matters. *Technology Review*, 6.

Jensen, R. (1999). *Dream Society: How the Coming Shift from Information to Imagination Will Transform Your Business*. New York: McGraw-Hill.

Keller, K. L. (1993). Conceptualizing, measuring, and managing customer-based brand equity. *Journal of Marketing*, *57*(1), 1–22. doi:10.2307/1252054

Kotler, P., Kartajaya, H., & Setiawan, I. (2010). *Marketing 3.0. From Products to Consumers to the Human Spirit*. Hoboken, NJ: John Wiley & Sons, Inc. doi:10.1002/9781118257883

Maffesoli, M. (1996). *The time of the tribes*. London, GB: Sage.

McGonigal, J. (2007). *Why I Love Bees: A Case Study in Collective Intelligence Gaming*. Paper.

Mistilis, N. (2012). Challenges and potential of the Semantic Web for tourism. *E-Review of Tourism Research*, *10*(2), 51–55.

Mödinger, W. (Ed.). (2011). *Marketing 3.0 – New Issues in Marketing: From Integrated Marketing Communication to the Marketing of Sustainable Leaders*. Stuttgart: Stuttgart Media University.

Morgan, M., Lugosi, P., & Ritchie, J. R. (Eds.). (2010). *The tourism and leisure experience* (pp. 117–136). Bristol, GB: Channel View Publications.

Mossberg, L. (2008). Extraordinary Experiences through Storytelling. *Scandinavian Journal of Hospitality and Tourism*, *8*(3), 195–210. doi:10.1080/15022250802532443

O'Sullivan, E. L., & Spangler, K. J. (1998). *Experience marketing. Strategies for the new millennium*. State College: Venture Publishing.

Pavlik, J. V., & Bridges, F. (2013). The Emergence of Augmented Reality (AR) as a Storytelling Medium in Journalism. *Journalism & Communication Monographs*, *15*(1), 4–59.

Picard, D., & Robinson, M. (Eds.). (2012). *Emotion in Motion. Tourism, Affect and Transformation*. Farnham: Ashgate.

Pine, B., & Gilmore, J. (1999). The experience economy: work is theatre & every business a stage. Boston, Harvard: Harvard Business School Press.

Prahalad, C. K., & Krishnan, M. S. (2008). *The New Age of Innovation: Driving Co-created Value through Global Networks*. New York, NY: Mc Graw-Hill.

Rincón, J. (2012). *XML y Web semántica: Bases de datos en el contexto de la Web semántica*. Universitat Oberta de Catalunya, 1-63.

Rose, F. (2011). *The Art of Immersion: How the Digital Generation Is Remaking Hollywood, Madison Avenue, and the Way We Tell Stories*. New York: W.W. Norton & Co.

Rosen, E. (2000). *The anatomy of buzz: how to create word-of-mouth marketing*. New York: Doubleday.

Salmon, C. (2008). *Storytelling. La fabbrica delle storie*. Roma: Fazi Editore.

Sassoon, J. (2012). *Web Storytelling. Costruire storie di marca nei social media*. Milano: Franco Angeli.

Schmitt, B. (1999). *Experiential Marketing*. New York: The Free Press.

Schmitt, B. (2003). *Customer Experience Management. New Jersey*. Hoboken: John Wiley & Sons.

Schmitt, B., & Simonson, A. (1997). *Marketing aesthetics. The strategic management of brands, identity, and image*. New York: The Free Press.

Scolari, A. (2009). Transmedia Storytelling: Implicit Consumers, Narrative Worlds, and Branding in Contemporary Media Production. *International Journal of Communication*, *3*, 586–606.

Sole, D., & Gray-Wilson, D. (1999). *Storytelling in Organizations: The power and traps of using stories to share knowledge in organizations. LILA*. Harvard University.

Stamboulis, Y., & Skayannis, P. (2003). Innovation strategies and technology for experience-based tourism. *Tourism Management*, *24*(1), 35–43. doi:10.1016/S0261-5177(02)00047-X

Stavrakantonakis, I., Gagiu, A., Toma, I., & Fensel, D. (2013). Towards Online Engagement via the Social Web (pp. 26-31). Proceedings of *WEB 2013: The First International Conference on Building and Exploring Web Based Environments*.

Sujan, M., Bettam, J., & Baumgartner, H. (1993). Influencing judgments using autobiographical memories: A self-referencing perspective. *JMR, Journal of Marketing Research*, *30*(4), 422–436. doi:10.2307/3172688

Tussyadiah, I. P., & Fesenmaier, D. R. (2009). Mediating tourist experiences. Access to places via shared videos. *Annals of Tourism Research*, *36*(1), 24–40. doi:10.1016/j.annals.2008.10.001

Zhou, Z., Cheok, A. D., Pan, J. H., & Li, Y. (2004, June). Magic Story Cube: An Interactive Tangible Interface for Storytelling. *ACE*, 3–5.

KEY TERMS AND DEFINITIONS

Alternate Reality Game (ARG): Is a game that links the web to the real word through transmedia storytelling. The players can change the story, normally a mysterious story, with their actions, interacting directly with the game characters. The alternate reality game uses different media, such as emails, blogs and telephone, but the centrality is that of the Internet. Normally it has a promotional scope.

Augmented Reality (AR): Is a virtual reality that represents a real-world environment augmented by means of computer-generated sensory elements such as sound, video, graphics or GPS data. The aim is to create a virtual environment with no difference with respect to the real world.

Digital Storytelling: Is a way of telling a story through the web (not only on companies' websites, but also on social media) with an active participation of Internet users.

Experiential Marketing: Is a marketing strategy that tries to immerse the customer in the product and to provide emotions and unforgettable experiences. It includes companies' marketing activities based on providing sensory experiences, with the aim of meeting hedonistic needs.

Multisensory Marketing: Are marketing activities based on providing multisensory experiences, which aim to meet hedonistic needs.

Social Media: Are digital entities that allow web users to create their own content, disseminate it, and receive in virtual communities and networks information of non-commercial nature about products / services, companies, brands. They are blogs, social networks, forums, newsgroups and communities, which represent independent information networks.

Transmedia Storytelling: Is a form of storytelling that uses multiple channels to spread the several components of a story. These parts have to be adapted to the specificity of the various media used and all together create a more complete and fascinating story.

User Generated Content: Is a digital content created by web users; they can share it online with great ease and without the need for specific technical skills.

Virtual Reality (VR): Is a simulated reality, a virtual simulation created through the use of the computer.

Web 2.0: Is an evolution of the Word Wide Web in which the communication becomes two-way and users can generate their own contents to put them on the Web. It represents the birth of an interactive platform, in which you can share information and feedbacks. It is not a technological evolution but a new way to make and use web content.

Web 3.0: It is also called *Semantic Web*. Its main characteristic is that the interaction is between computers and the aim is to process large quantities of data and information to obtain targeted knowledge. It has three main characteristics: to be ubiquitous, individualized, and efficient. The ubiquity is due to the possibility of being connected anywhere and in anytime. The individualized character refers to the information that is segmented and adapted to varied people and situations. The Web 3.0 is more an attitude than a technological evolution.

This research was previously published in Experimental Multimedia Systems for Interactivity and Strategic Innovation edited by Ioannis Deliyannis, Petros Kostagiolas, and Christina Banou, pages 1-15, copyright year 2016 by Information Science Reference (an imprint of IGI Global).

Chapter 12
Benefits of Using Social Media Commerce Applications for Businesses

Ardian Hyseni
South East European University, Kosovo

ABSTRACT

Social media commerce has changed the way of commerce globally; customers are affected more and more by social media, in decision making for buying a product or a service. While in the past people were affected by traditional marketing ways like newspapers, televisions and radios for buying a product, nowadays, through social media customers can find feedbacks and reviews on social media and can see thousands of photos of a single product with less a minute of searching in a social networking sites like. With the growth of social media's impact on businesses, social commerce has become a trending way of making commerce. In this paper it demonstrated a platform for businesses to make commerce through Facebook which is called Facebook commerce.

INTRODUCTION

Social media ecommerce is a trending way of making business over the internet, despite ecommerce that is made by websites, nowadays social media has made it available to buy and sell products over social networking sites like Facebook, twitter etc. Social media isn't just about posting a feed on Facebook or twitter, or putting like button or comment on your website, it is about connecting customer directly with your website and making visitors loyal customers. Ecommerce dates since 1994 when Jeff Bezos founded Amazon.com and in 1995 when Pierre Omidyar started P2P marketplace eBay (Shaefer, 2014). Both these sites were social networks seen as marketplaces for products with discount price. Customers could leave feedback, post reviews and comment for the products they bought. This was new era of commerce through internet was born. After eBay and Amazon, in 2004, Facebook was founded by a group of Harvard students. Facebook now is a leading social networking site based on the number of users and fan / business pages (Collier, 2012).

DOI: 10.4018/978-1-5225-5637-4.ch012

Businesses want to connect with people and customers which they do business, they want their customers opinion and reviews (Safko, 2009). By using social media, companies now can easily create interaction between company product and the customer. To understand and hear the voice of their customers, businesses need to keep up to date with the technology. Social media marketing is constantly evolving; sites like Facebook, Twitter, LinkedIn are leaders in the online networking which are the current communication trends (Corson-Knowles, 2013). Businesses need to combine new technologies with traditional marketing to increase the sales revenue (Varela, 2015). Social media is not just another way of marketing; it has to become a integrative part of a company. It is understandable that businesses should take more seriously the involvement and planning of social media for commercial gain.

Most of the ecommerce sites have started implementing social media networking site services in order to improve interaction and increase active participation of user in order to increase revenues (Kwahk & Ge, 2012). In a social networking sites users can get answers and interact with each other in order to get more information for a specific product or service. When user wants to order a product online, he or she can ask and find out more information on the social networking site. The aim is to examine how much people do use social media commerce and what is the impact of social media in people's decision making during the buying process in ecommerce.

Social networking sites consist of large number of users who are potential content generators and massive source of information (Underhill, 2008). Users generate new ideas, advertise and add a value for a little cost while increasing the effectiveness by understanding customer needs, identifying potential customers, and building customer loyalty (Kwahk & Ge, 2012). The increased number of users in social networks has led to a new shopping trend where people leverage social networks to make the right purchase. While businesses spend thousands of money in marketing, and it is considered as a temporary investment, in a TV or Newspaper, in social networking sites people who engage at your page they become a lifelong loyal customers (Kwahk & Ge, 2012). Businesses do not need to pay for advertising in social shopping, they can post products in their business page and all customers who follow that page are able to see it (Chaffey, 2011).

Problem Statement

Before discussing social media commerce, we need to analyze a bit of traditional marketplaces that were formally created in Europe around 1000 AD (Schaefer, 2014). Towns and villages were competing with each other towns and villages for commerce legal or illegal until few rules were applied usually by church or mosque leaders. Traditional marketplaces were highly personal and interactive between seller and customer. People usually were standing face to face with the seller, looked them in the eye saw also not only as a seller but also as a personality, and bought with a firm handshake (Schaefer, 2014). People purchased goods from people they knew and trusted or were recommended by a friend or relative. People visited or passed through workshop or farm on the way to market and expected transparency and loyalty from seller where they could buy products right in front of them (Mikalef, Giannokos & PAteli, 2012). If people felt cheated they knew where and whom they bought from and they could be knocking at seller's door.

In traditional marketplaces success of sellers depended on word of mouth or people's recommendation, feedback on quality, service and pricing was constant and immediate [6]. That time, there was no advertising so you needed to treat people right, it was sellers themselves who created their own authority of their shop or workshop. So if seller cheated a buyer, the word would spread throughout the marketplace like a plague, so that, the authority of the seller would be depended on buyer's feedback (Schaefer, 2014). In traditional marketplaces it wasn't just about buying and selling; it was also the social aspect of marketplaces where people talked about news, gossips and themselves. Than around 1400s things started to change, the invention of printing press and newspapers magazines flyers soon followed which was era of advertising, it was a new step away from traditional successes of sellers where advertising was word of mouth, people's recommendation and interactions between buyer and seller (Collier, 2012). Till 1920s still commerce was done through neighbors and small family-owned businesses on every town, until the first commercial broadcast radio station went on the air, and era of communication had begun. After radio came out Television, the internet and websites which made commerce easier and increased number of customers, but all of these traditional ways are evaporating. Newspapers are losing print circulation all around the world, people read online through web or social sites, television programs now are watched more likely through Netflix or Hulu, or buying movies and series for their iPads (Schaefer, 2014).

Traditional media channels are fading away, so where are people going? (Mikalef, Giannakos & Pateli, 2012) The social networking sites like Facebook Twitter LinkedIn Pinterest Google+ are new town squares for people to share news, photos, videos, and their personal life events. Latest trend is social media commerce, from where people through these social media networking sites are looking for products and finding answers to problems (Farooq & Jan, 2012). Research field is social media commerce, which is going to be new way, and most common way of making commerce through social media sites like Facebook and other social networking sites.

Motivation

Motivation of this thesis is based on social shopping trend that is taking a lead for commerce over the internet. Social shopping applications are new trending ways of commerce over the social media networking sites. At the moment there are only a few types of these applications that are circulating over the internet. The weakness of these applications is expensive membership per month. Small businesses want a cheap and flexible app for their own store.

There is a fact that 85% of orders from social media sites come from Facebook? Average orders 55$. According to US Social Commerce – Statistics & Trends it is expected that in 2015 social media commerce will represent five percent of all retail revenue in 2015 (Bennett, 2014). This five percent revenue is more than 15 billion, but according to Booz & Company (2011) it is predicted that social media commerce will revenue more than 30 billion dollar in 2015. These statistics tell us that social media commerce is rapidly raising and is a trend of commerce. Let's take a look some statistics for social media commerce:

- 90% of all orders are influenced according social media (Cheshire & Rowan, 2011).
- 90 percent of customers trust recommendations from people they know (Nielsen, 2009).
- 85% of orders from social media sites come from Facebook (Zephoria, n.d.).
- 9.5% of bump up price comes from positive product reviews (Booz & Company, 2011).
- 11.5% of negative reviews change person's intent of purchase (Zephoria, n.d.).
- 33% of costumers act on a promotion of brands from social media page (Statista, 2014).
- 30 million small business pages are active in Facebook and more than 1 billion active users (Bazaarvoice, n.d.).

Based on above statistics about impact of social media in commerce, it is concluded that in 2015 it is expected a huge increase of commerce through social media comparing to previous years. Social media is leading us to new way and trending way of commerce, just like in the past when Amazon and eBay started doing commerce. Firstly, it began just in USA, but few years later there was as a dramatic increase of sales over the internet all around the world (hou, Zhang & Zimmerman, 2013) . The trend of commerce in the past is going to be the same with social media commerce. People are looking for new trends of commerce, which is social media commerce (Yang, Kim & Dhalwani, 2008). It began with just a billion in 2010 and now it is increasing significantly.

LITERATURE REVIEW

Before social media networking sites emerged, lots of business activities existed in the online electronic world, which was called e-commerce. E-commerce websites existed in the past and people were able to buy and sell products and services over the internet through e-commerce websites (Yang, Kim & Dhalwani, 2008). Social media commerce is a combination of social media and e-commerce which together make social media commerce, which stands for buying and selling products over social media networking sites. Social media has changed and revolutionized the way that people communicate and share information. Globally, internet users spend more than four and a half hours per week on social networking sites, which make social networking sites huge potential market for customers and retailers (Booz & Company, 2011).

Related Work

Social commerce is not new, it began since 2005 when firstly Yahoo presented this word (Ysearchblog. com, 2005). But with the growing of e-commerce, social commerce started to enhance in different ways. Firstly were recommends, reviews and comments, but only in e-commerce sites. Afterwards there were needed to develop new ways for selling products through the social networking sites. Like and comment buttons connected to websites were implemented in e-commerce sites, that many people think it is social commerce, it is but not exactly (Guo, Wang, & Leskovic, 2011). Social media commerce is buying and selling directly from social networking sites like Facebook or twitter or any other social site (Marsden, n.d.). Social media commerce isn't just a trending way of business, it's the future and low cost commerce with not much advertising needed.

In Figure 1 it is shown the trend on how social media commerce has increased since 2010. And are based on this chart, one can see that it has at least 100-200% increase each year. In upcoming years, one can imagine how much of commerce will be done through social media sites.

Why Social Media?

There are many reasons why people should invest on social media, as there are thousands different purposes of using social media. In this thesis there are claimed some of the reasons why should be investing on social media, but not only for fun, mainly for business purposes. While social media has become a place for grouping people in one site for chatting, sharing photos and experiences, there are a few more reasons why social media can be good for business purposes.

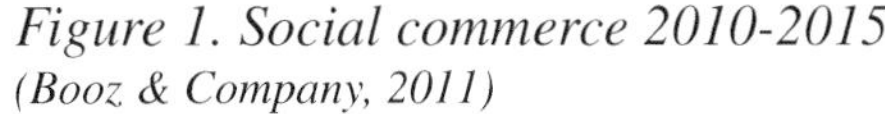

Figure 1. Social commerce 2010-2015
(Booz & Company, 2011)

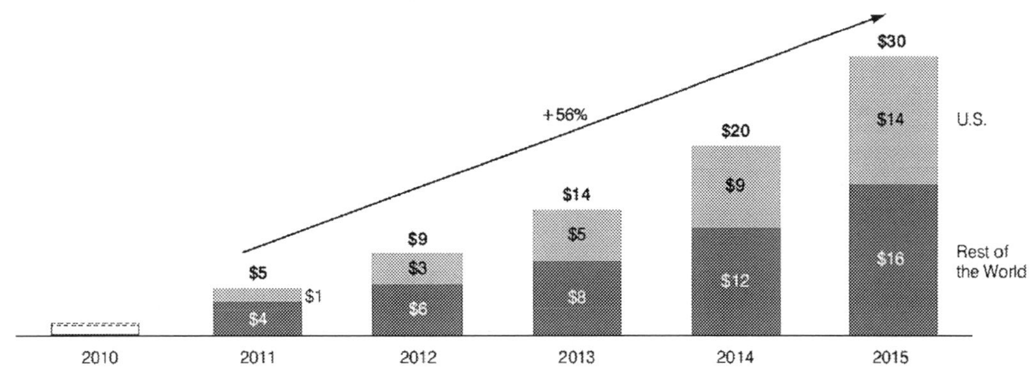

List of reasons why to invest in social media commerce:

1. Worldwide, there are over 1.39 billion monthly active Facebook users (MAUs) which is a 13 percent increase year over year (Zephoria, n.d.). This information helps our research to be concentrated on Facebook social networking site.
2. 4.5 billion likes generated daily as of May 2013 (Zephoria, n.d.). If there are 4.5 billion likes generated daily, even if there is only 1% for a product promoted this would be enough.
3. 890 million people log onto Facebook daily (DAU) for December 2014 (Zephoria, n.d.), If we provide a good app for business pages imagine having 890 million people daily active, it's like having 890 million customers available.
4. There are 1.9 billion mobile active users (MAU) (Zephoria, n.d.) .The use of Facebook advertising methods, business can get at any of these 1.9 billion mobile active users via Facebook.
5. Age 25 to 34, at 29.7% of users, is the most common age demographic (E-Marketer, 2014). Why it is important for a business the age? It is because most of online shoppers are between 18-35 years old.
6. Five new profiles are created every second. (Zephoria, n.d.) .The idea is to invest in any app for Facebook, imagine having 5 new potential customers every second in your store or app.
7. Photo uploads total 300 million per day (Chan, 2012). Imagine, from 300 million only 10% of these photos, to be photo of products, it is a huge marketing for free by social media for businesses.
8. Average time spent per Facebook visit is 20 minutes (Socialskinny, 2012). It's like having a potential customer that has 20 minutes to visit your store on Facebook.
9. Every minute on Facebook: 510 comments are posted, 293,000 statuses are updated, and 136,000 photos are uploaded (Hubspot, n.d.). Nowadays anyone who buys a product or a wear takes a picture and posts on Facebook so the key of marketing is to get to peoples eye and ea,r in the past was marketing of word of mouth no is word of social media.
10. 42% of marketers report that Facebook is critical or important to their business (Hubspot, n.d.). If in Facebook, there are around 1billion daily active users and your business doesn't have a page it's like being out of a huge potential market.

11. 16 Million Local business pages have been created as of May 2013 which is a 100 percent increase from 8 million in June 2012 (Zephoria, n.d.). If we have the latest statistics this number would be a lot bigger than this. 16 million local business pages in one website like Facebook make things much easier. Facebook seems to take a lead over Google Ads in aspect of marketing.
12. 7.5 million Promoted posts have been made from June 2012 to May 2013 (Zephoria, n.d.). Marketing way is changing; social media has become a powerful way of marketing. Newspapers, TVs and radios are going to fade away in aaspect of marketing.

After analyzing this statistics and explaining the business benefit from Facebook it is decided that for the application development to be concentrated on Facebook application (Corson-Knowles, 2013).

RESEARCH METHODOLOGY

In this chapter, the research methodology, research questions, hypothesis and survey questions will be presented in order to explore the way which will be taken for the purpose to test and examine the hypothesis and results of the research. Finally, how the data collected and results will be analyzed.

Research Methodology

In order to examine the questions for our research, in this thesis we raised few hypothesis. For the purpose of evaluating the hypotheses, some techniques will be used as quantitative approach through the questionnaire. To test the developed model and hypothesis, an effective research and methodology is required. It should be considered the conditions such as research questions, purpose of questions, and amount of time (Zhou, Zhang & Zimmerman, 2013). Quantitative and qualitative researches are the best way to explain and understand any phenomena. The research can be achieved by analyzing experiences and thoughts of individuals and groups. Quantitative research questions are the best strategy for gathering data, in this case survey/questionnaire. For this purpose, survey is the best strategy suggested for gathering data and finding the answers. Through survey, in short time can get bigger number of participants and data collected.

Research Questions

Research questions will be prepared according to the hypothesis which will be raised based on experiences and expectations of participants in this research. In this research questionnaire, there are 23 questions, which all of these have its own importance, its own purpose on the research. Through these questions that are prepared, results will be examined and find answers to the research findings. Results of the answers provided in the survey from participants will lead the thesis in which social networking site to be focused on preparing the application. Questions will be classified through a process, from which will lead to the adequate answers and steps will be taken to proceed with the questionnaire.

Survey contains of three parts of questions. First part contains three questions about participant's education level, department and gender they belong which are needed for profiling. Second part contains questions about social media commerce what knowledge do participants have and what do they think about the future of social media commerce. Third part contains questions about measuring how much impact does social media has in participant's decision making, and the last question is for estimating how much do participants do believe that social media commerce will be a leading way of commerce in the future.

Survey

In this research questionnaire, there are 10 questions, which all of these have its own importance, its own purpose on the research. Through these questions that are prepared, results will be examined and find answers to the research findings.

RESEARCH FINDINGS

In this chapter there are presented the research findings from survey taken by 100 participants. Participants are from Kosovo and Macedonia mostly, students from South East European University and others from different Universities around Europe who are friends and colleagues from different departments. From research results, one can get the demographics, such as the department that the participants belongs to, the gender of participants, education level, their shopping experience and expectations for social media commerce in the future.

Results

In this section are shown the results of the findings from the questionnaire taken by seven companies who have implemented social commerce application on their Facebook business page.

What is the Industry of the Company?

In Figure 2 are shown the sectors of the companies who participated on the research.

Table 1. Research questions

	Questions
1	What is the industry of the company?
2	Do you have e-commerce website?
3	How would you rate the benefits of Using Social Media Commerce apps on your business?
4	What is the number of sales that your company has made from social commerce apps since implementation?
5	What are the lacks of social commerce application?
6	Which are advantages of using Social Media Commerce?
7	Social Media Commerce will be a leading way of commerce in the future?

Figure 2. Sectors of the companies who participated on the research

Answer Choices	Responses	
Jewelry	14.29%	1
Electrical	0.00%	0
Lighting	28.57%	2
Clothing	0.00%	0
Sanitary	14.29%	1
Furniture	0.00%	0
Bookstore	0.00%	0
Flower Store	14.29%	1
Industrial Power tools	28.57%	2
Total		7

Do You Have E-Commerce Website?

In Figure 3 are shown the results whether companies who participated have e-commerce website in order to see how familiar companies are with online trading, Out of 7 companies who participated 4 companies have e-commerce website.

How Would You Rate the Benefits of Using Social Media Commerce Apps on Your Business?

In Figure 4, it clearly shown that social media commerce apps increase the effectiveness of the company on social media, but increase the sales revenue remains low in percentage.

What Is the Number of Sales That Your Company Has Made From Social Commerce Apps Since Implementation?

In Figure 5, it is clear that number of sales remains too low, in next question it will seen which are the reasons of low number of sales through social media.

Figure 3. Results whether companies who participated have e-commerce website

Answer Choices	Responses	
Yes	57.14%	4
No	42.86%	3
Total		7

Figure 4. Benefits of Using Social Media Commerce apps for a business

	1	2	3	4	5	N/A	Total	Weighted Average
Customer satisfaction on responding for prices	14.29% 1	14.29% 1	14.29% 1	14.29% 1	42.86% 3	0.00% 0	7	3.57
Increase the sales revenue	28.57% 2	0.00% 0	0.00% 0	14.29% 1	28.57% 2	28.57% 2	7	3.20
Increase the effectiveness of the company on social media	28.57% 2	0.00% 0	0.00% 0	0.00% 0	71.43% 5	0.00% 0	7	3.86
Catalog product and price-list on the social networking page	14.29% 1	14.29% 1	14.29% 1	14.29% 1	42.86% 3	0.00% 0	7	3.57

Figure 5. Number of sales that the company has made from social commerce apps since implementation

Answer Choices	Responses	
0-9	85.71%	6
10-49	14.29%	1
50-99	0.00%	0
100-999	0.00%	0
1000+	0.00%	0
Total		7

What Are the Lacks of Social Commerce Application?

In Figure 6, it is see that one of the main reasons that business think that customers do not buy through social media: is the lack of experience to do shopping via social media.

Which Are Advantages of Using Social Media Commerce?

In Figure 7, it is clear that Social Media Commerce has many advantages and benefits to businesses. All of above can be seen in Figure 7.

Figure 6. Lacks of social commerce applications

Answer Choices	Responses	
Price of platform for social commerce is expensive	14.29%	1
Customers aren't used to buy via social networking sites	100.00%	7
Social Media Commerce still remains new trend and needs time.	71.43%	5
Non of Above	0.00%	0
Total Respondents: 7		

Figure 7. Advantages of using social media commerce

Answer Choices	Responses	
Social Media Commerce is replacing E-Commerce sites?	71.43%	5
You have your own store on Facebook business page no need for a e-commerce website?	85.71%	6
Social media ads have a targeting people option which is more useful than traditional media like (TV, Radio, Newspaper) and it is much cheaper	71.43%	5
Your clients become potential customers once they become fan of your social media page and each product or promotion you make people are able to see on their news feed	100.00%	7
Total Respondents: 7		

Social Media Commerce Will Be a Leading Way of Commerce in the Future?

In Figure 8, It clear that businesses are skeptic that social media commerce will be a leading way of commerce in the future, so most of the companies are neutral.

DESIGN OF NEW SOCIAL MEDIA COMMERCE APP

The whole idea behind this application is to create an e-commerce website that will be integrated to Facebook for the sole purpose of selling. When one mentions e-commerce website, it should be clear that the idea is to allow for every user to create an account and to be able to have its own store. Each user will have its own admin area for managing the store and to have the possibility of publishing its store on Facebook business page. To do this there is needed for a good plan on developing this application.

The Idea

The idea for creating a social media commerce application is based on the new trending way of commerce which is a new topic for most of companies. While Facebook has 1.4 billion users and 300 million active users daily it makes us think what all those people are doing in a single web (Booz & Company, 2011). By using social media and e-commerce, a combination of these technologies, leads us to social media commerce. There are a few applications for buying and selling products through social media sites, but it hasn't emerged totally and people do not know much about this trending way of commerce. While looking at these few social commerce applications over the Internet, it is decided to come up with a new application and new idea. The application is going to be called SABOF.

Figure 8. Will social commerce be a leading way of commerce in the future?

Answer Choices	Responses	
Strongly Disagree	14.29%	1
Disagree	0.00%	0
Neutral	42.86%	3
Agree	28.57%	2
Strongly Agree	14.29%	1
Total		7

What Is SABOF?

SABOF is acronym of Selling And Buying Over Facebook – Sabof, is a new trend of shopping application (app) where you can create your page and post your products, from where you are able to sell and accept money via PayPal. The purpose of this app is to sell products through Facebook. It is simple to use and enough completed to set up a store and start selling. It is absolutely free! You don't need to pay for setting up a store and you can start selling from your Facebook business page for free.

How Does It Work?

The idea is simple, just pointing the browser to SABOF.com and click to a button create online store with Facebook, User will have to be signed up with Facebook through the login button, after which the user will be directed to his/her admin are. In admin area the user will have to give the name to the store and fill in the store with categories and products. After creating categories and products, the user will be able to write information about his/her company, payments, privacy policy, shipping and contact form.

Adding SABOF to Facebook

After filling the user store with the products and categories, in admin area there is the Facebook Tab, which when user clicks on it he/she will be redirected to the Facebook business page and the user will have to choose which Facebook business page wants to install the store in and start selling products online.

Before setting up the store, the user has PayPal link in admin area where he/she is supposed to enter his/her PayPal account details, in order payment's money to be transferred to user's PayPal account.

Design of UI Prototype

The design proposed for SABOF will look like Figure 9. Each user will have the store published in his/her Facebook business page within the shop tab. This is the prototype proposed, where in the next part it will be shown how it really looks like.

The Admin area prototype that is proposed looks like Figure 9. Here user will be able to manage its own store. In the next part of this chapter, there will be an example on how the user will create the store.

Proposed Technology

This application uses the PHP scripting language and the MySQL database application as the foundation of the websites (Ullman, 2013). Of course HTML is involved, as it is also CSS for any website. For design it will be used also Bootstrap and some free templates form Bootstrap technology.

Java script and jQuery framework are used to enhance the application, to add some extra functionalities. As long as our sign up and log-in in the system, it will use Facebook, therefore it is required to use Facebook SDK for PHP or JavaScript.

Figure 9. Design proposed for the store page

Figure 10. Proposed admin prototype

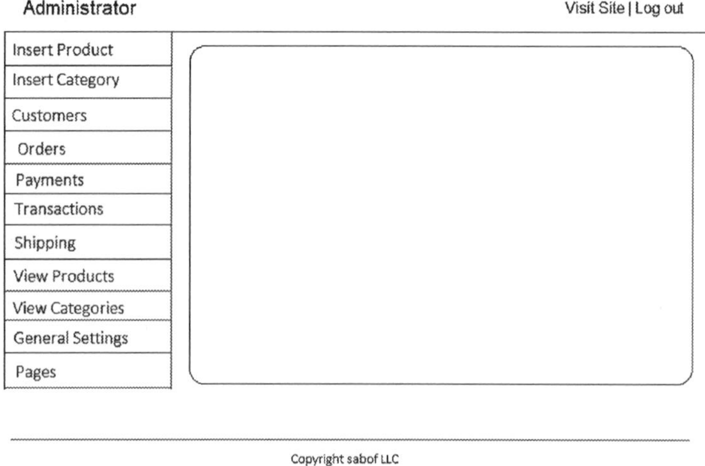

Developing the System and Integration with Facebook

After the User Interface design is proposed and final idea is finalized, next step is to write down HTML and SQL commands, or creating the application. But before that, few steps should be analyzed. Each step follows the other: From the beginning with planning till improving, as shown in the Figure 11.

After the programming part is finished, let's take a look at the server organization. In Figure 12 and Figure 13 are shown the files organized in the server side.

The Few Steps to Use SABOF

After everything is prepared, SABOF app is going to be tried. To see if everything is programmed well and the app is functional, a simple shop is going to be created. Firstly it is needed to sign up or login with Facebook credentials. After the user logs in, he is redirected to admin area where he/she should fill the store with the info and products. After filling the web data, the user should go to PayPal section to write his/hers PayPal account details that are required for receiving the payments. After the PayPal account is registered, the user must go to the Facebook tab, where he/she will be directed to his/her Facebook business page, and user can see the store on Facebook (user must have Facebook business page in order to publish its store to Facebook business page),

Figure 11. The development process

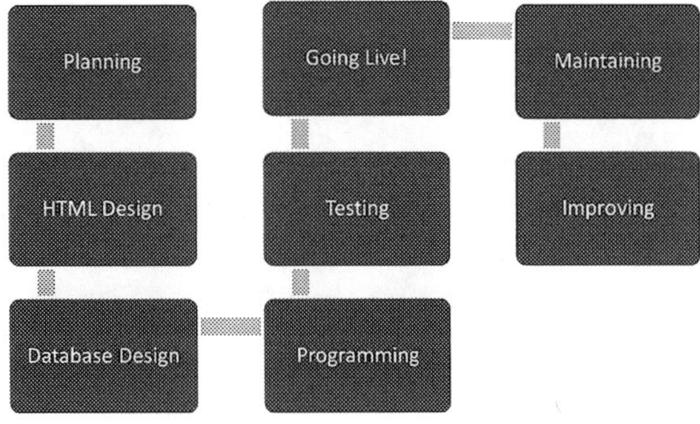

Figure 12. System organization: Files in the server side

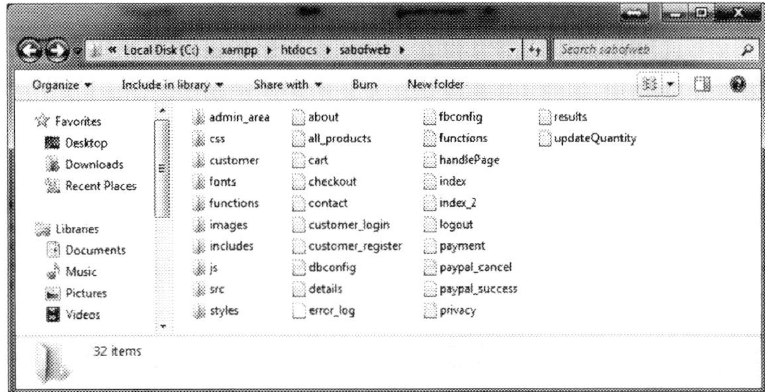

Figure 13. System organization: Files of admin area in the server side

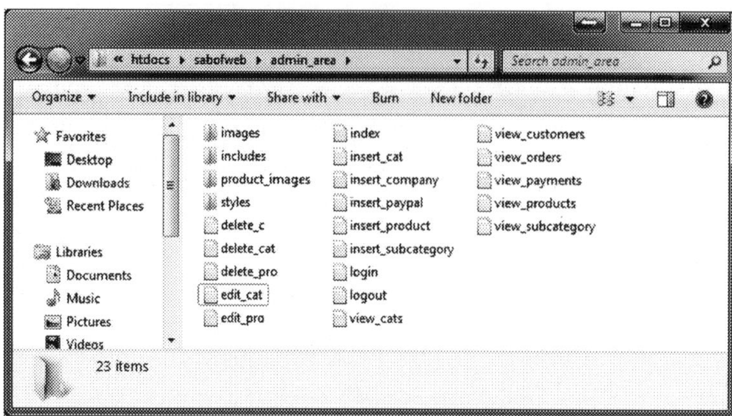

For creating a SABOF store and to post it to Facebook business page, user must go to www.sabof.com. In the front page there is a button "Create Store Now" as shown in Figure 14, which will direct user to Log In or Sign Up page, as shown on Figure 15.

After being redirected to Sign Up page, user must click to Login with Facebook button because the credentials and authentication are handled by Facebook (Figure 15). User must have Facebook account in order to sign up.

Figure 14. Create online store

Figure 15. Sign up or log in area

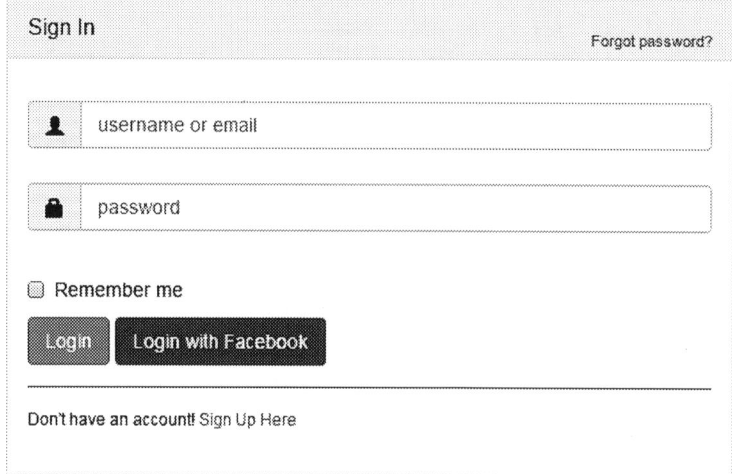

After the user is logged in, he/she will be redirected to Admin Area (Figure 16), where the user will be able to write company details, insert categories, insert products, insert PayPal account and insert the store into Facebook business page.

In Figure 16 is shown the company details page, where the user will be able to give a name to the store, write email address, put a logo of the company, and write about company and terms and conditions of payments of the company.

Where as in Figure 17 is shown the page that is used for inserting the categories for the products in the store.

In Figure 18 there is a screen of the categories that are created, and that can be edited or deleted by user in the future.

Figure 16. Admin area: Company details

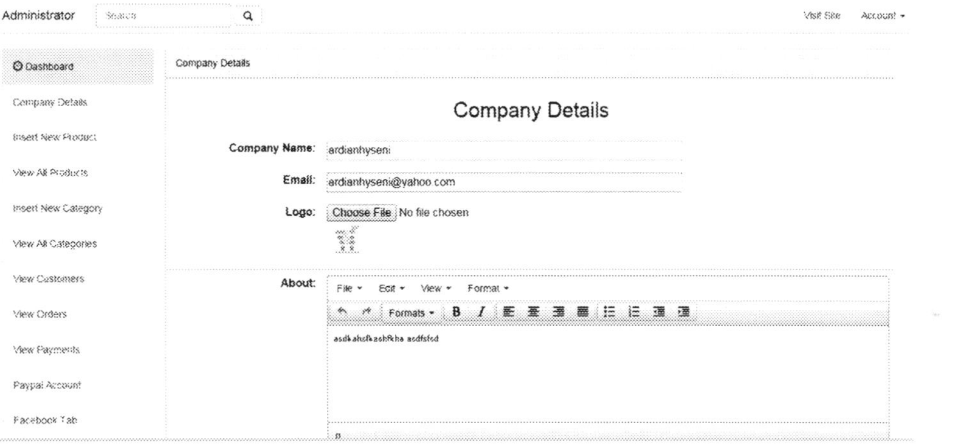

Figure 17. Inserting category

Figure 18. Categories

View All Categories

ID	Category Title	Edit	Delete
13	Fruits	Edit	Delete
14	Laptops	Edit	Delete
15	iPads	Edit	Delete
16	Mobile	Edit	Delete

The Figure 19 shows the page for inserting products to the store. In the product page, the user can write the name of the product, insert the category, insert subcategory, and insert product picture, product price, product details and keywords.

In Figure 20 is shown the page of the products which are created for our test store. In the view products page, are the number of products, product title, product image, product price, product edit button and delete button.

In Figure 21 is shown the page for inserting the PayPal email account, in order payment money to be delivered to users PayPal account. PayPal account should be written before the store is published in the Facebook business page.

In Figure 23 is shown the Facebook shop tab page. In this page user will be able to post the store to his/her Facebook business page. There is also 'Add Another Page Tab' link in case user has more than one Facebook business page.

In Figure 24 is shown the actual store, which is created for the test purpose for this thesis. As it is seen the design, is good and simple to use. All the categories and products which were created are shown in this test page.

In Figure 25 is shown the cart page. In the cart, quantity of the products can be updated, and also user can continue the shopping. After final order is decided, user can proceed with check out.

In Figure 26 is shown the check-out page, where is a PayPal button, which is for directing the user to the PayPal payment page.

In Figure 27 is shown the order summary and on the right is PayPal Login account.

In Figure 28 is shown the page, when user Logs In and continues with payment of the order.

In Figure 29 is shown the message that thanks for the order, and tells that the payment was finished successfully. Finally user will be redirected to the store.

In Figure 30 is shown the message that tells that payment was successful. And user can be directed to his account.

In Figure 31 is shown the invoice that is delivered to customer's account. User can see the invoice and has a link, which can direct user to his account to see other order details.

Future Development

The app provides the basic things for buying and selling products from a personal store with a PayPal payment method and shipping. For the future it will be worked on Currencies, Languages, Shipping, Membership, Payment methods and product gallery.

Currencies (Figure 31) will be put, to make possible for stores from different countries to be able to make payments with their own currencies and put the currencies in their personal store for their payment process.

Another future development that is proposed is going to be a membership (Figure 32), for the number of products per store. The reason is that servers need capacity for saving a huge data for many stores. The membership, it will not be too expensive and it will be calculated according to the number of products per store.

Another future that is proposed is integration of other payment methods like Credit Card. It is proposed for customers to be able to choose which payment method they want, PayPal or Credit Card (Figure 33).

Figure 19. Insert product

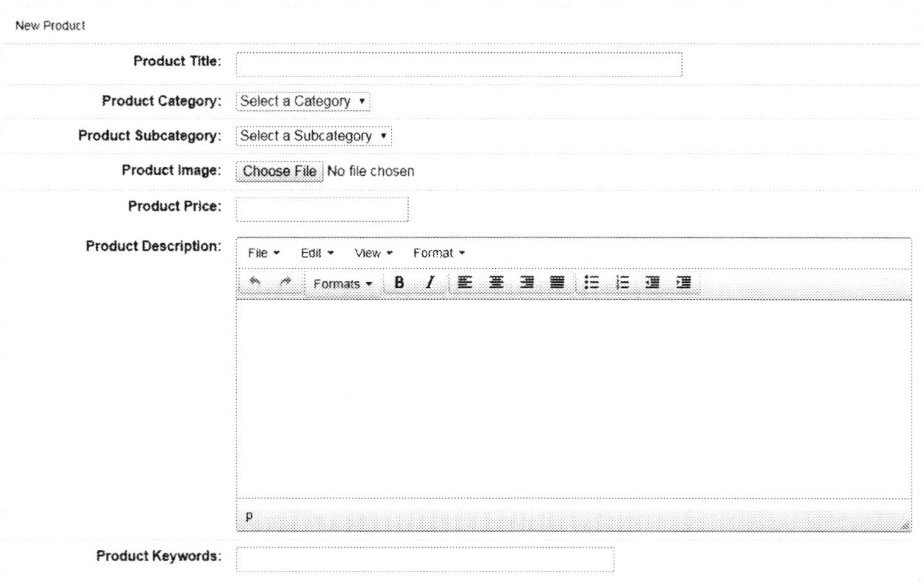

New Product

Product Title:

Product Category: Select a Category

Product Subcategory: Select a Subcategory

Product Image: Choose File No file chosen

Product Price:

Product Description: File Edit View Format

Formats B I

p

Product Keywords:

Figure 20. View products

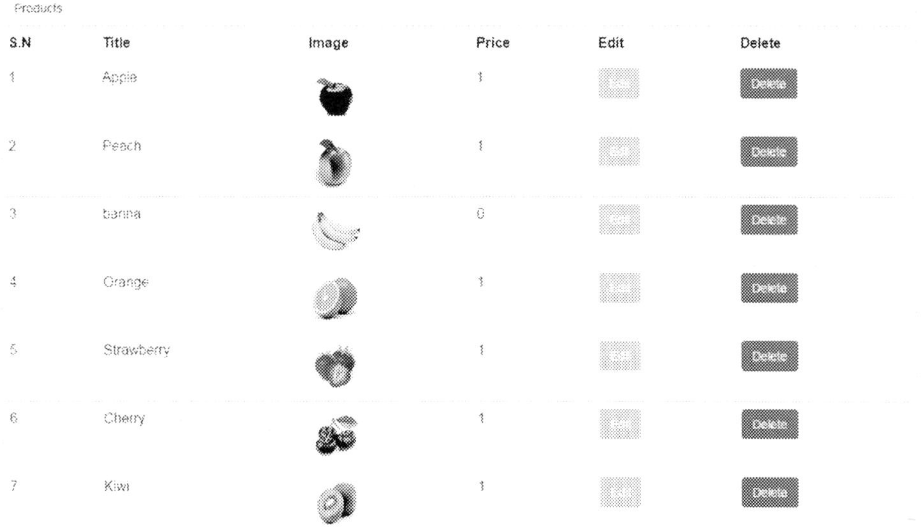

Products

S.N	Title	Image	Price	Edit	Delete
1	Apple		1	Edit	Delete
2	Peach		1	Edit	Delete
3	banna		0	Edit	Delete
4	Orange		1	Edit	Delete
5	Strawberry		1	Edit	Delete
6	Cherry		1	Edit	Delete
7	Kiwi		1	Edit	Delete

Figure 21. Insert PayPal account

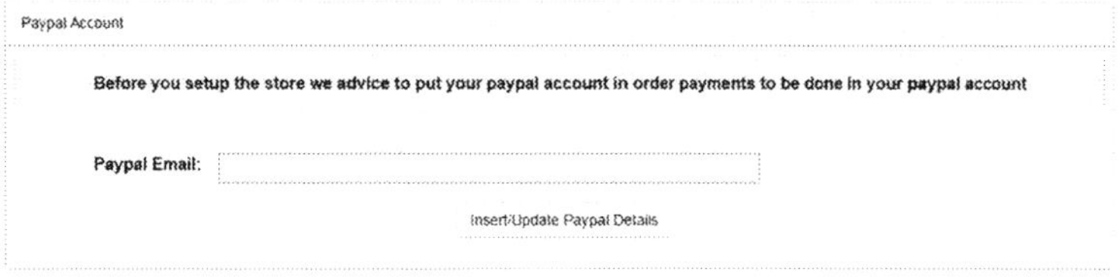

Paypal Account

Before you setup the store we advice to put your paypal account in order payments to be done in your paypal account

Paypal Email:

Insert/Update Paypal Details

Figure 22. Facebook shop tab

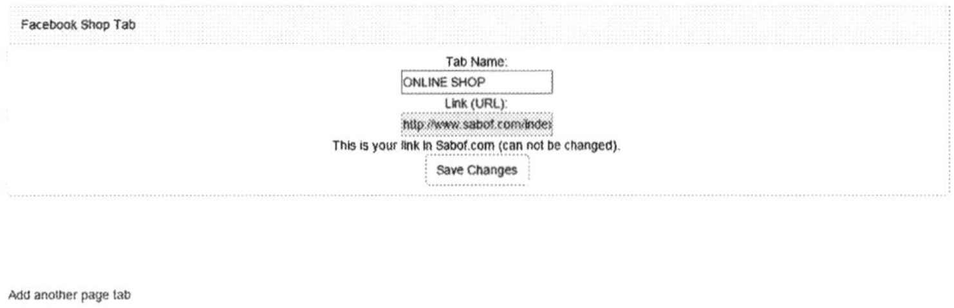

Facebook Shop Tab

Tab Name:
ONLINE SHOP
Link (URL):
http://www.sabof.com/inde
This is your link in Sabof.com (can not be changed).
Save Changes

Add another page tab

Figure 23. Store on Facebook business page

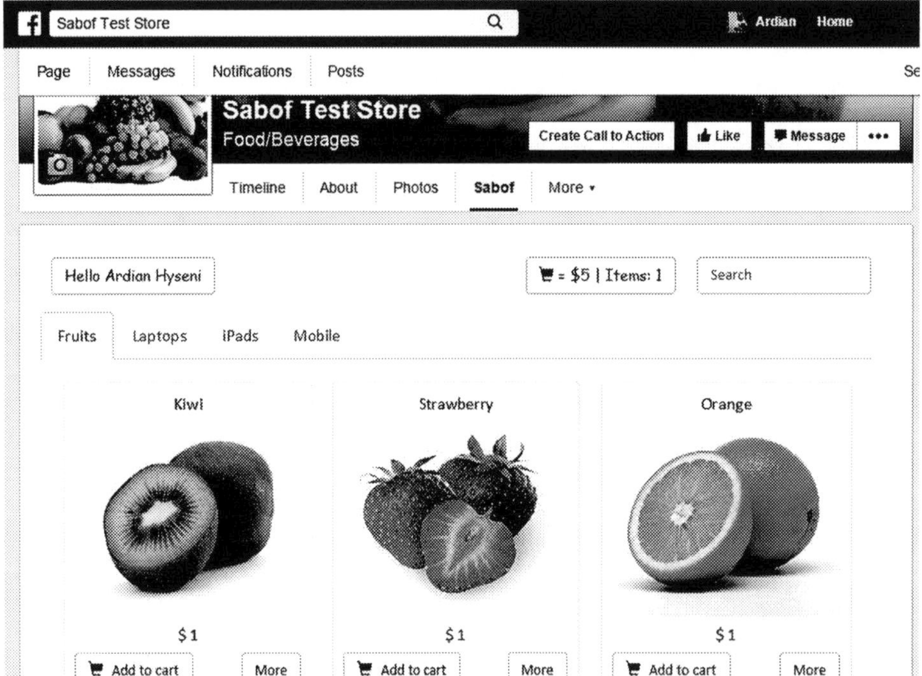

Another important feature that is proposed for the application is integration of other shipping methods to the application (Figure 34). As it is known, most useful shipping methods around the world are DHL, TNT, UPS, FedEx, EMS.

Another feature that is being under construction is the bazaar or shop.sabof.com, where all products from all shops created in SABOF application will be added in one page with its own category (Figure 35). And for the future it is being planned how to implement the payment system for all products from different stores in one store.

Figure 24. Cart page

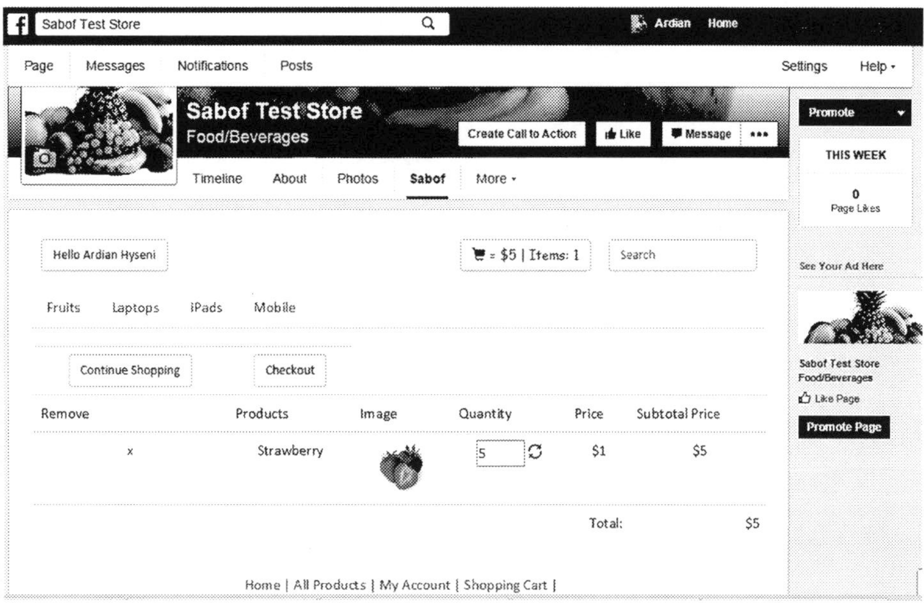

Figure 25. Payments by PayPal

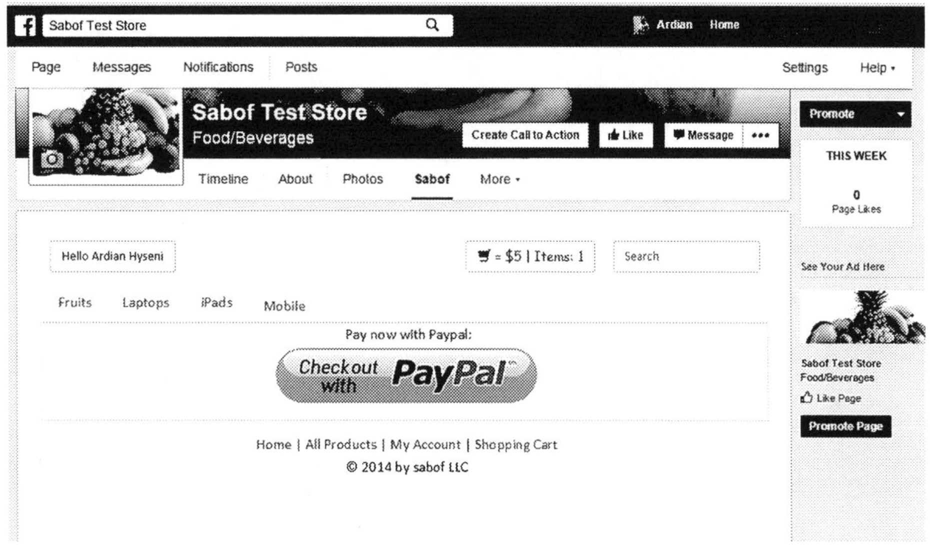

Figure 26. PayPal log in

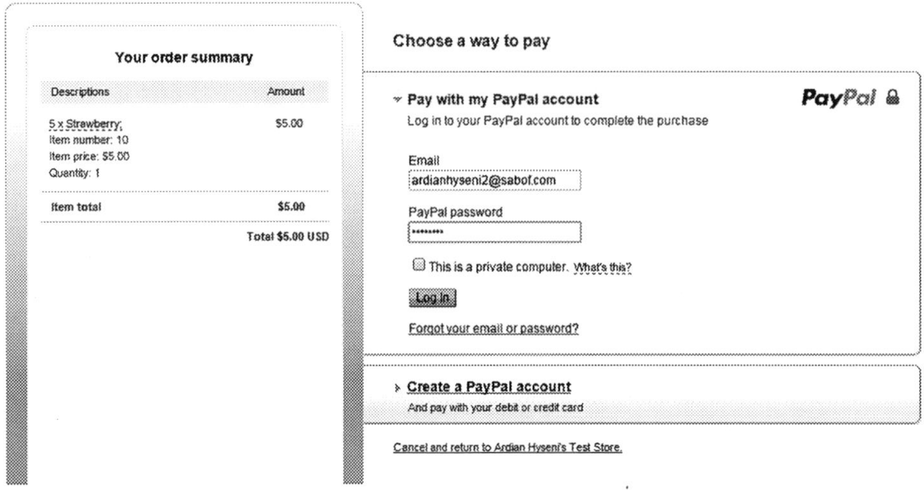

Figure 27. PayPal account logged in

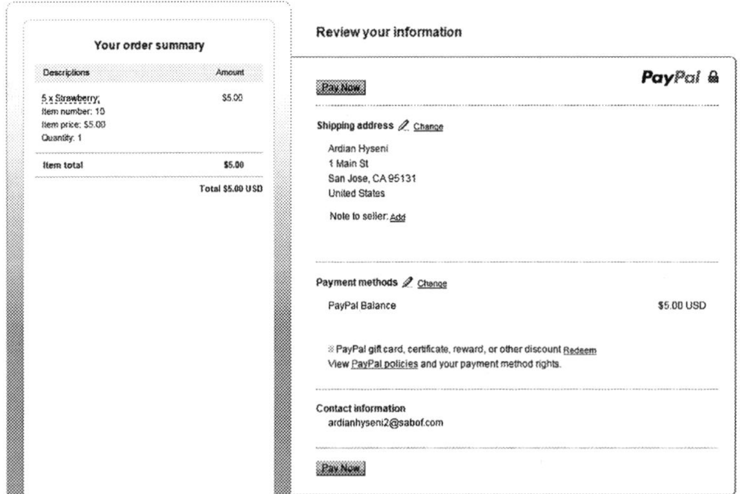

Figure 28. Payment completed

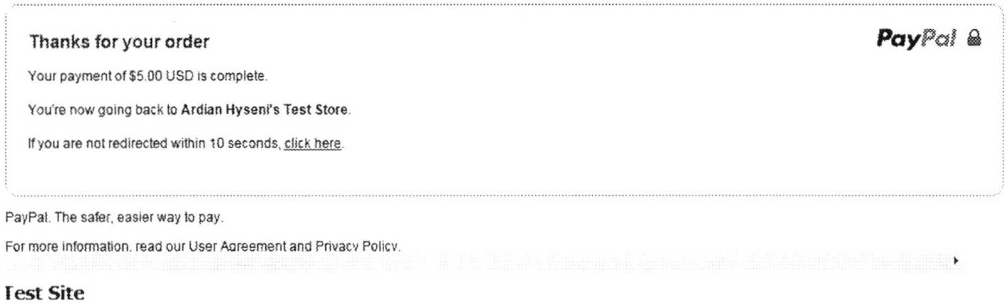

Ardian Hyseni's Test Store
Thanks for your order
PayPal
Your payment of $5.00 USD is complete.
You're now going back to Ardian Hyseni's Test Store.
If you are not redirected within 10 seconds, click here.
PayPal. The safer, easier way to pay.
For more information, read our User Agreement and Privacy Policy.
Test Site

Figure 29. Payment approval

Welcome:Ardian Hyseni
Your Payment was successful!

Go to your Account

Figure 30. Invoice delivered to customers account

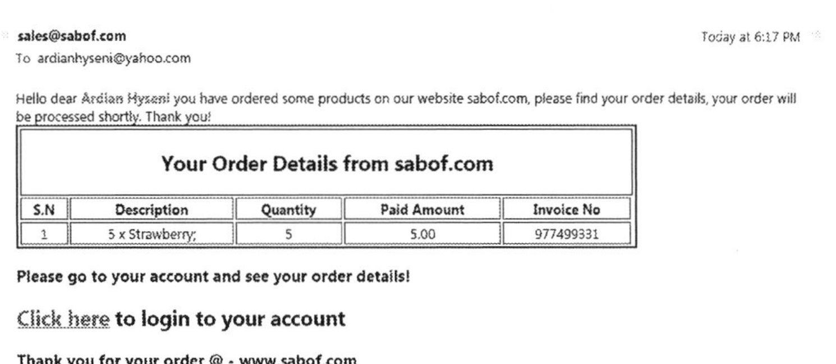

sales@sabof.com
To ardianhyseni@yahoo.com

Today at 6:17 PM

Hello dear Ardian Hyseni you have ordered some products on our website sabof.com, please find your order details, your order will be processed shortly. Thank you!

Your Order Details from sabof.com

S.N	Description	Quantity	Paid Amount	Invoice No
1	5 x Strawberry;	5	5.00	977499331

Please go to your account and see your order details!

Click here to login to your account

Thank you for your order @ - www.sabof.com

Figure 31. Currency

Select single currency - using radio buttons

€ $ £ ¥

Figure 32. Membership feature

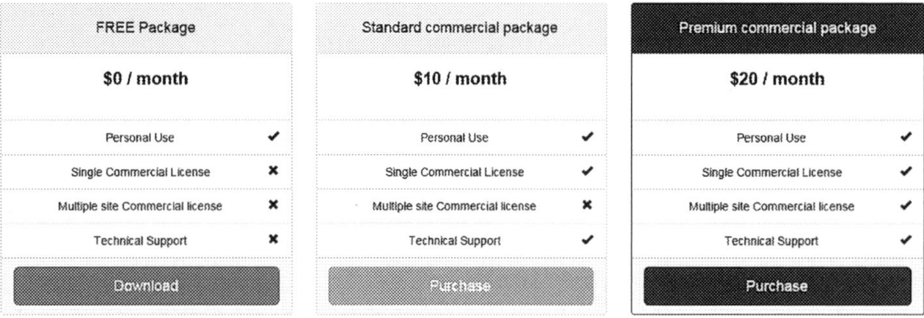

Figure 33. Credit card payment method

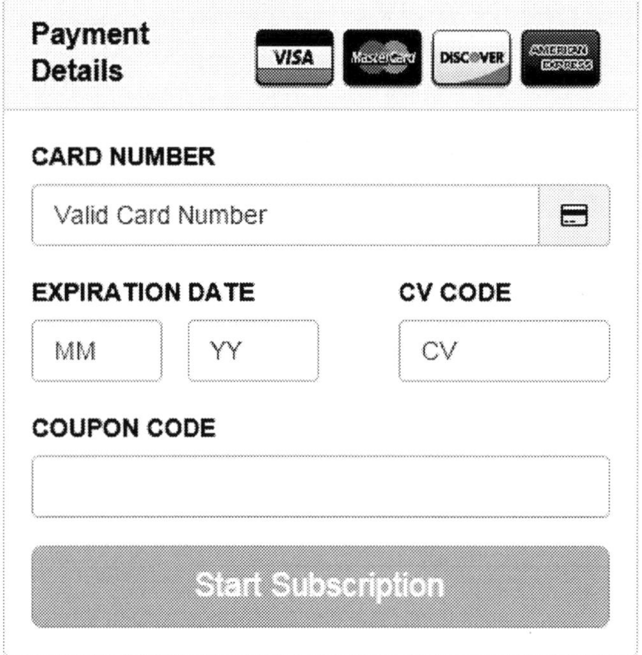

Figure 34. Integration of other shipping methods

Figure 35. Bazaar for all shops

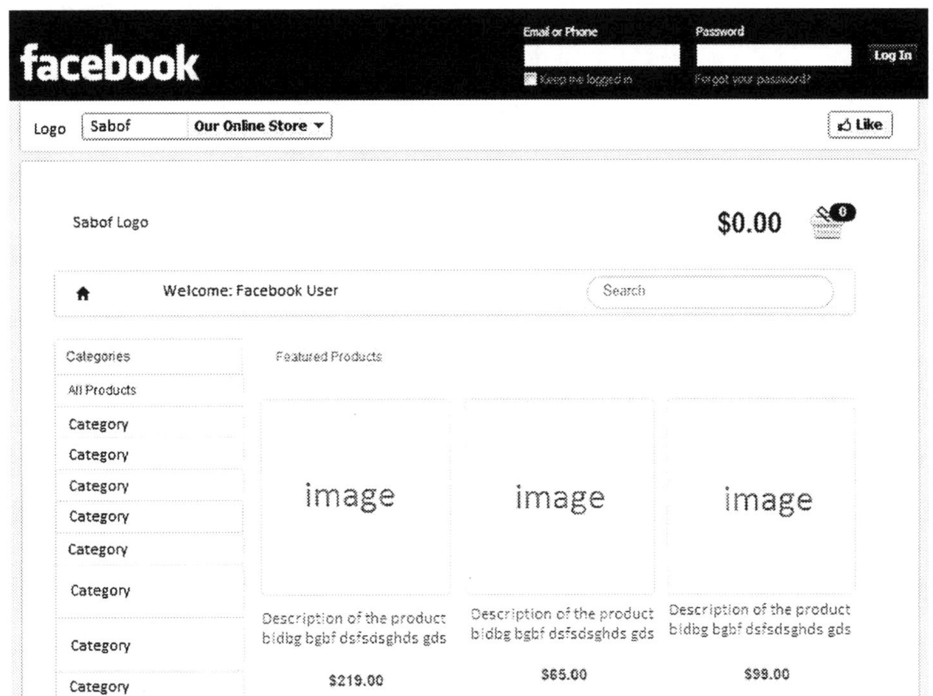

CONCLUSION

Generally social media commerce is an emerging shopping trend that is increasing significantly. So many apps for selling products through social networking sites are developed for a very short time. Based on the previous years the rise of social commerce it tends to be the leading way of commerce in the coming years.

Finally, based on the social trend and the app that is developed. It can be concluded that social commerce applications will have positive impact in businesses in all aspects of shopping experiences.

REFERENCES

Bazaarvoice. (n.d.). *Social commerce statistics*. Retrieved from: http://www.bazaarvoice.com/research-and-insight/social-commerce-statistics/

Bennett, S. (2014). U.S. social commerce – statistics & trends (infographic). *AdWeek*. Retrieved from: http://www.adweek.com/socialtimes/social-commerce-stats-trends/500895

Booz & Company. (2011). *Turning "Like" to "Buy" Social Media Emerges as a Commerce Channel*. Booz & Company Retrieved from: http://www.strategyand.pwc.com/reports/turning-like-social-media-emerges

Chaffey, D. (2011). *E-business and e-commerce management: strategy, implementation, and practice* (4th ed.). Upper Saddle River, NJ: Prentice Hall.

Chan, C. (2012). What Facebook Deals with Everyday: 2.7 Billion Likes, 300 Million Photos Uploaded and 500 Terabytes of Data. *Gizmodo*. Retrieved from: http://gizmodo.com/5937143/what-Facebook-deals-with-everyday-27-billion-likes-300-million-photos-uploaded-and-500-terabytes-of-data

Cheshire, T., & Rowan, D. (2011). Commerce gets social: How social networks are driving what you buy. *Wired Magazine UK*. Retrieved from: http://www.wired.co.uk/magazine/archive/2011/02/features/social-networks-drive-commerce

Corson-Knowles, T. (2013). *Facebook for Business Owners: Facebook Marketing For Fan Page Owners and Small Businesses (Social Media Marketing)* (vol. 2). TCKPublishing.com.

E-Marketer. (2014). Younger Users Spend More Daily Time on Social Networks. *E-Marketer*. Retrieved from: http://www.emarketer.com/Article/Younger-Users-Spend-More-Daily-Time-on-Social-Networks/1011592

Farooq, F., & Jan, Z. (2012). The Impact of Social Networking to Influence Marketing through Product Reviews. *International Journal of Information and Communication Technology Research*, *2*(8).

Guo, S., Wang, M., & Leskovec, J. (2011). The Role of Social Networks in Online Shopping: Information Passing, Price of Trust, and Consumer Choice. *EC '11 Proceedings of the 12th ACM Conference on Electronic Commerce*, 157-166.

Hubspot. (n.d.). *State of Inbound Marketing 2012: The ultimate list of marketing statistics*. Retrieved from: http://www.hubspot.com/marketing-statistics

Kwahk, K. Y., & Ge, X. (2012). The Effects of Social Media on E-commerce: A Perspective of Social Impact Theory. *2012 45th Hawaii International Conference on System Sciences*. IEEE.

Marsden, P. (n.d.). *Social Commerce: Monetizing Social Media*. Syzygy Group. Retrieved from: http://digitalintelligencetoday.com/downloads/White_Paper_Social_Commerce_EN.pdf

Mikalef, P., Giannakos, M., & Pateli, A. (2012). Shopping and Word-of-Mouth Intentions on Social Media. *Journal of Theoretical and Applied Electronic Commerce Research*, *8*(1), 17–34.

Nielsen. (2009). Global advertising consumers trust real friends and virtual strangers the most. *Nielsen*. Retrieved from: http://www.nielsen.com/us/en/insights/news/2009/global-advertising-consumers-trust-real-friends-and-virtual-strangers-the-most.html

Safko, L. (2009). *The Social Media Bible: Tactics, Tools, and Strategies for Business Success*. Hoboken, NJ: Wiley.

Schaefer, M.W. (2014). Social media explained: Untangling the world's most understood business trend. In *Social Media Commerce For Dummies*. Wiley.

Socialskinny. (2012). 100 social media statistics for 2012. *Social Skinny*. Retrieved from: http://thesocialskinny.com/100-social-media-statistics-for-2012/

Statista. (2014). *Social media and user-generated content tools used by omnichannel retailers in the United States as of 1st quarter 2014*. Retrieved from: http://www.statista.com/statistics/308539/us-omnichannel-retailer-social-media-tools/

Ullman, L. (2013). Effortless E-Commerce with PHP and MySQL (2nd ed.). New Riders.

Underhill, P. (2008). Why We Buy: The Science of Shopping--Updated and Revised for the Internet, the Global Consumer, and Beyond. Simon & Schuster.

Varela, C. (2015). *Facebook Marketing for Business: Learn to create a successful campaign, Advertise your Business, Strategies to generate traffic and Boost sales (Social Media)*. Amazon.

Yang, T. A., Kim, D. J., & Dhalwani, V. (2008). *Social Networking as a New Trend in e-Marketing. In Research and Practical Issues of Enterprise Information Systems II* (pp. 847–856). Boston: Springer.

Ysearchblog.com (2005). *Social Commerce via the Shoposphere & Pick Lists*. Retrieved from: Ysearchblog.com

Zephoria. (n.d.). The top 20 valuable Facebook statistics. *Zephoria*. Retrieved from: https://zephoria.com/top-15-valuable-Facebook-statistics/

Zhou, L., Zhang, P., & Zimmerman, H. D. (2013). Social Commerce Research: An integrated view. *Electronic Commerce Research and Applications*, *12*(2), 61–68. doi:10.1016/j.elerap.2013.02.003

This research was previously published in Mobile Platforms, Design, and Apps for Social Commerce edited by Jean-Éric Pelet, pages 322-346, copyright year 2017 by Business Science Reference (an imprint of IGI Global).

Chapter 13
The Usage of Social Media in New Product Development Process:
The Benefits and the Challenges

Rebecca Liu
Lancaster University, UK

Aysegul Eda Kop
University of Aberdeen, UK

ABSTRACT

This chapter contributes to a better understanding of the role of social media in the NPD process and a debate about the impact of social media on NPD success. Through a critical literature review, this chapter provides an insight into the impact of social media on incremental NPD and its contribution to NPD success, in the context of customer involvement. The review is mainly derived from 286 relevant papers published in top-ranked journals between 2005 and 2014. The results suggest that while social media provides an effective and efficient method for collecting information and knowledge about customers' expectations and experiences, it does not necessarily always lead to NPD success. The study shows that hidden customer needs, an advanced evaluation tool, the huge amount of information and a firm's absorptive capacity challenge the use of social media.

INTRODUCTION

Globalisation and the increasing speed of business force firms to continuously innovate and develop new products to ensure long term competitiveness. A continuous stream of ideas has been recognised as essential fuel for new product development (NPD) (Reid & de Brentani 2004). There is clear evidence that customers play an important role in all stages of NPD from idea generation and concepts through development and design to testing and market launch (Dahan Hauser 2002). Customers are not only able to create their own products but also willing to participate in and provide their know-how during the

DOI: 10.4018/978-1-5225-5637-4.ch013

NPD process (von Hippel & Katz 2002; Franke & Shah 2003). Today, the use of social media brings the NPD process into another arena. However, evidence of the association between the use of social media and NPD is mixed. The majority (e.g. Colliander & Dahlen 2011; Corstjens & Umblijs 2012; Ernst, Brem & Voigt 2013) reports that to engage customers through social media positively impacts on NPD success. This contrasts with others (e.g. Bartl, Füller, Mühlbacher & Ernst 2012; Haavisto 2014) who show that customer involvement and the use of social media are not necessarily always beneficial to NPD performance. We argue that it is crucial for managers to look closely at the usage of social media in the NPD process. We therefore critically review the existing literature and provide a conceptual framework for future research.

The internet provides companies with an increased ability for making contact outside the company. There are various ways of using the internet for NPD and R&D, including online/virtual communities (discussion forums, blogs) and social networking websites. Web 2.0 technology is an important technology that supports online interaction and serves as a dynamic portal for actors to share information and collaborate with each other (Adebanjo & Michaelides 2010). More importantly, these portals ensure a mutual platform for customers to learn from each other (Franke, Keinz & Schreier 2008). Throughout this chapter, we use 'social media' to refer to these mediums. All the studies cited in this chapter use these platforms to refer to similar and common functions in social media in order to provide interactive communications between their users.

In this chapter, we divide NPD into two categories. Incremental NPD concerns minor changes and modifications to products and technologies, whereas radical NPD represents major departures from existing capabilities in the firm and constitutes the basis for completely new products and services (see Garcia & Calantone 2002). It is argued that incremental NPD improvements may benefit significantly from user feedback while this feedback has little relevance in the case of radical NPD (Kelly et al. 2013). This difference in nature between these two NPD types suggests divergent roles for customer inputs in NPD. The involvement of customers in incremental NPD through social media is the main topic of this chapter. We focus on firms identifying market needs, determining previously unmet customer needs, and adopting the expectations and needs of customers in the manufacturing and launching of a product, as well as attributing necessary features to the product. Interactive communication platforms, like social media channels, have become an important way of contacting customers during the innovation process of companies. The success of the knowledge exchange created by online social portals in relation to innovation and NPD is an important topic for the literature. Scholars have called for further research on the role of social media in product innovation and development (Björk & Magnusson 2009). This chapter seeks to provide some insights into this important issue by conducting a wide-ranged research on previous studies. The next section details the research method we used. It then presents a literature review on customers and NPD, followed by a critical review of the use of social media and the benefits and challenges to NPD. This chapter concludes with a summary of theoretical and practical implications, the limitations and the directions for future research.

Research Method

To better understand the topic, we conducted a critical literature review. The sources of the review are mainly derived from scholarly journal publications. In particular, we reviewed three and four star journals (based on the ABS ranking of 2010) in the area of Innovation, Marketing and Production. The following is a complete list of the journals chosen: "Journal of Product Innovation Management", "Technovation",

"R&D Management", "Journal of Marketing", "Journal of Marketing Management", "European Journal of Marketing", "Journal of Marketing Research", "Journal of Operations Management", "Production and Operations Management", "Journal of Advertising Research", "International Journal of Production Research", "Journal of International Marketing", "Industrial Marketing Management", "Journal of Business Research", "International Journal of Operations and Production Management" and "Production Planning and Control".

Data collection was conducted through the Electronic Database of Ebsco Business Source. The publication timeframe was determined as 2005 – 2014. In addition to the Ebsco Database, Google Scholar was used to reach "Technovation", "Journal of Operations Management", "Industrial Marketing Management", "Journal of Business Research", "International Journal of Operations and Production Management", and "Production Planning and Control" since they could not be accessed through Ebsco Business Source. Also, Google Scholar was used for those years of the publications (especially 2013 and 2014) where access is limited because of a 12- or 18-month delay due to publisher restrictions for EBSCO, such as "Journal of Product Innovation Management", "Journal of Marketing Management", "R&D Management", "International Journal of Production Research" and "Production and Operations Management". Even though we wished to obtain the most recent 10 years of publications, because of the limitations for 2013 and 2014, only eight years (from 2005 to 2012) could be reached in all volumes of the publications. As a result, 44 papers on "social media" and 242 papers on "new product development" were identified. Thirty-nine of them were accepted as more relevant to this chapter. Table 1 shows a list of the articles that were read and used for this chapter according to their publications.

In addition, some essential articles from the references were checked according to their publications and dates. They were included if they belonged to three or four star publications after 2005. For instance, articles from the "Journal of Service Research" were found in this way. In addition to the articles from three and four star scholarly journals (based on ABS ranking of 2010), books and websites about innovation and NPD were used for definitions and general overviews of the topic. Finally, to assist the consistency of the usage of terms in this study, Appendix One provides a definition of some important concepts.

Customer and New Product Development

A considerable amount of literature has been published on product development (e.g. Garcia & Calantone 2002; Liu & Hart 2011; Calantone & Rubera 2012; Slotegraaf 2012). It appears from the literature that researchers have shown an increased interest in customer input for new product innovation (e.g. Edvardsson, Kristensson, Magnusson & Sundström 2012). They have analysed the influence and the success of customer input during new product development processes. Not only is technology know-how important in these processes, but also information about the market, including customer needs, ideas and expectations is essential. Drechsler, Natter & Leeflang (2013) claim that, during the new product development process, marketing research is conducted in order to decrease uncertainty and risks by obtaining accurate information on customer needs and their ideas about new products so that this information can be transferred into the new product's features. This increases the company's overall innovation performance. Thus, being connected with customers during the new product development process decreases the failure rates of new products by increasing the satisfaction of customers' needs. In this section, we review relevant studies regarding customer inputs/voice, involvement, collaboration and co-creation. We provide various insights from both positive (benefits) and negative (challenges) perspectives.

Table 1. Papers with title of the subjected models from the 3 and 4 star journals

4 Star Journal*	Number of Papers on Social Media	Number of Papers on NPD
Journal of Product Innovation Management	7	141
Journal of Marketing	9	15
Journal of Marketing Research	-	1
Journal of Operations Management	-	1
3 Star Journal*	**Number of Papers on Social Media**	**Number of Papers on NPD**
Journal of Marketing Management	8	9
European Journal of Marketing	2	3
R & D Management	2	27
Technovation	7	32
Industrial Marketing Management	-	2
Journal of Business Research	-	2
International Journal of Operations & Production Management	-	2
Production and Operations Management	-	4
Journal of Advertising Research	9	-
International Journal of Production Research	-	1
Production Planning & Control	-	1
Journal of International Marketing	-	1
Total number of papers from 3 start journals	28	84
Total number of papers from 4 start journals	16	158
Total Scholarly Journals (2005 - 2014)**	44	242

* 3 and 4 start ranking based on the ABS ranking 2010.
** Results from the Ebsco Business Resource for the period: January 2005 – April/May 2014 (except some delays for 12-18 months of some publications) and full text articles from Google Scholar for the period January 2005 - April 2014 for the journals that have no access from Ebsco and for the delayed years in Ebsco.

Benefits

There is a large volume of published studies describing the role of customer input in the NPD (e.g. Hoyer et al. 2010; Slotegraaf 2012). For example, Björk & Magnusson (2009) argue that successful innovative companies are those which are capable of evaluating customer ideas and developing them in a further process of innovation better than their competitors. In their study, Björk and Magnusson (2009) show that the high-quality innovative ideas and implementations which bring a competitive advantage over other competitors are those that result from a good connectivity between the company and its group of customers. Customer involvement open to ideas from outside the company is important and beneficial to the new product process as is the research carried out by the R&D departments inside the company. They claim that a good interactive communication between customers leads to enhancement in the quality of innovative ideas. Battor & Battor (2010) examine the role of Customer Relationship Management (CRM) in a company's innovation performance and capabilities. They hold the view that a close relationship between customers improves the company's abilities for innovation, and highlight the importance of understanding customers. Battor & Battor (2010) emphasise that successful innovation cannot be achieved with just the company's financial resources; companies also need to hear the voice of their customers, as well as to understand their customers' requirements and choices. Bharadwaj, Nevin & Wallman (2012) conclude that listening to the voice of its customers has a positive impact on a company's creativity and service delivery. In addition, they remind us about the benefit that listening to the customers' voice has on obtaining a competitive advantage. A deep understanding of customer needs and the market environment leads companies to increase the quality of their products and decreases their expenses and cycle time (Bharadwaj et al. 2012).

In studying customer involvement, the transfer and the transformation of customer knowledge are vital in NPD (Liu 2014). Su, Chen, & Sha (2006) focus on developing a model (E-CKM) that is able to manage the transformation of customer knowledge to product innovation. Knowledge from different segments is used successfully for empirical research with the help of E-CKM in order to decrease possible risk in the NPD process and increase the NPD success rate. They argue that customers' knowledge is essential for product innovation. It is needed to analyse and better understand market needs. In this sense, technologies (e.g. CRM, data-mining, and web-based questionnaires) are essential to evaluate customer information effectively and efficiently. In their research, Yannopoulos, Auh & Menguc (2012) support the idea that companies should involve their customers in the innovation process by creating a proactive communication channel to help customers identify their hidden needs, preferences and problems with the products so that the companies might gain a competitive advantage. Liu (2014) demonstrates empirically that transfer and transformation of customer knowledge speed up the product launch in the NPD process. The findings observed in Raasch's (2011) study mirror those of previous studies that have examined the positive influence of customer collaboration on new product development. He claims that manufacturing companies should go beyond traditional methods in terms of manufacturing and innovation. This group of scholars emphasises that knowledge transfer and transformation help companies develop more innovative and high-quality products.

In a study on consumer co-creation and NPD, Hoyer et al. (2010) conclude that customers' ideas for new product creation play an important role during the NPD process. It is important for companies to provide opportunities for customers to express their unmet needs, from which companies may generate innovative new products. Hoyer et al. (2010) also note that the process of customer co-creation enhances the chance of a product's adoption in the targeted market. This view is further enhanced by Faems, De Visser, Andries & Van Looy (2010). Faems et al. (2010) highlight that a firm's collaboration with external partners (e.g. customers) increases the diversity of knowledge, so enhancing its product innovation performance. Furthermore, Slotegraaf (2012) emphasises the importance of customer collaboration by referring to the fact that there are numerous companies that communicate with external sources to create new ideas for the NPD process. As Slotegraaf (2012) notes, a company may need external knowledge to gain a competitive advantage in the market by obtaining rich and more efficient knowledge than just a single company can produce. Al-Zu'bi & Tsinopoulos (2012) have claimed that collaboration brings the company many benefits in terms of finance and technology, as well as in the management and strategy-making of the company. Moreover, collaboration with external sources helps a company to decrease the cost of innovation, increase the speed and efficiency of the process, and to develop product options for the market. Customers may provide new ideas or modifications for the existing products. This group of scholars shows that the creativity and quality of new products more accurately predict and meet customer demands and needs. Furthermore, scholars also note that the tolerance levels of customers who contribute to the innovation process is higher. These customers are more eager to help the company in the correction of any new product faults (Raasch 2011).

Poetz & Schreier (2012) corroborated the ideas of previous research that claimed that customer co-creation brings benefits to a company. They emphasised that new product ideas which are produced by company employees, such as engineers and designers, generally are successful. Some researchers study good new ideas from the customer co-creation process. Poetz & Schreier (2012) conducted a study by asking for new product ideas from both internal (such as employees e.g. engineers, researchers) and external sources (such as customers); then, they would compare and analyse the quality of the ideas generated. The results of their experimental research show that the users are better at creating new high-level ideas for a new product and that customer ideas bring success in terms of customer benefits and innovativeness. In the same vein, Lau, Tang, & Yam (2010) highlight the impact of customer integration (such as information exchange and product innovation in co-operation with customers) on new product innovation and its performance. The results indicate that supplier and customer co-creation positively and directly influence the product's innovation and its performance. It is stated that product innovation co-operation with customers leads to improvements in product performance. The study conducted by Roberts, Hughes & Kertbo (2013), which aimed at finding the factors that motivate customers to engage in the innovation process, shows the importance of customer motivation for innovation. They emphasised that companies should create co-creation environments to give opportunities to their customers to join in on the co-creation of innovative products or allow them to contribute directly to the creation process. Derived from the concept of customer co-creation, Fuchs & Schreier (2011) searched for customer empowerment creating ideas for NPD and the product decisions for launching. In an experimental study, they divide customer input during the innovation process into two: one helps with the new product design while the other selects the product design for launching. It is found that those companies allowing customers to contribute to the NPD process benefit from a lower cost for a better product. They also notice that these two kinds of customer input increase customers' perceived attitudes towards the company; that it engenders a more positive tendency towards the company; and that it increases more powerful intentions to help the company for innovation. The results of this study contribute to our understanding of customer empowerment and encourage companies to empower customers in the NPD process. Moreover, it is noted that the internet enables customers to take an active role in the innovation process of a company by building online platforms such as social media.

Challenges

While most studies support the benefits of customer involvement, some argue the possible disadvantages of customer input to the NPD process (e.g. Weber et al. 2012). For example, Fredberg & Piller (2011) challenge the common wisdom of strong association of customer knowledge on product innovation (such as Yli-Renko & Janakiraman 2008; Athaide & Klink 2009; Björk & Magnusson 2009; Hoyer et al. 2010; Lau, Tang & Yam 2010; Fuchs & Schreier 2011). Based on a seven-year study on Adidas and its customers, Fredberg & Piller (2011) examine the effect of strong ties with customers on product innovation. They found that although companies may create a co-creation platform based on mutual knowledge exchange between the company and its customers, strong relations with customers do not necessarily ensure that customer input is always helpful to the innovation process. In contrast, they evidence that strong customer involvement may sometimes harm NPD. Unfortunately, they did not give further details on this aspect. Un, Cuervo-Cazurra, & Asakawa (2010) also challenge the positive association between customer inputs and NPD performance. Un et al. (2010) analyse the impact of collaboration of external sources with R&D departments of companies. This study focused on various external sources that impact on product innovation. Interestingly, they found that the most significant effect is obtained from suppliers (not customers). They found that the ideas provided by suppliers provide newer information for the company than customers do. Their research challenges the view that customer collaboration is the most important part of external sources in innovation as most previous studies indicated.

While a group of scholars challenges the positive association between customer input and NPD performance, another group of scholars emphasises the pros and cons of customer involvment in NPD. For example, Weber, Weggeman, & Van Aken (2012) argue that customer involvement in the NPD process has both benefits and drawbacks. They pointed out that changes in technology on the economy, society, and the market modify the role of customers. Today, companies have become more open to customer co-creation, co-innovation and co-design. Firms are expected to be more collaborative, more dynamic, more motivated and have closer relations with external partners (such as customers). Weber et al. (2012) listed various advantages of customer involvement in the product innovation process, such as reducing the costs of products and services, improving the quality of products and services, reducing uncertainty, easy adoption of the new product, being loyal, and obtaining psychological and personal benefits (e.g. feeling of belonging). Despite these prominent advantages, they call for attention to the possible drawbacks of engaging customers in the NPD process, such as the high cost that the company has to pay in order to encourage customer participation in NPD activities. They advise that company efforts do not always lead to equality in the return on their investment. Nijssen, Hillebrand, de Jong, & Kemp (2012) further endorse this assertion. Based on a study in the high-tech sector, Nijssen et al. (2012) found that companies often face a dilemma in managing NPD. Their study shows that the financial benefits of customer interaction in the short term may lead to a competitive market disadvantage in the long term. While firms are busy satisfying customer needs and solving customers' immediate problems, they may need to compromise on effort and time for more advanced product innovation, which sustains long term competitiveness. Christensen (1997) also reminds us that although a company can be managed well in satisfying the customers, this good management may cause failures in innovation that lead to losing their leader/top positions in the market or the aggressive investment of new products, or not producing innovative new products that are equal to or more than meeting customers' needs and expectations. This group of scholars challenges us to think again on the investment in innovation that only listens to the customers' voice. Satisfying customer needs may bring a high return on investment in the short run, but may lead to loss of their leading position in the market in the long term.

Subramaniam (2006) draws attention to research on the issue of transfer of knowledge gained from customers and argues that there has been a lack of studies that focus on the ways this knowledge should be transferred into new product innovation. He points out that not all information can be transferred into the innovation process. The significant thing is creating a good and effective method of achieving this. He emphasised that effective customer input requires not only a successful method of obtaining knowledge, but also a successful method of transferring knowledge into new products. Fang (2008) also points out the challenges of managing external knowledge in new product innovation co-projects and highlights the problematic tacit knowledge issue. The customer's role in new product innovation is evaluated as being a good knowledge source and co-developer. This study however finds that this participation may not lead to successful innovations. Various and adverse information may be obtained in cooperative projects with customers. Furthermore, excessive customer information does not always seem necessarily to be beneficial to the new product development process. In this regard, another school of thought provides some explanation to this drawback. We summarise below.

Open innovation has traditionally been regarded as beneficial for new product performance (Chesbrough 2006). However, some studies have pointed out the drawbacks of excessive collaboration (e.g. Calantone & Rubera 2012). Because collaboration simultaneously presents costs and benefits that vary with conditions, a contingent view of managerial practices suggests that the optimal level of integration should vary according to some factors that indicate when high levels of collaboration are preferable to lower levels. Firms can develop new products either by using their existing technological or customer knowledge, or by exploring new solutions far removed from the current capability endowment (Kyriakopoulos and Moorman 2004). In a study of the US auto industry, Calantone & Rubera (2012) investigated exploitative and explorative NPD and have shown that strong collaboration with customers when firms are pursuing explorative innovation programmes has a negative impact on new product programme performance. It seems that when companies develop new products that require a different market or technological knowledge, collaboration with customers does not necessarily generate postive results. This is a surprising result, which contradicts previous NPD literature (Ruekert & Walker, 1987; Olson et al. 1995, 2001). In the literature, there are arguments that organisational units involved in the exploration process should be kept separate from others, in an effort to guarantee them the freedom to develop new competencies (Levinthal & March 1993). Only when new competencies are developed should these units be reintegrated within the organisation to transfer their knowledge to others. This theory may explain the adverse effects of customer knowledge on NPD. In other words, customer voice or customer co-creation may benefit exploitative NPD, yet for explorative NPD, customer involvement may bring negative impact.

Social Media and New Product Development

Based on a survey of more than 3,000 senior executives across industries, geographies, and functions, a recent McKinsey report indicated that companies qualified as "networked" (those that used collaborative Web 2.0 technologies intensively to connect the internal efforts of employees and extend the organisation's reach to customers, partners, and suppliers) outperformed other companies in terms of market share, profitability, and market leadership (Bughin & Chui 2010). The car manufacturer Audi creates a "Virtual lab" for customers to contribute to the innovation process. This is followed by 1,662 participants who are chosen among online Audi communities to support the development team of Audi by developing ideas. Ducati and Harley-Davidson use social media communities for the purpose of developing new products. Nike allows customers to design their own shoes and choose the features that they wish to see in company products by means of online portals. Apple iPod also benefits from the improvements made to existing company products by online communities who, in addition, also give ideas for new designs.

In a study on the usage of social media, Naylor, Lamberton & West (2012) have found that the use of different forms of social media by top companies for the purpose of connecting with customers is around 83%. It is widely recognised that early adopters who integrated customers' voice via social media into their NPD strategy are well placed to capture new opportunities (Shearman 2011). Nowadays, the development of technologies has brought many opportunities for companies, one of them being social media. It allows companies to follow consumer needs and provide an easier way to filter and analyse these needs (Shearman 2011). Social media provides a medium that allows anyone to reach information without any time or geographical limits (Paid Social Media Advertising, Nielsen 2013 Report). Social platforms provide companies with the ability to create a unique portal between them and their customers. However, there are both positive and negative views in the existing literature. In this section, we review the arguments on the benefits and challenges of using social media for NPD, and summarise below.

Benefits

The majority of studies (e.g. Füller, Matzler & Hoppe 2008; Droge, Stanko & Pollitte 2010; Colliander & Dahlen 2011) considers social media as interactive communication channels that provide members with a relationship platform between customers and the company. Füller, Matzler & Hoppe (2008) examine the influence of communities in social media channels on the innovation process. They conduct a study on a sample of 550 members of the Volkswagen Golf GTI car community. They found that customers who belong to social media communities are much more willing to contribute to the innovation process. These customers are those who have positive tendencies towards the brand, who have an interest in the innovation process that they are allowed to take part in, who have more experience and knowledge about the brand, and who have a talent for innovation. They claim that companies, through social media, provide members with a chance to share their experiences, give suggestions for product improvements and modifications, solve problems and produce ideas. Füller et al. (2008) also note that the members in social media are more eager to contribute and create value by identifying the needs. This customer willingness helps companies to be more creative and profitable by developing new innovative ideas. Similarly, in a study of e-commerce websites, Droge, Stanko & Pollitte (2010) point out the close online relations between the customer and the company and highlight the role of social media channels in NPD. Social media channels, as portals, are essential to provide customers with a virtual community for contributing ideas and reading comments, and creating links between each other about an idea, a brand, a product or an activity. Droge et al. (2010) also stress that social media play a vital role for a company for value co-creation in the NPD process and contribute to marketing mix. This group of scholars highlights the importance of social media in marketing strategy. This view is enhanced by another group of scholars.

Colliander & Dahlen (2011) who study seven blogs and seven online magazines, compare the influence of social media and traditional marketing methods. The results show that social media is significantly more effective than traditional marketing methods in connecting with customers. In another study which set out to determine the power of social media, Lipsman, Mudd, Rich & Bruich (2012) found the positive effectiveness of social media in creating interrelations between customers and companies. They further emphasise that social media encourages customers to share their experiences and ideas more intensely by providing better accessibility and competency. Another study which argues in favour of the possible benefits of the internet for collaborative innovation was done by Sawhney, Verona & Prandelli (2005). Based on two exploratory case studies, Sawhney et al. (2005) claim that social media allows companies to be more interactive, to connect with more people, to be consistent and flexible, and to benefit from the opportunity of speed. They further highlight that internet-based customer integration affects the NPD process positively in terms of knowledge transfer. They advocate that being connected to companies through social media increases their encouragement to share knowledge and increases their eagerness to contribute. In addition, they found that being able to connect with the company directly creates a positive influence on their trust and involvement with the company.

Another group of scholars study social media from different angles such as co-creation, knowledge sharing and uncertainty reduction. For example Füller, Hutter & Faullant (2011), who study customer integration in design process through media, hold the view that social media allows customers to contribute positively from all over the world. The results show that co-creation experience through social media significantly influenced the quantity and quality of customer input more than any single idea from other marketing channels. They suggest that fully featured online platforms encourage creative consumers to offer new opinions through these platforms. Bartl, Füller, Mühlbacher & Ernst (2012) further support previous studies and point out that customers are capable of innovating new products and are good at adding their know-how to the innovation process and participating voluntarily. Furthermore, Al-Zu'bi & Tsinopoulos (2012) have found that social media is important in reducing uncertainty in the NPD process. Creating online platforms, virtual labs, and monitoring millions of blogs and websites are some of the methods that companies such as Audi, Adidas, BMW, Ducati, Procter & Gamble, and 3M prefer to utilise for the purpose of interacting with customers more regularly, efficiently and effectively (Füller et al. 2008; Fuchs & Schreier 2011). These techniques allow companies to follow customers' preferences during the development of new products (Füller et al. 2008). This process largely bridges the knowledge gap about customer and market information. As a result, customers' integration into the company's NPD scheme encourages them to buy the company's products and to remain loyal.

Piller & Walcher (2006) hold the view that asking external opinions is an efficient way of increasing the success of an innovation and emphasise the importance of inputs that are obtained through the internet. This increases the quality and creativity of the company's ideas (ibid). The results of their study suggest that the problems and uncertainties of a new product's development process may be decreased by online idea gathering tools. Tickle, Adebanjo & Michaelides (2011) further enhance this assertion and point out that social media work as communities of people who share common interests and who are able to come together without location limits, thereby having the advantages of being faster and cheaper. Haavisto (2014) studied the effect of social media on creating customer value in product innovation. The results of the study show that social media channels consist of innovative ideas and customers' desire for participation; they then bring success to the company in their new product innovation process. Haavisto (2014) highlights the possibility of discovering the unmet needs of customers through the analysis of social media channels. This group of scholars also highlight the fact that customers trust the information they obtain through social media about products with which they are unfamiliar (Athaide & Zhang 2011). From a company's perspective, the contribution of customers' knowledge is considered as being reliable for its product development process because customer knowledge generally provides the company with the opportunity to better predict the future behaviour of customers. These researchers support the usage and benefits of social media for innovating new products because of its ability to enable companies to listen to the voice of their customers. Finally, Björk & Magnusson (2009), who investigate the relationship between the use of social media and the quality of the innovative ideas, have found that more network connections would bring more successful ideas into the NPD networks.

Social media has been claimed as one of the best technologies for supplying users with open communication and free markets (Björk & Magnusson 2009). The development of social media provides new chances to companies for learning, innovating, and connecting to open innovation platforms which would provide them with the ability to reach external sources of knowledge about technologies and markets (Björk & Magnusson 2009; Adebanjo & Michaelides 2010). Together, these studies demonstrate that the usage of social media channels provides many advantages for the NPD of companies, providing them with easy, cheap, dynamic and limitless communication with customers that, in turn, has the ability to increase the efficiency and adoption of a new product. However, these benefits are challenged by another group of scholars.

Challenges

Social media is mostly used for communication between customers, business partners, internal employees and the company itself (Ernst, Brem & Voigt 2013). Tickle et al. (2011) advise that online social communities help companies to reach external knowledge, which is an important and competitive indicator for open innovation without the limits of organisational resources. However, it has been argued that using social media is not suitable for every company and does not bring success to all. For example, while Edvardsson et al. (2012) support the idea that a close relationship with customers is needed for an effective NPD, they find that just following customers is no longer sufficient. Edvardsson et al. (2012) also find that the ideas and experiences of customers obtained from social media are useful only when they are relevant. Corstjens & Umblijs (2012) also raise a similar point. Stressing the importance of being engaged with customers, they argued that just being able to hear the voice of customers is insufficient and suggest that companies need to go beyond just listening to their customers.

Another study further enhances the understanding of this issue. In studying customer input, Bartl et al. (2012) questioned the covertness of customer input in NPD decisions for product innovation. They claim that although the benefits of virtual customer integration methods (including better understanding of customer needs as well as the quality of the information obtained) are widely accepted, the issue of using social media remains problematic. Bartle et al. (2012) found that many companies have still not achieved the advantages expected from interaction between themselves and their customers through online portals. They conclude that this may be because of disadvantages of using social media. They then study potential disadvantages and raise the issue of customers' inability to articulate, unbalanced target group orientation, intellectual property problems, disturbance of internal processes, lack of secrecy and incremental innovations. These challenges are further supported by Haavisto (2014) who argues that a huge amount of information, or vague and irrelevant information, may create problems during the innovation process. This further supports the argument that listening to customer voice is simply insufficient for NPD success (Corstjens & Umblijs 2012; Edvardsson et al. 2012). Bartle et al. (2012) conclude that companies wanting to create and follow their communities through social media channels need to evaluate both advantages and disadvantages. Using social media for NPD success is not an easy task. It challenges scholars as well as practitioners. We discuss the implications in the next section.

Discussion

We study the usage of social media in NPD process. In particular, we focus on customer/user inputs obtained from the use of social media for incremental NPD. The literature has revealed that social media is one of the most effective channels for keeping in touch with customers (e.g. Ernst et al. 2013). The effects of social media, by means of creating interactive online platforms, are mentioned in the literature as: interacting regularly with customers; building close relations with customers and; acquiring new and accurate knowledge from them. Meeting customer expectations and needs is suggested as the main success factor for using social media in NPD. Because of this, considering the voice of the customer has increased the chances for success of a new product's development. However, it is also argued that the company needs to balance customer input to avoid the risk of obtaining excessive and irrelevant information and knowledge from customers.

As mentioned in the literature review, listening to what the customer has to say is essential for the success of a company, especially for NPD. To be able to see the influence of customers on the NPD process, we have highlighted the role of the customer in NPD from the perspectives of customer interaction, collaboration and co-creation. The literature review also advances our understanding of the drawbacks of customer involvement, such as the risk of losing long-term competiveness, the difficulty derived from excessive information and the issue of tacit knowledge. Thus, it is suggested that customer input does not always benefit NPD performance and that companies need to be more careful when using customer knowledge and involvement in the NPD process as highlighted by Calantone & Rubera (2012). Furthermore, although most studies agree with the positive effects of customer input on NPD, its possible failures are mentioned by various researchers (e.g. Subramaniam 2006; Nijssen et al. 2012). Even though companies should encourage their customers to co-develop new products with them, they need to take into consideration that an excess of information may complicate the process because of its being too vague and inconvenient, thereby increasing the costs that the company might accrue. Moreover, since industries differ, we argue that whether or not customer information is useful may depend on the type of industry.

We also find that most of the topics on social media were determined as relating to product content (e.g. Droge et al. 2010). It is well evidenced that the online community is able to coordinate the marketing agenda for new product success (Matzler & Hoppe 2008; Tickle et al. 2011). Social media seems capable of positioning the product in target consumers' minds. Scholars also emphasise that contributors through social media are often volunteers who enrich the quantity and quality of design ideas. Their research indicates that community atmospheres positively stimulate customers to participate in the co-creation experience in social media channels. Customers have the chance to communicate with each other interactively, thereby allowing them to write comments about each other's ideas. This participation, in turn, creates more constructive and positive communication. However, there are challenges that companies need to tackle. Companies need to evaluate projected returns and input levels from utilising these communities before starting to use them.

We argue that before taking advantage of external sources, a company needs to consider the benefits and drawbacks. In some cases, companies have to decide to what extent they will utilise customer collaboration for their NPD processes. For instance, the industry, the size of the company, their reliability, and the amount and cost of the information may be possible determinants for companies. Although most researchers agree with the benefits of co-operation between their R&D departments and customers, they stress the importance of input levels. On the other hand, some studies emphasise the possible disadvantages of a remarkable amount of inputs, such as cost implications and decreasing the new product success levels. Although various inputs may exist, future customers and those of competitors may have a negative impact on the competitive position of the company in the market.

The Implications

The role of social media in customer input during the NPD process is providing more experienced and willing customers with the opportunity to join in the process. Social media allows companies to benefit from portals through which customers can express their ideas, experiences, and knowledge freely, interactively and intensely. When customers belong to social media channels, these channels encourage customers to join and contribute to the NPD process. Belonging to a social media community awakens a willingness to make contributions. However, using social media can create problems when customer input to the NPD process is considered as being irrelevant or when the amount of information is too huge for the company to easily manage.

As most researchers agree, the contribution of external sources brings success to the company. These external sources include customers, suppliers, competitors and universities. Customer input is determined as being very beneficial in terms of creating a competitive advantage, high quality product innovation, better quality of innovative ideas, good interactive communication, the ability to predict and determine customers' unmet needs, decrease risks and uncertainty, decrease the cost of innovation, increase the speed of obtaining information, and enhance the chances of a product being adopted in the market. As a result, customer input brings many advantages which R&D departments cannot achieve by themselves. However, the diversity of information and the cost and finding methods for evaluating and accessing it can be seen as the negative results of customer inputs. There is an urgent need to better understand these issues.

Benefitting from customers' experiences and utilising their willingness to provide information via social media platforms are essential for the short term growth and long term survival of companies. Nevertheless, companies need to find ways of managing this information well. On the one hand, sectoral differences should not be ignored when studying the usage of social media for NPD. On the other hand, it must not be forgotten that customers are unable to identify all of their unmet needs. The hidden needs tend to be a challenge when using social media for product ideas, which requires further research.

Finally, the amount of customer inputs should be controlled in order to keep disadvantages at bay. Researchers have suggested and examined the implications of some methods for managing customer inputs, but a generally accepted method has not yet been identified. Further research is required.

CONCLUSION

This chapter studies the usage of social media for collecting customer inputs during the NPD process and its impact on product success by means of a critical literature review. The results of the relevant literature suggest that allowing external sources to help the new product development process brings more benefits than drawbacks. In this chapter, we have highlighted that customer input is mostly analysed as being one of the most important elements from external sources. The evidence suggests that customer input to the NPD process is essential and necessary for the success of new products. Although some drawbacks are mentioned by some researchers, the results of most studies support the idea that customer input brings advantages to the NPD process, including a better understanding of customers' unmet needs and expectations, a rich amount of information about the market, faster access to information, and the ability to minimise uncertainties. Social media is an effective, useful and fast channel for obtaining this customer information through interactive online channels. This interactive communication improves the quality and variety of ideas for new products. However, it is criticised for providing an enormous amount of (often irrelevant) information which is hard to manage and use for the development of a new product. In general, therefore, it seems that customer input through social media channels is used successfully by many top innovative companies. This result leads us to propose that further research is needed to encourage the usage of social media, especially when bearing in mind the ease with which it is able to provide customer information. However, more advanced methods are needed to examine and evaluate the customer inputs obtained through social media. Furthermore, the absorptive capacity of firms, the cost of this co-working, and the amount of hard-to-manage information are critical issues for managers and marketers to consider in a firm's NPD processes. Finally, the extent to which the information collected from social media is able to be used creates another challenge for product developers.

To conclude, the NPD process has been determined to be a very important process for the success or failure of a new product. R&D departments need to co-operate with customers during the NPD process in order to better understand customers' unmet needs and expectations and in order to allow them to obtain more innovative and better quality ideas from customers. This will be able to provide the company with a competitive advantage among competitors. A conceptual framework (See Figure 1) summarises the findings from this critical literature review and suggests some important topics for further research.

Limitations and Future Research

Several limitations to this pilot study need to be acknowledged. The most important limitation lies in the fact that one of the most important deficiencies of NPDs which are helped with social media is about consumers' hidden needs. Especially in the technology market, the innovation department needs to go beyond market research and consumer feedback and thoughts. For technological products, consumers are usually not able to define their needs unless someone else reveals them. Therefore, to analyse what consumers want and what they will tend to use is a constant challenge in innovation. Most customers are not able to identify whether they need a new innovation. Companies consider effective communication and intense knowledge exchange as beneficial solutions for changing this on behalf of the company. Because of this, the ability to find out what customers' hidden needs are by using social media awaits to be discovered by innovative companies. Also, in this context, the study is limited by the lack of methods

Figure 1. The usage of social media in new product development process: The benefits and the challenges

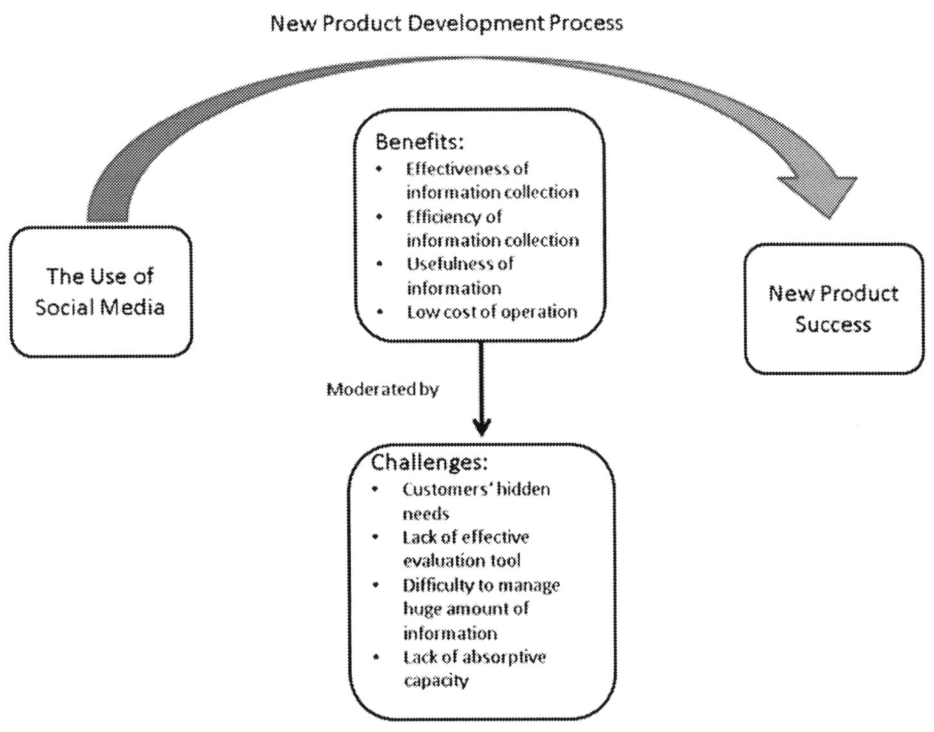

for evaluating customer inputs in the literature. It is also noteworthy that this review mainly focuses on incremental NPD. This is because customer input is closely associated with incremental NPD. However, the use of social media should not only be limited to incremental NPD and we encourage further research on the association of using social media and radical NPD. Finally, this study did not evaluate the use of customer inputs in different sectors which may show different results when supplied with customer inputs about NPD. The most researched sectors are the technology, automotive and clothing industries. More research in other sectors is needed in order to better understand the effect of customer input on the NPD process. Last but not least, the possible differences and benefits of customer input between the different stages of the new product development process may be one of the limitations of this research. The differences in the various stages of the NPD process have not yet been examined properly.

REFERENCES

Adebanjo, D., & Michaelides, R. (2010). Analysis of Web 2.0 enabled e-clusters: A case study. *Technovation*, *30*(4), 238–248. doi:10.1016/j.technovation.2009.09.001

Al-Zu'bi, Z. M. F., & Tsinopoulos, C. (2012). Suppliers versus lead users: Examining their relative impact on product variety. *Journal of Product Innovation Management*, *29*(4), 667–680. doi:10.1111/j.1540-5885.2012.00932.x

Athaide, G. A., & Klink, R. R. (2009). Managing seller–buyer relationships during new product development. *Journal of Product Innovation Management*, *26*(5), 566–577. doi:10.1111/j.1540-5885.2009.00681.x

Athaide, G. A., & Zhang, J. Q. (2011). The determinants of seller-buyer interactions during new product development in technology-based industrial markets. *Journal of Product Innovation Management*, *28*(s1S1), 146–158. doi:10.1111/j.1540-5885.2011.00867.x

Bartl, M., Füller, J., Mühlbacher, H., & Ernst, H. (2012). A manager's perspective on virtual customer integration for new product development. *Journal of Product Innovation Management*, *29*(6), 1031–1046. doi:10.1111/j.1540-5885.2012.00946.x

Battor, M., & Battor, M. (2010). The impact of customer relationship management capability on innovation and performance advantages: Testing a mediated model. *Journal of Marketing Management*, *26*(9–10), 842–857. doi:10.1080/02672570903498843

Bharadwaj, N., Nevin, J. R., & Wallman, J. P. (2012). Explicating hearing the voice of the customer as a manifestation of customer Focus and Assessing its Consequences. *Journal of Product Innovation Management*, *29*(6), 1012–1030. doi:10.1111/j.1540-5885.2012.00954.x

Björk, J., & Magnusson, M. (2009). Where Do Good Innovation Ideas Come From? Exploring the Influence of Network Connectivity on Innovation Idea Quality. *Journal of Product Innovation Management*, *26*(6), 662–670. doi:10.1111/j.1540-5885.2009.00691.x

Bughin, J. & Chui, M. (2010, December). The Rise of the Networked Enterprise: Web 2.0 Finds Its Payday. *McKinsey Quarterly*.

Calantone, R., & Rubera, G. (2012). When Should RD&E and Marketing Collaborate? The Moderating Role of Exploration–Exploitation and Environmental Uncertainty. *Journal of Product Innovation Management, 29*(1), 144–157. doi:10.1111/j.1540-5885.2011.00884.x

Cambridge Advanced Learner's Dictionary & Thesaurus. (n.d.). Cambridge University Press. Retrieved from: http://dictionary.cambridge.org/dictionary/british/social-media?q=social+media

Chesbrough, H. (2006). Open innovation: a new paradigm for understanding industrial innovation. In H. Chesbrough, W. Vanhaverbeke, & J. West (Eds.), *Open Innovation: Researching a New Paradigm* (pp. 1–14). Oxford: Oxford University Press.

Christensen, C. M. (1997). *The Innovators' Dilemma: When New Technologies Cause Great Firms to Fail*. Boston: Harvard Business School Press.

Colliander, J., & Dahlen, M. (2011). Following the fashionable friend: The power of social media - weighing publicity effectiveness of blogs versus online magazines. *Journal of Advertising Research, 51*(1), 313–320. doi:10.2501/JAR-51-1-313-320

Corstjens, M., & Umblijs, A. (2012). The Power of Evil: The Damage of Negative Social Media Strongly outweigh Positive Contributions. *Journal of Advertising Research, 52*(4), 433–449. doi:10.2501/JAR-52-4-433-449

Dahan, E., & Hauser, J. (2002). Managing a dispersed product development process. In B. Weitz & R. Wensley (Eds.), *Handbook of marketing* (pp. 179–222). Thousand Oaks, CA: Sage. doi:10.4135/9781848608283.n9

Drechsler, W., Natter, M., & Leeflang, P. S. H. (2013). Improving Marketing's Contribution to New Product Development. *Journal of Product Innovation Management, 30*(2), 298–315. doi:10.1111/j.1540-5885.2012.01010.x

Droge, C., Stanko, M. A., & Pollitte, W. A. (2010). Lead Users and Early Adopters on the Web: The Role of New Technology Product Blogs. *Journal of Product Innovation Management, 27*(1), 66–82. doi:10.1111/j.1540-5885.2009.00700.x

Edvardsson, B., Kristensson, P., Magnusson, P., & Sundström, E. (2012). Customer Integration within Service Development– A review of methods and an analysis of insitu and exsitu contributions. *Technovation, 32*(7–8), 419–429. doi:10.1016/j.technovation.2011.04.006

Ernst, M., Brem, A., & Voigt, K.-I. (2013). Social Media in Strategic Management. In M. R. Olivas-Lujan & T. Bondarouk (Eds.), *Advanced Series in Management. Emerald Group Publishing Limited* (pp. 169–195).

Faems, D., De Visser, M., Andries, P., & Van Looy, B. (2010). Technology Alliance Portfolios and Financial Performance: Value-Enhancing and Cost-Increasing Effects of Open Innovation. *Journal of Product Innovation Management, 27*(6), 785–791. doi:10.1111/j.1540-5885.2010.00752.x

Fang, E. (2008). Customer Participation and the Trade-Off Between New Product Innovativeness and Speed to Market. *Journal of Marketing, 72*(4), 90–104. doi:10.1509/jmkg.72.4.90

Franke, N., Keinz, P., & Schreier, M. (2008). Complementing mass customization toolkits with user communities: How peer input improves customer self-design. *Journal of Product Innovation Management, 25*(6), 546–559. doi:10.1111/j.1540-5885.2008.00321.x

Franke, N., & Shah, S. (2003). How communities support innovative activities: An exploration of assistance and sharing among innovative users of sporting equipment. *Research Policy, 32*(1), 157–178. doi:10.1016/S0048-7333(02)00006-9

Fredberg, T., & Piller, F. T. (2011). The paradox of tie strength in customer relationships for innovation: A longitudinal case study in the sports industry. *R & D Management, 41*(5), 470–484. doi:10.1111/j.1467-9310.2011.00659.x

Fuchs, C., & Schreier, M. (2011). Customer Empowerment in New Product Development. *Journal of Product Innovation Management, 28*(1), 17–32. doi:10.1111/j.1540-5885.2010.00778.x

Füller, J., Hutter, K., & Faullant, R. (2011). Why co-creation experience matters? Creative experience and its impact on the quantity and quality of creative contributions. *R & D Management, 41*(3), 259–273. doi:10.1111/j.1467-9310.2011.00640.x

Füller, J., Matzler, K., & Hoppe, M. (2008). Brand Community Members as a Source of Innovation. *Journal of Product Innovation Management, 25*(6), 608–619. doi:10.1111/j.1540-5885.2008.00325.x

Garcia, R., & Calantone, R. (2002). A critical look at technological innovation typology and innovativeness terminology: A literature review. *Journal of Product Innovation Management, 19*(2), 110–132. doi:10.1016/S0737-6782(01)00132-1

Haavisto, P. (2014). Observing discussion forums and product innovation – A way to create consumer value? Case heart-rate monitors. *Technovation, 34*(4), 1–8. doi:10.1016/j.technovation.2013.12.001

Hoyer, W. D., Chandy, R., Dorotic, M., Krafft, M., & Singh, S. S. (2010). Consumer Cocreation in New Product Development. *Journal of Service Research, 13*(3), 283–296. doi:10.1177/1094670510375604

Kelley, D. J., Ali, A., & Zahra, S. A. (2013). Where Do Breakthroughs Come From? Characteristics of High-Potential Inventions. *Journal of Product Innovation Management, 30*(6), 1212–1226. doi:10.1111/jpim.12055

Lau, A. K. W., Tang, E., & Yam, R. C. M. (2010). Effects of Supplier and Customer Integration on Product Innovation and Performance: Empirical Evidence in Hong Kong Manufacturers. *Journal of Product Innovation Management, 27*(5), 761–777. doi:10.1111/j.1540-5885.2010.00749.x

Lipsman, A., Mudd, G., Rich, M., & Bruich, S. (2012). The Power of "Like" How Brands Reach (and Influence) Fans Through Social-Media Marketing. *Journal of Advertising Research, 52*(1), 40–52. doi:10.2501/JAR-52-1-040-052

Liu, R. (2014). Management Learning in Business Networks: The process and the impact. *Management Learning*. doi:10.1177/1350507614537019

Liu, R., & Hart, S. (2011). Does Experience Matter? A study of knowledge processes and uncertainty reduction in solution innovation. *Industrial Marketing Management, 40*(5), 691–698. doi:10.1016/j.indmarman.2011.05.004

Liu, R., & Rayman-Bacchus, L. (2014). Absorptive Capacity, Dynamic Capabilities and Product Innovation. *British Academy of Management.*

Naylor, R. W., Lamberton, C. P., & West, P. M. (2012). Beyond the "Like" Button: The Impact of Mere Virtual Presence on Brand Evaluations and Purchase Intentions in Social Media Settings. *Journal of Marketing*, *76*(6), 105–120. doi:10.1509/jm.11.0105

Nijssen, E. J., Hillebrand, B., de Jong, J. P. J., & Kemp, R. G. M. (2012). Strategic Value Assessment and Explorative Learning Opportunities with Customers. *Journal of Product Innovation Management*, *29*(S1), 91–102. doi:10.1111/j.1540-5885.2012.00960.x

Paid Social Media Advertising. (2013). *Nielsen 2013 Report*. Retrieved from: http://www.agence-indigo.com/articles/Nielsen-Paid-Social-Media-Adv-Report-2013.pdf

Piller, F. T., & Walcher, D. (2006). Toolkits for idea competitions: A novel method to integrate users in new product development. *R & D Management*, *36*(3), 307–318. doi:10.1111/j.1467-9310.2006.00432.x

Poetz, M. K., & Schreier, M. (2012). The value of crowdsourcing: Can users really compete with professionals in generating new product ideas? *Journal of Product Innovation Management*, *29*(2), 245–256. doi:10.1111/j.1540-5885.2011.00893.x

Raasch, C. (2011). Product Development IN Open Design Communities: A Process Perspective. *International Journal of Innovation and Technology Management*, *8*(4), 557–575. doi:10.1142/S021987701100260X

Reid, S. E., & de Brentani, U. (2004). The Fuzzy Front End of New Product Development for Discontinuous Innovations: A Theoretical Model. *Journal of Product Innovation Management*, *21*(3), 170–184. doi:10.1111/j.0737-6782.2004.00068.x

Roberts, D., Hughes, M., & Kertbo, K. (2013). Exploring consumers' motivations to engage in innovation through co-creation activities. *European Journal of Marketing*, *48*(1/2), 147–169. doi:10.1108/EJM-12-2010-0637

Saisho, T. (2008). In A. Ishikawa & A. Tsujimoto (Eds.), *Creative Marketing for New Product and New Business Development*. Singapore: World Scientific Publishing. doi:10.1142/9789812772190_0004

Sawhney, M., Verona, G., & Prandelli, M. (2005). Collaborating to Create: The Internet as a Platform for Customer Engagement in Product Innovation. *Journal of Interactive Marketing*, *19*(4), 4–17. doi:10.1002/dir.20046

Shearman, S. (2011, January). Proving Social Media's ROI. *Marketing Magazine*, 9 – 11.

Slotegraaf, R. J. (2012). Keep the Door Open: Innovating Toward a More Sustainable Future. *Journal of Product Innovation Management*, *29*(3), 349–351. doi:10.1111/j.1540-5885.2012.00905.x

Su, C., Chen, Y., & Sha, D. Y. (2006). Linking innovative product development with customer knowledge: A data-mining approach. *Technovation*, *26*(7), 784–795. doi:10.1016/j.technovation.2005.05.005

Subramaniam, M. (2006). Integrating Cross-Border Knowledge for Transnational New Product Development. *Journal of Product Innovation Management*, *23*(6), 541–555. doi:10.1111/j.1540-5885.2006.00223.x

Tickle, M., Adebanjo, D., & Michaelides, Z. (2011). Developmental approaches to B2B virtual communities. *Technovation*, *31*(7), 296–308. doi:10.1016/j.technovation.2011.04.002

Trott, P. (2005). *Innovation management and new product development* (3rd ed.). Harlow, UK: Financial Times/Prentice Hall.

Un, C. A., Cuervo-Cazurra, A., & Asakawa, K. (2010). R&D Collaborations and Product Innovation. *Journal of Product Innovation Management*, *27*(5), 673–689. doi:10.1111/j.1540-5885.2010.00744.x

von Hippel, E., & Katz, R. (2002). Shifting innovation to users via toolkits. *Management Science*, *48*(7), 821–833. doi:10.1287/mnsc.48.7.821.2817

Weber, M. E. A., Weggeman, M. C. D. P., & Van Aken, J. E. (2012). Developing What Customers Really Need: Involving Customers in Innovations. *International Journal of Innovation and Technology Management*, *9*(3), 1250018–1250033. doi:10.1142/S0219877012500186

Yannopoulos, P., Auh, S., & Menguc, B. (2012). Achieving Fit between Learning and Market Orientation: Implications for New Product Performance. *Journal of Product Innovation Management*, *29*(4), 531–545. doi:10.1111/j.1540-5885.2012.00923.x

Yli-Renko, H., & Janakiraman, R. (2008). How Customer Portfolio Affects New Product Development in Technology-Based Entrepreneurial Firms. *Journal of Marketing*, *72*(5), 131–148. doi:10.1509/jmkg.72.5.131

ADDITIONAL READING

Athaide, G. A., & Klink, R. R. (2009). Managing Seller–Buyer Relationships during New Product Development. *Journal of Product Innovation Management*, *26*(5), 566–577. doi:10.1111/j.1540-5885.2009.00681.x

Bonner, J. M., & Walker, O. C. (2004). Selecting Influential Business-to-Business Customers in New Product Development: Relational Embeddedness and Knowledge Heterogeneity Considerations. *Journal of Product Innovation Management*, *21*(3), 155–169. doi:10.1111/j.0737-6782.2004.00067.x

Clarke, I. III, & Flaherty, T. B. (2003). Web-based B2B portals. *Industrial Marketing Management*, *32*(1), 15–23. doi:10.1016/S0019-8501(01)00199-7

Coviello, N. E., & Joseph, R. (2012). Creating Major Innovations with Customers: Insights from Small and Young Technology Firms. *Journal of Marketing*, *76*(6), 87–104. doi:10.1509/jm.10.0418

Dahan, E., Soukhoroukova, A., & Spann, M. (2010). New Product Development 2.0: Preference Markets—How Scalable Securities Markets Identify Winning Product Concepts and Attributes. *Journal of Product Innovation Management*, *27*(7), 937–954. doi:10.1111/j.1540-5885.2010.00763.x

Dahl, A., Lawrence, J., & Pierce, J. (2011). "Building an Innovation Community". *Research & Technology Management*, September—October 2011, 19-27.

Dowling, M., & Helm, R. (2006). Product development success through cooperation: A study of entrepreneurial firms. *Technovation*, *26*(4), 483–488. doi:10.1016/j.technovation.2005.06.015

Evanschitzky, H., Eisend, M., Calantone, R. J., & Jiang, Y. (2012). Success Factors of Product Innovation: An Updated Meta-Analysis. *Journal of Product Innovation Management*, *29*(S1), 21–37. doi:10.1111/j.1540-5885.2012.00964.x

Füller, J., Matzler, K., & Hoppe, M. (2008). Brand Community Members as a Source of Innovation. *Journal of Product Innovation Management*, *25*(6), 608–619. doi:10.1111/j.1540-5885.2008.00325.x

Hammedi, W., van Riel, A. C. R., & Sasovova, Z. (2011). Antecedents and Consequences of Reflexivity in New Product Idea Screening. *Journal of Product Innovation Management*, *28*, 662–679.

Kuester, S., Homburg, C., & Hess, S. C. (2012). Externally Directed and Internally Directed Market Launch Management: The Role of Organizational Factors in Influencing New Product Success. *Journal of Product Innovation Management*, *29*(S1), 38–52. doi:10.1111/j.1540-5885.2012.00968.x

Van Eck, P. S., Jager, W., & Leeflang, P. S. H. (2011). Opinion Leaders' Role in Innovation Diffusion: A Simulation Study. *Journal of Product Innovation Management*, *28*(2), 187–203. doi:10.1111/j.1540-5885.2011.00791.x

West, J., & Bogers, M. (2014) "Leveraging External Sources of Innovation: A Review of Research on Open Innovation" (January 2, 2013). Journal of Product Innovation Management, 31 (4), doi: . Available at SSRN: http://ssrn.com/abstract=219567510.1111/jpim.12125

KEY TERMS AND DEFINITIONS

Customer Co-Creation: It concerns markets as platforms for firms and active customers to share, combine and renew each other's resources and capabilities to create value through new forms of interaction, service and learning mechanisms. It differs from the traditional passive consumer market of the past.

Customer Relationship Management (CRM): A system for managing a company's interactions with current and future customers. It often involves using technology to organize, automate and synchronize sales, marketing, customer service, and technical support.

Incremental NPD: Concerns minor changes and modifications to products and technologies.

Innovation: The management and implementations of new ideas and novelty.

New Product Development (NPD): The process of innovating new products or services from idea generation to product commercialization.

Radical NPD: Represents major departures from existing capabilities in the firm and constitutes the basis for completely new products and services.

Social Media: Interactive online platforms that allow people to connect each other interactively through internet.

This research was previously published in the Handbook of Research on Integrating Social Media into Strategic Marketing edited by Nick Hajli, pages 120-139, copyright year 2015 by Business Science Reference (an imprint of IGI Global).

Chapter 14
Marketing on Tumblr:
Where It Helps to Be Honest (And Weird)

Kristen Smirnov
Whittier College, USA

ABSTRACT

Despite many demographic, behavioral, and technical features that should make it an appealing destination for social media marketers, the Tumblr platform has lagged in marketing adoption. This chapter discusses the site features that drive its potential, while also acknowledging the challenges that Tumblr presents. Contrasts are offered between the limited flexibility but easier adoption curve of other platforms such as Facebook and Twitter, with the phenomenon known as choice overload discussed as a possible explanation for non-Tumblr preferences. Three Tumblr case studies are presented in depth to illustrate best practices (Denny's diner chain and the musician Taylor Swift) and to warn against certain common pitfalls (Nordstrom). The chapter concludes with potential future research directions to pursue on this growing but underutilized platform.

INTRODUCTION

From a marketing perspective, Tumblr is the dark horse of the major social media platforms. Most corporate sites link to their Facebook, Twitter, and Instagram. If they're especially adventurous or dutiful, one might see Pinterest or LinkedIn. Although Tumblr's user base is valuable, it is also notably and uniquely difficult to market to. Despite having many user statistics that should put it in the same discussions as Pinterest and Instagram as a youthful social network on the rise, Tumblr is largely ignored in discussions of social media marketing.

This chapter offers methods to improve customer engagement and the likelihood of successful marketing efforts on the Tumblr platform. First, an examination is made of Tumblr's background, along with its user base and technical capabilities. Relevant academic theories about social media branding and consumer engagement are also introduced. A discussion of the marketing potential offered on the platform follows. Next, three case studies are presented with multiple supporting examples, with an analysis of two well-performing Tumblr accounts and one underperforming company. Lastly, conclusions and future research directions are offered.

DOI: 10.4018/978-1-5225-5637-4.ch014

It should be noted that Tumblr is rarely discussed in both the commercial and academic spheres. Accordingly, theories and references used in this chapter are largely about social media platforms in general, rather than findings specific to Tumblr. Accordingly, it is hoped that this chapter will make a significant contribution to the literature about the Tumblr platform.

As might be expected from this chapter's title, Tumblr allows for more flexibility in one's marketing presentation than many other platforms. Companies can be "weird" to stand out, to connect with an audience that distrusts typical marketing voices, or as a way to rebrand a staid image. Simply being weird, however, is not a coherent strategy. To understand how to best, promote consumer engagement and loyalty on a historically challenging platform, it's important to first discuss those consumers and the platform itself.

BACKGROUND

In the introduction, Tumblr was referred to as one of the major social media platforms. That label would surprise many people, who often leave it out of discussions of the most important social media players. Tumblr was founded in 2007 by David Karp and Marco Arment. In 2013, Yahoo acquired Tumblr for $1.1 billion (Statista, 2015). Tumblr is known as a microblogging platform, and accordingly, each user is described as having his or her own blog. An early assessment of the site described it thusly:

It's a happy medium between a tidbit posting service, such as Twitter, and a full-fledged blogging tool, such as WordPress or Blogger. Tumblr is aimed at folks who feel they may not have enough content or time to write a full blog, yet still want to write and share links and media. (Lowensohn, 2007)

This platform style, off-the-cuff but media-rich, proved popular. Tumblr is one of the fastest-growing major platforms (along with Pinterest), with nearly 100% active user growth between 2014 – 2015 (Cohen, 2015). During 2014, it registered nearly twice Instagram's growth rate for active users (Luden, 2014). Higher growth rates are easier for smaller companies, of course. Tumblr's information page (http://www.tumblr.com/about) states that it hosts approximately 260 million blogs with 122 billion posts, as of late 2015. Individual users may own multiple blogs, so the number of users would be somewhat smaller than that 260 million figure. While that is a large group of users, there are bigger platforms yet. Here stands one understandable reason for Tumblr's historic lack of attention compared to the even larger platforms of Instagram, Twitter, or the true behemoth, Facebook.

However, Tumblr has two major appealing features beyond its growth rate that should earn it more attention from marketers: its technical flexibility and its userbase. Those same two appealing features also pose challenges to marketers. With Tumblr's comparatively smaller userbase, the perceived negatives have outweighed the positives for many. For companies who wish to benefit from this growing platform in the future, however, a discussion of both elements is warranted. Before that, a context for all of these challenges is offered.

Paradoxically, we may say that we like flexibility but experience a paralyzing phenomenon known as choice overload when we actually encounter it. In theory, having more choice is preferable. We may feel a sense of freedom in high-choice environments, or that we are more assured of finding an optimal solution for some problem. However, larger number of options can instead lead to dissatisfaction with the decision we ultimately make, as we have now experienced a greater opportunity cost with our selection. It can even lead to a state of paralysis where we simply choose not to participate at all (Iyengar & Lepper, 2000).

Choice overload is not common knowledge. People perform more creatively under restricted choice even as they perceive greater choice to benefit them (Sellier & Dahl, 2011). Users with lower knowledge in a field will also prefer greater choice, with the perception that more options must be better (Hadar & Sood, 2014). With this in mind, Tumblr would seem appealing to a novice marketer who is uncertain of how to approach social media. On the surface, its enormous flexibility looks appealing. However, these same novice marketers would be poorly equipped to manage the challenges of such a technically sprawling platform. Conversely, well-informed social media marketers may look at the range of possibilities provided by Tumblr and decide that some given amount of effort will return better results in a more constrained environment.

To further make this point, a contrast is offered with another platform. Instagram gives little flexibility to its users. They may upload a user icon, pick an account name, and write a short profile description, but everything else is decided for them. Every account has the same layout; every header banner displays a selection of previous posts; every post is of a photograph or video that must be uploaded from a mobile device. All photos used to be uploaded only in square formats. Although Instagram recently allowed for photographs that are in portrait or landscape ratios, this ratio flexibility only shows up after opening individual posts or in the feed of current posts. Looking at anyone's profile page displays an identical layout of squares. When a marketer launches an Instagram account, they are immediately aware of these firm boundaries. Their work, then, becomes a fairly straightforward task of optimizing performance within those limits.

Tumblr lies on the far opposite end of the flexibility spectrum. The only standardization comes from the "dashboard," the default destination for seeing new posts, similar to the Facebook wall or Twitter timeline. Individual blogs, however, are wholly customizable. Unlike every other major social network, Tumblr gives full HTML code access to its users. Because of this, companies have nearly as much control over their blog's appearance as they would with a self-hosted WordPress setup. (The only major operational differences in the two blogging platforms, in fact, are the lack of top-level categories on Tumblr and the functionalities offered by external WordPress plug-ins). With this HTML access, users can install major commercial analytics packages like Clicky or Google Analytics, add e-commerce capabilities, host external advertisements, or embed service chat windows or Google Maps on their sidebar. Users have enormous flexibility in appearance and functionality, can maintain branding consistency to unmatched levels, and yet still have immediate access to more than a hundred million existing Tumblr users.

As well, the type of content posted is far more varied than on other major social networks, and is again comparable to the WordPress blogging platform. Tumblr posts can consist of text (with or without embedded graphics for illustration), images (static or animated) in any size ratio, photo sets that display all images simultaneously rather than needing to first open a gallery, formatted chats & sourced quotations, and audio and video clips (either hosted by Tumblr or through an external site like Soundcloud or YouTube). Users can even replace the default username.tumblr.com address with a custom domain. This offers the chance to integrate a Tumblr blog with a company's online presence, or even use it as the home page for a business. A Tumblr-hosted blog could be used like a typical homepage by attaching it to *yourbusinessname.com*, or could be more narrowly used to post product updates and stories to blog.yourbusinessname.com.

There is a surfeit of choice available to Tumblr users, and as discussed this choice can lead to confusion or paralysis. The strategic marketing questions posed by an Instagram account are kept within its strict boundaries: *Do we upload videos, or only still photographs? What content do we have in our photographs? How often do we post?* The questions posed by a Tumblr account are broader, and far more complex: *Which blog theme should we use? Should we hire a designer to make a custom branded theme? What elements should it include? Should we add in links to all our other social accounts? Do we want to integrate this into our main website? Should this* be *our main website? Should we make graphical posts or allow text-only posts? If we do allow text-only, what about quotes? What do our readers want among all these options? Why are they following us? What do they hope to see?*

Indeed, it's much simpler to use other platforms. On Instagram, marketers can feel confident that someone is following them to see a regular feed of photographs—and the occasional video—in standard sizes, on a standard presentation. The barriers to entry are lower than Tumblr's on every other major social network, as it's faster and easier to gain a working knowledge of Pinterest's technical capabilities or the user expectations on Twitter. The marketers who do try Tumblr, fascinated by the expanse of choice it offers, may become discouraged when their initially muddled efforts go unrewarded or simply unnoticed by consumers. With this in mind, Tumblr's relative lack of popularity among marketers becomes easier to understand.

Making smart, tough decisions on the company end becomes key, rather than relying on constraints provided by the platform. "Anything" is not a smart approach for any company, and on Tumblr "anything" is quite possible. It is vital to self-limit an account to a certain posting approach, or a certain type of visual, or a certain voice, and maintain that consistency and honest, believable image. Otherwise, it becomes all too easy to look like a child with an overflowing toy chest.

Constructing a coherent strategy on Tumblr becomes even more difficult when the relative novelty of social media marketing, in any form and on any platform, is considered. Though even a majority of managers who do not currently place importance on social media believe it will be of future importance (Kiron et al. 2012), the precise structure of how that use will play out is unclear. The capabilities and norms of various platforms are constantly shifting and overlapping; for one example, the shift away from square-only Instagram pictures, as discussed above. There are even starker challenges that abruptly arise, such as when changes to Facebook's algorithms limited companies' abilities to reach their customers without paid placement (Kumar et al., 2016). However, on a more positive note, another "challenge" is the creative potential for new interaction strategies that would be impossible using traditional marketing approaches (Majchrzak 2009). This chapter deals largely with the latter.

Companies who wish to try something new and innovative may be enticed by Tumblr's technical flexibility discussed above, despite the challenge it presents. Others may need further convincing that it's worth the effort to enter those deep and strategically complex waters. For many, Tumblr's user base would indeed be worth the effort. Tumblr has some of the most attractive demographics of any social media site. Its userbase is young, wealthy, and well-educated (Sloane, 2014; Statista, 2015). Users' average time spent per visit (or "dashboard session" in the company's own terminology) is a meaty 28 minutes (Fitzgerald, 2014). These two facts dovetail into one particularly intriguing fact for marketers: Tumblr users are the most valuable e-retail click of any major platform, spending a dollar more on average than Facebook, the next most fruitful userbase (Sloane, 2014).

The young and educated userbase makes for a notably relaxed environment. Casual interactions are the norm, and quirky pop culture jokes and easy vulgarity can succeed here when they might fall flat or offend on Facebook. College students are commonly encountered, with both the passion and social awareness that entails. Tumblr is somewhat famous (or infamous) for having a liberal and socially aware outlook. Companies with socially responsible practices may find a natural, enthusiastic fit with Tumblr's userbase. Conversely, less socially responsible companies attempting to capitalize on these attractive consumers have met with outright hostility and sabotage. At this point, the chapter moves to examples from specific accounts, both with major case studies and shorter discussions. Popular non-corporate Tumblrs are also discussed to identify some best practices that companies could adopt.

MARKETING CASE STUDIES ON TUMBLR

With such a flexible platform that has received relatively little formal marketing attention, it is difficult to give hard and fast rules for success. A method useful for finding appropriate strategies for the Tumblr consumer base is to critically examine success stories, as well as discuss where weaker accounts have made missteps. In this section, the chapter looks first at two popular accounts that make intelligent decisions for their brand and for the platform's users: Denny's and Taylor Swift. The accounts are examined with an eye toward brand strategy and consumer relationship management. Following this, another account—Nordstrom—is examined in depth to discuss its missteps, and how it and other marketers could correct these common Tumblr mistakes. Other accounts and advertising campaigns are also discussed as appropriate.

Before focusing on specific accounts, a few more key points about Tumblr's consumer base are raised. So far, this chapter has discussed facts and figures about the consumer base. Tumblr is like most social networks in that certain cultural and behavioral trends dominate. Pinterest is famous for its craft-focused, feminine, and social behaviors; Snapchat for extreme youth, humor, and a lack of pretension. Tumblr, too, has dominant trends. As one might expect on such a flexible platform with visual posts, there are many creative users and creative companies. Disney Pixar (http://disneypixar.tumblr.com), for example, typically makes one graphic-intensive post per day, which gets anywhere from several hundred to several thousand "likes" or "reblogs." It's also a politically aware and progressive site, where posts about environmentalism, feminism, or Bernie Sanders' presidential campaign all find easy traction.

However, these same playful, progressive, and curious customers reject some traditional marketing efforts with a vehemence seldom seen on other platforms. Nike recently ran a paid campaign on Tumblr with a slogan that would not have looked out of place on Facebook or Instagram posts. It encouraged readers to "embrace their uncomfort zone" and push themselves to greater athletic performance, rather than stay with what is comfortable and easy. Tumblr users reacted negatively to the new presence on their dashboard. One notable reaction (see Figure 1) overlaid the advertisement onto photography of workers in one of Nike's factories. This was an "uncomfort zone" for Nike, indeed. The ad campaign soon ended.

Jumpy, gory horror movie ads are criticized for sparking some users' anxiety disorders without any option to hide the post. Cover Girl earned hostility for the wording of a promotional post that was perceived to favor lighter eyes over brown, with associated cries of racism. And Nike again made a misstep with a recent animated GIF post that suggested women should "earn" the right to a relaxing bath by first sweating over exercise. Poorer attempts at Tumblr marketing don't always fail so dramatically, but they often share common themes: they are more traditional paid messages poorly suited for iconoclastic millennial and post-millennial consumers. They rely on stereotypes that progressive consumers reject, or they are offered by companies that those consumers would never embrace. There are trends to success on Tumblr as well, though.

Figure 1. Nike's attempt to advertise to Tumblr users failed, as demonstrated by one post that overlaid their paid message on a picture taken at a Nike factory. As of October 2015, this post had more than 150,000 likes or reblogs

Denny's

Denny's (http://dennys.tumblr.com) is an account that truly lives up to this chapter's title: it's flat-out weird. Visiting the Denny's Tumblr is akin to a hallucinogenic experience, filled with random text posts and surreal GIF animations. Someone familiar with Denny's, a classic American diner known for its Grand Slam breakfast platters, might find this to be an unexpected decision for the brand. Yet, Tumblr is the showcase of Denny's current social media strategy. They are perhaps the only corporation in America that links to Tumblr before Twitter, Instagram, or even Facebook from their homepage (http://www.dennys.com). Their Tumblr may also be visited by using a URL related to their homepage (http://blog.dennys.com), implying that it should be viewed as part of their overall corporate website.

Denny's is in the middle of a rebranding and repositioning effort, part of which focuses on attracting more millennial customers. These efforts have been successful, resulting in their biggest sales jump in more than a decade and stock price growth that outpaces the general restaurant market by more than five hundred percent (Giammona, 2015). The cited article, however, demonstrates the blinders that many practitioners have toward Tumblr as a platform. When examining Denny's modern social media presence, Bloomberg nodded to both Twitter and a collaboration with College Humor, a humor website that produces original videos. Despite Tumblr being the first social media link on the Denny's homepage, it went unmentioned. At this point a direct comparison between the performance of Denny's Twitter and Tumblr accounts is warranted.

The Denny's Twitter (http://www.twitter.com/dennys) is also aimed squarely at a younger market that enjoys surrealistic humor. As seen in Figure 2, the humor is highly random. A specific call-out to college freshmen suggests the specific target audience for the social media account and demonstrates their commitment to reaching millennials. By any measure, the Twitter account is successful. The displayed tweets were all liked and shared at least a thousand times, and even their less popular tweets receive a minimum of several hundred interactions from users. However, this does not compare to the consumer engagement on their Tumblr account.

Figure 2. Three of the most popular tweets from Denny's Twitter from the month of September, 2015

Denny's most popular Tumblr post for the same month was written in response to a structural change in how comments are displayed on the site's dashboard. They made the following stream-of-consciousness complaint, echoing the sentiments of many site users:

what in the HECK Tumblr what is this streamlined NONSENSE with the dang comments maybe we don't want everything spick-and-span CLEAN for crying out loud give us some CHAOS give us a whole block of misaligned nonsensical reply conversations just SHOVED into every which way in the bottom of a post just BURY US IN UGLY GREY LINES we yearn for bedlam, for pandemonium, for PURE BLOGGING MAYHEM got dang it the only thing we want streamlined is our menus you put the appetizers in the FRONT and the desserts in the BACK and the reblog comments ALL OVER THE FLIPPIN' PLACE SHEESH or whatever it's fine. (Denny's, 2015c)

By the end of September, approximately 70,000 notes were left while liking or reblogging this near-incoherent but impassioned opinion. The next most popular posts—a graphical edit of a saxophone made of pancakes and series of puns about corn on the cob—had roughly 40,000 and 50,000 notes respectively by the end of the month (Denny's, 2015a, 2015b). Tumblr posts have not been studied to the extent of Twitter posts, but they appear to have a notably longer shelf life than tweets. The "half-life" of a tweet (meaning the average point at which a tweet has received half the engagement it will ever get) has been found to be only 16 minutes (Rohlfs, 2015). In contrast, Tumblr posts regularly circulate for days, weeks, months, or even years after their original publication. (This chapter's author sees this happen on a regular basis, and in fact has made several posts which surface on occasion after months of inactivity to receive another few thousand notes.) In part, this longevity may be due to the blog structure for individual profiles, where it is easy to pull up posting archives by specific month or use the tagging system to browse old posts on any topic. It's comparatively difficult to find older posts on platforms that rely on an infinitely scrolling profile page, such as Facebook, Twitter, or Instagram. If someone discovers Denny's surrealistic Tumblr humor and wishes to see more, it is easy for them to browse the complete archives. Unlike on many other platforms, generating a rich cache of Tumblr content can pay long-term dividends.

This also points to another contributor to the higher engagement with Denny's Tumblr. The site culture heavily supports reposting content that was original to another user. Even a popular user like The Frogman (http://thefrogman.me), who has a large enough follower base to justify branding himself with a custom domain and offers his own merchandise for sale, has a tag specific to his own original posts. Everything else posted by this popular user, who posts dozens or even hundreds of times per month, is being shared from someone else. Tumblr is a communal culture, where users collect entertaining, useful, or appealing bits from their dashboard feed like electronic magpies. More vitally for high-engagement companies like Denny's, it is also a platform that supports the dispersal and expansion of previous conversations when this sharing occurs.

Compare this to Facebook. If a user sees a news story or video posted by another Facebook user and shares it to his/her own account, any new comments are unique to that sharing. A post by CNN's official account may receive hundreds or thousands of comments, but those conversations do not persist away from CNN's post on its own page. Similarly, when a pin is re-pinned on Pinterest, a new comment string begins on that new account. Re-tweeting a tweet will show any replies when the tweet is expanded, but they are hidden by default.

Tumblr's software is different. If Tumblr user A leaves a comment on a post, and Tumblr user B reblogs it from them, then user A's comment follows along as part of the post content. Another user could eventually reblog this expanded post and leave their own input added to the bottom of the current discussion, even if they do not follow user A and have never interacted with them. Asynchronous, public, and dispersed conversations are a core part of Tumblr culture and the site's code. This allows Denny's to not only engage with their customers, but for their engagement to be highly visible to other users. One need not visit the Denny's Tumblr to see the conversations being held there, or to become aware that Denny's is an approachable and entertaining Tumblr personality. Another popular September post began with Denny's asking its followers one question: "truth or dare?" Users made their decision when they reblogged the post, and Denny's then reblogged their answer with a new reply.

As the Tumblr platform is largely unstudied, these behaviors have seldom been described in formal theoretical language. Borgatti and Foster (2003) proposed an early framework for social media research that specified four key technical axes on which to examine a network's structure. One of these areas was Contagion, or how content spreads through a network. The examples above demonstrate how Tumblr's particular software coding promotes organic and unstructured content sharing and reuse. Posts may change markedly from their original forms, and with multiple branching versions. With a basic understanding of Tumblr's unique technical features, companies must be prepared to be nimble and reactive on it relative to their marketing plans on other networks.

Figure 3. Denny's engages their customers with a game of Truth or Dare

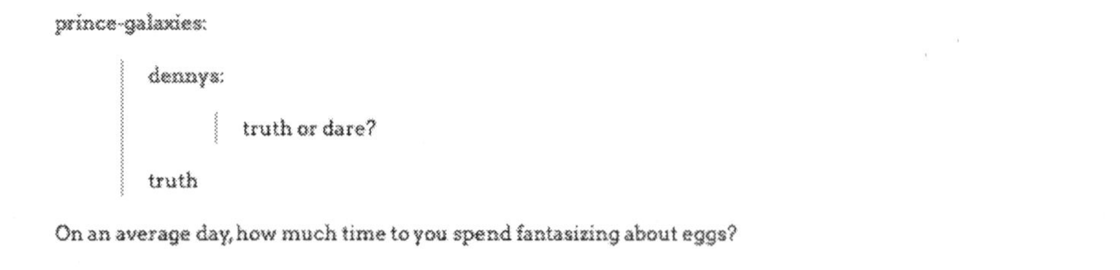

Building on Borgatti and Foster's work, Kane et al. (2014) described a dual-directional effect of the technical features of each social network. In one direction, a platform selection effect induces social homogeneity. (For a simple clarifying example, visually oriented users will presumably be more drawn to Instagram than to Twitter.) In the other direction, however, individual variation occurs based on how users chose to utilize a platform's capabilities. (To continue the example: among the visually oriented Instagram userbase, there will be those who prefer to post exclusively videos, those who post exclusively still photographs, and those who post a mixture of both.)

As discussed in the introduction, Tumblr has the greatest amount of technical flexibility of any major social media platform. Under the Kane et al. framework, there will be the greatest amount of user behavior variation, thanks to this relatively complicated range of post options. Recalling the earlier discussion of choice overload, this may all seem intimidating to marketers, and perhaps more trouble than it is worth. Recall another earlier point, however: under the Majchrzak (2009) view, this also allows for more creativity for innovative marketers who take the time to understand the software and the individuals who are drawn to this flexible outlet. Denny's has demonstrated that it is possible to harness the flexibility of how content spreads on Tumblr, and flourish among the platform's highly heterogeneous user behavior rather than becoming overwhelmed.

Denny's also lives up to the other half of this chapter's title: they're honest. In this case, honesty equals a sense that the person behind the account uses Tumblr on a regular basis and is familiar with its cultural norms. Their posts often display a keen awareness of discussions that are being held on the site, such as the quoted example of their outrage over the change in comment structure. They act like a loyal user of the site, and that act is believable. Their surrealistic humor is also consistent in tone and appearance, giving the impression that this truly is who they are. Although the odd tone may have been a hard sell in the account's early days, by this point, Tumblr knows who the Denny's account is and accepts it whole-heartedly. It's weird, and it's honest.

Denny's clearly recognizes the importance of Tumblr to their social media strategy, given the link's prominence on their home page. They are an early, surrealistic pioneer in a largely untouched landscape. Tumblr offers them unique posting opportunities and levels of engagement that cannot be duplicated on any other platform, and they have used it to see more intense and sustained consumer reactions than they receive on the larger Twitter platform.

Taylor Swift

Marketing not aimed at selling traditional goods and services is well suited for Tumblr. Causes and charities may find willing audiences in the young, socially aware userbase. A variety of media styles provide a variety of potential ways to get users engaged and excited for specific events. Perhaps the type of non-company marketing that is best suited for Tumblr, however, is for individuals.

Both celebrities and politicians have made good use of Tumblr. In the time surrounding Barack Obama's 2012 re-election campaign, a Tumblr account (http://barackobama.tumblr.com) was set up to alert users to campaign news, give them glimpses into the campaign process, and humanize the candidate. The author Neil Gaiman (http://neil-gaiman.tumblr.com) uses his account to share his work, related inspirations, and anything that he finds personally interesting, inspirational, or amusing. He also responds frequently to messages from individual users (known as "asks" on Tumblr, due to the default page URL for the messaging system). Fans may get in touch directly with an author they love to ask for insight on his novels (Gaiman, 2015a) or on broader questions of e-publishing payments (Gaiman, 2015b).

Due to the general lack of nuance in relationship labels on social networks, a social flattening effect occurs. Depending on the vocabulary chosen by a platform, everyone followed becomes elevated to the status of "friend," is a professionally distant "connection," and so on. Everyone sharing the same social label becomes homogenized into also holding the same social status and perceived social distance (Gilbert and Karahalios 2009; Kane et al. 2014). Because of this, social media is well suited for humanizing brands. Such branding efforts for individuals can make them especially open. They are, after all, someone "friended" or "followed" like any other user.

The singer Taylor Swift is a particularly popular Tumblr celebrity, and an excellent demonstration of best practices for the platform. Ms. Swift—or "Taylor," as seems more appropriate for her deliberately approachable brand image—has a strong presence on many social networks. Her Twitter (http://www.twitter.com/taylorswift13) has over sixty-five million followers; her Instagram (http://www.instagram.com/taylorswift), over fifty-two million. Visiting her Instagram showcases a pop star at the top of her game, in the midst of a global tour paired with one of the most successful pop albums in recent music history. Instagram posts in late 2015 are largely of scenes from the 1989 tour, whether on-stage or backstage, teasers for media appearances such as her cover of GQ magazine, or glimpses into Taylor's personal life with photos of pets and interior design decisions. Her Instagram's popularity befits her stardom, with posts typically earning a million likes and thousands of comments.

Tumblr allows for a more personal touch with her communication with fans. With the Denny's example, there was a clear winner in consumer engagement between their Twitter and their Tumblr. Denny's Tumblr had bigger numbers, more conversations, and a broader variety of engagement styles. Analyzing Taylor's portfolio, however, does not reveal one clear star above all the others. Rather, Taylor's Tumblr serves as a complement to the other parts of the social portfolio. In this, it is likely a closer example to what many companies would experience if they did properly develop their own Tumblr account: smaller raw numbers, but with greater engagement.

Borgatti and Foster's (2003) Contagion analysis method is once again relevant. The flow of information on the platforms is the key difference between these accounts and how they can be used to market her individual brand. Personal communication on Instagram generally equates to leaving a comment on someone else's post, waiting to see if they reply on that post, and perhaps leaving another comment. Taylor's Tumblr (http://taylorswift.tumblr.com) gets nowhere near the volume of engagement of her Instagram. Tumblr posts typically get engagement numbers in the thousands or tens of thousands, not over a million. However, the depth of that engagement differs. When a "like" shows up on Instagram, it is a quick user engagement that only requires a finger tap. Comments stay on Taylor's own photos, rather than following users to their own accounts. The much smaller engagement numbers on Taylor's Tumblr do include people who simply liked a post, but they also include all users who like a post so much that they chose to reblog it, adding it to their own blog's content in front of all their followers.

Tumblr is perfectly suited for generating electronic word-of-mouth among young consumers. One's preferences become aggressively public, shared to every follower's individual dashboard. In a site culture that thrives on the sharing of existing content, seeing one's friends repeatedly reblog content from Taylor Swift's Tumblr is a constant reminder that she is popular in those social circles. On Instagram, following someone who is a Taylor Swift fan means that they might occasionally post pictures of themselves captioned with her songs' lyrics, or that they will post pictures of themselves going to their local 1989 tour concert. On Tumblr, following someone who is a Taylor Swift fan means that they will share Taylor's own personal content with you on a regular basis.

Her strategy also utilizes how reblogging a post shares not only its content, but also all captions added by the previous reblogging chain. Taylor will leave a reply to some fan, and this reply is then shared across thousands of other accounts and all the users who subsequently reblog from them. She has reblogged fans' photos of themselves to leave encouraging comments, or even made herself into the gentle punch line for a joke. Her fans not only respond positively to this, but happily share her interactions with everyone who follows them. Although many sites are designed to make content go viral with shares and retweets, no other site is as well designed to make ongoing strings of interaction go viral, too.

Despite being a global superstar, Taylor's personal brand image is that of a quirky, approachable twenty-something who is as likely to stay in with her cats and browse Tumblr as to headline an arena concert. She often posts gentle disparagement of herself, appearing closer to her everyday fans in the process. Her single best Tumblr practice is to reblog posts originally made by her fans, cultivating a sense that she is practically a friend to any fans on the platform. One user directed a post to Taylor (using a notification system when an account name is used in a post) asking what she should name a pet pig, and Taylor reblogged the post to offer her a list of suggestions (Swift, 2015a). Another user posted that she had gotten the financial aid she needed to attend college and Taylor reblogged the post to add effusive encouragement:

FELICIA I AM SO PROUD OF YOU!!!!!!

This is why I love coming on here, reading an update on your life and getting tears in my eyes and feeling like sometimes hard work pays off and good things happen to good people.

This is so amazing, babe. (Swift, 2015b)

With respect to the current literature, her account reflects an interesting confluence between consumer-generated content and firm-generated content. Consumer-generated content on social networks is better studied (Kumar et al., 2016). Among other effects, it has been found to indicate product quality (Tirunillai and Tellis, 2014) and to more generally serve as positive word-of-mouth (Godes, 2011). Content generated by firms may be successfully used as part of an equity-building effort (Gensler et al., 2013). Corporate content posted on social media, if implemented well, can have a notably positive effect on consumers' receptivity toward a particular brand (Kumar et al., 2016). Through the ability to reblog user-generated content and add her own content to these existing posts, Taylor Swift presents both of these content types in her own account.

Taylor Swift has perfectly capitalized on Tumblr's unique software features to promote consumer engagement and fierce loyalty. Though she has more fans on Instagram and Twitter, Tumblr allows her to present herself as a friend to the users on Tumblr. She's pushed engagement one step beyond Denny's, where she not only posts her own content, but also regularly seeks out original content from other users to share with all her followers. Her image is gently quirky, if nothing to compare to Denny's bizarre account, but Taylor Swift's brand image on Tumblr is as honest as one could hope for. She is accessible, relatable, friendly, and open to the people buying her albums and concert tickets.

Users who once mocked Taylor's breakup-centered lyrics now defend her, and a diner chain is cultivating a whole new generation of fans. In both cases these successful marketing strategies were open and honest, avoided hard selling and blatant advertising, and recognized both the technical and offbeat cultural aspects of the site. Innovative startups and small companies have found traction on Tumblr, as well, when users became interested in the product itself without any further marketing effort. Liftware, a company that adapted camera stabilization technology to make utensils for people with Parkinson's disease, had hundreds of thousands of reblogs about what users saw as a valuable, interesting, and compassionate new product. (Liftware has since been acquired by Google, and the demo model Tumblr was excited about is now in active production.) The Liftware post was straightforward, socially aware, and used the multimedia capabilities of the site to make its benefits apparent. It appeared honest as it appealed to the user base, as did Taylor Swift and, in its own surrealistic way, Denny's.

Nordstrom

Not all companies on Tumblr have figured out how to utilize the site properly. The luxury retailer Nordstrom is a well-viewed company, with long-term trends placing it among the most beloved retail chains world-wide (Mannes, 2012). Nordstrom's home page links to many of their social media accounts. The typical presences of Facebook, Twitter, Pinterest, YouTube, and Instagram are all featured. So is their account on Wanelo (Want, Need, Love), a specialty social media platform centered on shopping activities. They do not, however, even link to their underperforming Tumblr account.

Nordstrom seems ideally suited to match up with Tumblr as a marketing platform. Tumblr users have a high household income, and Nordstrom is an upscale retailer. Tumblr provides for valuable e-retail clicks, and Nordstrom has a large online storefront. Tumblr rewards engagement and personal connections, and Nordstrom is famous for its personal touch and service levels. Tumblr applauds socially responsible companies, and Nordstrom has its own program for socially responsible actions (Nordstrom Cares). It receives popular word-of-mouth from Tumblr users themselves around Thanksgiving, as it's pointed to as a company that doesn't require its workers to come in on the holiday and should thus be rewarded with shopping dollars. Yet, its account flounders.

Examining Nordstrom's account (http://nordstrom.tumblr.com) gives some indications as to why they have not succeeded on the platform. From a strategic side, its mission is unclear. In some posts they showcase their products in traditional glamour shots; in others, they show behind-the-scenes shots from fashion shows; in others, they have seemingly random imagery to entice people to shop at a sale or enjoy life in a big city. A sense of randomness works for the Denny's Tumblr, as there is a consistent visual identity and surrealistic sense of humor as one scrolls down the page there. The jokes are random, but not the strategy. Nordstrom lacks this consistency. Many posts appear divorced from those around them. Stylized, graphical ads similar to a Target commercial sit next to traditional runway shows. About the only connecting thread on the page is "these products are sold at Nordstrom," and some posts don't even include that.

Perhaps even more damningly, the graphics are not up to the standards of the site's users. GIF files can currently be uploaded at a maximum of 2 megabytes on the Tumblr platform. For large-scale images like Nordstrom favors, that means that the animation cycles are short and choppy. Many of their GIFs attempt to play with this as a stop-motion effect, but the short loops make for a disorienting viewing session. They also fail to show off movement in the clothes they are attempting to sell.

Some posts actually actively hinder efforts to examine the products. A recent post showcasing a dress from an Ann Demeulemeester runway show at Paris Fashion Week used an animated GIF to do so (Nordstrom, 2015). The GIF is very large and lasts less than a second. In that time it flashes back and forth between a close-up of the front of the gown and a more distant view as the model walks away. It's impossible to get a good look at any part of the dress in that time. Only 256 colors can be used in a GIF, which causes a stippled corrective effect known as "dithering" on images that cover a wide spectrum of hues and values (such as the Demeulemeester dress). In two weeks, the post received 9 likes and only three reblogs. It was not content that people responded to positively, and did not want to post to their own blog.

Nordstrom's failings with their Tumblr account raise two different versions of the most common challenge with using the platform: with so much flexibility, it's hard to know what to do. The first challenge has to do with the types of posts used. They have made two major decisions that help to narrow their focus here, so choice overload is less damaging on this point. One: all posts involve pictures, rather than being links, text, or public answers to customer questions. Two: all posts are original to them, rather than being reblogs. Both of these decisions are different than what is seen with the positive examples of Taylor Swift and Denny's, who reblog other users' content or answer questions they pose. This may suggest that the ultimate goal of a popular Tumblr is variety and direct user engagement.

However, a look at other Tumblr blogs suggests that it is perfectly possible to succeed with only original photo posts. Tumblr users are well primed to respond to beautiful images, including fashion photography. A fan-run fashion blog (Fashion Runways, http://fashion-runways.tumblr.com) is used for contrast. A post of close-up images of accessories from a Dolce & Gabbana show, made just one day before Nordstrom's Demeulemeester post, has nearly 5,000 notes in a similar time (Fashion Runways, 2015a). Dolce & Gabbana is sold at Nordstrom. The "Featured Brands" listed on Nordstrom's online storefront include Givenchy, Chloé, Christian Louboutin, Fendi, Saint Laurent, and Valentino. The same Fashion Runways blog has a tagged category for posts about Valentino. All posts received at least a hundred notes. Many received several thousand. A few star performers passed one hundred thousand likes and reblogs from the fashion lovers of Tumblr (Fashion Runways, 2015b).

This contrast points to the core of Nordstrom's choice overload issue. Looking at their blog gives the impression of seeing many different companies' visual strategies on Tumblr, and going for a grab bag version of those efforts. To use the comparison from earlier in the chapter, the Nordstrom account is an overflowing toy chest. Even though they've put limits on the types of content, the style of that content lacks unity. The creative, malleable Tumblr culture supports random humor, stop-motion animation, still photography, strong graphic design, and many other kinds of content. Using all of those at once, though, cultivates an image that is less "weird" than "confused." A luxury retailer may not even wish to aim for a weird image, but one gets the feeling looking at the Nordstrom account that they feel it's (painfully) mandatory for Tumblr.

This chapter argues that "weird" is one way to succeed on Tumblr. However, one must also be honest. Nordstrom's Tumblr does not align with its existing brand image, as does Taylor Swift's Tumblr. Nor does its scattershot approach suggest one clear and honest (if unexpected) voice, like Denny's. Instead, it gives the impression of seeing a parent trying and failing to use various slang terms favored by their teenage children. "Weird" can certainly be an avenue to success on this platform, but it is not necessary. Simple commitment to an open, honest brand presentation can be strong, as well.

Nordstrom did not use a variety of post types to engage their readers, such as answering customer service questions directly or reblogging posts of successful shopping trips. (Although, these approaches could certainly be tried.) While Taylor Swift and Denny's suggest this type of interaction as a major contributor to successful consumer engagement, Fashion Runways' success counters the idea that it is absolutely necessary. Their reader engagement indicates that Nordstrom could see much better success with strong, confident presentations of their merchandise in ways customers would enjoy seeing. Aspirational high-end luxury, collections of tortoiseshell accessories, or dream rooms are all plausible photosets they could make while staying true to their brand and aligning well with more fashionable Tumblr users' interests.

A competitor in the fashion market, Gap (http://gap.tumblr.com), paid to have a simple, static post occasionally appear on users' dashboards. It contains two images: the elements of a man's outfit, and then a man wearing that same outfit (Gap, 2015). Though few Internet users would say they actually like advertising, the Gap's promotional post has been liked or reblogged more than thirty-five thousand times by fans of the look. The post is clean, classic, all-American, and slightly urban: all the markers of the Gap's brand. The photographs aren't exciting, but they're attractive. This ad isn't weird in the slightest, but it's entirely honest. (And, unlike Nike's simple paid slogans with no accompanying content, users didn't feel as if their dashboards had been seized by the Gap.) Nordstrom's first step on Tumblr should be to achieve a similar level of honesty. Weirdness, if they still wish to pursue it, can come later.

A final comparison further addresses Nordstrom's challenges with finding appropriate, Tumblr-specific content. As discussed, Denny's and Taylor Swift found success on Tumblr by regularly engaging with the users in innovative ways. For some marketers, these particular paths to success may be used as a template if they wish to truly commit to reaching the attractive Tumblr audience. However, many marketers may be unwilling to invest this effort into their Tumblr account when they have more confidence in other social media platforms, using more traditional marketing approaches. Denny's and Taylor are good models for committed Tumblrs, but for novices, the equivalent of training wheels can help avoid Nordstorm's creative missteps.

Content need not be original to the Tumblr platform. Even Taylor Swift's account regularly cross-posts content from other sources. The same shot of her onstage at a concert is likely to appear on Twitter, Instagram, and Tumblr. Beginning this way, with inherently appealing posts that users would actually want to engage with, can serve as a gentle introduction to the site and slowly build a follower base with little additional effort over existing social media marketing strategies. It's not innovative or highly engaging, but it's a reasonable first step for learning to use a platform outside of one's comfort zone (while avoiding the pitfalls of Nike's un-comfort zone). Once a marketer sees which sort of posts gain traction on Tumblr, they can begin to strategically customize their approach there without feeling overwhelmed by the site's flexibility.

An example: the Corcoran Group, a New York City-based luxury real estate company that also handles listings in the Hamptons and south Florida, has an established Facebook page (http://www.facebook.com/thecorcorangroup). Approximately 125,000 users have liked the page and see their updates on

Corcoran's listings, the real estate market, and New York City. Despite Facebook's much larger userbase than Tumblr, Corcoran's 10 A.M. Special Tumblr (http://thecorcorangroup10amspecial.tumblr.com) sees generally higher engagement with users. On Facebook, Corcoran seeks out interesting articles to share, produces original content featuring a pair of French bulldogs, and links to current real estate listings. On Tumblr, they simply take existing real estate photos of one beautiful luxury house and upload them as a photoset with a short caption. The Facebook dog posts are the most popular (with several dozen to several hundred likes), but as original content, also the most time-intensive. The Tumblr photosets, on the other hand, regularly get several dozen likes and often reach triple-digit engagement numbers with no expended effort but moving the photos off their real estate website and onto social media. Non-dog Facebook posts come nowhere near the Tumblr engagement numbers, and are often not shared at all.

DISUSSION AND FUTURE RESEARCH DIRECTIONS

There is no replacement for experience, and relatively few marketers have experience with Tumblr. A slow and steady approach that does not rely on original content creation can serve as an initial entry to the site, as well as staying true to a company's existing brand image. (In other words, staying honest.) Corcoran expends much less effort to run their Tumblr than Nordstrom's surrealistic or animated efforts, but gets better engagement numbers. Fashion Runways, which simply reposts existing fashion photography, also gets better engagement numbers than Nordstrom. These unpaid fashion fans have developed a more consistent and popular Tumblr presence than a major retailer.

Accordingly, the first step toward Tumblr success is to determine how to remain honest to one's brand in a site that makes it easy to do anything. If marketers translate their existing content onto Tumblr, the likelihood of a confused (and confusing) account drops significantly. Later, once Tumblr becomes a regular update alongside more traditional platforms, the companies running those accounts may feel more confident about engaging with users, expanding their post types, or even generating content entirely original to Tumblr. The risks of choice overload are averted, while still receiving the benefits of choice.

Just as Tumblr is underutilized by marketers compared to many other social media platforms, it is understudied by academics. Earlier, it was mentioned that the lifespan of tweets has been identified as being quite short. Although general trends on Tumblr are indicative of much longer engagement periods per post, there is a lack of similar data-driven research on the platform. Practitioners and academics alike would benefit from an understanding of how Tumblr's synthesis of blogging organizational structure with social media sharing capabilities affects post lifespan.

Tumblr's tagging system has differences from other sites' hashtags. On Twitter, Facebook, Tumblr, or Instagram, fans of the band One Direction all might check the tag "#1d" to see what others have posted about them. However, Tumblr's tags can also be longer than on other sites, and include spaces and most punctuation. This allows for richer and more flexible communications for people interested in a topic, as they are able to use longer and more complex hashtags to talk with similarly interested users. The construction and use of these longer hashtags is essentially unstudied, as is their use in tagging content for others' use versus when tags are used only to organize content on one's own blog.

As noted, earlier comments are carried along in reblogs in perpetuity. This feature, unique to Tumblr, has the potential to generate several fundamentally different versions of a post that then get their own reblog chains with ever-growing conversations. Consider a hypothetical photoset posted by Fashion Runways, in which one popular reblog chain is given an aesthetics-driven focus with a top-level comment of "This was my favorite runway show of the season. Such innovative construction." Another early commenter, however, reblogs the post with a discussion of how the company used African textile inspirations in their collection, but did not source materials from any African companies nor use any non-white models. Future discussions under this particular reblog chain would likely follow with a focus on social justice. From the perspective of the site owners, their original post with a straightforward fashion photoset is getting more engagement (likes and reblogs) no matter which version is seen. This poses obvious questions about the process of electronic word-of-mouth on the site, or even about broader questions of communication processes.

Lastly, more research is warranted on Tumblr users themselves. They pose many intriguing contradictions: young, but giving the most valuable retail clicks, Creative and progressive, yet often sharing others' content instead of their own, able to run many different blogs (with no visible connection) under one account, offering the chance for multiple interests or even identities to flourish under a single login. Tumblr's unique culture has served as a wall to many marketers. It's also kept many academics off Tumblr, choosing instead to focus on the more mainstream platforms. The research possibilities for Tumblr, whether more theory or practice-driven, are therefore numerous.

CONCLUSION

In this chapter's title, honesty was named as the first way to promote customer loyalty and engagement. It appears to be a nonnegotiable point, but there are many different ways to be "honest" on the platform. Like the Gap, one may simply showcase one's products in beautiful ways without doing a hard sell on other brand attributes, with a strategy of reaching out to users who would enjoy sharing that appealing content. Like Taylor Swift, one may regularly interact with users and remove perceived barriers to create a feeling of approachability and friendship. Or, like Denny's, one may construct an entirely new and different brand image for the platform, but absolutely maintain a sense of clarity and consistency for that new voice.

Weirdness is optional, and not something that must be pursued if it's a poor fit with a company like Nordstrom. Though weirdness is not mandatory, it's still a possibility. Tumblr allows for companies to let their hair down, so to speak, and attempt new and creative marketing approaches that they would be hesitant to try elsewhere.

Brands that have found the most success on Tumblr have seldom done so via direct marketing spending. Successful paid advertising, such as the Gap, has generally presented appealing imagery front and center to the viewer, rather than a branded message like Nike's unfortunate un-comfort zone. The very top performers don't operate via this route, but use organic growth based on engagement with users' interests, selves, or both. They understand the platform's culture and pursue a path of appealing content coupled with direct user interaction. They recognize the quirks and desires of this particular culture, respect that culture, and in the process gain loyal consumer advocates in wealthy, educated segments. They've stayed honest, and occasionally, they've gotten a little weird.

REFERENCES

Borgatti, S., & Foster, P. C. (2003). The Network Paradigm in Organizational Research: A Review and Typology. *Journal of Management*, *29*(6), 991–1013. doi:10.1016/S0149-2063(03)00087-4

Cohen, D. (2015). *Infographic: Explosive Active User Growth for Pinterest, Tumblr*. Retrieved from http://www.adweek.com/socialtimes/infographic-gwi-pinterest-tumblr/620098

Denny's. (2015a). *CORN ON THE*. Retrieved from http://blog.dennys.com/post/129381733083/corn-on-the

Denny's. (2015b). *STACKSOPHONE, BABY!* Retrieved from http://blog.dennys.com/post/128364753433/stacksophone-baby

Denny's. (2015c). *Untitled*. Retrieved from http://blog.dennys.com/post/128214110323/what-in-the-heck-tumblr-what-is-this-streamlined

Fashion Runways. (2015a). *Dolce & Gabanna at Milan Fashion Week Spring RTW 2016 - Headwear.* Retrieved from http://fashion-runways.tumblr.com/post/130351439421/dolce-gabbana-at-milan-fashion-week-spring-rtw

Fashion Runways. (2015b). *Valentino*. Retrieved from http://fashion-runways.tumblr.com/tagged/valentino

Fitzgerald, B. R. (2014). *Yahoo: Tumblr to Make Over $100 Million in Revenue Next Year*. Retrieved from http://blogs.wsj.com/digits/2014/10/21/yahoo-tumblr-to-make-over-100-million-in-revenue-next-year/

Gaiman, N. (2015a). *July 5th, 2015 at 12:43 PM*. Retrieved from http://neil-gaiman.tumblr.com/post/123294903396/neil-gaiman-can-you-give-me-a-lengthy-answer-about

Gaiman, N. (2015b). *July 7th, 2015 at 8:40 PM*. Retrieved from http://neil-gaiman.tumblr.com/post/123509154296/what-are-your-thoughts-about-amazons-decision-to

Gap. (2015). *New York photographer Brian Morr wears his Gap 1969 Japanese selvege denim for a day of exploring*. Retrieved from http://gap.tumblr.com/post/128736242093/new-york-photographer-brian-morr-wears-his-gap

Gensler, S., Völckner, F., Liu-Thompkins, Y., & Wiertz, C. (2013). Managing Brands in the Social Media Environment. *Journal of Interactive Marketing*, *27*(4), 242–256. doi:10.1016/j.intmar.2013.09.004

Giammona, C. (2015). *Denny's Revival Provides Blueprint for McDonald's Turnaround*. Retrieved from http://www.bloomberg.com/news/articles/2015-06-03/denny-s-revival-provides-blueprint-for-mcdonald-s-turnaround

Gilbert, E., & Karahalios, K. (2009). Predicting Tie Strength with Social Media. *Proceedings of the 27th International Conference on Human Factors in Computing Systems.*

Godes, D. (2011). Opinion Leadership and Social Contagion in New Product Diffusion. *Marketing Science*, *30*(2), 224–229. doi:10.1287/mksc.1100.0605

Hadar, L., & Sood, S. (2014). When Knowledge Is Demotivating: Subjective Knowledge and Choice Overload. *Psychological Science*, *25*(9), 1739–1747. doi:10.1177/0956797614539165 PMID:25037963

Iyengar, S. S., & Lepper, M. R. (2000). When Choice is Demotivating: Can One Desire Too Much of a Good Thing? *Journal of Personality and Social Psychology*, *79*(6), 995–1006. doi:10.1037/0022-3514.79.6.995 PMID:11138768

Kane, G. C., Alavi, M., Labianca, G., & Borgatti, S. P. (2014). What's Different About Social Media Networks? A Framework and Research Agenda. *Management Information Systems Quarterly*, *38*(1), 275–304.

Kiron, D., Palmer, D., Phillips, A. N., & Kruschwitz, N. (2012). Social Business: What Are Companies Really Doing? *MIT Sloan Management Review*.

Kumar, A., Bezawada, R., Rishika, R., Janakiraman, R., & Kannan, P. (2016). From Social to Sale: The Effects of Firm-Generated Content in Social Media on Customer Behavior. *Journal of Marketing*, *80*(1), 7–25. doi:10.1509/jm.14.0249

Lowensohn, J. (2007). *Tumblr: Microblogging done right*. Retrieved from http://www.cnet.com/news/tumblr-microblogging-done-right/

Luden, I. (2014). *Tumblr Overtakes Instagram As Fastest-Growing Social Platform, Snapchat Is The Fastest-Growing App*. Retrieved from http://techcrunch.com/2014/11/25/tumblr-overtakes-instagram-as-fastest-growing-social-platform-snapchat-is-the-fastest-growing-app/

Majchrzak, A. (2009). Comment: Where Is the Theory in Wikis? *Management Information Systems Quarterly*, *33*(1), 18–20.

Mannes, T. (2012). *Nordstrom, Kohl's among most beloved retail brands*. Retrieved from http://www.sandiegouniontribune.com/news/2012/may/16/poll-nordstrom-kohls-among-most-beloved-retail-bra/

Nordstrom. (2015). *Ann Demeulemeester at Paris Fashion Week*. Retrieved from http://nordstrom.tumblr.com/post/130401742690/ann-demeulemeester-at-paris-fashion-week-images

Rohlfs, A. (2015). *The Half-Life of Social Media Posts: How to Improve Engagement on Twitter*. Retrieved from http://www.pagemodo.com/blog/the-half-life-of-social-media-posts-how-to-improve-engagement-on-twitter/

Sellier, A.-L., & Dahl, D. W. (2011). Focus!! Creative Success Is Enjoyed Through Restricted Choice. *JMR, Journal of Marketing Research*, *48*(6), 996–1007. doi:10.1509/jmr.10.0407

Sloane, G. (2014). *Tumblr's Top Draw as a Marketing Platform Is Its Wealthier User Base: Ringing up revenue for retailers*. Retrieved from http://www.adweek.com/news/technology/tumblr-s-top-draw-marketing-platform-its-wealthier-user-base-160103

Statista. (2015). *Statistics and facts about Tumblr*. Retrieved from http://www.statista.com/topics/2463/tumblr/

Swift, T. (2015a). *Untitled 1*. Retrieved from http://taylorswift.tumblr.com/post/125996514805/treacherousswiftie-taylorswift-im-getting-a

Swift, T. (2015b). *Untitled 2*. Retrieved from http://taylorswift.tumblr.com/post/121252728745/seeyouinmywildestdreamsts-taylor-i-know-you

Tirunillai, S., & Tellis, G. J. (2012). Does Chatter Really Matter? Dynamics of User-Generated Content and Stock Performance. *Marketing Science*, *31*(2), 198–215. doi:10.1287/mksc.1110.0682

KEY TERMS AND DEFINITIONS

Analytics: Software designed to track data for a site's users, such as browsing time or geographical location, and present it as information useful to the site owner.

Blogging: A method for publishing online content that is dated and archived. This content is usually longer than typical posts on most social media platforms. Blogging is a process label, rather than its own platform like Facebook or Pinterest.

Choice Overload: The concept that rather that benefitting from high levels of choice, we become overwhelmed with so many options and instead become less satisfied or choose suboptimally.

Microblogging: A term for content presented in a blog-like manner, but that is typically shorter than posts made on traditional blogging platforms. There may be more of an emphasis on multimedia rather than on text.

Notes: A collective term for user engagement measures on Tumblr. It refers to both "likes" (which do not share content to another user's blog) and to "reblogs" (which do share content).

Photoset: A term used on Tumblr for a photo gallery in which all pictures are displayed simultaneously to the user in a sequential or mosaic-like arrangement.

Reblog: An original post on Tumblr may be reposted to other users' blogs, where they may add additional comments and tags.

Sharing: Most social media networks have some capability for re-posting content from one user's account to a second user's. The name tends to be specific to each platform: reblogging on Tumblr, retweeting on Twitter, repinning on Pinterest, etc. Sharing is Facebook's terminology and is also a general, generic descriptor for the process.

Tags: An organizational feature common to blogging platforms such as Tumblr and Wordpress. Clicking on a certain tag for a post will return all other posts made using that tag. They may be used to organize one's own blog or to find content made by others on some topic.

This research was previously published in Strategic Uses of Social Media for Improved Customer Retention edited by Wafaa Al-Rabayah, Rawan Khasawneh, Rasha Abu-shamaa, and Izzat Alsmadi, pages 59-83, copyright year 2017 by Business Science Reference (an imprint of IGI Global).

Chapter 15
Marketing With Twitter: Challenges and Opportunities

Alena Soboleva
University of Western Sydney, Australia

Suzan Burton
University of Western Sydney, Australia

Aila Khan
University of Western Sydney, Australia

ABSTRACT

The increasing use of Twitter by businesses has created the challenge of how to measure its effectiveness for marketing communications. Using data based on two years of Twitter activity by leading global brands in the Auto, FMCG and Luxury industries, this chapter presents measures which can be used by practitioners and researchers to assess the effectiveness of marketing communications on Twitter. It discusses the factors that predict consumer engagement with organizational tweets, and different Twitter strategies that have been successfully (and less successfully) used by leading global brands. We also consider the implications for marketing with Twitter, for these and for smaller organizations.

INTRODUCTION

Over the past ten years the increasing use of social media by businesses has re-defined the way businesses connect and communicate with customers (Hennig-Thurau et al., 2010; Rapp et al., 2013). Twitter is one of the most popular social media platforms, attracting around 255 million active monthly users, with around 500 million tweets sent per day (Twitter, 2014a). Twitter users tend to visit the platform more frequently than Facebook users, with 46% being daily visitors and 29% visiting the platform multiple times a day (Duggan & Smith, 2013).

In response to the rise of social media such as Twitter, marketers are actively incorporating social media into their programs, since social media can facilitate customer and user engagement with the organization (e.g. Hollebeek et al., 2014). By the end of 2013, more than 80% of Fortune 500 companies were active

DOI: 10.4018/978-1-5225-5637-4.ch015

on Twitter, with the top brands averaging 20% follower growth over the last quarter of 2013 (Shively, 2014). But as consumers' use of social media increases, their expectations also rise (Labrecque, 2014) – adding to the dramatic changes which social media bring to marketing (Hennig-Thurau et al., 2013).

This chapter discusses the potential for marketing with Twitter, and outlines its key challenges. We propose different measures that can be used to gauge the effectiveness of a Twitter strategy, and using Twitter data from leading global brands from two consecutive years, we discuss tweet features that have been identified as increasing follower engagement. We then examine similarities and differences in the Twitter strategies of these leading global brands and discuss the implications for brand communications on Twitter. Our objectives are to demonstrate how different measures can be used to assess the effectiveness of marketing with Twitter, identify the different Twitter strategies used by leading global brands, and discuss the potential implications for smaller organizations marketing with Twitter.

Potential Benefits of Marketing With Twitter

The large audience that can potentially be reached with Twitter makes it a very attractive tool for brands to interact with their customers. Twitter says that its research indicates that users want to hear from organizations on Twitter, as they typically follow five or more brands (Twitter, 2014b). Business executives are said to believe that Twitter has greater potential than other social networks for delivering sales growth (Barnes & Lescault, 2013). Businesses have used Twitter to report financial results (e.g. Alexander & Gentry, 2014) and for firm disclosures in order to increase market liquidity (Blankespoor et al., 2013). Increasingly, however, Twitter is being used both for marketing (e.g. Burton et al., 2013; Yadav et al., 2013), and advertising (e.g. Fulgoni & Lipsman, 2014; Lambrecht et al., 2014).

Increased Audience Reach

One of the obvious benefits that Twitter offers is exposure to wide audiences. Twitter is the seventh most-visited website in the US (eBizMBA, 2014), and offers the potential to reach a multitude of audiences because its technological features assist in the discovery of posted content. A user does not have to log in to read the tweets of a public Twitter account or 'Twitter handle' – the name selected by the user when they register with Twitter. As a result, it is easy to read content and start following someone on Twitter as there is no technical (and often no social) requirement for reciprocity (Marwick & boyd, 2011). The presence and popularity of celebrities on Twitter also draws people to the medium, with many marketers now adding celebrity tweeting to their range of endorsement strategies, increasing the ways that brand content can appear in users' Twitter feeds (Burkhalter et al., 2014). As we discuss later, other Twitter conventions can also facilitate propagation of Twitter messages, such as the practice of retweeting, which can attract new audiences (boyd et al., 2010) and inclusion of hashtags, which can increase content discovery (Huang et al., 2010). Possibly due to such features, Twitter has become so effective for disseminating content that it has been referred to as a broadcasting network (Shi et al., 2014) – and for newspapers, has been found to be more effective than Facebook for distributing content (Ju et al., 2013).

A Powerful Additional Channel

The growth of Twitter has meant that it has become an important part of the marketing mix for both B2B and B2C businesses (e.g. Swani et al., 2014). A Twitter presence generates exposure, can drive traffic to a brand's website, and allows a brand to connect with its customers directly (Kwon & Sung, 2011). With 24/7 connectivity, Twitter also provides a critical digital channel for executing promotions, stimulating sales and driving market share (Culnan et al., 2010). A number of industry reports suggest that customer relationship management systems that integrate Twitter data from customers and prospects help to increase the percentage of sales leads that result in actual sales, relative to traditional CRM approaches (Heggestuen, 2013b). Interacting on Twitter is especially relevant for companies which target younger adults in the 'millennial generation', who expect a two-way, mutual relationship with companies and require a brand to be present across a full range of media (Barton et al., 2014).

Twitter's potential for rapid response and message propagation means that brand tweets can potentially reach an audience that is far larger than the brand's followers. But brands need to convey authentic personalities through their Twitter presence in order to be noticed and liked by young adults (Sashittal et al., 2014). As a result, creating content that responds to trending themes is crucial to increase interest and word of mouth (Lieb & Groopman, 2013; Wells, 2014). One example of the power of Twitter was a tweet by Snickers during a 2014 World Cup match, when Luis Suarez, Uruguay's star forward, was believed to have bitten a defender on Italy's team. Snickers' US Twitter handle tweeted "*Hey @luis-16suarez. Next time you're hungry just grab a Snickers. #worldcup #luissuarez #EatASNICKERS*", with an embedded image of a Snickers, the caption "More Satisfying than Italian", and the widely followed hashtag '#LuisSuarez'. The tweet was retweeted nearly 50,000 times and favorited more than 20,000 times, demonstrating how a brand can use topical content to reach a very large audience on Twitter.

Engagement With Consumers and Word of Mouth

As more and more people sign up with Twitter, in part triggered by popular events such as the World Cup (Goel, 2014), the medium becomes more valuable as an avenue for brands to engage with customers. Twitter can facilitate consumer engagement with a brand in different ways: by including weblinks and hashtags to increase retweeting (Suh et al., 2010); by monitoring and responding to consumer comments online (Canhoto & Clark, 2013); by using popular hashtags such as #FF (Follow Friday) to promote organizational products or outlets (Page, 2012), or by including celebrities in brands' conversations to draw attention to unfamiliar brands (Wood & Burkhalter, 2013).

Twitter has also become a platform that stimulates brand conversations (e.g. Kietzmann et al., 2011; Smith et al., 2012) and as a result, facilitates consumers' willingness to engage in word of mouth (e.g. Jansen et al., 2009; Kim et al., 2014). Although some word of mouth will be outside the control of brands, regular tweeting of appropriate content can boost positive word of mouth (Zhang et al., 2011). Twitter can also be used to respond to negative word of mouth, either directly to a customer (e.g. Page, 2014), or to counter sudden surges of outrage by activating existing fan networks (Pfeffer et al., 2013).

Monitoring and Responsiveness

Listening in on social media can give an indication of sentiment towards a brand (Schweidel & Moe, 2014), and as discussed above, can provide a mechanism for responding to negative word of mouth. Monitoring can be used to track and respond to mentions of the brand's Twitter handle (Canhoto & Clark, 2013), and during a crisis, Twitter can be used to spread information and engage in discussion with stakeholders. For example, when a volcanic explosion in Iceland caused havoc for airlines in 2010, Air France-KLM used Twitter to communicate with 'huge waves' of customers (Kane, 2014).

Challenges of Using Twitter for Marketing

Twitter also presents challenges for marketers, as we discuss in the following section. One recent industry research study has even questioned the use of Twitter as a marketing channel, pointing to evidence of the low impact of social media on consumer purchase decisions (Swift, 2014). As with any other channel, brand communications on Twitter need to cut through the clutter of marketing communications, and need to do so in a way which is cost-effective for the brand. Below, we summarize three key challenges in marketing with Twitter.

Rapid Evolution of Technologies

Part of the challenge in marketing with Twitter is that the platform is constantly evolving. For example within the past year Twitter has introduced a range of innovations: embedded photos and/or videos within the tweet, so the tweet expands to show the content, rather than the user having to click a link to see the image, and thus leave Twitter (Cooper, 2014); 'big tweets' (highly retweeted or favorite tweets which appear in a larger font than those around them), and pinned tweets (tweets that a user has chosen to pin to their profile page) (Washeck, 2014). Twitter has also been said to be testing a 'buy now' button which allows users to pay by tweet, rather than repeatedly tapping to enter their card details on a mobile phone (Kuchler, 2014). These incremental changes in the way Twitter can be used could potentially have a significant impact on individual and organizational behavior on the platform. The evolution of Twitter features and the way that organizations are using Twitter are likely to make previous research and practice redundant, and thus require marketing managers to continually revise their marketing strategies to use Twitter most effectively.

Potential for Negative WOM

One of the obvious challenges of using any social media for marketing is that social media have the potential to make even strong brands vulnerable due to consumer empowerment (Rokka et al., 2013). As discussed above, Twitter can be a valuable medium for positive word of mouth (WOM) propagation, but it also potentially exposes brands to negative commentary and complaints from consumers (Pfeffer et al., 2013). For example in late 2014 a tweet increased the attention to an incident where an NFL player was shown on video knocking his wife unconscious, followed by what was generally seen to be limited response from the NFL. Both Covergirl (a P&G brand and NFL sponsor) and the NFL became the subject of widespread criticism after a Covergirl ad of a model with the slogan 'Get your game face on' was photo shopped and tweeted showing the model with a large black eye (Richards, 2014). This form of negative WOM can be particularly damaging, because negative WOM appears to have a much greater effect on consumers' choices than positive WOM (Hennig-Thurau et al., 2014). There is also a risk that negative WOM may spread further and faster: two studies have found that negative sentiment can increase propagation of tweets (Hansen et al., 2011; Naveed et al., 2011).

Uncertain Return on Investment

Establishing the ROI of social media marketing is a well-known problem with social media (e.g. Hoffman & Fodor, 2010). In one survey, 96.2% of brands reported challenges in using Twitter to achieve specific goals – in particular, in measuring the ROI and results of using Twitter as a marketing tool (Howen, 2014). 48% of social media marketers have been reported to be planning to create metrics that demonstrate the value of social media (Solis & Li, 2013). However such a goal will be difficult given the lack of standardized metrics across different social networks (Kelly, 2014). Measures such as replies, retweets, mentions and favorites can be used to estimate customer engagement (Furubayashi, 2014). But tweets can be effective due to a combination of factors such as an attractive call to action, embedded rich media, hashtags, or the time of the day the tweet is posted (Salesforce Marketing Cloud, 2012). In addition, the effect of these factors is likely to vary according to the consumer's relationship with the brand and its offerings, so determining the best tweet strategy will never be easy.

Despite the difficulties in establishing the ROI of Twitter use, there is some evidence that customers who use Twitter are likely to engage with a brand: Twitter says that its research reveals that 54% of consumers who use Twitter during primetime TV hours take action (such as visiting a brand's website) after seeing a brand mention in a tweet (Midha, 2014). Increasingly, however, brands are said to be moving away from the idea that they can track the ROI of social media, and are instead evaluating their social media strategies in terms of audience building, brand awareness and customer relations (Heggestuen, 2013a). In the next section we therefore review potential measures of the success of Twitter communication, and discuss tweet features which can be used to increase customer engagement with a brand's tweets.

Measures of Activity, Success, and Tweet Content

Various measures of Twitter activity and success have been proposed in the literature (Bruns & Stieglitz, 2013; Burton et al., 2013; Neiger et al., 2013; Sterne, 2010). In the following section, we classify Twitter measures into four categories, as shown in Figure 1: 1) *Brand activity,* 2) *Follower engagement,* 3) *Brand engagement* with the network, and 4) features of the *Message content.*

Brand Activity

The two most basic measures of Twitter activity are the number of tweets posted and number of followers, since together they provide an (imperfect) indicator of the time invested in Twitter activity, and of effectiveness in reaching followers.

Tweets per Day

The number of tweets sent provides a proxy - if crude - for the organizational time allocated to Twitter (Burton et al., 2013). Analysis of the number of tweets sent per day and follower numbers can also help to determine if there is an optimal number of tweets that should be sent per day (Zarella, 2013).

Number of Followers

The most basic and obvious measure of a Twitter handle's success is the number of followers, because it shows the size of the audience to whom tweets will be distributed. The number of followers is thus an indicator of a Twitter handle's potential influence (Kwak et al., 2010), but too often, marketers focus only on this metric (Furubayashi, 2014). Having more followers does not automatically translate into greater social influence (Cha et al., 2010). Followers can be inactive and never view tweets, so a Twitter handle may be more effective with fewer, more engaged followers who retweet its tweets. The number

Figure 1. Measures of Twitter success and activity

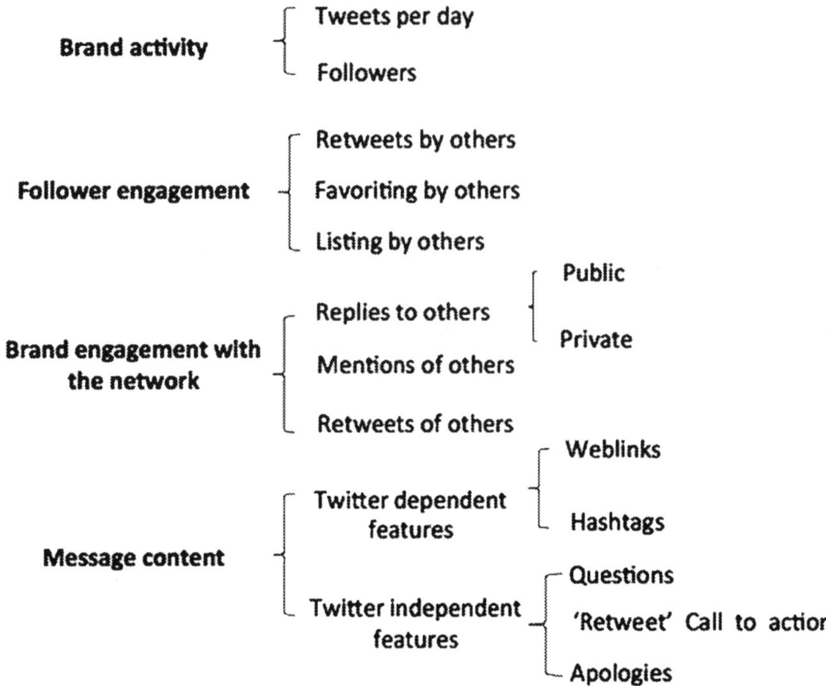

of followers can also be inflated by robot' (or fake) followers purchased to inflate a brand's follower count (Stringhini et al., 2013), thus highlighting the importance of measures of follower engagement, rather than just follower numbers.

Follower Engagement

Given the problems of using follower numbers to assess Twitter success, a critical measure of Twitter effectiveness is the extent to which a brand engages its Twitter followers. To be influential, a Twitter handle needs to do more than have followers: it also needs to overcome user passivity, so that users engage with its tweets (Romero et al., 2010). User engagement can therefore be assessed in three ways; by the frequency of retweeting, tweet favoriting and listing.

Retweets by Others

The most important measure of engagement with a tweet is retweeting, since retweeting shows that a follower has read a tweet and implies a personal endorsement of the tweet (except in the relatively rare circumstances where a follower retweets a message with negative commentary). Retweeting demonstrates user engagement with a brand, and is correlated with brand identification, brand trust, community commitment, and community membership intention (Kim et al., 2014). Retweeting is also important because it represents electronic word of mouth to the networks of the brand's followers (Zhang et al., 2011), and thus increases the potential reach of a brand's tweet to followers' networks. Although there are some recent reports that robot Twitter handles can be programed to retweet (Ferrara et al., 2014), at least until robot handles are routinely used to retweet, retweeting is likely to largely reflect actual follower activity, so is therefore a better measure of Twitter success than follower numbers, which may be inflated by inactive users or robot followers.

Favoriting by Others

As well as, or instead of retweeting, followers (or others who see a tweet) can show engagement by favoriting a tweet, by clicking a star icon underneath the tweet. The reasons for favoriting are diverse, but favoriting generally reflects content endorsement or demonstration of positive sentiment towards the tweet content or sender (Meier et al., 2014). Favoriting thus represents user engagement with the tweet, but is also different from retweeting, because unlike retweeting, favoriting does not extend the reach of the tweet to the user's own network.

Listing by Others

Lists are curated groups of Twitter handles which can be created and subscribed to (Twitter, 2012). The number of times a Twitter handle is listed can be interpreted as an indication of its authority (e.g. Duan et al., 2010), as a way of measuring influence (Pullen, 2009), and a form of recommendation (e.g. Krutkam et al., 2010). The frequency that a brand Twitter handle is listed is therefore an additional measure of user engagement with the brand.

Brand Engagement With the Network

A brand's Twitter handle can also show its own engagement with its followers in several ways: by replying, by mentioning and by retweeting others.

Replying to Others

A brand's replies to other Twitter users (signified by a tweet which begins with '@' or '.@') reflect a direct conversation between the brand and one or more followers. Replies have been said to be important in building rapport with followers through mutual engagement (Furubayashi, 2014). A default reply (indicated by a tweet starting with '@'), does not go to the sender's entire following. These tweets are visible to the recipient, to anyone who follows both sender and receiver, and are also visible on the sender's Twitter profile page. We call these replies 'private' to reflect that they are largely private, though a more accurate term might be 'less public', reflecting that 'private' replies are not confined to sender and recipient. Replies can also be 'public' (signified by a tweet beginning with '.@'), and these are visible to all followers of the sender. Both public and 'private' replies thus provide a measure of a brand's engagement with its network, either with one user (through @ replies) or with many (through .@ replies).

Mentions of Others

A Twitter user can refer to another user by including their Twitter handle in the message – a 'mention'. As with retweets and replies and, this metric allows assessment of the extent of a user's public interactions, in contrast with a potentially passive follower network (Yang & Counts, 2010).

Retweets of Others

Users can also engage with the Twitter network by retweeting others' tweets. As the name suggests, retweeting indicates interaction with other users, as well as a way to find out which tweets are seen as worthy of passing along (e.g. Ehrlich & Shami, 2010).

Message Content

Tweet content can be evaluated for inclusion of features designed to increase user engagement. These features have been divided into Twitter independent and Twitter dependent features (Castillo et al., 2011). Twitter-dependent features include weblinks or hashtags, and Twitter independent features relate to the presence of punctuation marks (e.g. question and exclamation marks) and other linguistic elements signaling emotions and/or content. A very large number of tweet features can and have been coded (e.g. Castillo et al., 2011; Misopoulos et al., 2014; Naveed et al., 2011) but those studies have not focused on brand tweets. In this analysis, we focus on two Twitter-dependent and three Twitter-independent features: weblinks and hashtags because they have been shown to increase retweeting, and questions, inclusion of a call to action ('Retweet') and apologies, because they are likely to be particularly important for brands attempting to create a user response (for questions and a call to action) and for responding to customer problems (with apologies).

Use of Weblinks

Tweets with weblinks have been found to be more likely to be retweeted (Suh et al., 2010), but what a user can do with weblinks has been rapidly evolving. Previously, clicking on a weblink meant that a user would be directed to a website (and thus leave Twitter). Although some weblinks in tweets still take users to an external website, weblinks can now be used to embed photos and/or videos (using 'Twitter Cards'), where instead of the user having to leave Twitter, the tweet itself expands to show the content (Cooper, 2014). One study of the impact of different tweet features found that photos increase the retweet rate by 35%, and videos by 28% (Rogers, 2014), though that study did not specifically analyze organizational tweets, nor differentiate between links to embedded content and those which direct the user to an external site.

Use of Hashtags

Like weblinks, inclusion of a hashtag in a tweet has been found to increase the retweet rate (Suh et al., 2010), with one recent estimate that inclusion of a hashtag increases the retweet rate by 16% (Rogers, 2014). Hashtags also increase the discoverability of the tweet outside the user's followers, because people who are not followers, but who search for the hashtag, can see tweets containing that hashtag.

Questions

Tweets can also be coded for the presence of linguistic elements which might increase retweeting. The use of questions in tweets is particularly interesting, because by their nature, questions are intended to elicit a response (Naveed et al., 2011). However there is conflicting research on the effect of questions in tweets: one study found that the use of questions increased retweeting (Naveed et al., 2011), while another found that tweets with question marks were associated with lower credibility (which, in turn, would be expected to be associated with lower retweeting) (Castillo et al., 2011). Neither study, however, examined the effect of questions in brand tweets.

Retweet Call to Action

A retweet request has been identified as one of the factors which can lead users to retweet (boyd et al., 2010). There are varying reports of the effectiveness of direct appeals for retweeting, with different studies reporting increases ranging from 34% (Malhotra et al., 2012) to 1,200% (Salesforce Marketing Cloud, 2012). However the effect of a direct call to action in the form of a request to retweet is likely to be lower for commercial tweets, and may also decrease as more Twitter users adopt the practice in an attempt to be retweeted. We therefore examined the effect of a 'Retweet' call to action for these leading brands.

Apologies

Twitter can also be used as a channel to identify and respond to customer problems. Problems can be identified by both direct complaint tweets to the brand, and also by monitoring brand mentions on Twitter. However responding to complaints using Twitter has the potential for exposing customer problems to a wider audience and (if apologies are not confined to private replies) creating a Twitter feed which is uninteresting to other followers. There has been some analysis of apologies (Burton & Soboleva, 2011; Page, 2014), but neither of those studies differentiated between public and 'private' replies, so the extent to which companies apologize publicly (if at all) is not clear.

So, in summary, Twitter has both benefits and challenges when used as a marketing tool: it can allow brands to reach larger groups of consumers, and spread brand messages beyond the brand's direct followers through Twitter features such as retweeting and mentions. However, there are also challenges in associating Twitter activities with desired financial outcomes, a risk that Twitter can expose the brand to negative word of mouth, and a constant challenge in revising the Twitter strategy in response to its evolving capabilities. In the following sections we analyze the Twitter practices of leading global brands using the measures outlined above, and draw out implications for them and for other businesses.

Can We Learn From What the Leading Brands Are Doing?

Given the challenges of marketing with Twitter, we analyzed the Twitter practices of 33 leading global business to consumer (B2C) brands. These brands are likely to have some of the largest social media marketing budgets, so should provide exemplars of marketing practice. In the following section, we detail the brands and how the data was collected and analyzed.

METHODOLOGY

Sample

The industries and companies were initially identified from Interbrand's Best Global Brands report (Interbrand, 2012), and then updated using the revised list one year later (Interbrand, 2013). Interbrand is a brand consultancy firm that publishes an annual list of the 100 most valued brands, using a broadly accepted brand valuation method (Haigh & Perrier, 1997). Interbrand's 2012 list contained entries for 18 industry categories, with the number of brands in each category ranging from 13 (for the Auto category) to 1 (for Transportation, Home furnishings and Energy). Since the aim of the study was to examine Twitter activity by leading B2C brands, two industry categories with a large B2B presence were excluded (Financial services and Technology), leaving a sample of three of the largest Interbrand industries (Automotive, FMCG/CPG[1] and Luxury).

All brands within the three selected industries on the Interbrand list had Twitter handles except for one luxury brand (Hermes), resulting in a 2013 sample of 13 Auto brands, 11 FMCG brands and 6 luxury brands. Many companies have more than one Twitter handle, so the central Twitter handle for each organization (and in the absence of an obvious central handle, the one with the largest number of followers) was chosen for analysis. Two additional brands (Chevrolet and Duracell) were included on the 2013 Interbrand list, so were added to the 2014 analysis, and one brand was excluded in each study period due to very low or no Twitter activity (Cartier in 2013 and Heinz in 2014). Despite the relatively small number of brands within each industry category, the analysis therefore includes a Twitter handle from the entire population of active Twitter users among top-ranked brands in the three industries being analyzed.

A list of the Twitter handles for the brands, their Twitter followers and their most commonly used hashtags is shown in Table 1. As of September 2014, all brands except Colgate and Danone, had 'verified' Twitter handles. (A handle can be 'verified' by Twitter to show that it represents the real brand (or person) and not an imposter. Verification is indicated on the brand's Twitter page by a blue checkmark icon next to the handle name.)

Data Collection

All tweets by the chosen Twitter handles for the period from November 2012 to 30 April 2013 were downloaded in csv format using Twitonomy's premium subscription service[2]. One year later, comparable data for the updated Interbrand list of brands was obtained, providing a comparable sample to assess change in activity over a year. Additional information on each Twitter handle was obtained from Twitonomy's analytics reports. Some analysis of the 2013 sample has been published elsewhere (Soboleva et al., 2013) so in this chapter, we focus primarily on the 2014 sample and on changes in activity from 2013 to 2014.

Measurements

Details of how measures were calculated are given below.

Brand Activity

Tweets per day: The number of tweets posted by each Twitter handle per day was calculated by taking the total tweets posted over the six month study period and dividing by 181 (i.e. the days in the six month period).

Number of followers: The number of followers for each Twitter handle was obtained from Twitonomy analytics reports downloaded within a week of the end of each data analysis period, thus reflecting the number of followers at the end of each six month study period. Table 1 gives updated follower numbers, as of September 2014.

Table 1. Brands examined, number of followers and most frequently used hashtags

Twitter handle	Followers('000s)[1]	3 most used hashtags (where >1)
Auto		
@Audi	884.0	#wantanr8 (68), #a3 (45), #quattro (38)
@BMWUSA	187.0	#bmw (227), #bmwbobsled (58), #bmwi8 (22)
@chevrolet[2]	503.0	#chevysxsw (798), #thenew (256), #purpleyourprofile (162)
@FerrariUSA	48.1	#ferrari (58), #ff (12), #tbt (11)
@Ford	527.0	#fordearnings (79), #fordmustang (50), #fordnaias (39)
@harleydavidson	224.0	#photooftheday (171), #potd (171), #daytonbikeweek (43)
@Honda	397.0	#hondalove (1996), #lovetoday (104), #bestyourself (53)
@Hyundai	166.0	#nextgenesis (112), #laautoshow (40), #hyundailaas (32)
@Kia	176.0	#kiak900 (171), #kiasoul (87), #kiakey (78)
@MercedesBenz	641.0	#amg (194), #mercedesbenz (192), #cclass (61)
@NissanUSA	402.0	#nissannyias (51), #nissan (47), #namethatnissan (46)
@Porsche	657.0	#porsche (19), #porschemacan (11), #naias (7)
@Toyota	351.0	#letsgoplaces (69), #toyotaft1 (54), #noroomforboring (51)
@VW	307.0	#vwcares (273), #vw (122), #dasauto (32)
FMCG		
@AvonInsider	83.4	#fabin5 (89), #beauty (62), #nyfw (55)
@Colgate	11.1	#nodeforestation (17)
@Duracell[2]	70.5	#powerasmile (29), #dwts (19), #trustyourpower (16)
@DanoneGroup	5.6	#danone (53), #agm14 (31), #fy2013(26)
@Gillette	59.6	#gillette4life (124), #sochi2014 (32), #byahair (30)
@HJHeinzCompany[3]	6.0	#earnings (17), #heinz (8), #dividend (3)
@JNJNews	74.2	#jnj (268), #jnjasm14 (41), #ntds (27)
@KelloggCompany	10.3	#startwithcereal (52), #cereal (10), #walmartexpo (7)
@Kleenex	16.2	#kleenex (288), #cooltouch (104), #kleenexstyle (41)
@Loreal	49.7	#finance (98), #lorealafrica (31), #hacklorealdpp (29)
@Nestle	56.5	#nestle (137), #employment4youth (83), #wef2014 (48)
@Pampers	114.0	#pampersgameface (115), #pampersrewards (41), #pamperslove (34)
Luxury		
@Burberry	3,180.0	#burberry (218), #lfw (132), #lcm (78)
@LouisVuitton	3,810.0	#louisvuitton (166), #lvpass (27), #lvlive (25)
@Cartier[4]	102.0	#cartier (46), #sihh (10), #cartierexhibition (7)
@Prada	143.0	#backstage (14), #castellocavalcanti (11), #ss14 (8)
@gucci	1,200.0	#gucci (99), #mfw (23), #guccifringe (23)
@RalphLauren	893.0	#teamusa (75), #ralphlauren (35), #meetteamusa (28)
@TiffanyAndCo	1,040.0	#tiffanyweddings (54), #tiffanybluebook (40), #tiffanyvalentine (26)

[1]Followers as of September 2014[2] New to Interbrand list in 2013 [3] Excluded in 2014 due to low activity
[4]Excluded in 2013 due to low activity

Follower Engagement

Retweets and favorites by others: The number of retweets and favorites for each tweet was obtained from the downloaded csv files, allowing comparison of retweets and favorites per tweet.

Times listed: The number of times each brand Twitter handle was listed by others was obtained from the Twitonomy analytics reports. Since listing is for the Twitter handle, listing is per brand, not per tweet.

Brand Engagement

Replies to others: Tweets with replies were identified from the csv files using a Microsoft Excel search function. Replies were separately coded into public (.@) and 'private' (@) replies.

Mentions of others: Mentions were also identified using a Micosoft Excel search for tweets containing '[space]@' outside the first two characters of the tweet (where @ signifies a public or private reply). (The space before the '2' sign is necessary to separate mentions from email addresses.)

Retweets of others: The proportion of tweets by each brand that are retweets of others' tweets was obtained from Twitonomy analytics reports.

Message Content

Twitter dependent features: Weblinks and hashtags were identified using a Microsoft Excel search formulas.

Twitter independent features: Questions, 'Retweet' calls to action and apologies were respectively identified using Microsoft Excel search formulas, searching for '?', 'Retweet', 'sorry', and 'apologize/apologise'. 'Sorry/Apology' tweets were reviewed to ensure that they predominantly reflected a customer response. The review indicated a very small percentage of tweets that were not linked to service recovery (e.g. 'sorry for your loss' and 'sorry to hear that you are sick'). However instead of coding all tweets to separate out this very small percentage which did not relate to service recovery, we report on total use of the terms 'apologi(z)e' and 'sorry' since automatic search allows efficient analysis of large data sets, and provides a very strong (though imperfect) representation of tweets reflecting service recovery. Similarly, the automated search for 'Retweet' identified two tweets (out of 133) containing the word 'retweet' which were other calls-to-action (that is, appeals to 'check out' something). These were retained in the analysis, since they represented calls to action, though using 'check out' other than 'retweet'.

Analysis

Since the samples for each industry represented the population of active Twitter users among the top global brands in the three industries being studied, the use of statistical tests is theoretically unnecessary, because any observed differences between industries are not due to sampling error, and reflect real differences between the industries during the study period. Nevertheless, since an analysis of any one time period reflects a sample of the activity during all possible time periods, we applied statistical tests, as some readers will be used to seeing them for comparisons between groups, and also to provide some assessment of the size of observed variability between groups, relative to the variability within groups.

Some of the statistics (e.g. number of followers) are very skewed, so for small sample sizes (i.e. comparison of summary industry performance) we used non-parametric tests to compare differences in median measures across industries. Where there were outliers in the data, we used Mood's median test (which is more robust than other tests against the presence of outliers) for comparisons across the industries. Where no outliers were present, we used the Kruskal-Wallis test, which is more powerful than Mood's median test in the absence of outliers. Where the Mood's or Kruskal-Wallis test was significant, we used follow-up Mann-Whitney tests for pairwise comparisons. For comparisons of proportions (hashtags, weblinks and retweets of others) we used the normal approximation (which is appropriate given the sample size). For differences in retweet rate of tweets with and without different message features (as in Table 7) we used T-tests, which are robust against non-normality of the data for the large sample sizes involved. Since the number of statistical tests was moderately large, we report results as 'significant' for p values of ≤ 0.01, report the exact value for p values between 0.01 and 0.05 without commenting on significance, and consider values of ≥ 0.05 as not significant, but report the size of p values between .05 and .1 to give an indication of the size of observed differences. [3]

RESULTS

The following section presents the results from the analysis under four sections, investigating 1) the activity and audience of the Twitter handles of the selected leading brands, 2) the effectiveness of their Twitter communication, as indicated by their success in engaging their Twitter audience, 3) the brands' engagement with their networks, and 4) the impact of message content features.

What Are the Leading Brands Doing?

Brand Activity

Tweets per Day

Most leading brands are tweeting less than ten times a day, on average (see Table 2). The Luxury brands tweeted far less than those in other industries, with a median of only 1.36 tweets per day over the six-month period, compared to a median of 7.48 tweets per day in the Auto industry. However within each industry, there were brands that tweeted less than once a day on average (Ferrari, Porsche, Colgate, Kellogg's, Cartier and Prada). Even the highest tweeting brands (Volkswagen and Honda) were respectively sending only 17.7 and 17.2 tweets per day, so Twitter communications would not seem to require a large amount of corporate time for these Twitter handles. For these brands, sending more tweets (or fewer) doesn't appear to influence the number of followers: there was no association between the number of tweets sent per day and the number of followers ($p > 0.1$). Some brands are even tweeting less: Luxury brands are typically sending fewer tweets than a year earlier (see Figure 2), but over the same period, have experienced a large increase in the number of followers (see Figure 3). These low-tweeting, very popular Luxury brands show that even very low Twitter activity can be successful in accumulating a large following.

Followers

Unsurprisingly, there was considerable variation in the number of followers between industries, with Luxury ($p < 0.003$) and Auto brands ($p < 0.001$) having significantly more followers than FMCG brands (see Table 3). Three Luxury brands (Louis Vuitton, Burberry and Gucci) had more than a million follow-

Table 2. Tweets sent per day 2014

		Tweets per day		
Industry	**N**	**Mean**	**Median**	**Std**
Auto	14	8.93	7.48	5.78
FMCG	11	4.93	5.10	3.99
Luxury	7	2.62	1.36	2.28
All	32	6.17	5.55	5.20
Sig: Overall: Follow up:		H = 7.59, $p = 0.023$ Luxury vs FMCG: p = ns Luxury vs auto: $p = 0.01$ Auto vs FMCG: $p = 0.09$		

Figure 2. Change in tweets per day 2013-14

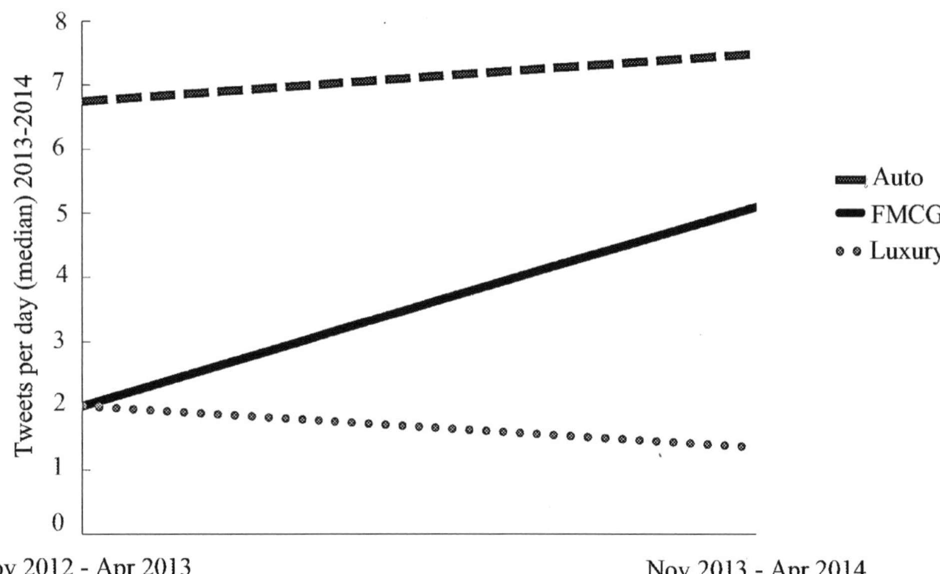

Table 3. Number of followers 2014

Industry	N	Number of followers: Mean	Median	Std
Auto	14	311.69	285.30	181.86
FMCG	11	44.74	47.30	33.65
Luxury	7	1,284.82	926.81	1,266.22
All	32	432.80	149.51	740.63
Sig: Overall: Follow up:		H = 18.04, $p < 0.001$ Luxury vs FMCG: $p = 0.003$ Luxury vs Auto: $p = 0.09$ Auto vs FMCG: $p < 0.001$		

ers each. While it is not unexpected that Luxury brands would have more followers than FMCG brands, the best performing FMCG brand (Pampers) had more than 100,000 followers – a higher number than Cartier, Prada, or in the Auto industry, Ferrari. The success of Pampers and other FMCG brands (such as Duracell and Avon, both with over 70,000 followers), shows that even low involvement product brands can obtain a large Twitter audience. All industries had experienced an increase in the number of followers over the year (see Figure 3), with Luxury brands having the largest increase, despite sending fewer tweets than a year earlier (see Figure 2). In contrast, the number of tweets sent had increased most for FMCG brands, but those brands had experienced the smallest increase in number of followers.

Figure 3. Change in followers 2013-14

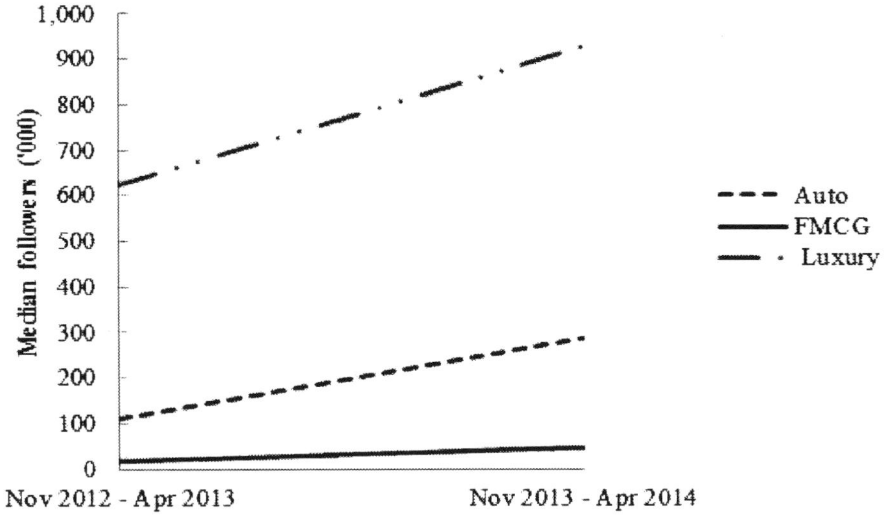

Follower Engagement:

Retweeting

There were large and significant differences in the extent to which industries' tweets were retweeted (by followers and their followers) (see Table 4). Luxury tweets were retweeted far more often; with a median retweet rate of 107.0 per tweet, compared to Auto (med = 21.6) and FMCG (med = 2.6). However, the best performing FMCG brand, Duracell, had retweet rates more than double that of three of the Auto companies - Hyundai, Honda and Kia. While those Auto brands represent Asian car companies (albeit their US Twitter handles), their low retweet rate is not explained by the country of origin of the brand, with other Asian auto brands (Nissan and Toyota) achieving high retweet rates. Compared to a year earlier, retweet rates of Luxury tweets had risen most sharply (from a median of 58 retweets per tweet to 107) (see Figure 4). FMCG retweets had doubled over the year (from a median of 1.3 to 2.6 retweets per tweet) but remained small in absolute terms.

Favoriting

Though tweets were less likely to be favorited than retweeted, frequency of favoriting was highly correlated with retweeting ($r = 0.98$), so unsurprisingly, results for favoriting mirrored those of retweeting, with Luxury tweets favorited significantly more than Auto tweets ($p = 0.005$) and FMCG ($p < 0.001$), and Auto tweets favorited significantly more than FMCG tweets ($p < 0.001$) (see Table 5). As with retweeting, Luxury tweets had experienced the highest increase in favoriting compared to one year earlier (see Figure 5). The FMCG industry, while experiencing the largest relative increase in favoriting (from a median of 0.3 to 1.6 favorites per tweet) continued to have a much smaller proportion of tweets favorited.

Table 4. Retweets per tweet 2014

		Retweets per tweet		
Industry	**N**	**Mean**	**Median**	**Std**
Auto	14	38.51	21.63	36.19
FMCG	11	3.48	2.57	3.46
Luxury	7	139.67	106.99	121.75
All	32	48.60	18.10	77.90
Sig: Overall: Follow up:		Chis = 19.14, $p < 0.001$ Luxury vs FMCG: $p < 0.001$ Luxury vs Auto: $p = 0.004$ Auto vs FMCG: $p < 0.001$		

Figure 4. Change in retweets rate 2013-14

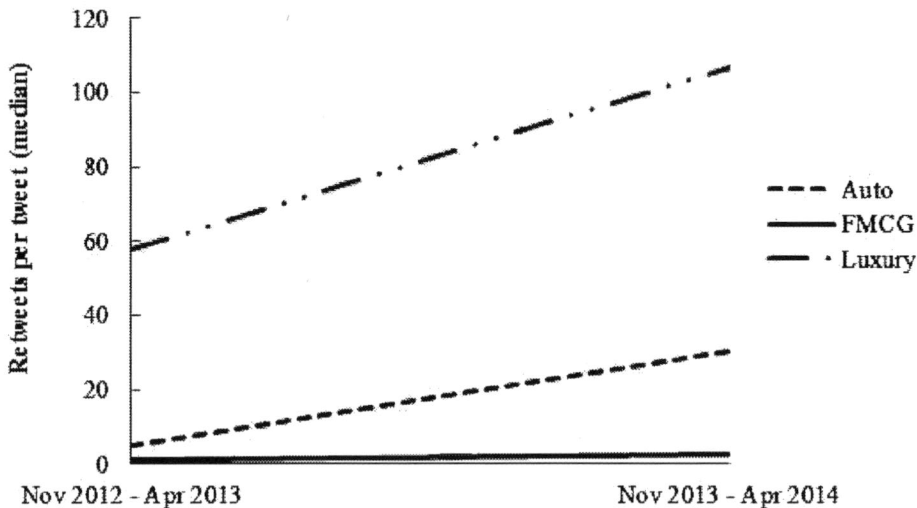

Table 5. Favorites per tweet 2013-14

		Favorited per tweet		
Industry	**N**	**Mean**	**Median**	**Std**
Auto	14	41.30	21.60	40.10
FMCG	11	3.80	1.61	5.45
Luxury	7	171.20	82.70	148.30
All	32	56.80	18.20	94.90
Sig: Overall: Follow up:		Chis = 14.65, $p = 0.001$ Luxury vs FMCG: $p < 0.001$ Luxury vs Auto: $p = 0.005$ Auto vs FMCG: $p < 0.001$		

Figure 5. Change in favoriting 2013-14

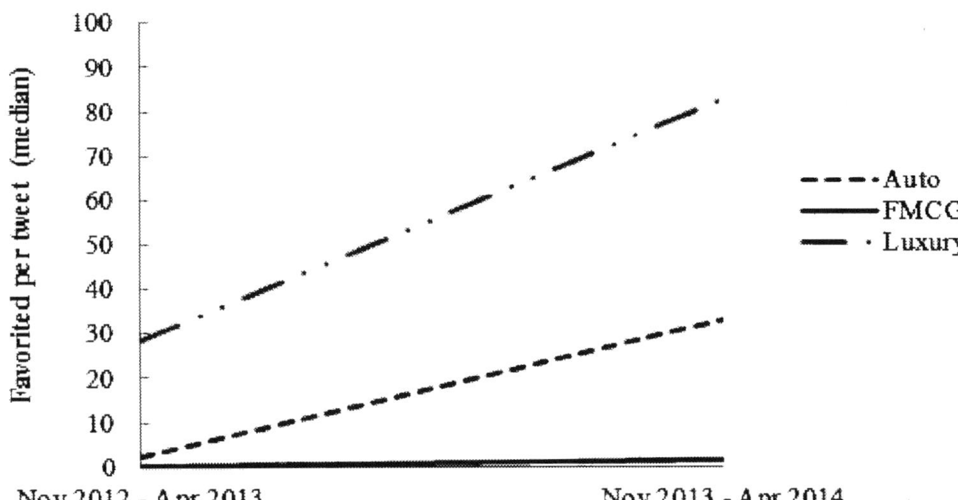

Listing

There were also significant differences in the frequency of listing ($p < 0.001$), with both Auto and Luxury Twitter brands listed significantly more often than FMCG brands, but no significant difference in the frequency of listing between Auto and Luxury ($p > 0.1$) (see Table 6). While non-followers can list a Twitter handle, following would be expected to be associated with the frequency of listing, since those who are sufficiently interested to list a Twitter handle are likely to become followers. Despite the increase in the number of followers in every industry from 2013 to 2014, the Auto industry was the only one to experience any meaningful increase in the number of times its brands were listed (from a median of 1513 to 2174 listings) (see Figure 6). Luxury brands, despite having the largest increase in followers, were listed only an additional 75 times from 2013 to 2014.

Table 6. Frequency of listing 2014

		Times listed		
Industry	**N**	**Mean**	**Median**	**Std**
Auto	14	3,592	2,174	5,427
FMCG	11	473	439	408
Luxury	7	4,085	3,146	3,549
All	32	2,628	1,440	4,170
Sig: Overall: Follow up:		Chis = 16.86, $p < 0.001$ Luxury vs FMCG: $p = 0.004$ Luxury vs Auto: p = ns Auto vs FMCG: $p < 0.001$		

Figure 6. Change in listing 2013-14

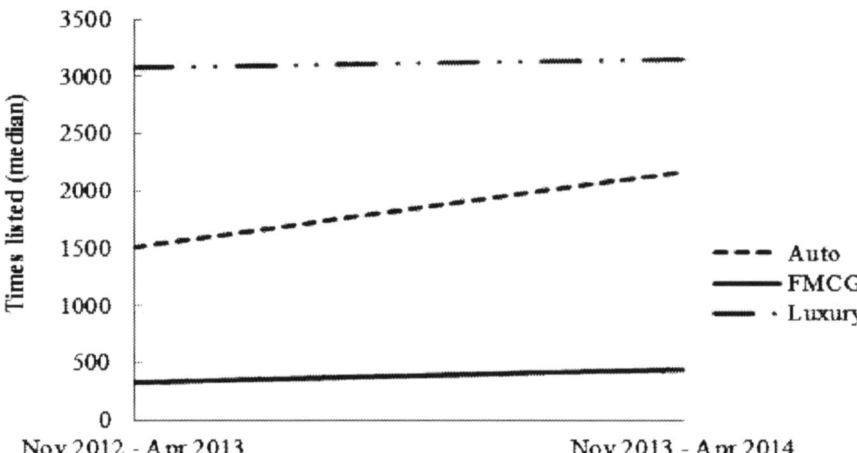

What Predicts Follower Engagement?

Certain tweet features were associated with higher levels of retweeting, but what worked varied between the industries, with weblinks being the only feature of tweets which consistently increased retweet levels. Table 7 summarizes the differences in average retweet level for tweets with and without various tweet features. As discussed previously, follower engagement can also be assessed by favoriting, but since favoriting and retweeting were highly correlated ($r = 0.98$, as discussed previously), we report only on retweeting in Table 7. In the following sections, we discuss each of these factors separately, after removing 'private' replies, which would be expected to be retweeted much less frequently, since as discussed above, they are visible to fewer people.

Replies to Others

Most brands included only a very small percentage of their replies in their Twitter feed – the more visible replies which we call 'public replies'. For example 98.3% of replies by the Auto industry were of the 'less public' form – replies which we call 'private' replies – tweets which are visible on the brand's Twitter home page and visible to the recipient and followers of both Twitter handles, but which do not appear on the Twitter feed of other followers. In comparison with the other two industries, Auto brands were replying more to their followers: in 2014, 73% of their total tweets were replies, up from 57% a year earlier. However because most of those replies were 'private', Auto brand followers would only see a small percentage of (presumably carefully selected) replies in their Twitter feeds. In contrast, Luxury brands made a much higher proportion of their replies public in 2014 (32.1%). However Luxury brands were also replying in far fewer tweets compared to a year earlier; in 2013, 35% of all Luxury tweets contained replies (of which 2.3% were public), but in 2014, only 9% were replies (of which 32.1% were public). Ideally, public replies will be those which will be of interest to other followers, but for every industry the average retweet rate of public reply tweets was lower than for tweets which were not replies. The difference was not large, and was of marginal significance only for the Auto industry, (as shown in Table 7) but does suggest that tweets without replies were more interesting to the followers of these brands - and thus more likely to be retweeted.

Mentions of Others

All industries mentioned others in roughly similar proportions of tweets – from a low of 33.6% for the Luxury industry to a high of 37.3% in the FMCG industry, but including a mention in a tweet did not increase the average retweet rate; to the contrary, in the Auto industry there was marginal evidence that mentioning others *decreased* the retweet rate ($p = .078$). Further analysis investigating whether an increased number of mentions led to higher retweet rates was consistent with that result; there was no evidence that including one or more mentions increased the retweet rate – and for the Auto industry, there was weak evidence that it decreased the retweet rate. The result is perhaps not surprising, since the major effect of mentions is likely to be to bring a Twitter handle to the notice of users who are mentioned. This strategy might result in increased followers, and longer term, increased retweet rates, but would not be expected to increase retweet rates for the tweet with the mention.

Retweets of Others

FMCG brands were distinguished by a significantly higher proportion of retweets of others in their tweets (20.6%), significantly higher than either Auto (8.6%) or Luxury brands (8.3%) (both $p < 0.001$). There were no significant differences in the frequency of retweets of others between Auto and Luxury ($p > .1$). Since further retweets of a retweeted tweet are credited to the original sender, we did not conduct further analysis on retweeted tweets.

Weblinks

Weblinks appear to be the single most effective feature for increasing retweets. For every industry, tweets with weblinks had significantly more retweets (see Table 7). All industries were using weblinks more than a year earlier – with weblinks in 81.6% of Luxury tweets in 2014, up from 58.2% a year earlier.

Hashtags

Hashtags were used extensively by all brands, and compared to a year earlier, all industries were using hashtags significantly more, with hashtag use ranging from a low of 48.5% in FMCG companies to a high of 56% for Auto companies. Table 1 shows the most commonly used hashtags for each brand. Tweets with hashtags were, like weblinks, retweeted more often, but there were differences between the industries in the effect of hashtags, with the increase only significant for FMCG ($p < 0.001$, see Table 7). There was a weak nonlinear relationship between the number of hashtags used and the level of retweets for the FMCG industry only, with retweet levels increasing with additional hashtags, up to a maximum of four hashtags. Though there were not many tweets with more than four hashtags, if five or more hashtags were included, the retweet level dropped in every industry.

Questions

The most retweeted tweet in the 2013-14 period dataset (with 12,604 retweets) was from VW, with a picture of the new VW GTI car, accompanied by the question '*What would you do to drive the Design Vision #VWGTI for a day?*'. Nevertheless, tweets with questions were, on average, retweeted less often in all industries, though the difference was only significant for Luxury brands, where tweets containing questions were retweeted at around half the rate of tweets without questions (see Table 7). Auto had the highest use of question marks, in 17.5% of its tweets in 2014, compared to FMCG (12.2%) and Luxury

(3.2%) (all differences significant at $p < 0.001$). However the Auto industry was using significantly fewer question marks compared to a year earlier, when questions appeared in 20.7% of Auto tweets ($p < 0.001$), with the decrease in part due to an apparent change in strategy by Harley Davidson, where the use of '?' decreased from 33% of tweets to 9%.

Retweet Call to Action

Only 0.4% of tweets included the word 'retweet' (usually in the form 'Retweet if…'), but those tweets had a much higher frequency of retweeting (see Table 7). Tweets including 'retweet' were retweeted more than 5 times as often for FMCG brands, 9 times for Auto brands, and 15 times more for Luxury compared to tweets without this call-to-action. While this very large boost in retweeting due to inclusion of the word 'retweet' is likely to decrease if more tweets appeal for retweets, the results suggest that a direct call-to-action to 'retweet' or 'favorite' can lead to a very large increase in the frequency of retweeting.

Service Recovery

Both the Auto and FMCG industries had a significant proportion of tweets addressing customer problems, as assessed by inclusion of the words 'sorry' or 'apologise/apologize'. For example

FMCG brands had one or both words in 4.5% of tweets, and Auto in 3.5%, with one or both words in 30.7% of tweets from Duracell, and 14.8% from VW. Luxury brands had *no* tweets containing the words 'sorry' or 'apologise/apologize' in either 2013 or 2014. However with the exception of two tweets (from Nestlé and Kleenex) all tweets with 'sorry' or 'apologise' appeared in 'private' replies. As a result, we did not examine the impact of 'sorry' on retweet rate.

So what can we learn from analyzing what the leading brands are doing on Twitter? The next sections discuss the results, and the implications for other brands.

DISCUSSION

Despite significant differences between and within industries, the results show that most of these leading brands have large Twitter followings. Three Luxury brands had more than a million followers, but even some FMCG brands achieved high follower numbers: the best performing FMCG brands (Pampers, Johnson & Johnson and Gillette) had higher or similar numbers of Twitter followers than the worst performing Luxury brand, Cartier. The number of direct followers may also under-estimate the reach of a popular tweet: the most retweeted original tweet (by VW: '*What would you do to drive the Design Vision #VWGTI for a day?* http://t.co/h6cPQJUo0N') was retweeted 12,604 times, thus reaching a far wider audience than followers of the VW handle. Such wide reach of organizational messages also seems to be very efficient: while we could not determine the organizational resources allocated to Luxury brands' Twitter activity, none were tweeting much, with the brand with the largest numbers of followers and retweets, Louis Vuitton, sending only 1.3 tweets per day on average.

For Luxury brands, Twitter is also becoming more cost-effective. All industries have grown their Twitter audiences, with the largest increase for Luxury brands, despite those brands tweeting less than a year earlier. While, as discussed earlier, the number of followers will over-estimate the number who receive a brand's messages due to inactive and/or fake followers, this increase in followers is also evidence that Twitter is becoming a more important channel for brand communication, albeit with a selected group of

Table 7. Tweet content and retweet levels

	Retweets with:	Retweets without:	
	Mean (SD)	**Mean (SD)**	**Sig**
Public replies			
Auto	52 (188)	77 (287)	0.056
FMCG	5.0 (16.5)	7.5 (28.6)	ns
Luxury	136 (247)	182 (479)	ns
Mentions			
Auto	69 (159)	80 (333)	0.078
FMCG	6.7 (35.8)	7.8 (22.7)	ns
Luxury	191 (550)	174 (426)	ns
Weblinks			
Auto	82 (296)	21.0 (128)	< 0.001
FMCG	8.7 (34.3)	5.1 (11.2)	< 0.001
Luxury	189 (485)	33.0 (79.8)	< 0.001
Hashtags			
Auto	77 (285)	73 (280)	ns
FMCG	8.4 (33.0)	5.1 (10.3)	< 0.001
Luxury	181.0 (525)	178 (391)	ns
Question marks			
Auto	72.0 (427)	77 (252)	ns
FMCG	6.0 (31.3)	7.6 (27.7)	ns
Luxury	87.0 (164)	183 (479)	< 0.001
Retweet CTA			
Auto	677 (1803)	73.0 (254)	0.068
FMCG	36.7 (70.6)	6.8 (26.5)	< 0.001
Luxury	2576 (3113)	168 (378)	0.016

followers, and with the secondary audience intermittently reached by retweets or discovered due to the inclusion of popular hashtags (such as 'TeamUSA'). For these leading brands, a sizable Twitter audience can be obtained by sending occasional, but engaging, tweets to followers.

Although user engagement can be assessed using retweets, favorites and the frequency of listing, our results suggest that one measure – retweet frequency – will usually be sufficient. Retweeting and favoriting are highly correlated, so including both in any measurement scheme provides little additional information, and as an indicator of potential secondary reach, retweeting is more important than favoriting because it is a form of electronic WOM. Our results also indicate that the frequency of listing is not a useful measure of user engagement: despite large increases in followers, retweeting and favoriting over the one year comparison period, the frequency of listing had only increased in any meaningful way in the Auto industry, which on measures of followers, retweeting and favoriting, was less successful than the Luxury brands. Only a very small percentage of Twitter users list Twitter handles, and after allowing for the industry type, the frequency of listing was not associated with other more important measures of user engagement (that is, retweeting or favoriting). It may be time to abandon listing as a measure of Twitter engagement.

There were indications that the Twitter strategies of these brands are evolving, possibly as more evidence emerges about the factors which appear to increase consumer engagement with Twitter. Consistent with evidence that tweets with hashtags are more likely to be retweeted (e. g. Rogers, 2014; Suh et al., 2010), and also with the greater potential for tweets with hashtags to be found by non-followers, all industries had markedly increased their use of hashtags. At the same time, however, the value of hashtags appears to be decreasing: after removing private replies, (which are seen by far fewer people and thus are less likely to be retweeted) inclusion of a hashtag only resulted in a significant increase in retweeting in the FMCG industry.

For weblinks, which increase the potential for user engagement with the brand and which have also been shown to be associated with higher rates of retweeting (Rogers, 2014; Suh et al., 2010), the pattern was more mixed: luxury brands had markedly increased their use of weblinks compared to a year earlier (with weblinks increasing from 58.2% to 81.6% of tweets) but the increase in weblinks by FMCG brands was much smaller – and the Auto brands were using weblinks in fewer tweets than a year earlier. Our results confirm that inclusion of weblinks is associated with higher levels of retweeting, and the benefit of weblinks is likely to increase as brands increasingly use weblinks to embed photos and videos.

While there were large differences in performance and tweet composition within industries, there were larger differences between industries. Luxury brands generally tweeted infrequently, had a very high proportion of weblinks displaying branded products, and rarely engaged with their followers (with very few replies and few retweets, largely restricted to influential sources such as fashion magazines promoting the brands' products). While Luxury brands used hashtags extensively, the most commonly used hashtags were strongly related to the brand names, with limited use of non-brand related hashtags (see Table 1). Auto and FMCG brands were much more engaged with their followers, with much higher proportions of tweets containing replies, retweets of others and for some brands, promotional efforts (competitions or tweets referring to sponsored and/or popular events, such as the Winter Olympics and Superbowl final). Auto brands, like Luxury, largely used brand-related hashtags, but FMCG companies were more likely to use non-brand related hashtags (see Table 1). These hashtags sometimes referred to sponsored events ('sochi2014') or campaigns ('nodeforestation', 'employment4youth'), but others were popular hashtags (e.g. 'beauty, and 'nyfw' (New York fashion week)), thereby increasing the chance that the tweets would be discovered by a broader audience. While different Twitter activities will be appropriate for different product categories, the relative similarity in Twitter strategies within industries, and differences between – especially for the high involvement industries of Luxury and Auto – suggests that some brands may be using a risk-reduction approach of copying their competitors' Twitter strategies. Thus, compared to a year earlier, Auto brands are engaging more with their followers with replies, retweets and mentions, while in contrast, Luxury brands are engaging less, instead using weblinks heavily to promote visually appealing branded content.

Differences in strategies between industries, and in the level of consumer engagement, are not surprising: a consumer's involvement with a product has been shown to be associated with their likelihood of engaging in electronic word-of-mouth (Wolny & Mueller, 2013). As a result, we would expect lower levels of consumer interaction with FMCG brands than with the higher involvement categories of Luxury or Auto. However despite some similarities in tweet composition within industries, as discussed above, there were marked differences in success within industries, as measured by consumer engagement (retweets and favorites) and follower numbers. We therefore examined the strategies of the best performers within each industry for retweeting (Louis Vuitton, BMW and Duracell) and for the number of followers (Louis Vuitton, Audi and Pampers). The tweets of the best performers within each industry were retweeted more than twice as often as the second best in the industry, and those with the most followers had follower numbers ranging from 11% more than the second best in the industry (Louis Vuitton) to 50% more than the second best (Audi). So what were these best performers doing? To find out, we examined overall statistics for the brands, and examined a random sample of 100 tweets from each of the high engagement and high follower brands more closely, focusing on usage of embedded photos, videos, and tweet content, in an attempt to identify any differences in tweet construction and content between the best performers in the industries and their less successful peers.

Strategies of the Best Performers

Product Based Broadcasting: Louis Vuitton

Louis Vuitton was the best performer across all three industries, with the highest number of followers and the highest level of retweeting. It had the lowest proportion of replies (with only three replies in the second six month time period, all public replies to celebrities) and only limited mentions of other Twitter handles. While it sometimes retweeted others, those retweets appeared to be largely limited to retweets of authoritative fashion sources promoting Louis Vuitton products (such as @VogueParis and @wallpapermag). In contrast with this lack of interaction with followers, the Louis Vuitton handle made heavy use of weblinks, with embedded photos and videos to display branded products. However in contrast with recommendations that brands should be interactive on Twitter (e.g. Fidelman, 2013), the Louis Vuitton handle decreased its engagement with its followers over the one year comparison period, using fewer replies and retweets of others. Instead, the brand appeared to be following a strategy of one-way communication, heavily focused on product promotion – and its high follower numbers and retweet rate show that such a strategy can be very rewarding for a high involvement brand.

Product Based Interaction: BMW and Audi

Despite having only 20% of the followers of Audi (the Auto brand with the largest number of followers) the BMW Twitter handle had the highest retweet rate within the Auto industry, and like Louis Vuitton, sent few tweets – an average of only 4.2 per day. Again like Louis Vuitton, its tweets were heavily product based, with extensive use of embedded photos of BMW cars, and BMW related hashtags. But in contrast with Louis Vuitton, BMW engaged far more with its followers, with a high proportion of replies (35%) and strategies designed to increase follower engagement. For example, the brand achieved more than 4,600 retweets after calling on recipients to retweet a tweet in order to add their names to a good luck banner for the US Winter Olympics team.

Audi, the Auto brand with the highest number of followers, has been singled out as an example of effective tweet strategy following a widely retweeted tweet during the 2013 Superbowl final poking fun at Mercedes, an event sponsor, during a blackout (Shively, 2013). But despite its much larger audience, follower engagement with Audi's tweets was much lower than BMW's, with Audi having a retweet rate only one third of BMW's – despite having five times the numbers of followers. So what might explain this greater retweeting by BMW followers? Like BMW, Audi engaged heavily with followers, with 47%

of its original tweets being replies (though only 4.8% of those were public replies) and 24.4% retweets of others. BMW's retweet rate was undoubtedly increased by Winter Olympic themed tweets (in part, promoting the BMW sponsorship of the US team bobsled). But Audi also had far fewer embedded photos than BMW, with photos in only 19% of the sample coded tweets, compared to photos in 59% of BMW's sampled tweets, suggesting that BMW's heavier use of embedded photos may have contributed to its high retweet rate.

Events and Celebrity Affiliation: Duracell

As discussed above, luxury products and cars are high involvement products, so it is not surprising that many people follow Twitter handles related to such products. The success of FMCG brands is therefore particularly interesting, because the product category is far lower involvement, so less likely to attract followers. Even within the FMCG category, some brands are likely to be higher involvement and offer more potential for engaging Twitter content - for example Avon, which had the highest percentage of 'retweet' calls to action, and Pampers, with promotions encouraging parents to tweet photos of their babies. Yet the most frequently retweeted FMCG brand was Duracell, with retweet rates more than double the second best performer in this area, Avon. So what was Duracell – a brand best known for batteries - doing to achieve such high retweet rates for such a low involvement product?

Duracell had very high engagement with its followers, with 49% of its original tweets consisting of replies, and 29% retweets of others. It also made frequent real-time references to popular sporting events (the Superbowl final and the Winter Olympics), and included extensive coverage of three Duracell sponsored athletes who have all overcome adversity, Amy Purdie (a Paralympian who lost both legs at age 19), and two popular and successful NFL players – Derrick Coleman, who is legally deaf, and Patrick Willis, who grew up in abject poverty. Portrayal of all three athletes is associated with Duracell's theme of 'will and power', and brand tweets relating to these athletes achieved very high retweet rates. Duracell also obtained very high retweet rates with tweets related to its campaign of donations for the 'Toys for Tots' appeal, backed by celebrity Ellen DeGeneres. In contrast with Louis Vuitton and BMW, Duracell also made extensive use of video, with 14% of the sampled tweets using embedded videos related to its sponsored athletes and Toys for Tots campaigns.

Promotion: Pampers

Like Audi and Louis Vuitton, Pampers had the highest number of followers in its category, with 44% more followers than the second most followed FMCG brand, Avon. Like Duracell, Pampers had high levels of engagement with followers, with one of the highest percentages of replies (75%), and high levels of mentions. The brand also used multiple tactics to create user engagement, with a high proportion of hashtags, and was one of the highest users of questions, though as shown in Table 7, using questions was associated with a (non-significant) decrease in retweeting for FMCG tweets. Like Duracell, Pampers highlighted sponsorship of the Winter Olympics by its parent company (Procter & Gamble) in its tweets, but instead of focusing on athletes, Pampers encouraged parents to tweet their babies' photos as part of its 'Pampers Game Face' promotion, showing photogenic babies purportedly reacting to Olympic performances. Pampers also encourages and rewards its followers through a loyalty program where they can gain coupons by posting, retweeting and following Pampers on Twitter. Compared to Duracell, Pampers was a much lower user of photos and videos (with no video links in the sampled 100 tweets).

Less Effective Strategies

Customer Engagement With Questions

Auto industry brands appeared to be attempting to engage customers by asking questions in tweets, with an industry average of 17.5% of tweets with questions, in sharp contrast with FMCG and Luxury brands, with respective averages of 12.2% and 3.2%. Nine out of the 14 Auto brands had questions in more than 10% of their tweets, led by Nissan, with questions in 27% of tweets, although the Auto brands with the highest number of followers (Audi) and the highest retweet rate (BMW) had markedly lower rates of questions (4.2% and 6.9% respectively). Tweets with questions had significantly lower retweet rates for Luxury brands, and lower (though not significantly lower) rates in the other two industries. Questions may draw follower attention to a tweet, but do not appear to be an effective way to increase retweeting – and may in fact decrease retweeting, consistent with evidence that tweets with questions are seen as less credible (Castillo et al., 2011).

Complaint Handling

Some brands (particularly Duracell, VW, Audi and Pampers) had a high percentage of tweets with apologies, although all except two were in 'private' replies, which while not appearing in followers' Twitter feeds, would still be visible on the brands' Twitter home page. VW made some complaints even more visible, by asking VW owners with problems to 'Tweet #VWCares for assistance' – thus directing them to a hashtag referencing a large number of complaints from irate VW customers, for example:

#VWCares @VW do you care my 2011 #jetta (leased) is dead for the 6th time? Less than 3 months since last breakdown! pic.twitter.com/0cf6nP7CCL

@VW #vwcares NOT. Did you know #vw warranties is administered by @Allstate no wonder nothing is covered. AVOID @VW and @Allstate scams!

Broadcasting Corporate Communications

Two FMCG brands (Danone and Colgate) appeared to be following a very different strategy, primarily using their tweets to communicate corporate information, with little apparent attempt to interact with users or increase follower engagement (few tweets with weblinks, mentions, retweets or replies). They had the lowest retweet rate of all brands and (with Kellogg's) the lowest number of followers (4,588 for Danone and 9,452 for Colgate, compared to an average 44,744 followers for FMCG brands). Colgate was also the lowest user of hashtags, with only one hashtag (#nodeforestation) used more than once. Both Colgate and Danone were also among the lowest tweeting brands, and appeared to be using their Twitter handles primarily to disseminate limited and specific company information. However when contrasted with the large number of followers of other FMCG brands such as Pampers (with over 108,000 followers) and Duracell (with 70,000 followers), the failure of Colgate and Danone to develop larger Twitter audiences suggests a lost opportunity to interact with their customers.

Implications for Practice

So what lessons can be learned from the Twitter strategies of the leading global brands? Few companies will have a marketing budget or staff to rival these leading brands, but we list below some suggestions for lower profile brands.

- *You don't have to be highly engaged with your audience to be very successful.* The success of the luxury brands, which largely used Twitter to broadcast promotional information, shows that if your brand is well known and your product is important to followers, you can achieve a large Twitter audience with a broadcast strategy. For example, Louis Vuitton is very successful in getting considerable consumer engagement (as shown by followers retweeting and favoriting) with a tweet strategy which is primarily product based broadcasting:

Discover the new colors in this season's #LouisVuitton small leather goods collection at http://t.co/bYYH3t3Wiq http://t.co/J2l88nBnYE (retweeted 6,199 times)

But products which are less important to customers (like these FMCG brands), and less well-known brands will generally need to use other strategies (as discussed below) to build follower numbers and increase follower engagement.

- *You don't need to tweet a lot to get a large Twitter audience.* More is not better. The most successful Twitter handles were sending fewer than two tweets a day. It's probably better to send fewer more interesting tweets than to send a lot of tweets which don't interest your followers. For example, nine of the 20 most retweeted tweets within the 2014 period were sent by either Ralph Lauren or Louis Vuitton, which respectively only tweeted 3.3 and 1.3 tweets per day in the period examined. Their tweets frequently featured a captivating call to action, or (for Louis Vuitton) mentioned an influential Twitter handle (that is, one with large number of followers) along with interesting embedded images, e.g.

For every retweet, Polo Ralph Lauren FDN will donate $1 to @MichaelJFoxOrg (up to$25K) in support of #Parkinsons http://t.co/oMtSwH14Z3 (retweeted 10,271 times)

Among FMCG brands, Duracell achieved the second highest number of followers despite having one of the lowest frequencies of tweeting, with, as discussed above, frequent references to popular events and celebrities.

- *Don't use your central Twitter handle as a service recovery channel.* While you should respond to customer complaints, use a separate Twitter handle for apologies unless you think your apology is important to many of your followers (for example, if a service is down, and you want to notify all followers). Don't use a hashtag to reference customer service issues (like Volkswagen), because it means that both potential buyers and unhappy customers can see other people's complaints. The best strategy may be to use a dedicated customer service Twitter handle for back and forth communication with followers, promote this handle in the form of a mention when answering customer queries, and list it in the bio section of your Twitter profile.

- *Think about whether to reply privately or publicly.* Even if it's not a response to a customer complaint or problem (where you should never reply publicly, as discussed above), think about how you should reply to tweets. If your reply isn't likely to be interesting to other followers, it's almost certainly better to use the less public form of reply. But effectively done, replies can obtain high retweet rates. For example Burberry often used 'private' replies to respond individually to followers, but also achieved high retweet rates with public replies to celebrities, as shown by a reply to Jamie Bower, an English actor, singer and model:

.@JamieBower wearing #Burberry sunglasses from The Trench Collection at the Menswear A/W14 show on Wednesday #LCM http://t.co/tnfSJYtD2p (retweeted 1282 times)

- *Use popular hashtags, but use them judiciously.* Tweets with hashtags were retweeted more often, though the result was only significant for the FMCG industry. For example Duracell achieved high tweet rates with a tweet referring to popular NFL star Derrick Coleman and the Seattle Seahawks, and containing an embedded YouTube video.

We trust your power, Derrick. Congrats to you and your team. #Seahawks http://t.co/0evcV90c1E (retweeted 534 times)

However the results also suggest that having too many hashtags can actually decrease the retweet rate: tweets with five or more hashtags had lower retweet rates than tweets containing four or fewer hashtags – and also lower retweet rates than no hashtags.

- *Use mentions if appropriate, but don't expect them to increase the retweet rate short-term.* The study found no evidence that including a mention increases the retweet rate for an individual tweet. This doesn't mean that including mentions can't be an effective strategy, however: particularly for less well-known Twitter handles, including relevant mentions can be effective at bringing a brand's Twitter handle to the notice of the people mentioned – with the potential for them to follow and retweet the brand's future tweets. Including mentions of interesting Twitter handles may also add value for a Twitter handle's own followers, but if the mentions aren't seen as relevant by followers, a mention could decrease follower engagement – and potentially even lead to lower retweet rates, as we saw with the marginally lower rate of retweeting for Auto industry tweets with mentions.
- *Weblinks and images create interest.* More than anything else, weblinks increased retweeting for these brands. For example Tiffany and many of the other luxury brands sent tweets with highly attractive product images, supplemented by positive messages, often referencing Tiffany's distinctive blue box:

The best surprises come wrapped in blue: http://t.co/Y8xVQZfkuj (retweeted 5,814 times)

Links with photos and videos embedded in tweets can be particularly effective in making tweets stand out for followers, or you can use weblinks to increase customer traffic to your website.

- *Celebrities create interest.* Duracell's strategy of sponsoring less well-known sportspeople (such as a Paralympian such like Amy Purdy, rather than an Olympian), and associating them with Duracell's theme of 'power', is a good example of cost-effective sponsorship. For example Duracell continued its coverage of Amy Purdy after the Winter Olympics with references to her appearance on Dancing with the Starts:

@AmyPurdyGurl: From #Sochi2014 to @DancingABC w/ @DerekHough here's to living life without limits. Her story: http://t.co/0CQF1tfwi5#DWTS (181 reteweets)

Small businesses won't be able to afford to sponsor a national team or high-profile athlete, but might be able to cost-effectively sponsor an emerging local athlete, team or musician.

- *Questions don't seem to create interest.* Many Twitter handles use questions in an apparent attempt to create user engagement. Tweets with questions can achieve high retweet rates –as discussed above the most retweeted tweet contained a question mark - but on average, tweets with questions were retweeted less than tweets without questions e.g.

Confession time: what's the strangest food craving you've had during #pregnancy? (Pampers, only 1 retweet)

And the winners are? #hacklorealdpp http://t.co/GVf5anqYD3 via @begeek (Loreal, zero retweets)

- *Including a 'retweet' request can increase retweeting.* A call to action to 'retweet' was associated with large increases in retweeting for every industry, e.g.

Retweet if you love heated seats in the winter. http://t.co/u0m3vykff5 (VW, retweeted 8938 times)

Consumers may quickly become immune to a suggestion to 'retweet' if too many tweets use this tactic, but for now, asking followers to 'retweet' can increase response rates. It is likely that a comparable appeal such as 'Favorite if…' could have similar results.

Limitations

While the results provide insight into the Twitter strategies of leading consumer brands, they must be interpreted in the light of some limitations. We examined only one Twitter handle from each company, albeit the highest profile handle. A study which attempts to identify and analyze all Twitter handles under a company's name may show that different handles are used for different purposes (e.g. for corporate communications, complaints handling, and customer engagement). As discussed, the results show the effect of different Twitter strategies for brands with high consumer awareness, so different strategies may be needed for less well-known brands, as discussed below.

FUTURE RESEARCH DIRECTIONS

This chapter has examined different uses of Twitter, but the global brands explored in this research have a natural advantage on Twitter because they are well-known, and are therefore likely to be able to more easily obtain Twitter followers. Future research could explore what smaller firms are doing on Twitter, and investigate those which are successful in obtaining high follower and retweet rates. Other useful directions for research include dedicated purpose Twitter handles (such as customer service handles) in order to investigate how Twitter can be used as a focused communication channel. Yet another avenue for research could be to examine how organizations are using new Twitter features (such as promoted tweets or a 'buy now' button), and investigate the extent to which these features increase follower engagement. Finally, analyzing consumer tweets about brands can provide further insights into what drives customer engagement on Twitter.

CONCLUSION

The results show that for premier brands, Twitter can be a very effective way to communicate with consumers, with the best performing Luxury brands achieving millions of followers – for Louis Vuitton, with only 1.3 tweets per day. More surprisingly, the results show that even low involvement products can obtain very large follower numbers, with the best performing FMCG brand (Pampers) having more than a 100,000 followers with fewer than thirteen tweets per day – and receiving more than 400 retweets for its most popular tweet, so through retweets, reaching an even wider audience.

The results also show evolution of Twitter tactics over the comparison period, with much higher use of hashtags across all industries, but diverging practice in other areas. Although social media is often argued to be an interactive medium, Luxury brands' Twitter handles – the industry with the largest number of followers – had become significantly *less* engaged with their followers over the year, with fewer replies, mentions and retweets of others, but those brands had still experienced a large increase in the number of followers. In contrast, Auto brands were replying much more in their tweets (73%, up from 57%), but had not achieved the same increase in retweeting. Some brands can clearly be very successful on Twitter with very limited interaction with followers.

The comparison across industries also revealed divergent strategies: Luxury brands were primarily broadcasting favorable company information using weblinks and embedded photos, while Auto and FMCG brands were primarily interactive. Some FMCG brands primarily posted corporate communications news, with very little interaction.

While these results relate to leading companies with high market visibility and presumably with significant social media budgets, the results suggest some directions for less prominent brands on Twitter. Firstly, leveraging on popular events with timely tweets, like some of these successful FMCG brands, can increase follower engagement and expose tweets to wider audiences. Secondly, while interaction is often argued to be an important part of social media strategy, the results show that a brand can be successful with a one-way broadcasting strategy on Twitter, although this approach is likely to be more difficult for brands without an established reputation. Alternatively, a brand can choose to interact with its followers, retweet selected tweets, respond to replies and use mentions in an attempt to increase follower engagement. Whatever the brand's strategy, selected use of weblinks to create interest and hashtags to expose tweet content to non-followers, is likely to assist in increasing the retweet rate.

Finally, the results show that among these leading brands, different companies are following, and being successful with, very different strategies. As with any marketing action, deciding on the communication strategy, and using appropriate measures to determine the results of that strategy will give the organization the best chance of effective Twitter use – and of modifying Twitter practice as the platform changes to allow new methods of marketing communication and advertising.

ACKNOWLEDGMENT

We'd like to acknowledge the contribution of Frank Burton, who provided invaluable help in developing our Microsoft Excel coding schemes.

REFERENCES

Alexander, R. M., & Gentry, J. K. (2014). Using social media to report financial results. *Business Horizons*, *57*(2), 161–167. doi:10.1016/j.bushor.2013.10.009

Barnes, N. G., & Lescault, A. (2013). *LinkedIn rules but sales potential may lie with Twitter: The 2013 Inc. 500 and social media*. Retrieved January 24, 2014, from http://www.umassd.edu/cmr/socialmedia research/2013inc2500/

Barton, C., Koslow, L., & Beauchamp, C. (2014). *How millennials are changing the face of marketing forever: The reciprocity principle*. Retrieved May 2, 2014, from https://www.bcgperspectives.com/content/articles/marketing_center_consumer_customer_insight_how_millennials_changing_marketing_forever/

Blankespoor, E., Miller, G. S., & White, H. D. (2013). The role of dissemination in market liquidity: Evidence from firms' use of Twitter™. *Accounting Review*, *89*(1), 79–112. doi:10.2308/accr-50576

boyd, d., Golder, S., & Lotan, G. (2010). *Tweet, tweet, retweet: Conversational aspects of retweeting on Twitter.* Paper presented at the 2010 43rd Hawaii International Conference on System Sciences, Kauai, HI.

Bruns, A., & Stieglitz, S. (2013). Towards more systematic Twitter analysis: Metrics for tweeting activities. *International Journal of Social Research Methodology*, *16*(2), 91–108. doi:10.1080/13645579.2012.756095

Burkhalter, J. N., Wood, N. T., & Tryce, S. A. (2014). Clear, conspicuous, and concise: Disclosures and Twitter word-of-mouth. *Business Horizons*, *57*(3), 319–328. doi:10.1016/j.bushor.2014.02.001

Burton, S., Dadich, A., & Soboleva, A. (2013). Competing voices: Marketing and counter-marketing alcohol on Twitter. *Journal of Nonprofit & Public Sector Marketing*, *25*(2), 186–209. doi:10.1080/10495142.2013.787836

Burton, S., & Soboleva, A. (2011). Interactive or reactive? Marketing with Twitter. *Journal of Consumer Marketing*, *28*(7), 491–499. doi:10.1108/07363761111181473

Canhoto, A. I., & Clark, M. (2013). Customer service 140 characters at a time: The users' perspective. *Journal of Marketing Management*, *29*(5-6), 522–544. doi:10.1080/0267257X.2013.777355

Castillo, C., Mendoza, M., & Poblete, B. (2011). *Information credibility on Twitter*. Paper presented at the International World Wide Web Conference, Hyderabad, India.

Cha, M., Haddadi, H., Benevenuto, F., & Gummadi, K. (2010). *Measuring user influence in Twitter: The million follower fallacy*. Paper presented at the 4th International AAAI Conference on Weblogs and Social Media (ICWSM'10), Washington DC.

Cooper, B. B. (2014). *How Twitter's expanded images increase clicks, retweets and favourites*. Retrieved June 20, 2014, from http://blog.bufferapp.com/the-power-of-twitters-new-expanded-images-and-how-to-make-the-most-of-it

Culnan, M. J., McHugh, P. J., & Zubillaga, J. I. (2010). How large U.S. companies can use Twitter and other social media to gain business value *MIS Quarterly Executive, 9*(4), 243-259.

Duan, Y., Jiang, L., Qin, T., Zhou, M., & Shum, H.-Y. (2010). *An empirical study on learning to rank of tweets*. Paper presented at the 23rd International Conference on Computational Linguistics, Beijing, China.

Duggan, M., & Smith, A. (2013). *Social media update 2013*. Retrieved February 25, 2014, from http://www.pewinternet.org/2013/12/30/social-media-update-2013/

eBizMBA, G. (2014). *Top 15 most popular websites | July 2014*. Retrieved June 30, 2014, from http://www.ebizmba.com/articles/most-popular-websites

Ehrlich, K., & Shami, N. S. (2010). *Microblogging inside and outside the workplace*. Paper presented at the 4th International AAAI Conference on Weblogs and Social Media (ICWSM 2010), Washington, DC.

Ferrara, E., Varol, O., Davis, C., Menczer, F., & Flammini, A. (2014). *The rise of social bots*. Retrieved August 6, 2014, from http://arxiv.org/abs/1407.5225

Fidelman, M. (2013). *3 Twitter engagement tricks you should do every day (from #1 most engaged band on Twitter)*. Retrieved March 24, 2014, from http://www.forbes.com/sites/markfidelman/2013/06/05/3-twitter-engagement-tricks-you-should-do-every-day-from-the-1-most-engaged-brand-on-twitter/

Fulgoni, G., & Lipsman, A. (2014). Digital game changers: How social media will help usher in the era of mobile and multi-platform campaign-effectiveness measurement. *Journal of Advertising Research, 54*(1), 11–16. doi:10.2501/JAR-54-1-011-016

Furubayashi, J. (2014). *The complete guide to Twitter analytics: How to analyze the metrics that matter.* Retrieved May 20, 2014, from http://simplymeasured.com/blog/2014/03/04/complete-guide-to-twitter-analytics/

Goel, V. (2014). Twitter's growth shifts to developing countries. *The New York Times*. Retrieved June 2, 2014, from http://bits.blogs.nytimes.com/2014/05/27/twitters-growth-shifts-to-developing-countries/?_php=true&_type=blogs&_r=0

Haigh, D., & Perrier, R. (1997). Valuation of trademarks and brand names. In R. E. Perrier (Ed.), *Brand Valuation* (pp. 35–42). London: Premier Books.

Hansen, L., Arvidsson, A., Nielsen, F., Colleoni, E., & Etter, M. (2011). Good friends, bad news - Affect and virality in Twitter. In J. Park, L. Yang, & C. Lee (Eds.), *Future Information Technology* (Vol. 185, pp. 34–43). Berlin: Springer. doi:10.1007/978-3-642-22309-9_5

Heggestuen, J. (2013a). *The death of social ROI -- Companies are starting to drop the idea that they can track social media's dollar value*. Retrieved December 12, 2013, from http://www.businessinsider.com.au/the-myth-of-social-roi-2013-10

Heggestuen, J. (2013b). *How companies are using social media to becomer more customer centric*. Retrieved April 27, 2014, from http://www.businessinsider.com.au/a-guide-to-social-crm-2013-8

Hennig-Thurau, T., Gwinner, K. P., Walsh, G., & Gremler, D. D. (2004). Electronic word-of-mouth via consumer-opinion platforms: What motivates consumers to articulate themselves on the Internet? *Journal of Interactive Marketing*, *18*(1), 38–52. doi:10.1002/dir.10073

Hennig-Thurau, T., Hofacker, C. F., & Bloching, B. (2013). Marketing the pinball way: Understanding how social media change the generation of value for consumers and companies. *Journal of Interactive Marketing*, *27*(4), 237–241. doi:10.1016/j.intmar.2013.09.005

Hennig-Thurau, T., Malthouse, E. C., Friege, C., Gensler, S., Lobschat, L., Rangaswamy, A., & Skiera, B. (2010). The impact of new media on customer relationships. *Journal of Service Research*, *13*(3), 311–330. doi:10.1177/1094670510375460

Hennig-Thurau, T., Wiertz, C., & Feldhaus, F. (2014). Does Twitter matter? The impact of microblogging word of mouth on consumers' adoption of new movies. *Journal of the Academy of Marketing Science*. doi:10.1007/s11747-014-0388-3

Hoffman, D., & Fodor, M. (2010). Can you measure the ROI of your social media marketing? *MIT Sloan Management Review*, *52*(1), 41–49.

Hollebeek, L. D., Glynn, M. S., & Brodie, R. J. (2014). Consumer brand engagement in social media: Conceptualization, scale development and validation. *Journal of Interactive Marketing*, *28*(2), 149–165. doi:10.1016/j.intmar.2013.12.002

Howen, A. (2014). *The marketing challenges of Twitter*. Retrieved May 20, 2014, from http://www.websitemagazine.com/content/blogs/posts/archive/2014/03/21/the-marketing-challenges-of-twitter.aspx

Huang, J., Thornton, K., & Efthimiadis, E. (2010). *Conversational tagging in Twitter.* Paper presented at the 21st ACM Conference on Hypertext and Hypermedia Toronto, Canada. doi:10.1145/1810617.1810647

Interbrand. (2012). *Best global brands 2012*. Retrieved December 20, 2012, from http://www.interbrand.com/en/best-global-brands/2012/Best-Global-Brands-2012.aspx

Interbrand. (2013). *Best global brands 2013*. Retrieved December 28, 2013, from http://www.interbrand.com/en/best-global-brands/2013/Best-Global-Brands-2013.aspx

Jansen, B. J., Zhang, M. M., Sobel, K., & Chowdury, A. (2009). Twitter power: Tweets as electronic word of mouth. *Journal of the American Society for Information Science and Technology*, *60*(11), 2169–2188. doi:10.1002/asi.21149

Ju, A., Jeong, S. H., & Chyi, H. I. (2013). Will social media save newspapers? *Journalism Practice*, *8*(1), 1–17. doi:10.1080/17512786.2013.794022

Kane, G. C. (2014). Reimagining customer service at KLM using Facebook and Twitter. *MIT Sloan Management Review*. Retrieved August 8, 2014 from http://sloanreview.mit.edu/article/reimagining-customer-service-at-klm-using-facebook-and-twitter/

Kelly, B. (2014). *Enterprise social media management software 2014: A marketer's guide*. Retrieved May 28, 2014, from http://downloads.digitalmarketingdepot.com/rs/thirddoormedia/images/MIR_1305_EntSocMd13.pdf?mkt_tok=3RkMMJWWfF9wsRons63LZKXonjHpfsX77%2BksUa%2BwlMI%2F0ER3fOvrPUfGjI4DTsNnI%2BSLDwEYGJlv6SgFTbLCMbpx37gNXxU%3D

Kietzmann, J. H., Hermkens, K., McCarthy, I. P., & Silvestre, B. S. (2011). Social media? Get serious! Understanding the functional building blocks of social media. *Business Horizons*, *54*(3), 241–251. doi:10.1016/j.bushor.2011.01.005

Kim, E., Sung, Y., & Kang, H. (2014). Brand followers' retweeting behavior on Twitter: How brand relationships influence brand electronic word-of-mouth. *Computers in Human Behavior*, *37*, 18–25. doi:10.1016/j.chb.2014.04.020

Krutkam, W., Saikeaw, K., & Chaosakul, A. (2010). *Twitter accounts recommendation based on followers and lists*. Paper presented at the 3rd Joint International Information and Communication Technology Conference, Mumbai, India.

Kuchler, H. (2014). *Twitter to launch a 'buy now' button*. Retrieved September 24, 2014, from http://www.ft.com/intl/cms/s/0/d6e077c8-3736-11e4-8472-00144feabdc0.html#axzz3ESliS67Q

Kwak, H., Lee, C., Park, H., & Moon, S. (2010). *What is Twitter, a social network or a news media?* Paper presented at the 19th International World Wide Web (WWW) Conference, Raleigh, NC. doi:10.1145/1772690.1772751

Kwon, E. S., & Sung, Y. (2011). Follow me! Global marketers' Twitter use. *Journal of Interactive Advertising*, *12*(1), 4–16. doi:10.1080/15252019.2011.10722187

Labrecque, L. I. (2014). Fostering consumer–brand relationships in social media environments: The role of parasocial interaction. *Journal of Interactive Marketing*, *28*(2), 134–148. doi:10.1016/j.intmar.2013.12.003

Lambrecht, A., Tucker, C., & Wiertz, C. (2014). *Should you target early trend propagators? Evidence from Twitter*. Retrieved August 7, 2014 from http://ssrn.com/abstract=2419743

Lieb, R., & Groopman, J. (2013). *Real-time marketing: The agility to leverage "now"*. Retrieved March 12, 2014, from http://www.altimetergroup.com/research/reports/real-time-marketing-agility-to-leverage-now

Malhotra, A., Malhotra, C. K., & See, A. (2012). How to get your messages retweeted. *MIT Sloan Management Review*, *53*(2), 61–66.

Marwick, A. E., & boyd, . (2011). I tweet honestly, I tweet passionately: Twitter users, context collapse, and the imagined audience. *New Media & Society*, *13*(1), 114–133. doi:10.1177/1461444810365313

Meier, F., Elsweiler, D., & Wilson, M. L. (2014). *More than liking and bookmarking? Towards understanding Twitter favouriting behaviour*. Paper presented at the 8th International Conference on Weblogs and Social Media, Ann Arbor, MI.

Midha, A. (2014). *Study: Exposure to brand tweets drives consumers to take action - both on and off Twitter*. Retrieved May 20, 2014, from http://blog.twitter.com/2014/study-exposure-to-brand-tweets-drives-consumers-to-take-action-both-on-and-off-twitter

Misopoulos, F., Mitic, M., Kapoulas, A., & Karapiperis, C. (2014). Uncovering customer service experiences with Twitter: The case of airline industry. *Management Decision*, *52*(4), 705–723. doi:10.1108/MD-03-2012-0235

Naveed, N., Gottron, T., Kunegis, J., & Alhadi, A. C. (2011). *Bad news travel fast: A content-based analysis of interestingness on Twitter*. Paper presented at the 3rd International Web Science Conference, Koblenz, Germany. doi:10.1145/2527031.2527052

Neiger, B. L., Thackeray, R., Burton, S. H., Giraud-Carrier, C. G., & Fagen, M. C. (2013). Evaluating social media's capacity to develop engaged audiences in health promotion settings: Use of Twitter metrics as a case study. *Health Promotion Practice*, *14*(2), 157–162. doi:10.1177/1524839912469378 PMID:23271716

Page, R. (2012). The linguistics of self-branding and micro-celebrity in Twitter: The role of hashtags. *Discourse & Communication*, *6*(2), 181–201. doi:10.1177/1750481312437441

Page, R. (2014). Saying 'sorry': Corporate apologies posted on Twitter. *Journal of Pragmatics*, *62*, 30–45. doi:10.1016/j.pragma.2013.12.003

Pfeffer, J., Zorbach, T., & Carley, K. M. (2013). Understanding online firestorms: Negative word-of-mouth dynamics in social media networks. *Journal of Marketing Communications*, *20*(1-2), 117–128. doi:10.1080/13527266.2013.797778

Pullen, L. (2009). *Twitter lists: Frequently asked questions*. Retrieved April 20, 2013, from http://mashable.com/2009/11/03/twitter-lists-faq/

Rapp, A., Beitelspacher, L., Grewal, D., & Hughes, D. (2013). Understanding social media effects across seller, retailer, and consumer interactions. *Journal of the Academy of Marketing Science*, 1–20.

Richards, K. (2014). This photoshopped CoverGirl ad is the most powerful protest against the NFL we've seen. *Business Insider Australia*. Retrieved September 23, 2014, from http://www.businessinsider.com.au/photoshopped-nfl-covergirl-ad-2014-9

Rogers, S. (2014). *What fuels a Tweet's engagement?* Retrieved April 12, 2014, from http://blog.twitter.com/2014/what-fuels-a-tweets-engagement

Rokka, J., Karlsson, K., & Tienari, J. (2013). Balancing acts: Managing employees and reputation in social media. *Journal of Marketing Management*, *30*(7-8), 802–827. doi:10.1080/0267257X.2013.813577

Romero, D., Galuba, W., Asur, S., & Huberman, B. (2010). *Influence and Passivity in Social Media*. Retrieved August 4, 2014, from http://www.hpl.hp.com/research/scl/papers/influence/influence.pdf

Salesforce Marketing Cloud. (2012). *Strategies for effective tweeting: A statistical review*. Retrieved October 26, 2013, from http://www.salesforcemarketingcloud.com/wp-content/uploads/2013/03/Strategies-for-effective-tweeting.pdf

Sashittal, H. C., Hodis, M., & Sriramachandramurthy, R. (2014). Is your brand a living entity? *MIT Sloan Management Review*, *55*(3), 95–96.

Schweidel, D. A., & Moe, W. W. (2014). Listening in on social media: A joint model of sentiment and venue format choice. *JMR, Journal of Marketing Research*, *51*(4), 387–402. doi:10.1509/jmr.12.0424

Shi, Z., Rui, H., & Whinston, A. B. (2014). Content sharing in a social broadcasting envrionment: Evidence from Twitter. *Management Information Systems Quarterly*, *38*(1).

Shively, K. (2013). *What can Audi teach you about your Twitter metrics?* Retrieved March 20, 2014, from http://unbounce.com/social-media/twitter-metrics-lessons-from-audi/

Shively, K. (2014). *How top brand marketers used Twitter during Q4 of 2013*. Retrieved March 3, 2014, from http://simplymeasured.com/blog/2014/01/20/twitter-study/

Smith, A. N., Fischer, E., & Yongjian, C. (2012). How does brand-related user-generated content differ across YouTube, Facebook and Twitter? *Journal of Interactive Marketing*, *26*(2), 102–113. doi:10.1016/j.intmar.2012.01.002

Soboleva, A., Burton, S., & Khan, A. (2013). *Consumer engagement with organisational tweets: Measuring Twitter effectiveness*. Paper presented at the Australia and New Zealand Marketing Academy Conference (ANZMAC), Auckland, New Zealand.

Solis, B., & Li, C. (2013). *The state of social business 2013: The maturing of social media into social business*. Retrieved November 24, 2013 from http://www.altimetergroup.com/2013/11/research-on-the-state-of-social-business-2013/

Sterne, J. (2010). *Social Media Metrics: How to Measure and Optimise your Marketing Investment*. Hoboken, NJ: John Wiley and Sons.

Stringhini, G., Wang, G., Egele, M., Kruegel, C., Vigna, G., Zheng, H., & Zhao, B. Y. (2013). *Follow the green: Growth and dynamics in Twitter follower markets*. Paper presented at the 13th Internet Measurement Conference (IMC), Barcelona, Spain. doi:10.1145/2504730.2504731

Suh, B., Hong, L., Pirolli, P., & Chi, E. (2010). *Want to be retweeted? Large scale analytics on factors impacting retweet in Twitter network*. Paper presented at the Second IEEE International Conference on Social Computing Minneapolis MN. doi:10.1109/SocialCom.2010.33

Swani, K., Brown, B. P., & Milne, G. R. (2014). Should tweets differ for B2B and B2C? An analysis of Fortune 500 companies' Twitter communications. *Industrial Marketing Management*, *43*(5), 873–881. doi:10.1016/j.indmarman.2014.04.012

Swift, A. (2014). *Americans say social media have little sway on purchases*. Retrieved July 16, 2014, from http://www.gallup.com/poll/171785/americans-say-social-media-little-effect-buying-decisions.aspx?ref=image

Twitter. (2012). *Using Twiter Lists*. Retrieved October 12, 2012, from http://support.twitter.com/articles/76460-using-twitter-lists#

Twitter. (2014a). *About Twitter*. Retrieved May 3, 2014, from http://about.twitter.com/company

Twitter. (2014b). *Who's on Twitter*. Retrieved May 7, 2014, from http://business.twitter.com/whos-twitter

Washeck, A. (2014). *6 new Twitter features you should know about* (P. Magazine, Trans.). Retrieved May 16, 2014, from http://www.pastemagazine.com/blogs/lists/2014/04/6-new-twitter-features-you-should-know-about.html

Wells, G. (2014). *Unleashing innovation: Big data (A special report) - Real-time marketing in a real-time world: How advertisers are using social media to promote their brands at a moment's notice* (Eastern ed.). Retrieved March 23, 2014, from http://online.wsj.com/news/articles/SB10001424052702303801304579407284034257414?mod=dist_smartbrief

Wolny, J., & Mueller, C. (2013). Analysis of fashion consumers' motives to engage in electronic word-of-mouth communication through social media platforms. *Journal of Marketing Management*, *29*(5-6), 562–583. doi:10.1080/0267257X.2013.778324

Wood, N. T., & Burkhalter, J. N. (2013). Tweet this, not that: A comparison between brand promotions in microblogging environments using celebrity and company-generated tweets. *Journal of Marketing Communications*, *20*(1-2), 129–146. doi:10.1080/13527266.2013.797784

Yadav, M. S., de Valck, K., Hennig-Thurau, T., Hoffman, D. L., & Spann, M. (2013). Social commerce: A contingency framework for assessing marketing potential. *Journal of Interactive Marketing*, *27*(4), 311–323. doi:10.1016/j.intmar.2013.09.001

Yang, J., & Counts, S. (2010). *Predicting the speed, scale, and range of information diffusion in Twitter.* Paper presented at the 4th International AAAI Conference on Weblogs and Social Media, Washington, D.C., USA.

Zarella, D. (2013). *The Science of Marketing: When to Tweet, What to Post, How to Blog, and Other Proven Strategies*. Somerset, NJ: Wiley.

Zhang, M., Jansen, B. J., & Chowdhury, A. (2011). Business engagement on Twitter: A path analysis. *Electronic Markets*, *21*(3), 161–175. doi:10.1007/s12525-011-0065-z

ADDITIONAL READING

Burton, S., Dadich, A., & Soboleva, A. (2013). Competing voices: Marketing and counter-marketing alcohol on Twitter. *Journal of Nonprofit & Public Sector Marketing*, *25*(2), 186–209. doi:10.1080/10495142.2013.787836

Cha, M., Haddadi, H., Benevenuto, F., & Gummadi, K. (2010). *Measuring user influence in Twitter: The million follower fallacy*. Paper presented at the 4th International AAAI Conference on Weblogs and Social Media (ICWSM'10), Washington DC.

Furubayashi, J. (2014). The complete guide to Twitter analytics: How to analyze the metrics that matter. Retrieved May 20, 2014, from http://simplymeasured.com/blog/2014/03/04/complete-guide-to-twitter-analytics/

Hennig-Thurau, T., Wiertz, C., & Feldhaus, F. (2014). Does Twitter matter? The impact of microblogging word of mouth on consumers' adoption of new movies. *Journal of the Academy of Marketing Science*. doi:10.1007/s11747-014-0388-3

Swani, K., Brown, B. P., & Milne, G. R. (2014). Should tweets differ for B2B and B2C? An analysis of Fortune 500 companies' Twitter communications. *Industrial Marketing Management*, *43*(5), 873–881. doi:10.1016/j.indmarman.2014.04.012

KEY TERMS AND DEFINTIONS

Electronic Word of Mouth (EWOM): 'Any positive or negative statement made by potential, actual, or former customers about a product or company, which is made available to a multitude of people and institutions via the Internet.' (Hennig-Thurau et al., 2004)

'Embedded' Content/Media in Tweets: Photos or video that are 'embedded' show directly within Twitter, saving users from needing to click on the link to view the media.

Favorite: Favoriting is a feature on Twitter that allows a user to mark a tweet as a favorite (and thus easily see it later). To favorite a tweet, a follower clicks on the small star icon beneath the tweet. The star will turn gold, confirming that the tweet has been 'favorited'.

Hashtag: A Twitter hashtag refers to a topic, keyword or phrase preceded by the '#' symbol. Hashtags are used to categorize messages on Twitter, and thus make them easily findable by people who search for the hashtag.

Interbrand Best Global Brands: Interbrand brand consultancy publishes an annual ranking of the best global brands, chosen based on the brands' financial performance, role, and strength. Global brands qualify for the list if they have a presence on at least three major continents, as well as broad geographic coverage in growing and emerging markets. Thirty percent of revenues must come from outside the home country, and no more than 50% of revenues should come from any one continent. (Source: www.interbrand.com).

Mention: A mention refers to a tweet that includes a reference to another Twitter user, by placing the @symbol in front of that user's handle or username (e.g. '@username').

Public Reply: If a user wants their followers to see their replies to another user or brand, they use '.@reply' instead of '@reply'. The tweet will show up in the sender's timeline and the timeline of anyone who follows them, in contrast with an '@reply' (i.e. one which does not start with a period), which while showing on the Twitter page of the sender, only appears in the Twitter feed of the recipient and anyone who follows both the sender and recipient.

Return on Marketing Investment (ROMI): The profit from a particular activity compared with the amount spent on marketing it in a particular period. This shows how effectively the company is spending money on marketing. (source: http://dictionary.cambridge.org/dictionary/business-english/return-on-marketing-investment).

Retweet: A retweet is a tweet which has been forwarded or 'resent' on Twitter by someone other than the sender. To 'retweet' is thus to send someone else's tweet to one's own followers. Retweeting is a common activity on Twitter and the frequency of retweeting reflects the popularity of individual tweets.

Twitter Username/Handle: A Twitter username is an alternative name for a Twitter handle, and represents the name each user has selected to be known as on Twitter. Usernames are limited to a maximum of 15 characters, and each Twitter username has a unique url, with the username added after twitter.com (i.e. www.twitter.com/username).

ENDNOTES

1. The terms FMCG (fast moving consumer goods) and CPG (consumer packaged goods) are often used interchangeably, with the term CPG more common in the U.S., and FMCG more common in Europe. The Interbrand report uses both terms, but more commonly uses the term FMCG, so we use that term throughout this chapter.
2. www.twitonomy.com
3. For readers who are not statistically minded, in our comparisons, a p value assesses the probability of obtaining a result as extreme as ours if there is no difference between the groups being studied (usually, between industries, or in some cases, in retweet rate between tweets with and without certain features). A high p value (by convention, described as 'ns' or 'not significant') provides little or no evidence of any (non-random) difference between the groups being studied.

This research was previously published in Maximizing Commerce and Marketing Strategies through Micro-Blogging edited by Janée N. Burkhalter and Natalie T. Wood, pages 1-39, copyright year 2015 by Business Science Reference (an imprint of IGI Global).

Chapter 16
Facebook Experience Is Different:
An Empirical Study in Indian Context

Punita Duhan
Meera Bai Institute of Technology, India

Anurag Singh
Banaras Hindu University, India

ABSTRACT

Though the concept of experience was propounded decades ago, the terms such as Customer Experience Management, Brand Experience etc. have started gaining currency only recently. Renewed focus on the concept is the result of positive impacts of brand experience as evidenced by researches. Emergence of Social Media has provided the organizations with supplementary platforms to enhance customer experiences. The experiences of customers with various social media platforms may rub on to their experiences with the brands being promoted through these. Accordingly, present research studies the experience of select social media platforms in Indian context. Result revealed that the experience of Facebook was significantly favorable in comparison to the rest three platforms; however, a scope of improvement is evident. Result is important for platform developers as it helps them to improve their platforms and for Marketing managers as it guides them to associate their brands with the more favourable platforms in order to reap concomitant benefits.

INTRODUCTION

Bifurcation between buying and consumption of products and services brought to the fore various mental activities associated with the act of consumption. Though, the need to focus on multisensory experiences related to consumption had become evident decades back (Alderson, 1957; Boyd & Levy, 1963), yet the subjective aspects of consumption were sacrificed on the altar of logical and bounded rationality till very late (Olshavsky & Granbois, 1979; Sheth, 1979; Holbrook & Hirschman, 1982). Termed as "experiential view" by Holbrook & Hirschman (1982), these conscious and subjective aspects of consump-

DOI: 10.4018/978-1-5225-5637-4.ch016

tion essentially explore the emotional responses of the consumers inherent in the act of consumption (Holbrook et al., 1982). Consumers attribute certain symbolic (Levy, 1959), syntactic (structure and style of message content), hedonic, psychotemporal, psychobiological meanings to the products they consume and these attributed subjective meanings facilitate researchers and marketers to explore the multisensory relationships in consumer behavior (Levy, 1959; Holbrook et al., 1982). Researches on customer's brand experiences and the antecedent impact of positive experiences on brand attitude, brand loyalty, brand commitment, brand performance, brand satisfaction, brand trust and brand attachment has led the focus of marketers on managing and enhancing Customers' Experience. All this has resulted in the incorporation of the terms like Experience Marketing, Experiential Marketing, Customer Experience Management, Experience Economy and Brand Experience in marketing glossary.

Dawn of era of digital economy is another factor, which has necessitated the study of brand experience (Chui, Manyika, Bughin, Dobbs, Sarrazin, Sands & Westergen, 2012). Digitization, by leveraging the power of Internet, has paved way for new business models, in which business communications, interactions and transactions between Consumers and marketers are carried over web (Kalakota & Robinson, 2001), facilitated by new media channels in the form of Social Media or Web 2.0 (Edelman, 2010). Absence of temporal and geographic boundaries in virtual experiences warrants for ongoing, real time analysis of customers' expectations, experiences (Kalakota et al., 2001) and effective handling of web experience, as inept web experiences can severely influence online as well as offline reputation of the firm (Constantinides, 2004). Web 2.0 has led to the emergence of new influencers in consumer decision journey such as strong online advocacy and discussions in brand communities (Edelman, 2010).

Social media's propagation and acceptance among masses across the globe is unprecedented (Stanley, 2009; Hughes, 2010; Nielsen, 2012; Vehr, 2012). Level of realism provided by an experience leads to more enduring attitudes towards the experience. Characteristics such as "telepresence" and "flow experience" have enabled Internet to exhibit a higher level of realism even in comparison to television. Researchers have indicated that enhanced interactivity and vividness of digital media leads to stronger perceptions of simulated experience (Schiffman, Kanuk& Kumar, 2010). This has prompted the organizations to use Social media platforms for variety of marketing purposes (Stelzner, 2012; Stelzner, 2013). Moreover, as per the Congruity theory of attitudes, changes in the evaluations of a source and a concept can be linked together by an associative assertion (Osgood & Tannenbaum, 1955). Hence, the experiences of customers with various social media platforms may rub on to their experiences with the products and services being promoted through these platforms.

Accordingly, present chapter is an attempt in this direction as to comprehend the customers' experience in relation to four popular social media platforms *viz.* Facebook, Google+, LinkedIn and Twitter in the Indian context. This comprehension of brand experience of given social media platforms will help marketers to devise effective marketing strategies to enhance the experience of these platforms for customers and in turn will help them to derive more value from these platforms. These media channels though not in entire control of manufacturers and retailers (Edelman, 2010), but can be utilized by organizations as the supplementary platforms to influence and enhance customer experiences. The objectives, which study attempts to explore, are to assess Facebook, Google+, LinkedIn and Twitter's experience, to assess Facebook, Google+, LinkedIn and Twitter's sensory experience, to assess Facebook, Google+, LinkedIn and Twitter's affective experience, to assess Facebook, Google+, LinkedIn and Twitter's behavioral experience and to assess Facebook, Google+, LinkedIn and Twitter's intellectual experience.

The Chapter has been structured around six sections. First section deals with the conceptual framework detailing the concept and advantages of the brand experience. Second section gives the literature review about brand experience in the wake of digitization and the need of the present research. This section also deals with the research questions, objectives and hypotheses of the research. Third section elaborates on the research methodology undertaken by the researchers. Focus of the fourth section is on analysis and interpretation of the results. Fifth section caters to the implications of the research and the concluding section of the chapter talks about limitations and future research possibilities.

CONCEPTUAL FRAMEWORK

Brand Experience

Concept of customer experience is not a novel concept as researchers have emphasized upon it since long time (Pine & Gilmore, 1998; Pine & Gilmore, 1999; Carbone & Haeckel, 1994; Johnston, 1999). Renewed focus on the concept is the result of the need for standardization for both products as well as services, as commoditization leaves lesser scope for competing in market on the basis of features alone (Pine et al., 1998). Experienced utility, subjective notions of value accorded to the brands, is a better differentiator than expected utility, the utilitarian notions of value, in today's highly competitive markets (Zaichkowsky, 1985; Schmitt, 2011).

In marketing parlance, two meanings have been attributed to the term "Experience". One meaning connotes the accumulated knowledge and experiences over time, whereas the other connotes the ongoing perceptions and feelings and direct observation. However, for the present chapter researchers go by the second connotation i.e. the perceptions, feelings and thoughts consumers attribute to the brands they encounter and consume.

Braunsberger and Munch (1998) define experience as *"displaying a relatively high degree of familiarity with a certain subject area, obtained through some type of exposure."* According to Brakus, Schmitt and Zarantonello (2009), "*Brand experience refers to subjective, internal consumer responses (sensations, feelings, and cognitions) and behavioral responses evoked by brand-related stimuli that are part of a brand's design and identity, packaging, communications, and environments.*"

Any interaction – direct or indirect, of the customer with the brand results in brand experience (Aaker & Maheswaran, 1997). It is the sum total of the various experiential aspects resulting from all the points of contact with the brand (wikipedia.com). Various stimuli related to the brand, such as unique identifications (viz. name, logo, symbols, signs), colors, shapes, packaging, typefaces, background design elements, slogans, mascots and brand characters communication (viz. print, electronic, audio, visual, audio-visual) and marketing environments (viz. stores, events, social media, websites) have symbolic meanings for the customers (Ha & Perks, 2005; Brakus et al., 2009; Ofir & Simonson, 2007; Bellizzi & Hite 1992; Meyers-Levy & Peracchio 1995; Joy & Sherry, 2003;Mandel & Johnson, 2002; Johar, Sengupta, & Aaker, 2005). These symbolic meanings assist consumer in brand evaluation through the formation of subjective and internal responses towards the brand. (Arnold, Reynolds, Ponder & Lueg, 2005; Chinomona, 2013).

ADVANTAGES OF POSITIVE BRAND EXPERIENCE

Although the concept of experience is novel and research on the concept is in nascent stages, yet it has emerged as a powerful and exciting concept in marketing (Schmitt, 2011). The statement that "Benefits are not in the products but in consumer experiences" underlines this importance (Zaichkowsky, 1985). As per Berry (2000), it is the most vital and powerful aspect of branding strategy. Unique brand experiences become unique selling propositions and help the brand stay ahead of competition (Pine et al., 1998; Pine et al., 1999; Voss 2003; Prahalad & Ramaswamy, 2004; Meyer & Schwager, 2007). Positive brand experiences lead to favorable brand image, customer satisfaction and loyalty (Yulianti & Tung, 2013; Chinomona, 2013). Satisfied customers repurchase the brands and repurchases, in turn, result in brand trust, brand loyalty and brand attachment (Koufaris, 2002; Kim, 2005; Wang & Emurian, 2005; Ercis, Unal, Candan & Yildrinm, 2012;Chinomona, 2013).

Satisfaction, trust, loyalty, and attachment with the brand influences repurchases and results in enhanced sales and profits (Chinomona, 2013; Liljander & Strandvik 1997; Yu & Dean, 2001; Pullman & Gross, 2004). Brand experience thus influences expectations (Johnson & Mathews 1997), brand perception (Cliffe & Motion, 2005), instills confidence (Flanagan, Johnston & Talbot, 2005), supports the brand (Berry & Carbone, 2007) and creates emotional bonds with customers (Pullman et al., 2004). As the Brand experience tends to become a prior as well as personal source of information for future purchase decisions of consumer (Brakus, Schmitt & Zhang, 2008; Sahin, Zehir & Kitapç, 2011), it becomes imperative for marketers to analyze and comprehend brand experience in order to frame effective marketing strategies (Smith & Wheeler, 2002;Schmitt, 2003; Yulianti et al., 2013). Advantages of the positive brand experience have been summarized in the Figure 1.

LITERATURE REVIEW

Brand Experience in the Era of Digitization

Induction of information technology in the organizations has mandated e-based structural reconfigurations, as e- business is the new path to profitability (Kalakota et al., 2001). "Virtual Trendsetters" (Guadagni & Tommaso, 2007) are adding new dimensions to the purchases and influencing consumers through virtual networks and informed groups (Bellini, Ascenzo, Ghi, Spagnoli & Traversi, (n. d.)). Digitization has altered the consumer decision journey by adding new touch points such as Web, Internet channels, Blogs, Forums and Social Networks (Edelman, 2010). This has mandated organizations to keep a tab on the opinions of the "netizens" about their brand by combing through the "voice of customers" to gain competitive advantages. New digital analytical tools such as "Opinion mining", "Sentiment Analysis", "Social media monitoring and analysis" are enabling the organizations to comprehend the types of interactions- quantitative and qualitative, emotional valence - positive or negative and emotional intensity for their brands in an unprecedented manner. Analysis and comprehension of unadulterated consumer sentiments can be instrumental in creating unforgettable customer experiences (Schmitt, 2003; Bellini et al., (n. d.))

Due to digitization, it has become obligatory on the part of organizations to interact and correlate with the market (Morace, 2002; Bellini et al., (n. d.)). Traditional 4P (Product, Price, Place & Promotion) marketing model is making way for 4E (Engagement, Experience, Enhance and Emotion) model of "ex-

Figure 1. Advantages of Brand Experience

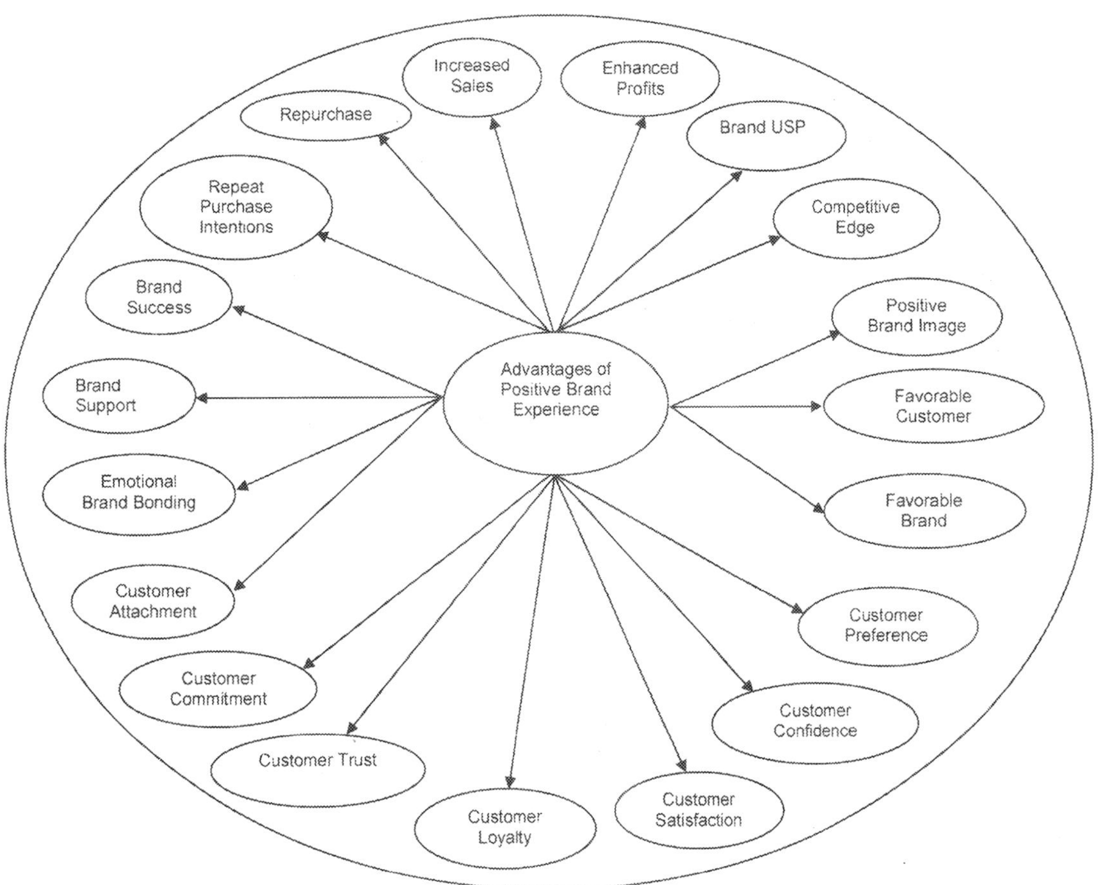

perience economy" (Gelter, 2007a) in order to deliver meaningful experiences to the customers (Bellini et al., (n. d.)).Customer Experience Management (CEM) being a concurrent approach with emotional dimensions is gaining currency over Customer Relationship Management (CRM) to manage customer encounters with the organizations (Schmitt, 2003; Meyer et al., 2007). "Strategic Experiential Module" is being advocated in order to provide "hybrid" and "holistic" experiences to customers (Schmitt, 2003; Ferraresi & Schmitt, 2006). Concomitant benefits of brand experience such as brand familiarity, customer satisfaction and brand trust has necessitated the creation and delivery of customer experience in case of e-brands as well (Reichheld & Schefter, 2000; Kenny & Marshall, 2000; Mcwilliam, 2000; Shankar et al., 2000; Ha, 2004; Kania, 2001; Ha et al., 2005). Brand trust is one of the most important factors in Internet based transactions (Quelch & Klein, 1996; Corbitt, Thanasankit & Yi, 2003) and positive brand experience can play a crucial role in inculcating trust in e-transactions and can ensure the participation of the individuals (Ha et al., 2005).

Dynamic digital arena demands a bottom-up approach to customer experience management- an approach based on detailed road map of customer's end-to-end journey in which customer experiences are managed at multiple touch points across multiple channels in a cumulative fashion (Rawson, Duncan & Jones, 2013). One such touch point facilitated by Internet is website brand experience, which has been defined as "*a consumer's positive navigations (i.e. using web-based communities and participating in events) and perceptions (i.e. the attractiveness of cookies, variety and uniqueness of visual displays and value for money) with a specific website*" (Ha et al., 2005). A website, which delivers relevant, well-organized and engaging information, offers positive experience (Chen &Wells, 1999) to the users and is successful in luring the customer to stay for a longer period, to explore further (Menon& Kahn, 2002) and in retaining the customer traffic (Ha et al., 2005). Most consumers on Internet are price seekers and positive brand experiences have a positive reaction to pricing as well. Hence, positive brand experiences on Internet can turn such price seekers into loyal customers (Ha et al., 2005). As such, there is a need for organizations to invest in community-building infrastructure (*viz.* chat rooms, bulletin boards and interactive events) to facilitate the interactions and support the brand experiences. Amazon's 'customer recommendation' content page is an oft quoted and successful instance in the case. Understanding customer's virtual experience is vital as it only influences virtual interactions but also the online and offline decision making of the customer (Constantinides, 2004).

RESEARCH GAP

Literature review has evidenced that brand experience- both offline as well as online, is a critical aspect of brand marketing strategy due to its wide-ranging concomitant impacts. However, the number of studies undertaken to study customer's brand experience is limited. Number of researches looking into the web experiences is even lesser and such studies in Indian context are hard to find. Added to this is the fact that despite the augmented usage of social media worldwide, there is almost nil research available exploring the experience concomitant to various social media platforms, same being true in Indian context. Hence, this study is an attempt to explore and comprehend customers' overall experience as well to study their experiences along the four dimensions *viz.* Sensory, Affective, Behavioural and Intellectual in relation to select social media platforms in Indian context and thereby fill the research void on this academic and research turf.

Research Questions

1. What ratings customers give to the experience of some select brands of social media platforms *viz.* Facebook, Google+, LinkedIn and Twitter?
2. Are the experiences related to these brands different from each other?
3. What ratings customers give to the four dimensions of experience *viz.* Sensory, Affective, Behavioral and Intellectual- in relation of Facebook, Google+, LinkedIn and Twitter?
4. Are the experiences of four dimensions different from each other for Facebook, Google+, LinkedIn and Twitter?

OBJECTIVES

In accordance with the research questions the objectives of the study are:

1. To assess Facebook, Google+, LinkedIn and Twitter's experience
2. To assess Facebook, Google+, LinkedIn and Twitter's sensory experience
3. To assess Facebook, Google+, LinkedIn and Twitter's affective experience
4. To assess Facebook, Google+, LinkedIn and Twitter's behavioral experience
5. To assess Facebook, Google+, LinkedIn and Twitter's intellectual experience.

RESEARCH AND STATISTICAL HYPOTHESES

$\mathbf{H_{01:}}$ There is no significant difference between Facebook, Google+, LinkedIn and Twitter's experience
$\mathbf{H_{a1:}}$ There is a significant difference between Facebook, Google+, LinkedIn and Twitter's experience
$\mathbf{H_{01:}}$ $\mu_{FB} = \mu_{GL} = \mu_{LN} = \mu_{TW}$
$\mathbf{H_{a1:}}$ $\mu_{FB} \neq \mu_{GL} \neq \mu_{LN} \neq \mu_{TW}$

where

$\boldsymbol{\mu_{FB}}$: Mean value of FaceBook Experience
$\boldsymbol{\mu_{GL}}$: Mean value of Google+ Experience
$\boldsymbol{\mu_{LN}}$: Mean value of LinkedIn Experience
$\boldsymbol{\mu_{TW}}$: Mean value of Twitter Experience
$\mathbf{H_{02:}}$ There is no significant difference between Facebook, Google+, LinkedIn and Twitter's Sensory experience
$\mathbf{H_{a2:}}$ There is a significant difference between Facebook, Google+, LinkedIn and Twitter's Sensory experience
$\mathbf{H_{02:}}$ $\mu_{FBSD} = \mu_{GLSD} = \mu_{LNSD} = \mu_{TWSD}$
$\mathbf{H_{a2:}}$ $\mu_{FBSD} \neq \mu_{GLSD} \neq \mu_{LNSD} \neq \mu_{TWSD}$

where

$\boldsymbol{\mu_{FBSD}}$: Mean value of FaceBook's Sensory Experience
$\boldsymbol{\mu_{GLSD}}$: Mean value of Google+'s Sensory Experience
$\boldsymbol{\mu_{LNSD}}$: Mean value of LinkedIn's Sensory Experience
$\boldsymbol{\mu_{TWSD}}$: Mean value of Twitter's Sensory Experience
$\mathbf{H_{03:}}$ There is no significant difference between Facebook, Google+, LinkedIn and Twitter's affective experience
$\mathbf{H_{a3:}}$ There is a significant difference between Facebook, Google+, LinkedIn and Twitter's affective experience
$\mathbf{H_{03:}}$ $\mu_{FBAD} = \mu_{GLAD} = \mu_{LNAD} = \mu_{TWAD}$
$\mathbf{H_{a3:}}$ $\mu_{FBAD} \neq \mu_{GLAD} \neq \mu_{LNAD} \neq \mu_{TWAD}$

where

μ_{FBAD}: Mean value of Facebook's affective Experience
μ_{GLAD}: Mean value of Google+'s affective Experience
μ_{LNAD}: Mean value of LinkedIn's affective Experience
μ_{TWAD}: Mean value of Twitter's affective Experience
$H_{04:}$ There is no significant difference between Facebook, Google+, LinkedIn and Twitter's behavioural experience
$H_{a4:}$ There is a significant difference between Facebook, Google+, LinkedIn and Twitter's behavioural experience
$H_{04:}$ $\mu_{FBBD} = \mu_{GLBD} = \mu_{LNBD} = \mu_{TWBD}$
$H_{a4:}$ $\mu_{FBBD} \neq \mu_{GLBD} \neq \mu_{LNBD} \neq \mu_{TWBD}$

where

μ_{FBBD}: Mean value of Facebook's behavioural Experience
μ_{GLBD}: Mean value of Google+'sbehavioural Experience
μ_{LNBD}: Mean value of LinkedIn's behavioural Experience
μ_{TWBD}: Mean value of Twitter's behavioural Experience
$H_{05:}$ There is no significant difference between Facebook, Google+, LinkedIn and Twitter's intellectual experience
$H_{a5:}$ There is a significant difference between Facebook, Google+, LinkedIn and Twitter's intellectual experience
$H_{05:}$ $\mu_{FBID} = \mu_{GLID} = \mu_{LNID} = \mu_{TWID}$
$H_{a5:}$ $\mu_{FBID} \neq \mu_{GLID} \neq \mu_{LNID} \neq \mu_{TWID}$

where

μ_{FBID}: Mean value of FaceBook's intellectual Experience
μ_{GLID}: Mean value of Google+'s intellectual Experience
μ_{LNID}: Mean value of LinkedIn's intellectual Experience
μ_{TWID}: Mean value of Twitter's intellectual Experience.

RESEARCH METHODOLOGY

Both primary as well as secondary data have been used in the research. Secondary data were used majorly for literature review, to develop the theoretical concept, to identify the research gap and to corroborate the research findings. Secondary sources of the data used were the available and published literature, such as research papers published in journals (both offline and online), other proprietary data in the form of reports, whitepapers etc. available at their websites and the relevant books.

For primary data collection, an online questionnaire was developed on Google docs. The questionnaire consisted of Brand Experience scale developed by Brakus, Schmitt & Zarantonello (2009). Items used in the scale for measuring various components of the experience as well as the overall brand experience are as under:

Sensory Dimension:

1. This brand makes a strong impression on my visual senses or other senses.
2. I find this brand interesting in a sensory way.
3. This brand does not appeal to my senses.

Affective Dimension:

4. This brand induces feelings and sentiments.
5. I do not have strong emotions for this brand.
6. This brand is an emotional brand.

Behavioral Dimension:

7. I engage in physical actions and behaviors when I use this brand.
8. This brand results in bodily experiences.
9. This brand is not action oriented.

Intellectual Dimension:

10. I engage in a lot of thinking when I encounter this brand.
11. This brand does not make me think.
12. This brand stimulates my curiosity and problem solving.

(The word "this brand" in each statement was replaced by the words Facebook, Google+, LinedIn and Twitter respectively in order to obtain responses for all the four brands of social media platforms)

The scale measured Brand experience of the respondents on a seven- point (with "1" for Strongly Agree and "7" for Strongly Disagree) Likert scale. Data were collected by means of an online national survey using snowball-sampling technique. Online survey instrument was distributed among Indian Social Media users via e-mail, Face Book, Twitter and other social media platforms. Collected data were analyzed using One-Way Repeated Measures ANOVA.

ANALYSIS AND INTERPRETATION

Reliability Testing of the Scale Items

The value of the Cronbach's alphas for the entire scale of Facebook, Google+, LinkedIn and Twitter are .830, .874, .724 and .841 respectively for 12 items in each scale. The values of α for the four platforms indicated the scale to be highly reliable.

BASIC SAMPLE ANALYSIS

Out of the received 117 responses, 09 were not using Social Media Platforms and excluded from the analysis. Out of the remaining 108 responses, all 108 were using Facebook, while 89, 87 and 87 were active on Google+, LinkedIn and Twitter respectively. As the One-Way Repeated Measures ANOVA was used for comparing means, only those respondents who were active on all the four platforms were selected, in order to control for individual differences (Field, 2009). Accordingly, 87 responses, which remained for the final analysis, were checked for data duplication and missing values. 04 numbers of missing values in the data were replaced by average response for that particular field. Demographic composition of the sample has been summarized in Table 1.

ONE-WAY REPEATED MEASURES ANOVA

Analysis for H_{01}:$\mu_{FB} = \mu_{GL} = \mu_{LN} = \mu_{TW}$

As Mauchly's test was non-significant, χ^2 (5) = 8.031, $p > .05$, hence data did not violate the assumptions of sphericity and indicated that the variances of differences are homogenous. F (3, 258) = 30.41, $p < .05$, for the Tests of Within-Subjects Effects, indicated that there is a significant difference between Facebook, Google+, LinkedIn and Twitter's experience. In addition, multivariate tests also support the result as the Pillai's Trace $V = 0.489$, F (3, 84) = 26.840, $p < .05$, $\omega^2 = .16$, the value of ω^2 indicates large effect (Field, 2009). Hence, H_{01} is rejected and H_{a1} is accepted that there is a significant difference between Facebook, Google+, LinkedIn and Twitter's experience.

As the experience of select social media platforms was statistically significant, repeated contrast results were interpreted to determine which platforms contributed to the overall difference. First contrast between Level 1 (FB) vs. Level 2 (GL) was significant, F (1, 86) = 72.926, $p<.05$, $r_{FBvs.GL} = .68$ (Medium Effect explaining 46.2% of the total variance), meaning thereby that there is a significant difference between Facebook experience and Google+ experience. Second contrast between Level 2 (GL) and Level 3(LN), F (1, 86) = 6.980, $p<.05$, $r_{GLvs.LN} = .27$ (small effect explaining 7.3% of the total variance) again indicates thatthere is a significant difference between Google+ experience and LinkedIn experience. However, the third contrast between Level 3 (LN) and Level 4(TW), F (1, 86) = 0.828, $p>.05$, $r_{LNvs.TW} = .10$ (small effect explaining 0.95% of the total variance) was not significant and only difference in means is due to chance. Same was also indicated by the Bar Graph (Figure 2) of the Mean values of various social media platforms, which evidences that respondents find FaceBook experience (μ_{FB} = 3.00) best and Google+ experience (μ_{GL} =4.30) worst out of the four. LinkedIn experience (μ_{LN} = 3.92) and Twitter experience (μ_{TW} = 4.03) are somewhat similar to each other.

Post-hoc analysis for Pairwise Comparison (with Bonferroni correction) indicated that the Facebook Experience is significantly different and better in comparison to Google+ ($\mu_{FB} - \mu_{GL}$ = -1.299, p<.05), LinkedIn ($\mu_{FB} - \mu_{LN}$ = -0.918, p<.05) and Twitter experience ($\mu_{FB} - \mu_{TW}$ = -1.027, p<.05). Other Experiences i.e. of Google+ from LinkedIn ($\mu_{GL} - \mu_{LN}$ =0.380, p>.05), of Google+ from Twitter ($\mu_{GL} - \mu_{TW}$ =0.271, p>.05) and of LinkedIn from Twitter ($\mu_{LN} - \mu_{TW}$ =-0.109, p>.05) though were different from each other, were not significant. Pairwise analysis too corroborated the above conclusion that Facebook experience is significantly better in comparison to Google+, LinkedIn and Twitter experience. Other three platforms, though differ in the experience, mean values being different from each other, the difference is not significant.

Table 1. Summary of Demographic Details of Respondents

Demographic Variable	Classifications	Frequency	Valid Percent	Cumulative Percent
Gender	Male	64	73.6	73.6
	Female	23	26.4	100.0
Marital status	Married	41	47.1	47.1
	Unmarried	46	52.9	100.0
Age (in Years)	18-24	5	5.7	5.7
	24-30	44	50.6	56.3
	30-36	11	12.6	69.0
	36-42	13	14.9	83.9
	42 and above	14	16.1	100.0
Education	Diploma	1	1.1	1.1
	Graduate	7	8.0	9.2
	Post- Graduate	49	56.3	65.5
	Ph. D. & higher	30	34.5	100.0
Profession	Student	19	21.8	21.8
	Private Job	29	33.3	55.2
	Govt. Job	33	37.9	93.1
	Self-employed	5	5.7	98.9
	Homemaker	1	1.1	100.0
Annual household income (in Rupees)	1- 4 Lakhs	36	41.4	41.4
	4-7 Lakhs	29	33.3	74.7
	7 lakhs & above	22	25.3	100.0
Net use per day (in Hours)	1-4 Hrs	31	35.6	35.6
	4-7 Hrs	33	37.9	73.6
	7 Hrs & above	23	26.4	100.0
Social Media usage per day (in Hours)	1-4 Hrs	69	79.3	79.3
	4-7 Hrs	16	18.4	97.7
	7 Hrs & above	2	2.3	100.0

Analysis for H_{01}:$\mu_{FBSD} = \mu_{GLSD} = \mu_{LNSD} = \mu_{TWSD}$

Results from analysis of Mauchly's test, χ^2 (5) = 2.376, $p > .05$, being non-significant, data did not violate the assumptions of sphericity. F (3, 258) = 18.52, $p < .05$, for the Tests of Within-Subjects Effects, and multivariate test -Pillai's Trace $V = 0.400$, F (3, 84) = 18.673, $p < .05$, $\omega^2 = .12$ (Large effect), indicated that there is a significant difference between Facebook, Google+, LinkedIn and Twitter's sensory experience. Hence, H_{02} is not supported and H_{a2} is supported that there is a significant difference between Facebook, Google+, LinkedIn and Twitter's sensory experience.

Interpretation of repeated contrast results revealed that first contrast between Level 1 (μ_{FBSD}) vs. Level 2 (μ_{GLSD}) was significant F (1,86) = 41.634, $p<.05$, $r_{FBSDvs.GLSD}= .57$ (Medium Effect explaining

Figure 2. Mean Values of Experience of Different Platforms

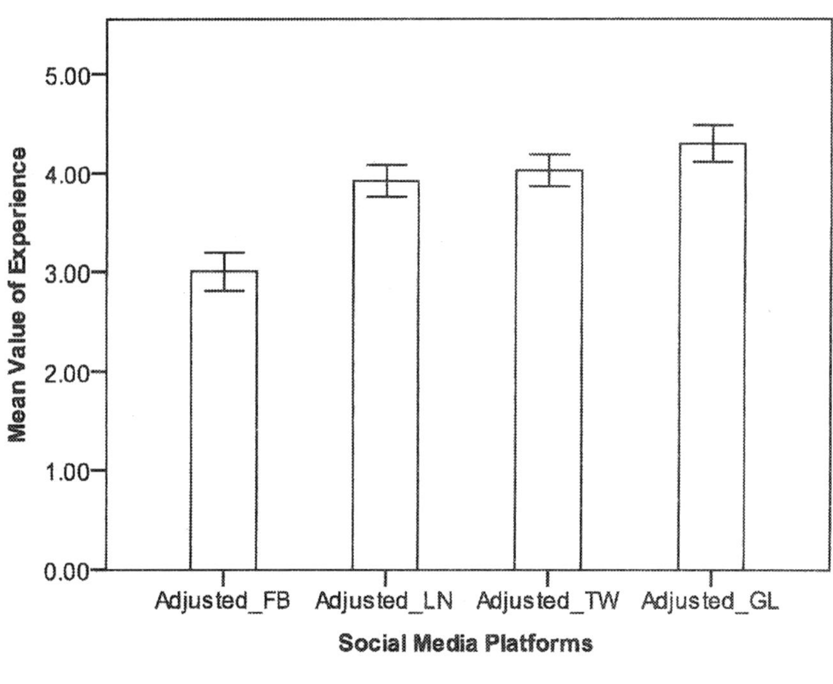

32.62% of the total variance) meaning thereby that there is a significant difference between Facebook sensory experience and Google+ sensory experience. Second contrast between Level 2 (μ_{GLSD}) and Level 3(μ_{LNSD}), F (1, 86) = 3.304, *p>.05*, $r_{GLSDvs.LNSD}$= .19 (small effect explaining 3.7% of the total variance) and the third contrast between Level 3 (μ_{LNSD}) and Level 4 (μ_{TWSD}), F (1,86) = 1.738, *p>.05*, $r_{LNSDvs.TWSD}$= .14 (small effect explaining 1.98% of the total variance) were not significant. This means that there is not a significant difference between Google+ sensory experience and LinkedIn sensory experience and between LinkedIn sensory experience and Twitter sensory experience. Differences in mean values are purely coincidental.

Same was pointed out by the Bar Graph (Figure 3) of the Mean values of sensory experiences of various social media platforms. Graph evidenced that respondents find Facebook sensory experience (μ_{FBSD} = 2.57) best, LinkedIn sensory experience (μ_{LNSD} = 3.56) second best, Twitter sensory experience (μ_{TWSD} = 3.81) third best and Google+ sensory experience (μ_{GLSD} =3.93) has been rated worst out of the four.

Post-hoc analysis for Pairwise Comparison (with Bonferroni adjustment) indicated that the Facebook sensory experience is statistically significant and better in comparison to Google+ (μ_{FBSD} - μ_{GLSD} = -1.367, p<.05), LinkedIn (μ_{FBSD} - μ_{LNSD} = -0.988, p<.05) and Twitter's sensory experience (μ_{FBSD} - μ_{TWSD} = -1.241, p<.05). Other sensory experiences i.e. of Google+ from LinkedIn (μ_{GLSD} - μ_{LNSD} =0.380, p>.05), of Google+ from Twitter (μ_{GLSD} - μ_{TWSD} =0.126, p>.05) and of LinkedIn from Twitter (μ_{LNSD} - μ_{TWSD} =-.253, p>.05) though were different from each other, were not significant. Pairwise analysis too corroborated the above conclusion that Facebook sensory experience is significantly better in comparison to Google+, LinkedIn and Twitter's sensory experience. Differences between the sensory experiences of other three platforms are not significant.

Figure 3. Mean Values of Sensory Experience of Different Platforms

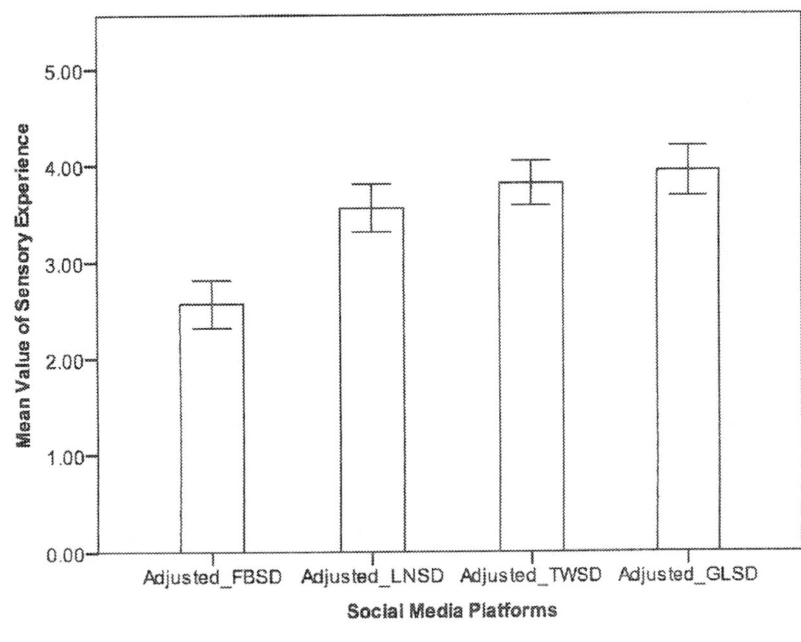

Analysis for H_{03}:$\mu_{FBAD} = \mu_{GLAD} = \mu_{LNAD} = \mu_{TWAD}$

χ^2 (5) = 10.927, $p > .05$, being non-significant, assumptions of sphericity was not violated. F (3, 258) = 36.74, $p < .05$, for the Tests of Within-Subjects Effects, along with multivariate test -Pillai's Trace V = 0.504, F(3, 84) = 28.461, $p < .05$, $\omega^2 = .18$ (Large effect), indicated that there is a significant difference between Facebook, Google+, LinkedIn and Twitter's affective experience. Hence, H_{03} is not supported and H_{a3} is supported that there is a significant difference between Facebook, Google+, LinkedIn and Twitter's affective experience.

Interpretation of repeated contrast results exhibited that first contrast between Level 1 (μ_{FBAD}) vs. Level 2 (μ_{GLAD}) is significant F (1, 86) = 78.710, $p<.05$,$r_{FBADvs.GLAD}$= .69 (Medium Effect explaining 47.80% of the total variance) meaning thereby that there is a significant difference between affective experience of Facebook and Google+. Second contrast between Level 2 (μ_{GLAD}) and Level 3(μ_{LNAD}), F (1, 86) = 0.502, $p>.05$, $r_{GLADvs.LNAD}$= .08 (small effect explaining 0.64% of the total variance) and the third contrast between Level 3 (μ_{LNAD}) and Level 4(μ_{TWAD}), F (1, 86) = 0.495, $p>.05$,$r_{LNADvs.TWAD}$= .08 (small effect explaining 0.64% of the total variance) are not significant. This means that there is not a significant difference between affective experience of Google+ and LinkedIn and between affective experience of LinkedIn and Twitter, and any differences in mean values of affective experience are purely by chance.

Bar Graph (Figure 4) of the mean values of affective experiences of various social media platforms, also evidences that respondents find affective experience of Facebook (μ_{FBAD} = 2.51) better than the rest three. Affective experience of Google+ (μ_{GLAD} =4.17) once again is last in experience ratings. Affective experience of Twitter (μ_{TWAD} = 3.94) is only marginally better than LinkedIn (μ_{LNAD} = 4.05).

Figure 4. Mean Values of Affective Experience of Different Platforms

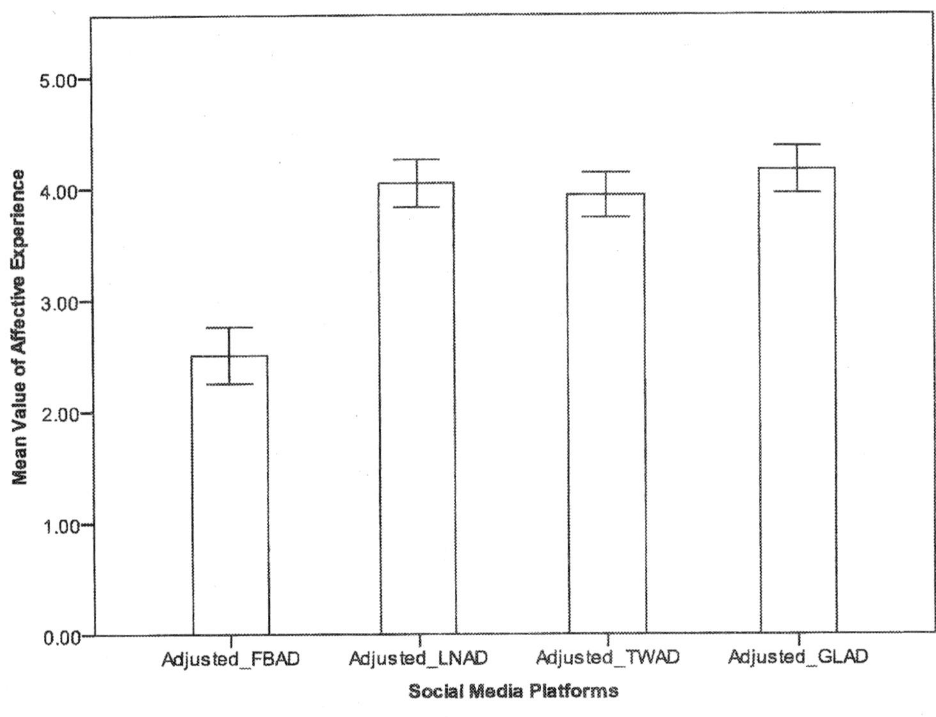

Post-hoc analysis for Pairwise Comparison (with Bonferroni adjustment) indicated that the affective experience of Facebook is statistically significant and better in comparison to Google+ (μ_{FBAD} - μ_{GLAD} = -1.662, p<.05), LinkedIn (μ_{FBAD} - μ_{LNAD} = -1.541, p<.05) and Twitter's affective experience (μ_{FBAD} - μ_{TWAD} = -1.433, p<.05). Other affective experiences i.e. of Google+ from LinkedIn (μ_{GLAD} - μ_{LNAD} =0.122, p>.05), of Google+ from Twitter (μ_{GLAD} - μ_{TWAD} =0.229, p>.05) and of LinkedIn from Twitter (μ_{LNAD} - μ_{TWAD} =0.107, p>.05) though were different from each other, were not significant. Hence, Pairwise analysis too supported the above conclusion that affective experience of Facebook is significantly better in comparison to Google+, LinkedIn and Twitter's affective experience. Other three platforms, though differ in the affective experience from each other, these differences are not statistically significant.

Analysis for H_{04}:$\mu_{FBBD} = \mu_{GLBD} = \mu_{LNBD} = \mu_{TWBD}$

As Mauchly's test, χ^2 (5) = 33.564, $p < .05$, was significant, hence data violated the assumptions of sphericity and the variances of the differences between behavioural experience of the four social media platforms were not equal. However, the value of Greenhouse-Geisser's epsilon being .835 that is away from the lower bound limit i.e. .333 and closer to upper limit 1; data were closer to being spherical. Value of Huynh-Feldt epsilon .862 was also high, which reaffirmed that variance of differences are homogenous.

The Tests of Within-Subjects Effects F (2.505, 215.403) = 11.102, $p < .05$ for Greenhouse-Geisser correction, and F (2.586, 222.384) = 11.102, $p < .05$ for Huynh-Feldt correction, indicated that there is a significant difference between Facebook, Google+, LinkedIn and Twitter's behavioural experience. In addition, multivariate tests also support the result as the Pillai's Trace $V = 0.255$, $F(3, 84) = 9.599$, $p < .05$, $\omega^2 = .01$, the value of ω^2 indicates small effect. Hence, H_{04} is rejected and H_{a4} is accepted that there is a significant difference between Facebook, Google+, LinkedIn and Twitter's behavioural experience.

Interpretation of repeated contrast results revealed that first contrast between Level 1 (μ_{FBBD}) vs. Level 2 (μ_{GLBD}) is significant $F(1, 86) = 26.278$, $p<.05$, $r_{FBBDvs.GLBD} = .48$ (small effect explaining 23.04% of the total variance) meaning thereby that there is a significant difference between Facebook behavioural experience and Google+ behavioural experience. Second contrast between Level 2 (μ_{GLSD}) and Level 3(μ_{LNSD}), $F(1, 86) = 2.725$, $p>.05$, $r_{GLSDvs.LNSD} = .18$ (small effect explaining 3.24% of the total variance) and the third contrast between Level 3 (μ_{LNSD}) and Level 4(μ_{TWSD}), $F(1,86) = 0.650$, $p>.05$, $r_{LNSDvs.TWSD} = .09$ (small effect explaining 0.81% of the total variance) are not significant. Hence, there is not a significant difference between behavioural experience of Google+ and LinkedIn and between behavioural experience of LinkedIn and Twitter.

Bar Graph (Figure 5) of the mean values of behavioural experiences of various social media platforms also supported the above assertion as respondents rated behavioural experience of FaceBook ($\mu_{FBBD} = 3.82$) highest and once again, behavioural experience of Google+ ($\mu_{GLBD} = 4.53$) is rated least. Behavioural experience of LinkedIn ($\mu_{LNBD} = 4.31$) and Twitter ($\mu_{TWBD} = 4.38$) marginally differ from each other.

Pairwise Comparison (with Bonferroni correction) evidenced that the Facebook behavioural experience is statistically significant and better in comparison to Google+ ($\mu_{FBBD} - \mu_{GLBD} = -0.705$, $p<.05$), LinkedIn ($\mu_{FBBD} - \mu_{LNBD} = -0.490$, $p<.05$) and Twitter's behavioural experience ($\mu_{FBBD} - \mu_{TWBD} = -0.558$, $p<.05$). Other behavioural experiences i.e. of Google+ from LinkedIn ($\mu_{GLBD} - \mu_{LNBD} = 0.214$, $p>.05$), of

Figure 5. Mean Values of Behavioural Experience of Different Platforms

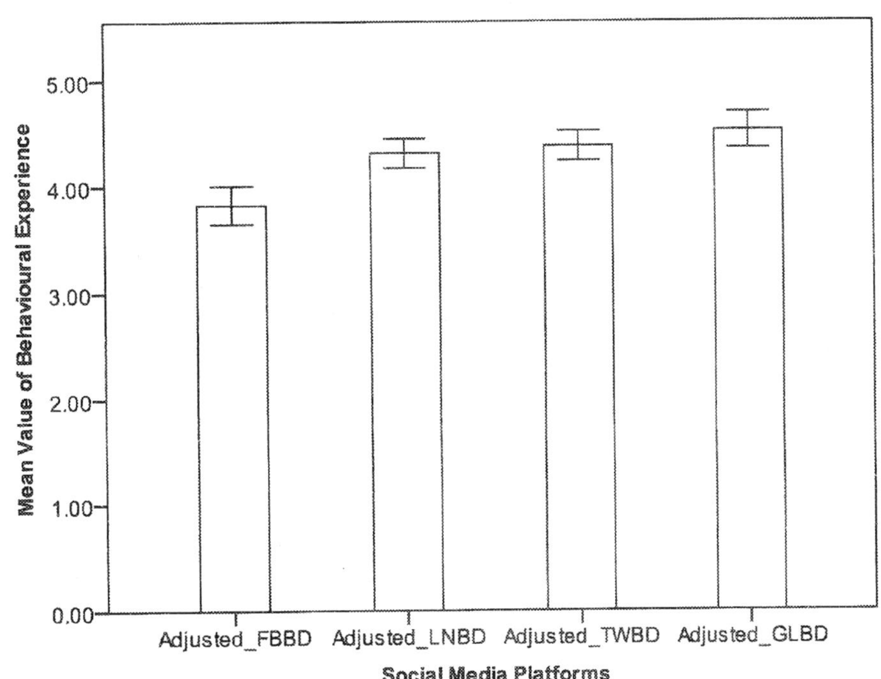

Google+ from Twitter (μ_{GLBD} - μ_{TWBD} =0.147, p>.05) and of LinkedIn from Twitter (μ_{LNBD} - μ_{TWBD} =-0.068, p>.05) though were not significantly different from each other. Pairwise analysis too substantiated the conclusion that Facebook's behavioural experience is significantly better in comparison to Google+, LinkedIn and Twitter's behavioural experience.

Analysis for H_{05}:$\mu_{FBID} = \mu_{GLID} = \mu_{LNID} = \mu_{TWID}$

As Mauchly's test, χ^2 (5) = 10.266, $p > .05$, was non-significant, hence data does not violate the assumptions of sphericity and the variances of differences are homogenous. The results for the Tests of Within-Subjects Effects indicated that there is a significant difference between Facebook, Google+, LinkedIn and Twitter's intellectual experience, F (3, 258) = 13.37, $p < .05$. In addition, multivariate tests also supported the result as the Pillai's Trace V = 0.301, F (3, 84) = 12.053, $p< .05$, $\omega^2 = .08$, the value of ω^2 indicates medium effect. Hence, H_{05} is not supported and H_{a5} is supported that there is a significant difference between Facebook, Google+, LinkedIn and Twitter's intellectual experience.

Tests of Within-Subjects repeated contrast demonstrated that first contrast between Level 1 (μ_{FBID}) vs. Level 2 (μ_{GLID}) was significant, F (1, 86) = 27.916, $p<.05$,$r_{FBIDvs.GLID}$= .49 (small effect explaining 24.01% of the total variance), meaning that there is a significant difference between Facebook intellectual experience and Google+ intellectual experience. Second contrast between Level 2 (μ_{GLID}) and Level 3(μ_{LNID}), F (1, 86) = 5.081, $p<.05$, $r_{GLIDvs.LNID}$= .24 (small effect explaining 5.83% of the total variance), being significant indicate that there is a significant difference between intellectual experience of Google+ and LinkedIn. The third contrast between Level 3 (μ_{LNID}) and Level 4(μ_{TWID}), F (1, 86) = 2.215, $p>.05$,$r_{LNIDvs.TWID}$= .16 (small effect explaining 2.56% of the total variance) is not significant i.e. there is not a significant difference between intellectual experience of LinkedIn and Twitter.

Significant difference between Facebook, Google+, LinkedIn and Twitter's intellectual experience necessitated post-hoc analysis (with Bonferroni's correction). Pairwise comparisons evidenced that the Facebook intellectual experience is statistically significant and better in comparison to Google+ (μ_{FBID} - μ_{GLID} = -1.092, p<.05), LinkedIn (μ_{FBID} - μ_{LNID} = -0.652, p<.05) and Twitter's intellectual experience (μ_{FBID} - μ_{TWID} = -0.878, p<.05). Other intellectual experiences i.e. of Google+ from LinkedIn (μ_{GLID} - μ_{LNID} =0.440, p>.05), of Google+ from Twitter (μ_{GLID} - μ_{TWID} =0.215, p>.05) and of LinkedIn from Twitter (μ_{LNID} - μ_{TWID} =-0.225, p>.05) were not significantly different from each other.

Bar Graph (Figure 6) of the mean values of intellectual experiences of various social media platforms too substantiated that intellectual experience of Facebook (μ_{FBID} = 3.12) is better than the intellectual experience of the other three platforms *viz.* Google+ (μ_{GLID} =4.21), LinkedIn (μ_{LNID} = 3.77) and Twitter (μ_{TWID} = 4.00).

Result at a Glance

Results of the One-way Repeated Measure ANOVA have been summarized in the Table 2 for a quick glimpse.

Figure 6. Mean Values of Intellectual Experience of Different Platforms

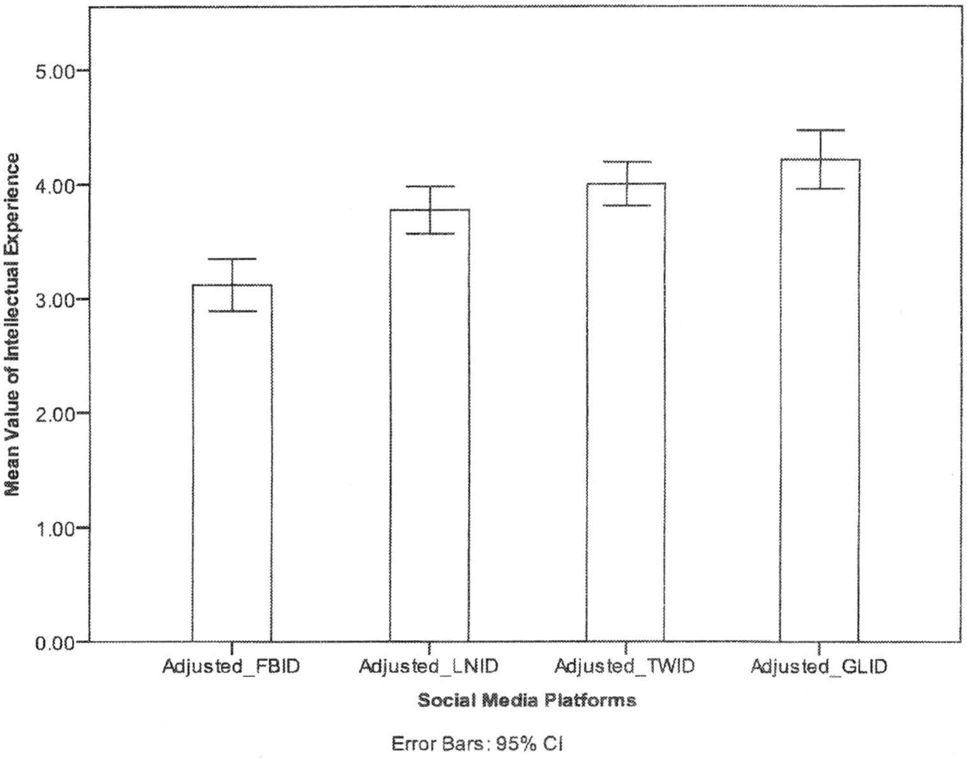

Table 2. Summary of One-way Repeated Measure ANOVA

Hypotheses	Result
H_{01}	Not Supported
H_{02}	Not Supported
H_{03}	Not Supported
H_{04}	Not Supported
H_{05}	Not Supported

IMPLICATIONS OF RESEARCH

Obtained results are important for social media platform developers as the results indicate how Indian Social Media users rate the experience of select platforms. Results demonstrate that Facebook is a clear winner as far as overall experience and experiences along various dimensions *viz.* Sensory, Affective, Behavioural and Intellectual are concerned. Higher absolute number of people using Facebook in India is a testimony to the fact that people prefer Facebook to other platforms (Kemp, 2014). However, this should not make developers of Facebook complacent. All the mean values i.e. of overall experience (μ_{FB} = 3.00) and of various dimensions (μ_{FBSD} = 2.57, μ_{FBAD} = 2.51, μ_{FBBD} = 3.82, μ_{FBID} = 3.12) lie between almost 3.00 and 4.00, which when interpreted result in ratings between Somewhat agree and neither agree nor disagree along a continuum of 1-Strongly agree to 7- strongly disagree. This is a clear indication to the developers of Facebook that they have miles to go before they sleep.

Developers of remaining three social media platforms have more reasons to worry as not only their platforms have been rated lower, results indicate that experiences of these platforms do not differ significantly from each other. Hence, they not only need to incorporate the features that lead to better user experiences, but also must take steps to differentiate their experiences from the others. Though the developers are adding new features such as Facebook facility of video calling using Skype, social games, facility to the organizations to have their Facebook pages (Pogue, 2012), enabling local language feature, messaging products like Whatsapp (Thomas, 2014) and Google+'s 'circles', facility to integrate with other Google products, 'huddle' and Hangout'(Pogue, 2012). However, as the results of the study indicate, a lot is yet to be achieved in Indian market. Continuous up gradation of features is mandated by the fact that better and unique experiences will not only keep one ahead of the competition by attracting more "virtual footfalls", it will also attract more advertisers/marketers to the platform. More number of visitors to the platform will result in enhanced access to demographic data in the shape of virtual footprints that can be diced and sliced (Sarkar, 2014) variously for behavioral targeting (Schiffman et al., 2010). All this will ensure more revenue generation for the platforms on one hand and the marketers on the other hand.

Customer experience production is all about engaging a customer (Pine et al., 1999) and it may be facilitated by Social Media in a very effective way as social web represents an increasingly important point of interaction between businesses and consumers (Fauser, Wiedenhofer & Lorenz, 2011). Opinion seekers are willing to accept and adopt online consumer reviews. e-Word of mouth communication can be treated as the extension of traditional interpersonal communication into this era of Web-based technologies and it is a great impact on the purchasing decisions of online Consumers (Cheung, Lee &Rabjohn, 2008). Marketers can employ advanced analytical techniques like "Opinion mining", "Sentiment Analysis", "Social media monitoring and analysis" to comb through the "voice of customers", available at these new generation touch point (Web, Internet channel, Blog, Forum and Social Network). This will help them to track the emotional valence (positive or negative) and emotional intensity for their brands that can be used for effectively managing the customer experiences (Bellini et al., (n.d.)).

Various activities undertaken by organizations on social media (Zailskaite-jakste & Kuvykaite, 2012) produce experience for the customers, which in turn lead to either Watching or Sharing or Commenting or Producing or Curating stage of Engagement pyramid (Owyang, 2010; Zailskaite-jakste et al., 2012). Depending upon the stage of engagement pyramid, either Involvement or Interaction or Intimacy or Influence is generated (Haven, 2007), which further results in benefits such as brand awareness, brand associations, brand loyalty, brand trust, brand advocacy etc. for the brands (Zailskaite-jakste et al., 2012).

Marketing managers can take a cue from here and can advertise, communicate and associate their products, services and brands with those platforms, which consumers rate high on brand experience scale in order to reap concomitant benefits. This is advantageous from various facets:

1. The platforms, which are better rated, will attract more "netizens" and will result in more exposure for the brands being advertised on these platforms.
2. Comprehension of experiences of social media platforms is important as Customer's virtual experience influences the virtual interaction and online as well as offline decision-making process of the customer (Constantinides, 2004), meaning thereby that better the experience, favourable the impression on the customer and favorable decision making.
3. Associations with favored platforms (in terms of experience) may result in positive attitude towards the products and services that have been advertised through these platforms (Duhan & Singh, 2013) as per the Congruity theory of attitudes (Osgood et al., 1955)
4. As many of the consumers on the Internet are price seekers, positive experience of social media platform together with the positive brand experience might lead to a affirmative reaction to the pricing (Ha et al., 2005).

Last, but not the least, research may prove to be a value addition to the existing body of knowledge, as there is a paucity of literature, more specifically in Indian context, in the area of brand experience, online brand experience and social media brand experience.

LIMITATIONS, FUTURE RESEARCH AVENUES, AND CONCLUSION

Limitations

The major limitations of the study encompass the possibilities of self-reported bias, repeat responses and most responses from more active social media users. The study may have given better and probably different results with a larger sample size selected using non-random sampling. Similarly, controlled experimental design may have yielded different results.

Future Research Avenues

As, the study is possibly the first of its kind in Indian perspective, it opens abundant research opportunities like exploring the experiences of Indian consumers with various brands of social media platforms across different age groups, different income groups, different genders, different marital status and different social media usage in order to formulate more competitive strategies to woo the customers. As the Indian consumers and markets, in comparison to other developed nations, are still warming up to the usage of ever evolving social media platforms, longitudinal research can aid marketers and social media marketing firms to keep track of the emerging development in this market. In addition, qualitative research such as Focus group interviews may result in better insights regarding consumer preferences. Future research focus can be on studying the impact of favourable experience on loyalty, satisfaction, commitment, future purchase intentions, repurchases etc.

Conclusion

Observing the significance of positive consumer experiences in today's dynamic digital business environment and the paucity of research in the area, more specifically in the Indian context, researchers undertook the study. Research attempted to study over all brand experience of consumers as well as the experience along the four dimensions (viz. Sensory, Affective, Behavioural and Intellectual) of experience with respect to select social media platforms. Results of One-way Repeated Measure ANOVA indicated that Indians consumers find Facebook experience, overall as well as along the four dimensions, significantly better and different from the other social media platforms. Obtained results are important for social media platform developers, as the results guide them to possibilities for improvement in brand experiences. The similarities and dissimilarities of one platform vis-a-vis the others reveal the potential and scope for differentiating one platform from others. Research may be useful guide to the marketing managers by helping them to select the most appropriate platform for promoting their products, services and brands.

REFERENCES

Aaker, J. L., & Maheswaran, D. (1997). The effect of cultural orientation on persuasion. *The Journal of Consumer Research*, *24*(3), 315–328. doi:10.1086/209513

Alderson, W. (1957). *Marketing Behavior and Executive Action*. Homewood, Illinois: Richard D. Irwin, INC.

Arnold, M. J., Reynolds, K. E., Ponder, N., & Lueg, J. E. (2005). Customer Delight in a Retail Context: Investigating Delightful and Terrible Shopping Experiences. *Journal of Business Research*, *58*(8), 1132–1145. doi:10.1016/j.jbusres.2004.01.006

Bellini, F., Ascenzo, F. D., Ghi, A., Spagnoli, F., & Traversi, V. (n.d.). *The Role of the Prosumer in Social Networks and the Sentiment Analysis for the Customer Experience Management*. Retrieved on January 10, 2014 from http://www.cersi.it/itais2012/pdf/066.pdf

Bellizzi, J. A., & Hite, R. E. (1992). Environmental Color, Consumer Feelings, and Purchase Likelihood. *Psychology and Marketing*, *9*(5), 347–363. doi:10.1002/mar.4220090502

Berry, L. L. (2000). Cultivating service brand equity. *Journal of the Academy of Marketing Science*, *28*(1), 128–137. doi:10.1177/0092070300281012

Berry, L. L., & Carbone, L. P. (2007). Build Loyalty Through Experience Management. *Quality Progress*, *40*(9), 26–32.

Boyd, Harper W., J., & Levy, S.J. (1963). New Dimensions in Consumer Analysis. *Harvard Business Review*, *41*(November-December), 129–140.

Brakus, J. J., Schmitt, B. H., & Zarantonello, L. (2009). Brand Experience : What Is It? How Is It Measured? Does It Affect Loyalty? *Journal of Marketing*, *73*(May), 52–68. doi:10.1509/jmkg.73.3.52

Brakus, J. J., Schmitt, B. H., & Zhang, S. (2008). Experiential Attributes and Consumer Judgments. In Handbook on Brand and Experience Management. Northampton, MA: EdwardElgar

Braunsberger, K., & Munch, J. M. (1998). Source expertise versus experience effects in hospital advertising. *Journal of Services Marketing*, *12*(1), 23–38. doi:10.1108/08876049810202348

Carbone, L. P., & Haeckel, S. H. (1994). Engineering Customer Experience. *Marketing Management*, *3*(3), 8–19.

Chen, Q., & Wells, W. D. (1999). Attitude toward the site. *Journal of Advertising Research*, *39*(5), 27–37.

Cheung, C. M. K., Lee, M. K. O., & Rabjohn, N. (2008). The impact of electronic customer communities. *Internet Research*, *18*(3), 229–247. doi:10.1108/10662240810883290

Chinomona, R. (2013). The Influence of Brand Experience on Brand Satisfaction, Trust And Attachment In South Africa. *International Business & Economics Research Journal*, *12*(10), 1303–1316.

Chui, M., Manyika, J., Bughin, J., Dobbs, R., Sarrazin, H., Sands, G., & Westergen, M. (2012). *The social economy: Unlocking value and productivity through social technologies*. McKinsey Global Institute Report. Retrieved on January 1, 2014 from http://www.mckinsey.com/insights/high_tech_telecoms_internet/the_social_economy

Cliffe, S. J., & Motion, J. (2005). Building contemporary brands: A sponsorship-based strategy. *Journal of Business Research*, *58*(8), 1068–1077. doi:10.1016/j.jbusres.2004.03.004

Constantinides, E. (2004). Influencing the online consumer's behavior: The Web experience. *Internet Research*, *14*(2), 111–126. doi:10.1108/10662240410530835

Corbitt, B., Thanasankit, T., & Yi, H. (2003). Trust and e-commerce: A study of consumer perception. *Electronic Commerce Research and Applications*, *2*(3), 203–215. doi:10.1016/S1567-4223(03)00024-3

Duhan, P., & Singh, A. (2013). Impact of Usefulness, Ease of Use, Enjoyment, Attitude and Subjective Norms on Behavioural Intentions and Adoption Of Virtual Communities: An Empirical Study. *Journal of IMS Group*, *10*(02), 19–31.

Edelman, D. C. (2010). Branding in the digital age. *Harvard Business Review*, *88*(12), 62–69.

Erciş, A., Ünal, S., Candan, F. B., & Yıldırım, H. (2012). The effect of brand satisfaction, trust and brand commitment on loyalty and repurchase intentions. *Procedia: Social and Behavioral Sciences*, *58*, 1395–1404. doi:10.1016/j.sbspro.2012.09.1124

Fauser, S. G., Wiedenhofer, J., & Lorenz, M. (2011). "Touchpoint social web": An explorative study about using the social web for influencing high involvement purchase decisions. *Problems and Perspectives in Management.*, *9*(1), 39–45.

Ferraresi, M., & Schmitt, B. H. (2006). *Marketing esperienziale*. Milano: FrancoAngeli.

Field, A. (2009). *Discovering statistics using SPSS* (3rd ed.). New Delhi: Sage Publications India Ltd.

Flanagan, P., Johnston, R., & Talbot, D. (2005). Customer confidence: The development of a "pre-experience" concept. *International Journal of Service Industry Management*, *16*(4), 373–384. doi:10.1108/09564230510614013

Gelter, H. (2007a). Towards an understanding of experience production. In Articles on Experiences 4 Digital Media & Games. University of Lapland Press.

Gelter, H. (2007b). Experience production in digital media and games. In Articles on Experiences 4 Digital Media & Games. University of Lapland Press.

Guadagni, P., & De Tommaso, V. (2007). *Ilnuovopoteredeiconsumatorisul web*. Hoepli.

Ha, H., & Perks, H. (2005). Effects of consumer perceptions of brand experience on the web : Brand familiarity, satisfaction and brand trust. *Journal of Consumer Behaviour*, *4*(6), 438–452. doi:10.1002/cb.29

Ha, H.-Y. (2004). Factors influencing consumer perception on brand trust on the online. *Journal of Product and Brand Management*, *13*(5), 329–342. doi:10.1108/10610420410554412

Haven, B. (2007). *Marketing's New Key Metric: Engagement*. Marketing. Retrieved on February, 07, 2013 from http://www.adobe.com/engagement/pdfs/marketings_new_key_metric_engagement.pdf

Holbrook, M. B., & Hirschman, E. C. (1982). The Experiential Aspects of Consumption: Consumer Fantasies, Feelings, and Fun. *The Journal of Consumer Research*, *9*(2), 132–140. doi:10.1086/208906

Hughes, R. (2010). *Enterprise Social Networking: Don ' t Be Afraid*. Retrieved on February 14, 2014 from http://www.clearvale.com/clearvale/mkt-nav/en/whitepapers/Enterprise_Social_Networking-Dont_Be_Afraid_2010_02_24.pdf

Johar, G. V., Sengupta, J., & Aaker, J. L. (2005). Two roads to updating brand personality impressions: Trait versus evaluative inferences. *JMR, Journal of Marketing Research*, *42*(4), 458–469. doi:10.1509/jmkr.2005.42.4.458

Johnson, C., & Mathews, B. P. (1997). The influence of experience on service expectations. *International Journal of Service Industry Management*, *8*(4), 290–305. doi:10.1108/09564239710174381

Johnston, R. (1999). Service transaction analysis: Assessing and improving the customer's experience. *Managing Service Quality*, *9*(2), 102–109. doi:10.1108/09604529910257876

Joy, A., & Sherry, J. F. Jr. (2003). Speaking of art as embodied imagination: A multisensory approach to understanding aesthetic experience. *The Journal of Consumer Research*, *30*(2), 259–282. doi:10.1086/376802

Kalakota, R., & Robinson, M. (2001). e-Business 2.0 Roadmap for Success (2nd ed.). New Delhi: Pearson Education.

Kania, D. (2001). *Branding. com*. Lincolnwood, IL: NTC Business Books.

Kemp, S. (2014). *Digital in India*. Retrieved on October 12, 2014 from http://www.slideshare.net/wearesocialsg/social-digital-mobile-around-the-world-january-2014

Kenny, D., & Marshall, J. F. (2000). Contextual marketing: The real business of the Internet. *Harvard Business Review*, *78*(6), 119–125. PMID:11184966

Kim, H. S. (2005). Consumer profiles of apparel product involvement and values. *Journal of Fashion Marketing and Management*, *9*(2), 207–220. doi:10.1108/13612020510599358

Koufaris, M. (2002). Applying the technology acceptance model and flow theory to online consumer behavior. *Information Systems Research, 13*(2), 205–223. doi:10.1287/isre.13.2.205.83

Levy, S. J. (1959). Symbols for sale. *Harvard Business Review, 37*(4), 117–124.

Liljander, V., & Strandvik, T. (1997). Emotions in Service Satisfaction. *International Journal of Service Industry Management, 8*(2), 148–160. doi:10.1108/09564239710166272

Mandel, N., & Johnson, E. J. (2002). When web pages influence choice: Effects of visual primes on experts and novices. *The Journal of Consumer Research, 29*(2), 235–245. doi:10.1086/341573

Mayfield, A. (2008). *What is Social Media*. Retrieved on May 06, 2013 from http://www.icrossing.com/ebooks

Mcwilliam, G. (2000). Building strong brands through online communities. *Sloan Management Review, 41*(Spring), 43–54.

Menon, S., & Kahn, B. (2002). Cross-category effects of induced arousal and pleasure on the internet shopping experience. *Journal of Retailing, 78*(1), 31–40. doi:10.1016/S0022-4359(01)00064-1

Meyer, C., & Schwager, A. (2007). Understanding customer experience. *Harvard Business Review, 85*(2), 116–126. PMID:17345685

Meyers-Levy, J., & Peracchio, L. A. (1995). Understanding the effects of color: How the correspondence between available and required resources affects attitudes. *The Journal of Consumer Research, 22*(2), 121–138. doi:10.1086/209440

Morace, F. (2002). *European Asymmetries*. Milano: Scheiwiller.

Nielsen nmIncite. (2012). *State of the Media: The Social Media Report 2012*. Retrieved on May 5, 2013 from http://postmediavancouversun.files.wordpress.com/2012/12/nielsen-social-media-report-20122.pdf

Ofir, C., & Simonson, I. (2007). The effect of stating expectations on customer satisfaction and shopping experience. *JMR, Journal of Marketing Research, 44*(1), 164–174. doi:10.1509/jmkr.44.1.164

Olshavsky, R. W., & Granbois, D. H. (1979). Consumer decision making-fact or fiction? *The Journal of Consumer Research, 6*(2), 93–100. doi:10.1086/208753

Osgood, C. E., & Tannenbaum, P. H. (1955). The Principle of Congruity in the Prediction of Attitude Change. *Psychological Review, 62*(1), 42–55. doi:10.1037/h0048153 PMID:14357526

Owyang, J. (2010). *Socialgraphics Help You to Understand Your Customers: Slides and Webinar Recording*. Retrieved on September 04, 2013 from http://www.web-strategist.com/blog/category/socialgraphics/

Pine, B. J. II, & Gilmore, J. H. (1998). Welcome to the Experience Economy. *Harvard Business Review, 1998*(July-August), 97–105. PMID:10181589

Pine, B. J. II, & Gilmore, J. H. (1999). *The Experience Economy: Work is Theatre and Every Business a Stage*. Cambridge, MA: Harvard Business School Press.

Pogue, D. (2012, July 18). Why Face Book should begin to worry. *Economic Times*, p. 8

Prahalad, C. K., & Ramaswamy, V. (2004). *The Future of Competition - Co-Creating Unique Value with Customers*. Boston: HarvardBusinessSchool Press.

Pullman, M. E., & Gross, M. A. (2004). Ability of experience design elements to elicit emotions and loyalty behaviors. *Decision Sciences*, *35*(3), 551–578. doi:10.1111/j.0011-7315.2004.02611.x

Quelch, J. A., & Klein, L. R. (1996). The Internet and International Marketing! *Sloan Management Review*, *37*(3), 60–75.

Rawson, A., Duncan, E., & Jones, C. (2013). The truth about customer experience. *Harvard Business Review*, *91*(9), 90–98. PMID:23593770

Reichheld, F. F., & Schefter, P. (2000). E-loyalty: Your secret weapon on the web. *Harvard Business Review*, *78*(4), 105–113.

Sahin, A., Zehir, C., & Kitapçı, H. (2011). The effects of brand experiences, trust and satisfaction on building brand loyalty; an empirical research on global brands. *Procedia: Social and Behavioral Sciences*, *24*, 1288–1301. doi:10.1016/j.sbspro.2011.09.143

Sarkar, R., (2014, October 8). Mobile doing to e-Commerce what e-Commerce did to retail, *Business Standard,* p. 1.

Schiffman, L. G., Kanuk, L. L., & Kumar, S. R. (2010). Consumer Behaviour (10th ed.). New Delhi: DorlingKindersley (India) Pvt. Ltd.

Schmitt, B. (2011). Experience marketing: Concepts, frameworks and consumer insights (Vol. 5, No. 2). Now Publishers Inc.

Schmitt, B. H. (2003). Customer Experience Management: A Revolutionary Approach to Connecting with Your Customers. John Wiley & Sons, Inc.

Shankar, V., Smith, A. K., & Rangaswamy, A. (2003). Customer satisfaction and loyalty in online and offline environments. *International Journal of Research in Marketing*, *20*(2), 153–175. doi:10.1016/S0167-8116(03)00016-8

Sheth, J. N. (1979). The Surpluses and Shortages in Consumer Behaviour Theory and Research. *Journal of the Academy of Marketing Science*, *7*(4), 414–427. doi:10.1007/BF02729689

Smith, S., & Wheeler, J. (2002). *Managing the customer experience: Turning customers into advocates*. Pearson Education.

Stanley, M. (2009). *Mobile Internet Report*. Retrieved on December 24, 2012 from www.ms.com/techresearch

Stelzner, M. A. (2012). Social Media Marketing Report, 2012. *Social Media Examiner*. Retrieved on January 3, 2013 from http://www.socialmediaexaminer.com/SocialMedia MarketingIndustryReport2012.pdf

Stelzner, M. A. (2013). *2013 social media marketing industry report: How marketers are using Social Media to Grow Their Businesses*. Retrieved on August 2, 2013, from http://www.socialmediaexaminer.com/SocialMedia MarketingIndustryReport2013.pdf

Thomas, T. K. (2014, October 10). Benefits of bringing connectivity to India are going to be profound: Zuckerberg. *The Hindu*, p. 11.

Vehr, N. J. (2012). *Vehr Communications, 2012 Social Media Usage Survey*. Retrieved on May 05, 2013 from http://www.vehrcommunications.com/wp-content/uploads/2012/02/2012-Social-Media-Usage-Survey-PRINT-FINAL.pdf

Voss, C. A. (2003). Rethinking paradigms of service - service in a virtual environment. *International Journal of Operations & Production Management*, *23*(1), 88–104. doi:10.1108/01443570310453271

Wang, Y. D., & Emurian, H. H. (2005). An overview of online trust: Concepts, elements, and implications. *Computers in Human Behavior*, *21*(1), 105–125. doi:10.1016/j.chb.2003.11.008

Yu, Y.-T., & Dean, A. (2001). The contribution of emotional satisfaction to customer loyalty. *International Journal of Service Industry Management*, *12*(3), 234–251. doi:10.1108/09564230110393239

Yulianti, I., & Tung, W. (2013). The Relationship Among Brand Experience, Brand Image and Customer Satisfaction of Facebook Users in Indonesia. *World Applied Sciences Journal*, *28*, 100–113. doi:10.5829/idosi.wasj.2013.28.efmo.27017

Zaichkowsky, J. L. (1985). Measuring the involvement construct. *The Journal of Consumer Research*, *12*(3), 341–352. doi:10.1086/208520

Zailskaite-jakste, L., & Kuvykaite, R. (2012). Consumer Engagement in Social Media by Building the Brand. In *Electronic International Interdisciplinary Conference 2012* (pp. 194–202). Academic Press.

KEY TERMS AND DEFINITIONS

Brand Experience: Refers to sum total of the perceptions, feelings and thoughts, resulting from all the points of contact, which consumers attribute to the brands they encounter and consume. Various responses such as emotional, subjective, internal and behavioural of the customer due to his/her interaction with the brand through various touch points are collectively termed as Brand experience.

Customer Experience Management: Refers to the management of customer experiences, in a cumulative manner, at multiple touch points across multiple channels based on a detailed road map of customer's end-to-end journey. The approach is based on, the hitherto largely ignored, emotional and internal aspects of the consumer behavior to manage customer encounters with the organizations.

Digitized Business Model: A Business model, leveraging the power of internet and characterized by business communications, interactions and transactions between Consumers and marketers being carried over web.

Expected Utility of the Brand: Refers to the value accorded to the brand by the customers based on their utilitarian and functional evaluations of the brand.

Experience: Refers to the familiarity, with some object/subject/area of interest, generated due to knowledge acquired and accumulated through some exposure to the object/subject/area of interest.

Experienced Utility of Brand: Refers to the value accorded to the brand by the customers based on their subjective and emotional evaluations of the brand.

Experiential View of Consumer Behavior: Refers to the exploration of the symbolic, syntactic, hedonic, psycho-temporal, and psychobiological meanings attributed to the products/brands by the consumers based on their conscious and subjective evaluations of the products/brands.

Web 2.0: Can be termed as the ideological and technical architecture, result of participatory and collaborative tools such as Adobe Flash, Really Simple Syndication (RSS), and Asynchronous Java Script (AJAX), of social media.

Website Brand Experience: Encompasses a consumer's navigational experiences and perceptions about the various features such as attractiveness of cookies, variety, currency, quality and uniqueness of visual display and/or graphical user interfaces of a specific website.

This research was previously published in Capturing, Analyzing, and Managing Word-of-Mouth in the Digital Marketplace edited by Sumangla Rathore and Avinash Panwar, pages 188-212, copyright year 2016 by Business Science Reference (an imprint of IGI Global).

Chapter 17
Examining the Role of WeChat in Advertising

Qi Yao
University of Macau, China

Mei Wu
University of Macau, China

ABSTRACT

WeChat, the most popular social networking service mobile app in China, enables users to contact friends with text, audio, video contents as well as get to know new people within a range of a certain distance. Its latest version has gone beyond the pure social function and opened a window into marketing. This study applies activity theory as a framework to explore new features of WeChat as a new platform for advertising. Then the authors qualitatively analyze the implications that marketers adapted and appropriated WeChat to engage with their customers and in turn how these implications modified the ways of advertising. The significance of this study is that it applied activity theory as an attempt to complement the theoretical pillars of communication study. Activity theory focuses on the activity itself rather than the interaction between WeChat and the users. Second, activity theory reveals a 2-way process which emphasizes both on how advertisers adapt WeChat based on everyday practice; and how WeChat modifies the activities which the advertisers engage in.

INTRODUCTION

Integrated with multimedia and Internet functions, a smartphone allows people to access diverse social communication spaces, where the existing types of conventional communication (calling and texting) mix with types of internet communication (email and social networking service). Smartphone makes the online space available 24/7, and thus develops ubiquitous sociality (Lee, 2013). Moreover owing to the fast growth of information technology, more types of mobile social media have been created, such as WhatsApp, Line, and WeChat. These mobile social networking services have been growing their influence among people, especially youth, around the world. Their user-friendly interfaces conveniently

DOI: 10.4018/978-1-5225-5637-4.ch017

present recent information with text, photos, and videos (Pelet, 2014). All of these benefit marketing practitioners to wage their campaigns and engage the audiences.

The prevalence of smartphones in people's daily life has critically changed the consumer's decision-making process (Pelet, 2014). The consumers now could easily access professional opinions, others' reviews, price comparisons and other convenient functions, which help consumers to make full-scale evaluation on products and services. This suggests marketers to take account of new ways to influence consumers and to carefully implement social networking service as a marketing tool (Pelet, 2014).

WeChat is the most popular mobile application in relation to social networks in current China. It was developed by Tencent company in China and released in January 2011.WeChat provides users with multimedia communication function including speaker phone, photo and mood sharing, text message, corporation official account, location sharing, location based searching and service. The latest version of WeChat added more functions such as game center, online payment, emoticon shop, street view scanning and scanning for translation. It served different countries, languages, operating systems and network formats. It took 56 months for Facebook to reach 100 million users and 30 months for WhatsApp. But when it comes to WeChat, it took only 15 months to reach 100 million users (Wu, Jakubowicz & Cao, 2013). Nowadays in China, WeChat users reached around 500 million. Moreover, the overseas user amount has broken through 100 million by the end of 2014 (Tencent, 2015).

While academic studies have been focusing on usage, society, behavior and other particular issues in the mobility context, advertisers also started to pay attention to the advantage offered by mobile social media such as WeChat. Compared with conventional mobile advertising methods such as sending SMS and MMS, now advertising through apps became the trend. As discussed before, the advertising on WeChat is based on user's strong-tied social connectedness. The marketers cannot depend on mass messaging to WeChat users, but take advantage of the users' social connectivity for propagation.

For the companies and advertisers, the official accounts of WeChat enable them to engage with their customers with a new method. Through WeChat official account, the company is able to approach the customers privately since all the conversation between them cannot be seen or commented on by others. Since WeChat official account is smart phone-based, consumers could read the messages anytime as well as forward them to Weibo, Moments (Peng You Quan[1]), friends and save them in WeChat. Since its 5.0 version, one of the most significant changes is that WeChat has separated the official account into two different forms: service account[2] and subscription account[3]. Owing to these new features, the customers seized the initiative to receive the messages only if they want to. Meanwhile, the new situation reminds advertisers not to use WeChat as a broadcast tool, which has been widely applied in other social media such as Qzone and Weibo. Instead of message bombardment, companies are demanded to offer more valuable contents as well as a high level of interactive experience with its audience (Leung, 2013).

The academia and industry are always sensitive to any new-born advertising media. However WeChat, which has already attracted almost one tenth of the population on this planet, has not brought enough attention to the marketing communication area. This study applied activity theory (AT) as framework to explore new features of WeChat as a new platform for advertising. Then we qualitatively analyzed the implications that marketers adapted and appropriated WeChat to engage with their customers and in turn how these implications modified the ways of advertising.

MOBILE SOCIAL MEDIA AND WECHAT IN CHINA

Mobile social media is always applied by companies and advertisers in areas such as promotions, communication, relationship development and marketing research (Kaplan & Haenlein, 2011). Both Facebook and Twitter are world-famous media platform for target-oriented advertising and online business communication. Although these two biggest mobile social media are blocked by the government of China, there are several native mobile social media which are very similar to them--Renren and Weibo, which could be deemed as the Chinese version of Facebook and Twitter respectively. Especially Weibo, which has already owned 249 million users, is beloved by companies and advertisers in China (CNNIC, 2015).

On April 11, 2014, Tencent QQ, the first instant messaging and social media software in China, has reached a new concurrent user record of 200 million. Tencent took advantage of QQ's huge volume of users and allowed users to sign in WeChat using QQ ID. Until May, 2014, Tencent announced that WeChat climbed to 396 million monthly active users. Beside the quantity advantage, WeChat is able to achieve this business model as its parent company Tencent already owns a complete line of e-commerce and e-payment services including QQ Online Shop and Yixun.com. These facilities and expertise will provide strong backing for the future growth of WeChat. Moreover, with the rise of E-business such as Taobao, Jumei and Jingdong, the companies and advertisers could no longer ignore the power of mobile social media as marketing communication platform. Meanwhile, people also became aware of the different online marketing communication strategies applied for different kinds of social media.

WeChat is more conducive to information diffusion than former social media because of its unique functions and information flow mechanism, it combines mobile phone, social media and Internet in one platform (Wu, Jakubowicz & Cao, 2013). Since its intrinsic instant messaging nature WeChat's users keep relatively strong ties. The friends in one's WeChat are mostly their family members, schoolmates and colleagues who are familiar with them in real life. It is also why people will believe the information which was shared on WeChat moment rather than Weibo or blogs. Companies and advertisers have found that it is increasingly important to promote their company on WeChat not only for its strong word of mouth effect but also for its various supported service (Figure 1).

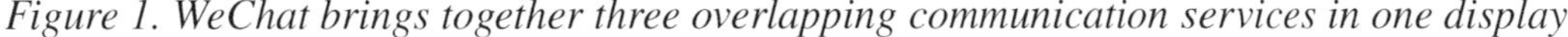

Figure 1. WeChat brings together three overlapping communication services in one display

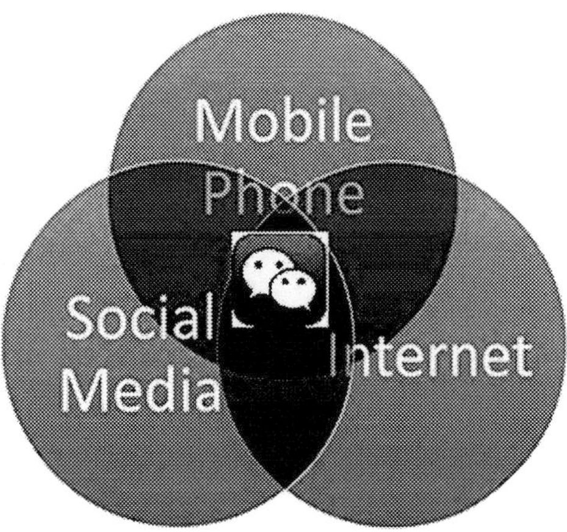

Compared with blogs and Weibo users, WeChat users are more equal, more interconnected and better able to establish relationships with those who are outside their original social networks. Beside the acquaintance mentioned above, some companies also utilize WeChat to engage their customers: customers can get useful information through instant interaction. Under such circumstances, the information flow is not superincumbent but mutual. WeChat, which combines SNS application and instant messaging application, not only possesses the common features of former mobile social media, but also has its own new highlights. Its combination deserves deeper consideration and study.

MOBILE SOCIAL MEDIA STUDY

It is not easy to draw a clear definition of mobile social media because nowadays social media tools are getting more merged into diverse facets of mediated communication (Lüders, 2008). Therefore mobile social media can be roughly defined as a kind of software, application, or service which could be accessed via mobile devices such as PDA, tablet PC and smartphone. Mobile social media enables users to connect with others people as well as to generate, exchange and share various contents (Lee, 2013).

What is the changing characteristic of sociality through mobile social media? In the early stage, mobile social media was designed to emphasize the presumed mobility of users, usually via location-based service: through various wireless communication technologies, mobile device users are able to recognize others within certain vicinity (Wu & Yao, 2014). Dodgeball (Boyd & Ellison, 2007), Foursquare (Frith, 2012), Digu and Momo (Wu & Yao, 2014) are the examples of location-based mobile social media. Many cross-platform social media, such as Facebook and QQ, have specific locative functions like check-in and searching people nearby, however this cannot define its mobile presence. Actually according to a study of Facebook (Protalinski, 2012), among 901 million monthly active users, more than half of them (488 million) logged in Facebook by a mobile phone or tablet. Nowadays more and more people are accessing social media on mobile devices. Same phenomenon also happens in China. According to Nielsen, until June 2014 the number of mobile netizens in China has reached 530 million, which means 83.4% of the netizens chose to access the Internet through a mobile device. Among these people, 60.2% spend on average 1.5 hours every day using mobile social networking services. This report also revealed that 67% of the users consider mobile social networking services to be very important to them (Nielsen, 2014).

Users perform social interactions and develop social connections through adding or forwarding text, photo and other multimedia contents with peers on the mobile social media. These activities can be deemed as the extension of conventional sociality to online space. When accessing mobile social media, the users' workflow includes matching and integrating social functionalities, messaging, online contents and publishing tools within a complicated ecosystem of online social behavior. Therefore one should be cautious when studying the characterizations and usage of mobile social media, since mobile social media is defined by functions and uses instead of designs or forms (Brusse, Gardner, McAullay, & Dowden, 2014).

SOCIAL MEDIA ADVERTISING STUDY

Traditionally the process of advertising is often marketer-controlled. Based on one-way communication, the marketers decide on the way of communication and channels (face-to-face, survey, online panel and etc.) depending on demographic setting within a pre-determined space and time. However the social media altered the process, creating a new system where consumers are the core of content-generation process (Singh, Veron-Jackson, & Cullinane, 2008). The biggest difference between advertising on traditional media and social media is the development of technology has shifted from the passive consumers (in the context of traditional media) into positive and creative talent (in the context of social media). For marketers, the power has been altered from the company to the consumers (Pierre, 2012). Today's consumers complete the purchase activities with various stages, ranging from the first engagement with a brand, understanding a product, to hear about the product from social circles (Powers, Advincula, Austin, Graiko, & Snyder, 2012).

Speaking of social circles, consumers now possess more power than ever before: the accessibility of online social networks and digital devices like smartphone, PDA and tablet PC enables consumers to share with others discussing brands, services and products as well as interacting with brands conveniently and efficiently (Powers, Advincula, Austin, Graiko, & Snyder, 2012).

In order to make advertisement effective, the advertisers are aware of how to deliver the message to customers on the market. Academics and experts created several theories and models which demonstrate how customers react to the advertising message they are exposed to (Ciadvertising, 2007). AIDA model, one of the earliest as well as the most popular effect of advertising models, was designed to describe the different stages through which an advertiser should take an outlook. "A" refers to draw the *attention* of the customer. "I" means to raise customers' *interest* by concentrating and presenting advantages and benefits of a product. "D" is *desire*; it is the stage that the advertisement successfully persuades customers to desire the product or service which could satisfy their needs. The last "A" means *action*: the advertisement finally conducts customers making certain action or purchasing (Wijaya, 2012).

Table 1. The difference of traditional media, Weibo and WeChat

	Traditional Media	**Weibo**	**WeChat**
Communication Channel	One-way communication	Two-way communication	Two-way communication
	Opaque[4]	Transparent	Opaque
	Centralized[5]	Decentralized	Decentralized
Content	One-to-many	One-to-many	One-to-one
	Company-generated content	User/company -generated content	User/company -generated content
Influencers	Elites & Celebrities	Big Vs[6]	Users with large numbers of friends circle
Platform	Paid	Free	Free
	Pre-scheduled	Real-time	Real-time
Evaluation	Reach and frequency	Interaction	Interaction

In the following part, activity theory will be introduced as the analytical framework to explore new features of WeChat as a new platform for advertising and how the AIDA model works within WeChat.

ACTIVITY THEORY

Since this study is among the first which introduces activity theory into communication study, it is critical to explain the reason why a psychology theory could be applied to smartphone app research. To elaborate the reasons, first this study will examine the most popular theories in communication study and their weakness. Then activity theory will be presented and explained for its complementary role in communication study.

To date, mobile services have been widely studied by the various theories. Among these, technology acceptance model (TAM), use & gratification theory are the most applied. TAM was developed to fulfill the need to understand users' satisfaction rate, and in turn to apply this rate to predict the success of a system (Davis, 1989). TAM mainly contains 2 attitudinal dimensions: Perceived Ease of Use and Perceived Usefulness, which are considered as direct factors related to the use of information system. Perceived Ease of Use refers to users' self-evaluations on the relationship between their cognitive work and the use of the system. Perceived Usefulness means how a particular system could improve users' job performance (Davis, 1989).

However despite its frequent application, TAM has been widely criticized. One part of the criticism is that TAM failed to consider the influence of social organization. Second is the insensitivity to diverse contexts of usage. TAM did not consider the probability that certain technology would be accepted in the beginning and then abandoned, or vice versa (Chuttur, 2009). The third and the most important reason is the studies that applied TAM are based on the fundamental premise that the scholars have the right to decide what shall be evaluated, even it is not certain whether the users indeed represent that type of use. In the real context, the relationship between the functionalities of the system and the tasks may be different among users and thus the ends would be completely different than scholars' anticipation (Salovaaraa & Tamminenb, 2008).

Use and gratification theory (U&G) was firstly developed in the studies of effectiveness of radio communication in the 1940s, when researchers were interested in different forms of media behaviors (Wimmer & Dominick, 1994). The primary goal of the U&G theory is to seek the psychological desires that shape users' choice for applying the mass media and the motivations which encourage them to take advantage of certain media for gratifications which satisfy people's inherent desires and needs (Elliott, 1974; Ruggiero, 2000; Zhu, 2004). However U&G faces various critics. One of them is that the data behind the theory is difficult to conclude and sometimes cannot be found (Littlejohn, 2002). Another problem is U&G is inclined to neglect the "dysfunctions of media in both culture and society" (Littlejohn, 1989). Lastly, U&G tends to consider media in positive ways and as able to provide audiences' needs. Less attention was paid on how the media cast negative cultural influences on society (Griffin, 2009). Such criticism makes U&G hard to analyze in the larger societal context (Severin & Tankard, 1997).

Therefore as mentioned above, communication study requires a theory that understands the users' real behaviors by investigating social-cultural contexts as users engage in media. Also attention should be drawn on how different parts of a community or organization could influence the implementation of the media. Moreover the communication study needs to understand that the media may be assimilated by the users and then in turn, the real practices could be modified when users are looking for adapting their activities with newly perceived possibilities of the media (Wu & Lin, 2011; Wu & Li, 2011).

Activity theory stems from a historical and cultural psychology originated by Vygotsky (1978) and Leont'ev (1978) from the former Soviet Union. Activity theory has been defined as a framework for understanding various forms of human activities and practices (Kuutti, 1996). Activity theory provides a broad range of conceptual frameworks that facilitate the research and design of Human Computer Interaction (HCI). Meanwhile it is also applied to determine how to provide users with the necessary tools to work with the interface to obtain the needed outcomes without participating in a long period of training (Gould, Verenikina, & Hasan, 2000).

An activity is comprised of subject, object and tools. According to Vygotsky (1978), human activity can be interpreted as a mediation process triggered by tools. The relations between subject and object are not direct but mediated. Tools play the part of mediating between them. Activity is a long-term formation, thus the outcome would not be transformed from object immediately, but through a procedure including several phases. Engeström (1987) improved this system and added 3 new relations: community, rules and division of labor. All of these components are mediated as shown below. Tool is applied by subject to complete an object, in order to fulfill a goal. Rules are then required between subject and other members within a community, meanwhile a division of labor is also indispensable between members of the community (Pang & Hung, 2001) (Figure 2).

- **Subject:** An actor (usually someone) who is involved in the activity and is chosen as the perspective in the analysis. In this study subject refers to the supervisor of social marketing from Company C, whom was interviewed.
- **Object**: Anything which could be manipulated or transformed by actors in an activity; an object could be material, rarely tangible (such as a plan), or totally intangible (such as a thought). The object for the supervisor as well as the company is to persuade more consumers to purchase its products.
- **Tool:** Anything utilized in the process of transformation. In Yamagata-Lynch's study (2001), the author pointed out that there are two kinds of tools available in the social environment: artifacts

Figure 2. Activity system

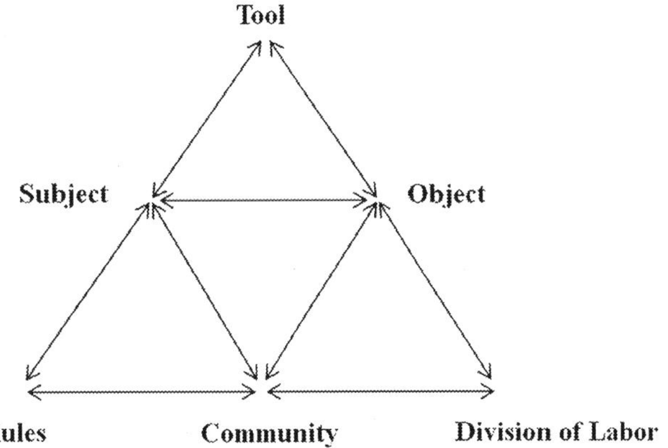

(also called "technical tools") and signs (or "psychological tools"). This study focuses on WeChat and its new features as a new tool for advertising.

- **Community**: A group of persons who pursue the same object. Here community means the social marketing team.
- **Rules**: Consist of laws, both implicit and explicit criterions, social relations and regulations within a community.
- **Division of Labor:** Involves both the vertical division of status and power, and the horizontal division of roles and tasks within a community.

Hence the activity system of this study can be shown as below (Figure 3).

Another important concept of activity theory is contradiction, because it is the motive for the development of activity system. Activities are not inert but dynamically developing and changing, thus activities play as nodes within hierarchies and networks. The nodes are affected by other changes and activities in the work context and cause inequality between them (Kuutti, 1996). Therefore "contradiction" is introduced to understand these changes within and among components.

The primary contradiction found within a sole node of an activity. This contradiction appears from the tension between value of use and value of change. It exists in every corner of the triangle structure of activity and is the essential source of unsteadiness and development. The secondary contradiction emerges between the compositive nodes such as between the subject and the tool or between the tools and rules[7] (Engeström, 1993).

The reason this study applied activity theory to evaluate the advertising on WeChat is its focus on the real field usage. Rather than other new technology researches, activity theory does not emphasize on the history of adoption, but on how such technology is applied in practice and how it fits into peoples' everyday life.

Previous studies have pointed out that the strength of applying activity theory is because of the concept "tool meditation as the core to all human activities". Activity theory focuses on tools, such as WeChat in

Figure 3. Activity system of the study

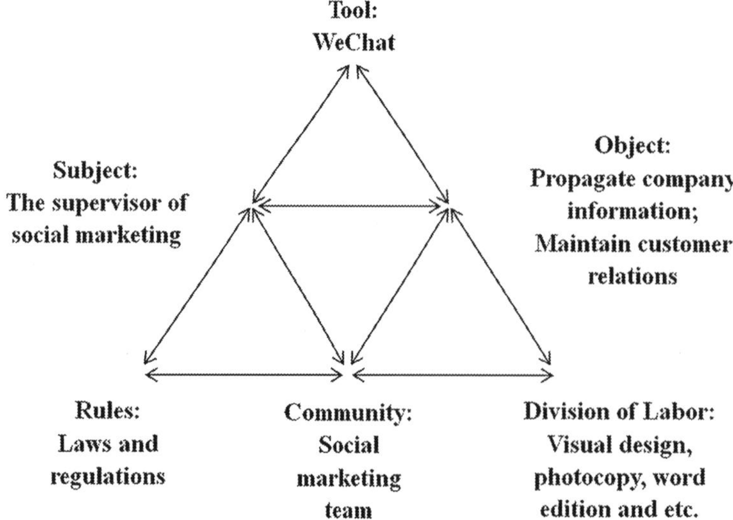

this study, as the meditators; and meanwhile instead of simply interaction, it emphasizes on the activity itself. In another word, the users here are deemed to be doing something rather than just using WeChat: WeChat is the tool through which users could fulfill or accomplish their goals. Therefore in this study, the focus is not only on the evaluation of WeChat as an advertising tool, but also on its usability and how well WeChat integrated into advertisers' activity to achieve their objective.

CASE STUDY: WECHAT OFFICIAL ACCOUNT OF COMPANY C

A case study of a WeChat official account has been conducted since winter 2014. The information provided in this part is according to a series of interviews with the supervisor of social marketing team of Company C[8]. The two interviewees were selected from the management level of Company C. The person who provided the majority of information was the Supervisor of Social Marketing Team, the other one was the manager of WeChat Operation Team.

The Background of the Company, Its WeChat Official Account and the Team

Located in a Southern province, Company C is one of the top smartphone manufacturers in China. The WeChat official account of Company C was established on Nov. 13, 2013. Its updating frequency is stochastic: usually 1-7 days per post. However, different from Weibo or Twitter, everyday WeChat official account could only send users one post, which may contain up to 8 columns of messages. Aside from traditional SNS, WeChat provides not only advertisement, but also includes other information such as store introduction, promotion, new arrival, etc. Moreover Company C irregularly launches events on WeChat such as bonus quizzes and games.

Social marketing Team, which is responsible for designing, updating and pushing content on WeChat, has 10 staff members. All of them graduated from electronic engineering major thus are well-acquainted with soft/hard ware knowledge. The operation of this community is very flexible. There is no particular division of labor, everyone who has time, or idea will be put in charge of the job.

Except WeChat, this team is also in charge of Weibo, QZone, Lofter[9] and web radio. Among all of these, Weibo is the most eye-catching because they invest most of the energy and resource in it. However they noticed that Weibo is declining because of a decrease of user numbers and degree of activity. More and more young people shift their attention to WeChat, which is more suitable for mobile devices. It seems Weibo is trying to find another business model because its business model is highly dependent on advertisements and is unable to get benefits from other channels. On the other hand, the advertisement bombardment severely ruins the user experience. Compared to Weibo, WeChat is a still in its developing stage, thus they dare not invest too much in WeChat due to its uncertainty.

The Object of WeChat Official Account

The WeChat official account provides 2 kinds of services. First is about the product, such as product introduction, A/S service and reservation. Second is to satisfy the consumers with living information, chatting service, games and etc. Therefore the purpose of WeChat and Weibo is the same: to solve customer's problems and form a positive image of the company. Compared to Weibo, WeChat is a combination of instant messaging and SNS. Its features enable the company to foster intimate relationships with customers as friends, because it is more private, more direct and more efficient in communication.

The supervisor mentioned "we hope after purchase consumers could still remember our company and we are happy if consumers are happy." In order to make consumers feel that they and the company have the same pursuit as well as to encourage consumers to spread the content, the official account sometimes rewards consumers with material objects like earphones, virtual bonus such as E-coupons and psychological consolation from the company.

The Process of Making Content for WeChat

First the team would have a meeting to set up the goal, exchange visual effects; after this the supervisor will arrange different jobs to the members, as mentioned above. An email will be sent to everyone to confirm the division of work, time, and resource distribution. If anything changed, they will use email to inform everyone. For example before the press conference, they will first, according to the official website, design a WeChat page with a link to the official website for reserving the product. The visual effect and style are consistent on the website, which contains more information; then they will extract the most essential and important things as the source material. The content including photos and texts are customized and optimized to fit in the screen of mobile devices. In another words, the work of the social marketing team is to integrate all the resources from website and other departments.

Referring to the rules, during this process except for professional ethics and laws, the team deems privacy protection the most. Since WeChat is a messaging app, it contains a lot of users' private information. The events they hold on WeChat always require user's authorization such as requiring gender, age and nick name. When reward or gift is provided, they also need users' address, phone number and the real name.

The Target Audience and the Content Pushing

According to the supervisor, generally they do not set the target audience specifically nor separate user groups when pushing contents, because according to their statistics (the official account server could tell the operating system of subscribers' smartphone) most people who subscribed to their official account are currently using their products. In another words the audience and the consumer group have been already prefixed both for the company and the official account. Although the marketing department has a total investigation data for all the consumers and they can use the data directly, they do not separate users in detail any further. The contents on WeChat are just for their product users.

When pushing the content, the time is very crucial. Usually the contents are pushed at 5-10 pm during weekends, and 3-4 pm and 7-9 pm on weekdays. "We must be careful to avoid message bombardment, which we usually do on Weibo. If the timing is wrong, the intimate relationship between customers and company will be ruined, since no one wants to hear the vibration or ringtone when they are busy with work or enjoy leisure." said the supervisor.

Viral Marketing Strategy

Mobile social media have shown as a powerful platform particularly in both helping new product launches (Kaplan & Haenlein, 2012) and developing viral marketing phenomena (Kaplan, 2011). Speaking of the offline strategy, the company pays a lot of attention to its "fan culture" and has a group of hard-core fans. Once the company pushes content on WeChat, these hard-core fans are the first wave that voluntarily spread out the message. In order to cultivate more fans, the company has dozens of "Home of C's Friend" (C stands for the name of the company) located in big cities such as Beijing, Shanghai, Chengdu and etc. These homes would hold offline events regularly, for example they would invite its loyal consumers to watch "Avengers" right after the movie was released. The aim of such offline activities is to encourage consumers to spread more online.

The online strategy to spread the virus is the game on WeChat (a flash game which could be operated directly on WeChat without downloading or redirection), which would be pushed to audience before the press conference. Even the game itself has nothing to do with the product or the conference, it attracts more than 100 thousand people to play, to win gift and, most important to forward the game to Moments.

Referring to the content design, the most popular content is interestingness. The team would combine the hot topic with its product. For example, when "Big Hero Six" was popular, the team designed a post with Baymax to promote its voice assistant as "your sincere life companion as Baymax". The usefulness is also the key to spread the virus, such as the information of the operating system upgrade, A/S service notice, smartphone insurance and etc.

Interaction and Evaluation

Different from Weibo and other social media, the interaction in WeChat is very limited. The users could comment on the content. However the comments would not be seen by the public until the company checks every comment (or comments) through the server and then gives permission to communicate them. Actually WeChat provides company a premium channel to build custom features, interact with customers and get the feedback, only if the company programs a set of API (Application Programming Interface). However such situation will be improved as the supervisor said they will develop a real-person and AI customer service within this year. The evaluation of the pushing content is also finite--the social circle of WeChat is relatively closed, thus the communication effect is not so prominent as Weibo, for instance the company does not know who reads or re-posts the content since WeChat only offers the number of reading hits without providing any details.

Problem and Challenge

The problems mainly come from WeChat. Since even the WeChat official does not know its course for the future, WeChat is inconsistent in its policy. For example Since July 2013, the subscription account could push one message per day and did not have a customized menu. The service account could push one message per month. But in the beginning of 2014, WeChat allowed the subscription accounts of government and charity organizations to have a customized menu. On April 15th, 2014, the service account was allowed to push four messages per month. Another example is since March 2014, some businesses started a marketing campaign: if the user called in his/her friends to "like" a message, when the "like" achieved a certain amount the user would receive reward such as a gift or even a tour. But on June 9th 2014, WeChat pronounced that such campaign was not permitted.

Therefore they have to both keep close contact with officials and predict the next step from even circumstantial sources. On the technical level, the functions of official account server have certain limits which impede them offering more diversified visual effects in photo and text. Moreover the life span of the content in WeChat is short, audiences tend to forget or ignore the messages quickly. Therefore the messages require a high level of time effectiveness.

FINDINGS

Technical advantages and the relentless march of technology offer unprecedented convenience for corporations to engage with their customers. In light of Activity Theory, this study investigated new features of WeChat as a new platform for advertising. Then we qualitatively analyzed the implications that marketers adapted and appropriated WeChat to engage with their customers and in turn how these implications modified the ways of advertising. In this part, concepts of activity system would be used to investigate WeChat as a new platform for advertising.

According to the interview, we can conclude that WeChat is still deemed an auxiliary method in the whole propagation system. It is mainly used to support the official website and Weibo. Under most situations, the advertising and propaganda in WeChat are based on the content of their official website. The process of making content is as follows (Figure 4).

Figure 4. The process of making content

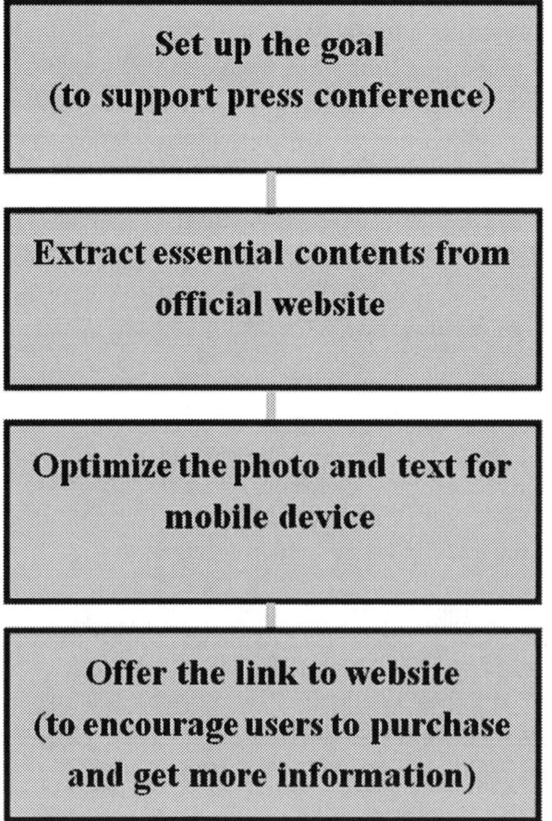

The Subject

In the activity system, the activities are based on the unique combination of past experience and personal preferences. In this case, the supervisor and his team are building WeChat as an advertising and relationship managing platform. Since WeChat is a totally new app and has its own unique features, the past experiences with other SNS media would not be very helpful in operating WeChat. Everything they have done with it is somehow conservative–"crossing the river while feeling the stones". However the supervisor still, based on his experience dealing with Weibo and Qzone, deems WeChat to be a powerful broadcasting tool, the most obvious example is the majority of messages in WeChat were about the products.

The Community and the Division of Labor

In terms of community, none of the members of the social marketing team was specially trained for operating WeChat. The divisions of labor are flexible, and the sources for WeChat come second-hand from other departments or the website, the highly homogenized information made WeChat sterile. Compared with Weibo, Company C invested too little in WeChat and developed WeChat as a broadcasting tool just as other social media.

The Object

According to activity theory, object motivates and directs different activities and the activities are coordinated around the object. In this case we can conclude that the object of the official account is, except for broadcasting, to form positive impressions, develop affinity, and reduce interpersonal uncertainty—in another words "to be good friend with the customers". Sharing is the key to extend the influence within WeChat, because different from Weibo or Renren, WeChat does not have a broadcasting function. The content, comment and "like" are only visible to the subscribers, thus only by sharing with subscribers' "Moment", could the content be seen by other users (subscribers' friends).

The Contradiction

Contradiction is important in Activity theory because it is deemed as the source of development–contradictions are always involved in the process of real activities. From a practical perspective, exploring the contradictions helps us to understand the characteristics of each node in an activity system, and indicates to us how to further develop and improve it. WeChat, as an advertising platform, both resolved and introduced contradictions in the activity system. In this case, WeChat resolved the contradiction of the tool: given the number of smartphone users is now 500 million (eMarketer, 2014), portability and mobility make the content on WeChat more accessible to the audience. On the other hand, however, it also introduced a contradiction that the tool is limited since compared with a website it contains less information, functions and has poor visual effects. This contradiction somehow explains why the marketer has to put the link of its website in every WeChat message.

Another contradiction is between the rule and the tool. The affordance of WeChat as an advertising platform is open to new marketing strategies, for example, to win the reward by accumulating "likes". On the other hand, the unstable policies (rules) of WeChat prevent marketers from innovating new methods to engage with their customers. Thus a new activity was introduced--to both keep close contact with officials and predict its next step from even circumstantial sources.

The third contradiction is between the rule and the object. The rule (privacy protection) here is a double-edged sword: the closed social circle made WeChat a perfect place to communicate privately with selected people. This private space enables one-to-one communication and is beneficial to creating a better, intimate relationship between customers and the company (the object). But such closed circle also prevents the company from reaching more audiences and evaluating their influence.

The Tool

1. **Subsidiary Role of WeChat:** Although more people access the Internet via mobile devices than computers, WeChat still serves as a subsidiary tool. The first reason is due to the limited size of the smartphone, the message has to be designed to fit into the screen. During this process, only the most important information would be selected to present on WeChat. The link to the official website indicates that the web is what the advertisers want to show the audiences. Moreover the rules—the bad usability of official account server also highly limit the expression of the content.

Second reason is the insufficient customer service. WeChat officials claimed that it should be used as a tool providing services and encouraging companies to offer value-added services for the customers. However instead of offering a service, the present official account serves merely as a shop window that exhibits its products.

2. **Broadcast Pushing as Existing Social Media:** In this case the use of "networkedness" has been found, the company intentionally takes advantage of social circles to expand the messages. However we noticed that such usage is very limited in its influence. WeChat was made as a two-way communication platform, but referring to the official account the communication is unidirectional. Scarcely could comments be seen in the posts, and all of them have already been inspected thoroughly by the "gatekeepers"—the social marketing team.

The official account did not divide its audiences demographically. It is more like a tool to spread the messages among already-fixed audiences. WeChat here is used as a tool to maintain the relationship with its fans, not the tool to expand its influence. It is like a gig where advocates are standing there and listening to the messages from their idol. Within this asymmetric communication, the outsiders could hardly step into the company's circle and become the potential customers due to the lack of impression formation. This problem is determined by its nature of closed social circle, but still the company innovated a new strategy to "bridge" outsiders to its social circle. This will be discussed later.

3. **Lack of Innovative Strategy:** Compared to Weibo, which broadcasts to the public, the dissemination circle of WeChat is confidential to everyone except among its friends. Therefore "water army", "zombie fans" and other traditional e-marketing strategies, which are widely used in other social media to boost advertising effect, were not found in this study. Even though some new methods

could be applied to enhance its effect, Yao (2014) pointed out that positive emotions such as surprise, joy and other virusworthy elements like nationalism, livelihood and timely topic are useful to spread the virality, to entice audiences forwarding and sharing with others. But what we found in this was merely copy and paste from the official website with no innovative strategies.

4. In terms of AIDA model, usually on the traditional media, a brand starts drawing people's attention through highly popular celebrities in the commercials, so that the message could catch people's eyeballs and provide a distinct benefit (Thomas & Howard, 1990). But WeChat is a closed social media; it is very hard to penetrate into the outsiders' social circle. Therefore the company sometimes holds collective events to "bridge" 2 previously separated social circles together. For example one of their events was associated with a bank. If the WeChat audiences of Company C open an account of the bank within the event period, they would gain a chance to win a gift such as a smartphone, earphones or coupons. In like manner, if the WeChat audiences of the bank purchase a smartphone of Company C, they would be rewarded with some gifts from the bank and the company too. Referring to "interest", we found that presenting advantages and features of the product along could not consistently keep audiences' interests. In contrast, if audiences are exposed too much to such information, they would probably unsubscribe the account. Thus as the "friend" of the audiences, the company holds various events irregularly. In the existing social media such as blog and cyber community, the administrator would give its users a "psychological reward[10]" to draw their interest. However, as a closed social community, any psychological reward would be useless to its users in WeChat since nobody else could see such a reward. Therefore in this case Company C has to offer material rewards.

CONCLUSION AND DISCUSSION

This study applied activity theory as a framework to investigate WeChat and analyzed the implications that marketers adapted and appropriated WeChat to engage with their customers and in turn how these implications modified the ways of advertising. We came up with three conclusions as follows:

Weibo is used as a broadcasting tool; its content is visible to everyone no matter if he/she is the follower of an account. Thus the dissemination structure of Weibo is extensive--the re-post, comment, feedback and "like" could be easily observed and measured. However the dissemination mechanism of WeChat is only available for the strong tie relationship and the content is closed to outsiders, which means the interactivity in WeChat is unobservable and hard to measure. The difference of advertising dissemination mechanism between Weibo and WeChat can be illustrated as follows (Figures 5 and 6).

The privacy protection has been treated more seriously in WeChat. As discussed above, the social circle of Weibo is accessible to everyone due to its openness. In another words, it is easy to know new friends, although most of them probably are only based on weak ties. But in WeChat in order to be the friend of the user, the account has to be very cautious with every user's information. Most users WeChat ID are just their QQ ID or cellphone number, which may contain a lot of personal information. Moreover the events held on WeChat also require users' real names, address and etc. Any misuse of such information would grievously jeopardize both user's privacy and company's reputation.

Figure 5. The extensive structure of Weibo (the interactivity and dissemination are visible)

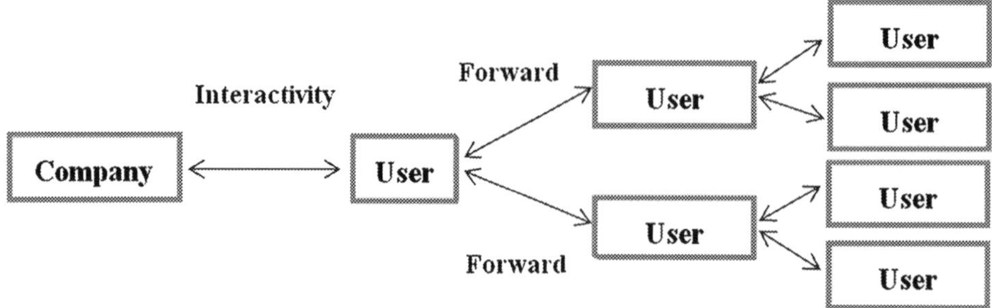

Figure 6. The restricted structure of WeChat

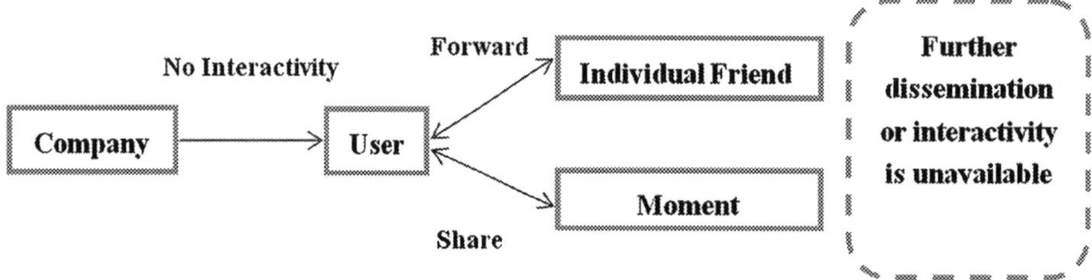

Low pushing frequency is another finding in this study. Compared to Weibo, which could send limitless messages every day, WeChat allows only one message per day. This called out a new challenge to the marketers–how to grab users' attention and interest with exquisitely designed content. However as WeChat is a smartphone-based app, the small screen, poor editing server and limited information largely obstruct the advertising dissemination. Therefore a new form of advertising is demanded to meet the needs. Unfortunately no new strategy has been found in this case.

The limitation of this study is first we cautiously claim the representativeness since only one official account was involved in this study. As an app WeChat evolves quickly, the official account in this study would be more sophisticated in the future since the supervisor claimed they will introduce customer service into it in this year. By then some of the conclusions in this study may not be applicable anymore. Second filed observation could be a complementary method to self-report methods. However since the company once encountered the issue of leakage of information, any form of observation was prohibited.

For the future study, more sophisticated studies are required to understand not only the company but how audiences interact with the official account and how its contents influence the perception of the advertisements and the decisions to forward or share. Comparative studies among different media platforms are also needed to investigate how activity system varies with different media and how the system could be applied not only in advertising but also in other aspects such as online-purchasing.

REFERENCES

Barker, M., Donald, N., & Krista. (2008). *Social Media Marketing: A Strategic Approach*. Cengage Learning.

Boyd, D., & Ellison, N. (2007). Social Network Sites: Definition, History, and Scholarship. *Journal of Computer-Mediated Communication*, *13*(1), 210–230. doi:10.1111/j.1083-6101.2007.00393.x

Brusse, C., Gardner, K., McAullay, D., & Dowden, M. (2014). Social media and mobile apps for health promotion in Australian Indigenous populations: Scoping review. *Journal of Medical Internet Research*, *16*(12), e280. doi:10.2196/jmir.3614 PMID:25498835

Chuttur. (2009). Overview of the Technology Acceptance Model: Origins, Developments and Future Directions. *Information Systems*. Indiana University.

Ciadvertising. (2007). *Hierarchy-of-effects models*. Retrieved from Ciadvertising: http://www.ciadvertising.org/studies/student/97_fall/theory/hierarchy/modern.html

CNNIC. (2015). *China Internet Network Information Center*. Retrieved from CNNIC: http://www.cnnic.cn/gywm/xwzx/rdxw/2015/201502/t20150203_51631.htm

Davis. (1989). Perceived usefulness, perceived ease of use, and user acceptance of information technology. *MIS Quarterly*, 319–340.

Elliott. (1974). Uses and gratifications research: A critique and a sociological alternative. In *The Uses of Mass Communications: Current Perspectives on Gratifications Research* (pp. 249-268). Beverly Hills, CA: Sage.

eMarketer. (2014). Retrieved from technews.cn: http://technews.cn/2014/12/25/china-will-top-500-million-smartphone-users-for-the-first-time-see-more-at-httpwww-emarketer-comarticle2-billion-consumers-worldwide-smartphones-by-20161011694sthash-1do3dlqq-dpuf/

Engeström. (1987). *Learning by expanding*. Cambridge University Press.

Engeström. (1993). Developmental studies of work as a test bench of activity theory: the case of primary care medical practice. In *Understanding Practice: Perspescives on Activity and Context*. Cambridge, UK: Cambridge University Press.

Frith. (2012). Location-based social networks and mobility patterns: An empirical examination of how Foursquare use affects where people go. *Mobilities Conference: Local & Mobile.*

Gould, Verenikina, & Hasan. (2000). *Activity Theory as a Basis for the Design of a Web Based System of Inquiry for World War 1 Data. Department of Information Systems*. Wollongong: Academic Press.

Griffin, E. M. (2009). *A first look at communication theory*. New York: McGraw-Hill Companies, Inc.

Huang, J. (2015). *Building Brand-Consumer Relationships on WeChat: the Case of IKEA*. Unpublished Master dissertation.

Ito, & Okabe. (2005). Technosocial situations emergent structuring of mobile e-mail use. In *Personal, portable, pedestrian: Mobile phones in Japanese life* (pp. 257–273). The MIT Press.

Kahle, & Valette-Florence. (2012). *Marketplace Lifestyles in an Age of Social Media: Theory and Method.* Academic Press.

Kaplan, A. (2012). If you love something, let it go mobile: Mobile marketing and mobile social media 4x4. *Business Horizons*, *55*(2), 129–139. doi:10.1016/j.bushor.2011.10.009

Kaplan, A. M., & Haenlein, M. (2011). The early bird catches the news: Nine things you should know about micro-blogging. *Business Horizons*, *54*(2), 105–113. doi:10.1016/j.bushor.2010.09.004

Kaplan, & Haenlein. (2011). Two hearts in three-quarter time: How to waltz the social media/viral marketing dance. *Business Horizons*, 253—263.

Kaplan, & Haenlein. (2012). The Britney Spears universe: Social media and viral marketing at its best. *Business Horizons*, 27-31.

Kuutti, K. (1996). Activity Theory as a Potential Framework for Human-computer Interaction Research. In Context and Consciousness: Activity Theory and Human-computer Interaction (pp. 17-44). Cambridge, MA: MIT Press.

Lee, D.-H. (2013). *Smartphones, mobile social space, and new sociality in Korea*. Mobile Media & Communication.

Leont'ev. (1978). *Activity, consciousness, and personality*. Englewood Cliffs, NJ: Prentice-Hall.

Leung, R. (2013). *WeChat Official Accounts and What This Means for Marketers*. Retrieved from ClickZ: http://www.clickz.com/clickz/column/2307141/wechat-official-accounts-and-what-this-means-for-marketers

Littlejohn. (1989). *Theories of Human Communication.* Belmount: Wadsworth.

Littlejohn. (2002). *Theories of human communication* (7th ed.). Belmont: Wadsworth.

Lüders. (2008). Conceptualizing personal media. *New Media & Society*, 683–702.

Nielsen. (2014). *Report of China Mobile SNS Users' Needs and Behaviors*. Retrieved from 199it.com: http://www.199it.com/archives/272681.html

Pang, P., & Hung, D. (2001). Activity Theory as a Framework for Analyzing CBT and E-Learning Environments. *Educational Technology*, 36–42.

Pelet, J. B. (2014). *Determinants of effective learning through social networks systems: An exploratory study*. IGI Global.

Pelet, J.-E., & Papadopoulou, P. (2014). Consumer behavior in the mobile environment: An exploratory study of M-commerce and social media. *International Journal of Technology and Human Interaction*, *10*(4), 36–48. doi:10.4018/ijthi.2014100103

Pierre, L. K. (2012). Marketing meets Web 2.0, social media, and creative consumers: Implications for international marketing strategy. *Business Horizons*, 261–271.

Powers, T., Advincula, D., Austin, M. S., Graiko, S., & Snyder, J. (2012). Digital and Social Media In the Purchase Decision Process. *Journal of Advertising Research*, *52*(4), 479–489. doi:10.2501/JAR-52-4-479-489

Protalinski. (2012). *Facebook has over 901 million users, over 488 mobile users*. Retrieved from ZDNet: http://www.zdnet.com/blog/facebook/facebook-has-over-901-million-users-over-488-million-mobile-users/12105

Ruggiero. (2000). Uses and gratifications theory in the 21st century. *Mass Communication & Society*, 3-37.

Salovaaraa, A., & Tamminenb, S. (2008). Acceptance or appropriation? A design-oriented critique on technology acceptance models. In *Future Interaction Design II* (pp. 157–173). London: Springer.

Severin, & Tankard. (1997). *Communication theories: Origins, methods, and uses in the mass media* (4th ed.). New York: Longman.

Shrum, L. (2004). *The Psychology of Entertainment Media: Blurring the Lines Between Entertainment and Persuasion*. Lawrence Erlbaum.

Singh, V.-J., Veron-Jackson, L., & Cullinane, J. (2008). Blogging: A New Play in Your Marketing Game Plan. *Business Horizons*, *51*(4), 281–292. doi:10.1016/j.bushor.2008.02.002

Tencent. (2015). *The New Milestone of WeChat*. Retrieved 12 20, 2015, from Techweb: http://www.techweb.com.cn/internet/2015-08-12/2188504.shtml

Thomas, B., & Howard, D. (1990). A Review and Critique of The Hierarchy of Effects in Advertising. *International Journal of Advertising*, 98–111.

Tuten, T., & Solomon, M. (2012). *Social Media Marketing*. Englewood Cliffs, NJ: Prentice Hall.

Vygotsky. (1978). *Mind in society: The development of higher psychological processes.* Cambridge, MA: Harvard University Press.

Walther, J. B. (2002). Cues filtered out, cues filtered in. In *Handbook of interpersonal communication*. Thousand Oaks, CA: Sage Publications.

Walther, J. B. (2005). Let Me Count the Ways: The Interchange of Verbal and Nonverbal Cues in Computer-Mediated and Face-to-Face Affinity. *Journal of Language and Social Psychology*, *24*(1), 36–65. doi:10.1177/0261927X04273036

Wijaya, B. S. (2012). *The Development of Hierarchy of Effects Model in Advertising*. International Research Journal of Business Studies.

Wimmer, & Dominick. (1994). *Mass media research: An introduction.* Belmont: Wadsworth.

Wu, M., Jakubowicz, P., & Cao, C. (2013). *Internet Mercenaries and Viral Marketing: The Case of Chinese Social Media*. IGI Global.

Wu, M., & Li, H. (2011). The Triumph of Shanzhai:No Name Brand: Mobile Phones and Youth Identity in China. In D. Y. Jin (Ed.), Global Media Convergence and Cultural Transformation: Emerging Social Patterns and Characteristics (pp. 213-232). IGI Global.

Wu, M., & Lin, H. (2011). Office on the move. In E. Coakes (Ed.), Knowledge Development and Social Change through Technology: Emerging Studies (pp. 232-246). IGI Global. doi:10.4018/978-1-60960-507-0.ch018

Wu, M., & Yao, Q. (2014). Location-Aware Mobile Media and Advertising: A Chinese Case. In X. Xu (Ed.), Interdisciplinary Mobile Media and Communications: Social, Political, and Economic Implications (pp. 228-244). IGI Global. doi:10.4018/978-1-4666-6166-0.ch013

Yamagata-Lynch, L. (2001). *Using activity theory for the sociocultural case analyses of a teacher professional development program involving technology integration.* (Doctoral dissertation). Indiana University.

Yao, Q. (2014). How Virusworthy Elements Affect Viral marketing Patterns in WeChat. 6th Chinese News and Communication Association.

Zhu. (2004). Competition between alternative sources and alternative priorities: A theory of weighted and calculated needs for new media. *China Media Report*, 16-24.

ENDNOTES

1. Moments or Peng You Quan, refers to "friends' circle", is one of the social functions on WeChat. Users could share text, photo, article and music to Moment. "Comment" or "like" about the sharing is only visible to user's friends.
2. Service account aims to offer various services such as online payment and customer service. The company could apply customized menu and connect to third-party platforms. Service account could only push four broadcast messages per month.
3. Subscription account only pushes the updated information about the company. Subscription account could push one broadcast message per day.
4. The dissemination route, which is unknown within traditional media, however is visible within social media such as Facebook and Weibo.
5. In the context of centralized traditional media, company is the only authority to offer the information or the services and to control users' data. However with the decentralized social media, the information is produced in several different places concurrently.
6. Big V refers to the popular microbloggers whose accounts have been verified and thus stamped with a "V" next to their names.
7. There are also tertiary and quaternary contradictions, but they are not involved in this study.
8. The company demanded to be anonymous for privacy protection. Therefore all names and brands used in this study are pseudo or acronyms names.
9. Lofter is the Chinese version of "Tumblr". Lofter is to provide a simple, easy-to-use microblogging platform which encourages users to post original content to a short-form blog.
10. For example in the cyber community, a new user would get the rank as "private". With his or her involvement in the community, the rank will be upgraded. According to the interview, such strategy is very effective to motivate users to participate.

This research was previously published in the Handbook of Research on Human Social Interaction in the Age of Mobile Devices edited by Xiaoge Xu, pages 386-405, copyright year 2016 by Information Science Reference (an imprint of IGI Global).

Chapter 18
The Application of Instagram as a Promotional and Communication Tool by Productive Families in the Kingdom of Bahrain

Amera H. Abdulrazzaq
University of Bahrain, Bahrain

Sharifa Hamad
University of Bahrain, Bahrain

Marwa Ali
University of Bahrain, Bahrain

Fatima Mohammed
University of Bahrain, Bahrain

Walaa S. Kamal
University of Bahrain, Bahrain

ABSTRACT

This study aims to investigate Instagram potentialities in the family business sector in Bahrain known as "Productive families". The intention to adopt and use the tool to promote their products and support information sharing, cooperation, and actual communication, the actual benefits and use derived as a stand-alone tool, and the socio-economic payoffs for their businesses. An analytical and quantitative approach is used throughout the study. A survey was distributed to 253 participants consisting of a standard questionnaire divided in to two main parts: the first part covered the demographic elements while the second part focused on two factors (Performance Expectancy and Effort Expectancy) of the Unified

DOI: 10.4018/978-1-5225-5637-4.ch018

Theory of Acceptance and Use of Technology model (UTAUT). The analysis reveals that: (1) Instagram can be an important means of creating valuable opportunities for productive families to achieve their missions and goals in promoting and advertising their products; (2) the two factors analyzed (Performance expectancy and Effort expectancy) directly influence the families' intention to use form which leads directly to the actual usage; (3) the families' age, gender and level of education have indirect effects on their intention to adopt and use the platform; (4) most of the families use Instagram to promote their businesses, specifically handcrafts and services and have doing so for over two year; (5) The main financially supporter is Tamkeen, which backs 53% of the surveyed families. To our knowledge, this is the first in-depth study of the use of Instagram by Productive Bahraini families.

1. INTRODUCTION

Everywhere, families are considered the building blocks of society; the stability of later strongly correlated that of the former. In response to disparities and harsh conditions that some families struggle upon, countries prioritized strategies to help families overcome such barriers.

Like other Gulf countries, the Kingdom of Bahrain, and under the supervision of the Ministry of Social Development, was able to achieve its goal of maintaining the stability and happiness of its families through economic empowerment.

The native Bahraini who lived on this very land thousands of years ago were dependent on crafting and agricultural activities, such as farming, fishing, pearl hunting, sewing and so on to make a living. Based on this tradition, the Ministry of Social Development initiated the "Productive Families" project, which allows families use these inherited skills in harmony with the modern lifestyle in the ever-changing world, in order to earn a living from the time-honored activities carried out by their time-honored ancestors.

The project provides the participating families owned businesses with vocational and technical training, financing, production units, marketing for products, registering and licensing of productive families and seeking to introduce a design and innovation Centre.

The Ministry of Social Development strives through this project to achieve several objectives, which on a larger scale would contribute to the establishment of a production-friendly environment that encourages entrepreneurs and self-employed citizens to become active members of the community under the protection of a legal cover, with traditional production being given ample support.

Over the past few years, the Ministry has organized a number of "Productive Families' fairs in various parts of the country, offer to sell their products to as many purchasers as possible.

There are also subprojects under the main heading of "Productive Families", including "Made in my Home", "Family Bank", "Khatwa Home-Based Businesses" and "Inma'a Initiative". All these initiatives complement each other in reaching towards a unified target of empowering productive families and improving their living standards.

HRH Princess Sabeeka bint Ibrahim Al Khalifa, President of the Supreme Council for Women, personally supports and admires the concept of families being productive and innovative in the community. As a sign of her encouragement and reassurance for such families, who put in effort and add value to the community, HRH Princess Sabeeka plans to promote these families through an approach that combines creativity, innovation, efforts and expertise reward outstanding families from all Arab world.

Looking closely at the current list of domestic entrepreneurs provided by the Ministry of Social Development, it may be noticed that it includes a total of 651 concerns of which 99 are owned by males while the remainder are in the hands of females. The types of activities range from handicraft, such as sewing, pottery, agricultural endeavors, such as fishing, farming, cooking dishes, preparing peppers and mixtures and finally to provision of services such as the distribution of tea and Arabic coffee on occasions, playing traditional music and folkloric dancing and so on.

Although productive families in the Kingdom of Bahrain are supported by the government, they must still expend efforts to assure their sustainability and success. Certainly, Instagram is one of the key tools that can positively enhance the families' businesses and provide them with different opportunities to develop their relationships with their new clients, to approach more customers and to provide all with better services. In this study, a short literature review is presented in section II while the objectives of the study are expounded, in section III. A description of the survey was informed this analytical investigation and the model is given in section IV, taking in to account the responses of the productive families (the study population) who are actively involved in promoting their businesses on Instagram. The analyses, hypotheses and results are covered in sections V and VI, while conclusions and recommendations are provided in section VII.

2. LITERATURE REVIEW

Today's electronic world facilitates communication, the processing of information, the marketing of businesses and so on. Shirky in his book (2008) declares how social tools, such as blogging software like Word Press and Twitter, file sharing platforms like Flickr, and online collaboration platforms like Wikipedia, support group conversation and group action in a way that previously could only be achieved through institutions and with the advent of online social tools, groups can form without previous restrictions of time and cost. Edosomwan et al (2011) stated that styles, means and trends of communication have changed on a global scale, due to the introduction of social media. Social media is type of electronic communication that enables its users to share views and information online via video, audio, pictures or texts. In the eighteenth century, this idea was born with the invention of telegraph which was chiefly used for the purpose of receiving and transmitting messages from distant places. Kietzmann (2011) stated that social media has attracted a vast number of users faster than any other online medium used for the purpose of personalization and interaction. Chen et al. (2011) also stated that social network marketing is the best strategy for promoting one's business, and that the traditional newspaper and television avenues no longer have a great influence on consumers. Hassan (2014) clarified that social media has emerged as a highly feasible and favored medium for marketing. In addition, Endres & Harper (2013) stated that when conducting marketing in a social forum, three things should be taken in to account. First, it should reach the intended users or customers. Second, the most suitable should be used to interact with those customers. Finally, the marketer should to focus on the needs and wants of the customers rather than the random knowledge. Smith and Mogos (2010) stated that social media has a great impact on the performance of a business. Kietzmann (2011) demonstrated that people are required to engage with Instagram through its usage and the formation of societies as well as with determining the levels of other users. Naaman (2010) explained the Instagram features enables its users to be active and in sharing their opinions, ideas and other contents content. Dennis (2014) showed how comments in Instagram enable customers understand the nature of things they need and how this will help to improve the relationship and the level of communication between them and the business owner. Furthermore, Modimogale and Kroeze (2011) stated further that globalization and digitalization have changed the way business is done and competes in the marketplace, and that the Information and Communication technology (ICT) is the lifeblood of this change. Massimo et al (2013) analyzed the impact of the adoption of broadband Internet technology on the productivity performance of small and medium enterprises (SMEs), and distinguished access to the broadband infrastructure from the adoption of complementary services. Alam and Noor (2009) examined the relationship between ICT adoption and its five factors, which are perceived benefits, perceived cost, ICT knowledge, external pressure and government support. The results of this study show that three of these factors are significant to the adoption of ICT; perceived cost and external pressure were the factors found to be insignificant. Schubert et al. (2007) accepted that small business owners are less likely to embrace innovation and have a well-defined business strategy. Given the importance of this sector, there is a need for governments and policy- makers to understand innovation in small business particularly in terms of ICT implementation and use, in order to formulate appropriate programs and policies. Babb and Nelson (2013) stated that, with the advent of analytics and other sophisticated measurement tools, entrepreneurs are finding that they can now not only take advantage of social media as a marketing tool but can also use data to optimize their social media marketing campaigns. Their study was conducted to examine trends in social media marketing and the resources available to entrepreneurs to jumpstart their marketing strategy by embrace social media. Instagram is an important marketing tool for every small business. Herman, (2014) stated that its use in any business helps to improve its performance, achieve its goals, and reach more customers. Herman (2010) stated that by using Instagram, it is easy to upload photos or videos that reflect the nature of the business. Ting (2015) mentioned that Instagram is widely used as a mobile application for personal reasons. Salomon (2013) lauded Instagram as the venue where people are currently having the most rewarding interactions; it has breathed new life into our social media activities. Abbott (2013) highlighted on the popularity of Instagram and how it can provide an appropriate channel to listen to one's audience and engage with one's followers.

3. STUDY OBJECTIVES

The primary objectives of this study are to:

1. Determine the factors that directly impact productive families' use of Instagram in Bahrain.
2. Determine the extent to which performance expectancy and effort expectancy enhance these families' businesses, as determined by gender, age and education.
3. Determine the impact of support provided by the Ministry of Social Development on these families use of Instagram.
4. Determine the extent of Instagram support the sharing, cooperation and promotion of these families businesses.

4. RESEARCH METHOD AND DATA MODEL

The target populations of this quantitative and analytical study were productive families who are listed under the Ministry of Social Development project in the Kingdom of Bahrain. The study tool was an online questionnaire posted on the web as a Google application tool. The questionnaire consisted of two parts: first, the families' demographic information; second, their perceptions of Instagram and its effect on the enhancement of their productivity and the support of the higher authorities, with a total of 20 statements. A five likert scale was applied from 1 (strongly disagree) to 5 (strongly agree); in the result, high scores meant that positive perceptions were structured and distributed for the purpose of investigating the above questions and the formulation of the following three hypotheses.

H1: There is a significant relationship between performance expectancy and effort expectancy in the respondents' intention to use Instagram.
H2: There is a significant relationship between the intention to use Instagram and the respondents' usage behavior.
H3: The controlled variables: age, gender, and education significantly affected the intention to use and the actual usage of productive families.

The study was conducted between February and September 2015 and the measurement is based on UTAUT model' which was proposed by Venkatesh, Morris, Davis and Davis (2003) as an extension of the Technology Acceptance Model (TAM) to study information technology adoption, intention, and use. UTAUT is a model of individual acceptance compiled from eight models and theories TRA, TAM, MM, TPB, C-TAM-TPB, MPCU, IDT and SCT. Juinn (2013) justified the use of UTAUT as reasonable for studying the acceptance and use of English learning websites. We therefore introduced a subjective task value to UTAUT when addressing our research questions. Figure1 below demonstrate the linkage between different variables; performance expectancy, effort expectancy, age, gender, and education. This was used to study and investigate the relationship between the independent and dependent variables and, consequently, resolve the study problem. 253 questionnaires (the sample size, selected from 648) were distributed to various productive families in an attempt to discover their views regarding the effect of Instagram on their productivity and businesses. They were also asked whether they had indeed adopted Instragram and the reasons behind. The model contains two main sections. The first section is the independent variables: performance expectancy (perceived usefulness) and effort expectancy (perceived ease of use); the second is the controlled variables (dependent variables): age, gender and level of education.

Figure 1. Factors influencing the use of Instagram by productive families

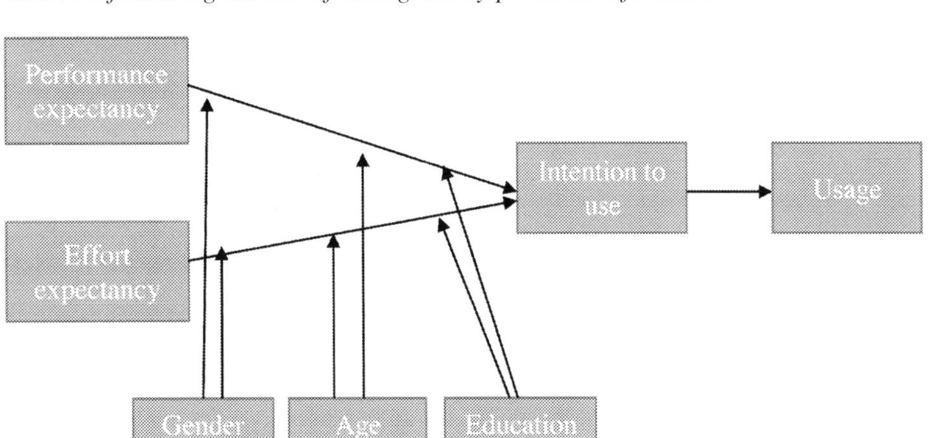

Table 1. Demographic characteristics of the participants

<table>
<tr><th>Percentages</th><th>Frequencies</th><th colspan="4">Categories</th><th>Measure</th></tr>
<tr><td>71%</td><td>179</td><td colspan="4">Female</td><td rowspan="2">Gender</td></tr>
<tr><td>29%</td><td>74</td><td colspan="4">Male</td></tr>
<tr><td>58%</td><td>147</td><td colspan="4">18-29</td><td rowspan="4">Age</td></tr>
<tr><td>19%</td><td>47</td><td colspan="4">30-39</td></tr>
<tr><td>12%</td><td>31</td><td colspan="4">40-49</td></tr>
<tr><td>11%</td><td>28</td><td colspan="4">50 and over</td></tr>
<tr><td>9%</td><td>23</td><td colspan="4">Non- educated</td><td rowspan="3">Level of education</td></tr>
<tr><td>44%</td><td>110</td><td colspan="4">Secondary education</td></tr>
<tr><td>47%</td><td>120</td><td colspan="4">Bachelor or higher</td></tr>
<tr><td>34%</td><td>85</td><td colspan="4">Services</td><td rowspan="4">Business type</td></tr>
<tr><td>33%</td><td>83</td><td colspan="4">Handicraft</td></tr>
<tr><td>27%</td><td>69</td><td colspan="4">Cooking</td></tr>
<tr><td>6%</td><td>16</td><td colspan="4">Agriculture</td></tr>
<tr><td>53%</td><td>25</td><td>Tamkeen</td><td rowspan="4">19%</td><td rowspan="4">47</td><td rowspan="4">Yes</td><td rowspan="5">Institution (supporters)</td></tr>
<tr><td>7%</td><td>3</td><td>Ministry of Labor</td></tr>
<tr><td>21%</td><td>10</td><td>Bahrain Development Bank</td></tr>
<tr><td>19%</td><td>9</td><td>Ministry of Agriculture</td></tr>
<tr><td>-</td><td>-</td><td colspan="2">81%</td><td>206</td><td>No</td></tr>
<tr><td>27%</td><td>50</td><td>Less than 1year</td><td rowspan="3">73%</td><td rowspan="3">184</td><td rowspan="3">Yes</td><td rowspan="4">(Instagram) use</td></tr>
<tr><td>30%</td><td>57</td><td>1-2 years</td></tr>
<tr><td>43%</td><td>80</td><td>More than 2 years</td></tr>
<tr><td>-</td><td>-</td><td colspan="2">27%</td><td>69</td><td>No</td></tr>
</table>

5. DATA ANALYSIS AND RESULTS

As shown in Table 1, 71% of the respondents were females while males contributed 29% In addition, 58% were between 18 to 29 years old and 47% held a bachelor or higher degree. As for business type, services and handicrafts are the most common types run by the productive families, with service represent 34% and handicrafts 33% Concerning the (supporters) that financially support the productive families' businesses, 53% are supported by Tamkeen, (21%) by Bahrain Development Bank, 19% by the Ministry of Agriculture, and the remainder 7% by the Ministry of Labour. The results also reveal that the majority 73% of the productive families used Instagram to promote their business, 43% of whom had been using Instagram for over two years, 30% for over one year and the rest less than a year. Regarding the analyses of each item of the model's variables, the results of the first group of questions focus on the variable effort expectancy (ease of use); 65% of the respondents strongly agreed that Instagram is user-friendly as their answer for one item among seven. The results of the second group of questions focused on the variable Performance Expectancy (usefulness) of Instagram; respondents' answers were all positive in terms of Instagram being a useful tool in enhancing their businesses, accomplishing tasks, increasing efficiency and raising their income. This is justifiable because the respondents are seeking better stable businesses, 62% of the respondents strongly agrees with one of the ten items, namely that Instagram was useful for their businesses. Regarding the concerns of behavioral intention, 60% of respondents strongly agreed on two of the four items: the intention to keep dealing with clients and business colleagues through Instagram and that it is a good communication tool in general. As for usage behavior, 60% of respondents strongly agree with one item out of four, namely that prior experience with Instagram was very helpful for their business career and helped them to provide better services for their clients.

6. TESTING THE HYPOTHESES

It is important to determine the significance of the relationships between the independent and dependent items of the model variables, Table 2 below, along with Figure 2 shows that the correlation is significant at the 0.01 level. The three hypotheses were tested concerning the respondents' intention to adopt and use Instagram. Hypothesis 1 was tested using chi-square to check the level of significance of the relationship between the independent variables. The chi-squared test was used to determine whether there was a significant difference between the expected and observed frequencies in one or more categories. Did the number of individuals or objects that fall in each category differ significantly from the number we would expect? Is this difference due to sampling variation, or is it a real difference? Table 3 below, shows that there is a strong relation between effort expectancy and performance expectancy which means H0 is accepted and there are no significant differences between ease of use and usefulness. To check the dependent variables' Table 4 below shows that there is a strong relationship between intention to use Instagram and usage behavior. H0 is accepted; there is no significant difference between them.

Chi-square analysis was used to test the third hypotheses above as it was an applied analytic technique to predict the usage behavioral of respondents.

Table 2. Summary of Pearson Correlation analyses for testing the relationship between variable items

		1	2	3	4	5		
		SA	A	U	D	SD	AVG	STD
(1) Instagram requires specific resources to use.	X	82	43	77	25	26	50.6	27.391605
(2) Instagram requires specific knowledge.	Y	64	72	73	19	25	50.6	26.425367
(3) Instagram is not compatible with other social media tools.	Z	68	47	60	37	41	50.6	13.049904
(4) Experts are needed to solve Instagram difficulties.	W	71	57	64	28	33	50.6	19.086645
(5) I feel comfortable using the Instagram in selling my products/services.	H	117	76	31	12	17	50.6	44.880954
(6) I have no problems to use Instagram in my business.	F	118	76	31	14	14	50.6	45.418058

Rx,y	0.7903064	Positive Strong Relationship between X and Y
Rz,w	0.9376548	Positive Strong Relationship between Z and W
Rx,w	0.9358972	Positive Strong Relationship between X and W
Ry,w	0.9294735	Positive Strong Relationship between Y and W
Rz,f	0.736543	Positive Strong Relationship between Z and F

Figure 2. Summary of Pearson Correlation analyses for testing the relationship between variable items

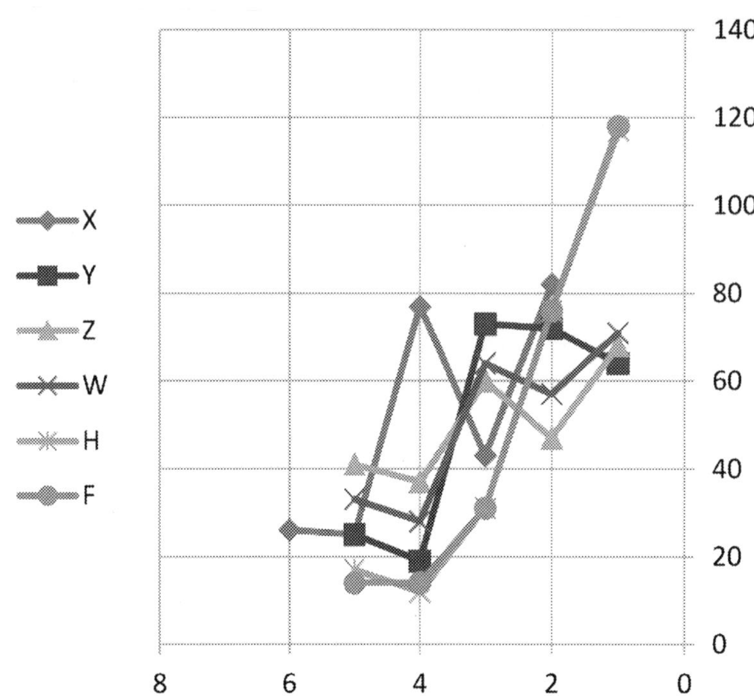

Table 3. Significance between independent variables

Hypothesis testing			
H0:	Ease of use	Eq	Usefulness
H1:	Ease of use	Neq	Usefulness
Observed values			
	Ease of use	Usefulness	Total
Agree	128	178	306
Disagree	125	75	200
Total	253	253	506
Expected values			
	Ease of use	Usefulness	Total
Agree	153	153	306
Disagree	100	100	200
Total	253	253	506
Chi-Value	5.45661E-06		
df	1		
Alpha	0.05		
P-Value	0.998136192		
Chi-crit	3.841459149		

3.841459149 > 00000545661

Acceptance of H0 and Rejection of H1

There is no Significant difference between ease of use and usefulness

Table 4. Significance between dependent variables

Hypothesis Testing			
H0:	Ease of use	Eq.	Intention to use
H1:	Ease of use	Neq.	Usage Behavioral
Observed Values			
	Intention to use	Usage Behavioral	Total
Agree	205	209	414
Disagree	48	44	92
Total	253	253	506
Expected Values			
	Intention to use	Usage Behavioral	Total
Agree	207	207	414
Disagree	46	46	92
Total	253	253	506
Chi-Test	0.644767958		
Df	1		
Alpha	0.05		
P-Value	0.421989506		
Chi-crit	3.841458821		

3.841459149 > 0.644767959
Acceptance of H0 and rejection of H1
There is no Significant difference between intention to use and usage behavioral

Table 5 indicates that effort expectancy and performance expectancy have a great impact on usage behavior when they are controlled by gender and this is justifiable as individual differences such as gender, age and level of education' significantly affect the way information technology is used.

To predict the behavioral intention of the respondents, regression analysis was employed. The coefficient of the model determines to what extent information estimation were trusted and the significance determined whether the information was accepted or rejected. Referring to the model, intention to use is the dependent variable while effort expectancy and performance expectancy are the independent variables. Table 6 below shows the beta of both independent variables that positively affect the intention to use with the significance of less than 0.01; the factors are then significant at 99%... which indicate that the first hypothesis is accepted.

Table 7 illustrates the investigation of the third hypothesis which indicates effort expectancy and performance expectancy have a great impact on intention and usage behavior when controlled by age with significance less than 0.01; the factors are then significant at 99% which indicates that the hypothesis is accepted.

Table 8 indicates that effort expectancy and performance expectancy affect the intention and usage behavior when both controlled by gender, with a significance less than 0.05; the factors are then significant at 95%, which indicates that the hypothesis is accepted.

In examining the effect of the two variables effort expectancy and performance expectancy on intention and usage behavior when controlled by education,

Table 5. Significant between gender and usage behavior

Hypothesis testing
H0: Gender No significant differences Usage
H1: Gender Significant differences Usage
Observed values
Ease of use Usage Total
Male 95 80 175
Female 158 173 331
Total 253 253 506
Expected values
Ease of use Usage Total
Male 87.5 87.5 175
Female 165.5 165.5 331
Total 253 253 506
Chi-Value 0.160929242
df 1
Alpha 0.05
P-Value 0.688302424
Chi-crit 3.841458821
3.841459149 > 0.1609239
Acceptance of H0 and rejection of H1
There is no significant difference between gender and usage

Table 6. Significance between effort expectancy, performance expectancy and intention to use

Model Unstandardized coefficients Standardized coefficients t Sig. 95.0% Confidence interval for B
B Std. error Beta Lower bound Upper bound
1 (Constant) 2.951 .237 12.431 .000 2.484 3.419
Effort expectancy .295 .084 .334 3.495 .001 .129 .462
Performance expectancy .131 .064 .180 2.041 .042 .005 .257

Table 7. Effort expectancy and performance expectancy significantly affect usage controlled by age

Model	Unstandardized coefficients		Standardized coefficients	t	Sig.
	B	Std. Error	Beta		
(Constant)	2.951	.237	.334	12.431	.000
Effort expectancy	.295	.084	.180	3.495	.001
Performance expectancy	.131	.064		2.041	0.42
Age	.024	.053	.029	.451	.652

Table 8. Effort expectancy and performance expectancy significantly affects usage controlled by gender

Model		Unstandardized coefficients		Standardized coefficients	t	Sig.
		B	Std. Error	Beta		
1	(Constant)	2.951	.237		12.431	.000
	Effort expectancy	.295	.084	.334	3.495	.001
	Performance expectancy	.131	.064	.180	2.041	.042
	Gender	-.068	.114	-.035	-.592	.554

Table 9. Effort expectancy and performance expectancy significantly affects usage controlled by education

Model		Unstandardized coefficients		Standardized coefficients	t	Sig.
		B	Std. Error	Beta		
1	(Constant) Effort expectancy Performance expectancy	3.635 .203 .138	.466 .124 .100	.180 .149	7.802 1.633 1.381	.000 .105 .170
	Education	-.022	.110	-.018	-.202	.840

Table 9 indicates that education, as a controlled variable, has no significant effect on intention and usage behavior, and is therefore rejected.

7. CONCLUSION AND RECOMMENDATIONS

This study identified various factors that contribute to the adoption and usage of Instagram by productive families in Bahrain. Two of the UTAUT theoretical model's variables were incorporated to help in analyses: "effort expectancy" and "performance expectancy". The analysis revealed that both factors influenced the families' intention to adopt and use Instagram, which directly correlated to the actual usage. Meanwhile, the three controlled variables, age, gender and level of education, had an indirect affect.

The results also showed that effort expectancy and performance expectancy, as controlled by age, gender and level of education, had a great influence on productive families' intention to adopt and use Instagram. Therefore, it is concluded that these families highly intend to use Instagram, which has in turn resulted in the adoption and use of this technology.

We recommend that the productive Bahraini families should focus on adopting and using Instagram for their businesses. In addition, institutional backers such as The Ministry of Social Development should focus on increasing the usefulness level of Instagram through the creation of accounts for productive families who do not have them or have difficulty using the technology due to their age or low level of education. In addition, workshops and training sessions are needed to spread social awareness of the usefulness and ease of use of Instagram how this technology could help productive families to build strong relationships with their customers and gain more profit.

REFERENCES

Abbott, W., Donaghey, J., Hare, J., & Hopkins, P. (2013). An Instagram is Worth a Thousand Words: An Industry Panel and Audience Q&A. *Library Hi Tech News, 30*(7), 1–6. doi:10.1108/LHTN-08-2013-0047

Babb, A., & Nelson, A. (2013). Instagram and the ethics of privacy. Retrieved from http://www.scu.edu/ethics-center/ethicsblog/globaldialog.cfm?c=15267

Bakhshi, S., Shamma, D. A., & Gilbert, E. (2014). Faces Engage Us: Photos with Faces Attract More Likes and Comments on Instagram. *Proceedings of CHI 2014* (pp. 965-974). ACM Press. doi:10.1145/2556288.2557403

Boyd, D., & Ellison, N. (2007). Social network sites: Definition, History, and Scholarship. *Journal of Computer-Mediated Communication, 13*(1), 210–230. doi:10.1111/j.1083-6101.2007.00393.x

Chen, J., Xu, H., & Whinston, A. B. (2011). Moderated online communities and quality of user-generated content. *Journal of Management Information Systems, 28*(2), 237–268. doi:10.2753/MIS0742-1222280209

Dennis, D. (2014). Successfully social: A non-profit's guide to modern social media marketing. Senior Honors Theses. Retrieved from http://digitalcommons.liberty.edu/honors/454

Edosomwan, S. (2011). The History of Social Media and its Impact on Business. *The Journal of Applied Management and Entrepreneurship*, 16(3).

Endres, A. M., & Harper, D. A. (2013). 'Wresting meaning from the market': A reassessment of Ludwig Lachmann's entrepreneur. *Journal of Institutional Economics*, *9*(3), 303–308. doi:10.1017/S174413741300009X

Gupta, V. (2000). SPSS for Beginners: Regression explained in simple terms. VJBooks Inc.

Hassan, A. (2014). Do brands targeting women use instamarketing differently: A content analyses, *Proceedings of the Marketing Management Association* (p. 62).

Herman, J. (2014). How to use Instagram to improve your marketing. *Maximizesocialbusiness.* Retrieved from http://maximizesocialbusiness.com/use-instagram-improve-marketing-13043/

Jang, J., Han, K., Shih, P., & Lee, D. (2015). Generation like: Comparative Characteristics in Instagram. *Proceedings of the 33rd Annual ACM Conference on Human Factors in Computing Systems* (pp. 4039-4042). Retrieved from http://www.pbs.org/wgbh/pages/frontline/generation-like/

Juinn, P., & Bing Tan. (2013) Applying the UTAUT to Understand Factors Affecting the Use of English E-Learning Websites in Taiwan. DOI:10.1177/2158244013503837

Kietzmann, J. (2011). Social media? Get serious! Understanding the functional building blocks of social media. *Business Horizons*, 54(3).241-251.

Massimo, G., Croce, A., & Grilli, L. (2013). ICT services and small businesses' productivity gains: An analysis of the adoption of broadband Internet technology. *Information Economics and Policy*, *25*(3), 171–189. doi:10.1016/j.infoecopol.2012.11.001

Modimogale, L., & Kroeze, J. (2011). The Role of ICT within Small and Medium Enterprises in Gauteng. *Communications of the IBIMA*. Retrieved from http://www.ibimapublishing.com/journals/CIBIMA/cibima.html

Naaman, M. (2012). Social multimedia: Highlighting opportunities for search and mining of multimedia data in social media applications. *Journal of Multimedia Tools and Applications.*, *56*(1), 9–34. doi:10.1007/s11042-010-0538-7

Salomon, D. (2013). Moving on from Facebook: Using Instagram to connect with undergraduates and engage in teaching and learning. *College & Research Libraries News*, *74*(8), 408–412.

Schubert, P., Fisher, J., & Leimstoll, U. (2007) ICT and Innovation in Small Companies. *Proceedings of ECIS 2007.* Retrieved from http://aisel.aisnet.org/ecis2007/117

Shah Alam, M., & Mohammad Noor, K. (2009). ICT Adoption in Small and Medium Enterprises: An Empirical Evidence of Service Sectors in *Malaysia. International Journal of Business and Management*, *4*(2), 112–125. Retrieved from www.ccseret.org/Journal.html

Shirky, C. (2009). Here comes everybody: The power of organizing without organizations.

Smits, M., & Mogos, S. (2010). The impact of social media on Business performance. *Proceedings of the 21st European Conference on Information Systems.*

Ting, H. (2015). Beliefs about the Use of Instagram: An exploratory. *International Journal of Business and Innovation.*, *2*(2), 15–31.

Venkatesh, et al.. (2003). User Acceptance of Information Technology: Toward a Unified View. *Management Information Systems Quarterly*, *27*(3), 425–478. Retrieved from http://www.jstor.org/stable/30036540

Yuheng, H., Manikonda, L., & Kambhampati, S. (2014). What we Instagram: A first analysis of Instagram photo Content and User types. *Proceedings of the eighth International AAAI Conference on Weblogs and Social Media.*

This research was previously published in the International Journal of Technology Diffusion (IJTD), 7(3); edited by Ali Hussein Saleh Zolait, pages 21-32, copyright year 2016 by IGI Publishing (an imprint of IGI Global).

Section 2
Branding, Consumer Engagement, and CRM

Chapter 19
Social Media Intelligence for Business

Sérgio Maravilhas
University of Porto, Portugal & Salvador University, Brazil

ABSTRACT

Social Media intelligence allow the knowledge of competitor's moves and the analysis of trends from the communications exchanged in the networks of individual consumers, making it easy for companies to develop solutions according to their clients and prospects desires. There are several characteristics that describe the quality of information that will allow the analysis of the value of the information used. Information is an important aid in the decision making process and must be of quality to improve its value. Marketing trends and competitive information is needed to clear decision-making about what products develop, for what customers, at what cost, through which distribution channels, reducing the uncertainty that a new product/service development always brings. Learning how to extract quality information, unbiased, valuable for business, from these social tools is the aim of this work, sharing with the interested parties some ways of using it for their profit and competitive sustainability.

INTRODUCTION

After World War II, in 1948, Claude Shannon formulated "The Mathematical Theory of Communication", better known by "Theory of Information" (Gleick, 2011). At the same time two almost simultaneous inventions, the transistor and the digital computer came to reveal themselves with an enormous revolutionary potential when the social effects of their application, producing new goods and services were discovered, especially in the production and distribution of a new immaterial good and service: the information (Castells, 2000). Information, opposite to material goods, is infinitely expandable, doesn't waste itself (meaning that we can give an information without losing it, which may allow us to give it to several people, something we can't do with a material good), and once created difficult to vanish (although its economical value may decrease). It's easy to transport and distribute and the costs of keeping it in data warehouses is lesser every day. The speed and easiness in processing and transporting information electronically, it's almost instantaneous ability in feed itself, start to subvert the traditional

DOI: 10.4018/978-1-5225-5637-4.ch019

ways of labour division, fragmentation, expertise and centralization of the human experience and its sociological configuration (Cleveland, 1983, 1985).

Some authors (Brown & Duguid, 2000; Castells, 2000, 2004; Webster, 2000) observed that a huge transformation is taking place; that we are moving towards a society that is no longer dependant in a massive industrialization or agriculture. They often talk about the knowledge and information based transformation of the world economy we are living in, with flux and flows of information gaining advantage to the exchange of goods. This notion is interconnected with the birth of the information technology, characterized by computers and electronic means of producing and transmitting information at the speed of light through a network of other technological apparatus (Godeluck, 2000).

We are living in an information society (IS) (Webster, 2000) where organizational and personal life are mediated by information and knowledge (Castells, 2000; Negroponte, 1995), with the help of technologies that gather, disseminate and deliver that raw material to support our decisions (McGee & Prusak, 1995; Penzias, 1995; Tapscott, 1995; Tapscott & Williams, 2008; Ward & Peppard, 2002).

Nowadays, we tend to call information society to the constraints we move in, sociologically interpreted. An IS, tend to describe a society no longer based in the production of materials, goods, production means, but in the production of knowledge.

Information, as a tool to reduce uncertainty and to develop knowledge in organizations (Best, 1996b; Kahaner, 1997; Porter & Millar, 1985), is an important aid in the decision making process and must be of quality to improve its value (Best, 1996b; Beuren, 1998; Choo, 2003; Davenport, Marchand, & Dickson, 2004; Marchand & Horton Jr., 1986; Tapscott, 1999; Wilson, 1985, 1987).

In the globalized world we are living in, quality information warrants best results when competing with other organizations (Brophy & Coulling, 1996; Redman, 1996; Wormell, 1990). Its value is related to the results that it will allow obtaining and it's dependable on its context (Best, 1996b; Davenport, 1997; Marchand & Horton Jr., 1986; Orna, 1999; Penzias, 1989; Tapscott, 1995; Tapscott, Ticoll, & Lowy, 2000).

Quality information is needed to clear decision-making about what products develop, for what customers, at what cost, through which distribution channels, reducing the uncertainty that a new product/service development always brings with it (Garber, 2001; Kotler, Armstrong, Saunders, & Wong, 1999; Mohr, Sengupta, & Slater, 2010; Scott, 2008; Trott, 2008).

Competitive Intelligence (CI) aims to monitor a firm's external environment for information relevant to its decision-making process (Choo, 2003).

Intelligence activities are based on the intelligence cycle. The intelligence cycle involves accurately identifying your information needs, collecting relevant information, analysing it, communicating the results to the people who need it, and taking rapid and appropriate action (Besson & Possin, 1996; Martinet & Marti, 1995; Taborda & Ferreira, 2002).

As an excellent information source, the Internet provides significant opportunities for CI (Sage, 2013).

Internet search engines have been widely used to facilitate information search on the Internet (Gomes & Braga, 2001; Taborda & Ferreira, 2002). However, many problems minimize their effective use in CI research (Bedell, 2011; Kahaner, 1997).

Many major companies, such as Ernst & Young, Motorola, Xerox, and almost all the pharmaceutical companies, have formal and well-organized CI units that enable managers to make informed decisions about critical business matters such as investment, marketing, and strategic planning (Prescott & Miller, 2002).

Traditionally, CI relied upon published company reports and other kinds of printed information. In recent years, Internet has rapidly become an extremely good source of information about the competitive environment of companies (Hawthorne & Cromity, 2012; Ojala, 2012; Revelli, 2000; Sage, 2013).

Although the Internet represents significant CI opportunities, it has also many technical, cognitive, and organizational challenges. The amount of information available on the Internet is gigantic, so, CI professionals are constantly facing the problem of information overload (Barbosa & O'Reilly, 2011; Dearlove, 1998). "Information overload is a real phenomenon, but progress is being made in tapping into social media to increase marketing intelligence" (Hawthorne & Cromity, 2012, p.38).

Much time and effort is required for CI professionals to search for relevant information on the Internet and then analyze the information collected in the correct context.

Internet search engines have been useful in helping people search for information on the Internet. Nevertheless, the exponential growth of information sources on the Internet and the unregulated and dynamic nature of many Web sites are making it increasingly difficult to locate useful information using these search engines (Scott, 2008).

Social Media tools allow the knowledge of competitor's moves and the analysis of trends from the communications exchanged in the networks of individual consumers (Russell, 2011; Tsvetovat & Kouznetsov, 2011), making it easy for companies to develop solutions according to their clients and prospects desires (Berthon, Pitt, Plangger, & Shapiro, 2012; Bramston, 2009; Burgelman, Christensen, & Wheelwright, 2009; Canhoto, 2013; Christensen, Anthony, & Roth, 2004; Kotze, 2013).

Web 2.0 and Social Media are more than tools where you can keep track of your old school and college friends (Bedell, 2011). Due to the amount of information exchanged in these platforms, companies can look at Web 2.0 tools like Wikis, Blogs, Social Networking sites and so forth, to check for some pieces of information that come in first hand to these communication tools (Berkman, 2008; Brown, 2012; Canhoto, 2013; Kotze, 2013). If we have enough patience, it will pay off the time spent in this activity because it will be possible to identify micro-trends that have not yet gained momentum (Sage, 2013).

Companies can use this information, from these social tools, for competitor surveillance, consumer satisfaction monitoring, trend development and technology watch.

There are not, yet, many bibliographic resources dealing with this subject, because it's still a new medium that needs to be proved and tested, that is being currently used to perform competitive strategies so companies can excel in their areas of business (Berthon, Pitt, Plangger, & Shapiro, 2012).

Learning how to extract quality information, unbiased, valuable for business, from these social tools is the aim of this work, sharing with the interested parties some ways of using it for their profit and competitive sustainability.

If properly done, this monitoring activity even allows a company to measure the level of satisfaction of its own employees by the analysis of the content of what they post online about their employer (Ojala, 2012).

That gives you clues about improvements and changes to be made.

We will start explaining the value of information for businesses, and afterwards describing CI and Social Networking, identifying some tools that will ease monitoring requirements, and conclude with a few ideas for analyzing Blogs, Wikis and Tag Clouds to identify consumer signals and trends (Barbosa & O'Reilly, 2011; Canhoto, 2013; Higham, 2010; Kotze, 2013; Rasquilha, 2010; Scott, 2008).

We will survey the applications of Web 2.0 relative to CI and consumer trends, and explore approaches of gathering information for CI through Web 2.0. Some applications of Web 2.0 (Blog, Wiki, RSS and Tag Clouds) are discussed for CI and business intelligence use.

THE VALUE OF ACCURATE INFORMATION FOR BUSINESS

According to Best it's not easy to assign a value to information and there is no "commonly accepted and universally applicable way of valuing the information resource" (1996a, p. 14).

Burk and Horton define information value as "the value attributed to information produced or acquired by organizations, entities and persons, and delivered in the form of an information product or service". For them, this value can be perceived immediately but, sometimes, this valuation occurs only several years later like in the case of "the values attached to information created by scientific research" that "are often realized long after it is created" (Burk Jr. & Horton Jr., 1988, p. 79).

Orna also points out the fact that information has no implicit value in itself since it depends on its use, purpose and context (1996, p. 20).

Wagner states that the "terms value and quality share a common meaning: the degree of excellence, but the former also denotes an economic exchange worth" (1990, p. 69), being the value of information and not the quality of information the preferred concept.

For Orna, the functional part of valuing can be defined as "the process of determining and applying appropriate criteria for estimating the value of things" (1996, p. 19).

An indirect valuation occurs, and the measures used are the value of the investment in information technologies used to hold the information, the costs associated with staff that collects and maintains the information resources, or the value the information has when it's put to a specific use.

To explain why the process of valuing is so difficult, we must remember that "fixing a value is always an indirect process that involves finding appropriate equivalents and standards, not necessarily or always in money terms, and the estimation of those who use it has to be taken into account as well" (Orna, 1996, p. 19).

McPherson (1994, pp. 207, 208) proposes three models for information valuing. The first one is related with the cognition process, in which the value is dependent on the contribution of information to the achievement of organizational goals. The second relates to the value of information when it enhances the knowledge not only in the user's brain but also in external, operational and recognizable actions that are observable. The third deals with traditional accounting, highly cost oriented that does not recognize the value of information unless it can be sold externally as a good or product.

Orna, to make this clearer, says that "to have value, information has to be transformed by human minds into knowledge, without which no products of tangible value can be created or exchanged" (1999, p. 141). That occurs because the valuation has three parts, the value triangle: i) object; ii) human judgement; iii) use to which person judging puts the object. It's a three way relationship, involving human judgment, based on the relationship between the object valued and the person that judges and evaluates, and the relationship between that object and the uses that the human will put the object into. It also involves criteria, which imply thinking and feeling (1999, pp. 143, 144).

What we can observe is that it's not easy to apply to information the traditional economic and accounting measures applied to tangible products, the cost-benefit analysis.

Nevertheless, it's important to do so in order to avoid "failure to spot potential threats in time because of lack of intelligence gathering and correlations; failure in attempts to innovate; (…) and failure to recognize opportunities for using information resources more productively" (Orna, 1996, p. 25).

Information is called the 'glue' that holds the organizational structure together, and there are four ways of using information to create value for a business: i) minimize risks; ii) reduce costs; iii) add value, orienting the output to the market and customers; iv) innovation, through the creation of new realities (Davenport, 1997; Davenport et al., 2004).

Characteristics of Valuable Information

Information has some characteristics that differentiate it from tangible products, such as: "If information is exchanged and traded, the value from using it can increase for all parties to the transaction. The value of information is not diminished by being used; it can be (...) used many times by many users for adding value to many activities and outputs" (Orna, 1999, p. 141).

Cleveland (1985, pp. 29-33) highlights the value of information and its characteristics, saying that information is: i) expandable – the more we have, the more we use and more valuable it gets; ii) compressible – can be concentrated, integrated, summarized, miniaturized for easier handling; iii) substitutable – replaces land, labour and capital; iv) transportable – at the speed of light, using e-mail or video-conference we can be anywhere like if we were there; v) diffusive – it tends to leak and the more it leaks the more we have and the more of us have it, making it available to a growing number of people; vi) shareable – allows exchange and sharing transactions because giving or selling a information lets the seller to keep it anyway, unlike physical goods.

For Grant (2002, pp. 242; 245, 246; 516), information is the medium through which an organization relates to its environment and allows the individuals to know how to react and adapt to external changes. For him, the value of information is related to what he designates "imperfect availability of information" and "imperfection of information". If, in a given market, not all the players have access to all the information available, or it's difficult to identify all the information needed to decide effectively in accordance to other competitor's moves, then the ones who possess or know the sources where the information needed exists, have a competitive advantage in that market.

This is going to be very important because even if all the players have access to the same information, again it will be the use that they make of it that is going to distinguish the success that they can obtain. It's only after the information gets inside someone's mind and is applied and put to use in something useful, like a product or a process that has the preference of the consumers in that market, that it becomes valuable and originates a big return on investment to his owner, the "value for money" valuation (Best, 1996a; Grant, 2002; Kotler et al., 1999; Mohr et al., 2010; Orna, 1996, 1999).

Even if everybody can access quality patent information, not everyone will innovate thanks to that. Furthermore, not everyone that does innovate will be successful because the results will be dependent on the output obtained and the accession of the consumers to the solution found, that is to say, it will depend on the product's characteristics, on its adequacy to the market and its consumers' needs, and on consumer satisfaction.

Again, a method to value information can be "through seeking indirect evidence of its value to businesses in promoting competitiveness, productivity, or innovation and successful marketing of the results" (Orna, 1996, p. 26), "and in avoiding risk and reducing uncertainty" (Orna, 1999, p. 142).

Although an information can be valuable for a long period of time, certain types of information are only valuable within a given time frame limit (Huang, Lee, & Wang, 1998). Information may lose its value because its timing has passed, like if you could knew the lottery numbers in advance for a certain week, after that week those numbers would be useless, or "a tip on the fourth race at Belmont might be valuable at lunchtime and valueless by dinnertime. Yesterday's weather forecast is of merely historical interest tomorrow" (Cleveland, 1985, p. 29). Nevertheless, some information retains its value and can be applied in the same field or in complementary fields, enhancing the final result obtained with this strategy.

COMPETITIVE INTELLIGENCE AND BUSINESS MANAGEMENT

CI is the use of public sources to develop information about the competition, consumers, and market environment (Miller & Business Intelligence Braintrust, 2002).

CI is different from espionage (Bergier, 1970; Fialka, 1997; Guisnel, 1997; Rustmann Jr., 2002; Winkler, 1997), which implies illegal means of information gathering. CI is restrained to the gathering of public information (Kahaner, 1997; Mordecai, 2013c).

One of the main differences between CI and general business information, such as business growth rate and operating ratios, is that CI is of strategic importance on the organization. It is not only the collection of information from a variety of sources, but also the analysis and synthesis of such information, which could help the company decide the course of action to improve its position (Choo, 2003).

Because of the broad reach and potential of CI, involvement in intelligence activities can provide first-class training for managers and marketers. In fact, an increasing number of leading companies insist that their best people spend some time in intelligence operations prior to promotion to the highest ranks (Miller & Business Intelligence Braintrust, 2002; Prescott & Miller, 2002; Taborda & Ferreira, 2002).

Intelligence must be passed to decision makers in a timely manner, and in a style and format that will encourage them to take appropriate measures and decisions. Intelligence reports and briefings should aim, above all, for clarity and brevity, and should provide the decision maker with suggestions or recommendations for action (Besson & Possin, 1996; Choo, 2003; Garber, 2001; Martinet & Marti, 1995).

Figure 1. The competitive intelligence process (http://www.sajim.co.za/index.php/SAJIM/article/view/559/667)

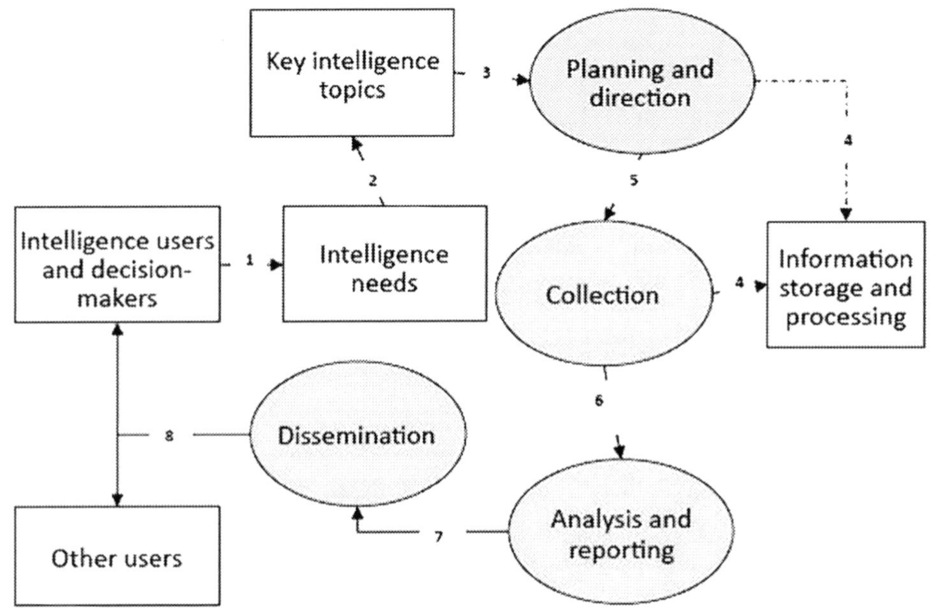

Executives have a major part to play in ensuring the success of your intelligence activities. Among other things, they must offer commitment, involvement, and support (Johnson, 2005; Prescott & Miller, 2002). Managers have a part to play in making intelligence activities successful because they already spend lots of time talking with others and that enables them to collect information. However, it is essential that they keep their intelligence manager informed of any significant change in the business environment (Miller & Business Intelligence Braintrust, 2002; Prescott & Miller, 2002).

A typical CI process consists of a series of business activities that involve identifying, gathering, developing, analyzing and disseminating information (Besson & Possin, 1996; Martinet & Marti, 1995; Taborda & Ferreira, 2002).

Every competitor broadcasts a large amount of data to you in their advertising and their product itself. Every feature that they have in their products and every special technique that's part of their service is data you can use. (Mordecai, 2013c)

The following list shows a typical sequence in which these activities take place: i) identify competitors, markets, customers, suppliers, or other variables in the environment to be monitored. Identify what information is to be collected; ii) specifically identify possible sources of information and collect the information from these sources; iii) evaluate the validity, reliability, and usefulness of the information collected; iv) gather information collected from different sources and integrate them; v) interpret and analyze the information for strategic or tactical significance. Draw conclusions and recommend actions; vi) disseminate and present analyzed findings to management; vii) respond to ad hoc inquiries for decision support (Ribault, Martinet, & Lebidois, 1995).

According to Goldman (2011), three tools deserve a visit to enlighten us about what our competitors are doing: AdGooroo (https://www.adgooroo.com/), SpyFu (http://www.spyfu.com/), and The Search Monitor (http://www.thesearchmonitor.com/). Also, in social media some tools are available for free (http://www.socialmediaexaminer.com/4-free-tools-to-analyze-your-social-media-competitors/?awt_l=4Yt0yp&awt_m=3Y_vqm1Acgr.ILT&utm_source=Newsletter&utm_medium=NewsletterIssue&utm_campaign=New).

Information gathering and information analysis are the key areas of the CI process.

Competitive Intelligence and the Internet

The Internet is currently the most popular medium for gathering information and it has enormous advantages for that function (Russell, 2011; Tsvetovat & Kouznetsov, 2011). At the same time, it calls for a minimum level of expertise if it is to be effective. For instance, you need to be able to find specific information (Berkman, 2008), and that calls for familiarity with search engines and sophisticated retrieval techniques (Prior, 2006, 2007).

Nevertheless, "search engines are severely lacking in the realm of exploratory search. (...) If you want to find new things with which you're unfamiliar, the online world has a market gap" (Hawthorne & Cromity, 2012, p. 36). Social Media can reduce that gap (Safko, 2010).

With very few exceptions, standards for citing and classifying information are poor, unenforceable or non-existent, and there is a distinct absence of identifying information (metadata) (Chen, Chau, & Zeng, 2002). "Content often lacks depth and substance, and it is almost impossible to distinguish be-

Figure 2. The Intelligence Cycle (Taborda & Ferreira, 2002, p. 36)

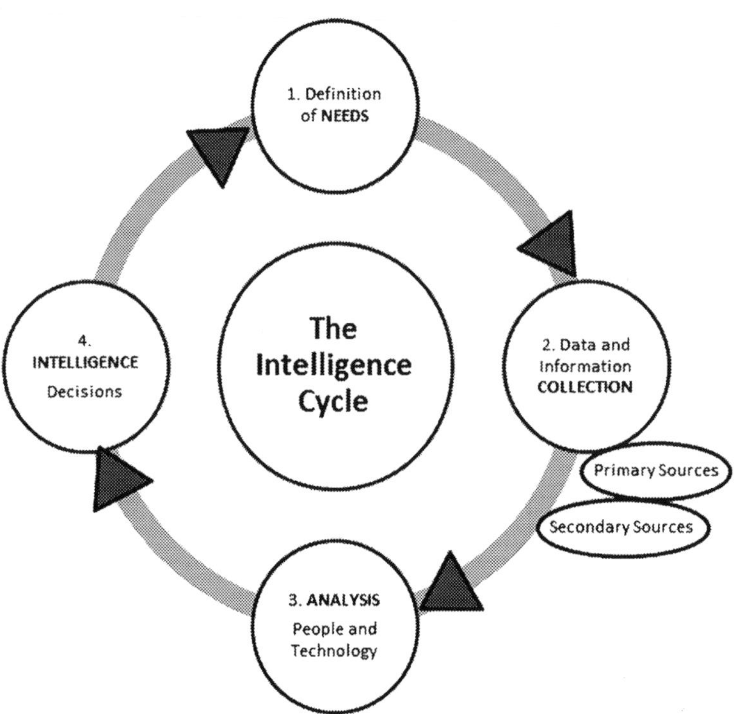

tween fact, editorial, advertising and news. But, many of these disadvantages will be overcome with time" (Prior, 2007).

Commercial online databases, such as Dialog (http://www.dialog.com) and Lexis-Nexis (http://www.lexisnexis.com), contain a large amount of well-organized information on a variety of subjects, storing information ranging from company annual reports to US patent documents, and from history journals to chemistry periodicals (Chen et al., 2002; Taborda & Ferreira, 2002). These commercial databases are among the major sources used by CI professionals (Herring, 2002).

"Recent years have seen the tremendous growth of the Internet. Many commercial online databases are now accessible through the Internet. The Internet also enables organizations to monitor and search the websites of their competitors, alliances, and possible collaborators" (Chen et al., 2002). Internet-based information sources are becoming increasingly important in the CI process (Guisnel, 1997). "In the old days, corporate intelligence gathering meant painstakingly gleaning information from experts and competitors' reports, subscribing to expensive online data aggregators such as Factiva or Dialog, and scanning unstructured documents from the media" (Kotze, 2013).

Corporate Web sites usually contain useful information, including company history, corporate overviews, business visions and missions, product overviews, financial data, sales figures, annual reports, press releases, biographies of top executives, locations of offices, hiring ads, among others (Godeluck, 2000; Weiss, 2008).

The data is "valuable in providing direct or indirect contextual information and enable the CI professionals to analyze corporate strategies. Another reason attracting CI professionals to use the Internet is that most of the contents available on the Internet are free of charge" (Chen et al., 2002). In fact, Internet is now one of the most important resources for CI information collection (Deng & Luo, 2007; Kirsch, Gregory, Brown, & Charley, 2006).

Corporate or employees Wikis and Blogs also contain a vast amount of useable information because everybody likes to tell in what they are working, what are they good at, the results that they were capable of reaching with their work, the goals and objectives they provided and so on (Turchi, 2012).

As Kotze (2013) declares "none of the employee's actions were 'leaks' and taken alone they are all innocuous. But taken together they may reveal more than the company wants. For the competitive intelligence professional at the competitor they are a vital stream of information".

Managers tend to think that more information is better. In today's business environment, however, it is not necessarily true. CI professionals could be spending too much time and effort on data collection rather than data analysis. For CI professionals to manually access the Internet, extract and analyse the information on every single Web page at a company Web site to locate the useful information, and to synthesize information is very exhausting and time consuming.

Fuld alerts that "tracking social media activity can provide many benefits", being five the main reasons to use social media for competitor insight: i) Identify key influencers; ii) Measure Marketing metrics; iii) Illuminate investment decisions; iv) Determine share of voice; v) Develop early warning indicators (http://insights.fuld.com/hs-fs/hub/17073/file-1376907966-pdf/Resources/5_Reasons_to_Use_Social_Media_for_Competitor_Insights.pdf).

To address this information and cognitive overload problem, research has been conducted in developing techniques and tools to analyze, categorize, and visualize large collections of Web pages, among other text documents. (Chen et al., 2002)

In turn, a variety of tools have been developed to assist searching, gathering, monitoring and analyzing information on the Internet (Guisnel, 1997; Prescott & Miller, 2002; Revelli, 2000)[1].

Figure 3. Information Gathering on the Internet (http://www.fuld.com/resources/ - adapted)

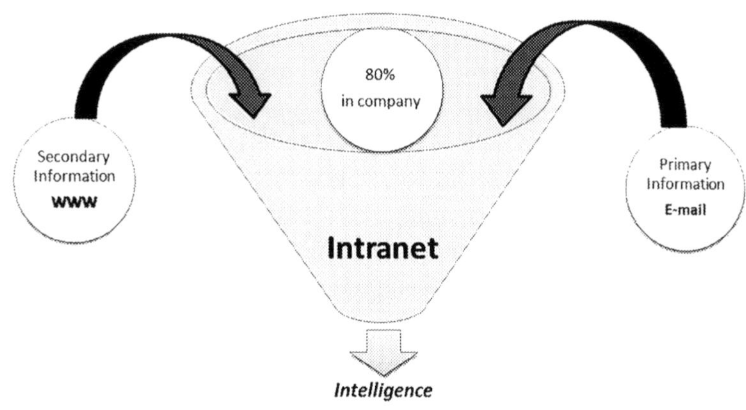

SOCIAL MEDIA NETWORKING

Social Networks, made possible by Web 2.0, are one of several next generation communications and collaboration tools that include Blogs, Wikis and Social Bookmarking.

Participants worldwide contribute to and collaborate in readily available online discussions, creating new knowledge bases that can become recognized as information sources (https://dro.deakin.edu.au/eserv/DU:30049105/scheepers-understandingtherole-2012.pdf).

Kane declares that "Social Media technologies may be particularly disruptive for business because they undermine some of the key reasons why companies survive or thrive" (http://sloanreview.mit.edu/article/why-social-media-will-fundamentally-change-business/).

Web 2.0 technologies transform broadcast media monologues (one to many) into social media dialogues (many to many). Social media is the product of internet-based applications that build on the technological foundations of Web 2.0. (Berthon, Pitt, Plangger, & Shapiro, 2012, p. 263)

Social networks are free to join, to search for a vast amount of reference questions, and to find experts for all kinds of requirements and research projects (Qualman, 2010).

The concept of a social network, meaning a social structure made of nodes (which are generally individuals or organizations) that are tied by one or more specific types of interdependency, is as valuable as the number of nodes that constitute it (Castells, 2004; Tapscott & Williams, 2008).

This means that, the bigger the number of nodes, the more valuable that network becomes (Godeluck, 2000).

With this in mind, it's easy to perceive that this trend in modern communication and interaction among humans will be very important to achieve results that it will be very difficult with other non-interactive means (Tapscott, 1995, 1999; Tapscott et al., 2000; Tapscott & Williams, 2008).

The relation of confidence among each node will open a number of possibilities that a traditional media, like TV or Newspapers, couldn't impose simply because we don't know who those people are or, if we do, we know that they are trying to earn something at our expenses (Tapscott et al., 2000).

With this new possibility, either we know the person communicating with us, or we know someone who knows him/her. That condition gives us the confidence and trust that will induce the preference on a certain product or service and makes us discard others. That's basic consumer behaviour (Scott, 2008).

For companies, this new possibility can be the most important decision of all times. It will allow to transform our brand in a major player among the preferences of customers (Carrera, 2012b; Hortinha, 2002; Mohr et al., 2010).

With Social Media companies can gain a better knowledge of their business environment, using visual tools that can enhance the analysis of the huge amount of posts, comments, and shares (Mordecai, 2013b).

Also for employees, that can be a major source of information and knowledge, because we can now access the information we need among a network of thousands of specialists in a certain subject that can answer us almost immediately saving us precious time in the searching process (Libert & Spector, 2009; Surowiecki, 2007).

If someone thought that social networking was only for the youngsters, like with MySpace (http://www.myspace.com), or with Facebook (https://www.facebook.com), that is a huge mistake. Web 2.0 introduced many new types of applications for users to express their thoughts, concerns, needs, desires and level of satisfaction with what they buy (Berthon, Pitt, Plangger, & Shapiro, 2012; Hawthorne & Cromity, 2012; Shapiro, & Varian, 1999).

This allows, in a very fast and inexpensive manner, to scan the trends of a market, understand consumer motivation and the actual preferences in the business area where companies act and compete (Rasquilha, 2010)[2].

New applications of Web 2.0 provide new opportunities for CI, such as Web Blogs (Blogs) which are created by thousands of individuals (Blood, 2004; Deng & Luo, 2007), Wikis (ex. Wikipedia) which allow public group creation, RSS (Rich Site Summary or Really Simple Syndication) using XML (Extensible Markup Language) to classify and organize the information (Tsvetovat & Kouznetsov, 2011) making it more transparent and open (Carrera, 2012b; Hortinha, 2002; Scott, 2008).

All of them bring convenience for CI especially in collecting information. "In the view of CI, Web 2.0 paved new ways and channels for gathering information" (Deng & Luo, 2007).

All this tools, like Blogs and Wikis, provide intelligence for consumer trend monitoring (Barbosa & O'Reilly, 2011; Higham, 2010; Rasquilha, 2010; Sage, 2013).

In conjunction with existing consumer intelligence and CI resources, Social Networks can highlight significant issues that affect your brands, identify competitor weaknesses, opportunities in the marketplace and those specific to a brand (Qualman, 2010).

Monitoring Blogs and Podcasts can help develop actionable solutions to fuel organizations (Carrera, 2009, 2012a, 2012b; Hortinha, 2002)

When looking at Blogs and Wikis, we must also look at some of the networking sites, like LinkedIn.com, Xing.com, Facebook.com, Myspace.com, and search tools for people such as Zoominfo.com for company and competitor employees. Sites like these will mention what people are doing, their interests and past achievements. This information is very valuable because contacts can be found easily. "Sites such as LinkedIn.com and Xing.com allow you to see where people used to work as well as where they are now. The networking sites can also be searched using tools such as yoname.com and wink.com" (Weiss, 2008).

Figure 4. The Social Media Landscape (http://wiki.telfer.uottawa.ca/ci-wiki/index.php/CI_and_my_generation:_Competitive_intelligence_and_social_media)

Also, creative consumers help companies developing new and better products by their feedback on using them and what to improve for better results (Berthon, Pitt, Plangger, & Shapiro, 2012).

Although Social Media includes Blogs, Podcasts, Wikis and more, we will just explore some of them, and will demonstrate how monitoring and analyzing what consumers create on Blogs and Wikis can enrich our understanding of their needs and desires (Higham, 2010; Hortinha, 2002; Kotler et al., 1999; Rasquilha, 2010; Scott, 2008), and thus support our CI efforts.

Online Social Networking for Business Intelligence

Online Social Networking enables us to find people who may not be familiar with our organisation, becoming quality prospects and then effective clients, creating an opportunity to connect with them and sell them our products and services (http://www.knime.org/files/knime_social_media_white_paper.pdf).

Social Networking offers a high level of integration, and focuses on the sharing elements of the various applications. Sharing resources can increase the possibility of finding relevant information, like sharing our favourite bookmarks or photos and in return having access to the favourite resources of others who share our interests. It can mean being able to read comments and chat with people on topics of shared interest and being able to tap into collective knowledge (Russell, 2011)[3].

If we already know someone in that network, we can feel more comfortable that they can become quality prospects. And, because of that mutual connection, we can overcome difficulties and begin a business relationship with more trust (Bolander, 2015).

These "new tools, based on social networking and deployed on mobile devices, are enabling companies to streamline operations, enhance customer satisfaction and improve financial performance across their entire businesses" (Bedell, 2011), allowing to accurately perform a SWOT (Strengths, Weaknesses, Opportunities and Threats) analysis to scan the macro-environment where the company develops its activity (Mordecai, 2013a).

Some advantages are that you can contact people or companies in your network to: i) Regenerate old connections; ii) Maximise value in your weak connections; iii) Build business relationships with clients or hiring managers; iv) Find and meet prospective job seekers; v) Grow a referral network; vi) Enlarge your corporate and personal brand; vii) Make new connections and grow your sphere of influence; viii) Open doors to future career opportunities, increased salary or promotions; ix) Increase visibility, which improves influence and effectiveness internally with your organisation as well as externally; x) Educate yourself and ask questions about other organisations; xi) Conduct competitive intelligence on companies, industries or individuals; xii) Make fewer cold calls and better prepare for them; xiii) Leverage contacts you already have (Steckerl, 2007).

Although a major opportunity for business, companies with brands in the luxury market are failing to take advantage of these tools (Dickins, 2013).

As some authors declare, "better social searching tools will enable information professionals to find reliable sources for sentiment or common knowledge for word-of-mouth coverage" (Hawthorne & Cromity, 2012, p. 36), what is already being performed by some companies that analyze attitudes, emotions, brand evangelism, and its sponsor correlation present in the Social Media conversation share (Focalytic, 2013).

Social Interactions and Communities of Practice

The advantage of Blogs is that they facilitate the growth of Social Networks into true communities of practice (Blood, 2004). Much of the value of these networks is in their advantage for the "social capital required for effective decision support to grow based on relationships between analytically opinionated minds" (Johnson, 2005).

This defies the control hierarchies that still define most businesses where top-down decision making is still the rule of the day (Scott, 2008). Here, the reputations of writers are built on the value of their ideas, their ability to convince others that their ideas are valid and therefore develop the most respect and authority (Curtis, 2006; Kassel, 2008; Miller, 2007).

Collaboration applications that build such communities of practice socialize critical business decisions in an open forum based on the social capital of merit.

Concerns with Networking Sites

"There's a tension between the audience participation model of Web 2.0 and business need for confidentiality and verification" (Miller, 2007). Some questions must be addressed like: i) If an employee is blogging, what are they saying about the firm? ii) In a world where Wikis or Social bookmarks and tags are popular research tools, who is responsible for the accuracy and quality of information? iii) If you create an online community, how will you moderate what should be an open and free forum? iv) If you let your employees access Facebook at work, how can you be sure that they will remain alert to whether it's a work or social conversation they're having? (Steckerl, 2007).

According to some authors (Miller, 2007; Steckerl, 2007), other issues that raise some questions are: i) Privacy - The more we share the more we are exposed. But, we will increase our benefit from the network with more exposure. This concept involves a little trust. For the network to be most useful to us there needs to be a little reciprocity. People very secretive about their privacy may not get great results from using these tools; ii) Barriers to entry - Getting started means investing time to put your information into the application. This can take a few minutes or a few hours, it depends on how much we want to disclose to the network. The more we share about us the easier it will be to make new connections. If we only upload a few contacts, we get little benefit since these systems only search for connections through people we already know; iii) Maintenance - If we have a large network we can get to a point where we are receiving lots of requests. We can turn off e-mails about our connections, and with some networks we can even change our settings to accept requests from specific levels. We may get requests from people we don't know or don't remember. We shouldn't add everyone because we are a reflection of our networks; iv) Cost - Many of these services may begin to charge membership fees.

Sage (2013) warns that the "speed and volume of information that is published on social media can cause significant damage. (...) A misleading comment can damage a company's reputation in seconds". He also points out to the problem of hackers and cyber security because Social Media can be used by hackers to acquire "personal information about employees, then use it to befriend them. Having built a relationship, the criminal may be able to deceive the employee into revealing how to access to their company's systems, and so opening the door to cyber-attacks" or Phishing.[4]

Ojala warns that "in minding our own business, we need to know what information about our employer can be gathered from social media and whether it is what *should* be publicly available" (2012, p. 53).[5]

The weakness in these new Social Networking sites is that "if users do not trust the system to protect their relationships, then they will not use the application effectively and gain very little incremental advantage from their connections" (Steckerl, 2007)[6].

In the end, the quality and value of this information will be dependent on the user and related to the results that it will allow obtaining, always integrated on its context.

SOCIAL TOOLS FOR THE WORKPLACE

The high number of social tools indicates an enthusiastic acceptance of this new media by individuals and companies (Steckerl, 2007).

Organisations cannot afford to ignore Social tools. If they don't know how they can use these tools, maybe they have already lost opportunities to faster competitors. For example, a business can help its staff save time searching if it encourages them to bookmark useful sites and share them with their co-workers.

We must remember that participation drives traffic. "Wikipedia is far more popular than Encarta, and Flikr is used more than Kodak Gallery. If you want people to use a tool, letting them contribute to it will engage their interest" (Miller, 2007).

For individuals, the benefits of using social tools often feel obvious but difficult or even impossible to measure. But, for most organisations, there's a need to demonstrate return on investment. "Those responsible for proving value have a dilemma: on the one hand, hard targets such as page hits or number of posts are easier to collect but have relatively little meaning" (Miller, 2007). On the other hand, measurements such as the ability of an organisation to innovate are hard to measure or directly attribute but are of fundamental importance to its financial health[7].

The idea that social tools are of interest to companies is unquestionable. As long as collaborators have basic Internet knowledge, the problem is the time needed to be actively involved. The more you use these new tools the more obvious the advantages become. To ignore these new tools is to ignore the unique benefits that they can offer (Zarrella, 2013).

Those companies who have opened their organisation to social tools had more positive results than they expected. The strategy is to treat your networked individuals as intelligent adults and minimize the need to be in control. Open and honest support is more constructive and usually works. However, we must stay involved and assume that the community can't grow without some time and attention (Curtis, 2006; Kassel, 2008; Steckerl, 2007).

Some of the Biggest Tools and How They Operate

For most of the services, the initial sign up is free. Users begin by filling out a form with personal data and then inviting friends. Some networks allow uploading current contacts, but others ask users to invite contacts directly through the application's interface. The connections then invite their own contacts, and that's how the network grows (Steckerl, 2007).

There are several Social Networking sites. Most of the applications competing for your attention offer a combination of professional and personal networking. Some of them are seriously oriented to business. From the top 20 players, three of them stand out: i) LinkedIn.com (http://www.linkedin.com) - Profiles look very much like a CV, excellent mix of people from different levels in the organisation, and many industries (Schaffer, 2011). Used mostly as a business research tool without the noise and redundant information that occurs in other social media platforms (Ojala, 2012). A fast growing business network with more than 200 million members worldwide. The most concrete application of LinkedIn is developing a network of associates, an excellent way to stay connected with current and past friends and clients (Kawasaki, 2007). Search for: industry experts, potential employees, hiring managers, deal-makers, people from specific geographies, or people with particular keywords in their profiles; ii) Plaxo.com (http://www.plaxo.com) - Keeps all of your current contacts' information updated automatically thus is extremely useful in repair old relationships and staying in touch. Not a tool to build your network yet, though it does have a very useful 'mini Blog' feature to help you keep friends informed. More than 40 million people use Plaxo; iii) Spoke.com (http://spoke.com) - Focused on providing sales prospects. Deeply integrated, extracts contact data from enterprise applications (Outlook, Notes, etc.) to establish and leverage connections. Provides more than 30 million contacts.

There are so many Social Networks that they are too numerous to list here. Most of them, like friendster.com, flickr.com, among hundreds of others tend to serve only social categories like dating, common interests, finding friends, photo sharing and others not directly related to business. Nevertheless, they might contain important information about their users like brands they wear, satisfaction, or not, with the products they own, special needs and interest in solve their problems with new technologies, products or services, among others (Mordecai, 2013a).

Some web sites can also be networking sites, like MySpace.com, Windows Live Spaces, LiveJournal.com, and Blogger.com.

Other networks with a decidedly business or professional purpose, ranked by number of users, are: i) Hi5.com (http://www.hi5.com/) – more than 330 million users. General social networking and business; ii) Passado.com (http://passado.com) – more than 4 million users (already had more than 7 million). Europe's largest business network, now called Wasabi (http://www.wasabi.com/signup) – More than 13 million users, about 6 million of whom are based in German-speaking countries. Business networking; iv) Ryze.com (http://www.ryze.com/) – More than 500,000 users. Business networking; v) Ecademy.com (http://www.sunzu.com/) – Became Sunzu in January 2013. More than 100,000 users before the name change. Business networking.

Two other networks reflect some specialty in social networking: i) BiomedExperts (http://www.biomedexperts.com) - "The first literature-based scientific social network - brings the right researchers together and allows them to collaborate online. Collexis provides the BiomedExperts social network free of charge to researchers worldwide in an effort to increase collaborative biomedical research for the common good". More than 434.000 experts; ii) globalEDGE (http://globaledge.msu.edu/) - "Sponsored and developed by the International Business Center at Michigan State University includes more than 350.000 registered users from across the globe and connects users to prospective collaboration partners and industry experts."

Social Networks for Business Use

Social Networks are one source, among many others, to consider in everyday reference and research work. There are tools like SlideShare (http://www.slideshare.net) that makes possible to share slide presentations, and includes the text of the slides in a format called a transcript. We can use the search box to find relevant topics, watch the presentation slides at the SlideShare site, or download them for future use. Some require registration based on the poster's preference before downloading is permitted, and Vidipedia (http://www.vidipedia.org) which is a selection of a multimedia picture social networking. Similarly to Wikipedia, Vidipedia is a free encyclopaedia that anyone can edit, search for key terms or browse by category. The results are encyclopaedic answers that link to relevant videos. When only one result is available, the video is automatically launched and all videos can be downloaded. Running a search on a given term produces an extensive description with definitions and videos.

A great advantage of Social Networking is connecting anyone who needs with those who have direct experience with companies, products, or services and are experts in some field (Kassel, 2008).

Businesses can use social tools to improve creativity, productivity, collaboration and visibility in certain markets, as well as engaging clients and partners in more fruitful collaboration (Berkman, 2008; Brown, 2012; Holloman, 2012).

There are a huge range of tools and sites (Russell, 2011; Tsvetovat & Kouznetsov, 2011), including: i) Wikis, ii) Blogs, iii) Mash-ups[8], iv) Social Tagging, v) Instant Messaging, vi) Video, vii) Social Bookmarking, viii) Podcasts, and ix) Services, like Facebook, Twitter, NetVibes, Flock and others (Miller, 2007).

There are practical examples of how geographically dispersed organisations could improve networking (Chang, 2016)[9], knowledge sharing and collaboration using these tools (Tapscott & Williams, 2008).

The biggest benefit of such social tools for business is that this ongoing social contact with a colleague or client can mean that face-to-face meetings start with a deeper personal trust and understanding (Berkman, 2008; Brown, 2012; Zarrella, 2009).

If a person posts in his or her Social Networking community something like "I'm walking my dog to the dog park and his leash just broke. It was brand new. I'm so frustrated" (Leonard, 2013), we get to know several important things that can be used on the behalf of our company. This person has a need, the need to purchase a new leash for the dog. We also know that there is frustration with a new leash that just got broke leaving a bad evaluation and opinion about the manufacturer of that product. That person shows a real love and care for its animal friend so he must want the best for it. A dog needs food, toys, veterinarian care, among other things and we may know where that person lives, which dog park uses and the stores where he passes to reach the park[10].

For a company in the pet business this is great because we have a behavioural segmentation (Kotler et al., 1999; Scott, 2008) that allows contacting the owner with a full range of services and products adapted to the animal, the climate where it lives and other specific needs. Perhaps the dog breed, name and birth date of the animal are posted also in the network and the offers can be personalized to target the prospect with some empathy.

Leonard (2013) calls this "the Anatomy of an Expression of Intent" and this can be used in a large sort of situations like animals, children, jobs, marriages and other businesses if we pay attention and learn how to read between the lines.

Blogs

According to Blog search engine Technorati (http://www.technorati.com), more than 180 million Blogs are being written in the public cyberspace known as the Blogosphere, up from just 100,000 in late 2002. Technorati's '2013 Digital Influence Report' shows that "consumers are turning to blogs when looking to make a purchase. In fact, blogs rank favorably with consumers for trust, popularity and even influence" (Leonard, 2013).

The report states that blogs are now the third-most influential digital resource (31%) when making overall purchases, behind retail sites (56%) and brand sites (34%), making it a useful resource to watch for consumer behavior and needs.

Ojala states that "blogs – or at least some blogs – gained the status of reputable sources for reporting and informed commentary. Curated blog content of interest to business researchers is part of online services such as ProQuest (in its Entrepreneurship product), LexisNexis, and Factiva." (2012, p.53).

Some Blogs with interest in CI like Traction (http://traction.tractionsoftware.com), MovableType (http://www.movabletype.org), and Manila (http://manila.userland.com) are used to streamline dissemination and collection[11] (Johnson, 2005). Now, enterprises in every industry are learning the power and risks of unleashing their employees' ideas on both their colleagues and the marketplace (Blood, 2004; Qualman, 2010).

Blogs have also taken on a greater role in CI practice within the enterprise, alongside Blogs in product, R&D, information technology, legal and financial teams, sales and marketing and even executive management (Johnson, 2005). Today, blogging is helping to create real communities of practice within organizations large and small (Curtis, 2006).

To obtain information about "which Blogs are reliable and worthy, the content aggregator and distributor Newstex (http://newstex.com/)" (Ojala, 2012, p.53) is the right place to start.

Wikis

The Wiki is a new collaboration tool in the corporate environment and is gaining significance in organizational information sharing. Borrowed from the Hawaiian word for quick, the first Wiki was originally developed by Ward Cunningham in 1995. Today they take the form of dozens of software applications that have Wiki-like capabilities (Johnson, 2005). Like Blogs, Wikis allow for very easy publishing and commenting on topics of collective interest to the community. Its unique social dynamics, allowing all contributors to change anything on any or all of the documents available, subjects the entire community to consensus-building (Carrera, 2012b).

Many of these tools are open-source and available free of charge, such as OpenWiki, Kwiki and Twiki. The best example of a Wiki is the Wikipedia. It begun in 2001 to build a free, multi-lingual encyclopaedia of knowledge on every subject in the human knowledge (Johnson, 2005). It has now more than 4.000.000 individual articles and serves as the laboratory for what Wikis can ultimately become given time and attention in the enterprise (Libert & Spector, 2009; Qualman, 2010; Surowiecki, 2007).

Wikis are just like Blogs. With Wikis, the same social interaction happens, but much faster and with far more intense collaboration (Tapscott & Williams, 2008). "They are based on the notion that the best results come from allowing decision-making to emerge from the bottom up with minimal editorial control from the top down (Johnson, 2005).

Wikis are great tools because of their editing and contribution characteristics. Wikis are made of hypertext documents linked together and edited collectively by the community in a web browser interface (Qualman, 2010). It is a very open medium where all authors can add to, change, or delete other people's work. "To prevent the damaging effects of creative destruction this can obviously lead to, Wikis have a means of comparing two states of a page, known as a *diff*, so that revisions can be viewed and rolled back and mistakes can be corrected" (Johnson, 2005).

The only way anyone can write something that will survive is if it's written with such quality that even its opponents can agree that it has value (Carrera, 2009, 2012a; Tapscott & Williams, 2008).

In CI, focus must be on the analysis of options available and the arguments that make one course stand apart from its alternatives as superior. This ascertains the quality of the information retrieved, allowing for a sustainable business decision making in organisations.

RSS

The technology that made all this possible is RSS (Rich Site Summary or Real Simple Syndication). It is an XML specification for distributing published media files to a web address that can be read by a RSS feed reader[12].

RSS has become the modern example for what XML can do for the user. It is also the most widespread form of XML in use today. RSS could very well become the principal mean by which all data, structured or unstructured, is broadcasted and applied (Johnson, 2005). This includes applications such as change-detection in Weblogs, retrieving spam-free email, or passing transactional data through a complex workflow environment (Carrera, 2009, 2012a).

In addition to receiving posts from news sites and other Weblogs, RSS feeds can contain data from corporate systems: sales information, financial data, inventory or vendor information, data from partner or distribution systems, competitor events, and all manner of real-time data relevant to the enterprise. (Johnson, 2005)

The challenge now is to disseminate examples where collaborative social community applications have an impact on competitive intelligence efficiency and/or effectiveness (Carrera, 2012b; Hortinha, 2002).

Tag Clouds

Analysis of Blogs, Wikis and Web pages is an excellent way to gain an understanding of the individuals who use those particular tools of Social Media, and thus put the information into context.

Social Media search engines provide important data through Tag Clouds and through lists, such as the week's top ten tags and/or Blogs. Tags are words that content creators use to describe their works (http://en.wikipedia.org/wiki/Tag_cloud). In effect, they are keywords, guides that lead content users to the posts of content creators. Analyzing Tag Clouds, groups of tags within content, provides powerful insights into what Blog and other Social Media content creators and users are interested in (Curtis, 2006).

Tag Clouds can be used to build up a picture of the demographics of particular sites as a Wordle[13]. If we look at a Tag Cloud and we see a big number of technology-related words, such as: Ajax, Apple, CSS, Linux and Web 2.0, this helps us to analyze what type of consumer uses that site, segmenting them in psychographic means, and correlate it to the site's popular tags.

To begin monitoring, we must match keywords with the tags created by active consumers. Content creators are active consumers that rely on tags to help other consumers find them. Tags connect content creators with the readers, and are an important tool for monitoring consumer trends.

Over time, the use of tags results in a folksonomy, "a user-defined, keyword system in which tags are defined by users rather than by a provided vocabulary. Unfortunately, folksonomies often diverge from keywords that researchers might use" (Curtis, 2006).

Tag Clouds provide an excellent way to identify the most popular trends and can be used in reverse. "Rather than matching keywords you choose in advance, let them lead you to toward what seems popular" (Curtis, 2006).

Squidoo (http://www.squidoo.com/browse/top_lenses) allows users to set up a web page where they control the content. Squidoo has a number of tags that will help you. Each web page (Squidoo calls them lenses) has the tags prominently displayed. In addition, the site has a number of tags compiled based on popularity, and category. After some examination we will have a better understanding of tags and consumer interests and needs disclosed in Social Media.

By watching tags carefully you can monitor and correlate product category, brands, uses, interests and needs. Tag Clouds will show consumer interests integrated in the social media space (Kassel, 2008; Miller, 2007; Steckerl, 2007).

This way, consumer trends can be revealed.

DISCUSSION

1. Information is the strategic resource of the organizations. Competition became a race to information, a race of discovery and learning (Choo, 2003). That's why we live in a so called 'Information Society'. To be aware of what is happening in the macro-environment of the organization is essential to its survival and growing. The value of the information resources must be fully appreciated by organization members to gain advantages amongst other offers in the markets where they compete. Information has a value, but it must be of high quality to be able to aid in the decision making process.
2. The value of the information resource rests in its characteristics: i) expandable – the more we have, the more we use and more valuable it gets; ii) compressible – can be concentrated, integrated, summarized, miniaturized for easier handling; iii) substitutable – replaces land, labour and capital; iv) transportable – at the speed of light, using e-mail or video-conference we can be anywhere like if we were there; v) diffusive – it tends to leak and the more it leaks the more we have and the more of us have it, making it available to a growing number of people; vi) shareable – allows exchange and sharing transactions because giving or selling a information lets the seller to keep it anyway, unlike physical goods (Cleveland, 1985, pp. 29-33).
3. Information is the medium through which an organization relates to its environment and allows the individuals to know how to react and adapt to external changes. The value of information is related to the "imperfect availability of information" and "imperfection of information" (Grant, 2002, pp. 242; 245, 246; 516). That's why companies must perform CI. CI is the use of public sources to develop information about the competition, consumers, and market environment (Miller & Business Intelligence Braintrust, 2002).
4. Internet is a gigantic source of information. Some tools help in the information harvesting to acquire the valuable resources and avoid time lost in that activity so people can focus in the analysis process, the real important one to perform positively.
5. Social Media are communication and collaboration tools that include Blogs, Wikis and Social Bookmarking. Participants worldwide contribute to and collaborate in readily available online discussions, creating new knowledge bases that can become recognized as information sources. It's easy to perceive that this trend in modern communication and interaction among humans will

be very important to achieve results that it will be very difficult with other non-interactive means (Tapscott, 1995, 1999; Tapscott et al., 2000; Tapscott & Williams, 2008). Monitoring Blogs and Podcasts can help develop actionable solutions to fuel organizations (Carrera, 2009, 2012a, 2012b; Hortinha, 2002).

6. These social interactions develop real communities of practice transforming critical business decisions in an open forum based on the social capital of merit. Nevertheless, some security measures must be taught to employees and collaborators so they don't give away trade secrets or other information that could look innocuous to them but a 'gold mine' to competitors. Other malicious elements can use that openness to launch cyber-attacks or Phishing.
7. Some of the bigger Social Media tools that can be used and must be monitored are: Facebook, Twitter, LinkedIn, Plaxo, Spoke, Hi5, Passado (now called Wasabi), Ryze, Sunzu (prior called Ecademy), BioMedExperts, GlobalEDGE, SlideShare, Vidipedia, amongst several others.
8. Blogs are now the third-most influential digital resource (31%) when making overall purchases, behind retail sites (56%) and brand sites (34%), making it a useful resource to watch for consumer behavior and needs, according to Blog search engine Technorati (http://www.technorati.com). Some Blogs with interest in CI like Traction (http://traction.tractionsoftware.com), MovableType (http://www.movabletype.org), and Manila (http://manila.userland.com) are used to streamline dissemination and collection (Johnson, 2005). To obtain information about "which Blogs are reliable and worthy, the content aggregator and distributor Newstex (http://newstex.com/)" (Ojala, 2012, p.53) is the right place to start.
9. The Wiki is a new collaboration tool in the corporate environment and is gaining significance in organizational information sharing. Wikis allow for very easy publishing and commenting on topics of collective interest to the community. Its unique social dynamics, allowing all contributors to change anything on any or all of the documents available, subjects the entire community to consensus-building (Carrera, 2012b). Many of these tools are open-source and available free of charge, such as OpenWiki, Kwiki and Twiki. The best example of a Wiki is the Wikipedia.
10. RSS (Rich Site Summary or Real Simple Syndication) is an XML specification for distributing published media files to a web address that can be read by a RSS feed reader. RSS could very well become the principal mean by which all data, structured or unstructured, is broadcasted and applied (Johnson, 2005).
11. Social Media search engines provide important data through Tag Clouds and through lists, such as the week's top ten tags and/or Blogs. Tags are words that content creators use to describe their works (http://en.wikipedia.org/wiki/Tag_cloud). In effect, they are keywords, guides that lead content users to the posts of content creators. Analyzing Tag Clouds, groups of tags within content, provides powerful insights into what Blog and other Social Media content creators and users are interested in (Curtis, 2006). Analysis of Blogs, Wikis and Web pages is an excellent way to gain an understanding of the individuals who use those particular tools of Social Media, and thus put the information into context. Consumer trends can be revealed by watching tags carefully. You can monitor and correlate product category, brands, uses, interests and needs. Tag Clouds will show consumer interests integrated in the social media space (Kassel, 2008; Miller, 2007; Steckerl, 2007). That's how information monitoring can be a strategic tool for any organization that wishes to stay competitive in the fast changing business environment of the XXI century.

CONCLUSION

In the globalized world quality information warrants best results when competing with other organizations, enabling a competitive advantage.

After describing what CI is and what is it good for, we have mentioned the advantages of being involved in CI projects. How to receive information for competitive decisions and the benefits of continually scan the business environment are some issues also analysed.

We have described several web tools available for information retrieval purposes and some features of each one, after showing the relations and benefits of the Internet for CI.

Social Networking is getting involved and getting your brand name being discussed every time you can. With the Internet we have the ability to reach more people and make more money in a highly personalized manner, knowing their needs and desires and the trends that are getting more attention (Kassel, 2008; Miller, 2007). Nevertheless, Ethics and good practice still play a major part.

Companies look at Social Media as a way of attracting and retaining customers (Brown, 2012; Ojala, 2012; Schaffer, 2011; Zarrella, 2009, 2013) but are not taking benefit (Dickins, 2013) of its major advantage in obtaining feedback from the market and be aware of competitors moves and market trends discussed by the clients (Berkman, 2008; Holloman, 2012). Customer and employee satisfaction is another invaluable information scanning that social tools allow to perform (Hawthorne & Cromity, 2012; Ojala, 2012; Sage, 2013).

Being connected is an incredible leverage, invaluable in your business development (Steckerl, 2007). Connections can have many unexpected positive results (Carrera, 2009; Kawasaki, 2007).

Also, creative consumers help companies developing new and better products by their feedback on using them and what to improve for better results (Berthon, Pitt, Plangger, & Shapiro, 2012).

We've concluded with a short description of some of the social network tools that can be adopted to gain current awareness about all the unexpected events in the macro environment of the companies, allowing the anticipation of what's going on with trends among specific market segments (Higham, 2010; Sage, 2013).

Web 2.0 tools are impacting the definition, collection and dissemination of CI but there is still much more untapped potential (Canhoto, 2013; Ojala, 2012).

CI professionals must redefine their roles in terms of strategic analysis (Kotze, 2013). Regardless of whether you show enthusiasm or scepticism in the face of these new Internet collaborative and communication tools, there is no excuse to be uninformed.

Consumers have always wanted to be heard, have always wanted their desires to be taken into account in the creation of new products and services. Consumer trends begin life through a series of small or big signals (Rasquilha, 2010). Through monitoring and analyzing the Social Media space, information professionals can provide a valuable analysis within consumer trend monitoring, knowing the consumer's interests and needs directly from the consumer posts and commentaries (Curtis, 2006), building the adequate solution to those clients' problems[14].

Like much of the web, corporate Blogs of Social Network web sites can be a good place to keep track of what the company is exploring for future products and services (Ojala, 2012). Blogs also provide excellent flags in response to consumer needs (Blood, 2004; Carrera, 2012a; Hortinha, 2002). BlogPulse point us toward the direction of trends we might otherwise let go (Curtis, 2006)[15].

In a fast moving business world, like the one we are living in, it should be a competitive edge having the chance of monitoring the market trends, the competition moves and still improve internal communication to flat the channels and downsize the hierarchy inside companies.

We must watch closely what the competitor employees are posting online and also keep an eye on what our employees are posting and check if they are, unconsciously, giving away valuable information to the competitors. We are not the only ones looking at the competition; they are doing the same thing with us and our company. Be aware.

Sage (2013) explains that social intelligence is better than traditional market research because it provides answers that companies consider critical to business strategy.

Only future research will tell if this is effectively true and the real value obtained by companies that perform this task accurately.

It's our expectation to contribute to take this relevant subject further in ulterior research to disseminate all the advantages in adopting Web 2.0 tools in companies.

Let's hope CEO's learn how to leverage all this advantages and know how to make a good use for them all.

REFERENCES

Barbosa, P., & O'Reilly, A. (2011). *Harvard Trends: Tendências de Gestão*. Porto: Vida Económica.

Bedell, D. (2011). Business Intelligence. *Global Finance, March*, 46-47.

Bergier, J. (1970). *A Espionagem Industrial*. Porto: Editorial Inova.

Berkman, R. (2008). *The Art of Strategic Listening: Finding Market Intelligence in Blogs and Social Media*. Paramount Market Pub.

Berthon, P., Pitt, L., Plangger, K., & Shapiro, D. (2012). Marketing meets Web 2.0, social media, and creative consumers: Implications for international marketing strategy. *Business Horizons*, *55*(3), 261–271. doi:10.1016/j.bushor.2012.01.007

Besson, B., & Possin, J. (1996). *Do serviço de informação à inteligência económica: detectar as ameaças e oportunidades da empresa*. Instituto Piaget.

Best, D. (1996a). Business Process and Information Management. In D. Best (Ed.), *The Fourth Resource: Information and its Management*. Hampshire: Aslib/Gower.

Best, D. (1996b). *The Fourth Resource: Information and its Management*. Hampshire: Aslib/Gower.

Beuren, I. M. (1998). *Gerenciamento da informação: um recurso estratégico no processo de gestão empresarial*. São Paulo: Atlas.

Blood, R. (2004). O Livro de Bolso do Weblogue: Conselhos Práticos para Criar e Manter o seu blogue (1ª ed.). Porto: Campo das Letras.

Bolander, et al (2015). Social networks sales organizations: their development and importance for salesperson performance. *Journal of marketing: A quarterly publication of the American marketing association, 79*(6), 1-16.

Bramston, D. (2009). Basics Product Design: Idea Searching (1st ed.). Lausanne: Ava Publishing.

Brophy, P., & Coulling, K. (1996). *Quality Management for Information and Library Managers*. Guildford: Aslib/Gower.

Brown, E. (2012). Working the Crowd: Social Media Marketing for Business (2nd ed.): British Informatics Society.

Brown, J., & Duguid, P. (2000). The Social Life of Information (1st ed.). Boston: Harvard Business School Press.

Burgelman, R., Christensen, C., & Wheelwright, S. (2009). Strategic Management of Technology and Innovation (5ª ed.). Singapore: McGraw-Hill.

Burk, C. Jr, & Horton, F. Jr. (1988). *InfoMap: A Complete Guide to Discovering Corporate Information Resources*. New Jersey: Prentice Hall.

Canhoto, A. (2013). Social media as a source of competitive intelligence. Retrieved from http://anacanhoto.com/2013/01/18/social-media-as-a-source-of-competitive-intelligence/

Carrera, F. (2009). Networking: Guia de Sobrevivência Profissional (1st ed.). Lisboa: Sílabo.

Carrera, F. (2012a). Comunicar 2.0: a Arte de bem Comunicar no Século XXI (1st ed.). Lisboa: Sílabo.

Carrera, F. (2012b). Marketing Digital na Versão 2.0: o que não pode ignorar (2nd ed.). Lisboa: Sílabo.

Castells, M. (2000). *The Information Age: The Rise of the Network Society* (2nd ed.). London: Blackwell.

Castells, M. (2004). *A Galáxia Internet: Reflexões sobre Internet, Negócios e Sociedade*. Lisboa: Fundação Calouste Gulbenkian.

Chang, V. (2016). A Cybernetics Social Cloud. *Journal of Systems and Software*. Retrieved from http://www.sciencedirect.com/science/article/pii/S0164121215002939

Chen, H., Chau, M., & Zeng, D. (2002). CI Spider: A tool for competitive intelligence on the Web. *Decision Support Systems*, *34*(1), 1–17. doi:10.1016/S0167-9236(02)00002-7

Choo, C. W. (2003). *Gestão de informação para a organização inteligente: a arte de explorar o meio ambiente*. Lisboa: Editorial Caminho.

Christensen, C., Anthony, S., & Roth, E. (2004). *Seeing What's Next: Using the Theories of Innovation to Predict Industry Change*. Harvard Business School Press.

Cleveland, H. (1983). A Informação como um Recurso. *Diálogo*, 16, 7-11.

Cleveland, H. (1985). The Knowledge Executive: Leadership in an Information Society (1st ed.). New York: Dutton.

Curtis, P. (2006). Gleaning consumer intelligence from blogs and podcasts. Retrieved from http://www.freepint.com/issues/040506.htm#tips

Davenport, T. (1997). *Information Ecology: Mastering the Information and Knowledge Environment*. New York: Oxford University Press.

Davenport, T., Marchand, D., & Dickson, T. (2004). *Dominando a gestão da informação*. Porto Alegre: Bookmann.

Dearlove, D. (1998). *Key Management Decisions: Tools and Techniques of the Executive Decision-Maker* (1st ed.). Wiltshire: Financial Times/Pitman.

Deng, Z., & Luo, L. (2007). An Exploratory Discuss of New Ways for Competitive Intelligence on WEB 2.0. In Wang (Ed.), Integration and Innovation Orient to E-Society (pp. 597-604). Boston: Springer.

Dickins, J. (2013). Social media is an underused opportunity for luxury brands [Electronic Version]. *Digital Marketing Hub: The Guardian*. Retrieved from http://www.guardian.co.uk/media-network/media-network-blog/2013/jun/14/social-media-opportunity-luxury-brands

Fialka, J. (1997). War by other means: Economic espionage in America (1ª ed.): Norton.

Focalytic. (2013). Social Media Content Analysis of the 2013 Masters Golf Tournament. *Focal Point*. Retrieved from http://www.focalytic.com/Portals/182440/docs/themastersgolfebook.pdf

Garber, R. (2001). Inteligência competitiva de mercado: como capturar, armazenar, analisar informações de marketing e tomar decisões num mercado competitivo. São Paulo: Madras.

Gleick, J. (2011). The Information: a History, a Theory, a Flood (1st ed.). St. Ives: 4th Estate.

Godeluck, S. (2000). *A Explosão da Economia na Internet*. Lisboa: Livros do Brasil.

Goldman, A. (2011). *Tudo que sei sobre Marketing aprendi com o Google*. S. Paulo: Saraiva.

Gomes, E., & Braga, F. (2001). *Inteligência competitiva: como transformar informação em um negócio lucrativo*. Rio de Janeiro: Campus.

Grant, R. M. (2002). *Contemporary strategy analysis: concepts, techniques, applications*. Wiley-Blackwell.

Guisnel, J. (1997). *Espionagem na Internet: As Guerras no Ciberespaço*. Lisboa: Difusão Cultural.

Guynn, J. (2013). Facebook releases information on NSA requests for user data. *Los Angeles Times*. Retrieved from http://www.latimes.com/business/technology/la-fi-tn-facebook-releases-first-information-on-fisa-requests-20130614,0,3315731.story

Hawthorne, K., & Cromity, J. (2012). Social Search for Market Intelligence. *Online: Exploring Technology & Resources for Information Professionals, March/April*, 36-38.

Herring, J. P. (2002). Tópicos fundamentais de inteligência: processo para identificação e definição de necessidades de inteligência. In Prescott & Miller (Eds.), Inteligência competitiva na prática. Rio de Janeiro: Campus.

Higham, W. (2010). The Next Big Thing: Spotting and Forecasting Consumer Trends for Profit (1st ed.). Bodmin: Kogan Page.

Holloman, C. (2012). The Social Media MBA: Your Competitive Edge in Social Media Strategy Development and Delivery (1st ed.). John Wiley & Sons.

Hortinha, J. (2002). X-Marketing (1ª ed.). Lisboa: Sílabo.

Huang, K., Lee, Y., & Wang, R. (1998). Quality Information and Knowledge (1st ed.). Prentice Hall.

Johnson, A. (2005). Blogs, Wikis & RSS: Colaborative social communities and the value of distributed CI. *Competitive Intelligence Magazine*. Retrieved from http://www.aurorawdc.com/blogswikisrss_scipcimag_20050102.pdf

Kahaner, L. (1997). Competitive Intelligence: How to gather, analyze, and use information to move your business to the top (1st ed.). New York: Simon & Schuster.

Kassel, A. (2008). Social Networking: A Research Tool. Retrieved from http://web.fumsi.com/go/article/find/3196

Kawasaki, G. (2007). Ten Ways to Use LinkedIn. Retrieved from http://blog.guykawasaki.com

Kirsch, Gregory, J., Brown, & Charley, F. (2006). Using Patents in Competitive Intelligence. *Competitive Intelligence Magazine*, *9*(1), 17–21.

Kotler, P., Armstrong, G., Saunders, J., & Wong, V. (1999). Principles of Marketing (2nd ed.). Cambridge: Prentice Hall.

Kotze, L. (2013). Social media increasingly important in competitive intelligence. Retrieved from http://www.ibis.co.za/Competitive-Intelligence-Blog/social-media-increasingly-important-in-competitive-intelligence.html

Leonard, H. (2013). Blogs Outrank Social Networks In Influence. Retrieved from http://www.businessinsider.com/blog-influence-outranks-social-networks-2013-3

Libert, B., & Spector, J. (2009). Muitas Cabeças Pensam Melhor: Como mobilizar o poder das multidões para o seu negócio (1ª ed.). Porto: Lua de Papel.

Marchand, D., & Horton, F. Jr. (1986). *Infotrends: Profiting from your Information Resources*. John Wiley & Sons.

Martinet, B., & Marti, Y. (1995). *A Inteligência Económica: os olhos e os ouvidos da empresa*. Instituto Piaget.

McGee, J. V., & Prusak, L. (1995). *Gerenciamento estratégico da informação: aumente a competitividade e a eficiência de sua empresa utilizando a informação como uma ferramenta estratégica*. Rio de Janeiro: Campus.

McPherson, P. (1994). Accounting for the Value of Information. *Aslib Proceedings*, *46*(9), 203–215. doi:10.1108/eb051366

Miller, A. (2007). Social Tools for Business Use: Messages from a Web 2.0 Conference. 12-12-2012, from http://web.fumsi.com/go/article/find/3916

Miller, J., & Business Intelligence Braintrust. (2002). *O milênio da inteligência competitiva*. Porto Alegre. *The Bookman*.

Mohr, J., Sengupta, S., & Slater, S. (2010). Marketing of High-Technology Products and Innovations (3rd ed.). New Jersey: Pearson.

Mordecai, V. (2013a). 4 Things Social Media Analysis Can Tell You About Your Business *Focal Point: Focalytic*. Retrieved from http://www.focalytic.com/focal-point/bid/291330/4-Things-Social-Media-Analysis-Can-Tell-You-About-Your-Business

Mordecai, V. (2013b). What Businesses Can Gain from a Custom Social Media Listening Tool *Focal Point: Focalytic*. Retrieved from http://www.focalytic.com/focal-point/bid/291331/What-Businesses-Can-Gain-from-a-Custom-Social-Media-Listening-Tool

Mordecai, V. (2013c). What Is Competitive Intelligence? *Focal Point: Focalytic*. Retrieved from http://www.focalytic.com/focal-point/bid/297577/What-Is-Competitive-Intelligence

Negroponte, N. (1995). *Being Digital*. New York: Knopf.

Ojala, M. (2012). Minding Your Own Business: Social Media Invades Business Research. *Online: Exploring Technology & Resources for Information Professionals, July/August*, 51-53.

Orna, E. (1996). Valuing Information: Problems and Opportunities. In D. Best (Ed.), *The Fourth Resource: Information and its Management*. Hampshire: Aslib/Gower.

Orna, E. (1999). Practical Information Policies (2ª ed.). Cambridge: Gower.

Penzias, A. (1989). *Ideas and Information: Managing in a High-Tech World*. New York: W. W. Norton.

Penzias, A. (1995). *Harmony: Business, Technology & Life After Paperwork*. Harper Collins.

Porter, M. E., & Millar, V. E. (1985). How information gives you competitive advantage. *Harvard Business Review*, *63*(4), 149–160.

Prescott, J. E., & Miller, S. H. (2002). *Inteligência competitiva na prática: técnicas e práticas bem sucedidas para conquistar mercados*. Rio de Janeiro: Campus.

Prior, V. (2006). Competitive Intelligence: An Introduction. Retrieved from http://www.freepint.com/issues/050106.htm#feature

Prior, V. (2007). DIY Detection: Competitive Intelligence for SMEs. Retrieved from http://web.freepint.com/go/features/2483

Qualman, E. (2010). Socialnomics: Como os media sociais estão a transformar o modo como vivemos e como fazemos negócios (1st ed.). Lisboa: Presença.

Rasquilha, L. (2010). *Tendências e Gestão da Inovação: como aplicar as tendências na estratégia de inovação empresarial*. Lousã: Verlag Dashöfer.

Redman, T. (1996). *Data Quality for the Information Age*. Norwood: Artech House.

Revelli, C. (2000). *Inteligência estratégica na Internet: como desenvolver eficazmente actividades de monitorização e de pesquisa nas redes*. Instituto Piaget.

Ribault, J.-M., Martinet, B., & Lebidois, D. (1995). A Gestão das Tecnologias (1st ed.). Lisboa: D. Quixote.

Russell, M. (2011). Mining the Social Web: Analyzing Data from Facebook, Twitter, LinkedIn, and Other Social Media Sites (1st ed.). O'Reilly Media.

Rustmann, F., Jr. (2002). CIA, Inc.: Espionage and the Craft of Business Intelligence (1st ed.). Dulles: Brassey's.

Safko, L. (2010). The Social Media Bible: Tactics, Tools & Strategies for Business Success. (2nd ed.). Hoboken: John Wiley & Sons.

Sage, N. (2013). How to create business value from social intelligence. *Computer Weekly*. Retrieved from http://www.computerweekly.com/opinion/How-to-create-business-value-from-social-intelligence

Schaffer, N. (2011). *Maximizing LinkedIn for Sales and Social Media Marketing: An Unofficial, Practical Guide to Selling & Developing B2B Business on LinkedIn*. CreateSpace Independent Publishing Platform.

Scott, D. (2008). *As Novas Regras de Marketing e Relações Públicas: Como usar os blogues, o podcasting, os media online e as notas informativas para chegar directamente aos consumidores*. Porto: Ideias de Ler.

Shapiro, C., & Varian, H. (1999). Information Rules: A Strategic Guide to the Network Economy (1st ed.). Boston: Harvard Business School Press.

Steckerl, S. (2007). Survival Guide: Online Social Networking. Retrieved from http://web.fumsi.com/go/article/use/2346

Surowiecki, J. (2007). A Sabedoria das Multidões: Como a inteligência colectiva transforma a economia e a sociedade (1st ed.). Porto: Lua de Papel.

Taborda, J. P., & Ferreira, M. D. (2002). *Competitive intelligence: conceitos, práticas e benefícios*. Pergaminho.

Tapscott, D. (1995). *The Digital Economy: Promise and Peril in the Age of Networked Intelligence*. New York: McGraw-Hill.

Tapscott, D. (1999). *Creating Value in the Network Economy*. Boston: Harvard Business School Press.

Tapscott, D., Ticoll, D., & Lowy, A. (2000). *Digital Capital: Harnessing the Power of Business Webs*. Boston: Harvard Business School Press.

Tapscott, D., & Williams, A. (2008). Wikinomics: A Nova Economia das Multidões Inteligentes (1st ed.). Matosinhos: Quidnovi.

Trott, P. (2008). *Innovation Management and New Product Development* (4th ed.). Essex: Prentice Hall.

Tsvetovat, M., & Kouznetsov, A. (2011). Social Network Analysis for Startups: Finding connections on the social web (1a ed.): O'Reilly Media.

Turchi, S. (2012). Estratégias de Marketing Digital e E-Commerce. (1st ed.). S. Paulo: Atlas.

Wagner, G. (1990). The Value and the Quality of Information: the Need for a Theoretical Synthesis. In Wormell (Ed.), Information Quality: Definitions and Dimensions. London: Taylor Graham.

Ward, J., & Peppard, J. (2002). Strategic Planning for Information Systems (3a ed.). Chichester: John Wiley & Sons.

Webster, F. (2000). *Theories of the Information Society*. Cornwall: Routledge.

Weiss, A. (2008). If They Only Knew: Finding Competitive Intelligence from the Web Sites of Your Competitors. Retrieved from http://web.fumsi.com/go/article/find/3355

Wilson, T. (1985). Information Management. *The Electronic Library*, *3*(1), 62–66. doi:10.1108/eb044644 PMID:2498741

Wilson, T. (1987). Information for business. The business of information. *Aslib Proceedings*, *39*(10), 275–279. doi:10.1108/eb051066

Winkler, I. (1997). *Corporate Espionage: What it is, why it's happening in your company, what you must do about it. Rocklin*. Prima Publishing.

Wormell, I. (1990). *Information Quality: Definitions and Dimensions*. London: Taylor Graham.

Zarrella, D. (2009). The Social Media Marketing Book (1st ed.): O'Reilly Media.

Zarrella, D. (2013). *The Science of Marketing: When to Tweet, What to Post, How to Blog, and Other Proven Strategies*. John Wiley & Sons.

ENDNOTES

1 For a list of CI software, Cf. (http://www.thecisource.com/resources/software). For a list of tools and how to use them for Social Media monitoring and competitor awareness, Cf. (http://www.business.com/social-media-marketing/people-are-talking-are-you-listening-the-importance-of-social-media-monitoring/), plus (http://www.socialmediaexaminer.com/how-to-perform-a-detailed-analysis-of-your-social-media-competitors/?awt_l=4Yt0yp&awt_m=3ggscWx3BAr.ILT&utm_source=Newsletter&utm_medium=NewsletterIssue&utm_campaign=New), and (https://www.brandwatch.com/2015/02/marketing-understanding-social-media-intelligence-stack/#.VO4M5IP-tlI.twitter).

2 Cf., also, (http://trendwatching.com/).

3 Cf. Flock (http://www.flock.com/) and StumbleUpon (http://www.stumbleupon.com/).

4 In Bold in the original text. "Phishing is the attempt to acquire sensitive information such as usernames, passwords, and credit card details (and sometimes, indirectly, money), often for malicious reasons, by masquerading as a trustworthy entity in an electronic communication" (https://en.wikipedia.org/wiki/Phishing).

5 In Bold and *Italic* in the original text.

6 Facebook releases information on NSA requests for user data (Guynn, 2013).

7 For information in Marketing metrics and analytics, Cf. (http://blog.eloqua.com/marketing-analytics/?utm_source=feedburner&utm_medium=email&utm_campaign=Feed%3A+ItsAllAboutRevenue+%28It%27s+All+About+Revenue%29). For calculating Return on Investment, Cf. (http://businesscenter.eloqua.com/roi-calculator/).

8 For good examples of Mash-ups, Cf. (Tapscott & Williams, 2008).

9 In the words of the author himself, "In social media, each person is a dot. Each action, whether clicking likes, commenting anything, it creates each link. The more links we have, the more interactions we have. So there are figures with dots and links. The links between each dot represent the strength of relationship. So this principle can be applied to businesses to study and understand the relationship between customers, stakeholders, suppliers, allies etc. Different types of technologies can be used to find out the dynamics of each network group." (e-mail discussion about the subject: 07-01-2016 – 1h45m)

10 "Julie Doe posts (…): "I love this particular brand of soda, though I really wish they had a diet option!" Social media analysis can then add this (…) to the group of opportunities that your business can pursue" (Mordecai, 2013a).

11 See, for example: IceRocket (http://www.icerocket.com), Technorati (http://www.technorati.com), Google (http://blogsearch.google.com/blogsearch), NM Incite (http://nmincite.com), Blogger (Google-owned) (http://www.blogger.com/start), Bloglines (http://www.Bloglines.com), Feedster (http://www.feedster.com), del.icio.us (http://del.icio.us/), and Podcast Alley (http://www.podcastalley.com).

12 For a list of several news readers for Mac and Windows, Cf. RSS Info (http://blogspace.com/rss/readers) . You can subscribe to an RSS feed for each individual term, simplifying your monitoring.

13 "Wordle is a toy for generating 'word clouds' from text that you provide. The clouds give greater prominence to words that appear more frequently in the source text. You can tweak your clouds with different fonts, layouts, and color schemes. The images you create with Wordle are yours to use however you like. You can print them out, or save them to the Wordle gallery to share with your friends". Retrieved 03-11-2008 from (http://www.dailyack.com/2008/06/worlde.html).

14 Retrieved 02-11-2012 from http://www.buzzlogic.com/press/news.html?postdate=1225203064 now Twelvefold Media (http://www.twelvefold.com/splash/?postdate=1225203064).

15 Cf. (http://blog.blogpulse.com/).

This research was previously published in the International Journal of Organizational and Collective Intelligence (IJOCI), 6(4); edited by Victor Chang and Dickson K.W. Chiu, pages 19-44, copyright year 2016 by IGI Publishing (an imprint of IGI Global).

Chapter 20

Does Successful Social Media Marketing Affect Brand Value?
An Empirical Investigation

Stefan Koch
Bogazici University, Turkey

Asli Dikmen
Bogazici University, Turkey

ABSTRACT

Brand management has been moving towards making use of multiple channels in order to engage customers, especially through social media, and sustain a more intense experience around the brand instead of depending merely on advertising. This paper will investigate the effectiveness of social media marketing activities on brand value through comparison of brand value rankings with brand engagement scores, determined by social media marketing activities. Data from a list of companies was collected and evaluated, and the authors found evidence for a relationship in some cases, especially for social networks in the form of Facebook, and for Twitter on global level. They found clear differences between Global and Turkish brands, in that Facebook is relatively and absolutely more important for brands in that country. In addition, clear differences showed up between some industries in importance of different channels for brand value.

INTRODUCTION

Brand is no longer simply a symbol of the product and brand management has been moving towards making use of multiple channels in order to engage customers and sustain a more intense experience around the brand instead of depending merely on advertising (Arvidsson, 2006). This paper will investigate the effectiveness of social media marketing activities on brand value through comparison of brand value rankings with brand engagement scores, determined by social media marketing activities. Quite often it is assumed that these two constructs are related, but no study has so far shown or analyzed this relationship. The paper begins with brief definitions of social media, brand engagement and brand

DOI: 10.4018/978-1-5225-5637-4.ch020

value concepts, followed by a literature review on social media marketing and measures of effectiveness. Related data from a list of chosen companies is collected and evaluated, and the paper concludes with a discussion of findings.

LITERATURE REVIEW AND HYPOTHESIS

Social Media

Social media enables individuals to create, collaborate and share content among each other through Internet-based applications, including but not limited to; content sharing, video sharing, photo sharing, social networking, rating, bookmarking, and games (Kaplan & Haenlein, 2010; Safko & Brake, 2009). Different from the traditional communication channels, social media not only enables top-down communications, but also encourages and enhances communication among individuals or customers, independent of the corporations (Thackheray et al., 2012).

Social media use has been rapidly increasing, and research suggests that by 2015, the total number of individuals and corporations with at least one social networking account will reach 3 billion (Radicati, 2011). This communication channel is important in the sense that it has the power to create conversations with the target audience, which in turn results in deeper connections and longer-term relations with them (Kent & Taylor, 1998). If incorporated into social marketing strategies correctly, use of social media can increase the involvement level of customers, and enhance customer loyalty.

Microblogging

Microblogging was defined as a communication service, where its users can post short messages into an undirected stream by Riemer, Richter, and Bohringer (2010). Users of the service can later choose to subscribe to specific users' messages, which enables them to create and follow directed streams.

A recent study by Naaman, Boase, and Lai (2010) on usage patterns of microblogging suggests that there are four main types of communication: '*Me Now*' (e.g. personal status messages) with 41%, '*Statements and Random Thoughts*' with 25%, '*Opinions/Complaints*' with 24%, and true '*Information Sharing*' with 21% of all posts.

Social Networks

Social network sites are defined as web-based services which allow its users to create a public/semi-public profile in a defined system, set up a list of other users they are connected to and view and/or alter their and other users' connections lists inside the system (Boyd & Ellison, 2007).

Social network sites not only enable their users to meet strangers, but also to articulate and display their social networks. This system sometimes results in connections that would not be made outside social networks; however, the importance is that most of the time these connections are of "latent ties" between individuals who also share an offline connection (Haythornthwaite, 2005). Very commonly, users are not trying to meet new people or network, but rather communicating with acquaintances that are already in their extended social networks (Boyd & Ellison, 2007).

Video and Photo Sharing

As the access to computers and Internet connection gets easier continuously, the recreational media sharing has also expanded significantly to a point where there are plenty of services relying purely on end-user contributions (Skageby, 2008). It was found in 2008 by The Pew/Internet & American Life Project that while 14% of online teens have posted videos, 57% have watched videos on video sharing websites. Fredrick (2008) discusses that the experience has immediacy, serendipity, fun, the chance to search specifically for what interests you, and the chance to share your creations with your friends and the world, which make the video sharing websites as compelling to teens as they are.

Skageby (2008) claims that the digital content being in sharing communities or networks is undirected; it is aimed at a broad audience, but not to a particular group or individual. However, in addition to 'public domain donations' (Cha, 2005), there is also an increasing amount of individually owned content provided by end-users (Lenhart & Madden, 2005), which result in an emerging number of content sharing networks. Those networks create an environment for social sharing practices by combining both several multimedia sharing features and relationship-oriented features.

Social Media Marketing

In one study, Probst (2012) discusses that the brands' orientation for higher influence and connecting with customers has shifted from engagement with individual recipients towards dissemination of information through interactive social media platforms.

One example from the luxury retail world of how brands differentiate themselves by means other than price include five ways of leveraging social influence through the use of: Social Communities, Viral Recommendations, Online Reviews & Rankings, the Mobile Network, and Social-networking Platforms. Studies indicate that followers are more likely to become "brand advocates" when they can directly communicate with the company, more than half of the consumers make an online research prior to purchase, product reviews by customers are highly influential and significantly increase brand loyalty and sales, most consumers use and perceive mobile sites and applications as the quickest and most convenient way for research and purchase, and finally social media along with mobile and in-store experiences are well connected and build up to a total brand experience (Probst, 2012).

Integrating Social Media and Social Marketing

Thackheray et al. (2012) suggest a four-step process to integrate social media and social media marketing strategies. They describe the first step as defining the audience, and their preferred use of social media. This step should also include how the audience uses the preferred social media in terms of frequency, time of use and the actions taken during use as well as their purposes; content sharing, content creation, browsing content, involvement for discounts, or coupons etc.

The second step is to set the purpose of the engagement with the audience. Li and Bernoff (2010) suggest five reasons to represent the strategic thinking behind the need to engage with the audience: 1) for feedback and insights about products, services, behaviors, or the organization, 2) to trigger communication and sharing among the audience about the organization's products or services, or simply enhancing WOM, 3) to identify most loyal and/or influential individuals and invite them to be official advocates for the products or services offered, 4) to offer the audience with a platform to support each other, extending customer services, and 5) to include the audience in the design process of the products or services.

The third step in the process is to outline the strategy in order to accomplish the purposes set in step two. In this step the organization should communicate the audience the benefits associated with connecting and having a relationship with the organization. The communication can be done through the use of certain rewards and incentives. The outline in the step should also include related procedures and evaluation criteria for successful implementation. For example, procedures to respond to negative outcomes, and to ensure ethical operations, as well as the appointment of responsible parties to respond and moderate the communications etc.

The final step in the process is choosing the appropriate technology, the media used for the strategy. The content and the media chosen are crucial for the success of the strategy; the content should be meaningful, relevant, and important for the audience, and should initiate and encourage response and willingness to share. The media chosen should ensure that the message grasps the attention of and reaches the target audience.

Measures of Effectiveness of Social Media Marketing

According to an article by Hoffman and Fodor (2010), the effective measurement of social media marketing for both short and long term purposes, should begin with taking into account customer motivations to use social media and measuring customers' investments made as they engage with marketers' brands. The authors discuss that the traditional ways of measurement would not apply to social media marketing and the correct form of measurement should have a rather consumer-oriented approach as the conversations and relations built with social media marketing activities take time, whereas the traditional ROI approach demands shorter-term measurements. The returns from social media marketing activities should not only be measured in dollars, but also in terms of customers' behaviors and investments; including measures such as number of visits and the time spent with social media applications, as well as number of comments, or updates related to the brand. With these investments, notable marketing outcomes such as changes in awareness levels or increases in WOM can be measured.

Brand Value and Engagement

Brand value is defined as "the money value attached to an established brand name by consumer goods companies" (Collins Dictionary of Business) and is increasingly becoming more important in determining overall corporate wealth.

Arvidsson (2006) discusses that in contemporary management, 'brand equity', a brand's capacity to generate future value stream, is thought to reflect brand value. A brand may have the ability to extract a premium price from consumers, to attract capital or to facilitate relations with interested parties. Recently, however, 'customer-based brand equity', customers' set of associations and attitudes with the brand which contributes to its value for them, has become more important (Kellner, 1993). Brand management tries to ensure that a particular brand is a part of each consumer's life in such a way that what customers do with the brand and how they experience it distinguishes that brand and increases its brand equity.

From a sociological perspective, consumption is seen as a collective, not an individual, practice and within a consumer society the use value of most goods come from their "ability to construct and reinforce social relations and shared meanings and experiences". As a result, in order to support brand equity, contemporary brand management should aim to maintain a certain pattern of mass affect; repeated in different situations and through a wide variety of actions performed by different actors (Arvidsson, 2006).

According to an engagement study by Targetbase Claydon Heeley, a research agency, although 78% of marketers think they employ effective engagement strategies, 77% of consumers think that brands cannot engage with them (Costa, 2010).

Hollebeek (2011) defines customer brand engagement as "the level of an individual customer's motivational, brand-related and context-dependent state of mind characterized by specific levels of cognitive, emotional and behavioral activity in brand interactions," while Achterberg et al. (2003) and Tsai et al. (2009) has defined social engagement as "a high sense of initiative, involvement and adequate response to social stimuli, participating in social activities, interacting with others." Mollen and Wilson (2010) on the other hand, defined brand engagement in online contexts; which they described as "the cognitive and affective commitment to an active relationship with the brand as personified by the website or other computer-mediated entities designed to communicate brand value." The aforementioned description extends the engagement concept from mere involvement to an interactive relationship; resulting in the emergence of the perceived experiential value (level of emotional congruence) and the instrumental value (utility and relevance) obtained from brand interactions (Brodie et al., 2013).

Costa (2010) points out a study conducted by Hall and Partners which shows that effective consumer engagement can bring about up to two-thirds of a brand's profits.

Hypothesis

Based on the extant literature, there seems to be a close connection between brand value and social media engagement. On the other hand, the measurement of both constructs are problematic and not uniformly defined in literature. Our aim is to contribute to this literature by establishing whether a relationship exists between brand value and social media engagement. Our hypothesis therefore is formulated as follows:

H1: Brands to have a higher social media engagement will have a higher brand value.

METHODOLOGY AND DATA COLLECTION

Methodology

In order to compare the effectiveness of social media marketing activities on brand engagement with brand value standing; a social media brand engagement score will be calculated for each brand in the top and bottom 10 from a top 100 ranking on brands. These scores will later be evaluated to see whether there is a correlation with brand value.

Top 100 Brands

A recent report by BrandFinance shows Top 100 Turkish and Top 500 Global brands as of 2012, based on brand value and brand ratings. Brand Finance Plc., founded in 1996 and headquartered in London, is a leading brand valuation consultancy; advising strongly branded organizations (including international brand owners, tax authorities, Intellectual Property (IP) lawyers and investment banks) on how to maximize their value through the effective management of their brands and intangible assets. BrandFinance reaches the brand value by using a discounted cash flow technique in which estimated future royalties are discounted at an appropriate discount rate in order to arrive at a net present value of the trademark and associated intellectual property. Brand ratings, on the other hand, are based on analysis that benchmarks "the strength, risk and potential of a brand, relative to its competitors, on a scale ranging from AAA to D."

Data Collection

For this study, data will be collected from the most popular representatives of three main social media applications: Microblogging, Social Networks, and Video and Photo sharing. Twitter, Facebook and YouTube are chosen as the representatives of each application respectively. We mostly employed the measures suggested by Hoffman and Fodor (2010).

For microblogging scores, the number of followers from each brands' verified Twitter accounts were combined. Proactive verification of accounts is used to ensure authenticity of identities on Twitter, as well as helping users to find exactly what they look for - verified accounts have a blue verified badge on their profile. The numbers include related sub brands as well as the main brands in the rankings. As for the social networks scores, only the main brands' Facebook pages are considered, as there is no such verification system used. For Facebook scores, the numbers reflect the active users of the related page as of December 25, 2012. Finally, for YouTube, the scores indicate the number of subscribers for each account used by the brand, including sub brands.

Twitter, Inc.

Twitter is a real-time information network, building upon small pieces of information, maximum 140 characters long; 'tweets'. However, 'tweets' are not limited to words; photos, videos or conversations can be shared as 'tweets' as well. Twitter gives its users the option not just to contribute, but also to observe and reach secondary information.

For businesses, Twitter can be used as a tool to connect to customers in real-time. It can be used to share information with their current and potential customers, to collect feedback, to keep track of current market intelligence, and to build relationships with customers, partners or influences. It can help businesses to enhance their customer relationship management (CRM), or aid their direct sales.

Users' messages create a real-time, undirected information stream, which can later be personalized by individual users by subscribing ('following') to others' posts (Riemer et al., 2010). The system also includes features that enable users to reference other users (through the '@username' tag), to reference other users' posts (by 'retweet'ing), and to use tags in messages for search queries (with the use of '#keyword') (Java et al., 2007). Twitter can be used anytime, anywhere from almost any device that has Internet connection.

Facebook

Facebook was founded in 2004 with the mission to make a more open and connected world. People use the social network for the purposes of staying connected with family and friends, discovering worldwide news and events going on, and sharing information they care about and expressing themselves. With 584 million daily active users on average and 604 million monthly active users of Facebook mobile products in September 2012, as of October 2012, Facebook has one billion active users in total.

YouTube

Founded in early 2005 by three ex-PayPal employees, YouTube has the vision "to give everyone a voice, to evolve video, and to make their partners and advertisers successful." With hundreds of millions of users from around the world, partnerships with established and new media companies, and available in more than 30 languages, YouTube is uploaded with 48 hours of video every minute meaning 8 years of content every day.

ANALYSIS AND RESULTS

From the top 100 rankings of both Turkish and global brands, data was collected for the top 10 and bottom 10 brands. See Tables 1 and 2 for the breakdown of data of both groups.

Turkish vs. Global Brands

Among the three measures used to represent the engagement of Turkish brands, despite the lack of verified Twitter accounts for more than half of the sample, Twitter is the social media application that reaches the widest audience on average. The case is similar for global brands; the average audience of verified Twitter accounts is six times more than that of Facebook pages and YouTube accounts combined.

When the reach of the three social media applications by Turkish and global brands was compared, the results indicate that the YouTube audience for global brands is more than two hundred times more than that of Turkish brands, while the Twitter and Facebook audience is twenty and almost ten times more, respectively.

In order to test for a statistically significant correlation between the brand engagement measures and the brand value scores of the brands, as well as its strength, Pearson's correlation coefficient (r) was calculated and Student's t distribution was used. The null hypothesis is that no linear relationship between each of the random variables (number of followers for Twitter, number of active users for Facebook and number of subscribers for YouTube) and the brand value score exists: H_0: $\rho = 0$. Table 3 shows the calculated values t and r for both Turkish and global brands. In the case of Turkish brands, the null hypothesis is rejected for Facebook. In other words, for Turkish brands, there is a statistically significant correlation between the number of active users of the brands' Facebook pages and their brand value ranking. For global brands, both the number of active users of the brands' Facebook pages and the number of followers on Twitter for verified accounts of the brand show a statistically significant correlation with the brands' scores for brand value.

By further analyzing the correlation between the variables, it can be said that the correlation between the values of global brands and the number of active users of Facebook pages is stronger than that of Turkish brands. However, all three: the number of active Facebook users of Turkish brands, the number of active Facebook users of global brands and the numbers of followers of global brands on Twitter have strong positive correlations with the brands' value (see Table 4).

Table 1. Turkish brands data

Top 10	Name	Twitter # of followers	Facebook # of active users	Youtube # of subscribers	Brand Value Score
1	Turk Telekom	19,265	549	111	100
2	Turkish Airlines	461,049	83,481	15,527	99
3	Akbank	20,977	43,658	117	98
4	Isbank	25,651	8,180	116	97
5	Turkcell	433,108	30,510	3,530	96
6	Efes	45,461	37,252	136	95
7	Garanti	77,020	41,592	80	94
8	Arcelik	N/A	987	80	93
9	Yapi Kredi	21,337	11,280	32	92
10	Petrol Ofisi	N/A	32	N/A	91
90	Marshall Boya	N/A	0	N/A	10
91	Eczacibasi Ilac	N/A	0	10	9
92	Arzum	N/A	4,918	14	8
93	Aviva Sigorta	38,805	475	1,221	7
94	YKB Finansal Kiral.	N/A	N/A	N/A	6
95	Ege Profil	N/A	10	N/A	5
96	Kutahya Porselen	N/A	1,247	N/A	4
97	Penguen Gida	N/A	0	6	3
98	Adopen	N/A	904	N/A	2
99	Ray Sigorta	N/A	90	N/A	1
100	Net Turizm	N/A	N/A	N/A	0
Bottom 10	Name	# of followers Twitter	# of active users Facebook	# of subscribers Youtube	Brand Value Score
	Mean	126,964	13,956	1,614	48

Table 2. Global brands data

Top 10	Name	Twitter # of followers	Facebook # of active users	Youtube # of subscribers	Brand Value Score
1	Apple	7,050,843	86,737	828,896	100
2	Google	13,149,028	157,973	2,884,522	99
3	Microsoft	7,563,025	30,340	613,441	98
4	IBM	51,592	3,286	68,529	97
5	Wal-mart	547,821	812,461	8,322	96
6	Samsung	8,071,828	307,928	376,447	95
7	GE	382,607	14,855	14,585	94
8	Coca-Cola	1,396,896	683,775	138,000	93
9	Vodafone	562,467	3,475	59,832	92
10	Amazon.com	3,092,963	220,849	14,770	91
90	CVS	112,259	4,493	2,212	10
91	ASDA	89,279	57,404	321	9
92	Goldman Sachs	30,291	324	1,330	8
93	Canon	N/A	6,823	66,693	7
94	Panasonic	35,253	2,013	27,954	6
95	Time Warner Cable	9,991	35,934	1,975	5
96	SAP	98,339	1,379	28,254	4
97	Boeing	N/A	492	26,738	3
98	eBay	284,530	86,111	12,367	2
99	Lowe's	96,837	30,529	65,408	1
100	Sumitomo	N/A	21	598	0
Bottom 10	Name	# of followers Twitter	# of active users Facebook	# of subscribers Youtube	Brand Value Score
	Mean	2,368,103	121,295	249,581	48

Table 3. t and r values for Turkish and global brands

Turkish Brands		Global Brands	
Student's t Distribution (t)		**Student's t Distribution (t)**	
Twitter	2.065	Twitter	3.136
Facebook	3.215	Facebook	2.344
YouTube	1.351	YouTube	1.932
Correlation Coefficients (r)		**Correlation Coefficients (r)**	
Twitter	0.428	Twitter	0.584
Facebook	0.594	Facebook	0.474
YouTube	0.296	YouTube	0.405

Table 4. Correlation between measures and brand value for both groups of brands

		Null Hypothesis		
		Twitter	Facebook	Youtube
Relationship	Turkish Brands	Accepted **n/a**	r = 0.59 **Strong Positive**	Accepted **n/a**
	Global Brands	r = 0.58 **Strong Positive**	r = 0.47 **Strong Positive**	Accepted **n/a**

Industry Based Analysis

The brands in the two groups can be categorized in twenty-four subsectors (see Table 5) in nine industries. When grouped in subsectors, nine of these categories include more than one brand, which enables the analysis for correlation.

For those nine categories in the subsectors, and for the nine industries, the r and t values were calculated to test for the null hypothesis. Table 6 and 7 show the results.

It can be seen from the results that the number of active users of a brand's Facebook page is strongly (and positively) correlated with that brand's value ranking for brands in the financials sector. However, the number of followers on Twitter and the number of subscribers on YouTube do not have a statistically significant correlation with the brand value in any sector. In the case of subsectors, the null hypothesis was accepted for all cases except for the correlation between the numbers of subscribers on YouTube in the banks subsector and the brand value ranking. The correlation between two variables was a very strong negative relationship.

Table 5. Breakdown of brands into industries

Industry	Subsector	Name
Basic Materials	*Chemicals*	Marshall Boya
Consumer Goods	*Auto Parts & Equipment*	Sumitomo
	Beverages	Efes
		Coca-Cola
	Food	Penguen Gida
	Home Furnishings	Arcelik
		Panasonic
	Household	Kutahya Porselen
	Housewares	Arzum
	Office/Business Equipment	Canon
Consumer Services	*Airlines*	Turkish Airlines
	Media	Time Warner Cable
	Retail	Petrol Ofisi
		Net Turizm
		Wal-mart
		CVS
		ASDA
		Lowe's
Financials	*Banks*	Akbank
		Isbank
		Garanti
		Yapi Kredi
		Goldman Sachs
	Insurance	Aviva Sigorta
		Ray Sigorta
	Diversified Financial Services	YKB Finansal Kiral.
Healthcare	*Pharmaceuticals*	Eczacibasi Ilac
Industrials	*Aerospace & Defense*	Boeing
	Building Materials	Ege Profil
		Adopen
Miscellaneous	*Miscellaneous*	GE
Technology	*Computers*	Apple
	Internet	Google
		Amazon.com
		eBay
	IT Services	IBM
	Semiconductors	Samsung
	Software	Microsoft
		SAP
Telecommunications	*Telecommunications*	Turk Telekom
		Turkcell
		Vodafone

Table 6. Correlation between measures and brand value, categorized in industries

		Null Hypothesis		
	Industries	Twitter	Facebook	Youtube
Relationship	Basic Materials	Accepted	Accepted	Accepted
	Consumer Goods	Accepted	Accepted	Accepted
	Consumer Services	Accepted	Accepted	Accepted
	Financials	Accepted	r = 0.75 **Very Strong Positive**	Accepted
	Healthcare	Accepted	Accepted	Accepted
	Industrials	Accepted	Accepted	Accepted
	Misc.	Accepted	Accepted	Accepted
	Technology	Accepted	Accepted	Accepted
	Telecommunications	Accepted	Accepted	Accepted

CONCLUSION

Results and Implications

In this paper we tried to ascertain whether higher social media engagement is associated with higher brand value. We found that this holds true for Facebook and for global brands also for Twitter, and as well as for banks for Youtube and financials subsector for Facebook. The hypothesis could not be con-

Table 7. Correlation between measures and brand value, categorized in subsectors

		Null Hypothesis		
	Subsectors	Twitter	Facebook	Youtube
Relationship	Banks	Accepted	Accepted	r = -0.99 **Very Strong Negative**
	Beverages	Accepted	Accepted	Accepted
	Building Materials	Accepted	Accepted	Accepted
	Home Furnishings	Accepted	Accepted	Accepted
	Insurance	Accepted	Accepted	Accepted
	Internet	Accepted	Accepted	Accepted
	Retail	Accepted	Accepted	Accepted
	Software	Accepted	Accepted	Accepted
	Telecommunications	Accepted	Accepted	Accepted

firmed for other aspects of social media engagement, or subsectors. This has important implications for measuring, as well as marketing management. Currently, only Facebook seems to be a strong predictor of high brand value. That could be interpreted in two ways: Either the impact of Facebook is sufficiently high, or it became so wide-spread that it essentially equals and mirrors some aspects of brand value.

Limitations and Future Research

There are three main issues limiting the accuracy of the results of the research. Firstly, the sample size is small considering the existing numbers of brands both in Turkey and globally. The lack of sample size and thus diversity, also in industries, limited the industry based correlation analysis and returned questionable results. Secondly, as the use of social media applications by brands as a means to engage with their consumers has not been fully developed yet, the data collected may not correctly reflect the full potential, or the value of the brand in the eyes of the consumers which may have resulted in unsatisfactory findings (i.e. very low numbers of subscribers, lack of verified accounts etc.). Lastly, the natural immediacy of the social media applications and their use is an important issue in terms of data consistency as all the data collected can change within a matter of seconds and analysis may have been proven to be undependable after a very short amount of time.

REFERENCES

Achterberg, W., Pot, A. M., Kerkstra, A., Ooms, M., Muller, M., & Ribbe, M. (2003). The effect of depression on social engagement in newly admitted Dutch nursing home residents. *The Gerontologist*, *43*(2), 213–218. doi:10.1093/geront/43.2.213 PMID:12677078

Arvidsson, A. (2006). Brand value. *Journal of Brand Management*, *13*(3), 188–192. doi:10.1057/palgrave.bm.2540261

Boyd, D. M., & Ellison, N. B. (2007). Social Network Sites: Definition, History, and Scholarship. *Journal of Computer-Mediated Communication, 13*(1), 210–230. doi:10.1111/j.1083-6101.2007.00393.x

Brodie, R. J., Ilic, A., Juric, B., & Hollebeek, L. (2013). Consumer engagement in a virtual brand community: An exploratory analysis. *Journal of Business Research, 6*(1), 105–114. doi:10.1016/j.jbusres.2011.07.029

Cha, A. E. (2005). Creative commons is rewriting the rules of copyright. *Washington Post.*

Costa M. (2010). ENGAGEMENT: Customer engagement improves brand profits. *Marketing Week,* 22-23.

Fredrick, K. (2008). Streaming consciousness: Online video sharing. *School Library Media Activities Monthly, 24*(10), 44–46.

Haythornthwaite, C. (2005). Social networks and Internet connectivity effects. *Information Communication and Society, 8*(2), 125–147. doi:10.1080/13691180500146185

Hoffman, D. L., & Fodor, M. (2010). Can you measure the ROI of your social media marketing? *MIT Sloan Management Review, 52*(1), 41–49.

Hollebeek, L. (2011). Exploring customer brand engagement: Definition and themes. *Journal of Strategic Marketing, 19*(7), 555–573. doi:10.1080/0965254X.2011.599493

Java, A., Song, X., Finin, T., & Tseng, B. (2007). Why we twitter: understanding microblogging usage communities. *Proceedings of the 9th WebKDD and 1st SNA-KDD 2007 workshop on web mining and social network analysis*, 56–65. doi:10.1145/1348549.1348556

Kaplan, A. M., & Haenlein, M. (2010). Users of the world, unite! The challenges and opportunities of social media. *Business Horizons, 53*(1), 59–68. doi:10.1016/j.bushor.2009.09.003

Kellner, K. L. (1993). Conceptualizing, measuring and managing customer-based brand equity. *Journal of Marketing, 57*(1), 1–23. doi:10.2307/1252054

Kent, M. L., & Taylor, M. (1998). Building dialogic relationships through the World Wide Web. *Public Relations Review, 24*(3), 321–334. doi:10.1016/S0363-8111(99)80143-X

Lenhart, A., & Madden, M. (2005). *Teen Content Creators and Consumers*. Washington, DC: Pew Internet & American Life Project.

Li, C., & Bernoff, J. (2010). *Groundswell: Winning in a world transformed by social technologies*. The Herald.

Mollen, A., & Wilson, H. (2010). Engagement, telepresence and interactivity in online consumer experience: Reconciling scholastic and managerial perspectives. *Journal of Business Research, 63*(9-10), 919–925. doi:10.1016/j.jbusres.2009.05.014

Naaman, M., Boase, J., & Lai, C. (2010). *Is it really about me? Message content in social awareness streams*. Savannah, USA: Computer Supported Cooperative Work.

Probst, E. (2012). The top 5. *CustomRetailer, 11*(5), 14–14.

Radicati S. (2011). *Email statistics report, 2011-2015.*

Riemer, K., Richter, A., & Bohringer, M. (2010). Enterprise microblogging. *Business & Information Systems Engineering*, *2*(6), 391–394. doi:10.1007/s12599-010-0129-1

Safko, L., & Brake, D. K. (2009). *The social media bible: Tactics, tools and strategies for business success*. Hoboken, NJ: Wiley.

Skageby, J. (2008). Semi-public end-user content contributions – A case study of concerns and intentions in online photo sharing. *International Journal of Human-Computer Studies*, *66*(4), 287–300. doi:10.1016/j.ijhcs.2007.10.010

Thackeray, R., Neiger, B. L., & Keller, H. (2012). Integrating Social Media and Social Marketing. *Health Promotion Practice*, *13*(2), 165–168. doi:10.1177/1524839911432009 PMID:22382492

Tsai, C. F., Ouyang, W. C., Chen, L. K., Lan, C. F., Hwang, S. J., Yang, C. H., & Su, T. P. (2009). Depression is the strongest independent risk factor for poor social engagement among Chinese elderly veteran assisted-living residents. *Journal of the Chinese Medical Association*, *72*(9), 478–483. doi:10.1016/S1726-4901(09)70411-3 PMID:19762316

This research was previously published in the Journal of Electronic Commerce in Organizations (JECO), 13(1); edited by Pedro Isaías, pages 15-26, copyright year 2015 by IGI Publishing (an imprint of IGI Global).

Chapter 21
The Roles of Social Media Marketing and Brand Management in Global Marketing

Kijpokin Kasemsap
Suan Sunandha Rajabhat University, Thailand

ABSTRACT

This chapter explains the roles of social media marketing and brand management in global marketing, thus describing the theoretical and practical concept of social media marketing, the overview of brand management, the significance of social media marketing, and the application of social media-related brand management in global marketing. The creation of social media marketing and brand management is necessary for modern organizations that seek to serve suppliers and customers, increase business performance, enhance competitiveness, and gain routine success in global business. Thus, it is vital for modern organizations to acknowledge their social media marketing and brand management utilization, establish a strategic plan to consistently evaluate their effective promotions, and immediately respond to social media marketing and brand management needs of customers. The chapter argues that applying social media marketing and brand management in global marketing has the potential to enhance organizational performance and achieve strategic goals in the digital age.

INTRODUCTION

The development of social media has facilitated communication of consumer to each other in global marketing (Abzari, Ghassemi, & Vosta, 2014). Due to the rising level of global competition as well as a fast-growing number of innovations organizations are forced to find new ways to attract, gain, and sustain loyal customers in order to stay competitive (Lorenzo-Romero, Constantinides, & Brünink, 2014). Social media has changed the power structures in the global marketplace (Constantinides, 2014). Social media is used as a platform to access potential customer and implement marketing campaign (Rawat

DOI: 10.4018/978-1-5225-5637-4.ch021

& Divekar, 2014). Social media offers opportunities to stimulate and to measure social interrelations among customers in global marketing (Chen, Chen, & Xiao, 2013).

The evolution of social media is challenging the ways that marketing academics and practitioners effectively conceptualize and manage the brands in modern organizations (Davis, Piven, & Breazeale, 2014). Brands have become instruments of status signaling, that satisfy consumer prevalence of a need for status (Han, Nunes, & Dreze, 2010). Understanding how brands should operate on social media is very important for contemporary marketing researchers and managers (Habibi, Laroche, & Richard, 2014). Brands have the power to communicate valuable information and can be used and perceived in many different ways by consumers (Catalin & Andreea, 2014). Concerning the advantages of social networks, brand management is practically able to implement brand communities with less time and financial effort (Zaglia, 2013).

The strength of this chapter is on the thorough literature consolidation of social media marketing and brand management. The extant literature of social media marketing and brand management provides a contribution to practitioners and researchers by describing a comprehensive view of the functional application of social media marketing and brand management to appeal to different segments of social media marketing and brand management in order to maximize the business impact of social media marketing and brand management in global marketing.

BACKGROUND

The use of social media has immensely grown over the past decade, with technological and Internet innovations like Facebook, Twitter, and YouTube achieving massive adoption in a few years. Social media is increasingly important in daily life and is an especially important social interaction mechanism for young people (Luchman, Bergstrom, & Krulikowski, 2014). Social media includes countless sites with very different functions or uses that fulfill different personal needs (Brandtzeg & Heim, 2009). Social media is defined as the perspective of technological innovations in terms of both hardware and software that facilitate inexpensive content creation, interaction, and interoperability by online users (Berthon, Pitt, Plangger, & Shapiro, 2012).

Labrecque et al. (2013) stated that the predictions of growing consumer power in the digital age are fueled by the rise of the Internet and reignited by social media With the proliferation in Web 2.0 technologies, many marketing educators are experimenting with new teaching and learning tools (i.e., Facebook, Twitter, YouTube, and Second Life) (Lowe, D'Alessandro, Winzar, Laffey, & Collier, 2013). A typical classification of social media includes collaborative projects (i.e. Wikipedia), blogs, user-generated content communities (i.e., Flickr, YouTube, and Youku/Toduo), virtual game worlds (i.e. EverQuest), and virtual social worlds (i.e. Second Life) (Kaplan & Haenlein, 2010).

SOCIAL MEDIA MARKETING AND BRAND MANAGEMENT IN GLOBAL MARKETING

This section describes the theoretical and practical concept of social media marketing, the overview of brand management, the significance of social media marketing, and the application of social media-related brand management in global marketing.

Concept of Social Media Marketing

The advent of the 21st century is marked by the introduction of a new generation of media in consumer's everyday life (Giannakis-Bompolis & Boutsouki, 2014). There is a growing use of the Internet for social interactions with a business purpose (Bauer, Grether, & Leach, 2002; Boyd & Spekman, 2004; Kandampully, 2003). Most popular social networks are Facebook, Youtube, and Twitter (Vásquez & Escamilla, 2014). Leeflang et al. (2014) stated that Internet usage continues to explode across the world with digital becoming an increasingly important source of competitive advantage. Kietzmann et al. (2011) indicated that Facebook is the most popular social media application, which offers many capabilities associated with social media toward sharing texts, pictures, videos, and blogging with other people.

Social media marketing is most prominent and plays a huge role in the fundamental level (Wen, 2013). Social media marketing establishes presence, increases brand exposure, and expands market size, thus opening up a room of opportunities for businesses to create and maintain their brand and consumer relationships (Wen, 2013). Social media facilitates marketing of products and services (Kaplan & Haenlein, 2010). Businesses utilize social influence marketing and advertisement programs to identify customers and communicate their philosophy (Jang, Sim, Lee, & Kwon, 2013). Businesses run social media pages to build familiarity and advertise their goods through steady communication with their customers (Mangold & Faulds, 2009). Consumers from diverse backgrounds are communicating more and exchanging abundant amount of information through social media (Piccoli, 2010).

Social media provides a forum for word-of-mouth (WOM) as an effective marketing strategy (Jang et al., 2013). WOM takes place within a variety of online environments, allowing information exchanges to be immediately available to a multitude of people and institutions (Hennig-Thurau, Gwinner, Walsh, & Gremler, 2004). Twitter has received increasing attention as a unique communication tool that facilitates electronic word-of-mouth (eWOM) (Kim, Sung, & Kang, 2014). The eWOM has materialized as a phenomenon of critical interest to global marketers (Williams, Crittenden, Keo, & McCarty, 2012).

Social media provides a sharing platform with its tools, such as social networks, forums, e-mails, and blogosphere (Uzunoglu & Kip, 2014). The shared views, experiences and opinions of online users are eWOM (Cheung & Thadani, 2012; Filieri & McLeay, 2014) which are more trusted compared to other corporate messages, since these messages directly communicate what are perceived to be consumers' own experiences (Wu & Wang, 2011). Trusov et al. (2009) provided a precise perception of the relation between WOM and traditional media.

Social media is a suitable option to access and collect information from other consumers (Godes & Mayzlin, 2004). Bruyn and Lilien (2008) studied the effect of consumer communications to each other in the process of decision-making in the context of viral marketing. Social media provides an unparalleled platform for consumers to publicize their personal evaluations of purchased products and to facilitate WOM communication (Chen, Fay, & Wang, 2011). Computers are regarded as commonplace and the Internet serves as the main method for communication for the younger generations (Piccoli, 2010).

Social media represents a new trend, as it changes the rules of communication with customers by allowing firms to engage in timely and direct end-consumer contact at a relatively low cost and higher efficiency levels than with more traditional communication tools (Martini, Massa, & Testa, 2014). Social media shortens the distance between the company and users, thereby strengthening user involvement and engagement in the innovation process (Piller, Vossen, & Ihl, 2012).

Social media is a new way through which people are able to search and share information (Akar, 2011). Social media tools play an important role in transforming the characteristics of front-end innovation, changing its boundaries and knowledge distances, and making it more efficient and effective in certain circumstances (Afuah & Tucci, 2012; Bogers, Afuah, & Bastian, 2010; Jespersen, 2010). There is a distinction made between customer-initiated social media (i.e., reviews and blogs) and organization-initiated social media (i.e. brand communities) (de Vries, Gensler, & Leeflang, 2012).

The growing power of bloggers to influence their connected network has emerged as a new communication venue for brands (Uzunoglu & Kip, 2014). Marketing communications should be considered as an important determinant of brand equity (Simon & Sullivan, 1993). Marketing communications have a positive influence on brand equity, brand loyalty, brand awareness and brand value (Yoo, Donthu, & Lee, 2000). Positive and negative communications of user through social media as well as traditional advertising of the companies can influence consumers' attitudes toward a particular brand (Abzari et al., 2014).

Overview of Brand Management

Brands tend to influence more the high-involvement resolutions because they provide a valid method of identification (Catalin & Andreea, 2014). An economic perspective focuses on the brand's value (Motameni & Shahrokhi, 1998; Yoo et al., 2000), while a strategic perspective emphasizes understanding consumer-based market segments to improve overall marketing campaigns. The growing small and medium-sized enterprises (SMEs) have adopted market and brand orientations to a greater extent than have the stable or declining ones (Reijonen, Laukkanen, Komppula, & Tuominen, 2012).

Establishing a good brand relationship is necessary for brand management in emerging markets (Kasemsap, 2015a). Individuals who identify with a particular brand experience a positive psychological result in the form of improved self-esteem and are more likely to act favorably toward effective brand management (Donavan, Janda, & Suh, 2006). Brand primarily serves as the basis for the interactions and the benefits generated in high-quality customer-to-customer (C2C) interactions (Muniz & O'Guinn, 2001). Implementing the branding practices will increase the likelihood that consumers perceive the brand in question as fair, leading to an increase in brand loyalty and positive WOM (Chen, Nguyen, & Klaus, 2013).

As business-to-business (B2B) companies face large customer purchase volumes, it is essential for long-term B2B brand success to maintain and manage brand loyalty (Rauyruen, Miller, & Barrett, 2007). An increasing emphasis on branding activities is evident in B2B markets (Kalafatis, Riley, & Singh, 2014). B2B branding has received increasing attention from researchers in the last few years (Cassia & Magno, 2012). Continuous pioneering with a new brand leads to greater brand preferences when technological uncertainty is high (Chang & Park, 2013).

Theoretical and practical terms related to brand management in global marketing (i.e., brand equity, brand awareness, brand associations, perceived brand quality, brand loyalty, brand community, brand alliances, brand trust, and brand identification) are described.

Brand Equity

Most conceptualizations of brand equity come from a consumer's perspective considering consumers often drive a brand's success (Aitken & Campelo, 2011). Brand equity is a resource that influences the consumer's response to a branded organization's efforts to differentiate one brand from other (Lee & Griffith, 2012). Lieven et al. (2014) stated that brand personality has been suggested as an important source of consumer-based brand equity.

Consumer-based brand equity usually is evaluated for four dimensions: brand awareness, brand associations, perceived brand quality, and brand loyalty (Buil, Martinez, & de Chernatony, 2013). Brand managers utilize existing consumer-based brand equity scales (Yoo et al., 2000) in order to conduct holistic research into all of the brand equity elements via deployment to myriad stakeholder groups, thus transforming knowledge into marketing improvements.

Brand Awareness

Brand awareness indicates how well consumers recall the brand (Buil et al., 2013) and is a component of overall brand knowledge (Keller, 1993). Different studies stress the importance of advertising in brand awareness (Aaker, 1996; Buil et al., 2013; Kirmani & Wright, 1989), as well as the importance of brand awareness in the perception of brand quality (Aaker, 1996; Buil et al., 2013; Keller & Lehmann, 2003). Adolescents appear to have an awareness of the role of branding and advertising to form the brand consumption attitudes (Isaksen & Roper, 2012).

Brand Associations

Brand associations are the cognitive connections that a person has with the brand (Zavattaro, Daspit, & Adams, 2015). The most important step in creating and delivering a superior value to customers is by adding brand associations that create value beyond the intrinsic characteristics of a product. One of the most important characteristics of a brand is the self-expressive function (Keller, 2008).

Perceived Brand Quality

While consumers draw conclusions about the quality of a brand based on their evaluation of its intrinsic attributes (Shaharudin, Mansor, & Elias, 2011; Sule Alonso, Paquin, & Levy Mangin, 2002), its packaging (Lavenka, 1991) or its price (Cronley, Posavac, Meyer, Kardes, & Kellaris, 2005; Kardes, Cronley, Kellaris, & Posavac, 2004), one of the main elements concerning perception of a product's quality is brand name (Dawar & Parker, 1994). Perceived brand quality relates to a person's view of one brand or product versus another (Zavattaro et al., 2015).

Perceived value forms as a result of the consumer's experiences purchasing and consuming a brand (Cronin, Brady, & Hult, 2000). One of the key issues influencing the perceived quality of a brand is its brand awareness (Aaker, 1996; Buil et al., 2013; Keller & Lehman, 2003). Consumers assign high quality to prestigious brands (Rubio, Oubina, & Villasenor, 2014). Brands appreciate greater credibility and brand value for the consumer (Erdem & Swait, 1998; Erdem, Swait, & Louviere, 2002).

Brand Loyalty

Brand loyalty has developed into diverse areas from brand preference to brand community (Yoo & Bai, 2013). Brand loyalty is a long-term commitment to the brand, which is based on awareness, perceived brand quality, and brand associations (Zavattaro et al., 2015). Brand loyalty is a pre-economic target value and indicator of corporate as well as brand community success (Algesheimer, Dholakia, & Herrmann, 2005; Chaudhuri & Holbrook, 2001).

Customer value, customer satisfaction, and brand loyalty have the strengths to mediate positive effect on customer relationship management (CRM) performance (Kasemsap, 2015b). Attaching consumers to a brand is a cornerstone of relationship marketing as brand attachment effectively increases brand loyalty (Schmalz & Orth, 2012).

Brand Community

The concept of a brand community stems from the sociological notion of what constitutes an early community (Muniz & O'Guinn, 2001). Brand communities represent valuable marketing, innovation management, and CRM tools (Zaglia, 2013). Brand community consists of socially networked groups of individuals with mutual interests, who inhabit a common area in order to cope with routine tasks (Muniz & O'Guinn, 2001). Brand communities exist in the real world as well as in the virtual space of the Internet, utilizing chat, e-mail, and discussion forums as the virtual forms of communication and interaction media (Andersen, 2005; Muniz & O'Guinn, 2001; Schau, Muñiz, & Arnould, 2009).

Brand community can exist everywhere (Thompson & Sinha, 2008). Social interactions between brand community members effectively influence customers' relationship with brand (McAlexander, Schouten, & Koenig, 2002). The social formations offer many advantages (Brown, Kozinets, & Sherry, 2003), and serve as a tool to build strong relationships with customers (Algesheimer et al., 2005). The consumer engagement process comprises a range of sub-processes reflecting consumers' interactive experience within online brand communities among community participants (Brodie, Ilic, Juric, & Hollebeek, 2013). Businesses need to engage consumers in brand communications, which consumers perceive to be non-commercially driven within brand communities (Brodie et al., 2013).

The interactions between customers are characterized by mutual trust, which is of pivotal importance to B2B brand communities (Bruhn, Schnebelen, & Schäfer, 2014). Brand communities are characterized by the three constituent components: consciousness of kind; rituals and traditions; and a sense of moral responsibility (Muniz & O'Guinn, 2001). The opportunities that interactions in B2B brand communities offer companies as well as brand community members have been recognized by B2B firms, but are still an underexplored field of marketing research (Bruhn et al., 2014).

Brand Alliances

Brand alliances in the B2B domain are becoming popular (Kalafatis et al., 2014). Brand alliances benefit the business partners through reputation endorsement and access to resources and competencies, such as distribution and technology (Bengtsson & Servais, 2005; Cooke & Ryan, 2000; Erevelles, Horton, & Fukawa, 2008). Norris (1993) presented a case study of Intel, highlighting the benefits of its component branding strategy of Intel-inside. Bucklin and Sengupta (1993) indicated that successful brand alliances involve partners with equal power and managerial resources. Dahlstrom and Dato-on (2004) stated that both asymmetry and complementarity of company assets are the positive determinants of a firm's decision to co-brand.

Ghosh and John (2009) utilized the transaction cost economics to describe that original equipment manufacturers are more likely to use branded components when the brand name of components provides them with opportunities for important market differentiation. Gammoh and Voss (2013) explained that a company's propensity to engage in brand alliance activities is contingent on the extent and quality of related past experiences, managerial competence, and attitude toward brand alliance.

In the business-to-customer (B2C) brand alliance studies, context effects are recognized in the form of brand leveraging (Ghosh & John, 2009), resource allocation (Heide & John, 1990), feedback effect (Park, Jun, & Shocker, 1996), quality signals (Rao, Qu, & Ruekert, 1999), and are revealed to affect preference for familiar stimuli (Cooke & Mellers, 1998; Simonson & Tversky, 1992) and to help interpretation of unfamiliar stimuli (Sen, 1998; Wright & Rip, 1980).

Brand Trust

Brand trust is viewed as the essence of brand's value to consumers (Berry, 2000). Trust in the online environment is characterized by greater complexity (i.e., trust in the website versus trust in technology), need for structural assurances of security and privacy, and the lack of tangible brand cues (Pentina, Zhang, & Basmanova, 2013). Trust in the online community members should motivate the sharing of information (Ridings, Gefen, & Arinze, 2002). Previous studies on eWOM communication have indicated that people are more likely to pass along information when the source of it is perceived as trustworthy (Brown, Broderick, & Lee, 2007; Chiu, Hsieh, Kao, & Lee, 2007; Yeh & Choi, 2011).

An essential catalyst for establishing and maintaining long-term relationships is brand trust, defined as confidence in the brand's consistency, reliability, and honesty (Wang & Emurian, 2005). Trust facilitates customer satisfaction with a brand (Chaudhuri & Holbrook, 2001; Morgan & Hunt, 1994), thus determining customer intentions to maintain the relationship with other associated brands (Stewart, 2003). Morgan and Hunt (1994) identified trust and the resulting commitment as key mediators of successful buyer–seller relationships that lead to cooperation and reduce conflict and uncertainty in the B2B context. In the end-consumer domain, brand trust represents a manifestation of relationship quality (Crosby, Evans, & Cowles, 1990).

Previous studies found positive effects of trust on the likelihood of continuing the buyer–seller relationships (Crosby et al., 1990), long-term orientation of the trustor (Ganesan, 1994), and consumer intent to make a purchase (Doney & Cannon, 1997). Trust is critical for attracting traffic and completing successful online interactions, as well as maintaining online communities and virtual groups (Coppola, Hiltz, & Rotter, 2004).

Brand Identification

A brand's identity should be a clear and concise narrative that defines the brand's values and ideals (Reed & Botts, 2014). Brand relationships have traditionally been theorized as simulating interpersonal relationships, which are reflected in self-identity or self-expansion theory (Huang & Mitchell, 2014). The idea of brand identification suggests that community members identified with a brand tend to engage in pro-brand activities through their affiliation with the community and interactions with peer members (Algesheimer et al., 2005; Bagozzi & Dholakia, 2006; Carlson, Suter, & Brown, 2008).

Significance of Social Media Marketing in Global Marketing

The introduction of social media platforms has contributed to the development of a new era of customer empowerment enabling customers to interconnect worldwide and easily share and exchange personal, social, and scientific knowledge in the global marketplace (Lee, Olson, & Trimi, 2012). By having more information and alternatives where to buy a product or service, customers take a more influential role in the process of value creation forcing organizations to step away from their traditional organization-centric view to a more customer-centric view in order to be competitive (Prahalad & Ramaswamy, 2004; Sashi, 2012).

Social media tools that include social networking features are being utilized to allow users both inside and outside the organization to easily communicate and collaboratively design, manage, and launch new products and services (Marion, Barczak, & Hultink, 2014). The unique aspects of social media and its immense popularity have revolutionized marketing practices (Hanna, Rohm, & Crittenden, 2011) and consumer behavior from information acquisition to post purchase behavior (Mangold & Faulds, 2009; Powers, Advincula, Austin, & Graiko, 2012). The networked and social nature of social media allows like-minded people to gather in groups and subgroups with a specific common interest (Mangold & Faulds, 2009).

Social media makes customers more sophisticated and help them develop new marketing tactics in searching, evaluating, choosing and buying goods and services (Albors, Ramos, & Hervas, 2008). While social media and its marketing applications proliferate, developing distinctive strategies for effectively targeting and engaging users on each platform remains a work-in-progress (Pentina et al., 2013). Companies considering the Internet as a strategic communication tool have recognized the power of influential members of social media platform who frequently share their brand experiences on a regular basis (Uzunoglu & Kip, 2014).

Firms need to be connected to their technological business environment through social media because interacting with external sources of knowledge can improve their capabilities about industry benchmark and competitive advantage (Kasemsap, 2014a). The determinants of social media participation take a utility-based approach and investigate gratifications obtained (Park, Kee, & Valenzuela, 2009), perceived value, satisfaction, and habit (Barnes & Bohringer, 2011). Other studies utilize the technology acceptance model (TAM) (Pookulangara & Koesler, 2011) and the theory of planned behavior (Pelling & White, 2009) to explain participation and loyalty of social media users.

Social networking sites (SNSs) (i.e., Facebook, Twitter, Flickr, and MySpace) lead to increased brand reputation, a more open, transparent culture, and a more effective and efficient way of working (Kasemsap, 2014b). Among other online platforms, communities in SNSs have received much attention in recent years for their ability to accelerate eWOM for brands (Kim et al., 2014). SNSs serve as a powerful and ideal venue for eWOM, a marketing venue where consumers disseminate and seek out information from their established social networks through interpersonal interactions online (Boyd & Ellison, 2007; Vollmer & Precourt, 2008). Brand-related information and opinions that are shared among personal contacts in SNSs may be perceived as more credible and trustworthy than other forms of eWOM communication (Chu & Kim, 2011).

Social media has intensified instant personal interaction between the brand and its community (Nambisan & Watt, 2011). The ease of participating in online social communities removes both the physical and temporal barriers, increasing the likelihood of participation from consumers who may not have been able or inclined to do so previously (Davis et al., 2014). Social media access has moved beyond the fixed physical space of the computer screen to the ubiquitous mobile channel of the smartphone: instant consumption and interactivity is fueled by brand-related content from other connected channels of communication (i.e., radio and television) (Davis & Sajtos, 2008).

Companies utilize interpersonal messages in their Twitter posts to develop close relationships with their consumers (Kwon & Sung, 2011; Lin & Pena, 2011). Consumers generate brand-related tweets on Twitter to express their sentiments, complaints, and opinions concerning brands (Jansen, Zhang, Sobel, &

Chowdhury, 2009). Twitter is used as a social channel to promote communication and to help companies develop mutually beneficial relationships with consumers (Jansen et al., 2009). In SNS environments where consumers display themselves publicly to others, a consumer engaging in eWOM shapes and expresses brand identity (Taylor, Strutton, & Thompson, 2012).

Social media offers opportunities to create the brand trust and reach a large audience at a low cost (Leeflang et al., 2014). The effects of social networks on customer adoption have been recognized in multiple studies (Nitzan & Libai, 2011; Rahmandad & Sterman, 2008; Yoganarasimhan, 2012). Marketing users disseminate and share information via Twitter (Zhang, Jansen, & Chowdhury, 2011). Twitter has been found to offer relational benefits by allowing users to build perceptions of one another and establish common ground for future conversations, and by promoting a feeling of connectedness with one another (Zhao & Rosson, 2009), thus enhancing the power of eWOM. Marketing behaviors occurring on SNSs are considered customer investments in response to marketers' social media efforts (Hoffman & Fodor, 2010).

Application of Social Media-Related Brand Management in Global Marketing

Managing a brand in the 21st century is more complex than ever before due to the advancement in technology (Abratt & Kleyn, 2012; Balmer, 2012; Kaufmann, Vrontis, Czinkota, & Alvin Hadiono, 2012), faster innovation, growing competition, complexity and more demanding consumers (Kaufmann et al., 2012; Klaus, 2013; Maklan & Klaus, 2011). As a business moves toward globalization, shifting from marketing (product brand) to corporate branding becomes essential (Balmer, 2012; Hatch & Schultz, 2009; Kapferer, 2012).

Brands represent the instances of socially constructed identities, created by marketers and consumers (Muniz & O'Guinn, 2001), that reflect characteristics associated with the typical user, as well as with advertising images and associations (Poddar, Donthu, & Wei, 2009). Brands with high-intensity placements should encourage consumers to view with friends (Coker, Altobello, & Balasubramanian, 2013). The development of Internet technology enables service firms to obtain a high capability for brand information transmission as well as relative customer feedback data collection (Shirahada & Kosaka, 2012). Consumers possess almost unlimited opportunities to engage with brands (Christodoulides, Jevons, & Bonhomme, 2012; Helm & Jones, 2010). The results of the brand access practically mandate the changes in branding strategies toward engagement platforms (Naylor, Lamberton, & West, 2012; Verhoef, Reinartz, & Krafft, 2010).

A brand's Facebook page is a marketing communication tool (Brodmerkel & Carah, 2013). González-Benito et al. (2014) stated that retailers have worked to advance store-brand strategies, leading to greater success and higher congruence with the retailer's positioning. Consumers reflect their personalities by the brands they use, but the relationship between brand choice and symbolic dimensions (i.e., extraversion, agreeableness, neuroticism, and openness to experience) is much stronger than the relationship with functional dimensions (i.e. conscientiousness) (Huang, Mitchell, & Rosenaum-Elliott, 2012).

Corporate brand value is the brand promise of an organization which provides sameness and credibility about its organization to all its stakeholders (Balmer, 2012; Balmer & Gray, 2003; Knox, 2004). Consumers demand a great deal of information from a company before committing to a buying decision, thus leading a company to show greater transparency and integrity when delivering its services (Rowley, 2004). Brand consumption value is an uninterrupted social process of stakeholder interactions

(Merz, He, & Vargo, 2009). Brand consumption becomes the social co-production of shared meanings (de Chernatony & Segal-Horn, 2001; Tuominen, 2007).

Brands are perceived as social entities by consumers (Pentina et al., 2013). Consumers prefer brands with personality traits that are congruent with the social situations (Sung, Choi, & Lin, 2012). Consumers achieve the business meaning through their relationships with brands (Bagozzi, Bergami, Marzocchi, & Morandin, 2012; Brown et al., 2003; McAlexander et al., 2002). Aaker (1997) stated that consumers attribute human personality qualities to brands. Fournier (1998) identified the stages of interpersonal relationships toward developing brands.

The emergence of the Internet has a positive impact on building corporate brand (Kapferer, 2012; Shultz & de Chernatony, 2002; Stuart & Jones, 2004). Klaus et al. (2013) stated that the Internet is important as it influences the way businesses operate and people's lifestyles. Learning how to manage corporate brand through how consumers experience corporate websites will develop a long-term brand relationship (Klaus, 2013; Klaus & Maklan, 2013; Morgan-Thomas & Veloutsou, 2013).

The Internet is recognized as a useful way of delivering brand value to all stakeholders (Argyriou, Kitchen, & Melewar, 2006). The Internet responds to the dynamic environment, thus allowing greater involvement of brand experience and brand engagement in the brand communities through business interaction (de Chernatony & Christodoulides, 2004; Klaus et al., 2013; Stuart & Jones, 2004). By communicating corporate brand value on the Internet, the brand value is concise and defined (Balmer & Gray, 2003).

Marketing attempts have been made to describe online brand personalities (Okazaki, 2006), electronic brand personalities (Park, Choi, & Kim, 2005), and website personalities (Chen & Rodgers, 2006) using both pre-existing personality scales and lists of adjectives derived from qualitative research. The symbolic meaning of brands reflects attributes associated with groups using the brand and is used to enhance self-concept through brand adoption (McCracken, 1988). Brands recognize the power of bloggers, to directly influence their connected network by making suggestions, which result in the use of products (Flynn, Goldsmith, & Eastman, 1996).

Regarding social media marketing, online corporate brand is an important source of positioning and differentiation within the industry to effectively reach customers (de Chernatony, 2002; Melewar & Navalekar, 2002; Parasuraman, Zeithaml, & Malhotra, 2005). Corporate brand requires a dynamic interface between the actions of organization and the interpretation of customers (Balmer & Gray, 2003; de Chernatony, 2002).

Brand communities in social media have positive effects on the brand (Laroche, Habibi, Richard, & Sankaranarayanan, 2012). Choosing the appropriate brand community type, cultivating consumers' interaction, and staying tuned to social engagement are critical factors to gain brand outcomes (Zaglia, 2013). B2B brand communities offer great opportunities to promote profitability, brand loyalty, and economic success (Bruhn et al., 2014). B2B brand communities are able to meet the demands of customers in providing them with brand-related information through their interactions with other experienced customers (Andersen, 2005). Brand communities lead to improved value creation processes and service quality (Ellahi & Bokhari, 2013).

Marketers have been able to bring brands and their messages to the awareness of consumers, possessing full control over the message, but social media has changed this (Väisänen, 2015). Managers are creating their brands together with consumers by sharing experiences and opinions. Because this new type of branding process is dependent on consumers' opinions and perceptions of the brand image, managers need to listen what their customers are saying and engage consumers into the co-creation of their brands. This two-way communication has changed the ideology of branding online completely (Corstjens & Umblijs, 2012; Singh & Sonnenburg, 2012).

The biggest brands on Facebook within the area are media groups, closely followed by e-commerce and airlines (Prakash, 2012). Brand managers should begin thinking of social media as a massive data repository, a digitized focus group with millions of unpaid participants. This repository consists of huge amounts of unstructured data, which hold valuable insights about customer shopping habits, lifestyle interests, product use cases, even aspirations (Hamedi, 2014). Brand managers need to direct the channel toward achieving a specific marketing and brand goal, such as increasing brand awareness, brand loyalty and engagement, intelligence gathering, and new product development (Mount & Martinez, 2014).

Social media marketing can improve global business in terms of increased brand recognition, better brand loyalty, higher brand authority, more opportunities to convert, higher conversion rates, increased inbound traffic, decreased marketing costs, better search engine rankings, and improved customer insights (Forbes, 2014). Kraak and Story (2015) conducted a systematic review of five electronic databases (2000–2014) to identify experimental studies that measured how food companies' mascots and entertainment companies' media characters influence up to 12 diet-related cognitive, behavioral and health outcomes for children under 12 years. Eleven studies met the inclusion criteria. Studies used 21 media characters, but no brand mascots. Results suggest that cartoon media character branding can positively increase children's fruit intake compared with no character branding (Kraak & Story, 2015).

Ashley and Tuten (2015) studied the creative strategies in social media marketing are shared by a sample of top brands. The results reveal that social media channels and creative strategies in social media marketing are applied. Despite the value of creative approaches in social media marketing, most branded social content can be categorized as functional (Ashley & Tuten, 2015). Singh et al. (2012) documented global social media usage patterns based on a large-scale survey of 4,630 social media users around the world. Singh et al. (2012)'s empirical study provides the insights into how users in the European Union, United States, and BRIC (Brazil, Russia, India, and China) regions use social media for business and personal use. Social media is increasingly becoming the vehicle for the voice of people and consumers worldwide. From a business perspective, companies are actively leveraging social media to create brand communities, gain consumer insights, and enhance brand awareness in global marketing (Singh et al., 2012).

FUTURE RESEARCH DIRECTIONS

The strength of this chapter is on the thorough literature consolidation of social media marketing and brand management. The extant literature of social media marketing and brand management provides a contribution to practitioners and researchers by describing a comprehensive view of the functional application of social media marketing and brand management to appeal to different segments of social media marketing and brand management in order to maximize the business impact of social media marketing and brand management. The classification of the extant literature in the domains of social media marketing and brand management will provide the potential opportunities for future research. Future research direction should broaden the perspectives in the implementation of social media marketing and brand management to be utilized in the knowledge-based organizations.

Practitioners and researchers should recognize the applicability of a more multidisciplinary approach toward research activities in implementing social media marketing and brand management in terms of knowledge management-related variables (i.e., knowledge-sharing behavior, knowledge creation, organizational learning, learning orientation, and motivation to learn). It will be useful to bring additional disciplines together (i.e., strategic management, marketing, finance, and human resources) to support a more holistic examination of social media marketing and brand management in order to combine or transfer existing theories and approaches to inquiry in this area. The investigation of linkages among social media marketing, brand management, and business intelligence would seem to be workable for future research efforts.

CONCLUSION

This chapter explained the roles of social media marketing and brand management in global marketing, thus describing the theoretical and practical concept of social media marketing, the overview of brand management, the significance of social media marketing, and the application of social media-related brand management in global marketing. Social media marketing provides organizations with a way to connect with their customers. Social media marketing programs usually center on efforts to create content that attracts attention and encourages readers to share it across their social networks toward competition in the global marketplace. However, organizations must protect their business information as well as closely watch comments and concerns on the social media they use.

Companies on a global scale should recognize that one of the most promising paths to long-term longevity, a prosperous organization, and healthy profits is to create and manage strong brands for their products and services. Brand management is the analysis and planning on how that brand is perceived in the market. Knowing how consumers perceive a brand is essential to effective marketing. Executives and brand managers need to understand how customers perceive and select brands in specific product categories and market segments. Developing a good relationship with the target market is essential for brand management in global marketing.

The utilization of social media marketing effectively promotes and develops brand management in global marketing. The strategic uses of social media marketing and brand management can offer a greater competitive advantage in modern organizations. The creation of social media marketing and brand management is necessary for modern organizations that seek to serve suppliers and customers, increase business performance, enhance competitiveness, and gain routine success in global business. Thus, it is vital for modern organizations to acknowledge their social media marketing and brand management utilization, establish a strategic plan to consistently evaluate their effective promotions, and immediately respond to social media marketing and brand management needs of customers.

REFERENCES

Aaker, D. A. (1996). Measuring brand equity across products and markets. *California Management Review*, *38*(3), 102–120. doi:10.2307/41165845

Aaker, J. L. (1997). Dimensions of brand personality. *JMR, Journal of Marketing Research*, *34*(3), 347–356. doi:10.2307/3151897

Abratt, R., & Kleyn, N. (2012). Corporate identity, corporate branding and corporate reputations: Reconciliation and integration. *European Journal of Marketing*, *46*(7–8), 1048–1063.

Abzari, M., Ghassemi, R. A., & Vosta, L. N. (2014). Analysing the effect of social media on brand attitude and purchase intention: The case of Iran Khodro company. *Procedia: Social and Behavioral Sciences*, *143*, 822–826. doi:10.1016/j.sbspro.2014.07.483

Afuah, A., & Tucci, C. L. (2012). Crowdsourcing as a solution to distant search. *Academy of Management Review*, *37*(3), 355–375. doi:10.5465/amr.2010.0146

Aitken, R., & Campelo, A. (2011). The four Rs of place branding. *Journal of Marketing Management*, *27*(9–10), 913–933. doi:10.1080/0267257X.2011.560718

Akar, E., & Topçu, B. (2011). An examination of the factors influencing consumers' attitudes toward social media marketing. *Journal of Internet Commerce*, *10*(1), 35–67. doi:10.1080/15332861.2011.558456

Albors, J., Ramos, J. C., & Hervas, J. L. (2008). New learning network paradigm: Communities of objectives, crowdsourcing, wikis and open source. *International Journal of Information Management*, *28*(3), 194–202. doi:10.1016/j.ijinfomgt.2007.09.006

Algesheimer, R., Dholakia, U. M., & Herrmann, A. (2005). The social influence of brand community: Evidence from European car clubs. *Journal of Marketing*, *69*(3), 19–34. doi:10.1509/jmkg.69.3.19.66363

Andersen, P. H. (2005). Relationship marketing and brand involvement of professionals through web-enhanced brand communities: The case of Coloplast. *Industrial Marketing Management*, *34*(1), 39–51. doi:10.1016/j.indmarman.2004.07.002

Argyriou, E., Kitchen, P., & Melewar, T. C. (2006). The relationship between corporate websites and brand equity. *International Journal of Market Research*, *48*(5), 575–599.

Ashley, C., & Tuten, T. (2015). Creative strategies in social media marketing: An exploratory study of branded social content and consumer engagement. *Psychology and Marketing*, *32*(1), 15–27. doi:10.1002/mar.20761

Bagozzi, R. P., Bergami, M., Marzocchi, G. L., & Morandin, G. (2012). Customer-organization relationships: Development and test of a theory of extended identities. *Journal of Applied Psychology*, *97*(1), 63–76. doi:10.1037/a0024533 PMID:21766998

Balmer, J. M. T. (2012). Corporate brand management imperatives: Custodianship, credibility, and calibration. *California Management Review*, *54*(3), 6–33. doi:10.1525/cmr.2012.54.3.6

Balmer, J. M. T., & Gray, E. R. (2003). Corporate brands: What are they? What of them? *European Journal of Marketing*, *37*(7-8), 972–997. doi:10.1108/03090560310477627

Barnes, S. J., & Bohringer, M. (2011). Modeling use continuance behavior in microblogging services: The case of Twitter. *Journal of Computer Information Systems*, *51*(4), 1–10.

Bauer, H. H., Grether, M., & Leach, M. (2002). Building customer relations over the Internet. *Industrial Marketing Management*, *31*(2), 155–163. doi:10.1016/S0019-8501(01)00186-9

Bengtsson, A., & Servais, P. (2005). Co-branding on industrial markets. *Industrial Marketing Management*, *34*(7), 706–713. doi:10.1016/j.indmarman.2005.06.004

Berry, L. L. (2000). Cultivating service brand equity. *Journal of the Academy of Marketing Science*, *28*(1), 128–137. doi:10.1177/0092070300281012

Berthon, P. R., Pitt, L. F., Plangger, K., & Shapiro, D. (2012). Marketing meets Web 2.0, social media, and creative consumers: Implications for international marketing strategy. *Business Horizons*, *55*(3), 261–271. doi:10.1016/j.bushor.2012.01.007

Bogers, M., Afuah, A., & Bastian, B. (2010). Users as innovators: A review, critique, and future research directions. *Journal of Management*, *36*(4), 857–875. doi:10.1177/0149206309353944

Boyd, D. M., & Ellison, N. B. (2007). Social network sites: Definition, history, and scholarship. *Journal of Computer-Mediated Communication*, *13*(1), 210–230. doi:10.1111/j.1083-6101.2007.00393.x

Boyd, D. E., & Spekman, R. E. (2004). Internet usage within B2B relationships and its impact on value creation: A conceptual model and research propositions. *Journal of Business-To-Business Marketing*, *11*(1–2), 9–34. doi:10.1300/J033v11n01_03

Brandtzaeg, P. B., & Heim, J. (2011). A typology of social networking sites users. *International Journal of Web Based Communities*, *7*(1), 28–51. doi:10.1504/IJWBC.2011.038124

Brodie, R. J., Ilic, A., Juric, B., & Hollebeek, L. (2013). Consumer engagement in a virtual brand community: An exploratory analysis. *Journal of Business Research*, *66*(1), 105–114. doi:10.1016/j.jbusres.2011.07.029

Brodmerkel, S., & Carah, N. (2013). Alcohol brands on Facebook: The challenges of regulating brands on social media. *Journal of Public Affairs*, *13*(3), 272–281. doi:10.1002/pa.1466

Brown, J., Broderick, A. J., & Lee, N. (2007). Word-of-mouth communication within online communities: Conceptualizing the online social network. *Journal of Interactive Marketing*, *21*(3), 2–19. doi:10.1002/dir.20082

Brown, S., Kozinets, R. V., & Sherry, J. F. Jr. (2003). Teaching old brands new tricks: Retro branding and the revival of brand meaning. *Journal of Marketing*, *67*(3), 19–33. doi:10.1509/jmkg.67.3.19.18657

Bruhn, M., Schnebelen, S., & Schäfer, D. (2014). Antecedents and consequences of the quality of e-customer-to-customer interactions in B2B brand communities. *Industrial Marketing Management*, *43*(1), 164–176. doi:10.1016/j.indmarman.2013.08.008

Bruyn, A., & Lilien, G. L. (2008). A multi–stage model of word of mouth through viral marketing. *International Journal of Research in Marketing*, *25*(3), 143–225. doi:10.1016/j.ijresmar.2008.03.004

Bucklin, L. P., & Sengupta, S. (1993). Organizing successful co-marketing alliances. *Journal of Marketing*, *57*(2), 32–46. doi:10.2307/1252025

Buil, I., Martinez, E., & de Chernatony, L. (2013). The influence of brand equity on consumer responses. *Journal of Consumer Marketing*, *30*(1), 62–74. doi:10.1108/07363761311290849

Carlson, B. D., Suter, T. A., & Brown, T. J. (2008). Social versus psychological brand community: The role of psychological sense of brand community. *Journal of Business Research*, *61*(4), 284–291. doi:10.1016/j.jbusres.2007.06.022

Cassia, F., & Magno, F. (2012). Business-to-business branding: A review and assessment of the impact of non-attribute-based brand beliefs on buyer's attitudinal loyalty. *Canadian Journal of Administrative Sciences*, *29*(3), 242–254. doi:10.1002/cjas.235

Catalin, M. C., & Andreea, P. (2014). Brands as a mean of consumer self-expression and desired personal lifestyle. *Procedia: Social and Behavioral Sciences*, *109*, 103–107. doi:10.1016/j.sbspro.2013.12.427

Chang, D. R., & Park, S. B. (2013). The effects of brand strategy and technological uncertainty on pioneering advantage in the multigenerational product market. *Journal of Product Innovation Management*, *30*(1), 82–95. doi:10.1111/j.1540-5885.2012.00988.x

Chaudhuri, A., & Holbrook, M. B. (2001). The chain of effects from brand trust and brand affect to brand performance: The role of brand loyalty. *Journal of Marketing*, *65*(2), 81–93. doi:10.1509/jmkg.65.2.81.18255

Chen, X., Chen, Y., & Xiao, P. (2013). The impact of sampling and network topology on the estimation of social intercorrelations. *JMR, Journal of Marketing Research*, *50*(1), 95–110. doi:10.1509/jmr.12.0026

Chen, Y., Fay, S., & Wang, Q. (2011). The role of marketing in social media: How online consumer reviews evolve. *Journal of Interactive Marketing*, *25*(2), 85–94. doi:10.1016/j.intmar.2011.01.003

Chen, J., Nguyen, B., & Klaus, P. (2013). Public affairs in China: Exploring the role of brand fairness perceptions in the case of Mercedes-Benz. *Journal of Public Affairs*, *13*(4), 403–414. doi:10.1002/pa.1493

Chen, Q., & Rodgers, S. (2006). Development of an instrument to measure web site personality. *Journal of Interactive Advertising*, *7*(1), 47–64. doi:10.1080/15252019.2006.10722124

Cheung, C. M. K., & Thadani, D. R. (2012). The impact of electronic word-of-mouth communication: A literature analysis and integrative model. *Decision Support Systems*, *54*(1), 461–470. doi:10.1016/j.dss.2012.06.008

Chiu, H. C., Hsieh, Y. C., Kao, Y. H., & Lee, M. (2007). The determinants of e-mail receivers' disseminating behaviors on the Internet. *Journal of Advertising Research*, *47*(4), 524–534. doi:10.2501/S0021849907070547

Christodoulides, G., Jevons, C., & Bonhomme, J. (2012). Memo to marketers: Quantitative evidence for change. How user-generated content really affects brands. *Journal of Advertising Research*, *52*(1), 53–64. doi:10.2501/JAR-52-1-053-064

Chu, S. C., & Kim, Y. (2011). Determinants of consumer engagement in electronic word-of-mouth (eWOM) in social networking sites. *International Journal of Advertising*, *30*(1), 47–75. doi:10.2501/IJA-30-1-047-075

Coker, K. K., Altobello, S. A., & Balasubramanian, S. K. (2013). Message exposure with friends: The role of social context on attitudes toward prominently placed brands. *Journal of Consumer Behaviour*, *12*(2), 102–111. doi:10.1002/cb.1423

Constantinides, E. (2014). Foundations of social media marketing. *Procedia: Social and Behavioral Sciences*, *148*, 40–57. doi:10.1016/j.sbspro.2014.07.016

Cooke, A. D., & Mellers, B. A. (1998). Multiattribute judgment: Attribute spacing influences single attributes. *Journal of Experimental Psychology. Human Perception and Performance*, *24*(2), 496–504. doi:10.1037/0096-1523.24.2.496

Cooke, S., & Ryan, P. (2000). Brand alliances: From reputation endorsement to collaboration on core competencies. *Irish Marketing Review*, *13*(2), 36–41.

Coppola, N. W., Hiltz, S. R., & Rotter, N. G. (2004). Building trust in virtual teams. *IEEE Transactions on Professional Communication*, *47*(2), 95–104. doi:10.1109/TPC.2004.828203

Corstjens, M., & Umblijs, A. (2013). The power of evil: The damage of negative social media strongly outweigh positive contributions. *Journal of Advertising Research*, *52*(4), 433–449. doi:10.2501/JAR-52-4-433-449

Cronin, J. J. Jr, Brady, M. K., & Hult, G. T. M. (2000). Assessing the effects of quality, value, and customer satisfaction on customer behavioral intentions in service environments. *Journal of Retailing*, *76*(2), 193–218. doi:10.1016/S0022-4359(00)00028-2

Cronley, M. L., Posavac, S. S., Meyer, T., Kardes, F. R., & Kellaris, J. J. (2005). A selective hypothesis testing perspective on price-quality inference and inference-based choice. *Journal of Consumer Psychology*, *15*(2), 159–169. doi:10.1207/s15327663jcp1502_8

Crosby, L. A., Evans, K. R., & Cowles, D. (1990). Relationship quality in services selling: An interpersonal influence perspective. *Journal of Marketing*, *54*(3), 68–81. doi:10.2307/1251817

Dahlstrom, R., & Dato-on, M. (2004). Business-to-business antecedents to retail co-branding. *Journal of Business-To-Business Marketing*, *11*(3), 1–22. doi:10.1300/J033v11n03_01

Davis, R., Piven, I., & Breazeale, M. (2014). Conceptualizing the brand in social media community: The five sources model. *Journal of Retailing and Consumer Services*, *21*(4), 468–481. doi:10.1016/j.jretconser.2014.03.006

Davis, R., & Sajtos, L. (2008). Measuring consumer interactivity in response to campaigns coupling mobile and television media. *Journal of Advertising Research*, *48*(3), 375–391. doi:10.2501/S0021849908080409

Dawar, N. J., & Parker, P. (1994). Marketing universals: Consumers' use of brand name, price, physical appearance and retailer reputation as signals of product quality. *Journal of Marketing*, *58*(2), 81–95. doi:10.2307/1252271

de Chernatony, L. (2002). Would a brand smell any sweeter by a corporate name? *Corporate Reputation Review*, *5*(2-3), 114–132. doi:10.1057/palgrave.crr.1540169

de Chernatony, L., & Christodoulides, G. (2004). Taking the brand promise online: Challenges and opportunities. *Interactive Marketing*, *5*(3), 238–251. doi:10.1057/palgrave.im.4340241

de Chernatony, L., & Segal-Horn, S. (2001). Building on services' characteristics to develop successful service brand. *Journal of Marketing Management*, *17*(7–8), 645–669. doi:10.1362/026725701323366773

de Vries, L., Gensler, S., & Leeflang, P. S. H. (2012). Popularity of brand posts on brand fan pages: An investigation of the effects of social media marketing. *Journal of Interactive Marketing*, *26*(2), 83–91. doi:10.1016/j.intmar.2012.01.003

Donavan, T. D., Janda, S., & Suh, J. (2006). Environmental influences in corporate brand identification and outcomes. *Journal of Brand Management*, *14*(1–2), 125–136. doi:10.1057/palgrave.bm.2550057

Doney, P. M., & Cannon, J. P. (1997). An examination of the nature of trust in buyer–seller relationships. *Journal of Marketing*, *61*(2), 35–51. doi:10.2307/1251829

Ellahi, A., & Bokhari, R. H. (2013). Key quality factors affecting users' perception of social networking websites. *Journal of Retailing and Consumer Services*, *20*(1), 120–129. doi:10.1016/j.jretconser.2012.10.013

Erdem, T., & Swait, J. (1998). Brand equity as a signaling phenomenon. *Journal of Consumer Psychology*, *7*(2), 131–157. doi:10.1207/s15327663jcp0702_02

Erdem, T., Swait, J., & Louviere, J. (2002). The impact of brand credibility on consumer price sensitivity. *International Journal of Research in Marketing*, *19*(1), 1–19. doi:10.1016/S0167-8116(01)00048-9

Erevelles, S., Horton, V., & Fukawa, N. (2008). Understanding B2C brand alliances between manufacturers and suppliers. *Marketing Management Journal*, *18*(2), 32–46.

Filieri, R., & McLeay, F. (2014). E-WOM and accommodation: An analysis of the factors that influence travelers' adoption of information from online reviews. *Journal of Travel Research*, *53*(1), 44–57. doi:10.1177/0047287513481274

Flynn, L. R., Goldsmith, R. E., & Eastman, J. K. (1996). Opinion leaders and opinion seekers: Two new measurement scales. *Journal of the Academy of Marketing Science*, *24*(2), 137–147. doi:10.1177/0092070396242004

Forbes. (2014). *The top 10 benefits of social media marketing.* Retrieved from http://www.forbes.com/sites/jaysondemers/2014/08/11/the-top-10-benefits-of-social-media-marketing/

Fournier, S. (1998). Consumer and their brands: Developing relationship theory in consumer research. *Journal of Consumer Research*, *24*(4), 343–353. doi:10.1086/209515

Gammoh, B. S., & Voss, K. E. (2013). Alliance competence: The moderating role of valence of alliance experience. *European Journal of Marketing*, *47*(5/6), 964–986. doi:10.1108/03090561311307029

Ganesan, S. (1994). Determinants of long–term orientation in buyer–seller relationships. *Journal of Marketing*, *58*(2), 1–19. doi:10.2307/1252265

Ghosh, M., & John, G. (2009). When should original equipment manufacturers use branded component contracts with suppliers? *JMR, Journal of Marketing Research*, *46*(5), 597–611. doi:10.1509/jmkr.46.5.597

Giannakis-Bompolis, C., & Boutsouki, C. (2014). Customer relationship management in the era of social web and social customer: An investigation of customer engagement in the Greek retail banking sector. *Procedia: Social and Behavioral Sciences*, *148*, 67–78. doi:10.1016/j.sbspro.2014.07.018

Godes, D., & Mayzlin, D. (2004). Using online conversations to study word-of-mouth communication. *Marketing Science*, *23*(4), 545–560. doi:10.1287/mksc.1040.0071

González-Benito, Ó., Martos-Partal, M., & Fustinoni-Venturini, M. (2014). Retailers' price positioning and the motivational profiling of store-brand shoppers: The case of Spain. *Psychology and Marketing*, *31*(2), 115–125. doi:10.1002/mar.20680

Habibi, M. R., Laroche, M., & Richard, M. (2014). Brand communities based in social media: How unique are they? Evidence from two exemplary brand communities. *International Journal of Information Management*, *34*(2), 123–132. doi:10.1016/j.ijinfomgt.2013.11.010

Hamedi, J. (2014, April 25). How social media will transform brand management. *Direct Marketing News*. Retrieved from http://www.dmnews.com/how-social-media-will-transform-brand-management/article/343917/

Hamzah, Z. L., Syed Alwi, S. F., & Othman, M. N. (2014). Designing corporate brand experience in an online context: A qualitative insight. *Journal of Business Research*, *67*(11), 2299–2310. doi:10.1016/j.jbusres.2014.06.018

Han, Y. J., Nunes, J. C., & Dreze, X. (2010). Signaling status with luxury goods: The role of brand prominence. *Journal of Marketing*, *74*(4), 15–30. doi:10.1509/jmkg.74.4.15

Hanna, R., Rohm, A., & Crittenden, V. L. (2011). We're all connected: The power of the social media ecosystem. *Business Horizons*, *54*(3), 265–273. doi:10.1016/j.bushor.2011.01.007

Hatch, M. J., & Schultz, M. (2009). Of bricks and brands: From corporate to enterprise branding. *Organizational Dynamics*, *38*(2), 117–130. doi:10.1016/j.orgdyn.2009.02.008

Heide, J. B., & John, G. (1990). Alliances in industrial purchasing: The determinants of joint action in buyer–supplier relationships. *JMR, Journal of Marketing Research*, *27*(1), 24–36. doi:10.2307/3172548

Helm, C., & Jones, R. (2010). Brand governance: The new agenda in brand management. *Journal of Brand Management*, *17*(8), 545–547. doi:10.1057/bm.2010.20

Hennig-Thurau, T., Gwinner, K. P., Walsh, G., & Gremler, D. D. (2004). Electronic word-of-mouth via consumer-opinion platforms: What motivates consumers to articulate themselves on the Internet? *Journal of Interactive Marketing*, *18*(1), 38–52. doi:10.1002/dir.10073

Hoffman, D. L., & Fodor, M. (2010). Can you measure the ROI of your social media marketing? *MIT Sloan Management Review*, *52*(1), 41–50.

Huang, H. H., & Mitchell, V. W. (2014). The role of imagination and brand personification in brand relationships. *Psychology and Marketing*, *31*(1), 38–47. doi:10.1002/mar.20673

Huang, H. H., Mitchell, V. W., & Rosenaum-Elliott, R. (2012). Are consumer and brand personalities the same? *Psychology and Marketing*, *29*(5), 334–349. doi:10.1002/mar.20525

Isaksen, K. J., & Roper, S. (2012). The commodification of self-esteem: Branding and British teenagers. *Psychology and Marketing*, *29*(3), 117–135. doi:10.1002/mar.20509

Jang, H. J., Sim, J., Lee, Y., & Kwon, O. (2013). Deep sentiment analysis: Mining the causality between personality-value-attitude for analyzing business ads in social media. *Expert Systems with Applications*, *40*(18), 7492–7503. doi:10.1016/j.eswa.2013.06.069

Jansen, B. J., Zhang, M., Sobel, K., & Chowdury, A. (2009). Twitter power: Tweets as electronic word of mouth. *Journal of the American Society for Information Science and Technology*, *60*(11), 2169–2188. doi:10.1002/asi.21149

Jespersen, K. R. (2010). User-involvement and open innovation: The case of decision-maker openness. *International Journal of Innovation Management*, *14*(3), 471–489. doi:10.1142/S136391961000274X

Kalafatis, S. P., Riley, D., & Singh, J. (2014). Context effects in the evaluation of business-to-business brand alliances. *Industrial Marketing Management*, *43*(2), 322–334. doi:10.1016/j.indmarman.2013.09.002

Kandampully, J. (2003). B2B relationships and networks in the Internet age. *Management Decision*, *41*(5), 443–451. doi:10.1108/00251740310479296

Kapferer, J. N. (2012). *The new strategic brand management: Advanced insights and strategic thinking*. London, UK: Kogan Page.

Kaplan, A. M., & Haenlein, M. (2010). Users of the world, unite! The challenges and opportunities of social media. *Business Horizons*, *53*(1), 59–68. doi:10.1016/j.bushor.2009.09.003

Kardes, F. R., Cronley, M. L., Kellaris, J. J., & Posavac, S. S. (2004). The role of selective information processing in price-quality inference. *The Journal of Consumer Research*, *31*(2), 368–374. doi:10.1086/422115

Kasemsap, K. (2014a). The role of social media in the knowledge-based organizations. In I. Lee (Ed.), *Integrating social media into business practice, applications, management, and models* (pp. 254–275). Hershey, PA: IGI Global. doi:10.4018/978-1-4666-6182-0.ch013

Kasemsap, K. (2014b). The role of social networking in global business environments. In P. Smith & T. Cockburn (Eds.), *Impact of emerging digital technologies on leadership in global business* (pp. 183–201). Hershey, PA: IGI Global. doi:10.4018/978-1-4666-6134-9.ch010

Kasemsap, K. (2015a). The role of brand management in emerging markets. In *Marketing and consumer behavior: Concepts, methodologies, tools, and applications* (pp. 2006–2023). Hershey, PA: IGI Global. doi:10.4018/978-1-4666-7357-1.ch099

Kasemsap, K. (2015b). The role of brand loyalty on CRM performance: An innovative framework for smart manufacturing. In *Marketing and consumer behavior: Concepts, methodologies, tools, and applications* (pp. 413–446). Hershey, PA: IGI Global. doi:10.4018/978-1-4666-7357-1.ch019

Kaufmann, H. R., Vrontis, D., Czinkota, M., & Alvin Hadiono, A. (2012). Corporate branding and transformational leadership in turbulent times. *Journal of Product and Brand Management*, *21*(3), 192–204. doi:10.1108/10610421211228810

Keller, K. L. (1993). Conceptualizing, evaluating, and managing customer–based brand equity. *Journal of Marketing*, *57*(1), 1–22. doi:10.2307/1252054

Keller, K. L. (2008). *Strategic brand management: Building, measuring and managing brand equity*. Upper Saddle River, NJ: Prentice Hall.

Keller, K. L., & Lehmann, D. R. (2003). How do brands create value? *Marketing Management*, *12*(3), 27–31.

Kietzmann, J. H., Hermkens, K., McCarthy, I. P., & Silvestre, B. S. (2011). Social media? Get serious! Understanding the functional building blocks of social media. *Business Horizons*, *54*(3), 241–251. doi:10.1016/j.bushor.2011.01.005

Kim, E., Sung, Y., & Kang, H. (2014). Brand followers' retweeting behavior on Twitter: How brand relationships influence brand electronic word-of-mouth. *Computers in Human Behavior*, *37*, 18–25. doi:10.1016/j.chb.2014.04.020

Kirmani, A., & Wright, P. (1989). Money talks: Perceived advertising expense and expected product quality. *Journal of Consumer Research*, *16*(3), 344–353. doi:10.1086/209220

Klaus, Ph. (2013). The Case of Amazon.com: Towards a conceptual framework of online customer service experience (OCSE) using emerging consensus technique (ECT). *Journal of Services Marketing*, *27*(6), 443–457. doi:10.1108/JSM-02-2012-0030

Klaus, P., Gorgoglione, M., Buonamassa, D., Panniello, U., & Nguyen, B. (2013). Are you providing the "right" experiences? The case of Banca Popolare di Bari. *International Journal of Bank Marketing*, *31*(7), 506–528. doi:10.1108/IJBM-02-2013-0019

Klaus, Ph., & Maklan, S. (2013). Towards a better measure of customer experience. *International Journal of Market Research*, *55*(2), 227–246. doi:10.2501/IJMR-2013-021

Knox, S. (2004). Positioning and branding your organization. *Journal of Product and Brand Management*, *13*(2), 105–115. doi:10.1108/10610420410529735

Kraak, V. I., & Story, M. (2015). Influence of food companies' brand mascots and entertainment companies' cartoon media characters on children's diet and health: A systematic review and research needs. *Obesity Reviews*, *16*(2), 107–126. doi:10.1111/obr.12237 PMID:25516352

Kwon, E. S., & Sung, Y. (2011). Follow me! Global marketers' Twitter use. *Journal of Interactive Advertising*, *12*(1), 4–16. doi:10.1080/15252019.2011.10722187

Labrecque, L. I., vor dem Esche, J., Mathwick, C., Novak, T. P., & Hofacker, C. F. (2013). Consumer power: Evolution in the digital age. *Journal of Interactive Marketing*, *27*(4), 257–269. doi:10.1016/j.intmar.2013.09.002

Laroche, M., Habibi, M. R., Richard, M. O., & Sankaranarayanan, R. (2012). The effects of social media based brand communities on brand community markers, value creation practices, brand trust and brand loyalty. *Computers in Human Behavior*, *28*(5), 1755–1767. doi:10.1016/j.chb.2012.04.016

Lavenka, N. M. (1991). Measurement of consumers' perceptions of product quality, brand name, and packaging: Candy bar comparisons by magnitude estimation. *Marketing Research*, *3*(2), 38–46.

Lee, H., & Griffith, D. (2012). Transferring corporate brand image to local markets: Governance decisions for market entry and global branding. *Advances in International Marketing*, *23*(1), 39–65. doi:10.1108/S1474-7979(2012)0000023006

Lee, S. M., Olson, D. L., & Trimi, S. (2012). Co-innovation: Convergenomics, collaboration, and co-creation for organizational values. *Management Decision*, *50*(5), 817–831. doi:10.1108/00251741211227528

Leeflang, P. S. H., Verhoef, P. C., Dahlstrom, P., & Freundt, T. (2014). Challenges and solutions for marketing in a digital era. *European Management Journal*, *32*(1), 1–12. doi:10.1016/j.emj.2013.12.001

Lieven, T., Grohmann, B., Herrmann, A., Landwehr, J. R., & van Tilburg, M. (2014). The effect of brand gender on brand equity. *Psychology and Marketing*, *31*(5), 371–385. doi:10.1002/mar.20701

Lin, J. S., & Pena, J. (2011). Are you following me? A content analysis of TV networks' brand communication on Twitter. *Journal of Interactive Advertising*, *12*(1), 17–29. doi:10.1080/15252019.2011.10722188

Lorenzo-Romero, C., Constantinides, E., & Brünink, L. A. (2014). Co-creation: Customer integration in social media based product and service development. *Procedia: Social and Behavioral Sciences*, *148*, 383–396. doi:10.1016/j.sbspro.2014.07.057

Lowe, B., D'Alessandro, S., Winzar, H., Laffey, D., & Collier, W. (2013). The use of Web 2.0 technologies in marketing classes: Key drivers of student acceptance. *Journal of Consumer Behaviour*, *12*(5), 412–422. doi:10.1002/cb.1444

Luchman, J. N., Bergstrom, J., & Krulikowski, C. (2014). A motives framework of social media website use: A survey of young Americans. *Computers in Human Behavior*, *38*, 136–141. doi:10.1016/j.chb.2014.05.016

Maklan, S., & Klaus, Ph. (2011). Customer experience: Are we measuring the right things? *International Journal of Market Research*, *53*(6), 771–792. doi:10.2501/IJMR-53-6-771-792

Mangold, W. G., & Faulds, D. J. (2009). Social media: The new hybrid element of the promotion mix. *Business Horizons*, *52*(4), 357–365. doi:10.1016/j.bushor.2009.03.002

Marion, T. J., Barczak, G., & Hultink, E. J. (2014). Do social media tools impact the development phase? An exploratory study. *Journal of Product Innovation Management*, *31*(S1), 18–29. doi:10.1111/jpim.12189

Martini, A., Massa, S., & Testa, S. (2014). Customer co-creation projects and social media: The case of Barilla of Italy. *Business Horizons*, *57*(3), 425–434. doi:10.1016/j.bushor.2014.02.003

McAlexander, J. H., Schouten, J. W., & Koenig, H. F. (2002). Building brand community. *Journal of Marketing*, *66*(1), 38–54. doi:10.1509/jmkg.66.1.38.18451

McCracken, G. (1988). *Culture and consumption*. Bloomington, IN: Indiana University Press.

Melewar, T. C., & Navalekar, A. (2002). Leveraging corporate identity in the digital age. *Marketing Intelligence & Planning*, *20*(2), 96–103. doi:10.1108/02634500210418518

Merz, M. A., He, Y., & Vargo, S. L. (2009). The evolving brand logic: A service-dominant logic perspective. *Journal of the Academy of Marketing Science*, *37*(3), 328–344. doi:10.1007/s11747-009-0143-3

Morgan, R. M., & Hunt, S. D. (1994). The commitment-trust theory of relationship marketing. *Journal of Marketing*, *58*(3), 20–38. doi:10.2307/1252308

Morgan-Thomas, A., & Veloutsou, C. (2013). Beyond technology acceptance: Brand relationships and online brand experience. *Journal of Business Research*, *66*(1), 21–27. doi:10.1016/j.jbusres.2011.07.019

Motameni, R., & Shahrokhi, M. (1998). Brand equity valuation: A global perspective. *Journal of Product and Brand Management*, *7*(4), 275–290. doi:10.1108/10610429810229799

Mount, M., & Martinez, M. G. (2014, June 17). Rejuvenating a brand through social media. *MIT Sloan Management Review*. Retrieved from http://sloanreview.mit.edu/article/rejuvenating-a-brand-through-social-media/

Muniz, A. M. Jr, & O'Guinn, T. C. (2001). Brand community. *The Journal of Consumer Research*, *27*(4), 412–432. doi:10.1086/319618

Nambisan, P., & Watt, J. H. (2011). Managing customer experiences in online product communities. *Journal of Business Research*, *64*(8), 889–895. doi:10.1016/j.jbusres.2010.09.006

Naylor, R. W., Lamberton, C. P., & West, P. M. (2012). Beyond the like button: The impact of mere virtual presence on brand evaluations and purchase intentions in social media settings. *Journal of Marketing*, *76*(6), 105–120. doi:10.1509/jm.11.0105

Nitzan, I., & Libai, B. (2011). Social effects on customer retention. *Journal of Marketing*, *75*(6), 24–38. doi:10.1509/jm.10.0209

Norris, D. G. (1993). Intel inside: Branding a component in a business market. *Journal of Business and Industrial Marketing*, *8*(1), 14–24. doi:10.1108/08858629310027560

Okazaki, S. (2006). Excitement or sophistication? A preliminary exploration of online brand personality. *International Marketing Review*, *23*(3), 279–303. doi:10.1108/02651330610670451

Parasuraman, A., Zeithaml, V. A., & Malhotra, A. (2005). e-SERVQUAL: A multiple-item scale for assessing electronic service quality. *Journal of Service Research*, *7*(3), 213–233. doi:10.1177/1094670504271156

Park, S. E., Choi, D., & Kim, J. (2005). Visualizing e-brand personality: Exploratory studies on visual attributes and e-brand personalities in Korea. *International Journal of Human-Computer Interaction*, *19*(1), 7–34. doi:10.1207/s15327590ijhc1901_3

Park, C. W., Jun, S. Y., & Shocker, A. D. (1996). Composite branding alliances: An investigation of extension and feedback effects. *JMR, Journal of Marketing Research*, *33*(4), 453–466. doi:10.2307/3152216

Park, N., Kee, K., & Valenzuela, S. (2009). Being immersed in social networking environment: Facebook groups, uses and gratifications, and social outcomes. *CyberPsychology & Behavior*, *12*(6), 729–733. doi:10.1089/cpb.2009.0003 PMID:19619037

Pelling, E. L., & White, K. M. (2009). The theory of planned behavior applied to young people's use of social networking web sites. *CyberPsychology & Behavior*, *12*(6), 755–759. doi:10.1089/cpb.2009.0109 PMID:19788377

Pentina, I., Zhang, L., & Basmanova, O. (2013). Antecedents and consequences of trust in a social media brand: A cross-cultural study of Twitter. *Computers in Human Behavior*, *29*(4), 1546–1555. doi:10.1016/j.chb.2013.01.045

Piccoli, G. (2010). Information technology and the future of hospitality brand management. Retrieved from http://content.ebscohost.com.ezproxy.library.unlv.edu/pdf25 26/pdf/2010/

Piller, F. T., Vossen, A., & Ihl, C. (2012). From social media to social product development: The impact of social media on co-creation of innovation. *Die Unternehmung*, *66*(1), 7–27. doi:10.5771/0042-059X-2012-1-7

Poddar, A., Donthu, N., & Wei, Y. (2009). Web site customer orientations, web site quality, and purchase intentions: The role of web site personality. *Journal of Business Research*, *6*(4), 441–450. doi:10.1016/j.jbusres.2008.01.036

Pookulangara, S., & Koesler, K. (2011). Cultural influence on consumers' usage of social networks and its impact on online purchase intentions. *Journal of Retailing and Consumer Services*, *18*(4), 348–354. doi:10.1016/j.jretconser.2011.03.003

Powers, T., Advincula, D., Austin, M. S., & Graiko, S. (2012). Digital and social media in the purchase-decision process: A special report from the advertising research foundation. *Journal of Advertising Research*, *52*(4), 479–489. doi:10.2501/JAR-52-4-479-489

Prahalad, C. K., & Ramaswamy, V. (2004). Co-creation experiences: The next practice in value creation. *Journal of Interactive Marketing*, *18*(3), 5–14. doi:10.1002/dir.20015

Prakash, N. (2012, December 8). How the Middle East, North Africa are using Facebook for marketing. *Mashable*. Retrieved from http://mashable.com/2012/12/07/facebook-middle-east-africa/

Rahmandad, H., & Sterman, J. D. (2008). Heterogeneity and network structure in the dynamics of diffusion: Comparing agent-based and differential equation models. *Management Science*, *54*(5), 998–1014. doi:10.1287/mnsc.1070.0787

Rao, A. R., Qu, L., & Ruekert, R. W. (1999). Signaling unobservable product quality through a brand ally. *JMR, Journal of Marketing Research*, *36*(2), 258–268. doi:10.2307/3152097

Rauyruen, P., Miller, K. E., & Barret, N. J. (2007). Relationship quality as a predictor of B2B customer loyalty. *Journal of Business Research*, *60*(1), 21–31. doi:10.1016/j.jbusres.2005.11.006

Rawat, S., & Divekar, R. (2014). Developing a social media presence strategy for an e-commerce business. *Procedia Economics and Finance*, *11*, 626–634. doi:10.1016/S2212-5671(14)00228-7

Reed, A., & Botts, S. (2014). Building identity loyalty through social media. *Think with Google*. Retrieved from https://www.thinkwithgoogle.com/columns/building-identity-through-social-media.html

Reijonen, H., Laukkanen, T., Komppula, R., & Tuominen, S. (2012). Are growing SMEs more market-oriented and brand-oriented? *Journal of Small Business Management*, *50*(4), 699–716. doi:10.1111/j.1540-627X.2012.00372.x

Ridings, C. M., Gefen, D., & Arinze, B. (2002). Some antecedents and effects of trust in virtual communities. *The Journal of Strategic Information Systems*, *11*(3–4), 271–295. doi:10.1016/S0963-8687(02)00021-5

Rowley, J. (2004). Online branding. *Online Information Review*, *28*(2), 131–138. doi:10.1108/14684520410531637

Rubio, N., Oubina, J., & Villasenor, N. (2014). Brand awareness–Brand quality inference and consumer's risk perception in store brands of food products. *Food Quality and Preference*, *32*, 289–298. doi:10.1016/j.foodqual.2013.09.006

Sashi, C. M. (2012). Customer engagement, buyer-seller relationships, and social media. *Management Decision*, *50*(2), 253–272. doi:10.1108/00251741211203551

Schau, H. J., Muñiz, A. M. Jr, & Arnould, E. J. (2009). How brand community practices create value. *Journal of Marketing*, *73*(5), 30–51. doi:10.1509/jmkg.73.5.30

Schmalz, S., & Orth, U. R. (2012). Brand attachment and consumer emotional response to unethical firm behavior. *Psychology and Marketing*, *29*(11), 869–884. doi:10.1002/mar.20570

Sen, S. (1998). Knowledge, information mode and the attraction effect. *Journal of Consumer Research*, *25*(1), 64–77. doi:10.1086/209527

Shaharudin, M. R., Mansor, S. W., & Elias, S. J. (2011). Food quality attributes among Malaysia's fast food customer. *International Business and Management*, *2*(1), 198–208.

Shirahada, K., & Kosaka, M. (2012). Evaluation method for service branding using word-of-mouth data. *Electronics and Communications in Japan*, *95*(12), 21–28. doi:10.1002/ecj.11442

Shultz, M., & de Chernatony, L. (2002). Introduction the challenges of corporate branding. *Corporate Reputation Review*, *5*(2/3), 105–112. doi:10.1057/palgrave.crr.1540168

Simon, C. J., & Sullivan, M. W. (1993). The measurement and determinants of brand equity: A financial approach. *Marketing Science*, *12*(1), 28–52. doi:10.1287/mksc.12.1.28

Simonson, I., & Tversky, A. (1992). Choice in context: Trade-off contrast and extremeness aversion. *JMR, Journal of Marketing Research*, *29*(3), 281–295. doi:10.2307/3172740

Singh, N., Lehnert, K., & Bostick, K. (2012). Global social media Usage: Insights into reaching consumers worldwide. *Thunderbird International Business Review*, *54*(5), 683–700. doi:10.1002/tie.21493

Singh, S., & Sonnenburg, S. (2012). Brand performances in social media. *Journal of Interactive Marketing*, *26*(4), 189–197. doi:10.1016/j.intmar.2012.04.001

Stewart, K. J. (2003). Trust transfer on the World Wide Web. *Organization Science*, *14*(1), 5–17. doi:10.1287/orsc.14.1.5.12810

Stuart, H., & Jones, C. (2004). Corporate branding in market space. *Corporate Reputation Review*, *7*(1), 84–93. doi:10.1057/palgrave.crr.1540213

Sule Alonso, M. A., Paquin, J. P., & Levy Mangin, J. P. (2002). Modelling perceived quality in fruit products: Their extrinsic and intrinsic attributes. *Journal of Food Products Marketing*, *8*(1), 29–49. doi:10.1300/J038v08n01_03

Sung, Y., Choi, S. M., & Lin, J. S. (2012). The interplay of culture and situational cues in consumers' brand evaluation. *International Journal of Consumer Studies*, *36*(6), 696–701. doi:10.1111/j.1470-6431.2011.01047.x

Taylor, D. G., Strutton, D., & Thompson, K. (2012). Self-enhancement as a motivation for sharing online advertising. *Journal of Interactive Advertising*, *12*(2), 13–28. doi:10.1080/15252019.2012.10722193

Thompson, S. A., & Sinha, R. K. (2008). Brand communities and new product adoption: The influence and limits of oppositional loyalty. *Journal of Marketing*, *72*(6), 65–80. doi:10.1509/jmkg.72.6.65

Trusov, M., Bucklin, R. E., & Pauwels, K. (2009). Effects of word-of-mouth versus traditional marketing, findings from an internet social networking site. *Journal of Marketing*, *73*(9), 90–102. doi:10.1509/jmkg.73.5.90

Tuominen, P. (2007). Emerging metaphors in brand management: Towards a relational approach. *Journal of Communication Management*, *11*(2), 182–191. doi:10.1108/13632540710747398

Uzunoglu, E., & Kip, S. M. (2014). Brand communication through digital influencers: Leveraging blogger engagement. *International Journal of Information Management*, *34*(5), 592–602. doi:10.1016/j.ijinfomgt.2014.04.007

Väisänen, J. (2015, January 15). Threats of brand management in social media why strong social media presence magnifies brand weaknesses and how international brand managers can address this: Part 1. *Brand Management for a Wired World*. Retrieved from http://www.brandba.se/blog/2014/8/14/threats-of-brand-management-in-social-media-why-strong-social-media-presence-magnifies-brand-weaknesses-and-how-international-brand-managers-can-address-this-part-1

Vásquez, G. A. N., & Escamilla, E. M. (2014). Best practice in the use of social networks marketing strategy as in SMEs. *Procedia: Social and Behavioral Sciences*, *148*, 533–542. doi:10.1016/j.sbspro.2014.07.076

Verhoef, P. C., Reinartz, W. J., & Krafft, M. (2010). Customer engagement as a new perspective in customer management. *Journal of Service Research*, *13*(3), 247–252. doi:10.1177/1094670510375461

Vollmer, C., & Precourt, G. (2008). *Always on: Advertising, marketing, and media in an era of consumer control*. New York, NY: McGraw–Hill.

Wen, Q. (2013, July 2). Using social media for brand management. *Megaphone Marketing*. Retrieved from http://megaphonemarketing.com.au/using-social-media-for-brand-management/

Williams, D. L., Crittenden, V. L., Keo, T., & McCarty, P. (2012). The use of social media: An exploratory study of usage among digital natives. *Journal of Public Affairs*, *12*(2), 127–136. doi:10.1002/pa.1414

Wright, P., & Rip, P. (1980). Product class advertising effects on first-time buyers' decision strategies. *Journal of Consumer Research*, *7*(2), 776–788. doi:10.1086/208805

Wu, P. C. S., & Wang, Y. (2011). The influences of electronic word-of-mouth message appeal and message source credibility on brand attitude. *Asia Pacific Journal of Marketing and Logistics*, *23*(4), 448–472. doi:10.1108/13555851111165020

Yeh, Y. H., & Choi, S. M. (2011). Mini-lovers, maxi-mouths: An investigation of antecedents to eWOM intention among brand community members. *Journal of Marketing Communications*, *17*(3), 145–162. doi:10.1080/13527260903351119

Yoganarasimhan, H. (2012). Impact of social network structure on content propagation: A study using YouTube data. *Quantitative Marketing and Economics*, *10*(1), 111–150. doi:10.1007/s11129-011-9105-4

Yoo, M., & Bai, B. (2013). Customer loyalty marketing research: A comparative approach between hospitality and business journals. *International Journal of Hospitality Management*, *33*, 166–177. doi:10.1016/j.ijhm.2012.07.009

Yoo, B., Donthu, N., & Lee, S. (2000). An examination of selected marketing mix elements and brand equity. *Journal of the Academy of Marketing Science*, *28*(2), 195–211. doi:10.1177/0092070300282002

Zaglia, M. E. (2013). Brand communities embedded in social networks. *Journal of Business Research*, *66*(2-2), 216–223. doi:10.1016/j.jbusres.2012.07.015 PMID:23564989

Zavattaro, S. M., Daspit, J. J., & Adams, F. G. (2015). Assessing managerial methods for evaluating place brand equity: A qualitative investigation. *Tourism Management*, *47*, 11–21. doi:10.1016/j.tourman.2014.08.018

Zhang, M., Jansen, B. J., & Chowdhury, A. (2011). Business engagement on Twitter: A path analysis. *Electronic Markets*, *21*(3), 161–175. doi:10.1007/s12525-011-0065-z

Zhao, D., & Rosson, M. B. (2009). How and why people Twitter: The role that microblogging plays in informal communication at work. Paper presented at the ACM 2009 International Conference on Supporting Group Work, New York, NY. doi:10.1145/1531674.1531710 doi:10.1145/1531674.1531710

ADDITIONAL READING

Antorini, Y. M., Muniz, A. M., & Askildsen, T. (2012). Collaborating with customer communities: Lessons from the Lego group. *MIT Sloan Management Review*, *53*(3), 73–79.

Bao, Y., Bao, Y., & Sheng, S. (2011). Motivating purchase of private brands: Effects of store image, product signatureness, and quality variation. *Journal of Business Research*, *64*(2), 220–226. doi:10.1016/j.jbusres.2010.02.007

Gensler, S., Völckner, F., Liu-Thompkins, Y., & Wiertz, C. (2013). Managing brands in the social media environment. *Journal of Interactive Marketing*, *27*(4), 242–256. doi:10.1016/j.intmar.2013.09.004

Hansen, D. L., Shneiderman, B., & Smith, M. A. (2011). *Analyzing social media networks with Nodexl*. Burlington, MA: Elsevier.

Healy, J. C., & McDonagh, P. (2013). Consumer roles in brand culture and value co-creation in virtual communities. *Journal of Business Research*, *66*(9), 1528–1540. doi:10.1016/j.jbusres.2012.09.014

Hollebeek, L. D., Glynn, M. S., & Brodie, R. J. (2014). Consumer brand engagement in social media: Conceptualization, scale development and validation. *Journal of Interactive Marketing*, *28*(2), 149–165. doi:10.1016/j.intmar.2013.12.002

Hsu, Y. H., & Tsou, H. T. (2011). Understanding customer experiences in online blog environments. *International Journal of Information Management*, *31*(6), 510–523. doi:10.1016/j.ijinfomgt.2011.05.003

Kalafatis, S. P., Remizova, N., Riley, D., & Singh, J. (2012). The differential impact of brand equity on B2B co-branding. *Journal of Business and Industrial Marketing*, *27*(8), 623–634. doi:10.1108/08858621211273574

Kuksov, D., Shachar, R., & Wang, K. (2013). Advertising and consumers' communications. *Marketing Science*, *32*(2), 294–309. doi:10.1287/mksc.1120.0753

Lee, T. Y., & BradLow, E. T. (2011). Automated marketing research using online customer reviews. *JMR, Journal of Marketing Research*, *48*(5), 881–894. doi:10.1509/jmkr.48.5.881

Lipsman, A., Mudd, G., Rich, M., & Bruich, S. (2012). The power of ''like'': How brands reach (and influence) fans through social-media marketing. *Journal of Advertising Research*, *52*(1), 40–52. doi:10.2501/JAR-52-1-040-052

Liu, F., Li, J., Mizerski, D., & Soh, H. (2012). Self–congruity, brand attitude, and brand loyalty: A study on luxury brands. *European Journal of Marketing*, *46*(7–8), 922–937.

Mann, B. J. S., & Kaur, M. (2013). Exploring branding strategies of FMCG, services and durables brands: Evidence from India. *Journal of Product and Brand Management*, *22*(1), 6–17. doi:10.1108/10610421311298650

Marzocchi, M., Morandin, G., & Bergami, M. (2013). Brand communities: Loyal to the community or the brand? *European Journal of Marketing*, *47*(1-2), 93–114. doi:10.1108/03090561311285475

Mayzlin, D., & Yoganarasimhan, H. (2012). Link to success: How blogs build an audience by promoting rivals. *Management Science*, *58*(9), 1651–1668. doi:10.1287/mnsc.1110.1510

Moe, W. M., & Schweidel, D. A. (2012). Online product opinions: Incidence, evaluation, and evolution. *Marketing Science*, *31*(3), 372–386. doi:10.1287/mksc.1110.0662

Noble, C. H., Bing, M. N., & Bogoviyeva, E. (2013). The effects of brand metaphors as design innovation: A test of congruency hypotheses. *Journal of Product Innovation Management*, *30*, 126–141. doi:10.1111/jpim.12067

Olsen, L. E., & Lanseng, E. J. (2012). Brand alliances: The role of brand concept consistency. *European Journal of Marketing*, *46*(9), 1108–1126. doi:10.1108/03090561211247874

Onishi, H., & Manchanda, P. (2012). Marketing activity, blogging and sales. *International Journal of Research in Marketing*, *29*(3), 221–234. doi:10.1016/j.ijresmar.2011.11.003

Pongsakornrungsilp, S., & Schroeder, J. (2011). Understanding value co-creation in a co-consuming brand community. *Marketing Theory*, *11*(3), 303–324. doi:10.1177/1470593111408178

Quintal, V., & Phau, I. (2013). Brand leaders and me-too alternatives: How do consumers choose? *Marketing Intelligence & Planning*, *31*(4), 367–387. doi:10.1108/02634501311324852

Romaniuk, J., & Nenycz-Thiel, M. (2013). Behavioral brand loyalty and consumer brand associations. *Journal of Business Research*, *66*(1), 67–72. doi:10.1016/j.jbusres.2011.07.024

Schnittka, O., Sattler, H., & Zenker, S. (2012). Advanced brand concept maps: A new approach for evaluating the favorability of brand association networks. *International Journal of Research in Marketing*, *29*(3), 265–274. doi:10.1016/j.ijresmar.2012.04.002

Sharifi, S. S. (2014). Impacts of the trilogy of emotion on future purchase intentions in products of high involvement under the mediating role of brand awareness. *European Business Review*, *26*(1), 43–63. doi:10.1108/EBR-12-2012-0072

Smock, A. D., Ellison, N. B., Lampe, C., & Wohn, D. Y. (2011). Facebook as a toolkit: A uses and gratification approach to unbundling feature use. *Computers in Human Behavior*, *27*(6), 2322–2329. doi:10.1016/j.chb.2011.07.011

Stahl, F., Heitmann, M., Lehmann, D. R., & Neslin, S. A. (2012). The impact of brand equity on customer acquisition, retention, and profit margin. *Journal of Marketing*, *76*(4), 44–63. doi:10.1509/jm.10.0522

Wang, X., Yu, C., & Wei, Y. (2012). Social media peer communication and impacts on purchase intentions: A consumer socialization framework. *Journal of Interactive Marketing*, *26*(4), 198–208. doi:10.1016/j.intmar.2011.11.004

KEY TERMS AND DEFINITIONS

Brand: An identifying symbol, words, or mark that distinguishes a product or company from its competitors.

Brand Loyalty: The extent of the faithfulness of consumers to a particular brand, expressed through their repeat purchases.

Brand Management: The process of maintaining, improving, and upholding a brand so that the name is associated with positive results.

Brand Strategy: The long-term marketing support for a brand, based on the definition of the characteristics of the target consumers.

Facebook: The name of a social networking service and website, launched in 2004.

Marketing: The management process through which goods and services move from concept to the customer.

Marketing Strategy: An organization's strategy that combines all of its marketing goals into one comprehensive plan.

Social Media: The Internet or cellular phone based applications and tools to share information among people.

Twitter: A social networking website, which allows users to publish short messages that are visible to other social media users.

This research was previously published in Competitive Social Media Marketing Strategies edited by Wilson Ozuem and Gordon Bowen, pages 173-200, copyright year 2016 by Business Science Reference (an imprint of IGI Global).

Chapter 22
Determinants of Brand Recall in Social Networking Sites

Kaan Varnali
Istanbul Bilgi University, Turkey

Vehbi Gorgulu
Istanbul Bilgi University, Turkey

ABSTRACT

This research aims to contribute to the understanding of how brand impressions in social networking sites influence brand recall. Further, the relationship between the built-in metrics offered by social networking sites and brand recall are also examined to assess the validity of these metrics as measures of advertising effectiveness. Results indicate a positive relationship between brand recall and self-brand congruence, tie-strength with, trust toward, and perceived popularity of the profile associated with the post, and clicking a link embedded in the post / ad in which the brand appears. On the other hand, there is not a significant difference between the levels of brand involvement, homophily with the profile associated with the post / ad, like-count, and four types of built-in user-interaction options including liking, sharing, posting a comment and tagging among the brands that were successfully retrieved from the memory and those were not.

INTRODUCTION

Today, consumers are more than passive buyers and audience members; they are also creators and distributors of media content (Vanden Bergh et al., 2011). Social network sites (SNS), which are sets of individuals, organizations and social entities connected by a set of social relationships such as friendship, co-working or information exchange (Garton, Haythornthwaite, & Wellman, 1997) also take part in the distribution of marketing information by allowing users to actively engage with branded-content delivered to them via sponsored stories, stories about friends, page publishing or ads coupled with social connotations. Since consumers typically judge information regarding the marketplace provided by other consumers to be more trustworthy and credible (Pornpitakpan, 2004), leveraging user-generated or -distributed content in social media is imperative for marketers (Liu-Thompkins, 2012; Schivinski

DOI: 10.4018/978-1-5225-5637-4.ch022

& Dabrowski, 2014). The value of these practices has been well documented in the context of word of mouth, or referral effects (Chu & Kim, 2011; Keller & Fay, 2012; Lee & Youn, 2009).

More recently the breadth of the domain of inquiry expanded to include more detailed issues such as the antecedents of consumer perceptions and responses toward advertisements on social networks (Soares & Pinho, 2014), motivations for consumer engagement with brand pages (Kabadayi & Price, 2014; Logan, 2014), the effects of likes and friends' likes on Facebook brand pages in influencing brand related outcomes (Phua & Ahn, 2014; Tsai & Men, 2013), and development of a typology of Facebook fans (Wallace, 2014). However, despite the managerial relevance, the impact of delivering brand impressions [i.e., exposure to the brand elements in a manner that strengthens overall brand evaluation (Dillon et al., 2001)] in social media on the state of brand-related knowledge stored in the memory (i.e., brand awareness) has been largely missing in the relevant literature. The main reason for this conspicuous lack of researcher interest on this issue conceivably lies in the practical difficulties of employing a full-scope experimental research (preferably live on platforms such as Facebook) capturing the essential components of social media experience, which constitutes the dominant approach in assessing brand awareness in the literature. One of the most interesting researches on this area was conducted by Alves and Antunes (2015), who found out that consumers expect to personal advantages through proximity to the brands on the Internet and that the activity of following brands on social networks impacts on purchase decision processes of customers.

Thus it can be stated that as this new marketing medium unfolds, brands enthusiastically race to establish a presence in SNs (Malhotra *et al.*, 2013; Rohm *et al.*, 2013), however with a very limited understanding of the true impact of their activities on brand-awareness. Today, the key metrics developed to measure effectiveness of brand communications in SNS are based on simple interaction counts and *talk-about* (e.g., the number of mentions, likes, shares, comments, views, re-tweets), saying very little about the extent to which these incidences positively contribute to brand awareness (Lipsman et al., 2012; Phua & Ahn, 2014). Over-reliance on such metrics adds to the difficulty of grasping the full promise of social media marketing. As such, current practice and research lacks evidence to what extent brand impressions delivered via social media influences brand recall.

Facebook is a useful platform to conduct such practice, which is the dominant social networking site with more than 1 billion monthly active users. An important attempt to build a reliable method for calculating the engagement rate of the Facebook brand pages was carried out by Vadivu and Neelamalar (2015), who aimed to identify the extent to which the moderators' post influences the engagement rate of its audience in terms of its content, frequency and the number of fans present for a particular brand page. Through observing and probing Facebook users as they are being exposed to branded content while spending time in their own Facebook accounts, the present study aims to provide exploratory insights for the following questions:

- Can users retrieve the brand impressions delivered via SNs from their memory?
- What factors associated with delivering brand impressions in SNs facilitate the retrieval of brand name from memory?
- Does engaging with a branded content encountered in SNs enhance the retrieval of the associated brand name from memory?
- Can SNs-provided simple interaction counts be used as reliable indicators for the impact of brand impressions on brand awareness in SNS?

THEORETICAL BACKGROUND

Brand awareness denotes a state of brand-related knowledge stored in the memory of the consumer (Hoyer & Brown, 1990). Memory affects brand consideration and thus influences choice (Nedungadi, 1990). The expectation is that awareness will keep the brand in the consumer's consideration set, thereby increasing the probability that the brand will subsequently be purchased (Hoyer & Brown, 1990). Especially in low involvement decisions, even a minimum level of brand awareness, such as the mere familiarity with the brand name, may be sufficient for product choice, even in the absence of a well-formed attitude (Bettman & Park, 1980; Keller, 1993; Park & Lessig, 1981).

The memorability of a brand name, therefore, is critical for the success of a brand impression (Jungsun & Ferle, 2008). A brand's accessibility in memory is strongly associated with the strength of activation of the brand node, which is a function of the frequency, recency, and salience of brand instantiation and of brand evaluation (Barsalou, 1985; Kintsch & Young, 1984). In theory, a brand node is activated, or primed, by a direct reference to the brand name. Therefore, the true potential of an SNS brand impression depends on its ability to prime the brand and cue retrieval.

Recall, which refers to the ability to reproduce previously presented items, occurs when memory is searched and a word is independently retrieved (Jungsun & Ferle, 2008; Lerman & Garbarino, 2002). Recall is often used as a measure for memorability (Gillund & Shiffrin, 1984; Lerman & Garbarino, 2002; Lowrey, Shrum, & Dubitsky, 2003). As such, in the present study it is conceived as the indicator of the extent to which an SNS brand impression succeeds in enhancing the accessibility of the brand in memory.

Items that are attended are more likely to be stored in memory and recalled at a later time (Greenberg, 2012). Building upon the decades of research on the effect of task and context congruity on advertising effectiveness (e.g., Norris & Colman, 1992; Novak et al., 2003), we focused our attention on two theoretical accounts in explaining the selective attention toward advertising messages in SNS. First, at the core of any message that aims to prime a brand lays the brand itself, and hence, as in all types of ads, brand-related characteristics (i.e., brand involvement, self-brand congruence) may account for the differences in brand recall in SNS.

Second account is related with the inherent nature of SNS use, in other words the effect of the context in which brand impression is delivered. The primary motivations of SNS use stem from social needs, such as self-expression, belongingness, seeking meaningful relationships, identity formation, impression management, and subjective norms (Acquisti & Gross, 2006; boyd, 2007; Christofides, Muise, & Desmarais, 2009; Donath & boyd, 2004; Zuckerberg, 2008). Therefore, as an inherent characteristic of SNS use, users should be highly aware of their surroundings and their actions in terms of how they relate to their social agenda. In a similar vein, a recent survey-based study demonstrated that social influence captured by group norms and social identity do indeed influence group intentions and perceived ad relevance in online social networks (Soares & Pinho, 2014). Accordingly, we conceive that social connotations of the post / ad (perceived characteristics and the identity of the profile associated with a post) may also influence observers' attention and information processing motivations in SNS. Drawing upon the framework of social network theory, tie strength (Brown & Reingen, 1987), homophily (Gilly et al., 1998), trust (Nisbet, 2006) and popularity (Tong et al., 2008) are explored as focal dimensions that characterize the perceived social characteristics of the person whose profile is associated with a post / ad in SNS, and consequently influence brand recall.

Additionally, following prior research on this domain (i.e., Phua & Ahn, 2014) the impact of two medium specific factors is also examined. SNS enable observers to interact with the messages (clicking the links within a post, liking or sharing a post, tagging, posting a comment underneath a post). Interaction is a type of conscious behavior, hence by definition requires a user to at least notice a particular content and engage in some level of cognitive processing to be able to take a deliberate action. A deeper processing of information enhances recall of the information (Muter, 1984). Therefore, interaction, although in most of the cases in SNS involve a minimal level of cognitive effort, may enhance the impact of a brand impression. Accordingly, the potential influence of users' interaction with posts / ads in SNS on brand recall is assessed. Furthermore, "like count", the coefficient representing the number of people who clicked the "like" button underneath a post, may serve as a behavioral cue regarding the popularity of the post (not the person who owns the post). As such, it may influence selective attention processes, thus is also considered as a potential predictor of brand recall.

In case of Facebook, brand impressions are delivered to Facebook users through four channels. First, marketers can acquire and engage "fans" through establishing Fan pages and deliver unpaid brand impressions by *page publishing*. Facebook users become "fans" by clicking the "like" button on these pages. Then, brand related content published in these pages appear on the Fan Page wall and may also appear in the News Feeds of the fans, which is a constantly updating list of stories from people and Pages that users follow on Facebook. Second, when a user actively engages with a brand, the story of this engagement becomes visible either on the user's wall or in the Newsfeeds of the friends of that user as *stories about friends*. These unpaid impressions, therefore, may reach Fans and friends of Fans. Third, as a paid brand impression type, *sponsored stories* can be actively distributed more broadly to Fans and friends of Fans to appear not in the Newsfeed but in the right hand column of Facebook interface. Fourth, *ads with social* cues (i.e., the ad includes the name of a user's friend) that come directly from advertisers can also be delivered to friends of fans (Lipsman et al., 2012).

A study by Nielsen revealed that Facebook ads, both paid and unpaid versions, were successful in increasing brand awareness on average by 4%, and purchase intention by 2% between exposed and control audiences after exposure (Nielsen, 2010). Further, a study by Mariani and Muhammed (2014) demonstrate, rather relying on descriptive data that people notice brand communication on Facebook and friends' likes influence future purchasing intentions. Although these findings provide some evidence on the positive impact of Facebook ads on brand awareness, it provides no explanation on how this influence occurs. Drawing on advertising and sociology literatures, the present study attempts to contribute to the understanding of how SNS brand impressions might be influencing brand recall. Further, the relationship between the metrics offered by SNS and brand recall will also be explored to assess the reliability of these metrics as measures of advertising effectiveness. Next, we discuss these accounts in detail and develop propositions.

DEVELOPMENT OF RESEARCH PROPOSITIONS

Brand Related Characteristics

Brand Involvement

The most pervasively used brand-related characteristic in the brand recall literature is the concept of involvement. The concept of involvement characterizes a state of motivation and of interest specific to an individual, which involves individual characteristics (e.g. needs, interests, goals), situational factors (e.g., purchase occasion or perceived risk associated with the purchase decision), and characteristics of the stimulus (e.g. the type of media or the product class) (Andrews & Shimp, 1990; Laurent & Kapferer, 1985; Zaichowsky, 1986). Although there exist many different conceptualizations of involvement in the relevant literature, they all relate to the feeling of self-relevancy.

This study adopts a perspective on involvement similar to that of Celsi and Olson (1988) and Broderick and Mueller (1999), conceptualizing involvement as a consumer's subjective experience or feeling of personal relevance towards a brand. Advertising is apt to have more general relevance for those perceiving the brand as personally important. As such, those who are highly involved with a brand should be more selectively attentive and willing to process information included in a brand-related post / ad (Cohen, 1983; Mitchell, 1979), which would consequently increase the likelihood of a successful brand prime.

Proposition 1: Brand involvement positively relates to brand recall in brand impressions delivered via Facebook.

Self-Brand Congruity

The motivation to express one's own self is among the primary forces that drive consumers to purchase goods or services (Sirgy, 1982). Self-congruity theory proposes that consumer decision making is determined, in part, by the congruence resulting from a psychological comparison involving the user image of a brand and the consumer's self-concept (Escalas & Bettman, 2003; Sirgy, 1986). User-image of a brand reflects the stereotype of the generalized users of that brand and is determined by a host of factors such as advertising, price, and other marketing and psychological associations (Sirgy, 1982; Sirgy, 1985). Consumers perceive high self-congruity when the product-user image matches that of his or her self-image. Self-brand congruity affects consumer behavior through self-concept motives such as the need for self-consistency, self-esteem, and self-expression (Escalas & Bettman, 2005; Sirgy, 1982).

Facebook's basic site structure is deliberately designed to gratify self-disclosure behavior (Zuckerberg, 2008), which is significantly driven by the need to convey self-image to other people (Buss & Briggs, 1984). In line with this argument, deliberate and strategic self-disclosure has been recognized as one of the core SNs behaviors (Acquisti & Gross, 2006). People, specifically young people, ''write themselves into being'' through their actions in SNs (boyd, 2007, p. 129). From this perspective, strategically associating one's profile with posts /ads involving self-congruent brands in SNs, may serve as a carefully calculated way to brand oneself and impress others (boyd & Ellison, 2008), as part of a larger social phenomenon of using social media instrumentally for self-conscious commodification (Marwick & boyd, 2011). Taylor et al. (2011) found that self-brand congruity is an important factor in facilitating greater attitudinal acceptance of advertisements designed to appear in the SNs context. We posit that people would actively seek posts / ads involving self-congruent brands in SNs and spend more time and cognitive resources to evaluate such posts / ads in order to identify content that by associating with their own profiles they can strategically benefit from the brand user-image to emit desired identity signals about themselves. Altogether these processes would underlie the positive relationship between self-brand congruity and enhanced brand recall in SNS.

Proposition 2: Self-brand congruity positively relates to brand recall in brand impressions delivered via Facebook.

SOCIAL CONNOTATIONS

Tie-Strength

The strength of an interpersonal tie (i.e. strong, weak, or absent) is a linear combination of the amount of time, the emotional intensity, the intimacy, and the reciprocal services, which characterize each tie (Granovetter, 1973). Strong-ties, such as family and close friends, constitute stronger and closer relationships that are within an individual's personal network. Strength of a tie helps formation of trust and provides social motivations to be cooperative (Hansen, 1999; Reagans & McEvily, 2003), hence strong-ties are more likely to be activated for the flow of referral behavior and influence interpersonal decision making within small groups and dyads (Brown & Reingen, 1987; Chu & Kim, 2011). Weak-ties on the other hand, consist of less personal social relationships that are composed of a wider set of acquaintances and colleagues, and facilitate dissemination of information across wider networks (Brown & Reingen, 1987; Pigg & Crank, 2004). As such, tie strength indicates 'the potency of the bond between members of a network (Mittal, Huppertz, & Khare, 2008: 196), and even in an online context, influences behavior (De Bruyn & Lilien, 2008).

Facebook shows each user a customized News Feed in which stories related with stronger ties (determined by the frequency of past interaction) are prioritized and appear on top their feed. However, other criteria such as the number of likes a post receives, recency of a post, or the promoted status of a post also enable posts associated with weaker ties to be shown to a user, sometimes located at the very top of their feed. Since social motives (i.e., to keep track of activities of significant others and preserve the status as a close friend) precede utilitarian motives (i.e., searching for marketplace information) in driving Facebook use, we put forth that people would be more attentive toward posts associated with strong-ties. It has also been documented that information shared by a strong-tie in an online context is more likely to be noticed (De Bruyn & Lilien, 2008). Therefore, we conceive that brand impressions embedded in the posts associated with strong ties will be more effective in terms of priming brands in memory, when compared to those embedded in posts associated with weak ties.

Proposition 3: The strength of the social tie between the observer and the person associated with the brand impression positively relates to brand recall in brand impressions delivered via Facebook.

Homophily

Source similarity or homophily refers to the degree to which individuals are similar in terms of certain shared social characteristics (Rogers, 1983). Festinger's (1954) theory of social comparison may provide a theoretical ground explaining how perceived source similarity may influence effectiveness of brand impressions in SNs. This theory proposes that people tend to compare their attitudes and capabilities with those of others. According to Festinger (1954), the tendency to compare oneself with another person increases as that person is seen to be similar to oneself, because individuals assume that similar people have similar needs and preferences. Several studies have found a positive relationship between homophily and persuasiveness and credibility of the information transmitted in the online contexts (Brown, Broderick, & Lee, 2007; Prendergast, Ko, & Yuen, 2010). Following this logic, a post / ad that is associated with a person whose personal characteristics are perceived as similar to the viewer should draw more attention and trigger a higher level of cognitive processing than a post / ad associated with a person who is perceived as dissimilar, hence result in higher brand recall performance.

Proposition 4: Homophily between the observer and the person associated with the brand impression positively relates to brand recall in brand impressions delivered via Facebook.

Trust

The literature in a variety of fields from philosophy to sociology and marketing is replete with studies on trust (Morgan & Hunt, 1994; Sullivan & Transue, 1999; Warren, 1999) and numerous definitions of trust have been offered (Corritore, Kracher, & Wiedenback, 2003). The unifying theme has always been the expectation that one can rely on the words or promises of another (Rotter, 1971). It is a mechanism for reducing complexity and for dealing with uncertainty (Luhmann, 1988). As such, trust is usually regarded as a catalyst in general consumer-marketer relationships, especially in online relationships (Lee, 2005), and influences message processing and attitudes toward advertising (Palka, Pousttchi, & Wiedemann, 2009; Sternthal, Dholakia, & Leavitt, 1978).

Trust in the context of SNs facilitates users' reliance on the usefulness of information attained from other registered SNs members to justify and evaluate personal decisions (Pigg & Crank, 2004; Ridings, Gefen, & Arinze, 2002). In situations where individuals do not yet have credible and meaningful information about the other party, initial trust formation occurs (McKnight, Cummings, & Chervany, 1998). Gradually through experience and familiarity knowledge-based and respect-based trust develops and it offers the highest form of commitment in relationships (Koehn, 2003). SNs friendships often involve such parties with whom trust perceptions are at the initial stages of formation, and thus are goal-based or calculative-based that rely on assessments of benefits versus costs. Drawing on the literature on motivations of SNs use, benefits and costs associated with trusting the other party in the context of

SNs should be largely perceived and assessed with respect to the social agenda of the user, driven by impression management needs. Therefore, we posit that, in order not to risk missing important pieces of information that may have social value (social statuses of people, places, brands, ideas) and to minimize the risk of associating one's profile with content that may inflict undesired effects on the delicate matter of impression management, a post / ad associated with a more trustworthy Facebook friend should be given priority in attentive and cognitive processes.

Proposition 5: Trust toward the person associated with the brand impression positively relates to brand recall in brand impressions delivered via Facebook.

Perceived Popularity

Both the source-attractiveness model of McCracken (1989) and the law of attraction of Byrne (1971) suggest that message effectiveness depends chiefly on the perceived attractiveness of the source. Receivers can better identify with and understand sources that are perceived as more attractive and therefore perceived source attractiveness increases the persuasiveness of the information transmitted. Extant research in interpersonal judgments suggests that there exists a positive and reciprocal relationship between perceived popularity and perceived attractiveness in terms of a variety desired characteristics, such as self-confidence, social appeal, and extraversion (Berry & Miller, 2001; Eagly et al., 1991). This reciprocal relationship also implies that perceived popularity may contribute to perceived source attractiveness.

In Facebook, the network size of an individual is revealed by a coefficient showing the number of friends. This coefficient may well serve to establish how well-liked an individual is, and also to provide clues about the profile owner's social status, physical attractiveness, or credibility, consequently serve as an indicator of popularity (Tong et al., 2008). In line with this argument, Ellison, Steinfeld and Lampe (2007) found that "Friending" large numbers of people is one of the (if not the) main activities of Facebook. The fact that behavioral residues (i.e., posts left on the wall, ratings) generated by friends on Facebook are used by observers in impression formation processes has already been documented by Walther et al. (2008). Accordingly, it seems plausible an individual who appears to have lots of friends in Facebook is likely to be seen as a more attractive source, and hence his or her posts or ads associated with his or her profile would draw more attention from viewers and trigger a higher level of cognitive processing, consequently resulting in an increased brand recall performance.

Proposition 6: Perceived popularity of the person associated with the brand impression positively relates to brand recall in brand impressions delivered via Facebook.

METHODOLOGY

Procedure

The algorithm of Facebook uses several factors to determine top stories relevant for each user, including the number of comments, who posted the story, and what type of post it is. Accordingly, each user receives a different set of stories in their News Feed. Therefore, generating and using experimental stimuli (e.g., delivering users' stories about fictitious brands via fictitious friends) and establishing a factorial design (which would have been the preferable experimental setting for the overarching research goals) were not attainable. In our pilot studies, which involved in-depth interviews and observations, we saw that users feel a sense of embeddedness within their social networks and experience medium-specific instant gratifications while using Facebook. Therefore, conducting the research live in Facebook was crucial for the realism and the applicability of our findings. We designed the following data collection method to reconcile our goals and limitations.

Subjects, in groups of 20 (the maximum number of people the computer lab could accommodate at a given time), were individually seated in front of personal computers in a computer lab. Once all the subjects were seated, they were asked to log in to their Facebook accounts. They were informed that a study will be conducted about their Facebook use, and no personally identifiable information will be collected or recorded. They were specifically asked not to leave Facebook, and if they somehow are directed to other landing pages via clicking links in Facebook posts, they should return back to their Facebook News Feed. They were allowed to spend 5 minutes freely on Facebook unsupervised. At the back of the lab, three research assistants carefully observed the screens of the computers to ensure that subjects were doing what they were instructed. Following the 5 minute period (the duration of the experiment), the subjects were asked to shut-down their screens and to write down all of the brand names they could recall in 4 minutes for the brands they saw during the time they spent using Facebook. The research assistants asked participants to randomly select 3 of the brands from their list of recalled brands. Then, they were asked to turn-on their screens and scroll-up to find the posts related to these 3 brands they randomly selected from their lists. Subjects answered all the questionnaire items for each of these three specific posts / ads (i.e., brand-related characteristics, social connotations, like count, and interaction). Then, participants were asked to search for posts / ads in their News Feeds that: 1) involve brands that are not included in the recalled brands list, and 2) they remember paying attention to. Among the list of non-recalled brands the participants again randomly selected 3 brands. Finally, they answered the same set of questions for each of the 3 specific posts / ads which involve a randomly selected non-recalled brand. Summated scores were calculated for each of the questionnaire items for both *brands that were recalled* and *brands that were not recalled*. In order to avoid potential response biases, we tried to ensure that subjects did not know the purpose of the study prior to their participation.

Sample

The sample of the study consisted of 291 university students, recruited by banners posted on both public boards and on a variety of online media used by university students. Applicants were filtered based on their familiarity with SNs and Facebook in particular. Those who are active users of Facebook were included in the sample. The subjects were primarily urban youth, of which 149 were male (51.2%) and 142 were female (48.8%). Their ages ranged from 18 to 26. Subjects' number of friends on Facebook ranged from 52 to 2217, with an average of 540.

Measures and Measurement Validation

Following the procedure employed by Jungsun and Ferle (2008) and Lerman and Garbarino (2002), brand name recall was measured by providing the subjects with a four-minute time period in which to write down all of the brand names they could recall for the brands they saw during the time they spent using Facebook. Brand involvement ($\alpha = .92$), self-brand congruity ($\alpha = .85$), tie-strength ($\alpha = .91$), homophily ($\alpha = .90$), and trust ($\alpha = .91$) were measured by using 5-point Likert scales adapted from the relevant literature. Scale items and their sources are shown in the Appendix. The number of Facebook Friends coefficient is used as a proxy for perceived popularity of the profile associated with a post / ad. The number of Likes coefficient provided the like-count of each post. Finally, five Yes/No questions were used for the interaction options provided in Facebook: clicking a link within the post, Liking, sharing, tagging, and writing a comment.

Additionally, a set of control variables were also recorded to capture individual Facebook behavior during the experiment to aid interpretation of the results: the number of posts seen, number of brands available for recall in posts reviewed, number of posts with multiple mentions of a brand name, number of brands that are mentioned in multiple posts.

A confirmatory factor analysis involving all multi-item constructs is conducted in order to assess the psychometric properties of the measures. The fit statistics indicated a good fit for the measurement model (chi-square = 1301.76; df = 620; IFI = 0.93; TLI = 0.92; CFI = 0.93; RMSEA = 0.062) (Hu & Bentler, 1999). All standardized factor loadings were significant ($p < 0.001$) and higher than .60 (Anderson & Gerbing, 1988), average variance extracted estimates for all factors were well above 0.50 and composite reliability figures for all factors were above 0.75 ($CR_{Inolvement} = 0.92$, $CR_{Self\text{-}Brand\ Congruence} = 0.90$, $CR_{Tie\text{-}Strength} = 0.76$, $CR_{Homophily} = 0.90$; $CR_{Trust} = 0.83$). These figures provide evidence for the convergent validity and internal consistency of measurement items (Hair et al., 2006). In addition, for all constructs the variance extracted values were higher than squared correlations with other factors, providing evidence for discriminant validity (Fornell & Larcker, 1981).

Data Analysis

Before attempting to assess the differences between the means of the theoretical predictors of brand recall in SNs between the brands that were successfully recalled and were failed to be recalled, the potential effects of several confounding factors are controlled for. First, the effect of recency and primacy of exposure was controlled by examining the vertical positions of the post in which the brand appeared within the News Feed for both recalled and non-recalled brands. Only 22 percent of the recalled brands were located in the top five posts and the last five posts reached by the user by scrolling down in the News Feed. Further analyses showed that the effect of vertical position in the News Feed on brand recall was not statistically significant. Second, we have regressed the number of posts seen, number of brands available for recall in posts reviewed, number of posts with multiple mentions of a brand name, number

Table 1. Reliability and validity

Constructs	A	CR	AVE	1	2	3	4	5
1. Brand Involvement	0.92	0.92	0.61	0.78				
2. Self-Brand Congruity	0.85	0.90	0.59	0.57	0.77			
3. Tie-Strength	0.91	0.76	0.82	0.16	.019	0.91		
4. Homophily	0.90	0.90	0.75	0.29	0.34	0.67	0.87	
5. Trust	0.91	0.83	0.77	0.22	0.19	0.69	0.59	0.88

Notes: The analysis was performed with maximum likelihood method. Diagonal elements in bold are the square root of AVE. Off-diagonal elements are correlations between the constructs. α, Cronbach's Alpha, CR, composite reliability; AVE, average variance extracted.

of brands that are mentioned in multiple posts on brand recall. None of the factors were significant. It was also interesting to see that in none of the cases there were more than 3 posts that mention the same brand.

Our research design limits the available options for subsequent data analysis to only paired-sample t-tests and Wilcoxon Signed Ranks Tests (associated drawbacks are discussed in the limitations section). A series of paired-sample t-tests were conducted to assess the differences between the mean values of the theoretical predictors of brand recall in SNS. Next, a series of Wilcoxon Signed Ranks Tests are conducted to assess the differences between the levels of "Like count", "Number of friends / fans" as a proxy for popularity, and five interaction options offered by Facebook among recalled and non-recalled brands.

RESULTS

The number of brands recalled ranged between 1 and 12, with a median of 4 brands. The frequency of number of brands recalled is shown in Figure 1. 81.4 percent of the recalled brands have appeared within the News Feed, while 18.6 percent appeared in the side bar embedded within *ads with social* and *sponsored stories*. Among the recalled impressions occurred in the News Feed, 39.2 percent came from *page publishing* (i.e., the owner of the post was a Fan Page, not a personal account), and the rest (60.8%) were in the form of *stories about friends*.

The mean values, paired-samples correlations, and associated t-values are shown in Table 2. Although all the mean differences were in the expected direction, only the levels of self-brand congruence ($t = 2.67$; $p < 0.01$), trust ($t = 2.60$; $p < 0.01$), and tie-strength ($t = 2.18$; $p < 0.05$) differed significantly between

Figure 1. Frequency of number of brands recalled

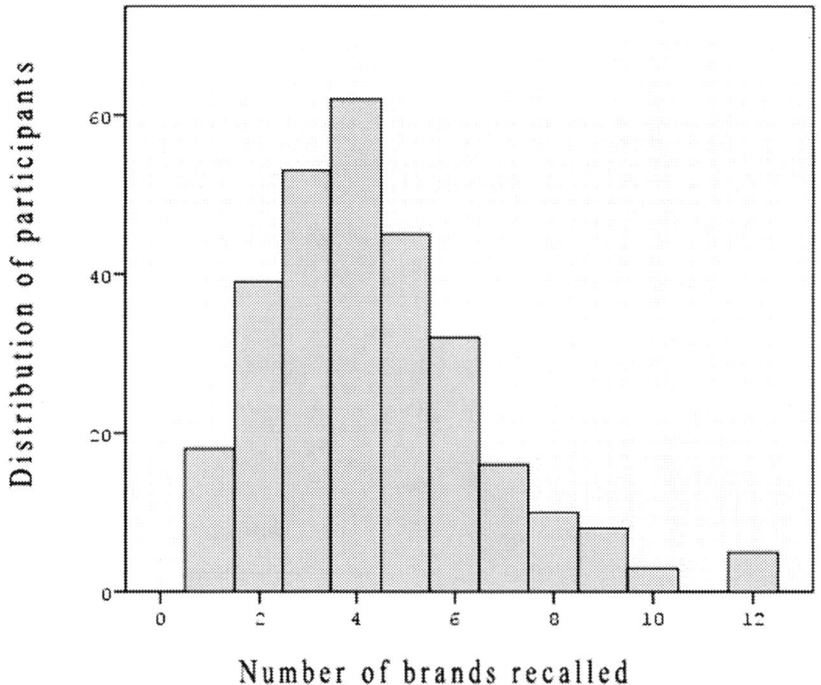

Table 2. Comparison of group means

Construct	df	M_{Recall}	$M_{No\ Recall}$	Paired Correlation	*t*-value
Brand Involvement	290	3.11	3.01	0.25	1.20
Self-Brand Congruence	290	3.14	2.92	0.13	2.67 **
Tie-strength	290	2.97	2.76	0.10	2.18 *
Homophily	290	2.82	2.71	0.17	1.28
Trust	290	2.88	2.66	0.21	2.60 **

* p < 0.05
** p < 0.01

the recalled brands and non-recalled brands. In order to reduce the chances of obtaining false-positive results (type I errors), a Bonferroni correction is performed, which revealed that with a more conservative error-rate only self-brand congruence and trust significantly relates to brand recall.

As shown in Table 3, Wilcoxon Signed-rank tests revealed that, although with relatively small effect sizes, popularity ($Z = -3.36$, $p < 0.05$, $r = 0.20$) and clicking a link in the post / ad in which the brand appears ($Z = -2.29$, $p < 0.05$, $r = 0.13$) significantly effects brand recall. On the other hand, the effects of "Like count" ($Z = -0.29$, $p = 0.78$, $r = 0.02$), and the other four engagement options including Liking ($Z = -0.84$, $p = 0.40$, $r = 0.05$), Sharing ($Z = -0.63$, $p = 0.53$, $r = 0.04$), posting a comment ($Z = -0.63$, $p = 0.53$, $r = 0.04$), and tagging ($Z = -0.82$, $p = 0.41$, $r = 0.05$) were insignificant. Overall, findings supported propositions 2, 3, 5 and 6, whereas propositions 1 and 4 were rejected.

LIMITATIONS

There are several limitations of the present study. In line with our exploratory intentions, we collected data while respondents were live on their Facebook accounts, experiencing their regular Facebook screen. This approach not only reduced our ability to control the effects of many unrecognized factors [see a detailed discussion on the effects of unobserved heterogeneity (Becker et al., 2013)], but the practical impossibility of delivering experimental stimuli to predetermined groups of people (i.e., employing a

Table 3. Results of the Wilcoxon Signed Rank Test

Construct	Z	R
Popularity	-3.36 *	0.20
Clicking a Link	-2.29 *	0.13
Like Count	-0.29	0.02
Liking	-0.84	0.05
Sharing	-0.63	0.04
Posting a Comment	-0.63	0.04
Tagging	-0.82	0.05

* p < 0.05

factorial design) also constrained the scope of statistical analyses available and forced us to use a series of paired-sample t-tests and Wilcoxon Signed Ranks Tests (instead of more stringent statistical tests to examine effects such as ANOVA). Therefore, from a theoretical perspective, the exploratory nature of the analyses in the present study precludes us from offering causal explanations for the observed relationships. Acknowledging this major drawback of the present study, we believe the study is capable of contributing substantially to research in the domain of advertising on online social networks.

Another limitation relates to the issue of attention paid to the posts. We were unable to record how much attention, if any, was paid to the posts, specifically where the non-recalled brands appeared. Direct observation would have jeopardized the realism of the experiment and retrospective self-report questions would have been misleading. The sample characteristics (291 university students) also limit the generalizability of the findings to other demographic groups.

Lastly, it is important for marketing that a brand is recalled when the actual decision to buy is being made. The ability to retrieve a brand during the decision process depends on how strongly the brand is linked in memory with the need. Unfortunately, since each user receives a different set of stories in their News Feed, we were unable to use an experimental stimulus and hence had to measure recall independently of the need. Future research may adopt a scenario approach to overcome this weakness, which will inevitably jeopardize the external validity of the empirical setting.

DISCUSSION AND AVENUES FOR FUTURE RESEARCH

Results of the present research indicate a positive relationship between brand recall:

1. Self-brand congruence,
2. Tie-strength with,
3. Trust toward, and
4. Perceived popularity of the profile associated with the post, and
5. Clicking a link embedded in the post / ad in which the brand appears.

On the other hand, we failed to find a significant difference between the levels of brand involvement, homophily with the profile associated with the post / ad, like-count, and four types of built-in user-interaction options including liking, sharing, posting a comment and tagging among the brands that were successfully retrieved from the memory and those were not.

The findings of the present research, although exploratory in nature, provide interesting insights regarding the four overarching research questions. Regarding the first research question, the fact that each of our subjects successfully retrieved at least one brand impression freely from their memory, suggests brand impressions in Facebook have the potential to affect short-term memory. This finding when combined with the results of the survey-based study conducted by Mariani and Muhammed (2014) in which 87% of every-day Facebook users reported noticing brand advertisement in Facebook, supports the practice of advertising in social media.

Regarding the second research question, our findings provide exploratory evidence regarding how an array of literature-based theoretical predictors of brand awareness in social media relates to brand recall in a realistic setting. Self-brand congruence, tie-strength with, trust toward, and perceived popularity of the profile associated with the post, and clicking a link embedded in the post / ad in which the brand positively relate with brand recall. On the other hand, we failed to find a significant difference between the levels of brand involvement, homophily with the person associated with the post / ad, like-count, and four types of built-in user-interaction options including liking, sharing, posting a comment and tagging among the brands that were successfully retrieved from the memory and those were not. Although the exploratory nature of our research design forbids us to make strong generalizations, these findings may have interesting theoretical and practical implications for marketing in SNs.

The theoretical foundation of the hypothesized relationships between self-brand congruence, tie-strength, trust, and popularity and brand recall rests on the assumption that SNS use is primarily driven by social needs such as self-expression and impression management (boyd, 2007; boyd & Ellison, 2007; Marwick & boyd, 2011). When people are highly involved with a task, their attention can be directed toward an item because it is relevant to the task at hand (Jessen & Rodway, 2010). Driven by their preoccupation with impression management, it may be plausible that SNs users orient themselves toward or process information from only those posts / ads that may in the future serve as desirable identity signals when associated with their profiles. Brands that are congruent with users' desired self-images, may serve as excellent aids for identity construction; hence those posts that involve such brands may be selected for deeper processing. These findings resonate well with the findings of the study conducted by Soares and Pinho (2014), in which they found that group norms and social identity significantly and positively influences perceived advertising relevance in online social advertising. When coupled with results of the Soares and Pinho (2014), our findings indicate that brand communication in social media may aid the motivation to publicly announce social identity and group memberships.

Perceptions regarding trustworthiness and popularity of the person associated with a post/ad are also found to relate positively with brand recall. It seems that the task-at-hand, strategic impression management, not only influences how SNs users select the content they interact with, but may also affects to whom they tune-in to. It is plausible that in order not to miss important chunks of socially important and social identity-relevant information, people seek for and carefully evaluate the posts / ads associated with popular and trustworthy sources.

Conversely, brand involvement was not associated with brand recall in SNs. In accordance with the logic presented above, a possible explanation for this outcome may be grounded on the fact that people do not search for brand-related information on SNs, instead they are attentive toward socially-relevant cues and behavioral residues. SNs users are more concerned with the content associated with the people they are involved with, not the brands. They are more involved with the brands to the extent that the associations of the brand cater to their desired self-images. In drawing this explanation we also relied on the notes we took during the in-depth interviews. Many of the respondents either directly or indirectly stated that interacting with brands on social media is actually a social act full of cultural meanings and values. They emphasized that interaction with branded content is actually a form of consumer-to-consumer interaction that occurs around sharing of brand-related values. This inference fits well with Kozinets' (2014) definition of social brand engagement as "a meaningful connection, creation and communication between one consumer and one or more other consumers, using brand or brand-related language, images and meanings" (p. 10). Cumulatively, this outlook suggests that targeting and segmentation of users in SNs should focus on social needs and gratifications, instead of utilitarian needs or interest-based characteristics. Further, the results suggest that the meaning of "being a Fan" in SNs may diverge from conventional settings, because perceptions related with image-related congruency of a brand seems to weigh heavier than other dimensions of brand involvement (i.e., personal interests, goals, product category) in the context of SNs in influencing cognitive processing of brand-related messages.

Regarding our third research question, among the four built-in interaction options provided by Facebook examined in the present study (liking, sharing, tagging, and posting a comment), none could cognitively engage our subjects enough to facilitate brand recall. Our results showed that only clicking a link placed within a post is associated with brand recall, which is probably due to the fact that clicking a link takes the user away from the Facebook News Feed and lands the user to a more brand-focused page. When the Facebook-specific interaction options are considered, the actions of liking, sharing and tagging can be enacted by a single mouse click, which often do not require elaborate cognitive processing. The comments underneath a post may sometimes be totally unrelated with the original content. People converse via posting comments underneath posts, and the topic of the conversation quickly shifts away from the post itself. Similarly, liking and tagging a particular content may serve as means to interact with the owner of the post, not the post itself. All these provide potential explanations as for why the relationship between these actions and brand recall was insignificant. Therefore, marketers should be cautious when relying on the ability of the number of the incidences of these actions associated with their content in assessing the true marketing impact of their activities in SNs.

Finally, "Like-count", a frequently used success metric in the industry, does not seem to qualify as a reliable measure for brand awareness. Our failure to find a relationship between brand recall and Like-count raises an additional issue: What is the meaning of 'like' is in these environments? It can be speculated that the meaning of 'like' is broader than conventional understandings. It seems that the Like button serves many purposes. Thus, the meaning of a 'like' in SNs remains a mystery, which calls for future research.

The study of marketing communications in social media is still in an early stage. The present study provides insights regarding the impact of brand impressions in SNs on brand awareness and probably produces more questions than it elucidates concrete answers. There also exist many other relevant and important questions yet to be answered associated with brand impressions in SNs. For example, since our findings suggest that trust toward and tie-strength with the profile / page associated with the post are important predictors of brand recall, it a strategic imperative to shed light on the processes through which trust toward and tie-strength with a Fan Page are enhanced in SNs? Does media format (i.e., video, picture, text-based posts) affect brand recall in SNs? Is it possible to create new kinds of built-in interaction options that can improve the accessibility of brands in memory? Similar to the marketing effects of product and brand placements (Balasubramanian, Karrh, & Patwardhan, 2006), can brand impressions in SNs exert an influence on implicit memory? How do the four different methods of delivering brand impressions on Facebook (i.e., sponsored stories, stories about friends, page publishing, and ads with social) differ in terms of their marketing impacts? Each of these issues is practically significant to advertisers, media planners and marketing theorists, yet remains untapped in the relevant literature and hence points toward an interesting direction for future research.

REFERENCES

Acquisti, A., & Gross, R. (2006, June). Imagined communities: Awareness, information sharing, and privacy on the Facebook. In *Privacy enhancing technologies* (pp. 36–58). Springer Berlin Heidelberg. doi:10.1007/11957454_3

Alves, G., & Antunes, J. (2015). New paradigm in communication — The social networks between Brands and Consumers. In *Information Systems and Technologies (CISTI), 2015 10th Iberian Conference*.

Anderson, J. C., & Gerbing, D. W. (1988). Structural equation modeling in practice: A review and recommended two-step approach. *Psychological Bulletin*, *103*(3), 411–423. doi:10.1037/0033-2909.103.3.411

Andrews, J. C., & Shimp, T. A. (1990). Effects of involvement, argument strength and source characteristics on central and peripheral processing in advertising. *Psychology and Marketing*, *7*(3), 195–214. doi:10.1002/mar.4220070305

Balasubramanian, S. K., Karrh, J. A., & Patwardhan, H. (2006). Audience Response to Product Placements: An Integrative Framework and Future Research Agenda. *Journal of Advertising*, *35*(3), 115–141. doi:10.2753/JOA0091-3367350308

Barsalou, L. W. (1985). Ideals, central tendency, and frequency of instantiation as determinants of graded structure. *Journal of Experimental Psychology. Learning, Memory, and Cognition*, *11*(4), 629–654. doi:10.1037/0278-7393.11.1-4.629 PMID:2932520

Becker, J. M., Rai, A., Ringle, C. M., & Völckner, F. (2013). Discovering unobserved heterogeneity in structural equation models to avert validity threats. *Management Information Systems Quarterly*, *37*(3), 665–694.

Berry, D. S., & Miller, K. M. (2001). When boy meets girl: Attractiveness and the five-factor model in opposite-sex interactions. *Journal of Research in Personality*, *35*(1), 62–77. doi:10.1006/jrpe.2000.2304

Bettman, J. R., & Park, C. W. (1980). Effects of prior knowledge and experience and phase of the choice process on consumer decision processes: A protocol analysis. *The Journal of Consumer Research*, *7*(3), 234–248. doi:10.1086/208812

boyd, d., & Ellison, N. B. (2008). Social network sites: Definition, history, and scholarship. *Journal of Computer-Mediated Communication, 13*, 210-230.

boyd, d. (2007). Why youth heart social network sites: The role of networked publics in teenage social life. In D. Buckingham (Ed.), *Youth, identity, and digital media: The John D. and Catherine T. MacArthur Foundation series on digital media and learning*. Cambridge, MA: The MIT Press.

Broderick, A., & Mueller, R. D. (1999). A theoretical and empirical exigesis of the consumer involvement construct. *Journal of Marketing Theory and Practice*, *7*, 97–108. doi:10.1080/10696679.1999.11501855

Brown, J., Broderick, A. J., & Lee, N. (2007). Word of mouth communication within online communities: Conceptualizing the online social network. *Journal of Interactive Marketing*, *21*(3), 2–20. doi:10.1002/dir.20082

Brown, J. J., & Reingen, P. H. (1987). Social ties and word-of-mouth referral behavior. *The Journal of Consumer Research*, *14*(3), 350–362. doi:10.1086/209118

Buss, A. H., & Briggs, S. R. (1984). Drama and the self in social interaction. *Journal of Personality and Social Psychology*, *47*(6), 1310–1324. doi:10.1037/0022-3514.47.6.1310

Byrne, D. E. (1971). *The attraction paradigm*. New York: Academic Press.

Celsi, R. L., & Olson, J. C. (1988). The role of involvement in attention and comprehension processes. *The Journal of Consumer Research*, *15*(2), 210–224. doi:10.1086/209158

Cho, C. H. (2003). Factors influencing clicking of banner ads on the www. *Cyberpsychology & Behavior*, *6*(2), 201–215. doi:10.1089/109493103321640400 PMID:12804033

Christofides, E., Muise, A., & Desmarais, S. (2009). Information disclosure and control on Facebook: Are they two sides of the same coin or two different processes? *Cyberpsychology & Behavior*, *12*(3), 341–345. doi:10.1089/cpb.2008.0226 PMID:19250020

Chu, S., & Kim, Y. (2011). Determinants of consumer engagement in electronic word-of-mouth (eWOM) in social networking sites. *International Journal of Advertising*, *30*(1), 47–75. doi:10.2501/IJA-30-1-047-075

Cohen, J. B. (1983). Involvement and you; 1000 great ideas. *Proceedings: Association for Consumer Research*, *10*, 325–328.

Corritore, C. L., Kracher, B., & Wiedenback, S. (2003). On-line trust: Concepts, evolving themes, a model. *International Journal of Human-Computer Studies*, *58*(6), 737–778. doi:10.1016/S1071-5819(03)00041-7

De Bruyn, A., & Lilien, G. L. (2008). A multi-stage model of word-of-mouth influence through viral marketing. *International Journal of Research in Marketing*, *25*(3), 151–163. doi:10.1016/j.ijresmar.2008.03.004

Dillon, W. R., Madden, T. J., Kirmani, A., & Mukherjee, S. (2001). Understanding what is in a brand rating: A model for assessing brand and attribute effects and their relationship to brand equity. *JMR, Journal of Marketing Research*, *38*(4), 415–429. doi:10.1509/jmkr.38.4.415.18910

Donath, J., & Boyd, D. (2004). Public displays of connection. *BT Technology Journal*, *22*(4), 71–82. doi:10.1023/B:BTTJ.0000047585.06264.cc

Eagly, A. H., Makhijani, M. G., Ashmore, R. D., & Longo, L. C. (1991). What is beautiful is good, but: A meta-analytic review of research on the physical attractiveness stereotype. *Psychological Bulletin*, *110*(1), 109–128. doi:10.1037/0033-2909.110.1.109

Ellison, N. B., Steinfeld, C., & Lampe, C. (2007). The benefits of Facebook ''friends'': Exploring the relationship between college students' use of online social networks and social capital. *Journal of Computer-Mediated Communication*, *12*(4). doi:10.1111/j.1083-6101.2007.00367.x

Escalas, J. E., & Bettman, J. R. (2003). You are what they eat: The influence of reference groups on consumer connections to brands. *Journal of Consumer Psychology*, *13*(3), 339–348. doi:10.1207/S15327663JCP1303_14

Escalas, J. E., & Bettman, J. R. (2005). Self-construal, reference groups and brand meaning. *The Journal of Consumer Research*, *32*(3), 378–389. doi:10.1086/497549

Festinger, L. (1954). A theory of social comparison processes. *Human Relations*, *7*(2), 117–140. doi:10.1177/001872675400700202

Fornell, C., & Larcker, D. F. (1981). Evaluating structural equation models with unobservable variables and measurement error. *JMR, Journal of Marketing Research*, *18*(1), 39–50. doi:10.2307/3151312

Garton, L., Haythornthwaite, C., & Wellman, B. (1997). Studying online social networks. *Journal of Computer-Mediated Communication*, *3*(1).

Gillund, G., & Shiffrin, R. M. (1984). A retrieval model for both recognition and recall. *Psychological Review*, *91*(1), 1–67. doi:10.1037/0033-295X.91.1.1 PMID:6571421

Gilly, M. C., Graham, J. L., Wolfinbarger, M. F., & Yale, L. J. (1998). A dyadic study of interpersonal information search. *Journal of the Academy of Marketing Science*, *26*(2), 83–100. doi:10.1177/0092070398262001

Granovetter, M. S. (1973). The strength of weak ties. *American Journal of Sociology*, *78*(6), 1360–1380. doi:10.1086/225469

Greenberg, A. S. (2012). The role of visual attention in Internet advertising. *Journal of Advertising Research*, *52*(4), 400–404. doi:10.2501/JAR-52-4-400-404

Hair, J. F., Black, W. C., Babin, B. J., Anderson, R. E., & Tatham, R. L. (2006). *Multivariate data analysis* (6th ed.). Pearson Prentice Hall.

Hansen, M. T. (1999). The search-transfer problem: The role of weak ties in sharing knowledge across organization subunits. *Administrative Science Quarterly*, *44*(1), 82–111. doi:10.2307/2667032

Hoyer, W. D., & Brown, S. P. (1990). Effects of brand awareness on choice for a common, repeat purchase product. *The Journal of Consumer Research*, *17*(2), 141–148. doi:10.1086/208544

Hu, L., & Bentler, P. M. (1999). Cutoff criteria for fit indexes in covariance structure analysis: Conventional criteria versus new alternatives. *Structural Equation Modeling*, *6*(1), 1–55. doi:10.1080/10705519909540118

Jessen, T. L., & Rodway, P. (2010). The effects of advertisement location and familiarity on selective attention. *Perceptual and Motor Skills*, *110*(3), 941–960. doi:10.2466/pms.110.3.941-960 PMID:20681345

Jungsun, A., & La Ferle, C. (2008). Enhancing recall and recognition for brand names and body copy a mixed-language approach. *Journal of Advertising*, *37*(3), 107–117. doi:10.2753/JOA0091-3367370308

Kabadayi, S., & Price, K. (2014). Consumer–brand engagement on Facebook: Liking and commenting behaviors. *Journal of Research in Interactive Marketing*, *8*(3), 203–223. doi:10.1108/JRIM-12-2013-0081

Keller, E., & Fay, B. (2012). Word-of-mouth advocacy: A new key to advertising effectiveness. *Journal of Advertising Research*, *52*(4), 459–464. doi:10.2501/JAR-52-4-459-464

Keller, K. L. (1993). Conceptualizing, measuring and managing consumer-based brand equity. *Journal of Marketing*, *57*(1), 1–22. doi:10.2307/1252054

Kintsch, W., & Young, S. R. (1984). Selective recall of decision-relevant information from texts. *Memory & Cognition*, *12*(2), 112–117. doi:10.3758/BF03198424 PMID:6727632

Koehn, D. (2003). The nature of and conditions for online trust. *Journal of Business Ethics*, *43*(3), 3–19. doi:10.1023/A:1022950813386

Kozinets, R. V. (2014). Social media engagement: A new idea. *GFK Marketing Intelligence Review*, *6*(2), 8–15. doi:10.2478/gfkmir-2014-0091

Laurent, G., & Kapferer, J. N. (1985). Measuring consumer involvement profiles. *JMR, Journal of Marketing Research*, *22*(1), 41–53. doi:10.2307/3151549

Lee, M., & Youn, S. (2009). Electronic word of mouth (eWOM): How eWOM platforms influence consumer product judgment. *International Journal of Advertising*, *28*(3), 473–499. doi:10.2501/S0265048709200709

Lee, T. (2005). The impact of perceptions of interactivity on customer trust and transaction intentions in mobile commerce. *Journal of Electronic Commerce Research*, *6*(3), 165–181.

Lerman, D., & Garbarino, E. (2002). Recall and recognition of brand names: A comparison of word and non-word name types. *Psychology and Marketing*, *19*(7/8), 621–639. doi:10.1002/mar.10028

Lipsman, A., Mudd, G., Rich, M., & Bruich, S. (2012). The power of "like": Brands reach (and influence) fans through social-media marketing. *Journal of Advertising Research*, *52*(1), 40–52. doi:10.2501/JAR-52-1-040-052

Liu-Thompkins, Y. (2012). Seeding viral content: Lessons from the diffusion of online videos. *Journal of Advertising Research*, *52*(4), 465–478. doi:10.2501/JAR-52-4-465-478

Logan, K. (2014). Why Isn't Everyone Doing It? A Comparison of Antecedents to Following Brands on Twitter and Facebook. *Journal of Interactive Advertising*, *14*(2), 60–72. doi:10.1080/15252019.2014.935536

Lowrey, T. M., Shrum, L. J., & Dubitsky, T. M. (2003). The relation between brand-name linguistic characteristics and brand-name memory. *Journal of Advertising*, *32*(3), 7–17. doi:10.1080/00913367.2003.10639137

Luhmann, N. (1988). Familiarity, confidence, trust: Problems and alternatives. In D. Gambetta (Ed.), *Trust: Making and breaking cooperative relations* (pp. 94–197). New York: Basil Blackwell.

Malhotra, A., Malhotra, C. K., & See, A. (2013). How to create brand engagement on Facebook. *MIT Sloan Management Review*, *54*(2), 18–20.

Mariani, R., & Mohammed, D. (2014). "Like" A Global Endorsement. How Clicking "Like" Influences Facebook Users Brand Recall and Future Purchasing Intentions. *Journal of Management Policy and Practice*, *15*(4), 51.

Marwick, A., & boyd, . (2011). I tweet honestly, I tweet passionately: Twitter users, context collapse and the imagined audience. *New Media & Society*, *13*(1), 96–113. doi:10.1177/1461444810365313

McCracken, G. (1989). Who is the celebrity endorser? Cultural foundation of the endorsement process. *The Journal of Consumer Research*, *16*(3), 310–321. doi:10.1086/209217

McCroskey, J. C., Richmond, V. P., & Daly, J. A. (1975). The development of a measure of perceived homophily in interpersonal communication. *Human Communication Research*, *1*(4), 323–332. doi:10.1111/j.1468-2958.1975.tb00281.x

McKnight, D. H., Cummings, L. L., & Chervany, N. L. (1998). Initial trust formation in new organizational relationships. *Academy of Management Review*, *3*(23), 473–490.

Mitchell, A. A. (1979). Involvement: A potentially important mediator of consumer behavior. *Proceedings: Association for Consumer Research*, *6*, 191–196.

Mittal, V., Huppertz, J. W., & Khare, A. (2008). Customer complaining: The role of tie strength and information control. *Journal of Retailing*, *84*(2), 195–204. doi:10.1016/j.jretai.2008.01.006

Morgan, R. M., & Hunt, S. D. (1994). The commitment-trust theory of relationship marketing. *Journal of Marketing*, *58*(3), 20–38. doi:10.2307/1252308

Muter, P. (1984). Recognition and recall of words with a single meaning. *Journal of Experimental Psychology. Learning, Memory, and Cognition*, *10*(2), 198–202. doi:10.1037/0278-7393.10.2.198

Nedungadi, P. (1990). Recall and consumer consideration sets: Influencing choice without altering brand evaluations. *The Journal of Consumer Research*, *17*(3), 263–276. doi:10.1086/208556

Nielsen. (2010). *State of the media: The social media report*. Nielsen, NM Incite.

Nisbet, E. C. (2006). The engagement model of opinion leadership: Testing validity within a European context. *International Journal of Public Opinion Research*, *18*(1), 3–30. doi:10.1093/ijpor/edh100

Norris, C. E., & Colman, A. M. (1992). Context Effects on Recall and Recognition of Magazine Advertisements. *Journal of Advertising*, *21*(September), 37–46. doi:10.1080/00913367.1992.10673374

Novak, T. P., Hoffman, D. L., & Duhachek, A. (2003). The Influence of Goal-Directed and Experiential Activities on Online Flow Experiences. *Journal of Consumer Psychology*, *13*(January), 3–16. doi:10.1207/S15327663JCP13-1&2_01

Palka, W., Pousttchi, K., & Wiedemann, D. G. (2009). Mobile word-of-mouth: A grounded theory of mobile viral marketing. *Journal of Information Technology*, *24*(2), 172–185. doi:10.1057/jit.2008.37

Park, C. W., & Lessig, V. P. (1981). Familiarity and its impact on decision biases and heuristics. *The Journal of Consumer Research*, *8*(2), 223–230. doi:10.1086/208859

Phua, J., & Ahn, S. J. (2014). Explicating the 'like' on Facebook brand pages: The effect of intensity of Facebook use, number of overall 'likes', and number of friends ''likes' on consumers' brand outcomes. *Journal of Marketing Communications*, 1-16.

Pigg, K. E., & Crank, L. D. (2004). Building community social capital: The potential and promise of information and communications technologies. *Journal of Community Informatics*, *1*(1), 58–73.

Pornpitakpan, C. (2004). The persuasiveness of source credibility: A critical review of five decades of evidence. *Journal of Applied Social Psychology*, *34*(2), 243–281. doi:10.1111/j.1559-1816.2004.tb02547.x

Prendergast, G., Ko, D., & Yuen, S. Y. V. (2010). Online word of mouth and consumer purchase intentions. *International Journal of Advertising*, *29*(5), 687–708. doi:10.2501/S0265048710201427

Reagans, R., & McEvily, B. (2003). Network structure and knowledge transfer: The effects of cohesion and range. *Administrative Science Quarterly*, *48*(2), 240–267. doi:10.2307/3556658

Ridings, C. M., Gefen, D., & Arinze, B. (2002). Some antecedents and effects of trust in virtual communities. *The Journal of Strategic Information Systems*, *11*(3&4), 271–295. doi:10.1016/S0963-8687(02)00021-5

Rogers, E. M. (1983). *Diffusion of innovations* (3rd ed.). New York: Free Press.

Rohm, A., Kaltcheva, V. D., & Milne, G. R. (2013). A mixed-method approach to examining brand-consumer interactions driven by social media. *Journal of Research in Interactive Marketing*, *7*(4), 295–311. doi:10.1108/JRIM-01-2013-0009

Rotter, J. B. (1971). Generalized expectancies for interpersonal trust. *The American Psychologist*, *26*(5), 443–452. doi:10.1037/h0031464

Schivinski, B., & Dabrowski, D. (2014). The effect of social media communication on consumer perceptions of brands. *Journal of Marketing Communications*, 1-26.

Sirgy, M. J. (1982). Self-concept in consumer behavior: A critical review. *The Journal of Consumer Research*, *9*(3), 287–300. doi:10.1086/208924

Sirgy, M. J. (1985). Self-image/product-image congruity and consumer decision-making. *International Journal of Management*, *2*(4), 49–63.

Sirgy, M. J. (1986). *Self-congruity: Toward a theory of personality and cybernetics*. New York: Praeger.

Sirgy, M. J., Grewal, D., Mangleburg, T. F., Park, J., Chon, K., & Claiborne, C. B. et al. (1997). Assessing the predictive validity of two methods of measuring self-image congruence. *Journal of the Academy of Marketing Science*, *25*(3), 229–241. doi:10.1177/0092070397253004

Soares, A. M., & Pinho, J. C. (2014). Advertising in online social networks: The role of perceived enjoyment and social influence. *Journal of Research in Interactive Marketing*, *8*(3), 245–263. doi:10.1108/JRIM-01-2013-0004

Sternthal, B., Dholakia, R., & Leavitt, C. (1978). The persuasive effect of source credibility: Tests of cognitive response. *The Journal of Consumer Research*, *4*(4), 252–260. doi:10.1086/208704

Sullivan, J. L., & Transue, J. E. (1999). The psychological underpinnings of democracy: A selective review of research on political tolerance, interpersonal trust, and social capital. *Annual Review of Psychology*, *50*(1), 625–650. doi:10.1146/annurev.psych.50.1.625 PMID:15012465

Taylor, D. G., Lewin, J. E., & Strutton, D. (2011). Friends, fans and followers: Do ads work on social networks? *Journal of Advertising Research*, *51*(1), 285–296. doi:10.2501/JAR-51-1-258-275

Tong, S. T., Van Der Heide, B., Langwell, L., & Walther, J. B. (2008). Too much of a good thing? The relationship between number of friends and interpersonal impressions on Facebook. *Journal of Computer-Mediated Communication*, *13*(3), 531–549. doi:10.1111/j.1083-6101.2008.00409.x

Tsai, W. H. S., & Men, L. R. (2013). Motivations and antecedents of consumer engagement with brand pages on social networking sites. *Journal of Interactive Advertising*, *13*(2), 76–87. doi:10.1080/15252019.2013.826549

Vadivu, V. M., & Neelamalar, M. (2015). Digital brand management — A study on the factors affecting customers' engagement in Facebook pages. In *Smart Technologies and Management for Computing, Communication, Controls, Energy and Materials (ICSTM), 2015 International Conference*. doi:10.1109/ICSTM.2015.7225392

Vanden Bergh, B. G., Lee, M., Quilliam, E., & Hove, T. (2011). The multidimensional nature and brand impact of user-generated ad parodies in social media. International Journal of Advertising, 30(1), 103–131.

Wallace, E. (2014). Who Likes You and Why? A typology of Facebook Fans. *Journal of Advertising Research*, (March), 93–109.

Walther, J. B., Van Der Heide, B., Kim, S., Westerman, D., & Tong, S. T. (2008). The role of friends' behavior on evaluations of individuals' Facebook profiles: Are we known by the company we keep? *Human Communication Research*, *34*, 28–49. doi:10.1111/j.1468-2958.2007.00312.x

Warren, M. E. (1999). *Democracy and trust*. Cambridge University Press. doi:10.1017/CBO9780511659959

Zaichowsky, J. L. (1986). Conceptualizing involvement. *Journal of Advertising*, *15*(2), 4–14. doi:10.1080/00913367.1986.10672999

Zuckerberg, M. (2008). *Thoughts on the evolution of Facebook*. Facebook Blog. Retrieved from http://blog.facebook.com/blog.php?post=31033537130

This research was previously published in Strategic Uses of Social Media for Improved Customer Retention edited by Wafaa Al-Rabayah, Rawan Khasawneh, Rasha Abu-shamaa, and Izzat Alsmadi, pages 124-153, copyright year 2017 by Business Science Reference (an imprint of IGI Global).

APPENDIX

Final Items Used in Testing and Analyses

Brand Involvement: (Jungsun & La Ferle, 2008; Cho, 2003)

1. The brand is important to me.
2. I get involved with the brand.
3. The brand is relevant to me.
4. I am going to use / buy a product of the brand in the next six months.
5. I am interested in the brand in general.

Trust: (Chu & Kim, 2011)

1. I trust the owner of the profile / page associated with the post / ad.
2. I have confidence in the owner of the profile / page associated with the post / ad.
3. I can believe in the owner of the profile / page associated with the post / ad.

Self-Brand Congruence: (Sirgy et al., 1997)

1. The brand is consistent with how I see myself.
2. The brand caters to people like me.
3. The brand reflects who I am.
4. The typical customers of the brand are very much like me.

Homophily: (McCroskey et al., 1975). The owner of the profile / page associated with the post / ad …

1. Thinks like me.
2. Behaves like me.
3. Similar to me.
4. Is like me.

Tie-Strength: (Chu & Kim, 2011; Brown & Reingen, 1987)

1. I frequently communicate with the owner of the profile / page associated with the post / ad.
2. Overall, the owner of the profile / page associated with the post / ad is important for me.
3. Overall, I feel close to the owner of the profile / page associated with the post / ad.

Chapter 23
The Effects of Consumer Social Media Marketing Experiences on Brand Affect and Brand Equity

Tugba Orten Tugrul
Izmir University of Economics, Turkey

ABSTRACT

A limited number of studies have shown that social media marketing activities positively contribute to brand performance. In this chapter, therefore, a conceptual framework elucidating how consumer social media marketing experiences lead to more favorable brand affect, and in turn, enhanced brand equity is proposed. Importantly, perceived social media marketing activities are identified as a key moderator influencing the effects of consumer social media marketing experiences on brand equity. Repeated measures ANOVA and regression analyses were conducted to test the proposed model in a study consisting of three phases. The results provide support for (a) the main effects of consumer social media marketing experiences on brand affect and brand equity, (b) the mediating effect of brand affect, and (c) the moderating effect of perceived social media marketing activities. The chapter concludes with a discussion of the theoretical and managerial implications of the research findings, and recommendations for future studies.

INTRODUCTION

Effective social media management is one of the central interests and demands of today's business world (Kaplan & Haenlein, 2010). The current consumer trend toward increasingly frequent social media usage provides new opportunities, but also challenges. This growing popularity of social media requires the traditional communication medium to be revised according to the new market conditions and customer expectations (Hennig-Thurau et al., 2010; Hensel & Deis, 2010; Qualman, 2013). The two main factors in this context are customers' desire for direct two-way direct communication when engaging with brands

DOI: 10.4018/978-1-5225-5637-4.ch023

(Kaplan & Haenlein, 2010), and companies' ability to exploit social media's facilitation of immediate and low cost access to target consumers through a variety of channels (Luke, 2009). By incorporating social media in their existing marketing strategies, firms can reach their branding, customer service and relationship management objectives (Tuten & Solomon, 2013). Research has demonstrated that social media provide a range of advantages to firms, such as better customer relations and enhanced customer equity (Trainor, Andzulis, Rapp, & Agnihotri, 2013; Kim & Ko, 2012). Specifically, social media marketing activities have positive impacts on brands in terms of awareness, attitude, loyalty and equity (Erdoğmuş & Çiçek, 2012; Kim & Ko, 2012; Mangold & Faulds, 2009). In spite of these potential benefits, a systematic understanding of how social media marketing activities affect brand equity remains elusive.

In the current competitive marketing environment, brand equity is one of the keystones of a firm's long term success. It has a significant effect on consumer responses to branding strategies and supporting marketing programs (Keller, 1993). According to the brand value chain, marketing activities associated with target-oriented programs influence what customer think and feel about the brand (Keller & Lehmann, 2003). If the firm has a strong brand value, its customers are likely to have repurchase intentions and be more willing to generate and spread positive word-of-mouth (Vogel, Evanschitzky, & Ramaseshan, 2008). From a broader perspective, positive brand equity may create opportunities for higher revenues, lower costs, and greater profits (Keller, 1993). These positive effects of brand equity demonstrate the returns of marketing investments in brand value development (Yoo & Donthu, 2001). Therefore, brand equity is as a key strategic asset that firms should monitor to maximize long-term brand performance. Although researchers have devoted a considerable amount of attention to brand equity concept, marketing activities that can create equity need to be further investigated (Faircloth, Capella, & Alford, 2001). For instance, brand experiences preserved in the minds of customers have the potential to trigger the creation of brand value process and lead to successful market performance in the long run (Keller & Lehmann, 2003). Thus, profitable brand management requires building consistent and distinctive customer brand experiences, which takes into account the impacts of all marketing mix elements (Mosley, 2007). Prior research revealed that customer experience has a significant and positive influence on brand equity (Biedenbach & Marell, 2010; Sheng & Teo, 2012). In addition, the interaction between brands and customer experiences has also an emotional dimension. Previous studies have highlighted the importance of enlightening the emotional aspects of consumption experiences in the study of consumer behavior (Chaudhuri & Holbrook, 2001; Holbrook & Hirschman, 1982). It has been shown the favorable customer experiences may lead to emotional responses and interactions, providing opportunities for creating brand value (Gentile, Spiller, & Noci, 2007). However, only recently a limited number of studies explore the relationship between customer experiences and brands (Verhoef et al., 2009).

As discussed previously, there have been a limited number of studies which examine how brand equity is impacted by social media marketing activities and consumer experiences. Moreover, two factors are treated as independent in these studies. In contrast, the current study embraces a holistic approach, examining the impact of consumer social media marketing experiences on brand equity with an emphasis on understanding the role played by perceived social media marketing activities. Additionally, considering the emotional aspect of experiences, the relationship among consumer social media marketing experiences, affect elicited by brands and brand equity is explored.

In the following section, the literature review and hypotheses derived from prior studies are presented. The methodology section which follows provides the details of the sample and the procedure of data collection, the measurements of the constructs, the tests of hypotheses and the results. Conclusions and implications for practice are next discussed, and finally, the limitations and possible directions for future research are discussed.

THEORETICAL BACKGROUND AND CONCEPTUAL MODEL

Traditional forms of communication and marketing need to be revised to address the impacts and demands of social media (Hennig-Thurau et al., 2010; Hensel & Deis, 2010; Qualman, 2013). It replaced the old-fashion one-way communication with a two-way direct communication, free of time, place or medium restrictions (Kim & Ko, 2012). Social media is an online way of communicating, conveying, collaborating, and cultivating among connected people through multiple channels, each of which has a different focus (Tuten & Solomon, 2013). Examples of social media include social communities, which focus on socializing with other users sharing unique interests; social publishing sites, which address the dissemination and promotion of content such as words, videos or photos; social entertainment, which features the fun and shared uses of social media; and social commerce zone, which concentrates on the online shopping experience supported by social media applications and tools. One of the key requirements of social media success is "being active" (Kaplan & Haenlein, 2010). Hence, customers expect companies to actively use specific social media platforms to share and discuss products, services or business related contents with other participants (Evans & McKee, 2010). Thus, social media should also be managed in an honest and transparent way in order to communicate relevant, updated and accurate branded content (Erdoğmuş & Çiçek, 2012). However, it seems that communication about brands in social media context may occur with or without the permission or initiative of the companies in question (Kietzmann, Hermkens, McCarthy, & Silvestre, 2011). Therefore, it is critical that strategies for monitoring, understanding, and responding to different social media activities are developed, and are well-integrated with other communication and marketing strategies (Kaplan & Haenlein, 2010; Kietzmann et al., 2011; Mangold & Faulds, 2009).

Social media presents a promising environment for pursuing advertising and marketing goals (Hensel & Deis, 2010). Different social media applications can fulfill many different social media marketing objectives such as brand awareness, engagement and word-of-mouth (Hoffman & Fodor, 2010). In the context of the marketplace, social media can be defined as a medium which allows the sharing of consumers' thoughts and experiences of brands, products or services with people with similar interests, allowing better informed choices to be made (Evans, 2012). Therefore, by using social media platforms, marketers can communicate promotional messages that have the potentials to be disseminated to thousands or even millions of consumers. In addition, by conducting social media marketing activities, companies can communicate directly with customers and receive feedback, observe customer-to-customer conversations, create favorable customer experiences by providing customized and entertaining services, and, in turn, lead customers to share promotional branded-contents with others. Social media marketing refers to the use of social media technologies, channels and software to create, communicate and promote exchange offerings that are valuable for a company's stakeholders (Tuten & Solomon, 2013). The nature and dynamics of social interactions between organizations and consumers in the current new media environment are particularly important for managing and enhancing customer relations (Hennig-Thurau et al., 2010), because these interactions enable firms to build deeper customer intimacy by understanding, anticipating, and fulfilling declared and hidden customer needs. As companies develop their social media marketing presence, they have an opportunity to discover the experiences and desires of their target customers, and to tailor their products and services accordingly (Evans & McKee, 2010). Social media marketing activities includes introducing products, services or brands sincerely, and also interacting and engaging consumers by providing variety of services through social media channels as means of marketing communications (Kim & Ko, 2012).

Social media may impact consumer behavior in various ways, including brand awareness creation, information acquisition, opinion and attitude formation, purchase behavior, and post-purchase communication (Mangold & Faulds, 2009). According to DEI Worldwide report (2008), 70% of consumers have used social media sites for product or brand information; 49% have made a purchase decision based on the information on social media sites; and 60% have used social media sites to pass on information to others. The opinion of an individual has now reached hundreds or even thousands, in contrast to the few contacts that were possible before the advent of social media (Swedowsky, 2009). Another recent study by Ipsos OTX and Ipsos Global Advisor (2012) mentioned that 22% of internet users worldwide said they buy a brand because a friend "likes" or follows it on a social network. This is not surprising considering the fact that over 90% of consumers trust peer recommendations, while only 14% trust advertisements (Qualman, 2013). These statistics demonstrate that firms and brands may benefit from the opportunities provided by social media in their marketing strategies aimed at creating value for customers and capturing value in return.

Previous studies provided evidence that social media technology investments enhance a firm's social customer relationship management capabilities and customer relationship performance (Trainor et al., 2013). Similarly, attracting new customers and cultivating customer relationships were found to be small and medium business-to-business brands' most prominent marketing reasons for using social networking sites (Michaelidou, Siamagka, & Christodoulides, 2011). Moreover, research demonstrated that social media marketing activities strengthen customer relations, create purchase intention, and enhance brand and customer equity (Kim & Ko, 2012).

Brand equity refers to "the differential effect of brand knowledge on consumer response to the marketing of the brand" (Keller, 1993: 8). In contrast, brand value embraces a company perspective, and is defined as "the sale or replacement value of a brand" (Raggio & Leone, 2007: 380). However, these two constructs have been frequently considered to be identical in the literature, and thus are used interchangeably (Faircloth et al., 2001; Keller, 1993; Keller & Lehmann, 2003; Yoo & Donthu, 2001). The customer-based conceptualization of brand equity represents the individual consumer level, subjective and intangible assessment of brand value derived from the long-term marketing invested into a brand (Yoo & Donthu, 2001). A strategy based on brand equity enables firms to create positive, strong, and unique brand associations that can lead favorable consumer perceptions, preferences and behaviors (Keller, 1993). In other words, if a brand has high awareness and favorable image, customers are likely to experience high brand equity and, in turn, choose that particular brand rather than competing offerings (Vogel et al., 2008). Crucial to building such a valuable asset is an understanding of how marketing mix elements create brand equity (Faircloth et al., 2'001; Keller & Lehmann, 2003). For instance, undertaking marketing activities that can lead to consumers' experience of or exposure to the brand have the potential to enhance familiarity and awareness (Keller, 1993).

Brand value may also come from the building of a successful relationship between a brand and its online customer communities, formed in the social media landscape. In such a case, those online customers are more likely to be loyal to the brand's existing products, and try its new marketing offers, and be less vulnerable to unfavorable company or brand information (Culnan, McHugh, & Zubillaga, 2010), because brand trust was found to be one of the most significant antecedents of brand loyalty among social media-based brand communities (Laroche, Habibi, Richard, & Sankaranarayanan, 2012). Brand loyalty is also affected positively by the relevancy of the content of social media, the popularity of the content among users and their contacts, and the variety of platforms and applications provided on social media (Erdoğmuş & Çiçek, 2012). In addition, social media marketing activities that entertain customers, enable customized information searching, and lead to word-of-mouth enhance brand equity and purchase intention (Kim & Ko, 2012).

In spite of the findings of recent research, there is still much to learn about the interaction between brand perceptions and customer experiences (Verhoef et al., 2009). Customer experience can be defined as the internal and subjective customer response to contact from companies, whether direct (e.g., buying or using products or services) or indirect (e.g., word-of-mouth recommendations and criticisms, or advertising) (Meyer & Schwager, 2007). This experience is composed of customer-company interactions that provoke a reaction (Shaw & Ivens, 2005). Customers perceive each experience as a complex and multidimensional construct, including sensorial, emotional, cognitive, pragmatic, lifestyle and relational components (Gentile et al., 2007). Therefore, it is critical for companies to understand the holistic nature of customer experiences to remain successful in today's highly competitive marketplace (Verhoef et al., 2009). The concept of customer experience has received significant attention in the experiential marketing literature as a new lever which can create value for both the company and the customer (Gentile et al., 2007). On the company side, the value generated from the interactions between a company and its customers has a potential impact on intangible assets of the company. Marketing activities that lead to consumers' positive brand experience may establish stronger, more favorable and unique brand associations in the memory and enhance customer-based brand equity (Keller, 1993), as demonstrated by previous studies (Biedenbach & Marell, 2010; Sheng & Teo, 2012). Insights from existing research suggest that providing a compelling online environment can produce the setting for the desired customer experiences to emerge, leading to several positive consequences for companies (Novak, Hoffman, & Yung, 2000). Thus, consumers' social media marketing experiences are expected to lead to enhanced brand equity.

H1. Consumer social media marketing experiences have a positive effect on brand equity.

Marketing scholars have long advocated the recognition of the importance of the emotional aspects of consumer experiences (Holbrook & Hirschman, 1982). However, research in the marketing and consumer behavior fields leaves some important questions unanswered, such as brand-elicited emotions in consumption experiences (Chaudhuri & Holbrook, 2001). Brands serve as emotional ties between firms and customers (Lemon, Rust, & Ziethaml, 2001). A good consumer experience, thus, is expected to create emotional interactions and affective customer relations with the company, its brands or products (Gentile et al., 2007). As an example, satisfied consumers may develop a passionate emotional attachment to particular brands (Carroll & Ahuvia, 2006). "A brand's potential to elicit a positive emotional response in the average consumer as a result of its use" is defined as brand affect. (Chaudhuri & Holbrook, 2001: 82). In addition, the value generated from emotional aspects of consumer experiences has a potential impact on brand equity and customer equity (Gentile et al., 2007). The generation of consumer moods, feelings or emotions originated from consumer-brand relations was found to be associated with improved brand loyalty and positive word-of-mouth (Carroll & Ahuvia, 2006). Similarly, brands which produce positive affect in consumers are associated with high levels of brand loyalty (Chaudhuri & Holbrook, 2001; Dick & Basu, 1994). In line with such findings, the present study proposes that consumers' social media marketing experiences will be positively related to brand affect, and thus, brand equity.

H2. Consumer social media marketing experiences have a positive effect on brand affect.
H3. Brand affect mediates the effect of consumer social media marketing experiences on brand equity.

Consumer experiences in online communities are related to exploratory consumer behaviors that are also linked to important marketing objectives (Novak et al., 2000). Anything that leads to consumer brand experience has the potential to build or increase customer-based brand equity (Keller, 1993). As described previously, social media marketing activities are aimed at creating brand knowledge, awareness, image, engagement, which are all aspects of brand value. For instance, consumers who perceive activities on a brand's social media platforms as entertaining, fashionable, interactive, and customized, are more likely to attach higher values to that brand (Kim & Ko, 2012). Thus, consumer social media experiences are likely to have a greater impact on brand equity when consumers have more favorable perceptions of the brand's social media marketing activities.

H4. Perceived social media marketing activities moderates the effect of consumer social media marketing experiences on brand equity.

To summarize, this research explores the relationships among social media marketing experience, brand affect and brand equity. Drawing from prior research, the results are expected to indicate that positive experiences with a brand's social media sites are likely to lead more favorable brand affects, and in turn, enhanced brand equity. In addition, consumer perceptions of the social media marketing activities is identified as a moderator of consumer social media marketing experience effect on brand equity. The conceptual model of this study is depicted in Figure 1.

METHODOLOGY

Participants

68 undergraduate students from Izmir University of Economics participated in this study for extra course credit (ages 20–24, Md = 22; 63% female). University students were selected because the current generation of young adults has been described as being the frequent users of social networks (Wilcox &

Figure 1. Conceptual model

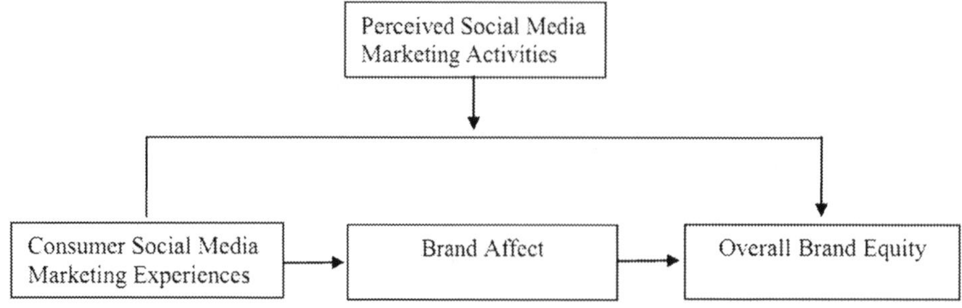

Stephen, 2013). Moreover, student consumers are generally familiar with fashion products, and therefore more likely to provide reliable and valid data in this area (Yoo & Donthu, 2001).

Since this study focuses on consumer social media marketing experience, respondents were restricted to consumers who had previously purchased a product from Mudo, a long-established brand in the Turkish clothing and decoration retailing industry, but had no experience of its social media sites. Mudo positions itself as a pioneering clothing brand shaping the fashion perceptions of especially young people. It actively uses many social media platforms including Facebook, Twitter, Pinterest, Vimeo, Google Plus and Youtube. Thus, Mudo makes a particularly suitable case for the examination of a brand's social media marketing practices and related performance.

According to TUIK statistics (2013), the internet usage rate for the population of Turkey is 48.9 percent, with the highest rate of engagement for the 16-24 age group, at 68 percent. The Internet is estimated to have contributed 22 billion TL to the Turkish economy in 2011, of which consumer spending on e-commerce is the largest contributor, accounting for 4.5 billion TL (BCG, 2013). 24.1 percent of Internet users shop online, and 48.6 percent of purchased clothing products and sports equipment in 2013 (TUIK, 2013). In terms of social media engagement, Turkey ranks at the fourth in the world, with an average 10.2 hours spent on social networking sites per month (Comscore, 2011). Facebook is the most popular social media platform, with around 30 million users spending an average of 56 minutes per day (Facebook Ads, 2011). Twitter is another popular social media channel with around 9 million users (Alexa, 2014). Given their high involvement in social media (BCG, 2013), a Turkish sample can be considered particularly suitable for the study of the effects of consumer social media marketing experiences.

Procedure

The study was conducted in three parts. Participants came to the lab for a study titled "Social Media". They were told the purpose of the study was to suggest new ideas for the successful management of social media for brands. In the first phase of the study, after answering questions about brand purchase experience, brand social media sites experience, social media usage frequency and product category involvement, respondents were asked to complete other survey questions about brand affect and overall brand equity constructs. Then, they were given unrelated filler tasks to minimize the possibility that the recall of their prior brand evaluations would impact the subsequent stage of the study. Next, participants were administered a social media marketing experience task. In a room with computers provided, they were asked to browse each of the brand's social media sites for 10 minutes. Afterwards, participants were asked to complete the brand affect and brand equity part of the questionnaire that was used in the first stage, as well as additional questions about the perceived social media marketing activities under concern.

Measures

Brand purchase experience and brand social media sites experiences were measured with yes or no items. Product category involvement (PCI) was measured with four five-point items (Yoo & Donthu, 2001). Social media usage frequency (SMUF) was measured using a five-point frequency scale with "almost never" and "very often" endpoints (Dabholkar, 1996).

Brand affect (BA) was measured with three items developed by Chaudhuri and Holbrook (2001): "I feel good when I use Mudo brand," "Mudo brand makes me happy," and "Mudo brand gives me pleasure." Overall brand equity (OBE) was measured by four items adopted from Yoo and and Donthu (2001):"It makes sense to buy Mudo brand instead of any other brand," "Even if another brand has the same features as Mudo brand, I would prefer to buy Mudo brand," "If there is another brand as good as Mudo brand, I would prefer to buy Mudo brand," and "If another brand is not different from Mudo brand in any way, it seems smarter to purchase Mudo brand." Borrowed from Kim and Ko (2012), the eleven-item scale was used to measure perceived social media marketing activities (SMM). The dimensions of SMM were entertainment, interaction, trendiness, customization and word of mouth. The first construct was related to the enjoyment created by Mudo's social media platforms, the second expressed interaction, opinion exchange and information sharing among users, the third construct focused on the trendiness and the recency of information release, and the fourth represented the customized information searching service aspect, and the fifth included customer's intentions to pass on information seen in these platforms and upload online branded-contents to their personal social media accounts. All of the above items were evaluated using five-point Likert scales anchored at 1 = "strongly disagree" and 5 = "strongly agree."

Results and Discussion

Findings indicated that respondents, university student consumers, were heavy users of social media platforms (M_{SMUF} = 4.51, SD $_{SMUF}$ = .80) and highly involved with clothing product category (M_{PCI} = 3.95, SD_{PCI} = .42). These results implied that students participating in this study were effective surrogates for a social media marketing study.

The reliability of the items of each construct was assessed using Cronbach's alpha (Nunnally & Bernstein, 1994). The results showed that all the constructs have adequate reliability as being higher than 0.70 Cronbach's α coefficient (α_{SMM} = .88; $\alpha_{\text{preexperience-BA}}$ = .90 and $\alpha_{\text{postexperience-BA}}$ = .87; $\alpha_{\text{preexperience-OBE}}$ = .80 and $\alpha_{\text{postexperience-OBE}}$ = .86).

Results for Brand Equity

A repeated-measures ANOVA test was employed to measure the effect of consumer social media marketing experiences on brand equity. The results revealed that there was a significant difference in brand equity scores measured before and after participants engaged in a social media sites experience ($M_{\text{preexperience-OBE}}$ = 2.72, SD $_{\text{preexperience-OBE}}$ = .64 vs. $M_{\text{postexperience-OBE}}$ = 3.18, SD $_{\text{postexperience-OBE}}$ = .70; $F(1, 67) = 118.467$, $p < .05$). Thus, Hypothesis 1 is supported.

Results for Brand Affect

To examine the influence of consumer social media marketing experiences on brand affect, a one-way within subjects ANOVA test was conducted. As expected, consumer social media marketing experiences created a significant difference for brand affect ($M_{\text{preexperience-BA}}$ = 3.28, SD $_{\text{preexperience-BA}}$ = .52 vs. $M_{\text{postexperience-BA}}$ = 3.67, SD $_{\text{postexperience-BA}}$ = .56; $F(1, 67) = 81.562$, $p < .05$); therefore, Hypothesis 2 is supported. Results for H1 and H2 are shown in Figure 2, and are further detailed in Tables 1 and 2.

Figure 2. Profile plots for the consumer SMM experience effects on brand affect and brand equity

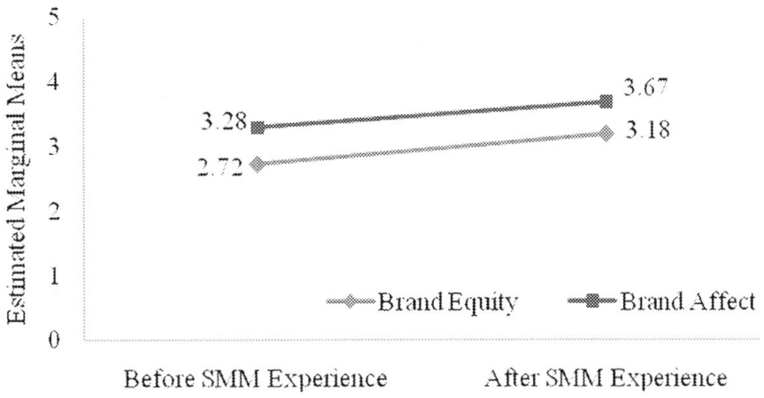

Estimated Marginal Means
5
4
3
2
1
0
3.28
2.72
3.67
3.18
Brand Equity
Brand Affect
Before SMM Experience
After SMM Experience

Table 1. Descriptive statistics for brand equity and brand affect

	Brand Equity			Brand Affect		
	N	**Mean**	**SD**	**N**	**Mean**	**SD**
Before SMM Experience	68	2.7206	.63559	68	3.2846	.51599
After SMM Experience	68	3.1765	.70454	68	3.6713	.56276

Table 2. Repeated-measures ANOVA results

	df	F	Sig.
Brand Equity	1	118.467	0.000
Brand Affect	1	81.562	0.000

Results for Mediation Effect of Brand Affect

The mediation analysis developed by Judd, Kenny and McClelland (2001) was applied to test for mediation effect in a within-subject design. Firstly, each brand equity measure on the brand affect measure from the same condition (before vs. after social media marketing experience) was regressed. As expected, brand affect levels in each condition are significantly related to brand equity levels ($t_{preexperience}$ (66) = 5.09, $B_{preexperience}$ = .65, $SE_{preexperience}$ =.13; $t_{postexperience}$ (66) = 5.99, $B_{postexperience}$ =.74, $SE_{postexperience}$ =.12; $p < .05$). When the brand equity difference was regressed on the brand affect centered sum and difference, the brand affect difference was a significant predictor of the brand equity difference, $t_{BA\_difference}$ (65) = 3.47, $B_{BA\_difference}$ =.39, $SE_{BA\_difference}$ =.11, $p < .05$, but the brand affect centered sum was not. This finding provides support for Hypothesis 3.

Results for Moderating Effect of Perceived Social Media Marketing Activities

Firstly, the perceptions of social media marketing activities were investigated. Findings demonstrated that respondents have positive perceptions of Mudo's marketing activities on its social media sites ($M_{SMM} = 3.82$, $SD_{SMM} = .59$). Next, the moderating effect of the perceived social media marketing activities on the relationship between consumer social media marketing experiences and brand equity was measured, according to the recommendations of Judd et al. (2001). Moderation due to the perceived social media marketing activities was estimated by regressing the brand equity difference on the centered perceived social media marketing activities. The result showed a significant interaction between perceived social media marketing activities and consumer social media marketing experiences, $t_{centeredSMMA}(66) = 2.27$, $B_{centeredSMMA} = .13$, $SE_{centeredSMMA} = .06$, $p < .05$. Thus, Hypothesis 4 is supported. Results for H3 and H4 are shown in Tables 3 and 4.

CONCLUSION AND MANAGERIAL PRACTICAL IMPLICATIONS

Companies increasingly use social media channels to meet the demands of the current online marketing environment. Specifically, all brand activity within the social media landscape is aimed at developing enhancing brand value. In this regard, by using social media marketing techniques, firms try to promote stronger customer engagements and more favorable brand evaluations. The creation and management of successful customer experience by brands is also critical for the development of emotional ties with customers. Thus, the purpose of this study is to examine the effects of consumer social media marketing experiences on brands, namely, brand affect and brand equity. Additionally, this study investigates the moderating effect of consumer perceptions of social media marketing activities on the relationship between brand equity evaluations and media marketing experiences. The findings of this study have several important practical and theoretical implications.

Table 3. Regression analysis results for mediation effect

	t	B	SE	Sig.
Constant	.974	.194	.199	.334
BA_Sum	.585	.016	.028	.560
BA_Difference	3.466	.385	.111	.001
Dependent Variable: BE _Difference				

Table 4. Regression analysis results for moderating effect

	t	B	SE	Sig.
Constant	-.117	-.025	.216	.908
SMMA	2.267	.134	.059	.027
Dependent Variable: BE _Difference				

Results reveal that consumers attach more value to a brand after experiencing the brand's marketing activities on its social media sites. This finding has two important implications. Firstly, from a business executive point of view, it highlights the benefits of building a social media presence. Secondly, this result draws attention to the significance of creating positive customer experiences in branding. Hence, this study showed that consumer social media marketing experiences enhance brand equity. Thus, managers should consider social media as a strategic marketing tool integrated to the brand value creation process.

Findings have also illustrated that consumer social media marketing experiences influence brand affect positively. For brand managers, this result suggests that social media marketing is a way of creating affective relations with their customers. Therefore, while developing social media marketing strategies, companies should consider the emotional aspects of consumer experiences, and manage their social media landscapes accordingly.

Beyond the identification of the effect of consumer experiences on brand value, this study provides evidence for the underlying process. According to the results, brand affect mediates the effect of consumer social media marketing experiences on brand equity. This finding supports the argument that social media marketing activities that facilitate superior customer experiences lead to the development of emotional consumer-brand ties, which, in turn, enhances brand value. Thus, marketing managers can use the present finding to advocate increased investments in social media marketing activities aimed at creating favorable long-term effects on brands.

Finally, as this study shows, perceived social media marketing activities play a moderating role in consumer experience-based brand equity enhancement. In other words, the effect of consumer social media marketing experiences on brand equity is greater when consumers have more favorable perceptions of the social media marketing activities. Consequently, marketing activities on social media platforms that entertain customers, enable customized information searching, create interaction among users and enable content and information sharing can be considered as creating a competitive advantage, positively contributing to the brand value generation derived from consumer experiences.

LIMITATIONS AND FUTURE RESEARCH

The research is not without limitations, and the three important are addressed in this section. Firstly, the heavy social use of the sample can be seen as a limitation, and future studies attempting to replicate this study should choose samples with different social media habits. Secondly, in view of the discussion over personality differences and social media usage (Hughes, Rowe, Batey, & Lee, 2012), an exclusive focus on young consumers, with similar characteristics may limit the generalizability of the findings regarding older generations. The final major limitation relates to the use of the four-item unidimensional measure of consumer-based brand equity, which may be less efficient than a multidimensional scale in examining the relationships between brand equity and its antecedents or consequences (Yoo & Donthu, 2001).

This study points to a number of productive opportunities for future research. First of all, the conceptual model developed in this study helps to explicitly investigate the effects that customer social media marketing experience has on brand affect and brand equity. Additional studies could expand this view by including other key variables that may have significant influences on the development of brand equity. Drawing on prior research (Biedenbach & Marell, 2010), the potential role of brand attitude in the relationship between consumer experience and brand equity may shed light on the reasons for specific consumer responses to branding activities on social media, and also their effects on brand performance.

Moreover, based on the model developed by Verhoef et al. (2009), future works that take into account several determinants of customer experience have the potential to enlarge the current state of knowledge in social media marketing focused branding research. Specifically, incorporating the previously suggested bi-directional interaction of customer expectations and experiences in branding studies may provide new evidence, demonstrating the importance of creating positive brand experiences on social media platforms (Meyer & Schwager, 2007; Ofir & Simonson, 2007; Verhoef et al., 2009).

The role of emotions have received considerable attention in the advertising literature related to marketing and consumer behavior studies; however, emotional aspects of consumer experiences in branding research have received for less (Chaudhuri & Holbrook, 2001). Thus, further research is needed to develop a deeper understanding of the causes and effects of feelings or affect elicited by brands in the social media marketing environment.

Social media marketing is also a fruitful avenue for future research. Previous studies argued that a firm's customer relationship performance is impacted by its capability to manage and promote customer interactions facilitated by social media technologies (Trainor et al., 2013). Future research should therefore explore other firm-based factors that might improve or limit the effectiveness of social media marketing applications. In addition, researchers recently used ad hoc measures to evaluate the effectiveness of social media marketing activities (Michaelidou et al., 2011). However, finding appropriate ways of measuring the return on investment of social media marketing is a common issue for many companies today (Hoffman & Fodor, 2010). It is essential to conduct research that develops a comprehensive scale to measure the yields of social media marketing investments, considering different social media applications and brand objectives.

Finally, the dynamics and strategic effects of social interactions between customers and organizations enabled and facilitated by social media marketing are important areas for future research. In this regard, companies' reactions to negative electronic word-of-mouth or customer complaints communicated through corporate social media platforms and their impacts on brands such as decreased customer retention and brand equity are interesting research directions (Hennig-Thurau et al., 2010).

REFERENCES

Alexa. (2014). *Top sites in Turkey*. Retrieved from http://www.alexa.com/topsites/countries/TR

Biedenbach, G., & Marell, A. (2010). The impact of customer experience on brand equity in a business-to-business services setting. *Journal of Brand Management*, *17*(6), 446–458. doi:10.1057/bm.2009.37

Carroll, B. A., & Ahuvia, A. C. (2006). Some antecedents and outcomes of brand love. *Marketing Letters*, *17*(2), 79–89. doi:10.1007/s11002-006-4219-2

Chaudhuri, A., & Holbrook, M. B. (2001). The chain of effects from brand trust and brand affect to brand performance: The role of brand loyalty. *Journal of Marketing*, *65*(2), 81–94. doi:10.1509/jmkg.65.2.81.18255

Comscore. (2011). *It's a social world: Social networking leads as top online activity globally, accounting for 1 in every 5 online minutes*. Retrieved from http://www.comscore.com/Insights/Press_Releases/2011/12/Social_Networking_Leads_as_Top_Online_Activity_Globally

Culnan, M. J., McHugh, P. J., & Zubillaga, J. I. (2010). How large U.S. companies can use Twitter and other social media to gain business value. *MIS Quarterly Executive*, *9*(4), 243–259.

Dabholkar, P. A. (1996). Consumer evaluations of new technology-based self-service options: An investigation of alternative models of service quality. *International Journal of Research in Marketing*, *13*(1), 29–51. doi:10.1016/0167-8116(95)00027-5

Dean, D., Karabey, B. S., Stevens, A., Tansan, B., Tonguc, A. S., & Vos, M. (2013). *Turkey online - How the internet is transforming the Turkish economy*. Retrieved from http://www.turkiye-e-konomi.com/en/Turkey-Online-English.pdf

Dick, A. S., & Basu, K. (1994). Customer loyalty: Toward an integrated conceptual framework. *Journal of the Academy of Marketing Science*, *22*(Spring), 99–113. doi:10.1177/0092070394222001

Erdoğmuş, İ. E., & Çiçek, M. (2012). The impact of social media marketing on brand loyalty. *Procedia: Social and Behavioral Sciences*, *58*, 1353–1360. doi:10.1016/j.sbspro.2012.09.1119

Evans, D. (2012). *Social media marketing: An hour a day*. Indianapolis: Wiley.

Evans, D., & McKee, J. (2010). *Social media marketing: The next generation of business engagement*. Indianapolis: Wiley.

Facebook Ads. (2011). *Güncel Facebook Türkiye istatistikleri*. Retrieved from http://tr-tr.facebook.com/notes/promoqube/g%C3%BCncel-facebook-t%C3%BCrkiye-istatistikleri/230108337030128

Faircloth, J. B., Capella, L. M., & Alford, B. L. (2001). The effect of brand attitude and brand image on brand equity. *Journal of Marketing Theory and Practice*, *9*(3), 61–75.

Gentile, C., Spiller, N., & Noci, G. (2007). How to sustain the customer experience: An overview of experience components that co-create value with the customer. *European Management Journal*, *25*(5), 395–410. doi:10.1016/j.emj.2007.08.005

Hennig-Thurau, T., Malthouse, E. C., Friege, C., Gensler, S., Lobschat, L., Rangaswamy, A., & Skiera, B. (2010). The impact of new media on customer relationships. *Journal of Service Research*, *13*(3), 311–330. doi:10.1177/1094670510375460

Hensel, K., & Deis, M. H. (2010). Using social media to increase advertising and improve marketing. *The Entrepreneurial Executive*, *15*, 87–97.

Hoffman, D. L., & Fodor, M. (2010). Can you measure the ROI of your social media marketing? *MIT Sloan Management Review*, *52*(1), 41–49.

Holbrook, M. B., & Hirschman, E. C. (1982). The experiential aspects of consumption: Consumer fantasy, feelings and fun. *The Journal of Consumer Research*, *9*(2), 132–140. doi:10.1086/208906

Hughes, D. J., Rowe, M., Batey, M., & Lee, A. (2012). A tale of two sites: Twitter vs. Facebook and the personality predictors of social media usage. *Computers in Human Behavior*, *28*(2), 561–569. doi:10.1016/j.chb.2011.11.001

Ipsos OTX and Ipsos Global Advisor. (2012). *The ripple effect of following a brand on social media.* Retrieved from http://www.emarketer.com/Article/Ripple-Effect-of-Following-Brand-on-Social-Media/1009177

Judd, C. M., Kenny, D. A., & McClelland, G. H. (2001). Estimating and testing mediation and moderation in within-subject designs. *Psychological Methods*, *6*(2), 155–134. doi:10.1037/1082-989X.6.2.115 PMID:11411437

Kaplan, A., & Haenlein, M. (2010). Users of the world, unite! The challenges and opportunities of Social Media. *Business Horizons*, *53*(1), 59–68. doi:10.1016/j.bushor.2009.09.003

Keller, K. L. (1993). Conceptualizing, measuring, and managing customer-based brand equity. *Journal of Marketing*, *57*(1), 1–22. doi:10.2307/1252054

Keller, K. L., & Lehmann, D. R. (2003). How do brands create value? *Marketing Management*, *12*(3), 27–31.

Kietzmann, J. H., Hermkens, K., McCarthy, I. P., & Silvestre, B. S. (2011). Social media? Get serious! Understanding the functional building blocks of social media. *Business Horizons*, *54*(3), 241–251. doi:10.1016/j.bushor.2011.01.005

Kim, A. J., & Ko, E. (2012). Do social media marketing activities enhance customer equity? An empirical study of luxury fashion brand. *Journal of Business Research*, *65*(10), 1480–1486. doi:10.1016/j.jbusres.2011.10.014

Laroche, M., Habibi, M. R., Richard, M., & Sankaranarayanan, R. (2012). The effects of social media based brand communities on brand community markers, value creation practices, brand trust and brand loyalty. *Computers in Human Behavior*, *28*(5), 1755–1767. doi:10.1016/j.chb.2012.04.016

Lemon, K. N., Rust, R. T., & Zeithaml, V. A. (2001). What drives customer equity? *Marketing Management*, *10*(1), 20–25.

Luke, K. (2009). Marketing the new-fashioned way: Connect with your target market through social networking sites. *Practice Management Solutions,* 18-19.

Mangold, W. G., & Faulds, D. J. (2009). Social media: The new hybrid element of the promotion mix. *Business Horizons*, *52*(4), 357–365. doi:10.1016/j.bushor.2009.03.002

Meyer, C., & Schwager, A. (2007). Understanding customer experience. *Harvard Business Review*, *85*(2), 117–126. PMID:17345685

Michaelidou, N., Siamagka, N. T., & Christodoulides, G. (2011). Usage, barriers and measurement of social media marketing: An exploratory investigation of small and medium B2B brands. *Industrial Marketing Management*, *40*(7), 1153–1159. doi:10.1016/j.indmarman.2011.09.009

Mosley, R. W. (2007). Customer experience, organizational culture and the employer brand. *Journal of Brand Management*, *15*(2), 123–134. doi:10.1057/palgrave.bm.2550124

Novak, T. P., Hoffman, D. I., & Yung, Y. (2000). Measuring the customer experience in online environments: A structural modeling approach. *Marketing Science*, *19*(1), 22–42. doi:10.1287/mksc.19.1.22.15184

Nunnally, J. C., & Bernstein, I. H. (1994). *Psychometric theory*. New York: McGraw-Hill.

Ofir, C., & Simonson, I. (2007). The effect of stating expectations on customer satisfaction and shopping experience. *JMR, Journal of Marketing Research*, *44*(February), 164–174. doi:10.1509/jmkr.44.1.164

Qulman, E. (2013). *Socialnomics: How social media transform the way we live and do business*. Wiley.

Raggio, R. D., & Leone, R. P. (2007). The theoretical separation of brand equity and brand value: Managerial implications for strategic planning. *Brand Management*, *14*(5), 380–395. doi:10.1057/palgrave.bm.2550078

Shaw, C., & Ivens, J. (2005). *Building great customer experiences*. New York: McGraw-Hill.

Sheng, M. L., & Teo, T. S. H. (2012). Product attributes and brand equity in the mobile domain: The mediating role of customer experience. *International Journal of Information Management*, *32*(2), 139–146. doi:10.1016/j.ijinfomgt.2011.11.017

Swedowsky, M. (2009). *Improving Customer experience by listening and responding to social media*. Retrieved from http://www.nielsen.com/us/en/insights/news/2009/improving-customer-experience-by-listening-and-responding-to-social-media.html

Trainor, K. J., Andzulis, J., Rapp, A., & Agnihotri, R. (2013). Social media technology use and customers relationship performance: Capabilities-based examination of social CRM. *Journal of Business Research*, *67*(6), 1201–1208. doi:10.1016/j.jbusres.2013.05.002

TUIK. (2013). *Hanehalkı bilişim teknolojileri kullanım araştırması*. Retrieved from http://tuik.gov.tr/PreHaberBultenleri.do?id=13569

Tuten, T. L., & Solomon, M. R. (2013). *Social media marketing*. Pearson Education Inc.

Verhoef, P. C., Lemon, K. A., Parasuraman, A., Roggeveen, A., Tsiros, M., & Schlesinger, L. A. (2009). Customer experience creation: Determinants, dynamics and management strategies. *Journal of Retailing*, *85*(1), 31–41. doi:10.1016/j.jretai.2008.11.001

Vogel, V., Evanschitzky, H., & Ramaseshan, B. (2008). Customer equity drivers and future sales. *Journal of Marketing*, *72*(6), 98–108. doi:10.1509/jmkg.72.6.98

Wilcox, K., & Stephen, A. T. (2013). Are close friends the enemy? Online social networks, self-esteem, and self-control. *The Journal of Consumer Research*, *40*(1), 90–103. doi:10.1086/668794

Worldwide, D. E. I. (2008). *Engaging consumers online - The impact of social media on purchasing behavior*. Retrieved from www.deiworldwide.com/files/DEIStudy-Engaging%20ConsumersOnline-Summary.pdf

Yoo, B., & Donthu, N. (2001). Developing and validating a multidimensional consumer-based brand equity scale. *Journal of Business Research*, *52*(1), 1–14. doi:10.1016/S0148-2963(99)00098-3

KEY TERMS AND DEFINITIONS

Brand Affect: Positive emotions elicited by brands in consumers.

Brand Equity: The individual consumer level, subjective and intangible assessment of value of a brand.

Brand Value: The sale or replacement value of a brand.

Consumer Experience: The subjective consumer responses to any contacts from companies.

Consumer Social Media Marketing Experience: The reactions of consumers to a company's offerings created, communicated and exchanged on social media.

Social Media: A method of online communication which allows the conveying of information, collaboration, and the cultivation of relationships among connected people.

Social Media Marketing: The use of social media technologies, channels and software to conduct marketing activities aimed at exchanging offerings between consumers and companies.

This research was previously published in the Handbook of Research on Integrating Social Media into Strategic Marketing edited by Nick Hajli, pages 73-87, copyright year 2015 by Business Science Reference (an imprint of IGI Global).

Chapter 24
Brands and Media Gatekeeping in the Social Media:
Current Trends and Practices – An Exploratory Research

Georgia-Zozeta Miliopoulou
DEREE – The American College of Greece, Greece

Vassiliki Cossiavelou
University of the Aegean, Greece

ABSTRACT

The purpose of this paper is to examine current trends and practices regarding brand communication through the social media, as brand activation in the online social environment rises and proliferates rapidly. Believing that further interdisciplinary contributions are needed to bridge the gap between brand management on the one hand and ICT potential on the other, the authors designed and implemented an exploratory research. They interviewed middle and senior-management executives, working either in companies who promote brands in the social media or in agencies who undertake social media projects and tasks. The authors' results indicate that gatekeeping remains an integral and very important aspect of social media brand management. Most brands consider what to release rather than what not to. They withhold information based on a narrow campaign-oriented mindset which reflects traditional marketing and public relations' practices and has not embraced the requirements for transparency and openness that prevail in the digital and social media environment.

INTRODUCTION

Brands today create competitive content for most media platforms, including all social media channels, gradually becoming media outlets themselves (Solis, 2010). They are using multimedia storytelling modeled websites, corporate blogs, Facebook, Twitter, Google+, YouTube, etc. as channels to share content over a wide range of virtual communities and to stimulate potential clients. As brands are becoming

DOI: 10.4018/978-1-5225-5637-4.ch024

online publishers, they tend to enrich social media conversations and then use content marketing tools like Search Engine Optimization (SEO) (Castronovo, Huang, 2012), or tools that facilitate purchase decisions (McDowell, 2011) so as to convert leads to customers and achieve Return On Investment (ROI). This appears to be a more transparent approach to achieve and measure ROI in comparison with traditional media. The greater the ROI, the more a brand acquires the ability to engage in new media platforms. According to a recent Forrester Research report, this is an opportunity for the brands to build a human, authentic image, and to raise brand awareness promoting the quality of their products and services (Wizdo et al., 2016).

Even 3 years ago, 46% of online users were relying on social media when making a purchase decision. Furthermore, more than a third of the members of Chief Marketing Officer (CMO) Council declared that digital marketing will account for 75% or more of their spending within the next 5 years (Brenner, 2012) underlying a tendency for most brands to own the touch points where they place their advertisements, and agreed that this approach is far more effective than traditional promotion (Bonn, 2012), (Kane et al., 2009). In this economic-societal context, predictions indicate that "by 2016 60% of companies will have an executive in their organization that is directly responsible for an overall content marketing strategy" (Curata, 2015, pp. 14).

In 2010, there were 4 billion subscribers to mobile services over a diversity of content-capable devices. This new landscape forever changes the brand-consumer relationship, challenging brands to enable multi-screen viewing for omni-connectivity and to offer synergistic content tailored to user location and personal preferences. Users already demand high quality condensed information -like TV snacking- with little scrolling or key input (Haikel-Elsabeh, 2013).

LITERATURE REVIEW

In this new, still fluid landscape where new terms and ideas like "brand journalism" emerge (Bull, 2013), the media gatekeeping filters ought to be reexamined. For more than fifty years, media gatekeeping has been among the most influential contributions in communication theories. Articulated by Shoemaker and Reese, this model outlines five dimensions of content filters, namely: individual influences, professional routines, organizational influences, extra-media influences and the cultural environment. Digital technologies have a profound effect on each of these filters because they enable interaction on a "many-to-many" scale and strengthen extra publisher influences (Cossiavelou, Bantimaroudis, 2009).

The approach of brands as publishers calls for a reexamination of the agenda-setting for potential customers, especially for product and service content that will manage to inspire trust and lead to purchase (Hermida *et al.*, 2012). The relationship among content generator -the brand- and content retriever -the consumer- is crucial for this agenda- setting.

Specifically, it is noted that the individual filter seems to become a fuzzy concept as new practices emerge and need to be redefined and researched. For the second dimension of gatekeeping, evidence shows that brands allowing highly critical comments from both individuals and lobbying groups constitute an exception, while new skills are required to understand and manage online communities (McWilliam, 2012). As the quality of the conversations could matter more than the quantity of followers and as the social media constitute an opt-in environment, new requirements emerge that create complexity and affect the business models of big brands. As a result new strategies and solutions have to be adopted, and this also affects budgeting decisions.

For the third filter, the intra-organizational dimension of gatekeeping, a number of changes are observed: famous brands are hosting online, social media communities, allowing individuals to establish their own virtual interest-based sub-communities and to share knowledge or simply exchange information on product experience (McWilliam, 2012). Managing such communities is a strategic challenge. Leadership issues arise as well as questions regarding measurement of engagement, rather than just raw impressions (Kozinets et al., 2010). Organizational reputation, brand emotions and behavioral intentions are under constant renegotiation: using short hyperlinks to compete with text limitations on Twitter, devising new media crisis communication models (Siah Ann Mei, Bansal, Pang, 2010), integrating mobile features, dealing with legal issues like cybersquatting (usernames' reservation or tags) or even keeping up with the ever-changing Facebook and Twitter policies to ensure an account's authenticity (Curtin, 2010) are only some of the potentially harmful issues for trademark owners.

The intra-brand gatekeeping filter also includes the evolving ROI strategies for investments in constantly advanced content management systems (CMS), in updating business models that may include elements of 'shared' resources and apportioned rewards both in terms of reputation and monetary value.

Gradually, the duties of both PR practitioners and journalists have become interdependent, thus their job descriptions have to be also renegotiated. Meanwhile, although followers constitute a cornerstone of the digital media culture (Böttcher, 2014), they lack time and motivation for gatekeeping or even gatewatching. Marketers are getting more and more interested in analyzing their virtual communities in popular social media platforms, assessing motivations and understanding how user activity influences brand engagement.

The literature regarding the extra-organization gatekeeping dimension reveals a closer relationship between content developers, content platform enablers and device developers (Siah Ann Mei, Bansal, Pang, 2010). They all act as gatewatchers as there is an acute dissimilarity in the core benefits of instant anytime messaging, or other real-time functions between wired and wireless broadband networks. Thus social media strategies embrace this new potential, adjusting to the instantaneous requirements for short information on mobile screens. The customers' shift towards mobile screens paves the way for different platform models for mobile service delivery: the portal-based models (telco-centric or aggregator-centric model) and device-centric models (closed or open technology approach); in all these models, the mobile operators' new gatekeeping roles are already being examined (Ballon, Walravens, 2008). The reconfiguration of mobile service provisions towards platform business models that stimulates third-party service offering or sponsoring (West, Mace, 2010), blurs the boundaries between the organizational and the extra-brand's social media gatekeeping dimensions.

As far as the fifth gatekeeping dimension is concerned, in today's so called "cultural chaos" (McNair, 2006) research reveals less defined and more complex cultural relationships among brands and social media users-customers: novel contextual and institutional elements, related to the nature of virtual communities as networks, no-hierarchy structures, and co-production of messages in a narrative style. A promise is implied here, that in the future there will be ongoing dialectical conversations, in the context of continuous holistic campaigns. These cultural relationships progressively develop between brands, products, opinion leaders and relevant communities where open source marketing, Wikinomics (Tapscott, William, 2008), brand communities and consumer tribes (Bruns, 2008) are leading the way (McNair, 2006). Gatewatchers share all these new roles thus potentially turning to gatejumpers or at least alternating the nature of the gates, precisely because of the influence of technology on culture and the cultural dimension of gatekeeping (Bruns, 2008; Cossiavelou, Bantimaroudis, 2009). Half of the earth's population now shares this "participatory culture" (Jenkins, 2006, pp. 1). Web 2.0 is gradually described as an attitude, not a technology; a loss of control is constantly discussed; convergence in digital environments is now more about culture than technology.

Brands are a node into a very complex ecosystem of mobile infrastructure, which they also come to use in order to communicate with their online communities. Key features such as mobility management, wide geographical coverage, transmission quality, privacy, and spectrum efficiency impose diverse designs and diverse alliances (Ballon, Walravens, 2008) on the mobile value chain systems (Peppard, Rylander, 2006). Research on future social media features already explores viral digital conversations, user-generated content and tags in high bandwidth, even on real-time settings, which facilitate the transition from viral communities to face-to-face simultaneous conversation. Such conversations among buyers, sellers and the press, give the brands-mobile industry dipole a kick off role on the research and innovation alliances. The new landscape comprises brands as publishers and mobile industries as infrastructure providers (Bisker *et al.*, 2008). These alliances however are far from neutral. The corporate-owned participatory social media are largely controlled by the dominant internet companies that constrain participation via terms of use, funnel traffic against net neutrality rules to their proprietary nodes, more easily mine users' personal data and could even shape users' subjectivity (Milberry, Anderson, 2009) imposing a hardly detectable new-fashion new media gatekeeping model.

RESEARCH HYPOTHESIS AND METHOD

Based on experience and observation, we hypothesized that online brand gatekeeping has emerged as a broader organizational issue affecting not only branded content and communities, but also organizational structures and processes that might lead to more transparent and interactive communication approaches. Due to lack of prior evidence, we chose to first explore whether our observations are valid, select qualitative data, discover trends and gain insight so as to then proceed with concrete null hypotheses and evidential approaches:

H-1: Despite the multitude of tools & media platforms that enable brands to share rich content with their audiences directly and engage in dialogue, most brand management still relies on a lot of gatekeeping.

H-2: This gatekeeping is a result of the established mindsets, practices, organizational structures and cultures that still affect decision-making in middle and senior management.

To test these hypotheses, we conducted 10 in-depth interviews with middle and senior managers in the field of communication, five of which work for advertisers and the other half for advertising agencies (see sample of interviewees in Appendix A and the questions asked in Appendix B). Our interviewees from the brand perspective all work for multinational corporations or handle global brands in Greece, except one: a digital manager working for a Greek NGO included an NGO digital manager. Our interviewees from the agencies either belong to a multinational network of companies or have a client portfolio comprising multinational accounts. We preformed both quantitative and qualitative analysis of the collected data, spotting common patterns and pinpointing unique differences. The findings ought to be tested in a larger sample and cross-analyzed by industry, country, and even social media channel.

FINDINGS

To present our findings, we analyze the interviewees' answers per each filter of the media gatekeeping model, starting with the brand's point of view and then moving to present in a comparative way the agency's point of view.

First Gatekeeping Filter: Individuals

Starting with the brand's side, only one interviewee clearly stated that they already allow content and community managers more freedom and initiative over content and interaction (see Table 1).

Two out of five interviewees believe that their brand is not open enough and should open up, enabling interaction based on users' requests, interests and demands. However they did acknowledge that this is a major change. An interviewee observes:

It is important to have people that are well educated and informed about social media and also have some specific guidelines that help them to be part of the social media ecosystem effectively.

Two more interviewees believe that the brand ought to maintain control of the content released online and believe their colleagues would also see it that way. One claims that gatekeeping processes are necessary to ensure control over brand image and tonality. The second raises the issue of ethical and appropriate marketing that protects corporate and brand reputation, claiming that:

Our reputation as a company and as an industry requires great responsibility, strict controlling processes, and great caution in casual conversations or humorous statements.

From the agency's point of view, all interviewees state that transparency should be preferred and gatekeeping should be minimized:

The less the gatekeeping the more 'true' and thus human a company is... people like talking to people – not entities.

Another agency executive states that:

Table 1. Advertisers and agencies on brands' social media gatekeeping filter on individual level

Advertisers	Agencies
1/5: We allow content and community managers a lot of initiative.	• Transparency should be preferred. • Gatekeeping should be minimized. • Clients restrain openness by following tight processes and strict requirements. • All agencies fear negative consumer reactions and use gatekeeping to preserve client-agency relations. • Community managers do not have authorization to discuss with users, cross-sell or up-sell.
2/5: Our brands should open up but it is a huge leap	
2/5: The brand ought to maintain control of content for image and tonality or for ethical marketing.	

We promote uniqueness and creativity. That means one can go as far as ethical borders and strategy are not violated.

However this appears more like a wish rather than a mid- or long-term plan; as one interviewee put it:

We truly believe that transparency is more important than brand gatekeeping in general but there are certain sectors [where] this is really not feasible.

The interviewee claims that agencies are constantly restrained by their clients' tight processes and requirements, thus being unable to promote a culture of openness and transparency.

One reason behind the personal tendency towards gatekeeping from the agency's point of view lies in the unpredictability of consumers' reaction that might cause incidents or crises affecting client-agency relations:

Ultimately, someone does talk real time to a consumer… But most time [this] exists over a bureaucratic war-zone.

Facing that 'war-zone', agencies and their executives at all layers opt for the safety that comes from a healthy client-agency relationship rather than undertake personal risk:

Agencies don't want freedom. Freedom comes with risk. Global brands get angry when accidents happen. So what we do is have answer scripts and answer only what is trivial and expected... There are consumer questions we forward to the client even if we know the answer.

The personal filter of gatekeeping is evident here, as agency people do not discuss users' needs, nor do they promote more or diversified clients' products and services without authorization.

To minimize such risks and pave the way for more initiatives in the future, one interviewee made the following remark:

We play the man, not the odds. That means we hire people we trust their sense of logic and empathy.

Second Gatekeeping Filter: Practices

A number of standardized procedures in social media management, content release and community management indicate that traditional marketing prevails if not on principle, at least in action. To trace new practices, we analyzed structure and processes separately (see Table 2).

Regarding structure:

- One out of five interviewees describes a big and still growing investment in a new department equipped with advanced monitoring infrastructure and reporting tools, whose leader reports to the marketing head. Staffed by low-rank well-trained personnel, this department monitors and engages in conversation while their agency still undertakes day-to-day calendar based content management. This interviewee acknowledges that:

Table 2. Advertisers and agencies on brands' social media gatekeeping filter on practices

<table>
<tr><th></th><th>Advertisers</th><th>Agencies</th></tr>
<tr><td>Rregarding structure</td><td>• 1/5: Benchmark new department – reports to the marketing head
• 2/5: One new employee
• 2/5: No change</td><td rowspan="2">• They advocate for different practices regarding interactivity, real time conversation and dialogue.
• Their internal structures have changed considerably. They follow campaign based client requirements.
• Most strategic proposals emerge after assessment of the competition and 'type of client' in terms of social media openness. Strategy follows traditional steps.</td></tr>
<tr><td>Regarding process</td><td>• 1/5: Benchmark processes
• 4/5: Calendar-based processes mainly with content produced in the global headquarters.
• Only two interviewees do not rely on predefined scripts in community management.</td></tr>
</table>

Strict and time-consuming processes of the past cannot be implemented in the social media era... social media now have become the core of one of our four principles: to become social at heart.

Pre-defined scripts are used and if they do not apply, further approval is sought:

- Two interviewees have hired one person to undertake social media management;
- One interviewee implemented no organizational change: social media management is now added to the marketing department's agenda. The fifth interviewee only describes changes in processes listed below.

Regarding processes:

- The interviewee that invests in process explains that they gradually engage brand ambassadors and convert employees to ambassadors through training; that they build communities, seek feedback and capitalize their ecosystem by using different types of content in different social networking sites or other online environments. They allocate budget specifically for digital and social media campaigns, hire agencies to refresh their ideas and aggregators to curate content;
- The rest of the interviewees work based on a calendar and interact based on pre-defined scripts. Among those:
    - In one case, decisions are made in quarterly meetings between: the General Manager, the Marketing manager, and the Digital Marketing specialist to decide the overall frame, while staying alert in case something happens;
    - In another case there have been no previous processes and the social media manager builds interaction from scratch as no marketing activities take place;
    - Two more interviewees receive material created in the headquarters that do not consider size or other parameters in each local market and collaborate with the agency to manage it through the use of calendars. One of them has no liberty to create local content and also outsources community management; the other has some liberty to introduce local content and manages communities internally.

Interviewees representing agencies always emphasize interactivity, real time conversation and direct communication with the brand. This has led to a number of new agencies, business units and skill-sets:

a number of changes most agencies do not see on their clients' side either due to old-fashioned mentalities or to a lack of freedom and funding.

Most of their strategic proposals emerge after assessment of the competition and 'type of client' in terms of social media openness; then they define a strategy following typical steps. Some diffuse the same content in all touch points while others set up their touch points differently to address different audiences. One interviewee mentioned that most clients in Greece follow mechanized paths for touch point set-up and content diffusion.

Both sets of interviewees describe practices that include:

- A very limited selection of potential touch-points that only cover popular social media;
- An avoidance of participation in non-owned touch-points, for example forums or blogs;
- A lack of content up scaling that would maximize communication impact;
- A limited palette of Key Performance Indicators (KPIs) that emphasize diffusion versus engagement or dialogue.

All of the agencies interviewed mention the use of a pre-approved calendar for content planning. Working with a calendar means that having a pre-defined marketing strategy to implement, the social media experts allocate received content to all potential touch points and then outsource implementation to the agency, ensuring internal approvals. One agency mentions that certain clients pre-approve each and every post. Calendars go through periodic revisions and updates to cover unexpected events.

Content and community managers are allowed initiative that is mostly confined to pre-defined scripts; in some cases they are free to come up with suggestions. One interviewee attributes this approach to the fact that social media managers are not part of the senior management.

Third Gatekeeping Filter: Intra-Organization

According to our interviewees, in the corporate and structural level, gatekeeping follows pre-established practices. Three out of five mention that one department is not aware of the other department's actions and agenda unless there is a very specific reason (see Table 3). One of them states that:

Senior managers do know in advance (most of the times). Key stakeholders (i.e. product managers) participate in the pre-process. Employees are being informed immediately after an action takes place. But there is no regular pre-communication internally.

One of our interviewees, attesting that corporate gatekeeping is indeed an issue in the organization, said they attempt to tackle the issue by engaging in training programs to enable the social media team to harvest stories from within the organization and develop content out of them. Still, the social media department is supposed to have control over the process and to limit harvesting to a number of topics relevant to their agenda.

Two interviewees have announced internal training programs for all employees, aiming to provide instructions on how they should manage corporate content as individuals. However, another two out of five claim that engaging employees remains an issue, as most are either unaware or not interested. One even complains that they have to put pressure on employees to even "like" the company page.

Table 3. Advertisers on intra -organization filter of brands' social media performance

Advertisers	Agencies
5/5: Senior management has no relevant training. Involved executives are low-middle management, whose supervisor usually reports to a CMO / CCO.	Restrained by confidentiality agreements they claim if clients were more open, the agency would follow.
3/5: Senior management is not involved	
2/5: Senior management approves all campaigns	
3/5: One department is not aware of the other's agenda unless there is a reason.	
2/5: They have announced training for all employees on how to manage corporate content as individuals.	

Furthermore, senior management appears to be un-involved in three out of the five organizations examined. The employees responsible for the social media are low to middle management, whose supervisor usually reports to a marketing or communications' officer at the C-level suite. Top management has received no training and, as a business unit general manager observed:

Only the Digital Marketing person has attended a couple of short terms conferences/trainings. All the rest who are involved, get only 'life' trainings...This is basically due to the fact that money spent on such trainings is not well justified yet by the business results / requirements. But it has to change pretty soon in order for us to become more effective in the new era.

Two interviewees said that senior management approves social media campaigns before they are released, among which, one handles sensitive brands and the other handles new technology brands.

From the agency's point of view, this issue is different: agencies are supposed to safeguard their clients' data and information, therefore transparency appears to be less relevant. The client determines how open his team in the agency will be:

In our agency we are open on principle but we don't always know what everyone else is doing.

Most agencies' interviewees appear to believe if their clients were more open, the agency would follow:

Some marketing departments fully coordinate internally, talking to different departments, asking for content like PR events etc. For some of our clients we have an open online spreadsheet and they all add there and see what others have added. However if we handle one brand for a client who represents many different brands in the Greek market, then one brand very rarely knows what the other brand is doing.

This comment by an interviewee sums up the issue well:

Some people are aware of what they could create if there was more collaboration and less compartmentalization but they won't pay for it eventually. And stakeholders are never involved in the process; from fear control will be lost.

Fourth Gatekeeping Filter: Extra-Organization

An essential extra-organization partner is the agency who handles the social media. Based on the practices described above, gatekeeping should not be observed in this collaboration as openness, readiness and alignment are necessary for both parties. However two of the five interviewees who assign their social media to agencies as well as all the five agencies that participated in this research, confirm that client-agency relations are built on a need-to-know basis. Gatekeeping is not defined as such but does appear in the form of concrete, task-based briefings or regular calendars disclosed only to those who are directly involved.

Our interviewees did not describe any kind of process or practice that aims at openness, full disclosure, free discussion or initiatives coming from suppliers –the agency being the closest of them all. Agencies, on the other hand, are confined by confidentiality agreements and would not extend dialogue beyond the scope of given campaigns or other tasks. More over our interviewees did not mention any direct or indirect gatekeeping factor regarding mobile operators, their main concern being content gatekeeping in popular touch points.

Fifth Gatekeeping Filter: Culture

According to our interviewees, gatekeeping still prevails in the corporate culture mainly because of compartmentalization. Although some efforts do focus on engaging 'consumers' or 'users', the emphasis remains on planning, diffusing and then perhaps responding, rather than co-creating or enabling un-restricted user-generated content and spontaneous interaction. 'Tampering' with the brand is, of course, out of the question and negative aspects of consumer engagement appear to be more frightful than absolute lack of engagement. Only one of the ten interviewees, belonging in the new technologies' sector, claims that gatekeeping is to be avoided, that broad employee training should enable everyone to openly participate on behalf of the company thus promoting ambassadorship and that the only barrier left is this training to penetrate the entire organization. Still, there is no evidence yet that those companies embrace a techno-culture mentality that would alter their strategies. On the contrary, they appear to follow pre-established marketing practices excluding important elements like dialogue and freedom regarding user generated content.

DISCUSSION

The clearest of findings in our research is that most of the global brands examined tend to heavily apply gatekeeping in all their attempts to communicate through the social media. Associating brands with gatekeeping already came as a surprise for some interviewees. The culture of transparency and openness to information seems irrelevant to the marketing communication departments that are used to carefully diffuse information in the mass media, counting every word and seeking approval by the top management and the legal departments. The idea of giving control to the users, their consumers, appears unlikely and undesirable both in the advertisers' and the agencies' point of view; as one of the interviewees from the agencies' side mentioned:

Traditional media campaigns could have zero impact or positive impact. On the other hand, social media campaigns could have a negative impact and this possibility, no matter how little or manageable, makes companies reluctant to invest.

A second reason for this gatekeeping lies in traditional structures and processes that can be enriched but not easily altered in a profound way. Only two of our interviewees described profound changes in structure, process and training to respond to the social media ecosystem. The other eight -and in this case the agencies described the plethora of their other clients as well- mention that social media management falls under the respective marketing departments who merely incorporate content diffusion in their routines and watch out for negative comments. Even if agencies try to limit gatekeeping, they end up following client requirements.

The gatekeeping processes for social media and touch-points' management are manifested in:

- A lack of dedicated teams in advertisers' companies;
- A number of standardized practices aiming at diffusion limited to popular channels and platforms;
- An outsourcing of community management to the agency, though most advertisers tend to point out that internal social media management -often avoided for financial reasons- would provide important insight and the agencies' side acknowledges complexities or delays associated with this practice;
- The fact that community managers are in most cases entry level professionals who are not able to convey important information back to the organization.

Thus quantitative reporting is not accompanied by qualitative findings that would enhance understanding and improve practices. Furthermore, interviewees often state that senior executives who are not familiar with social media appear reluctant and more defensive regarding the new opportunities, feeling safer to treat the new ecosystem, literally, as 'new media', in the sense that they simply constitute opportunities for free placement.

Another important finding overall is the relative disproportion of freedom between the administrative center and the subsidiaries. While a company's headquarters might plan using advanced know-how and creative skills, they do not consider local particularities. Still, quantity of response overruns quality of engagement as a KPI and one-way content diffusion is considered more important than dialogue. Future research could determine whether this approach is at least partly due to the fact that KPIs are decided by senior marketing executives who still apply mass media quantitative goals unaccompanied by engagement objectives.

Future research might also determine whether Greek subsidies are more limited in comparison to other small markets, in terms of resources and access to training, because of the country's financial downturn and turmoil, or other potential reasons, that could intensify the restraints and the enhanced gatekeeping processes that this research showcases.

Experience and know-how do not only involve ICT technologies' and social media platforms' management but also profound insights that would enable the brand to trace and address specific target-clusters among consumers and key-stakeholders, thus better understanding the local market's needs and desires and responding accordingly by modifying offering and communication messages.

We believe, however, that future research might reveal differences, relative to company size and industry. For example, traditional, historic brands, or fast moving consumer goods, might continue to express a tendency for strict gatekeeping, contrary to the manifested trends and best practices. Furthermore, industries that rely on strict codes of ethics to market their goods or promote their organizational activities will include gatekeeping in their set of best practices, as it is an imperative for successful activations. This gatekeeping could be loosened if community managers and content managers in all markets and subsidiaries receive better training and experience, as they move from entry level to middle management. This has been the tradition for many brands that did not rely in the past on traditional marketing processes but instead were open to user communities even before the web, like Harley-Davidson or a lot of open source software companies. To make best use of new technologies, after all, we must develop new mindsets.

ACKNOWLEDGMENT

Our greatest thanks to the interviewees who dedicated time and sincerely answered all our questions; we are committed to preserving their anonymity.

REFERENCES

Ballon, P., & Walravens, N. (2008, July). Competing platform models for mobile service delivery: the importance of gatekeeper roles. In *Mobile Business, 2008. ICMB'08. 7th International Conference on* (pp. 102-111). IEEE. doi:10.1109/ICMB.2008.17

Bisker, S., Ouilhet, H., Pomeroy, S., Chang, A., & Casalegno, F. (2008, April). Re-thinking fashion trade shows: creating conversations through mobile tagging. In CHI'08 Extended Abstracts on Human Factors in Computing Systems (pp. 3351-3356). ACM. doi:10.1145/1358628.1358856

Bonn, R. (2012, October, 22). As brands become publishers, are they getting their content right? *The Gardian*. Retrieved July 30, 2015 from The Gardian: http://www.theguardian.com/media-network/media-network-blog/2012/oct/22/brands-becoming-publishers-content-marketing

Böttcher, A. V. (2014). *Twitter, News Aggegators & Co: Journalistic Gatekeeping in the Age of Digital Media Culture*. Academic Press.

Brenner, M. (2012, October 10) Is content marketing the new advertising? *Forbes*. Retrieved July 30, 2015 from Forbes: http://www.forbes.com/sites/sap/2012/10/10/is-content-marketingthe-new-advertising/

Bruns, A. (2008). *3.1. The Active Audience: Transforming Journalism from Gatekeeping to Gatewatching*. Academic Press.

Bull, A. (2013). *Brand journalism*. Routledge.

Castronovo, C., & Huang, L. (2012). Social media in an alternative marketing communication model. *Journal of Marketing Development and Competitiveness*, *6*(1), 117–134.

Cossiavelou, V., & Bantimaroudis, P. (2009). Revisiting the gatekeeping model: Gatekeeping factors in European wireless media markets. *International Journal of Interdisciplinary Telecommunications and Networking*, *1*(4), 37–53. doi:10.4018/jitn.2009092803

Curata. (2015). The content marketing pyramid: A framework to develop & execute your content marketing Strategy. *Curata*. Retrieved October 8, 2015 from Curata: http://www.curata.com/resources/ebooks/content-marketing-pyramid

Curtin, T. J. (2010). The Name Game: Cybersquatting and Trademark Infringement on Social Media Websites. *Journal of Law and Policy*, *19*, 353.

Haikel-Elsabeh, M. (2013). Understanding Brand Implication and Engagement on Facebook. *User Behavior in Ubiquitous Online Environments*, 216.

Hermida, A., Fletcher, F., Korell, D., & Logan, D. (2012). Share, like, recommend: Decoding the social media news consumer. *Journalism Studies*, *13*(5-6), 815–824. doi:10.1080/1461670X.2012.664430

Jenkins, H. (2006). *Convergence culture: Where old and new media collide*. New York University Press.

Kane, G. C., Fichman, R. G., Gallaugher, J., & Glaser, J. (2009). Community relations 2.0. *Harvard Business Review*, *87*(11), 45–50. PMID:19891388

Kozinets, R. V., De Valck, K., Wojnicki, A. C., & Wilner, S. J. (2010). Networked narratives: Understanding word-of-mouth marketing in online communities. *Journal of Marketing*, *74*(2), 71–89. doi:10.1509/jmkg.74.2.71

McDowell, W. S. (2011). The brand management crisis facing the business of journalism. *The International Journal on Media Management*, *13*(1), 37–51. doi:10.1080/14241277.2010.545364

McNair, B. (2006). *Cultural chaos: journalism and power in a globalised world*. Routledge. doi:10.4324/9780203448724

McWilliam, G. (2000). Building stronger brands through online communities. *MIT Sloan Management Review*, *41*(3), 43.

Milberry, K., & Anderson, S. (2009). Open Sourcing Our Way to an Online Commons Contesting Corporate Impermeability in the New Media Ecology. *The Journal of Communication Inquiry*, *33*(4), 393–412. doi:10.1177/0196859909340349

Peppard, J., & Rylander, A. (2006). From value chain to value network: Insights for mobile operators. *European Management Journal*, *24*(2), 128–141. doi:10.1016/j.emj.2006.03.003

Siah Ann Mei, J., Bansal, N., & Pang, A. (2010). New media: A new medium in escalating crises? *Corporate Communications: An International Journal*, *15*(2), 143–155. doi:10.1108/13563281011037919

Solis, B. (2010). *Why brands are becoming media*. Retrieved July 30, 2015, from Mashable: http://mashable.com/2010/02/11/social-objects/

Tapscott, D., & Williams, A. D. (2008). *Wikinomics: How mass collaboration changes everything*. Penguin.

West, J., & Mace, M. (2010). Browsing as the killer app: Explaining the rapid success of Apple's iPhone. *Telecommunications Policy*, *34*(5), 270–286. doi:10.1016/j.telpol.2009.12.002

Wizdo, L., O'Neill, P., Camuso, M., & Birrell, R. (10 May 2016). *Gauging your progress and success*. Retrieved May 11, 2016, from Forrester Research: https://www.forrester.com/report/Gauging+Your+Progress+And+Success/-/E-RES95303

This research was previously published in the International Journal of Interdisciplinary Telecommunications and Networking (IJITN), 8(4); edited by Michael R Bartolacci and Steven R. Powell, pages 51-64, copyright year 2016 by IGI Publishing (an imprint of IGI Global).

APPENDIX A: SAMPLE OF INTERVIEWEES

Brand's Side

1. Coca-Cola Southern Europe (Beverage);
2. Diageo Hellas (Alcohol);
3. Intersys Hellas (Electric and electronic products' representatives, for brands like Canon, Océ, Pioneer, NEC, Haier, Hisense, Duracell, TomTom, Telefunken and Gorenje);
4. Microsoft Hellas (Technology);
5. "Mazi gia to paidi" (Together for the children) (NGO).

Agency's Side

1. Tempo OMD (Media shop);
2. Frank & Fame (Advertising agency);
3. Mindworks (Digital agency);
4. Social Mellon (Digital agency);
5. Pollen (Advertising agency).

APPENDIX B: GUIDE FOR SEMI-STRUCTURED INTERVIEW

1. How has the social media landscape affected your communication practices?
2. How do you plan & release content in the web & social media?
3. How do you define content strategy & touch-points?
4. How transparent is your content plan &strategy?
5. Where is the decision-making center for all the above?
6. How much initiative is allowed to the content managers & community managers?
7. Do you ever consider the fact of absolute freedom in content release, based on employee initiatives or consumer requirements?
8. How do you rate transparency versus gatekeeping in your company's set of values?
9. Have internal structures and processes been changed so as to respond to the social media environment? At what level? How have employees, middle management & top level executives responded to these changes?
10. Have you implemented training programs? At what level? (low, middle, top management)
11. Would you personally consider the lack of your brand's gatekeeping a positive or negative element regarding consumer engagement? How do you think your peer colleagues would see this?

Chapter 25
Creating Brand Ambassadors:
Strategic Online Engagement in a Nonprofit Association

Erin K. Nemenoff
University of Memphis, USA

Julia Schenk
National Panhellenic Conference, USA

ABSTRACT

Membership associations can face specific challenges when it comes to marketing and brand recognition. This case describes how the National Panhellenic Conference (NPC), a membership association for 26 national and international women's fraternal organizations, or "sororities," addresses these challenges. NPC's mission is to be the premiere advocacy and support organization for the advancement of the sorority experience. However, NPC has traditionally struggled with brand recognition and identity, hampering their mission fulfillment. This chapter illustrates the social media techniques used to engage and inform NPC's key constituents through a virtual event, using a two-pronged approach. The first prong involves deepening engagement to move stakeholders to higher levels of interaction with the association. NPC must effectively communicate with its vast network of members and stakeholders to help generate greater awareness of NPC and promote sorority life in general. The second prong involves using its existing network to amplify NPC's key messages and spread it to those beyond its current network. Outputs and outcomes for the virtual event were used to determine that a defined strategy, as provided in the organization's strategic plan and logic model, impacted overall outcomes.

INTRODUCTION

This chapter examines the social media use of one nonprofit membership association, the National Panhellenic Conference (NPC). In the late 1800s and early 1900s, women were unequal on college campuses, unequal under the law, and in need of an organization to help them band together through a critical time in the development of any young person. Women's fraternal organizations were formed

DOI: 10.4018/978-1-5225-5637-4.ch025

to fit those needs. NPC was founded in 1902 as a membership association for campus-based women's fraternal organizations (member groups). It was formed on the premise that, similar to the need for women's fraternal organizations, member organizations would better succeed in a male-dominated, and at times hostile, campus culture if they banded together under a collective interest.

Today, NPC is one of the world's oldest and largest membership associations for women. It is comprised of 26 national and international women's fraternal organizations, with a total membership of over 4 million women. Of note, although its members number in the millions, NPC can be considered a medium-sized nonprofit, and faces similar challenges to other similarly-sized organizations: a relatively small staff, an operating board, and a relatively small budget (Virtual, Inc., 2013). The mission of NPC is to be the premier advocacy and support organization for the advancement of the sorority experience. However, it has faced some challenges in mission fulfillment, particularly in its marketing and advocacy roles, due to a complex structure and the intergenerational nature of its stakeholders.

The purpose of this chapter is to highlight the marketing and branding challenges that can exist for nonprofit membership associations, as well as nonprofit organizations with a federated structure. Organizations with a federated structure must adapt to potential barriers with organizational messaging, as they may not reach beyond the institutional affiliates to engage or inform the average member of the organization. Also, both associations and federated organizations can have a diverse set of stakeholders across all levels of the organization. These stakeholders can be diverse geographically, generationally, and can also have diverse (and sometimes divergent) interests. The case will highlight how strategy-driven communication helps membership associations not only communicate across multiple layers of an organization, but also with diverse groups, using various social media tactics. What is needed to develop brand ambassadors, or those who will leverage their social media presence to educate their networks about the organization? How does NPC move those within the organization's existing network to a deeper level of participation and engagement, and how does the organization perpetually broaden that network?

This chapter also examines an association's ability to accomplish key organizational objectives using social media as a strategy. The primary driver of the work will be to highlight an association's ability to better advocate for its members and mission when organizational priorities and strategy drive social media tactics. Further, data from multiple years is used to examine the impacts of a specific multi-platform online event on stakeholder engagement through social media. Did NPC's strategic focus on advocacy and branding via social media yield better results than previous years?

This chapter will contribute to what we know about social media use in the nonprofit sector, and will speak specifically to issues encountered in membership associations. Using examples from the NPC, this chapter illustrated the impact of connecting strategy to social media use. Specifically, readers will see the influence of the strategic planning process, and the importance of developing a logic model to articulate not only a theory of change for the marketing program, but also to determine a series of measurable outcomes to benchmark the success of the initiative. In addition, readers will see how an organization can create a corps of brand ambassadors among stakeholders using a two-pronged approach to social media strategy: deeper engagement and widened networks.

This chapter is organized into four sections. In the first section, a theoretical framework is discussed highlighting the "why" behind the strategic choices NPC made during its most recent online campaign. The second section provides an overview of the methods used to collect data for this case study. Third, the case of the NPC is presented including the impact of a recent strategic plan, a more intentional outcomes measurement process, as well as the organization's background in using emergent technology with key stakeholders—a particularly interesting point, since their key stakeholders are between 18 and

22 years of age. We will also look at the actual implementation of the social media strategy through a specific online event: International Badge Day. What social media tactics were used by NPC and what were the results? Did the strategy implemented in 2014 yield different results than in 2013? The final section discusses challenges encountered by NPC and the lessons learned to inform future campaigns.

CONCEPTUAL/THEORETICAL FRAMEWORK

What do the key elements of an effective social media strategy look like in a nonprofit organization? Strategy should be the conduit between organizational mission and organizational choices, and help a nonprofit understand the activities an organization should undertake to attain stated goals and best fulfill their mission (Bryson, 2010). This section looks at the connection between organizational strategy and marketing efforts. In addition it discusses the function of a logic model, as well as theories of social media marketing, to determine preferred tactics in an online campaign. Specifically, it will highlight two specific strains of thought that stem from dialogic theory of public relations (Kent & Taylor, 1998; Kent & Taylor, 2002).

An organization's marketing plan should have measurable outcomes as defined by organizational strategy. For example, if a strategic goal of an association is to better engage and connect with members, the organization needs to not only determine how the marketing program will directly impact that goal, but also decide what the desired outcomes of that marketing tactic will be in reference to the stated goal. One of the ways nonprofits understand whether their tactics have made an impact is through the use of a logic model. Logic models help articulate and visually illustrate the organization's theory of how its available resources will be used to attain intended outcomes and impacts for a particular program (Kanter & Delahaye Paine, 2012; W. K. Kellogg Foundation, 2004). The use of logic models in social media marketing is growing, but the practice is not yet commonplace (Cici, 2010). However, funders are encouraging organizations to evaluate social media efforts, and are providing tools and resources to do so (John S. and James L. Knight Foundation, 2011; Robert Wood Johnson Foundation, 2012; among others).

Social media strategies must be targeted to best achieve objectives, but also to wisely use scarce organizational resources, as nonprofits tend to have little capacity to engage in social media marketing (Briones, Kuch, Liu, & Jin, 2011). Another challenge in using social media strategically is finding the best platforms for the organization's content, as the social media landscape changes rapidly, offering new platforms each year. Hanna, Rohm and Crittenden (2011) have suggested that organizations make the best use of their resources when they understand the social media platforms available to them, and effectively integrate them into the broader marketing strategy. Organizations need to understand who their target audience is, what social media platforms their audience uses in their online communication, and what story the organization needs to tell using those platforms (Hanna et al., 2011). Once a nonprofit can answer these questions, they will be better prepared to determine the best avenues for online engagement across all stakeholder groups. But the strategy does not end with identifying the different stakeholder segments and their platforms of choice. Not only does the organization need to determine the best method of reaching the stakeholders who already have a vested interest in the nonprofit, they also need to determine the steps to deepen that engagement and interaction, as well as garner additional interest in their organization. In this regard, nonprofits should consider their social media strategy to be a deep and wide approach that builds deepened engagement and wider audiences.

Kent and Taylor (1998; 2002) noted that the online environment, in particular, can be an ideal place to encourage dialogue, in this case, between an organization and its stakeholders. They suggest that dialogic communication is created through five key components: maintaining a dialogic loop by allowing opportunities for the audience to provide feedback and ask questions; providing useful information, both of general interest to all, but also of interest to specific audiences; generation of return visits, by creating incentive to return to a particular site or profile over time; intuitiveness of the interface, noting that the site should be easy to use; and conservation of visitors, indicating that visitors should be retained on your page (Kent & Taylor, 1998).

Researchers have confirmed this line of theory, in discovering that organizations tend to utilize social media to share information, and to engage in dialogue and build relationships with stakeholders (Jansen, Zhang, Sobel & Chowdury, 2009; Lovejoy & Saxton, 2012; Rybalko & Seltzer, 2010; Waters, 2007; Waters, Burnett, Lamm & Lucas, 2009), although the use of social media does not always yield a true dialogic engagement for nonprofit organizations due in part to issues of organizational capacity, as mentioned earlier (Linville, McGee & Hicks, 2012; Lovejoy & Saxton, 2012; Lovejoy, Waters & Saxton, 2012; Waters et al., 2009).

Deepened Engagement

Lovejoy and Saxton (2012) built on dialogic theory by articulating a spectrum of social media communications. One function of communication is to spread information about the organization that is of interest to followers. A second function is creating a dialogue with online followers to build relationships and community among the organization's stakeholders. The third function of communication is to mobilize followers to take action on behalf of the organization, whether it is signing a petition, donating to an organization, or attending an event. In this regard, dialogue isn't necessarily the final step of online communication, but certainly an important aspect in a spectrum of communications tactics.

Guo and Saxton (2013) translated Lovejoy and Saxton's (2012) research into a ladder of engagement for social media communications. They discovered that nonprofits use these tactics to deepen stakeholder interaction and engagement with the organization. Their ladder of engagement consists of three steps that correspond to Lovejoy & Saxton's communication functions: reaching out to people (information), keeping the flame alive (dialogue), and stepping up to action (action).

In the first step, the nonprofit simply uses social media platforms to educate stakeholders about the organization and its mission. Communication at this level is typically one-way and informational. The second step involves keeping the flame alive where a nonprofit begins to deepen engagement among its online community by starting a light dialogue (Guo & Saxton, 2013; Lovejoy & Saxton, 2012). Examples of this type of interaction could include: responding directly to a follower who asks a question; asking questions of stakeholders to generate dialogue; or strengthening ties to the online community by retweeting posts of organizational affiliates.

The final step on the ladder of engagement is stepping up to action, where the nonprofit uses social media to mobilize stakeholders. This level of engagement often involves a call to action, which can take the form of participation in online events or another type of direct action in support of the organization's mission (Guo & Saxton, 2013; Lovejoy & Saxton, 2012). An example of this type of social media post is asking stakeholders to support a public service campaign, providing links to additional information about the campaign, or asking for followers to volunteer for the organization.

In following the ladder of engagement (Guo & Saxton, 2013), nonprofits are encouraged to regularly communicate with their stakeholders and online "followers" to further deepen engagement to help the organization attain strategic goals and mission fulfillment. However, a nonprofit must also recruit new online followers. This is typically seen through the dissemination of an organization's message through existing online networks (Ciszek, 2013; Kim & Rhee, 2011).

Wider Audiences

Ciszek (2013) also expanded the dialogic framework by suggesting that dialogue is not only relegated to what occurs between the organization and its publics, but can also occur *between* publics, about or on behalf of the organization and its mission. In particular this form of interaction can, "...humanize the work of the organization from the ground up" (Cisek, 2013, p. 206), and demonstrates a way that publics are able to build community among themselves through dialogue with and about the organization.

As suggested above, the key to increased amplification of an organization's message is in allowing stakeholder voices to help tell the story of the nonprofit's mission (Briones et al., 2010; Ciszek, 2013; Kim & Rhee, 2011). Not only does this message amplification allow increased participation and engagement of existing stakeholders, it also helps build additional awareness of the nonprofit to those outside of their existing online network. This form of marketing encourages stakeholders to help fulfill the organization's strategic goals, particularly goals surrounding mission awareness. Ciszek (2013) proposed a model of amplification, shown below (Figure 1), which places an organization at the "hub" of communications activity. The model illustrates the central nature of the organization, as well as the two-way dialogue between the organization and its online stakeholders. Additionally, there are interconnected relationships between the various publics, defined below, showing a likely overlap in communication. As multiple stakeholder groups amplify the nonprofit organization's message, it leads to increased organizational and mission awareness.

A nonprofit must effectively communicate with its network of stakeholders to help generate mission awareness, and market the organization in general. Federated associations, in particular, have challenges in not only determining the ideal target audience, but also in engaging the various levels of the organization either directly, or through the federated structure (Briones et al., 2010). Briones and colleagues (2010) recommended that federated organizations provide key players with essential information and tools to do it on the association's behalf. For the NPC, this entails assisting College and Alumnae Panhellenic Associations, as well as the various member groups, effectively tailor communications to their sub-networks.

In order to best leverage the networks of its online followers, a nonprofit needs to segment its online stakeholders, much like its fundraising prospects, to determine how to best communicate with in order to share the organization's message and broaden its existing network. Wilson (2000) identified three specific publics who are participants in an organization's strategic communications: key publics, influentials, and intervening publics. Key publics are those whose participation in the organization is fundamental to accomplishing organizational goals, or the group of people that the organization works on behalf of (Ciszek, 2013). For NPC, the key publics are the collegiate and alumnae individual members. Influentials are "celebrities" within the organization's field of interest, and whose participation can have a substantial impact on the success of the nonprofit's social media efforts (Ciszek, 2013). "Influentials" include the 26 NPC member groups, board members of NPC, and board members of NPC's member groups. Finally, intervening publics are a particular mission's opinion leaders, and serve as a pass-through for organizational information (Ciszek, 2013; Rawlins, 2006). In the case of the NPC, these individuals

Figure 1. NPC's amplification model
Note: Adapted from: Ciszek, 2013.

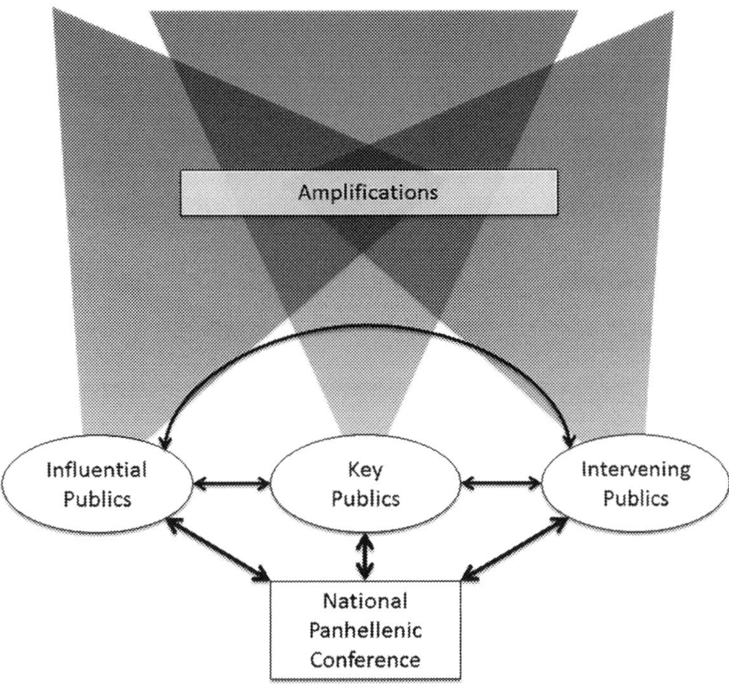

would be the College and Alumnae Panhellenic Associations, as well as various interest groups that regularly disseminate sorority-related content. It is important to note that both influentials and intervening publics can be groups or individuals whose missions aren't congruent with that of the nonprofit, and as such, their amplification of organizational messages can have negative consequences for the nonprofit.

In summary, an organization engaging in strategic social media use outlines a specific strategy for its marketing efforts, including both outcomes and related benchmarks to determine effectiveness. The nonprofit then determines the appropriate audience for its messaging, and identifies the appropriate social media platforms to communicate with its various publics. The communication itself should not only deepen ties to existing stakeholders, and leverage their social media activity in support of the organizational mission, but also leverage their social media networks to broaden the organization's online audience.

Research questions informed by these theoretical perspectives are:

1. What challenges does the National Panhellenic Conference face in using social media to build relationships with stakeholders?
2. Did strategic social media activities for the International Badge Day campaign lead to an increase in stakeholder engagement?
3. Did strategic social media activities for the International Badge day campaign lead to greater message amplification?

METHODS

Each year on the first Monday in March, NPC hosts International Badge Day, a virtual event which asks sorority women to wear their sorority's membership badge wherever they are that day. Many campus-based affiliates participate by not only encouraging their members to wear their badges, but also by hosting on-campus events designed to promote the sorority experience. Because the event is designed to provide a sense of community to members across the country and internationally via social media, several platforms were used to disseminate NPC's message and engage members in different ways. Specifically, NPC utilized Facebook events, its Facebook page, and Twitter to promote the event and engage members. Data were collected from both the 2013 and 2014 events, and are highlighted below.

Data for Facebook use were collected for the month surrounding International Badge Day 2013 and International Badge Day 2014, as metrics for that day alone do not speak to posts in the time surrounding the event, when it is being heavily promoted. Amplification was measured by the number of Facebook page fans, the number of invitations extended to join the International Badge Day Facebook event, as well as metrics from Facebook's web analytics tools: Insights Weekly Reach metrics, which measure the number of people who have seen any content associated with the organization's Facebook page during a given time.

Facebook engagement was measured by the number of individuals who clicked "going" on the International Badge Day Facebook event, as well as key metrics provided by Facebook Insights; specifically, the number of people talking about NPC, the number of people creating stories about NPC, and the number of people engaged with NPC's Facebook page. A final analysis of Facebook data compares amplification and engagement statistics from 2013 to 2014, to determine whether messaging surrounding International Badge Day is having a similar impact from year to year, or if amplification and engagement on this platform are increasing or decreasing.

Data for Twitter use were also collected for the month surrounding International Badge Day 2013 and International Badge Day 2014, for the reasons outlined above. Twitter amplification for International Badge Day was measured for 2013 and 2014 by measuring the number of followers, the number of retweets of each type of public, as well as the change in percent of unique tweets from each of the three publics mentioned above: influential, intervening, and key publics.

Twitter engagement was measured by overall hashtag use corresponding to each year's International Badge Day event (#badgeday13 and #badgeday14), as well as the number of tweets that include photos of members wearing their badges, which was part of the call to action for participants. Engagement was also measured by the number of tweets that included Panhellenic-branded content, as those tweets demonstrate higher levels of engagement than simply using the corresponding event hashtag.

It is important to note that the primary author of this chapter is a board member of NPC, and the secondary author is employed by the organization. As such, some biases may be present in the collection and interpretation of data. To minimize any bias present, the researchers analyzed data at the census level to eliminate any selection bias. Further, both positive and negative results have been included in this chapter, to eliminate reporting bias.

CASE

Organization Background

NPC was formed on the premise that, similar to the need for women's fraternal organizations mentioned earlier, member organizations would better succeed in a male-dominated, and at times hostile, campus culture if they banded together under a collective interest: "Possessing an unshakable belief in the power of women's friendship, they (member groups) came to understand that the one thing they could not afford was to be at odds with each other" (National Panhellenic Conference [NPC], 2012a, p. 1).

Today, the NPC is a membership association comprised of 26 member organizations, totaling 4 million members across the U.S. and the globe. It is one of the oldest and largest organizations for women. Although the complex structure of the organization will be discussed in greater detail below, the primary constituents are women who are 18-22 years of age, although members can stay active and involved at any age through alumnae programming. As a result, NPC's constituents span multiple generations, and each generation has particular needs that the organization must strategically meet.

Although NPC has been in existence for over a century, it is only recently that it has made a concerted effort to plan for the future, with an understanding that its previous organizational form may no longer be relevant for today's stakeholders. In 2009, the staff was comprised of an administrative director, a communications and programs coordinator, and a business operations coordinator, with most operational decisions occurring at the board level. NPC determined that its traditional volunteer-driven structure was no longer relevant for the needs of the organization's stakeholders, nor was it practical for addressing the intergenerational needs of its stakeholders or their differing preferences for time commitment. As a result, in 2010, NPC hired its first executive director to lead the organization to a more staff-driven model of operations, and rely less on the potentially inconsistent implementation of programs that can occur with a volunteer-led model.

In 2013, the expanded its office staff to include an executive director, marketing and events manager, business operations coordinator, training and curriculum design coordinator, and Panhellenic support coordinator, as well as two or three paid interns each academic semester. The financial capacity of the organization also grew during that time, from $600,000 in revenues and $550,000 in expenses in 2009, to approximately $700,000 in revenues and $600,000 in expenses in 2013, as indicated by the organization's IRS Form 990 for the corresponding years.

One of the significant changes to the organization, beyond an increased staff and budget, was the transition from an operating board to a governing board. This shift has paired with an increased emphasis on organizational effectiveness and strategy. In 2011, the board of directors adopted new mission and vision statements: "The National Panhellenic Conference is the premier advocacy and support organization for the advancement of the sorority experience" and "Advancing the Sorority Experience Together," respectively. Reflecting on the new organizational mission, the board adopted its most recent strategic plan in 2012, focusing on the areas of advocacy, support and collaboration for organizational stakeholders. Of particular interest to readers is the organizational strategy to enhance NPC's position as the expert on and premier advocate for the sorority movement (NPC, 2012b). The intent of this organizational strategy was to create a more formalized marketing plan, including a strategic online presence.

The organizational strategies drive NPC's programs and services through a complex federated structure with multiple stakeholders. NPC must advocate for the sorority experience on behalf of the member groups, as well as the individual members. NPC encourages collaboration among member groups, and engages in collaborative partnerships with host campuses, industry partners, and other stakeholder groups such as the U.S. Department of Education and the White House Council on Women and Girls. NPC provides support to both member groups and local Panhellenic Associations by providing them with industry-level news and data to help them be individually successful. NPC also supports College and Alumnae Panhellenic Associations by providing them with information to be successful on their own as advocates for the sorority experience.

As outlined in Figure 2, NPC's members include over 325,000 women on 666 college campuses in the U.S. and Canada, as well as nearly 4 million alumnae all over the world. Collegians are part of one NPC member group, but form collaborative Panhellenic communities when more than one chapter of an NPC member group is present on a college campus. Similarly, alumnae retain their membership in their member group and the national conference upon graduation, and have an opportunity to stay active in one of over 3,000 alumnae chapters or 197 Alumnae Panhellenic associations in communities across the U.S., Canada, and the United Kingdom.

Over the past four years, NPC has created strategic priorities that reflect the changing landscape of their operating environment. These priorities have directly influenced its strategic marketing plan, and specifically, its utilization of social media as a marketing tool. NPC's target audience of college-aged women, combined with a federated structure and multiple layers of stakeholders, makes social media use a necessity for this type of membership association. The next section will identify how NPC uses strategic social media to reach the organizational goals defined in its strategic plan: "Refine and implement a clear and easily identifiable marketing platform that evolves as our stakeholders and the needs of the Conference evolve" and "Cultivate relationships with stakeholders to develop a corps of brand ambassadors" (NPC, 2012b).

Figure 2. NPC organization structure and membership

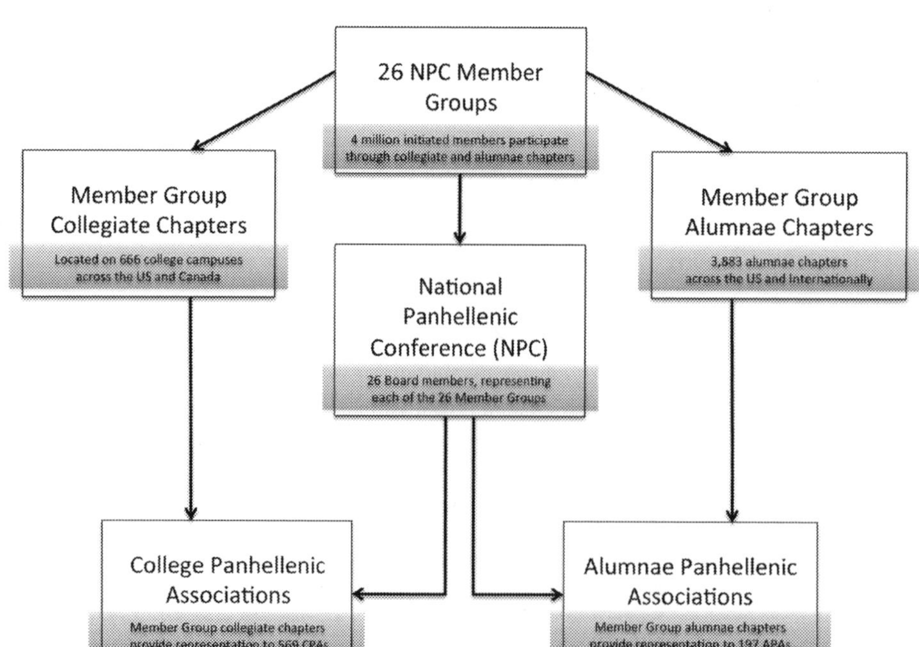

Project and Experience

As social media are an emerging technology, it is only recently that NPC has become more focused and strategic in its social media use. In 2008, the organization developed its Facebook presence and launched its first virtual event for International Badge Day on December 18, 2008. In the first 12 hours 400 people said "yes" to participating in the event and 1,400 invites were sent. For International Badge Day 2009, Facebook "flair" was a major part of the strategy. NPC joined Twitter in April 2009 and moved from a Facebook group to a "fan" page in June 2009. They also created a presence on Linkedin, Pinterest, Instagram, and Blogger. The initial strategy being that the members are using social media platforms to communicate, so NPC also needs to communicate using the platforms.

NPC's current social media use is defined by the 2012 strategic plan. It hopes to enhance its position as an expert on, and premier advocate for, the sorority movement. It intends to do so by continuing to refine and implement clear marketing strategies that meet the needs of stakeholders and the organization. . Keeping the organizational strategy in mind, as well as its primary constituent base of 18-22 year-old women, the NPC uses social media to engage various stakeholder groups and best advocate for its member groups. One piece of the marketing plan was to devise a logic model, which articulates all organizational resources to be utilized in fulfilling the strategic organizational goals. The logic model, shown below, articulates all organizational resources, including staff, volunteers, equipment, and finances, that will be used to reach the intended outcomes of increased engagement and increased reach. The logic model focuses primarily on one campaign for International Badge Day, but that campaign employs similar resources and expects the same outcomes as the larger organizational social media strategy, but on a smaller scale.

NPC uses social media to engage its diverse stakeholder groups and provide relevant information to each type of member. It is not possible to connect with members worldwide in person, which is why an online platform is so important for stakeholder and member engagement. Currently, social media is used to highlight the practices and accomplishments of exceptional College and Alumnae Panhellenic Associations, as well as individual members. This content is typically about academic excellence of a particular Panhellenic Association, available scholarships for members, or promoting successful philanthropic efforts. NPC also uses social media to highlight events and issues of importance or relevance to stakeholders. Examples include facts about National Women's History Month (#nwhm), Advisor Appreciation Month (#tyadvisors), the campaign to ban bossy, and NPC's Month of the Scholar (#npcscholar). Finally, the NPC also disseminates educational content about its 26 member organizations by celebrating all organizational Founders' Days, providing facts and posts about the different member organizations, and by hosting International Badge Day each year.

NPC utilizes Facebook, Twitter, Pinterest, Instagram, and YouTube in its social media marketing efforts, although they are employed in specific ways. Facebook and Twitter, for example, are used in more conversational communication, and provide a fair bit of interaction between the association and its affiliates. Although there has been a spike in alumnae participation on Facebook, NPC engages college-age members primarily on Twitter. YouTube, Instagram, and Pinterest are used to generate informational content, which is then cross-posted on Facebook and Twitter for dissemination. Video content on YouTube is designed to be informational and motivational, providing education about the association, its mission, and its members. Pinterest and Instagram are used to share information and content related to the member groups, NPC initiatives and insight into the activities of member groups, local Panhellenic Associations and NPC volunteers and staff.

Figure 3. NPC logic model

Although NPC uses multiple social media outlets this chapter focuses only on how NPC has used Twitter and Facebook to both deepen and broaden engagement with various stakeholders via International Badge Day. Using Gou and Saxton's (2013) ladder of engagement, NPC has engaged in reaching out to people primarily to through information dissemination about mission of the organization. Low-engagement tweets were generally sent toward the beginning of the campaign, with deepening engagement closer to the actual event. Simply posting the International Badge Day event on Facebook accomplishes reaching out to people. Similarly, NPC tweeted a link to the Facebook event to its followers, and posted photos of member group badges, as well as videos of NPC board members talking about their badges on Twitter. NPC posted 34 tweets reaching out to people, primarily at the beginning of the campaign to increase awareness of the campaign itself.

The next step in the ladder of engagement is keeping the flame alive (Guo & Saxton, 2013); in other words, NPC needs to deepen engagement with its audience through dialogue and building community. In order to engage followers, posts from College Panhellenic Associations were retweeted with comments such as *@NPCWomen: Check out why members of the NPC Board of Directors wear their badge to get ready for #badgeday14* ow.ly/tDAQn. NPC also engaged its constituents by holding weekly International Badge Day trivia contests during the month leading up to, on the day of, and for several weeks following the event. NPC posted 21 tweets to keep the flame alive, generally at the middle and later stages of the campaign. This is an example of a tweet from the campaign: *@NPCWomen: Great idea! RT @ PennStatePHC: 100 reasons why we are proud to wear our letters #badgeday14.*

In addition, NPC engaged its Facebook audience in deeper communication by highlighting various board members and their affiliations, with links to view videos about why those women wear their badges. These posts tagged the various member organizations, which typically resulted in likes and pages shares, with a few comments from followers of both NPC's page, as well as the member groups. For example one post read: "The NPC blog has officially launched with the first installment of 'Why I Wear My Badge.' Today, Ana Miller of Pi Beta Phi and Lynne Chambers of Alpha Sigma Alpha share their badge stories. Check it out, and celebrate your badge by participating in International #badgeday14."

Finally, the NPC developed International Badge Day, branded as #badgeday14 online, as a way to ask stakeholders to step up to action (Guo & Saxton, 2013) on behalf of the organization. Through various tweets and Facebook posts, NPC created a call to action for followers to support the mission, and subsequently, help fulfill organizational goals through 13 high-engagement tweets toward the middle and end of the campaign. For example, NPC tweeted a request for organizational members to wear their badges on International Badge Day, and send photos to NPC via social media. Additionally, NPC retweeted a call to action from the organization's board chairman: *@NPCWomen: RT @NPCChairman I challenge you to stand tall, wear your badge with pride and let your voice be heard #badgeday14.*

NPC also engaged Facebook followers by posting a link to the International Badge Day event on its page, and encouraging followers to invite Panhellenic members within their networks to the event. In addition, the association asked followers to share on their own Facebook pages why they wear their membership badges, as well as post photos of the members in their badge on the International Badge Day event page.

Although NPC has seen success in engaging their online audience via social media it is important for the association to continually develop interest in the organization and its mission, and look to amplify its message beyond the existing network. Amplification of a message is a particularly interesting idea for a federated membership association. In a slight deviation from what Ciszek (2013) posited, the influentials and intervening publics are the primary points of dissemination to key publics, as the average member holds the strongest affinity for the Panhellenic Associations and NPC member organizations. It is through the Panhellenic Associations and their member groups that they most likely hear about International Badge Day and other content regarding NPC and its mission. For that reason, the association concentrates its amplification efforts within these two groups, and relies heavily on key publics in specific instances. However, in order for NPC's message to be amplified to new audiences, it still must create content that is engaging enough for existing followers to retweet or share to their networks of followers.

The influential are the "celebrities" within the industry (Ciszek, 2013). These may include NPC's 26 member organizations, NPC's board of directors, as well as the individual member organizations' boards of directors. One tactic to reach message amplification through these publics was to mention member groups in International Badge Day-related Facebook posts, like information about their membership badge, or a link to a video with the NPC board member that represents their organization. These tagged posts may then be seen in news feeds of the member group's followers. Member groups and others from this category tend to retweet and share NPC's content regularly, and already serve as supporters of the organization's mission, both online, and in-person.

The intervening publics are the affiliates of NPC—the College and Alumnae Panhellenic Associations. These entities helped spread awareness of the organization and increase followers by creating content about NPC or retweeting NPC-generated content to their followers. They also do so by sharing the link for International Badge Day on Facebook, or posting original content to generate excitement and awareness about NPC and their Panhellenic Association's support of and participation in NPC's mission. College Panhellenic Associations frequently supplemented NPC's online event with on-campus events, and utilized #badgeday14 to promote those events as well.

The key publics, or the average collegiate or alumnae member, are essential in spreading the word about the Facebook International Badge Day event. It is primarily the key publics, and frequently, the alumnae, who invite their friends (other members) to the Facebook event. Additionally, the individual collegiate members were very active in using #badgeday14 on Twitter.

In this section, various strategies and tactics for the NPC's social media marketing plan were discussed. In the sections below, challenges and successes of those strategies and tactics will be identified using data from the 2014 International Badge Day event.

Challenges and Opportunities

NPC has seen several challenges in its social media use that are common to most organizations, but are likely exacerbated by its federated membership association structure, as well as its publics who span generations and geography. Research Question 1 asked what particular challenges NPC faces in using social media to build relationships with stakeholders. Through this case study 4 challenges have been identified: diluted messaging, influential and intervening publics lacking social media know-how, a limited resource pool, and stakeholders migrating to other platforms.

Diluted Messaging

Looking specifically at International Badge Day, one major challenge is the idea of diluted messaging caused by the structure of NPC. NPC does not have a direct connection to the key publics, and must rely on the influentials and intervening publics to share their message with those key publics. Panhellenic Association affiliates are encouraged to spread the message of International Badge Day to their constituents using the logo and resources provided by the larger organization, and are encouraged to host their own celebration events. By doing so, Panhellenic Associations create Facebook events with the same name and event photo, and potentially drive attendees away from the national Facebook event. In addition, some groups use the hashtag incorrectly in their own promotions, for example using #badgeday2014 instead of #badgeday14.

Influential and Intervening Publics Lack Social Media Know-How

Another challenge within the structure of NPC is educating influential publics on how to best advocate online. Each of the NPC member groups, an influential public, has its own marketing strategy and goals, and aren't beholden to NPC's marketing requests or requirements. Although they benefit from membership, they may not have a desire (or in some cases, capacity) to participate in the marketing goals of the association. The second challenge in educating the influential publics is the intergenerational nature of the board of directors. The board ranges in generation from Generation X to the Baby Boomers. Older generations may not be willing to adopt new technology in the fashion needed for them to share their influence, and younger generations may be willing, but lack knowledge or skill to use social media as a marketing tool.

The intervening publics, or the Panhellenic Associations, also lack knowledge of how to effectively use social media as a marketing tool for NPC. The Alumnae Panhellenic Associations may have a modest Facebook presence, but have very little time and knowledge to effectively use one platform, much less multiple platforms, to serve as brand ambassadors for NPC. The College Panhellenic Associations, on the other hand, are digital natives, but still require guidance and reminders that they are likely the strongest potential brand ambassadors that NPC has. Both lack the skill to harness their enthusiasm for NPC in a social media marketing activity.

Limited Resources

A challenge that NPC faces, like most nonprofit organizations, is a limited resource allocation for maintaining an online brand. Specifically, there is no staff solely dedicated to creating and executing social media strategy. With one person managing the bulk of the social media as only a portion of her assigned duties, there is often only time to think about the tactics, but not ask how they are related to strategic goals. In addition, with limited staff and resources, deepening engagement is challenging. Responding to comments, posts and messages on pages is time- and labor-intensive, and can become less of a priority on particularly hectic days.

Migration to Other Platforms

As with all practitioners of social media marketing, NPC faces the challenge of migration to other online platforms. This is especially difficult when your key audience (18 to 22 year-olds) adopts new technology early. It truly is impossible to stay ahead of the curve, and as a result NPC works to stay *with* the curve.

Social media use has provided NPC with several opportunities to continue its organizational learning and development. As you will read below, NPC is addressing some of these challenges through board development, both in terms of trends and issues in technology. More broadly however, this topic has encouraged more conversations about generational differences and needs. The board has been challenged to think about how social media and other tools can help NPC strategically address generational needs, given current resources (both fiscal and human). This has also allowed and encouraged the staff to be more strategic in implementing both strategy and tactics employed.

Though there are many challenges with social media, the organizational opportunities far outweigh them. It provides an association with member organizations the opportunity to have a direct link to the individuals, the key publics. Those key publics are the ones who can really spread the message and serve as the brand ambassadors called for in NPC's strategic plan.

Solutions and Outcomes

Although NPC handles the social media challenges presented above as best they can, there will always be new challenges requiring new solutions when the social media landscape is changing so rapidly, and in some cases, so drastically. In the section below, the tactics NPC used to address the above challenges are discussed as are the outcomes it is seeing from its social media use.

Solutions

Diluted Messaging

The first challenge discussed above is the issue of potentially diluted messages, as caused by multiple competing events and "unofficial" hashtag use. Competing events held by local College and Alumnae Panhellenic Associations actually benefit NPC, rather than create a hindrance. Guo & Saxton (2013) have suggested that as individuals form a deeper connections with organizations via social media, they will act on the mission's behalf. In this regard, local Associations' events are helping NPC educate others about its mission. Competing events reflect a "stepping up to action," and represent a specific way in which intervening publics can amplify the association's message. The affiliates are using resources provided by the association to promote the mission of the overall association. In this case, rather than competing events, perhaps they can be better thought of as complementary to the organization's "parent" event. NPC posted links to the affiliate events on its primary event page to help develop connections between key publics (i.e. Facebook event invitees) and intervening publics, or Panhellenic Associations, who are hosting virtual, and possible in-person International Badge Day events in their area.

The use of unofficial or incorrect hashtags for International Badge Day may dilute messaging for event, but the greater impact is on the organization's ability to effectively measure the impact of its online event. A quick search of tweets using competing hashtags (#npcbadgeday, #badgeday, and #badgeday2014) yielded about 150 mis-tagged tweets. However, like the complementary events discussed above, these stakeholders are still participating in the organization's call to action, just not quite as prescribed. These stakeholder groups are still informing their audiences about the association, and are celebrating their membership in NPC via social media. NPC's strategy in addressing the incorrect hashtags is straightforward: striving to continually put out the right message. For example, in cases where a stakeholder tweets using the incorrect hashtag or no hashtag for International Badge Day or another event, NPC responds with: *@NPCWomen: If you're tweeting about International Badge Day, be sure to use the hashtag #badgeday14!*

Better Educate Influential and Intervening Publics

Another challenge outlined above is the need to provide better education to the influential and intervening publics, so that they can better spread NPC's message to their networks. The influentials were determined to be NPC's board of directors, as well as the member groups. One strategy employed by NPC's board of directors was to provide an educational workshop on the importance of using social media to advocate for NPC, and techniques to best engage and inform followers using social media. During this session, the NPC staff shared social media usage statistics with both the board and high-level volunteers, in order to help emphasize social media's role among key stakeholders. Volunteers were given simple ways to become more engaged on social media: primarily through sharing, liking, and retweeting. Involving high-level volunteers in the training was an important step, since they tend to be a bit younger and more engaged on social media than the majority of the board members. These individuals are influential, as they tend to be high-level volunteers in their respective NPC member group, and have a broad network. By including high-level volunteers, NPC staff trained an additional 78 brand ambassadors.

Since the training session, those who embraced the simple elements of engagement have increased the traffic to specific messaging promoted by NPC. 38 board members and high-level volunteers (36.5%) currently have Twitter accounts, and of those, 13 (12.5%) actively tweeted for International Badge Day. Sixteen of those influentials (15.38%) regularly tweet on behalf of NPC using retweets, shares, and self-generated content directly promoting the organization. Of note, this proportion almost parallels the proportion of younger (Millennial and Generation X) board members and high-level volunteers, suggesting a generational influence on Twitter adoption and use within the organization. Still, this leaves room for opportunity and additional participation by key volunteers.

Additionally, activity on Facebook has increased among board members and high-level volunteers. 97 board members and high-level volunteers (93.27%) use Facebook, and of those, 60 (61.86%) attended the International Badge Day Facebook event, with many liking and commenting on event posts made by those considered "key publics." Further, 38 (39.18%) posted content about the Facebook event or International Badge Day generally, on their personal Facebook page. Again, the higher level of participation on Facebook is not surprising, as many individuals across several generations now use Facebook as a form of online communication. For both Facebook and Twitter, however, it is important for NPC to continue providing training to board members and high-level volunteers to ensure both new and continued use of these tools in marketing efforts.

Other influentials of importance are the NPC member groups. To engage these publics NPC provided them with curated content about themselves, thus creating a return on investment for helping spread messaging. NPC social media staff decided to tag member groups in posts connecting the member group or its individual members (in this case, affiliated NPC board members and high-level volunteers) to NPC in some way. To incent member groups into sharing content specifically for International Badge Day, NPC shared photos and facts on different social media about the individual member group badges, and used the #badgeday14 hashtag. These tactics provided needed incentive for member groups to engage, participate, and spread NPC's message. The NPC staff and key volunteers, in turn, like content generated by the Panhellenic Associations to help reinforce these activities throughout the year.

Both College and Alumnae Panhellenic Associations, the intervening publics in our case, required additional education and support to best help the NPC spread its message. In order to do this, NPC set up a Facebook to disseminate information to Alumnae Panhellenic Associations and allow them to share ideas and best practices for operations with each other. This page was also utilized to invite individual alumnae members and the Alumnae Panhellenic Associations to the online International Badge Day event. The various Alumnae Panhellenic Associations used this group page to share photos and stories about how they were celebrating International Badge Day in their local communities. This tool has increased engagement surrounding International Badge Day, Alumnae Panhellenic Associations, and NPC. Because very few, if any, Alumnae Panhellenic Associations have Twitter accounts, NPC decided Facebook is where they will connect with this particular group most effectively.

Members of College Panhellenic Associations, as early adopters, know how to use social media to communicate. However, affiliates still required some guidance on how to effectively advocate for the sorority experience. To address this, NPC provided educational sessions during various regional leadership conferences. These conferences are held immediately prior to International Badge Day each year, so the timing is excellent to ask Panhellenic Association leaders to use their social media accounts (both personal and Panhellenic Association) to post information about International Badge Day. NPC asked Panhellenic Association leaders to join the Facebook event and use #badgeday14, and provided them with information to take action and spread the word about International Badge Day on their local campuses. In addition, NPC provided affiliate leaders with techniques to be stronger advocates for the sorority experience, broadly, and the National Panhellenic Conference, specifically, by asking them to regularly post about the impact the Associations have on their campuses and in their local communities. The NPC staff and key volunteers, in turn, retweets, likes, and shares content generated by the Panhellenic Associations to help reinforce these activities throughout the year.

Limited Resources

The issue of limited staff and financial capacity is an issue that is not unique to NPC. However, including brand management in the most recent strategic plan formalized the organization's commitment and desire to move forward with a well-developed marketing plan that included social media marketing. As a result, the board of directors dedicated funding to hire interns to help with the social media engagement, and also directed funding for the use of HootSuite Pro, which provides detailed analytics to help measure online engagement, among other things. In other words, they put their money where their strategy was, acknowledging that unfunded strategies aren't, in fact, strategic.

HootSuite, a social media management system, has been a helpful tool for NPC staff to better manage the time and effort required to maintain its social media presence. Using HootSuite, NPC is able to send between 1 and 3 original tweets per day, excluding direct communication with its online audience. NPC can also monitor multiple keywords, across multiple platforms, simultaneously. This is particularly helpful for events like #badgeday14, where staff can readily see all tweets using that hashtag in one place. Although searches on Facebook and Twitter can achieve the same result, HootSuite does this much more efficiently. NPC also uses HootSuite to schedule tweets and Facebook posts in bulk, which allows staff to plan a month (or more) of tweets, or an entire marketing campaign, in advance, and simply monitor online traffic during the event to engage and respond to their online audience. In addition, HootSuite provides basic analytics for a small fee, allowing relatively quick measurement of NPC's online impact for about $10 per month (at the time of writing).

Another key component of using limited resources is using them effectively. The marketing and events manager, alongside the communications and marketing interns, conduct full-day planning sessions sporadically to set goals and create tactics for specific online initiatives like International Badge Day. In doing this, they not only create an effective strategy, they are also able to identify specific tasks for the influential publics to help the Conference amplify NPC's messages during those campaigns. In effect, this planning helps with social media marketing, as well as some pieces of the organization's volunteer management program.

Migration to Other Platforms

As stated elsewhere in this chapter, the key public is comprised of women between the ages of 18 and 22, resulting in a need for heightened awareness of changes and trends in the social media landscape. As a result, NPC staff maintains membership in other associations focused on communications and social media, and regularly follows practitioners and educators who talk about effective social media use. Doing so allows them to be prepared for "the next big thing." However, NPC also employs strategy before diving in to a new platform, since doing so adds more to the workload for already scarce staff time. Staff looks to whether the key publics are active on those platforms, how they are using those platforms, and how those platforms can be tied in to upcoming initiatives. Once NPC has satisfactorily answered those questions, the platform will be built in to the existing social media marketing plan. Recently, NPC added

Instagram, as many of the key publics were already using it, liking and sharing content, and participating in NPC's online campaigns through it. NPC adopted Instagram as a tool, but also implemented it at a strategic time. The platform was launched in conjunction with the organization's annual meeting, where there were many opportunities for photos to be taken and subsequently posted.

Campaign Outcomes

When using social media strategically, an organization must clearly define the desired end-goal of that strategy, since it will need to assign resources accordingly, and define benchmarks for success. Earlier, it was identified that NPC created a logic model to help guide its strategic social media use. For NPC, the desired impacts of its marketing efforts are an increased awareness of the NPC brand among its members, to be the premier voice for the sorority experience, and to be the premier advocate for the sorority experience. However, those aren't easily measured in the short-term. Instead, NPC focused on specific more easily measured outcomes in its first year of assessment. For International Badge Day, outcomes included heightened social media engagement with stakeholders, as measured by the number of original posts generated by NPC's online audience (Research Question 2), and an increase in amplification through the number of followers across Twitter and Facebook (Research Question 3). But the question is: has NPC achieved higher engagement and amplification of messages because of its strategic social media use?

Facebook

Amplification via Facebook was measured by the number of Facebook page fans, the number of invitations extended to join the Facebook event, as well as Facebook Insight's Weekly Reach metric, which measures the number of people who have seen any content associated with an organization's Facebook page. NPC elected to measure amplification and engagement for the week surrounding International Badge Day, as metrics for that day alone do not speak to posts in the days surrounding the event. As Table 1 shows, the number of Facebook page fans increased by about 20% between March 2013 and March 2014, and over 500 joined between February 1 and March 31, 2014, the period during International Badge Day's heaviest promotion and traffic. Additionally, there was a slight increase in the number of people invited to the International Badge Day online event. However, and perhaps more interesting to see, is the marked decrease in reach, which is the number of people who have seen any content from NPC's page, from 2013 to 2014. Some have speculated that Facebook's recent algorithm change is impacting page reach (Post, 2014; Tobin, 2014; among others).

It is also clear that there is a change in engagement alongside the decline in amplification. Engagement was measured by the number of individuals who clicked "going" on the International Badge Day Facebook event, and data provided by Facebook Insights on the number of people talking about NPC, the number of people creating stories about NPC, and the number of people engaged with NPC's Facebook page. In each of these instances, there is a marked increase in engagement, particularly among those "talking about" NPC. "Talking about" NPC includes liking the page; posting to NPC's timeline; liking, commenting, or sharing NPC's posts; responding to an event; or mentioning or tagging NPC's page in an original post. Individuals in 2014 were creating nearly 50% more content about NPC than in 2013, and are "talking about" or engaged with NPC's page in some regard nearly 50E more.

Table 1. Amplification and engagement of stakeholders via Facebook

	Change by Year		
	2013	**2014**	**% Change 2013-2014**
Facebook, General			
# Page Fans	11,844	14,901	20.52%
% Change in fans, Jan	1.90	2.50	24.00%
% Change in fans, Feb	4.60	4.60	0.00%
% Change in fans, March	3.20	3.70	13.51%
Facebook Amplification Metrics			
# Invited to International Badge Day	87,209	99,113	12.01%
Badge Day Week Reach	360,199	306,026	-17.70%
Facebook Engagement Metrics			
# Badge Day Event Attendees	30,083	31,522	4.57%
# People talking about NPC's page	1,171	2,324	49.61%
# People creating stories about NPC	1,734	3,347	48.19%
# People engaged with NPC's Facebook page	9,071	16,780	45.94%

Twitter

Amplification via Twitter was measured by the number of followers, the number of retweets by each type of public, as well as the change in number of unique tweets from each of the three publics: influential, intervening, and key publics. Table 2 shows that the number of Twitter followers increased by just over 25% between March 2013 and March 2014, 1,100 of whom joined between February 1 and March 31, 2014. Although the influential and intervening publics retweeted less frequently, there was an increase in the number of retweets by key publics. This may indicate that the message is reaching the key publics and creating buzz among them. Additionally, there was an increase in the number of influentials and intervening publics producing International Badge Day-related content on Twitter, and thus, reaching a wider audience. Unique tweets from College Panhellenic Associations increased by 50%, indicating that there are more affiliates generating content using the appropriate International Badge Day hashtag. Similarly, there were twice as many board members and high-level volunteers who tweeted on behalf of 2014 International Badge Day event compared to the 2013 iteration. Although amplification is decreasing in certain regards, it is somewhat offset by the number of new participants.

Twitter engagement was measured by overall hashtag use corresponding to each year's International Badge Day event, as well as the number of tweets that include photos of members wearing badges, which was part of the call to action for the event. Engagement was also measured by the number of tweets that included Panhellenic-branded content. Twitter engagement for International Badge Day, when assessing overall hashtag use, dropped 15% between 2013 and 2014. In other words, the number of event-related tweets declined. What is interesting, though, is that the type of tweet changed indicating better engagement. For example, the call to action asks members to use their social media to promote International

Table 2. Amplification and engagement of stakeholders via Twitter

	Change by Year		
	2013	2014	% Change 2013-2014
Twitter, General			
# Followers	10,634	14,211	25.17%
Twitter Amplification, Retweets			
# Retweets, NPC-generated content	1,100	753	-46.08%
# Retweets, Influential-generated content	2,500	1,969	-26.97%
# Retweets, Intervening public-generated content	393	252	-55.95%
# Retweets, Key publics-generated content	677	1,074	36.96%
Twitter Amplification, Unique tweets			
% Unique tweets, Influentials	14.18	25.47	44.33%
% Unique tweets, Intervening publics	35.62	71.43	50.13%
% Unique tweets, Key publics	83.81	87.07	3.74%
Twitter Engagement Metrics			
Uses of #badgeday(year)	1,211	1,053	-15.00%
% Posts with photos	51.11	64.96	21.32%
% Posts with PH-branded message	14.7	17.19	14.49%

Badge Day, but also to celebrate in person. In 2014, the number of images of members wearing their badges increased by 20%. Additionally, there was a 14% increase in the number of posts having some Panhellenic-branded theme. Although many tweets still often reflected an individual's respective member group, the awareness of International Badge Day's attachment to NPC, as well as NPC, in general grew.

Summary

Research Question 1 asked what challenges the NPC faced in using social media to build relationships with stakeholders. Its primary challenges were diluted messaging, influential and intervening publics lacking social media know-how, a limited resource pool, and stakeholders migrating to other platforms. Research Questions 2 and 3 asked whether social media activity for the International Badge Day campaign led to heightened stakeholder engagement and increased message amplification, respectively. The data indicates some interesting movement in both engagement and amplification, signifying a possible impact of the social media campaign.

Not only did key publics generate quite a bit of unique content, they consistently retweeted indicating movement toward becoming advocates for the NPC brand. As such, it seems as though the International Badge Day campaign led to heightened stakeholder engagement, confirming Research Question 2. Amplification on both Facebook and Twitter provide an interesting blend of perhaps tempered success, indicating mixed results for Research Question 3. Certain metrics saw an increase in amplification, while others saw a decrease. Overall, with heightened engagement, even in light of decreases in amplification, it seems like the ratio of "signal to noise" might be increasing. In other words, the messages being sent about NPC may be slightly lower in quantity, but are higher in quality and impact. NPC's social media marketing, by becoming more targeted, by educating important publics on serving in a brand ambassador role, and by being more strategic, has become more effective.

CONCLUSION

In the case above, strategy played an important role in improving overall social media marketing effectiveness, even for a single online campaign. In determining an overall strategy, identifying resources, and setting goals, NPC chose appropriate tactics to tie resources to goals. These tactics led to deepened engagement with existing publics and stakeholders, as well as additional amplification. Social media has been an effective tool in fulfilling the mission and strategic goals of the organization. First, social media is used to communicate with a wide variety of organizational members across a federated structure, and has not only increased communication with more members, it has also allowed for deeper communication with those members farthest from the top of the organization. In addition, because of the strategic engagement of the various levels of affiliates and members, they are now helping communicate on behalf of NPC at large, publicly celebrating their membership as Panhellenic women.

The literature review and this case have provided evidence that nonprofits face some tough challenges in implementing social media as part of their marketing efforts, and many of those challenges stem from a lack of dedicated resources. What can organizations do to create successful social media marketing plans, in light of this issue?

First, strategy is essential for success. Including social media marketing as an organizational priority, particularly through a strategic plan, will help give it the attention and resources needed to be effective. Implementing a strategy before taking on any social media activity leads to a more effective use of resources, as goals and tactics for the marketing program are stated, objective, and measurable. In short, you know when your organization has hit the mark. Strategy informs tactics, not the other way around.

Second, planning helps use scarce resources effectively. A logic model provides a roadmap for the organization to determine resources needed, specific tactics, and desired outcomes. In other words, planning allows staff to be more effective with their time and the organization's finances when they are focused on targets, not just "seeing what sticks." NPC created its first logic model for this project, which helped articulate how they planned to utilize resources toward their goals. However, they did not include specific metrics of success, and instead used more broad terms, like "increase" and "heightened." In future planning and logic modeling, however, NPC and other nonprofits would be advised to include specific metrics for the various outputs and outcomes at the onset, so they can have a better-defined set of goals for their marketing efforts. An example would be to increase the number of Twitter followers by 10 percent, following the Badge Day campaign. One important note on scarce human resources, which is outside the scope of this chapter, but important nonetheless—although NPC utilized the time and talent of interns to manage their online brand, this isn't always advisable. For NPC, the interns were association members, with an interest in the success of the organization. Weigh the pros and cons before outsourcing your online brand management to an intern.

Third, leverage internal and external resources to accomplish social media goals. Consider using your organization's board and trusted volunteers as brand ambassadors, and ask them to share your organization's message with their networks. After all, they (should!) have a vested interest in the success of your organization. However, make sure you provide them with the tools to do so effectively. In a federated organization, include your affiliates as brand ambassadors to help share your message at the local level. Again, provide these stakeholders with tools to do so effectively—missing this step not only results in inconsistent messaging, but could result in incorrect messaging. Finally, use technology to your advantage, and use an online social media manager like HootSuite or TweetDeck to help manage the workload.

Fourth, if you can't stay ahead of the curve, at least stay with the curve. Marketing via social media can be a moving target, with the Latest New Platform emerging on a regular basis. To best understand the environment, at the very least, consider subscribing to any of the major nonprofit social media blogs to help you identify trends and effective uses for online tools (BethKanter.org and AllisonFine.com are well-known, and a personal favorite from a nonprofit marketing professional in the field is Duane's Dartboard at DuaneHallock.com). If you have a modest budget, consider joining an association or attend seminars or webinars that can provide you with trends on the horizon, as well as new platforms and new capabilities. But, before you implement a new platform, make sure it fits into your overall strategy, and that your publics are actually using it. After all, it's an awfully dull conversation when nobody is on the other end.

Moving forward, it will be interesting to see the impact that adding more social media platforms will have on measures of marketing program and social media effectiveness. Will the additional platforms result in smaller pools of audiences across all platforms, or will they stay consistent? Further, what does the cross-over look like between the platforms, and which are particularly effective for message dissemination across the various publics? What additional tools will be developed to help organizations manage their online presence more effectively? Finally, what are the impacts of this campaign? By wearing their badges and sharing its meaning with others online, have members helped increase awareness of the organization and its mission? Measuring outcomes of an effective nonprofit social media strategy is still a relatively new concept, with the majority of research occurring after 2010. With the newness of this line of practice and inquiry, there is a wealth of learning opportunities ahead of us.

REFERENCES

Briones, R. L., Kuch, B., Liu, B. F., & Jin, Y. (2010). Keeping up with the digital age: How the American Red Cross uses social media to build relationships. *Public Relations Review*, *37*(1), 37–43. doi:10.1016/j.pubrev.2010.12.006

Bryson, J. M. (2010). Strategic planning and the strategy change cycle. In D. O. Renz (Ed.), *The Jossey-Bass handbook of nonprofit leadership and management* (pp. 230–261). San Francisco, CA: Jossey-Bass.

Cici, K. (2010). *Social media evaluation: A survey of Minnesota nonprofit organizations*. Minneapolis, MN: Minnesota Council of Nonprofits.

Ciszek, E. (2013). Advocacy and amplification: Nonprofit outreach and empowerment through participatory media. *The Public Relations Journal*, *7*(2), 187–213.

Guo, C., & Saxton, G. D. (2013). Tweeting social change: How social media are changing nonprofit advocacy. *Nonprofit and Voluntary Sector Quarterly*, *43*(1), 57–79. doi:10.1177/0899764012471585

Jansen, B., Zhang, M., Sobel, K., & Chowdury, A. (2009). Twitter power: Tweets as electronic word of mouth. *JASIST*, *60*(11), 2169–2188. doi:10.1002/asi.21149

John, S., & James, L. (2011). Impact: A practical guide to evaluation community information projects. Miami, FL: Knight Foundation.

Kanter, B., & Delahaye Paine, K. (2012). *Measuring the networked nonprofit: Using data to change the world*. San Francisco, CA: Jossey-Bass.

Kent, M. L., & Taylor, M. (1998). Building dialogic relationships through the World Wide Web. *Public Relations Review*, *24*(3), 321–334. doi:10.1016/S0363-8111(99)80143-X

Kent, M. L., & Taylor, M. (2002). Toward a dialogic theory of public relations. *Public Relations Review*, *28*(1), 21–37. doi:10.1016/S0363-8111(02)00108-X

Kim, J.-N., & Rhee, Y. (2011). Strategic thinking about employee communication behavior (ECB) in public relations: Testing the models of megaphoning and scouting effects in Korea. *Journal of Public Relations Research*, *23*(3), 243–268. doi:10.1080/1062726X.2011.582204

Linville, D. L., McGee, S. E., & Hicks, L. K. (2012). Colleges' and universities' use of Twitter: A content analysis. *Public Relations Review*, *38*(2), 636–638. doi:10.1016/j.pubrev.2012.05.010

Lovejoy, K., & Saxton, G. D. (2012). Information, community, and action: How nonprofit organizations use social media. *Journal of Computer-Mediated Communication*, *17*(3), 337–353. doi:10.1111/j.1083-6101.2012.01576.x

Lovejoy, K., Waters, R. D., & Saxton, G. D. (2012). Engaging stakeholders through Twitter: How nonprofit organizations are getting more out of 140 characters or less. *Public Relations Review*, *38*(2), 313–318. doi:10.1016/j.pubrev.2012.01.005

National Panhellenic Conference. (2012a). *Adventures in friendship: A history of the National Panhellenic Conference*. Retrieved from https://www.npcwomen.org/resources/pdf/Adventures%20in%20Friendship.pdf

National Panhellenic Conference. (2012b). *Strategic plan of the National Panhellenic Conference*. Indianapolis, IN: National Panhellenic Conference.

Post, S. (2014, January 7). Facebook algorithm changes impacting small businesses. *The Columbus Metropreneur*. Retrieved from http://www.themetropreneur.com/columbus/facebook-algorithm-changes-impacting-small-businesses/

Rawlins, B. L. (2006). *Prioritizing stakeholders for public relations*. Gainesville, FL: Institute for Public Relations.

Robert Wood Johnson Foundation. (2012, May 1). *Evaluating the impact of social media at the Robert Wood Johnson Foundation*. Retrieved from http://www.rwjf.org/en/about-rwjf/newsroom/newsroom-content/2012/05/evaluating-the-impact-of-social-media-at-the-robert-wood-johnson.html

Rybalko, S., & Seltzer, T. (2010). Dialogic communication in 140 characters or less: How Fortune 500 companies engage stakeholders using Twitter. *Public Relations Review*, *36*(4), 336–341. doi:10.1016/j.pubrev.2010.08.004

Tobin, J. (2013, December 10). *Facebook brand pages suffer 44% decline in reach since December 1*. [Web log comment]. Retrieved from http://www.ignitesocialmedia.com/facebook-marketing/facebook-brand-pages-suffer-44-decline-reach-since-december-1/

Virtual, Inc. (2013). *2013 Association operations survey*. Wakefield, MA: Virtual, Inc.

W. K. Kellogg Foundation. (2004). *Logic model development guide: Using logic models to bring together planning, evaluation, and action*. Battle Creek, MI: W. K. Kellogg Foundation.

Waters, R. D. (2007). Nonprofit organizations' use of the Internet: A content analysis of communication trends on the Internet sites of the organizations on the Philanthropy 400. *Nonprofit Management & Leadership*, *18*(1), 59–76. doi:10.1002/nml.171

Waters, R. D., Burnett, E., Lamm, A., & Lucas, J. (2009). Engaging stakeholders through social networking: How nonprofit organizations are using Facebook. *Public Relations Review*, *35*(2), 102–106. doi:10.1016/j.pubrev.2009.01.006

Wilson, L. (2000). *Strategic program planning for effective public relations campaigns* (3rd ed.). Dubuque, IA: Kendall/Hunt.

KEY TERMS AND DEFINITIONS

Amplification: The process of allowing stakeholder voices to help disseminate organizational content online. This can range from retweeting or sharing organization-generated content to curating and sharing original content about the organization via social media platforms. In amplifying the organization's messaging, new audiences are reached, potentially increasing the organization's reach.

Federated Organization: An organizational structure consisting of a centralized office that creates organization-wide policy that is carried out at the local, or affiliate/chapter, level.

Ladder of Engagement: The process of cultivating relationships and creating deeper levels of online communication with stakeholders via social media. Similar to donor development, the ladder of engagement engages stakeholders in communication that ranges from simple and informational at its lowest level, to a call to action on behalf of the organization at its highest level.

Logic Model: A visual depiction of a program's theory of change. A logic model clearly identifies the resources needed and activities undertaken to achieve stated programmatic and organizational outcomes or goals.

Membership Association: A type of nonprofit organization that connects people via a shared interest, whose primary stakeholders are its dues-paying members. Membership associations can join individuals from a particular profession, an activity like a sports league, or a particular issue or interest like women's rights.

National Panhellenic Conference: The National Panhellenic Conference is one of the oldest and largest membership associations for women in the world, representing over 4 million collegiate and alumnae sorority women from 26 International and National member organizations.

Virtual Event: An event held via social media that allows individuals who are in different locations to collectively engage with an organization in a coordinated effort.

This research was previously published in Cases on Strategic Social Media Utilization in the Nonprofit Sector edited by Hugo Asencio and Rui Sun, pages 153-183, copyright year 2015 by Information Science Reference (an imprint of IGI Global).

Chapter 26

Brand Loyalty and Online Brand Communities:
Is Brand Loyalty Being Strengthened Through Social Media?

Katherine Barnet
William Paterson University, USA

Sharmila Pixy Ferris
William Paterson University, USA

ABSTRACT

This research explores the use of the online social media network Pinterest in brand-to-consumer engagement and brand loyalty. The basis of the study was formed upon previous research on brand loyalty, online brand communities, brand experiences, and emotional connections to brands. Brand loyalty is defined in this study as pins, likes, or comments on a post by one of three food brands: Cooking Light, Food Network, and Kraft Foods. Content analyses were conducted over a two-week period to observe the number and types of posts by the three brands and the interaction with their Pinterest followers. It was found that consumers who engage with brands on social networks sites, such as Pinterest, do have positive brand experiences, which has been previously linked to increased brand loyalty.

INTRODUCTION

Some of the most common, and important, questions that brand marketers ask today are in regards to brand loyalty. How do I make my customers' brand loyal? What should I consider when evaluating brand loyalty? What are my competitors doing to increase brand loyalty among their customers? What marketing tactics should I utilize that may help increase brand loyalty to my product or brand? To address these questions, brand loyalty has been researched by scholars across a variety of disciplines for some time. Researchers have found that brand loyalty can be formed or enhanced through positive brand experiences (Iglesias, Singh, & Batista-Foguet, 2011), targeted and effective communication (Duncan

DOI: 10.4018/978-1-5225-5637-4.ch026

& Moriarty, 1998; Kaplan & Haenlein, 2010; Vinerean, Cetina, Dumitrescu & Tichindelean, 2013), affective commitment or emotional connections (Chaudhuri & Holbrook, 2001; Iglesias et al., 2011), and the use of online brand communities (Kim, Choi, Qualls, and Han, 2008; Naveed, 2012). Now, if marketers incorporate these aforementioned findings in marketing or promotional tactics, will brands or products be able to reach consumers on a higher level and impact brand loyalty?

In today's over-stimulated and over-saturated consumer marketplace, it is up to the marketers to sell more than just the physical attributes or capabilities of a product or brand – it is about selling the emotional or personal experiences that come with connecting with a brand. Pine and Gilmore (1998) state that companies have realized over the last several decades that consumers are looking for more than just a product or a brand; they are seeking a brand experience. They also identified two parts of such an experience: customer participation and connection. Studies have found that consumers today are engaging with not only a brand or a product, but also companies, other customers, marketers, and communities (Muñiz & O'Guinn, 2001; McAlexander, Schouten, & Koenig, 2002; Mangold & Faulds, 2009; Schau, Muñiz, & Arnould, 2009). This paper will examine how utilizing certain online brand communities, specifically social media, can help a brand or company to foster positive brand experiences and emotional relationships and how those relationships can affect brand loyalty.

LITERATURE REVIEW

Brands are a pervasive entity in our world today. Everywhere we look, we are inundated with countless brands and brand choices. From the cars we drive to the food we eat to the electronics we use and the paper this is printed on, everything that we use and consume today is tied to a brand. Marketers and researchers alike have studied how people choose brands and what factors influence brand choices. The idea that consumers form relationships with certain brands (Fournier, 1998) and that positive, or negative, brand experiences influence brand relationships (Chaudhuri & Holbrook, 2001; Algesheimer, Dholakia, & Herrmann, 2005), can then lead to the holy grail of marketing: brand loyalty. Loyalty or commitment to a brand is a result of the decision made by a consumer that a specific brand is better than its competitors and is reinforced through repeated purchases (Day, 1969; Naveed, 2012; Oliver, 1999). Furthermore, Oliver (1999) notes that loyalty occurs "despite situational influences and marketing efforts having the potential to cause switching behavior" (p. 34). Marketers realize that true brand loyalty and a connection with a brand will be more valuable than any other marketing, advertising or promotional tactics.

As there are countless brands for every item in our marketplace, fostering relationships and encouraging brand loyalty, particularly when connecting through brand experiences, is vital for brands to stand out from the competition. One important aspect of both brand experiences and brand loyalty is affective commitment, or the emotional connection between a consumer and a brand. Allen and Meyer's 1990 study (as cited in Iglesias et al., 2011) defined affective commitment as "the customers' emotional attachment to a particular brand or store based on their identification with that store or brand" (p. 572). Additionally, affective commitment is vital for both brand experience and brand loyalty (Iglesias et al., 2011) and brand love (Albert & Merunka, 2013), which can then lead to increased buying behaviors and greater brand advocacy (Turri, Smith, & Kemp, 2013, p. 209). Greater brand advocacy, or word-of-mouth marketing, has been easier for consumers to engage in through the formation and openness of brand communities.

The idea that brand communities contribute to brand loyalty is a relatively new concept, discussed in-depth by Muñiz and O'Guinn in 2001. Hur, Ahn, and Kim (2011) take the concept of brand community one step further and explored online brand communities. They found that "well-managed brand community communication leading commitment toward a brand community will most likely enhance various types of brand loyalty" (p. 1206). Hur et al.'s definition of a brand community will be used as the basis in this study. They note that a brand community is "a group of people who possess a particular brand or who have a strong interest in a brand, and who are active both online and offline" (2011, p. 1196). One area that has become a minefield for companies, brands, and marketers interested in brand communities and brand loyalty is social media.

Social Media and Brand Communities

Over the last several years, our society has seen a great influx of social media sites and channels. Kaplan and Haenlein (2010) provide a definition for social networking sites that will be the basis for this research. "Social networking sites are applications that enable users to connect by creating personal information profiles, inviting friends and colleagues to have access to these profiles, and sending emails and instant messages between each other" (Kaplan & Haenlein, 2010, p. 63). From Facebook, LinkedIn, Twitter, and Vine, to Pinterest, Instagram, and Tumblr, every day has the potential for a new social media site to emerge, and another one to fall off our radar. Weinberg and Pehlivan (2011) found that social networks are "useful for influencing and tracking consumer beliefs and attitudes toward a product or brand" (p. 280). Some brand marketers realized early on that they needed to figure out a way to be present in these new consumer communities, as they provide unmatched new opportunities to reach their audiences. Hanna, Rohm, and Crittenden (2011) had found that "consumers are dictating the nature, extant and context of marketing exchanges" (p. 265). As a result of the more available and open dialogue forum, social media sites have provided a new and unique way for brands and companies to engage back with consumers.

Marketers realized that social media allows them to promote brands and build and cultivate brand relationships and enhance brand experiences (Chen, Fay, & Wang, 2011; Kim et al., 2008; Naveed, 2012). These new, and far-reaching, platforms now allow companies to facilitate and encourage conversations with consumers, something that is extremely unique and very different than any marketing of the past. "The quantity, quality, and speed of feedback today is another area that separates relationship marketing from traditional marketing" (Duncan & Moriarty, 1998, p. 4). Some researchers have found that utilizing social media as a supplemental program to an overall integrated marketing plan will yield the best results in terms of brand engagement, influence, and awareness (Bruhn, Schoenmueller, & Shäfer, 2012; Hanna et al., 2011; Hensel & Deis, 2010).

It is relevant and important to further explore how social media affects consumers brand experiences and loyalty because studies have found consumers who engage with brands on social networking sites report higher levels of brand attitude, brand commitment, purchasing behavior, word-of-mouth marketing, or consumer interaction (Jang, Olfman, Ko, Koh, & Kim, 2008; Jin, 2012; Kim et al., 2008). Online brand communities, specifically those formed and developed through social media, and the potential influence on brand loyalty will be explored through this research.

Online Brand Communities and Brand Experiences

Online communities have grown tremendously over the last several years as the internet has become more readily available in people's homes, and now through the use of mobile devices. However, there is limited research on how online communities can affect the brands we interact with in our daily lives. Kim et al. (2008) found that "online communities represent a growing class of marketplace communities where participants can provide and exchange information on products and services, or common interests" (p. 410). Thus, online brand communities can serve as a great resource for marketers looking for information on their consumers. Kim et al. also state that online brand communities provide important information for marketing research, can be recognized as distinctive market segments, and play an important role in enhancing brand loyalty, market share, sales, and communications (2008). If online communities can play a role in enhancing brand communities, how can or how do companies partake in the discussions? Are they helping or hindering the conversation? This research addresses these questions.

Brand site developers, as well as the brands and companies that use them, are trying to figure out how to engage with consumers on the site to keep them there and interested. Gillespie, Krishna, Oliver, Olsen, and Thiel's 1998 concept of "stickiness" (as cited in Holland & Baker, 2001) refers to "the sum of all the website qualities that induce visitors to remain at the site rather than move on to another site" (p. 37). Holland and Baker (2001) then apply the idea of 'stickiness' to brand loyalty in that length of time on a site, depth of visit, and repeat visits may indicate affective or emotional commitment or brand loyalty. Furthermore, "a site must build relevant and valuable content…to warrant customer involvement" (p. 38). Two areas that can increase 'stickiness' are personalization and community building (Holland & Baker, 2001). There is countless ways that social media users are able to both personalize their pages and interact with the social community they are part of. Brands and companies need figure out how to encourage users to continue to personalize and promote their interests, which can include their favorite brands and products. In managing and encouraging consumer participation through personalization and community building, site brand loyalty can increase and can thusly lead to affective relationships and positive brand experiences from consumer's social media is unique because it allows consumers to actively participate with their favorite brands and companies (Jin 2012).

Previous research has shown that brand loyalty can be increased through the use of online brand communities (Kim et al., 2008) and through the establishing and fostering an emotional connection between consumers and brands (Iglesias et al., 2011). Based on the above, the following problem was advanced for research: What is the relationship between brand loyalty and online brand communities?

METHODOLOGY

This research focused on engagement with Pinterest as an online brand community and how it affects brand loyalty through a potentially positive brand experience. Pinterest is an online social media site launched in 2010 that allows users, or "pinners," to 'pin' images to a virtual pinboard and follow and share with other users and brands. Pinboards are created by each user depending on his or her interests or hobbies. Pinners can follow brands, people, or companies and pin, like, or send any posts that interest them. Pinterest is a very attractive platform for brands and companies since it is "a highly visual medium that gives businesses a chance to catch the eye of consumers with compelling images and colorful infographics" (Griswold, 2013, p. 1). It is also important to note that the ShareThis *Consumer Sharing*

Trend Report for third quarter 2013 on the amount of content that people shared noted that Pinterest grew 19.22%, LinkedIn grew 15.11%, Facebook grew 14.78% and Twitter declined -7.66% (Wolfrom, 2013). As discussed earlier, achieving affective commitment, or an emotional connection with a brand, through brand experiences in online communities can affect brand loyalty.

Description of Methodology

Content analysis was selected as the appropriate research method for this study. Vogt (as cited in Reinard, 2007) defined content analysis as "any several research techniques used to describe and systematically analyze the content of written, spoke, or pictorial communication" (2005, p. 59). The steps of content analysis include (1) defining and limiting the communication population to be studied, (2) selecting coding units and classification systems, (3) selecting a sampling of messages from the communication population, (4) coding the content or treatment of the messages, (5) analyzing the data, and (6) interpreting the results as it relates to the research question (Reinard, 2007).

Content analysis allows a researcher to efficiently move through large amounts of data and simplify the details and information. It also serves as a tool for both description and explanation. Content analyses are particularly useful when studying nontraditional setting, such as monitoring mass media communication (Reinard, 2007), and in the case of this research, Pinterest. Limitations of content analyses include that the researcher is unable to draw cause-and-effect conclusions, it can be difficult to find representative samplings of the communication message or content, and the results of one content analysis generally cannot be applied to others that use different categories (Reinard, 2007). In relation to this specific study, the results were only applicable to the area of brand marketing being studied, which is food brands, and those active on Pinterest.

Research Design

This study's research question outlined its two variables as online brand communities and brand loyalty, or more specifically, how using an online brand community (Pinterest) and how it affected brand loyalty. Pinterest was previously defined as an online social media site that allows pinners to pin images to a virtual pinboard and follow and share with other users and brands. Brand loyalty, as it relates to brand engagement or a brand experience with Pinterest, referred to pins, likes, and comments by a pinner.

The research was conducted by following the Pinterest pages of three major food brands for two weeks to observe the amount of pins that a brand created in one day and the subsequent consumer/follower interaction with the brands, which included "likes" and comments. The interaction was recorded after one day of the initial posting and again after one week of the posting. The types of pins were categorized into the following categories: recipe pins, brand or chef pins, cooking tip pins, and other. Comments were also reviewed and categorized to observe any feedback from users. Categorizations for comments included positive, negative, both, and other. See Table 1 for details on comment categorization.

The brands that were studied were a food magazine brand (Cooking Light), a food consumer company (Kraft Recipes), and a food television network (Food Network). The total number of followers, total number of boards, and total number of pins was considered when selecting the three brands. As of December 15, 2013, Cooking Light has 136,200 followers, 98 boards, and 5,808 pins; Kraft Recipes has 143,123 followers, 60 boards, and 3,184 pins; Food Network has 166,111 followers, 67 boards, and

Table 1. Categorization of comments

Comment	Explanation	Example
Positive	Positive in nature	"This looks yummy!"; "I can't wait to try this!"; "I make this all the time"
Negative	Negative in nature	"I wasn't a fan of this"; "I made this but it didn't turn out the way I wanted"; "Too salty for me"
Both	Has both positive and negative parts	"I don't like "spicy" but it is a good start on a concept I could customize to my taste"
Other	Neither positive nor negative	#Kraftrecipes; "@Food Network - Hello, I have a lot of appetizers on my boards and would love to be a contributor on your Let's Game Day board. Thank you."

4,098 pins. These three segments were selected because they are common areas that consumers look for cooking or recipe tips – magazines, television, and the brands they buy.

A pretest was conducted over a period of three days prior to the designated two weeks of data collection to ensure that all coding categories were exhaustive. Reliability was checked through the use of another coder to confirm the proper categorization of data. The data was then entered into Microsoft Office Excel, which allowed for succinct and sufficient data recording. After data was entered, the researcher studied the data summary to observe any patterns across the types of pins, number of interactions with pinners/followers, and the types of interactions with pinners/followers.

RESULTS

Data collection was completed over the course of two weeks, from February 9, 2014 through February 23, 2014. The three brands were initially selected two months prior to data collection because they are common brands that consumers look for cooking or recipe tips and had a similar range of followers. By the time the data collection began, Cooking Light increased by 14,097 followers and 717 pins, Kraft Recipes increased by 10,522 followers and 584 pins, and Food Network increased by 104,517 followers and 417 pins.

Further review of the Pinterest brand boards showed that some boards were contributor allowed boards, meaning that certain people that were approved by the brand to contribute to boards were able to add pins to the boards. 48 out of the 98 Cooking Light boards, 2 out of the 60 Kraft Recipes boards, and 34 out of the 67 Food Network boards were contributor allowed boards and were excluded from analysis. Only brand specific boards were followed and observed for data collection. Of the remaining brand only board, not all boards were posted on daily. Food Network was the only brand that had one specific board that was contributed to daily – their "Let's Cook: Recipe of the Day" board. In addition, there were some boards across all three brands that were not pinned to at all during the two-week period. The majority of these were seasonal boards, such as boards focused on fall or winter holidays or seasonal boards.

Over the two-week period, Cooking Light posted 195 pins, Kraft Recipes posted 231 pins, and Food Network posted 107 pins (Figure 1). Cooking Light posted an average of 14 pins per day, with the highest daily pins at 23 and the lowest daily pins at 3; Kraft Recipes posted an average of 17 pins per day, with

Figure 1. Increase in Pins

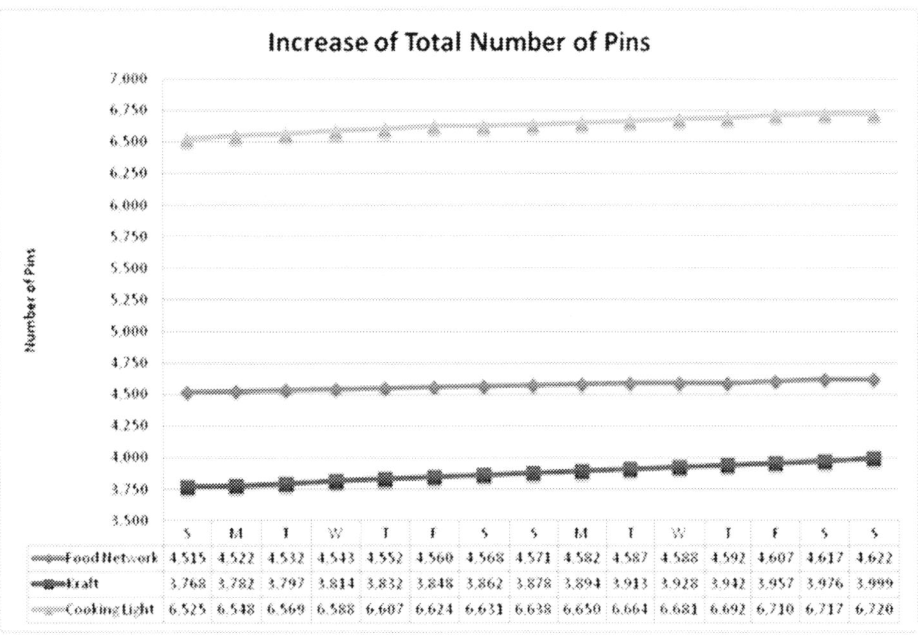

	S	M	T	W	T	F	S	S	M	T	W	T	F	S	S
Food Network	4,515	4,522	4,532	4,543	4,552	4,560	4,568	4,571	4,582	4,587	4,588	4,592	4,607	4,617	4,622
Kraft	3,768	3,782	3,797	3,814	3,832	3,848	3,862	3,878	3,894	3,913	3,928	3,942	3,957	3,976	3,999
Cooking Light	6,525	6,548	6,569	6,588	6,607	6,624	6,631	6,638	6,650	6,664	6,681	6,692	6,710	6,717	6,720

the highest daily pins at 27 and the lowest daily pins at 14; Food Network posted an average of 7 pins per day, with the highest daily pins at 15 and the lowest daily pins at 1 (Figure 2).

Each pin was further coded into specific food or brand categories: entrée, side, dessert, brand, or tip. Out of the total 533 of pins across the three brands, 435 were coded as entrées, 28 were coded as sides, 50 were coded as dessert, 10 were coded as brand, and 10 were coded as tips.

In addition to tracking the number of pins per day, the amount of interaction between the brands and Pinterest users was tracked. The number of re-pins, likes, and comments per brand pin were collected and coded. Data was reviewed one day after the initial post and 7 days after the initial post. The highest number of re-pins after one day of the initial posting was a for a Food Network Valentine's Chocolate Molten Lava Cake post with 655 pins, which tied with another Food Network Dessert post (How to Make a Perfect Chocolate Souffle) for the highest number of likes (52) after one day. The highest number of re-pins after one week of the initial posting was for a Cooking Light post (28 Baked Chicken Recipes) with 897 re-pins, an increase of 668 re-pins versus the initial 229 re-pins. This Cooking Light Baked Chicken Recipe post tied with another Cooking Light post (Chipotle Bean Burritos) with the highest increase in likes (+39) after one week of the initial posting.

DISCUSSION

The years 2003 to present have been marked as the era of social media, with notable launches of social media platforms including Friendster in 2002, MySpace and LinkedIn in 2003, Facebook in 2004, YouTube in 2005, Twitter in 2006, Tumblr in 2007, Pinterest in 2010, and Google+ in 2011 (Bennett, 2013). What is even more interesting is the amount of social media platforms that launched alongside the

Figure 2. Daily pins across the three brands in February 2014

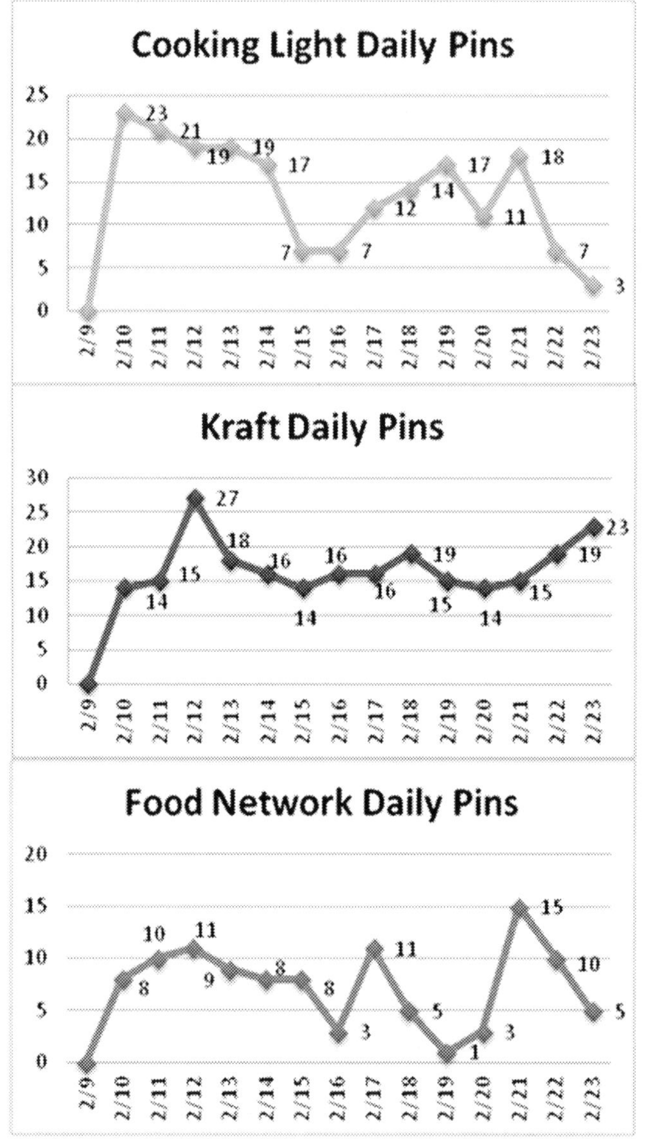

prominent ones that are no longer part of the mainstream conversation, or the ones that will be launched in the future. With all these new communication channels that consumers have access to, companies and brands have been trying to figure out the best way to penetrate these markets and connect with their audiences. Some brands have learned faster than others, but one thing that has emerged is that identifying your target audience and using the right platform for your consumers are big drivers of success.

Social Media Examiner has produced an annual Social Media Marketing Industry Report for the last five years to review the biggest platforms, consumer trends, and goals of marketers as it relates social media. The Report identified five key areas where marketers are looking for information: social tactics, engagement, measurement, tools, and strategies (Stelzner, 2013). There are also nine key benefits of using social media marketing that were identified through the research: increased exposure, increased traffic, provided marketplace insight, developed loyal fans, generated leads, improved search rankings, grown business partnerships, reduced marketing expenses, and improved sales.

The same Social Media Examiner report (Stelzner, 2012) found that, of the 14 major social media networks or platforms, Pinterest ranked #7, with 41% of marketers saying they used the platform (Stelzner, 2013). This is even more noteworthy for my study considering in the previous year's report, Pinterest was categorized as a photo-sharing site and lumped with Instagram and Flickr (Stelzner, 2012). More notable was that 51% of marketers in the 2013 report planned to increase their use of Pinterest in marketing efforts. When breaking it out even further in marketing segments, business-to-consumer marketers were 57% more likely to increase their Pinterest use versus business-to-business marketers at 44% (Stelzner, 2013). These insights are particularly interesting when the results of the current study are applied to the key areas and key benefits.

In the current study, the use and engagement of Pinterest by consumers with three brands was tracked over a two-week period, coded, and analyzed to study brand loyalty. The most effective social marketing tactics and tools and the best ways to engage with consumers are relevant for this study as engagement with the brands was studied using a particular social media platform. The majority of the key benefits, if not all of them, as outlined by Stelzner (2013) can be identified as present when reviewing the engagement of a consumer with a brand's Pinterest board, or any other social media page. Each Pinterest post or brand board increases the exposure and connection of the brand to the consumer, can lead to increased traffic on a brand website as a result of links included with each post, can provide marketplace insight if trends are identified, generate leads considering consumers are interacting directly with the brands and improve search rankings organically as it is rich content being posted and shared among users. It can also be argued that partnerships can be formed between brands and other brands or bloggers, reduced marketing expenses as a result of marketing digitally as opposed to in print or broadcast media, and improved sales as a result of content shared. All of these areas can be seen as aiding in the development of brand loyalty among consumers because brands are increasing their overall reach and engaging with consumers in a unique and meaningful way.

This study, over the course of a two-week period, found that there were 533 pins that were added to the three brand boards, with Kraft Recipes as the most active brand in regards to postings, followed by Cooking Light and Food Network. Kraft received the highest number of comments at 18, followed by Cooking Light at 16 and Food Network at 4. When reviewing the content of the comments, there was minimal interaction, if at all, with the brands with majority of the comments, with the exception of Cooking Light. Several Cooking Light followers asked the brand to be added to their contributor boards. Cooking Light responded to each post thanking the follower for the request but denying access as the boards are reserved for bloggers. This shows that the consumers are engaged with the brands and their social media presence and wanted to become even more engaged. This can be interpreted as a positive brand experience and high brand loyalty, as reviewed previously.

In regards to the content and types of posts by the brands, recipe posts were the most widely posted content type, with minimal cooking tip or branded posts. Many of the pins revolved around consumer trends and events, such as Valentine's Day, the Olympics and American pride, National Margarita Day, winter comfort food, and desserts. These overall themes, or the ideas behind the themes, are relevant for marketers who are looking to connect with consumers. Particular dates or events such as Valentine's Day or the Super Bowl or providing winter comfort food recipes during the cold months may seem like the obvious choices, but lesser known ones such as National Margarita Day or recipes that highlight American pride can also generate high consumer involvement and interest.

Another interesting finding was that many of the pins that Cooking Light posted on Pinterest were later featured in their next month's magazine print issue. For example, the posts were tracked for two weeks in February, which aligns with the on-sale period of the March issue of the magazine. This is a great effort by the brand to produce similar, cohesive, and connected messages across their platforms. It should also be pointed out that the need for fresh content is important. Brands that are able to do so should make sure that they are sharing different types of content across platforms, but also maintaining a singular brand image and message consistently.

Limitations and Suggestions for Future Research

The current study reviewed the use of a singular and growing social media platform for a specific group of brands over a two-week period. Additional information such as posting patterns of brands, overall yearly trends, over what period of time the frequency and increase in posts and engagement with consumers is greatest, and information regarding potential brand penetration and lifts in sales, particularly for those with e-commerce capabilities, could be gathered if the length of time and brand pool is increased. Future research could also expand the monitoring to social media platforms. The current study provides a solid foundation for future research on the use of social media for brand engagement and consumer loyalty.

CONCLUSION

The overall goal of this study was to review the relationship of online brand communities with brand loyalty. The study focused on one particular online community, Pinterest, and three cooking related brands that are active on the site. The brands were connected with their target audience, who was already previously engaged with the brands, and created a positive brand experience in each post. This brand experience was measured through the number of re-pins, likes, and comments. The study confirms with industry data that the use of Pinterest in business-to-consumer (B2C) relationships has increased and can result in numerous benefits, including increased exposure, increase online traffic, marketplace insight, and brand loyalty.

REFERENCES

Albert, N., & Merunka, D. (2013). The role of brand love in consumer-brand relationships. *Journal of Consumer Marketing*, *30*(3), 258–266. doi:10.1108/07363761311328928

Algesheimer, R., Dholakia, U. M., & Herrmann, A. (2005). The social influence of brand community: Evidence from European car clubs. *Journal of Marketing*, *69*(3), 19–34. doi:10.1509/jmkg.69.3.19.66363

Bennett, S. (2013). A brief history of social media (1969 – 2012). Retrieved from https://www.medi-abistro.com/alltwitter/social-media-1969-2012_b45869

Bruhn, M., Schoenmuller, V., & Schäfer, D. B. (2012). Are social media replacing traditional media in terms of brand equity creation? *Management Research Review*, *35*(9), 770–790. doi:10.1108/01409171211255948

Chaudhuri, A., & Holbrook, M. B. (2001). The chain of effects from brand trust and brand affect to brand performance: The role of brand loyalty. *Journal of Marketing*, *65*(2), 81–93. doi:10.1509/jmkg.65.2.81.18255

Chen, Y., Fay, S., & Wang, Q. (2011). The role of marketing in social media: How online consumer reviews evolve. *Journal of Interactive Marketing*, *25*(2), 85–94. doi:10.1016/j.intmar.2011.01.003

Day, G. S. (1969). A two-dimensional concept of brand loyalty. *Journal of Advertising Research*, *9*(3), 29–35.

Duncan, T., & Moriarty, S. E. (1998). A communication-based marketing model for managing relationships. *Journal of Marketing*, *62*(2), 1–13. doi:10.2307/1252157

Fournier, S. (1998). Consumers and their brands: Developing relationship theory in consumer research. *The Journal of Consumer Research*, *24*(4), 343–373. doi:10.1086/209515

Griswold, A. (2013, November 5). Pinterest is now the fastest growing content-sharing platform. *Business Insider.* Retrieved from http://www.businessinsider.com/pinterest-is-fastest-growing-content-sharing-platform-2013-11

Hanna, R., Rohm, A., & Crittenden, V. L. (2011). We're all connected: The power of the social media ecosystem. *Business Horizons*, *54*(3), 265–273. doi:10.1016/j.bushor.2011.01.007

Hensel, K., & Deis, M. H. (2010). Using social media to increase advertising and improve marketing. *The Entrepreneurial Executive*, *15*, 87–97.

Holland, J., & Baker, S. M. (2001). Customer participation in creating site brand loyalty. *Journal of Interactive Marketing*, *15*(4), 34–45. doi:10.1002/dir.1021

Hur, W., Ahn, K., & Kim, M. (2011). Building brand loyalty through managing brand community commitment. *Management Decision*, *49*(7), 1194–1213. doi:10.1108/00251741111151217

Iglesias, O., Singh, J. J., & Batista-Foguet, J. M. (2011). The role of brand experience and affective commitment in determining brand loyalty. *Journal of Brand Management*, *18*(8), 570–582. doi:10.1057/bm.2010.58

Jang, H., Olfman, L., Ko, I., Koh, J., & Kim, K. (2008). The influence of on-line brand community characteristics on community commitment and brand loyalty. *International Journal of Electronic Commerce*, *12*(3), 57–80. doi:10.2753/JEC1086-4415120304

Jin, S. A. (2012). The potential of social media for luxury brand management. *Marketing Intelligence & Planning*, *30*(7), 687–699. doi:10.1108/02634501211273805

Kaplan, A. M., & Haenlein, M. (2010). Users of the world, unite! The challenges and opportunities of social media. *Business Horizons*, *53*(1), 59–68. doi:10.1016/j.bushor.2009.09.003

Kim, J. W., Choi, J., Qualls, W., & Han, K. (2008). It takes a marketplace community to raise brand commitment: The role of online communities. *Journal of Marketing Management*, *24*(3), 409–431. doi:10.1362/026725708X306167

Mangold, W. G., & Faulds, D. J. (2009). Social media: The new hybrid element of the promotion mix. *Business Horizons*, *52*(4), 357–365. doi:10.1016/j.bushor.2009.03.002

McAlexander, J. H., Schouten, J. W., & Koenig, H. F. (2002). Building brand community. *Journal of Marketing*, *66*(1), 38–54. doi:10.1509/jmkg.66.1.38.18451

Muñiz, A. M. Jr, & O'Guinn, T. C. (2001). Brand community. *The Journal of Consumer Research*, *27*(4), 412–432. doi:10.1086/319618

Naveed, N. (2012). Role of social media on public relation, brand involvement, and brand commitment. *Interdisciplinary Journal of Contemporary Research in Business*, *3*(9), 904–913.

Oliver, R. L. (1999). Whence Consumer Loyalty? *Journal of Marketing*, *63*, 33–44. doi:10.2307/1252099

Pine, B. J. II, & Gilmore, J. H. (1998). Welcome to the experience economy. *Harvard Business Review*, *76*(4), 97–105. PMID:10181589

Reinard, J. C. (2007). *Introduction to communication research* (4th ed.). New York, NY: McGraw-Hill.

Schau, H. J., Muñiz, A. M. Jr, & Arnould, E. J. (2009). How brand community practices create value. *Journal of Marketing*, *73*(5), 30–51. doi:10.1509/jmkg.73.5.30

Stelzner, M. (2012). 2012 social media marketing industry report: How marketers are using social media to grow their businesses. Retrieved from http://www.socialmediaexaminer. com/SocialMediaMarketingIndustryReport2012.pdf

Stelzner, M. (2013). 2013 social media marketing industry report: How marketers are using social media to grow their businesses. Retrieved from http://www.socialmediaexaminer. com/SocialMediaMarketingIndustryReport2013.pdf

Turri, A. M., Smith, K. H., & Kemp, E. (2013). Developing affective brand commitment through social media. *Journal of Electronic Commerce*, *14*(3), 201–214.

Vinerean, S., Cetina, I., Dumitrescu, L., & Tichindelean, M. (2013). The effects of social media marketing on online consumer behavior. *International Journal of Business and Management*, *8*(14), 66–79. doi:10.5539/ijbm.v8n14p66

Weinberg, B. D., & Pehlivan, E. (2011). Social spending: Managing the social media mix. *Business Horizons*, *54*(3), 275–282. doi:10.1016/j.bushor.2011.01.008

Wolfrom, M. (2013, November 1). Consumer sharing trends report. *ShareThis*. Retrieved from http://www.sharethis.com/blog/consumer-sharing-trends-report/#more-9308

This research was previously published in the International Journal of Online Marketing (IJOM), 6(3); edited by Hatem El-Gohary, pages 50-61, copyright year 2016 by IGI Publishing (an imprint of IGI Global).

Chapter 27
Advertising in the World of Social Media-Based Brand Communities

Mohammad Reza Habibi
California State University – Fullerton, USA

Michel Laroche
Concordia University, Canada

Marie-Odile Richard
State University of New York Polytechnic Institute, USA

ABSTRACT

Social media has revolutionized marketing practices and created many opportunities for smart marketers to take advantage of its unique characteristics. The purpose of this chapter is to introduce the concept of Social Media-Based Brand Communities to advertisers and show how they can use these communities to work for them in creating and distributing favorable communication messages to masses of consumers. The authors underscore that consumers in a brand community can be employed as unpaid volunteer ambassadors of the brand who diligently try to create favorable impressions about the brand in the external world. Social media has also empowered them to do so through participating in brand communities based in social media. These communities, however, are different from conventional brand communities on at least five dimensions: social context, structure, scale, storytelling, and myriad affiliated communities. Therefore, marketers should treat such communities differently. This chapter provides the essentials all marketers should know before facilitating brand communities in social media.

INTRODUCTION

It was not long ago when Muniz and Schau (2007) applied and studied the concept of "vigilant marketing" in the brand community context. Observing the power of user generated content technologies in enabling consumers to have a stronger and more creative voice as well as the power of brand communi-

DOI: 10.4018/978-1-5225-5637-4.ch027

ties to gather thousands of brand devotees together, they stated that brand communities could be a holy grail for advertisers. Members of a brand community resemble unpaid evangelists that spread marketing communication messages with high levels of creativity on behalf of the brand.

Borrowing the term "vigilante marketing" from Ives (2004), Muniz and Schau (2007, p. 35) defined it as "unpaid advertising and marketing efforts, including one-to-one, one-to-many, and many-to-many commercially oriented communications, undertaken by brand loyalists on behalf of the brand." They conducted a qualitative study on an Apple's web-based (web 1.0) community and showed that consumers (members of the community) collectively create, disseminate, and absorb effective communication messages within a brand community context, which is strictly controlled by volunteer members. They also showed that consumers are highly sophisticated in and adept at mimicking advertising messages and creating symbolic meanings for the brand.

Based on their findings and in line with other advertising gurus (Garfield, 2005; Shultz, 2005), they predicted that the future of advertising will be dramatically different and will face substantial challenges: "Meeting these challenges will require a major shift in the way advertising is defined and practiced." (Muniz & Schau 2007, p. 36). Although they were right in their prediction about the challenges of advertising and the necessity of shift in advertising practices, what perhaps they did not expect at that moment was the enormous explosion of social media as the platform on which billions of consumers can easily access content creation capabilities, keep in touch with each other, and easily communicate with a strong voice (Fournier & Avery, 2011; Kaplan & Haenlein, 2010). This explosion gave consumers a great power as brand messengers not seen in the history of consumer research. As a result the power of advertising has become limited recently in the age of social media (Kohli, Suri, & Kapoor, 2015).

The purpose of this chapter is to show a way that can be helpful to advertisers in order to harness the enormous power of social media in favor of their advertising and communication goals. Therefore, the chapter introduces the concept of Social Media Based Brand Community (SMBBC) to advertisers and shows how they can use these communities to play an important role, on their behalf, in creating and distributing favorable communication messages to masses of consumers. Using the latest research and empirical findings, the chapter elaborates on essential characteristics of such communities that marketers and advertisers should know while facilitating brand community practices. We also elaborate on future research implications.

WHAT IS A BRAND COMMUNITY?

Initially, brand communities were recognized as a proper alternative for performing relationship marketing (Berry, 1995). The main idea behind relationship marketing was keeping one-on-one relationships with customers to enhance their loyalty and satisfaction; however, developing such relationships was not cost efficient (Iaccobucci, 1994). It would be more difficult for a firm to keep a distinct relationship with each one of its customers than having agents who would do so on the behalf of the firm. Therefore, brand communities, in which consumers perform many tasks on a brand's behalf, can efficiently actualize relationship marketing (Muniz & O'Guinn, 2001). In a brand community each customer has a set of relationships with the brand and other customers.

A brand community is defined as a "specialized, non-geographically bound community based on a structured set of social relations among admirers of a brand" (Muniz & O'Guinn, 2001, p. 412). It is essentially a place (physical or virtual) in which brand aficionados and devotees gather together. The first reason that these people gather together is perhaps similar to liking a topic but it is definitely not the only one. Members gain a lot of other benefits from participating in such communities. Mainly they somehow fulfill the social need to be identified with symbols of and attached to social groups (Tajfel & Turner, 1985) and to develop their self-concept (Muniz & Schau, 2002). Moreover, consumers gain some utilitarian values (McAlexander, Schouten, & Koenig, 2002). For instance consumers gain required skills to better use the brand. For brands, in addition to being an alternative for relationship marketing, brand communities are a source of innovation and new product development (Fuller, Matzler, & Hoppe, 2008; Von Hippel, 2005). This is because brand community members are committed to the welfare of the brand community members and of the brand as a whole.

The texture of a brand community involves four different relationships among customers and brand community elements (McAlexander, Schouten, & Koenig, 2002). This is called the customer centric model of brand community which is illustrated in Figure 1. Compared to previous models of brand community which assumed relationships only among members, this model is more comprehensive and includes all the relationships among all the players in a community. McAlexander and his colleagues (2002) not only showed that customers build relationships with the product, the brand, other customer, and the company, but they also indicated that these relationships enhance customer loyalty to the brand as well.

Is Any Collective a Brand Community?

Since the inception of brand community research, two main questions have always been probed by researchers: how can one call a brand related collective a brand community? And whether a brand community can exist on different platforms. These questions are highly relevant since the presence of brand communities on different platforms means that marketers can magnify the success and benefits of brand communities by leveraging the capabilities and advantages of different platforms. As mentioned, one of the advantages of brand communities is having members to participate in vigilante marketing. For example, McAlexander and his colleagues (2002) identify the brand community markers in a temporary brandfest among admirers of a brand. They show that even facilitating a temporary brand community can involve customers in unpaid marketing and advertising activities, and also transcend their experi-

Figure 1. Customer centric model of brand community (Source: McAlexander, Schouten, and Koenig, 2002)

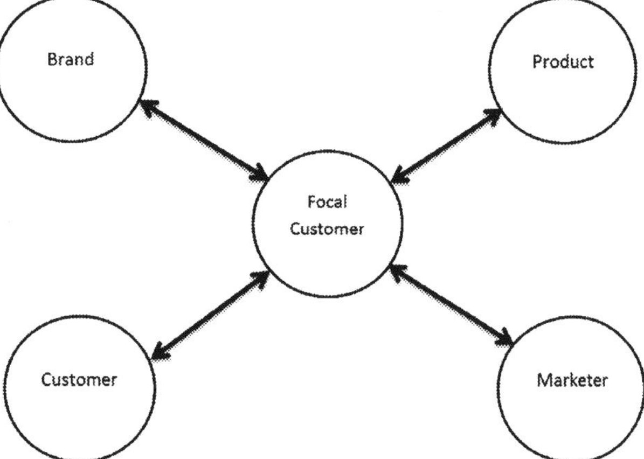

ence and consequently make them feel more obligated to the brand. Now let us have a quick discussion on how researchers have answered the above questions.

How can we call a collective a brand community? All brand communities have three markers that should be manifested in the collective in order to be called a community. These three markers are shared consciousness, rituals and traditions, and obligations to society (Muniz & O'Guinn, 2001). *Shared consciousness* is the feeling of unity among members. It is because of shared consciousness that members feel like family members toward each other and also distinguish themselves from outsiders especially from rival communities (Bagozzi & Dholakia, 2006*a*; Muniz & O'Guinn, 2001). It is shared consciousness that leads members of a community to defend their borders and try to preserve their collective identity from being affected (Habibi, Laroche, & Richard, 2014).

The second indicator of a brand community is *rituals and traditions*. These are usually symbolic practices that aim to preserve the identity, meanings, and history of the brand (Muniz & O'Guinn, 2001). For example, members of a community develop and use a common jargon that is meaningful only inside the borders of the community. Finally, the third marker is called *obligations to society*. It incites members to be conscious of being responsible toward welfare of their fellow members and the community. That is why in many occasions they do not hesitate to provide assistance to each other on behalf of the brand (Muniz & O'Guinn, 2001; Schau, Muniz, & Arnould, 2009).

Although there are some research articles that provide measures for these indicators (Habibi, Laroche, & Richard, 2014b), qualitative observation is perhaps the most common method to identify these indicators and qualify a brand related collective as a brand community. Fortunately, there is research that directly or indirectly examines if brand communities are present on the basis of different platforms. This research stream shows that brand communities can be physical or offline (Algesheimer, Dholakia & Herrmann, 2005; Muniz & O'Guinn, 2001), virtual or online (Adjei, Noble, & Noble, 2010; Muniz & Schau, 2007; Thompson & Sinha, 2008), social media-based (Habibi, Laroche, & Richard, 2014a; Zaglia, 2013), of different sizes (Bagozzi & Dholakia, 2006*b*; McAlexander & Koenig, 2010), within different temporal situations (Schouten, McAlexander, & Koenig, 2007), and also can form around different products from high involving to convenience products (Cova & Pace, 2006).

Marketers and advertisers should note that only after these indicators are identified, can one apply the brand community concepts and practice them. Therefore, confronting collectives that do not manifest these indicators, marketers perhaps should better emphasize community building approaches (Kilambi, Laroche, & Richard, 2013). There are several studies in this regard elaborating on them but this is beyond the scope of this chapter. Also note that members of a community have different motivations and levels of passion in a community. Perhaps, the meaning of the community and the felt sense of connectedness and commitment toward the community is not equal for all members. Conventional brand communities, either online or offline, have some sort of hierarchical mechanisms to separate devotees from less devotees (Schouten & McAlexander, 1995; Sicilia & Palazon, 2008). Marketers should know that devotees are more willing to spread the word about the brand and engage in vigilante marketing.

How a Brand Community Can Be an Environment for Brand Evangelists?

As mentioned, members of a brand community tend to defend their community and to preserve their identity. They are motivated in creating their own meanings and love for the brand even in the absence of marketers and brand representatives (Muniz & Schau, 2005; 2007). One particular research that shows how brand community members act as brand ambassadors was conducted by Schau and his colleagues

(2009). They studied all practices in a brand community that generate some sort of added value for the brand and members of its community. They categorized these activities into 12 different practices which then were clustered into four thematic groups. One of these groups is called "impression management" which includes two different practices consumers perform in order to create a favorable impression on outsiders. This is exactly where members commit themselves to vigilante marketing as unpaid advertisers and altruistic emissaries of the brand to the external world, to non-users, and to potential customers (Schau, Muñiz, & Arnould, 2009).

Impression management is actualized via "evangelizing" and "justifying." Evangelizing refers to situations where members purposefully share good news about the brand, and try to inspire others to use the brand. Similar to the advertiser who take a one-to-many approach, evangelizing members try to convince masses of people like "preaching from the mountain top" (Schau, Muñiz, & Arnould, 2009, p. 43). On the other hand, through justifying practices, members of the community rationalize their devotion to the brand and explain to outsiders and marginal members why they spend so much time and effort for the benefit of the community. Again, similar to advertisers, they try to convince essentially potential customers why what they care about a lot is worthy and valuable.

The emergence of social media has given extraordinary tools to brand aficionados in order to practice evangelizing and justifying practices (Habibi, Laroche, & Richard, 2014a). Consumers now can easily communicate with their dense network of connections in social media (Hennig-Thurau, Hofacker, & Bloching, 2013) and therefore pass along information very quickly within their interconnected networks (Kohli, Suri, & Kapoor, 2015). But this does not necessarily guarantee that consumers would pass along positive news about the brand or act as brand evangelists. Remember evangelizing and justifying happens within brand communities. Thus, one should first check if brand communities exist on social media and if so how different they are. Then their implications for advertisers are developed.

SOCIAL MEDIA BASED BRAND COMMUNITIES AS ADVERTISING CHANNELS

Social media has penetrated all aspects of our lives on a daily basis. Consider these numbers; Facebook alone has about more than 1.2 billion active users and the number is growing rapidly; the age range of social media users is anywhere between 13 to 65+ (Jones, 2013); people spend about one third of their waking day on social media activities (Lang, 2010), which range from entertainment to professional practices (Jones, 2013). These vast numbers–in addition to the potential power of social media to change marketing and consumer behavior–has incited most marketers to jump on the social media bandwagon with the hope of gaining more customer, sales, and brand awareness. In fact, more than 93% of marketers have already used social media for business purposes (Jones, 2013). However, marketing on social media is highly complicated considering the social media's turbulent environment.

To symbolically illustrate the turbulent environment of social media communication and advertising, Hennig-Thurau, Hofacker, & Bloching, (2013) use the "pinball" metaphor as opposed to the "bowling" metaphor for advertising before the emergence of social media. In contrast to bowling which is a linear and one-directional game, pinball is a highly interactive game in which the ball can change its path unpredictably at any moment depending on what element in the game hits the ball. It was due to this unpredictability of social media that many scholars argued, anecdotally, that social media is not a natural environment for brands and they warned them to stay away or be very cautious while using social media (Fournier & Avery, 2011).

However, sophisticated research and empirical findings show that social media is a natural environment for brands and especially for community building practices (Habibi, Laroche, & Richard, 2014a; Zaglia 2013). We earlier mentioned that consumers are in a network of firm-customer-customer relationships within a brand community. This network is supported by the new paradigm of communications in the context of social media; marketer-customer-customer (Kohli, Suri, & Kapoor, 2015). Habibi, Laroche, and Richard, (2014*a*) argue that brand communities, their markers and building blocks exist on social media and that using the brand community perspective to conduct marketing practices in the social media environment is appropriate. They study two different brand related collectives and show that not only brand community markers are manifested but also practices such as evangelizing and justifying are strongly practiced by members of the brand community. Moreover, the interactive features of social media such as photo sharing, video sharing, liking, and commenting have empowered members in telling their stories differently to impress outsiders and the external world.

Considering these studies, one can safely consider SMBBCs as communication and advertising channels in which marketers and members together and interactively communicate brand messages. Consumers through vigilante marketing and impression management practices play the role of unpaid, devoted advertisers for the brand. These free advertisers can be even more influential than paid and sponsored advertisements. What advertising practitioners should consider is to facilitate conversations and foster the feelings of unity as a family or community among members. This however should be done keeping in mind the unique dimensions associated with brand communities that are established on social media.

Unique Aspects of Social Media Based Brand Communities

SMBBCs have at least five unique dimensions that make them distinguishable from previous brand communities studied in the brand community literature (Habibi, Laroche, & Richard, 2014*a*). Marketers have to keep these dimensions in mind for they mandate different approaches while facilitating brand communities in social media. The first dimension is *social context* (Habibi, Laroche, & Richard, 2014*a*). The social context of SMBBCs in which members socialize is completely different from previous online and offline brand communities; it can be located somewhere between conventional online and face-to-face communities. In SMBBCs, usually most members use their real identities (Ross et al., 2009) so they can gain a great deal of information such as age, gender, location, life status, profession, and interests by clicking on a fellow's profile. Also they can instantly start conversations. According to McAlexander and his colleagues (2002) the social context can be one of the main differentiators among communities yet it is an under-studied factor in brand communities. A related study implies that this unique social context can influence members' evaluation of the brand (Naylor, Lamberton, & West, 2012). The research shows that members prefer like-minded and similar people in their community.

The second dimension is called *structure* (Habibi, Laroche, & Richard, 2014*a*). Unlike conventional brand communities, SMBBCs lack some sort of structure or hierarchy through which one can distinguish devotees from newbies or newcomers. In physical brand communities there is usually an explicit hierarchy that distinguishes hard core members from pretenders (Schouten & McAlexander, 1995). Also, in conventional online communities there is a system implemented that ranks members based on their participation volume for instance (Brodie, Ilic, Juric, & Hollebeek, 2013). But, in SMBBCs, such ranking system does not exist and considering the scale of these communities, organizers of the page are a small fraction of the community. This lack of hierarchy might create some confusion among members when they communicate together (Habibi, Laroche, & Richard, 2014*a*).

The third dimension is *scale*. The scale in SMBBCs is often extraordinary, containing more than millions of members from different areas of the globe. Such mega sized brand communities are unique in the history of brand communities. Although this might be perceived as a very good opportunity for marketers and advertisers to have numerous fans at the same place and time, the implications of this dimension are yet to be explored empirically.

The fourth unique dimension is *content and storytelling* (Habibi, Laroche, & Richard, 2014*a*). Storytelling is perhaps the most commonly used vehicle members use to transmit symbolic meanings and their experiences with the brand to other members as well as the community as a whole. In contrast to the text-based medium of storytelling in other communities, in SMBBCs consumers mainly use a mix of photos, videos, and text to narrate their stories. Also other members can instantly react to the stories and provide support or emotional empathy with the storyteller. This way of storytelling is unique and can make stories much more interesting to the audience. Advertisers can look at this approach of storytelling as a creative way consumers are involved in evangelizing the brand by linking the brand to their personal lives. Stories usually make a lasting impression on the audience.

Finally, the fifth dimension is the *myriads of affiliated brand communities* (Habibi, Laroche, & Richard, 2014*a*). Social media enables consumers to initiate communities around their favorite topics with minimal cost and high ease of use. Therefore, in their study Habibi and his colleagues observed numerous brand communities which were established around a given brand. This can increase chance issues such as multiple memberships and identities (McAlexander, Schouten, & Koenig, 2002). Although these communities admire the same brand, their approaches, goals, and specific interests might be different. Therefore, advertisers should consider the specific characteristics of each community.

Advantages and Challenges of the New Channel Over Previous Channels

For marketers and advertisers there are many advantages associated to SMBBCs. Considering their unique dimensions, the SMBBCs can be considered as wide public advertising and communication channels with millions of brand aficionados together at the same time and place. These channels not only provide one-to-many communication capability to the advertisers, they also provide many-to-many communications and advertising messages, as members of the community are involved in impression management practices. This gives advertisers a historical opportunity to interact with consumers. However, they should be highly cautious since the social media environment can be highly volatile and sometimes improper communication messages can backfire on the firms (Fournier & Avery, 2011).

The unique aspects of SMBBCs mandate advertiser to behave as a part of the brand communities, not the organizers, to share meanings and values with customers. They should respect the norms of storytelling in the community and facilitate conversations among members. Also they should emphasize the community aspects of the collective and try to cement the bonds among members. Conducting proper brand community practices in social media is shown to be positive in enhancing brand trust and loyalty to the brand, which are among most important marketing and advertising objectives (Laroche, Habibi, & Richard, 2013; Laroche et al., 2012).

There are several challenges that advertisers might face while getting involved with SMBBCs. First, due to the novelty of social media and consequently related research, the understanding of SMBBCs is insufficient. As described there are several dimensions that make SMBBCs unique, which should be addressed by researchers. The other challenge is to gain consumers' engagement in the communities. It is shown than engagement moderates the effect of brand community elements on brand trust. Also highly engaged customers build stronger relationship with their community (Habibi, Laroche, & Richard, 2014*b*). Perhaps the main challenge is building the community around a specific brand. This requires a lot of attention, efforts and community building practices. To do so, advertisers should consider current established brand community notions and invest in long term efforts to enhance the community.

FUTURE RESEARCH DIRECTIONS

There are several avenues for future research studies regarding SMBBCs. First and foremost is to investigate the effects of the differentiating dimensions of SMBBCs. For example, what are the implications of multiple memberships? How do the unique social contexts of SMBBCs create differential results for the brand? How does the size of such communities influence consumers' behavior within SMBBCs?

Also the literature lacks longitudinal studies regarding brand communities. Except for a few seminal studies (e.g., McAlexander, Schouten, & Koenig, 2002), most studies are cross sectional while brand communities are dynamic phenomena. To have a better understanding of the dynamics of brand communities the field needs longitudinal studies. For example, we need to know how the personal feelings about a community develop over time in SMBBCs (Kilambi, Laroche, & Richard, 2013). How do value creation practices and their incremental effects develop over time?

One more interesting research avenue is a cross cultural one. Most studies about brand communities have been conducted in the western cultures. In fact, in the contemporary consumption oriented American culture, brand communities were introduced as a substitute to neighborhood-based communities which were common decades ago (Muniz & O'Guinn, 2001). Therefore, it would be interesting to observe whether brand communities have the same value, role, and position in Eastern cultures. What are the alternative forms of brand communities in Eastern cultures?

CONCLUSION

The goal of this chapter was to introduce brand communities based on social media as a unique advertising opportunity to advertising practitioners and marketing managers. The specific proposition of this chapter is that marketers can employ brand communities on social media to have an army of unpaid advertisers and ambassadors who are devoted to distribute favorable messages about their brand. There are several main points about such communities that marketers should know before facing them. First, consumers function as unpaid ambassadors of the brand through vigilante marketing and impression management practices in brand communities. Second, social media has endowed consumers with content creation and sharing capabilities which they can employ in favor of their attempts in vigilante marketing. Third, marketing managers should facilitate the development of SMBBCs by considering their unique dimensions. These endeavors would pay off not only by spreading the word in favor of the brand but also by enhancing important marketing objectives such as brand trust and loyalty.

REFERENCES

Adjei, M., Noble, S., & Noble, C. (2010). The influence of C2C communications in online brand communities on customer purchase behavior. *Journal of the Academy of Marketing Science*, *38*(5), 634–653. doi:10.1007/s11747-009-0178-5

Algesheimer, R., Dholakia, U. M., & Herrmann, A. (2005). The social influence of brand community: Evidence from European car clubs. *Journal of Marketing*, *69*(3), 19–34. doi:10.1509/jmkg.69.3.19.66363

Bagozzi, R. P., & Dholakia, U. M. (2006a). Open source software user communities: A study of participation in Linux user groups. *Management Science*, *52*(7), 1099–1115. doi:10.1287/mnsc.1060.0545

Bagozzi, R. P., & Dholakia, U. M. (2006b). Antecedents and purchase consequences of customer participation in small group brand communities. *International Journal of Research in Marketing*, *23*(1), 45–61. doi:10.1016/j.ijresmar.2006.01.005

Berry, L. L. (1995). Relationship marketing of services: Growing interest, emerging perspectives. *Journal of the Academy of Marketing Science*, *23*(Fall), 236–245. doi:10.1177/009207039502300402

Brodie, R. J., Ilic, A., Juric, B., & Hollebeek, L. (2013). Consumer engagement in a virtual brand community: An exploratory analysis. *Journal of Business Research*, *66*(1), 105–114. doi:10.1016/j.jbusres.2011.07.029

Cova, B., & Pace, S. (2006). Brand community of convenience products: New forms of customer empowerment: The case of 'My Nutella the community'. *European Journal of Marketing*, *40*(9/10), 1087–1105. doi:10.1108/03090560610681023

Fournier, S., & Avery, J. (2011). The uninvited brand. *Business Horizons*, *54*(3), 193–207. doi:10.1016/j.bushor.2011.01.001

Füller, J., Matzler, K., & Hoppe, M. (2008). Brand community members as a source of innovation. *Journal of Product Innovation Management*, *25*(6), 608–619. doi:10.1111/j.1540-5885.2008.00325.x

Garfield, B. (2005). Listenomics. *Advertising Age*, *76*(41), 1–35.

Habibi, M. R., Laroche, M., & Richard, M.-O. (2014a). Brand communities based in social media: How unique are they? Evidence from two exemplary brand communities. *International Journal of Information Management*, *34*(2), 123–132. doi:10.1016/j.ijinfomgt.2013.11.010

Habibi, M. R., Laroche, M., & Richard, M. O. (2014b). The roles of brand community and community engagement in building brand trust on social media. *Computers in Human Behavior*, *37*, 152–161. doi:10.1016/j.chb.2014.04.016

Hennig-Thurau, T., Hofacker, C. F., & Bloching, B. (2013). Marketing the pinball way: Understanding how social media change the generation of value for consumers and companies. *Journal of Interactive Marketing*, *27*(4), 237–241. doi:10.1016/j.intmar.2013.09.005

Iacobucci, D. (1994). Toward defining relationship marketing. In J. N. Sheth & A. Parvatoyar (Eds.), *Relationship marketing: Theory, methods and applications* (pp. 89–97). Atlanta, GA: Center for Relationship Marketing, Roberto C. Goizueta Business School, Emory University.

Ives, N. (2004, December 23). Unauthorized campaigns used by unauthorized creators to show their creativity become a trend. *New York Times*, p. C3.

Jones, K. (2013). The growth of social media v2.0 [INFOGRAPHIC]. *Search Engine Journal*. Retrieved March 15, 2014, from http://www.searchenginejournal.com/growth-social-media-2-0-infographic/77055/

Kaplan, A. M., & Haenlein, M. (2010). Users of the world, unite! The challenges and opportunities of social media. *Business Horizons*, *53*(1), 59–68. doi:10.1016/j.bushor.2009.09.003

Kilambi, A., Laroche, M., & Richard, M.-O. (2013). Constitutive marketing: Toward understanding brand community formation. *International Journal of Advertising*, *32*(1), 45–64. doi:10.2501/IJA-32-1-045-064

Kohli, C., Suri, R., & Kapoor, A. (2015). Will social media kill branding? *Business Horizons*, *58*(1), 35–44. doi:10.1016/j.bushor.2014.08.004

Kotler, P., Armstrong, G., & Cunnigham, P. (2007). *Principles of marketing* (Seventh Canadian edition). Toronto, Canada: Pearson.

Lang, B. (2010, September 20). *Ipsos OTX study: People spend more than half their day consuming media*. Retrieved from http://www.thewrap.com/node/21005

Laroche, M., Habibi, M. R., & Richard, M.-O. (2013). To be or not to be in social media: How brand loyalty is affected by social media? *International Journal of Information Management*, *33*(1), 76–82. doi:10.1016/j.ijinfomgt.2012.07.003

Laroche, M., Habibi, M. R., Richard, M. O., & Sankaranarayanan, R. (2012). The effects of social media based brand communities on brand community markers, value creation practices, brand trust and brand loyalty. *Computers in Human Behavior*, *28*(5), 1755–1767. doi:10.1016/j.chb.2012.04.016

McAlexander, J. H., & Koenig, H. F. (2010). Contextual influences: Building brand community in large and small colleges. *Journal of Marketing for Higher Education*, *20*(1), 169–184. doi:10.1080/08841241003788086

McAlexander, J. H., Schouten, J. W., & Koenig, H. F. (2002). Building brand community. *Journal of Marketing*, *66*(1), 38–54. doi:10.1509/jmkg.66.1.38.18451

Muniz, A. M. Jr, & O'Guinn, T. C. (2001). Brand community. *The Journal of Consumer Research*, *27*(4), 412–432. doi:10.1086/319618

Muñiz, A. M. Jr, & Schau, H. J. (2005). Religiosity in the abandoned Apple Newton brand community. *The Journal of Consumer Research*, *31*(4), 737–747. doi:10.1086/426607

Muñiz, A. M. Jr, & Schau, H. J. (2007). Vigilante marketing and consumer-created communications. *Journal of Advertising*, *36*(3), 35–50. doi:10.2753/JOA0091-3367360303

Naylor, R. W., Lamberton, C. P., & West, P. M. (2012). Beyond the "Like" button: The impact of mere virtual presence on brand evaluations and purchase intentions in social media settings. *Journal of Marketing*, *79*(6), 105–120. doi:10.1509/jm.11.0105

Ross, C., Orr, E. S., Sisic, M., Arseneault, J. M., Simmering, M. G., & Orr, R. R. (2009). Personality and motivations associated with Facebook use. *Computers in Human Behavior*, *25*(2), 578–586. doi:10.1016/j.chb.2008.12.024

Schau, H. J., & Muniz, A. M. Jr. (2002). Brand communities and personal identities: Negotiations in cyberspace. *Advances in Consumer Research. Association for Consumer Research (U. S.)*, *29*(1), 344–349.

Schau, H. J., Muñiz, A. M. Jr, & Arnould, E. J. (2009). How brand community practices create value. *Journal of Marketing*, *73*(5), 30–51. doi:10.1509/jmkg.73.5.30

Schouten, J. W., & McAlexander, J. H. (1995). Subcultures of consumption: An ethnography of the new bikers. *The Journal of Consumer Research*, *22*(1), 43–61. doi:10.1086/209434

Schouten, J. W., McAlexander, J. H., & Koenig, H. F. (2007). Transcendent customer experience and brand community. *Journal of the Academy of Marketing Science*, *35*(3), 357–368. doi:10.1007/s11747-007-0034-4

Shultz, D. E. (2005). *Foreword to Life after the 30-Second Spot, by Joseph Jaffe*. Hoboken, NJ: John Wiley.

Sicilia, M., & Palazón, M. (2008). Brand communities on the internet: A case study of Coca-Cola's Spanish virtual community. *Corporate Communications: An International Journal*, *13*(3), 255–270. doi:10.1108/13563280810893643

Tajfel, H., & Turner, J. C. (1985). The social identity theory of intergroup behavior. In S. Worchel & W. G. Austin (Eds.), *Psychology of intergroup relations* (pp. 7–24). Chicago: Nelson Hall.

Von Hippel, E. (2005). *Democratizing innovation*. Boston, MA: MIT Press.

Zaglia, M. E. (2013). Brand communities embedded in social networks. *Journal of Business Research*, *66*(2), 216–223. doi:10.1016/j.jbusres.2012.07.015 PMID:23564989

KEY TERMS AND DEFINITIONS

Advertising: "Any paid form of non-personal presentation and promotion of ideas; goods or services by an identified sponsor" (Kotler & Armstrong, 2007, p. 486).

Brand Community: "A specialized, non-geographically bound community, based on a structured set of social relations among admirers of a brand" (Muniz & O'Guinn, 2001, p. 412).

Communication: "The specific blend of promotion tools that the company uses to persuasively communicate customer value and build customer relationships" (Kotler & Armstrong, 2007, p. 456).

Social Media: "A group of Internet-based applications that build on the ideological and technological foundations of Web 2.0, and allow the creation and exchange of User Generated Content" (Kaplan & Haenlein, 2010, p. 61).

Vigilante Marketing: "Unpaid advertising and marketing efforts, including one-to-one, one-to-many, and many-to-many commercially oriented communications, undertaken by brand loyalists on behalf of the brand" (Muniz & Schau, 2007, p. 35).

This research was previously published in the Handbook of Research on Effective Advertising Strategies in the Social Media Age edited by Nurdan Öncel Taşkıran and Recep Yılmaz, pages 160-170, copyright year 2015 by Business Science Reference (an imprint of IGI Global).

Chapter 28
The Effects of Consumer Engagement Behavior on the Growth of Social Media Brand Community:
Evidence From an SME

Xiaoyun He
Auburn University at Montgomery, USA

Arash Negahban
California State University, USA

ABSTRACT

In recent years, there has been increasing attention to how consumers' roles and behaviors can shape and affect social media based brand communities. In this study the authors examine the dynamic relationships between specific consumer engagement behaviors and the growth rate of social media brand community over time. The results of their study suggest that the overall consumer engagement behavior has a significant predictive relationship with the growth rate of brand community in both short term and long term. While each type of positive consumer engagement behavior alone is not a significant indicator of the growth rate of brand community, a combination of them, as a whole, has a positive predictive relationship with the growth rate of brand community. When the effect of promotional posts is taken into consideration, consumer sharing is found to have relatively stronger and faster predictive relationship with the growth rate of brand community, followed by commenting and liking, than other consumer engaging activities. Negative consumer engagement behaviors in general do not play a significant role in predicting the growth rate of brand community in long term, but it does lead to adverse effect in the short term. This study sheds insights on the dynamic effects of consumer engagement behavior in building and growing social media based brand communities.

DOI: 10.4018/978-1-5225-5637-4.ch028

INTRODUCTION

Social media are fundamentally impacting the way we communicate and interact with each other. They are shifting the paradigm of information flow and consumer interactions (Kaplan & Haenlein, 2010). Some well-known social media platforms include Facebook, Twitter, LinkedIn, and YouTube. These social media platforms have rapidly grown in size over the last few years. For example, as of June 30, 2016, the online social networking site Facebook has over 1.7 billion monthly active users and this number continues to grow rapidly (Facebook, 2016). Individuals and businesses can create a Facebook page for free. These pages allow firms to connect with their customers, market their products and services, create a two-way communication channel to send messages to and receive feedbacks from their customers, and build their online brand community (e.g., Aral et al., 2013; Goh, Heng, & Lin, 2013).

Brand community has been widely recognized for its significant role in achieving organizational benefits (e.g., Muniz & O'Guinn 2001; McAlexander, Schouten, & Koenig, 2002; Schau, Muñiz, & Arnould, 2009). These include learning customers' perceptions of product offerings, influencing community members' evaluations and actions, gaining and enhancing customer loyalty, increasing market efficiency, etc. To take advantage of the capabilities of both social media and brand community, organizations have started using social networking sites to support the creation and development of online brand communities (Fournier & Lee, 2009; Kaplan & Haenlein, 2010; Goh, Heng, & Lin, 2013; Park & Kim, 2014). There are brand fan pages on Facebook with millions of users. For example, Jeep has more than 1.5 million members as of May 10, 2013. The potential benefits of having a strong online brand community have been widely recognized for building customer loyalty, lowering marketing costs, enhancing brand images, and attracting new customers to grow the business (Kim, Choi, Qualls et al., 2008; Schau, Muñiz, & Arnould, 2009; Laroche et al., 2012).

Recent studies suggest that consumers are becoming pivotal in engaging in the conversations between firms and consumers and among consumers themselves in social media brand communities (Habibi, Laroche, & Richard, 2014; Hollebeek, Glynn, & Brodie, 2014). Such conversations enable consumers to integrate their own brand-related experiences and thoughts into the process of brand community building. Traditionally, firms have most control on their marketing messages and brand management. However, in the current digital era, consumers are now more empowered than ever before to create and share their own brand stories through liking, commenting, and sharing activities on the social media. The consumer-generated content can be instantly passed onto thousands of other online users through consumers' social networks. As Scott Cook, the co-founder of Intuit, emphasizes: "A brand is no longer what we tell the consumer it is – it is what consumers tell each other it is." (Savitz, 2012).

Traditionally, customers are considered as exogenous to the firm and as passive recipients of the firm's active value creation efforts (Deshpande, 1983). In recent years a new perspective of customers has emerged, based on which, customers can co-create value and even become endogenous to the firm (Schau, Muñiz, & Arnould, 2009). In this new shift, online brand communities play the role of a catalyst and provide a platform for co-creation of value and customer engagement (e.g., Fournier & Lee, 2009; Laroche et al., 2012).

Customer engagement has been viewed as a behavioral construct that expands beyond purchase behavior. Customer engagement behavior is specifically defined as a customer's behavioral manifestations, beyond purchase, that have a brand or firm focus (Van Doorn, Lemon, Mittal et al., 2010). Customer engagement is important in building a long-term, sustainable competitive advantage and is tied to a firm's ability to retain, sustain, and nurture its customer base (Gruca & Rego, 2005). With the new perspective of co-creation between a firm and its customers, customer engagement is expected to play a vital role in growing and nurturing the firm's customer base, particularly in social media based brand communities (Gummerus, Liljander, Weman et al., 2012; Hollebeek, Glynn, & Brodie, 2014). Few studies have examined how consumer engagement behavior may affect the building and growth of a social media brand community over time.

In the context of social media brand communities, consumers are empowered to create and share their own brand stories through posting, commenting, sharing, and other engagement behaviors (Fournier & Lee, 2009). Prior studies have used metrics, such as: number of likes, number of comments, and number of shares, to measure customer engagement (e.g, Cvijikj & Michahelles, 2013; Lee, Hosanagar, & Nair, 2014; Murdough 2009). The goal of this study is to shed light on the dynamic effects of consumer engagement behavior on the growth rate of social media brand community. Specifically, this study seeks to address the following questions:

1. Is there a significant relationship between consumer engagement behavior and the growth rate of social media brand community?
2. Among the various metrics of consumer engagement behavior, which metric best relates to the growth rate of social media brand community?
3. What are the dynamics of the relationship between them over time?

To address the research questions, we use data from Facebook brand community (i.e., fan page) of an SME (Small and Medium Enterprise) that offers flower delivery services. SMEs are significant creators of employment and contributors to national economies. In the U.S., SMEs employ half of all private sector employees and create more than half of the nonfarm private GDP (Basefsky & Sweeney, 2006). As one of the most popular social network sites and a hallmark of social media on the Internet, Facebook is also one of the most adopted social media platforms by both large and small organizations (DiStaso & McCorkindale, 2013; Habibi, Laroche, & Richard, 2014).

We used a time series technique called vector-autoregressive model with exogenous covariates (VARX) to examine the dynamic effects of consumer engagement behavior on the growth rate of brand community over a period of time. We find that the overall consumer engagement behavior has a significant predictive relationship with the growth rate of brand community in both short term and long terms. Our results also indicate that positive and negative consumer engagement behaviors have different effects on the growth rate of brand community, which will be discussed in more details.

The rest of the paper is organized as follows: First, we present the theoretical background and hypotheses for our study followed by research design and methodology. We will then discuss the results, findings, and implications of this study. Finally, we will discuss the limitations and draw the conclusion of the paper.

THEORETICAL BACKGROUND AND HYPOTHESES

Relationship Between Consumer Engagement Behavior and the Growth Rate of Social Media Brand Communities

As creation and sharing of content becomes a hallmark of social media platform, social media has enabled and facilitated the realizations of the most important aspect of brand community – creation and sharing of meanings (Habibi, Laroche, & Richard, 2014). Thus, the intersection of the two – social media brand community - would be an ideal environment for creating and sharing of content, meaning, and values (Habibi, Laroche, & Richard, 2014; Shahrokh & Poursaeed, 2015). We expect that the overall consumer engagement behavior may predict the growth rate of social media brand communities for several reasons.

First, according to observational (social) learning theory (Bandura, 1977), learning could occur through the simple processes of observing someone else's activity. Social media brand community provides a platform for engaged consumers to express their opinions and experiences about the products and services offered by firms. The actual behavior manifestations are in the form of creating and sharing a brand story, commenting on a brand story, answering a question, and generating new content. With social media gaining more popularity, consumers are more empowered than ever to create and disseminate content on such online platforms as social media brand communities. By observing others' online engagement activities and postings, a new prospect may learn more about the brand and be influenced to join the community. In addition, prior studies have shown that these user-generated content have more persuasive power and are more effective than marketer-generated content in attracting new signups, leading to significant increase in sales and consumer purchases, and contributing to better stock performance (e.g., Stephen & Galak, 2012; Tirunillai & Tellis, 2012; Goh, Heng, & Lin, 2013; Ding et al., 2014). Since these user-generated-content are resulted from the various consumer engagement behaviors (e.g. posting and sharing), we expect that consumer engagement behavior has the similar effect of user-generated content on attracting new signups and growing online brand community.

Second, it has been argued that social media, and subsequently social media based brand community, can be an effective vehicle for credible Word-of-Mouth (WOM) (Chevalier & Mayzlin 2006; Liu 2006; Fournier & Lee 2009; King et al., 2014). Once consumers are aware and engaged, they are in a good position to communicate their opinions to others. Satisfied and loyal customers communicate their positive attitudes toward the brand itself and its products to prospective customers both online and offline (Anderson 2004; Hoffman & Fodor 2010). It appears that the positive impacts can be associated with the effects of Electronic-WOM (E-WOM) that online brand community generates. Recent research has shown such positive effects of E-WOM as shaping consumers' brand perceptions, acquiring new clients, and boosting sales (e.g., Godes & Mayzlin, 2004; Chevalier & Mayzlin, 2006; Liu, 2006; Sonnier, McAlister, & Rutz, 2011; Stephen & Galak, 2012; Kazienko, Szozda, Filipowski et al., 2013). Along this stream of research, the E-WOM derived from consumers' commenting and sharing behaviors in social media brand community is expected to expand the brand reach to new prospects that may then join the firm's brand community.

Moreover, one of the motivations for consumers to join online brand communities on social media is to support their favorite brand (Habibi, Laroche, & Richard, 2014; Park & Kim, 2014). People are more interested in social links and interactions that come from brand affiliations than in the brands themselves (Fournier & Lee, 2009). Social interactions can be categorized by the associated level of engagement reflected in consumer behaviors. For example, a customer may take time to answer a question; comment on a story, or share a story posted by other customers, etc. These "engagement" levels share certain similarity to what marketing research predicts for theoretically derived involvement aspects that drive consumer actions (Peters, Chen, Kaplan et al., 2013). Through these engaging actions, the participants essentially enhance and expand their social connections, which are expected to contribute to the continued growth of their affiliated brand community (Ding, Phang, Lu et al., 2014). In other words, consumer engagement behavior signals the future growth rate of brand community. Thus, we posit:

Hypothesis 1: Consumer engagement behavior has a significant predictive relationship with the growth rate of brand community.

Effects of Positive vs. Negative Engagement Behaviors

The behavioral manifestations by consumers, other than purchases, can be both positive (e.g., posting a positive brand message) and negative (i.e., organizing public actions against a firm) (Van Doorn, Lemon, Mittal et al., 2010; Hollebeek & Chen, 2014). The continuum of behaviors can range from pure voice (complaint behavior, positive or negative recommendation, positive or negative WOM) to pure exit (decrease consumption, nonrenewal of a contract) and many behaviors in between (Van Doorn, Lemon, Mittal et al., 2010). Social media based brand community is a place where consumers are willing to share and relate their product experience with other members in the community and voicing their opinions and sentiments (Fournier & Lee 2009; Habibi, Laroche, & Richard, 2014). If consumers are satisfied with a brand or product, they may exhibit favourable attitudes and behaviors toward it. For example, they may post positive information about the brand or share a brand story. On the other hand, if they do not have a good experience, they may take actions to express their negative experiences or opinions such as unlike a page or hide the stories from a page. Therefore, the feedback behaviors from consumers in social media brand community can be either overall positive or overall negative. Accordingly, Facebook classifies user behaviors into positive and negative feedback (Facebook, 2016). Positive feedback includes like a story, comment on a story, share a story, answer a question, claim an offer, and respond to an event; whereas negative feedback includes hide all stories from a Page, hide a particular story, unlike a page, and report an object as a spam.

The type of consumer engagement behavior can affect the growth rate of a brand community differently for the following reasons. Behavioral manifestations by consumers may send out signals about the quality of products and services that the focal firm of the brand community provides. According to signal theory (Connelly, Certo, Ireland et al., 2011), quality in general refers to the underlying and unobservable ability of the signaler to meet the needs of an observing outsider. The notion of quality can be socially constructed depending on the context. In many cases, a signal is able to change stakeholders' perceptions (Spence 1973; Connelly, Certo, Ireland et al., 2011). On social media platforms, signals from consumers are typically considered as more effective in changing others' perceptions than those from a firm itself (Ding, Phang, Lu et al., 2014).

On the one hand, positive engagement behavior such as sharing a positive brand story may send out a positive signal about the brand or product qualities. Such positive signals from a brand community may enhance others' positive perception or change their perception and thus attract them to join the community (Connelly, Certo, Ireland et al., 2011). On the other hand, negative behaviors may send out negative signals about the brand. Such negative signals may become a deterrent for others to join the community. In other words, the negative behaviors may prevent people from joining the community.

Furthermore, due to negativity bias, negative signals may elicit stronger response than positive ones (Rozin & Royzman, 2001). Thus, we hypothesize:

Hypothesis 2: Positive vs. negative consumer engagement behaviors exhibit different predictive relationships with the growth rate of brand community. In particular, positive behaviors signal higher growth rate; whereas negative behaviors signal lower growth rate.

Dynamics of Predictive Effects in Consumer Engagement Behaviors

Prior studies have examined the dynamics of responses to online user-generated content in such contexts as firm sales and stock prices (e.g., Sonnier, McAlister, & Rutz, 2011; Tirunillai & Tellis, 2012; Luo, Zhang, & Duan, 2013). For example, Tirunillai and Tellis (2012) show that negative user reviews are related to stock returns with wear-in effect, which is defined as how much time it takes before the stock market response to user reviews reaches the peak. Luo, Zhang, & Duan (2013) demonstrate that social media metrics have a shorter wear-in effect in predicting firm equity value than conventional online behavioral metrics. A shorter wear-in effect means a faster predictive value, which indicates the urgency of the predictive relationships. Therefore, the wear-in time period is useful for managers to adjust their social media strategies in a timely manner. For example, wear-in time may serve as valuable information for managers to decide when to eliminate ineffective practices while introducing new ways to engage consumers.

We expect that some types of consumer engagement behaviors (e.g., sharing a story) have a shorter wear-in effect than the others (e.g., commenting on a story or responding to an event) in predicting the growth rate of brand community. This is because when a community member shares a story, the story and its associated brand can be transmitted at an unprecedented speed and diffused fast through the wide reach of social media (Fournier & Lee, 2009; DiStaso & McCorkindale, 2013). In addition, the content shared can be reproduced, linked, broadcasted, voted on, and spread quickly, thus generating significant buzz and information richness (Luo, Zhang, & Duan, 2013). On the other hand, the reach of commenting on a story or responding to an event is typically limited to the participants of the community at the beginning, unless they are shared afterwards. In other words, it will take longer for them to reach their predictive value than sharing. Therefore, compared to other behavioral metrics, sharing can reach more new prospects and spread the words more quickly in an online environment. This leads to the following hypothesis:

Hypothesis 3: Among all the ten types of consumer engagement behaviors, sharing has the shortest wear-in effect in predicting the growth rate of brand community.

RESEARCH METHODOLOGY

Research Context

We conducted our research within the context of a business fan page brand community on Facebook by an SME (Small and Medium Enterprise) firm, which wishes to remain anonymous. The firm primarily provides flower delivery services to the northeastern region of the U.S. In November 2009, the firm started their Facebook page as a community platform to engage and interact with their consumers, and also to facilitate interactions among consumers. The firm also indicated that Facebook page is its only social media presence. This provides us a fairly thorough setting to examine the impact of consumer engagement in social media brand community. By February 2013, the firm had garnered about 6,400 page likes. Facebook Insights tool provides page manager daily data on various Page Engagement metrics. We were provided the access to the firm's Facebook page data collected through this Insights tool.

The dataset spans the period from April 2012 to February 2013. It contains 48 weeks of data on consumer engagement along with the information of promotional offers on a daily basis. With the focus of this study, we are particularly interested in the two types of Page Engagement metrics available from Facebook Insights, namely positive feedback and negative feedback that are exhibited in consumers' behaviors. The Positive Behaviors (PBs) is comprised of six measures (the overall measure of positive behaviors is the sum of these six measures): the number of liking a story (short as LKS), the number of commenting on a story (CMS), the number of sharing a story (SHR), the number of answering a question (ANS), the number of claiming an offer (CLM), and the number of responding to an event (RES); whereas the Negative Behaviors (NBs) include four measures (the overall measure of negative behaviors is the sum of these four measures): the number of hiding all stories from a Page (HDS), the number of hiding a particular story (HID), the number of unliking a page (UNK), and the number of reporting an object as a spam (REP). The overall consumer engagement behavior (CEB) is measured by the sum of PBs and NBs. We use fan base that is measured by page likes as a proxy for community size, which is then used to calculate the growth rate (GR) of the firm's brand community. That is, suppose the community size is n_1 at day t_1 and it is n_2 at day t_2, then the growth rate is $(n_2 - n_1)/n_1$ over the period of $(t_2 - t_1)$.

In addition, prior research suggests that the higher levels of aggregation of temporal data (e.g., monthly or quarterly) may lead to biased estimate, whereas lower levels of aggregation (e.g., hourly) may result in sparse data (Tirunillai & Tellis, 2012). Therefore, we chose the daily level of analysis. Table 1 presents the descriptive statistics of the data for this study.

Empirical Model

In order to examine the dynamic effects of consumer engagement on the growth rate of social media brand community over time, we use a time series technique known as vector-autoregressive model with exogenous covariates (VARX) (Dekimpe & Hanssens, 1999; Lütkepohl & Krätzig, 2004; Adomavicius, Bockstedt, & Gupta, 2012). VARX, which has several advantages over other time series models, is suitable for our study for several reasons. First, it allows us to examine the immediate, short-term as well as the long-term, cumulative effects of commenting activities on building an engaging community. Second, it accounts for biases such as endogeneity, serial correlation, and reverse causality. The endogenous treatment in VARX model implies that it captures both carry-over effects (explained by the past of a variable itself) and cross effects (explained by the past of each other). Third, it allows us to account for direct and indirect feedback effects, i.e., it can model complex chained effect in a complete cycle - feedback loop.

The general reduced-form VARX model with lag order *k* is:

$$Y_t = \alpha + \delta_t + A_1 Y_{t-1} + A_2 Y_{t-2} + \dots + A_k Y_{t-k} + \varepsilon_t \quad (1)$$

Table 1. Descriptive Statistics

Variable	Mean	Max	Min	Median	Std. Dev.
GR (Growth rate)	8.17	29.00	1.00	8.56	1.59
LKS (Like a story)	4.26	32.00	0.00	4.15	1.62
CMS (Comment on a story)	1.92	25.00	0.00	2.23	1.31
SHR (Share a story)	3.18	35.00	0.00	3.26	1.67
ANS (Answer a question)	0.87	12.00	0.00	0.91	1.14
CLM (Claims an offer)	4.07	26.00	2.00	3.82	1.29
RES (Respond to an event)	3.91	31.00	3.00	4.04	1.53
PBs (Positive Behaviors)	16.65	104.00	6.00	17.03	11.92
HDS (Hide all stories)	0.76	5.00	0.00	0.79	0.61
HID (Hide a story)	0.95	9.00	0.00	0.92	1.10
UNK (Unlike a page)	0.58	7.00	0.00	0.59	0.73
REP (Report a spam)	0.21	3.00	0.00	0.24	0.42
NBs (Negative Behaviors)	1.38	14.00	0.00	1.41	1.25
CEB (Engagement Behavior)	8.14	111.00	6.00	9.07	10.86

where $Y_t = (y_{1t,}\ y_{2t}, \ldots, y_{nt})'$ denotes an $(n \times 1)$ vector of time series variables, α is an $(n \times 1)$ vector of constant terms, δ_t is $(n \times 1)$ vector of coefficients, A_k is an $(n \times n)$ coefficient matrices, and ε_t is an $(n \times 1)$ vector of disturbances that have zero mean and are serially uncorrelated.

To answer our research questions, we specifically examine the predictive relationships between the number of liking a story (short as LKS), the number of commenting on a story (CMS), the number of sharing a story (SHR), the number of answering a question (ANS), the number of claiming an offer (CLM), the number of responding to an event (RES), the overall measure of positive behaviors (PBs), the number of hiding all stories from a Page (HDS), the number of hiding a particular story (HID), the number of unliking a page (UNK), and the number of reporting an object as a spam (REP), the overall measure of negative behaviors (NBs), the overall measure of consumer engagement behavior (CEB), and the growth rate in brand community (GR). Therefore, it is natural for us to choose these fourteen variables (i.e. the corresponding time series) to make up the VARX system.

In addition, we adapt the general form in Equation (1) to fit into our research context by adding the vectors of exogenous control variables that include: a deterministic-trend variable T to capture the effects of the gradually changing variables; indicator variable D for days of the week; seasonal (e.g., holidays) dummy variable H, and variable P for days when a promotional offer is posted. Thus, the Equation (1) is adapted to the following general Model 1.

$$Y_t = \alpha + \delta_t T + \theta_t D + \lambda_t H + \beta_t P + A_1 Y_{t-1} + A_2 Y_{t-2} + \ldots + A_k Y_{t-k} + \varepsilon_t \quad (2)$$

The above adapted VARX model allows us to capture the dynamic interactions among the consumer engagement variables and growth rate of brand community in the general case. Yet, considering that promotional offers that are posted on the firm's Facebook Page can be an important incentive for consumers to comment, share and like, we also evaluate how promotional posts (e.g., removing them from control) may impact the dynamic effects of consumer engagement. This leads to the following model, named as Model 2.

$$Y_t = \alpha + \delta_t T + \theta_t D + \lambda_t H + A_1 Y_{t-1} + A_2 Y_{t-2} + \ldots + A_k Y_{t-k} + \varepsilon_t \quad (3)$$

The underlying rationale for determining the appropriate lag order k of a VARX model is to choose the lag length so that it maximizes the fit between the observed time series and the estimated predicting process (Lütkepohl & Krätzig 2004). Two commonly used measures for selecting lag order are Bayesian Information Criterion (SIC) and Final Prediction Error (FPE). The selection criteria for the optimal lag length are presented in Table 2. In the specification of our VARX model with the time series in our data set, the SIC and FPE agreed that the optimal lag length was two.

In order to illustrate the ability of the VARX model to represent the data, we plot predicted values versus actual values of daily growth rate. Figure 1 depicts the plot. As we can see from the figure, the predicted values track the actual growth rate in a pretty close manner.

The estimates of VARX regression coefficients typically are not as informative as analyzing relationships among variables because of complicated dynamics inherent in VARX model (Dekimpe & Hanssens 1999; Lütkepohl & Krätzig 2004). Instead, Granger-causality tests, impulse response functions, and generalized forecast error variance decompositions are used in the analysis (Adomavicius et al., 2012).

Table 2. Lag selection criteria

Lag	FPE	BIC
0	2.09E-21	-13.45
1	1.84E-22	-14.56
2	1.68E-22*	-15.01*
3	1.75E-22	-14.78
4	1.94E-22	-14.43
5	2.33E-22	-13.89
6	2.91E-22	-13.72
7	3.28E-22	-13.35
8	3.51E-22	-13.26
9	4.24E-22	-13.01

Note: * indicates the optimal lag order that minimizes the FPE or BIC criterion.

Figure 1. Plot of Model Fit Test

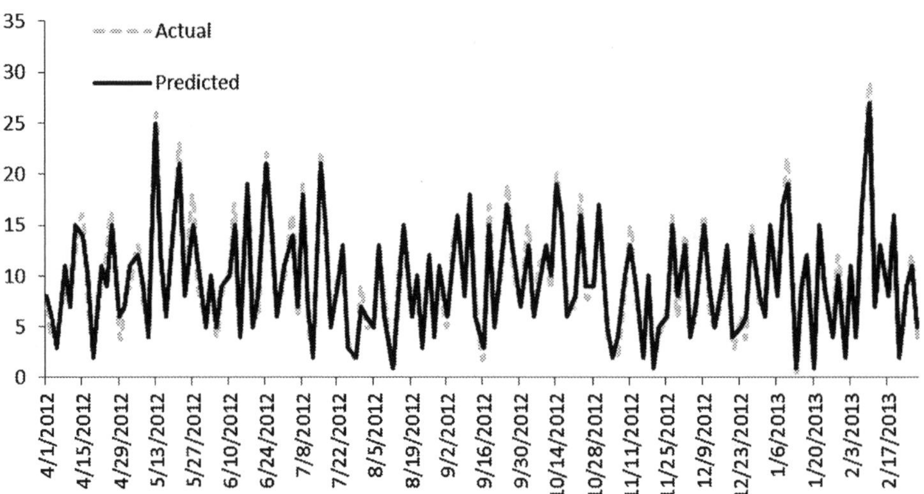

In particular, we conduct the Granger-causality tests to test for the presence and direction of a predictive relationship between each metric of consumer engagement and the growth of brand community. Then, in order to model the dynamics (i.e., the short-term and long-term or accumulated relationships) in the VARX system, we resort to the impulse response function. This is because it is not sensitive to the causal ordering of the variable entering the system. Further, the relative impact of the metrics of consumer engagement on the growth rate of brand community is assessed by using generalized forecast error variance decompositions. We report model estimation and the results of the analysis in the next section.

MODEL ESTIMATION AND MAIN RESULTS

The process of estimating VARX model starts with the unit-root tests. These unit-root tests examine if the variables entering the system evolve continually or are stationary. If a variable is stationary, then its effect dissipates eventually, despite that an unexpected change in endogenous variables in VARX can induce fluctuations over time. The variance of stationary variables is finite and time-invariant. We conduct the Augmented Dickey-Fuller (ADF) tests to check stationary so as to ensure that our results are robust to alternative formulations of the null hypothesis (Dekimpe & Hanssens, 1999). The ADF tests of all metrics in our data are less than the critical value -2.28 and thus it can reject the null hypothesis of a unit root with a 95% confidence level. Also, the Engel-Granger test suggests that the variable series do not cointegrate in equilibrium, and therefore our VARX model is appropriate (Hamilton, 1994; Lütkepohl & Krätzig, 2004). Then, we conduct Granger causality tests for the presence and direction of a causal relationship between each metric of consumer engagement behaviors and the growth rate of brand community.

Granger causality tests are used to determine whether the lagged values of one variable help predict values of another variable in the VARX system (Granger, 1969). For example, in our case, the positive engagement behaviors from consumers is said to "Granger cause" the growth rate of brand community if the lags of the positive engagement behaviors predict the growth rate of community even after controlling for lags of the growth rate of brand community. Table 3 reports the *p*-values of the tests for both Model 1 and Model 2.

The results in Table 3 indicate that, in both Model 1 and Model 2, the overall consumer engagement behavior (CEB) does significantly "Granger cause" the growth rate of brand community. Specifically, in Model 1, each type of the positive behaviors alone does not significantly "Granger cause" the growth rate of brand community; but a combination of them (as an overall measure of positive behaviors from consumers) does significantly "Granger cause" the growth rate of brand community ($p = 0.046$). However, when the effect of promotional events is not controlled (i.e., in Model 2), like a story, comment on a story, and share a story are the major metrics that are found to significantly "Granger cause" the growth rate of brand community at the 5% significance level, but the other metrics in the category of positive behaviors do not significantly "Granger cause" the growth rate of brand community. The overall measure of positive behaviors does significantly "Granger cause" the growth rate of brand community as well ($p = 0.019$). As expected in both models, neither each of the negative behaviors metrics alone nor the combination of them as a whole (as an overall measure of negative behaviors from consumers) significantly "Granger cause" the growth rate. In addition, the reverse predictive relationship from the growth rate of community size to each of the positive behaviors as well as the overall positive behaviors is statistically significant. These results provide initial evidence that there are temporal predictive relationships between some, but not all, of the consumer engagement behaviors and growth rate of brand community. Thus, these results provide initial support of both Hypothesis 1 and Hypothesis 2.

The short term and long term dynamics between consumer engagement behaviors and the growth rate of community size are estimated through simulations of the Generalized Impulse Response Function (GIRF) (Pesaran & Shin, 1998; Dekimpe & Hanssens, 1999). GIRF is an alternative means of measuring the influence of one variable in the VARX system on another variable. The GIRF uses the VARX

Table 3. The p-values of granger causality tests

Response to	Growth Rate (GR)	
	Model 1	**Model 2**
LKS	0.053	0.034**
CMS	0.055	0.041**
SHR	0.050	0.028**
ANS	0.096	0.083
CLM	0.068	0.050
RES	0.072	0.051
PBs	0.046**	0.009***
HDS	0.062	0.053
HID	0.110	0.073
UNK	0.060	0.058
REP	0.084	0.072
NBs	0.066	0.057
CEB	0.048**	0.025**

Note: $^{**}p < 0.05$; $^{***}p < 0.01$.

estimates to trace the effect of a unit shock (one standard deviation) in any of the variables (measures of consumer engagement) on the other variable (the growth rate of brand community) in the model over subsequent periods. The short-term effect is derived from the estimates of the VARX system for the first seven time periods, the average time taken for the effect of consumer engagement measures to reach their peak effect. The long term or accumulative effect is defined as the accumulated effect of GIRF to reach its asymptote. Most of the accumulated effect on the growth rate of brand community reaches asymptotic levels within fourteen time periods. In order to ensure that we have captured the total effects of consumer engagement on the growth rate of brand community, we set the accumulated duration as a period of twenty days. In addition, the dynamics of the system is also measured by wear-in time or the number of periods before the peak predictive value is reached. The largest (in absolute value) impulse response coefficients determine the peak value.

Table 4 presents the results from GIRF tests. The results indicate that the overall consumer engagement behavior (CEB) has a significant predictive relationship with the growth rate of brand community in terms of both short and long terms at 95% significance level. In the case of Model 1, positive behaviors as a whole has a significant predictive relationship with the growth rate of brand community in terms of both short and long terms. Specifically, one unit increase in PBs (positive behaviors) at time zero results on average in a 3.052 unit increase in the growth rate of brand community in the short run. The increase is statistically significant ($p < 0.05$). The immediate effect of share a story and answer a question on the growth rate is 2.351 and 1.214 units respectively, and the magnitude of both effects is statistically weak ($p < 0.10$). In the long run, a one unit increase in PF at time zero results in a 5.770 unit increase in the growth rate. It is statistically significant ($p < 0.01$). Also, the long run effect of each type of the positive behaviors on the growth rate is marginally significant ($p < 0.10$). On the other hand, while the negative behaviors as a whole does not significantly influence the growth rate in the long run, it does

Table 4. The results of generalized impulse response functions (GIRFs)

	Model 1			Model 2		
	Immediate	**Accumulative**	**Wear-in Time (days)**	**Immediate**	**Accumulative**	**Wear-in Time (days)**
LKS	1.033	1.871	7.3	1.175	2.566**	5.1
CMS	1.196	2.932	5.4	1.229**	3.841**	3.8
SHR	2.351	3.374	3.6	3.215***	5.023***	2.4
ANS	1.214	1.893	5.2	1.464	2.018	4.0
CLM	0.972	2.537	4.6	1.507	2.775	3.6
RES	1.138	2.841	3.9	1.732	3.417	3.2
PBs	**3.052****	**5.770*****	**5.2**	**4.326*****	**6.801*****	**3.7**
HDS	-0.029	-0.067	5.8	-0.031	-0.118	6.1
HID	-0.052	-0.084	6.4	-0.025	-0.073	5.3
UNK	-0.058	-0.132	7.4	-0.076	-0.169	5.6
REP	-0.166	-0.250	7.7	-0.131	-0.194	6.5
NBs	**-0.143****	**-0.231**	**6.8**	**-0.087****	**-0.158**	**5.9**
CEB	**2.837****	**4.904****	**6.1**	**3.983****	**5.692****	**4.4**

Note: $^{**}p < 0.05$; $^{***}p < 0.01$.

affect the growth rate negatively in the short term (0.143 unit decrease, $p < 0.05$). In particular, hide all stories from a page and unlike a page each exhibits a slightly negative effect on the growth rate in the short term (0.029 and 0.058 unit decrease respectively; $p < 0.10$).

With Model 2, the positive behaviors as a whole shows a strong predictive relationship with the growth rate of brand community in the short and long terms. Notably different from the results in Model 1, comment on a story and share a story each alone exhibit significant association with the growth rate in the short and long run; like a story does not impact the growth rate immediately, but it does affect the growth rate in the long term. Specifically, one unit increase in PBs (positive behaviors) at time zero results on average in a 4.326 and 6.801 unit increase in the growth rate of brand community in the short and long run respectively. Both increases are statistically significant ($p < 0.01$). On average, share a story leads to a 3.215 and 5.023 unit increase in the short term and long term respectively ($p < 0.01$). The effect of comment on a story is significant as well ($p < 0.05$). Regarding the negative behaviors, we see similar results as those in the case of Model 1. These results further support Hypothesis 2.

In addition, Table 4 also reports the wear-in time results. As we mentioned earlier, wear-in time measures how long it takes for each of the metrics to reach the peak of the predictive relationship with growth rate of brand community (i.e., the dynamics of the relationships). The results show that, among all the individual metrics, share a story has a shortest wear-in time (3.6 days in Model 1 and 2.4 days in Model 2), followed by respond to an event (3.9 days and 3.2 days respectively), while report an object as a spam has the longest wear-in time (7.7 days and 6.5 day respectively). Also, positive engagement behaviors have a shorter wear-in time than negative engagement behaviors in both models. These results support Hypothesis 3.

The above results suggest that the overall consumer engagement behavior has a significant predictive relationship with the growth rate of brand community in terms of both short and long terms. On the one hand, positive consumer engagement behaviors as a whole is strongly associated with the growth rate of brand community in the short term as well as in the long run, while each type of the positive behaviors alone is not a significant indicator. On the other hand, negative behaviors do negatively affect the growth rate in the short term. Such results of the GIRF tests largely corroborate those of the aforementioned Granger causality tests.

While the results from Granger causality tests and GIRFs indicate the significance of interactions among variables in the VARX model, generalized forecast error variance decomposition provides us the magnitude of effect by specifying the percentage of forecast error variance that is accounted for by each metric in the model. In other words, it is like a partial R^2 for the forecast error by forecast horizon. Table 5 reports the results from the variance decompositions for the first period. The results provide the illustration of the relative power of each type of the metrics in explaining the variance of the growth rate of brand community. Specifically, positive consumer behaviors have higher predictive power than negative consumer behaviors in both models (6.37% vs. 1.74% in Model 1; 7.16% vs. 2.03% in Model 2). Among the major metrics in the category of positive behaviors, the results suggest the relative order of share a story (1.76% and 1.95% in Model 1 and 2 respectively), comment on a story (1.26% and 1.49% respectively), like a story (1.01% and 1.17% respectively) in predicting their long-term effects on the growth rate of brand community. Also, their overall effects in Model 2 are relatively stronger than those in Model 1.

In addition, Figure 2 provides a graphical representation of the variance decompositions, illustrating the proportions of forecast error variance, up to fourteen days ahead, accounted for by shocks in each of three major metrics – like a story, comment on a story, and share a story in Model 1. These are

Table 5. The results of variance decomposition

Variance Explained by	Growth Rate (GR)	
	Model 1	**Model 2**
LKS	1.01%	1.17%
CMS	1.26%	1.49%
SHR	1.76%	1.95%
ANS	0.82%	0.85%
CLM	0.68%	0.73%
RES	0.87%	0.92%
PBs	**6.37%**	**7.16%**
HDS	0.45%	0.53%
HID	0.31%	0.38%
UNK	0.62%	0.70%
REP	0.36%	0.42%
NBs	**1.74%**	**2.03%**
CEB	**5.02%**	**6.21%**

Figure 2. The forecast horizon of variance decomposition (Major metrics)

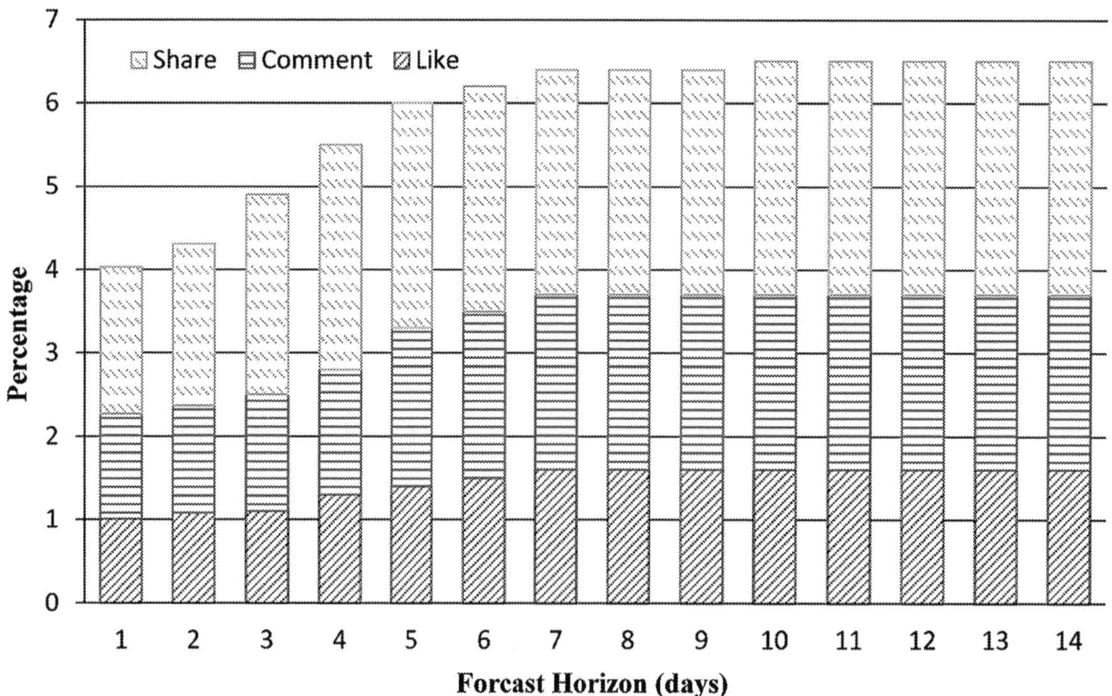

consistent with the prior results. For example, the effect of like a story persists for about 7 days. The influence of share a story is relatively stronger and persists for about 4 days. We note that, at each time point, the contributions from all the variables including the growth of brand community in the system sum to 100%. In this case, the growth rate of brand community accounts for the largest proportion of its own forecast error variance, which is not shown for better readability of the graph.

DISCUSSION

The results suggest that consumer engagement behavior has a significant predictive relationship with the growth rate of brand community in both short term and long terms. Positive consumer engagement behavior, as a whole, is a leading indicator of the growth rate of brand community; however, each type of positive behaviors alone does not exhibit significant predicative relationship with the growth rate. When the effect of promotional posts is taken into consideration, sharing is found to have relatively stronger and faster predictive relationship with the growth rate of brand community, followed by commenting and liking respectively, than other consumer engaging activities. This suggests that consumer engagement exhibited in sharing, commenting, and liking activities may serve as an indicator of the effectiveness of a firm's strategies in attracting new customers and consequently growing brand community at a faster pace. It also suggests that promotional events play a role in stimulating the consumer engaging activities and thus strengthening their predictive power. On the other hand, negative consumer engagement behaviors as a whole does not play a significant role in predicting the growth of brand community in the long run, but it does lead to adverse effect in the short run. Thus, firms especially SMEs need to take into consideration of the role of consumer engagement behavior when formulating and assessing their brand community strategies.

Implications for Research

This study contributes to the literature in brand communities across MIS and marketing areas. Firms are now able to leverage social media for shaping brand-centric communities in ways previously impractical with traditional marketing media (McAlexander, Schouten, & Koenig, 2002; Stephen & Glak, 2012; Kazienko, Szozda, Filipowski et al., 2013; O'Reilly & Lancendorfer, 2013). This research provides a better understanding of the effect of consumer engagement behaviors on building and growing social media based brand communities. Our study highlights potential impacts of engaging customers that is beyond simple exploitation in today's dynamic, increasingly consumer-dominated social media environment (Schau, Muñiz, & Arnould, 2009; Van Doorn, Lemon, Mittal et al., 2010; Wirtz et al., 2013). Extant literature has argued that, with vital characteristics of brand communities such as the richness of social context and geo-temporal concentrations, the evolution of these communities should be treated as dynamic rather than static phenomena (McAlexander, Schouten, & Koenig, 2002; Verhoef et al., 2009). Built upon such dynamic view, we use time-series models to examine the dynamic effects of consumer engagement behaviors and growth rate of brand community. Our models not only focus on short-term value, but also the enduring effects of consumer engagement behaviors. It fits into the overall demand in web analytics research that more attention is being directed to the long-term and cumulative effects of social media (Luo et al., 2013).

Online brand communities, as topic-specific media outlets, are usually appealing to high-involvement consumers who want to socially interact and discuss topic of mutual interest with like-minded others (Stephen & Galak, 2012). These communities are believed to be more effective than traditional marketing outlets in influencing others' behavior and generating buzz for a niche brand like the flower delivery business in this study. It appears that positive impact of consumer engagement behaviors can be associated with the effect of E-WOM that online brand community generates, e.g., by sharing positive brand-related content through consumers' online social network (e.g., Chevalier & Mayzlin, 2006; Liu, 2006; Sonnier, McAlister, & Rutz, 2011). Therefore, better understanding of the effects of consumer engagement behaviors may stimulate further research on the role of social media brand communities in shaping consumers' brand perceptions and boost sales through E-WOM.

Furthermore, prior studies suggest that IT-related intangibles provide productivity benefits and performance advantages to firms (Brynjolfsson et al., 2002). For example, investments in business processes that facilitate and monitor customer engagement may represent valuable IT intangible assets. Online community built on social media has particularly been considered as a possible intangible asset for driving firm value (Kaplan & Haenlein 2010; Larson & Watson 2011; Laroche, Habibi, Richard, 2012). Empirical evidence provided in this study confirms the role of consumer engagement in affecting the growth of firms' online brand community as an asset. To effectively leverage such asset, firms should be mindful on how to coordinate resources, balance activities, and guide efforts in social media based brand community-building strategies.

Practical Implications

This study also informs managers in several ways. First, social media brand community provides a public platform for firms to enable their customers engage in various behavior. Through various engaging behaviors, such as making comments, sharing posts, liking a page, etc., customers often send out powerful messages and feedback about their experiences and opinions to firms as well as to other consumers. Our findings on the predictive relationships between the overall consumer engagement behavior and the growth rate of their fan base in brand community provide supporting evidence that in order to further grow their brand fan base at a fast pace, managers should leverage their social media brand community to foster customers participation and positive interactions (Verhoef et al., 2010). This will eventually lead to a new way of nurturing and sustaining their customer base (Gruca and Rego 2005; Van Doorn, Lemon, Mittal et al., 2010), which, in turn, is related to looking beyond the traditional approach in measuring and managing customer value in the new social media age (Hollebeek, Glynn, & Brodie, 2014; Anderl et al., 2015). The measurement and management of customer value has traditionally focused on purchase behavior, i.e., increasing customers' spending with a company over time (e.g., Reinartz et al., 2004; Kumar 2007). Nevertheless, it has come to realization that long-term and sustainable competitive advantage is tightly associated with a firm's ability to attract, retain, and nurture its customer base (Gruca & Rego 2005; Van Doorn, Lemon, Mittal et al., 2010). In today's social media enabled networking era, nurturing and sustaining customer base requires firms to look beyond transactional purchase behavior alone. Social media based brand community offers a great tool and new opportunities for firms to do so. This research provides empirical evidence to corroborate the value of leveraging these new opportunities in consumer engagement.

Second, our study reveals the differential effects of different types of consumer engagement behaviors. This suggests that, in order to quickly grow their fan base, managers should take different actions in response to the different consumer behavioral manifestations. Specifically, firms may want to go a step further by actively stimulating and promoting positive consumer engagement. For instance, in a recent study by de Vries, Gensler, and Leeflang (2012), the authors studied the types of firm-generated brand posts that stimulate consumers to react and found that vividness and interactivity of brand posts are important for consumers to like, comment, and share. These proactive actions from firms will increase customer satisfaction and reduce customer churn. Prior studies indicate that a minor increase in customer satisfaction can lead to a major increase in a firm's overall value (Anderson et al., 2004; Larivière et al., 2016; Sorescu & Sorescu 2016). Also, it has been suggested that consumers who actively participate and engage in the brand community are willing to pay higher prices for the brand (Laroche, Habibi, Richard, 2012; Park & Kim 2014). Thus, timely and appropriate actions from managers may potentially impact firms' financial performance in the long run.

Third, firms should be aware of the important factors that may affect the dynamics in the growth of brand community. The decision to express an opinion may be influenced by posts and sentiment that were previously posted. However, negative feedback manifested in consumers' behaviors does not necessarily mean that a firm's brand or product is uniformly disliked despite some adverse effects in the short term. A careful analysis of the dynamics between consumer engagement behaviour and growth rate of brand community can help identify when a firm should act accordingly to address an issue raised by a negative feedback (Moe, Schweidel, & Trusov 2011). In this study, we have examined wear-in effects exhibited in the dynamic relationships between consumer engagement behavior and growth of brand community. In particular, a shorter wear-in effect means a faster predictive value, which indicates the urgency of the predictive relationships. Therefore, the wear-in time period is useful for managers to adjust their strategies of managing online brand communities in a timely manner (Verhoef et al., 2009; Wirtz et al., 2013).

Research Limitations and Future Research

The findings of this study should be interpreted within limitations of the empirical data analysis. First, this researched focused on only online brand communities on a specific social network. Although online communities can have high diversity in cultural backgrounds, geography, ethnicity, etc., the lack of face-to-face interaction in these communities creates a different dynamic than traditional that make them difficult to compare with each other. In this study, we did not consider such differences. Second, there are many factors outside the ones we investigated that can influence consumer engagement behaviors and the growth rate of social media brand communities. For instance, trust is critical for converting social media "followers" to "customers", which can ultimately increase consumer engagement and extend the reach of social media brand communities. Third, in our research we assumed that consumer's empowerment through social media leads to more online activities and ultimately higher consumer engagement and stronger online brand community. However, there can be potential negative consequences, such as brand hijacking (Cova & Pace 2006; Cova et al., 2007). We did not consider such negative consequences in our research.

With respect to external validity and generalizability, it should be noted that the adoption of social media based brand community was still in its fast evolving stage during the examination window (2012-2013). Whether its effects found in this study extend beyond this period is a question that future research may explore. Also, the sample represents a U.S.-based SME in a certain region, thus it would be interesting to test the impacts of social media in other types of organizations and in other geographic regions.

In this study, we have directly used the classification of positive feedback (i.e., behaviors) and negative feedback (i.e., behaviors) provided by Facebook Insights tool. Comments are viewed as a positive feedback because they can reflect that at least the customers cared to write and post them. Future research may conduct content analysis of consumer comments (Cvijikj & Michahelles 2013; Lee, Hosanagar, & Nair, 2014). For example, the comments posted by consumers in a brand community can be either overall positive or overall negative (i.e., taking into consideration of the valence of comments). While research on consumers-generated content in social media have primarily focused on the valence of positive and negative, Sonnier, McAlister, & Rutz (2011) recently suggest that, in addition to positive and negative online communications, neutral ones also have significant effect on firms' daily sales performance. Hence, further research on clarifying the role of neutral comments is needed.

Another related attribute to note in consumer engagement is the mix of both qualitative measures (e.g., discussion topics and sentiment) and quantitative measures (e.g., count of shares) (Murdough 2009). Social media is unique in bringing both types of insight together to characterize performance and the value derived from social media efforts. In this research, we only considered quantitative measures. Taking into account both qualitative and quantitative measures by future research would provide more insights on the impacts of consumer engagement.

CONCLUSION

As consumers are becoming more vocal and engaged than ever before by participating and generating messages in brand communities, it is often less clear for firms on how community members' online engagement behavior may dynamically affect the growth rate of their brand communities. In this study, we take initial steps to empirically examine the dynamic effects of consumer engaging activities on the growth rate of social media based brand community. The results suggest that consumer engagement behavior has a significant predictive relationship with the growth rate of brand community in both short term and long terms. The potential benefits of having a strong and fast-growing online brand community include enhance customer loyalty, lower marketing costs, increase brand awareness, and attract new customers to grow the business (e.g., Kim, Choi, Qualls et al., 2008; Schau, Muñiz, & Arnould, 2009; Laroche, Habibi, Richard, 2012). However, we would like to re-emphasize that online communities, due to their inherent lack of communication, create a very different dynamic than traditional communities, which may limit the findings of studies that only focus on one these communities. We hope future research efforts will further uncover new insights on how firms are able to strategically stimulate positive engagement among their community members by utilizing traditional and online communities.

REFERENCES

Adomavicius, G., Bockstedt, J., & Gupta, A. (2012). Modeling Supply-Side Dynamics of IT Components, Products, and Infrastructure: An Empirical Analysis Using Vector Autoregression. *Information Systems Research*, *23*(2), 397–417. doi:10.1287/isre.1120.0418

Anderl, E., März, A., & Schumann, J. H. (2015). Nonmonetary customer value contributions in free e-services. *Journal of Strategic Marketing*.

Anderson, E. W., Fornell, C., & Mazvancheryl, S. K. (2004). Customer satisfaction and shareholder value. *Journal of Marketing*, *68*(4), 172–185. doi:10.1509/jmkg.68.4.172.42723

Aral, S., Dellarocas, C., & Godes, D. (2013). Social Media and Business Transformation: A Framework for Research. *Information Systems Research*, *24*(1), 3–13. doi:10.1287/isre.1120.0470

Bandura, A. (1977). *Social learning theory*. New York: General Learning Press.

Basefsky, S., & Sweeney, S. (2006, November 28-29). Employment relations in SMEs: The United States. Proceedings of the Workshop of Industrial Relations in the EU, USA and Japan and Other Global Economies, Berlin, Germany.

Chevalier, J. A., & Mayzlin, D. (2006). The Effect of Word of Mouth on Sales: Online Book Reviews. *JMR, Journal of Marketing Research*, *43*(3), 345–354. doi:10.1509/jmkr.43.3.345

Connelly, B. L., Certo, S. T., Ireland, R. D., & Reutzel, C. R. (2011). Signaling theory: A review and assessment. *Journal of Management*, *37*(1), 39–67. doi:10.1177/0149206310388419

Cova, B., & Pace, S. (2006). Brand community of convenience products: New forms of customer empowerment - the case "My Nutella The Community". *European Journal of Marketing*, *40*(9/10), 1087–1105. doi:10.1108/03090560610681023

Cova, B., Pace, S., & Park, D. J. (2007). Global brand communities across borders: The Warhammer case. *International Marketing Review*, *24*(3), 313–329. doi:10.1108/02651330710755311

Cvijikj, I. P., & Michahelles, F. (2013). Online engagement factors on Facebook brand pages. *Social Network Analysis and Mining*, *3*(4), 843–861. doi:10.1007/s13278-013-0098-8

de Vries, L., Gensler, S., & Leeflang, P. (2012). Popularity of brand posts on brand fan pages: an investigation of the effects of social media marketing. *Journal of Interactive Marketing*, 26(2), 2012, 83-91.

Dekimpe, M., & Hanssens, D. (1999). Sustained spending and persistent response: A new look at long-term marketing profitability. *JMR, Journal of Marketing Research*, *36*(4), 397–412. doi:10.2307/3151996

Deshpande, R. (1983). "Paradigms Lost": On Theory and Method in Research in Marketing. *Journal of Marketing*, *47*(4), 101–110. doi:10.2307/1251403

Ding, Y., Phang, C. W., Lu, X., Tan, C. H., & Sutanto, J. (2014). The Role of Marketer-and User-Generated Content in Sustaining the Growth of a Social Media Brand Community. *Proceedings of the 2014 47th Hawaii International Conference on System Sciences* (pp. 1785-1792). IEEE. doi:10.1109/HICSS.2014.226

DiStaso, M. W., & McCorkindale, T. (2013). A benchmark analysis of the strategic use of social media for Fortune's most admired U.S. companies on Facebook, Twitter and YouTube. *The Public Relations Journal*, *7*(1).

Facebook. (2016). Company Info. Retrieved From http://newsroom.fb.com/company-info/

Fournier, S., & Lee, L. (2009). Getting brand communities right. *Harvard Business Review*, *87*(4), 105–111. PMID:19736854

Godes, D., & Mayzlin, D. (2004). Using online conversations to study word-of-mouth communication. *Marketing Science*, *23*(4), 545–560. doi:10.1287/mksc.1040.0071

Godes, D., Mayzlin, D., & Verlegh, P. et al.. (2005). The Firm's Management of Social Interactions. *Marketing Letters*, *16*(3/4), 415–428.

Goh, K., Heng, C., & Lin, Z. (2013). Social Media Brand Community and Consumer Behavior: Quantifying the Relative Impact of User- and Marketer-Generated Content. *Information Systems Research*, *24*(1), 88–107. doi:10.1287/isre.1120.0469

Granger, C. (1969). Investing causal relations by econometric models and cross-spectral methods. *Journal of Econometric Society*, *37*(3), 424–438. doi:10.2307/1912791

Gruca, T., & Rego, L. (2005). Customer satisfaction, cash flow, and shareholder value. *Journal of Marketing*, *69*(July), 115–130. doi:10.1509/jmkg.69.3.115.66364

Gummerus, J., Liljander, V., Weman, E., & Pihlström, M. (2012). Customer engagement in a Facebook brand community. *Management Research Review*, *35*(9), 857–877. doi:10.1108/01409171211256578

Habibi, M. Z., Laroche, M., & Richard, M. (2014). Brand communities based in social media: How unique are they? Evidence from two exemplary brand communities. *International Journal of Information Management*, *34*(2), 123–132. doi:10.1016/j.ijinfomgt.2013.11.010

Hamilton, J. (1994). *Time Series Analysis*. Princeton University Press.

Hoffman, D. L., & Fodor, M. (2010). Can you measure the ROI of your social media marketing? *Sloan Management Review*, *52*(1), 41–49.

Hollebeek, L. D., & Chen, T. (2014). Exploring positively-versus negatively-valenced brand engagement: A conceptual model. *Journal of Product and Brand Management*, *23*(1), 62–74. doi:10.1108/JPBM-06-2013-0332

Hollebeek, L. D., Glynn, M. S., & Brodie, R. J. (2014). Consumer Brand Engagement in Social Media: Conceptualization, Scale Development and Validation. *Journal of Interactive Marketing*, *28*(2), 149–165. doi:10.1016/j.intmar.2013.12.002

Kaplan, A., & Haenlein, M. (2010). Users of the world, unite! The challenges and opportunities of social media. *Business Horizons*, *53*(1), 59–68. doi:10.1016/j.bushor.2009.09.003

Kazienko, P., Szozda, N., Filipowski, T., & Blysz, W. (2013). New business client acquisition using social networking sites. *Electronic Markets*, *23*(2), 93–103. doi:10.1007/s12525-013-0123-9

Kim, J. W., Choi, J., Qualls, W., & Han, K. (2008). It takes a marketplace community to raise brand commitment: The role of online communities. *Journal of Marketing Management*, *24*(3-4), 409–431. doi:10.1362/026725708X306167

King, R. A., Racherla, P., & Bush, V. D. (2014). What we know and don't know about online word-of-mouth: A review and synthesis of the literature. *Journal of Interactive Marketing*, *28*(3), 167–183. doi:10.1016/j.intmar.2014.02.001

Kumar, V. (2007). Customer lifetime value: The path to profitability. *Foundations and Trends in Marketing*, *2*(1), 1–96. doi:10.1561/1700000004

Larivière, B., Keiningham, T. L., Aksoy, L., Yalçin, A., Morgeson, F. V. III, & Mithas, S. (2016). Modeling Heterogeneity in the Satisfaction, Loyalty Intention, and Shareholder Value Linkage: A Cross-Industry Analysis at the Customer and Firm Levels. *JMR, Journal of Marketing Research*, *53*(1), 91–109. doi:10.1509/jmr.12.0143

Laroche, M., Habibi, M. Z., Richard, M., & Sankaranarayanan, R. (2012). The effects of social media based brand communities on brand community markers, value creation practices, brand trust and brand loyalty. *Computers in Human Behavior*, *28*(5), 1755–1767. doi:10.1016/j.chb.2012.04.016

Larson, K., & Watson, R. (2011). The value of social media: toward measuring social media strategies. *Proceedings of the International Conference on Information Systems (ICIS)*, Shanghai, China.

Lee, D., Hosanagar, K., & Nair, H. (2014). The Effect of Social Media Marketing Content on Consumer Engagement: Evidence from Facebook (Working Paper). Wharton School.

Liu, Y. (2006). Word of mouth for movies: Its dynamics and impact on box office revenue. *Journal of Marketing*, *70*(3), 74–89. doi:10.1509/jmkg.70.3.74

Luo, X., Zhang, J., & Duan, W. (2013). Social media and firm equity value. *Information Systems Research*, *24*(1), 146–163. doi:10.1287/isre.1120.0462

Lütkepohl, H., & Krätzig, M. (2004). *Applied Time Series Econometrics*. Cambridge University Press. doi:10.1017/CBO9780511606885

McAlexander, J. H., Schouten, J. W., & Koenig, H. F. (2002). Building brand community. *Journal of Marketing*, *66*(1), 38–54. doi:10.1509/jmkg.66.1.38.18451

Moe, W., Schweidel, D., & Trusov, M. (2011). What influences customers' online comments. *MIT Sloan Management Review*, *53*(1), 14–16.

Muniz, A. M. Jr, & O'Guinn, T. C. (2001). Brand Community. *The Journal of Consumer Research*, *27*(4), 412–432. doi:10.1086/319618

Murdough, C. (2009). Social media measurement: It's not impossible. *Journal of Interactive Advertising*, *10*(1), 94–99. doi:10.1080/15252019.2009.10722165

O'Reilly, K., & Lancendorfer, K. M. (2013). Consumers as "Integrators" of Marketing Communications: When "Like" is as Good as "Buy". *International Journal of E-Business Research*, *9*(4), 1–15. doi:10.4018/ijebr.2013100101

Park, H., & Kim, Y. (2014). The role of social network websites in the consumer–brand relationship. *Journal of Retailing and Consumer Services*, *21*(4), 460–467. doi:10.1016/j.jretconser.2014.03.011

Pesaran, H., & Shin, Y. (1998). Generalized impulse response analysis in linear multivariate models. *Economics Letters*, *58*(1), 17–29. doi:10.1016/S0165-1765(97)00214-0

Peters, K., Chen, Y., Kaplan, A. M., Ognibeni, B., & Pauwels, K. (2013). Social media metrics — a framework and guidelines for managing social media. *Journal of Interactive Marketing*, *27*(4), 281–298. doi:10.1016/j.intmar.2013.09.007

Reinartz, W., Krafft, M., & Hoyer, W. (2004). The customer relationship management process: Its measurement and impact on performance. *JMR, Journal of Marketing Research*, *41*(3), 293–305. doi:10.1509/jmkr.41.3.293.35991

Rozin, P., & Royzman, E. B. (2001). Negativity Bias, Negativity Dominance, and Contagion. *Personality and Social Psychology Review*, *5*(4), 296–320. doi:10.1207/S15327957PSPR0504_2

Schau, H., Muñiz, A. Jr, & Arnould, E. (2009). How brand community practices create value. *Journal of Marketing*, *73*(5), 30–51. doi:10.1509/jmkg.73.5.30

Shahrokh, Z. D., & Poursaeed, M. M. (2015). Managing Non-Organic Virtual Brand Communities in Social Networking Sites. *International Journal of E-Business Research*, *11*(4), 47–62. doi:10.4018/IJEBR.2015100104

Sonnier, G. P., McAlister, L., & Rutz, O. J. (2011). A dynamic model of the effect of online communications on firm sales. *Marketing Science*, *30*(4), 702–716. doi:10.1287/mksc.1110.0642

Sorescu, A., & Sorescu, S. M. (2016). Customer Satisfaction and Long-Term Stock Returns. *Journal of Marketing*, *80*(5), 110–115. doi:10.1509/jm.16.0214

Spence, M. (1973). Job market signaling. *The Quarterly Journal of Economics*, *87*(3), 355–374. doi:10.2307/1882010

Stephen, A. T., & Galak, J. (2012). The effects of traditional and social earned media on sales: A study of a microlending marketplace. *JMR, Journal of Marketing Research*, *49*(5), 624–639. doi:10.1509/jmr.09.0401

Tirunillai, S., & Tellis, G. (2012). Does chatter really matter? Dynamics of user-generated content and stock performance. *Marketing Science*, *31*(2), 198–215. doi:10.1287/mksc.1110.0682

Van Doorn, J., Lemon, K. N., Mittal, V., Nass, S., Pick, D., Pirner, P., & Verhoef, P. C. (2010). Customer engagement behavior: Theoretical foundations and research directions. *Journal of Service Research*, *13*(3), 253–266. doi:10.1177/1094670510375599

Verhoef, P., Reinartz, W., & Krafft, M. (2010). Customer engagement as a new perspective in customer management. *Journal of Service Research*, *13*(3), 247–252. doi:10.1177/1094670510375461

Wirtz, J., den Ambtman, A., Bloemer, J., Horváth, C., Ramaseshan, B., van de Klundert, J., & Kandampully, J. (2013). Managing brands and customer engagement in online brand communities. *Journal of Service Management*, *24*(3), 223–244. doi:10.1108/09564231311326978

This research was previously published in the International Journal of E-Business Research (IJEBR), 13(1); edited by Payam Hanafizadeh and Jeffrey Hsu, pages 25-43, copyright year 2017 by IGI Publishing (an imprint of IGI Global).

Chapter 29
Emotional Branding and Social Media:
Positive and Negative Emotional Appeals

Nicholas Mathew
Cleveland State University, USA

Ashutosh Dixit
Cleveland State University, USA

ABSTRACT

Emotional branding is increasingly being used by marketers to win customers for their products or services. And, social media has become a growing and popular forum where marketers use emotional branding. This paper/chapter explores the concept of emotional branding and the role of emotional branding in marketing contexts such as in social media. Positive and negative emotions are explored with practical examples of advertisements that use emotional appeals. The paper provides a literature review on emotions and emotional branding and offers theoretical perspectives on the emotional branding concept. The paper also provides a brief discussion on the theoretical and practical implications of emotional branding in the realm of marketing.

INTRODUCTION

In the current competitive marketplace, it is important for businesses to capture the attention of potential customers. But, how can businesses successfully gain the attention of customers and make them buy goods and services? Creativity and the generation of new ideas are essential in helping businesses to successfully compete and acquire new customers. As the business landscape evolves, marketers are generating new ideas and helping businesses find creative ways to successfully compete by highlighting the *emotional* aspect of products or services. The highlighting of this emotional aspect falls under a concept known as emotional branding, which has been conceptualized as the successful attachment of a specific emotion to a brand (Rossiter & Bellman, 2012).

DOI: 10.4018/978-1-5225-5637-4.ch029

Emotional branding is about a brand's engagement with consumers on the level of senses and emotions; how a brand comes to life for people and forges a deeper, lasting connection (Gobe, 2009). Marketers can use emotional connections to develop a sense of loyalty and passion among consumers towards a brand (Gobe, 2009). This loyalty and passion can help brands to compete successfully in the marketplace. Researchers have argued that emotional branding usually appeals to consumers not through rational arguments related to the positives and negatives of using a product or service (Gobe, 2009). However, it appeals to consumers through the use of storytelling, narratives, and other tactics that demonstrate an empathetic understanding of customers' inspirations, aspirations, and life circumstances (Thompson, Rindfleisch, & Arsel, 2006).

Research has suggested the importance of branding that takes into account people's emotions or feelings (Holbrook & Hirschman, 1982). From the mid- 2000s on, influential brand consultants, researchers, and writers such as Kevin Roberts and Marc Gobé began educating marketers on the fact that brand awareness and loyalty are not enough and managers now need to seek emotional commitment and create brand love among customers (Koiznets, 2014). Therefore, this chapter seeks to further develop and understand the role and usage of emotional branding in the marketing context. The objectives of this chapter are:

1. To gain an understanding of emotional branding in the realm of social media marketing.
2. To explore the usage of positive and negative emotions by marketers through practical examples.
3. To provide theoretical and practical implications on the usage and role of emotional branding.

This chapter is organized into three sections. The first section of the paper provides a literature review on emotional branding, emotions, and emotional branding and social media. The next section offers practical and theoretical implications, followed by a section that provides concluding thoughts on emotional branding appeals.

LITERATURE REVIEW

This section provides a literature review and discussion on emotions, emotional branding, and emotional branding and social media. It also explores the positive and negative emotions that marketers often use to appeal to consumers. In addition, the section provides practical examples of advertisements that use these positive and negative emotions.

Emotional Branding

Emotional branding is defined as the consumer's attachment of strong, specific, usage-relevant emotions such as love, hate or fear towards a brand (Roberts, 2004; Rossiter & Bellman, 2012). It suggests that customers form a strong bond with brands, which are meaningful to them, captivate them, and compellingly enrich their lives (Merz, He, & Vargo, 2009). The emotional branding appeal generally involves the generation of warm feelings among customers for the brand. Emotional branding is based on the idea that beyond a product's functional benefits, people wish to buy an emotional experience (Peterson, 2006). Beyond promoting and building awareness and loyalty for the brand, emotional branding is about the creation of brand love among consumers. Emotional branding is based on emotions, which are an affective state of consciousness distinguished from cognitive and volitional states of consciousness

(Holbrook & Hirschman, 1982). The full range of relevant emotions a person can experience includes love, hate, fear, joy, boredom, anxiety, pride, anger, disgust, sadness, sympathy, lust, ecstasy, greed, guilt, elation, shame, and awe (Holbrook & Horschmann, 1982).

Emotions

In order to understand emotional branding in detail, it will be useful to understand the concept of emotions. Emotions have been defined as a state of physical and mental readiness that involves valence (directional force), evaluative appraisal, a target (or object or stimulus), and behavioral tendencies (Morrison & Crane, 2007). Researchers have agreed that emotions alter how people perceive the environment and appear to motivate behavior (Morrison & Crane, 2007).

When discussing emotional branding, it is important to understand the concept of attachment. The attachment theory from the field of psychology has been used to explain emotional branding. The theory suggests that the degree of emotional attachment to an object predicts the nature of an individual's interaction with the object. For example, individuals who are strongly attached to a person are more likely to be committed to, invest in, and make sacrifices for that person (Bowlby, 1980; Hazan & Shaver, 1994; Thomson, MacInnis, & Park, 2005). Consumers' emotional attachments to a brand might predict their commitment, repurchase intention, loyalty, and their willingness to make financial sacrifices in order to obtain it (Thomson, MacInnis, & Park, 2005). These emotional attachments can have implications for emotional branding. As part of emotional branding, marketers can use emotional appeals to capitalize on consumers' emotional attachments towards a brand.

Emotional branding can be used by marketers to develop a sense of true loyalty among consumers towards a brand. Some theorists distinguish "truly loyal" repurchase from other repurchasing (Dick & Basu, 1994). Truly, loyal repurchase emanates from strong affective ties to the brand in contrast to other underlying causes (e.g., "spurious loyalty" due to high switching costs) (Pham, 1998). Hence, there is a link between a consumer's true loyalty to a brand and his/her affective ties to the same brand. To better understand these affective ties, it is necessary to understand the concept of affect. Affect is the conscious subjective aspect of feeling or emotion and it plays a central role in consumer decision making (Pham, 1998). In the "How-do-I-feel-about-it?" heuristic, affect is the essential decision input. In relation to affect, researchers have argued that when consumers "feel like" engaging in certain consumption episodes, they act on the information contained in their feelings (Pham, 1998). When discussing affect in relation to consumer consumption patterns, it is important to consider the medium of social media. Social media is an important medium through which marketers connect with consumers. It offers an effective way to develop affective ties with and convey emotional messages to consumers. For instance, research has suggested that by impacting people emotionally with content on a brand's Facebook page, a brand owner is likely to increase the chance of a person forming or increasing an attachment with a brand, and so increase the likelihood of people revisiting brand content on Facebook and communicating with it. Crucially, this attachment is also likely to manifest itself in talk about and recommendations of the brand and its products both off and online (Smith, 2013).

The Two Faces of Emotion: Positive and Negative

Positive emotions include pleasant or desirable situational responses, ranging from interest and contentment to love and joy. These emotions are markers of people's overall well-being or happiness, but they also enhance future growth and success. This has been demonstrated in work, school, relationships, mental and physical health, and longevity (Cohn & Fredrickson, 2009). Positive emotional messages (such as happiness and gratitude) can assuage people's fears and help build trust among people (Dunn & Schweitzer, 2005). Thus, introduction of positive feelings in the consumer may increase the chances that they will select a particular service provider (Morrison & Crane, 2007).

Negative emotions include anger, hate, and sadness and are associated with events that hinder the fulfillment of objectives (Namkung, & Jang, 2010). Advertisers have found that negative emotions appeal to different types of consumers (Cotte & Ritchie, 2005). Desensitized or indifferent customers may find negative emotions (such as fear) appealing. Consumers who feel the need to belong to a certain group (also known as tribal consumers) may also find negative emotions (such as guilt) appealing (Cotte & Ritchie, 2005). Appeals using guilt or fear can motivate consumers who may feel doubtful or uncertain about a purchasing decision to finally make the decision. Thus, the negative appeals (involving fear, guilt, etc.) could result in outcomes where consumers undertake a purchase decision. Thus, authors have listed negative appeals such as those related to fear and sadness (among others) in the chapter. Besides, they have also listed examples of positive appeals such as love and happiness.

The use of positive and negative emotions with practical examples, which have appeared in advertisements, are described below:

1. **Compassion/Caring:** Guinness (Beer). Guinness, a famous beer brand, was promoted in an advertisement where a group of men playing wheelchair basketball makes the viewer of the advertisement feel a sense of admiration and respect for their drive. That is until the game ends and everyone one stands up, save for one guy who is really wheelchair-bound. The realization that his friends stand by him no matter what delivers the ultimate emotional punch line. This advertisement attempts to show the camaraderie and compassion of the wheelchair-bound person's friends and has the potential to strike a strong emotional chord with customers. Beer drinking is sometimes a social activity with people bonding over a few drinks and thus, the strong and friendly relationship among friends shown in the advertisement can have a positive impact on potential consumers (Hum, 2015).
2. **Guilt:** *Save the Children's "Most Shocking Second a Day Video"*. Save the Children is an international non-governmental organization (NGO) that aims to promote children's rights. It provides relief and helps support children in developing countries and conflict zones. Save the Children's video advertisement reimagines how a relatively peaceful country such as Britain would be affected by war, through the eyes of a little girl. It paints a picture of how children (especially those caught in the ongoing Syrian civil war) are the biggest victims of conflict. The ending message: "Just because it isn't happening here doesn't mean it isn't happening" is a powerful motivator that encourages us to act. This advertisement tries to show that we should not be indifferent to what is happening around us. The advertisement can be seen as playing on people's feelings of guilt and spurring them into action to help the children. The advertisement also attempts to develop a certain level of compassion among viewers in order to motivate them to act (Hum, 2015).
3. **Love:** *Tinder/ Domino's Pizza.* Tinder is a very popular dating app that is used in many countries around the world. As of early 2016, it had 25 million registered users (Tinder Information, Statistics, Facts, and History, n.d.). And, many of these users belong to the 18-34 age group. Many companies/ organizations are using Tinder to promote their products or services and raise awareness of social issues. On Valentine's Day, Domino's Pizza began a promotional campaign on Tinder, which gave

users the chance of getting free pizza and discounts. The campaign involved engaging users in the pun-filled Valentine's Day conversations; those users having the best conversations were sent delicious rewards. Their tag line was "Fancy a date with Domino's?"

The campaign had a potential social reach of more than 200,000 users. It was considered a success as its content blended well with the Valentine's Day message of love and romance (Ohanessian, 2016).

4. **Hate:** *Marmite.* Marketers can sometimes use hate or other negative emotions in advertisements to position their brand. They use these emotions to elicit positive feelings towards the brand. British condiment Marmite's distinctive taste evokes strong and polarizing feelings. People either love the taste or hate it. The company embraced these two distinct feelings by developing a "Love It or Hate It" promotional campaign. The campaign has had a strong impact on Marmite's branding and positioning strategies. In fact, Marmite's tagline is "Love it or Hate it." In 2010, Marmite debuted Marmite XO—an extra-strength version and began targeting those consumers who loved the brand. The company used social media to identify 30 consumers who were particularly devoted to the brand, invited them to taste testings (complete with Marmite-flavored cocktails), and set up a Facebook group. The promotion generated more than 54,000 visits to the company's website and 300,000 Facebook page views, and retailers sold out of Marmite XO as soon as it arrived on their shelves (Luo, Wiles, & Raithel, 2014).
5. **Gratitude:** *Uber.* The app-enabled taxi service, Uber, has been positioning itself as brand that is convenient, easy, effective, and trustworthy. A customer would have feelings of gratitude when they are able to use a product or service that they can trust. This sense of gratitude may translate into a loyal customer base for the product or service. Uber is trying to find areas where they have the opportunity to build a deeper connection with customers; they want their customers to feel secure and trusting in their feelings towards the Uber service. For instance, there was a customer who left a $200 umbrella in an Uber car. The obligation for Uber was to return the umbrella to the customer; a customer service representative got hold of the umbrella, boxed it up with Uber sunglasses and a hat, and posted it over her lunchbreak back to the customer (Cameron, 2016). Uber plans to highlight these customer experiences in their promotional campaigns as it tries to emotionally connect with customers. Also, as part of its promotional campaigns, Uber actively uses social media to showcase the real-life stories of its drivers and riders with the aim of inspiring potential customers and employees.
6. **Doubt:** *Under Armour.* American sports clothing and accessories company, Under Armour's "I Will What I Want" campaign tells the story of a ballet candidate who is rejected for not having the right body and for being too old. Anyone facing rejection will experience emotions related to doubt; we would start doubting ourselves and start losing confidence. The campaign which has been widely shared on social media has a positive twist when we see that the rejected ballet candidate grows up to be Misty Copeland, a well-known professional ballet soloist for the American Ballet Theatre (Hum, 2015). Within a few weeks of the advertisement's release, the "IWILLWHATIWANT" hashtag had been used in over 3000 tweets and the video had been viewed more than 4.2 million times on YouTube and had over 1600 likes on Instagram (Hulting, 2014). Under Armour has actively promoted the campaign on social media and made good use of the digital content marketing space

7. **Bravery/Hope:** *Dabur Vatika ad.* Dabur Vatika, a hair oil and shampoo product manufactured by the well-known Indian brand Dabur is promoted in a campaign that highlights hope and bravery (Indus Net Techshu, 2015) Dabur's "Brave and Beautiful" campaign salutes female cancer survivors. The advertisement shows a bald woman who has just recovered from cancer. She has survived the disease but is not confident of how her neighbors or colleagues would look at her. Then we see her getting ready for her first day at office after the cancer treatment. She ties a head wrap first but then removes it. She looks at herself in the mirror after wearing a saree – with doubt written all over her face. Then, her husband places a small bindi on her forehead - an act that gives her the needed support to go out into the world. She enters her office with apprehension but is soon well-received and warmly welcomed by her colleagues. The emotions are visible in the expressions and behavior of the actors in the advertisement. The advertisement's message might leave the viewer in tears; not tears of sadness but of hope" (Indus Net Techshu, 2015). The advertisement garnered 2.4 million views on YouTube and went viral on many social media sites; the campaign gained a couple of million likes on Facebook and many followers on Twitter (Gururani, 2015).
8. **Fear:** *Public Anti-Smoking commercial.* Many public health anti- smoking advertisements show the negative effects of smoking and thus strike a certain degree of fear in the hearts and minds of people viewing those advertisements. For example, the "Heartbreak" anti-bidi smoking campaign launched by the Government of India showcases the negative implications of smoking. The campaign has been promoted through social media and has the potential to reach a wide group of people. The campaign shows the adverse effects of smoking on the smoker's family and overall health (WHO Framework Convention on Tobacco Control, 2011). These campaigns/advertisements can have a strong emotional impact on people and can motivate them to act.
9. **Happiness:** *British Airways.* British Airways has created promotional campaigns with strong emotional undertones for their Indian target market. In the "A Ticket to Visit Mum" promotional campaign, the airline helps a New Yorker named Ratnesh fly back to Mumbai to share a meal with his mother. And, in the "Go Further to Get Closer" campaign, a married Indian couple Sumeet and Chetna, who work so tirelessly that they rarely get to see one another, reconnect on a trip to London. The couple also appears on a "How Close Are You?" Facebook quiz that includes personalized vacation suggestions. Both these campaigns have garnered millions of views on social media. British Airways customers include many Indian expatriates who live thousands of miles away from home; these expats often like to remember their home country. Thus, British Airways developed a campaign/content marketing experience that tries to create among their Indian customers positive memories of their homeland. "This content marketing experience doesn't do anything to resolve flight-related questions, but they attempt to link British Airways to happy and positive memories of home, family, and the people we love—the kind of feeling that can compel someone to share a video or buy a plane ticket" (Braun, 2015).
10. **Sadness:** *Metlife Hong Kong.* Insurance company Metlife Hong Kong developed the "Dream for My Child" integrated advertising campaign centered on a very emotional commercial, "My Dad's Story". The advertisement features a young girl reading aloud her reflections on her father. She moves from sentimental admiration of the sweetest daddy in the world through to her struggles to come to terms with his dual life. The father shows himself to his daughter as having a job, money, and not being hungry. However, it becomes clear that the father is taking a wide range of menial jobs to earn money for his daughter's education and to provide for her more generally. As the commercial draws to a close, the viewer can feel the sadness experienced by both father and daughter.

The final message is "A child's future is worth every sacrifice". MetLife then invites viewers to visit a website where they can submit their dreams for their children for a chance to win a 3-year endowment plan, and find out about MetLife's EduCare saving plans for parents to save money for their children's higher education (Macleod, 2015).

11. **Pleasure/Fun:** *Frooti.* Frooti is one of the largest-selling mango flavored drinks in India and has been very popular in the country. The #TheFrootilife campaign marked the rebranding of the Frooti drink. The campaign's aim was to create a miniature world of pleasure and fun where Frooti was the focus. The campaign created plenty of visual play around mangoes as well as the actual product, keeping it fun and colorful. The brand made use of the nostalgia element, as many Indians relate to Frooti being a memory from their childhood days. They created engaging videos that told a story and instantly connected with everyone, touching upon the idea of nostalgia. The campaign drove great numbers with content that was not only enjoyable but also shareable, especially on social media. This campaign helped to re-establish the brand and bring it closer to the intended target. The brand began engaging with consumers on a personal level by sending cartons of Frooti to offices around the country. This engagement generated much user-generated content (such as tweets and videos) that further built the reach and increased the visibility of the brand across social media platforms (Mindshift Interactive, 2016). The campaign also made use of Bollywood stars such as Shah Rukh Khan to better connect with the audience and enhance the brand's appeal.
12. **Frustration/Anger:** *Naukri.com.* Jobs and recruitment site Naukri.com created an advertisement set in a professional company office where an angry boss named Hari Sadu is dealing with two of his employees when a phone call comes through. One of the employees attempts to help his boss with the call by speaking to the caller. While helping, the employee takes shots at his boss by spelling out to the caller in a particular way the boss' name; the name Hari Sadu is spelled out as H for Hitler, A for Arrogant, R for Rascal and I for Idiot….. The boss is clearly embarrassed/upset and possibly begins to realize that he has been treating his employees badly. Many people may have had rude and arrogant bosses in their working careers and they would have felt very frustrated working for such bosses. This advertisement highlighted the frustration experienced by employees in their daily working lives and thus struck an emotional chord with many people. (Indus Net Techshu, 2015). The advertisement which has been widely shared on social media has helped increase Naukri's brand profile.

Emotional Branding and Social Media

Social media has become an important area for marketers to consider when promoting goods and services. Marketers can think of social media platforms as creative outlets — and as an opportunity to provide fresh, fun messages in an easily digestible manner for their customers and target audiences (Helmes, 2016). Popular social media platforms include Facebook, Twitter, LinkedIn, Google Plus, Instagram, YouTube, WhatsApp, Pinterest, and Reddit. Many businesses – big and small– have social media pages dedicated to engaging with their customers.

For instance, on Facebook, existing or potential customers can simply "like" a company page and start receiving regular updates regarding its products and services. Facebook is currently the biggest social media network on the Internet, both in terms of the number of users and name recognition (Maina, 2016). It has around 1.59 billion monthly active users, thus making it one of the best mediums for businesses to connect with people from all over the world (Maina, 2016).

Twitter has around 320 million active monthly users while YouTube has over 1 billion website visitors per month and is the second most popular search engine behind Google (Maina, 2016). WhatsApp is a very popular messaging service and is very popular in countries such as India and Brazil; more than one billion people use WhatsApp worldwide. Other social media sites such as Instagram and Pinterest are fast becoming popular and are used by millions of people around the world. It is clear that marketers can use social media platforms to reach audiences far and wide. And, marketers can use emotional branding in social media to build relationships with and create loyalty among customers (Kozinets, 2014).

Social media is about connecting, building, and maintaining relationships between and among people. Similarly, emotional branding is about connecting, building, and maintaining relationships with customers. Marketers can effectively use social media to encourage customers to talk about how they're thinking and feeling — especially, about a particular company/business. It is important for marketers to keep this dialogue open to generate word of mouth (Patel & Puri, 2016). And, word of mouth has credibility as it is based on someone's personal experience; it is emotional branding at its best (Gobe, 2009).

Social media sites such as Twitter and Facebook are effective emotional branding tools for word of mouth marketing. In Twitter, with just 140 characters, people can tweet very easily their feelings, emotions, or thoughts about a product or service. Given the 140-character tweet limit, Twitter also forces people to be concise and succinct when communicating their thoughts and feelings. This succinctness presents an excellent opportunity for companies to develop small-sized catch phrases to connect with customers emotionally. Phrases such as "British Airways: Fueled by Love" - which is part of an advertisement campaign aimed at British Airways' India customers - are catchy and have generated plenty of attention on social media. The phrase has become a hashtag *(#Fuelledbylove);* such hashtags are often used on social media sites to convey messages and are a quick and concise way of getting the brand across to millions of people worldwide.

Social media can be used by both companies and customers to express many positive feelings about a particular brand. On the downside, however, when customers are angry about a negative experience, they can easily vent their anger through social media (Patel & Puri, 2016). And, companies must be careful in responding to such customers via social media as any response could attract a certain level of publicity – either negative or positive. While there are many positives to using social media for emotional branding, marketers should also be aware of some negatives.

When communicating with customers, marketers may encounter "Trolls" on social media. Trolls are people who usually post negative comments on social media not because they are genuinely unhappy with a particular company and want to find a solution (Nelson, 2016). They post mainly because they want to get a negative emotional response out of anyone who reads their posts. They do not want a solution to their "problem"– they just want an argument or fight (Nelson, 2016). The ways in which companies respond to customers on social media can have an impact – positive or negative – on their emotional branding strategy. Nevertheless, social media can be an excellent tool for businesses to engage with customers; such engagement can also result in the development of a feedback loop involving customers and businesses.

Feedback loops result in the exchange of ideas between businesses and their customers; such exchanges can help businesses improve their product or service offerings. Companies such as the famed café, Starbucks, leverage social media to develop feedback loops and build/or maintain relationships with their customers. And, the building and maintenance of such relationships is an important aspect of emotional branding.

Emoticons is another aspect of emotional branding social media usage that is worth considering. An emoticon is a digital icon or a sequence of keyboard symbols that serves to represent a facial expression, as:-) for a smiling face or as:- (for despair or sad face. They are used in a digital message or text to convey the writer's emotions or clarify intent (Robb, 2014). The use of emoticons varies across cultures with different emoticons used in Western and Eastern cultures. In fact, on a broader level, the use of emoticons varies by geography, age, gender, and social class—similar to language dialects or regional accents (Robb, 2014).

Emoticons are sometimes used to overcome awkward situations as people usually feel more comfortable disclosing their positive or negative emotions through virtual communication (as in over the Internet and social media) rather than face to face. For example, in South Korea where people are major users of emoticons, pictorial representations appeal not just to the young but also to middle-aged office workers looking to smooth awkward or delicate situations with bosses, colleagues, and family members (Studer, 2016).

Brands are increasingly using emoticons to get their message across to customers. Emoticons help brands to define emotions they want to be associated with and evoke specific responses from users. They enable brands to add an element of fun, enthusiasm, and personalization in their communication (Khetarpal, 2016). Companies are using emoticons to target certain demographics, especially consumers in the 13 – 25 age group (Khetarpal, 2016).

Emoticons have become an important part of the marketing campaigns of some brands with some companies even trademarking/patenting their use. Pepsi in India launched its #PepsiMoji campaign during the popular sporting event, IPL. The soft drinks major developed thirty eight patented emojis and used them across media streams such as outdoor and digital films. These patented emojis were also put on the packaging of Pepsi and Diet Pepsi cans, and on PET bottles. The idea of the campaign was to let consumers buy Pepsi based on their mood and use it to express what they are feeling (Khetarpal, 2016). While emoticons have clearly become popular in marketing campaigns, there is a danger that their increased usage can result in communication becoming too impersonal for some consumers. Thus, companies need to be balanced and strategic in their use of pictorial representations such as emoticons in their promotional campaigns.

Companies using social media in their promotional campaigns need to be aware that everything on social media can be checked and monitored but not controlled (Gobe, 2009). For instance, consumers can easily post negative comments about a certain brand with companies unable to do much to control such negative publicity. Companies can sometimes use such negative publicity as an opportunity to better connect with customers and build stronger relationships – building relationships being one of the most important elements that make up emotional branding. They need to be open and transparent about what they can offer to customers; this openness can help build trust in a certain brand.

IMPLICATIONS

The primary purpose of the chapter is to explore the role of emotional branding in the context of social media. As part of this exploration, authors have provided practical examples of the usage of positive and negative emotional appeals by marketers. Also, the attachment theory has been employed to explain the use of emotional branding by marketers (Thomson et al., 2005). The theory provides an insight into why marketers use emotional branding to appeal to consumers.

The concept of emotional branding can also be connected to the theories on brand loyalty and organizational commitment. Truly loyal purchases by consumers are based on strong affective (i.e. related to moods, feeling, and attitudes) ties and commitments to the brand. The emotional core of these affective ties is emotional attachment, which is the foundation for the consumers' commitment to a certain organization, its products or brands. This commitment will result in persistent and desire-driven brand purchase, repurchase, and loyalty. The emotional attachment (as described in the attachment theory) is what marketers hope to build on with consumers when they deploy emotional appeals in marketing campaigns. Thus, through real-life emotional branding advertisement examples, this study attempts to connect theory to practice.

On a practical level, the logical outcome of deep emotional attachment is extreme brand loyalty—repurchase "against all odds and at all costs," despite situational incentives and enticements aimed at inducing switching (Oliver, 1999). Marketers can thus build emotional attachment to brands as a strategy to realize the financial rewards of true loyalty (Grisaffe & Nguyen, 2011). An emotional attachment could take customers beyond brand loyalty to brand evangelism (Riorini, 2016; VanAuken, 2016). And, people who experience an emotion tend to start a communication process to share this emotion with others. In fact, the more disruptive the emotional event, the sooner and more frequently it will be shared. (VanAuken, 2016). Thus, emotional appeals can also diffuse sooner among people and potentially be more effective.

CONCLUSION

Social media affords great opportunities for marketers to develop brands that focus on people's emotions or feelings. Many companies around the world have made a tremendous impact through emotional branding strategies in the realm of social media. Emotional branding in social media can have two sides – positive and negative. The positive or bright side can result in the elicitation of strong and passionate feelings among consumers towards a brand. However, too much positivity with little action is what marketers need to be cautious about. If a company makes positive claims on social media, then it needs to be ready to back them up with good product quality or customer service.

Marketers should also not hesitate to use negative emotions in their campaigns. Sometimes, negative emotions can be used with humor in an advertisement; humor can soften the negative feelings and create a positive impact on potential consumers. Negative appeals can evoke an uncomfortable state that makes consumers want the "solution" offered by the advertiser (Aaker, Stayman &Hagerty 1986; Cotte & Ritchie, 2005). Marketers usually use negative emotional appeals to: (a) capture their audience's attention, (b) induce an intended set of emotions, and (c) motivate them to purchase the marketer's product or service (Richins 1997; for a review see Cohen & Charles, 1991; Cotte & Ritchie, 2005).

For marketers, it is important to self-regulate when involved in emotional branding. Since the branding is based on emotions, there is a chance that consumers may not be making a fully rational consumption decision (when purchasing a brand that was promoted through emotions). As a result, marketers need to be cautious about capitalizing too much on people's emotions; they should be careful about any negative social consequences that might result from their marketing campaigns. Thus, emotional branding needs to be balanced and strike the right tone.

REFERENCES

Aaker, D. A., Stayman, D. M., & Hagerty, M. R. (1986). Warmth in advertising: Measurement, impact, and sequence effects. *The Journal of Consumer Research, 12*(4), 365–381. doi:10.1086/208524

Bowlby, J. (1980). *Attachment and loss*. New York, NY: Basic books.

Braun, A. (2015). *Emotional Branding: The Missing Piece In Your Content Strategy*. Retrieved September 1, 2016 from http://www.cmo.com/opinion/articles/2015/9/1/emotional-branding-the-missing-piece-in-your-content-strategy.html#gs.=TI9Q7w

Cameron, N. (2016). *How brands are tackling the emotional heart of customer experience*. Retrieved August 12, 2016 from http://www.cmo.com.au/article/603503/how-brands-tackling-emotional-heart-customer-experience/

Cohen, J. B., & Charles, S. A. (1991). Affect and Consumer Behavior. In T. S. Robertson & H. H. Kassarjian (Eds.), *Handbook of Consumer Behavior* (pp. 188–240). Englewood Cliffs, NJ: Prentice-Hall.

Cohn, M. A., & Fredrickson, B. L. (2009). Positive emotions. Oxford Handbook of Positive Psychology, 2, 13-24.

Cotte, J., & Ritchie, R. (2005). Advertisers' theories of consumers: Why use negative emotions to sell? In *NA-Advances in Consumer Research* (Vol. 32, pp. 24–31). Duluth, MN: Association of Consumer Research.

Daye, D. (2016). *Insights for Emotional Branding. Branding Strategy Insider*. Retrieved September 7, 2016, from https://www.brandingstrategyinsider.com

Dick, A. S., & Basu, K. (1994). Customer loyalty: Toward an integrated conceptual framework. *Journal of the Academy of Marketing Science, 22*(2), 99–113. doi:10.1177/0092070394222001

Dunn, J. R., & Schweitzer, M. E. (2005). Feeling and believing: The influence of emotion on trust. *The Journal of Applied Psychology, 88*, 736–748. PMID:15898872

Gobe, M. (2010). Emotional Branding, Revised Edition: The New Paradigm for Connecting Brands to People. New York, NY: Skyhorse Publishing, Inc.

Grisaffe, D. B., & Nguyen, H. P. (2011). Antecedents of emotional attachment to brands. *Journal of Business Research, 64*(10), 1052–1059. doi:10.1016/j.jbusres.2010.11.002

Gururani, V. (2015, October 30). *Top 3 Social Media Campaigns That Went Viral in 2014! - Just Poked!*. Retrieved August 31, 2016, from https://www.linkedin.com/pulse/top-3-social-media-campaigns-went-viral-2014-just-poked-gururani

Hazan, C., & Shaver, P. R. (1994). Attachment as an organizational framework for research on close relationships. *Psychological Inquiry, 5*(1), 1–22. doi:10.1207/s15327965pli0501_1

Helmes, S. (2016). *Email marketing in the age of social media: Marketing Land*. Retrieved September 25, 2016, from http://marketingland.com/email-marketing-age-social-media-190205

Holbrook, M. B., & Hirschman, E. C. (1982). The experiential aspects of consumption: Consumer fantasies, feelings, and fun. *The Journal of Consumer Research*, *9*(2), 132–140. doi:10.1086/208906

Hulting, N. (2014, September 10). *Under Armour's #IWillWhatIWant Campaign Finds Its Audience*. Retrieved September 24, 2016, from http://www.brittonmdg.com/the-britton-blog/under-armours-iwillwhatiwant-campaign-finds-its-audience/

Hum, S. (2015, June 9). *Right In The #Feels – 13 Examples of Emotion-Focused Marketing*. Retrieved September 25, 2016, from http://www.referralcandy.com/blog/feels-13-examples-emotion-centric-marketing/

Indus Net Techshu. (2015, January 30). *Emotional Branding – 7 Indian Brands Tapping Into Emotions*. Retrieved September 7, 2016, from http://www.techshu.com/blog/emotional-branding-7-indian-brands-tapping-emotions

Khetarpal, S. (2016). *The Smiley Way -Business Today*. Retrieved September 20, 2016, from http://www.businesstoday.in/magazine/features/brands-are-increasingly-using-emojis-in-their-messaging/story/234247.html

Kozinets, R. V. (2014). Social brand engagement: A new idea. *GfK Marketing Intelligence Review*, *6*(2), 8–15. doi:10.2478/gfkmir-2014-0091

Luo, X., Wiles, M., & Raithel, S. (2014, August 18). *Make the Most of a Polarizing Brand*. Retrieved August 1, 2016, from https://hbr.org/2013/11/make-the-most-of-a-polarizing-brand

Macleod, D. (2015, February 19). *MetLife shares My Dad's Story*. Retrieved August 6, 2016, from http://theinspirationroom.com/daily/2015/metlife-shares-my-dads-story/

Maina, A. (2016). *20 Popular Social Media Sites Right Now, Small Business Trends*. Retrieved August 12, 2016, from http://smallbiztrends.com/2016/05/popular-social-media-sites.html

Merz, M. A., He, Y., & Vargo, S. L. (2009). The evolving brand logic: A service-dominant logic perspective. *Journal of the Academy of Marketing Science*, *37*(3), 328–344. doi:10.1007/s11747-009-0143-3

Mindshift Interactive. (2016, January 19). *Content marketing that makes the cut on social media | Forbes India Blog*. Retrieved September 25, 2016, from http://forbesindia.com/blog/business-strategy/content-marketing-that-makes-the-cut-on-social-media/#ixzz4KTN9X5ke

Morrison, S., & Crane, F. G. (2007). Building the service brand by creating and managing an emotional brand experience. *Journal of Brand Management*, *14*(5), 410–421. doi:10.1057/palgrave.bm.2550080

Namkung, Y., & Jang, S. C. (2010). Effects of perceived service fairness on emotions, and behavioral intentions in restaurants. *European Journal of Marketing*, *44*(9/10), 1233–1259. doi:10.1108/03090561011062826

Nelson, S. (2016). *Social Listening: How to Create Feedback Loops Between Your Company and Your Community- DigitalMarketer*. Retrieved August 12, 2016, from http://www.digitalmarketer.com/social-listening/

Ohanessian, B. (2016, April 12). *7 Creative Tinder Marketing Campaigns that will Inspire Your Brand to Think Outside the Box*. Retrieved September 7, 2016, from https://www.sprinklr.com/the-way/7-creative-tinder-marketing-campaigns/

Oliver, R. (1997). Satisfaction: A Behavioral Perspective on the Consumer. New York: McGraw–Hill.

Patel, N., & Puri, R. (2016). *The complete guide to understanding consumer psychology, Quicksprout*. Retrieved September 15, 2016, from https://www.quicksprout.com/the-complete-guide-to-understand-customer-psychology-chapter-2/

Peterson, J. E. (2006). Qatar and the world: Branding for a micro-state. *The Middle East Journal*, *60*(4), 732–748. doi:10.3751/60.4.15

Pham, M. T. (1998). Representativeness, relevance, and the use of feelings in decision making. *The Journal of Consumer Research*, *25*(2), 144–159. doi:10.1086/209532

Richins, M. L. (1997). Measuring Emotions in the Consumption Experience. *The Journal of Consumer Research*, *24*(2), 127–146. doi:10.1086/209499

Robb, A. (2014). *How Using Emoji Makes Us Less Emotional- New Republic*. Retrieved August 15, 2016, from https://newrepublic.com/article/118562/emoticons-effect-way-we-communicate-linguists-study-effects

Roberts, K. (2004). *Lovemarks: The Future Beyond Brands*. New York: Powerhouse Books.

Rossiter, J., & Bellman, S. (2012). Emotional branding pays off. *Journal of Advertising Research*, *52*(3), 291–296. doi:10.2501/JAR-52-3-291-296

Smith, S. (2013). Conceptualising and evaluating experiences with brands on Facebook. *International Journal of Market Research*, *55*(3), 357–374. doi:10.2501/IJMR-2013-034

Studer, S. (2016). *The Curious Adventures of Con and Frodo - The Economist*. Retrieved September 24, 2016, from https://www.1843magazine.com/technology/the-curious-adventures-of-con-and-frodo

Thompson, C. J., Rindfleisch, A., & Arsel, Z. (2006). Emotional branding and the strategic value of the doppelgänger brand image. *Journal of Marketing*, *70*(1), 50–64. doi:10.1509/jmkg.2006.70.1.50

Thomson, M., MacInnis, D. J., & Park, C. W. (2005). The ties that bind Measuring the strength of consumers emotional attachments to brands. *Journal of Consumer Psychology*, *15*(1), 77–91. doi:10.1207/s15327663jcp1501_10

Tinder Information, Statistics, Facts, and History. (n.d.). *Dating Sites Reviews*. Retrieved September 10, 2016, from http://www.datingsitesreviews.com/staticpages/index.php?page=Tinder-Statistics-Facts-History

VanAuken, B. (2016). *How Brands Make Emotional Connections*. Retrieved September 24, 2016, from https://www.brandingstrategyinsider.com/2015/09/how-brands-make-emotional-connections.html#.WLHmtH9HRld

WHO Framework Convention on Tobacco Control. (2011, June). *India – "Heartbreak" anti-bidi smoking campaign launched.* Retrieved September 24, 2016, from http://www.citationmachine.net/bibliographies/208207296?new=true

KEY TERMS AND DEFINITIONS

Brand Loyalty: A type of consumer behavior where consumers develop a strong commitment to a particular brand expressed through repeat purchases of the brand irrespective of factors such as price, competition or convenience.

Emotional Attachment: Emotional attachment is characterized by profound feelings of connection, affection, and desire between two persons or between a person and a brand/product/service.

Emotional Branding: Branding which results in consumers developing a profound attachment to a particular brand based on emotions such as love, hate, happiness or fear.

Emotions: Emotions are a state of physical and mental readiness that involves a) directional force (positive or negative), b) making evaluations or assessments, c) a particular object or stimulus, and c) certain behavioral tendencies.

Negative Emotions: Negative emotions involve feelings such as anger, hate, and sadness. Negative emotions are usually associated with events that hinder the fulfillment of objectives.

Positive Emotions: Positive emotions involve pleasant or desirable situational responses, ranging from interest and happiness to love and joy.

Social Media: Website and application platforms on which users network with each other, exchange information, and create and share content.

This research was previously published in Driving Customer Appeal Through the Use of Emotional Branding edited by Ruchi Garg, Ritu Chhikara, Tapan Kumar Panda, and Aarti Kataria, pages 289-302, copyright year 2018 by Business Science Reference (an imprint of IGI Global).

Chapter 30
Engaging Your Global Social Media Audience: A Framework for E-Retailers

Leila Samii
Aurora University, USA

ABSTRACT

The global reach of social media provides opportunities for e-Retailers. Implementing a global social media strategy maximizes the efficiency of the exchange of information between the target audience and the brand. Information acquisition provides e-Retailers with knowledge about their target audience, while information dissemination spreads awareness about the brand to the target audience. As a result, e-Retailers leveraging user content on social media enable the development of strategic global engagement to reduce cultural complexities. The REALLY framework develops a foundation to leverage user-generated content using standardization for multilayered social media campaigns for e-Retailers. Roxy's global social media campaign is used as a case example to analyze global social media strategy and internationalization.

INTRODUCTION

There is no question of the vast size and global reach of social media. The potential for e-Retailers to spread content on social media is limitless across applications and country borders. In fact, in the US 52% of adults are using at least two social media platforms (Duggan, Ellison, Lampe Lenhart & Madden, 2015). There is a need for a foundational understanding of social media concepts to leverage global strategy independent of social media channels.

The extensive reach of social media has changed the way people communicate across countries and cultures. The range and speed of social media supports e-Retailers in the efficient exchange of information with consumers across markets through a global strategy. Marketing has evolved from traditional one-way and two-way broadcasting strategies to a more dynamic social strategy creating multi-way communication between the brand and consumer (Piskori, 2010).

DOI: 10.4018/978-1-5225-5637-4.ch030

The multi-way communication is not limited to channels or borders. Opportunities are created for e-Retailers to listen to the content being posted from the social media community. The exchange of information between the consumer and e-Retailer creates a dialogue for both sides to learn about one another. Many brands have been utilizing social media; however they do so from a country to country perspective, limiting the full potential of social media. Social media should be standardized to reach a global audience. Using a global strategy on social media enables e-Retailers to maximize their efficiency and social media community.

Social media applications are global platforms with limitless barriers to enter into the space. The optimal approach to global social media strategy has created complexity amongst brands. There are mixed results as to the optimal approach for implementing either a global or multi-domestic social media strategy. There is gap in the literature discussing social media strategy from a global lens however extending theory from multiple disciplines creates a holistic understanding of global social media strategy. For example, global strategy versus multi-domestic strategy has been discussed in the international business literature with support for both. A global strategy emphasizes standardization across countries to increase economies of scale (Levitt, 1983) while a multi-domestic strategy emphasizes adaptation from country to country to customize for the specific market (Ohmae, 1989). Both multi-domestic and global strategies have their benefits and drawbacks; however adapting and standardizing parts of the business units seems most reasonable (Quelch & Hoff, 1993). Looking specifically at social media, it is beneficial for e-Retailers to leverage the global reach of their social media message through a comprehensive strategy.

Through a global social media strategy, complexities of culture will become a challenge. Therefore, there is a need for strategies to be developed to leverage user generated content and reduce cultural complexities. Many brands have leveraged user generated content to efficiently spread brand awareness around their company. In fact, listening to the content being spread on social media provides learning opportunities for e-Retailers to understand more about their community in their specific industry. Through the careful listening and analysis of user posts e-Retailers can develop engagement strategies for their community. An e-Retailer's brand image can be reflected through a strategic social media campaign leveraging user global engagement.

This chapter develops a model for social media strategy after surveying internationalization research. A global social media model is presented to capitalize on user generated content for a global strategy. The proposed REALLY framework developed by the author is a holistic approach for managing cultural challenges while maximizing the true global reaches on social media. This chapter is organized in the following: first an introduction into the theoretical concepts that guide global social media are presented, then a framework for successful global e-Retailing on social media is proposed. Next, Roxy Quicksilvers' Dare Yourself campaign is analyzed as a case example and finally the new social internationalization process is revealed to guide the process.

BACKGROUND

Global Social Media

In a report conducted by Nielsen, it was discovered that personal computer and mobile phone users spend more time on social media sites than on any other site (Nielsen, 2012). Alongside search engine optimization, social media leads the promotional marketing strategy mix in lead generation for companies

(Hubspot, 2013). Social media sites are formed by user generated content (UGC) added to a specific Web 2.0 application (Kaplan & Haenlein, 2010). Social media leverages the online community to create UGC on the dynamic global platform. In an effort to increase traffic on the Web 2.0 about a specific brand, users share content about their own perceptions of the brand. The information that is shared varies between positive or negative, short or long, with or without visual content. There are multiple types of content that users create that are all dependent on their experience with the brand. In some cases, consumers are creating or adding to conversations about a brand without ever having an interaction with the brand. UGC is inevitable on social media.

Social media content is shared on various platforms to people with similar interests. Due to social media, the first touch point a consumer experiences with a brand may or may not originate from the brand. In many instances, a consumer will have pre-conceived notions that guide their brand experience from another customer's experience with the brand (Bruhn, Schoenmueller & Schafer, 2012). The landscape of social media is a global borderless platform and if UGC is not managed it will be detrimental to e-Retailers. Successful brands leveraging the multi-way communication use strategies which enlist users to create content around the e-Retailer with a clear message to help with the brand image.

The generation of a brand with full control of their image fully is long gone (Barwise & Meehan, 2010). Social media users from across the globe have a larger say in an e-Retailers brand image. Customer demand and business imperatives are truly global with the increase in Web 2.0 (Iacobucci, Arabie, & Bodapati, 2000) and even more so with the rise of social media applications and usage. Social media users adopt and colonize on each one of the platforms to develop communities including members from all over the world. According to the Internet World Stats (2015) Facebook has over 1 billion subscribers with over 93% daily active users from 210 different countries and territories. Social media applications have been commonly compared to population sizes of countries from around the world. The one difference between physical countries and social media applications are the limitless size and minimal barriers to enter onto the social media sites for people from various cultures. Comparatively, China and India are the only countries that surpass the population of Facebook, the leading social media site, in terms of "citizens" (United States Census, 2015).

The vast range and speed of information spreading through the Web 2.0 is as fast as any consumers connection speed. Thus, the virality or sharing of content quickly spreads from country to country through social media. The global reach of social media sites has blurred the geographic lines that differentiate countries due to the openness of communication and spread of information on the Web 2.0. Social media applications encourage a large marketplace for exchange of goods, services and ideas across the borderless world. The Web 2.0 has created "an invisible continent" (Ohmae, 2000) enabling firms to reveal information about their brand prior to entering the market, while obtaining market knowledge and acquiring information about consumers in a given country (Prashantham, 2005).

The openness of social media on the Invisible Continent not only has limited barriers for users to enter, but also for firms to create a strong presence to communicate brand messages. Therefore, once on social media sites, a brand is now open to most countries on the online marketplace which is facilitated by the Web 2.0 (Ohmae, 2000). For e-Retailers, the openness of social media creates many opportunities as an e-Retailer brand becomes global with no barriers for a brand or consumer to become a part of the social media continent. E-Retailers posting on social media should focus their social media marketing on a global strategy to maximize the spread of a message.

In an effort to minimize cultural blunders, many e-Retailing firms have focused their attention on dividing their social media accounts on a country to country basis or through a fragmented organizational structure. Research has shown language is an important cultural factor for consumer acceptance of social media content (Singh, Lenhert, & Bostick, 2012) and supports the fragmented social media organization structure. However, the efficiency of social media is lost if the firm does not implement a centralized social media organizational strategy. E-Retailing firms should focus on implementing a global social media strategy to leverage all of the benefits of social media for a competitive advantage in the global marketplace (Etgar & Rachman-Moore, 2010).

Internationalization

Johanson and Vahlne (1977) first introduced the Uppsala model of internationalization as an incremental approach to selling abroad. Traditionally, internationalization is explained as gradual transition into foreign markets based upon the market knowledge, market commitment, commitment decisions and current activities of the firm. The gradual international process was thought to be vital factor in decreasing the liability of foreignness and the costs associated with uncertainty of doing business in foreign markets (Zaheer, 1995). However, since the Uppsula model was introduced the business environment has changed and the borderless world has decreased the importance of foreign market entry and expansion strategies (Johanson & Vahlne, 2009). The growth of the internet and social media infrastructure has generated highly connected global businesses. Highly connected brands in the marketplace are interconnected with a brand presence on social media building consumer brand awareness. On the other hand, brands have more knowledge about the consumer and the industry. The information a brand learns through social media decreases a brand's liability of foreignness with the details of the marketing environment.

The Invisible Continent has changed the process in which brands move abroad and learn about the markets' they are entering. Internationalization is important for position-building in a foreign network, not only for market entry (Axelsson & Johanson, 1992). The exchange of content on the internet has strengthened information acquisition about the market so e-Retailing businesses develop stronger positioning strategies. Firms leverage the Internet to acquire knowledge and for resource building for a better understanding of the market (Loane, 2006), while social media provides a deeper layer of consumer knowledge. The e-Retailer acquires a more individualized perspective of the target audience to have a better understanding of their consumers. By expanding an e-Retailers' social media presence for researching the marketing environment, consumers are more likely to passively notice the brand on social media through their personal community more than on the Web 2.0.

Social media facilitates a large exchange of personal and brand related information in developing connections. On social media, observable exchanges of information and conversations are the norm which leads to relationship building between the brand and its social media community. The information processed by the brand aids in understanding the environment of a country. As a result, the internet has increased network relationships (Mathew, Healy & Ali, 2006) and has become a prominent factor for internationalization (Coviello & Munro, 1997). The parallel between network relationships and communities reveal the constant formation of social media sites and social networks. Social media communities have created network relationships with the various levels of the brand's social media community, which will be discussed in more detail later in the chapter. A social media community includes the users that are a prominent driving factor of the information that populates a brand's social media page.

The exchange of information and the relationship building is vital to the success of a global brand and should be utilized to market brand products. International marketing knowledge, cross border customer knowledge and customer acquisition are facilitated by the internet (Mathew et al., 2006). E-Retailing brands using search engine portals leverage the access of international customers towards a pathway for internationalization. The process of internationalization through the internet is beneficial for selling products. On the other hand, brands learn specifically about the marketplace while consumers can learn about certain products and services through a brand's owned social media site.

Information Exchange

Social media enables brands to access cultural and market knowledge despite the cultural and geographical proximity or psychic distance (Arenius, 2005; Child, Ng & Wong, 2003). Facilitation of brand knowledge is made possible with social media applications on the internet for information dissemination, information about their brand, and information acquisition, market knowledge for the brand (Prashantham, 2005). Information acquisition and information dissemination create efficiency for marketing teams in e-Retailing.

Information dissemination enables consumers to be familiar with a brand prior to them entering the country's market. The knowledge about the brand is not necessarily communicated through brand related content, yet a person may learn about the company by coincidence on social media through the users' community. Since social media is borderless, users constantly are stumbling on content without intending to do so. Although important for the consumer to learn about the brand, if the message is not clear or if the message is misinterpreted by the consumer the brand could lose a customer. In the worst case scenario, the consumer would spread negative content due to mixed messages. Therefore, brands need to prepare for unintentional views of their social media content, on top of intentional views.

The information transfer on social media has many benefits, however problems can arise from the large exchange of user generated content on social media. In a local context, a social media campaign can be executed with minimal brand complexity due to similarities in culture. The cultural values and meaning are more simplistic for brand congruence within the mind of the consumer in a local context. However in a global setting, the message has a large potential to create brand complexity with the varying cultural factors despite language barriers.

Social media thought has focused on the need for a decentralized social media organization structure. Language has been suggested to be an important component for social media success (Singh et al., 2012). There leaving the organizational structure of social media within companies fragmented on a country to country basis based on language. However, with the advancements in technology, web browsers automatically translate websites, therefore although language is an important factor for consideration it is adjusted for by the web browser. Moreover, social media sites adjust for the language barrier to the users preferred language, such as Twitter (Twitter, 2015). Therefore, the more important factor to address on social media is the cultural context and the message that is communicated through the global platform to leverage a centralized organizational structure. The message and meaning on social media is interpreted by users based on factors including communal norm, marketing promotion element, character narrative and communication forum (Kozinets, Valck, Wojnicki, & Wilner, 2010). Thus, the interpretation of the message by the consumer, when communicated through social media, has the possibility of misinterpretation if the cultural message is not in sync with the cultural norms. Social media communication through the spread user-produced content creates a complex cultural process with many voices. A global strategy with a centralized social media organization structure is the best method of leveraging the efficiency of social media, if and only if the brand capitalizes on consumer posts.

Adding another layer to the cultural marketing mix is the proliferation of user generated content (UGC) posted on social media. The free flow of information now has given consumers more control

(Ohmae, 2000). Companies that listen to their community are leading the social media revolution for three reasons: first, brands understand their consumers' wants and needs through information acquisition, second, brands are using the user generated content to create a brand image, and third, via information dissemination brands are communicating with their consumers. E-Retailing brands that capitalize on information acquisition and dissemination are successful.

UGC can create complexity for brand management. Negative brand comments on social media left unaddressed have the potential to go viral on the internet (Burmann, 2010). For example, on a United flight a passenger watched one of the employees accidentally break his guitar. The passenger went through many channels within United for reimbursement. The passenger never was compensated and as a result he created a YouTube video with over 14 million views to date titled "United Breaks Guitars"[1] . On the other side, positive comments are vital to the success of e-Retailing brands on social media with generating information around the brand.

E-Retailers capitalizing on information acquisition through consumer posts on social media have the potential to learn about their target audience. The information acquisition about the consumer provides vital knowledge for the best approach for communicating a message to the target audience. For example, UGC that is posted by consumers helps e-Retailers determine their positioning strategy both on- and offline.

The message and positioning strategy for a brand becomes dynamic once content is posted on social media channels, even with a global marketing strategy. The global presence on social media channels presents a challenge to manage all of the various cultural factors for a cohesive brand image. The global brand image must be strategically positioned to spread the brand message and capture the cultural idiosyncrasies. Therefore, brands that encourage user generated branding disentangle the potential cultural problems that arise with a global marketing strategy. The e-Retailing brand using UGB is now communicating messages to the target audience in the accurate cultural context. The meaning associated with the messages developed through UGB capitalizes on relatable content to a specific country.

GLOBAL SOCIAL MEDIA STRATEGY

REALLY Framework

As a result of the evolution of information transfer through the openness of social media, e-Retailers are still learning how to leverage content and their resources. As a result of the advances in social media channels and data, the author has developed a framework to be used at various stages of the social media strategy. The proposed framework was developed to maximize the efficiency of posting social media content through the REALLY social media framework. The framework should constantly be referred to during all parts of the social media strategy, whether introducing a social media strategy or campaign or during the maturity phase of a social media strategy. The REALLY framework is a holistic framework which leverages each of its factors for social media success utilizing a global strategy. Social media is global with information exchange from all over the world. The REALLY framework develops a foundation for strategic global social media campaigns.

The REALLY framework is an acronym that stands for Research, Engagement, Analysis, Listening, Learning and You and each part of the framework has interchangeable factors that complement one another. For example, information is acquired about the target audience and the industry which shape the social media campaign. The information about the target audience can pin point users to help leverage and spread the campaign message. Furthermore, social media opportunities are determined from industry voids in the marketplace that e-Retailing brands can capitalize on. The REALLY framework can be adapted to all social media channels which is important with the changes in popularity of social media for a global strategy.

Research, is one of the most important aspects of social media. Figure 1 reveals the various parts of the REALLY framework. Research is acquiring information about the industry and the target audience to develop an understanding of the marketplace. The Research portion incorporates the rest of the framework and should consistently be evolved to change with the advancements in technology channels. During the Research phase, e-Retailers should listen, learn and analyze information about the target audience, influencers, competitors, set goals and objectives, define a message and finally analyze their own brand. Through Listening on social media e-Retailers are acquiring information from user generated content about their brand. As a result, e-Retailers are learning information about their target audience, industry and their own brand through the eyes of the consumers. The Listening and Learning piece is invaluable to e-Retailers because it provides unsolicited feedback from the consumers. The Research, Listening and Learning should be analyzed to have a deeper understanding about the UGC so e-Retailers can leverage the content for engagement. E-Retailers now have the appropriate information to engage the customers on the right channels and with the right message. Finally, e-Retailers should create a message for the social media campaign that encompasses the brand image or the You of the REALLY Framework.

Moreover, the REALLY framework has many varied parts of the framework that are included throughout the 5 factors of the framework. Each factor of the REALLY framework should be referred to throughout the entirety of the process. To truly understand the e-Retailers global audience, it is important to constantly update the REALLY framework and extend the best process for your specific brand. Since social media success is specific to the online target audience, what works for one brand, may not always work for another brand and vice versa. Therefore, the REALLY framework was created for brands to recognize the peculiarities of their specific social media community and tactics, despite cross- cultural differences. The holistic approach to social media needs to be utilized for success on social media.

Figure 1. REALLY framework

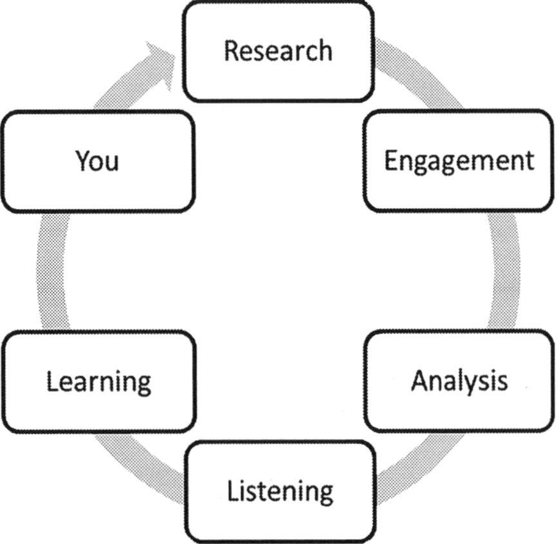

The REALLY framework has dynamic factors that reveal the peculiarities of the target audience to create segments based on the behaviors of the social media community. Table 1 reflects the specific factors within the REALLY framework that should be leveraged to develop a comprehensive strategy or campaign. For instance, the Target Audience should be researched and analyzed to reveal opportunities for content and social media channels to develop a global message. The research of the target audience should reflect the commonality of what is deemed as important for the target audience. The communication and etiquette of the specific community should be researched to determine the message that should be communicated. In some instances, it may seem that the cultural factors are important, however the audience will discount the cultural differences in the message if it positioned correctly based on the community standards. Therefore, understanding the community through research is much more vital and telling than defining cross cultural factors.

e-Retailers can observe the best positioning for a global message through their research analysis and listening to the interactions that occur in the community. Influencers in the community should be researched, analyzed and listened to learn trends in the e-Retailing industry from content to new channels being used for communication. Moreover, brands should engage with Influencers to develop relationships to create a larger network and to spread a larger message. Table 1 reveals the different factors that should be incorporated throughout the REALLY framework.

The information in the table reveals action items that should be analyzed when implementing the REALLY framework. Though the factors will be specific to the organization, all of the factors should be a focus to stay relevant.

Target Audience

Research is fundamental to any social media strategy and should be incorporated throughout all levels of a social media strategy. Through Research, the community will reveal the communication mediums that the e-Retailer should utilize, content that is valued and the overall etiquette amongst the community members. As discussed, social media messages should be positioned with a global audience and have a dynamic voice to resonate with all of the community.

Starting with the target audience, e-Retailing brands should research the information to successfully communicate and engage on social media. Engaging with the target audience is one of the most involved tasks since one misstep could cause detrimental problems to the brand. The customer is king (Okanawo, 2009) reflects the need for brands to fully understand their target audience to deliver them the current

Table 1. REALLY framework with factors to address

Research	Engagement	Analysis	Listening	Learning	You
e-Retailing Industry	Influencers	Target Audience	e-Retailing Industry	Positive WOM	Brand Image
Target Audience	Brand Advocates	Influencers	Influencers	Negative WOM	UGB
Influencers	Consumers	Brand	Consumers	Influencers	Social Responsibility
	Empowering			Competitor TA Posts	Objectives/Goals
	UGB				

information. The analysis of the target audience is vital for positioning the brand message to connect with the global consumer.

One approach to understand the many various global voices of the target audience is to analyze the consumers from a dynamic approach that moves beyond primarily traditional demographic analysis. Defining the target audience has shifted to segmenting the market through holistic classifications of the target audience including psychographics and behavioral factors (Kaplan & Haenlein, 2010; Li &Bernoff, 2008; Mangold & Faulds, 2009; Muntinga, Moorman & Smit, 2011). The increase in data capturing through social media allows for sophisticated segmentation allowing for messages that resonate with the consumers with similarity in their lifestyles. Employing information such as user behaviors and characteristics deepens the focus of user information more than primarily population statistics and cultural factors.

Demographics are defining factors about a person however they are static or slow to change features. Some examples of demographics include age, gender and income level. Next, psychographics are descriptive factors about an individual person that is usually generalized to a group. Some examples of psychographics include personality, lifestyle and attitude. Finally, behaviors relates to the consumer's usage pattern of a product. The behaviors include, but are not limited to loyalty, purchase behavior and rate of use. Typically, geography is included in the list however geographic distances have been decreased by modern technology (Child, Ng and Wong, 2003) especially with social media. The consumers' motivation to interact with the e-Retailer rewards the brand with appropriate messaging and content. The brand now knows more about the customer and their lifestyle that is deeper than a generalization of cultural norms of a group of individuals. Social media has provided a more definitive knowledge base of the dynamic consumer across cultures.

Social media usage is a popular determinant of the target audience on social media. Typologies of users social media interaction was developed and created a deeper understanding of the consumers (Li & Bernoff, 2008). The Social Technographic Profile, commonly referred to as the Groundswell Tools reveals 6 typologies of social media users. From the most active and influential to the ones non-active on social media are: creators, critics, joiners, collectors, spectators and inactives. The Groundswell tool reveals social media usage by general demographics determined by Age, Country and Gender. The Groundswell tool creates a snapshot of the user base determined by their usage of social media, despite the cultural differences. Analyzing the usage of social media is vital to a social media strategy. An e-Retailer overlooking the type of social media user could fail to engage with the users by requesting the users to interact with the e-Retailer's social media channel in a method that is unfamiliar to them. One step further than interactions of social media use is determining the motivations driving social media use by the community. Expanding on the Groundswell typologies, the Consumers' Brand Related Activity, COBRA, develop motivations of social media use. Table 2 shows the three drivers of engagement from the COBRA Motivations are consumers (low engagement), contributors (middle engagement) and creators (high engagement) of users based upon motivations of use (Muntinga, et al., 2011). Motivations provide e-Retailers a deeper understanding of how to leverage the different types of social media users from across the globe.

In instances that e-Retailing companies do not have access to the actual Groundswell data for their company, the tool has general data per age, gender and country. Therefore, it is possible to deduce a general understanding of the motivations of their target audience. Table 2 is a template for generalizing the Groundswell tools information into the COBRA typologies.

Table 2. Groundswell social technographic profiles to COBRA typologies

	Groundswell Social Technographic Profiles
Creator	Creator
	Critic
Contributor	Collector
	Joiner
Consumer	Spectator
	Inactive

Determining motivations of your social media users becomes easier when generalized in terms of the Groundswell tool in comparison to the COBRA typologies. The Groundswell tool and COBRA typologies should be used as a starting guide for your research and engagement, however it is a general resource.

Finally, the behaviors of the target audience should be taken into consideration. Target audience behaviors on social media should focus on loyalty to the e-Retailing brand as referenced in Table 1. Brand loyalty facilitates engagement and recommendation of the e-Retailing company by the consumer (Capozzi & Zipfel, 2012). The increased engagement through social media enables the e-Retailing brand to nurture relationships and build deeper relationships with its consumers. In fact, a deeper relationship with the e-Retailer is expected by the customer (Falkow, 2010). Brand loyalty fosters trust between the brand and the consumer with the deeper relationship (Capozzi & Zipfel, 2012). Since social media develops community networks, e-Retailing brands should capitalize on the information dissemination of the consumer to their community about the e-Retailer, creating brand advocates (Booth & Matic, 2011). As a result, brands should determine the loyalty of their customers to their e-Retailing brand to leverage the brand advocates.

Moreover, it is recommended that e-Retailing brands use listening tools to learn and analyze the target audience. There are many listening tools on the market today including Hootsuite, Google Alerts, TweetDeck and Talk Walker (Safko, 2010). Each tool provides information to learn more about keyword searches and context of the conversation related to e-Retailing brands on social media sites. By listening to the target audience e-Retailers have the ability to develop a global message that resonates with many social media users. The information provided from the listening tools develops a holistic understanding of the target audience to determine voids the company can fill.

Once listening tools are set in place, research should be conducted and analyzed based on some of the following factors being discussed by the target audience: keywords, frequency of posts, sentiment and popular channels. More detailed information on factors to analyze can be found on ReallyLeila.com under "e-Retailing Challenges and Opportunities in the Global Marketplace" with the Password: REALLY. The target audience information of behaviors on social media will present opportunities for e-Retailers on social media.

To stay relevant on social media, it is important to constantly track the target audience demographics, psychographics and behavioral factors.

Table 3. Target audience factors to measure

	Factors to Measure
Demographic Factors	Age
	Gender
	Income
	Marital Status
	Geographic Location
Psychographic Factors	Social Media Usage
	Social Media Motivations
Behavioral Factors	Loyalty
	Keywords
	Frequency of Posts
	Sentiment
	Popular Channels

Research has consistently explained success factors of social media marketing strategy (i.e. Kaplan & Haenlein, 2010; Mangolds & Faulds, 2009; Piskorski, 2011; Safko, 2012) and specifically on the social network site, Facebook (Vries, Gensler & Leeflang, 2012). Certain characteristics have been examined to attract more interactivity with the brand on social media sites. The number of likes, vividness, interactivity, content and position all have relationships with the number of likes and comments on a page. Through the analysis of engagement of the community and the brand, it efficiently determines the positioning of social media for a global audience.

INFLUENCER MARKETING

Influencers are typically thought leaders creating content on social media and therefore are commonly also known as Creators and/or Mavens (i.e. Foster, West & Francescucci, 2011; Yang, 2013). For the scope of this chapter we will use the term Influencers to address the group of people creating content and have social media clout. Influencers typically are up with the new trends in the industry and have large communities on social media. The Influencers are vital for e-Retailing social media for a few reasons: trust, clout, knowledge of community and trends.

Influencers should be observed to discover advancements in the industry both on- and offline. E-Retailers should listen to Influencers to understand trends in the industry and monitor the norms of the culture on social media channels (Kumar & Mirchandani, 2012). Similar to the Consumer target audience, some important factors to analyze the Influencer on include their target audience, content, themes and community. After the information is analyzed for the Influencers in the industry, voids and opportunities should be noted for the e-Retailer to implement.

Once the e-Retailers analyze the Influencers, they should leverage Influencers to spread a brand's message to the Influencer's community (Booth & Matic, 2011; Kaplan & Haenlein, 2011; Kumar & Mirchandani, 2012). Typically, Influencers will have a larger community and know how to communicate with their audience, therefore the global message will resonate more so with the Influencers gloal audience. Consumers trust information spread from peers through word of mouth more than from advertisements in general (Senecal & Nantel, 2004). Moreover, Influencers spread targeted messages through knowledge of their community culture. For e-Retailing brands, targeting Influencers are vital to help spread the message to the Influencers network. Since the Influencer already has a strong community, the call to action for the e-Retailer fosters a dialogue between the Influencers community and the Influencer. As a result, the community is hearing from a familiar voice in a relatable cultural context (Kumar and Mirchandanu, 2012). The Influencers clout and knowledge of their community will increase brand congruence through trust and recognition of appropriate message context.

Objectives and Goals

Objectives and goals define the brand goal and the various tactics to use. The opportunities presented by the target audience and the Influencers will provide a clear pathway to moving forward with social media. The strategic objectives and goals should reflect the research of the social media landscape in the industry (Keller, 1993), as well as the typologies of users and motivations. Defining the objectives and a clear message should parallel the brand image to support the vision of the company. Enlisting Influencers to communicate the message will preserve the e-Retailers brand image.

As discussed, social media is dynamic and attracts various types of users with different motivations to participate online. Successful social media strategies and campaigns leverage the various types of social media users. Having a one-size-user-fits-all approach to a social media campaign will not be as successful at imprinting the brands message onto the consumer. E-Retailers would be most successful with a multilayered social media campaign to create a greater affinity to the brand. As the campaign strategy is determined the e-Retailer should take into consideration the lack of control around the conversation. Therefore, the e-Retailer should leverage UGB to shift the social media community's conversation around a specific topic.

User Generated Branding

Although brands cannot control messages on social media entirely, they can influence the message with stimulation of consumer-related content about the brand. E-Retailers leveraging consumer generated content around the brand efficiently develop the brand image and message with the help of the community (Gensler, Völckner, Thompkins & Wiertz, 2013). Strategic campaigns efforts and sponsoring content aimed at influencing user generated content creates a central point for conversation on social media to create User Generated Branding (UGB) (Burmann, 2010). User generated branding has been successful for many brands. For example, the ALS Challenge was a successful example of a brand leveraging UGC to create a UGB. The ALS challenge was an effort to spread awareness about ALS by stimulating consumer related content around the non-profit. The ALS challenge dared consumers to dump buckets of ice over their head to raise awareness around the ALS disease. Participants then would tag their network of friends on social media and challenge them to dump buckets of ice water over their head and then tag their friends. The challengers whom did not follow through with the ALS challenge were required to make a donation. According to the ALS Association (2015), the ALS challenge raised $21.7mllion, became a household name throughout the campaign and created more awareness around ALS. Moreover, the campaign focused the users around a central point for conversation to leverage their UGC and develop a UGB.

Social media campaigns enlist many different types of social media users to participate. Many e-Retailer leverage the various types of social media users and motivations to spread targeted contextual messages. For instance, the Influencers are the ones constantly creating content online and are the users that participate with the most engagement. Therefore, Influencers should be targeted to help spread the word around a social media campaign (Kaplan & Haenlein, 2011; Kumar & Mirchandani, 2012). The clout of the Influencers will motivate other Creators and Consumers to participate with a social media campaign.

Social Responsibility

Observations of social media campaign reflect the execution and perceived objectives aiming to better the community or a cause typically are successful. Emotional arousal is triggered by e-Retailing brands improving the community. It is important for the message of the social media campaign to be clear and meaningful to the user for participation. Multilayered social media campaigns with a socially responsible component have been successful. As an example, discussed earlier, the ALS challenge #IceBucketChallenge went viral with 17 million videos created by users for the challenge with 10 billion views and on Facebook along 28 million Facebook users were talking about the challenge in less than 3 months (ALS, 2015). The emotional arousal coupled with the social responsibility objective created a clear message to support ALS.

Social media has changed selling strategies (Mangold & Faulds, 2009). In e-Retailing, the importance of using social media for selling should not be isolated from the social responsibility. In fact, the social media objectives should align with the social responsibility of the e-Retailer, as will be discussed later in a case. Therefore, marketing objectives are somewhat different on social media than on traditional marketing channels, as with social media the purchase decision is heavily weighted on the brand image versus the actual product. The approach to marketing has become more implicit with social media. Brand's that have a positive image and are known to do "good" for society are typically successful brands.

The social media campaign must have a clear contextual message resonating with many cultures and the varying types of social media users. Very limited brands have created a successful truly global social media campaign. Quicksilver's brand Roxy has created a global campaign that has targeted 80 countries.

ROXY #DareYourself GLOBAL SOCIAL MEDIA STRATEGY

Introduction

Social media produces the exchange of information and many companies have leveraged the use of content spread around a brand. Roxy Quiksilver capitalized on the global social media user generated content to spread a positive brand image. Similar to many other e-Retailing brands, Roxy has disrupted the internationalization process with a strong global brand image prior to entering the specific country market with physical locations or products. Brands can refer to Roxy's global social media implementation as a framework to determine the country market potential prior to fully investing in the market.

Roxy is a subsidiary of Quiksilver and sells primarily girls and women clothing for extreme sports such as surfing, swimming and skiing. Quiksilver, the parent company of Roxy, has trend setting brands including DC Shoes, Silver Edition, Fidra, Raisons, Radio Fiji labels, Roxy and Quiksilver. As one of the top players in action sportswear, Quiksilver brands focus on clothing for outdoor sports. Since 1969, Quiksilver has been changing the action sports lifestyle from the type of fabric used in their clothes to their social media marketing success.

Quiksilver introduced Roxy to fill a void in the niche market of active wear for women, specifically action sports clothing. The name Roxy is known as a trendy brand among active women for the outdoors. Roxy brand is limited to primarily sports clothing, while selling some shoes, boots and hand bags. When Roxy was first introduced in 1990, Quiksilver noticed the need for a women's line with the proliferation of women surfers. Action sportswear was never the same for women after Roxy entered the retail landscape.

REALLY Framework Strategy

Social media is one of Roxy's strengths. Roxy conveys the brand image of an active lifestyle coupled with emotional messages daring women to push themselves to the limits. As a result, Roxy determined an opportunity in the marketplace to leverage social media. The *Dare Yourself* campaign was launched as a multilayered social media campaign to promote the Roxy brand image. The campaign attracted various types of social media users.

Research

The information acquired through research of the target audiences' behaviors and psychographics facilitated a high arousal and empowering campaign. The Dare Yourself campaign was targeted to women aged 18-28. Interestingly, a Pew report by Brennar and Smith (2013) compared social media usage by age group in a sample of countries. In every country that was analyzed, the 18-29 year olds participated in social media considerably more that 30-49 and 50+. The differentiation of social media usage by age changes the message being communicated. Age segmentation towards marketing is a more rational and better approach to marketing than traditional ideas of country to country. Therefore, empowering women in the 18-28 age group was important and on target, especially when referring to the COBRA typologies as noted in Table 5 (Munting et al., 2010). Roxy's research of the target audience presented opportunities for solid social media objectives and a targeted message.

The global social media campaign was inspirational to women from all over the world and all walks of life. The Dare Yourself campaign aimed to challenge and fill the void of women athletes. Roxy capitalized on the opportunity to encourage women to reach their goals beyond their limits and to think about the future. Further, it inspired women to change the world and dismiss gender roles, culture, language and geography. Roxy did not put limits on the campaign, so women would not put limits on their entry.

The Roxy Dare Yourself campaign examined from the Research perspective of the REALLY framework reveals the type of e-Retailing Industry and the defined Target Audience in terms of age, gender, location and keywords.

Table 4. Roxy's research for the Dare Yourself campaign from the REALLY framework

Research	Roxy
e-Retailing Industry	Women's Active Wear
Target Audience	18-29 year olds, the Americas, Europe, Latin America, South Asia and North Asia, active women, athletic, competitive, high achievers.

Engagement

The Engagement of the REALLY framework that was created through the Roxy *Dare Yourself* campaign was dependent on the research and analysis of the community. Roxy created the *Dare Yourself* multilayered UGB campaign and attracted various types of social media users while empowering women. As referenced in Table 5, the Roxy Dare Yourself campaign was a 2-Phased campaign. In the first phase of the campaign, women were encouraged to enter the contest two ways by submitting 1) a one-minute video or 2) writing a 150-word essay with pictures showing how they "Dare" themselves every day. The premise of the contest was to make women aware of their lives and their potential. In the second phase of the campaign, the rest of the community was encouraged to vote on their favorite video and/or pictures and essays. The 2 phases or multilayered campaign attracted many participants to create content from all over the world with different social media behaviors and motivations.

The *Dare Yourself* campaign was launched in key countries in the Americas, Europe, Latin America, South Asia and North Asia. Moreover, the contestants of the campaign were only permitted to be submitted in 11 languages: English, French, German, Russian, Japanese, Traditional Chinese, Korean, Indonesian, Thai, Portuguese and Spanish.

The explanation of the Roxy Dare Yourself campaign in terms of the Engagement of the REALLY framework reveals the level of engagement of the social media user and the action item based on the motivation.

Analysis, Listening and Learning

The Dare Yourself campaign had a clear message and was successfully targeted to the defined audience. Alexa a credible site for website analysis defines website and online demographics and psychographics. Based on Alexa's ranking system, Roxy website visitors are primarily females with a large portion having a college degree and some having some type of college for Roxy. The Alexa ranking is in line with the target audience that was selected for the *Dare Yourself* campaign. The *Dare Yourself* campaign had 4,000 submissions as noted in Table 6. The number of entries was substantial for girls aged 18-28 to be

Table 5. Roxy's engagement for the Dare Yourself campaign from the REALLY framework

Engagement	Roxy
Creators	Video submission; Personal identity, integration and social interaction, empowerment and entertainment
Consumers	Voting; Information, entertainment and remuneration
Empowering	Creators increasing their voice through their submissions

curating original content. These women created content about themselves and sent in videos on how they challenge themselves every day. The creation of information is difficult to do and it reflects that there are a large number of women aged 18-28 years that are creating content on social media.

Roxy's Dare Yourself campaign could be concluded as successful. For one, Roxy's communities all consist of tens of thousands and hundreds of thousands of users. Further, the large Roxy community reveals a robust social media strategy creating a solid foundation for a social media campaign. Klout a widely used social media tool that determines the influence a brand has on social media through social network analysis (Klout, 2015). Roxy has a Klout score of 66. According to Klout, any user that has a score of 65 or higher is in the top 5% of social media users. Therefore Roxy is considered an Influencer on social media revealing their strength of engaging users.

The *Dare Yourself* campaign was launched to create a community for women aged 18-28. With 75 countries being represented in the campaign, while it was only launched in a group of countries in 11 languages, it stimulated a large number of users to generate content. During the second phase of the campaign, there were 100,000 votes in the first week of the voting phase and 750,000 views of the contest. Interestingly, the numbers and the strategy of the launch of the campaign attracted each type of social media user and their motivations for using social media. The Roxy brand looked into the voids that were present in the active wear clothing space and determined there was a need to empower women to challenge their daily routine.

The analysis of the Roxy case in terms of the Analysis, Listening and Learning of the REALLY framework details the results of the campaign as a result of the Dare Yourself Campaign.

Interestingly, when looking at the motivations of social media users the *Dare Yourself* campaign parallels the motivations of social media users. Creators are motivated in social media for personal identity, integration and social interaction, empowerment and entertainment. The *Dare Yourself* campaign drove personal identity, integration and empowerment in their creators that submitted their videos. Women were empowered through their personal identity by showing the world how they dare themselves on a daily basis.

The number of people that voted in the first week of the consumer voting contest was 100,000. There were 100,000 community members that were interested in the *Dare Yourself* campaign and wanted to contribute, yet did not want to create original content. Users that are contributors want to join social media and share information. There is a large number of contributors on social media and it is vital to any social media campaign to include them in your social media strategy. Through listening, Roxy learned the different types of social media users.

Table 6. Roxy's analysis, listening and learning for the Dare Yourself campaign from the REALLY framework

Analysis	Roxy
Target Audience	75 countries, 11 languages Creators- 4,000 entries Contributors- 100,000 votes Creators, Consumers and Contributors- 750,000 views
Influencers	Klout score is 66 (top 5%)
Brand	Active, fun, women oriented, pushing women to the limit.
Positive WOM	Spread of the campaign revealed positive WOM

Roxy targeted the contributors in social media by asking the users to vote on the creators that submitted to the *Dare Yourself* campaign. The contributors have social media motivations that include personal identity, integration and social interaction and entertainment. Through the *Dare Yourself* campaign, Roxy targets the contributors by asking the Contributors to involve themselves through voting for the best *Dare Yourself* videos and pictures. Although Contributors did not create original content, they were still motivated by the entertainment factor and identifying with the Creators.

The *Dare Yourself* contest was extremely large. For a company of its size, the success of having 4,000 contest contestants and 100,000 contributors that voted is quite substantial. However, there were a number of consumers that did not want to contribute or create, yet they were still interested in the campaign. Although most of these Consumers are not possible to identify, the sheer number of views of the *Dare Yourself* campaign, 750,000 views, reflect the strong need to also appeal to the motivations of the Consumer. Based on the success of the Dare Yourself campaign, Figure 2 reflects the different type of users and their motivations: Creators, Contributors and Consumers and Action items for an e-Retailer to implement for a social media campaign.

You

Roxy set out to accomplish four objectives in their Dare Yourself campaign (C.Beeson, personal communication, January 28, 2013):

Figure 2. Social media users, roles and action items for a social media campaign

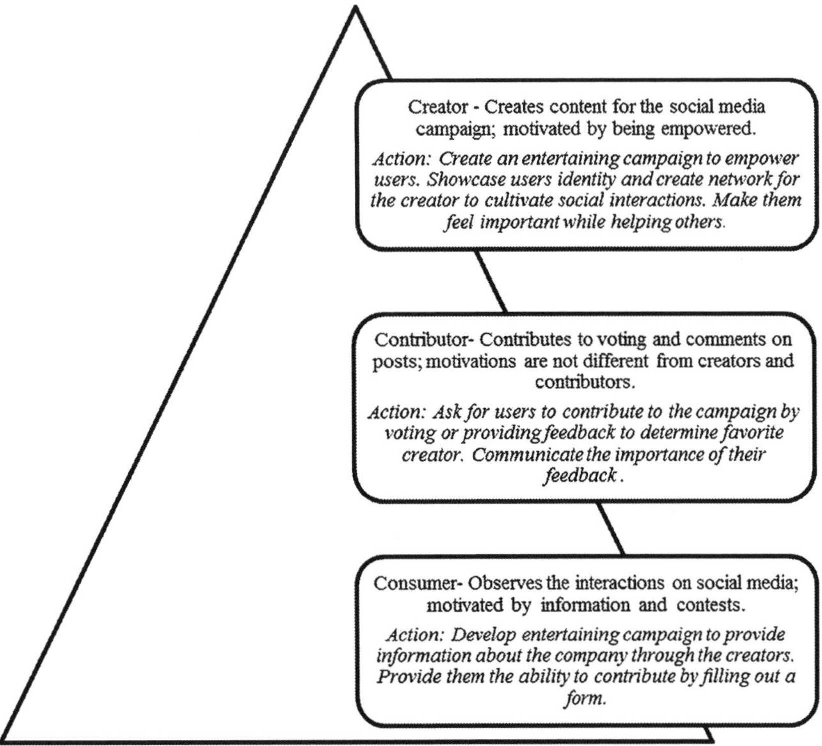

1. To connect with their audience globally.
2. To build and broaden their online, and global community primarily through their nearly 3 million followers on Facebook.
3. To complement the surf and snow categories and lifestyles.
4. To inspire girls.

The objectives were important to empower girls creating an emotional connection to the brand. Moreover, the objectives were in line with the brand image and included a sense of social responsibility. The Roxy Dare Yourself campaign message was: "what it means to live every day as an adventure to show the mark you want to leave on the world" (Roxy, 2013).

As spoken about earlier, Roxy took a multilayered approach to target the various motivations of the target audience to satisfy their objectives. The multilayered approach to the campaign was shown to be imperative to the success of the campaign and to the UGB strategy. In the first phase of the campaign there were 4,000 entries submitted from all over the world. The content created on social media around the Roxy was quite substantial as detailed in Table 7.

The explanation of the Roxy Dare Yourself campaign from the "You" perspective is shown in Table 7. The information reflects Roxy's brand image, leveraging UGB, social responsibility and their objectives and goals.

Roxy standardized their promotional strategy of the *Dare Yourself Campaign.* Roxy limited their campaign to 11 languages and launched the same campaign throughout their key markets. Roxy communicated the same message to their global market of 18-28 year old women. Moreover, Roxy promoted their campaign through print advertising, social/online advertising, retail marketing and PR with the same message and brand image across the globe. Interestingly, there was no need to change their campaign from country to country based on cultural differences.

Consequently, the organizational structure on social media was centralized to one social media account per channel. During the time of the campaign, Roxy had only one social media channel per application (i.e. one Facebook account in English, one YouTube account in English). They did not have various social media accounts per language or country. Interestingly, they have a large social media community on each of the channels supporting the centralized social media structure. Contrary to previous research, the success of the campaign was not dependent on the social media channel language, the UGB controlled for the cultural and community differences.

Finally, at the time of the campaign, Roxy was only selling in 19 countries (United States, Argentina, Australia, Canada, Chile, Colombia, Costa Rica, Ecuador, French Polynesia, Guam, Guatemala, Honduras, Mexico, New Zealand, Nicaragua, Panama, Peru, Puerto Rico and Venezuela), however they had an

Table 7. Roxy's You for the Dare Yourself campaign from the REALLY framework

You	Roxy
Brand Image	Consistent across all marketing channels, print and digital.
UGB	Leveraging the target audience to create content with video submissions and asking consumers' to vote.
Social Responsibility	Challenging women to better and dare themselves.
Objectives/Goals	Connecting with global audience, build and broaden social media community, complement brand and inspire girls.

overwhelmingly large response from 75 countries. The sheer number of responses from countries outside of their authorized retailers signals another phenomenon that is occurring in social media, a change in the internationalization process. In many countries that were represented in the campaign, the brand Roxy was not present. However, with the virality of content and UGB, users are learning about brands through social media. Roxy has created a market through their positive brand image and successful global social media campaign prior to physically entering the market by stimulating conversation through UGB.

SOCIAL INTERNATIONALIZATION

We define social internationalization as a process of the exchange of information and ideas through social media. Social media has changed e-Retailing through social internationalization. Traditional international business theory suggests internationalization and location selection as incremental with specific stages for determining the best market for expansion (Vahlne and Johanson, 1977). However with the rise of social media usage has evolved the internationalization process. The information exchanged on social media between users and the e-Retailer is more dynamic and descriptive. Firms should be flexible and evolve based on the customers' needs (Tallman and Shenkar, 1992). Consumers can be analyzed in more depth on social media since there is a platform for users to reveal information about themselves. The Web 2.0 as a platform connects e-Retailers and consumers, but social media provides more insight to the e-Retailer about the consumers. Social internationalization facilitates discussion and information dissemination around the e-Retailer to develop a market with a social media campaign. Moreover, information acquisition is leveraged for location selection by e-Retailers based on customer needs.

Prior to social media and the internet, brand awareness was limited to the retailer having a physical presence in a country. However, the *Dare Yourself* campaign supports the revelation of the change in internationalization. Social Internationalization is only in it's the beginning phases as more e-Retailers learn the methods to leverage information dissemination and acquisition. Future research should look into social internationalization in more detail.

CONCLUSION

Social Internationalization has changed the e-Retailing process. The traditional internationalization process has evolved from bricks-and-mortar sequential expansion to e-Retailing and developing market potential through social media. The potential of social media should be leveraged for the success of the e-Retailer. Through following the REALLY framework, e-Retailers can capitalize on the target audience to develop multilayered UGB social media campaign.

This chapter focused on global strategic approaches to social media campaigns to leverage UGC across all social media channels across various countries. To capitalize on the efficiency of social media and its global reach, e-Retailers should use a global strategy instead of looking at social media contrasts in an individual country approach. It must be noted, social media channels are constantly changing and foundational knowledge of global social media is important to understand the emerging patterns. Therefore the information presented is applicable to all channels and countries. Technology is ever changing, thus e-Retailers that are nimble will be successful by having knowledge in the underlying frameworks that guide global social media.

REFERENCES

Arenius, P., Sasi, V., & Gabrielsson, M. (2006). Rapid Internationalization enabled by the Internet: The case of a knowledge intensive company. *Journal of Entrepreneurship*, 279-290.

Axelsson, B., & Johanson, J. (1992). *Foreign market entry: The textbook vs the network view*. London: Routledge.

Barwise, P., & Meehan, S. (2010). The one thing you must get right when building a brand. *Harvard Business Review*, December, 80–84.

Berger, J. (2012). *Contagious: Why things catch on*. New York: Simon and Schuster.

Bodapati, Arabie, & Palmer, R. A. (2004). How managers perceive the impacts of information technologies on contemporary practices: Reinforcing, enhancing or transforming? *Journal of Relationship Marketing*, 3(4), 7–26.

Booth, N., & Matic, J. (2011). Mapping and leveraging influencers in social media to shape corporate brand perceptions. *Corporate Communications*: An *International Journal (Toronto, Ont.)*, 16(3), 184–191.

Brennar, J., & Smith, A. (2013). *Social Networking*. Washington, D.C.: Pew Internet.

Bruhn, M., Schoenmueller, V., & Schäfer, D. B. (2012). Are social media replacing traditional media; is brand equity creation? *Management Research Review*, 770-790.

Burmann, C. (2010). *A call for user-generated branding*. Brand Management.

Capozzi, L., & Zipfel, L.B. (2012). The conversation age: the opportunity for public relations. *Corporate Communications: An International Journal*, 17(3), 336 – 349.

Carroll, D. (2015, January 9). United Breaks Guitars. *Dave Carrol Music.* Retrieved from http://www.davecarrollmusic.com/music/ubg/

Child, J., Ng, S. H., & Wong, C. (2002). Psychic Distance and Internationalization: Evidence from Hong Kong Firms. *International Studies of Management & Organization*, 32(10), 36–56.

Duggan, M., Ellison, N., Lampe, C., Lenhart, A., & Madden, M. (2015, January 9). Social Media Site Usage 2014. *Pew Research Center*. Retrieved from http://www.pewinternet.org/2015/01/09/social-media-update-2014/?utm_content=buffer68e1e&utm_medium=social&utm_source=twitter.com&utm_campaign=buffer

Erikson, E. (1968). *The Psychosocial stages of development*. London: Norton & Company.

Etgar, M., & Rachman-Moore, D. (2010). Geographical Expansion by International Retailers: A Study of Proximate Markets and Global Expansion Strategies. *Journal of Global Marketing*, *23*(1), 5–15. doi:10.1080/08911760903439560

Evans, L. (2010). *Social media marketing: Strategies for engaging in Facebook, Twitter & other social media*. Indianapolis: Que Publishing.

Facebook users of the world. (2015, May 4). *Internet World Stats*. Retrieved from http://www.internetworldstats.com/facebook.htm

Falkow, S. (2010). PR Trends 2010: Branded Content. *The Proactive Report*.

Foster, M., West, B., & Francescucci, A. (2011). Exploring social media users segmentation and online brand profiles. *Journal of Brand Management*, 19(1), 4-17.

Gensler, V., Völckner, F., Liu-Thompkins, Y., & Wiertz, C. (2013). Managing brands in the social media environment. *Journal of Interactive Marketing*, *27*(4), 242–256. doi:10.1016/j.intmar.2013.09.004

Hubspot. (2013). Revealing charts from the 2013 state of inbound marketing. *Hubspot*.

Iacobucci, D., Arabie, P., & Bodapati, A. V. (2000). Recommendation Agents on the Internet. *Journal of Interactive Marketing*, *14*(3), 2–11. doi:10.1002/1520-6653(200022)14:3<2::AID-DIR1>3.0.CO;2-J

Impact of the Ice Bucket Challenge. (2015, April 15). *ALS Association*. Retrieved from http://www.alsa.org/news/archive/impact-of-ice-bucket-challenge.html

Johanson, J. & Vahlne, J. (1977). The internationalization of the firm- A model of knowledge development and increasing foreign market commitments. *Journal of International Business*, 8, 22-32.

Johanson, J. & Vahlne, J. (2009). The Uppsala internationalization process revisited: From liability of foreignness to liability to outsidership. *Journal of International Business Studies*, 40(9), 1411-1431.

Kaplan, A., & Haenlein, M. (2010). Users of the world, unite! The challenges and opportunities of social media. *Business Horizons*, *53*(1), 59–68. doi:10.1016/j.bushor.2009.09.003

Keller. (1993). Conceptualizing, measuring, and managing customer-based brand equity. *Journal of Marketing*, 1993, 1-22.

Klout. (2013). *Klout*. Retrieved from Klout: www.klout.com

Kozinets, V., de Valck, K., Wojnicki, A. C., & Wilner, S. J. S. (2010). Networked narratives: Understanding word-of-mouth marketing in online communities. *Journal of Marketing*, *74*(2), 71–89. doi:10.1509/jmkg.74.2.71

Kumar, V., & Mirchandi, R. (2012). Increasing he ROI of Social Media Marketing. *Sloan Management Review*, 54(1), 55.

Levitt, T. (1983). The globalization of markets. *Harvard Business Review*, 1983.

Li, C., & Bernoff, J. (2011). *Groundswell*. Cambridge: Forrester.

Loane, S. (2006). The Role of the Internet in the Internationalisation of small and medium sized companies. *Journal of International Entrepreneurship*, 33(4), 263–277.

Mangold, W. G., & Faulds, D. J. (2009). Social Media: The new hybrid element of the promotion mix. *Business Horizons*, *52*(4), 357–365. doi:10.1016/j.bushor.2009.03.002

Mathews, S., Healy, M., & Ali, Y. (2006). A comparative evaluation of the Internet's influence on international market penetration and development growth strategies of Australian SME's. *Proceedings of the Australia & New Zealand Marketing Academy Annual Conference.* Brisbane.

Muntinga, D. G., Moorman, M., & Smit, E. G. (2011). Introducing COBRAs Exploring motivations for brand-related social media use. *International Journal of Advertising*, *30*(1), 13–46. doi:10.2501/IJA-30-1-013-046

Coviello, N., & Munro, H. (1997). Network relationships and the internationalisation process of small software firms. *International Business Review.*

Ohmae, K. (1989, June). Managing in a Borderless World. *Harvard Business Review.*

Ohmae, K. (2000). *The Invisible Continent.* New York, NY: Harper Business.

Okonkwo, U. (2009). Sustaining the luxury brand on the Internet. *Journal of Marketing*, 16, 303–310.

Piskorski, M. J. (2011). Social Strategies That Work. *Harvard Business Review*. PMID:22111430

Prashantham, S. (2005). Toward a Knowledge-Based Conceptualization of Internationalization. *Journal of International Entrepreneurship*, *3*(1), 37–52. doi:10.1007/s10843-005-0304-5

Quelch, J.A., & Hoff, E.J. (1993). Customizing Global Marketing. In R.Z. Aliber, & R.W. Click (Eds.), *Reading in international business: A decision approach.* Cambridge: Massachusetts Institution of Technology.

Roxy. (2015). Retrieved from www.roxy.com

Safko, L. (2012). *The Social Media Bible.* Hoboken: John, Wiley & Sons.

Samii, L. (2015). e-Retailing Challenges and Opportunities in the Global Marketplace. *ReallyLeila.* Retrieved from http://reallyleila.com/2015/05/31/e-retailing-challenges-and-opportunities-in-the-global-marketplace/

Senecal, S., & Nantel, J. (2004). The influence of online product recommendations on consumers' online choices. *Journal of Retailing*, 80(2), 159-169.

Singh, N., Lenhert, K., & Bostick, K. (2012). Usage: Insights into reaching consumers worldwide. *Thunderbird International Business Review*, 54(5), 683-700. doi:10.1002/tie.21493

The State of the media: The social media report 2012. (2012). *Nielsen.*

Twitter, Inc. (2012). Retrieved from www.twitter.com

U.S. and World Population Clock. (2015, May 30). *US Census Bureau.* Retrieved from http://www.census.gov/popclock/

Vries, L., Gensler, S., & Leeflang, P. (2012). Popularity of brand posts on brand fan pages: An investigation of the effect of social media marketing. *Journal of Interactive Marketing*, 26(2), 83-91.

Yang, H. (2013). Market mavens in social media: Examining young Chinese consumers' viral marketing attitude, eWOM and behavior. *Journal of Asia-Pacific Business*, *14*(2), 154–178. doi:10.1080/10599231.2013.756337

Zaheer, S. (1995). Overcoming the Liability of Foreignness. *Academy of Management Journal*, *38*(2), 341–363. doi:10.2307/256683

KEY TERMS AND DEFINITIONS

Centralized Social Media Organizational Strategy: Creating a social media strategy with only one account per social media application (i.e. Twitter, Facebook, Pinterest) in one language.

Culture: A group of people with similar ideas and beliefs to the exchange of information, behaviors and norms that guides their understanding of messages.

Global Social Media Strategy: A social media strategy maximizing the potential of social media with standardization of messages.

Information Acquisition: Knowledge transfer from an industry, market, country and/or consumer to a company to decrease liability of foreignness and complexities.

Information Dissemination: Knowledge transfer about a company to a market, country and/or consumer to create awareness.

Internationalization: The process of cross border movements of a company.

Multilayered Strategy: Attracting various types of social media audiences based on their patterns of social media usage and motivations.

Social Internationalization: Creating awareness around a brand through information dissemination on social media prior to selling products overseas.

User Generated Branding: Leveraging social media users to spread user generated content around a brand by the brand strategically stimulating discussion through a social media campaign.

User Generated Content: Social media participants creating unsolicited content on social media applications.

This research was previously published in E-Retailing Challenges and Opportunities in the Global Marketplace edited by Shailja Dixit and Amit Kumar Sinha, pages 206-228, copyright year 2016 by Business Science Reference (an imprint of IGI Global).

Chapter 31
Using Social Media to Influence CRM and Loyalty:
Case Study of Restaurant Industry

Rozita Shahbaz Keshvari
Islamic Azad University, Iran

ABSTRACT

This chapter explores the influence of social media in Customer Relationship Management that leads to Customer loyalty. The social media in restaurant is recognized as an essential component of the customer satisfaction and therefore it is a cornerstone of the success of CRM and customer loyalty through social media nowadays. The purpose of this chapter is to investigate how Restaurant industry can harness the power of social media by utilizing CRM that leads to Customer loyalty. The problem is approached applying both the restaurants perspective and the customer perspective. The recent explosion in social media usage, combined with the transformation of the consumer into a "consume' activist", has permanently changed the relationship between a restaurant and its customers. There were two interviews conducted for 384 restaurants collected and analyzed for the research. The results proved that Social media can be an excellent channel for building long-lasting customer relationships in restaurants.

1. INTRODUCTION

Many years ago, most businesses were local brick-and-mortars that relied on door-to-door marketing to engage the public. As technology developed rapidly, motion pictures, radio and television opened up new avenues for business marketing, eventually expanding to include direct mail, telemarketing, print advertising, trade shows and e-mail blasts. While these practices have proven successful over the years, many of today's consumers now view them as intrusive, and have consequently become quite savvy at ignoring traditional marketing attempts. Nowadays, communication has taken on new era and adapted to new mediums evolved to reflect the society in which they were developed.

DOI: 10.4018/978-1-5225-5637-4.ch031

1.1. Area of Interest

The customer experience in restaurants is paramount. It impacts retention rates, referrals, our brand, and ultimately our success or failure. Negative experiences are inevitable. It's how the restaurants handle recovery that makes all the difference. This determines if their customers will give them a second chance or embark on a negative word of mouth campaign that could reach thousands. Understanding and addressing the factors that negatively impact restaurant customer's experiences is both critical and challenging. Menuitems and promotions change regularly. Staff schedules rotate. Employees come and go. Their customers' traffic is high-volume sometimes, variable at others. And in addition to keeping tabs on day-to-day operations, franchisees must stay on top of corporate issues and cost concerns. So when it comes to effectively attracting, retaining and handling customers in restaurants to manage their needs, feedback and experiences, the need for an especially powerful and flexible solution (Utilizing social media as a powerful CRM tool) will become clear.

The social media in restaurant is recognized as an essential component of the customer satisfaction and therefore it is a cornerstone of the success of CRM and customer loyalty through social media in nowadays which is no denying the influence of social media on the way that we as human beings communicate on a daily basis. The motivation for writing this paper on the topic of social media is to gain better understanding of the phenomenon that is influencing CRM and customer loyalty, as it is needy today. Enterprises in different filed of business such as financial, banking, services, production and so on should utilize the Social Media management to provide a number of singular challenges to the restaurant owner, not the least of which is trying to stay on top of multiple platforms as they shift and dip in a seemingly constant game of musical chairs. Pinterest is on top, no Instagram, Foursquare is trending on Twitter, now it's not, wait it's changed again – and now hashtags on Facebook.

The restaurants as service industry should try to marshal their marketing resources in an effective, and fiscally practical, manner can appear nearly impossible. The authors try to find a few quick ways in which they can improve their efforts at little or no cost in restaurant industry. The other reason that motivate the author to choose this subject for this research is the restaurant field of business which is B2C (Business to Customer) & B2B (Business to Business) marketing. Further, research conducted by Dataforeningen (2010) show that businesses operating on the B2C market are experiencing an explosion in managing customer relationships on social media platforms, and on Facebook in particular (Dataforeningen, 2010). As there is limited or no academic research in the area of social media in CRM in this context, the researcher wish to address the gap by contributing to the social media research by applying marketing theory, limited to theories of customer relationship management and customer loyalty, to the concepts of social media in Iranian Restaurant industry. Moreover, the researcher attempt to show that Social media is changing customer loyalty programs also by identifying problems through monitoring what people are saying about their brands.

1.2 Key Terms and Definitions

1.2.1 Social Media

Social media tools are computer and web-based tools and softwares that people use them to share, exchange and create information and files, photos and videos in visual networks. People use computer, laptop, tablet and mobile for creating or sharing a subject, idea or picture, and sometimes other people, see that and comment their opinion or viewpoint about it. Social media is an inexpensive tool for communicate with people and promotion. You can use this tool for broadcasting news in a very short time to a large number of audiences.

Social media is defined as a new marketing channel for customer care and customer retention due to its remarkable popularity among a vast majority of both customers and enterprise. Enterprises are using social media platforms such as Facebook, Twitter and blogs as important solution to address and try to resolve any customer complaint or concerns posted on these social media sites in a timely manner to retain and improve their brand value. Customer Relationship Management performed on social media is called Social CRM (S. Mohan, E. Choi & D. Min, 2008). Social media are social software platforms that allow for two-way communication between one or many individuals, for the purpose of sharing, collaborating and interacting (Lein & Ugstad, 2011)

1.2.2 CRM

CRM or Customer Relationship Management is a field of management that uses strategies, methods and softwares to keep, manage and process customer data and records to improving and growing the quality of relation between the organization and their customers in order to keeping present customers and increasing customer loyalty. It works with recognizing the customer needs, and making products and services matching their needs, and also providing good customer services.

For any business, managing the relationship with customers is of paramount importance. According to a 2002 Goldman Sachs study, CRM is considered the second most important initiative after security for businesses (Marouan El Bernoussi, 2012). Indeed, customers are the core of businesses and the success of a company relies on customers' satisfaction degree and on its ability to manage its relationship with them. Therefore, the most important objective for any enterprise is to make their customers satisfied because the durability of their business depends on them. Customer relationship management is the use of technology in attracting, retaining and enhancing customer relationships (Berry 2002)

1.2.3 Customer

A customer of your organization is a person or organization that expect to be interested in, wants or benefits the products or services prepared by your organization. As this definition suggests, a customer is not necessarily someone who is currently purchasing from the marketer. Every person who enters the business is a potential customer. Even though they may not purchase something today, they may purchase something tomorrow.

1.2.4 Customer Loyalty

Customer loyalty can be said to have occurred if people choose to use a particular shop or buy one particular product, rather than use other shops or buy products made by other companies. Customer loyalty is the key objective of customer relationship management and describes the loyalty which is established between a customer and companies, persons, products or brands. The individual market segments should be targeted in terms of developing customer loyalty.

Customer loyalty is an important metric of your business' success. It gives enterprises insight into issues ranging from whether they are serving the right customers, to the quality of their products/services, to the level of their customer service. Loyal customers also have the potential to dramatically increase the enterprises profits over time. But loyal customers don't just happen; they're cultivated as part of a conscious process that's built into the business' DNA. So, Customer loyalty is the continued and regular patronage of a business in the face of alternative economic activities and competitive attempts to disrupt the relationship (Toporek, 2014).

1.2.5 Marketing

Discovering and identifying customers' needs and make product and services according to covering their needs at the right time, right price and right place.

1.2.6 Customer Service

Customer service is the act of taking care of the customer's needs by providing and delivering professional, helpful, high quality service and assistance before, during, and after the customer's requirements are met. Customer service is meeting the needs and desires of any customer.

1.2.7 Purchasing

The activity of achieving products or services from an external provider/supplier.

1.2.8 Industry

The manufacturing or technically productive enterprises in a particular field, country, region, or economy viewed collectively, or one of these individually. A single industry is often named after its principal product. Every business that can be isolated from others, is an industry.

1.3 RESEARCH OBJECTIVES

In this paper, the researcher will try to explain and critically analyze how restaurants and customers perceive their mutual virtual relationship on social media. And also in a general meaning, how social media are integrated into CRM and Customer loyalty business strategies. On the other hand, this study will help to identify factors contributing to the success or failure of utilizing social media in restaurant positioning efforts and determine the influential elements of this phenomenon on CRM and loyalty of the customers. Those factors can be used by restaurants to reposition the marketing strategy of restaurant to improve or change the restaurant revenue in the respective target market. The specific objectives of the study are:

1. To derive the dimensions of the social media in restaurant and the dimensions of CRM and Customer Loyalty towards it;
2. To examine how the Social media in restaurant affects customers' decision to return to the restaurant in the future;
3. To examine how customer satisfaction affects customers' loyalty in restaurant by enhancing social media tools;

4. To provide recommendations to the restaurant managers for increasing loyal customers through modern marketing tools especially social media.

1.4 RESEARCH HYPOTHESES

The study includes *3* hypotheses as following:

H1: By improving technology aligned with new and various social media tools, the level of CRM acceptance in customers in restaurants increase and leads to loyalty.
H2: The ability to understand customers' needs, desires, and orders and comment messages has a direct relationship with the trustworthy customer service channels.
H3: Having control on receiving needs, desires, and orders and comment of the customers through different social media communication channels in restaurant affect the acceptance of the consumers' attitude about social media as CRM tool for creating customer loyalty.

2. LITERATURE REVIEW

In this section, the author presents background information on the topic. As, the author explained before, the restaurant industry has an important role as a job creator in the Iranian economy in addition to its social impact on communities nationwide, and there are no scientific researches which concentrated on Social Media, CRM and Customer loyalty together in restaurant industry, the author focuses this industry to provide an implication of the Social Media that are of greatest importance to improve the restaurant relationship with customers through customer services and attraction of more loyal customers. On the other hand, for the restaurant business to meet the needs and desires of the targeting customers, the business must investigate the needs and desires of the customers. The information of this paper is vital not only for sustaining successful restaurant business, but also for understanding and improving CRM and Customer loyalty by using Social media.

Pontus Boström studied about CRM through Social Media and its effect on Brand Loyalty. He discussed about this fact that media is simply a communications channel. In the old days, business relationships were built one-to-one through personal communications, but 'Mad Men' took over these channels in the 50′s and used mass media to shout messages at customers to get their attention and encourage them to buy. Mass marketing has become less effective as the volume of messaging has mushroomed and overwhelmed the customer. Social Media is an evolution of the Media channel. The purpose of his research was to gain a deeper understanding of the different dimensions of attitudinal loyalty. As well to understand how mobile providers could take advantage of social media in their CRM work. A case study was chosen with four students in each focus group. One focus group had an international perspective with exchange students and the second group was made up of Swedish students. An interview was held with Telenor to receive information on how companies use social media as a customer relationship management tool. Four concepts were investigated to answer the research questions. The empirical data provides evidence that social media have an effect on attitudinal loyalty and therefore needs careful consideration from companies. Most companies are using social media to some degree and if utilized correctly it can provide a competitive advantage. In this study, he has developed a deeper understanding for the area of social media (SCRM) and the three dimensions of attitudinal loyalty (trust, commitment and recommendation). This research improved that attitudinal loyalty can be affected by SCRM to some extent. The empirical data suggest that trust and recommendation is affected by social CRM. Trust is the antecedent that social CRM have the greatest effect on. If social media is done poorly it can result in decreasing levels of trust, for example low and slow response rates. On the other side a good and efficient managed social media site where customers receive fast responses can result in a higher level of trust. This could also result in a willingness to recommend subscriptions to others. A satisfactory customer support can lead to a better overall impression of the service which has a tendency to result in customer recommendations. (Boström & Svensson, 2013)

In other study, the researchers attempted to understand the guest's needs and desires are invaluable when determining methods for improving the restaurant image. A lack of understanding of customer preference leads to problems in both product and service design (Schall, 2003). Research showed that the most successful restaurants are the ones which are fully aware of customer preferences and develop their services in line with targeted market needs. The researchers suggested restaurant operators should understand the impact of both the customers' level of satisfaction and the restaurant image on the customers' loyalty. The operators should also investigate the driving force for each component of the customer loyalty. Customers may vary in the way they become loyal to a restaurant; for some customers restaurant image may be important, whereas for others quality of service and food are more important. The results of this study regarding the customer's satisfaction level and the image attributes could help the operators of the fine dining restaurant operators to develop customers' loyalty (Victorino et al, 2005). The restaurant must focus on delivering food quality and services and a high level of dining satisfaction that will lead to increased customer return and greater market share. (Zeithaml & Bitner, 1996)

In 2012, Eric Lévy-Bencheton worked on Social CRM towards enhanced Customer Relationship Management. He mentioned the customer experience was often made public: "consum'activists" no longer hesitates to use social media to voice their views. Their views have a major impact on the purchasing decisions of others within their social circle and companies are unable to control them. This loss of management and control means that companies must change in order to stay in touch with their customers. The main idea of his research was to survive the rapid upheavals created by social media and to capitalize on these opportunities, how companies must ask themselves serious questions and update their technology accordingly to ensure they are ready for this new revolution - Social CRM. The study demonstrated that management emerged from three main perspectives: service marketing, industrial marketing, and general management. In perspective of service marketing, the way to retain customers is to improve customer service quality and satisfaction. The need for Marketing, Sales and Customer Service jobs will certainly be questioned, and these will perhaps become the first positions to come under scrutiny. But more generally, it is the entire management structure of the company that must be reconsidered. Companies must take the evolving and technological landscape of CRM into account and adopt a coherent, alert and engaging social media strategy (Lévy-Bencheton, 2012).

Furthermore, Magnini and Honeycutt studied that customer emotions play an important role in driving customer satisfaction and loyalty; they discussed the importance of face recognition and name recall to customers and its effect on customer loyalty (Magnini & Honeycutt, 2005). In 1987, Gummesson proved that in case of service providers the quality of relationships between customers and front line employees, which provides both a professional and social dimension, can strongly contribute to customers' loyalty (Gummesson, 1987). Signicant amount of work has been done on using social media data for getting insights about customers and their views about an enterprise. Monitoring and predicting user behavior and events over social media data has been explored in detail in. There has also been some recent work on analyzing social media content on brand pages for monetization purposes. Work like focuses on the former CRM process of using social data to identify potential leads for enterprises. The surge of social data has recently prompted researchers to envision conceptual models for social CRM systems that incorporate Web 2.0 technologies and user driven collaborative paradigms. Using social media data for business intelligence etc. are also relevant in this context.

In 2011 Hurtola and Jenny researched about the importance of social media in building customer loyalty. They mentioned that social media marketing was a new form of marketing that was currently generating a lot of interest. They believed the introduction of the internet and social media had changed marketing, bringing both possibilities and challenges. The ever-evolving field of social media had also challenged the use of traditional marketing models and theories. The client of their research was company which was activated as a multinational clothing company. The purpose of this article was to investigate the possibilities that social media had to offer for Company X. The company was connected to social media in many ways, and the purpose of this study was to explore the differences between the people connected to Company X via social media and those who were not connected. The aim of the questionnaire in this research was to gather information about the characteristics of the Finnish social media users who were interested in the company and to establish what their consumption patterns were in comparison with the ones who were not connected to the company via social media. They reached to this conclusion that internet questionnaire form was a successful way to gather information about social media users. The questionnaire form was accessible for a month and links were posted to several social media sites and the questionnaire form was available both in English and Finnish. As the aim was to collect data from Finnish social media users, this proved to be a wise decision; only five of the replies were in English. Respondents were also able to attend a drawing of lots for a gift certificate to Company X"s stores if they wished and this might have helped in gaining results (Hurtola & Jenny, 2011).

Marouan El Bernoussi studied the value of social media in CRM. Through this study, the researcher wanted to deeply study CRM and the value of linking social media to it. Specifically, the researcher wanted to determine if there is a potential gap between customers' and companies' perception of social CRM. He reviewed many books and manuscripts as literature review about information systems, CRM, social media and marketing, the researcher gained considerable knowledge to tackle this topic. The researcher used quantitative and qualitative approach to conduct research. Finally, he reached to these findings: Social media add value to CRM and improve companies' businesses. Social CRM will not replace the classical model of CRM. Most importantly, there is a perception gap between customers' and companies' perception of social CRM. Outcomes and implications for practice resulting from this dissertation were that businesses wanting to adopt social CRM strategies must develop a real social CRM strategy and not contenting themselves of having a presence on social media (Marouan El Bernoussi, 2012).

As mentioned before, there is on direct research that covers these research areas in restaurant industry except the ones that explained above, in following this study identifies what other researchers evolved recently (last three years ago) and compares them with each other to find the knowledge gap, and defines the perceptual model of this study. So, the researcher summarized some of the key and relevant literature in Table 1.

Table 1. Summarized of the key and relevant literature (Source: compiled by the author, 2014)

Row	Author	Area of the research	Results & Findings of the research	Year
1	Eric Lévy-Bencheton,	To study how companies survive the rapid upheavals created by social media and to capitalize on these opportunities, companies must ask themselves serious questions and update their technology accordingly to ensure they are ready for this new revolution - Social CRM.	- Companies owe CRM to themselves to be reactive by fitting into this new social ecosystem, even if this means losing control in terms of their relationships with customers and prospects. - They found four steps in the field of Social CRM: 5) E-reputation 6) Strategy & organization 7) Coaching 8) Transformation & Technology	2011
2	Shamaila Marita Lein & Mette Ugstad	To conduct an analysis of how Norwegian management consultancy firms may apply social media in customer relationship management strategies. The problem is approached applying both the company perspective and the customer perspective. For the purpose of exploring the research topic, interviews are conducted with seven Norwegian management consultancy firms.	- The application of social media in CRM can be said to be in a planning-and wait- and- see phase. - Potential for social media was identified across the CRM process - Customers seem to not be ready for application of social media in CRM today, but show positive attitudes to such application in the future. - Facebook and LinkedIn were found to be most popular social media platforms.	2011
3	Marouan El Bernoussi	To study CRM and the value of linking social media to it besides determining if there is a potential gap between customers' and companies' perception of social CRM.	- Social media add value to CRM and improve companies' businesses - Social CRM will not replace the classical model of CRM. - There is a perception gap between customers' and companies' perception of social CRM.	2012
4	Pontus Boström & Oskar Svensson	To gain a deeper understanding of the different dimensions of attitudinal loyalty. As well to understand how mobile providers could take advantage of social media in their CRM work. A case study was chosen with four students in each focus group. One focus group had an international perspective with exchange students and the second group was made up of Swedish students.	- Attitudinal loyalty can be affected by SCRM. - Trust is the antecedent that social CRM have the greatest effect on. - A satisfactory customer support can lead to a better overall impression of the service. - Social media can have positive and negative effects for the company. - The use of social media as a CRM tool can affect trust in a positive manner if used in an efficient way. - To be able to provide efficient assistance and keep up with the digital development a company needs to invest heavily on resources in their social media department.	2013
5	Raymond Menne & Desislava Halova	To investigate how companies can harness the power of social media by utilizing Social CRM. We investigated how integrating social media channels into existing Client Relationship Management platforms can influence customer service and customer loyalty.	- Integrating social media in to CRM does influence customer service and customer loyalty. - The main effects are increased opportunity to collect instant feedbacks from customers and insights into their preferences to improve the service offered even further. - Customers tend to prefer to engage and communicate more with the company when they are entertained by the content or by the way the company approaches them – in a fun, witty and friendly way	2013

3. METHODOLOGY

The author purpose is to study that social media as new communication channel with existing customer in CRM systems influence the customer satisfaction and customer loyalty. To fulfill this aim, the author chooses a research design that considers the relation between Social Media, CRM, and Customer

Loyalty. As the researcher wants to test theoretical models by using them in real world situations, uses a case study which is an in depth study of a particular situation rather than a sweeping statistical survey. It is a method used to narrow down a very broad field of research into one easily researchable topic. Furthermore, the author use a mix of data collection methods (both quantitative and qualitative) in order to provide a more full perspective on how restaurants is incorporating social media into their customer relationship to achieve better satisfaction and ultimately loyalty.

The target population, (N), in this research was all the restaurants in capital of Iran (include Traditional restaurants and fast foods) operating in Tehran. The main reasons that author choose restaurants of Tehran referred to its role in PETS of the country. "PETS" is the abbreviation word defined by author; it is made of four key dimensions as foundation and developing elements of each country (P: Policy- E: Economy- T: Technology- S: Social) that each of its blames and blooms affect the other sub-dimension in country. It means, all of the new policy, economy, technology and social structure and planning was implemented initially in Tehran (due to this fact that the place, people, procedure and other needy factors of the mentioned items are exited and considered in Tehran), so we can see all of its effects and results soon in Tehran. The other reason for choosing Tehran as target population is mass of people who are living in there, "The more population is increased, the more development is created especially in social consequence." According to statistics of 118Food website as valid source in restaurant industry, there are 2230 restaurants in Tehran. In Table 2, you can see the map of Tehran and its twenty two regions includes each regions restaurant umbers.

The paper focus on the customer's viewpoint and how they perceive the restaurant customer relationship management, their work with social media and in turn the effect on attitudinal loyalty. For determining sample size, the author uses Cochran formula as follows:

$$n = \frac{Nz^2pq}{Nd^2 + z^2pq}$$

$$\mathbf{Z} = \mathbf{1.96} \qquad \mathrm{p} = \mathrm{q} = \mathbf{0.5} \qquad \mathrm{d} = \mathbf{0.05}$$

Regarding to the above formula, the sample size of this research is 328 restaurants in all twenty two regions of Tehran. As you see in Table 1, the numbers of restaurants are not equal in regions, so the researcher chooses randomly just one sample in each region and gather two customers opinion. This research has consisted of primary and secondary data that was collected from a number of sources. In primary research section, the author collected data from interviews, surveys and for secondary research part, most of our data was collected on the basis of literature source in the form of books, textbooks, articles, newspaper articles, internet research of news and articles published online and so on. For validity of this research, first of the author asked the viewpoint of restaurant industry plus social communication and made the questionnaire. After that, the researcher chose ten top restaurants and separated them to gain their standpoint. The data was directly exported from customers' viewpoint to SPSS. There are five clusters in the area of this study includes: social media, customer service, customer trust, customer satisfaction and customer loyalty. To test the reliability of this research, the author use Cronbach's alpha. The alpha is 0.9 that is more than 0.7 (a level considered acceptable in most science research) so, this research and constructs are reliable as shown in Table 3.

Table 2. Number of restaurants in Tehran regions (Source: http://www.118food.com, 2014)

Region	Number of Restaurants
1	405
2	341
3	406
4	133
5	82
6	323
7	104
8	54
9	12
10	35
11	66
12	23
13	56
14	25
15	13
16	11
17	5
18	12
19	37
20	20
21	7
22	6

Table 3. Reliability Statistics

Cronbach's Alpha	N of Items
.900	27

4. FINDINGS

4.1. Data Analysis for Descriptive

This section includes the data analysis and the results. The distributed questionnaires were 656 including traditional restaurant and fast foods. Table 4 provides a summary of the demographic rate. The descriptive statistics were used to identify the nature of all respondents such as demographics profiles.

Table 4. Result of first demographic question" What is your gender?"

		Frequency	Percent	Valid Percent	Cumulative Percent
Valid	Female	345	45.8	52.6	52.6
	Male	311	41.3	47.4	100.0
	Total	656	87.1	100.0	
Missing	System	97	12.9		
Total		753	100.0		

Figure 1. Chart of response gender

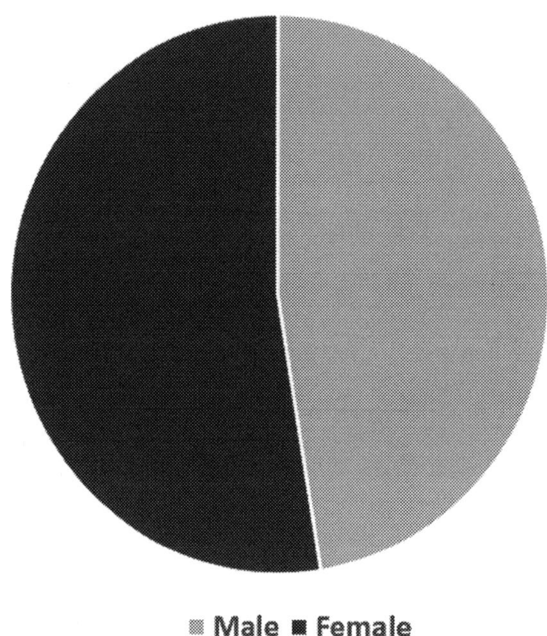

Over 45% of the respondents were females. As you see in table 5, the major age group pf the respondents was between 25 to 34 years old (41.4%). There were an almost close proportion of the age groups of 18-24 years old (40.6%). The rest of the respondents were more than 35 years old and they included small portion in this research.

Besides the two mentioned demographic questions, the author considered two main questions in the questionnaire to analyze the customers' standpoint about their preference device for social media interaction and also asked them which of social media is included their communications channel in the restaurant? The findings (Table 6) shows the majority of the respondents were used smartphone as their preference device in social media communication (29.9%). About 20% preferred to use laptop as social media for their interactions with restaurants.

Moreover, the results (Table 7) presents that about 33% of the restaurant customers used Facebook in their communication channel with their restaurants. About 30% of them used Twitter to communicate with the restaurants. Linkedin gained the third level in communication channel in restaurants (about 13%).

Table 5. Result of second demographic question "What is your age?"

		Frequency	Percent	Valid Percent	Cumulative Percent
Valid	18-24	306	40.6	46.6	46.6
	25-34	312	41.4	47.6	94.2
	35-44	20	2.7	3.0	97.3
	45-54	10	1.3	1.5	98.8
	More than 55	8	1.1	1.2	100.0
	Total	656	87.1	100.0	
Missing	System	97	12.9		
	Total	753	100.0		

Figure 2. Chart of response age

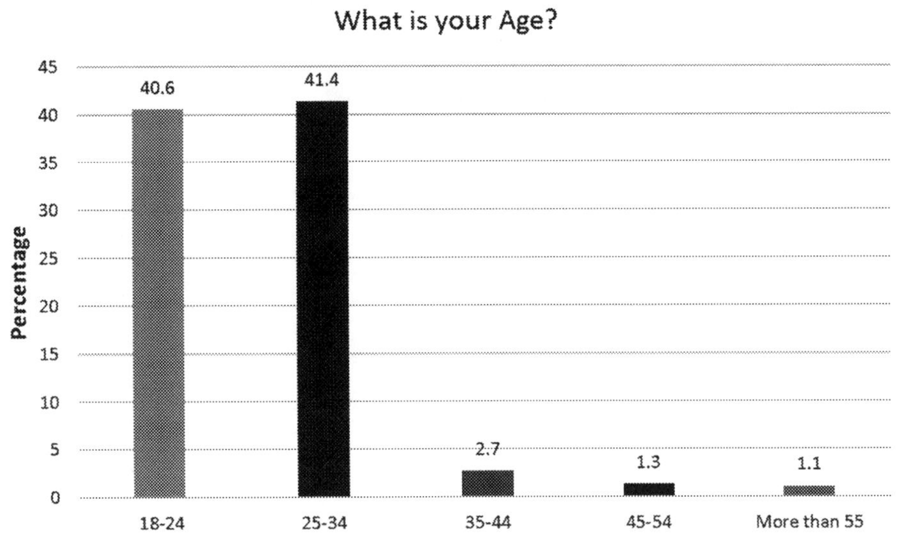

Table 6. Result of third demographic question" preference device for social media interaction"

		Frequency	Percent	Valid Percent	Cumulative Percent
Valid	Desktop	102	13.5	15.5	15.5
	Laptop	156	20.7	23.8	39.3
	Smartphone	225	29.9	34.3	73.6
	Tablet	173	23.0	26.4	100.0
	Total	656	87.1	100.0	
Missing	System	97	12.9		
	Total	753	100.0		

Figure 3. Preference device for social media interaction chart

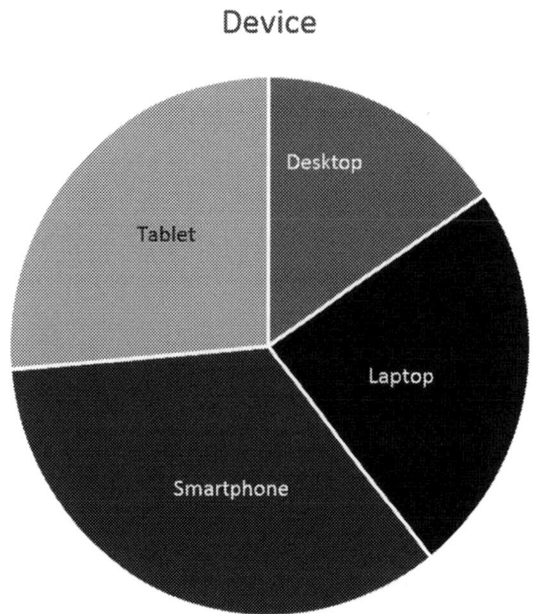

Table 7. Result of fourth demographic question "social media communication channel in restaurant"

		Frequency	Percent	Valid Percent	Cumulative Percent
Valid	Facebook	248	32.9	37.8	37.8
	Twitter	222	29.5	33.8	71.6
	Linkdin	96	12.7	14.6	86.3
	YouTube	68	9.0	10.4	96.6
	Google+	10	1.3	1.5	98.2
	Xing	8	1.1	1.2	99.4
	None of them	4	0.5	0.6	100.0
	Total	656	87.1	100.0	
Missing	System	97	12.9		
Total		753	100.0		

Before determining the dimensions of mentioned constructs, the researcher tested the customer service channels which are the most trustworthy and the most efficient ones in social communication in restaurants. The findings represent that the trustworthy customer service channel in restaurants are telephone with 46.7%, next is email with 36.9% and the last one is social media with 3.5%. When asked the customer who of these customer services are more efficient in restaurants, 57% answered telephone is the most efficient ones, then email and finally social media (table 8) & (table 9).

In last part of analyzing, the author used the Friedman test to analyze which indexes have the most impact on each of the mentioned constructs (Table 10).

Figure 4. Social media communication channel in restaurant chart

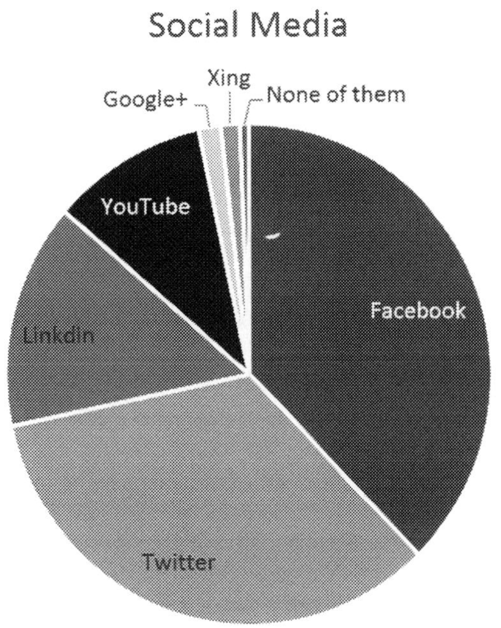

Social Media

Xing
Google+
None of them
YouTube
Facebook
Linkdin
Twitter

Table 8. The trustworthy customer service channels

		Frequency	Percent	Valid Percent	Cumulative Percent
Valid	Telephone	352	46.7	53.7	53.7
	Email	278	36.9	42.4	96.0
	Social Media	26	3.5	4.0	100.0
	Total	656	87.1	100.0	
Missing	System	97	12.9		
	Total	753	100.0		

According to Table 10, each factor that have lower mean rank in comparison the others in the contacts have more value and importance in customers viewpoint. Therefore, in construct of social media: efficiency of customer service channels, simplicity and several of communication channels are the most important indexes in this group. In construct of customer service, first of all familiarity with foods, restaurants, brands and secondly customer positive image of restaurant are important. For customer trust that is influential construct is social media, there are two main factors, one is restaurant data privacy and the other is receiving the needy attention to customers issue. About customer satisfaction, presenting satisfied community in restaurants is very important for the customer. In the last construct (customer loyalty), quality of services, trust and successful CRM are the three important factors that affect directly the loyalty of the customers in restaurants.

Figure 5. The trustworthy customer service channels chart

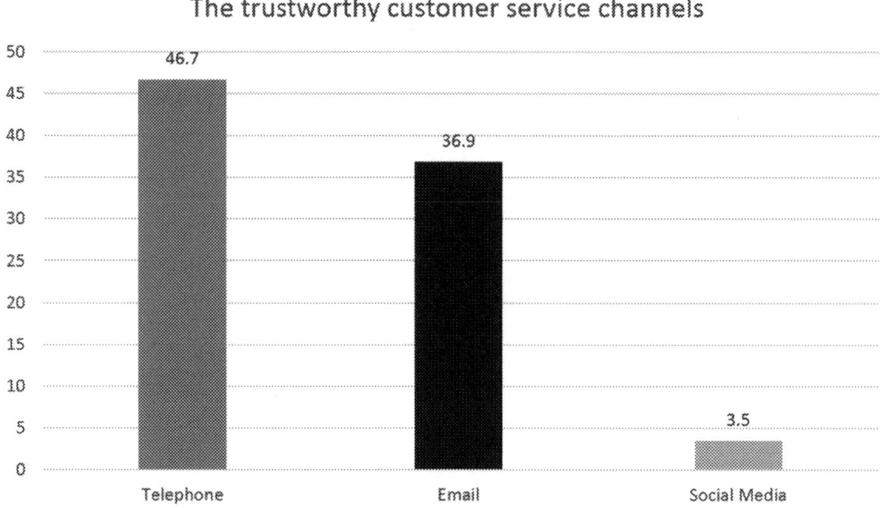

Table 9. The efficient customer service channels

		Frequency	Percent	Valid Percent	Cumulative Percent
Valid	*Telephone*	433	57.5	66.0	66.0
	Email	205	27.2	31.3	97.3
	Social Media	18	2.4	2.7	100.0
	Total	656	87.1	100.0	
Missing	*System*	97	12.9		
Total		753	100.0		

Figure 6. The efficient customer service channels chart

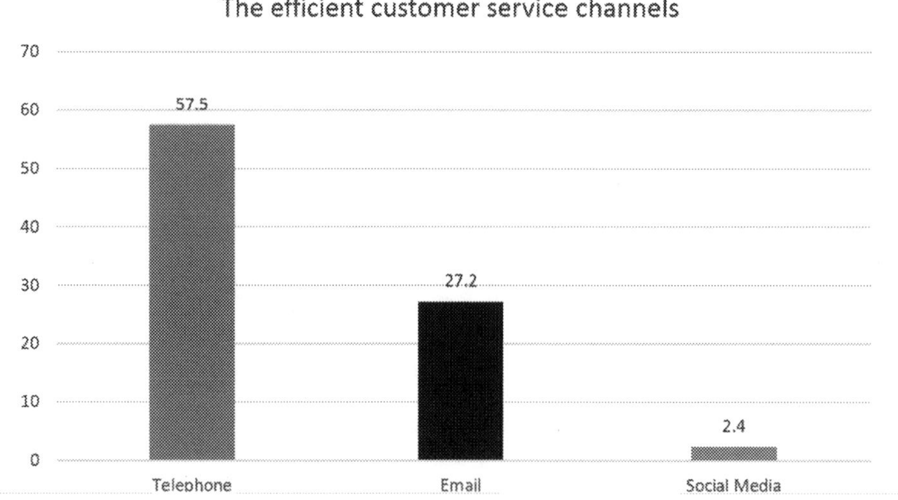

Table 10. The most significant factors in social media construct

Mean Rank	Asymp. Sig.	Factors	Constructs
3.28	.000	Rate of interaction	*Social Media*
3.14	.000	Various of communication channel	
3.85	.000	Trustworthy of customer service channels	
3.04	.000	Efficiency of customer service channels	
3.13	.000	Simplicity	
3.42	.000	Fast response time	
4.01	.000	Fun	
3.38	.000	Friendlier communication	
4.19	.000	Transparency	
3.28	.002	Positive image of restaurant	*Customer Service*
3.65	.000	Handling the customers question/concerns quickly	
3.71	.000	Handled the customers question/concerns by network(internet)	
3.22	.001	Familiarity with foods, restaurants, brands	
3.48	.000	Access news about everything	
3.98	.001	Sharing opinion about the foods and restaurant industry	
3.78	.000	Helping to solve customers' issue	*Customer Trust*
4.16	.000	Promise to solve the issues	
3.53	.000	Receive the needy attention to customers issue	
3.39	.000	Data privacy	
3.23	.000	Providing the needy services	*Customer Satisfaction*
3.19	.000	Solving my problems/issues/questions/concerns	
2.87	.000	Satisfied community	
2.29	.000	Quality of services	*Customer Loyalty*
3.47	.000	Meet new people	
3.03	.000	Service satisfaction	
2.38	.000	Trust	
2.88	.000	Successful CRM	

4.2. Data Analysis for Research Hypotheses

The correlational research is a descriptive research method (non-trial) that examines the relationship among the variables, based on the target of the study. Correlation studies can be classified into three categories based on the target:

- Two-variable Correlation
- Regression analysis
- Covariance analysis or correlation matrix

Once the data have been collected in ordinal rankings or been inverted into ranks, Spearman's rank correlation (rs) can be used, which is a nonparametric method. One of the advantages of Spitaman's correlation coefficient over Pierrson correlation coefficient is that if one or more than one of the data is very large, compare to other numbers, since it is only the rank of them that is considered, they do not affect other data. As in the first part of the research, the model of research and hypotheses were discussed, in this section, we attempt to see whether or not the proposed factors of using social media in conceptual model of the research, have any impact on CRM and customer loyalty in restaurants?

Hypothesis 1 - By improving technology aligned with new and various social media tools, the level of CRM acceptance in customers in restaurants increase and leads to loyalty.

H_0: There is no correlation between two variables of social media tools and acceptance of CRM in customers in restaurants and loyalty.
H_1: There is between two variables of social media tools and acceptance of CRM in customers in restaurants and loyalty.

The above mentioned hypothesis test (shown in Table 11) indicates that in %95 level of certainty, since the significance value is less than level of error, therefore Hypothesis H_0 is not valid and H_1 is valid. Therefore, with the error probability %5 in the main population the sample group can also be validated and in other words, there is no enough evidence to discredit the theory of the researcher on the mentioned hypothesis, and it must be mentioned that there is a significant relationship of (%67) between Social media tools and acceptance of CRM in customers in restaurants and loyalty. By improving technology aligned with new and various social media tools such as: desktop, laptop, smartphone and tablet, the level of CRM acceptance in customers in restaurants increase and leads to loyalty. In other words, improving technology aligned with new and various social media tools have direct relation with their level of customer CRM acceptance and loyalty in restaurants. According to this percentage (67%), the majority of customers prefer to use their own smartphone to order, talk about their needs and desires. Customers want to see the new technology they use integrated into their dining experience, a new study from techonomic on consumer-facing technology shows, especially if it will speed up the process of getting their meal or paying their bill. *(Acceptance of the hypothesis H_1)*

Hypothesis 2 - The ability to understand customers' needs, desires, and orders and comment messages has a direct relationship with the trustworthy customer service channels.

Table 11. Table of the results from Hypothesis test 1

Significant relation	α (level of error)	Number of significance (sig)	Spearman Correlation Coefficient	Name of the Variables
There is a significant relationship	.05	.001	.67	**Social media tools and acceptance of CRM in customers in restaurants and loyalty**

H_0: There is no correlation between two variables of understanding customers' needs, desires, and orders and comment messages and trustworthy customer service channels

H_1: There is a correlation between two variables of understanding customers' needs, desires, and orders and comment messages and trustworthy customer service channels.

The results of testing the hypothesis 2 (shown in table 12) indicates that in %95 level of certainty, since the significance value is less than level of error, therefore Hypothesis H_0 is not valid and H_1 is valid. Therefore, with the error probability %5 in the main population the sample group can also be validated and in other words, there is no enough evidence to discredit the theory of the researcher on the mentioned hypothesis, and it must be mentioned that there is a positive significant relationship of (%53) between the ability to understand customers' needs, desires, and orders and comment messages and trustworthy customer service channels. Restaurants can understand customers' needs, desires, and orders and comment messages through trustworthy customer service channels such as telephone, email, and social media. The findings demonstrate customers trust to telephone more than other service channels not only for explaining their needs and desires, but also their orders in the restaurants. It proves that nowadays, customers seek to warm voice instead of electronic customers' service tools. On the other hand, we can conclude our restaurants in Iran should focus more on improving social media culture to increase loyalty. Restaurants offering Voice of the Customer (VoC) by expert accountable staff to reply the customers are well aware of this, as they see thousands of customer comments every day, each containing this recurring thread of common-sense logic for ensuring customer satisfaction: "Be patient and friendly. Treat customers politely and respectfully. Keep products and services in stock and up to date." *(Acceptance of the hypothesis H_2)*

Hypothesis 3 - Having control on receiving needs, desires, and orders and comment of the customers through different social media communication channels in restaurant affect the acceptance of the consumers' attitude about social media as CRM tool for creating customer loyalty.

H_0: There is no correlation between two variables of having control on receiving needs, desires, and orders and comment of the customers and the acceptance of the consumers' attitude about social media as CRM tool for creating customer loyalty.

H_1: There is a correlation between two variables of having control on receiving needs, desires, and orders and comment of the customers and the acceptance of the consumers' attitude about social media as CRM tool for creating customer loyalty.

Table 12. Table of the results of Testing Hypothesis 2

Significant relation	α (level of error)	Number of significance (sig)	Spearman Correlation Coefficient	Name of the Variables
There is a significant relationship	.05	.000	.53	**The ability to understand customers' needs, desires, and orders and comment messages and trustworthy customer service channels**

Table 13. Table of the results of Testing Hypothesis 3

Significant relation	α (level of error)	Number of significance (sig)	Spearman Correlation Coefficient	Name of the Variables
There is a significant relationship	.05	.000	.71	**Having control on receiving needs, desires, and orders and comment of the customers and the acceptance of the consumers' attitude about social media as CRM tool for creating customer loyalty**

The results of testing the hypothesis 3 (shown in table 13) indicates that in %95 level of certainty, since the significance value is less than level of error, therefore Hypothesis H0 is not valid and H1 is valid. Therefore, with the error probability %5 in the main population the sample group can also be validated and in other words, there is no enough evidence to discredit the theory of the researcher on the mentioned hypothesis, and it must be mentioned that there is a positive significant relationship of (%71) between Having control on receiving needs, desires, and orders and comment of the customers and the acceptance of the consumers' attitude about social media as CRM tool for creating customer loyalty. The customers believe that the social media communication channels in restaurant such as Facebook, Twitter, LinkedIn, YouTube, Google+, Xing, then can control their needs and desires easier and faster. Using these social media communication channels as customer relationship management solution, the restaurant owner affairs representative can view a customer's complete interaction history, issues, addresses, loyalty information, and more - whether the interaction was initiated via phone, email or Web form. They can quickly identify guests, address concerns, resolve issues, and offer solutions that help to turn a negative experience into a positive one. *(Acceptance of the hypothesis H_3)*

5. CONCLUSION

Social Media is the name for the collection of tools (Facebook, LinkedIn, Twitter and many others) that any business uses to be Social via the Web. These tools are sweeping their world and are being adopted at an astonishing rate by individuals and businesses. Yet, many people still have misunderstandings about what these tools are and how they can or should be used. A common assumption is that "Facebook is for people looking to hook-up with their high school sweetheart, LinkedIn is for people looking for a job, and Twitter is for propeller heads". Do not make this mistake! All of these Social Media tools (and many that you have never heard of) are powerful tools that your competitors are using as part of their strategy to steal YOUR customers today. Businesses are using Social Media tools to re-establish and practice the old art of one-to-one communications on a global scale.

Restaurant CRM and Loyalty are two of the most important competitive survival tools for popular restaurants because loyal customers provide repeat business, higher market shares, referrals, and competitive advantages. Thereupon, it is strategically important to understand customers' standpoint and requests to attract, maintain, and satisfy those customers in order to maintain this continuous source of income. In this study, the researcher find out the restaurant managers should understand the impact of both the customers' level of satisfaction, customer trust, social media, and customer service on customers' loyalty. The managers should also pay attention to the driving force for each component of the customer loyalty. Customers may vary in the way they become loyal to a restaurant; for some customers restaurant image may be important, whereas for others quality of service and food are more important. The results of the present study regarding the customer's satisfaction level and customer trust, social media, and customer service could help the managers of the restaurant operators to develop customers' loyalty. The use of social media as a CRM tool can affect trust in a positive approach if used in an efficient way. While the majority of customer comments may be variations on the same theme, customers want to be heard individually and addressed personally. Restaurants who feel accountable to the people they serve will see that feedback can do more than inform and instruct. It creates a connection that drives better business practices, higher customer satisfaction and retention, and increased sales.

On the other hand, this study represents that most of Tehran restaurants customers are young with medium age of 26 years. It is good opportunity for the restaurants that utilize this group's new idea of communication to improve their services. Recommend to the restaurants to pay attention of this result that young people in Tehran have identified social media as a key element of communicating the message of the importance of safe food, new food, and various services.

Moreover, the findings indicate that new smartphone are customers' preference as social media to communicate with their favorite restaurant. Nowadays, in Tehran the number of smartphones is increasing and it will continue to increase. Everything people did online with their PCs they are doing on their smartphones. They are listening to music, reading ads, writing reviews, playing games, and looking up information. The only thing is now they are mobile. The mobile and social media revolution is well on its way. So, recommend the restaurants to update/create their profiles on google places, Facebook and other social media, optimize their website for mobile phones and tablets, and use mobile sites to educate their customers and create entertainment calendars and assign coupons.

According to findings, the author found though in Tehran the growth of using social media is increasing days in and days out, the customers trust neither are nor growth simultaneously. Most of the people preferred to use telephone to order their food to the restaurants. The main reason of this result referred to this fact that customers need warm or hot voice when calling the restaurants. They think this device is easy and efficient device to order and get services. They satiate to hear recorded voice on phone or an electronic email and response. Therefore, this study recommends the restaurants manger to consider telephone, email as CRM (Customer Relation Management) or E-CRM (Electronic Customer Relation Management) in today communication as new generation of social media communication channel.

The results proved that Social media can be an excellent channel for building long-lasting customer relationships in restaurants. Prompt and effective responses to requests for product information, praise or feedback about service, or complaints can result in improved customer support, quicker order fulfillment and faster lead qualification. Therefore, when using social media as a business tool it's important to take strategic steps to ensure restaurants can take full advantage of the opportunity. Here are some recommendations that can help you as restaurants' owner leverage the power of social media to build customer strong relationships. So far, restaurants have been slow to take to technology, there are some few recommendations and recent innovations aligned with the subject of this article that can break new ground in restaurant industry in Iran:

Select Your Social Channels Carefully in Restaurants

In addition to the old guard of Facebook, Twitter and LinkedIn, platforms such as Tumblr, Instagram and Pinterest are the new channels of digital influence, being used for everything from real-time engagement to customer service. Also don't forget that Google+ has excellent reach to the more technical audience and is also coming on strong with all the resources of Google at its disposal. This study suggests you to use Facebook initially. This may be the biggest technology leap coming in the next year, as nearly 90 percent of restaurant owners say they plan to have a Facebook presence by next year. This is a fairly low-cost add-on to make, and it has the potential to grow sales, which always gets a restaurateur's attention. Then Twitter and thirdly LinkedIn are the two most popular tools in restaurant of Iran. So, you can categorize your customers need for improving long-term relationship and offer the best choice to them and let them to choose the most prominent ones aligned with their needs, that make them happy and satisfy and trust to you easier.

Use Social Media Management Toolkits

Use tools that let restaurants quickly identify issues related to your restaurants from the massive pool of updates including blog comments, podcasts, pictures and videos. Take note of more advanced features available from toolkits including image recognition to identify photographs and videos that are relevant to your restaurants services and foods offering. As the results showed, the best social media tool that you can consider in your restaurants toolkits is supplying some application in your customers' smartphone. Digital menu boards besides smartphones are another opportunity for restaurants. Watch for fast-food restaurants to change menus more often, because digital menu boards make it so much easier than manually changing prices and items. Digital signage also allows quick-serve restaurants to provide entertainment and interactivity while you wait in.

Have an Integration Strategy

To provide value to enterprise users (e.g. sales, marketing, customer support), relevant social media content should be integrated with your CRM and other core IT systems, such as ERP, finance and logistics, creating a centralized enterprise portal. A systems integration platform with interfaces to social media and popular IT systems can provide the needed connectivity. As social media networks go in and out of favor, loosely coupled integration provided by an integration platform means that restaurants can easily add, remove or change social media channels as warranted. As you know, customers nowadays are already using social media to lodge complaints, give compliments and ask questions. It's imperative for businesses to meet their customers where they are and address any customer service or support issues as quickly as possible. A comprehensive system integration strategy and platform can help support the process and accelerate companies' ability to enjoy the benefits of social CRM.

Automate Processes Wherever Possible

Information from social media should be as actionable, such as automatically triggering alerts in cases of negative comments so they can be handled as quickly as possible. Although the processes should be automated, the interactions themselves should be personalized. Canned responses are obvious to customers and have a negative impact on the restaurants' image. Consumers want to see the new technology they use integrated into their dining experience.

Investigate Big Data Analysis and Manipulation

With so much data now at hand, there is great potential to better understand and manage customer relationships. This can include using image recognition to identify elements in posts and correlate it with other elements, but it's also key to being able to actively manage relationships with many customers and potential customers on a personal level in restaurants.

Mobile Ordering

This is one area where fast-food chains are in the forefront. Restaurants can use iPad order kiosks. Why wait in line if restaurants can file the customer's order at a kiosk immediately, and then sit down and relax? Expect more of this, since it could help prevent walk-aways and result in more orders. It's been noted that customers using a mobile ordering app tend to place larger orders than by phoning it in. Maybe it's because they have a visual guide that shows them just how delicious your fare is...kind of like having a great in-house menu and team that present an enticing vision to your in-house customers. Restaurants can't do that over the phone, and a phone book add is extremely limited at best in the amount of information they can present—but they can custom tailor your message perfectly with a restaurant ordering app. Show your customers how great your food is, give them an easy to use ordering interface, and watch your average order size grow. It really makes sense! On the other hand, when you have a mobile ordering for your restaurant, your competitors don't. It's that simple as well in the eyes of your customers. When they want to place a quick carry out or delivery order via the convenience of their mobile device, and they know that your business caters to their mobile savviness, you become the go to restaurant while your competition is left in the dark. Restaurant apps are catching on quickly in the industry, but you can still be first and lock in your position today.

Games While-U-Wait

Restaurants can project gesture-enabled games onto restaurant floors for kids to play while they wait for Happy Meals. That'll keep kids busy and we all know happy kids mean happy parents who come back to your restaurant.

Online Coupons

Restaurants should use digital coupons, and diners gobble them up. Offering online coupons for foods and restaurant's services can have numerous benefits. Restaurant can sell foods quickly, sell more foods on top of the discounted ones, and increase traffic on restaurant website. In addition, by providing internet coupons, restaurant can enhance their restaurants' brand and promote customer loyalty. Online coupons minimize advertising costs while maximizing your marketing flexibility. While a coupon business opportunity primarily advertises the restaurant, they are discounting, it can also advertise your restaurant. Their restaurant's name, address, and other pertinent information should be featured prominently on the coupon. Doing so will have prospects perceive their restaurant as one that offers deals, leading them to visit your website for other discounts.

This study offers strategic guidelines to restaurant management. The CRM perceptions and level of satisfaction are some of the factors that helps guide the positioning and repositioning strategies of the restaurant in the local market place. The relationships among customers' satisfaction, trust, services perceptions, and restaurant loyalty determined the magnitude of their relative importance to a specific market by linking customer behavior to the restaurant loyalty. The restaurants operators should make their customers aware of their offerings. Social media should be carefully developed based on the results of ongoing research. If the target market indicates that a major personality trait is up to date, the manager should develop social media, which feature a modernized layout of furnishings, colors, and logos in various devices and channels. New customers will try the restaurant based on an initial notion of perceived quality and if they are satisfied that will enhance their further intention to revisit the restaurant. Furthermore, Managers should put more efforts to facilitate the restaurant implementation planning to respond to the changing market and customer demands. Such a system requires a mix of strategic management, marketing, motivation, innovation, training, and financial techniques in social media that will be a good subject for future research.

REFERENCES

Berry, L. L. (2002). Relationship Marketing of Services- Perspectives from 1983 & 2000. *Journal of Relationship Marketing*, *1*(1), 59–77. doi:10.1300/J366v01n01_05

Boström & Svensson. (2013). *CRM through Social Media and its effect on Brand Loyalty*. Luleå University of Technology.

Dataforeningen. (2010). *Mellomrapport; Norske virksomheters bruk avsosiale medier*. Retrieved Jun 14, 2011, from: http://www.kommunikasjon.no/Foreningen/Nyheter/_attachment/7822?=true&_ts=127f21c4f8b

El Bernoussi, M. (2012). *The value of social media in CRM: from CRM 1.0 to CRM 2.0*. Dublin Business School.

Eric Levy-Bencheton. (2012). *Practice Sales & Marketing / Customer Relationship Management*. Atos Consulting, White paper translated from the French "Social CRM: vers la Relation Client augmentée.

Gummesson, E. (1987). *Quality: The Ericsson Approach*. Stockholm: Ericsson.

Hurtola & Jenny. (2011). *The importance of social media in building customer loyalty for Company X*. Laurea University of Applied Sciences.

Magnini, V., & Honeycutt, E. (2005). Face Recognition and Name Recall, Training Implications for the Hospitality Industry. *The Cornell Hotel and Restaurant Administration Quarterly*, *46*(1), 69–78. doi:10.1177/0010880404270881

Mohan, S., Choi, E., & Min, D. (2008). Conceptual modeling of enterprise application system using social networking & web 2.0 social CRM system. In *Proceedings of the International Conference on Convergence & Hybrid Information Technology, ICHIT '08*. IEEE Computer Society. doi:10.1109/ICHIT.2008.263

Rataree, G. (2003). *Measurement of Customer Satisfaction level of Hotel Food and Beverage Service at the Westin Hotel*. (Unpublished Thesis). Oklahoma State University.

Schall, M. (2003). Best practices in the assessment of hotel-guest attitudes. *The Cornell Hotel and Restaurant Administration Quarterly*, *44*(2), 51–65. doi:10.1016/S0010-8804(03)90018-8

Shamaila Marita Lein & Mette Ugstad. (2011). *Social Media in Customer Relationship Management - An analysis of Norwegian management consulting firms*. (Master thesis). Copenhagen Business School.

Soriano, D. (2002). Customers' expectations factors in restaurants: *The situation in Spain. International Journal of Quality & Reliability Management*, *19*(8/9), 1055–1067. doi:10.1108/02656710210438122

Toporek, A. (n.d.). *What is Customer Loyalty*. Retrieved 2014, from: http://customersthatstick.com

Victorino, L., Verma, R., Plaschka, G., & Dev, C. (2005). Service innovation and customer choices in the hospitality industry. *Journal of Managing Service Quality*, *15*(6), 555–576. doi:10.1108/09604520510634023

Wu, B., Ye, Q., Yang, S., & Wang, B. (2009). A new telecom CRM framework from social network perspective. In *Proceedings of the 1st ACM international workshop on Complex networks meet information and knowledge management*. ACM.

Zeithmal, V., & Bitner, M. (1996). Service Marketing. New York: McGraw-Hill.

This research was previously published in Strategic Customer Relationship Management in the Age of Social Media edited by Amir Khanlari, pages 244-267, copyright year 2015 by Business Science Reference (an imprint of IGI Global).

Chapter 32
The Role of Individual Behavior and Social Influence in Customer Relation Management

Jerzy Surma
Warsaw School of Economics, Poland

ABSTRACT

One of the crucial trends in business is to offer one-to-one personalized services. In this context, companies try to build customer relationship management systems based on the customer social relations and behavioral patterns. The key issue is predicting to which products or services a particular customer is likely to respond. Additionally, identifying peer-to-peer influence on social network sites is critical to a social media marketing strategies. That is why companies have to learn to understand their customer in the broader social context in order to build successful Customer Relationship Management (CRM) systems, which are described in this chapter. In those systems, the individual customer behavior patterns can be used to build an analytical customer profile. Based on the profile, a company might target a customer with a personalized message. In this chapter, the authors use four research studies in order to extensively present this issue.

INTRODUCTION

Living in contemporary world, we leave thousands of digital footprints behind us through usage of mobile phones, credit cards, electronic mail, browsing in social networks etc. Each footprint shows our real actions that we take in given time and place. The analysis of thousands of such footprints on large groups of people allow us to analyze human behavior on an unimaginable before scale in scientific studies concerning psychology and sociology (Lazer, 2009). The results of those analysis will have a significant influence on many disciplines such as medical prophylaxis, political elections or contemporary marketing in personalized customer relationship management. In this context it is interesting to look at the summary of historical development of customer management by Kumar (2008). It begins with direct relations with individual customers, then entire-market customers, segmented customers and finally the return

DOI: 10.4018/978-1-5225-5637-4.ch032

to the initial idea of personalized service usage of interactive marketing (Deighton, 1996). Additionally in light of the current social media marketing challenges the focus switched to digital word-of-mouth (WoM) communication and/or consumer-to-consumer campaigns. Based on this interactive marketing should be extended to use social networks in order to support achieving marketing objectives through social influence (Trusov, Bodapati, & Bucklin, 2010).

According to Kumar, interactive marketing can be described as follows (Kumar, 2008):

1. **The Range of Decisions:** Identification of interested customers and assuring on-going relations or relations at proper time.
2. **The Range of Analysis:** Elaborating the complete characteristics of the customer.
3. **Value Building Factor:** Personalization and adapting proper service at a proper time.

The usage of customer behavior in marketing has a relatively long history. Analytical customer relationship management systems have been used in telecommunications and banking sector since the 90s of the previous century (Shankar & Winer, 2006). In this perspective, new type of data about diversified customer behaviors introduces new opportunities in contemporary marketing. This new potential, related to the development of Business Intelligence systems (Surma, 2011), has contributed to the development of personalized marketing concept based on profound analysis of history of contacts with customer[1].

It is important to underline an impact of social influence on the customer behavior. Identifying peer-to-peer influence on social network sites is critical to new social media marketing strategies (Aral & Walker, 2011). Social influence studies are described extensively in Cialdini and Goldstein (2004) paper, and a potential marketing application in on-line social networks are presented in Trusov (2010) research. Social influence mechanisms are widely deployed by companies to develop advertising messages for mass media. Showing people who somehow resemble the message's recipient, or on the contrary – members of a group to which the recipient aspires, can be perceived as an example of the use of social influence mechanisms. Currently, it is possible to customize advertising messages, based on the given consumer's level of susceptibility to social influence. Social relationships maintained by the users in on-line social networks to a large extent reflect their personal relationships maintained in the real world. Users perceive other participants as a source of information and aim at identifying with the group (Deutsch & Gerard, 1995).

CUSTOMER PROFILING

From Segmentation to Personalization

In order to understand properly new analytical opportunities in marketing, it is crucial to differentiate correctly the classic approach based on customer segmentation (see Figure 1) in comparison to personalized approach related to interactive marketing (see Figure 2). In case of segmentation, the division of customers is done usually on the basis of social-demographic characteristics (e.g., sex, age, education, place of residence) and the analysis of the purchase history, using the RFM[2] analysis. In this approach, the customer is classified to the segment as a similar object to other members (objects) of the segment[3]. All customers in a given segment, in a given marketing campaign receive the identical message, irrespective of the differences between them. The time and the method of delivering the message is chosen arbitrarily by the manager of marketing campaign and is the same for the whole segment. In this approach we usually don't reflect value changes of customer characteristics in time and we treat the whole segment as static and homogeneous group of objects.

The interactive approach to customer management is significantly different (see Figure 2). Customer is treated as an independent person that has specific needs and preferences. The company wants to get to know the characteristics of the customer through conversations, maintaining the relationship (Kumar, 2008), as well as collecting and analyzing the digital footprints that customer leaves behind him in different interactions. It is well known that customer responds to a given marketing message is not happening in a vacuum. Many factors contributed to this decision, such as psychological variables (motivation, perception, learning, attitude, personality/lifestyle), social influence (family, social class, reference groups, culture), and purchase situation (purchase reason, time, surroundings) (Perreault, Cannon, & McCarthy, 2009). However, most factors that contribute directly to customer response cannot be captured and stored in corporate databases. The possible way to reflect these response factors is to relate them mainly to customer behavior patterns and available social relations data. As a result of this pattern analysis, it is possible to create the Analytical Customer Profile (Surma, 2012). On the basis of this profile, we can adjust the marketing offer to specific customer needs. The time and the method of delivering the message is determined by the customer preferences. As opposed to segmentation, the contact with customer is activated indirectly by the customer himself through the on-going process of the prediction of his needs. In this approach, it is crucial to observe the behavior of the customer in time and to analyze the dynamics of the values of the characteristics represented in the profile. Next we will demonstrate the phases of contact personalization with customer and the idea of the customer analytical profile concept.

Personalization Process

The process of personalization, which is based on the analytical customer profile, is shown on Figure 3. The whole process consist of four phases (Versanen & Raulas, 2006):

1. **Processing:** Transform transactional and external client data into analytical customer profile. Customer profile is generated based on the econometrical and data mining methods (Chiu & Tavella, 2008).
2. **Customization:** Is the production of personalized marketing output due to:
    a. Selection of the proper product/service offer based on the customer needs (*hyle*),
    b. Development of the personalized marketing message, that is adequate to the customer preferences (*morphe*).

Figure 1. Classical marketing based on the customer segmentation: "Propose a customer to a product"
Source: Author.

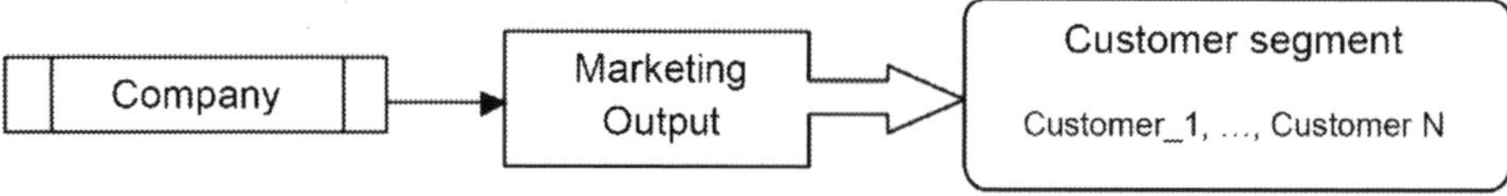

Figure 2. Interactive marketing based on the personalization: "Propose a product for a customer"
Source: Author.

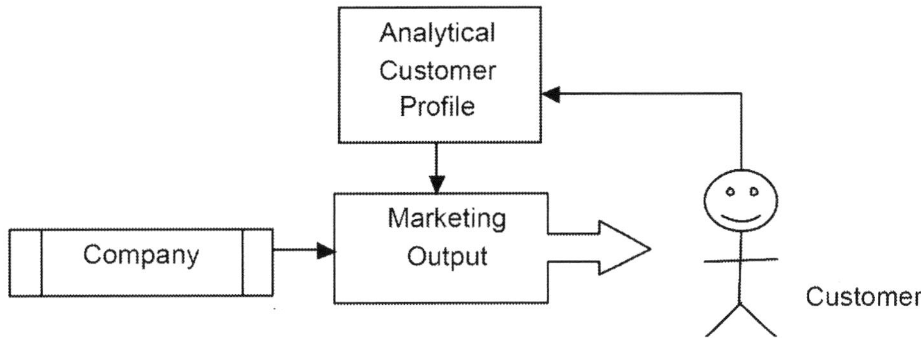

3. **Delivery:** Procedure how the personalized marketing output reaches the customer. During this phase an access channel and time of delivery is established. Those parameters are forecasting based on the customer preferences taken from customer profile.
4. **Interactions:** Recognized and registered customer behavior taken from two sources:
    a. **Internal:** Response for delivered marketing output, click stream on the company internet portal, personal data deliver into registration forms, contacts with call center, registered purchases, exchange opinion with others customers on the company blog, etc.
    b. **External:** Activities on the external online social networks [4], transactions in the loyalty programs with a business partners, customer data received from external marketing databases, etc.

The Structure of Analytical Customer Profile

The main aim of personalization process (see Figure 3) is to deliver adequate marketing messages to the customer in proper time. We assume that it is possible to predict customer behavior on the basis of the history of his behaviors and social influence. It is crucial to established which variables describing the customer should be processed and whether there is appropriate transactional data available.

The analytical customer profile is a result of abstraction (generalization[5] and aggregation[6]) of interactions (time series of customer transactional data, as well as other social-demographic data) in order to generate adequate marketing messages[7]. The characteristics (variables) stored in analytical profile generally belong to one of two perspectives (see Figure 4):

- **Demographic Perspective:** Built on the basis of data declared by customer and received from official contacts with customer. This data is mainly statistics (e.g., place of birth). However some of them are subject to change in time (e.g., place of residence, education).
- **Behavioral and Social Perspective:** Build on the basis of behavioral data left by customer during interactions with the company, other customers, and social environment. This data is mainly dynamic.

Figure 3. The process of personalization
Source: Versanen and Raulas (2006).

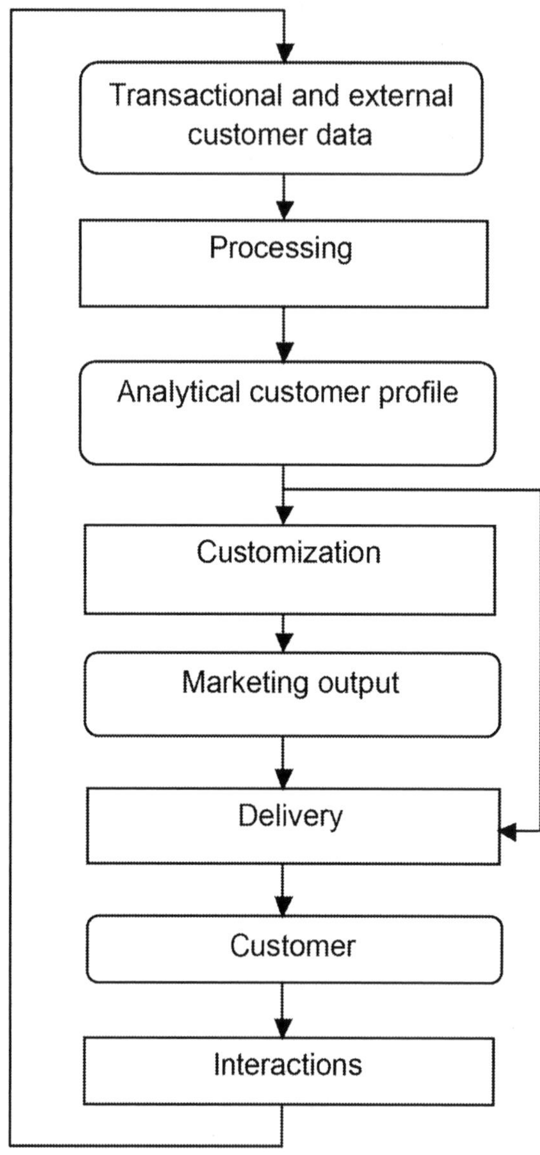

The successful prediction of customer behaviors is possible only when analytical profile really reflects motivations and attitudes that determine customer decisions. Those motivations and attitudes result from a human nature of analyzed person and are in reality responsible for her actions (Nisbet, Elder, & Miner, 2009). The interactions reflected in transactional data can be compared to shadows (*σκιά*) of Plato in the cave (Plato, 2007). If we continue this metaphor, the analytical profile is built on the basis of "shadows" and as defined it is rather imperfect attempt to model human behavior. However, we have to underline three conditions that are favorable to build profiles. First of all, transactional data represents real actions, as opposed to declared information. Secondly, it is the long term, often long-standing abstraction of transactional data that is the key of analytical profile. In this context, the level of credibility of knowledge about customer is increasing according to the length of data collecting period. Finally, the wide range of collected transactional data is also important: from the data available inside the company, through the public data available e.g., on on-line social networks, to data retrieved from customer profiles from other companies.

Profile Analysis

The business dimension of personalization requires a proper analysis of client profitability in time, i.e., the calculation of profits from sale per customer in comparison to average costs spent on his service. When every customer is unequivocally identified and monitored with the usage of analytical profile, it is possible to calculate the indicator of past customer value and to estimate the indicator of customer lifetime value (Kumar, 2008). The indicator of past customer value allows among others the precise monitoring of customer profitability, in which we can compare the positive cash flows earned thanks to the knowledge from analytical profile and the individual costs of building and maintaining the analytical profile. The usage of analytical profile allows us to calculate the indicator of lifetime value, which is related to prediction of future customer margins and future costs (taking into account changes in time value of money). The prediction of "what and when" customer is willing to buy is in this context a key element[8].

Prediction models determine which characteristics (variables) should be represented in analytical profile. This set of variables can differ according to type of products or sector etc. The usage of models that suggest a given customer the most probable purchase and its time allow the personalization management system (after the update of analytical profile) to pass on to customization phase. Afterwards it is possible to activate automatically the phase of delivering the marketing message to customer at proper time [9]. In this context we can talk about the activity of analytical profile whether the process was automatic or was directly monitored by marketing department. In this approach, the analytical profile (as a real customer representation) generates declaration of realization of personalized, 1-to-1 market-

Figure 4. The structure of analytical customer profile
Source: Author.

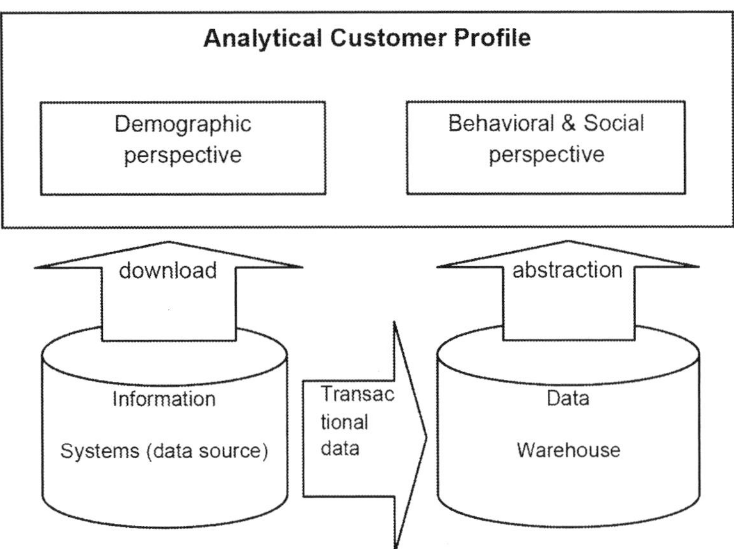

ing campaign. Everyday management of large volume of unique declarations is a new and nontrivial management problem, i.e., event driven process management.

RESEARCH STUDIES

In this chapter four research studies are presented. Those projects were carefully selected in order to present the recent research in customer profiles analysis and the social influence (see Table 1).

Proactive Customer Relationship Management

We have already shown the trend to transform customer relationship management activities from campaign-centric (static and old fashion approach) to customer-centric, where the company needs to develop detailed knowledge about customers. This approach requires the continuous development of customer profile, and then to apply marketing interventions that are relevant to the status and preference of each individual customer. In this context Sun, Li, and Zhou (2006) proposed the framework of proactive CRM based on the adaptive learning. Adaptive learning offers the company the opportunity to learn about customer preferences in an uncertain environment and adapt its strategies in a real-time fashion. Formally they formulate CRM intervention decisions as a solution to a stochastic dynamic control problem under demand uncertainty with built-in customer reactions. The adaptive learning component allows to derive an integrated sequence of CRM decisions about *when* to contact *which* customer with *what* product using which communication channel (*how*). This approach was empirically tested on the cross-selling campaign management for a retail banking services in a national bank (Li, Sun, & Montgomery, 2005). The data set consist of monthly account opening and transaction histories, cross-selling solicitations about the type of product promoted, communication channels, and demographic information of a randomly selected sample of 4000 households for 15 financial product groups during a total of 27 month.

The effectiveness of a cross-selling campaign was improved from 5,6% to 11,2%. The return on investment on performed campaigns was improved by 40,8%, and demonstrate the increase of long-term profit when the company shifts its cross-selling strategy from campaign centric to customer centric. This research justifies the approach in which the company is able to maximize long-term profit based on the dynamic and customized decisions generated from time series of information about the customer.

Table 1. Research studies characteristics

Study	Social Influence	Customer Profile Management	Source
Proactive Customer Relationship Management	No	Yes	Sun, Li, and Zhou (2006)
Social influence in on-line social networks: Cyworld	Yes	No	Raghuram, Han, and Gupta (2009)
Social influence in on-line social networks: Facebook	Yes	No	Aral and Walker (2012)
Customer referrals in financial services	Yes	No	Kumar, Petersen, and Leone (2010)

Source: Author.

Social Influence in On-Line Social Networks: Cyworld

Cyworld[10] is a South Korean social network service operated by SK Communications. With over 18 million users out of a 48 million population (with 33 million Internet users) Cyworld is South Korea's leading social network. Created in 1999 when the online advertising market was not enough to sustain a website, and when valuations of online communities was unheard of, Cyworld had to come up with innovative business models, services and pioneered many functions which are gradually being "rediscovered" elsewhere. Raghuram, Han, and Gupta (2009) performed the research on Cyword with three questions (a) do friends influence purchases of a user in a social network ? (b) which users are more influenced by social pressure ? and (c) what is the impact of this social influence in sales and revenues. To address these questions they developed a quantitative model that capture the effect of social influence on a member's decision purchase. The Cyworld users can decorate their own mini-home pages by purchasing virtual items[11]. Based on that the transactional (purchasing) data for building the model was taken by monitoring behavior of over 200 users for several months.

The final results show that there is a significant and positive impact of friends purchases on the purchase probability of users. They found significant heterogeneity among users. Deep examination reveals differences across three user groups: positive (40%), negative (12%), and zero (48%) social effect. Users who have limited connection to other members are not influenced by friends purchases. Positive social effect, translated into a 5% increase in revenue, was observed in moderately connected users. These users are imitating others behavior. In contrast to this group, highly connected users tend to reduce their purchases of items when they see their friends buying them. This negative social effect reduces the revenue for this group by more than 14%. These empirical results are relevant for social networking sites. The members in high status group have an influence on those in the middle status group for the diffusion of a new product.

Social Influence in On-Line Social Networks: Facebook

The econometrical identification of social influence is a difficult problem, especially in the case of which separation of correlation from causation in networked data is complicated (Aral, 2011). In the mentioned research on Cyworld this problem is not solved. Aral and Walker (2012) research based on experiments give an opportunity to identify influential and susceptible individuals in large social networks with a clear separation causation from correlation. They proposed an experiment on Facebook that was conducted over a 44-day period. At the beginning of the experiment, they ran an advertising campaign to recruit a representative population of Facebook users to the experimental application. Advertisements were subsequently displayed to users through advertising space within Facebook and within existing Facebook applications in such a way as to maximize the likelihood that representative proportions of the demographic characteristics of Facebook users were captured. The campaign was conducted in three waves throughout the duration of the experiment to recruit a population of experimental subjects that consisted of 7730 application users (continued to fully install and use the application sufficiently to grant permission for the application to send notifications on their behalf) and 1.3M distinct peers, resulting in 976 peer adoptions.

The main results were as follows: younger users are more susceptible to influence than older users, men are more influential than women, women influence men more than they influence other women, and married individuals are the least susceptible to influence in the decision to adopt the product offered.

Additionally experimental results show that the joint distributions of influence, susceptibility, and the likelihood of spontaneous adoption in the local network around individuals together determine their importance to the propagation of behaviors.

Customer Referrals in Financial Services

The social influence effect investigated in Cyworld and Facebook is crucial in a proper understanding of referral marketing. Referral marketing is a method of promoting products or services to new customers through referrals, usually word of mouth. Kumar, Petersen and Leone (2010) examined the monetary value of word of social relations, referral behavior and their role in consumer decision making and purchase behavior. The main research hypothesis was whether it is possible to predict customer's indirect impact (through referral behavior) on the firm's future profits. This hypothesis was empirically verified on the basis of data collected from 14160 customers in four years period. The data was obtained from the financial services company (ranks high among the global Fortune 1000 firms), and was related to a wide range of products and services, including banking, insurance, and investments. The data included each customer's own purchase behavior and the estimated marketing costs. The data set included also the findings from a survey given to each of the 14160 customers that provided information on their "willingness to refer" to new customers. In this sample 9492 of customers stated that they are intended to make referrals, however only 4204 actually made attempts at referrals.

The efficiency of the performed campaign management was measured by means of CLV (customer lifetime value) and CRV (customer referral value). For CLV, the average in performed experiments in the test group customers was $274 before and $291 after (the same for the control group is significantly lower and was respectively $270 and $271). For CRV, the average in performed experiments in the test group customers was $145 before and $164 after (the same for the control group is significantly lower and was respectively $145 and $146). The results show that each of the performed campaigns was successful in significantly increasing the average customer's CLV and CRV. Based on this research we can see that building a social network can be a long-term competitive advantage for both the customer and the firm because it enables the firm's relationship with each customer to evolve over time (Ganesan, 1994).

FINAL REMARKS

In order to build a successful customer relationship management systems companies must learn to understand their customer in a social context. The crucial problem is to the predict a customer response based on a behavioral modeling. To predict the action of customer response we must model human nature based on behavioral patterns and social relations. In this context we presented a model of an active analytical customer profile. In four research studies we showed the current research in this field.

The presented results are promising but showing a lack of models that integrate customer behavior and social influence. Nevertheless the question, what exactly does it mean for someone to influence or be influenced by their peers is an open and difficult research problem. The experimental approach is the best research framework available, but it is seems almost impossible to detect all factors in observational data in order to get a proper flow of influence.

ACKNOWLEDGMENT

This research was financially supported by National Science Centre in Poland NCN (2011/01/B/HS4/06630).

REFERENCES

Aral, S. (2011). Identifying Social Influence: A Comment on Opinion Leadership and Social Contagion in New Product Diffusion. *Marketing Science*, *30*(2), 1–7. doi:10.1287/mksc.1100.0596

Aral, S., & Walker, D. (2011). Identifying Social Influence in Networks Using Randomized Experiments. *IEEE Intelligent Systems*, *26*(5), 91–96. doi:10.1109/MIS.2011.89

Aral, S., & Walker, D. (2012). Identifying Influential and Susceptible Members of Social Networks. *Science*, *337*(6092), 337–341. doi:10.1126/science.1215842 PMID:22722253

Chiu, S., & Tavella, D. (2008). *Data mining and market intelligence for optimal marketing returns*. Amsterdam: Elsevier.

Cialdini, R. B., & Goldstein, N. J. (2004). Social influence: Compliance and Conformity. *Annual Review of Psychology*, *55*(1), 591–621. doi:10.1146/annurev.psych.55.090902.142015 PMID:14744228

Deighton, J. (1996). The Future of Interactive Marketing. *Harvard Business Review*, 11–12.

Deutsch, M., & Gerard, H. B. (1995). A study of normative and informational influence upon individual judgment. *Journal of Abnormal and Social Psychology*, *51*(3), 629–636. doi:10.1037/h0046408

Ganesan, S. (1994). Determinants of Long-Term Orientation in Buyer-Seller Relationship. *Journal of Marketing*, *58*(2), 1–19. doi:10.2307/1252265

Haimowitz, I., & Kohane, I. (1996). Managing temporal worlds for medical trends diagnosis. *Artificial Intelligence in Medicine*, *8*(3), 299–321. doi:10.1016/0933-3657(95)00037-2 PMID:8830926

Kelly, S. (2006). *Customer Intelligence. From Data to Dialoque*. Chichester, UK: Wiley.

Knott, A., Hayes, A., & Neslin, S. (2002). Next-Product-To-Buy Models for Cross-Selling Applications. *Journal of Interactive Marketing*, *16*(3), 9–75. doi:10.1002/dir.10038

Kumar, V. (2008). *Managing customers for profits: strategies to increase profits and building loyalty*. Wharton Scholl Publishing.

Kumar, V., Petersen, J., & Leone, R. (2010). Driving Profitability by Encouraging Customer Referrals: Who, When, and How. *Journal of Marketing*, *74*(5), 1–17. doi:10.1509/jmkg.74.5.1

Lazer, D. (2009). Life in the network: The coming age of computational social science. *Science*, *6*(323), 721–723. doi:10.1126/science.1167742 PMID:19197046

Li, S., Sun, B., & Montgomery, A. (2005). *Introducing What Financial Product to Which Customer at What Time - An Empirical Analysis of Customized and Dynamic Cross-selling Campaigns.* Tepper School of Business working paper, 2006-E66.

Nisbet, R., Elder, J., & Miner, G. (2009). *Handbook of Statistical Analysis & Data Mining Applications.* Amsterdam: Elsevier.

Perreault, J., Cannon, J., & McCarthy, E. (2009). *Essentials of Marketing.* New York: McGraw-Hill.

Plato, . (2007). *The Republic.* New York: Penguin Classics.

Prahalad, C. K., & Krishnan, M. S. (2008). *The New Age of Innovation (Analytics: Insight for Innovation).* New York: McGraw-Hill.

Raghuram, I., Han, S., & Gupta, S. (2009). *Do Friends Influence Purchases in a Social Network?* Harvard Business School Working Paper, no. 09-123.

Shankar, V., & Winer, R. (2006). When Customer Relationship Management Meets Data Mining. *Journal of Interactive Marketing, 20*(3-4), 2–4. doi:10.1002/dir.20062

Shibo, L., Sun, B., & Wilcox, R. (2005). Cross-Selling Sequentially Ordered Products: An Application to Consumer Banking Services. *JMR, Journal of Marketing Research, 42*(2), 233–239. doi:10.1509/jmkr.42.2.233.62288

Sun, B., Li, S., & Zhou, C. (2006). "Adaptive" Learning and "Proactive" Customer Relationship Management. *Journal of Interactive Marketing, 20*(3/4), 82–96. doi:10.1002/dir.20069

Surma, J. (2011). *Business Intelligence.* New York: Business Expert Press.

Surma, J. (2012). Modeling customer behavior and social relations with analytical profiles. In I-H. Ting (Ed.), Social Network Mining, Analysis and Research Trends: Techniques and Applications. New York: IGI Global.

Trusov, M., Bodapati, A. V., & Bucklin, R. E. (2010). Determining Influential Users in Internet Social Networks. *JMR, Journal of Marketing Research, 47*(4), 643–658. doi:10.1509/jmkr.47.4.643

Venkatesan, R., Kumar, V., & Bohling, T. (2007). Optimal Customer Relationship Management Using Bayesian Decision Theory: An Application for Customer Selection. *JMR, Journal of Marketing Research, 44*(11), 579–594. doi:10.1509/jmkr.44.4.579

Vesanen, J., & Raulas, M. (2006). Building bridges for personalization: A process model for marketing. *Journal of Interactive Marketing, 20*(1), 5–20. doi:10.1002/dir.20052

Wijsen, J. (2001). Trends in databases: Reasoning and mining. *IEEE Transactions on Knowledge and Data Engineering, 13*(3), 426–438. doi:10.1109/69.929900

ADDITIONAL READING

Attali, J. (2009). *Brief History of the Future: A Brave and Controversial Look at the Twenty-First Century*. Arcade Publishing.

Evans, M., Jamal, A., & Foxall, G. (2009). *Consumer Behavior*. Chichester: Wiley.

Evans, M., O'Malley, L., & Patterson, M. (2004). *Exploring Direct and Customer Relationship Marketing*. Thompson Learning.

Lace, S. (Ed.). (2005). *The Glass Consumer: Life in a Surveillance Society*. Policy Press, National Consumer Council.

Mitchell, T. M. (2009). Mining Our Reality. *Science*, *18*(326), 1644–1645. doi:10.1126/science.1174459 PMID:20019279

Petland, A. (2008). *Honest Signals. How They Shape our World*. Boston: MIT Press.

Petland, A. (2014). *Social Physics: How Good Ideas Spread—The Lessons from a New Science*. Penguin Press.

Piskorski, M. J. (2014). *A Social Strategy: How We Profit from Social Media*. Princeton University Press.

Solove, D. (2004). *The Digital Person. Technology and Privacy in the Information Age*. New York University Press.

Tapp, A. (2008). *Principles of Direct and Database Marketing. A Digital Orientation*. Harlow: Prentice Hall.

Williams, D. S. (2014). *Connected CRM: Implementing a Data-Driven, Customer-Centric Business Strategy*. Chichester: Wiley.

KEY TERMS AND DEFINITIONS

Analytical Customer Profile: A result of abstraction of interactions (time series of customer transactional data, as well as other social and demographic data) in order to generate adequate marketing messages.

Customer Relationship Management: The principles, practices, and guidelines that an organization follows when interacting with its customers.

Interactive Marketing: An identification of interested customers and elaborating the complete characteristics of the customer in order to achieve personalization and adapting proper service at a proper time.

Personalization: A process of analyzing (processing) customer data, customization and delivery of marketing output, and interactions with customers for increasing their lifetime value.

Social Influence: Occurs when one's emotions, opinions, or behaviors are affected by others.

ENDNOTES

1. The representative publications in this area are: presentation of the idea of Customer Intelligence (Kelly, 2006) and introducing "N=1" concept by Prahalad and Krishnan (2008).
2. RFM stands for Recency - How recently a customer has purchased?, Frequency - How often does he purchase ?, Monetary Value - How much does he spend ?
3. Usually it is segmentation a priori, in which market segments are determined arbitrarily on the basis of expert knowledge. The usage of data mining techniques allows segmentation post-hoc in which thanks to clustering algorithms, it is possible to discover real customer segments on the basis of the analysis of available transactional and social-demographic data.
4. See as an example functionality of the Open Graph protocol for Facebook: developers.facebook.com/docs/opengraph [2014.04.21].
5. An example of generalization would be defining customer interest on the basis of books purchased and viewed by him. Generalization requires defining and implementing the appropriate ontology model of the chosen field.
6. Aggregation is a standard procedure in data warehouse, it requires performing appropriate procedures on quantitative data such as sum or average.
7. The idea of abstraction of time series was presented by Haimowitz and Kohan (1996) as well as Wijsen (2001).
8. Exemplary purchase prediction models are logit models (Knott, Hayes, & Neslin, 2002), probit models (Shibo, Sun, & Wilcox, 2005), or Bayesian models (Venkatesan, Kumar, & Bohling Venkatesan, 2007). The studies of these models have shown that despite the limited access to transactional data, it was possible to achieve statistically accurate improvement of customer purchase prediction compared to expert prediction.
9. Of course it is also possible to stop delivering message to customer e.g. in case of negative prognosis in analyzed future.
10. http//:global.cyworld.com. [2014.04.21].
11. In 2007 Cyworld generated $65 million or almost 70% of its revenue from selling virtual items. The remaining revenue was generated from advertising and mobile services.

This research was previously published in the Handbook of Research on Managing and Influencing Consumer Behavior edited by Hans-Ruediger Kaufmann, pages 385-396, copyright year 2015 by Business Science Reference (an imprint of IGI Global).

Chapter 33
The Impact of Social Relationships on Online Word-of-Mouth and Knowledge Sharing in Social Network Sites:
An Empirical Study

Sherein Hamed Abou-Warda
Kafrelsheikh University, Egypt

ABSTRACT

This study provides insight into how social relationships perspective influence on online Word-of-Mouth and knowledge sharing on social networking sites (SNSs). By using the sample from 385 Egyptian college students - who spend more time on SNSs, this study investigates the relationship among the use of SNSs, users' social Relationships, online Word-of-Mouth, and knowledge sharing. Partial Least Square (PLS) was utilized to examine the hypotheses through a questionnaire designed on the Likert seven-point scale. The results indicated that the intensity of usage of SNSs is a positively related with social relationship factors which has a positive effect on online WOM; in addition, online WOM has positively significant influence on knowledge sharing. The results also indicated that male students are found to have more social relationship than female counterparts do. Male students feel more strongly about knowledge sharing when they perceive that online WOM communication is good.

1. INTRODUCTION

Social media has become an integral part of digital marketing (Heinonen, 2011). The marketing tools and approaches for communicating with customers have changed greatly with the emergence of social media. With the rapid growth in web users and everyone migrating online, companies are realizing the importance of having a social media presence to reach those millions of consumers (Parsons, 2013). Kaplan and Haenlein (2010, p. 61) defined social media as "a group of Internet based applications that

DOI: 10.4018/978-1-5225-5637-4.ch033

build on the ideological and technological foundations of Web 2.0, and allow the creation and exchange of user generated content". In terms of history, the first social networking site (SNSs) was launched in 1997. In 2004, the most successful current SNS, Facebook, was established as a part of a suite of Web applications and virtual community for Harvard students where users can create individual public profiles, interact with real-life friends, and meet other people based on shared interests. With the enormous interest in social media, SNSs are increasingly used to participating in discussions, share information with other peoples, to create relationships with others, and to keep up with close social ties. All these activities have established the phenomenon known as electronic word-of-mouth or online word-of-mouth (Brown, Broderick, and Lee, 2007; Dellarocas, 2003; Dwyer, 2007; Goldenberg, Libai, and Muller, 2001; Goldsmith and Horowitz, 2006) and knowledge sharing of products or brands (Choi and Scott, 2013).

Online WOM refers to a particular type of WOM which occurs in the online setting (Dwyer 2007); it is defined as "any positive or negative statement made by potential, actual, or former customers about a product or company, which is made available to a multitude of people and institutions via the Internet" (Hennig-Thurau, Gwinner, and Gremler, 2004, p. 39). Through a rigorous search of several mainstream IS and Marketing journals, as well as key electronic databases, Cheung & Thadani (2010) identified 25 papers using the individual-level analysis in the investigation of the effectiveness of electronic WOM communication; electronic WOM is comprised of four major elements: communicator, stimulus, receiver, and response which provides us with an overview of the current status of knowledge sharing. Knowledge sharing can be defined as "the combination of one or both parties seeking knowledge in response to the request, such that one or both parties are affected by the experience" (Ghosh and Scott, 2007, p. 4). Therefore, recently online WOM could take place via many different social media channels such as microblog, microsite, video sharing, social bookmarking, photo sharing, mobile apps, audio sharing, wikis, social games, virtual world and the social networking sites (e.g. Facebook, Twitter, and Myspace) (Goldsmith 2006; Goldsmith and Horowitz 2006; Vilpponen, Winter, and Sundqvist 2006). These sites can give people unlimited access to a great amount of information and a variety of brand choices (Negroponte and Maes, 1996). As a result, it has become apparent that people use the SNSs to exchange their experience and share their knowledge (Goldsmith and Horowitz 2006).

Researchers from various disciplines have examined SNSs, they have found that social relationships perspective is observed in SNSs (Shu-Chuan and Sejung, 2011; Choi et al., 2011; Burke, 2011; Utz, and Beukeboom, 2011; Di Gennaro and Dutton, 2007). The unique applications of SNSs provide marketers with various opportunities to maintain existing personal networks or to expand them, which simultaneously promote social relationships. Therefore, some researchers have examined the influence of social capital (Hung and Li, 2007); tie strength (Panovich et al., 2012; Steffes and, 2009); trust (Awad and Ragowsky, 2008); and interpersonal influence (Shu-Chuan and Sejung, 2011; Chu, 2009) on online WOM in SNSs. In addition, they have examined the influence of social capital (Huysman and Wulf, 2005; Inkpen and Tsang, 2005); tie strength (Coenen, 2006); and trust (Chow and Chan, 2008) on knowledge sharing in SNSs. In recent literature, Shu-Chuan and Sejung (2011) examined social relationship variables as potential predictors of electronic WOM communication in the online social channels between the United States and China. Moreover, Choi and Scott (2013) investigated the relationship among the users' social capital, knowledge sharing, and electronic WOM in SNSs. Despite such contributions from these studies, the relationship between online WOM and knowledge sharing has not been studied directly (Choi and Scott, 2013). As far as I know, it has until now been unclear the relation between the SNSs usage intensity and social relationships perspective on SNSs; in addition, no study has been studied directly the impact of social relationships (specifically, social capital, tie strength, trust, and interpersonal influence) on online WOM and knowledge sharing in the context of SNSs. I believe that social relationships perspective effects in online WOM and knowledge sharing on SNSs. Moreover, online WOM can play an important role in knowledge sharing in the context of SNSs. In this light, close examination of social relationship–related variables should provide useful insight to both online WOM and knowledge sharing among SNSs users. Therefore, we need to understand which social relationship variables are potential predictors of online WOM and knowledge sharing, and how online WOM leads to knowledge sharing in SNSs. Little is known about the potential predictors of online WOM or knowledge sharing in the virtual marketing or digital marketing, particularly a social media phenomenon is continuing to grow at a fast pace.

This paper closes these research gaps by exploring relationship between the SNSs usage intensity and social relationships perspective (social capital, tie strength, trust, and interpersonal influence); and examining the impact of social relationships perspective on online WOM and knowledge sharing in the context of SNSs. The major research question is determined in the following question: "Can we fill these gaps through building a conceptual model in SNSs, and examining the relation among SNSs usage intensity, users' social relationships, online WOM and knowledge sharing in the context of SNSs?", branches off this question, a group of sub-questions in the context of SNSs: (1) Does the SNSs usage intensity build users' social relationships?; (2) Are users' social relationships positively related to online WOM?; (3) Does users' social relationships facilitate knowledge sharing?; (4) Is online WOM positively related to knowledge sharing?. The overall purpose of this study is to examine the impact of users' social relationships (specifically, social capital, tie strength, trust, and interpersonal) on online WOM and knowledge sharing in the context of SNSs. The present study is different from previous studies on several grounds. *First*, this study was carried out on a new marketing dimension of digital marketing, the social relationships perspective. *Second*, this study contribute to the literature on social media marketing by delving into the relation between SNSs usage intensity and users' social relationships; in addition the impact of users' social relationships on online WOM and knowledge sharing in the up-and-coming online social networking environment. *Third*, this study introduced theoretical model and tested with empirical data for researchers to study the exploitation of SNSs; impact in the individual's life; organizational networking; and could provide rationale for practitioners to utilize SNSs for marketing purposes such as implementation of effective digital marketing strategies, the intelligent selling strategies etc. *Finally*, this study contributes to the literature on international marketing by delving into the cultural differences where this study was carried out on Egyptian SNSs users.

This paper is organized as follows. Section 2 provides a literature review and hypothesis development followed by the conceptual model that depends largely on logical links is provided. The methodology designed to test the hypotheses is presented in Section 3, followed by the results in Section 4. And then, discussion and conclusion are discussed in Section 5. The implications of this study are drawn and suggestions for further research are presented in Section 6. Finally, the references of this research are the end of this paper.

2. LITERATURER REVIEW AND HYPOTHESIS DEVELOPMENT

2.1. Usage of SNSs and Users' Social Relationships

SNSs has been examined along multiple dimensions including: demographics of the users (Duggan and Brenner, 2013; Hampton et al.,2011; Ahn, 2011; Sponcil and Priscilla, 2013; Lenhart et al.,2010; Tufekci, 2008); Extent of SNSs' usage (Kuss and Griffiths, 2011; Farooq and Jan, 2012; Ellison, Steinfield and Lampe, 2007; Ahn, 2011; Sponcil and Priscilla, 2013; Lenhart et al.,2010; Sheldon, 2008; Quan-Haase and Young, 2010; Pempek et al., 2009, Baym et al.,2007); and social relationships (Lenhart et al., 2010; Hampton et al.,2011; Kuss and Griffiths, 2011; Farooq and Jan, 2012; Ahn, 2011; Sponcil and Priscilla, 2013; Ellison, Steinfield and Lampe, 2007; Lampe, Ellison, and Steinfield, 2007; Donath and Boyd, 2004). Users use SNSs to keep up with close social relationships (Lenhart et al., 2010; Pempek, Yermolayev and Calvert, 2009; Hampton et al., 2011); to make new social relationships (Donath and Boyd, 2004); to maintain social relationships with family and friends; and to meet new people, passing time, and entertainment (Sheldon, 2008) in a fairly easy and convenient way (Quan-Haaseand and Young, 2010). Moreover, they spent much of the time reading other individuals profiles or news feeds or looking at photographs or viewing information without interacting in any way (Pempek et al., 2009). Some researchers have examined the relationship between intensity of students' use of Facebook and students' social relationships (Sponcil and Priscilla, 2013). Using of Facebook helped to improve the quality of relationships among users (Lampe, Ellison and Steinfield, 2007; Baker and Oswald, 2010; Farrugia, 2013). The current study focuses on the relational dimension of social relationships which related with SNSs usage intensity and concerns on online WOM and share knowledge among users on SNSs. Therefore, this study follows the manifestations of the relational dimension from (Yi Hsu and Chau, 2013), which are social capital; tie strength; trust; and interpersonal influence. Where, some researchers found a strong correlation between use of SNSs and social capital (Ahn, 2011; Kuss and Griffiths, 2011; Brandtzagand and Nov, 2011; Ellison, Steinfield and Lampe, 2007; Williams, 2006; Steinfield, Ellison and Lampe, 2008; Moira and Kraut, 2011); trust (Valenzuela, Park and Kee, 2009); Tie (Zhao, 2006); and interpersonal influence (Tyson, 2009).

2.1.1. Social Capital

Social capital has been studied in SNSs (Williams, 2006; Hung and Li, 2007; Huysman and Wulf, 2005; Inkpen and Tsang, 2005; Chiu, Hsu and Wang, 2006; Ellison, Steinfield, and Lampe, 2007; Ellison, Steinfield, and Lampe, 2011; Ellison et al., 2011; Steinfield, Ellison, and Lampe, 2008; Valenzuela, Park, and Kee, 2009; Levin et al., 2015; Laud et al., 2015). There have been many definitions of social capital. The definition about the social capital of Nahapiet and Ghoshal (1998) provides valuable implications for studying the knowledge integration and relationships in SNSs; they have suggested that social capital includes three dimensions: structural, relational, and cognitive. Putnam (2000) has indicated social capital refers to the "connections among individuals" social networks and the norms of reciprocity and trustworthiness that arise from them" (p.19). The current study focuses on individual-level social capital, in these, social capital has been defined as "the connections between people and the factors that tie people together" (Yi Hsu and Chau, 2013).

According to Putnam (2000) and Yi Hsu and Chau (2013) there are the most important distinction in social capital is bonding and bridging social capital. Bonding social capital is found between individuals in tightly-knit, emotionally close relationships and homogenous groups with similar background such as ethnic groups or country groups or close friends. On the contrary, bridging social capital refer to as "weak ties," which are loose connections between individuals who may provide useful information or new perspectives for one another but typically not emotional support or heterogeneous group, such as youth service groups or civil rights movement. Both two types of social capital can exist in social capital simultaneously, bridging social capital is associated with the loose or weak ties across communities and bonding social capital is associated with dense network or strong ties within a limited group (Leonard and Onyx, 2003). Ellison, Steinfield and Lampe, (2007) found that intensity of Facebook use was connected with both bonding social capital and bridging social capital among college students. Hence, this study hypothesizes that SNSs usage intensity increases social capital in SNSs.

H1a: The SNS usage intensity increases social capital in SNSs.

2.1.2. Tie Strength

Another dimension of social relationships directly relevant to SNSs usage is tie strength. In his 1973 paper, "The Strength of Weak Ties," Granovetter advanced the idea that weak ties are not a source of alienation, but rather connectors to different social circles and the resources of those circles (Granovetter, 1973). Granovetter identified this after observing friendships in an offline social network, and pointed toward the idea that one's weak ties might be an effective information source because they traveled in separate social circles, and so could better transmit new information. There have been many definitions of tie strength. This study concentrates on social tie strength in these, tie strength has been defined as "the strength of a friendship—close friends are strong ties, and acquaintances are weak ties" (Panovich et al., 2012). Therefore, tie strength has been examined in SNSs (Shu-Chuan and Sejung, 2011); Steffes and Burgee, 2009; Gupte and Rad, 2012; Panovich, Miller and Karger, 2012; Lee and Kim, 2011; Shu-Chuan, 2009). Further examination showed that individuals worked their social tie through four stages of relationships equating to higher levels of intimacy, strength, and depth within social relationship. According to LaSalle (2004), the four stages are best defined as follows: a) Orientation, it is a way for people to begin to develop a relationship by revealing basic information to others; b) Exploratory affective exchange, where the information has passed the basic phase and becomes more detailed by conversion among individual; c) Affective exchange is where the relationship becomes more intimate, the pair conversing is comfortable with the exchange; and d) Stable exchange, the final stage, is where the social tie is the strongest. Accordingly, this study hypothesizes that SNSs usage intensity increases tie strength in SNSs.

H1b: The SNS usage intensity increases tie strength in SNSs.

2.1.3. Trust

Trust is one of social relationship variables that effect on the SNSs usage and interaction in SNSs. Trust has been studied in various disciplines (Bhattacherjee, 2002), and there have been many definitions of trust (Hsu, Ju, Yen, and Chang, 2007). Trust can be defined as "an expectation that others one chooses to trust will not behave opportunistically by taking advantage of the situation" (Gefen, Karahanna, and Straub, 2003, p. 54). However, the current study focuses on individual-level trust, in these, trust has been defined as "behavioral intentions that result from specific beliefs in competence, integrity, and benevolence (McKnight, Choudhury, and Kacmar, 2002) that contributes to the value of relationship (Zahedi, Bansal, and Ische, 2010). Trust has been found to involve a willingness to take a risk in communication with others based on a sense of confidence that others will respond as expected and act in reciprocally supportive ways. Besides, in communication context, when consumers trust in their contacts, they no need to spend more time and money enforcing contracts, so trust makes people use and believe in information express from others easily (Bhattacherjee, 2002; Zahedi, Bansal, and Ische, 2010; Dwyer, Hiltz, and Passerini, 2007; Valenzuela, Park, and Kee, 2009; Chow and Chan, 2008; Shu-Chuan and Sejung, 2011; Awad and Ragowsky, 2008). One study has indicated that, highly consumers' usage of virtual communities might be more trusting of other group members than in face-to-face communities (Blanchard and Horan, 1998). In addition, the level of trust plays a role that determines the decision to bridge other networks to use and exchange information of an individual (Onyx and Bullen, 2000). Recently, one study has contributed to people to understand the role of trust in the SNSs usage (Choi and Scott, 2013). Accordingly, this study hypothesizes that SNSs usage intensity increases trust in SNSs.

H1c: The SNS usage intensity increases trust in SNSs.

2.1.4. Interpersonal Influence

Interpersonal influence has been studied in various disciplines, and there have been many definitions of interpersonal influence. In this study, informational influence can be defined as "the condition of credible evidence of reality, it mean the tendency of people to make informed decisions by accepting information from others" (Yi Hsu and Chau, 2013). Some researchers have identified two determinants of susceptibility to interpersonal influences; they are informational influences and normative interpersonal influences (Bearden, Netemeyer and Teel, 1989; Chu and Kim, 2011). Informational influence refers to the condition of credible evidence of reality, it mean the tendency of people to make informed decisions by accepting information from others; normative interpersonal influence relates to conformity with the pledges to achieve rewards and avoid punishment, it refers the tendency of consumers follow the expectation of others (Yi Hsu and Chau, 2013). Accordingly, this study hypothesizes that SNSs usage intensity increases interpersonal influence in SNSs.

H1d: The SNS usage intensity increases interpersonal influence in SNSs.

2.2. Social Relationships and Both Online WOM and Knowledge Sharing on SNSs

Given that relationship building is the primary objective of SNSs users, SNSs may be used to strengthen social relationships that already exist (Ellison, Steinfield, and Lampe, 2007). Therefore, marketers attempt to harness the power of online word-of-mouth in SNSs (Williamson 2006) for knowledge sharing of products and brands in virtual communities (Hung and Li, 2007). Bernard et al.(1989) indicated that the social networking sites could strongly influence on the consumers brand perception and purchasing decisions, because the consumers tend to find more information, insights and opinions from the trusted sources before they decide to choose the products or brands. Hence, this trend brings a new opportunity to the marketers to build the social relationships with the potential consumers. Moreover, the unique social nature of communications and the potential influence of social relationships developed can advance marketers' knowledge of the underlying process of Online WOM and Knowledge sharing in these sites (Shu-Chuan, 2009, p. 3).

2.2.1. Social Capital

Social capital is one of the concepts that have been frequently discussed in the WOM and knowledge sharing literatures. For example, Chu and Kim (2011) found that the potential of online networking sites as a powerful social venue that increase bridging among people, and the SNSs provide consumers opportunities to maintain existing personal networks and expand them that promote bonding and bridging social capital simultaneously. Finally, Hung and Li (2007) found that social capital plays an important role in the process of electronic WOM on virtual consumer communities. Accordingly, this study hypothesizes that social capital is positively related to Online WOM in SNSs.

H2a: Social capital is positively related to Online WOM in SNSs.

On the other side, the impact of social capital on information exchange and knowledge sharing in the virtual communities is still unclear. Although Putnam (2000) suggested that the Internet decreases social capital, Wellman et al. (2001) indicated that Internet use supplements social capital by extending existing levels of face-to-face. The social capital in SNSs is strong enough to stimulate members to overcome the barriers of complex knowledge sharing process, and then share valuable knowledge. Some studies suggested that individuals would share knowledge within virtual communities with the expectations of enriching knowledge, seeking support, making friends, etc. (Andrews, 2002; Zhang and Hiltz, 2003). Nahapiet and Ghoshal (1998) argued that social capital affects the conditions requisite for the knowledge creation and sharing favorably. Chiu, Hsu, and Wang (2006) investigated the motivations behind people's knowledge sharing in virtual communities by integration of social capital and social cognitive theories. One study found that social capital had a significant effect on knowledge transfer (Inkpen and Tsang, 2005). Other study empirically examines the relationship between social capital and knowledge sharing; the results found that social capital was significantly related to knowledge sharing (Huysman and Wulf, 2005; Inkpen and Tsang, 2005) and students' academic performance in higher education (Aslam et al., 2013). Accordingly, this study hypothesizes that social capital increases knowledge sharing in SNSs.

H2b: Social capital increases knowledge sharing in SNSs.

2.2.2. Tie Strength

Tie strength is often operationalized as number of messages exchanged between partners (Huberman et al., 2009; Huffaker, 2011), how many of those messages are reciprocated (Marlow, 2009), appearing in the same photo (Bakshy et al., 2011; Bond et al., 2011; Ugander et al., 2011) or number of comments on each other's work (Bakshy et al., 2011). The primary idea behind tie strength is that, amongst our network of friends (online or offline), we have friends with whom we are close (strong ties) and friends who are less close, acquaintances or weak ties (Panovich et al., 2012). Constant et al. (1996) found that, in cases where strong ties lacked the knowledge to answer questions, weak ties were able to provide good answers, given motivation. Finally, a recent study examined young peoples' tie strength on Facebook

(Wegge et al., 2015). Some researchers have examined the influence of tie strength on online WOM in SNSs; they found that tie strength was significantly related to online WOM in SNSs (Panovich et al., 2012; Steffes and Burgee, 2009). Accordingly, this study hypothesizes that tie strength is positively related to Online WOM in SNSs.

H3a: Tie strength is positively related to Online WOM in SNSs.

On the other side, Granovetter (1973) highlighted the role of tie strength in information exchange between people. Recent work by Gilbert and Karahalios (2009) looked at Granovetter's denotation of strong and weak ties within real-life offline SNSs and found a series of features such as number of mutual friends, number of words exchanged, and so on that can effectively predict tie strength between friends in SNSs. These models of tie strength online can help us to understand the exchange of information. Panovich et al. (2012) presented a study evaluating the role of tie strength in question answers in social media; They found while sociological studies have indicated that weak ties are able to provide better information, their findings are significant in that weak ties do not have this effect, and stronger ties (close friends) provide a subtle increase in information that contributes more to participants' overall knowledge, and is less likely to have been seen before. One study has examined the influence of tie strength on knowledge sharing in SNSs; it found that tie strength was significantly related to knowledge sharing in SNSs (Coenen, 2006). Accordingly, this study hypothesizes that tie strength increases knowledge sharing in SNSs.

H3b: Tie strength increases knowledge sharing in SNSs.

2.2.3. Trust

Trust is necessary for knowledge sharing and online WOM. Trust is the first essential to people both in face-to-face environments and online environments (Choi and Scott, 2013). Trust has been found to facilitate the exchange and use of information due to the increased perceived credibility of information when the partner as an information source is trusted in a social relationship (Robert, Dennis, and Ahuja 2008). Some researchers have examined the influence of trust on online WOM in SNSs; they concluded that trust in personal source could affect the nature and pattern of online WOM behavior (Awad and Ragowsky, 2008; Choi and Scott, 2013). Finally, a recent study found that the intensity of use of SNSs is positively related to trust and identification which have a positive effect on electronic WOM (Choi and Scott, 2013). Accordingly, this study hypothesizes that trust is positively related to Online WOM in SNSs.

H4a: Trust is positively related to Online WOM in SNSs.

On the other side, Nahapiet and Ghoshal (1998) have suggested that trust increase the perceived trustworthiness of information; the perceived trustworthiness are the important factor that influence on knowledge-sharing. Therefore, with the higher degree of trust, the amount and type of information exchanges enhances (Andrews and Delahaye, 2000). Some researchers have examined the influence of trust on knowledge sharing in SNSs (Chow and Chan, 2008; Choi and Scott, 2013). Trust has been found to facilitate the exchange, use of information and share of knowledge due to the increased perceived credibility of information and when the partner as an information source is trusted in a social relationship

(Robert, Dennis, and Ahuja, 2008).). Accordingly, this study hypothesizes that trust increases knowledge sharing in SNSs.

H4b: Trust increases knowledge sharing in SNSs.

2.2.4. Interpersonal Influence

Interpersonal influence is key determinant of such electronic WOM behavior and linked to the influence of social relationships on consumer reliance on social networking sites as a source of product-focused information. Researchers have suggested that interpersonal influences play an important role in influencing consumer decision making (Bearden, Netemeyer, and Teel 1989; D'Rozario and Choudhury 2000). Some researchers have examined the influence of interpersonal influence on online WOM in SNSs, they found although interpersonal influence has been conceptualized as a two dimensional construct, normative and informational influence, both influences may drive electronic WOM behaviors in social networking sites (Shu-Chuan and Sejung, 2011; Chu, 2009). Accordingly, this study hypothesizes that interpersonal influence is positively related to Online WOM in SNSs.

H5a: Interpersonal influence is positively related to Online WOM in SNSs.

On the other side, informational influence may be manifested through either consumers directly requesting information from knowledgeable others or indirectly making observations of the behavior of others; this occurs when consumers perceive that information from others increases their own knowledge, and thus exert impacts on product evaluations and choices (Bearden, Netemeyer, and Teel 1989). In essence, normative influences play a determining role in directing and controlling "evaluations, choices, and loyalties," (Chu, 2009). Therefore, the users of SNSs who are more susceptible to normative influences are more likely to comply with the expectations of close contacts and look for social approval; on the other sides, SNSs users who have informational influence are predicted to display a higher need to acquire valuable information from informed contacts (Chu and Kim, 2011). Accordingly, this study hypothesizes that interpersonal influence increases knowledge sharing in SNSs.

H5b: Interpersonal influence increases knowledge sharing in SNSs.

2.3. Online WOM and Knowledge Sharing on SNSs

Despite WOM has largely been studied in marketing, there is little research on online WOM (Choi and Scott, 2013). Online WOM has been viewed as the degree, to which the WOM platform on the Website is considered to be relevant, helpful, or useful (Awad and Ragowsky, 2008; Choi and Scott, 2013). Previously, we show that there are differences between two types of WOM. While traditional WOM usually involves information through an immediate conversation; online WOM involves more than information, it usually involves richness-reach trade-off through the written communication (Sweeney, Soutar, and Mazzarol, 2012). Richness means "the quality of information," and reach means "the number of people who participate in the sharing of that information" (Evans and Wurster, 2000: p. 23). Finally, written communication is more logical than oral communication. According to DeLone, Espinosa, Lee, and Carmel (2005), knowledge that richness-reach tradeoff, the quality of the information decreases with increasing the number of people who participate in the sharing of that information. Moreover, a word follows a word in an orderly manner in writing, and logic is embedded in the step-by-step linear process (Gulati, Nohria, and Zaheer, 2000). The relationship between electronic WOM and knowledge sharing has not been studied directly, except Choi and Scott' study (2013), they found that electronic WOM plays an important role to share knowledge, especially in online social networking environments. Accordingly, this study hypothesizes that online WOM is positively related to knowledge sharing in SNSs.

H6: Online WOM is positively related to knowledge sharing in SNSs.

Figure 1 shows the conceptual model.

3. METHODOLOGY

To answer the research questions, a survey approach was employed to address the research objectives focusing on those who use of SNSs, regardless of whether they are fully aware of knowledge sharing, social relationships, and online WOM in SNSs or not. The internet population comprises approximately 48 million (The Ministry of Communications and Information Technology, 2015); and Facebook had over 1.18 billion monthly active users as of August 2015 (Wikipedia, 2015). Social networking site users are characterized as young students (Duggan and Brenner, 2013; Lenhart et al., 2010; Pempek, Yermolayev and Calvert, 2009); better-educated (Lenhart et al., 2010); and are disproportionately composed of college students (Ellison, Steinfield, and Lampe 2007; Tufekci, 2008; Baym et al., 2007); moreover, Facebook is the most favored social media channels among students, so it would be interesting to the users who spread Facebook to the world and the users who have had longer experience in using SNSs (Ashley and Tuten, 2015; Brandtzag and Nov, 2011); in addition to the most significant demographic variables affecting SNSs' usage were gender, age and education (Duggan and Brenner, 2013). Therefore, the Facebook use of a college student sample was deemed appropriate for the current study, also controlled for gender, age, and education. The study sample was taken from students who were using Facebook attending a large north delta university campus during September 2015 in Egypt. Four hundred

Figure 1. Conceptual model

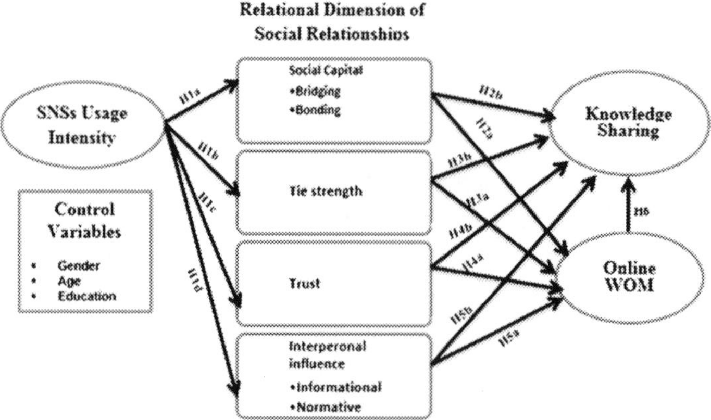

and sixteen volunteer students from various classes were selected to provide a convenient and stratified sample of gender, age, and education. Four hundred questionnaires were completed but 15 were unusable, so analyses were conducted on responses to 385 questionnaires, a response rate of 92.5%.

The study used a self-administered questionnaire. The questionnaire had been originally developed and distributed in Arabic to collect data. Questions in the survey included the following areas: demographics, extent of usage of Facebook, effect on social relationships, online WOM, and Knowledge sharing. The questions on the instrument were designed to satisfy the research questions as set forth in the introduction of this study. Therefore, the questionnaire was considered to have content validity. Tyson's (2009) scales were used to measure SNSs usage intensity. Shu-Chuan and Sejung's (2011) and Chu's (2009) were employed, with certain modifications, to measure dimensions of social relationships including, social capital, tie strength, trust, and interpersonal influence. Goyette, Ricard, Bergeron, and Marticotte's (2010) and Choi and Scott's (2013) scales were used to measure online WOM. Finally, Choi and Scott's (2013) scales were used to measure knowledge sharing. Prior to the main study, a pilot study was undertaken. Approximately three business administration professors and six marketing researchers evaluated the questionnaire in order to ensure that the questionnaire was not too complex and was easy to understand. The results of the pilot study, led to several minor wording, sequence modifications and twelve items were removed from the questionnaire. The questionnaire was subsequently distributed to a small sample of 20 graduate students. Further changes were made to the questionnaire according to the results obtained that involved shortening and simplifying the instrument. After verifying the validity of the questionnaire, the final version of questionnaire was used for primary data gathering. Researchers stood on campuses and asked students if they wanted to take the survey and if they were using Facebook, then handed them the survey to complete on paper and give back to researchers at that time. Participants reported the extent to which they agreed with items using a seven-point Likert scale with anchors ranging from Strongly Disagree (1), Neutral (4), to Strongly Agree (7).

4. RESULT

4.1. Assessment of Measurement Scale

The psychometric properties of the scales were analyzed in multiple ways. First, unidimensionality of measurement scales were tested by principal component analysis, whereas, principal component analysis helps in development of a quality of scale (Anderson and Gerbing (1988). Second, validity and reliability of the measurement model were tested by factor analysis and Cronbach's α, whereas, a confirmatory factor analysis (CFA) using the EQS 6.1 structural equation modelling software was performed for a more in depth validation of the scale's psychometric properties (Bentler, 1992) and helps validate the quality of the measurement tool (Baumgartner and Homburg, 1996). However, according to Baumgartner and Homburg's recommendation (1996), the reliability of measurement scales must be evaluated from different angles; therefore, three different types of analysis were performed to test the reliability of measurement scales, calculating the adjusted item-total correlations, subsequently calculating Cronbach's Alpha for measuring of internal consistency, also, calculating the reliability index of the CFI components. Finally, the causal structure of the proposed research model was tested using Amos 5.0 to test the structured equation modeling (SEM), whereas, structural equation modelling (SEM) holds great potential in measurement scale validation (Anderson and Gerbing, 1988). The results of analysis of unidimensionality, reliability and validity are summarized in Table 1. The goodness-of-fit measures for the structural model were shown in Table 2.

The results in Table 1 showed that the number of items for the core constructs was decreased to 46 items (from the original 87 items). The structure consisted of seven dimensions (SNSs usage intensity, social capital, tie strength, trust, interpersonal influence, online WOM, and knowledge sharing), measured by 3, 13, 3, 5, 9, 7 and 6 items, respectively. First column of results in Table 1 indicates that each dimension of the scale is unidimensional; Also, (CFA) indicates that the coefficients are all associated with their respective dimensions, that they are all greater than 0.50 and that they were statistically significant and they were meaningful (Hair et al., 2010). Second column of results in Table 1 shows that all dimensions have adjusted item-total correlations greater than 0.35, which is satisfactory (McKelvey, 1976). Third column of results in Table 1 support the internal consistency of constructs. The composite reliability (CR) ranges from .71 to .89, Therefore, the reliability of all constructs is adequate and satisfactory since they are above .7 (Peterson, 1994). Also, third column of results in Table 1 supports the reliability of component; component reliability indices (CFI) range between 0.63 and 0.84, exceeding the minimum of 0.60 suggested by Bagozzi and Yi (1988) and Fornell and Larcker (1981).

Table 1. Results of reliability and validity analyses

Dimensions	Principal Component Analysis/CFA	Adjusted Item-Total Correlations	Alpha (α)/CFI
SNS Usage Intensity (Number of items = 3 items)			0.71/0.65
I have many friends on Facebook.	0.76/0.59	0.48	
I spend more than an hour on Facebook per day.	0.75/0.57	0.47	
Facebook has become part of my daily routine	0.79/0.63	0.49	
Social Capital (Number of items = 13 items)			0.82/0.74
Bridging Social Capital			
Interacting on Facebook makes me interested in things that happen outside of my town.	0.67/0.84	0.42	
Interacting on Facebook makes me want to try new things.	0.82/0.76	0.47	
Interacting on Facebook makes me interested in what people different from me is thinking.	0.77/0.88	0.51	
Interacting on Facebook makes me feel like part of a larger community.	0.86/0.89	0.62	
Interacting on Facebook reminds me that everyone in the world is connected.	0.76/0.59	0.53	
I am willing to spend time to support general community activities on the Facebook.	0.83/0.68	0.49	
I come in contact with new people on the Facebook all the time.	0.85/0.78	0.50	
Bonding Social Capital			
There is a member of the Facebook I can turn to for advice about making very important decisions.	0.77/0.54	0.49	
When I feel lonely, there are members of the Facebook I can talk to.	0.79/0.67	0.57	
The people I interact with on the Facebook would put their reputation on the line for me.	0.82/0.77	0.77	
The people I interact with on the Facebook would be good job references for me.	0.84/0.67	0.76	
The people I interact with on the Facebook would help me fight an injustice.	0.86/0.88	0.72	
There is a member of the Facebook I can turn to for advice about making very important decisions.	0.79/0.89	0.69	
Tie Strength (Number of items = 3 items)			0.79/0.76

continued on following page

Table 1. Continued

Dimensions	Principal Component Analysis/CFA	Adjusted Item-Total Correlations	Alpha (α)/CFI
I contact with many friends on Facebook.	0.87/0.59	0.56	
I feel that, it is important to contact with my "friends" list on Facebook.	0.67/0.78	0.57	
I contact very close with my "friends" list on this Facebook.	0.77/0.76	0.61	
Trust (Number of items = 5 items)			0.72/0.77
Generally, most contacts with my "friends" list on the Facebook can be trusted.	0.78/0.89	0.55	
I feel confident about having discussions with the contacts on my "friends" list on the Facebook.	0.79/0.87	0.49	
I trust most contacts on my "friends" list on the Facebook.	0.81/0.76	0.50	
I have confidence in the contacts on my "friends" list on the Facebook.	0.85/0.59	0.62	
I can believe in the contacts on my "friends" list on the Facebook.	0.84/0.75	0.60	
Interpersonal Influence (Number of items= 9 items)			0.75/0.63
Normative			
It is important that others like the products and brands I buy.	0.77/0.85	0.67	
If other people can see me using a product, I often purchase the brand they expect me to buy.	0.76/0.78	0.82	
I achieve a sense of belonging by purchasing the same products and brands that others purchase.	0.72/0.68	0.71	
If I want to be like someone, I often try to buy the same brands that they buy.	0.81/0.58	0.69	
I often identify with other people by purchasing the same products and brands they purchase.	0.69/0.88	0.66	
Informational			
To make sure I buy the right product or brand, I often observe what others are buying and using.	0.78/0.59	0.76	
If I have little experience with a product, I often ask my friends about the product.	0.75/0.82	0.78	
I often consult other people to help choose the best alternative available from a product class.	0.84/0.87	0.61	
I frequently gather information from friends or family about a product before I buy.	0.81/0.65	0.59	
Online WOM (Number of items = 7 items)			0.89/0.84
Facebook content is relevant for me	0.86/0.98	0.79	
Facebook content is helpful	0.78/0.77	0.82	
Facebook content is usually the information I need.	0.79/0.59	0.74	
Facebook content is accurate	0.80/0.68	0.66	
Facebook content is complete.	0.84/0.78	0.69	
Facebook content is reliable	0.87/0.60	0.67	
Facebook content is timely	0.84/0.76	0.77	
Knowledge Sharing (Number of items = 6 items)			0.85/0.82
I enjoy sharing my knowledge with my Facebook friends	0.79/0.91	0.86	
It seems to me that my Facebook friends enjoy sharing their knowledge with others	0.77/0.89	0.85	
It seems to me that Facebook facilitates sharing knowledge among people	0.79/0.85	0.77	
It seems to me that my Facebook friends share the best knowledge that they have	0.78/0.77	0.69	
I come to my Facebook community to share knowledge I know about a particular subject.	0.85/0.63	0.84	
I come to my Facebook community to share my skills	0.84/0.73	0.76	

The result in Table 2 indicates that the goodness of fit of the data to the model is satisfactory whenever, the $\chi2/$ degrees of freedom df is under 5 (3.752); also, the majority of the indices GFI and AGFI are greater than 0.85 (0.916, 0.914 respectively); the indices IFI and CFI are greater than 0.9 (0.918, 0.925 respectively). Therefore, the result of the theoretical model has a very good fit (Figure 2).

4.2. Data Analysis and Finding

Descriptive analyses and the partial least squares (PLS) method was were the major statistical techniques used. First, various descriptive analyses were performed to examine the characteristics of the sample as well as use of social networking sites in general. Second, PLS was employed to examine the hypotheses, the data were analyzed with PASW version 18 and PLS-Graph build 1130. PLS is a second generation structural equation modeling (SEM) technique; it works well with structural equation models that contain latent variables and a series of cause-and-effect relationships (Gustafsson and Johnson, 2004). PLS method was used because of four major advantages. First, in most marketing studies, data tend to be distributed non-normally and PLS does not require any normality assumptions and handles non-normal distributions relatively well (Bontis, Booker, and Serenko, 2007). Second, PLS is a powerful technique for analyzing latent variable structural equation models with multiple indicators (Sirohi, McLaughlin, and Wittink, 1998). Third, Because of its robustness against distributional constraints as compared to covariance-based analysis methods (e.g. AMOS or LISREL) (Chin, 1998). Finally, PLS focuses on prediction of the constructs rather than explanation of the relationships between items (Hair, Black, Babin, and Anderson, 2010; Choi and Scott, 2013).

4.2.1. Sample Description

Table 3 shows demographic data. As it is shown, responses from 385 students were analyzed. 49.4% of the respondents were female students (190) and 50.6% of the respondents were male students (195). 29.1% of the respondents were younger than 20 (112), 62.6% of the respondents were between 20 and 30 years old (241), 5.7% of the respondents were between 31 and 40 years old (22), and 2.6% of the respondents were older than 40 (10). 74.0% of the respondents were undergraduate students (285), 5.7% of the respondents were bachelor students (22), 18.3% of the respondents were diploma students (70), 1.0% of the respondents were master degree students (4) and 1.0% of the respondents were PhD students (4).

Table 2. The goodness-of-fit measures for the structural model

Fit Indicators	Results	Recommended Value
Chi-square statistic, $\chi2/df$	3.752	< 5(Wheaton et al, 1977)
Goodness-of-Fit Index (GFI)	0.916	≥ 0.85(Bentler,1992)
Adjusted Goodness-of-Fit Index (AGFI)	0.914	≥0.85(Bentler,1992)
IFI	0.918	≥0.9(Bentler,1992)
Comparative Fit Index (CFI)	0.925	≥0.9(Bentler,1992)
Root Mean Square Error of Approximation (RMSEA)	0.065	<0.1 (Steiger, 1990)

Table 3. Sample demographic information

Demographic Variables		Frequency (n)	Percentage %
Gender	Female	190	49.4%
	Male	195	50.6%
Age	Younger than 20	112	29.1%
	20 to 30 years	241	62.6%
	31 to 40 years	22	05.7%
	More than 40 years	10	02.6%
Education	Undergraduate	285	74.0%
	Bachelor	22	05.7%
	Diploma	70	18.3%
	Master Degree	4	01.0%
	PhD	4	01.0%

4.2.2. Demographic Differences Testing

Before testing these hypotheses, for control variables, independent sample t-tests were conducted to examine whether there are gender, age, and education differences with regard to respondents' online WOM and knowledge sharing behaviors in SNSs. The results showed no substantial age differences in terms of online WOM behaviors on SNSs. There is no significant difference among education. Also, there is no significant difference between female and male, either. On the other side, gender, age, and education do not affect the relationship between the SNSs usage intensity and online Word of mouth. However, when examined if there are gender differences in the interest with social relationship variables, the results showed that female respondents (M = 75.91) have more strong ties in SNSs than do male participants (M = 56.81) ($t(1,256) = 1.84$, $p < .005$). Also, female respondents (M = .18) have a higher ratio of strong ties on SNSs than do male participates (M = .13) ($t(1,366) = 2.82$, $p < .001$). Since no notable demographic differences in terms of dependent variables were found, demographic differences were not considered as a contributing factor in further examinations of knowledge sharing in SNSs:

S = Significant Path

NS= Not Significant Path

We can see from Figure 2, that most the path coefficients in the inner model were significant; among the dimensions of social relationships, the top three strongest path coefficients with online WOM were shown by tie strength and interpersonal influence equally, followed respectively by trust. Social capital was identified as the lowest. In addition, the top strongest path coefficient was shown by online WOM and knowledge sharing.

The structural model (inner model) in PLS was assessed by examining the path coefficients, t-statistics, *P* Value and R^2 value (Chin, 1998). Hypothesis is accepted if t-statistic value exceeds critical value of 1.99 or if the p-value less than error level value (α) of 0.05 (Handoko, Setiawan, and Djumahir, 2013). Table 4 summarizes the results of the hypotheses supported. As it is shown, Path diagram test results

Figure 2. Structural model

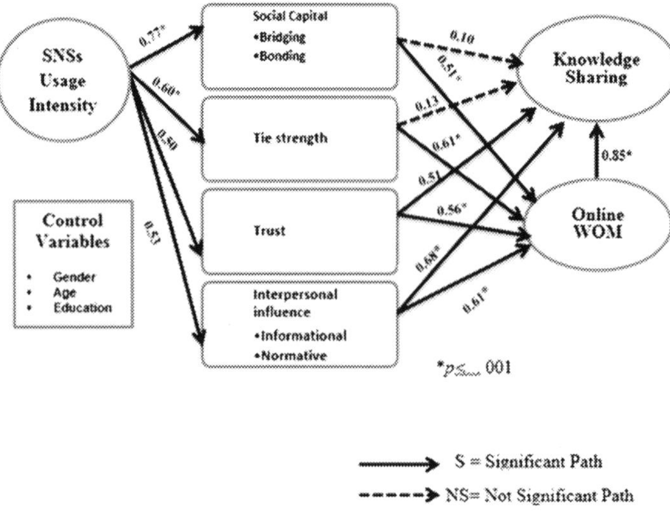

for effect of SNSs Usage Intensity on Social Capital, Tie strength, Trust and Interpersonal influence show t-statistics values of 11.41, 7.11, 9.90 and 5.49 respectively which exceed critical value of 1.99 and a p-value 0.00, 0.04, 0.01 and 0.04 respectively less than 0.05. Therefore SNSs usage intensity has significant effect to increase social capital, tie strength, trust and interpersonal influence. This suggests that H1a, H1b, H1c, and H1d are accepted and original sample estimate indicates positive value of 0.77, 0.60, 0.50, and 0.53 respectively thus proving an increase using SNSs could increase both bonding social capital and bridging social capital, tie strength and trust among college students in Egypt. Therefore when people usually use SNSs intensively, they likely to perceived effect of interactions with other, both strong ties and loose ties in social capital, building strength of a friendship—close friends; willingness to take a risk in communication with others and believe in information express from others easily. This result agrees with the Ellison, Steinfield and Lampe's study (2007) for social capital; Panovich et al.'s study (2012) for tie strength; Shu-Chuan and Sejung's study (2011) for trust; and Yi Hsu and Chau's study (2013) for interpersonal influence.

Testing result the relationship between Social Relationships (Social capital, Tie strength, Trust, and Interpersonal influence) and Online WOM show t-statistics value of 5.61, 6.41, 7.39, and 7.49 respectively which exceeds the critical value of 1.99 and a p-value of 0.00, 0.03, 0.02, and 0.02 respectively is less than standard error value of 0.05. It shows that social capital; tie strength; trust; and interpersonal influence has significant effect on improvement of Online WOM among college students in Egypt. This suggests that H2a; H3a; H4a; and H5a is accepted and original sample estimate with value of 0.51, 0.61, 0.56, and 0.61 respectively prove direction and significant relationships. High social capital, tie strength, trust, and interpersonal influence directly able to encourage and improve peoples' online WOM in Egypt, especially among freshness.

On the other side, testing result the relationship between Social Relationships (Trust and Interpersonal influence) and Knowledge Sharing show t-statistics value of 6.35 and 7.58 respectively which exceeds the critical value of 1.99 and a p-value of 0.01 and 0.04 respectively is less than standard error value of 0.05. It shows that trust and interpersonal influence has significant effect on improvement of knowledge sharing behavior among college students in Egypt. This suggests that H4b and H5b are accepted and original sample estimate with value of 0.51 and 0.68 respectively prove direction and significant relationships. High trust and interpersonal influence directly able to improve peoples' knowledge sharing behavior in Egypt, especially among freshness. However, testing result the relationship between Social Relationships (Social capital and Tie strength) and Knowledge Sharing show t-statistics value of 1.43 and 0.91 respectively which less than critical value of 1.99 and a p-value of 0.35 and 0.42 respectively is exceeds standard error value of 0.05, so it shows that social capital and tie strength had no significant effect on improvement of knowledge sharing behavior among college students in Egypt. This suggests that H2b and H3b are rejected and original sample estimate with very small value and positive at 0.10 and 0.13 respectively prove that the relationship is very weak and not significant.

Finally, Test results the effect of Online WOM on Knowledge Sharing show t-statistics value of 12.51 exceeds the critical value of 1.99 and a p-value of 0.00 is less than standard error value of 0.05. It shows that of Online WOM has significant effect on improvement of knowledge sharing behavior among college students in Egypt. This suggests that H6 is accepted and original sample estimate with very high value and positive at 0.85 prove that the relationship is very strong and significant relationship. Therefore, we can say that, Online WOM directly able to improve knowledge sharing behavior among peoples in Egypt, especially freshness. The R^2 values show also that Online WOM is explained the most (R^2 = .89), knowledge sharing the second most (R^2 = .55), interpersonal influence the third most (R^2 = .46), and Trust the fourth most (R^2 = .35).

5. DISSECTION AND CONCLUSION

In today's online environment, SNSs such as Facebook, Twitter, LinkedIn, CyWorld and MySpace etc. have made a significant impact on peoples' life. People nowadays prefer spending more time in gossiping,

Table 4. The results of the Partial Least Square (PLS) hypothesis testing

No.	Relationship	Original Sample Estimate	*t*-Statistics	*P* Value	Supported
H1a	SNSs Usage Intensity → Social capital	0.77	11.41	0.00	Yes
H1b	SNSs Usage Intensity → Tie strength	0.60	7.11	0.04	Yes
H1c	SNSs Usage Intensity → Trust	0.50	9.90	0.01	Yes
H1d	SNSs Usage Intensity → Interpersonal influence	0.53	5.49	0.04	Yes
H2a	Social capital → Online WOM	0.51	5.61	0.00	Yes
H2b	Social capital → Knowledge Sharing	0.10	1.43	0.35	No
H3a	Tie strength → Online WOM	0.61	6.41	0.03	Yes
H3b	Tie strength → Knowledge Sharing	0.13	0.91	0.42	No
H4a	Trust → Online WOM	0.56	7.39	0.02	Yes
H4b	Trust → Knowledge Sharing	0.51	6.35	0.01	Yes
H5a	Interpersonal Influence → Online WOM	0.61	7.49	0.02	Yes
H5b	Interpersonal Influence → Knowledge Sharing	0.68	7.58	0.04	Yes
H6	Online WOM → Knowledge Sharing	0.85	12.51	0.00	Yes

playing games, browsing friend's profiles and chatting with their friends on SNSs rather than meeting and face-to-face conversation. Therefore, the impact of online word-of-mouth and knowledge sharing on consumer purchase decisions has been an emerging topic of importance to marketing researchers as a new domain for marketing. The purpose of the present study was to investigate the relationship among the SNSs usage; social relationships; online WOM; and knowledge sharing on SNSs. As predicted, our findings suggest that the intensity of usage of SNSs is positively related to social relationships which do play a role in determining behavior of Online WOM and knowledge sharing in the online environment.

Our results demonstrate that SNSs usage intensity can help to address the social relationship development and maintenance needs the college-age populations; the results show that SNSs usage intensity increases social capital, tie strength, trust, and interpersonal influence. SNSs usage intensity can building bridging social capital and bonding social capital among users due to the way that technologies like distribution lists, photo directories, and search capabilities support online linkages with others. Moreover, SNSs usage intensity could increase the number of weak ties a user might be able to maintain large and heterogeneous networks of friends cheaply and easily. The results also show that SNSs usage intensity allows users to maintain large numbers of relationships at varying levels of closeness. Therefore, we can say that, SNSs appear to increase our innate carrying capacity for relationships; and tie strength can be used to improve the of personalization and the overall user experience on SNSs. In addition, the results show that SNSs usage intensity allows users connect without boundary limitations, where the flow of communication between individuals is comfortable, the true self should be apparent. Moreover, the results show that SNSs usage intensity's people, students in this study, do increase both informational interpersonal influence and normative interpersonal influence; this could be because students accept the information from others as credible evidence about reality. Previous studies found the same results related with social capital (Donath and Boyd's study, 2004; Ellison, Steinfield, and Lampe, 2007), tie strength (Burke, 2011), trust (Yi Hsu and Chau, 2013), and interpersonal influence (Yi Hsu and Chau, 2013).

The results also demonstrate that, although social capital, tie strength, trust, and interpersonal influence effect on Online WOM behaviors, they do not increase knowledge sharing on SNSs expect trust and interpersonal influence. The positive qualities of social relationships appeared in all online WOM activities; these positive of social relationships could help students to understand the exchange of information on SNSs. Moreover, social capital, tie strength appeared in knowledge sharing behavior on SNSs. Students in this study feel that the content in SNSs are relevant, helpful, accurate, reliable, or timely; they want their friends to have the same benefits. Consequently, they spread the benefits, and they perceive that they share knowledge in SNSs. However, students do not feel the need to share knowledge just because of trust or interpersonal influence; when they use their SNS. This also could be because they are using SNSs in their private environments.

Finally, the results demonstrate that, online WOM plays a vital role to share knowledge, especially on SNSs. One important result is that male students experience stronger relationship between online WOM and knowledge sharing in SNSs than female students. This result indicates that male students feel more strongly about online WOM when they use their SNS heavily, when they perceive that they belong to their SNS community, or when they trust others. Males emphasize maintaining relationships more and communicate with one another more than females. Males are more likely to share their information with others and change their behavior based on interactions with others. Moreover, male students feel more strongly about knowledge sharing when they perceive that online WOM is good. These results disagree with the results of Choi and Scott study's (2013); this may be because cultural differences which does play a role in determining social relations in the online environment (Shu-Chuan and Sejung, 2011).

6. IMPLICATIONS FOR FUTURE RESEARCH

From the marketing perspective, it is importance to understand the aspects in social relationships have influence on online WOM and knowledge sharing behaviors - a SNSs usage of current consumers, which lead the marketers or organizations get success to touch their consumers. This research finds that the SNSs usage intensity is positively related to some of the aspects of users' social relationship (social capital, tie strength, and trust) which have a positive effect on online WOM and knowledge sharing on SNSs. Moreover, this research also finds that online WOM has a positive effect on knowledge sharing. This gives practitioners a clear view about the consumers' online WOM behaviors and how to share knowledge on SNSs which enables marketers and organizations to provide inspiration for new product development or new services; to direct the marketing strategies; and to increase customers' loyalty toward its brand by communicating through SNSs. Moreover, it provides researchers a theoretical model about the relationship between the SNSs usage and the social relationships; the relationship between social relationships and both of online WOM and knowledge sharing; and the relationship between online WOM and knowledge sharing on SNSs to test the framework for modeling and examining SNSs in another culture.

Because of the limitations of the current study which exclusive Facebook use in private non-corporate environments using Egyptian students and focusing on the some dimension of social relationships (social capital, tie strength, trust, and interpersonal influence), future research should find out whether there are similar results in another culture; further research on this topic using the model would enable a theoretical understanding of the potential to online WOM and knowledge sharing on SNSs in other working environments (e.g. business, education and society); further research using the model would enable a theoretical understanding of the issues that need to be resolved between online WOM and knowledge sharing in SNSs; in addition, future research needs to explore other dimension of social relationships.

REFERENCES

Ahn, J. (2011). The Effect of Social Network Sites on Adolescents' Social and Academic Development. *Journal of the American Society for Information Science and Technology*, *62*(8), 1435–1445. doi:10.1002/asi.21540

Anderson, J. C., & Gerbing, D. W. (1988). Structural Equation Modeling in Practice: A Review and Recommended Two - Step Approach. *Psychological Bulletin*, *103*(3), 411–423. doi:10.1037/0033-2909.103.3.411

Andrews, D. (2002). Audience-specific online community design. *Communications of the ACM*, *45*(4), 64–68. doi:10.1145/505248.505275

Andrews, K. M., & Delahaye, B. L. (2000). Influences on Knowledge Processes on Organisational Learning: The psychosocial Filter. *Journal of Management Studies*, *37*(6), 797–809. doi:10.1111/1467-6486.00204

Ashley, Ch., & Tuten, T. (2015). Creative Strategies in Social Media Marketing: An Exploratory Study of Branded Social Content and Consumer Engagement. *Psychology and Marketing*, *32*(1), 15–27. doi:10.1002/mar.20761

Aslam, M. M. H., Shahzad, K., Syed, A. R., & Ramish, A. (2013). Social Capital and Knowledge Sharing as Determinants of Academic Performance. *Journal of Behavioral and Applied Management*, *15*(1), 25–41.

Awad, N. F., & Ragowsky, A. (2008). Establishing Trust in Electronic Commerce through Online word of mouth: An Examination across Genders. *Journal of Management Information Systems*, *24*(4), 101–121. doi:10.2753/MIS0742-1222240404

Bagozzi, R. P., & Yi, Y. (1988). On the Evaluation of Structural Equation Models. *Journal of the Academy of Marketing Science*, *16*(Spring), 74–94. doi:10.1007/BF02723327

Baker, L., & Oswald, D. (2010). Shyness and Online Social Networking Services. *Journal of Social and Personal Relationships*, *27*(7), 1–21. doi:10.1177/0265407510375261

Bakshy, E., Rosenn, I., Marlow, C., & Adamic, L. (2011, April 16–20). The Role of Social Networks in Information Diffusion. *Proceedings of WWW 2012*, Lyon, France.

Baumgartner, H., & Homburg, C. (1996). Applications of Structural Equation Modeling in Marketing and Consumer Research: A review. *International Journal of Research in Marketing*, *13*(2), 139–161. doi:10.1016/0167-8116(95)00038-0

Baym, N. K., Zhang, Y. B., Kunkel, A., Ledbetter, A., & Mei-Chen, L. (2007). Relational Quality and Media Use in Interpersonal Relationships. *New Media & Society*, *9*(5), 735–752. doi:10.1177/1461444807080339

Bearden, W. O., Netemeyer, R. G., & Teel, J. E. (1989). Measurement of Consumer Susceptibility to Interpersonal Influence. *The Journal of Consumer Research*, *15*(4), 473–481. doi:10.1086/209186

Bentler, P. M. (1992). *EQS: Structural Equation Program Manual*. New York: BMDP Statistical Software.

Bernard, H. R., Johnsen, E. C., Killworth, P. D., & Robinson, S. (1989). Estimating the Size of an Average Personal Network and of an Event Population. In M. Kochen (Ed.), *The Small World* (pp. 159–175). Norwood, NJ: Ablex Publishing.

Bhattacherjee, A. (2002). Individual trust in online firms: Scale development and initial test. *Journal of Management Information Systems*, *19*(1), 211–241.

Blanchard, A., & Horan, T. (1998). Virtual Communities and Social Capital. *Social Science Computer Review*, *16*(3), 293–307. doi:10.1177/089443939801600306

Bond, F. W., Hayes, S. C., Baer, R. A., Carpenter, K. M., Guenole, N., Orcutt, H. K., & Zettle, R. D. et al. (2011). Preliminary Psychometric Properties of the Acceptance and Action Questionnaire-II: A revised measure of psychological flexibility and experiential avoidance. *Behavior Therapy*, *42*(4), 676–688. doi:10.1016/j.beth.2011.03.007 PMID:22035996

Bontis, N., Booker, L. D., & Serenko, A. (2007). The Mediating Effect of Organizational Reputation on Customer Loyalty and Service Recommendation in the Banking Industry. *Management Decision*, *45*(9), 1426–1445. doi:10.1108/00251740710828681

Brandtzæg, P. B., & Nov, O. (2011). Facebook Use and Social Capital – A Longitudinal Study, Proceedings of the Fifth International AAAI Conference on Weblogs and Social Media, Association for the Advancement of Artificial Intelligence (www.aaai.org)

Brown, J., Broderick, A. J., & Lee, N. (2007). Word of Mouth Communication within Online Communities: Conceptualizing the Online Social Network. *Journal of Interactive Marketing*, *21*(3), 2–20. doi:10.1002/dir.20082

Burke, M. (2011, December 28). *Reading, Writing, Relationships: The Impact of Social Network Sites on Relationships and Well-Being* [Thesis]. Carnegie Mellon University, Pittsburgh, Pennsylvania.

Cheung, C. M. K., & Thadani, D. R. (2010). The Effectiveness of Electronic Word-of-Mouth Communication: A Literature Analysis. Proceedings of the 23rd Bled e Conference eTrust: Implications for the Individual, Enterprises and Society, Bled, Slovenia.

Chin, W. W. (1998). The partial least square approach to structural equation modeling. In M. Ga (Ed.), *Modern methods for business research* (pp. 295–336). Mahwah, London, New Jersey: Lawrence Erlbaum Associates.

Chiu, C.-M., Hsu, M.-H., & Wang, E. T. G. (2006). Understanding knowledge sharing in virtual communities: An integration of social capital and social cognitive theories. *Decision Support Systems*, *42*(3), 1872–1888. doi:10.1016/j.dss.2006.04.001

Choi, J. H., & Scott, J. E. (2013). Electronic Word of Mouth and Knowledge Sharing on Social Network Sites: A Social Capital Perspective. *Journal of Theoretical and Applied Electronic Commerce Research*, *8*(1), 69–82. doi:10.4067/S0718-18762013000100006

Choi, S. M., Kim, Y., Sung, Y., & Sohn, D. (2011). Bridging or Bonding? A Cross-Cultural Study of Social Relationships in Social Networking Sites. *Information Communication and Society*, *14*(1), 107–129. doi:10.1080/13691181003792624

Chow, W. S., & Chan, L. S. (2008). Social Network, Social Trust and Shared Goals in Organizational Knowledge Sharing. *Information & Management*, *45*(7), 458–465. doi:10.1016/j.im.2008.06.007

Chu, S.-C. (2009). Determinants of Consumer Engagement in Electronic Word-of-Mouth in Social Networking Sites [Thesis]. The University of Texas at Austin.

Chu, S.-C., & Choi, S. M. (2011). Electronic Word-of-Mouth in Social Networking Sites: A Cross-Cultural Study of the United States and China. *Journal of Global Marketing*, *24*(3), 263–281. doi:10.1080/08911762.2011.592461

Chu, S.-C., & Kim, Y. (2011). Determinants of Consumer Engagement in Electronic Word-of-Mouth (eWOM) in Social Networking Sites. *International Journal of Advertising*, *30*(1), 47–75. doi:10.2501/IJA-30-1-047-075

Coenen, T. (2006, October 29). Knowledge Sharing over Social Networking Systems [PhD dissertation]. Retrieved from http://creativecommons.org/licenses/by-nc-sa/2.0/be/

Constant, D., Sproull, L., & Kiesler, S. (1996). The Kindness of Strangers: The Usefulness of Electronic Weak Ties for Technical Advice. *Organization Science*, *7*(2), 119–135. doi:10.1287/orsc.7.2.119

D'Rozario, D., & Choudhury, P. K. (2000). Effect of Assimilation on Consumer Susceptibility to Interpersonal Influence. *Journal of Consumer Marketing*, *17*(4), 290–307. doi:10.1108/07363760010335321

Dellarocas, Ch. (2003). The Digitization of Word-of-Mouth: Promise and Challenge of Online Feedback Mechanisms. *Management Science*, *49*(10), 1407–1424. doi:10.1287/mnsc.49.10.1407.17308

DeLone, W., Espinosa, J. A., Lee, G., & Carmel, E. (2005). Bridging global boundaries for IS project success" System Sciences. HICSS'05. *Proceedings of the 38th Annual Hawaii International Conference*.

Di Gennaro, C., & Dutton, W. (2007). Reconfiguring Friendships: Social Relationships and the Internet. *Information Communication and Society*, *10*(5), 591–618. doi:10.1080/13691180701657949

Donath, J., & Boyd, D. (2004). Public displays of connection. *BT Technology Journal*, *22*(4), 71–82. doi:10.1023/B:BTTJ.0000047585.06264.cc

Duggan, M., & Brenner, J. (2013, February 14). The Demographics of Social Media Users — 2012. Pew Research Center's Internet & American Life Project. Retrieved from http://pewinternet.org/Reports/2013/Social-media-users.aspx

Dwyer, C., Hiltz, S. R., & Passerini, K. (2007). Trust and Privacy Concern within Social Networking Sites: A Comparison of Facebook and Myspace. *Paper presented at the Thirteenth Americas Conference on Information Systems*, Keystone, CO.

Dwyer, P. (2007). Measuring the Value of Electronic Word of Mouth and Its Impact in Consumer Communities. *Journal of Interactive Marketing*, *21*(2), 63–79. doi:10.1002/dir.20078

Ellison, N., Steinfield, C., & Lampe, C. (2011). Connection Strategies: Social Capital Implications of Facebook-enabled Communication Practices. *New Media & Society*, *13*(6), 873–892. doi:10.1177/1461444810385389

Ellison, N., Vitak, J., Gray, R., & Lampe, C. (2011). Cultivating Social Resources on Facebook: Signals of Relational Investment and their Role in Social Capital Processes. *Paper presented at the iCS-OII 2011 "A Decade in Internet Time" Symposium*, Oxford, UK.

Ellison, N. B., Steinfield, C., & Lampe, C. (2007). The Benefits of Facebook "Friends": Social Capital and College Students' Use of Online Social Network Sites. *Journal of Computer-Mediated Communication*, *12*(4), 1143–1168. doi:10.1111/j.1083-6101.2007.00367.x

Evans, P., & Wurster, T. S. (2000). *Blown to Bits: How the New Economics of Information Transforms Strategy*. Boston, USA: Harvard Business School Press.

Farooq, F., & Jan, Z. (2012). The Impact of Social Networking to Influence Marketing through Product Reviews, International. *Journal of Information and Communication Technology Research*, *2*(8), 627–637.

Farrugia, R. C. (2013). *Facebook and Relationships: A Study of How Social Media Use is Affecting Long-Term Relationships* [Thesis]. Rochester Institute of Technology.

Fornell, C., & Larcker, D. F. (1981). Evaluating Structural Equation Models with Unobservable Variables and Measurement Error. *JMR, Journal of Marketing Research*, *18*(1), 39–50. doi:10.2307/3151312

Gefen, D., Karahanna, E., & Straub, D. W. (2003). Trust and TAM in Online Shopping: An Integrated Model. *Management Information Systems Quarterly*, *27*(1), 51–90.

Ghosh, B., & Scott, J. E. (2007). Effective Knowledge Management Systems for a Clinical Nursing Setting. *Information Systems Management*, *24*(1), 73–84. doi:10.1080/10580530601038188

Gilbert, E., & Karahalios, K. (2009). Predicting Tie Strength with Social Media. *Presented at the Proc. 27th International Conference on Human Factors in Computing Systems (CHI '09)*. doi:10.1145/1518701.1518736

Goldenberg, J., Libai, B., & Muller, E. (2001). Talk of the Network: A Complex Systems Look at the Underlying Process of Word-of-Mouth. *Marketing Letters*, *12*(3), 211–223. doi:10.1023/A:1011122126881

Goldsmith, R.E. (2006). Electronic Word-of-Mouth. In Encyclopedia of E-Commerce, E-Government and Mobile Commerce. Hershey, PA: Idea Group Publishing.

Goldsmith, R. E., & Horowitz, D. (2006). Measuring Motivations for Online Opinion Seeking. *Journal of Interactive Advertising*, *6*(2), 2–14. http://www.jiad.org/article76 doi:10.1080/15252019.2006.10722114

Goyette, I., Ricard, L., Bergeron, J., & Marticotte, F. (2010). e-WOM Scale: Word-of-Mouth Measurement Scale for e-Services Context. *Canadian Journal of Administrative Sciences*, *27*(1), 5–23. doi:10.1002/cjas.129

Granovetter, M. S. (1973). The Strength of Weak Ties. *American Journal of Sociology*, *78*(6), 1360–1380. doi:10.1086/225469

Gulati, R., Nohria, N., & Zaheer, A. (2000). Strategic Networks. *Strategic Management Journal*, *21*(3), 203–215. doi:10.1002/(SICI)1097-0266(200003)21:3<203::AID-SMJ102>3.0.CO;2-K

Gupte, M., & Rad, T. E. (2012, June 22–24). Measuring Tie Strength in Implicit Social Networks. *Proceedings of WebSci 2012*, Evanston, Illinois, USA. doi:10.1145/2380718.2380734

Gustafsson, A., & Johnson, M. D. (2004). Determining Attribute Importance in a Service Satisfaction Model. *Journal of Service Research*, *7*(2), 124–141. doi:10.1177/1094670504268453

Hair, J. F. Jr, Black, W. C., Babin, B. J., & Anderson, R. E. (2010). *Multivariate Data Analysis*. Upper Saddle River, NJ: Prentice Hall.

Hampton, K. N., Goulet, L. S., Rainie, L., & Purcell, K. (2011, June 16). Pew Research Center's Internet & American Life Project. Retrieved from http://pewinternet.org/Reports/2011/Technology-and-social-networks.aspx

Handoko, Y., Setiawan, M., & Djumahir, S. (2013). Organizational Culture, Job Satisfaction, Organizational Commitment, the Effect on Lecturer Performance. *International Journal of Business and Management Invention*, *2*(12), 21–30.

Heinonen, K. (2011). Consumer Activity in Social Media: Managerial Approaches to Consumers' Social Media Behavior. *Journal of Consumer Behaviour*, *10*(6), 356–364. doi:10.1002/cb.376

Hennig-Thurau, T., Gwinner, K. P., Walsh, G., & Gremler, D. D. (2004). Electronic Word-of-Mouth Via Consumer Opinion Platforms: What Motivates Consumers to Articulate Themselves on the Internet? *Journal of Interactive Marketing*, *18*(1), 38–52. doi:10.1002/dir.10073

Hsu, M.-H., Ju, T. L., Yen, C.-H., & Chang, C.-M. (2007). Knowledge Sharing Behavior in Virtual Communities: The Relationship between Trust, Self-Efficacy, and Outcome Expectations. *International Journal of Human-Computer Studies*, *65*(2), 153–169. doi:10.1016/j.ijhcs.2006.09.003

Huberman, B. A., Romero, D. M., & Wu, F. (2009). Social Networks that Matter: Twitter under the Microscope. *First Monday*, *14*(1), 8.

Huffaker, D. A. (2011). The Impact of Group Attributes on Communication Activity and Shared Language in Online Communities. *First Monday*, *16*(4), 4. doi:10.5210/fm.v16i4.3450

Hung, K. H., & Li, S. Y. (2007). The Influence of eWOM on Virtual Consumer Communities: Social Capital, Consumer Learning, and Behavioral Outcomes. *Journal of Advertising Research*, *47*(4), 485–495. doi:10.2501/S002184990707050X

Huysman, M., & Wulf, V. (2005). IT to Support Knowledge Sharing in Communities, Towards a Social Capital Analysis. *Journal of Information Technology*, *21*(1), 40–51. doi:10.1057/palgrave.jit.2000053

Inkpen, A. C., & Tsang, E. W. K. (2005). Social Capital, Networks, and Knowledge Transfer. *Academy of Management Review*, *30*(1), 146–165. doi:10.5465/AMR.2005.15281445

Kaplan, A. M., & Haenlein, M. (2010). Users of the World, Unite! The Challenges and Opportunities of Social Media. *Business Horizons*, *53*(1), 59–68. doi:10.1016/j.bushor.2009.09.003

Kuss, D. J., & Griffiths, M. D. (2011). Online Social Networking and Addiction—A Review of the Psychological Literature. *International Journal of Environmental Research and Public Health*, *8*(12), 3528–3552. doi:10.3390/ijerph8093528 PMID:22016701

Lampe, C., Ellison, N., & Steinfield, C. (2007). A familiar Face (book): Profile elements as signals in an online social network. *Proceedings of Conference on Human Factors in Computing Systems*, New York (pp. 435-444). doi:10.1145/1240624.1240695

LaSalle, J. (2004). Social Penetration Theory. In R. West & L. Turner (Eds.), *Introducing Communication Theory Analysis and Application* (2nd ed.). New York, NY: McGraw-Hill.

Laud G., Karpen I. O., Mulye, R., & Rahman, K. (2015). The Role of Embeddedness for Resource Integration: Complementing S-D logic Research through a Social Capital Perspective. *Marketing Theory*.

Lee, J., & Kim, S. (2011). Exploring the Role of Social Networks in Affective Organizational Commitment: Network Centrality, Strength of Ties, and Structural Holes. *American Review of Public Administration*, *41*(2), 205–223. doi:10.1177/0275074010373803

Lenhart, A., Purcell, L., Smith, A., & Zickuhr, K. (2010). Social Media and Young Adults. Pew Internet and American Life Project. Retrieved from http://www.pewinternet.org/Reports/2010/Social-Media-and-Young-Adults.aspx

Leonard, R., & Onyx, J. (2003). Networking Through Loose and Strong Ties: An Australian Qualitative Study. *Voluntas*, *14*(2), 189–203. doi:10.1023/A:1023900111271

Levin D. Z., Walter J., Appleyard M. M., & Cross R. (2015). Relational Enhancement: How the Relational Dimension of Social Capital Unlocks the Value of Network-Bridging Ties. *Group Organization Management.*

Marlow, C. (2009). Maintained relationships on Facebook. Retrieved from http://overstated.net/2009/03/09/maintained-relationships-on-facebook

McKelvey, R. D. (1976). Intransitivities in Multidimensional Voting Models and Some Implications for Agenda Control. *Journal of Economic Theory*, *12*(3), 472–482. doi:10.1016/0022-0531(76)90040-5

McKnight, D. H., Choudhury, V., & Kacmar, C. (2002). Developing and Validating Trust Measures for Ecommerce: An Integrative Typology. *Information Systems Research*, *13*(3), 334–359. doi:10.1287/isre.13.3.334.81

Moira, B., Kraut, R., & Marlow, C. (2011, May 7–12). Social Capital on Facebook: Differentiating Uses and Users. *Proceedings of the CHI 2011*, Vancouver, BC, Canada.

Nahapiet, J., & Ghoshal, S. (1998). Social Capital, Intellectual Capital, and The Organizational Advantage. *Academy of Management Review*, *23*(2), 242–266.

Negroponte, N. & Maes P. (1996, October). Electronic Word of Mouth. *Wired.*

Onyx, J., & Bullen, P. (2000). Measuring Social Capital in Five Communities. *The Journal of Applied Behavioral Science*, *36*(1), 23–42. doi:10.1177/0021886300361002

Panovich, K., Miller, R. C., & Karger, D. R. (2012, February 11–15). Tie Strength in Question & Answer on Social Network Sites. *Proceedings of the CSCW '12*, Seattle, Washington, USA. doi:10.1145/2145204.2145361

Parsons, A. (2013). Using Social Media to Reach Consumers: A Content Analysis of Official Facebook Pages. *Academy of Marketing Studies Journal*, *17*(2), 27–36.

Pempek, T. A., Yermolayeva, Y. A., & Calvert, S. L. (2009). College Students' Social Networking Experiences on Facebook. *Journal of Applied Developmental Psychology*, 30(3), 227-238. doi:10.1016/j.appdev.2008.12.010

Putnam, R. (2000). *Bowling Alone: The Collapse and Revival of American Community*. New York: Touchstone. doi:10.1145/358916.361990

Quan-Haase, A., & Young, A. L. (2010). Uses and Gratifications of Social Media: A Comparison of Facebook and Instant Messaging. *Bulletin of Science, Technology & Society*, *30*(5), 350–361. doi:10.1177/0270467610380009

Robert, L. P. Jr, Dennis, A. R., & Ahuja, M. K. (2008). Social Capital and Knowledge Integration in Digitally Enabled Teams. *Information Systems Research*, *19*(3), 314–334. doi:10.1287/isre.1080.0177

Sheldon, P. (2008). Student Favorite: Facebook and Motives for Its Use. *Southwestern Mass Communication Journal*, *23*(2), 39–53.

Shu-Chuan Chu, (2009). *Determinants of Consumer Engagement in Electronic Word-of-Mouth in Social Networking Sites* [Degree of Doctor of Philosophy]. University of Texas at Austin.

Sirohi, N., McLaughlin, E. D., & Wittink, D. R. (1998). A Model of Consumer Perceptions and Store Loyalty Intentions for a Supermarket Retailer. *Journal of Retailing*, *74*(2), 223–245. doi:10.1016/S0022-4359(99)80094-3

Sponcil, M., & Priscilla, G. (2013). Use of Social Media by College Students: Relationship to Communication and Self-concept. *Journal of Technology Research*, *4*(July), 1–13.

Steffes, E. M., & Burgee, L. E. (2009, January 30). Social Ties and Online Word of Mouth. *Internet Research*, *19*(1), 42–59. doi:10.1108/10662240910927812

Steinfield, C., Ellison, N. B., & Lampe, C. (2008). Social Capital, Self-Esteem, and Use of Online Social Network Sites: A Longitudinal Analysis. *Journal of Applied Developmental Psychology*, *29*(6), 434–445. doi:10.1016/j.appdev.2008.07.002

Sweeney, J. C., Soutar, G. N., & Mazzarol, T. (2012). Word of Mouth: Measuring The Power of Individual Messages. *European Journal of Marketing*, *46*(1), 237–257. doi:10.1108/03090561211189310

The Ministry of Communications and Information Technology. (2015). Arab republic of Egypt. Retrieved from http://www.mcit.gov.eg/indicators/ar/ind_Communications.aspx

Tufekci, Z. (2008). Grooming, Gossip, Facebook, and Myspace. *Information Communication and Society*, *11*(4), 544–564. doi:10.1080/13691180801999050

Tyson, J. (2009). *Connecting through Facebook: The Influence of Social Networking Communication* [Thesis]. Wake Forest University, Winston-Salem, North Carolina, USA.

Ugander, J., Backstrom, L., Kleinberg, J., & Marlow, C. (2011). Structural Diversity in Social Contagion.

Utz, S., & Beukeboom, C. J. (2011). The Role of Social Network Sites in Romantic Relationships: Effects on Jealousy and Relationship Happiness. *Journal of Computer-Mediated Communication*, *16*(4), 511–527. doi:10.1111/j.1083-6101.2011.01552.x

Valenzuela, S., Park, N., & Kee, K. (2009). Is There Social Capital in a Social Network Site?: Facebook Use and College Students' Life Satisfaction, Trust, and Participation. *Journal of Computer-Mediated Communication*, *14*(4), 875–901. doi:10.1111/j.1083-6101.2009.01474.x

Vilpponen, A., Winter, S., & Sundqvist, S. (2006). Electronic Word-of-Mouth in Online Environments: Exploring Referral Network Structure and Adoption Behavior. *Journal of Interactive Advertising*, 6(2). Retrieved from http://www.jiad.org/article82

Wegge, D., Vandebosch, H., Eggermont, S., & Walrave, M. (2015). The Strong, the Weak, and the Unbalanced: The Link between Tie Strength and Cyber Aggression on a Social Network Site Social. *Science Computer Review*, *33*(3), 315–342. doi:10.1177/0894439314546729

Wellman, B., Quan-Haase, A., Witte, J., & Hampton, K. N. (2001). Does the Internet Increase, Decrease, or Supplement Social Capital? Social Networks, Participation, and Community Commitment. *The American Behavioral Scientist*, *45*(3), 437–456. doi:10.1177/00027640121957286

User Facebook in Egypt. (2015). *Wikipedia*. Retrieved from https://en.wikipedia.org/w/index.php?search=User+Facebook+In+Egypt&title=Special%3ASearch&fulltext=1

Williams, D. (2006). On and off the Net: Scales for Social Capital in an online era, *Journal of Computer- Mediated Communication*. 11(2), 593-628. Retrieved from http://jcmc.indiana.edu/vol11/issue2/williams.html

Williamson, D. A. (2006). Social Network Marketing: Ad Spending Update. *Emarketer.* Retrieved from http://www.emarketer.com/Report.aspx?code=em_soc_net_mktg_nov06&src=report_summary_reportsell

Yi Hsu & Chau, Thi Hong (2013). Social Relationship Factors Influence on eWOM Behaviors in Social Networking Sites: Empirical Study: Taiwan and Vietnam. *International Journal of Business, Humanities and Technology*, 3(3), 22-32.

Zahedi, F. M., Bansal, G., & Ische, J. (2010). Success Factors in Cooperative Online Marketplaces: Trust as the Social Capital and Value Generator in Vendors- Exchange Relationships. *Journal of Organizational Computing and Electronic Commerce*, *20*(4), 295–327. doi:10.1080/10919392.2010.516626

Zhang, Y., & Hiltz, S. R. (2003). Factors that Influence Online Relationship Development in a Knowledge Sharing Community. *Proceedings of the Ninth American Conference on Information Systems* (pp. 410–417).

Zhao, S. (2006). Do Internet Users have more Social Ties? A Call for differentiated analyses of internet use. *JCMC*, *11*(3), 844–862. doi:10.1111/j.1083-6101.2006.00038.x

This research was previously published in the International Journal of Online Marketing (IJOM), 6(1); edited by Hatem El-Gohary, pages 1-23, copyright year 2016 by IGI Publishing (an imprint of IGI Global).

Chapter 34
Gender Differences in Motivations to Use Social Networking Sites

Valeria Noguti
University of Technology Sydney, Australia

Sonika Singh
University of Technology Sydney, Australia

David S. Waller
University of Technology Sydney, Australia

ABSTRACT

This chapter investigates gender differences in motivations to use social networking sites (SNS), a subset of social media. The present research focuses on Facebook given its prominence among currently available SNS. Analysing a survey of university students in Australia, the results indicate that female consumers are more likely than male consumers to use Facebook to seek information (to research and learn new things and to discuss products and brands) and for convenience (to obtain things with little effort). Both of these reasons in turn relate positively to their degree of engagement on Facebook, where engagement is operationalized as cognitive absorption which is a state of deep involvement with an activity.

INTRODUCTION

Over the last 20 years the internet has resulted in significant changes in how we communicate, gather information, and purchase goods and services. Innovations in online social media have resulted in websites that not only allow users to retrieve information, but also encourage the interactive sharing of information and the creation of user-generated content (Kaplan & Haenlein, 2010; Mangold & Faulds, 2009). In particular, there has been an explosion in popularity of social networking sites (SNS) which is an online platform that has the main objective to facilitate regular communication among individuals. These include various social media sites such as Facebook, Twitter and LinkedIn, as well as photo and

DOI: 10.4018/978-1-5225-5637-4.ch034

video sharing sites such as YouTube, Tumblr, Instagram, Flickr and Pinterest. Facebook is a popular SNS where people can search for other people and businesses, and keep friends updated with the latest pictures, videos, news and information (Chi, 2011; Curran, Graham & Temple, 2011; Lukka & James, 2014). One of the reasons online social networks provide an important topic for research is that consumers' media habits have been consistently shifting away from traditional mass media, such as television, towards the internet (Deloitte, 2014) and notably social media. Hence, companies benefit from having their brands present on social media, including SNS, as it is where consumers spend more and more of their time.

Within a social networking context, the research objectives of our study are to: (1) determine what motivates people to use SNS; (2) discover the relationships between motives and engagement in SNS; and (3) ascertain any gender differences in the use of SNS. The analyses of responses to an online survey capturing the reasons for using Facebook provides insights on the gender differences in survey respondent motivations and related engagement with social media.

BACKGROUND

Motivations for Using Social Media

Until recently the types of media used worldwide remained mostly unchanged, dominated by traditional media such as newspapers, magazines, radio, television, cinema and books. For a long time traditional media have been playing a key role in our cultural development as they fulfil an important individual need to connect with society (Katz, Blumler & Gurevitch, 1974; Katz, Haas & Gurevitch, 1973). This connection with society, via traditional media, happens through the filter of a few; namely editors, writers and others who decide on what is to be widely communicated. The media type and these filters render such traditional media primarily unidirectional in that information and opinions flow from the media to the audience, with little interaction flowing in the reverse direction, limited for example to selected letters from readers that are published in specific sections of newspapers and magazines. The development of the internet and the creation of social media and in particular SNS, pushed by the mass adoption of Facebook, drastically changed the characteristics of media. The development of social media democratised communications, allowing people to interact with each other in new ways which were fast, low cost, and large scale, reaching people with ease almost anywhere in the world.

This new way to connect with other people has also catapulted the practice of multi-directional communication flows. Now consumers share their views not only with their own friends and communities, but also directly with businesses and governments both in public and private ways. By publicly participating in the conversation, people in turn create a large body of content that represents the views of society in a way that adds to the views disseminated by mass media, businesses and governments. Hence, social media has allowed individuals to more thoroughly fulfil their need to connect with society – not only by helping people to express themselves, but also by facilitating access to all sorts of information and opinions from others.

SNS are defined as "web-based services that allow individuals to construct a public or semi-public profile within a bounded system, articulate a list of other users with whom they share a connection, and view and traverse their list of connections and those made by others within the system" (Boyd & Ellison, 2007, p. 211). As a type of media, it is fruitful to look at motivations to use SNS by employing, as a starting point, the theory of uses and gratifications of media (Katz et al., 1974; Katz et al., 1973).

Katz and colleagues theorised three sources of media gratification: media content, exposure to media per se, and the social context. These different sources generate benefits such as fulfilment of surveillance, which links with the need for security, curiosity, and exploration; reinforcement to one's attitudes, which in turn may derive from the need for reassurance; social utility, which links to affiliation needs; and escape, which links to the need to reduce anxiety. The theory discusses how each type of media may relate differently to each type of need. For example, mentioning Enzenberger (cited by Katz et al., 1974) the authors discuss how the 8mm camera, as a type of media, offered benefits such as keeping the family together and atomising and depoliticising society. Similarly, social media has helped change society by democratising the dissemination of information, while SNS, as a type of social media, relate primarily to particular types of needs, notably social needs. Overall, while the uses and gratifications theory of media has been developed for traditional media, it is equally applicable to social media providing both similar and new gratifications in the social context.

One the most influential SNS is Facebook, with 1.35 billion users active monthly worldwide (Statista, 2014). Facebook stimulates high levels of user participation: 63% of American Facebook users visit the site at least once a day, and 40% do so multiple times a day (Duggan & Smith, 2013). A list of factors have been identified as motives for using Facebook including seeking friends, convenience, social support, information, and entertainment (Kim, Sohn & Choi, 2011). Facebook has also become a place to find general information about anyone, including those not known personally. Hence, a further relevant motive to use social media is to specifically research people (Lampe, Ellison & Steinfield, 2008).

While social media attracts both men and women, gender differences have been found in its usage. For example, a study on the use of MySpace indicated that teenage girls use more self-references, social words, and negative emotions than teenage boys (Pfeil, Arjan & Zaphiris, 2009). Women also tended to have more friends in MySpace. Men who are more emotionally unstable are more likely to use social media, whereas women's social media use does not differ based on emotional stability (Correa, Hinsley & De Zuniga, 2010). These findings suggest that women tend to use social media more for the social aspect than men and it is possible that this use leans to the emotional side. Indeed, women use more social media to communicate with peers than men (Barker, 2009) and use SNS more for relationship maintenance, whereas men tend to use SNS more for forging new relationships (Muscanell & Guadagno, 2012). It would then be expected that gender differences may relate to different motivations to use SNS.

Gender Differences in Information Search

Social media includes not only SNS but also other types of virtual environments such as blogs, product review enabled sites, consumer forums, and online communities, which may or may not be sponsored or affiliated to a company. Users would by definition be motivated to use social media sites where consumers exchange information about products and services because they facilitate information search. In comparison, users of SNS may consider them primarily from a social interaction point of view. Still, SNS fulfil information search needs. Pai and Arnott (2013) found that by browsing others' pages, SNS users satisfy their curiosity and gain useful insights. Besides discussions that users have about products and brands on SNS, advertising also provides information to consumers on SNS (Zeng, Huang & Dou, 2009); consumers can learn about events, promotions, and gather general information about brands and companies, and communicate with businesses and other users. Further, research in the area of tourism suggests that social media has become important for information search as a large number of social media sites is returned when using search engines (Xiang & Gretzel, 2010). This particular motive, i.e. seeking information, is important for marketers, companies and consumers themselves because seeking information is a fundamental step in the consumer buying process (Howard & Sheth, 1969). Moreover, it has been found that the more time consumers spend searching for information on the internet, in addition to the increased frequency in which they engage in such search, the more likely purchase decisions will be influenced by the information gathered (Bhatnagar & Ghose, 2004). Given that social media in recent years has emerged as an immense, free, and easy-to-access information resource, both through posts by advertisers, consumers, government and companies, information search should play a significant role as a reason for using social media. Prior research has already found evidence for such a link (Kim et al., 2011), and here we further investigate gender differences within this context.

The literature on information search has already established gender differences that shed light on the processes underlining the search process for women and men. When considering internet searches for five product categories, namely software, music CDs, clothing apparel, recreational equipment, and travel arrangements, Bhatnagar and Ghose (2004) found that men search for longer than women, even though they do not differ in search frequency. Early research commented on men's higher levels of computer aptitude and women having greater computer anxiety (Nelson & Watson, 1990; Rosen & Maguire, 1990), and that men tend to perceive internet and email as more useful than women (Gefen & Straub, 1997). They also found that consumers search for longer when looking for apparel (Bhatnagar & Ghose, 2004). The finding that men search for longer and that longer searches occurred for clothing apparel may seem at odds with the fact that women enjoy shopping more than men (Kotzé, North, Stols & Venter, 2012), especially for clothing (Guiry, Mägi & Lutz, 2006).

As these findings were reported in times when social media and easy-to-use mobile platforms were not yet mainstream, and many did not even exist, it is possible that the finding that men spend more time searching online may no longer hold true. Indeed, women were already more geared than men towards using the internet for personal communication before online social media use was widespread (Weiser, 2000). Furthermore, by 2004 the number of American women using the internet equalled the number of men (Kim, Lehto & Morrison, 2007). More recent research (Seock & Bailey, 2008) has reported that in the case of apparel, female college students are more active online, searching for information and making purchases.

Another gender difference in search behaviour is the fact that, in addition to the differences in searching for apparel reported above, women tend to search online more in general. For example, in studying different types of customer automobile purchases, Furse, Punj and Stewart (1984) found that women tended to be part of the cluster that spent the most time searching. Other research on the purchase of Christmas gifts found that women systematically search more for both general and specific in-store information, besides starting the task much earlier than men and doing more shopping trips (Laroche, Saad, Cleveland & Browne, 2000). When it comes to information search for travel, Vogt and Fesenmaier (1998) found that women have more functional needs than men, where functional needs refer to motivated efforts directed at contributing to a purpose. More specifically, women scored higher overall in the group of needs that included items such as 'learn about prices', 'find bargains', 'locate information that is concise', and 'reduce the likelihood of being disappointed'. No differences were found for hedonic, innovation, aesthetic, and social needs. This later piece of research suggests that women may search more extensively for travel information because they have higher needs to be both efficient and effective in their decision making process than men (Vogt and Fesenmaier, 2001). Cognitively, women process information differently from men (Putrevu, 2001). While men process information more hemispherically, focusing on individual elements that may have the greatest personal impacts, women process information more symmetrically and in a more integrated way, in an attempt to uncover relationships among several elements (Putrevu, 2001). One factor that may fuel women's more extensive information search is risk avoidance, as women have consistently been found to take less risk than men in a number of contexts (Byrnes, Miller & Schafer, 1999).

Further, in one culturally specific example, Japanese women are more active mobile internet users than their male counterparts, which is consistent with the idea that women tend to engage more in deeper information processing by searching all available media and use a more diverse range of information sources (Okazaki & Hirose, 2009). Interestingly, this research seems to corroborate earlier discussions suggesting that the fact that technology has become more accessible to society as a whole, including through the emergence of mobile technology, may have helped change the previous dominance of men in the use of computers. In conclusion, the fact that women tend to search more in general would suggest that they may search more information than men in SNS as well. This is the primary question we investigate in this research.

Social Media Engagement

The concept of engagement has proliferated in the literature in recent years (e.g. Calder and Malthouse 2008; Gambetti & Graffigna, 2010; Kabadayi & Price, 2014; Verhoef, Reinartz & Krafft, 2010). However, this process has generated rather different definitions and understandings (Gambetti & Graffigna, 2010). Within this ongoing debate, some view engagement as a behavioural manifestation beyond transactions and stemming from motivational drivers (Van Doorn et al., 2010; Verhoef, Reinartz & Krafft, 2010). Others view engagement as a psychological experience. Agarwal and Karahanna (2000) discuss cognitive engagement online as a state of deep involvement with new information technologies. In the subject area of media, Calder and Malthouse (2008) see media engagement as a fundamental factor for advertising effectiveness. The authors differentiate it from *liking*, theorising that engagement is a separate element determining an experience. It is one element that has a motivational nature, as opposed to the hedonic nature that *liking* has.

Research discussing behavioural engagement with social media that has appeared in the academic literature includes liking and commenting behaviour on Facebook (Kabadayi & Price, 2014), and consumer purchases as a function of brand engagement in online communities (Khim-Yong, Cheng-Suang & Zhijie, 2013). According to current research, engagement is taken from the psychological experience standpoint. This contributes to other research looking at psychological factors in social media, such as consumer attitudes toward social media marketing (Akar & Topçu, 2011; Kim et al., 2011), and perceptions of advertisements in Facebook, Twitter and YouTube (Pikas & Sorrentino, 2014). The inherent involvement that social media creates in users of a new technology, largely driven by new mobile developments and that mobile devices and media content can be viewed anywhere in the world, is another factor that highlights the relevance of considering engagement at the psychological level, and not just the behavioural level.

It is expected that, to the extent that social media delivers people's information needs, people would feel engaged with it. Hence, using social media with the clear purpose to seek information would positively relate to engagement with social media. Related literature has found that in the purchase of 'big ticket items' women benefit more than men from online environments because online media reduces the inefficiencies in price paid because gender identity need not be disclosed (Zettelmeyer, Morton & Silva-Risso, 2006). In line with this finding, women's purchase behaviour is also more influenced by online consumer reviews than men's (Bae & Lee, 2011). If women benefit from purchasing online, do they search/use more social media sources than men to search for information? This is one question that our research investigates in the context of online social media, as well as whether this information search relates to user engagement.

EMPIRICAL INVESTIGATION

Methodology

The data were collected from a convenience sample of undergraduate business students of a major metropolitan university in Australia. Given its dominance as a social media platform, it was decided to focus the data collection on Facebook. The qualifying question was whether a participant had a Facebook profile. Students were briefed about the purpose of the research and were asked to complete a self-administered online questionnaire. An incentive to complete the questionnaire was a chance to win one of ten $50 gift cards for a department store.

The online questionnaire took approximately 15 minutes to complete. To assess reasons for using Facebook, a five-dimensional scale (Kim et al., 2011) was employed that composed of: seeking friends ($\alpha = 0.81$), seeking convenience ($\alpha = 0.90$), seeking social support ($\alpha = 0.87$), seeking information ($\alpha = 0.90$), and seeking entertainment ($\alpha = 0.82$). A sixth dimension researching people ($\alpha = 0.73$) was included, adapted from Lampe et al. (2008). Participants were asked how many times they actively logged-on to Facebook each day and user engagement was measured using an adapted cognitive absorption scale (Agarwal & Karahanna, 2000). More specifically, because the scale is very long and respondents were already filling out other long scales related to their motivations for using Facebook, only items TD2, TD3, TD5, FI2, CO1 and CU3 of the original cognitive absorption scale, as appears in Agarwal and Karahanna (2000), were used in the survey. These items were deemed the most relevant for the context of social media use; one item that seemed most adapted to Facebook use was selected from each dimension, with the exception of the heightened enjoyment dimension as our focus was on information search. Three items were selected from the temporal dissociation dimension because these items were more heterogeneous, whereas items in the other dimensions were very similar to each other. In addition, the items were accordingly modified from the context of Web use to Facebook use. The measured construct presented satisfactory reliability ($\alpha = 0.83$). A measure of shopping enjoyment was adapted from Donthu and Gilliland (1996) using their three-item attitude toward shopping dimension. The three items are 'Buying things makes me happy', 'Shopping is fun', and 'I get a real "high" from shopping'. An additional item was included, namely 'Shopping is exciting' ($\alpha = 0.93$). Recognising the importance of new technologies, a question was also included focusing on a consumer innovativeness scale ($\alpha = 0.91$, Goldsmith & Hofacker 1991), modelled towards technology and apps/gadgets. Demographics were collected at the end of the survey. The survey was piloted after which some questions were revised prior to launching online.

A total of 169 questionnaires were received, of which 161 were retained for the analyses after removing data for those who did not use Facebook (8 respondents). Of the respondents, 60 (37%) were male and 101 (63%) were female, and the average age was 19.97 years old. Females on average spent more time on Facebook at 2.22 hours per day compared to 2.01 hours for males.

Model

Social media users generate content as well as consume content created by other users and marketers. Prior findings related to social media indicate that consumers benefit from easy access to word-of-mouth information, therefore social media is playing an increasingly important role in the marketing mix. However, there is scant literature that highlights gender based differences in the use of social media and its impact on engagement on social media. In this study we model the role of gender on reasons to use Facebook and examine how motivation to use Facebook impacts the behaviour of consumers (see Figure 1).

Consumers may use Facebook for several reasons such as to seek friends (y_1), for convenience (y_2), to seek social support (y_3), to seek information (y_4), seek entertainment (y_5), and learn more about others, i.e. research people (y_6). These are the dependent variables and each of these reasons can be analysed as a linear regression equation. However, there may be contemporaneous cross-equation correlations as, for example, factors that influence use of Facebook to seek friends may also influence use of Facebook to seek social support. To control for contemporaneous cross-equation correlations, we estimate a system of equations using seemingly unrelated regressions (SUR). The SUR model is represented in Equation 1.

$$\begin{pmatrix} y_1 \\ \vdots \\ y_6 \end{pmatrix} = \left(\begin{bmatrix} \beta_1' X_1 & \cdots & 0 \\ \vdots & \ddots & \vdots \\ 0 & \cdots & \beta_6' X_6 \end{bmatrix} \right) + \begin{bmatrix} \varepsilon_1 \\ \vdots \\ \varepsilon_6 \end{bmatrix} \quad (1)$$

The error variance matrix is dimension J x J and $\varepsilon_j \sim N(0,\Sigma)$, and Σ is the variance-covariance matrix. The dependent variable $y=(y_{1\ldots}\ y_6)'$ is a vector of the various reasons to use Facebook. The matrix X consists of the exogenous variables, such as gender, that are expected to influence the use of Facebook and $\beta=(\beta_{1\ldots}\ \beta_6)'$ represents the vector of coefficients that capture the impact of the exogenous variables. The exogenous variables are gender, consumer innovativeness, age, household size and shopping enjoyment. Innovativeness and shopping enjoyment are Likert scale measures, whereas gender is a dummy variable. Gender equals 1 for males and 0 for females. The estimation results are presented in Table 1 below.

Figure 1. Gender based differences on using Facebook and engagement

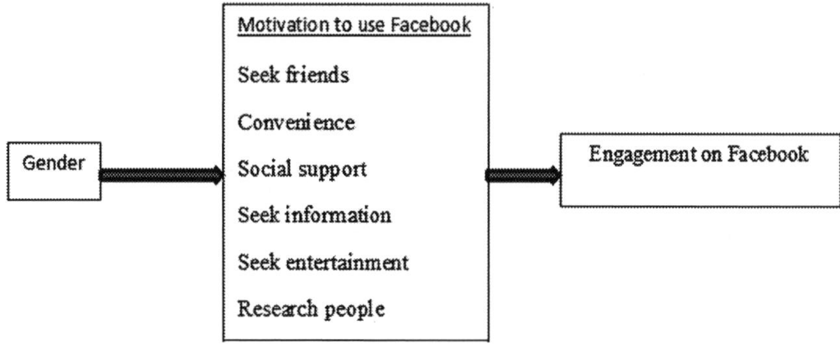

Table 1. Reasons for using Facebook

.	Equation	Obs	Parms	RMSE	R-sq	chi^2	P
.	Seek friends	161	5	5.484397	0.0681	11.76	0.0382
.	Convenience	161	5	4.331558	0.1677	32.45	0
.	Social support	161	5	5.675147	0.0308	5.12	0.4016
	Seek information	161	5	6.718109	0.1730	33.67	0
	Seek entertainment	161	5	4.622088	0.1502	28.46	0
	Research people	161	5	5.279683	0.0797	13.94	0.0160
		Coef.	**std.**	**z**	**P>|z|**	**[95% Conf. Interval]**	
DV	**Seek friends**						
	Gender	0.70	1.00	0.70	0.48	-1.26	2.67
	Innovativeness	**0.15**	0.06	2.66	0.01	0.04	0.26
	Shopping enjoyment	0.06	0.34	0.16	0.87	-0.62	0.73
	Age	-0.10	0.16	-0.62	0.54	-0.40	0.21
	Household size	0.30	0.28	1.07	0.29	-0.25	0.85
	Intercept	10.57	3.90	2.71	0.01	2.92	18.22
DV	**Convenience**						
	Gender	**-1.82**	0.79	-2.30	0.02	-3.37	-0.27
	Innovativeness	0.06	0.04	1.43	0.15	-0.02	0.15
	Shopping enjoyment	**0.87**	0.27	3.21	0.00	0.34	1.41
	Age	**-0.20**	0.12	-1.58	0.11	-0.44	0.05
	Household size	0.24	0.22	1.06	0.29	-0.20	0.67
	Intercept	20.43	3.08	6.63	0.00	14.39	26.48
DV	**Social support**						
	Gender	0.66	1.04	0.64	0.52	-1.37	2.69
	Innovativeness	0.07	0.06	1.15	0.25	-0.05	0.18
	Shopping enjoyment	0.40	0.36	1.11	0.27	-0.30	1.09
	Age	0.08	0.16	0.50	0.62	-0.24	0.40
	Household size	0.26	0.29	0.89	0.37	-0.31	0.83
	Intercept	3.72	4.04	0.92	0.36	-4.20	11.64
DV	**Seek information**						
	Gender	**-2.76**	1.23	-2.24	0.03	-5.16	-0.35
	Innovativeness	**0.32**	0.07	4.72	0.00	0.19	0.46
	Shopping enjoyment	0.43	0.42	1.02	0.31	-0.40	1.25
	Age	0.01	0.19	0.06	0.95	-0.37	0.39
	Household size	0.40	0.34	1.16	0.25	-0.28	1.07
	Intercept	8.41	4.78	1.76	0.08	-0.96	17.79
DV	**Seek entertainment**						
	Gender	-0.27	0.84	-0.32	0.75	-1.92	1.39
	Innovativeness	0.04	0.05	0.91	0.36	-0.05	0.14
	Shopping enjoyment	**1.25**	0.29	4.32	0.00	0.69	1.82
	Age	-0.04	0.13	-0.27	0.79	-0.30	0.22
	Household size	0.30	0.24	1.28	0.20	-0.16	0.77
	Intercept	12.24	3.29	3.72	0.00	5.79	18.69

RESULTS

The results indicate that males are less likely to use Facebook for convenience or to seek information (Table 1). Among other factors that influence the use of Facebook, we find that more innovative consumers use Facebook to seek friends, to seek information, and to research people, while consumers who enjoy shopping are more likely to use Facebook for convenience, to seek entertainment, and to research people. The results indicate that age is not a significant predictor of Facebook use. The coefficient of age is negative and significant for convenience. This result is consistent with prior findings that older people are less likely to use the Internet. In addition, our results indicate that household size is not a significant predictor of Facebook use.

Further, we investigate the impact of various reasons of using Facebook on consumer engagement as measured by the extent to which consumers immerse themselves or get involved on Facebook. The results of linear regression analysis of consumer engagement are indicated in Table 2.

As can be seen from Table 2, consumer motivation to use Facebook significantly impacts the extent to which consumers are engaged on Facebook. Those who use Facebook for convenience, social support, to seek information, and to seek entertainment are likely to use Facebook more than people who use Facebook for other purposes. While prior research finds that social media platforms are a useful source

Table 2. Consumer engagement on Facebook

Number of obs = 161							
Source	SS	df	MS				
Model	3801.63	8	475.21				
Residual	4546.93	152	29.91				
Total	8348.56	160	52.18				
Prob > F = 0.0000							
R-squared = 0.46							
Adj R-squared = 0.43							
Root MSE = 5.47							
F(8, 152) = 15.89							
		Coef.	**Std. Err.**	**t**	**P>|t|**	**[95% Conf. Interval]**	
DV	**Engagement**						
	Seek friends	-0.07	0.09	-0.74	0.46	-0.26	0.12
	Convenience	**0.45**	0.12	3.60	0.00	0.20	0.69
	Social support	**0.28**	0.09	3.25	0.00	0.11	0.45
	Seek information	**0.17**	0.07	2.46	0.02	0.03	0.31
	Seek entertainment	**0.49**	0.11	4.48	0.00	0.27	0.71
	Research people	-0.07	0.10	-0.73	0.47	-0.26	0.12
	Gender	-1.13	0.95	-1.20	0.23	-3.01	0.74
	Log-in frequency	0.46	0.58	0.80	0.43	-0.68	1.60
	Intercept	3.56	2.94	1.21	0.23	-2.25	9.37

to obtain word-of-mouth and to build a network of friends, our study highlights information seeking behaviour as a core driver for using Facebook.

Finally, the results of this study highlight that female consumers are more likely than male consumers to use Facebook for convenience and to seek information. The information seeking behaviour relates positively to the degree of engagement on Facebook. This is an interesting finding from the perspective that prior research has shown that females benefit from using online resources when making big ticket purchases as they are able to bargain without disclosing their gender (Zettelmeyer et al., 2006). Our results highlight that females are more likely to use online resources such as social media for purposes other than social engagement, i.e. to find information. This has important implications for retailers that use social media advertising to target consumers with relevant product related information.

IMPLICATIONS

The results indicating that women are more likely to use Facebook than men for convenience or to seek information suggest a number of implications. While women are more likely to search online for information than men in general, as discussed in the background section of this chapter, women are also interested in efficient and effective searching processes. Given the abundance of options regarding where to get information, ease-of-use is no longer an additional benefit but rather an imperative strategy for any business that desires to engage with and target their communications to their potential female customers. Effort should be made by businesses to clearly state their offerings and provide relevant information to attract the interest of prospective online consumers. Another insight from our research is that getting the attention of consumers amid the clutter of the online environment is very difficult, especially as the amount of online material has grown exponentially over the years. The fact that our study shows that women are more likely to research on SNS, such as Facebook, further suggests that social media is currently a key place not only to send information out but also to engage with consumers, especially women. Therefore, businesses are encouraged to build an online social media presence as part of their marketing communications strategy.

Relating to brands, women are more likely than men to share brand-related material based on things seen in social media ads (Burst Media, 2013), and are more likely than men to interact with brands in social media, to show support for brands they like, and access special offers, coupons, and/or promotions (Burst Media, 2013). This indicates an important role that women play in generating word-of-mouth, both positive and negative, which can be a form of product information that can be searched for by other women. While corroborating previous findings that women seek more functional benefits from their searches (Vogt & Fesenmaier, 1998), this also highlights the importance of the emotional aspect of the relationship of women with brands, which can be boosted through appropriate use of social media and electronic word-of-mouth.

The relationship between seeking information and convenience in social media and cognitive engagement also exemplifies how a sense of purpose, coupled with achieving this purpose, leads to higher involvement with media. The importance of cognitive engagement for marketers cannot be underestimated, notably its potential to result in higher information retention and use, higher satisfaction, and higher willingness to make recommendations to friends, all of which in turn lead to more interaction with the business and ultimately to increased purchases.

FUTURE RESEARCH DIRECTIONS

The fact that women are more inclined to use online environments for convenience than men, coupled with the fact that technology has changed from being inaccessible to a large number of people to being very accessible to all, suggests a world where women may have taken the lead when it comes to use of technological innovation, at least in relation to the search for related information and potentially online shopping. Take, for example, the numerous cases of new software for virtually trying products that have been reported in the news (Felsted, 2014). L'Oreal has created an app called Makeup Genius that allows users to see what the makeup looks like on their own face as they move by using the virtual mirror in their iPhones or iPads. While the marketing for the release of the app featured a man, notably L'Oreal's CEO, with the objective of creating a fun atmosphere around the product, the app is targeted at women, as are the majority of L'Oreal's cosmetic products. Another innovation has been implemented by the Japanese clothing company Uniqlo. They have installed a magic mirror in one store which allows shoppers to see the clothes they are trying on in different colours.

Given the rapid innovation in the use of social media, it would be fruitful to see future research which revisits previous gender gaps in terms of technology adoption (Jackson, Ervin, Gardner & Schmitt, 2001), especially when considering different domains. It is important to keep different contexts in mind because, for example, in contrast to shopping, it seems that products such as gaming consoles may remain appealing to men rather than women (Lenhart, Purcell, Smith & Zickuhr, 2010).

Other gender differences that deserve further research are those related to the use of different social media platforms. Considering American online adults, while a higher percentage of men use LinkedIn and Reddit than women, more women than men are users of Facebook, Instagram, and Pinterest (Burst Media, 2013; Duggan, 2013; Duggan & Smith, 2013). For Pinterest, women's usage is far in excess of men's usage (33% of women, 8% of men). These figures can be better interpreted when the reasons for using these networks are uncovered. Considering that Facebook is used more for social reasons and Twitter more for information (Hughes, Rowe, Batey & Lee, 2012), it would be interesting to explore if the gender differences found here for Facebook are present in Twitter as well. More research integrating these findings with consequences of social media use would be highly valuable for businesses, such as discovering the use of information gathered in social media, product/service choice, social media advertising effectiveness, and the potential psychological effects of social media use (e.g. anxiety).

Our research explored one facet of how women differ from men in their use of social media. Looking at motivations to use Facebook, the study here documented measured general reasons for using the social network, for example, to learn about new things. Given the nature of most of the conversations that permeate Facebook, it is fair to believe that a lot of the information learned relates to hedonic products and experiences such as movies, restaurants, clothing and travel. In turn, hedonic products also tend to be engaging and this may be a factor contributing to higher cognitive absorption. That is, consumers simply have fun while discussing such topics and this type of information exchange may be a determinant of engagement in social networks. Future research could further explore if information sought in social networks relates more to hedonic as opposed to utilitarian products and services, and, if so, whether women would be more likely to engage with social media than men for information gathering in certain product categories.

Finally, further research crossing potential cultural differences with our findings may render interesting findings. Kim et al. (2011) have studied motivations to use Facebook in America compared with Korea. It is possible that gender interacts with such findings, which would be of value to the international marketer.

CONCLUSION

The objectives of this study were to determine what motivates people to use SNS, discover the relationships between motives and engagement in social media, and ascertain any gender differences in the use of social media. Our research identifies the use of social media to seek information as an important factor leading to social media engagement, as well as seeking entertainment, social support, and convenience. A managerial implication of this finding is that advertising can be designed to better fit with these motivations in order to be more effective. For example, brands that create entertaining content on social media, and/or increase convenience for users (e.g. offer easy to use coupons via mobile technology to use when making a payment at a store), are likely to obtain higher user engagement and support.

While there are limitations to this study, including that the sample was of undergraduate business students, and that the findings are limited by the correlational nature of our cross-sectional data (hence causality cannot be claimed), we believe that the empirical support it provides for our conceptual model is substantive and aligns with previous literature. Therefore, more research is encouraged on gender differences in information search and buying behaviour related to online media. By having a better understanding of how differently men and women are interacting and affected by social media, marketers can better target them with the information they require in the form they want, to provide a clearer pathway to engagement, and ultimately purchases.

REFERENCES

Agarwal, R., & Karahanna, E. (2000). Time flies when you're having fun: Cognitive absorption and beliefs about information technology usage. *Management Information Systems Quarterly*, *24*(4), 665–694. doi:10.2307/3250951

Akar, E., & Topçu, B. (2011). An examination of the factors influencing consumers' attitudes toward social media marketing. *Journal of Internet Commerce*, *10*(1), 35–67. doi:10.1080/15332861.2011.558456

Bae, S., & Lee, T. (2011). Gender differences in consumers' perception of online consumer reviews. *Electronic Commerce Research*, *11*(2), 201–214. doi:10.1007/s10660-010-9072-y

Barker, V. (2009). Older adolescents' motivations for social network site use: The influence of gender, group identity, and collective self-esteem. *Cyberpsychology & Behavior: The Impact of the Internet, Multimedia and Virtual Reality On Behavior. Society*, *12*(2), 209–213.

Bhatnagar, A., & Ghose, S. (2004). Online information search termination patterns across product categories and consumer demographics. *Journal of Retailing*, *80*(3), 221–228. doi:10.1016/j.jretai.2003.10.001

Boyd, D. M., & Ellison, N. B. (2007). Social network sites: Definition, history, and scholarship. *Journal of Computer-Mediated Communication*, *13*(1), 210–230. doi:10.1111/j.1083-6101.2007.00393.x

Byrnes, J. P., Miller, D. C., & Schafer, W. D. (1999). Gender differences in risk taking: A meta-analysis. *Psychological Bulletin*, *125*(3), 367–383. doi:10.1037/0033-2909.125.3.367

Calder, B. J., & Malthouse, E. C. (2008). Media engagement and advertising effectiveness. In B. J. Calder (Ed.), *Kellogg on advertising and media* (pp. 1–36). Hoboken, NJ: Wiley.

Chi, H.-H. (2011). Interactive digital advertising vs. Virtual brand community: Exploratory study of user motivation and social media marketing responses in Taiwan. *Journal of Interactive Advertising*, *12*(1), 44–61. doi:10.1080/15252019.2011.10722190

Correa, T., Hinsley, A. W., & De Zuniga, H. G. (2010). Who interacts on the web?: The intersection of users' personality and social media use. *Computers in Human Behavior*, *26*(2), 247–253. doi:10.1016/j.chb.2009.09.003

Curran, K., Graham, S., & Temple, C. (2011). Advertising on Facebook. *International Journal of E-Business Development*, *1*(1), 26–33.

Deloitte. (2014). Media consumer survey. *Australian Media and Digital Preferences* (3rd ed.).

Donthu, N., & Gilliland, D. (1996). Observations: The infomercial shopper. *Journal of Advertising Research*, *36*(2), 69–77.

Duggan, M. (2013). It's a woman's (social media) world. Retrieved from www.pewresearch.org/fact-tank/2013/09/12/its-a-womans-social-media-world/

Duggan, M., & Smith, A. (2013). Social media update 2013: PEW Research Center's Internet & American Life Project. Retrieved from www.pewinternet.org/2013/12/30/social-media-update-2013/

Felsted, A. (2014, November 12). Apps bring web shopping to life, *Financial Times*.

Furse, D. H., Punj, G. N., & Stewart, D. W. (1984). A typology of individual search strategies among purchasers of new automobiles. *The Journal of Consumer Research*, *10*(4), 417–431. doi:10.1086/208980

Gambetti, R. C., & Graffigna, G. (2010). The concept of engagement a systematic analysis of the ongoing marketing debate. *International Journal of Market Research*, *52*(6), 801–826. doi:10.2501/S147078531020166

Gefen, D., & Straub, D. W. (1997). Gender differences in the perception and use of e-mail: An extension to the technology acceptance model. *Management Information Systems Quarterly*, *21*(4), 389–400. doi:10.2307/249720

Goldsmith, R. E., & Hofacker, C. F. (1991). Measuring consumer innovativeness. *Journal of the Academy of Marketing Science*, *19*(3), 209–221. doi:10.1007/BF02726497

Guiry, M., Mägi, A. W., & Lutz, R. J. (2006). Defining and measuring recreational shopper identity. *Journal of the Academy of Marketing Science*, *34*(1), 74–83. doi:10.1177/0092070305282042

Howard, J. A., & Sheth, J. N. (1969). *The Theory of Buyer Behavior*. New York: John Wiley & Sons.

Hughes, D. J., Rowe, M., Batey, M., & Lee, A. (2012). A tale of two sites: Twitter vs. Facebook and the personality predictors of social media usage. *Computers in Human Behavior*, *28*(2), 561–569. doi:10.1016/j.chb.2011.11.001

Jackson, L. A., Ervin, K. S., Gardner, P. D., & Schmitt, N. (2001). Gender and the internet: Women communicating and men searching. *Sex Roles*, *44*(5-6), 363–379. doi:10.1023/A:1010937901821

Kabadayi, S., & Price, K. (2014). Consumer–brand engagement on Facebook: Liking and commenting behaviors. *Journal of Research in Interactive Marketing*, *8*(3), 203–223. doi:10.1108/JRIM-12-2013-0081

Kaplan, A. M., & Haenlein, M. (2010). Users of the world, unite! The challenges and opportunities of social media. *Business Horizons*, *53*(1), 59–68. doi:10.1016/j.bushor.2009.09.003

Katz, E., Blumler, J. G., & Gurevitch, M. (1974). Utilization of mass communication by the individual. In J. G. Blumler & E. Katz (Eds.), *The uses of mass communications: Current perspectives on gratifications research* (Vol. III, pp. 19–32). Beverly Hills, CA: Sage.

Katz, E., Haas, H., & Gurevitch, M. (1973). On the use of the mass media for important things. *American Sociological Review*, *38*(2), 164–181. doi:10.2307/2094393

Khim-Yong, G., Cheng-Suang, H., & Zhijie, L. (2013). Social media brand community and consumer behavior: Quantifying the relative impact of user- and marketer-generated content. *Information Systems Research*, *24*(1), 88–107. doi:10.1287/isre.1120.0469

Kim, D.-Y., Lehto, X. Y., & Morrison, A. M. (2007). Gender differences in online travel information search: Implications for marketing communications on the internet. *Tourism Management*, *28*(2), 423–433. doi:10.1016/j.tourman.2006.04.001

Kim, Y., Sohn, D., & Choi, S. M. (2011). Cultural difference in motivations for using social network sites: A comparative study of American and Korean college students. *Computers in Human Behavior*, *27*(1), 365–372. doi:10.1016/j.chb.2010.08.015

Kotzé, T., North, E., Stols, M., & Venter, L. (2012). Gender differences in sources of shopping enjoyment. *International Journal of Consumer Studies*, *36*(4), 416–424. doi:10.1111/j.1470-6431.2011.01060.x

Lampe, C., Ellison, N. B., & Steinfield, C. (2008). Changes in use and perception of Facebook. *Paper presented at the 2008 ACM conference on Computer supported cooperative work*, San Diego, CA, USA. doi:10.1145/1460563.1460675

Laroche, M., Saad, G., Cleveland, M., & Browne, E. (2000). Gender differences in information search strategies for a Christmas gift. *Journal of Consumer Marketing*, *17*(6), 500–522. doi:10.1108/07363760010349920

Lenhart, A., Purcell, K., Smith, A., & Zickuhr, K. (2010). Social media & mobile internet use among teens and young adults. *PEW Research Center's Internet & American Life Project*.

Lukka, V., & James, P. T. J. (2014). Attitudes toward Facebook advertising. *Journal of Management and Marketing Research*, *14*, 1–26.

Mangold, W. G., & Faulds, D. J. (2009). Social media: The new hybrid element of the promotion mix. *Business Horizons*, *52*(4), 357–365. doi:10.1016/j.bushor.2009.03.002

Muscanell, N. L., & Guadagno, R. E. (2012). Make new friends or keep the old: Gender and personality differences in social networking use. *Computers in Human Behavior*, *28*(1), 107–112. doi:10.1016/j.chb.2011.08.016

Nelson, C. S., & Watson, J. A. (1990). The computer gender gap: Children's attitudes, performance and socialization. *Journal of Educational Technology Systems, 19*(4), 345–353. doi:10.2190/51CF-7CHE-DX52-E9F5

Okazaki, S., & Hirose, M. (2009). Does gender affect media choice in travel information search? On the use of mobile internet. *Tourism Management, 30*(6), 794–804. doi:10.1016/j.tourman.2008.12.012

Online insights: Expanding the conversation - leveraging social media for brand interaction. (2013). *Burst Media.* Retrieved from www.burstmedia.com/pdf/burst_media_online_insights_2013_04.pdf

Pai, P., & Arnott, D. C. (2013). User adoption of social networking sites: Eliciting uses and gratifications through a means–end approach. *Computers in Human Behavior, 29*(3), 1039–1053. doi:10.1016/j.chb.2012.06.025

Pfeil, U., Arjan, R., & Zaphiris, P. (2009). Age differences in online social networking – a study of user profiles and the social capital divide among teenagers and older users in Myspace. *Computers in Human Behavior, 25*(3), 643–654. doi:10.1016/j.chb.2008.08.015

Pikas, B., & Sorrentino, G. (2014). The effectiveness of online advertising: Consumer's perceptions of ads on Facebook, Twitter and YouTube. *Journal of Applied Business and Economics, 16*(4), 70–81.

Putrevu, S. (2001). Exploring the origins and information processing differences between men and women: Implications for advertisers. *Academy of Marketing Science Review, 10*(1), 1–14.

Rosen, L. D., & Maguire, P. (1990). Myths and realities of computerphobia: A meta-analysis. *Anxiety Research, 3*(3), 175–191. doi:10.1080/08917779008248751

Seock, Y. K., & Bailey, L. R. (2008). The influence of college students' shopping orientations and gender differences on online information searches and purchase behaviours. *International Journal of Consumer Studies, 32*(2), 113–121. doi:10.1111/j.1470-6431.2007.00647.x

Statista. (2014). *Number of monthly active Facebook users worldwide from 3rd quarter 2008 to 3rd quarter 2014 (in millions).* Retrieved 24 November 2014, from http://www.statista.com/statistics/264810/number-of-monthly-active-facebook-users-worldwide/

Van Doorn, J., Lemon, K. N., Mittal, V., Nass, S., Pick, D., Pirner, P., & Verhoef, P. C. (2010). Customer engagement behavior: Theoretical foundations and research directions. *Journal of Service Research, 13*(3), 253–266. doi:10.1177/1094670510375599

Verhoef, P. C., Reinartz, W. J., & Krafft, M. (2010). Customer engagement as a new perspective in customer management. *Journal of Service Research, 13*(3), 247–252. doi:10.1177/1094670510375461

Vogt, C. A., & Fesenmaier, D. R. (1998). Expanding the functional information search model. *Annals of Tourism Research, 25*(3), 551–578. doi:10.1016/S0160-7383(98)00010-3

Weiser, E. B. (2000). Gender differences in internet use patterns and internet application preferences: A two-sample comparison. *Cyberpsychology & Behavior, 3*(2), 167–178. doi:10.1089/109493100316012

Xiang, Z., & Gretzel, U. (2010). Role of social media in online travel information search. *Tourism Management, 31*(2), 179–188. doi:10.1016/j.tourman.2009.02.016

Zeng, F., Huang, L., & Dou, W. (2009). Social factors in user perceptions and responses to advertising in online social networking communities. *Journal of Interactive Advertising, 10*(1), 1–13. doi:10.1080/15252019.2009.10722159

Zettelmeyer, F., Morton, F. S., & Silva-Risso, J. (2006). How the internet lowers prices: Evidence from matched survey and automobile transaction data. *JMR, Journal of Marketing Research, 43*(2), 168–181. doi:10.1509/jmkr.43.2.168

KEY TERMS AND DEFINITIONS

Cognitive Absorption: A state of deep involvement with an activity to the point of losing track of time.

Convenience: To obtain things with little effort and without significant constraints.

Information Search: To seek any kind of information, this includes information about products and brands, and also finding out about anything that is new.

Motivation: Reasons that lead people to perform (or prevent people from performing) some act.

Social Media: Any online platform that facilitates communication among individuals and between individuals and organisations. This includes social networking sites, online brand and product communities, blogs, consumer forums, consumer advice websites (e.g. TripAdvisor), news sites reader comments sections, etc.

Social Networking Site (SNS): Any online platform that has as the main objective to facilitate regular communication among individuals. This includes social networking sites such as Facebook, Twitter, Instagram, LinkedIn, Vine, etc.

SUR Model: Seemingly unrelated regression model. It is a system of linear regression equations. The error terms of the equations are assumed to be correlated across the equations.

User Engagement: To commit cognitively to online activities within a social networking site, e.g. Facebook.

This research was previously published in Gender Considerations in Online Consumption Behavior and Internet Use edited by Rebecca English and Raechel Johns, pages 32-49, copyright year 2016 by Information Science Reference (an imprint of IGI Global).

Chapter 35
Purchase Intention of Males and Females Through Social Media

Chih-Chin Liang
National Farmosa University, Taiwan

ABSTRACT

Social media use pervades daily life, leading to a dramatic transformation in communication styles. Three factors affecting purchase intentions through SM modified from technology acceptance model include experience (experience on purchasing through social media, perceived usefulness on purchasing through social media, perceived ease of use on purchasing through social media), company (corporate credibility, product/service information), and social (social influence on purchasing through social media, electronic word of mouth on purchasing through social media). Three hundred and thirty-two respondents (male: 171, female: 161) from Taiwan were surveyed using a structure questionnaire. Analysis results indicate that significantly influence shopping intention with respect to social media. Additionally, males and females differ in purchasing intention. Social influence affects purchase intention for females, but not for males. Product/service information affects social influence for females, but not for males.

1. INTRODUCTION

Social media has emerged in the 21th century (Mangold and Faulds, 2009). From a business perspective, social media refers to various sources of online information that are created, initiated and used by consumers who are intent on influencing each other with respect to the purchase of products and services (Blackshaw, 1989; Pookulangara and Koesler, 2011). For marketing purposes, merchandisers must segment a market into different niches, allowing a company to promote goods to a target niche. Of these niches, genders are always targeted, owing to their different purchase intentions (Aspara and Van Den Bergh, 2014; Avery, 2012; Brangule-Vlagsma et al., 2002).

Social media use is intended mainly for personal communication. Social influence plays an important role in social media use. If information on social media is useful (commonly referred to as perceived usefulness) and helpful in customer decisions (commonly referred to as perceived ease of use), customers do not have to visit company websites to acquire information on a specific product or service. Instead,

DOI: 10.4018/978-1-5225-5637-4.ch035

users can log onto social media and find valuable comments and product information from companies and friends. Electronic word of mouth thus plays a pivotal role in customers selecting products and services. With social media, marketing communication becomes a two-way communication, rather than one-way communication used in traditional marketing (Eley and Tilley, 2009). Social media allows companies to share information and interact with customers via the Internet. As online shopping companies must provide customers with easy access and useful functions (Huang and Benyoucef, 2013; Hennig-Thrau et al., 2011; Pookulangara and Koesler, 2011), social media represents the most important marketing platform for companies to promote their products and services. The company must provide sufficient social media-related information to help customer purchases (Liang and Huang, 1998), making it easier for them to understand customer needs. Business companies have created Twitter accounts, set up Facebook fan pages, or posted YouTube videos to deliver product/ service information (Weinberg and Pehlivan, 2011), which represents the major promotion method that companies offer through social media. Obviously, company creditability is widely used in product/service information, too (Davis, 1989; Weinberg and Pehlivan, 2011). In sum, social media has provided organizations with innovative ways of satisfying customer demand and influencing consumer behavior, including purchasing behavior (Hsieh and Chu, 2009; Swaminathan et al., 1999).

Despite the aspirations of companies to promote products on social media, to our knowledge, exactly how the above factors affect the purchase intention of customers with different genders on social media has not been addressed (Bashar et al., 2012; Das, 2014; Ehrlichman and Eichenstein, 1992; Lee et al., 2013; Okazaki, 2007). The purchase intention of males and females on social media must also be understood to elucidate the human behaviors of both gender groups.

This study attempts to identify the purchase intention of males and females on social media by administering a questionnaire survey on their purchasing experiences. A pretest verified the questionnaire reliability and validity. Purchasing experiences of respondents through social media were also surveyed based on an author-verified questionnaire. The rest of this paper is organized as follows. Section 2 reviews relevant literature. Section 3 then details the research methodology and the proposed questionnaire. Next, Section 4 summarizes the analytical results. Section 5 illustrates individual marketing strategies for males and females. Conclusions are finally drawn in Section 5, along with recommendations for future research.

2. RELATED WORKS

2.1. Social Media Experience

As is well known, individuals have a more positive attitude towards a particular stimulus when they are more familiar with it (Carpeneter et al., 2011; Zajonc, 1968). Restated, greater familiarity that consumers have with an online medium owing to their frequent use implies a higher receptiveness towards that medium (Belanche et al., 2012). Restated, a more positive social media experience implies greater perceived ease of use on social media. We thus posit the following:

H1: Social media experience improves perceived ease of use on social media.

Based on the above Inference, increasing Internet usage increases the likelihood of online purchases (Aldridge et al., 1997; Liang and Huang, 1998). According to Camilla study (2010) users who understand what is required to use social media have positive social media experiences. Positive social media experiences lead to more favorable behavioral outcomes. From the above discussion, we can infer that overall social media experience and online shopping intentions of customers are closely related. The following question items are subsequently created (see Appendix).

2.2. Electronic Word of Mouth

Social media gathers individual comments on all topics in a platform format. People comment on products/services and distribute that information through a social media platform. Word of mouth (Choi and Kim, 2014; Khare et al., 2011; Sen and Lerman, 2007) refers to conversations between customers about different products or serices (Dellarocas, 2003). Word of mouth is given new meaning with the emergence of the Internet. Correspondingly, social media is an important communication venue that transmits word-of-mouth through online media. Customers often refer to online comments before their purchase (Sen and Lerman, 2007; Söderlund and Rosengren, 2007). As is consumer-generated information, electronic word of mouth describes a product or experience from a consumer perspective. Electronic word of mouth also refers to a consumer's feelings and satisfaction with a product, thus providing a valuable reference for other consumers to compare with marketer-generated information (Chen and Xie, 2008). Therefore, positive electronic word of mouth can increase the purchase intention of customers. The Appendix lists the questionnaire items.

2.3. Social Influence

As the main reason for consumers to use a social media platform, familiar individuals could be the reference group that one may inquire for assistance. Social influence allows individuals through engagement to obtain information from the reference group as evidence of purchase. A reference group refers to individuals whose values and attitudes that other individuals use as the basis for their purchasing behavior (Dholakia et al., 2004; Pookulangara and Koesler, 2011; Schiffman and Kanuk, 2007). A reference group may be parents, co-workers, teachers, and peers who can provide answers to consumers regarding questions (Bristol and Mangleburg, 2005). Communicating with a reference group can inform consumers, make them aware of specific product brands, and allow them to compare their own thinking with the attitudes and behaviors of a group (Brocato et al., 2012). We thus hypothesize the following:

H2: Social media experience enhances social influence.

Additionally, according to Lee et al. (2011), positive social influences strengthen online shopping intentions. Kim and Srivastave (2007) also found that social influence significantly affects consumer behavior and directly influences their ease of use on social media. We thus posit the following:

H3: Social influence improves perceived ease of use on social media.

Finally, among electronic word of mouths, comments from familiar individuals sound more trustworthy than from strangers. Namely, social influence improves electronic word of mouth. We thus hypothesize the following:

H4: Social influence improves electronic word of mouth.

In sum, the following question items are subsequently generated (see Appendix).

2.4. Perceived Usefulness and Perceived Ease of Use

Perceived usefulness and perceived ease of use affect customer intentions to use a new technology such as social media (Davis et al., 2014). Perceived usefulness refers to the extent to which individuals believes that using a particular information system enhances their job performance. In this context, 'performance' refers to the merits of purchasing a product through social media minus the tradeoff of retailing from physical stores. Different potential social media shoppers may present favorable or unfavorable responses towards engaging in online purchasing because their behavioral intention depends on their cognitive choice (Ramayah and Ignatius, 2005). Shoppers who feel that shopping references from social media are useful may considering adapting social media. We thus hypothesize the following:

H5: Social influence improves perceived usefulness.

Meanwhile, perceived ease of use reflects the extent to which an individual believes that using a particular system is free of actual and mental efforts (Davis et al., 2014). In another definition, perceived ease of use involves the "user-friendliness" of a website (Ramayah and Ignatius, 2005); in this case, the website represents a social media platform. Customers who recognize that the advantages of purchasing through social media outweigh its complexity may prefer social media channels.

Both perceived usefulness and perceived ease of use directly and positively affect consumer intentions to use e-commerce. Lin and Lu (2011) attempted to explain why individuals use SNSs. Apparently, perceived usefulness and perceived ease of use influence social media usage among other factors. That study also demonstrated that two constructs have a direct and positive relationship with an individual's intention to use a social network service. The following question items are subsequently created (see Appendix).

2.5. Product/Service Information

Product/service information refers to herein as features of products/services that a company posted on social media websites to facilitate transactions (Shim et al., 2001). Product information profoundly impacts digital marketing. Customers often locate product information with the emergence of social media strategies (Facebook, YouTube, etc.). Restated, product information on social media plays a prominent role in raising purchase intentions Product/service information is the main promotional strategy of many companies. Product/service information may affect comments from a reference group and further affect customer purchases. We thus hypothesize the following:

H6: Product/service information enhances social influence.

Product/service information significantly influences online consumer behaviors through social media. Shim *et al.* (2001) indicated that the intention to use social media for product information searching may increase the intention to use the Internet for online purchasing. We thus posit the following. The question items are designed based on references (see Appendix):

H7: Product/service information improves social media experiences.

2.6. Corporate Credibility

Corporate credibility refers to the perceptions of customers towards the trustworthiness, expertness and attractiveness of a company (Ronald et al., 2000). Restated, corporate credibility describes how customers evaluate the honesty and expertise of a company. Organizational credibility is viewed as essential for marketing success. While a lack of credibility leads customers to doubt the company, the disadvantage is that customers are less likely to buy its products.

Previous studies have demonstrated that corporate credibility significantly impacts the purchase intentions of consumers (Lafferty et al., 2002). A positive perception of consumers towards a company helps to form their positive purchase intention. Previous studies also indicate that corporate credibility influences product/service information because consumer perceptions of the trustworthiness and expertise of a company help them to evaluate product/service quality. We thus posit the following. The Appendix lists the question items:

H8: Corporate credibility enhances product/service information.

2.7. Purchase Intention

The online purchase environment is considered as a collection of different purchase orientations, which refer to a general predisposition of potential e-shoppers towards the act of shopping (Rohm and Swaminathan, 2004). With the emergence of online shopping activities, customers' online shopping behavior may be different due to their shopping orientations. Chanaka et al. (Chanaka et al., 2007) state that because individual consumers have different dispositions towards purchases, consumers' purchase orientations may affect both their purchase behavior and purchase intention in online shopping. This is similar to the findings of Swaminathan and colleagues (Ling et al., 2011; Swaminathan et al., 1999) who find that shopping orientations are one of important indicators of making online purchase. In their study, the effect of shopping orientations toward customers' online purchase intention is thoroughly evaluated by empirical approach. A total of 248 participants in Malaysia take part in their study. They find that purchase orientation is an important factor influencing online purchase intention and a positive relationship is found between them. The question items are designed based on literature review (see Appendix). Additionally, all factors should be related to purchase intention, therefore this study has the following hypotheses:

H9.1: Social media experience affects customer purchase intention.
H9.2: Electronic word of mouth affects customer purchase intention.
H9.3: Social influence affects customer purchase intention.
H9.4: Perceived ease of use affects customer purchase intention.
H9.5: Perceived usefulness affects customer purchase intention.
H9.6: Product/service information affects customer purchase intention.

H9.7: Corporate credibility affects customer purchase intention.

3. RESEARCH METHOD

Data for this study was collected using a questionnaire. The pretest shows the acceptable reliability of the measurement with Cronbach α value (α≥0.7 is acceptable, the minimum value of above constructs is 0.754) as the standard (George and Mallery, 2003) (see Table 1). A 5-point Likert scale is used.

The target respondents are males and females in Taiwan, and are interested in purchasing online. To enhance the effectiveness of the sample, an online survey method was used in this study. Data were collected using a convenience sampling method through surveying respondents from fans group of purchase communities. Totally 400 respondents participated in the survey. Following confirmation of the sample selection criteria, 332 responses were valid for data analysis. The respondents comprised approximately 52% males and 48% females. The respondents were 18 years or older. Most of them ranged from 18-25 years old (39%), and 36-45 years old (23%). The respondents who were 45 years or older accounted for 17% of the study sample.

Data in this study were analyzed using the statistical software SPSS 18. Additionally, the causality model was analyzed using AMOS 18. Confirmatory factor analysis considered the aforementioned factors. For the factor loading, a cut-off point of 0.5 was used for item inclusion in this study.

4. RESULTS

4.1. Descriptives

Analytical results indicate that among various social media platforms, Facebook is the most favorite one with 99% of users, and 79% of respondents ranking it as the top social media. Google+ ranks second with 65% of the respondents. Approximately 4% of respondents usually follow new updates of product launches and marketing campaigns from online retailers in social network sites, while 44% occasionally do so, and up to 52% never do so. Approximately 42% of the respondents had purchased products/services online from the promotion on social networking sites, and 30% confirmed purchasing 1-2 times over the

Table 1. Reliability test

Constructs	(α)	Qualified
Product/service information (PSI) with 4 items	0.913	Yes
Perceived ease of use (PEOU) with 3 items	0.908	Yes
Corporate credibility (CC) with 3 items	0.907	Yes
Electronic word of mouth (EWOM) with 4 items	0.783	Yes
SM experience (SME) with 3 items	0.874	Yes
Perceived usefulness (PU) with 3 items	0.880	Yes
Social influence (SI) with 3 items	0.754	Yes
Purchase intention (PI) with 3 items	0.812	Yes

past 12 months. Personal consumption products such as clothes, cosmetics, shampoo, and toothbrushes are the ones mostly selected by 22% of respondents, followed by computers (17%). In sum, the profile of respondents indicates that they might represent online shoppers.

4.2. Confirmatory Factor Analysis

In this study, first-order confirmatory factor analysis (single first–order CFA) has been adopted for the 8 factors (Joreskog and Sorbom, 1992; Doll, Xia, and Torkzadeh, 1994). Analytical results of the single first–order CFA model (model 1) indicate that question items of perceived ease of use, corporate credibility, perceived usefulness, and electronic word of mouth must be removed from the factors affecting purchase intention, owing to low factor load (<0.5) (Bagozzi and Yi, 1988; Dang, 2012; David et al., 2003). The analytical results show that purchase intention, social influence, product/service information, and social media experience are valid for the causality relationship test. Based on the analytical results, H1, H3, H4, H5, H6, and H8 are not supported. Hypotheses 9.2, 9.4, 9.5, and 9.7 are also not supported based on the above results of first-order confirmatory factor analysis. Figure 1 illustrates the modified research model, owing to the elimination of corporate credibility, electronic word of mouth, perceived ease of use and perceived usefulness after CFA.

4.3. Structure Equation Model

Based on the results of Bagozzi and Yi (1988), this study evaluates the theoretical models based on preliminary fit criteria, overall model fit, and internal structural model fit. As for preliminary fit criteria, the factor loading of the measure index of each latent construct reaches significance exceeding 0.5 for all, male, and female respondents (see Table 2). Furthermore, the observed variables contain no negative error variances. Therefore, this model satisfies the preliminary fit criteria. The overall model fit also reveals that the modified model can explain the validity of the analysis of causality relationship for all, male, and female respondents (see Table 3). Table 4 shows the discriminant validity. The results show that factors are valid for the analysis of causality relationship (Lucas et al., 1996). Finally, the test of fit of the internal structural model reveals acceptable (see Table 5) (Bentler, 1989; Blackshaw, 1989; Bollen, 1989).

Figure 2 shows the causal relationships among purchase intention, product/service information, social media experience, and social influence for all respondents. Analytical results indicate that for all respondents, H2, H6, H7, and H9.3 are supported. In this study, for the comparison of different

Figure 1. Research model

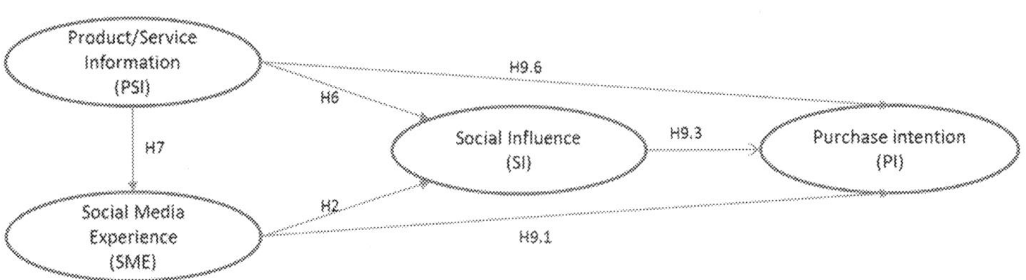

Table 2. Basic fit

Path	All			Male			Female		
	Std. Error	t-Value	Factor Load	Std. Error	t-Value	Factor Load	Std. Error	t-Value	Factor Load
PSI → PSI1	0.062	18.905***	0.867	0.065	15.790***	0.880	0.075	13.879***	0.857
PSI → PSI2	0.063	20.909***	0.890	0.063	15.367***	0.868	0.076	14.419***	0.912
PSI → PSI3	0.065	16.987***	0.794	0.064	12.789***	0.815	0.074	11.238***	0.764
PSI → PSI4	0.065	18.258***	0.824	0.067	15.414***	0.889	0.073	10.977***	0.756
SME→ SME1	0.066	17.592***	0.854	0.076	12.358***	0.844	0.068	12.431***	0.863
SME → SME2	0.074	16.177***	0.798	0.074	11.769***	0.813	0.071	11.369***	0.782
SME → SME3	0.075	17.712***	0.859	0.065	12.438***	0.849	0.069	13.036***	0.870
PI → PI1	0.045	19.310***	0.938	0.045	16.619***	0.937	0.065	14.670***	0.941
PI → PI2	0.047	16.166***	0.802	0.046	10.014***	0.797	0.061	10.751***	0.806
PI → PI3	0.045	12.351***	0.709	0.045	9.058***	0.714	0.059	9.011***	0.707
SI → SI1	0.121	8.554***	0.710	0.124	9.049***	0.712	0.101	6.011***	0.709
SI → SI2	0.120	8.720***	0.905	0.124	15.828***	0.907	0.122	6.495***	0.894
SI → SI3	0.139	8.640***	0.711	0.141	9.001***	0.708	0.168	6.039***	0.715

*** Represents the t-value of factor load is significant.

Table 3. Internal structural fit

Latent Variables	Constructs	All			Male			Female		
		Individual Item Reliability	Composite Reliability	Average Variance Extracted	Individual Item Reliability	Composite Reliability	Average Variance Extracted	Individual Item Reliability	Composite Reliability	Average Variance Extracted
PSI	PSI1	0.752	0.909	0.713	0.774	0.921	0.746	0.734	0.894	0.680
	PSI2	0.792			0.753			0.832		
	PSI3	0.630			0.664			0.584		
	PSI4	0.679			0.790			0.572		
SME	SME1	0.729	0.859	0.697	0.712	0.874	0.698	0.745	0.877	0.704
	SME2	0.637			0.661			0.612		
	SME3	0.738			0.721			0.757		
PI	PI1	0.880	0.860	0.675	0.878	0.860	0.674	0.885	0.862	0.678
	PI2	0.643			0.635			0.650		
	PI3	0.503			0.510			0.500		
SI	SI1	0.504	0.822	0.610	0.507	0.822	0.610	0.503	0.715	0.604
	SI2	0.819			0.823			0.799		
	SI3	0.506			0.501			0.511		

Table 4. Discriminant validity

	All				Males				Females			
	PSI	**SME**	**PI**	**SI**	**PSI**	**SME**	**PI**	**SI**	**PSI**	**SME**	**PI**	**SI**
PSI	0.909				0.921				0.894			
SME	0.171	0.859			0.205	0.874			0.139	0.877		
PI	0.110	0.209	0.860		0.084	0.185	0.860		0.147	0.247	0.862	
SI	0.002	0.004	0.017	0.822	0.000	0.001	0.004	0.822	0.006	0.011	0.043	0.715

Table 5. Model fit summary

Statistics	Mean	Criteria	Value
Absolute Fit Indices			
RMSEA	Root mean square error of approximation	< .08	0.065**
GFI	Goodness-of-fit index	> .90	0.945**
AGFI	Adjusted goodness-of-fit index	> .80	0.915**
Normed Fit Indices			
NFI	Normal fit index	> .90	0.950**
RFI	Relative fit index	> .90	0.933**
IFI	Incremental fit index	> .90	0.985**
TLI (NNFI)	Tacker-Lewis index (non-normal fit index)	> .90	0.979**
CFI	Comparative fit index	> .90	0.984**
Parsimony Goodness-of-Fit Indices			
PGFI	Parsimony goodness-of-fit index	> .50	0.613**
PNFI	Parsimony-adjusted NFI	> .50	0.718**
PCFI	Parsimony-adjusted CFI	> .50	0.745**
DF of χ^2	Degree of Freedom	< 3.00	1.414**

** Represents the index is significant.

Figure 2. The causal relationship among variables (all respondents)

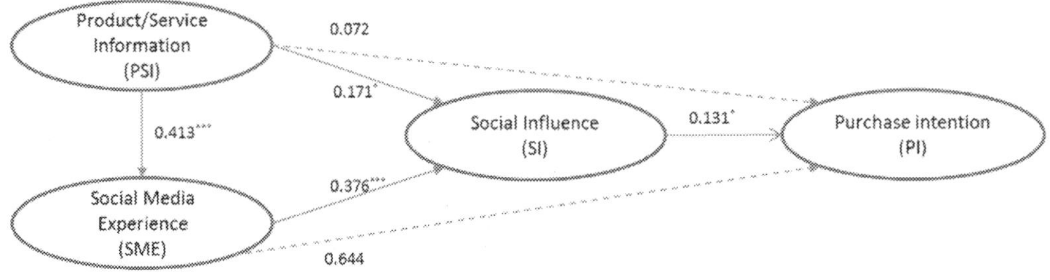

"*", or "***" represents the relationship between variables is significant.

purchase intentions between males and females, Figures 3 and 4 show the causal relationships of males and females, respectively.

Causality analysis yields the following results. social media has an indirect positive effect on purchase intention (i.e. the total value of the path coefficient between social media and purchase intention is 0.049), social media experience has a significant direct positive effect on social influence (i.e. the total value of the path coefficient between social media experience and social influence is 0.449), social influence has a significant direct positive effect on purchase intention (i.e. the total value of the path coefficient between social influence and perceived ease of use is 0.131), product/service information has a significant direct/indirect positive effect on social influence (i.e. the total value of the path coefficient between product/service information and social influence is 0.323), product/service information has a significant direct positive effect on social media experience (i.e. the total value of the path coefficient between product/service information and social media experience is 0.413), and product/service information has an indirect positive effect on purchase intention (i.e. the total value of the path coefficient between product/service information and perceived ease of use is 0.042). Generally, the female samples follow the total causal relationships. The male samples are different from female samples. Analytical results also show how male and female respondents differ. For males, the relationship between product/service information and purchase intention is insignificant (0.051, and p is larger than 0.05), the relationship between social media experience and purchase intention is insignificant (0.042, and p is larger than 0.05), the relationship between product/service information and social influence is insignificant (0.119, and p is larger than 0.05), and the relationship between social influence and purchase intention

Figure 3. The causal relationship among variables (male respondents)

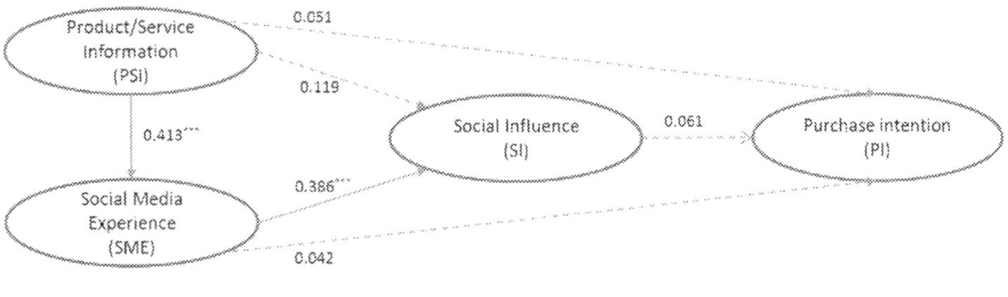

Figure 4. The causal relationship among variables (female respondents)

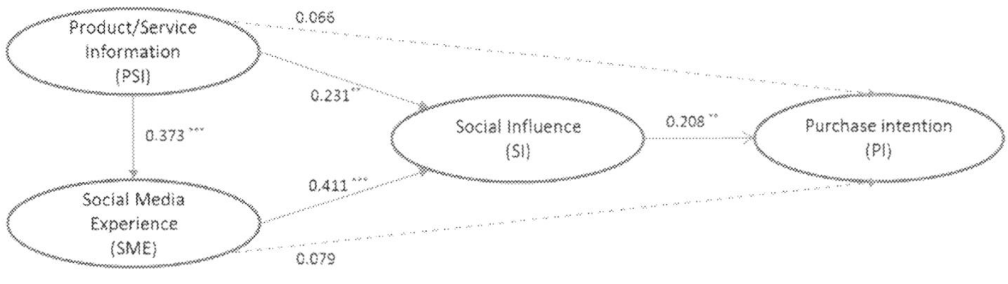

is insignificant (0.061, and p is larger than 0.05). Finally, the above results validate hypotheses H2, H6, H7, and H9.3 (see Table 6).

4.4. Gender Difference on Factors

This study describes analytical results of the differences between genders through T-test. The difference of each question item in causality relationship between different genders is insignificant. The differences of each factor in between different genders is insignificant (see Table 7). Restated, the respondents are insignificant in the replies on this questionnaire survey.

4.5. Implications

The differences of the answer of each question item and each factor between genders are insignificant. However, the males has no purchase intention through the stimulation from product/service information, social media experience, and social influence based on the analytical results of causality relationship. For males, product/service information affects social media experience and further affects social influence. However, the males just collect information for enhancing social influence only, but not for purchasing the goods. For females, product/service information and social media experience affect social influence and further enhance purchase intention. Restated, product information is useful for the females to purchase if their friends can help the positive comments on the goods. The company should focus on gender differences and find the proper way to attract the female's friend's eyeballs and further create the positive social influence. For females, the social media experience also help the enhancement

Table 6. The summary of causality relationship

Path	All				Male			Female		
	Direct	**Indirect**	**Total**	**Results**	**Direct**	**Indirect**	**Total**	**Direct**	**Indirect**	**Total**
SI → PI	0.131*	----	0.131	H9.3: **accept**	----	----	0	0.208**	----	0.208
PSI → SI	0.171*	0.152* (through SME)	0.323	H6: **accept**	----	0.159* (through SME)	0.159	0.231***	0.153* (through SME)	0.384
SME→ SI	0.449***	----	0.449	H2: **accept**	0.386***	----	0.386	0.411***	----	0.411
PSI → SME	0.413***	----	0.413	H7: **accept**	0.413***	----	0.413	0.373***	----	0.373
PSI → PI	----	0.020* (through SME, and SI) 0.022* (through and SI)	0.042	H9.6: PSI indirect affect PI	----	----	0	----	0.032* (through SME, and SI) 0.048* (through and SI)	0.080
SME → PI	----	0.049* (through SI, and SI)	0.049	H9.1:SME indirect affect PI	----	----	0	----	0.085* (through SI, and SI)	0.085

"*", "**", or "***" represents the relationship between variables is significant.

Table 7. t-test

Question Item/ Factor	Males		Females		t-Value	Significant
	Average	Std. Error	Average	Std. Error		
PSI	**0.02**	**1.023**	**-0.25**	**0.976**	**0.442**	**0.659**
PSI1	4.07	0.991	3.93	0.997	1.325	0.186
PSI2	4.01	0.988	3.99	0.980	0.223	0.824
PSI3	4.01	0.917	3.99	0.898	0.121	0.904
PSI4	4.23	0.954	4.22	0.880	0.102	0.919
SME	**0.05**	**0.99**	**-0.55**	**1.013**	**0.970**	**0.330**
SME1	3.16	1.120	3.06	1.116	0.827	0.409
SME2	3.35	1.087	3.29	1.092	0.545	0.586
SME3	3.46	1.189	3.29	1.232	1.282	0.201
SI	**0.07**	**1.019**	**-0.08**	**0.976**	**1.346**	**0.179**
SI1	2.86	1.077	2.93	1.113	-0.648	0.518
SI2	3.23	1.091	3.32	1.149	-0.724	0.469
SI3	3.59	1.050	3.54	1.031	0.440	0.660
PI	**-0.38**	**1.002**	**0.04**	**0.999**	**-0.741**	**0.475**
PI1	3.37	0.982	3.26	0.972	1.057	0.291
PI2	3.11	1.051	3.01	1.031	0.812	0.418
PI3	2.76	1.104	2.56	1.023	1.719	0.086

"*"represents the difference of the answer between genders is significant.

on social influence. The senior social media user can affect female's purchase intention. The company should cooperate with the senior users to promote goods through social media. In Taiwan, the senior social media users begin acting the spokesmen and promoting goods through social media (Shim et al., 2001; Schiffman and Kanuk, 2007). It is a good idea for the females to pay money for goods through social media platform, but not for the males.

Finally, this work presents marketing suggestions for companies who want to promote/sell products to consumers through social media platforms, based on the abovementioned analytical results. Those recommendations are as follows:

1. Analytical results indicate that for all respondents, product/service information affects social influence, social media experience directly, and purchase intention indirectly significantly. Additionally, social media experience affects social influence, and purchase intention indirectly and significantly. Restated, product/service information is essential for a company to promote products on social media. This is also the current situation. If a company wants to promote products to consumers through social influence, the company must form a website with attractive design for purchases aimed at generating positive social media experience. A positive social media experience increases social influence. Additionally, the company must provide adequate information of products/services on social media, subsequently causing social influence to increase along with the positive increase on product/service information;

2. Analytical results indicate that the marketing strategy for males should differ from females, owing to the differences between males and females with respect to how product/service information affects social influence and for the purchase intention. For males, product/service information only affects social influence through social media experience indirectly. Product/service information has no effect on purchase intention. Restated, if wanting to increase social influence by providing product/service information to males only, a company slightly these efforts. However, males show no purchase intention through social media. The company could provide males their required information merely, and try to enhance their purchase intention through other media. Alternatively, a company should focus on increasing social influences of males directly. Namely, providing required information makes males feel that the website is a valuable reference for purchases that male's friends recommend;
3. For females, the causal relationship among variables resembles that of total respondents. Product/service information should be of priority concern to the company. Additionally, for females, social media experience significantly affect social influence with large effects (0.411). Namely, if wanting to attract females to purchase products through social media, a company must provide functions that can provide females and their friends with a valuable social media purchasing experience.

5. CONCLUSION

This study attempted to identify the extent to which factors influence male and female customer intentions to make a purchase through social networking sites. Analytical results of a causal relationship indicate that for all respondents and females, product/service information affects social influence and social media experience positively, social influence affects purchase intention positively, social media experience affects social influence positively, and social media experience affects perceived ease of use positively. For males, product/service information positively affects social influence indirectly through social media experience and social influence has no effects on purchase intention. The marketing strategies for males and females should differ from each other. For instance, for a company that promotes products/services by providing advertising information on social networks, such information is useful for females, but maybe not so for males if they are not satisfied with their purchases through social network sites.

REFERENCES

Aldridge, A., Karen, F., & Pierson, J. (1997). Get Linked or Get Lost: Marketing Strategy for the Internet. *Internet Research: Electronic Networking Applications and Policy*, *7*(3), 161–169. doi:10.1108/10662249710171805

Aspara, J., & Van Den Bergh, B. (2014). Naturally designed for masculinity vs. femininity? Prenatal testosterone predicts male consumers choices of gender-imaged products. *International Journal of Research in Marketing*, *31*(1), 117–121. doi:10.1016/j.ijresmar.2013.09.001

Avery, J. (2012). Defending the markers of masculinity: Consumer resistance to brand gender-bending. *International Journal of Research in Marketing*, *29*(4), 322–336. doi:10.1016/j.ijresmar.2012.04.005

Bagozzi, R. P., & Yi, Y. (1988). On the evaluation of structural equation models. *Journal of the Academy of Marketing Science*, *16*(1), 74–94. doi:10.1007/BF02723327

Bashar, A., & Ahmad, I., & WASIQ, M. (2012). *Effectiveness Of Social Media As A Marketing Tool: An Empirical Study*. International Journal of Marketing. *Financial Services & Management Research*, *1*(11), 88–99.

Belanche, D., Casaló, L. V., & Guinalíu, M. (2012). Website usability, consumer satisfaction and the intention to use a website: The moderating effect of perceived risk. *Journal of Retailing and Consumer Services*, *19*(1), 124–132. doi:10.1016/j.jretconser.2011.11.001

Bentler, P. M. (1989). *EQS, Structural Equations, Program Manual, Program Version 3.0*. Los Angeles: BMDP Statistical Software, Inc.

Blackshaw, P., & Nazzaro, M. (2004). Consumer-Generated Media (CGM). 101-Nielsen Online. Retrieved from http://www.nielsenbuzzmetrics.com/whitepapers

Bollen, K. A. (1989). *Structural equations with latent variables*. New York: Wiley. doi:10.1002/9781118619179

Brangule-Vlagsma, K., Pieters, R. G., & Wedel, M. (2002). The dynamics of value segments: Modeling framework and empirical illustration. *International Journal of Research in Marketing*, *19*(3), 267–285. doi:10.1016/S0167-8116(02)00079-4

Bristol, T., & Mangleburg, T. F. (2005). Not Telling the Whole Story: Teen Deception in Purchasing. *Journal of the Academy of Marketing Science*, *33*(1), 79–95. doi:10.1177/0092070304269754

Brocato, E. D., Voorhees, C. M., & Baker, J. (2012). Understanding the influence of cues from other customers in the service experience: A scale development and validation. *Journal of Retailing*, *88*(3), 384–398. doi:10.1016/j.jretai.2012.01.006

Camilla, B. (2010). Engagement with SM & outcomes for brands. In *Proceedings of ANZMAC '10.*

Carpenter, J. M., Green, M. C., & LaFlam, J. (2011). People or profiles: Individual differences in online social networking use. *Personality and Individual Differences*, *50*(5), 538–541. doi:10.1016/j.paid.2010.11.006

Chanaka, J., Len, T. W., & Charles, D. (2007). Consumers online: Intentions, orientation and segmentation. *International Journal of Retail & Distribution Management*, *35*(6), 515–599. doi:10.1108/09590550710750377

Chen, Y., & Xie, J. (2008). Online Consumer Review: Word-of-Mouth as a New Element of Marketing Communication Mix. *Management Science*, *54*(3), 477–491. doi:10.1287/mnsc.1070.0810

Choi, J., & Kim, Y. (2014). The moderating effects of gender and number of friends on the relationship between self-presentation and brand-related word-of-mouth on Facebook. *Personality and Individual Differences*, *68*, 1–5. doi:10.1016/j.paid.2014.03.040

Dang, T. H. (2012). *Employees' Purchase Intention via Social Media* [Master Thesis]. National Formosa University, Taiwan.

Das, G. (2014). Impacts of retail brand personality and self-congruity on store loyalty: The moderating role of gender. *Journal of Retailing and Consumer Services*, *21*(2), 130–138. doi:10.1016/j.jretconser.2013.07.011

David, G., Elena, K., & Straub, D. W. (2003). Trust and TAM in Online Shopping: An Integrated Model. *Management Information Systems Quarterly*, *27*(1), 51–90.

Davis, F. D. (1989). Perceived usefulness, perceived ease of use, and user acceptance of information technology. *Management Information Systems Quarterly*, *13*(3), 319–340. doi:10.2307/249008

Davis, R., Piven, I., & Breazeale, M. (2014). Conceptualizing the brand in social media community: The five sources model. *Journal of Retailing and Consumer Services*, *21*(4), 468–481. doi:10.1016/j.jretconser.2014.03.006

Dellarocas, C. (2003). The Digitization of Word of Mouth: Promise and Challenges of Online Feedback Mechanisms. *Management Science*, *49*(10), 1407–1424. doi:10.1287/mnsc.49.10.1407.17308

Dholakia, U. M., Bagozzi, R. P., & Pearo, L. K. (2004). A social influence model of consumer participation in network-and small-group-based virtual communities. *International Journal of Research in Marketing*, *21*(3), 241–263. doi:10.1016/j.ijresmar.2003.12.004

Ehrlichman, H., & Eichenstein, R. (1992). Private wishes: Gender similarities and differences. *Sex Roles*, *26*(9-10), 399–422. doi:10.1007/BF00291551

Eley, B., & Tilley, S. (2009). *Online Marketing Inside Out. Melbourne: SitePoint* (European Edition). Edinburgh: Pearson Education Limited.

George, D., & Mallery, P. (2003). *SPSS for Windows step by step: A simple guide and reference. 11.0 update*. Boston: Allyn & Bacon.

Grewal, D., Roggeveen, A. L., Compeau, L. D., & Levy, M. (2012). Retail value-based pricing strategies: New times, new technologies, new consumers. *Journal of Retailing*, *88*(1), 1–6. doi:10.1016/j.jretai.2011.12.001

Hennig-Thrau, T., Malthouse, E. C., Friege, C., Gensler, S., Lobschat, L., Rangaswamy, A., & Skiera, B. (2011). The Impact of New Media on Customer Relationships. *Journal of Service Research*, *13*(3), 311–330. doi:10.1177/1094670510375460

Hsieh, N. C., & Chu, K. C. (2009). Enhancing consumer behavior analysis by data mining techniques. *International journal of information and management sciences*, *20*(1), 39-53.

Huang, Z., & Benyoucef, M. (2013). From e-commerce to social commerce: A close look at design features. *Electronic Commerce Research and Applications*, *12*(4), 246–259. doi:10.1016/j.elerap.2012.12.003

Khare, A., Labrecque, L. I., & Asare, A. K. (2011). The assimilative and contrastive effects of word-of-mouth volume: An experimental examination of online consumer ratings. *Journal of Retailing*, *87*(1), 111–126. doi:10.1016/j.jretai.2011.01.005

Kim, Y. A., & Srivastava, J. (2007). Impact of social influence in e-commerce decision making. In *Proceedings of the 9th International Conference on Electronic Commerce*, Minneapolis, MN, USA (pp. 293-302). doi:10.1145/1282100.1282157

Lafferty, B. A., Goldsmith, R. E., & Newell, S. J. (2002). The Dual Credibility Model: The Influence of Corporate and Endorser Credibility on Attitudes and Purchase Intentions. *Journal of Marketing Theory and Practice*, *10*(3), 1–12. doi:10.1080/10696679.2002.11501916

Lee, K.O., Shi, N., Cheung, M.K., Lim, K.H., & Sia, C.L. (2011). Consumer's decision to shop online: The moderating role of positive informational social influence. *Journal of International Management*, *48*, 158–191.

Lee, W., Tyrell, T., & Erdem, M. (2013). Exploring the behavioral aspects of adopting technology: Meeting planners use of social network media and the impact of perceived critical mass. *Journal of Hospitality and Tourism Technology*, *4*(1), 6–22. doi:10.1108/17579881311302329

Liang, T. P., & Huang, J. S. (1998). An Empirical Study on Consumer Acceptance of Products in Electronic Markets: A Transaction Cost Model. *Decision Support Systems*, *24*(1), 29–43. doi:10.1016/S0167-9236(98)00061-X

Lin, K. Y., & Lu, H. P. (2011). Why people use social networking sites: An empirical study integrating network externalities & motivation theory. *Computers in Human Behavior*, *27*(3), 1152–1161. doi:10.1016/j.chb.2010.12.009

Ling, K. C., Chai, L. T., & Piew, T. H. (2011). The effects of shopping orientations, online trust and prior online purchase experience toward customer's online purchase intention. *International Business Research*, *3*(3), 63. doi:10.5539/ibr.v3n3p63

Lucas, R. E., Diener, E., & Suh, E. (1996). Discriminant validity of well-being measures. *Journal of Personality and Social Psychology*, *71*(3), 616–628. doi:10.1037/0022-3514.71.3.616 PMID:8831165

Mangold, W. G., & Faulds, D. J. (2009). Social media: The new hybrid element of the promotion mix. *Business Horizons*, *52*(4), 357–365. doi:10.1016/j.bushor.2009.03.002

Okazaki, S. (2007). Exploring gender effects in a mobile advertising context: On the evaluation of trust, attitudes, and recall. *Sex Roles*, *57*(11-12), 897–908. doi:10.1007/s11199-007-9300-7

Pookulangara, S., & Koesler, K. (2011). Cultural influence on consumer's usage of social networks and its impact on online purchase intentions. *Journal of Retailing and Consumer Services*, *18*(4), 348–354. doi:10.1016/j.jretconser.2011.03.003

Ramayah, T., & Ignatius, J. (2005). Impact of Perceived Usefulness, Perceived Ease of Use and Perceived Enjoyment on Intention to Shop Online. *ICFAI Journal of Systems Management*, *III*(3), 36–51.

Rohm, A. J., & Swaminathan, V. (2004). A typology of online shoppers based on shopping motivations. *Journal of Business Research*, *57*(7), 748–757. doi:10.1016/S0148-2963(02)00351-X

Ronald, G., Barbara, L., & Stephen, N. (2000). The influence of corporate credibility on consumer attitudes and purchase intent. *Corporate Reputation Review*, *3*(4), 304–318. doi:10.1057/palgrave.crr.1540122

Schiffman, L. G., & Kanuk, L. L. (2007). *Reference Groups and Family Influences in Consumer Behaviour* (10th ed., pp. 310–352). London: Prentice Hall.

Sen, S., & Lerman, D. (2007). Why are you telling me this? An examination into negative consumer reviews on the web. *Journal of Interactive Marketing*, *21*(4), 76–96. doi:10.1002/dir.20090

Shim, S., Eastlick, M. A., Lotz, S. L., & Warrington, P. (2001). An online prepurchase intentions model: The role of intention to search. *The Journal of Consumer Affairs*, *35*(1), 28–49.

Söderlund, M., & Rosengren, S. (2007). Receiving word-of-mouth from the service customer: An emotion-based effectiveness assessment. *Journal of Retailing and Consumer Services*, *14*(2), 123–136. doi:10.1016/j.jretconser.2006.10.001

Swaminathan, V., Lepkowska-White, E., & Rao, B. P. (1999). Browsers or buyers in cyberspace? An investigation of factors influencing electronic exchange. *Journal of Computer-Mediated Communication*, *5*(2).

Weinberg, B. D., & Pehlivan, E. (2011). Social spending: Managing the social media mix. *Business Horizons*, *54*(3), 275–282. doi:10.1016/j.bushor.2011.01.008

Zajonc, R. B. (1968). The Attitudinal Effects of Mere Exposure. *Journal of Personality and Social Psychology Monograph*, *9*(2), 1–27. doi:10.1037/h0025848

This research was previously published in the International Journal of Customer Relationship Marketing and Management (IJCRMM), 8(3); edited by Riyad Eid, pages 1-17, copyright year 2017 by IGI Publishing (an imprint of IGI Global).

APPENDIX

Table 8. Question items

Social Media Experience		
Dimension	**Measurement**	**References**
Individual Attributes		
Social Media experience (SME)	SME1 - I am an experienced in purchasing goods through social network sites.	Aldridge et al., 1997; Camilla, 2010; Jiyoung, 2009
	SME2 - I am proficient in finding product or service information through social network sites.	
	SME3 - I understand how to make online purchases from my use of social network sites.	
Electronic Word of Mouth		
Electronic word of mouth (EWOM)	EWOM1 - When visiting a social network site containing product information, I find comments from other visitors on this site useful in helping me to make a purchase decision.	Chen & Xie (2008); Sen & Leman, 2007
	EWOM2 - I often persuade my friends through social network sites to purchase products/services that I like.	
	EWOM3 - I like to view my friends' opinions through social network sites before I purchase products.	
	EWOM4 - I feel more comfortable in choosing products/services when I view my friends' opinions about the products/services through social network sites.	
Social Influence		
Social Influence (SI)	SI1 - I use social network sites as a reference for shopping because my relatives, friends and colleagues can provide me with valuable advice.	Bristol & Mangleburg, 2005; Schiffman & Kanuk, 2007
	SI2 - I often consult with other individuals to select the best alternative products available.	
	SI3 - I often gather information about products from friends or family through social network sites before purchasing them.	
Perceived Usefulness		
Perceived usefulness (PU)	PU1 - Social network sites help me to make more efficient purchasing decisions.	Ramayah & Ignatius, 2005
	PU2 - Promotional events through social network sites make my life easier.	
	PU3 - Social network sites are useful in helping me to purchase products/services.	Lin & Lu, 2011
Perceived Ease of Use		
Perceived ease of use (PEOU)	PEOU1 - Learning to shop through social network sites is relatively easy.	Davis, 1989; Ramayah & Ignatius, 2005
	PEOU2 - Promotional events through social network sites should be clear and understandable.	
	PEOU3 - Products/services that are reviewed in social network sites are relatively easy to purchase.	
Product/Service Information		
Product/ service information (PSI)	PSI1 –Sufficient information is available through social network sites for me to assess the quality of products/ services.	Shim et al., 2001
	PSI2 - Product/service-related information through social network sites is easily understood.	
	PSI3 - A diverse array of products/services should be available to select from social network sites.	
	PSI4 - Social network sites clearly list the prices of products/services.	
Corporate Credibility		
Corporate credibility (CC)	CC1 - I would purchase a product/service mentioned through social network platforms if its provider is well known.	Lafferty et al., 2002
	CC2 - I would purchase product/service advertising through social network platforms if its provider has operated successfully for a considerable time.	
	CC3 - I would purchase product/service advertising through social network platforms if its provider has a permanent and physical address.	
Purchase Intention		
Purchase Intention (PI)	PI1 - I would consider purchasing through social network sites in the future	Ling et al., 2010; Chanaka et al., 2007
	PI2 - I plan to purchase using social network sites for products/services	
	PI3 - In general, I would buy products/services using social network sites rather than going to a physical store	

Chapter 36
Trust Management Issues in Social-Media Marketing

Vikas Kumar
Sharda University, India

Prasann Pradhan
Shri Venkateshwara University, India

ABSTRACT

Social Media provides a new channel to marketers and businesses to communicate with their customers and business partners and integrate this media in their business strategy. The large scale growth of the social media and its increasing users has opened up new marketing era for the businesses. However, with enormous growth of the social media and other online channels, the competition has increased worldwide. Correspondingly, the customer retention and satisfaction has come-up as the biggest challenge. It has become necessary to gain and retain the customer trust, so that the existing customers are retained and new customers are attracted. Trust management becomes the most important issue in the online environment to work closely with the existing and potential customers along with the business partners. Present work discusses the important aspects of entrusting, managing and maintaining user trust with the social media marketing strategies. The paper highlights the various prevailing models of the trust management and comes out with the strong arguments to facilitate the user trust for businesses using social media marketing techniques.

1. INTRODUCTION

The diverse changes in the online environment had forced people to give a rethink to their business strategy for selling and buying of products and services. Businesses are increasingly using the internet for commercial activities (Teo, 2005; As'ad et al., 2012; Ghouri et al., 2012; Anjum et al., 2012) as well as the communications at various levels. Social media marketing is a new concept, which allows people from all over the world to promote their products as well as to communicate and share ideas or opinions with each other on one platform. According to Chikandiwa et al. (2013), Social media marketing is described as a system, which allows marketers to engage, collaborate, interact and harness intelligent

DOI: 10.4018/978-1-5225-5637-4.ch036

crowd sourcing for marketing purposes. Social media marketing has given opportunity to vendors, organizations, business partners, purchasers, sellers, buyers or consumers to buy, sell or advertise their products and services through these social media platforms. Use of social media has also become very much popular as a marketing tool for the establishment and management of customer relationships and to influence the people shopping behaviour (Ruane et al., 2013; Lagrosen et al., 2014).

Social media not only provides a platform to disseminate information about the products and services offered by organisations, but it also provides a platform for conversations and attending to the customer expectations or views. Firms have the opportunity to shift relationships with the consumers from dialogue to trialogue, in which consumers engage in meaningful relationships with one another and with the firms (Hlavinka et al., 2011; Lipsmann et al., 2012; Mangold et al., 2009; Tsimonis et al., 2014). For example: Starbucks, Nike, Coca-Cola and Dell have successfully used social media to obtain customer feedback, create new products and offers, strengthen customer loyalty and engage in online dialogue with followers (Beuker, 2009; Gallaugher and Ransbotham, 2010; Mitic et al., 2012). Social Media Marketing is defined as any form of direct or indirect marketing that is used to build awareness, recognition, recall, and action for a brand, business, product, person, or other entity and is carried out using the tools of the social Web, such as blogging, micro-blogging, social networking, social bookmarking and content sharing (Gunelius, 2011).

Social media marketing industry report 2015 (Stelzner, 2015), which have studied over 3700 marketers with the goal of understanding how they are using social media to grow and promote their businesses, presents a number of significant facts:

- 96% of marketers indicated that they are participating in social media marketing;
- A significant 92% of marketers indicate that social media is important for their business;
- At least 91% of marketers want to know the most effective social tactics and the best ways to engage their audience with social media;
- A significant 57% of marketers use video in their marketing; however, 72% want to learn more about video marketing and plan on increasing their use of video;
- Facebook and LinkedIn are the two most important social network for marketers.

The top two benefits of social media marketing are increased exposure and increasing traffic. A significant 90% of all marketers indicated that their social media efforts have generated more exposure for their businesses. Increased traffic was the second major benefit, with 77% reporting positive results as shown in the Figure 1 (Stelzner, 2015).

Number of users in the social media sites is increasing very rapidly. According to Statista.com (http://www.statista.com), In 2010, the number of social media users was 0.97 billion which had increased in 2013 to 1.61 billion and is expected to reach 2.33 billion by 2017.Therefore, it is quite clear that the growth of social media marketing is enormous worldwide. Over the last 2 years in India, many people have been engaged directly or indirectly through theses social media sites. People in India are connected to these social media channels for chatting, making friends, blogging, tweeting, sharing their views, business promotions, marketing, etc. Many company brands like MTV India, Channel V, Tata Photon, Tata Docomo, etc. had engaged with these social media marketing sites. Many Indian top celebrities had also engaged with these social media marketing sites for the promotion of their albums or movies, serials, etc. Many Indian political parties have been involved in campaigning and engaging the people through these social media sites. Recently Bhartiya Janta Party (BJP), who won the 2014 Indian Lok

Figure 1. Benefits of social media marketing

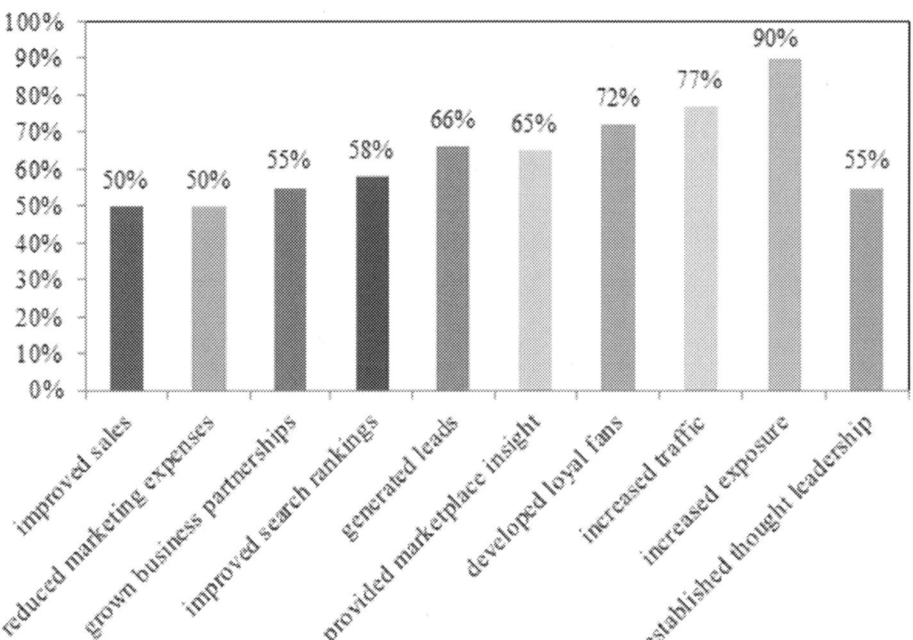

Sabha elections and became the number one party. BJP and their leaders including the Prime minister candidate have been engaged and communicated the people of India via the social media channels like Facebook, Twitter, etc. The BJP has been elected as the government of India is one example of the power of social media marketing popularity in India. The other example is the newly elected government of Delhi i.e. the AAP (Aam Aadmi Party) who has won the 67 seats out of 70 seats in 2015 (http://www.elections.in.). The AAP has accessed the different social media channels during Delhi Assembly elections to have a better connect with the people of Delhi. A study by the Associated Chambers of Commerce and Industry of India (ASSOCHAM) (http://assocham.org) states that the political parties spend around 3000-4000 million rupees for their publicity campaigns on social and digital media. The report by ASSOCHAM also states that social networking websites and similar technology giants will generate better revenue this year due to the digital campaigns. The spending on digital media has reached such a level that the Election Commission of India has made it compulsory for the political parties to disclose their advertising budgets on social and digital media (Dutta, 2014).

Inspired by the power of social media to engage users in virtual relationships, organizations began seeking ways to immerse into 'people's internet' and learn to leverage the 'likes', 'shares' and 'comments' for profit making (Andriole, 2010; Culnan et al., 2010; Mitic et al., 2012). People in this new era have not only shifted their interests to online shopping, but have also become active in social media to search information about the product or services before any purchase decision. From the social media marketing point of view, the root of any business to be successful will be gaining the customer trust and maintain their reputation in the competitive environment, So that the new users can also get engaged without any hesitation or risk.

According to Gartner (2012), "Consumers increased reliance on social media ratings and reviews will see an increase in enterprise spending on paid social media ratings and reviews, making up to 10-15%

of all reviews by 2014. However, analysts predict that increased media attention on fake social media and revives will result is strong litigations against many strong brands. Although the consumer trust in social media is currently low, consumer perception of tightened government regulations and increased media exposure of fake social media ratings and reviews will ultimately increase consumer trust in new and existing social media ratings and reviews. It indicates that trust entails a vital role in helping users overcome perceptions of risk and uncertainty in the use and acceptance of new technology (Gefen et al., 2003; Pavlou and Gegen, 2004; Li et al., 2008). According to Almenarez et al. (2011), trust is a measure that describes the trustworthiness of individual entities based on previous knowledge, common knowledge, and monitoring schemes. However, trust is not a static concept and changes over the time. Correspondingly, the trust management becomes important in maintaining and managing user trust. This paper focuses on the importance of trust management in social media marketing.

2. SOCIAL MEDIA MARKETING ASPECTS

Social media marketing has changed the pace of today's online world and has become an integral part of the online marketing campaign. Social media is all about the ways in which the user's or firm's can create, connect and share content online. It changes the people view on marketing for buying and selling of goods and services. Few years back, companies reached their consumers through trade shows, print advertising, or other traditional marketing methods like televisions, newspapers, magazines, etc. But today, consumers start their shopping experience by looking on the internet by using search engines, blogosphere and social media sites. All businesses aim for profits. Social media is not just as marketing tool, it has given a new way for running a business effectively. According to Gartner report by Sarner (2010), "While investments and growth in social marketing is assured during the next two years, the ultimate success of social marketing will depend on how well marketers can accelerate through the inevitable social expectation bust and make social marketing projects more than just 'engagement' objectives and then actually tie social activities to clear and measurable business objectives. Far too many companies are still following the hype of 'social' and have created or participated in social media without a plan". Social media sites like Facebook, Twitter, Myspace, LinkedIn, Orkut, Google+, etc., have taken a full advantage from their users like clients, business partners, firms or customers and provides them a platform, where they can communicate and share their ideas and content to each other. Social media marketing can be an inexpensive way to communicate and promote a company rather than putting together a huge marketing team or a prohibitive budget which becomes very much expensive and time consuming. Traditionally methods like Television, Phone, E-mail, Print media, etc. for promotion and advertising prove to be much costly as compared to social media marketing. Here, the marketers can pay for CPC (Cost per Click) or CPM (Cost per Mille) model and can even start with just few dollars as compared to thousands and millions of dollar when advertising in traditional media. The important aspects of the social media can be summarized as the following.

2.1. Social Media Marketing Channels

In today's online world, so many different social media marketing channels are available for marketing. The most famous social media marketing channels are:

- **Facebook (http://www.facebook.com):** Facebook provides a platform, where people come to socialize, talk, and share their views to each other. According to facebook.com, the business is made for the customers, build relationship with them, reach new people and drive sales using this channel. The Facebook said, when the user or business have a strong presence on facebook site, then their business has access to the most powerful kind of word-mouth-marketing recommendations between friends. Facebook offers the following steps for advertising:
    1. Build your page. Everything starts your page;
    2. Connect with the people, ads help you to reach the right peoples;
    3. Engage your audience, quality post keep people interested;
    4. Influence friends of fans, expand your reach through friends.
- **Twitter (http://www.twitter.com):** Twitter is another social networking website which allows organizations or companies to endorse their products and services information to a worldwide audience. It is the place where people are more inclined to listen than to speak. It has given opportunity to user to post articles in support of their business or advertise sale and link back to their website. The use of a product can be described in short messages (or tweet) particularly in 140 words, that followers are more likely to be read and understand. Twitter have some guidelines that are required to be followed by the advertisers:
    1. The users must understand the twitter terms and services, rules and all best practices;
    2. Marketers or advertisers are required to comply with legal requirements as shown in the twitter site and must keep the user's security;
    3. Don't distribute spam harmful code or other disruptive content. Advertisers should not put any type of content that may harm or disturb the others;
    4. It is advised that only promote honest, authentic and relevant content. Be transparent and accurate;
    5. Set high editorial standards for the twitter content you create;
    6. Set high standards for the off twitter connections you create.

Twitter has become a more popular and important marketing tool for many organizations, brands and individuals. Many brands use Twitter successfully for rapid customer service. It allows an immediate broadcast of news to the dedicated followers and fans. For example Dell lists several twitter channels like www.dell.com/twitter.

- **LinkedIn (http://www.linkedin.com):** LinkedIn is the world's largest professional social network site. It offers the platform where users or company's do B2B marketing. For example if some company looking to sell stationeries at a discounted rate to small-midsize companies, then it is the best platform to connect and use. It has also become a good platform to post professional jobs:
    1. This is a fast growing social network with over 300 million registered users in over 200 countries and territories. More than 2.8 million businesses with LinkedIn company Pages, and professional signing up at a rate of approximately two new member per-second (http://www.linkedin.com);
    2. A user can easily discover the people employed by a certain company, or the various types of businesses a certain persons have worked for. So if user or organization is looking to connect with industry professionals and generate leads in their businesses, LinkedIn is the best place

for that and it is recommended that user or organization should integrate this channel as an integral part of their social media marketing strategy.

- **Google+ (http://plus.google.com):** Google introduced in late 2011 its social networking site Google+, which aims to make sharing on the web more like sharing in real life. Check out circles, Events and Hangouts:
  1. Google Plus is a great way to promote a blog and really push the inbound marketing. By targeting 'circles' on Google Plus, user can share content and drive people to their own website;
  2. It hosts a large number of communities, where users can engage in conversation either publicly or privately. It has also offers Google Plus Business, which provides a great alternative to Facebook's pages;
  3. Google Hangouts (a part of Google+) provides users with a free video calling platform that they can use to connect. This platform can also be used by brands for inexpensive business seminars and open forums, which are great for connecting with clients and partners.

2.2. Social Media Monitoring Tools

When a business organization uses social media as a merk identified the social media platform where the audience or users spend most of the time, then it's time to start listening the audience, customers or users views and search out what kind of conversations they are having about the respective brand, or product(s) or service(s) and reflects the changes in the strategy of business implementation accordingly if necessary, through the help of the social media monitoring tools such as:

- **TweetDeck (https://web.tweetdeck.com):** It is a free desktop application that combines Twitter and Facebook monitoring with search for a multidimensional social application that also allows for publishing;
- **Viralheat (https://www.viralheat.com):** This is another social media monitoring tool, that tracks hundreds of video sharing sites, twitter, blogs, social networks, groups and forums in real time. It offers the capability to restrict the profiles by location and offers a great way to power regional marketing and monitoring campaigns;
- **Social Mention (http://www.socialmention.com):** It is a social media search and analysis platforms that aggregates user generated content from across the world into a single stream of information;
- **Google Alerts (https://www.google.co.in/alerts):** This is a free tool available on internet for monitoring millions of blogs and new sites using target keywords; receive streaming or batch reports;
- **Hootsuite (https://hootsuite.com):** It allows to monitor several social networks and post messages on Facebook, LinkedIn, Google+, and Foursquare via a single dashboard. Marketers can schedule messages, communicate with coworkers and assign tasks. It has a free version as well as a paid version that will allow you to manage the entire team of social media superstars;
- **TweetReach (https://tweetreach.com):** This tool analyzes your tweets by who is reading them and how they are being shared. It gives a basic picture of how far a particular tweet has traveled as well as how many people search a hashtag term;

- **Klout (https://klout.com):** Klout measures the "influencer" score by looking at various social media interactions such as followers, retweeters, sharers, +1's. This isn't just about who responds, but how many of your posts or tweets are shared or retweeted;
- **SocialPointer (http://www.socialpointer.com):** It allows you to monitor social mentions and respond in real-time. You can also monitor what your competitor is saying and get instant feedback on your company;
- **Agorapulse (https://www.agorapulse.com):** It focuses on Facebook and allows you to see side-by-side comparisons of your brand and others. It also offers contest and promotion applications as well. It is a paid tool and starts at $29/month;
- **GaggleAMP (https://gaggleamp.com):** This allows you to capitalize on your employees' friends and connections. You create a Gaggle within your organization and allow co-workers and employees to send out a social media message that you provide. You're reaching your own fans as well as their networks. It is a paid tool and starts at $25/month;
- **Sproutsocial (http://sproutsocial.com):** This is wonderful tool to help you in finding new customers and growing your social media presence. With this tool, you can monitor all your clients' social media profiles as well as schedule Twitter content. It is a paid tool and starts $39/month.

2.3. Different Domains of Social Media Marketing

Social media gives a platform to marketers or advertisers to interact, discuss, listen and respond to the users in an effective and timely manner. Correspondingly, the social media not only helps the businesses to promote their products and services to the direct customers. But, it can also help in other forms of marketing. The most widely used applications are:

1. **Business to Business (B2B) Marketing:** B2B marketing can take place between a vendor and a purchaser of goods and services through these online social media marketing sites. Social media has become a potential tool for this type of marketing as most of the big organizations are using the social media now days. The B2B channels can be used to secure procedures based on encryption and authorization level, with payment by predetermined credit terms. For example, Alibaba.com is the full B2B site, it used the Facebook (https://www.facebook.com/AlibabaUS), Twitter (https://twitter.com/AlibabaTalk), Linkedin (https://www.linkedin.com/company/alibaba.com), and Youtube (https://www.youtube.com/user/TeamAlibaba);
2. **Business to Consumer Marketing (B2C):** B2C marketing means that transaction can take place between an individual and a shop or firm selling goods and services through these online social media marketing channels. This is more like an extension of catalogue shopping, through mail order and telephone ordering using credit cards payments. The advantage of this type of marketing is convenience. For example, Shopclues.com where business products are directly provided to their users. Shopclues.com also uses the different social media channels for their marketing such as Facebook (https://www.facebook.com/ShopClues), Twitter (https://twitter.com/shopclues), Google+ (https://plus.google.com/+Shopclues-India/posts), Linkedin (https://www.linkedin.com/company/shopclues), Pinterest (https://www.pinterest.com/shopclues/) and Youtube (https://www.youtube.com/channel/UCnxPAa_6EL5ggl0_FRq6Zjw);

3. **Consumer to Consumer (C2C) Marketing:** The attention to the C2C interaction would be as useful as attention to the business-business (B2B) relations or business-customers (B2C) relations. This type of online marketing can take place directly between customers, without intervention of any business as middleman. One example of this type of transaction in social media marketing is Olx.in. The platform Olx.in uses social media channels such as Facebook (https://www.facebook.com/olxindia), Google+ (https://plus.google.com/113395767313404239895/posts) and Twitter (https://twitter.com/OLX_India). The different type of online marketing used social media channels not only for their profit or convenience but also for engaging more number of users trust in it. Since, more number of users trust in it, they discuss their experience with other people via social media sites which results more trust. Therefore, the trust ability of that company increase in the hearts of users, especially for the novel user.

2.4. Increasing Social Media Traffic

Number of people engaged the social media of company, basically reflects the success of Social Media Marketing (e.g. number of likes in the facebook, number of followers in the tweeter, number of connections in LinkedIn etc.). Social Media Marketing Managers do a lot to improve the network traffic towards their business site from social media marketing sites. Few such tasks are:

1. **Managing Conversations:** Conversation is the key for communicating. Conversation brings audience to your website from the social media sites. When you are engaged with your audience, they will be able to know you, like you and trust you. If they have trust on you, they could be more actively engaged in your website. The customers will then become participants in the conversations rather than a simple viewer. This will effectively increase the business potential. For example, good marketers always try to post replies to both positive and negative feedbacks and increase the effectiveness of conversations;
2. **Running Contests:** Marketers can offer a number of contest for the users on the social media sites, that can draw active attention of the users (e.g. Best Picture Contest on facebook, Lucky Draw on opinion polls, Maximum Tweets contest etc.). This helps a lot in getting the contact details of the contest participant as well as in acquiring new customers. This can significantly result in getting the details of people, who may be interested in your products and services. For example if you are a software developer, you could give away a free software redesign to prompt other to use your services. When people enter in your contest, you automatically have a list of potential customers;
3. **Testimonials:** They are the most powerful form of marketing. Whenever you do business with someone you ask for testimonial or better yet recommendation. The testimonials go a long ways in establishing the trust of new as well as existing users;
4. **Content:** Content is an important for driving force to attract the network traffic to your business website from your social websites. If the viewer does not find anything attractive, you will have a hard time getting them to come back. Content writing and content management has become a big business now a days;
5. **Offers:** Offers provide a wonderful tool to drive traffic and sales to your website. It enables businesses to reach customers with a promotion or advertisement, so that they can share with their friends or communities. Social media specific offers have become very much popular in the present day business scenario.

2.5. People Engagement and Success Stories

Anyone having an internet connection and account on any of the social media platform becomes directly or indirectly involved in the social media marketing. People can access these media via different digital devices like desktops, laptops, tablets, smart phones, mobiles, etc. The mobile users are continuously increasing mobile devices have become the most important tools for success of social media marketing sites. For example, a user can access the Facebook from their mobile phone on anytime, anywhere basis and this pushes up the social media marketing efforts. With the increasing engagement of people, a lot of success stories already exist, a few of them are:

- Banking sector has been using these social media marketing channels for their customer or user reviews. Indian banks such as ICICI Bank, Axis Bank and SBI are among the top 10 Banks with Social Media presence as per a survey by Financial Brand (http://thefinancialbrand.com) in the second quarter of 2015. Banks can communicate their users or customers via social media sites. Social media marketing enabled banks to regain the customer trust, which has been lost due to the recent economical crisis and the increased use of e-banking (Bonson et al., 2011; Ernest et al.,2011; Gritten,2011 and Chikandwa et al, 2013);
- News or media channels from all over the world have also accepted this online social media marketing concept. They have been using the social media channels like Facebook, Twitter, Youtube, and so on, for their promotion and marketing of their programs. They can also get the reviews from their users or viewers. So that some type trust is establish between the news or media channel and the user. Therefore, these social media sites are helpful in trust building in between the parties;
- Newspaper, magazines, journals, business organizations, industries, and so on, has been endorsing via the social media marketing channels. For example TimesofIndia newspaper company addresses their audience via facebook site account (https://www.facebook.com/TimesofIndia) or via twitter site account (https://twitter.com/timesofindia);
- Many colleges and universities are giving information to their students or users or viewers through these social marketing channels. For example, Banaras Hindu University (www.bhu.ac.in) in India who addresses their people via Facebook site account (https://www.facebook.com/Banaras.University);
- Different social welfare programs are also going on, in these social media sites. For example, Social media, particularly Twitter, have given a greater voice to Lesbian, Gay, Bisexual and Transgender (LGBT) communities around the world. Individuals and groups have used social media to gather, physically and virtually, to promote and support LGBT issues and rights — and they have done so in countries that are both are tolerant and intolerant of LGBT rights. The United States, Russia and Egypt — have used social media to give voice to those who have been previously quieted by society (http://www.salzburg.umd.edu/unesco/social-media-and-lgbt-community). Therefore, this types of programs give some level of trust between the people and the government or between the parties.

Markets try every bit and piece to attract customers to their social media platforms and retain them. The increased number of users help in the business promotions and hence in the business growth. However, with the increasing number of customers and users, more trust and trust establishing strategies are needed in order to retain and acquire the customers. Any breach of mutual trust can render the whole social media marketing strategy useless and hence the loss of goodwill and financial exchequer. Correspondingly, the trust management strategies become very much vital in the social media marketing.

3. STAKEHOLDERS PERSPECTIVE IN SOCIAL MEDIA MARKETING

Trust management in social media marketing plays a crucial role in retention and acquisition of the customers. The users tend to trust their circle of friends or colleagues much more than they trust the company's advertisements (Woodcock et al, 2010; Hamid et al, 2012). If social media is used correctly and efficiently, it can help businesses to grow quickly, easily and profitably, by building an essential emotional connection with people and establishing a trustworthy relationship. Since, users are enormously growing in these social sites, the responsibility of social media administrators has increased for maintaining and managing the trust between the users. Mayer et al. (1995), define trust as "the willingness of a party to be a vulnerable to the actions of another party based on the expectation that the other will perform a particular action important to the truster, irrespective of the ability to monitor or control that other party". In the relation of consumer trust in e-commerce, trust is also referred as "one believes in, and is willing to depend on, another party" (McKnight et al., 2002) and "trust is driven by past experience, long term orientations, positive trusting stance, and feelings of control" (Jarvenpaa et al., 1999). According to Bourkerche et al., (2008), trust can be described as a mutual relationship established between any two entities for a specific purpose or action. Trust is established based on prior dealings, knowledge and past transaction experiences with user. Through this trust, a trust relationship is built between the parties involved in transactions. In social media marketing, trust will be built based on conversation, listening and responding to the audience or users. Based on this trust, some kind of trustworthy relationship can be established between the parties involved. Trust management concept becomes very much important in managing and maintaining the trust record of the parties involved in successful transaction through these social media sites. Trust record contains the vast amount of trust information related to the user. For example the level of trust, prior successful transactions, trust value and so on.

Social media marketing and its relationship with different stakeholders such as customers, companies, government, and third party sites can be managed and maintained by using the trust management mechanisms. Different stakeholders of trust management in the social media marketing have been shown in the Figure 2 and each of these stakeholders may have their own perspectives and interests. For example the Government is interested to see that their law requirements were fulfilled or not, customers are interested to see that their privacy and security requirements are met or not, and so on. All these trust issues can be handled by the effective trust management.

Social media sites will require some type of trust management mechanism for retaining the users and attracting new customers. Marketers or advertisers, who understand the role of customers or users trust for their businesses better than their competitors are more likely to develop some kind of emotional or sentimental brand in the heart of a user and can begin a trustworthy relationship with them. This can happen only by gaining the trust of their parties or users involved in it and that can happen only by understanding the perspective of different stakeholders.

Figure 2. Different stakeholders in social media marketing channels

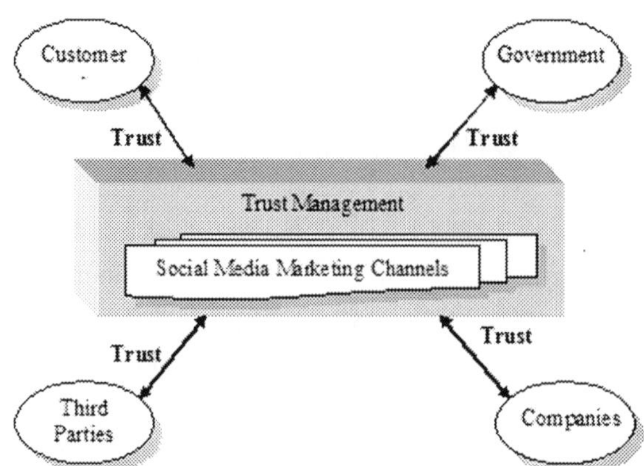

3.1. Customer Perspective

Social media customers can be broadly classified as: Direct customers and Indirect customers. Direct customers are those, who are directly involved as a user for these social media sites, e.g. if Bob had direct account on Facebook site. Indirect customers are those who are not the directly associated as member or user of these social media sites but they can be using these social media sites by their company or other friendly accounts. For example Dell company had an account on facebook site and the user of Dell has an account on their Dell company site but that user may access Facebook for their purpose without having an account on that site. So, those types of user are indirectly associated with the social media sites. There are many things that are expected by the customers from the social media sites to trust these sites:

- Customers see, whether the following social media websites will serve for his or her needs of the goods or services i.e. is social media site can help them in a trustworthy manner to select the goods or services;
- Whether the social media site can maintain the customer security and privacy is very much important? Customers want security about their personal information like photos from the social media sites. So, that information is not misused for any illegal purposes;
- Customers look for convenience in accessing their accounts and communicating with others from the social media marketing sites;
- It is important that whether the social provides a legal ability for any wrong attempts, such as hacking, fake accounts or faulty users. Customers are attracted towards those social media sites, which provide a structured way for controlling these things;
- Another thing that customers needs from these social media sites is the high performance like speed and accuracy. Although it depends upon the available internet speed, but does social media sites will provide more performance in slow speed internet?, becomes and important question for the customers. For example Facebook will open easily when the users have slow speed internet connection as compared to the heavy social media sites like LinkedIn, which takes more time to open.

3.2. Government Point of View of Trust to These Social Media Sites

Government is an important stakeholder for social media sites. What government wants from these social media sites to increase the trust between are:

- Is the social media site providing services according to law to the users? Government wants the social media sites to provide services according to the national, demographic area or local laws;
- The next thing that government wants from these social media sites is that they should provide the complete information for applicable laws in their sites to maintain transparency to the customers or users. So, that government can trust into the social media site and can mark in their records as trustable site;
- The social media site needs a proper mechanism for maintaining and managing the failures or violations of laws. Therefore, if anybody violates the law, they should take immediate action for that. This mechanism should be transparent to government. So, that government can increase their trust level to that social media sites. Therefore, proper transparency is required between the government and the social media site laws so that whenever these social media sites dealing with their online consumer or user they have to transparent with their government;
- The social media sites are required to be transparent to the government regarding the financial transactions between the clients or users. They need to provide accurate information regarding their financial transactions and business dealings;
- Governments also wants from these social media sites that they should have fair business practices with their users like customers, clients or business partners, and vice versa. Cheating should not be done from any side (i.e. user as well as social media site), to and from the government. So that the trust can be developed and maintained between the parties and the government.

3.3. Company's Point of View of Trust to These Social Media Sites

This is important to consider the expectations of the companies, which are directly associated with the social media site for their endorsement and promotion of their products and services. They may have a direct account to the social media site and may have a free or a paid account in the social media sites according to the company's need (but mostly paid accounts). They may have the following point of views:

- Is there any mechanism for social media site to maintain and prevent the company reputation from fake accounts or users? This means that what steps does social media site will take, if any user tries to damage their company reputation. For example, an unsatisfied or fake user can damage the company reputation through the social media. A fake user can make a fake account related to the name of a company, and deal wrongly with the consumer. Social media sites will be required to handle such type of threats. So that company can trust the social media sites;
- Do they provide any extra services, applications or tools for communication between the company and their employees feedback?
- What extra services and application they will provide for their paid accounts users? Does these services are mentioned in their legal agreement? Does social media site provide these services according to the agreements signed?

- What are the legal provisions if the there is a breach of contract by the social media sites;
- What kind of security and protection is available for the data of the company.

3.4. Third Party Point of View of Trust to These Social Media Sites and Vice Versa

Third parties are those who are not directly as a user or customer from these social media sites but they will be providing their services to these social media sites such as security, database management, etc. What third party wants from these social media site for trust building and vice versa are:

- Third parties want from these social media sites that their payment will be in time. Is payment will be going according to the SLA contract or not? Social media site wants that they will be paying according to the performance and quality as mentioned in the SLA contract;
- Social media site should regularly inform the third party about the services performance that they were providing. For example, is third party services performance providing continue as accurate or not? Is there any loss or gain in performance? Regular update about performance to third party providing will be beginning some level of relationship and trust among each other;
- The SLA (Service Level Agreement) contract is the main root of beginning the relationships between each other. So it must be carefully written and followed.

4. TRUST MANAGEMENT ISSUE IN SOCIAL MEDIA MARKETING

Trust Management acts as a mediator between the stakeholder and social media marketing site. It will manage all the trust records of different stakeholders from different viewpoints. It will be helpful for making business decisions. Based on different viewpoints from different stakeholders, trust management system must consider a number of trust issues.

4.1. Trust Issues in the Social Media Sites and Businesses

Social media sites can increase their trust among the business users by assuring the following:

- The range of services provided to the business users. e.g. The companies may be interested to learn more about their audience's likes and dislikes, behaviour etc. beyond their own specific products and services. E.g. in the format of market research. Correspondingly, the social media sites should ensure that such analysis and research tools and facilities will be available to the business users to enhance their productivity and hence the trust in the particular media site;
- Social media marketing sites provide third-party users experiences, but it is also required that social media site also provides assurances regarding these third-party users that they are all genuine. If third-party is not genuine, it generates lack of trust. So, marketers or social media site should consider this point before using third-party services;

- It is very easy for any malicious or anonymous user to use any social media platform without giving much detail and creates his fake account and by that fake account they will promote negativity for anyone related to person, product, business, company or country. How social sites will work to control such incidents. Because it is very difficult for social sites to identify and pick that user who promote negativity due to any personal or professional reasons. So, social sites will require to do work on these issues for trust building between their users. Presently, no social site answers this question publicly that how they will catch that culprit. What social site will do in these issues is that they only close that malicious user account but they never find the real identity of that user. So that user again open his another anonymous account in their or another social site and promote negativity. Hence, social media sites should use good identity management practices and the procedures must be documented well and assured to the corporate uses;
- Proper monitoring, listening and deployment will be required for individual user or customer by these social sites. If not, it may leads to the lack of trust among other users or parties;
- Social media sites should ensure that their user comply with the laws at local, state or national level regulations before they can promote their products and services;
- They also must ensure that their users private information should be not disclosed at any manner without their permission to anybody;
- Users accessing theses social sites from all over the world, so it is the duty for these social media sites to provide proper guidelines to their users regarding promotions, advertisements and so on. So that they cannot breach the security, privacy and law for any country regulations. Social media sites must also clarify the point that what appropriate actions can take place against an advertiser or promoter, if they violate the policies, rules, term and services?
- Social media sites should provide online help centers that will work in a 24x7, in a specified time limit to listen and to assure for solving the problems of their customers or users. Listening and responding from and to users are the two most useful tools for trust establishment;
- Account profile that includes username, profile picture, name, locations, websites and information regarding the product and services should be ensured to be accurate. So, that the user may get assurance regarding if anything goes wrong in buying or selling the products or services, a relevant action can be initiated from the side of social media site, against that user, vendor or company;
- Social sites should guarantee their users, vendors, and business partners that their private and confidential data and integrity is maintained;
- Social media site also assure the users for availability and recovery of data or services in case of failure occurs, it may be a natural disaster or software or hardware or network failure;
- Social sites must ensure their users that they will be able to help both online and offline, if necessary.

4.2. Building Customer Trust on Social Media Marketing Campaigns

Business companies or organizations involved in advertising or promoting their product and services through these social media sites must consider the following trust issues when they are dealing with online user via social media channel:

- Companies which ignore the voice of their customers will see diminishing loyalty, and a growing resentment among the online users. It loses the trust between them. So they have to hear the voice of their customers and must attend all the reviews and responses of the users. The marketing efforts should not be one sided;

- Businesses need to monitor and understand the customer needs and expectations and should plan their campaigns accordingly. Business organizations or individuals can increase their presence by offering discounts, schemes, various types of contests, social awareness programs and so on. So that stakeholders may engage in their offerings and if they like it. This will automatically increase the trust;
- Companies must understand that operating online business is much more different than the traditional offline methods, because only the business organization is directly responsible for everything that is written or advertised in social media sites. Consumers or users only saw or hear what the organizations write. If responsible persons from organizations misspell, misunderstood or mistakenly write a blog or tweet or advertise, then consumer or user is understands wrongly, which results in falling the business organization reputation and trust among the users or consumers. So, business organization must be very careful when writing or tweeting or blogging in the social sites;
- Companies will be required to continuously monitor and deploy their business through these social media sites that what feedback is given by the users. Feedback from social media sites helps drive both future business as well as marketing strategies. However, if the feedbacks are not responded well, they may create a breach of trust among the users;
- In the Social media sites, if users like the content they will share it with their own communities. So, the content before placing by a business company or individuals for advertising in these social media sites has to be carefully considered and checked. Content should be attractive, genuine and relevant to the particular promotion. The more valuable is the content, more value it will add to the business and consequently the more valuable users will increase and trust spread easily across the communities;
- Corporate Blogs must be written within the company and not by an outside agency. The personality and voice be both genuine and consistent. So stakeholders can have better familiarity and trust.

4.3. Establishing Brand Using Trust Management

Brands offers some level of inbuilt people trust, there is no doubt about it. According to Davis et al.,1999, brands are also important to the development of trust in web based relationship marketing. Brand is the trust mark that is the cue for all the past trust generating activity and in the absence of human touch; it can be a symbol of quality and assurance that is capable of building trust (Shankar et al, 2002). People have some level of inherent trust on the brands. Whenever they plan to buy any product or service, they first think about that brand in which they already maintain trust and customers always try to search items in a trusted brand. So, there is no question remaining about that - Can brand engage customers or users?

Brands may be a people, product or company or any other enterprise business. Branding may be done through advertisements, endorsements, and promotion via these social media sites. Trust is one of the most important factors associated with branding (Checksin Research, 2000). Marketers or businesses who understand the role and the value of customer or user engagement faster than their competitors are more likely to develop brands and more trustable customers. Identify engaged customers and start some kind of brand ambassador programme to further accelerate the relationship and energize their word of mouth. However, in social media marketing, the ideal customers or more valuable customer or user, does not necessarily mean to be someone who buys a lot. The ideal user or customer could be an influencer, who is a small irregular buyer or user but who posts rating and reviews, as the reviews could influence others people or user. In establishing trust, marketers need to know about the sentiment; views and affinity a user or person has towards a brand. Branding and trusting can make a reputation in the market; reputation can bring or attract new users toward it. Trusted user recommends other user for the brand that made a reputation in the market via social media sites. Hence, branding and trusting are closely related concerning the social media marketing and can have high impact on the business.

5. CONCLUSION

Businesses have been using the different social media marketing channels from the long period of time for the endorsement, advertisement and promotion of their goods and services and this has enormously grown with the growth of the internet. The main reason behind this is that businesses find a direct and easy communication mechanism with their customers or audiences. Since, satisfied customers are vital to a business to be successful and profitable, therefore it has becomes necessary to develop and maintain customer trust through satisfaction and assurances. The social media marketing efforts will be certainly more successful if the trust management is given high importance by both the social media sites and the marketing companies taking care of the different associated issues. A strong trust management effort will help to acquire, transmit and increase or decrease the level of trust between different stakeholders and will certainly go a long way in the business success. It will help the businesses or firms to grow more rapidly through social media viral effect by deploying the opinions of their users or audiences into their marketing strategy. On the other hand, a poorly managed trust can render the marketing efforts useless.

REFERENCES

Almenarez, F., Marin, A., Diaz, D., Cortes, A., Campo, C., & Garci-Rubio, C. (2011). Trust management for multimedia P2P applications in autonomic networking. *Ad Hoc Networks*, *9*, 687–697.

Analysts to Examine Key Issues Social CRM Issues at Gartner Symposium/ITxpo. (2012). Retrieved from http://www.gartner.com/newsroom/id/2161315

Andriole, S. J. (2010). Business impact of Web 2.0 technologies. *Communications of the ACM*, *53*(12), 67–79. doi:10.1145/1859204.1859225

Assaad, W., & Gomez, J. M. (2011). Social Network in marketing (Social Media Marketing) Opportunities and Risks *International Journal of Managing Public Sector Information and Communication Technologies*, *2*(1), 13–22.

As'ad, I., & Ahmad, F. (2012). An Empirical Study of E-Commerce Implementation among SME in Indonesia. *International Journal of Independent Research Studies*. *1*(1), 13–22.

Beuker, I. (2009). How digital brands can succeed and thrive in the engaged era. *Journal of Digital Asset Management*, *5*(6), 375–382. doi:10.1057/dam.2009.28

Bonson, E., & Flores, F. (2011). Social media and corporate dialogue: The response of global financial institution. *Online Information Review*, *35*(1), 34–49. doi:10.1108/14684521111113579

Bourkerche, A., & Ren, Y. (2008). "A trust-based security system for ubiquitous and pervasive computing environments", *Computer Communications. Elsevier Publication*, *31*, 4343–4351.

Checksin Research. (2000). Trust in the Wired Americas. Retrieved from http://www.cheskin.com/think/studies/trust2.html

Chikandiwa, S. T., Contogiannis, E., & Jembere, E. (2013). The adoption of social media marketing in South African banks. *European Business Review*, *25*(4), 365–381.

Culnan, M. J., McHugh, P. J., & Zubillaga, J. I. (2010). How large US companies can use twitter and other social media to gain business value. *MIS Quarterly Executie*, *9*(4), 243–259.

Dutta, M. (2014). Elections 2014 is all about social media. *The Times of India News*. Retrieved from http://timesofindia.indiatimes.com/news/Election-2014-is-all-about-social-media/articleshow/33835014.cms

Davis, R., Buchanan-Oliver, M., & Brodie, R. (1999). Relationship marketing in electronic commerce environment. *Journal of Information Technology*, *14*(4), 319–331. doi:10.1080/026839699344449

Ernest & Young. (2011). *African Attractiveness Survey*. Retrieved from http://www.ey.com/Publication/vwLUAssets/2011_Africa_Attractiveness_Survey/$FILE/11EDA187_attractiveness_africa_low_resolution_final.pdf

Gallaugher, J., & Ransbotham, S. (2010). Social media and customer dialogue management at Starbucks. *MIS Quarterly Executive*, *9*(4), 197–212.

Gefen, D. (2003). Assessing unidimensionality through Lisrel: An explanation and example. *Communication for the Information Systems*, *12*, 23–47.

Ghouri, A. M., & Khan, N. R. (2012). *Marketing Practices in Small and Medium Sized Catering and Restaurant Business of Pakistan*. Germany: LAP LAMBERT Academic Publishing GmbH & Co.

Global webIndex. (n. d.). Retrieved from http://www.emarketer.com

Gritten, A. (2011). New insights into consumer confidence in financial services. *International Journal of Book Marketing*, *29*(2), 90–106. doi:10.1108/02652321111107602

Gunelius, S. (2011). *30 Minute Social Media Marketing*. New York: McGraw Hill Publication.

Hamid, N. R. A., Akhir, R. M. and Cheng, A. Y. (2012). Social media: an emerging dimensions of marketing communication. *Journal of Market and Marketing Research*, 1-8.

Hlavinka, K., & Sullivan, J. (2011). Urban legends: word of mouth myths, madvocates and champions. Retrieved from http://www.colloquy.com/files/2011-COLLOQUY-Talk-Talk-White-Paper.pdf/

Koul, R. (2012). The Role of Social Media in Business. *Wipro Council for Industry Research Wipro Technologies*. Retrieved from http://wipro.com

Jarvenpaa, S. L., & Tractinsky, N. (1999). Consumer trust in an Internet store: A cross cultural validation. *Journal of Computer-Mediated Communication*, *5*(2), 1–5.

Lagrosen, S. O., & Grunden, K. (2014). Social media marketing in the wellness industry. *The TQM Journal*, *26*(3), 253–260.

Li, X., Hess, T. J., & Valacich, J. S. (2008). Why do we trust new technology? A study of initial trust formation with organizational information systems. *Journal of Strategic Information Systems*, *17*, 39–71.

Liao, C., Liu, C. C., & Chen, K. (2011). *Examining the impact of privacy, trust and risk perceptions beyond monetary transactions: An integrated model. Electronic Commerce Research and Applications*. Elsevier Publication.

Lipsman, A., Mudd, G., Rich, M., & Bruich, S. (2012). The power of 'like'. How brands reach (and influence) fans through social media marketing. *Journal of Advertising Research*, *52*(1), 38–52. doi:10.2501/JAR-52-1-040-052

Mangold, W. G., & Faulds, D. J. (2009). Social media: The new hybrid element of the promotion mix. *Business Horizons*, *52*(4), 357–366. doi:10.1016/j.bushor.2009.03.002

Mayer, R. C., Davis, J. H., & Schoorman, F. D. (1995). An Integrative model of organizational trust. *Academy of Management Review*, *20*(3), 709–734.

McKnight, D. H., & Chervany, N. L. (2002). What trust means in e-commerce customer relationships: An interdisciplinary conceptual typology. *International Journal of E-Commerce*, *6*(2), 35–59.

Mitict, M., & Kapoulas, A. (2012). Understanding the role of social media in bank marketing. *Marketing Intelligence and Planning*, *30*(7), 668–686.

Nair, A., & Sidhu, J. (n. d.). Social Media for B2B Marketing. *B2BENTO*. Retrieved from http://www.b2bento.com

New Forecast: Emerging Markets Lead World in Social Networking Growth. (n. d.). Retrieved from http://www.emarketer.com

Novani, S., & Kijima, K. (2013). Efficiency and Effectiveness of C2C Interactions and Mutual Learning for Value Co-Creation: Agent-Based Simulation Approach. *International Journal of Business and Management*, *8*(9), 1–13.

Pavlou, P. A., & Gefen, D. (2004). Building effective online marketplaces with institution-based trust. *Information Systems Research*, *15*(1), 37–59. doi:10.1287/isre.1040.0015

Pranter, C. A., & Martin, C. L. (1991). Compatibility Management: Roles in Service Performers. *Journal of Services Marketing*, *5*(2), 43–53. doi:10.1108/08876049110035530

Ruane, L., & Wallace, E. (2013). Generation Y females online: Insights from brand narratives. *Qualitative Market Research: An International Jouranal*, *16*(3), 43–56.

Sarner, A. (2010). Social Marketing in 2013. Retrieved from http://www.gartner.com/newsroom/id/2309616

Shankar, V., Urban, G. L., & Sultan, F. (2002). Online trust: A stakeholder perspective, concepts, implications, and future directions. *Journal of Strategic Information Systems*, *11*, 325–344.

Smith, P. R., & Zook, Z. (2011). Marketing Communications - Integrating offline and online with social media (Vol. 5, pp. 1-37).

Social Media and the LGBT Community, Finding a voice through Social Media: the LGBT Community. (n. d.). *Salzburg Academy on Media and Global Change*. Retrieved from http://www.salzburg.umd.edu/unesco/social-media-and-lgbt-community

Stelzner, M. A. (2015). *2015 Social Media Marketing Industry Report - How Marketers Are Using Social Media to Grow Their Businesses* (pp. 1–53). Social Media Examiner. Retrieved from http://www.socialmediaexaminer.com

Teo, T. S. H. (2005). Usage and Effectiveness of Online Marketing Tools among Business-to-Consumer (B2C) Firms in Singapore. *International Journal of Information Management*, *25*(3), 203–213. doi:10.1016/j.ijinfomgt.2004.12.007

The Financial Brand. (2015). Top 100 Banks Using Social Media. Retrieved from http://thefinancialbrand.com/52746

The State of Digital Marketing 2012 Report. (n. d.). Retrieved from http://go.webmarketing123.com/2012-State-of-Digital-Marketing-Report.html

Tsimonis, G., & Dimitriadis, S. (2014). Brand strategies in social media. *Marketing Intelligence and Planning*, *32*(3), 328–344.

Woodcock, N., & Green, A. (2010). *Social CRM as a Business Strategy*. The Customer Framework.

This research was previously published in the International Journal of Online Marketing (IJOM), 5(3); edited by Hatem El-Gohary, pages 47-64, copyright year 2015 by IGI Publishing (an imprint of IGI Global).

Chapter 37
Social Media and Customer Retention:
Implications for the Luxury Beauty Industry

Ellen Stokinger
London Metropolitan University, UK

Wilson Ozuem
University of Gloucestershire, UK

ABSTRACT

Social media has become an integrated part of everyday life, but its entry into the luxury goods industry has been far from easy. The use of social media in the luxury beauty industry has caused many heated debates as it is seen as a form of interference in the exclusivity of luxury brands by limiting the physical and sensual contact between brand and customer. The purpose of this chapter is to provide some insights into how social media impacts the cosmetics industry. Further, the authors provide evidence that the effective application of social media in the luxury beauty industry could lead to wider market share and customer retention. The chapter concludes with some strategies that practitioners and researchers can adopt to develop effective marketing communication strategies using social media platforms.

INTRODUCTION

The concept of social media and its relevance to effective marketing communications has gained much attention (Bolton et al., 2013; Brennan & Croft, 2012; Hamid, Akhir & Cheng, 2013; Hanna, Rohm & Crittenden, 2011; Hoffman & Fodor, 2010; Mangold & Faulds, 2009; Ozuem & Tan, 2014). The evolution of Social Media has led to the democratisation of corporate communications, with power shifting from advertising departments towards the opinions of individuals and communities, who like or dislike, comment upon and share content (Kietzmann, Hermkens, McCarthy & Silvestre, 2011; Dann & Dann, 2011). The online social landscape has converted the standard one-to-many media monologue into many-to-many dialogue. Social Media has increasingly become a product of consumers (Berthon, Pitt, Plangger & Shapiro, 2012). Online conversations have become the new fuel and forefront of customer-

DOI: 10.4018/978-1-5225-5637-4.ch037

firm relationships. Practitioners of the Cluetrain Manifesto (Levine, Locke, Searle &Weinberger, 2011) even describe conversations as "new products" that are part of a marketplace of organisations that permanently pitch to each other. As the rise of Social Media offers great opportunities to connect with consumers, Mangold and Faulds (2009) have made a case for the long-term incorporation of Social Media in a company's integral Marketing Communications strategy.

Bain and Company (2013), the leading strategy consultancy in the global luxury goods industry, expects the worldwide market of luxury goods to continue its double-digit growth, accounting for a total of £208 billion sales by 2015. In the UK specifically, the Walpole (2013), a non-profit association representing more than 180 British luxury brands such as Harrods, the Royal Opera House and Selfridges, reports an estimated growth of 12 per cent in the UK luxury industry, reaching an estimated record of £11.5 billion in the year 2017. With regard to beauty in particular, the global luxury beauty market outpaced mass-market beauty growth by 1.6 per cent in 2012 (BW Confidential). The luxury beauty industry in the UK is especially unique, as the nation's beauty market grew by 5 per cent to £2.2bn in 2012, propelling the UK to the third biggest luxury beauty market in Europe after France and Italy (Euromonitor International, 2013). The luxury beauty market in the UK is forecasted to be the fastest growing developed market in Western Europe with a growth rate of 6 per cent over the next five years, compared with an average growth of 2 per cent in the region (Euromonitor International, 2013).

The rise in the standard of living and consumer education about products has led to a democratisation of what were originally considered the most exclusive products (Garland, 2008). Globalisation has furthermore contributed to an increased level of competition, leading companies to create more exclusive products in order to differentiate from each other (Vickers & Renand, 2003). Many companies seek to add value to their brand by simply adding the term "luxury" or by extending their product portfolio with a luxury range, whilst others have created a truly luxury-oriented brand as their core business proposition. This study focuses on the last group, luxury brands that authentically carry the original meaning of luxury.

The growing desire of consumers for exclusivity and personalisation motivates luxury retailers to strongly invest in beauty. Evidence for this can be seen in for example the new "Beauty Workshop" area in Selfridges, the recently opened "Beauty Mart" section in Harvey Nichols in London or the new Luxury Beauty store on Amazon. Nowadays luxury beauty brands increasingly use Social Media to give consumers a more actively engaging brand experience. Despite the growing popularity of online shopping, so far only one in five women purchases beauty products via the Internet and many consumers are still uncomfortable about buying beauty products online, as the preference to explore, assess and test the products prior to purchase still holds true (YouGov, 2012).

Social Media has become an integrated part of everyday life, but its entry into the luxury goods industry has been far from easy. The use of Social Media in the luxury beauty industry has caused many heated debates as it is seen as interference to the exclusivity of a luxury brand by limiting the physical and sensual contact between the customer and the luxury brand (Choo, Moon, Kim & Yoon, 2012; Dall'Olmo Riley & Lacroix, 2003; Dubois & Paternault, 1995; Khang, Ki & Ye, 2012; Okonkwo, 2010; Seung-A, 2013; Smith, 2009). However, as the number of affluent customers purchasing online increases, luxury brands face the challenge of retaining their customer base in order to create more sustainable revenue streams (Bolton, 1998; Buttle, 2009). Companies have reacted to this recent evolution in the marketing landscape and almost every luxury brand has adopted Social Media to connect with customers (Kim & Ko, 2010). A survey by the Luxury Interactive Conference's research team reported that 78 per cent of digital marketing executives for luxury brands increased their spend on Social Media in 2012, with 73 per cent of those surveyed planning to further increase their Social Media spend in 2013 (Alston, 2012).

The last decade has seen the production of a vast range of literature about Social Media. Topics of preference have so far included communication (Ozuem, Howell & Lancaster, 2008; Quinton & Harridge-March, 2010; Powers, Advincula, Austin, Graiko & Snyder,2012), the impact of word of mouth (Kozinets, Valck, Wojnicki & Wilner, 2010; Hennig-Thurau, Gwinner, Walsk & Gremler, 2004, Prendergast & Yuen, 2010), purchase intentions (Naylor, Walker, Cait & West, 2012) and service creation (Jarvenpaa & Tuunainen, 2013; Onook, Manish & Raghave, 2013; Trainor, 2012). Some of the literature focuses on how Social Media influences customer relations (Katsioloudes, Grant & McKechnie, 2007; Kim & Ko, 2010; Clark & Melancon, 2013; Laroche, Habibi, & Richard, 2013; Hennig-Thurau et al., 2010).

Most of these studies have focused on customer loyalty (Clark & Melancon, 2013; Gummerus, Liljander, Weman & Pihlström, 2012; Hawkins & Vel, 2013; Laroche et al., 2013) yet Hennig-Thurau et al. (2010) considered customer retention as the outcome of engagement with new media. Their observations, however, were out-with the context of the UK luxury beauty industry. Blattberg, Getz and Thomas (2001) emphasised the need to clearly distinguish between customer loyalty and customer retention. Just because a customer is retained does not automatically imply that the individual is also loyal to a brand. Whereas customer loyalty is a customer reward that occurs once customers have changed their hearts and minds in favour of a particular product or service, customer retention is an organisational reward and focuses on how to keep customers without first having to change their hearts or minds (The Customer Institute, 2010).

Furthermore, Kim and Ko (2010) identified the impact of Social Media on customer equity, thereby emphasising the correlation between purchase intention and customer equity. Referring to the financially driven customer equity model as described by Blattberg et al. (2001), customer equity consists of three steps – customer acquisition, customer retention and add-on selling. It can thus be argued that evaluating the impact of Social Media marketing on customer equity jumps to the end without considering important hurdles in between such as customer retention. Therefore, instead of directly measuring customer equity or focusing on customer loyalty, this study recommends first analysing the extent to which Social Media impacts on customer retention. Whilst Social Media is often viewed as a positive lever in the customer-firm relationship, few studies refer to the luxury industry and fewer yet speak to the context of the UK luxury beauty industry.

Kim and Ko (2010; 2012) have made a substantial contribution to the literature on Social Media in the luxury market. However, as with many other studies, the researchers primarily focus on the luxury fashion industry (Choo et al., 2012; Kim & Ko, 2010; Kim & Ko, 2012; Jin, 2012; Moore & Doyle, 2010; Phan, Thomas & Heine, 2011). In contrast to the consumption of luxury fashion, buying luxury beauty products involves a high level of pre-purchase testing, which raises the question of whether or not Social Media provides an adequate tool to retain customers, as product testing is difficult and complex to implement online. This study therefore aims to identify the extent to which Social Media is a convenient tool to support the retention of luxury beauty customers and in which ways a brand's communication via Social Media can impact on customer retention.

BACKGROUND

The proliferation of Social Media is closely related to and facilitated by the development of Web 2.0 technologies (Berthon et al., 2012; Brennan & Croft, 2012; Fieseler & Fleck, 2013; Kaplan & Haenlein, 2010; Laroche et al., 2013; Tuten, 2008). The term "Web 2.0" was first introduced by the American media company O'Reilly and can be thought of as a set of technological innovations including hardware and software, which have the aim of empowering the user instead of the firm by allowing for content creation and increased interaction (Berthon et al., 2012; O'Reilly, 2005). While its predecessor, Web 1.0, had already laid the foundation for connecting people online via email and chat, Web 2.0 takes connectivity to another level by providing a variety of tools which enable the user to create, publish and share content and give recommendations to online friends and followers (Atta & Mahmoud, 2012; Evans & McKee, 2010).

This development has allowed for a new and disruptive marketing platform: Social Media and this was quickly identified as a revolution of the online generation and it has thus attracted the interest of researchers whose definitions bring Social Media into contact with different aspects such as the power of "social sharing" behaviour (Kaplan & Haenlein, 2010, Jevons & Gabbott, 2000; Nair, 2011; Safko & Brake, 2009; Stokes, 2008), interconnectivity (Dann & Dann, 2011; Hoffman & Novak, 2012; Laroche et al., 2013), influence (Brown & Fiorella, 2013), education (Blackshaw & Nazzarro 2004, Mangold & Faulds, 2009) and comparisons with traditional marketing (Mangold & Faulds, 2009; Zarella, 2010).

The most widespread definition of Social Media was originated by Kaplan and Haenlein (2010), who suggested that Social Media refers to a range of internet-based applications that build on the foundation of Web 2.0 and enable users to create and exchange User Generated Content (UGC). UGC is the engine of today's participative web and to "count" as UGC it must be published, creative and produced outside the professional context (Daugherty, Eastin &Bright, 2008; OECD, 2007). Many researchers emphasise the importance of exchanging and sharing UGC (Jevons & Gabbott, 2000; Nair, 2011; Safko & Brake, 2009; Stokes, 2008), after all the "social" in Social Media already promises a high degree of contact and exchange with other people.

Stokes (2008) sees the sense of Social Media in its ability to make users share content. Safko and Brake (2009) develop this further and define Social Media as a tool that allows users to share information, knowledge and opinions by engaging in online dialogues. On Social Media platforms, users have the opportunity to create a specific image of themselves, which is maintained through the sharing of posts, pictures, videos, liking certain posts and groups and extending the network of online friends. However, one might have the impression that some users pursue purely narcissistic interests (Nair, 2011), which can then quickly evoke negative attitudes towards users, brands or companies. In addition, the opportunity for self-expression might not be available to such an extent offline (Hoffman & Novak, 2012) and can thus result in some exaggeration of the personal self.

It is undisputed that Social Media can bring together like-minded people and businesses (Hagel & Armstrong, 1997; Wellman & Gulia, 1999) and hence it satisfies a need rooted deeply in human nature for a sense of belonging, (Maslow, 1943; Gangadharbhatla, 2008). Hoffman and Novak (2012) describe this as another revolutionising aspect of Social Media, as it is a tool that enables users to connect and re-connect even over long distances. Social Media allows for interconnectivity between users and between content and communication technologies (Dann & Dann, 2011). In the context of interconnectivity Tuten (2008) describes Social Media as an online community categorised as either social networks or virtual worlds that are participatory, conversational and fluid. Significantly, an online community "promotes the individual while also emphasizing an individual's relationship to the community" (Tuten, 2008, p.20). The motivation to engage in an online community derives from the need for contact comfort, also referred to as a need for affiliation, and a need for entertainment (Tuten, 2008). A brand community in particular is defined as a "specialised, non-geographically bound community, based on a structured set of relations among admirers of a brand" (Muniz & O'Guinn, 2001, p.412). Brands are referred to fundamentally as social entities (Muniz & O'Guinn, 2001) created through the inter-play of consumers and marketers (Firat & Venkatesh, 1995), which can thus be leveraged through the utilisation of Social Media.

Enabling users to talk to each other can be considered as an extension to traditional word-of-mouth communication (Divol, Edelman & Sarrazin, 2012; Mangold & Faulds, 2009). Amongst online users, some establish a more dominant position than others by sharing more information and opinions and thus procuring more buzz around them. Marketers have quickly discovered the power of targeting Social Media communities and they recognise that such groups gave rise to a new form of "influence marketing" (Williams & Cothrell, 2000; Brown & Fiorella, 2013). As well as exerting influence, Social Media also impacts upon persuasive acts, as persuasion is based on social connections and cultural assumptions (Noor Al-Deen & Hendricks, 2012).

Furthermore, the emergence of Social Media has led to a shift in power asymmetry from the marketer to the consumer, who now has a greater mandate over media consumption than ever before (Vollmer & Precourt, 2008). Social Media can spur consumer education about brands, products and services (Blackshaw & Nazzaro, 2004; Mangold & Faulds, 2009, Hoffman & Novak, 2012). Since Social Media is about sharing, consumers can use the web as a way to educate themselves and to contribute to the education of others within their network. In addition to collecting information from Social Media sources, users also see Social Media as a service channel that enables them to remain in easy touch with organisations (Leggat, 2010).

Whereas Social Media has all the hallmarks of the traditional paths of communication between company and consumer, it has also evolved as a new communication channel between consumer and consumer and it can thus be considered as a hybrid addition to the promotional mix (Mangold & Faulds, 2009). Mangold and Faulds (2009) therefore stress the permanent incorporation of Social Media in every company's Integral Marketing Communication's strategy. However, only implementing Social Media in the promotional mix does not guarantee success, as it is also crucial that public relations practitioners adapt their strategies to newly evolving media (Pavlik, 2007). Kietzmann et al. (2011) furthermore suggest that a firm's performance on Social Media (if done passionately and appropriately) can significantly impact upon reputations, turnover and even survival but it can cause damage if done half-heartedly (Kietzmann et al., 2011).

Dimensions of Social Media

The variety of Social Media allows for many different kinds of users and marketers have to distinguish between these different Social Media users if they want to target them effectively (Hanna et al., 2011). Sukoco and Wu (2010) have identified two kinds of interests groups in Social Media communities. One group seeks to fulfil a self-related interest including knowledge and enjoyment and another follows socially-related interests which refer to their search for affiliation and social status. Humans generally want to create a specific image of themselves and want to control how other people perceive this image (Goffmann, 1959) by disclosing selected pieces of their daily lives to the public.

Cavazza (2013) suggests another model to categorise the motivations of online consumers according to four categories (sharing, discussing, networking and publishing). Whereas these categories adequately describe the most common online behaviour of today's user, it is doubtful if users already know the exact action they undertake during a browsing session. This study argues that users are more likely to know only the general purpose of what they want from their Social Media visit instead of planning the exact action beforehand. Rather than already knowing what exactly to discuss with other users prior to

Figure 1. The trefoil model of social media users and tools
Source: researcher.

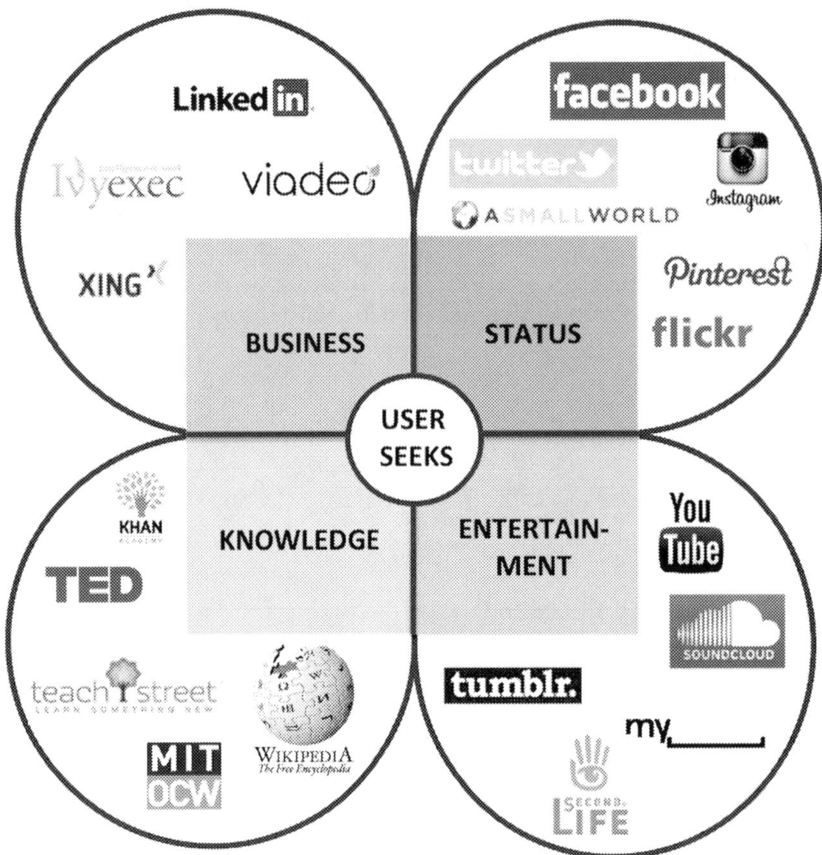

browsing, customers are more likely to first seek to satisfy general needs such as entertainment once only and find an inspiring article which they spontaneously decide to share. In examining Social Media platforms, the current paper identifies four different kinds of Social Media users and allocates the most appropriate Social Media tools aligned to each of these users.

The trefoil model distinguishes between four purposes of the users' online activity, their desire for status, entertainment, knowledge or business. In most cases the users' online activity has at least one and at maximum all four identified purposes. During browsing on Social Media the user might spontaneously switch between the purposes.

- **Status-Seekers:** Generally use social networking sites and visual Social Media, which allows them to construct a certain image through tweeting, sharing pictures with sophisticated filters and following particular brands. Examples include Facebook, twitter, Instagram, Pinterest and flickr.
- **Entertainment-Seekers:** Visit Social Media in order to have a good experience, to feel better through browsing. They seek platforms, which cover a certain topic of interest, such as music-focused Social Media platforms including Youtube, my space and Soundcloud, or, according to hobby and interest through organised blogs like tumblr.

- **Knowledge-Seekers:** Have the goal of extending their knowledge whilst using Social Media and so they target science-based learning platforms such as Wikipedia, TED or the Khan Academy.
- **Business-Seekers:** Generally use Social Media because they want to leverage their career perspectives, either indirectly, through extending their professional network and updating their online CV, or even directly by applying for positions using, for example, their LinkedIn profiles.

Social Media is growing at a phenomenal speed and the increasing number of platforms provides challenges for companies to decide which newly developed media are sustainable and which are not (Kaplan & Haenlein, 2010). Possibly the most successful example of a sustainable medium is Facebook. Founded in 2004 by Harvard student Mark Zuckerberg Facebook has become the world's number one social medium in just under 10 years with 1 billion active users (Kirckpatrick, 2010; Socialmediatoday, 2013). Another example of a Social Medium that successfully re-shaped the communication landscape of today is Twitter. This micro-blog was launched as a secondary project in 2006 by a San-Francisco-based podcasting company but it quickly turned into a major project when it reached 215 million monthly active users and 500 million tweets a day in 2013 (Geron, 2013; O'Reilly & Milstein, 2012). However, not every Social Medium is qualified to survive in the long-term and even Apple's music sharing platform Ping has not managed to find success (Hof, 2012).

With such a rich amount of Social Media types it is useful to categorise these in order to afford an overview. Kaplan and Haenlein (2010) divide Social Media into six types comprising of collaborative projects, blogs, content communities, social networking sites, virtual game worlds, and virtual social worlds. However, new Social Media tools frequently emerge and in this context Kaplan and Haenlein's (2010) categorisation seems to offer only a limited perspective of the vast array of Social Media types. Mangold and Faulds (2009) provide a more detailed understanding of different Social Media types and tools, and their list is broken down and allocated to the appropriate user in the previously identified trefoil model of Social Media users and tools.

For now the trefoil model of Social Media users and tools in combination with Mangold and Faulds' (2009) adjusted categorisation of Social Media tools and types provides a comprehensive overview about today's Social Media landscape. However, Social Media tools evolve quickly and the model therefore requires regular updates.

Critics have already raised the argument that text-based Social Media such as posts on Facebook and Twitter are out-dated and are being replaced by visual-based Social Media (Walpole, 2013; Moritz, 2012). The latest development in Social Media supports this critique. Instagram, the photo-sharing networking service, has garnered 7,302,000 users and overtook Twitter with 6,868,000 users in August 2012. Pinterest, another content sharing service, has emerged as the 4th largest driver of traffic worldwide (Moritz, 2012).

Mapping of Social Media for Marketing

The first predecessor of today's Social Media was introduced in 1979, when Tom Truscott and Jim Ellis from Duke University created "Usenet" (Kaplan & Haenlein, 2010). By allowing its users to post public messages this platform served asa Bulletin Board System (BBS) similar to today's forums (Kaplan & Haenlein, 2010). In addition to Usenet, the Internet ran a variety of protocols such as email, the chat system IRC and Gopher, a system to browse files (Rettberg, 2008). Towards the end of 1990 Tim Berners-Lee, a CERN scientist, implemented the first graphical web browser, which allowed for text with embedded

Figure 2. Examples of social media types and tools
Source: Mangold and Faulds, 2009, p.358.

Status-seekers

- Social networking sites (MySpace, Facebook)
- Invitation only social networks (ASmallWorld.net)
- Photo sharing sites (Flickr)

Entertainment-seekers

- Creative works sharing sites:
  - Video sharing sites (Youtube)
  - Music sharing sites (Soundcloud)
  - Content sharing combined with assistance (Piczo)
  - General intellectual property sharing sites (Creative Commons)
- Virtual worlds (Second Life)
- Commerce communities (Ebay, Amazon)
- Social bookmarking sites allowing users to recommend music, videos (Digg)
- Open Source Software communities (Linux)

Knowledge-seekers

- User-sponsored blogs (The Unofficial Apple Weblog, Cnet.com)
- Company-sponsored websites/blogs (Apple)
- Company-sponsored cause/help sites (click2quit)
- Collaborative websites (Wikipedia)
- Podcasts
- News delivers sites
- Educational materials sharing (MIT OpenCourseWare)

Business-seekers

- Business networking sites (LinkedIn)

images at the same time (Rettberg, 2008). This gave rise to the construction of the first webpages, both private and corporate, which (retrospectively considered) were the precursors of today's blogs (Rettberg, 2008). In 1998 Bruce and Susan Abelson launched the first social networking site "Open Diary", which connected online diary writers together in one community and gave them the opportunity to comment on other bloggers' opinions (Kaplan & Haenlein, 2010; Safko, 2012).

The development of high-speed Internet was the break-through of the constantly changing and evolving Social Media environment. Critics formulated doubts as to whether Social Media could survive in today's fast-paced media environment and labelled it as short-term trend. However, in 2012 there were 1.43 billion social network users worldwide (Arno, 2012) and many additional email and search engine users deliver sufficient proof that Social Media is a permanent, integrated part of life for young and old users. The serious advancement of Social Media leads to a shift in marketing thinking. Transactional marketing, which was identified by McCarthy's (1960) 4P model of Product, Price, Promotion and Place is now being replaced by the more relevant notion of relational marketing, which aims to satisfy the unique needs of each individual customer (Bhatnagar, 2012). To understand the different desires of every consumer, marketers need to involve them from early on in product development (Hoffman, Kopalle & Novak, 2010). Taking this into consideration, Lauterborn (1990) complements the concept of the 4Ps with the 4Cs including Consumer wants and needs, Cost to satisfy, Convenience to buy and Communication (Lauterborn, 1990). While the 4C concept provides a better fit with today's marketing environment, both the concepts were introduced before the take-off of Social Media.

In the meantime, the development of new technologies has challenged traditional ways of communication between companies and consumers (Ozuem et al., 2008). Instead of one-way communication directed by the company and with a passively receptive customer, consumers are now actively involved in a dialogue with companies. Brown and Fiorella (2013) acknowledge that the Internet and Social Media have disrupted direct communication between brands, its influencers and their followers. Nowadays, companies can no longer rely on the bandwagon effect of appealing directly to the influencers of a marketplace to win more consumers. The researchers conclude that the facilitation of word-of-mouth and the enormous amount of noise have proven to be critical to consumer trust in brands, which is the basis for a successful online marketing campaign. Brown and Fiorella (2013) thus suggest the 4As model, a concept specifically suitable for an increasingly word-of-mouth-based marketing environment.

Regardless of which kind of Social Media a company chooses it must ensure that the audience receives the message. Google's Pay Per Click and Facebook's Insight algorithm help to ensure that the right audience is targeted. In order to accept the message, the user must trust the chosen medium. This can be achieved by social influencer endorsements and a seamless application of the brand's message by planning every step. Amplification is a further success factor for Social Media marketing, as people thrive on the sharing and multiplication of messages. Brown and Fiorella (2013, p.43) furthermore state that Social Media have completely changed the "ballgame" of marketing to consumers. An important aspect thereof is the impact of Social Media on customer service. Companies can no longer afford to ignore criticism and customer apathy. The conversation-enabling nature of Social Media spreads negative word-of-mouth very rapidly, which, in the worst case, can lead to complete consumer detachment from a company with accompanying loss of revenue (Khammash & Griffiths, 2010; Sandes & Urdan, 2013).

Figure 3. Paradigm shifts in technologically-induced environments
Source: McCarthy,1960; Lauterborn, 1990; Brown and Fiorella, 2013.

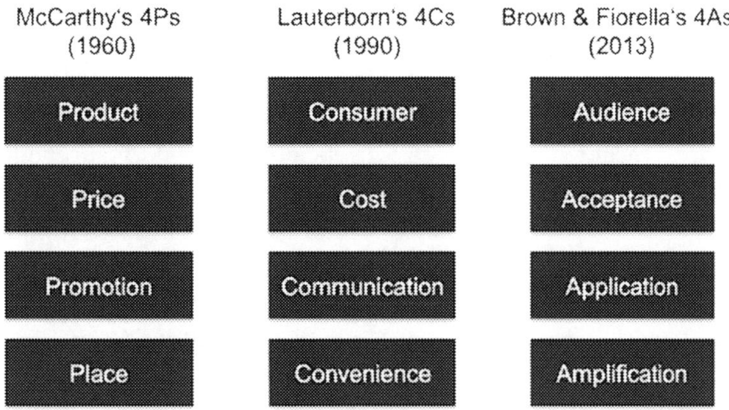

For marketers the emergence of Social Media implies one dominant benefit: the forming of close relationships with the consumer. Information exchange with a brand's followers and amongst followers themselves on Social Media uncovers the way consumers think and feel about a product. Gunelius (2011) remarks that online conversations between users are beneficial for companies in the sense that they build brand awareness, brand recognition and brand loyalty. Literature increasingly recognises the importance of co-creation and collaboration with customers online (Vargo & Lusch, 2004). Sharing details about the brand's history, lifestyle, product range and events keeps the consumer close and allows for the creation of emotional bonds (Quinton & Harridge-March, 2010). The researchers suggest that social bonding with the customer results in a sense of loyalty and the more participative the nature of these social bonds, the less the consumer is stimulated to look elsewhere. Trainor (2012) thus remarks that the utilisation of Social Media represents a competitive advantage for companies as it helps to generate superior customer value and increased profitability for the firm. Tuten (2008) identifies further advantages of a brand's presence on Social Media, including strengthening its personality and extending its ethos as well as providing a positive contribution to brand equity through internationalisation.

Many advocates of Social Media are convinced that the recent development has completely replaced traditional media. Whereas this can be confirmed to some extent, the 2012 CMO survey provides evidence of some contradiction (The CMO survey, 2013). Even though marketers can increase their Social Media spend in the next five years to around three times the current level, Social Media spend will only account for 20% of the Marketing budget with the remaining 80% still being spent on traditional media advertising (The CMO survey, 2013).

SOCIAL MEDIA AND CUSTOMER RETENTION INTERPLAY

Studies on the emergence of Social Media and its impact on customer retention are scarce. In analysing the effects of ten different kinds of new media, Hennig-Thurau et al. (2010) conclude that new media releases a higher level of brand engagement and thus positively impacts on customer retention. Liang, Chen and Wang (2008) focus on online, instead of offline, customer relationships and predict that online relationship marketing contributes to customer loyalty through perceived relationship investment and relationship quality. The researchers see customer loyalty as the precursor of customer retention and cross-buying. Blattberg et al. (2001) suggest that customer retention and customer loyalty are not the same, as a customer can be retained but does not necessarily need to be loyal. This contradicts the conception of Liang et al. (2008) and motivates this research to further elaborate on the impact of Social Media on customer retention.

In order to analyse the extent to which Social Media influences customer retention, it is crucial to understand the key drivers of customer retention. Buttle (2009) suggests measuring customer retention by tangible and intangible means. Tangible measures include key performance indicators such as raw customer retention rates, sales-adjusted retention rates, profit-adjusted retention rates or cost of customer retention (Buttle, 2009). Furthermore, he identifies four intangible drivers of customer retention as customer delight, customer perceived value, social and structural customer bonds and customer engagement. To create customer delight companies need to introduce detailed customer knowledge systems, which address and exceed the desire of each individual customer (Buttle, 2009). The emergence of Social Media provides an additional channel of communication and if integrated with other channels, marketers can more easily spread the word of value adding benefits like loyalty schemes and customer clubs. Social bonds are personal ties that are created during the interaction with others and the virtual world can be considered as distant at first, so companies need to consider their online interfaces with customers in order to transmit vividly what the brand stands for (Srinivasan, Anderson & Ponnavolu, 2002; Wilson, 1995). Structural bonds exist when the company and the customer dedicate resources to the relationship (Buttle, 2009). Moreover, customer engagement involves commitment and experience and significantly contributes towards the formation of competitive advantage (Buttle, 2009).

Referring to the tangible and intangible measures of customer retention, Hoffman and Fodor (2010) remark that many marketers still focus solely on return numbers, such as Buttle's (2009) tangible customer retention KPIs, which the researchers consider to be short-term oriented and only suitable for traditional media. The emergence of Social Media comes with a set of unconventional and more intangible characteristics and marketers need to adjust their measurement schemes to this. Hoffman and Fodor (2010) provide four strategic options to measure Social Media effectiveness and these are presented in Figure 4.

The aim for every company should be to move away from fuzzy measurement attempts to more quantifiable metrics in the direction of the upper right quadrant. At first sight, many intangible factors might seem immeasurable, but Hoffmann and Fodor (2010) stress that marketers need to implement metrics for intangible factors as well, such as brand awareness, brand engagement and word-of-mouth in order to create successful campaigns.

Literature on customer retention cannot be considered complete without citing further intangible drivers such as customer satisfaction and customer loyalty (Crosby, 1990). Satisfaction has been identified as one of the key influencing factors of customer retention (Gustafsson, Johnson& Roos2005; Liang et al., 2008; Sashi, 2012; Buttle, 2009) due to the long-term impact on customer behaviour (Oliver, 1980; Yi, 1990). Customer satisfaction generally refers to a customer's impression of product quality, service

Figure 4. Strategic options for social media measurement
Source: Hofmann and Fodor, 2010, p.47.

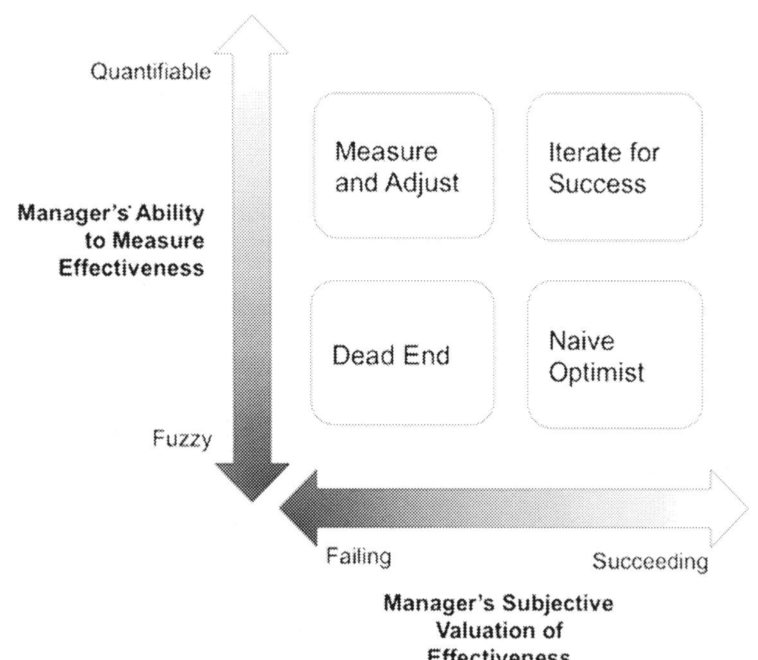

quality and price equity (Bolton & Lemon, 1999; Fornell, 1992). The more satisfied a customer is with a brand experience, the greater the retention rate (Anderson & Sullivan, 1993; Ranaweera & Prabhu, 2003).

The quality of a product can be divided into three levels; basic quality, which the customer routinely expects, linear quality, which the customer more or less wants and attractive quality, which surprises, delights and excites the customer (Kano, 1995). Delight, which can be traced back to satisfaction, therefore is another key driver of customer retention (Buttle, 2009). The advance of Social Media has found appeal in the literature of satisfaction as it gives customers the opportunity to communicate faster with a company, and likewise it allows companies to respond faster to customer complaints and thus enhances the level of customer service (Krishna, Dangayach & Jain, 2011; Clark & Melancon, 2013).

Morgan and Hunt (1994) define trust as one party's confidence in another party's reliability and integrity. Chaudhuri and Holbrook (2001) refer to trust as the willingness of consumers to rely on the brand to perform its intended function. Satisfaction alone is not enough to retain customers (Danesh, Nasab & Kwek, 2012), and it has been widely discussed in literature that satisfaction goes hand in hand with customer trust in a company (Crosby, Ewans & Cowles, 1990; Dwyer, Schurr & Oh, 1987; Hart & Johnson, 1999; Liang et al., 2008). According to Betrand (2013), the emergence of Social Media has had a strong impact on customer trust.

The level of online word-of-mouth is multiplied and as consumers generally trust personal sources to a higher extent than they trust non-personal sources (Weber, 2007), companies have an additional opportunity to influence their customers (Brown & Fiorella, 2013). Trust in online environments was found to reduce the cognitive uncertainty related to online purchasing (Dash & Saji, 2007) and instead increased customer retention (Abhamid, Akhir& Cheng, 2013). However, the uncertainty of the Internet in terms of e-commerce (Pavlou, 2003) and personal information (Flavian & Guinaliu, 2006; Kelly & Erickson, 2004) provides challenges to the long-term preservation of customer trust.

Social Media and Customer Engagement

Customer engagement seems to occupy the centre stage of Social Media literature and is often referred to as impacting customer loyalty (Brodie, Hollebeek, Biljana & Ilic, 2011; Clark & Melancon, 2013; Hoffman & Fodor, 2010; Quinton & Harridge-March, 2010). In addition, various studies have shed light on the positive impact of customer engagement on commitment and trust (Agnihotri, Kothandaraman, Kashyap & Singh, 2012; Bowden, 2009; Verhoef, 2003). Bowden (2009) suggests that customer engagement results from calculative commitment, which then leads to emotional commitment forming the foundation for customer loyalty and finally, increases trust through constant involvement. Gummerus et al.(2012, p.857) provide a simple definition of customer engagement as a "set of behavioural activities towards a firm", whereas Agnihotri et al. (2012, p.335) consider customer engagement in the new light of Social Media and base its existence on repeated buyer-seller interactions on Social Media, "in which positive (negative) feedback strengthens (weakens) buyer-seller relationships". Referring to the emergence of new media, Libai (2011) states that this not only gives customers the possibility to engage with a company through purchase, but also via non-purchase behaviour. Although all these definitions of customer engagement agree that it contributes to the customer-firm relationship to some extent, the extent to which it impacts on customer retention has so far not been extensively elaborated upon in literature (Hennig-Thurau et al., 2010).

In addition, Gummerus et al.'s (2012) research on consumer engagement behaviour suggests that by engaging in different ways in online communities, users accordingly harvest relationship benefits such as entertainment. Dholakia, Bagozzi, & Pearo (2004) and Nonnecke, Andrews & Preece (2006) credit the entertainment of customers to relaxation, fun, community participation and online services. Adding to customer engagement impact on entertainment, Prahalad and Ramaswamy (2004) and Brodie et al. (2011) consider customer engagement as something formed by interactive customer experiences and as an important step in the co-creation of value, which is especially promoted through the participative nature of Social Media (Atwal & Williams, 2009; Kumar et al., 2010).

MANAGERIAL IMPLICATIONS AND RECOMMENDATIONS

The current paper proposes a number of managerial implications. Before beginning with a Social Media presence, luxury beauty brands need to first reflect upon their core values and their vision and mission. They must develop a clear and succinct Social Media strategy based on these factors. This strategy needs to include not only obvious objectives such as sales, cost efficiencies and product development, but also needs to consider objectives such as brand awareness, customer engagement and word-of-mouth. It is important that all the objectives are assessable. In the future, retailing will increasingly follow an Omni-channel approach, focusing on a seamless provision of experiences through whichever channel, digital or offline, the brand participates in. In order to make this work, the Social Media strategy needs to be integrated within the corporate strategy. Every department and every employee has to be aligned with it in order to convey authentic experiences through every single touch point.

For a Social Media strategy to be successful, a continuous budget needs to be ensured. It is therefore crucial to equip every objective of the Social Media strategy with measurable key performance indicators. Every campaign on Social Media is different and in order to continuously improve their activities, luxury beauty brands need to measure the effect of each campaign on customer retention by looking at conversion rates, positive sentiment analysis and successful customer complaints rates amongst others. Picking up the Omni-channel trend cited above, luxury beauty brands would greatly benefit from integrating online and offline data about customers. Customers nowadays expect companies to know when they have previously purchased from them and combining these two databases does not only open up an entirely new dimension to customer experiences but also enables a more complete measurement of customer retention, which ultimately allows for a more personalised communication with customers.

Without investing in traditional media a luxury beauty brand cannot expect any form of engagement from its customers. Prior to a participating in Social Media, customers have to be made aware of the brand's existence. Therefore luxury beauty brands need to continue investing in advertising, whilst at the same time balancing this with content creation. Whereas under-investment in advertising and over-creation of content lead to a brand's unknown exposure in the market place, vice versa, over-investment in advertising and under-creation of content can provoke a customer expectation gap, ultimately leading to customer disappointment and rejection of the brand. Luxury beauty brands have to find the right balance between advertising and content creation to achieve maximum brand exposure.

Customers aspire to luxury beauty brands. The products are highly coveted for their exclusivity and this is influenced by the brand's story and price point. Therefore, luxury beauty brands should not engage their customers via promotions, as this removes part of the exclusivity from the brand and can even lead to customer disappointment, realising that the brand is not as luxurious as expected when the same promotion tools as in the mass market are applied. The luxury beauty customer is not a value-for-money customer and their involvement starts with the brand's roots, the story. Therefore, luxury beauty brands should engage customers via value-adding content, such as previews, 'How to'- videos, beauty expert interviews - giving customers exclusive content they cannot get anywhere else, delighting them by going the unexpected extra mile. Beauty is fun and so is Social Media, now the brands need to leverage this by being innovative and having the courage to try things out. Luxury beauty brands should not be afraid to fail; mistakes contribute to the learning curve and prevent becoming rooted in a comfort zone.

Luxury beauty brands participating on Social Media should be aware that growth is incredibly fast-paced. Some already consider the Facebook social network, founded in 2004, as out-dated. An array of new, visual-based Social Media tools is on the rise. Whereas text-based Social Media are convenient for customer service purposes, and therefore have to remain a part of the strategy, visual Social Media allow for a more vivid and luxurious presentation of the brand. A healthy mix of text and visual-based Social Media is necessary. Text-based Social Media communications should have the aim of leveraging customer dialogue via reviews and posts, whereas communication through visual Social Media should increase emotional engagement by encouraging customers to share photos of important and meaningful moments. To further humanise the image of luxury beauty brands it is important to relax the communication and to not always share perfectly retouched pictures but to allow for natural and more imperfect looks. The aim of every luxury beauty company should be to become truly customer-centred. The participative nature of Social Media implies that word-of-mouth, and especially negative word-of-mouth, can spread very fast. Therefore luxury beauty companies need to have sufficient resources at hand to follow what their customers say about the brand in each channel and to immediately react to issues in an authentic and transparent manner. Only when the company proves to be reactive and honest will customers feel valued and able to establish a feeling of trust towards the brand. A customer that trusts a brand will ultimately come back.

REFERENCES

Abhamid, N. R., Akhir, R. M., & Cheng, A. Y. (2013). Social media: An emerging dimension of marketing communication. *Journal of Management and Marketing Research*, *12*, 4–11.

Agnihotri, R., Kothandaraman, P., Kashyap, R., & Singh, R. (2012). Bringing 'Social' into Sales: The Impact of Salespeople's Social Media Use on Service Behaviours and Value Co-creation. *Journal of Personal Selling & Sales Management*, *32*(3), 333–348. doi:10.2753/PSS0885-3134320304

Alston, M. (2012). *78% of Luxury Marketers Spent More on Social Media in 2012 Than 2011, Luxury Interactive*. Retrieved from: http://finance.yahoo.com/news/78-luxury-marketers-spent-more-141500809.html

Anderson, E. W., & Sullivan, M. W. (1993). The antecedents and consequences of customer satisfaction for firms. *Marketing Science*, *12*(2), 125–143. doi:10.1287/mksc.12.2.125

Arno, C. (2012). *Worldwide Social Media Usage Trends in 2012, Search Engine Watch*. Retrieved from: http://searchenginewatch.com/article/2167518/Worldwide-Social-Media-Usage-Trends-in-2012

Atta, A., & Mahmoud, A. (2012). Web 2.0: A Movement within the Learning Community. *Information Management and Business Review*, *4*(12), 625–631.

Atwal, G., & Williams, A. (2009). Luxury brand marketing – The experience is everything! *Brand Management, 16*(5), 338–346. doi:10.1057/bm.2008.48

Bain & Company. (2013). *Worldwide luxury goods continues double-digit annual growth; global market now tops €200 billion, finds Bain & Company*. Retrieved from: http://www.bain.com/about/press/press-releases/worldwide-luxury-goods-continues-double-digit-annual-growth.aspx

Berthon, P. R., Pitt, L. F., Plangger, K., & Shapiro, D. (2012). Marketing meets Web 2.0, social media, and creative consumers: Implications for international marketing strategy. *Business Horizons, 55*(3), 261–271. doi:10.1016/j.bushor.2012.01.007

Bertrand, G. (2013). Socialmedia research: Developing a trust metric in the social age. *International Journal of Market Research, 55*(3), 333–335. doi:10.2501/IJMR-2013-032

Bhatnagar, N. (2012). Customer Relationship Marketing: Customer-Centric Processes for Engendering Customer- Firm Bonds and Optimizing Long-Term Customer Value. *Intechopen* [online]. Retrieved from: http://cdn.intechopen.com/pdfs/35309/InTech-Customer_relationship_marketing_customer_centric_processes_for_engendering_customer_firm_bonds_and_optimizing_long_term_customer_value.pdf

Blackshaw, P., & Nazzaro, M. (2004). Consumer-Generated Media (CGM) 101: Word-of-mouth in the age of the Webfortified consumer. *Intelliseek* [online]. Retrieved from: http://www.brandchannel.com/images/papers/222_cgm.pdf

Blattberg, R., Getz, G., & Thomas, J. S. (2001). *Customer Equity: Building and Managing Relationships as Valuable Assets*. Boston: Harvard Business School Press.

Bolton, R. N. (1998). A Dynamic Model of the Duration of the Customer's Relationship with a Continuous Service Provider: The Role of Satisfaction. *Marketing Science, 17*(1), 45–65. doi:10.1287/mksc.17.1.45

Bolton, R. N., & Lemon, K. N. (1999). Dynamic Model of Customers' Usage of Services: Usage as an Antecedent and Consequence of Satisfaction. *The Journal of Consumer Research, 36*(2), 171–186.

Bolton, R. N., Parasuraman, A., Hoefnagels, A., Migchels, N., Kabadayi, S., & Gruber, T. et al. (2013). Understanding Generation Y and their use of social media: A review and research agenda. *Journal of Service Management, 24*(3), 245–267. doi:10.1108/09564231311326987

Bowden, J. L. H. (2009). The process of customer engagement: A conceptual framework. *Journal of Marketing Theory and Practice, 17*(1), 63–74. doi:10.2753/MTP1069-6679170105

Brennan, R., & Croft, R. (2012). The use of social media in B2B marketing and branding: An exploratory study. *Journal of Consumer Behaviour, 11*(2), 101–115. doi:10.1362/147539212X13420906144552

Brodie, R. J., Hollebeek, L. D., Biljana, J., & Ilic, A. (2011). Customer engagement: Conceptual domain, fundamental propositions, and implications for research. *Journal of Service Research, 14*(3), 252–271. doi:10.1177/1094670511411703

Brown, D., & Fiorella, S. (2013). Influence Marketing. Que Publishing.

Buttle, F. (2009). *Customer relationship management – concepts and technologies* (2nd ed.). Oxford, UK: Elsevier.

Cavazza, F. (2013). *Social Media Landscape 2013, Fred Cavazza*. Retrieved from: http://www.fredcavazza.net/2013/04/17/social-media-landscape-2013/

Chaudhuri, A., & Holbrook, M. B. (2001). The chain of effects from brand trust and brand affect to brand performance: The role of brand loyalty. *Journal of Marketing*, *65*(2), 81–93. doi:10.1509/jmkg.65.2.81.18255

Choo, H., Moon, H., Kim, H., & Yoon, N. (2012). Luxury customer value. *Journal of Fashion Marketing and Management*, *16*(1), 81–101. doi:10.1108/13612021211203041

Clark, M., & Melancon, J. (2013). The Influence of Social Media Investment on Relational Outcomes: A Relationship Marketing Perspective. *International Journal of Marketing Studies*, *5*(4), 132–142. doi:10.5539/ijms.v5n4p132

CMO Survey. (2013). *Highlights and Insights February 2013*. Retrieved from: http://cmosurvey.org/files/2013/02/The_CMO_Survey_Highlights_and_Insights_Feb-2013-Final2.pdf

BW Confidential. (2013). *Europe's Prestige Beauty Market 2012, BW Confidential* [online]. Retrieved from: http://www.bwconfidential.com/en/europe-s-prestige-beauty-market-2012,article-1875.html

Crosby, L. A., Evans, K. R., & Cowles, D. (1990). Relationship quality in services selling: An interpersonal influence perspective. *Journal of Marketing*, *54*(3), 68–81. doi:10.2307/1251817

Customer Institute. (2010). *Loyalty Versus Retention - Is There a Difference? The Customer Institute*. Retrieved from: http://thecustomerinstitute.blogspot.co.uk/2010/04/loyalty-versus-retention-is-there.html

Dall'Olmo Riley, F., & Lacroix, C. (2003). Luxury branding on the internet: Lost opportunity or impossibility? *Marketing Intelligence & Planning*, *21*(2), 96–104. doi:10.1108/02634500310465407

Danesh, S. N., Nasab, S. A., & Kwek, C. L. (2012). The Study of Customer Satisfaction, Customer Trust and Switching Barriers on Customer Retention in Malaysia Hypermarkets. *International Journal of Business and Management*, *7*(7), 141–150.

Dann, S., & Dann, S. (2011). *E-marketing: theory and application*. Basingstoke, UK: Palgrave Macmillan.

Dash, S., & Saji, K. B. (2007). The role of consumer self-efficacy and website social presence in customers' adoption of B2C online shopping: An empirical study in the Indian context. *Journal of International Consumer Marketing*, *20*(2), 33–48. doi:10.1300/J046v20n02_04

Daugherty, T., Eastin, M., & Bright, L. (2008). Exploring Consumer Motivations for creating User-Generated Content. *Journal of Interactive Advertising*, *8*(2), 16–25. doi:10.1080/15252019.2008.10722139

Dholakia, U. M., Bagozzi, R. P., & Pearo, L. K. (2004). A social influence model of consumer participation in network- and small-group-based virtual communities. *International Journal of Research in Marketing*, *21*(3), 241–263. doi:10.1016/j.ijresmar.2003.12.004

Divol, R., Edelman, D., & Sarrazin, H. (2012). Demystifying social media. *The McKinsey Quarterly*, *2*, 66–77.

Dubois, B., & Paternault, C. (1995). Observations: Understanding the world of international luxury brands. *Journal of Advertising Research*, *35*(4), 69–76.

Dwyer, F. R., Schurr, P. H., & Oh, S. (1987). Developing buyer–seller relationships. *Journal of Marketing*, *51*(2), 11–27. doi:10.2307/1251126

Euromonitor International. (2013). *Luxury Beauty Having a Love Affair with the UK, Euromonitor International* [online]. Retrieved from: http://www.euromonitor.com/

Evans, D., & McKee, J. (2010). *Social Media Marketing – The Next Generation of Business Engagement*. Indianapolis, IN: Wiley Publishing Inc.

Fieseler, C., & Fleck, M. (2013). The Pursuit of Empowerment through Social Media: Structural Social Capital Dynamics in CSR-Blogging. *Journal of Business Ethics*, *118*(4), 759–775. doi:10.1007/s10551-013-1959-9

Firat, A. F., & Venkatesh, A. (1995). Liberatory Postmodernism and the Reenchantment of Consumption. *The Journal of Consumer Research*, *22*(3), 239–267. doi:10.1086/209448

Flavian, C. and Guinaliu, M. (2006). Consumer trust, perceived security and privacy policy: Three basic elements of loyalty to a web site. *Industrial Management + Data Systems, 106*(5), 601-620.

Fornell, C. (1992). A National Customer Satisfaction Barometer: The Swedish Experience. *Journal of Marketing*, *56*(1), 6–21. doi:10.2307/1252129

Gangadharbhatla, H. (2008). Facebook me: Collective self esteem, need to belong and Internet self efficacy as predictors of the I-generations attitudes toward social networking sites. *Journal of Interactive Advertising*, *8*(2), 5–15. doi:10.1080/15252019.2008.10722138

Garland, E. (2008). The experience economy: The high life of tomorrow. *The Futurist*. Retrieved from: http://mestovetra.files.wordpress.com/2008/06/experience-economy.pdf

Geron, T. (2013). *Twitter Reveals Long-Awaited IPO Plans With 215 Million Users, Forbes*. Retrieved from: http://www.forbes.com/sites/tomiogeron/2013/10/03/twitter-reveals-long-awaited-ipo-plans-253m-revenue-in-first-half-of-2013/

Goffman, E. (1959). *The presentation of self in everyday life*. New York: Doubleday Anchor Books.

Gummerus, J., Liljander, V., Weman, E., & Pihlström, M. (2012). Customer engagement in a Facebook brand community. *Management Research Review*, *35*(9), 857–877. doi:10.1108/01409171211256578

Gunelius, S. (2011). *30 minute Social Media Marketing: Step by Step Techniques to Spread the Words about your Business*. McGraw-Hill.

Gustafsson, A., Johnson, M. D., & Roos, I. (2005). The Effects of Customer Satisfaction, Relationship Commitment Dimensions, and Triggers on Customer Retention. *Journal of Marketing*, *69*(10), 210–218. doi:10.1509/jmkg.2005.69.4.210

Hagel, J., & Armstrong, A. G. (1997). *Net gain: Expanding markets through virtual Communities*. Boston: Harvard Business School Press.

Hanna, R., Rohm, A., & Crittenden, V. L. (2011). We're all connected: The power of the social media ecosystem. *Business Horizons*, *54*(3), 265–273. doi:10.1016/j.bushor.2011.01.007

Hart, C. W., & Johnson, M. D. (1999). Growing the trust relationship. *Marketing Management*, *8*(1), 8–19.

Hawkins, K., & Vel, P. (2013). Attitudinal loyalty, behavioural loyalty and social media: An Introspection. *Marketing Review*, *13*(2), 125–141. doi:10.1362/146934713X13699019904605

Hennig-Thurau, T., Gwinner, K., Walsh, G., & Gremler, D. (2004). Electronic word of-mouth via consumer-opinion platforms: What motivates consumers to articulate themselves on the Internet? *Journal of Interactive Marketing*, *18*(1), 38–52. doi:10.1002/dir.10073

Hennig-Thurau, T., Malthouse, E., Friege, C., Gensler, S., Lobschat, L., Rangaswamy, A., & Skiera, B. (2010). The Impact of New Media on Customer Relationships. *Journal of Service Research*, *13*(3), 311–330. doi:10.1177/1094670510375460

Hof, R. (2012). *Google+'s Success and Failure, in Two Images, Forbes*. Retrieved from: http://www.forbes.com/sites/roberthof/2012/02/09/googles-success-and-failure-in-two-images/

Hoffman, D. L., & Fodor, M. (2010). Can you measure the ROI of your social media marketing? *MIT Sloan Management Review*, *52*(1), 41–49.

Hoffman, D. L., Kopalle, P. K., & Novak, T. P. (2010). A New Marketing Paradigm for Electronic Commerce. *JMR, Journal of Marketing Research*, *47*, 854–865. doi:10.1509/jmkr.47.5.854

Hoffman, D. L., & Novak, T. P. (2012). Why Do People Use Social Media? Empirical Findings and a New Theoretical Framework for Social Media Goal Pursuit. *Social Science Research Network*. Retrieved from: http://ssrn.com/abstract=1989586

Jarvenpaa, S., & Tuunainen, V. K. (2013). How Finnair Socialized Customers for Service Co-Creation with SocialMedia. *MIS Quarterley Executive*, *12*(3), 125–136.

Jevons, C., & Gabbott, M. (2000). Trust, Brand Equity and Brand Reality in Internet Business Relationships: An Interdisciplinary Approach. *Journal of Marketing Management*, *16*(6), 619–634. doi:10.1362/026725700785045967

Jin, S. A. A. (2012). The potential of social media for luxury brand management. *Marketing Intelligence & Planning*, *30*(7), 687–699. doi:10.1108/02634501211273805

Kano, N. (1995). Upsizing the organization by attractive quality creation. In *Total Quality Management: Proceedings of the First World Congress*. London: Chapman & Hall. doi:10.1007/978-94-011-0539-2_6

Kaplan, A., & Haenlein, M. (2010). Users of the world, unite! The challenges and opportunities of Social Media. *Business Horizons*, *53*(1), 59–68. doi:10.1016/j.bushor.2009.09.003

Katsioloudes, M., Grant, J., & McKechnie, D. S. (2007). Social marketing: Strengthening company-customer bonds. *The Journal of Business Strategy*, *28*(3), 56–64. doi:10.1108/02756660710746283

Kelly, E. P., & Erickson, G. S. (2004). Legal and privacy issues surrounding customer databases and e-merchant bankruptcies: Reflections on Toysmart.com. *Industrial Management & Data Systems*, *104*(3), 209–217. doi:10.1108/02635570410525762

Khammash, M., & Griffiths, G. H. (2010). Arrivederci CIAO.com, Buongiorno Bing. Com - electronic word-ofmouth (eWOM), antecedences and consequences. *International Journal of Information Management*, *31*(1), 82–87. doi:10.1016/j.ijinfomgt.2010.10.005

Khang, H., Ki, E., & Ye, L. (2012). Social Media Research in Advertising, Communication, Marketing, and Public Relations. *Journalism & Mass Communication Quarterly*, *89*(2), 279–298. doi:10.1177/1077699012439853

Kietzmann, J. H., Hermkens, K., McCarthy, I. P., & Silvestre, B. S. (2011). Social media? Get serious! Understanding the functional building blocks of social media. *Business Horizons*, *54*(3), 241–251. doi:10.1016/j.bushor.2011.01.005

Kim, A. J., & Ko, E. (2010). Impacts of Luxury Fashion Brand's Social Media Marketing on Customer Relationship and Purchase Intention. *Journal of Global Fashion Marketing*, *1*(3), 164–171. doi:10.1080/20932685.2010.10593068

Kim, A. J., & Ko, E. (2012). Do Social Media marketing activities enhance customer equity? An empirical study of luxury fashion brand. *Journal of Business Research*, *65*(10), 1480–1486. doi:10.1016/j.jbusres.2011.10.014

Kirkpatrick, D. (2010). *The Facebook effect: The inside story of the company that is connecting the world*. New York: Simon & Schuster.

Kozinets, R., Valck, K., Wojnicki, A., & Wilner, S. (2010). Networked Narratives: Understanding Word-of-Mouth Marketing in Online Communities. *Journal of Marketing*, *74*(2), 71–89. doi:10.1509/jmkg.74.2.71

Krishna, A., Dangayach, G., & Jain, R. (2011). A Conceptual Framework for the Service Recovery Paradox. *The Marketing Review*, *11*(1), 41–56. doi:10.1362/146934711X565288

Kumar, V., Aksoy, L., Donkers, B., Venkatesan, R., Wiesel, T., & Tillmanns, S. (2010). Undervalued or Overvalued Customers: Capturing Total Customer Engagement Value. *Journal of Service Research*, *13*(3), 297–310. doi:10.1177/1094670510375602

Laroche, M., Habibi, M. R., & Richard, M. O. (2013). To be or not to be in social media: How brand loyalty is affected by social media? *International Journal of Information Management*, *33*(1), 76–82. doi:10.1016/j.ijinfomgt.2012.07.003

Lauterborn, B. (1990). New Marketing Litany: Four P's Passe: C-Words Take Over. *Advertising Age*, *61*(41), 26.

Leggatt, H. (2010). *Rebuild Brand Loyalty with Social Media, Bizreport*. Retrieved from: http://www.bizreport.com/2010/08/price-sensitiveshoppers- still-seeking-out-deals.html

Levine, R., Locke, C., Searle, D., & Weinberger, D. (2001). *The Cluetrain Manifesto: The end of business as usual*. New York: Basic Books.

Liang, C. L., Chen, H. J., & Wang, W. H. (2008). Does online relationship marketing enhance customer retention and cross-buying? *Service Industries Journal*, *28*(6), 769–787. doi:10.1080/02642060801988910

Libai, B. (2011). Comment: The perils of focusing on highly engaged customers. *Journal of Service Research, 14*(3), 275–276. doi:10.1177/1094670511414583

Mangold, W. G., & Faulds, D. J. (2009). Social media: The new hybrid element of the promotion mix. *Business Horizons, 52*(4), 357–365. doi:10.1016/j.bushor.2009.03.002

Maslow, A. H. (1943). A theory of human motivation. *Psychological Review, 50*(4), 370–396. doi:10.1037/h0054346

McCarthy, E. J. (1960). *Basic Marketing - A Managerial Approach*. Homewood, IL: Richard D. Irwin.

Moore, C. M., & Doyle, S. A. (2010). The evolution of a luxury brand: The case of Prada. *International Journal of Retail & Distribution Management, 38*(11), 915–927. doi:10.1108/09590551011085984

Morgan, R. M., & Hunt, S. (1994). The commitment-trust theory of relationship marketing. *Journal of Marketing, 58*(3), 20–38. doi:10.2307/1252308

Moritz, D. (2012). *The Shift to Visual Social Media – 6 Tips for Business, Socially Sorted*. Retrieved from: http://sociallysorted.com.au/shift-to-visual-social-media-6-tips-for-business-infographic/

Muniz, M. A. Jr, & O'Guinn, C. T. (2001). Brand community. *The Journal of Consumer Research, 27*(4), 412–432. doi:10.1086/319618

Nair, M. (2011). Understanding and Measuring the Value of Social Media. *Journal of Corporate Accounting & Finance, 22*(3), 45–51. doi:10.1002/jcaf.20674

Naylor, R., Walker, L., Cait, P., & West, P. M. (2012). Beyond the 'Like' Button: The impact of Mere Virtual Presence on Brand Evaluations and Purchase Intentions in Social Media Settings. *Journal of Marketing, 76*(6), 105–120. doi:10.1509/jm.11.0105

Nonnecke, B., Andrews, D., & Preece, J. (2006). Non-public and public online community participation: Needs, attitudes and behaviour. *Electronic Commerce Research, 6*(1), 7–20. doi:10.1007/s10660-006-5985-x

Noor Al-Deen, H. S., & Hendricks, J. A. (2012). *Social Media – usage and impact*. Plymouth, MA: Lexington Books.

O'Reilly, T. (2005). *What is Web 2.0? Design Patterns and Business Models for the Next generation of Software, O'Reilly*. Retrieved from: http://www.im.ethz.ch/education/HS08/OReilly_What_is_Web2_0.pdf

O'Reilly, T., & Milstein, S. (2012). *The Twitter Book*. Sebastopol, CA: O'Reilly Media Inc.

Okonkwo, U. (2010). Luxury Online. New York: Palgrave Macmillan.

Oliver, R. L. (1980). A Cognitive Model of the Antecedents and Consequences of Satisfaction Decisions. *JMR, Journal of Marketing Research, 17*(4), 460–469. doi:10.2307/3150499

Onook, O., Manish, A., & Raghave, R. H. (2013). Community intelligence and social media services: A rumor theoretic analysis of tweets during social crisis. *Management Information Systems Quarterly, 37*(2), 407–A7.

Organisation for Economic Co-operation and Development (OECD). (2007). *Working Party on the Information Economy – Participative Web: User-created content*. Retrieved from: http://www.oecd.org/sti/38393115.pdf

Ozuem, W., Howell, K. E., & Lancaster, G. (2008). Communicating in the new interactive marketspace. *European Journal of Marketing*, *42*(9/10), 1059–1083. doi:10.1108/03090560810891145

Pavlik, J. V. (2007). *Mapping the consequences of technology of public relations, Institute for public relations, Institute for Public Relations*. Retrieved from: http://www.instituteforpr.org/topics/mapping-technology-consequences/

Pavlou, P. A. (2003). Consumer acceptance of electronic commerce: Integrating trust and risk with the technology acceptance model. *International Journal of Electronic Commerce*, *7*(3), 101–134.

Phan, M., Thomas, R., & Heine, K. (2011). Social Media and Luxury Brand Management: The Case of Burberry. *Journal of Global Fashion Marketing*, *2*(4), 213–222. doi:10.1080/20932685.2011.10593099

Powers, T., Advincula, D., Austin, M., Graiko, S., & Snyder, J. (2012). Digital and Social Media in the Purchase Decision Process. *Journal of Advertising Research*, *52*(4), 479–489. doi:10.2501/JAR-52-4-479-489

Prahalad, C. K., & Ramaswamy, V. (2004). Co-creation experiences: The next practice in value creation. *Journal of Interactive Marketing*, *18*(3), 5–14. doi:10.1002/dir.20015

Prendergast, G., Ko, D., & Yuen, S. Y. V. (2010). Online word of mouth and consumer purchase intentions. *International Journal of Advertising*, *29*(5), 687–708. doi:10.2501/S0265048710201427

Quinton, S., & Harridge-March, S. (2010). Relationships in online communities: The potential for marketers. *Journal of Research in Interactive Marketing*, *4*(1), 59–73. doi:10.1108/17505931011033560

Ranaweera, C., & Prabhu, J. (2003). The influence of satisfaction, trust and switching barriers on customer retention in a continuous purchasing setting. *International Journal of Service Industry Management*, *14*(4), 374–395. doi:10.1108/09564230310489231

Rettberg, J. W. (2008). *Blogging – Digital Media and Society Series*. Malden, MA: Polity.

Safko, L. (2012). *The Social Media Bible– Tools, Tactics and Strategies for Business Success* (3rd ed.). John Wiley & Sons Inc.

Safko, L., & Brake, D. K. (2009). *The Social Media Bible*. John Wiley & Sons, Inc.

Sandes, F. S., & Urdan, A. T. (2013). Electronic Word-of-Mouth Impacts on Consumer Behaviour: Exploratory and Experimental Studies. *Journal of International Consumer Marketing*, *25*(3), 181–197. doi:10.1080/08961530.2013.780850

Sashi, C. M. (2012). Customer engagement, buyer-seller relationships and Social Media. *Management Decision*, *50*(2), 253–272. doi:10.1108/00251741211203551

Seung-A, A. J. (2012). The potential of Social Media for luxury brand management. *Marketing Intelligence & Planning*, *30*(7), 687–699. doi:10.1108/02634501211273805

Smith, T. (2009). The Social Media Revolution. *International Journal of Market Research, 51*(4), 559–561. doi:10.2501/S1470785309200773

Socialmediatoday (2013). *5 Surprising Social Media Statistics for 2013, Social Media today*. Retrieved from http://socialmediatoday.com/docmarkting/1818611/five-surprising-social-media-statistics-2013

Srinivasan, S. S., Anderson, R., & Ponnavolu, K. (2002). Customer loyalty in e-commerce: An exploration of its antecedents and consequences. *Journal of Retailing, 78*(1), 41–50. doi:10.1016/S0022-4359(01)00065-3

Stokes, R. (2008). *E-marketing: The essential guide to online marketing*. Quirk eMarketing (Pty) Ltd.

Sukoco, B., & Wu, W. (2010). The personal and social motivation of customers' participation in brand community. *African Journal of Business Management, 4*(5), 614-622.

Trainor, K. (2012). Relating SocialMedia Technologies to Performance: A Capabilities-Based Perspective. *Journal of Personal Selling & Sales Management, 32*(3), 317–331. doi:10.2753/PSS0885-3134320303

Tuten, T. L. (2008). *Advertising 2.0 – Social Media Marketing in a Web 2.0 World*. Westport, CT: Praeger Publishers.

Vargo, S. L., & Lusch, R. F. (2004). Evolving to a new Dominant Logic for Marketing. *Journal of Marketing, 68*(1), 1–17. doi:10.1509/jmkg.68.1.1.24036

Verhoef, P. C. (2003). Understanding the Effect of Customer Relationship Management Efforts on Customer Retention and Customer Share Development. *Journal of Marketing, 67*(4), 30–45. doi:10.1509/jmkg.67.4.30.18685

Vickers, J. S., & Renand, F. (2003). The Marketing of Luxury Goods: An exploratory study – three conceptual dimensions. *The Marketing Review, 3*(4), 459–478. doi:10.1362/146934703771910071

Vollmer, C., & Precourt, G. (2008). *Always on: Advertising, marketing, and media in an era of consumer control*. New York: McGraw-Hill.

Walpole. (2013). *British Luxury Showcase*. Author.

Weber, L. (2007). *Marketing to the Social Web: How Digital Customer Communities Build Your Business*. John Wiley & Sons Inc.

Wellman, B., & Gulia, M. (1999). Net-surfers don't ride alone: Virtual communities as communities. In Networks in the global village, (pp. 331-366). Boulder, CO: Westview.

Williams, L., & Cothrell, J. (2000). Four smart ways to run online communities. *Sloan Management Review, 41*(4), 81–91.

Wilson, D. T. (1995). An integrated model of buyer–seller relationships. *Journal of the Academy of Marketing Science, 23*(4), 335–345. doi:10.1177/009207039502300414

Yi, Y. (1990). A critical review of consumer satisfaction. In Review of Marketing, (pp. 68-123). Chicago: American Marketing Association.

Yougov. (2012). *Beauty Customer Journey, YouGov* [online]. Retrieved from: http://d25d2506sfb94s.cloudfront.net/cumulus_uploads/document/wa32oxme7c/Beauty%20Customer%20Journey.pdf

Zarella, D. (2010). *The social media marketing book*. O'Reilly Media Inc.

ADDITIONAL READING

Baer, J. (2013).Youtility, New York, Penguin Group.

Brown, D., & Fiorella, S. (2013). Influence Marketing, US: Que Publishing.

Clark, M., & Melancon, J. (2013). The Influence of Social Media Investment on Relational Outcomes: A Relationship Marketing Perspective. *International Journal of Marketing Studies*, *5*(4), 132–142. doi:10.5539/ijms.v5n4p132

Hoffman, D. L., & Fodor, M. (2010). Can you measure the ROI of your social media marketing? *MIT Sloan Management Review*, *52*(1), 41–49.

Sandes, F. S., & Urdan, A. T. (2013). Electronic Word-of-Mouth Impacts on Consumer Behaviour: Exploratory and Experimental Studies. *Journal of International Consumer Marketing*, *25*(3), 181–197. doi:10.1080/08961530.2013.780850

KEY TERMS AND DEFINITIONS

Cosmetics: A cosmetic product is applied on the human body with the purpose of cleaning, protecting, maintaining or perfuming it.

Customer Retention: A company's activities in order to ensure that the customer repeatedly comes back to repurchase from the company and does not move on to the competition.

Loyalty: Customer loyalty is expressed through an attitudinal and behavioural preference for one brand.

Luxury Beauty Industry: Belongs to the consumer products industry. It provides premium products in a set of different subcategories such as colour cosmetics, skin care, fragrances, sun care, hair care and men's grooming.

Marketing Communications: Coordinated messages through which a company reaches out to its target audience.

Social Media: The totality of different online channels and platforms, which enable online users not only to receive but also to create and share content.

Word of Mouth: A powerful form of advertising based on peer-to-peer recommendations.

This research was previously published in Computer-Mediated Marketing Strategies edited by Gordon Bowen and Wilson Ozuem, pages 200-222, copyright year 2015 by Business Science Reference (an imprint of IGI Global).

Chapter 38
Social Media, Customer Relationship Management, and Consumers' Organic Food Purchase Behavior

Evelyn Chronis
The University of Sydney, Australia

Qiang Lu
The University of Sydney, Australia

Rohan Miller
The University of Sydney, Australia

ABSTRACT

Extant research has been focusing on the effectiveness of social media in driving consumer engagement and interaction. However, little research has examined how social media influences firms' Customer Relationship Management. This chapter fills this gap by proposing a conceptual framework to capture the impact of social media on traditional Customer Relationship Management in the context of consumers' organic food purchasing. Specifically, this study investigates how social media influences the purchase behavior of loyalty program members and non-loyalty program members. This study also examines the effectiveness of different types of social media content on consumer purchase behavior of organic food.

INTRODUCTION

The adoption of social media into the business landscape in the past decade has transformed the nature of business communication, customer interaction and engagement. Many businesses are realizing the value of social media, but very few know how to truly harness its power. The implementation of social media strategies are becoming increasingly adopted in business boardrooms as academics debate over the definition of this 'social' phenomenon joining business practices and processes. The concept of 'Social

DOI: 10.4018/978-1-5225-5637-4.ch038

CRM' (Customer Relationship Management) has thus been introduced in the academic literature, aiming to encapsulate the essence and characteristics of social media's unique capabilities.

Social CRM is a logical extension to traditional CRM processes and approaches, drawing on a social media implementation to increase customer engagement, build customer relationships and ultimately, drive sales. Its true value lies in its facilitation of two-way flows of communication between businesses and consumers, thereby extending upon traditional CRM tools. As Social CRM becomes increasingly adopted by businesses using social media as a platform for building and enhancing consumer engagement and communication, it is becoming of increasing importance to understand its impact on firm performance and profitability.

This chapter aims to examine the impact of a Social CRM system on organic food expenditure to determine the effectiveness of Social CRM tools in driving sales. Existing research currently highlights the effectiveness of social media in driving consumer engagement and interaction (Miller & Tucker, 2013). However, research surrounding social media's influence on the purchase behavior of loyalty program and non-loyalty program members is in its infancy. As Social CRM extends upon CRM processes, it is necessary to understand its impact on loyalty program and non-loyalty program members. Furthermore, little is also known about the effectiveness of different types of social media content on sales. The research questions guiding the inquiry into this under-studied but highly relevant research area are: What is the impact of social media on the purchase expenditures of loyalty program members compared with non-loyalty program members? What different types of social media content are effective in driving organic food consumption?

The chapter is structured as follows. First, an overview of the changing nature of food consumption and increased consumer demand for organic food is provided, followed by the introduction, definition and explanation of the concept of Social CRM. Secondly, the organic food literature is discussed to give a prelude of the socio-demographic profile of the organic food consumer, and the motivations and barriers to organic food purchase, in order to set the scene for the research propositions. Third, the propositions of the research are discussed. Finally, the chapter concludes with the major contributions of the study, followed by a discussion of future research directions.

WHY THE ORGANIC FOOD INDUSTRY?

First, a note on the growing organic food or 'healthy eating trend.' Since the 1960s, food consumption has transformed alongside the breakdown of mass-consumerism in its replacement by a multi-dimensional, dynamic society (Beharrell & Crockett, 1992). Within this transformed society, individuals are constantly searching for ways to express their personal and collective identities, values and beliefs. One way in which individuals are achieving this new found self-expression is through their healthy food choices. Food consumption has essentially become an 'expression of personal identity and group affiliation within an increasingly fragmented social structure' (Beharrell & Crockett, 1992: 5).

Alongside the desire for individual and collective self-expression, external societal trends relating to the food related obesity epidemic have called upon increased inquiries into the area of healthy food choice. Obesity has overtaken smoking as the primary cause of preventable disease and illness in Australia and is now arguably, one of the most pressing issues ever facing humanity (Hoad, Somerford, & Katzenellenbogen, 2010). Fortunately, in light of the raised concerns over the obesity epidemic, many consumers are now acknowledging the connection between their diet and health, and are acting upon that knowledge through the consumption of organic food to bridge this connection (French & Hale, 2010; Langley, 2013). 'New age values' concerning individual health, diet, nature and the environment (Beharrell & Crockett, 1992) are propelling the increased demand for organic food products. This increasing consumer demand for organic food has resulted in the organic farming industry placing as one of the top three industries expected to 'fly' in 2014 (IBISWorld, 2014).

LITERATURE REVIEW

Social Media

Social media are internet-based applications that build on the technological foundations of Web 2.0 (e.g. internet forums, email, blogs, social networking sites and online communities) that have revolutionised how consumers and firms interact (Leiner, et al., 2000). As Web 2.0 has evolved to include the development of social media, businesses are using social media as a platform to disseminate information to consumers about brands, products and services. They have done so in a way that enables increased collaboration and engagement with consumers, without regard of geographical barriers. This increase in consumer collaboration and engagement with brands has dramatically changed the nature of 21st century relationship marketing (Leung, 2013). Furthermore, the nature of contemporary marketing has also fundamentally changed as a result of consumers' assuming greater control over their consumption decisions by using social media to seek information about brands, products and services (Greenberg, 2007).

At the individual level, social media has created an 'environment of unprecedented hyper-connectivity' between users (Leung, 2013). Many businesses are thus quickly learning the value of the hyper-connectivity facilitated through social media platforms and are implementing processes to monitor, respond, amplify and influence consumer behavior through these platforms (Divol, Edelman, & Sarrazin, 2012). For example, many businesses are using social media to build brand communities to monitor, respond, amplify and influence consumer behaviour, and also to disseminate information to increase consumer engagement, and ultimately, generate sales.

In today's cluttered marketing environment, many marketers believe that online brand communities are cost effective and powerful marketing tools that foster stronger consumer relationships with the brand (Algesheimer, Dholakia, & Herrmann, 2005). Online brand communities are a form of social media widely used by businesses. They are 'specialised, non-geographically bound communities based on a structured set of social relationships among admirers of a brand' (Muniz & O'Guinn, 2001). Businesses have created their own online brand communities to communicate with consumers in an inexpensive and timely fashion (Patino, Pitta, & Quinones, 2012) at each and every stage of the consumer journey (Divol, et al., 2012). Brand communities thus have the potential to positively influence elements of the customer centric model by strengthening brand loyalty, trust and engagement with brands (Laroche, Habibi, & Richard, 2013).

The creation of online brand communities has led to the rise of community-led marketing initiatives within the digital marketing strategies of businesses. This has created important implications in the area of relationship marketing as these community-driven marketing initiatives seek to enhance consumer/brand relationships, essentially transforming traditional CRM processes. Traditional CRM tools sought to manage customer relationships in a manner that aimed to extract the greatest revenue per customer throughout the customer's lifetime with the firm (Winer, 2001). This type of consumer/firm relationship management was largely dominated and dictated by the firm. However, the adoption of social media platforms, such as brand communities, has changed the nature of consumer/firm relationships. Consumers are now able to respond to firms and create their own conversations. This reciprocated engagement with the firm has therefore created consumer/firm interactions that are driven by two-way streams of dialogue and engagement. The concept of these redefined consumer/firm relationships has been introduced into the marketing literature as Social Customer Relationship Management (SCRM). SCRM draws on social media tools to engage in a strategy of consumer interaction to manage the consumer/brand relationship.

Consumers are using social media to voice their opinions, share their thoughts and experiences, seek advice and information and interact with others about brands (Smithee, 2011). Facebook is becoming an increasingly popular social media platform used by consumers to seek information about a brand or consumption activity, while feeling part of a community of like-minded consumers (Patino, et al., 2012). Social media sites, such as Facebook, are becoming increasingly popular information sources for consumers because the information disseminated via these platforms is perceived to be more trustworthy and credible. This can be explained by the less pervasive nature of social media channels in comparison to traditional marketing communications and tools (Schivinski & Dabrowski, 2013). Social media platforms facilitate dialogue with consumers as they are able to respond to brand-promoted material and participate in dialogue with the brand and other participants (Patino, et al., 2012). Social media has therefore enabled consumers to become 'expressers, informers, engagers, networkers and socialisers,' with brands and other consumers (Vinerean, Cetina, Dumitrescu, & Tichindelean, 2013).

It is the 'social' element inherent in social media platforms that extends upon traditional media, allowing consumers to seek advice and information from trusted social influences, such as friends, family or other like-minded individuals (Wilcox & Stephen, Forthcoming). As a result, the brand is no longer the only disseminator of information to consumers, rather consumers now also play a role in the creation of information on these platforms (Iyengar, Han, & Gupta, Working Paper).

The use of social media by consumers seeking information about brands raises important implications for marketers seeking to use social media to promote their brands, products and services. As social media is perceived as a trustworthy source of brand information, this insinuates that businesses can use social media as an effective marketing and communications tool. This thesis will investigate the use of social media as a platform of information dissemination by a company, and how this information impacts on consumer purchase behaviour. We will analyse a Facebook brand page that is used by the company to disseminate information about its products (organic food), and how this information impacts on the purchase expenditures of its consumers.

Customer Relationship Management (CRM)

A considerable body of academic and trade literature addresses the concept of Customer Relationship Management (CRM) approaches as a traditional marketing tool. Both academics and practitioners have explored the value and impact of building, maintaining and fostering relationships to enhance firm performance (Reinartz, 2004). The justification for CRM processes in traditional retail channels was that businesses should develop strong relationships with customers as increases in retention rates and customer longevity leads to increased firm profitability (Reichheld & Sasser, 1990).

CRM processes have also been linked to increased profitability through their capacity to enhance customer satisfaction levels and furthermore brand loyalty, which in turn results in an increase of the average revenue per customer (Dowling, 2002; Anderson, Fornell, & Lehmann, 1994;). CRM processes can also facilitate a customer-centric approach that helps businesses manage the consumer and brand relationships in order to extract the greatest value from consumers throughout the consumers' lifetime (Baird & Parasnis, 2011). However, since 2004, social tools and online processes have transformed CRM approaches. The result? Social joining the CRM- Social CRM.

What Is Social CRM?

The concept of social media, such as Facebook, joining traditional Customer Relationship Management tools and processes has been recently introduced into the academic literature as 'Social CRM' (SCRM). As the communicative empowerment of consumers is enhanced through social media, SCRM has been explained as a logical extension to traditional CRM processes, rather than a replacement (Baird & Parasnis, 2011). An extension insofar as it adds to the features, functions and characteristics of CRM tools (Greenberg, 2009).

SCRM has been defined as:

A philosophy and a business strategy, supported by a technology platform, business rules, workflow, processes and social characteristics, designed to engage the customer in a collaborative conversation in order to provide mutually beneficial value in a trusted and transparent business environment. It's the company's response to the customer's ownership of the conversation. (Greenberg, 2009)

The real value of SCRM therefore lies in its facilitation of two-way flows of communication between the firm and consumer, which was previously unattainable through traditional CRM tools. Through SCRM, consumers are able to engage in reciprocated conversations with the brand and other consumers and stakeholders. This has essentially changed the role of brands from 'directors' of one way streams of communications to consumers, to 'facilitators' of two way flows of dialogue between brand and consumer (Baird & Parasnis, 2011). Facebook, in particular, has received the 'lion's share of attention' in the social media space (Weinberg & Pehlivan, 2011).

As the very nature of social media enables consumers to engage and communicate with the brand on their *own* accord, in their *own* time and at their *own* control, the ownership of conversation has essentially shifted to the consumer (Greenberg, 2009). As a result, consumers are beginning to trust social media platforms as credible sources of knowledge and information acquisition as these platforms facilitate communication with like-minded consumers. Consumers are no longer the 'target' of business communications, rather facilitators of communication with other consumers and business stakeholders. This transformation has seen the demand for businesses to acknowledge this increased interaction with consumers, and accommodate it accordingly, without jeopardizing traditional business operations (Greenberg, 2009). The true value of SCRM lies in its capacity to therefore facilitate co-creation between business and consumer to arrive at a outcomes that are beneficial for both parties (Greenberg, 2009).

Social media platforms, such as Facebook brand pages, have broadened the nature of acquiring knowledge and disseminating information in real time for consumers (Seraj, 2012; Weinberg & Pehlivan, 2011). As individuals engage with brand pages online they are transforming the traditional communication mechanisms once typical of business processes (Jayanti & Singh, 2010). As individuals congregate on social media for the purpose of acquiring and disseminating information, they are simultaneously turning away from traditional advertising channels in favour of their increased control over their media consumption (Mangold & Faulds, 2009). Consequently, social media has become a popular advertising tool for businesses seeking to reap the benefits of increased consumer trust and attention (Xiang & Gretzel, 2010).

However, a question mark still remains in the boardroom surrounding social media's legitimacy in the marketing mix due to the ambiguity surrounding its economical impact on firm performance. Social media remains an 'enigma wrapped in a riddle for many executives' (Divol, et al., 2012). Many companies have adopted the social media to facilitate communications with their consumers, however the justification to devote resources to social media strategies remains a challenge for most marketing executives. The financial impact of social media as an element of the marketing mix is complex due to the qualitative, and thus nebulous, nature surrounding its financial metrics.

However, given the implementation of social media in business marketing strategies, and its popularity as a preferred, pervasive advertising medium by consumers, a stream of research has emerged investigating the return on investment of social media (Hoffman & Fodor, 2010; Kumar et al., 2013;). In particular, studies have since emerged pertaining to examine the relationship between online content and firm performance, namely as a function of sales (Goh, Heng, & Lin, 2013; Gopinath, Thomas, & Krishnamurthi, 2014). Gopinath, Thomas, and Krishnamurthi (2014) examined the impact of user-generated content (UGC) on sales by separating the volume of UGC from its valence, which has three dimensions- attribute, emotion and recommendation oriented messages. The study found that only the valence of recommendation has a direct impact on sales, indicating that UGC can be a very valuable asset to firms engaging with social media (Gopinath, et al., 2014). The study also found that the 'volume' of UGC does not have a significant impact on sales, indicating 'quality' is better than 'quantity' in terms of online WOM. Goh, Heng, and Lin (2013) found similar results in their evidence of social media contents affecting consumer purchase behavior through embedded information and persuasion. Further research has explored this positive effect as being facilitated by high quality, informative and trustworthy context providing social, intellectual and cultural value to consumers via social media platforms (Seraj, 2012; Smith, Fischer, & Yongjian, 2012).

Organic Food

What Is Organic Food?

Organic food refers to 'natural,' 'wholesome' and 'healthy' food (Beharrell & Crockett, 1992) produced through renewable sources, the best environmental practices, the application of high animal welfare standards, and without the use of synthetic fertilisers and pesticides (Magistris & Gracia, 2008). The contemporary 'organic food consumer' has emerged as a result of lifestyle changes reflective of wider environmental and societal shifts towards a healthy lifestyle approach (Beharrell & Crockett, 1992). Transformed healthy eating habits since the 1960s, reflective of positive health and environmental friendliness, have influenced the trend towards organic foods as a means of individual self-representation (Davies et al., 1995). The stream of research surrounding organic food constructs a socio-demographic profile of the organic food consumer and addresses the motivations and barriers toward organic food consumption.

A Socio-Demographic Profile of the Organic Food Consumer

The increased consumption of organically produced food, coupled with the rise of environmental concerns, lead to the proliferation of research aiming to better understand the typical profile of organic food consumers and their socio-demographic characteristics (Davies, Titterington, & Cochrane, 1995; Fotopoulos & Krystallis, 2002b). Research suggests that females hold more positive beliefs toward organic food consumption (Lea & Worsley, 2005) and are the primary purchasers of organic food within the household (Fotopoulos & Krystallis, 2002b; Byrne et al., 1992). Demographic reviews of organic food consumption have further found that age (Reicks, Splett, & Fishman, 1997), disposable income and the presence of children in the household all significantly influence organic food consumption (Davies, Titterington, & Cochrane, 1995).

However, other studies identify no relationship between organic food purchase and income (Goldman & Clancy, 1991). Adopting a different approach of profiling the organic food consumer based on their levels of knowledge and awareness of organic food, Fotopoulos and Krystallis (2002) identified three types of organic food buyers: the Unaware, the Aware non-buyers and the Buyers. Ultimately, a single profile of the organic food consumer has not been achieved, which reflects the complex motivational drives behind organic food consumption.

Motivations Towards Organic Food Consumption

Alongside the literature profiling the organic food consumer, there is extant research exploring the motivations underlying organic food consumption. There is generally a greater consensus surrounding the motives driving consumer purchase in comparison to attempts to profile the organic food consumer. It is generally accepted that the main drivers behind organic food consumption are health related, environmentally determined and ethically driven factors (Aertsens, Mondelaers, Verbeke, Buysse, & Huylenbroeck, 2011; Chinnici, D'Amico, & Pecorino, 2002; Davies, Titterington, & Cochrane, 1995).

Health

A considerable body of evidence argues that health related factors are the most important drivers for organic food purchases (Magistris & Gracia, 2008; Padel & Foster, 2005; Zanoli & Naspetti, 2002). Individuals' are motivated by their self-interests and the self-benefits of organic food; that is, organic food is considered as a 'way of life' representing values of wholesomeness and self-transcendence (Schifferstein & Ophuis, 1998; Lea & Worsley, 2005). The product characteristics identified with health motivation are 'better quality' and 'better taste' (Aertsens et al., 2011; Lea & Worsley, 2005), free of synthetic pesticide residues (Aertsens et al., 2011) and higher in vitamin and mineral content compared to conventionally produced food (Lea & Worsley, 2005). These strongly contribute to constructing the health motivations behind organic food consumption.

Environment

Concern over the environment has been found to be a further significant influence on organic food consumption (Schifferstein & Ophuis, 1998). It has been argued that that a concern for the environment can play a more important role in determining individual organic food consumption rather than health related motivations (Durham, 2007). Concern for the welfare of the environment has had a positive impact on organic food consumption as the process of organic farming is seen as an environmentally sustainable practice (Beharrell & Crockett, 1992). The environmental factors driving organic food consumption are motivated by the support of using renewable inputs through correct agricultural management techniques that in turn, optimize the background health of crops and maintain soil structure and fertility (Beharrell & Crockett, 1992).

Ethics

Food safety and concern for animal welfare are also considered major motivating factors towards organic food consumption (Harper & Makatouni, 2002). Ethical motivations concerning the welfare of animals have been commonly found amongst purchasers of organic food (Harper & Makatouni, 2002). The ethical dimension concerning the welfare of animals in organic food production serves to contribute to the perception of organic food being 'healthier' than conventional food, and also allows consumers to express their ethical concerns as extensions of their self-image (Harper & Makatouni, 2002)

Barriers Inhibiting Organic Food Consumption

Price

Organic food maintains a price premium compared to its conventional food counterpart, which inadvertently creates a price versus value trade-off in consumers' decision-making process to purchase organic food (Padel & Foster, 2005). This price versus value decision inhibits the consumption of organic food (Padel & Foster, 2005; Byrne et al., 1992; Roddy, Cowan, & Hutchinson, 1994; Fotopoulos & Krystallis, 2002a). However, it is also speculated that consumers may use price to inform their opinions about the taste and quality of organic food.

Availability

There can be a perception that locating specialty organic food outlets can be difficult; this lack of availability and inconvenience in turn, inhibits organic food purchases (Zanoli & Naspetti, 2002; Fotopoulos & Krystallis, 2002a). There is however, an increasing number of organic food outlets entering the market, and other food stores are also diversifying into organic foods, thereby making organic food more available for consumers.

Knowledge

Consumers' limited or lack of sufficient knowledge on the benefits of organic food consumption has been explored as another major barrier to organic food consumption (Demeritt, 2002). This lack of knowledge negatively influences organic food consumption as consumers are uninformed of the benefits of organic food, and consequently, cannot justify its price premium, leading to organic product avoidance (Padel & Foster, 2005). It is claimed that increasing consumers' organic food knowledge can in fact, positively influence organic food consumption (Magistris & Gracia, 2008; Aertsens et al., 2011) by transforming the 'unwilling consumer to a motivated organic supporter' (Fotopoulos & Krystallis, 2002a).

CONCEPTUAL FRAMEWORK

The extant research suggests consumers' lack of knowledge about organic food is a critical barrier to organic food consumption. Research suggests an increase in organic food knowledge positively influences ones likelihood to purchase and frequent use of organic food (Magistris & Gracia, 2008; Aertsens et al., 2011). As the nature of acquiring knowledge has evolved alongside the implementation of social media technologies, individuals are now engaging online to engage in knowledge transfer and information regarding products and services (Jayanti & Singh, 2010). Studies have found that social media platforms deliver value to consumers through providing intellectual value (goal driven and quality content), social value (an interactive environment for building relationships) and cultural value (a self-governed community culture that maintains trust and respect towards the community and among members) (Seraj, 2012).

The creation of intellectual value is characteristics of SCRM tools. SCRM has the capacity to facilitate the flow of information towards consumers and thereby increase consumers' knowledge on certain products or brands (Seraj, 2012; Jayanti & Singh, 2010). It therefore follows, those individuals who have 'liked' a company's Facebook page are receiving content that is rich in intellectual, social and cultural value, that can in turn, influence purchasing behavior. These individuals are also gaining knowledge about the company and its products. Facebook brand pages have been particularly praised for their ability to generate worth of mouth 'buzz' about a brand (Goh, et al., 2013), while also generating knowledge for consumers through their capability of sharing information through posts and other content, which in turn, have been proven to drive sales (Kozinets, 2002). The positive link between engagement in online brand communities and firm sales, profitability and performance has been studied and proven in the literature (Goh, et al., 2013; Gopinath, et al., 2014; Hoffman & Fodor, 2010; Kumar, Bhaskaran, Mirchandani, & Shah, 2013).

Findings from previous studies indicate that the decision making process of purchasing organic food involves various motivational factors, making it a complex psychological consumption process. Adding to this complexity is the additional array of perceived barriers to purchase, including a lack of knowledge about organic food and its benefits. Studies suggest that knowledge about organic food is an inhibitor to purchase, but when increased, pleased a pivotal role in the forming of positive attitudes towards organic food. This positive attitude formation in turn positively influences ones likelihood to purchase organic food (Magistris & Gracia, 2008).

It is therefore proposed that as social media is a trusted platform for knowledge acquisition for its consumers, it can serve to mitigate the negative effect of the 'knowledge' barrier to organic food consumption and thereby positively influence organic food sales (see Figure 1). As it has been supported that informative and high quality social media content (Seraj, 2012) can drive sales and firm profitability (Goh, Heng, & Lin, 2013; Kumar, et al., 2013; Gopinath, Thomas, & Krishnamurthi, 2014), we propose:

Proposition 1: Social media content will have a positive impact on organic food consumption

Studies in CRM literature show how CRM processes successfully yield greater average returns per consumer and thus, firm profitability (Dowling, 2002; Reinartz, 2004). In particular, streams of CRM literature have explored this link analyzing the positive impact of loyalty reward programs on increasing customer lifetime duration and share of wallet (Meyer-Waarden, 2007), repeat purchases (Taylor & Neslin, 2005) and customer retention and value (Bolton, Kannan, & Bramlett, 2000). This research supports the view a 'loyal' customer belonging the loyalty rewards program is more profitable.

Figure 1. Conceptual Framework

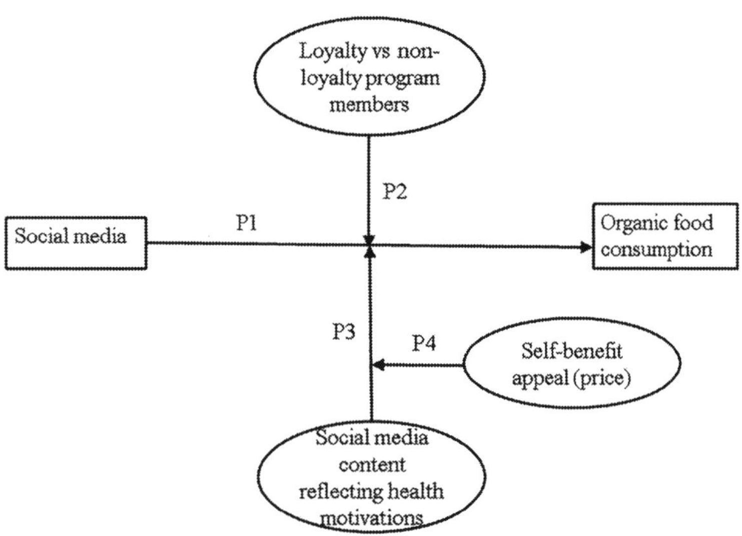

However, little is known about the effectiveness of SCRM processes in influencing loyalty program (LP) members' purchase behavior. It is accepted that LP members have existing loyalty to the company through the traditional CRM program, which begs the question- what value could SCRM processes additionally provide? SCRM processes could in fact, behave as a saturation point for these LP members, whereby additional advertising attempts via these SCRM processes will be of little to no effect on LP members. We argue, that customers who have initiated the process of joining the loyalty program recognize the benefits of organic food consumption and are frequent consumers of it. It therefore follows, that these consumers have a sufficient level of knowledge prompting them to consume organic food. We further argue that the LP members are therefore 'de-sensitised' to additional online promotion material through SCRM processes.

We further argue, that SCRM processes will therefore have a greater effect for non-members of the company's loyalty reward program. These customers are not yet fully integrated in the company's traditional CRM program and are therefore not as frequent in purchasing organic food, and perhaps, not as knowledgeable. They have however, self-selected their inclusion on the company's Facebook page, and thus have an interest in organic food.

As we have discussed the informative value of social media, these non-LP members will benefit significantly from the information and knowledge sharing nature of the organic foods' Facebook page. By keeping members of the company's Facebook community up to date with information regarding organic food, consumers will increase their knowledge and consumption of organic food. We therefore draw on organic food theory to claims an increase in consumers' knowledge about organic food will result in an increase in organic food consumption by non-LP members who are not as knowledgeable as LP members:

Proposition 2: Social media content will have a greater positive impact on organic food consumption for non-loyalty program members

Studies of social media suggest that different types of social media content have different impact on consumer engagement and sales (Goh, Heng, & Lin, 2013; Gopinath, Thomas, & Krishnamurthi, 2014). Minton et al. (2012) explored the different reasons in social media motives for sustainability in a cross-cultural study. Their findings cautioned advertisers from using generic sustainable advertising messages over social media. Instead, advertisers should target distinct sets of motives for sustainability that are industry and country specific. In individualist societies, they found responsibility and involvement motives consistently lead to organic food purchases. That is, individuals liked to feel 'responsible' for engaging in healthy eating behaviours and 'involved' with other consumers and companies in the process of doing so.

Drawing from the organic food literature, the two primary drivers of organic food consumption are health and environmental motivations. Combining this literature with the findings of Minton et al. (2012), 'health' motives are more closely in line with motives linked to a sense of responsibility and level of involvement, in comparison to environment motives, that are less individualist and more collective in nature. We therefore purport that social media content that reflect the health motivations towards organic food consumption will lead to a positive increase in organic food consumption:

Proposition 3: Social media content reflecting 'health motivations' will lead to a positive increase in organic food consumption

Health motivations refer to the individual's self-benefits of consuming organic food, which are mainly concerned with the increasing of one's personal health via the consumption of organic food (Magistris & Gracia, 2008). Health motivations are therefore reflective of 'self-benefit' appeals that promote the individual benefits of consuming organic food (White & Simpson, 2013). Should the self-benefits of organic consumption be strengthened in the social media content through an external self-benefit motivation, it therefore follows that influence of social media content on organic food consumption will be strengthened.

Social media content combining the health benefit factor of organic food consumption and a self-benefit factor external to organic food consumption, will lead to a greater significant impact on organic food consumption. Literature suggests normative appeals that activate the individual self are more responsive to self-benefit appeals (for example, cost savings) in influencing sustainable behaviours (White & Simpson, 2013). Linking to this theory, one of the most widely documented barriers to organic food consumption is the price premium of organic food products. Price acts as a barrier to organic food purchase to consumers who cannot justify the price premiums of organic food (Padel & Foster, 2005). However, it is also purported that by increasing ones knowledge about the health benefits of organic food consumption has twofold value; it creates positive attitudes regarding organic food which increases ones likelihood to purchase organic food, and, it serves to decrease the perceived barrier of price to purchase organic (Magistris & Gracia, 2008).

Ultimately, as social media platforms can act as trusted sources of knowledge acquisition for consumers as aforementioned, combining the self-benefit appeal of 'price' with the health benefits of organic food will increase ones knowledge about organic food and thus, increase organic food expenditure. The literature suggests that if the price barrier to organic food consumption be resolved in the consumers' decision-making process by promoting the health benefits of organic food consumption, the barriers effect will be mitigated. Therefore, we propose that if the price of an organic food product is included in the social media message in combination with the health benefits of the consumption of that product, there will be an increase in consumption of that product:

Proposition 4: Social media content that combines both the health benefits and price appeal of organic food will increase organic food consumption of that product

CONCLUSION AND FUTURE RESEARCH DIRECTIONS

By drawing on consumer motivations towards organic food consumption, and incorporating this theory to link a company's social media content and its effect on sales, our research is of significant contribution to the organic food literature. From a theoretical perspective, our study contributes significantly to the existing knowledge of CRM and emerging SCRM literature. It contributes to legitimizing the use of SCRM processes as new advertising tools in the marketing mix.

From a practical perspective, our research is of significant in identifying the ways in which marketers can communicate with consumers to increase healthy eating behaviors in response to the prevalent obesity epidemic. As society employs processes towards a holistic approach to health, whereby individuals are increasingly motivated to sculpt their lives through healthy eating, identifying how organic food consumption can be increased by the use of social media will have implications for organic food retailers, general food retailers at large, and policy makers who are seeking ways to reduce the effects of obesity related health issues.

While there is a considerable amount of research that addresses the impact of CRM customers on sales, there is a gap in addressing the impact of social media (SCRM) customers and CRM customers on sales. Little is also known about social media's influence on customers of a firm, and even less is understood about the effect social media has on sales. Currently, most social media tracking is done independently to sales, especially in a food retail environment, focusing on metrics such as consumer engagement and interaction. Linking social media to customer identities through a CRM program of an organic food company provides an opportunity to better understand the role of social media and CRM, relative to sales.

No study, to the best of our knowledge, has explored the link of SCRM and CRM, relative to sales, and furthermore, has not explored the impact of social media in the context of organic food. Organic food consumers represent a niche group of food consumers that have in recent years, formed a unique community to express their self-identity and values towards organic food consumption. Social media has provided a platform in which these consumers are able to promote their healthy way of living by connecting with businesses and other like-minded individuals online. We explore this niche by analyzing if these consumers are influenced by different types of social media posts that reflect typical motivations of organic food consumption, and whether this content has an effect on sales. This is just the first step to research this important area. More research is necessary to provide a full understanding of the issues in this important area.

REFERENCES

Aertsens, J., Mondelaers, K., Verbeke, W., Buysse, J., & Huylenbroeck, G. V. (2011). The influence of subjective and objective knowledge on attitude, motivations and consumption of organic food. *British Food Journal, 113*(11), 1353–1378. doi:10.1108/00070701111179988

Algesheimer, R., Dholakia, U. M., & Herrmann, A. (2005). The social influence of brand community: Evidence from European car clubs. *Journal of Marketing, 69*(3), 19–34. doi:10.1509/jmkg.69.3.19.66363

Anderson, E. W., Fornell, C., & Lehmann, D. R. (1994). Customer satisfaction, market share, and profitability: Findings from Sweden. *Journal of Marketing, 58*(3), 53–66. doi:10.2307/1252310

Baird, C. H., & Parasnis, G. (2011). From social media to social customer relationship management. *Strategy and Leadership, 39*(5), 30–37. doi:10.1108/10878571111161507

Beharrell, B., & Crockett, A. (1992). New Age Food! New Age Consumers! *British Food Journal, 94*(2), 5–13. doi:10.1108/00070709210018979

Bolton, R. N., Kannan, P. K., & Bramlett, M. D. (2000). Implications of Loyalty Program Membership and Service Experiences for Customer Retention and Value. *Journal of the Academy of Marketing Science, 28*(1), 95–108. doi:10.1177/0092070300281009

Byrne, P. J., Toensmeyer, U. C., German, C. L., & Muller, H. R. (1992). Evaluation of consumer attitudes towards organic produce in Delaware and the Delmarva region. *Journal of Food Distribution Research, 23*(1), 29–44.

Chinnici, G., D'Amico, M., & Pecorino, B. (2002). A multivariate statistical analysis on the consumers of organic products. *British Food Journal, 104*(3/4/5), 187-199. doi: 10.1108/00070700210425651

Davies, A., Titterington, A. J., & Cochrane, C. (1995). Who Buys Organic Food? A Profile of the Purchasers of Organic Food in Northern Ireland. *British Food Journal, 97*(10), 17–23. doi:10.1108/00070709510104303

Demeritt, L. (2002). *All things organic 2002: A look at the organic consumer.* Bellevue, WA: The Hartman Group.

Divol, R., Edelman, D., & Sarrazin, H. (2012). (*Producer*). Demystifying Social Media.

Dowling, G. (2002). Customer Relationship Management: In B2C Markets, Often Less is More. *California Management Review, 44*(3), 87–104. doi:10.2307/41166134

Durham, C. A. (2007). The impact of environmental and health motivations on the organic share of produce purchases. *Agricultural and Resource Economics Review, 36*(2), 304.

Fotopoulos, C., & Krystallis, A. (2002a). Organic product avoidance: Reasons for rejection and potential buyers' identification in a countrywide survey. *British Food Journal, 104*(3/4/5), 233-260. doi: 10.1108/00070700210425697

Fotopoulos, C., & Krystallis, A. (2002b). Purchasing motives and profile of the Greek organic consumer: A countrywide survey. *British Food Journal, 104*(9), 730–765. doi:10.1108/00070700210443110

French, S., & Hale, T. (2010). Are Healthy Thinkers Also Healthy Shoppers? Retrieved 22/5/14, from The Nielsen Company http://www.nielsenmediamonitor.com/content/corporate/us/en/newswire/2010/are-healthy-thinkers-also-healthy-shoppers.html

Goh, K.-Y., Heng, C.-S., & Lin, Z. (2013). Social Media Brand Community and Consumer Behavior: Quantifying the Relative Impact of User- and Marketer-Generated Content. *Information Systems Research, 24*(1), 88–107. doi:10.1287/isre.1120.0469

Goldman, B. J., & Clancy, K. L. (1991). A survey of organic produce purchases and related attitudes of food cooperative shoppers. *American Journal of Alternative Agriculture, 6*(2), 89–96. doi:10.1017/S0889189300003933

Gopinath, S., Thomas, J. S., & Krishnamurthi, L. (2014). Investigating the Relationship Between the Content of Online Word of Mouth, Advertising, and Brand Performance. *Marketing Science, 33*(2), 241–258. doi:10.1287/mksc.2013.0820

Greenberg, P. (2007). Welcome to the era of the social consumer (pp. 138-140): CRMProject.

Harper, G. C., & Makatouni, A. (2002). Consumer perception of organic food production and farm animal welfare. *British Food Journal, 104*(3/4/5), 287-299. doi: 10.1108/00070700210425723

Hoad, V., Somerford, P., & Katzenellenbogen, J. (2010). High body mass index overtakes tobacco as the leading independent risk factor contibuting to disease burden in Western Australia. *Australian and New Zealand Journal of Public Health, 34*(2), 214–215. doi:10.1111/j.1753-6405.2010.00509.x PMID:23331368

Hoffman, D. L., & Fodor, M. (2010). Can You Measure the ROI of Your Social Media Marketing? *Sloan Management Review, 52*(1), 40–50.

IBISWorld. (2014). IBISWorld reveals the industries set to fly and fall in 2014 (M. Centre, Trans.). In IBISWorld (Ed.), (pp. 1-5): IBISWorld.

Iyengar, R., Han, S., & Gupta, S. (2009). Do Friends Influence Purchases in a Social Network? Working paper

Jayanti, R. K., & Singh, J. (2010). Pragmatic learning theory: An inquiry-action framework for distributed consumer learning in online communities. *The Journal of Consumer Research, 36*(6), 1058–1081. doi:10.1086/648689

Kozinets, R. V. (2002). The field behind the screen: Using netnography for marketing research in online communities. *JMR, Journal of Marketing Research, 39*(1), 61–72. doi:10.1509/jmkr.39.1.61.18935

Kumar, V., Bhaskaran, V., Mirchandani, R., & Shah, M. (2013). Practice Prize Winner—Creating a Measurable Social Media Marketing Strategy: Increasing the Value and ROI of Intangibles and Tangibles for Hokey Pokey. *Marketing Science, 32*(2), 194–212. doi:10.1287/mksc.1120.0768

Langley, S. (2013). Australian consumers will pay more for 'eco-friendly' vegetables, study. Retrieved 29/5/2014, from Australian Food News http://ausfoodnews.com.au/2013/12/04/australian-consumers-will-pay-more-for-%E2%80%98eco-friendly%E2%80%99-vegetables-study.html

Laroche, M., Habibi, M. R., & Richard, M.-O. (2013). To be or not to be in social media: How brand loyalty is affected by social media? *International Journal of Information Management*, *33*(1), 76–82. doi:10.1016/j.ijinfomgt.2012.07.003

Lea, E., & Worsley, T. (2005). Australians' organic food beliefs, demographics and values. *British Food Journal*, *107*(11), 855–869. doi:10.1108/00070700510629797

Leiner, B. M., Cerf, V. G., Clark, D. D., Kahn, R. E., Kleinrock, L., Daniel, C. L., ... (2000). A brief history of the internet. 2000. *Web Page. URL: http://info. isoc/org/internet-history/brief. html, 18.*

Leung, L. (2013). Generational differences in content generation in social media: The roles of the gratifications sought of narcissism. *Computers in Human Behavior*, *29*(3), 997–1006. doi:10.1016/j.chb.2012.12.028

Magistris, T., & Gracia, A. (2008). The decision to buy organic food products in Southern Italy. *British Food Journal*, *110*(9), 929–947. doi:10.1108/00070700810900620

Mangold, W. G., & Faulds, D. J. (2009). Social media: The new hybrid element of the promotion mix. *Business Horizons*, *52*(4), 357–365. doi:10.1016/j.bushor.2009.03.002

Meyer-Waarden, L. (2007). The effects of loyalty programs on customer lifetime duration and share of wallet. *Journal of Retailing*, *83*(2), 223–236. doi:10.1016/j.jretai.2007.01.002

Miller, A. R., & Tucker, C. (2013). Active Social Media Management: The Case of Health Care. *Information Systems Research*, *24*(1), 52–70. doi:10.1287/isre.1120.0466

Muniz, A. M. Jr, & O'Guinn, T. C. (2001). Brand Community. *The Journal of Consumer Research*, *27*(4), 412–432. doi:10.1086/319618

Padel, S., & Foster, C. (2005). Exploring the gap between attitudes and behaviour: Understanding why consumers buy or do not buy organic food. *British Food Journal*, *107*(8), 606–625. doi:10.1108/00070700510611002

Patino, A., Pitta, D. A., & Quinones, R. (2012). Social media's emerging importance in market research. *Journal of Consumer Marketing*, *29*(3), 233–237. doi:10.1108/07363761211221800

Reichheld, F. P., & Sasser, W. E. (1990). *Zero Defeciions*. Quoliiy Comes To Services.

Reicks, M., Splett, P., & Fishman, A. (1997). *Shelf Labelling of Organic Foods: Effects on Customer Perceptions and Sales*. The Retail Food Industry Center.

Reinartz, W., Krafft, M., & Hoyer, W. D. (2004). The Customer Relationship Management Process: Its Measurement and Impact on Performance. *JMR, Journal of Marketing Research*, *41*(3), 293–305. doi:10.1509/jmkr.41.3.293.35991

Roddy, G., Cowan, C., & Hutchinson, G. (1994). Organic food–a description of the Irish market. *British Food Journal*, *96*(4), 3–10. doi:10.1108/00070709410060998

Schifferstein, H. N. J., & Ophuis, P. A. M. O. (1998). Health-Related Determinants of Organic Food Consumption in the Netherlands. *Food Quality and Preference*, *9*(3), 119–133. doi:10.1016/S0950-3293(97)00044-X

Schivinski, B., & Dabrowski, D. (2013). The impact of brand communication on brand equity dimensions and brand purchase intention throuhg Facebook. *GUT FME Working Paper Series A, 4*(4), 1 - 20.

Seraj, M. (2012). We Create, We Connect, We Respect, Therefore We Are: Intellectual, Social, and Cultural Value in Online Communities. *Journal of Interactive Marketing*, *26*(4), 209–222. doi:10.1016/j.intmar.2012.03.002

Smith, A. N., Fischer, E., & Yongjian, C. (2012). How Does Brand-related User-generated Content Differ across YouTube, Facebook, and Twitter? *Journal of Interactive Marketing*, *26*(2), 102–113. doi:10.1016/j.intmar.2012.01.002

Smithee, B. (2011). How social media is expanding the defitions of MR, and as leaders why it is largely your responsibility. *Alert, 51*(3).

Taylor, G. A., & Neslin, S. A. (2005). The current and future sales impact of a retail frequency reward program. *Journal of Retailing*, *81*(4), 293–305. doi:10.1016/j.jretai.2004.11.004

Vinerean, S., Cetina, I., Dumitrescu, L., & Tichindelean, M. (2013). The Effects of Social Media Marketing on Online Consumer Behavior. *International Journal of Business and Management*, *8*(14). doi:10.5539/ijbm.v8n14p66

Weinberg, B. D., & Pehlivan, E. (2011). Social spending: Managing the social media mix. *Business Horizons*, *54*(3), 275–282. doi:10.1016/j.bushor.2011.01.008

White, K., & Simpson, B. (2013). When Do (and Don't) Normative Appeals Influence Sustainable Consumer Behaviors? *Journal of Marketing*, *77*(2), 78–95. doi:10.1509/jm.11.0278

Wilcox, K., & Stephen, A. T. (Forthcoming). Are Close Friends the Enemy? Online Social Networks, Self-Esteem and Self-Control. *The Journal of Consumer Research*.

Winer, R. S. (2001). A Framework for Customer Relationship Management. *California Management Review*, *43*(4), 89–105. doi:10.2307/41166102

Xiang, Z., & Gretzel, U. (2010). Role of social media in online travel information search. *Tourism Management*, *31*(2), 179–188. doi:10.1016/j.tourman.2009.02.016

Zanoli, R., & Naspetti, S. (2002). Consumer motivations in the purchase of organic food: A means-end approach. *British Food Journal*, *104*(8), 643–653. doi:10.1108/00070700210425930

ADDITIONAL READING

Cicia, G., Del Giudice, T., & Scarpa, R. (2002). Consumers' perception of quality in organic food: a random utility model under preference heterogeneity and choice correlation from rank-orderings. *British Food Journal, 104*(3/4/5), 200-213.

Claussen, J., Kretschmer, T., & Mayrhofer, P. (2013). The Effects of Rewarding User Engagement: The Case of Facebook Apps. *Information Systems Research, 24*(1), 186–200. doi:10.1287/isre.1120.0467

Fisher, T. (2009). ROI in social media: A look at the arguments. *Journal of Database Marketing &. Customer Strategy Management, 16*(3), 189–195. doi:10.1057/dbm.2009.16

Hughner, R. S., McDonagh, P., Prothero, A., Shultz, C. J., & Stanton, J. (2007). Who are organic food consumers? A compilation and review of why people purchase organic food. *Journal of Consumer Behaviour, 6*(2-3), 94–110. doi:10.1002/cb.210

Loureiro, M. L., McCluskey, J. J., & Mittelhammer, R. C. (2001). Assessing Consumer Preferences for Organic, Eco-labeled, and Regular Apples. *Journal of Agricultural Resource Economics, 26*(2), 404–416.

Luo, X., Zhang, J., & Duan, W. (2013). Social Media and Firm Equity Value. *Information Systems Research, 24*(1), 146–163. doi:10.1287/isre.1120.0462

Magnusson, M. K., Arvola, A., Hursti, U.-K. K., Åberg, L., & Sjödén, P.-O. (2003). Choice of organic foods is related to perceived consequences for human health and to environmentally friendly behaviour. *Appetite, 40*(2), 109–117. doi:10.1016/S0195-6663(03)00002-3 PMID:12781160

Makatouni, A. (2002). What motivates consumers to buy organic food in the UK?: Results from a qualitative study. *British Food Journal, 104*(3/4/5), 345-352.

Patino, A., Pitta, D. A., & Quinones, R. (2012). Social media's emerging importance in market research. *Journal of Consumer Marketing, 29*(3), 233–237. doi:10.1108/07363761211221800

Rindfleisch, A., & Heide, J. B. (1997). Transaction cost analysis: Past, present, and future applications. *Journal of Marketing, 61*(4), 30. doi:10.2307/1252085

Rishika, R., Kumar, A., Janakiraman, R., & Bezawada, R. (2013). The Effect of Customers' Social Media Participation on Customer Visit Frequency and Profitability: An Empirical Investigation. *Information Systems Research, 24*(1), 108–127. doi:10.1287/isre.1120.0460

Rust, R. T., & Zahorik, A. J. (1993). Customer satisfaction, customer retention, and market share. *Journal of Retailing, 69*(2), 193–215. doi:10.1016/0022-4359(93)90003-2

Stephen, A. T., & Galak, J. (2012). The Effects of Traditional and Social Earned Media on Sales: A Study of a Microlending Marketplace. *JMR, Journal of Marketing Research, 49*(5), 624–639. doi:10.1509/jmr.09.0401

Torjusen, H., Lieblein, G., Wandel, M., & Francis, C. A. (2001). Food System Orientation and Quality Perception among Consumers and Producers of Organic Food in Hedmark County, Norway. *Food Quality and Preference, 12*(3), 207–216. doi:10.1016/S0950-3293(00)00047-1

KEY TERMS AND DEFINITIONS

Customer Loyalty: Tendency of a customer to purchase a product or service over a period of time. It is usually caused by positive previous experience.

Customer Relationship Management: A system that companies use to manage and evaluate interactions with their customers. An effective relationship management can deepen companies' relationships with their customers and build up customer loyalty.

Facebook Brand Page: A profile on Facebook which is different an actual User profile. It can used to generate worth of mouth 'buzz' about a brand and knowledge for consumers through its capability of sharing information through posts and other content.

Facebook: An online social networking website founded by Mark Zurckerberg on February 4, 2004. IT had an initial public offering in May 2012 with initial market value of $104 billion.

Loyalty Program: A reward program provided by companies to reward their loyal customers who frequently purchase from them. It also allows companies to collect detailed customer data.

Organic Food: Natural, wholesome and healthy food. It is produced through renewable sources, the best environmental practices, the application of high animal welfare standards, and without the use of synthetic fertilisers and pesticides.

Social Customer Relationship Management: A logical extension to traditional CRM processes, rather than a replacement. The real value of SCRM therefore lies in its facilitation of two-way flows of communication between the firm and consumer.

This research was previously published in Strategic Customer Relationship Management in the Age of Social Media edited by Amir Khanlari, pages 198-215, copyright year 2015 by Business Science Reference (an imprint of IGI Global).

Chapter 39
The Impact of Social Media on Customer Engagement With U.S. Banks

Arturo Haro-de-Rosario
University of Almería, Spain

Laura Saraite
University of Almería, Spain

Alejandro Sáez-Martin
University of Almería, Spain

María del Carmen Caba-Pérez
University of Almería, Spain

ABSTRACT

This chapter has two main aims. First, to investigate the Facebook practices used in the U.S. banking sector with the aim of enhancing customer engagement; second, to perform a comparative analysis of the use of Facebook in this respect, among different U.S. banks. In this comparative analysis, we apply the Federal Reserve charter classification (Nationally chartered member bank, State-chartered member bank and State-chartered nonmember bank). The findings of this study contribute significantly to our understanding of the influence of social media in enhancing customer engagement. Banks, and their community managers in particular, can make use of the conclusions drawn in this study to develop future strategies to foster citizen engagement via Facebook.

INTRODUCTION

Social media, based on Web 2.0 technologies, have elevated online communications to a new level (Constantinides & Fountain, 2008). According to Mitic and Kapoulas (2012), social media are becoming an integral part of consumers' lives and can enhance the understanding of their needs and preferences, on the basis of shared information. Therefore, social media could help organisations build up brand

DOI: 10.4018/978-1-5225-5637-4.ch039

awareness, visibility, reputation, knowledge sharing and customer acquisition and retention (Kaplan & Haenlein, 2010; Bolotaeva & Cata, 2010).

The fast rate of Social Media adoption, and their rapidly growing popularity, encourages speculation on the potential goldmine that lies within the complex network of user commentaries, testimonials and communities (Eccleston & Griseri, 2008; Hardey, 2009). In this respect, Mitic and Kapoulas (2012) observed that social media have quickly escalated to become a global phenomenon where connectedness to Facebook or Twitter is everything and the ability to acquire "follows", "likes" or "shares" means power. In consequence, inspired by the power of social media to engage users, organisations have begun to seek ways to learn to leverage these "likes", "shares" and "comments" for profit making (Andriole, 2010; Culnan et al., 2010).

In a banking context, social media allow customers to engage, collaborate and interact, and present an opportunity for those banks which strategically adopt Web 2.0 technologies into their organisation structure. Thus, social media provide a perfect platform for customer relationship management (Chikandiwa et al., 2013). Moreover, according to Bonsón and Flores (2011) and Gritten (2011), social media could enable banks to regain the customer trust that had been lost due to the recent economic crisis.

The most popular social media used by banks, for the purpose of communicating with their customers, are Facebook and Twitter (Chikandiwa et al., 2013; Goi, 2014). Samuels (2013) observed that banks are now using social media like Facebook far more intensively, as it affords them more space in which to post images, information and private messages. Similarly, Logvinov (2013) argued that banks are turning to social media to build and rebuild their customer relationships by inviting their customers to participate in the business, such as helping other customers and designing new products and services.

Taking the view that the appropriate use of social media can raise levels of customer feedback, loyalty and engagement (Beuker, 2009; Gallaugher & Ransbotham, 2010), pioneers in social media are emerging in the banking sector (Mitic & Kapoulas, 2012). In the U.S., banks such as Citibank, Bank of America and ING Direct now have an active presence in social media, oriented toward creating rapport with customers and providing interactive online service support (Stone, 2009; Cohen, 2010). However, according to Klimis (2010), European banks appear to be more reserved, and there are fewer examples of their presence in the social media. Therefore, although social media implementation in banking is emerging (especially in the U.S.), the sector is still at an early stage of establishing a social media presence and using Web 2.0 technologies to enhance engagement with customers (Cocheo, 2009; Hardey, 2009; Klimis, 2010).

The literature on the banking sector has abundant references to online and electronic services (e.g. e-banking), but has paid relatively little attention to the adoption and use of social media (Mitic & Kapoulas, 2012; Chikandiwa et al., 2013; Goi, 2014; Murray et al., 2014). Furthermore, most previous studies in this field have used interviews or questionnaires, although it has been argued that metrics measuring the effectiveness of social media engagement and its impact on customer relationships are still vague, and to date no hard evidence has been produced to prove the benefits of social media for the banking sector (Jaser, 2010; Vemuri, 2010). Therefore, there is a need to investigate, based on social media profiles, how certain banks adopt social media, why others resist the trend, and what could be learned from their practices and approaches.

Taking these considerations into account, this chapter has two main aims. First, to investigate the Facebook practices used in the U.S. banking sector with the aim of enhancing customer engagement; second, to perform a comparative analysis of the use of Facebook in this respect, among different U.S. banks. In this comparative analysis, we apply the Federal Reserve charter classification (Nationally chartered member bank, State-chartered member bank and State-chartered nonmember bank). The findings of this study contribute significantly to our understanding of the influence of social media in enhancing customer engagement. Banks, and their community managers in particular, can make use of the conclusions drawn in this study to develop future strategies to foster citizen engagement via Facebook. In addition, by exploring the differences among U.S. banks regarding their adoption of social media to increase customer engagement, we gain a better understanding of the possibilities of social media and their implementation in this sector of the economy. As a more general outcome, we hope that this research will spur reflection on the benefits offered by the adoption of social media in this sector and related industries.

Web 2.0 Technologies and Social Media in the Banking Sector

Due to increased competition, the greater homogeneity of financial products and services, globalisation and the recent economic crisis, financial institutions have had to increase the level of services provided in order to improve customer satisfaction, increase the degree of differentiation from the competition and, ultimately, involve the entire organisation in customer satisfaction (Liebana & Muñoz, 2013). This shift, known as Customer Relationship Management, has produced a transformation in financial institutions, both in their organisational model and in their business management model (Liebana et al., 2011). Thus, new technological solutions have been introduced into the banking sector via the internet, leading to the creation of 'electronic banking' (Gerrard et al., 2006;. Suriya et al., 2012; Liebana & Muñoz, 2013).

Electronic banking is defined as the combination of online banking activities (e-banking) and relational marketing through the internet (Mukhtar, 2015). E-banking allows services to be offered at lower cost, by eliminating intermediaries, and makes them easily accessible (Ozdemir & Trott, 2009; Flavián et al., 2006). Moreover, the internet provides an alternative marketing channel, one that banks can use to attract and maintain new customers (Mukhtar, 2015).

Banks' rising interest in retaining customers and strengthening their engagement has evolved in parallel with the growth of the internet (Wirtz et al., 2010). The social media, arising with the development of Web 2.0 tools, are considered the "next milestone" in the evolution and analysis of corporate information (Bonsón & Flores, 2011). The new possibilities of social interaction are considered a key aspect of achieving customer engagement and entering into close relations with stakeholders (Sashi, 2012). Social media also facilitate the creation of value between the company and the customer (Harrison & Barthel, 2009). Therefore, this new phase of the internet, in which users of social media are no longer restricted to consulting online information, but can actively participate in its creation, has opened the way to the quick and easy communicating, collaborating and sharing of information online (Bonsón & Rathaki, 2013).

Mitic and Kapoulas (2012) identified four possible ways in which banks can engage with their customers via social media: by creating up-to-date, interactive content; by encouraging customers to interact with the bank through social media; by encouraging customers to actively contribute ideas to improve the banks' offer of services and products, for mutual benefit; and by collaborating with the online community to raise awareness about social media programs. Chikandiwa et al. (2013) and Goi (2014), among others, have shown that Facebook and Twitter are the most commonly used forms of social media, while Samuels (2013) observed that Facebook offers the most space for the publication of images and information.

THEORETICAL FRAMEWORK AND PREVIOUS RESEARCH

Numerous theories have been proposed to explain how and why organisations implement their strategies and actions through social media. Thus, Wattal et al. (2010) referred to agency theory, noting that the social media have reshaped the relationship between stakeholders and organisations, offering the latter incentives to disclose information that enables their actions to be monitored. In accordance with the theory of rumour transmission, first proposed by Buckner (1965), it has been suggested that companies can improve their methods of promotion through the analysis of social media and organic word-of-mouth (Kazienko et al., 2011). In this line, too, and following stakeholder theory (Freeman, 1984), Bonsón and Ratkai (2013) examined how stakeholders' moods in the social media can change in response to companies' actions.

Referring to the theory of legitimacy, Bonsón and Ratkai (2013) suggested that society is a broader category than that of stakeholders because it contains entities that are not stakeholders in the company. Accordingly, a company must conduct its activities both through the social media and apart from them, in order to be considered socially acceptable. In other words, they must not only meet the expectations of, for example, present-day investors, but also those of future ones and of possible clients.

In any case, the impact and benefits of social media can only come after acceptance, adoption and continued usage. According to Kaplan and Haenlein (2010) and Clemons (2009), social media should be viewed as a tool for improving customer engagement, and therefore strategies should be determined to promote the adoption of social media. The literature in this field classifies models of social media adoption into two main groups (Chikandiwa et al., 2013). On the one hand is the social organising model (SOM), based on the strategic framework of the organisation. According to Owyang (2010), companies may be organised for social development in any of five ways: centralised, distributed, coordinated, multiple hub and spoke, and holistic.

The second group consists of four models based on the level of maturity in terms of the adoption of social media: the social media strategy learning curve (SMSLC), the social media adoption curve (SMAC), the social engagement journey (SEJ) and the social media maturity model (SMMM). The SMSLC model describes the emergence, tactics, integration and development of the process by which social media are adopted (Smiciklas, 2011). The SMAC model is composed of six successive steps: learning, observation, broadcast, participation, relationship and collaboration (MiXT Media, 2008). By means of the SEJ model, Carfi (2012) describes the five scenarios that an organisation must experience to become completely connected socially: traditional, experimental, operational, measurable and fully engaged. Finally, the SMMM model comprises the following phases: ad-hoc, experimental, functional and transformation (Luxembourg, 2011).

In addition to the above, the technology acceptance model (TAM) (Davis, 1989), which identifies the factors that lead people to accept or reject the use of technological applications, has been used by authors such as Curtis et al. (2010) to demonstrate the effectiveness of social media in the clear, precise disclosure of information, and in obtaining real-time feedback from stakeholders.

All of the above-mentioned theories and models are important, but the dialogic communication theory proposed by Taylor and Kent (1998) has been the most widely used over the last decade to explain the importance of the use of social media as a strategic tool for promoting communication and dialogue (Waters et al., 2009; Bortree & Seltzer, 2009; Rybalko & Selzter, 2010; McAllister, 2012; Bonsón & Ratkai, 2013; Bonsón et al., 2014; Sáez-Martín et al., 2015). This theory highlights the use of Web 2.0 technologies via the social media as a key element in improving organisations' interactivity and communication and in enhancing stakeholders' satisfaction and engagement. Thus, through increased transparency and participation, trust is reinforced between organisations and their stakeholders (Bonsón & Ratkai, 2013; Bonsón et al., 2014).

In relation to previous studies of banks' use of social media, an important paper was presented by Chikandiwa et al. (2013), who examined patterns of adoption of social media by banks in order to conduct marketing by this channel of communication. In this line, too, Mitic and Kapoulas (2012) investigated banks' requirements for adopting social media, and concluded that social media are more appropriate for smaller or younger banks that wish to use innovative ways to increase their market share.

Goi (2014) examined the impact of social media on banks with respect to aspects such as conversation, exchange, publication and participation, all of which are also relevant to market share. With regard to the acquisition and retention of customers, Murray et al. (2014) suggested that social media are used primarily to improve customer participation in the affairs of the bank.

Despite the importance of these studies and the relative absence of research into the use of social media in the banking sector, the metrics used previously have been criticised as using only surveys and interviews to investigate the effectiveness of participation in social media and their impact on relations with customers (Jaser, 2010; Vemuri, 2010). Therefore, there is a need for further research, to analyse bank profiles in the most popular forms of social media, such as Facebook. For this purpose, Bonsón and Ratkai (2013) provide a useful introduction. On the basis of dialogic communication theory, these authors propose a set of metrics with which to evaluate reactivity, dialogic communication and engagement through corporate profiles on Facebook (popularity, engagement and virality). These metrics provide a better understanding and measurement capability of social media, and thus can help improve the management of online communication between banks and their customers.

METHOD

Sample

The Federal Deposit Insurance Corporation, which is the U.S. government agency that protects customer deposits, has recorded the existence of 7,836 banking groups in the country. Most are State or local banks, while a few are nationwide banking giants, and play a major role in the economy.

According to the Federal Reserve, the U.S. banking system is composed of three types of banks: Nationally chartered member banks, which operate on the authority of Federal law and are members of the Federal Reserve; State-chartered member banks, which operate in accordance with the provisions of the banking laws of each State and are also members of the Federal Reserve; and State-chartered nonmember banks, which are private banks operating within a given State and which do not participate in the Federal Reserve System. In general, nonmember banks are less regulated than member banks, being subject only to the laws of the States in which they are chartered.

Our analysis is focused on the Facebook profiles of the largest U.S. banks. The study sample was obtained taking into consideration the Federal Reserve database, which compiles data on domestically chartered insured commercial banks that have consolidated assets of $300 million or more. We selected the 150 largest U.S. banks as the initial sample.

The approach used to determine the official Facebook page of the 150 banks was, first, to examine the official website of each bank. If no link was found to an official Facebook profile, "Facebook" was used as a search term on the bank's own website. If this approach failed to obtain a Facebook profile, a search was conducted in Google, specifying "Facebook" with the title of the bank. By conducting this procedure, of the 150 banks analysed, 83 were found to have an official Facebook page (37 Nationally chartered member banks, 25 State-chartered member banks and 21 State-chartered nonmember banks). Therefore, these 83 U.S. banks constituted the final study sample.

The study was conducted during the month of August 2015. The period of one month is considered an acceptable timeframe in which to analyse the information present in social media (Nah and Saxton, 2013). Altogether, 1,825 Facebook posts were analysed, together with 16,834 comments, 389,789 likes and 33,693 shares.

Analysis Procedure

The research for this chapter is structured in two phases. First, a descriptive analysis was conducted to determine the level of customer engagement through the Facebook profiles of U.S. banks. In the second phase, an analysis of differences of medians was performed to identify significant divergences between customer engagement in nationally chartered member banks, State-chartered member banks and State-chartered nonmember banks.

In the descriptive analysis, we examined the popularity, commitment and virality of U.S. banks' Facebook pages, following the metrics developed by Bonsón and Ratkai (2013) to measure the level of customers' engagement. In the financial world, the popularity of Facebook has led the majority of banks to create their own profiles, containing lists of other users, enabling them to scan and search through their connections (Boyd and Ellison, 2008). The effectiveness of a bank's Facebook page can be measured as the number of "likes" it obtains. Commitment reflects a more interactive engagement with customers, and is measured by the number of "comments". The virality parameter reflects the effectiveness of viral posts on Facebook, and thus customers' involvement in the active disclosure of posts. It is measured by the number of "shares", i.e., how many times a wall post is shared with others.

As shown in Table 1, the numbers of posts, likes, fans, comments and shares were collected for each Facebook profile in order to calculate the proposed metrics. The data were compiled manually by three researchers working independently. An initial meeting was held to specify the strategy to be adopted for each metric. At the end of the process, the results were reviewed to resolve any differences and to overcome possible bias.

In the second part of our analysis, the Mann-Whitney U test was applied to determine whether there are significant differences in customers' engagement among the three groups of U.S. banks, following previous research on social media and online information disclosure (Pfeil et al., 2009; Roblyer et al., 2010; Syhu & Kapoor, 2010). This test is considered the nonparametric equivalent of the t-test, and it is well suited for the analysis of two independent groups when the sample is small, when the assumptions of normality and homoscedasticity cannot be made, and when the discriminant variable for the two groups is ordinal (Sheskin, 2011). The hypotheses for this test are defined as follows:

H1: There are differences between customer engagement in Nationally-chartered member banks and State-chartered member banks.

H2: There are differences between customer engagement in Nationally-chartered member banks and State-chartered nonmember banks.

Table 1. Metrics used to measure customers' engagement

	Sign	Formula	Measures
Popularity	P1	Posts with likes/ total posts	Percentage of the total posts that have been liked
	P2	Total likes/total posts	Average number of likes per post
	P3	(P2/number of fans) * 1000	Popularity of messages among fans
Commitment	C1	Posts with comments/ total posts	Percentage of the total posts that have been commented on
	C2	Total comments/ total posts	Average number of comments per post
	C3	(C2/number of fans) * 1000	Commitment of fans
Virality	V1	Posts with shares/ total posts	Percentage of the total posts that have been shared
	V2	Total shares/ total posts	Average number of shares per post
	V3	(V2/number of fans) * 1000	Virality of messages among fans

Source: Bonsón and Ratkai (2013)

H3: There are differences between customer engagement in State-chartered member banks and State-chartered nonmember banks.

In all three cases the null hypothesis is that there is no difference between the medians.

RESULTS

Tables 2 and 3 show the data obtained in the comparative analysis for customer engagement in the U.S. banking sector. It can be seen that the form of participation that is most commonly used by these banks' customers is related to the popularity of the Facebook profiles analysed, measured by the "likes" received (see Table 2). The second commonly most used way of participating in Facebook is to "share" the publications of the bank, in what is known as virality. These data are consistent with the findings of other, similar studies (Wright, 2009; Bonsón & Ratkai, 2013), in which it is argued that these results can be explained by the fact that it is faster and easier to click "like" or "share" than to write a comment. Therefore, the least used form of interaction is that of commitment, which is measured by the comments made in response to the posts of each bank.

In general, however, bank customers present low levels of commitment, an outcome that can be explained by reference to the models referring to the adoption of social media. According to these models, banks are in the early stages of social media adoption, and therefore it is difficult to perceive or quantify the positive outcomes associated with their use, because these can only be generated after the adoption, integration and prolonged use of social media by U.S. banks.

With respect to the level of engagement achieved by each type of bank, the descriptive results reveal the existence of differences depending on the type of metric used (Table 2). Thus, the overall data indicate that U.S. customers are more engaged with State-chartered member banks than with the other types. Nevertheless, each measure should be analysed separately.

Beginning with the levels of popularity (P) of each Facebook profile, it appears that customers favour the State-chartered banks, whether member or nonmember banks (P1=96%). However, in terms of the average number of "likes" per post (P2), the Nationally chartered member banks outperform the rest (P2=239). If popularity is measured by the number of fans, i.e. the number of "likes" per post and per fan (P3), we see that the State-chartered member banks are the most popular of those studied. However, the values obtained when this metric is used are very low, and so, following Bonsón and Ratkai (2013), they are shown multiplied by a thousand in the table.

The data for levels of customer commitment (C) (see Table 2) indicate that 44% of the posts of Nationally chartered member banks receive at least one comment (C1), with an average of 17 comments per post (C2). In this respect, the two types of State-chartered banks performed more weakly; on aver-

Table 2. Customers' engagement in U.S. banks: Descriptive statistics

			Mean	Std. Dev.	Min.	Max.
Nationally chartered member banks	Popularity	P1	0.9420	0.1185	0.4615	1.0000
		P2	239.9860	725.4367	3.0000	4261.4444
		P3	3.2077	4.3867	0.0325	18.7140
	Commitment	C1	0.4433	0.3239	0.0000	1.0000
		C2	17.4956	44.0756	0.0000	199.0000
		C3	0.1470	0.2285	0.0000	1.0273
	Virality	V1	0.4682	0.3031	0.0000	1.0000
		V2	15.6709	37.0223	0.0000	169.8889
		V3	0.2149	0.2504	0.0000	0.9144
State-chartered member banks	Popularity	P1	0.9617	0.0840	0.6250	1.0000
		P2	200.4301	384.3458	2.8750	1680.8750
		P3	9.6377	11.2069	0.2325	40.1146
	Commitment	C1	0.3986	0.2972	0.0000	1.0000
		C2	7.3869	13.5653	0.0000	53.0625
		C3	0.3053	0.4336	0.0000	1.4705
	Virality	V1	0.4861	0.3190	0.0000	1.0000
		V2	18.4879	36.7003	0.0000	142.4583
		V3	1.1488	2.4383	0.0000	11.1524
State-chartered nonmember banks	Popularity	P1	0.9658	0.1090	0.5000	1.0000
		P2	112.5027	318.1018	1.1875	1456.8571
		P3	3.2655	3.1600	0.0408	9.8534
	Commitment	C1	0.3992	0.3321	0.0000	1.0000
		C2	5.1765	12.3240	0.0000	55.6000
		C3	0.6415	2.5748	0.0000	11.8753
	Virality	V1	0.3858	0.3241	0.0000	1.0000
		V2	5.5938	12.7592	0.0000	57.7857
		V3	0.2297	0.3306	0.0000	1.3029

age, 39% of posts received at least one comment, and there were an average of 7 comments per post for member banks, and 5 for the nonmember banks. On considering the number of fans of the Facebook profiles of each bank (C3), we see that the State-chartered nonmember banks have a higher level of customer commitment (0.64) than the others.

In the metrics that measure customer virality (V), the State-chartered member banks obtain the highest values. Thus, 48% of the posts made by these banks are shared at least once (V1), and each post is shared on average over 18 times (V2). With respect to fans (V3), too, the profiles of the State-chartered member banks are the most viral (see Table 2).

These results show that, whatever the form of participation (likes, shares or comments), the level of engagement presented by customers on the Facebook pages of U.S. banks is relatively low. Therefore, the banks' policy should be aimed at acquiring customer engagement via their social media. In this regard, banks should focus on their customers' engagement in terms of the comments made, an approach that will allow banks to interact directly with customers and to determine their preferences or complaints regarding the services provided.

The results of the Mann-Whitney U test are summarised in Table 3. As can be seen, the tests performed between pairs of types of banks (Nationally chartered member banks, State-chartered member banks and State-chartered nonmember banks) only reveal significant differences in the metrics that focus on fans to measure popularity, commitment and virality (P3, C3 and V3). Thus, the State-chartered member banks differ from the others, while there were no significant differences in terms of customer engagement between the Nationally chartered member banks and the State-chartered nonmember banks. Therefore, although these tests indicate that the use of Facebook, both by customers and by banks, varies from one type of bank to another, the results obtained only partly corroborate the descriptive differences detected between the levels of engagement for the three types of U.S. banks.

DISCUSSION AND CONCLUSION

The social media play an increasingly important role in the development of communication strategies in the banking sector, and make a decisive contribution to strategies, to attract and retain customers. In addition, social media offer many possibilities for promoting dialogic communication and thus for building up brand awareness, enhancing the bank's reputation and increasing customer engagement.

In the present study, we investigate the practices of U.S. banks in Facebook, from the perspective of the theory of dialogic communication, in order to measure the level of customer engagement. Descriptive data indicate, firstly, that popularity is the most widely used form of customer engagement and, secondly, that this engagement is more strongly present in State-chartered member banks.

Some authors, such as Mitic and Kapoulas (2012), have suggested that banks should develop strategies to encourage customers to actively contribute to the social media by providing ideas to improve the supply of products and services. Nevertheless, our results show that the implementation of this type of strategy is still at a low level. Moreover, few customers actually participate in banks' concerns by making comments in response to social media posts. Accordingly, banks are failing to take advantage of a unique opportunity to obtain the views of their customers. Therefore, in line with Mitic and Kapoulas (2012), we recommend that banks should undertake actions to encourage active participation and customer commitment, and to overcome the greater effort required for customers to write a comment.

Table 3. Comparative analysis of customers' engagement in U.S. banks: Mann-Whitney U test

		Hypotheses		
		H1 (Nationally banks vs State member banks)	H2 (Nationally banks vs State nonmember banks)	H3 (State member banks vs State nonmember banks)
		Z Statistic	**Z Statistic**	**Z Statistic**
Popularity	P1	-0.613	-1.030	-0.460
	P2	-0.380	0.607	1.202
	P3	-3.121***	-0.526	2.194**
Commitment	C1	0.460	0.502	0.177
	C2	0.301	0.817	0.695
	C3	-1.794*	0.089	1.621
Virality	V1	-0.287	1.174	1.269
	V2	0.022	1.141	1.092
	V3	-1.880*	0.283	1.820*

* Significant at the 0.10 level. ** Significant at the 0.05 level. *** Significant at the 0.01 level.

Regarding the comparative analysis, the Mann-Whitney U test shows that customer engagement for State-chartered member banks is only significantly different from that for the other types of banks in the metrics that include the number of fans. Although these results are consistent with the descriptive analysis, it is strange that no significant differences were found in levels of engagement between National banks and State-chartered nonmember banks, since, in general, these are banks with very different characteristics. All National banks belong to the Federal Reserve, and so they are more highly regulated than nonmember banks, private banks that constitute what has been termed 'shadow banking', and which are only subject to the laws of the State in which they conduct their activity. The United States, together with China, is one of the countries where this type of banking is most widespread. In 2014 alone, shadow banking operations to a value exceeding 71 billion dollars were recorded in the United States.

Therefore, the results obtained may be related to the size of the banks; both National banks and State-chartered nonmember banks are usually very large, while State-chartered member banks are generally smaller. This difference may account for the differences observed in customer engagement via Facebook. It should also be noted that State-chartered nonmember banks do not operate nationally because they would then be regulated by the Federal Reserve, while State-chartered member banks do not do so due to their small size.

In any case, these results help us to better understand the role played by the social media in increasing customer engagement. Consideration of these findings might help community managers to develop future strategies to encourage participation, and to attract and retain customers, through Facebook. However, it should be borne in mind that customer engagement through Facebook is not achieved simply by creating a Facebook profile; in addition, banks must define strategies to facilitate customer feedback (Bonsón & Flores, 2011). Moreover, the fact that a Facebook profile has a large number of fans does not automatically mean that the bank will have a highly engaged body of customers in this respect (Bonsón et al., 2014).

As areas for future research, it would be interesting to extend the study sample to other countries and to make comparisons between them. The present analysis is limited to measuring the level of customer engagement through interactions in the social media. It would be useful to extend the scope of analysis, by performing a content analysis of banks' Facebook profiles. This could be done taking as a starting point the previous research conducted in this field by authors such as Bortree and Seltzer (2009) and Rybalko and Seltzer (2010). Finally, in line with Stieglitz and Dang Xuan (2013), it would be interesting to analyse the mood of customers through social media, as this may influence their degree of engagement. The outcome of such an analysis could also be used to improve the online strategies and actions currently applied by banks.

REFERENCES

Andriole, S. J. (2010). Business impact of Web 2.0 technologies. *Communications of the ACM*, *53*(12), 67–79. doi:10.1145/1859204.1859225

Beuker, I. (2009). How digital brands can succeed and thrive in the engaged era. *Journal of Digital Asset Management*, *5*(6), 375–382. doi:10.1057/dam.2009.28

Bolotaeva, V. and Cata, T. (2010). Marketing opportunities with social networks. *Journal of Internet Social Networking and Virtual Communities*, 1-8.

Bonsón, E., & Flores, F. (2011). Social media and corporate dialogue: The response of global financial institution. *Online Information Review*, *35*(1), 34–49. doi:10.1108/14684521111113579

Bonsón, E., & Ratkai, M. (2013). A set of metrics to assess stakeholder engagement and social legitimacy on a corporate Facebook page. *Online Information Review*, *37*(5), 787–803. doi:10.1108/OIR-03-2012-0054

Bonsón, E., Royo, S., & Ratkai, M. (2014). Facebook Practices in Western European Municipalities: An Empirical Analysis of Activity and Citizens' Engagement. *Administration & Society*. Available at: http://aas.sagepub.com/content/early/2014/09/04/0095399714544945.abstract

Bortree, D., & Seltzer, T. (2009). Dialogic strategies and outcomes: An analysis of environmental advocacy groups' Facebook profiles. *Public Relations Review*, *35*(3), 317–319. doi:10.1016/j.pubrev.2009.05.002

Boyd, D., & Ellison, N. (2008). Social network sites: Definition, history and scholarship. *Journal of Computer-Mediated Communication*, *13*(11), 210–230.

Buckner, H. T. (1965). A theory of rumor transmission. *Public Opinion Quarterly*, *29*(1), 54–70. doi:10.1086/267297

Carfi, C. (2012). *Ant's Eye Vie*. The Social Engagement Journey. Available at: http://www.slideshare.net/antseyeview/social-engagement-journey-13578584/

Chikandiwa, S. T., Contogiannis, E., & Jembere, E. (2013). The adoption of social media marketing in South African banks. *European Business Review*, *25*(4), 365–381. doi:10.1108/EBR-02-2013-0013

Clemons, E. K. (2009). The complex problem of monetizing virtual electronic social networks. *Decision Support Systems*, *48*(1), 46–56. doi:10.1016/j.dss.2009.05.003

Cocheo, S. (2009). Banks wade into new media stream. *ABA Banking Journal, 101*(5), 14–29.

Cohen, L.S. (2010). CT banks delve into social media marketing. *Connecticut Banking*, 12-15.

Constantinides, E., & Fountain, S. J. (2008). Web 2.0: Conceptual Foundations and Marketing Issues. *Journal of Direct. Data and Digital Marketing Practice*, 9(3), 231–244. doi:10.1057/palgrave.dddmp.4350098

Culnan, M. J., McHugh, P. J., & Zubillaga, J. I. (2010). How large US companies can use twitter and other social media to gain business value. *MIS Quarterly Executive*, 9(4), 243–259.

Curtis, L., Edwards, C., Fraser, K. L., Gudelsky, S., Holmquist, J., Thornton, K., & Sweetser, K. D. (2010). Adoption of social media for public relations by nonprofit Organizations. *Public Relations Review*, *36*(1), 90–92. doi:10.1016/j.pubrev.2009.10.003

Davis, F. D. (1989). Perceived Usefulness, Perceived Ease of Use, and User Acceptance of Information Technology. *Management Information Systems Quarterly*, *13*(3), 319–340. doi:10.2307/249008

Eccleston, D., & Griseri, L. (2008). How does Web 2.0 stretch traditional influencing patterns? *International Journal of Market Research*, *50*(5), 591–616. doi:10.2501/S1470785308200055

Flavián, C., Guinaliu, M., & Gurrea, R. (2006). The role played by perceived usability, satisfaction and consumer trust on website loyalty. *Information & Management*, *1*(1), 1–14. doi:10.1016/j.im.2005.01.002

Freeman, R. E. (1984). *Strategic management: a stakeholder approach*. Boston: Pitman press.

Gallaugher, J., & Ransbotham, S. (2010). Social media and customer dialogue management at Starbucks. *MIS Quarterly Executive*, 9(4), 197–212.

Gerrard, P., Cunningham, J. B., & Devlin, J. F. (2006). Why consumers are not using Internet banking: A qualitative study. *Journal of Services Marketing*, *20*(3), 160–168. doi:10.1108/08876040610665616

Goi, C. L. (2014). The Impacts of Social Media on the Local Commercial Banks in Malaysia. *Journal of Internet Banking and Commerce*, *19*(1).

Gritten, A. (2011). New insights into consumer confidence in financial services. *International Journal of Bank Marketing*, *29*(2), 90–106. doi:10.1108/02652321111107602

Hardey, M. (2009). The social context of online market research: An introduction to sociability of social media. *International Journal of Market Research*, *51*(4), 562–564. doi:10.2501/S1470785309200785

Harrison, T. M., & Barthel, B. (2009). Wielding new media in Web 2.0: Exploring the history of engagement with the collaborative construction of media products. *New Media & Society*, *11*(1-2), 155–178. doi:10.1177/1461444808099580

Jaser, J. (2010). The case against social media in banking. *New Jersey Banker*, 26-33.

Kaplan, A. M., & Haenlein, M. (2010). Users of the world, unite! The challenges and opportunities of social media. *Business Horizons*, *53*(1), 59–68. doi:10.1016/j.bushor.2009.09.003

Kazienko, P., Musial, K., & Kajdanowicz, T. (2011). Multidimensional Social Network and Its Application to the Social Recommender System. *IEEE Transactions on Systems, Man, and Cybernetics. Part A, Systems and Humans*, *41*(4), 746–759. doi:10.1109/TSMCA.2011.2132707

Kent, M., & Taylor, M. (1998). Building dialogic relationships through World Wide Web. *Public Relations Review*, *24*(3), 321–334. doi:10.1016/S0363-8111(99)80143-X

Klimis, C. (2010). Digital marketing: The gradual integration in retail banking. *EFMA Journal*, *4*(226), 16–19.

Liébana, F., Martínez, M., & Rejón, F. (2011). The economic crisis in the European Union: The confidence in the Spanish financial sector. Workshop: Crisis, Lisbon, EU policies and member states, Granada.

Liébana, F. and Muñoz, F. (2013). Determinación de los perfiles de los usuarios de banca electrónica a partir de la satisfacción online: una aplicación empírica. Revista de Estudios Empresariales. *Segunda época, 2*, 84-113.

Logvinov, M. (2013). *Banks Aren't Social? Think Again*. Bank Tech. Available at: http://www.banktech.com/business-intelligence/banks-arent-social-thinkagain/240162041

Luxenmbourg, A. (2011). *Social Media Maturity Model.* M & I Partners. Available at: http://www.socialmediamodels.net/social-media-adoption-models-category/social-mediamaturity model/

McAllister, S. M. (2012). How the world's top universities provide dialogic forums for marginalized voices. *Public Relations Review*, *38*(2), 319–327. doi:10.1016/j.pubrev.2011.12.010

Mitic, M., & Kapoulas, A. (2012). Understanding the role of social media in bank marketing. *Marketing Intelligence & Planning*, *30*(7), 668–686. doi:10.1108/02634501211273797

MiXT Media. (2008). *Social Media Adoption Curve*. Available at: http://www.socialmediamodellen.nl/socialmedia-organisatie-volwassenheidsmodellen/social-media-adoption-curve-model/

Mukhtar, M. (2015). Perceptions of UK Based Customers toward Internet Banking in the United Kingdom. *Journal of Internet Banking and Commerce*, *20*(1), 1–38.

Murray, L., Durkin, M., Worthington, S., & Clark, V. (2014). On the potential for Twitter to add value in retail bank relationships. *Journal of Financial Services Marketing*, *19*(4), 277–290. doi:10.1057/fsm.2014.27

Nah, S., & Saxton, G. D. (2013). Modeling the adoption and use of social media by nonprofit organizations. *New Media & Society*, *15*(2), 294–313. doi:10.1177/1461444812452411

Owyang, J. (2010). *Social Businesses Forecast: 2011 The Year of Integration*. Available at: http://www.slideshare.net/jeremiah_owyang/keynote-social-business-forecast-2011-the-year-ofintegration

Ozdemir, S., & Trott, P. (2009). Exploring the adoption of a service innovation: A study of Internet banking adopters and non-adopters. *Journal of Financial Services Marketing*, *13*(4), 284–299. doi:10.1057/fsm.2008.25

Pfeil, U., Arjan, R., & Zaphiris, P. (2009). Age differences in online social networking–A study of user profiles and the social capital divide among teenagers and older users in MySpace. *Computers in Human Behavior*, *25*(3), 643–654. doi:10.1016/j.chb.2008.08.015

Roblyer, M., McDaniel, M., Webb, M., Herman, J., & Witty, J. V. (2010). Findings on Facebook in higher education: A comparison of college faculty and student uses and perceptions of social networking sites. *The Internet and Higher Education*, *13*(3), 134–140. doi:10.1016/j.iheduc.2010.03.002

Rybaiko, S., & Seltzer, T. (2010). Dialogic communication in 140 characters or less: How Fortune 500 companies engage stakeholders using Twitter. *Public Relations Review*, *36*(4), 336–341. doi:10.1016/j.pubrev.2010.08.004

Sáez-Martín, A., Haro-de-Rosario, A., & Caba-Pérez, M. D. C. (2015). Using Twitter for Dialogic Communication: Local Government Strategies in the European Union. *Local Government Studies*, *41*(3), 421–444. doi:10.1080/03003930.2014.991866

Samuels, T. (2013). *Banking on More Social Media*. Socialnomics. Available at: http://www.socialnomics.net/2013/08/20/banking-on-more-social-media

Sashi, C. M. (2012). Customer engagement, buyer-seller relationships, and social media. *Management Decision*, *50*(2), 253–272. doi:10.1108/00251741211203551

Sheskin, D. (2011). *Handbook of parametric and nonparametric statistical procedure* (5th ed.). Academic Press.

Smiciklas, M. (2011). *Social media learning curve strategy and framework*. Available at: http://www.socialmediaexplorer.com/social-media-marketing/social-media-strategy-learning-curveand- framework/

Stieglitz, S., & Dang-Xuan, L. (2013). Emotions and Information Diffusion in Social Media - Sentiment of Microblogs and Sharing Behavior. *Journal of Management Information Systems*, *29*(4), 217–247. doi:10.2753/MIS0742-1222290408

Stone, M. (2009). Staying customer-focused and trusted: Web 2.0 and Customer 2.0 in financial services. *Database Marketing & Customer Strategy Management*, *16*(2), 101–131. doi:10.1057/dbm.2009.13

Suriya, M., Mahalakshmi, V., & Karthik, R. (2012). A study on customer perception towards internet banking. *International Journal of Sales & Marketing Management Research and Development*, *2*(3), 15–34.

Syhu, H. S., & Kapoor, S. (2010). Corporate Social Responsibility Initiatives: An Analysis of Voluntary Corporate Disclosure. *South Asian Journal of Management*, *17*(2), 47–80.

Vemuri, A. (2010). Getting social: Bridging the gap between banking and social media. *Global Finance*, *24*(5), 20–21.

Waters, R. D., Burnett, E., Lamm, A., & Lucas, J. (2009). Engaging stakeholders through social networking: How non-profit organisations are using Facebook. *Public Relations Review*, *35*(2), 102–106. doi:10.1016/j.pubrev.2009.01.006

Wattal, S., Schuff, D., Mandviwalla, M., & Williams, C. B. (2010). Web 2.0 and politics: The 2008 U.S. Presidential Election and E-Politics Research Agenda. *Management Information Systems Quarterly*, *34*(4), 669–688.

Wirtz, B. W., Schilke, O., & Ullrich, S. (2010). Strategic development of business models: Implications of the Web 2.0 for creating value on the internet. *Long Range Planning*, *43*(2-3), 272–290. doi:10.1016/j.lrp.2010.01.005

Wright, S. (2009). Political blogs, representation and the public sphere. *Aslib Proceedings*, *61*(2), 155–169. doi:10.1108/00012530910946901

This research was previously published in Strategic Uses of Social Media for Improved Customer Retention edited by Wafaa Al-Rabayah, Rawan Khasawneh, Rasha Abu-shamaa, and Izzat Alsmadi, pages 154-172, copyright year 2017 by Business Science Reference (an imprint of IGI Global).

Index

C

H

I

K

L

M

N

O

P

Q

R

S

T

U

V

W

Y